WALKER'S MANUAL OF PENNY STOCKS

WALKER'S MANUAL OF PENNY STOCKS

Published by:

Walker's Manual, LLC
3650 Mt. Diablo Blvd., Suite 240
Lafayette, California 94549-3765

925-283-9993	Telephone
925-283-9513	Facsimile
www.walkersotc.com	Web Site
info@walkersotc.com	E-Mail

Harry K. Eisenberg	Editor in chief
Karen L. Johnston	Book design & production

Publisher's Cataloging-in-Publication
(*Provided by Quality Books, Inc.*)

Walker's manual of penny stocks — 2nd ed.
    p. cm.
    Includes index.
    ISBN: 0-9652088-1-8

    1. Penny stocks — United States — Handbooks, manuals, etc. 2. Securities —
    United States — Handbooks, manuals, etc. 3. Corporations — United States
    — Directories.

HG6041.W35 1999   332.63'228
                         QBI99-607

To Cindy
my loving wife and partner of 29 years
for her support, her wisdom and her interest
in bringing Walker's Manuals to reality

¢¢

Walker's Manual of Unlisted Stocks

picks up where *Walker's Manual of Penny Stocks* leaves off, concentrating on stocks priced at $5 or more at December 31, 1998. While this title focuses exclusively on the over-the-counter market, it features a great variety of US public companies. They come from virtually every industry, represent investment types that run the gamut from value to growth to income to speculative, and boast share prices ranging from $5 to well over $1,000.

This year we've added a new section showcasing 100 of the best community banks we could find. Of course, 1999's 4th edition of this widely referenced work includes 400 inactive securities on top of the banks, many of them new in this edition. As always, we are committed to providing the most complete and accurate picture possible of every company we profile. We hope you enjoy exploring all of Walker's Manuals.

¢¢

¢¢

Table of Contents

¢¢

Indices

¢¢

Preface to the Second Edition

¢¢

This year at Walker's Manual we know something that last year we merely suspected: behind any stock priced under $5 we *might* or might *not* find a company well worth investing in. Such an equivocal statement would hardly seem likely to ruffle any feathers. But low-priced stocks—also known as penny stocks—have long been treated as pariahs in the stock market. Pundits demonize them by suggesting that they are associated only with rogue companies: worthless shells or worse yet, criminal enterprises. You would have to be a fool to so much as glance at a penny stock after hearing such things from the experts!

But even on the face of it, this dogma seemed odd to us. Stock price by itself is no indicator of past or future performance or overall value, and so to rely on it as a yardstick of quality would appear unwise. By focusing on price instead of a broader set of financial criteria, quality stocks can be relegated to oblivion while poor ones end up in your portfolio. As investment strategies go, this one is clearly of questionable value.

Certainly that was our own suspicion when we undertook to publish the 1st edition of *Walker's Manual of Penny Stocks*. Now, a year later, we've revisited the 500 stocks that were included in last year's book. What we're seeing, not surprisingly, is a population as varied as it was when the book was first published, with many good-looking companies as well as a few failures. On the one hand, a couple of them—Aid Auto Stores, Inc. and Dakotah, Incorporated—went bankrupt. A few more went into Chapter 11 reorganization:

American Rice, Inc.
Martin Color-Fi, Inc.
Coded Communications Corporation

On the other hand, plenty of the companies saw their stock prices rise 50% or better—some tenfold or more—between December 31, 1997 and 1998...

	1997	1998		1997	1998
AMCON Distribution Company	$ 3.75	$ 6.94	Danskin, Inc.	$ .50	$ 1.00
Athanor Group, Inc.	2.37	3.56	Decora Industries, Inc.	4.44	7.68
AutoBond Acceptance Corporation	2.75	4.13	Dynatronics Corporation	1.00	2.56
BLC Financial Services, Inc.	1.47	2.25	Eagle Point Software Corporation	4.00	8.63
Ballistic Recovery Systems, Inc.	.31	.83	Eastco Industrial Safety Corp.		
Bluegreen Corporation	4.37	7.56	(now Worksafe Industries)	1.87	3.19
Cache, Inc.	3.03	4.88	EcoScience Corporation	1.56	4.13
Canterbury Park Holding Corporation	2.81	4.50	Evans Systems, Inc.	1.69	15.63
Commodore Holdings Limited	3.06	5.88	Fairmount Chemical Co., Inc.	.11	.19
CompuDyne Corporation	2.00	4.25	Fotoball USA, Inc.	1.25	3.38
Comtech Telecommunications Corp.	4.37	8.75	Frontier Airlines, Inc.	1.97	4.81
Concorde Gaming Corporation	.09	.16	Geerlings & Wade, Inc.	4.00	9.19
Costa Rica International, Inc.	1.13	7.88	GlobeNet International I, Inc.	.75	1.13
DCI Telecommunications, Inc.	1.81	2.83	Greg Manning Auctions, Inc.	1.25	9.38
Daedalus Enterprises, Inc.			Hansen Natural Corporation	1.81	5.38
(now Sensys Technologies)	3.00	4.50	Hauppauge Digital, Inc.	4.94	9.25
			Interfoods of America, Inc.	.63	1.50

	1997	1998		1997	1998
International Yogurt Company	$ 2.81	$ 5.25	QCS Corporation	$ .60	$ 6.50
JB Oxford Holdings, Inc.	.69	1.81	RADVA Corporation	.47	1.00
JJFN Services, Inc.			RMS Titanic, Inc.	.59	1.06
(now Strategic Capital Resources, Inc.)	.14	.35	Rent-A-Wreck of America, Inc.	1.00	1.50
L.A. T Sportswear, Inc.	.63	1.13	SVI Holdings, Inc.	4.22	9.19
La-Man Corporation			Sel-Leb Marketing, Inc.	.93	2.50
(now Display Technologies)	3.09	7.43	SETECH, Inc.	1.75	2.94
Lucille Farms, Inc.	1.22	2.88	Seventh Generation, Inc.	.47	.81
Market Guide, Inc.	2.38	11.88	Shop At Home, Inc.	3.69	7.38
Medical Advisory Systems, Inc.	.25	4.38	Sierra Monitor Corporation	.19	.88
Mentortech Inc.	.5	3.10	Spanlink Communications, Inc.	2.00	3.81
MicroFrame, Inc.	1.34	2.81	Sport Chalet, Inc.	4.75	7.00
MobilNetix Systems, Inc.	1.50	3.00	Suprema Specialties, Inc.	3.19	4.94
NBI, Inc.	.59	1.03	Swank, Inc.	1.06	1.81
Navarre Corporation	2.12	10.06	Tanknowlogy-NDE International, Inc.	.13	.88
Networks Electronic Corp.	1.00	3.25	Teknowledge Corporation		
Oakridge Holdings, Inc.	.81	2.75	(6.50 after a 1 for 5 reverse split)	.49	1.30
PVC Container Corporation	4.50	8.44	Telesoft Corp.	3.38	5.88
Pallet Management Systems, Inc.	1.81	7.81	The Topps Company, Inc.	2.22	5.00
Players International, Inc.	3.06	6.18	ValueVision International, Inc.	3.75	7.03
Polymer Research Corp. of America	2.12	3.25	Westmoreland Coal Company	1.25	3.82
Prime Cellular, Inc.	.50	1.00	Xyvision, Inc.	.26	.67
Publicker Industries, Inc. (now Publicard)	1.38	14.00	Z-Axis Corporation	.06	.25
			ZEON Corporation	.50	3.00

...while others with less dramatic percentage increases still broke the $5 price threshold...

	1997	1998		1997	1998
Air Transportation Holding Co., Inc.	$ 4.25	$ 5.13	Mechanical Technology Incorporated	$ 4.00	$ 8.13
Candela Corporation	4.25	5.56	O.I. Corporation	4.12	5.56
DHB Capital Group Inc.	3.91	5.13	Spiegel, Inc.	4.94	5.75
Delta Woodside Industries, Inc.	4.87	6.00	TRC Companies, Inc.	4.25	5.50
Edison Control Corporation	4.50	6.50	Technology 80 Inc.	3.62	5.00
H.D. Vest, Inc.	4.87	5.75	U.S. Home & Garden, Inc.	4.13	5.00
HEI, Inc.	4.62	5.44	U.S. Plastic Lumber Corporation	4.50	5.75
Hyde Athletic Industries, Inc.	4.87	5.13	Valley Forge Scientific Corp.	3.44	5.37
International American Homes, Inc.					
(1 for 3 reverse split)	1.50	5.75			

...and still others—a respectable number of them—were acquired at healthy premiums:

Aloette Cosmetics, Inc.	Greyhound Lines, Inc.
Ameriwood Industries International Corporation	Innovative Tech Systems, Inc.
Carnegie Group, Inc.	Katz Digital Technologies, Inc.
Digital Dictation, Inc.	The Lion Brewery, Inc.
Electronic Designs, Inc.	Lukens Medical Corporation
Fireplace Manufacturers, Incorporated	Magicworks Entertainment Incorporated
The Fresh Juice Company, Inc.	Ocal, Inc.
Gamma Biologicals, Inc.	RF Power Products, Inc.
Genetic Laboratories Wound Care, Inc.	Spurlock Industries, Inc.
GeoWaste Incorporated	Standard Funding Corp.
Golden Eagle Group, Inc.	Toastmaster Inc.

In between the best and the worst were most of the 500—some did well and some didn't. The only global conclusion we see in these results is that price is *not* a reasonable guide to the quality of a stock. Only by thoroughly acquainting yourself with a company's financial situation will you be able to judge whether or not it is a good prospect.

We have been very pleased by the enthusiastic reception of *Walker's Manual of Penny Stocks*, and are excited to present the 2nd edition. 243 of the companies from the 1st edition have been replaced, while the rest have been thoroughly updated. We hope that you'll find our book a helpful addition to your research library.

¢ ¢

¢ ¢

Introduction

¢ ¢

Your younger brother called yesterday and was waxing enthusiastic over some company he just invested in. He bought their stock, he tells you, for only $1.34 per share! At this you perk up your ears. A penny stock—what is he getting himself into? But before you call back to lecture him about prudent investing, consider this—exactly what does that low price tell you about the company your brother is now a shareholder of? Is it probably some risky high technology start-up, or is it possible that a well-established company would be priced so low? Does it have to be a tiny outfit with no real growth potential, or could it be a household name known nationwide? Can you infer how well the company is managed from the stock's price? What about its financial condition or recent performance? Do you know where you can buy the stock or how often it trades? Should an investment like this always be considered fundamentally speculative? Is it a scam? Does the low stock price itself tell you *anything* at all about the company or its prospects?

In a word—no. Sadly though, belief remains widespread that all cheap stocks are simply pariahs crowding the marginal over-the-counter market, investor swindles just waiting to happen. Assumed by many to be fly-by-night companies which will be gone tomorrow with your cash in tow, they are usually referred to as *penny stocks*, and they are perhaps the most misunderstood and maligned group of stocks in the entire marketplace.

Journalists in particular excel in this vilification, routinely dishing out cautionary tales of elderly retirees stripped of their life savings by shady figures peddling—you guessed it—penny stocks. Even legitimate business writers seem willing to take broadside aim at penny stocks along with the Pink Sheets®, the OTC Bulletin Board, over-the-counter stocks and unlisted stocks without so much as a nod towards over 1,000 reputable companies whose stock falls into one or more of those categories. This general lack of understanding is typified by a *New York Times* article called "Hoping For Green In The Pink Sheets, But Seeing Red." (August 25, 1996) Here are a few excerpts from the article, along with our comments (in parentheses):

> "...the pink sheets cover about 13,000 [companies], mostly foreign." (In fact, only 4% of Pink Sheet® stocks represent non-US companies).

> "Smallness carries several dangers, including thin cash reserves for future hard times..." (No matter what size a company is, thin cash reserves are a serious problem. That point aside, many small companies actually have quite generous cash reserves).

> "...[their] financials are often flimsy...You may not even know how flimsy the numbers are. Information on these companies is often scarce...Since [they] don't issue interim statements to shareholders, how would you know if anything turns lousy?" (Actually, information is often readily available on a

quarterly basis. Most Pink Sheet® companies issue quarterly reports both to their shareholders and to the Securities and Exchange Commission).

"The companies are also exempt from S.E.C. proxy rules—leaving open the possibility that shareholder rights will be trampled" (In fact, few of these companies are exempt from SEC proxy rules).

All of the misinformation aside, the singling out of penny stocks and the over-the-counter market for such attacks is simply unfounded. The misperception fostered is twofold: one, that all penny stocks are to be shunned, and two, that merely not being a penny stock is somehow a guarantee of greater investment safety, especially from fraud. But nothing could be further from the truth. While there is no doubt that investors have been swindled in penny stock schemes, fraud is hardly a stranger to higher-priced stocks, the national stock markets, or to other investment vehicles, for that matter. You don't need to be a daily reader of the *Wall Street Journal* to be aware that the 1980's and 90's alone have been fraught with insider trading, securities violations and other white-collar crime on a scale at times so grand that some of the largest and most reputable securities houses in the world have been utterly brought down by it. Penny stocks may not be immune, but neither are they the only or even the preferred vehicle for investor fraud.

Conversely, and despite the bad press, a great deal of legitimate business activity concerns itself with the many reputable companies that have low-priced stock. Across the United States, when you grab some fish & chips for lunch, stop at the corner store for a lottery ticket or fly to Hawaii for your dream vacation, you may well be doing business with a so-called penny stock company. Arthur Treacher's, Hawaiin Airlines, 7-Eleven (The Southland Corporation)—with stock prices ranging from $.62 to $3.25 on December 31, 1998, the shares of this diverse and reputable group fit squarely into some of the most common definitions of penny stocks.

Don't feel bad if you are confused as to the exact definition of this term. So many variants circulate these days that it appears everyone else is too. At its most literal, the term penny stock describes a stock that trades for one or a few pennies per share, but this is by no means the definition most widely employed. Also popular, for example, is the one with the price cutoff at exactly $1 per share. At an extreme, price isn't even the defining characteristic of penny stocks! To some, "...price is irrelevant. The most important part of the definition of penny stocks is that these companies have yet to put together a stable, dependable business" (Frick, Robert L., et al. *Keys To Risks And Rewards Of Penny Stocks*. Hauppauge, New York: Barron's Educational Series, Inc., 1990).

Well, we do agree that price *should be* irrelevant in determining the acceptability of an investment. Indeed, if Frick's criteria were adhered to, half of the listings on NASDAQ would be called penny stocks, and the standard against which all stocks are judged would change dramatically. But, we digress. Penny stocks are so labeled by almost everyone precisely because of the price of their stock. Unfortunately, this is unlikely to change anytime soon.

The Securities and Exchange Commission (SEC) is no help. Beginning in 1992 they amended The Securities Exchange Act specifically to address low-priced stocks. In doing so, they defined penny stocks as the shares of any company that are priced under $5 *and* that are not traded on a national securities exchange or quoted on NASDAQ. The SEC latched onto the term penny stock to describe the world of low-priced stocks trading over-the-counter. But why were they even focused on these stocks? An unusual increase during the 1980's of white-collar crime involving unlisted, often low-priced stocks had caught their regulatory eye. Whereas listed securities were considered well regulated since the passage of major federal legislation in both 1933 and 1934, unlisted securities in general and low-priced unlisted securities in particular seemed to have been literally designed to avoid that regulation. In an effort to protect individual investors, the SEC imposed a number of new rules involving penny stocks on the securities industry and the investing public.

So between SEC rules and listing requirements of the national exchanges, the focus *is* squarely on price. We sincerely wish the SEC would have minimized the importance of stock price by establishing instead standards for cash flow and working capital. These could have applied equally to *all* public companies, forcing them to achieve and maintain minimum performance in critical financial areas prior to having their stock freely traded, and as a continuing measure of their fiscal health. This, we feel, would have afforded far more real investor protection.

While the ill-advised focus on stock price isn't going anywhere, the label, at least, can be clarified. We have culled what we feel to be the relevant attributes of penny stocks in our attempt to put together a meaningful definition of the term and representation of the population. The result? While *Walker's Manual of Penny Stocks* conforms to the SEC's $5 price cutoff, it does not discriminate between unlisted and listed stocks—no matter which exchange(s) they do or do not call home, to us they are penny stocks simply if they trade under $5 per share.

And in fact, penny stocks do trade everywhere that higher-priced stocks trade. It is true that very few of them will be found in the national markets, simply because of listing requirements, previously mentioned, that include price restrictions. And while the vast majority do trade over-the-counter as a result, it is also true that alternative arrangements are sometimes made available by even the major exchanges to accommodate companies that do not meet these minimum requirements. Consequently, on December 31, 1998 you would have found a number of penny stocks listed on the NYSE and AMEX along with those in the over-the-counter market and on NASDAQ:

New York Stock Exchange (NYSE)	188
American Stock Exchange (AMEX)	326
National Association of Securities Dealers Automatic Quotation System (NASDAQ)	2,000
The over-the-counter market, including the Pink Sheets® and the OTC Bulletin Board	5,000

Our bottom line is that as criteria go, stock price and whether or not a stock is listed are not good indicators of a prospective investment's desirability. The label of penny stock is one of a number of flags, nothing more, reminding us of the importance of understanding a company's valuation before we trade in its stock. It's too bad that we aren't also reminded of the same principal when dealing with higher-priced stocks. On the one hand, there is no fundamental reason to avoid penny stocks or unlisted stocks in general. On the other, investors simply must learn about any investment they are making—or accept the consequences of investing with blind faith as their advisor.

While it is clearly not desirable in terms of public relations for a stock's price to be under $5, a number of possible reasons exist for this market valuation. Many of these revolve around the results of operations. A company may be a start-up, for example, lacking the history of revenues or profits on which so much investor confidence rests. Plenty of established firms also lack profitability, and the market may reflect this reality by lowering the stock price accordingly. Some companies might even have suffered substantial losses and may be hanging precariously onto financial solvency. In other types of situations, however, a low stock price indicates more about the structure of capital than about earnings or profits. A company may simply be small, for instance, too small to command large prices for the shares that it has outstanding. Whatever their overall market capitalization, other companies have so many shares outstanding that they are literally spread very thin in terms of price per share.

Which of the above scenarios was acceptable to us in making the selection for this book? Below is an outline of factors we considered in choosing companies for inclusion in *Walker's Manual of Penny Stocks*:

- **Existing revenue stream** is a key factor that separates the real players from the hopefuls. It also enables you to evaluate growth, a market niche and future financial condition. If we require a current revenue stream, are we eliminating research and development companies? Absolutely not. Many of the companies in this book are developing new products and new markets. They have substantial investments in research and development, acquisitions and strategic alliances.

- **Financial solvency** as measured by traditional ratios is important to us—we closely inspect debt/equity, current ratio and working capital. However, some companies struggle financially but because of other strengths can attract necessary capital infusions. There are a number of companies in this book whose auditors have issued going-concern qualifications in their opinions. There are also companies involved in bankruptcy proceedings. While the end of the road may be near for some these companies, others may recover beautifully. We make no assumptions one way or the other, but try to balance all factors. We do note all of the situations above when they have occurred.

- **Longevity** and history weigh a great deal in separating substantial companies from those that might not be for real. Often the smaller but older, more established companies are good value investments. The average age of the companies in this manual exceeds twenty years old.

- **Profitability** or trending towards profitability speaks to the viability of any concern. Huge losses are difficult for any company to sustain over prolonged periods of time.

- The **number of employees** an organization has is another example of a flag. A company with just a handful of employees should be evaluated with caution, not rejected outright. On the other hand, one with the infrastructure required to handle hundreds of employees would appear to have greater stability, but this should not be assumed without other supporting evidence.

Factors we did not consider include:

- **Where the stock is traded**, as was mentioned above, is not inherent to our definition of penny stock. Many over-the-counter penny stocks can no longer seriously be considered as investments, because they are only skeletons of their former entities. Once those are eliminated, we apply no rules of thumb to the remainder. Each must be evaluated on its own merits. We ended up selecting stocks from each of the markets for the final company mix that is in this book.

- The **size** of companies in this book varies considerably. We neither favor nor prejudice small companies, which certainly have their advantages as well as disadvantages. One look at the popularity of the small-cap segment of the marketplace should dispel any doubts about small company stocks. As with every other criteria, individual appetite applies.

- Every stock in this book was **priced** below $5 at December 31, 1998, but we have not favored any price segment within those parameters. It is fair to say that we wanted you to see a reasonable spread of prices between the two extremes of $.01 and $4.99, and we were pleased that this occurred quite naturally as we made our final selection.

Having spent no inconsiderable effort in the defense of penny stocks, we do take issue with some of the reasons that investors are attracted to them. There is a common but flawed belief, for example, that lower-priced stocks will likely have larger percentage gains than their higher-priced cousins. This concept is demonstrated by a scenario where stock is purchased for $.10 and sold not so far down the road for $5.00, a whopping 5,000% return. The only problem here is that very few penny stocks will ever produce that kind of return. The odds that you will pick the one that does are probably commensurate with those of Lame Eddy winning the Kentucky Derby.

Then there's the "it's something that I can afford" syndrome. This one boils down to simple math: if you have $500, you can buy 5 shares at $100 or 100 shares at $5. Whether you end up with the 5 shares or the 100, your investment is still $500. (if you're thinking the $5 shares will grow more or faster than the $100 ones will, please re-read the paragraph above). The way to make good investments, to make money, is by acquiring quality, not quantity. For $500 you may be able to buy a greater number of shares of penny stocks, but you also have other, often preferable investment options. In our view, the person who has only a small amount to invest should be conservative, not speculative. Start small and be careful: your nest egg will not likely mushroom or dissolve, but will steadily grow as a result.

Lastly, there's the tendency towards speculation, investing with the expectation of turning a quick profit. Wanting to believe in such miracles is what enables bogus brokers to operate—they want you to believe too. In them. Avoid them like the plague. This is not hard to do if you rely on your own homework and not the word of anyone, however well-intended, for unsupported investment advice. We are not suggesting that you avoid penny stocks. To the contrary, we hope that you will be open-minded to everything and will always be responsible no matter where or how you invest your money. In our own personal portfolios we have many of the most well-known companies in America, including Berkshire Hathaway, Disney, Compaq Computer and McDonalds. We also have a fabulous selection of inactive securities and community banks like those featured in *Walker's Manual of Unlisted Stocks*. Penny stocks? Yes, we have them too!

¢ ¢

We hope that this discussion has provided you with an understanding of penny stocks that is sufficient to evaluate the company profiles that follow. On the next page you will also find a glossary of specific financial terms used in the financial statement section of each company's page. Following our presentation of the 500 company profiles, we have also included indices ranking them by price per share, total revenues, market capitalization, return on average equity, price/earnings ratio, price/book value %, compound revenue growth % and compound earnings per share growth %. These will give you one quick way to see how the companies compare and to evaluate possible investment opportunities. Lastly, for your convenience we list informational indices such as all companies by their legal names, by the state in which they are located, and by their SIC code. We hope you enjoy the 2nd edition of *Walker's Manual of Penny Stocks*.

¢ ¢

Our objective is to bring our readers information on companies that are not well known or followed by institutional investors. We will continue our search for new material to include in future editions of our book. The information contained in this book has been obtained from company reports and documents. In most cases the financial information has been audited by the company's independent auditors and/or is a part of a required filing with a governmental agency. While we take significant measures to insure that the information which we present is objective and accurate, Walker's Manual, LLC does not take any responsibility for its underlying accuracy or reliability. Certain of the principals of Walker's Manual, LLC do, in some cases, have ownership positions in the profiled companies. The inclusion of particular companies in this book is not, however, an endorsement of their investment desirability.

¢ ¢

Glossary

Per Share Information

Stock Price Bid price for the stock at the end of the year or period presented unless otherwise noted. Amounts are adjusted for stock splits and stock dividends.

Earnings Per Share Net income after all items divided by average shares outstanding for the period.

Price / Earnings Ratio

Year-end stock price divided by earnings per share. The ratio is expressed as a multiple (a p/e of 7.25 means that shares are trading at 7.25 times earnings).

Book Value Per Share

Total common stockholders' equity divided by total shares outstanding at the end of the period.

Price / Book Value % The percentage relationship between stock price and book value per share.

Dividends Per Share

Dividends paid for the period, expressed on a per share basis.

Annual Financial Data

Total Revenues Total sales and revenues.

Costs & Expenses Current period costs and expenses.

Income Before Taxes and Other Total income less all expenses and costs before minority interest, accounting changes and extraordinary items.

Other Items Includes minority shareholders' interest in the earnings of a subsidiary, extraordinary items and the cumulative effect of accounting changes. If considered significant, these items will be discussed in the comments section.

Income Taxes Total income taxes for the period.

Net Income Income net of income taxes, extraordinary items and minority interests. Used to compute earnings per share.

Per Share Information	
Stock Price	0.75
Earnings Per Share	0.09
Price / Earnings Ratio	8.33
Book Value Per Share	1.25
Price / Book Value %	60.00
Dividends Per Share	0.0
Annual Financial Data	
Operating Results (000's)	
Total Revenues	20,297.7
Costs & Expenses	-19,700.5
Income Before Taxes and Other	597.2
Other Items	0.0
Income Tax	-256.0
Net Income	341.2
Cash Flow From Operations	-309.4
Balance Sheet (000's)	
Cash & Equivalents	192.7
Total Current Assets	6,433.4
Fixed Assets, Net	484.7
Total Assets	9,988.4
Total Current Liabilities	4,097.2
Long-Term Debt	624.0
Stockholders' Equity	5,213.2
Performance & Financial Condition	
Return on Total Revenues %	1.68
Return on Avg Stockholders' Equity %	7.15
Return on Average Assets %	4.15
Current Ratio	1.57
Debt / Equity %	11.97

Cash Flow From Operations Cash flow generated during the period. This is obtained from the Company's statements of cash flows, which are not presented.

Cash & Equivalents Represents all cash, items immediately convertible into cash, and marketable securities owned at the end of the year.

Total Current Assets Those assets available for use in operations during the current fiscal year.

Fixed Assets, Net

Investment in property plant and equipment, net of accumulated depreciation.

Total Assets The sum of all assets at the balance sheet date.

Total Current Liabilities

Liabilities at the balance sheet date that must be satisfied during the current fiscal year.

Long-Term Debt Obligations such as bonds, notes and capital lease obligations at the balance sheet date that are due more than one year from the balance sheet date.

Stockholders' Equity The amount by which total assets exceed total liabilities.

Return on Total Revenues % Net income divided by total revenues; a performance measure based on the year presented.

Return on Avg Stockholders' Equity % Net income divided by average stockholders' equity; a performance measure based on the year presented.

Return on Average Assets % Net income divided by average total assets; a performance measure based on the year presented.

Current Ratio Ratio of current assets to current liabilities.

Debt / Equity % Measurement of debt as a percentage of equity.

WALKER'S MANUAL OF

PENNY STOCKS

2ND EDITION

ACR Group, Inc.

3200 Wilcrest Drive, Suite 440   Houston, TX 77042-6019   Telephone (713)780-8532   Fax (713)780-4067

Company Description

The principal business of ACR Group, Inc. is the wholesale distribution of heating, ventilating, air conditioning and refrigeration (HVACR) equipment, parts and supplies in the southeastern United States, central and south Texas, and Las Vegas, Nevada. Recognizing a consolidation in the distribution segment of the HVACR industry, the Company has focused extensive efforts on rapid growth. Greater size allows the Company greater purchasing power to lower the cost of goods sold and to compete with the largest distributors. The Company acquired its first operating company in 1990. Since then, ACR Group has acquired or started eight additional HVACR distribution companies and now has 34 branch operations in nine states.

	02/28/98	02/28/97	02/29/96	02/28/95
Per Share Information				
Stock Price as of 12/31	1.06	2.19	1.87	0.50
Earnings Per Share	0.08	0.10	0.02	0.05
Price / Earnings Ratio	13.25	21.90	93.50	10.00
Book Value Per Share	0.75	0.68	0.55	0.53
Price / Book Value %	141.33	322.06	340.00	n.a.
Dividends Per Share	0.0	0.0	0.0	0.0
Annual Financial Data				
Operating Results (000's)				
Total Revenues	96,682.4	78,957.4	56,705.1	41,545.1
Costs & Expenses	-96,111.9	-78,070.9	-56,506.3	-40,983.4
Income Before Taxes and Other	570.5	886.5	198.8	561.7
Other Items	0.0	0.0	0.0	0.0
Income Tax	332.9	258.3	-15.0	-3.5
Net Income	903.4	1,144.8	183.8	558.2
Cash Flow From Operations	1,268.7	-1,804.7	-891.4	-1,428.9
Balance Sheet (000's)				
Cash & Equivalents	90.0	412.7	348.2	162.7
Total Current Assets	30,039.8	23,471.8	17,758.7	13,739.4
Fixed Assets, Net	3,713.8	3,435.4	2,111.0	1,268.8
Total Assets	41,107.8	30,557.6	22,010.3	17,131.7
Total Current Liabilities	16,492.8	12,391.7	9,640.6	7,921.5
Long-Term Debt	16,282.2	10,735.1	6,397.7	3,568.6
Stockholders' Equity	7,960.4	7,006.0	5,666.2	5,482.4
Performance & Financial Condition				
Return on Total Revenues %	0.93	1.45	0.32	1.34
Return on Avg Stockholders' Equity %	12.07	18.07	3.30	10.73
Return on Average Assets %	2.52	4.36	0.94	3.70
Current Ratio	1.82	1.89	1.84	1.73
Debt / Equity %	204.54	153.23	112.91	65.09

Compound Growth %'s	EPS %	16.96	Net Income %	17.41	Total Revenues %	32.52

Comments

Total revenues increased 22.7% during fiscal 1998. Same store sales grew 7% while acquisitions accounted for the balance. Tax loss carryovers enabled the Company to recognize income tax benefits in each of the last two fiscal years. $32.1 million of carryovers remain to offset future income. At February 28, 1998, the Company had $6 million of goodwill on the books which equates to approximately 75% of book value. For the nine months ended November 30, 1998, revenues and net income were $92.7 million and $1,981,136 ($.17 per share) as compared to $74.9 million and $1,790,693 ($.15 per share) for the same period of the preceding year.

Officers	Position	Ownership Information	
Alex Trevino, Jr.	President, CEO	Number of Shares Outstanding	10,634,017
Anthony R. Maresca	Senior VP, Treasurer	Market Capitalization	$ 11,272,058
		Number of Shareholders	515
		Where Listed / Symbol	NASDAQ / ACRG

Other Information			
Transfer Agent	ChaseMellon Shareholder Services Dallas, TX	SIC Code	5075
Auditor	Ernst & Young LLP	Employees	310

AM Communications, Inc.

100 Commerce Boulevard   Quakertown, PA 18951-2237   Telephone (215)536-1354   Fax (215)536-1475

Company Description

AM Communications, Inc. designs, manufactures and markets network monitoring systems, primarily cable television (CATV) systems and including hardware and software, to the broadband communications market. The Company's proprietary system allows CATV operators to monitor the performance and operation of the complete broadband distribution network, thereby enhancing network reliability and optimizing performance. The Company's principal activity from its formation in 1974 to 1989 was the construction of cable television systems. This production was discontinued in 1989. The Company's current products are the result of a diversification strategy undertaken in the late 1980's.

	03/28/98	03/29/97	03/30/96	04/01/95
Per Share Information				
Stock Price as of 12/31	0.12	0.44	0.45	2.19
Earnings Per Share	0.03	-0.09	-0.04	0.02
Price / Earnings Ratio	4.00	n.a.	n.a.	109.50
Book Value Per Share	0.02	-0.01	0.07	0.01
Price / Book Value %	600.00	n.a.	642.86	21,900.00
Dividends Per Share	0.0	0.0	0.0	0.0
Annual Financial Data				
Operating Results (000's)				
Total Revenues	16,854.0	10,525.0	8,407.0	5,290.0
Costs & Expenses	-15,887.0	-12,350.0	-9,496.0	-5,339.0
Income Before Taxes and Other	967.0	-1,825.0	-1,089.0	-49.0
Other Items	0.0	0.0	0.0	0.0
Income Tax	-30.0	-936.0	-12.0	816.0
Net Income	937.0	-2,761.0	-1,101.0	767.0
Cash Flow From Operations	546.0	211.0	-1,916.0	217.0
Balance Sheet (000's)				
Cash & Equivalents	710.0	620.0	664.0	454.0
Total Current Assets	4,697.0	3,954.0	4,927.0	2,896.0
Fixed Assets, Net	734.0	899.0	565.0	194.0
Total Assets	5,450.0	4,969.0	6,435.0	4,181.0
Total Current Liabilities	2,280.0	2,634.0	1,710.0	1,363.0
Long-Term Debt	2,583.0	0.0	0.0	0.0
Stockholders' Equity	548.0	2,186.0	4,615.0	2,818.0
Performance & Financial Condition				
Return on Total Revenues %	5.56	-26.23	-13.10	14.50
Return on Avg Stockholders' Equity %	68.54	-81.19	-29.62	31.81
Return on Average Assets %	17.99	-48.42	-20.74	22.33
Current Ratio	2.06	1.50	2.88	2.12
Debt / Equity %	471.35	n.a.	n.a.	n.a.

Compound Growth %'s	EPS %	14.47	Net Income %	6.90	Total Revenues %	47.15

Comments

Revenues increased 60% in fiscal 1998 due to increased demand for the Company's status and performance monitoring products and the Company's success in expanding its OEM and CATV customer relationships. Several new products were also introduced. Research and development expense totaled $3.9 million and $4.0 million in fiscal 1998 and 1997, respectively. Net operating loss carryforwards available for 1999 to 2012 total $22.5 million. For the nine months ended December 31, 1998, the Company reported revenues and a net loss of $7.0 million and $1,924,000 ($.06 per share) as compared to $12.2 million and a net profit of $832,000 ($.02 per share) for the same period of the preceding year.

Officers	Position	Ownership Information	
William H. Lambert	Chairman	Number of Shares Outstanding	31,072,296
Keith D. Schneck	President, CEO	Market Capitalization	$ 3,728,676
Michael L. Quelly	Vice President	Number of Shareholders	973
Joseph R. Rocci	Vice President	Where Listed / Symbol	OTC-BB / AMCM

Other Information			
Transfer Agent	Continental Stock Transfer & Trust Co. New York, NY	SIC Code	3663
Auditor	KPMG LLP	Employees	74
Market Maker	Paragon Capital Corporation	(800)521-8877	
	Mayer & Schweitzer, Inc.	(800)631-3094	

AMBI Inc.

771 Old Saw Mill River Road   Tarrytown, NY 10591   Telephone (914)347-5767   Fax (914)347-6370

Company Description

AMBI Inc. develops and commercializes nutrition products for cardiovascular and other conditions and develops pharmaceuticals for serious infectious diseases. The Company markets the nutrition products through a network of distributors. If the pharmaceutical products are approved by a regulatory authority, it is anticipated that such products will be commercialized by joint venture partners. On August 11, 1997, the Company acquired the entire beneficial interest in Nutrition 21, a partnership engaged in the business of developing, producing and marketing proprietary nutrition products and dietary supplements. AMBI was founded in 1983.

	06/30/98	06/30/97	06/30/96	06/30/95
Per Share Information				
Stock Price as of 12/31	1.00	1.78	3.00	4.00
Earnings Per Share	-0.04	-0.38	-0.34	0.01
Price / Earnings Ratio	n.a.	n.a.	n.a.	400.00
Book Value Per Share	0.36	0.27	0.50	0.42
Price / Book Value %	277.78	659.26	600.00	952.38
Dividends Per Share	0.0	0.0	0.0	0.0
Annual Financial Data				
Operating Results (000's)				
Total Revenues	20,829.0	11,713.0	16,342.0	11,874.0
Costs & Expenses	-19,661.0	-28,057.0	-20,776.0	-11,288.0
Income Before Taxes and Other	1,168.0	-16,344.0	-4,434.0	537.0
Other Items	0.0	9,683.0	0.0	0.0
Income Tax	-116.0	-152.0	-285.0	-254.0
Net Income	1,052.0	-6,813.0	-4,719.0	283.0
Cash Flow From Operations	1,891.0	-14,351.0	-6,602.0	-739.0
Balance Sheet (000's)				
Cash & Equivalents	2,109.0	8,615.0	8,431.0	3,337.0
Total Current Assets	6,625.0	10,015.0	17,749.0	9,359.0
Fixed Assets, Net	914.0	1,082.0	3,881.0	3,446.0
Total Assets	20,735.0	12,754.0	23,367.0	13,788.0
Total Current Liabilities	8,894.0	2,960.0	2,937.0	2,026.0
Long-Term Debt	1,543.0	2,184.0	2,935.0	770.0
Stockholders' Equity	10,298.0	7,610.0	17,146.0	10,625.0
Performance & Financial Condition				
Return on Total Revenues %	5.05	-58.17	-28.88	2.38
Return on Avg Stockholders' Equity %	11.75	-55.04	-33.99	2.02
Return on Average Assets %	6.28	-37.72	-25.40	1.57
Current Ratio	0.74	3.38	6.04	4.62
Debt / Equity %	14.98	28.70	17.12	7.25

Compound Growth %'s	EPS %	n.a.	Net Income %	54.91	Total Revenues %	20.60

Comments

Management attributes the increase in revenues and the return to profitability to the acquisition of Nutrition 21 and a reduction in marketing, sales and research costs. The acquisition was accounted for as a purchase. Therefore, operating results were combined starting with the date of the acquisition. Fiscal 1997 results include a nonrecurring gain of $9.7 million on the sale of a division. At June 30, 1998, patent costs and licensed technology relating to the acquisition of Nutrition 21 totalled $11.7 million and were included as assets on the balance sheet. This amount exceeds the book value of the Company. For the six months ended December 31, 1998, the Company reported revenues and earnings of $12.8 million and $3,807,000 ($.14 per share) as compared to $9.0 million and a net loss of $294,000 ($.07 per share) for the same period of the preceding year.

Officers	Position	Ownership Information	
Fredric D. Price	President, CEO	Number of Shares Outstanding	20,898,297
Alan V. Gallantar	Treasurer, Controller	Market Capitalization	$ 20,898,297
Jonathan de la Harpe	Vice President	Number of Shareholders	2,000
Victor Moreno	Vice President	Where Listed / Symbol	NASDAQ / AMBI

Other Information			
Transfer Agent	American Stock Transfer & Trust Company New York, NY	SIC Code	2836
Auditor	KPMG LLP	Employees	40
		Web Site	AMBIinc.com

AML Communications, Inc.

1000 Avenida Acaso   Camarillo, CA 93012   Telephone (805)388-1345   Fax (805)484-2191

Company Description

AML Communications, Inc. designs, manufactures and markets amplifiers and related products for the cellular, personal communication services (PCS) and other communication markets. AML's cellular products, introduced in late 1994, have historically been marketed mainly to cellular operators and are designed to enable them to significantly increase the quality and quantity of calls processed by new and existing cellular base stations. The Company has recently introduced products for the PCS marketplace. During fiscal 1997, the Company entered the satellite communication gateway market by offering a high power amplifier for data transmission applications in a low earth orbit satellite communication network. The Company was founded in 1986 and went public in 1995.

	03/31/98	03/31/97	03/31/96	03/31/95
Per Share Information				
Stock Price as of 12/31	1.28	4.12	13.37	10.37
Earnings Per Share	0.11	0.33	0.23	-0.01
Price / Earnings Ratio	11.64	12.48	58.13	n.a.
Book Value Per Share	2.18	2.09	1.67	0.12
Price / Book Value %	58.72	197.13	800.60	8,641.67
Dividends Per Share	0.0	0.0	0.0	0.0
Annual Financial Data				
Operating Results (000's)				
Total Revenues	13,155.0	14,327.0	7,083.0	2,606.0
Costs & Expenses	-12,087.0	-10,964.0	-5,163.0	-2,628.0
Income Before Taxes and Other	1,068.0	3,363.0	1,920.0	-22.0
Other Items	0.0	0.0	0.0	0.0
Income Tax	-382.0	-1,237.0	-723.0	0.0
Net Income	686.0	2,126.0	1,197.0	-22.0
Cash Flow From Operations	4,582.0	-1,306.0	475.0	n.a.
Balance Sheet (000's)				
Cash & Equivalents	8,608.0	4,766.0	6,312.0	257.0
Total Current Assets	13,114.0	12,099.0	10,506.0	1,145.0
Fixed Assets, Net	2,096.0	1,963.0	1,139.0	420.0
Total Assets	15,679.0	14,543.0	11,645.0	1,565.0
Total Current Liabilities	1,933.0	1,744.0	1,876.0	477.0
Long-Term Debt	0.0	0.0	360.0	621.0
Stockholders' Equity	13,708.0	12,737.0	9,409.0	467.0
Performance & Financial Condition				
Return on Total Revenues %	5.21	14.84	16.90	-0.84
Return on Avg Stockholders' Equity %	5.19	19.20	24.24	-0.63
Return on Average Assets %	4.54	16.24	18.12	-0.44
Current Ratio	6.78	6.94	5.60	2.40
Debt / Equity %	n.a.	n.a.	3.83	132.98

Compound Growth %'s	EPS %	-30.84	Net Income %	-24.30	Total Revenues %	71.54

Comments

The decline in fiscal 1998 sales is attributable to lower unit prices and increased volume due to increased competition. Sales outside the United States were lower than expected but increased from 5.3% of net sales in fiscal 1997 to 42.4% of net sales in fiscal 1998. However, 95.8% of fiscal 1998 foreign sales were to a single customer in Brazil. The Company continues to maintain a strong balance sheet. Research and development expenses totaled $1,962,000 and $1,510,000 in fiscal 1998 and 1997, respectively. For the nine months ended December 31, 1998, the Company reported revenues and a net loss of $6.7 million and $955,000 ($.15 per share) as compared to $8.9 million and a net profit of $497,000 ($.08 per share) for the same period of the preceding year.

Officers	Position	Ownership Information	
Jacob Inbar	President, CEO	Number of Shares Outstanding	6,291,930
Kirk A. Waldron	VP - Finance, CFO	Market Capitalization	$ 8,053,670
Tiberiu Mazilu	Vice President	Number of Shareholders	1,000
Edwin J. McAvoy	VP - Sales	Where Listed / Symbol	NASDAQ / AMLJ

Other Information			
Transfer Agent	ChaseMellon Shareholder Services Los Angeles, CA	SIC Code	3663
Auditor	Arthur Andersen LLP	Employees	101

ASA International Ltd.

10 Speen Street   Framingham, MA 01701   Telephone (508)626-2727   Fax (508)626-0638

Company Description

ASA International Ltd. provides networked automation systems and ongoing monthly support to approximately 900 businesses in the United States, Canada, and Australia. The Company designs and develops proprietary enterprise and point-solution software to the electronic time and labor recording market, for catalog direct marketers, for the automotive aftermarket and legal markets, and for wineries, chemical companies and furniture manufacturers. The Company installs this software on a variety of computers and networks, and provides implementation, training, and long-term software and hardware support to its clients. ASA was founded in 1969.

	12/31/98	12/31/97	12/31/96	12/31/95
Per Share Information				
Stock Price	2.25	2.25	0.97	1.44
Earnings Per Share	0.11	0.11	-0.17	0.11
Price / Earnings Ratio	20.45	20.45	n.a.	13.09
Book Value Per Share	2.63	2.56	2.51	2.67
Price / Book Value %	85.55	87.89	38.65	53.93
Dividends Per Share	0.0	0.0	0.0	0.0
Annual Financial Data				
Operating Results (000's)				
Total Revenues	35,609.0	25,597.5	25,471.0	31,043.3
Costs & Expenses	-34,539.4	-24,440.4	-26,040.0	-29,993.9
Income Before Taxes and Other	1,069.6	973.2	-891.3	1,049.3
Other Items	0.0	0.0	0.0	0.0
Income Tax	-653.0	-585.0	242.0	-592.0
Net Income	416.6	388.2	-649.3	457.3
Cash Flow From Operations	3,605.6	1,884.0	2,502.1	2,261.9
Balance Sheet (000's)				
Cash & Equivalents	4,262.4	1,282.8	674.2	404.0
Total Current Assets	11,467.1	8,098.9	5,226.1	6,476.0
Fixed Assets, Net	4,842.5	4,281.4	4,352.4	4,705.1
Total Assets	19,732.4	17,825.7	16,630.0	19,515.2
Total Current Liabilities	6,118.7	6,116.1	5,226.2	6,081.2
Long-Term Debt	4,067.8	2,696.0	3,012.0	2,707.5
Stockholders' Equity	8,809.1	8,397.6	8,011.8	10,109.6
Performance & Financial Condition				
Return on Total Revenues %	1.17	1.52	-2.55	1.47
Return on Avg Stockholders' Equity %	4.84	4.73	-7.17	4.63
Return on Average Assets %	2.22	2.25	-3.59	2.31
Current Ratio	1.87	1.32	1.00	1.06
Debt / Equity %	46.18	32.10	37.59	26.78

Compound Growth %'s	EPS %	0.00	Net Income %	-3.06	Total Revenues %	4.68

Comments

Revenues spurted upward by 39% in 1998. Approximately one-third of the increase was attributable to an acquisition with the balance derived from internal growth. In March 1999, the Company completed the disposition of a its CommercialWare Division which accounted for approximately 30% of Company revenue in each of the last two years. A gain on this transaction will be reported in 1999. The net loss in 1996 resulted from a decline in computer hardware sales and a corporate restructuring that included the sale of a division to a former employee. Approximately $6.7 million of 1996 revenue related to the division that was sold. Therefore compound growth rates in revenue are partially distorted.

Officers	Position	Ownership Information	
Alfred C. Angelone	President, CEO	Number of Shares Outstanding	3,348,462
Terrence C. McCarthy	Vice President, Treasurer	Market Capitalization	$ 7,534,040
William A. Kulok	Director	Number of Shareholders	1,277
James P. O'Halloran	Director	Where Listed / Symbol	NASDAQ / ASAA

Other Information			
Transfer Agent	American Securities Transfer, Inc. Lakewood, CO	SIC Code	7373
Auditor	BDO Seidman LLP	Employees	213
		Web Site	asaint.com

ATS Money Systems, Inc.

25 Rockwood Place   Englewood, NJ 07631   Telephone (201)894-1700   Fax (201)894-0958

Company Description

ATS Money Systems, Inc. is engaged in the development, sale and service of 1) currency counting systems and equipment for department and chain stores' cash offices and bank commercial vaults, and 2) specialized information communications systems primarily used by chain stores. The Company's customers are businesses that handle a large number of cash, check and credit transactions on a daily basis, such as banks, department stores and chain stores. The Company was founded in 1987.

	12/31/98	12/31/97	12/31/96	12/31/95
Per Share Information				
Stock Price	0.91	0.78	0.47	1.10
Earnings Per Share	0.10	0.11	0.05	0.06
Price / Earnings Ratio	9.10	7.09	9.40	18.33
Book Value Per Share	0.61	0.53	0.41	0.35
Price / Book Value %	149.18	147.17	114.63	314.29
Dividends Per Share	0.0	0.0	0.0	0.0
Annual Financial Data				
Operating Results (000's)				
Total Revenues	11,811.5	9,802.5	8,098.2	8,438.7
Costs & Expenses	-10,801.1	-8,693.0	-7,581.6	-7,881.2
Income Before Taxes and Other	1,010.4	1,109.5	516.6	557.5
Other Items	0.0	0.0	0.0	0.0
Income Tax	-437.4	-443.8	-199.3	-187.9
Net Income	573.0	665.7	317.4	369.7
Cash Flow From Operations	743.4	1,166.7	728.0	-58.8
Balance Sheet (000's)				
Cash & Equivalents	286.4	424.2	308.1	164.5
Total Current Assets	4,200.4	3,352.0	2,360.0	2,418.4
Fixed Assets, Net	132.4	163.9	134.6	84.6
Total Assets	6,100.7	5,088.2	3,453.9	3,199.7
Total Current Liabilities	2,494.7	1,836.4	847.9	937.1
Long-Term Debt	160.4	0.0	217.4	246.0
Stockholders' Equity	3,445.6	3,062.9	2,388.5	2,016.6
Performance & Financial Condition				
Return on Total Revenues %	4.85	6.79	3.92	4.38
Return on Avg Stockholders' Equity %	17.61	24.42	14.41	20.20
Return on Average Assets %	10.24	15.59	9.54	12.46
Current Ratio	1.68	1.83	2.78	2.58
Debt / Equity %	4.66	n.a.	9.10	12.20

Compound Growth %'s	EPS %	18.56	Net Income %	15.73	Total Revenues %	11.86

Comments

Revenues rose a dramatic 48.2% in 1998 primarily as the result of equipment and system sales and maintenance services to one major customer. But lower profit margins offset the benefit of the higher sales level and the Company finished the year with a small decline in net profit. Management believes that the economic conditions within the retail industry, from which the Company draws its largest customers, will continue to improve. Sales to three major customers made up approximately 63% of total revenues for 1998. In 1998, the Company commenced a program to repurchase 500,000 shares of its common stock. During 1998, 181,500 shares were purchased at an average price of $1.08 per share.

Officers	Position	Ownership Information	
Gerard F. Murphy	President, CEO	Number of Shares Outstanding	5,660,047
James H. Halpin	Exec VP	Market Capitalization	$ 5,150,643
Joseph M. Burke	VP - Finance, CFO	Number of Shareholders	392
Michael M. Smith	Treasurer	Where Listed / Symbol	OTC-BB / ATSM

Other Information			
Transfer Agent	American Stock Transfer & Trust Co. New York, NY	SIC Code	3578
Auditor	Deloitte & Touche LLP	Employees	55
Market Maker	Paragon Capital Corporation	(800)345-0505	Web Site	atsmoney.com
	M.H. Meyerson & Co., Inc.	(800)333-3113		

Aasche Transportation Services, Inc.

10214 North Mount Vernon Road   Shannon, IL 61078   Telephone (815)864-2421   Fax (815)864-2646

Company Description

Aasche Transportation Services, Inc., founded in 1939, operated primarily in the temperature-controlled segment of the transportation services industry until 1998. The Company transports a variety of foods and other products that require temperature-controlled service and "just-in-time" delivery. The "just-in-time" concept stresses the importance of precise delivery times and the need for dependability in order to control inventory levels and limit handling. A substantial portion of the Company's business is concentrated in target markets in the Midwest, Southeast, Northeast and South Central United States. The Company uses sophisticated satellite communication and advanced computer systems to increase operating and administrative efficiencies. On January 30, 1998, the Company acquired Specialty Transportation services, Inc. which is the only national and the largest for-hire carrier of municipal solid waste and special waste in transfer vehicles in the United States. Since that date the Company has operated in two industry segments.

	12/31/98	12/31/97	12/31/96	12/31/95
Per Share Information				
Stock Price	4.00	3.87	5.12	5.25
Earnings Per Share	0.01	0.06	-0.67	-0.35
Price / Earnings Ratio	400.00	64.50	n.a.	n.a.
Book Value Per Share	3.07	2.82	2.66	3.30
Price / Book Value %	130.29	137.23	192.48	159.09
Dividends Per Share	0.0	0.0	0.0	0.0
Annual Financial Data				
Operating Results (000's)				
Total Revenues	114,312.0	65,237.0	77,501.0	67,748.0
Costs & Expenses	-113,359.0	-64,461.0	-81,442.0	-68,275.0
Income Before Taxes and Other	953.0	776.0	-3,941.0	-527.0
Other Items	0.0	0.0	0.0	-261.0
Income Tax	-830.0	-506.0	1,321.0	-538.0
Net Income	123.0	270.0	-2,620.0	-1,326.0
Cash Flow From Operations	490.0	2,566.0	6,535.0	7,440.0
Balance Sheet (000's)				
Cash & Equivalents	2,761.0	0.0	0.0	503.0
Total Current Assets	24,655.0	8,140.0	8,715.0	8,588.0
Fixed Assets, Net	45,403.0	19,176.0	29,552.0	49,769.0
Total Assets	88,278.0	35,507.0	46,304.0	65,357.0
Total Current Liabilities	60,979.0	13,466.0	20,316.0	20,383.0
Long-Term Debt	2,237.0	3,745.0	5,767.0	7,000.0
Stockholders' Equity	14,429.0	12,809.0	10,531.0	12,905.0
Performance & Financial Condition				
Return on Total Revenues %	0.11	0.41	-3.38	-1.95
Return on Avg Stockholders' Equity %	0.90	2.31	-22.36	-12.50
Return on Average Assets %	0.20	0.66	-4.69	-2.35
Current Ratio	0.40	0.60	0.43	0.42
Debt / Equity %	15.50	29.24	54.76	54.24

Compound Growth %'s	EPS % n.a.	Net Income % n.a.	Total Revenues % 19.05

Comments

The increase in 1998 revenues as compared to 1997 is entirely attributable to the acquisition. Revenue from pre-existing operations declined by 6.8% in the same period. The Company has been marginally profitable for two consecutive years. Expenses related to acquisitions and reorganizations resulted in numerous non-recurring items in 1995 and 1996. At December 31, 1998, the Company had $14.2 million of goodwill recorded as assets which equated to approximately 98% of stockholders' equity and book value per share. The Company also had a substantial deficiency in working capital and was in violation of certain loan covenants. These factors caused a going concern qualification in the auditors report on the Company's financial statements.

Officers	Position	Ownership Information	
Larry L. Asche	Chairman, CEO	Number of Shares Outstanding	4,696,130
Kevin M. Clark	President	Market Capitalization	$ 18,784,520
Daniel R. Wright	COO	Number of Shareholders	2,700
Leon M. Monachos	CFO, Treasurer	Where Listed / Symbol	NASDAQ / ASHE

Other Information			
Transfer Agent	Continental Stock Transfer & Trust Co. New York, NY	SIC Code	4213
Auditor	Ernst & Young LLP	Employees	1,170
		Web Site	aschetransfer.com

Abatix Environmental Corp.

8311 Eastpoint Drive, Suite 400   Dallas, TX 75227   Telephone (214)381-1146   Fax (214)381-9513

Company Description

Abatix Environmental Corp., founded in 1983, is a full line supplier of durable and nondurable supplies to the asbestos and lead abatement, hazardous materials, industrial safety and construction tools industries. Eight distribution centers serve customers throughout the Southwest, Midwest, Pacific Coast, Alaska and Hawaii. Approximately 48% of the Company's sales are to asbestos and lead abatement contractors, 23% to the industrial safety market, 12% to construction-related firms, and 17% to other firms including hazardous material contractors. Management believes it has about a 15% to 20% market share in the markets it serves and that serving these industries will continue to be its primary emphasis in the near future.

	12/31/98	12/31/97	12/31/96	12/31/95
Per Share Information				
Stock Price	3.44	2.63	2.88	2.88
Earnings Per Share	0.60	0.43	0.36	0.36
Price / Earnings Ratio	5.73	6.12	8.00	8.00
Book Value Per Share	3.26	2.67	2.24	2.00
Price / Book Value %	105.52	98.50	128.57	144.00
Dividends Per Share	0.0	0.0	0.0	0.0
Annual Financial Data				
Operating Results (000's)				
Total Revenues	37,345.9	34,991.7	33,086.7	27,647.6
Costs & Expenses	-35,458.0	-33,639.7	-31,875.4	-26,335.2
Income Before Taxes and Other	1,887.8	1,332.7	1,195.3	1,306.9
Other Items	0.0	0.0	21.5	0.0
Income Tax	-720.4	-491.6	-460.9	-493.5
Net Income	1,167.4	841.1	755.9	813.4
Cash Flow From Operations	419.5	2,133.0	-1,064.5	1,187.8
Balance Sheet (000's)				
Cash & Equivalents	224.0	304.9	310.3	415.9
Total Current Assets	9,918.4	9,003.5	9,722.0	8,229.6
Fixed Assets, Net	451.0	632.1	763.6	593.1
Total Assets	10,595.5	9,854.2	10,678.0	8,976.9
Total Current Liabilities	4,408.3	4,676.6	6,219.4	4,659.2
Long-Term Debt	0.0	0.0	0.0	0.0
Stockholders' Equity	6,187.2	5,177.7	4,458.5	4,317.8
Performance & Financial Condition				
Return on Total Revenues %	3.13	2.40	2.28	2.94
Return on Avg Stockholders' Equity %	20.54	17.46	17.23	19.79
Return on Average Assets %	11.42	8.19	7.69	9.48
Current Ratio	2.25	1.93	1.56	1.77
Debt / Equity %	n.a.	n.a.	n.a.	n.a.

Compound Growth %'s	EPS %	18.56	Net Income %	12.80	Total Revenues %	10.54

Comments

The Company's sales have continued to increase as a result of its efforts to further expand and diversify its customer base. This diversification is also important since the asbestos abatement industry will likely diminish over time as building materials containing asbestos are removed from schools, houses and office buildings. The Company does not believe that the current and intermediate term effect of a diminishing market will have a material adverse effect on the Company. The Company's profitability has also been increasing which is linked to better margins. In January 1999, the Company acquired Keliher Hardware Company, an industrial supply distributor, which is expected to provide a larger customer base and the ability to cross sell products to customers of both Companies. Since November 1994, the Company has repurchased 517,700 shares of its common stock.

Officers	Position	Ownership Information	
Terry W. Shaver	President, CEO	Number of Shares Outstanding	1,896,114
Gary L. Cox	Exec VP, COO	Market Capitalization	$ 6,522,632
Frank J. Cinatl, IV	Vice President, CFO	Number of Shareholders	700
Donald N. Black	Director	Where Listed / Symbol	NASDAQ / ABIX

Other Information			
Transfer Agent	North American Transfer Co. Freeport, NY	SIC Code	5085
Auditor	KPMG LLP	Employees	103
		Web Site	abatix.com

Accuhealth, Inc.

1575 Bronx River Avenue   Bronx, NY 10460   Telephone (718)518-9511   Fax (718)824-2432

Company Description

Accuhealth, Inc. provides comprehensive home health care services, including administration of a wide array of infusion therapies, sales of oral medications and sales and rentals of durable medical equipment and related supplies. Much of the medical services are provided to critically ill home-bound patients. Services are provided to patients throughout the states of New York, New Jersey and Connecticut. The Company has acquired other related businesses over the last two years including Healix Healthcare, Inc., which was acquired on April 9, 1998. Accuhealth was formed in 1983.

	03/31/98	03/31/97	03/31/96	03/31/95
Per Share Information				
Stock Price as of 12/31	0.81	1.12	0.75	1.75
Earnings Per Share	-0.21	-0.03	-0.77	0.24
Price / Earnings Ratio	n.a.	n.a.	n.a.	7.29
Book Value Per Share	-0.61	-0.90	-1.09	1.30
Price / Book Value %	n.a.	n.a.	n.a.	134.62
Dividends Per Share	0.0	0.0	0.0	0.0
Annual Financial Data				
Operating Results (000's)				
Total Revenues	18,603.8	16,369.4	15,112.1	15,468.4
Costs & Expenses	-18,515.1	-16,242.6	-15,890.4	-15,806.6
Income Before Taxes and Other	-206.1	126.7	-778.3	676.1
Other Items	0.0	0.0	0.0	-325.6
Income Tax	0.0	0.0	0.0	0.0
Net Income	-206.1	126.7	-778.3	350.6
Cash Flow From Operations	-881.6	-438.8	-1,036.3	-2,034.9
Balance Sheet (000's)				
Cash & Equivalents	166.6	31.5	2.7	147.3
Total Current Assets	8,281.7	6,167.6	5,187.3	4,519.2
Fixed Assets, Net	1,788.3	2,144.4	2,429.0	2,640.6
Total Assets	12,193.6	8,500.2	7,651.0	7,294.9
Total Current Liabilities	9,564.7	6,104.2	5,868.0	4,582.5
Long-Term Debt	551.6	601.0	0.0	694.6
Stockholders' Equity	1,654.5	1,421.4	1,294.6	2,017.8
Performance & Financial Condition				
Return on Total Revenues %	-1.11	0.77	-5.15	2.27
Return on Avg Stockholders' Equity %	-13.40	9.33	-46.99	43.84
Return on Average Assets %	-1.99	1.57	-10.42	4.64
Current Ratio	0.87	1.01	0.88	0.99
Debt / Equity %	33.34	42.29	n.a.	34.42

Compound Growth %'s	EPS % n.a.	Net Income % n.a.	Total Revenues %	6.35

Comments

Approximately 39% of the increase in revenues is derived from acquisitions. Merger related costs totaled $295,000 and were expensed in fiscal 1998. At the end of fiscal 1998, the Company had a working capital deficit of $1,283,000. The Company discontinued its retail drugstore operations resulting in a charge to operations of $278,000 for fiscal 1995. Earnings per share are calculated after deduction of the preferred stock dividend. For the nine months ended December 31, 1998, the Company reported revenues of $27.5 million and a net loss $1,097,000 ($.32 per share) as compared to $13.4 million and a net profit of $218,569 ($.05 per share) for the same period of the prior year. The Company has demonstrated that it can continue to grow despite a relatively lean financial condition.

Officers	Position	Ownership Information	
Stanley Goldstein	Chairman	Number of Shares Outstanding	1,801,118
Glenn C. Davis	President, CEO	Market Capitalization	$ 1,458,906
Jeffrey S. Freed	Exec VP	Number of Shareholders	300
Mary Comerford	Senior VP, COO	Where Listed / Symbol	OTC-BB / AHLT

Other Information			
Transfer Agent	North American Transfer Co. Freeport, NY	SIC Code	8082
Auditor	Marcum & Kliegman LLP	Employees	96
Market Maker	Herzog, Heine, Geduld, Inc. (800)221-3600		
	Janney Montgomery Scott Inc. (215)563-8671		

Acme Electric Corporation

400 Quaker Road   East Aurora, NY 14052   Telephone (716)655-3800   Fax (716)655-3348

Company Description

Acme Electric Corporation designs, manufactures and markets power conversion equipment for electronic and electrical systems. Principal markets encompass computers, test equipment, information systems, military, aerospace, telecommunications and a variety of industrial, commercial and residential applications requiring conversion of electrical energy from one usable state to another. Approximately 7% of the Company's workforce is engaged in engineering design and product development. The Company was founded in 1917.

	06/30/98	06/30/97	06/30/96	06/30/95
Per Share Information				
Stock Price as of 12/31	4.75	4.87	6.75	9.12
Earnings Per Share	0.50	0.03	-0.06	0.20
Price / Earnings Ratio	9.50	162.33	n.a.	45.60
Book Value Per Share	3.78	3.27	3.18	3.22
Price / Book Value %	125.66	148.93	212.26	283.23
Dividends Per Share	0.0	0.0	0.0	0.0
Annual Financial Data				
Operating Results (000's)				
Total Revenues	90,916.0	94,062.0	96,551.0	91,127.0
Costs & Expenses	-86,822.0	-93,817.0	-96,949.0	-89,517.0
Income Before Taxes and Other	4,094.0	245.0	-398.0	1,610.0
Other Items	0.0	0.0	0.0	0.0
Income Tax	-1,565.0	-109.0	118.0	-618.0
Net Income	2,529.0	136.0	-280.0	992.0
Cash Flow From Operations	7,585.0	5,748.0	3,549.0	-605.0
Balance Sheet (000's)				
Cash & Equivalents	629.0	398.0	828.0	386.0
Total Current Assets	27,106.0	29,694.0	33,058.0	39,437.0
Fixed Assets, Net	15,115.0	16,039.0	16,469.0	14,657.0
Total Assets	45,495.0	50,144.0	54,180.0	56,178.0
Total Current Liabilities	11,864.0	12,975.0	11,963.0	14,447.0
Long-Term Debt	12,833.0	19,198.0	24,394.0	24,419.0
Stockholders' Equity	19,075.0	16,488.0	15,684.0	15,849.0
Performance & Financial Condition				
Return on Total Revenues %	2.78	0.14	-0.29	1.09
Return on Avg Stockholders' Equity %	14.22	0.85	-1.78	6.52
Return on Average Assets %	5.29	0.26	-0.51	1.91
Current Ratio	2.28	2.29	2.76	2.73
Debt / Equity %	67.28	116.44	155.53	154.07

Compound Growth %'s	EPS % 35.72	Net Income % 36.61	Total Revenues % -0.08

Comments

The Company has just finished a three year process of transforming its manufacturing operations, bringing them to a new level of performance that is expected to allow them to compete more effectively in the global marketplace. Manufacturing overheads were reduced substantially. Fiscal 1998 revenue declined due to a negative sales trend in the electronics business which was partially offset by an increase in sales to the military/aerospace market. But operating results were impressive and the debt/equity ratio has improved dramatically. Fiscal 1997 results include a one-time charge of $725,000 related to the Company's only known environmental problem which has now been settled. For the six months ended December 31, 1998, the Company reported revenues and net income of $41.2 million and $924,000 ($.18 per share) as compared to $44.9 million and $668,000 ($.13 per share) for the same period of the preceding year.

Officers	Position	Ownership Information	
Robert J. McKenna	President, CEO	Number of Shares Outstanding	5,050,745
John B. Drenning	Secretary	Market Capitalization	$ 23,991,039
Daniel K. Corwin	Vice President, General Manager	Number of Shareholders	1,206
Nicola T. Arena	Vice President, General Manager	Where Listed / Symbol	NYSE / ACE

Other Information			
Transfer Agent	American Stock Transfer & Trust Co. New York, NY	SIC Code	3629
Auditor	PricewaterhouseCoopers LLP	Employees	630
		Web Site	acmeelec.com

Adams Golf, Inc.

300 Delaware Avenue, Suite 548   Wilmington, DE 19801   Telephone (302)427-5892

Company Description

Adams Golf, Inc. designs, manufactures and markets premium quality, technologically innovative golf clubs. The Company's design objective is to produce golf clubs that deliver meaningful performance benefits and inspire player confidence. The Company believes that its most successful product line to date, the Tight Lies fairway woods, meets this objective by providing golfers with the ability to hit the ball from virtually any lie while maximizing distance. The patented Tight Lies fairway woods feature an upright trapezoidal head, a shallow face and a lower center of gravity as compared to conventional fairway woods. The Company went public in 1998.

	12/31/98	12/31/97	12/31/96	12/31/95
Per Share Information				
Stock Price	4.06	n.a.	n.a.	n.a.
Earnings Per Share	0.61	-0.37	0.0	-0.05
Price / Earnings Ratio	6.66	n.a.	n.a.	n.a.
Book Value Per Share	3.92	0.53	0.13	n.a.
Price / Book Value %	103.57	n.a.	n.a.	n.a.
Dividends Per Share	0.0	0.0	0.0	0.0
Annual Financial Data				
Operating Results (000's)				
Total Revenues	85,978.0	36,705.4	3,525.7	1,126.3
Costs & Expenses	-66,182.0	-40,729.1	-3,513.0	-1,369.0
Income Before Taxes and Other	19,693.0	-4,071.5	12.7	-242.7
Other Items	0.0	0.0	0.0	0.0
Income Tax	-7,183.0	-582.8	0.0	0.0
Net Income	12,510.0	-4,654.2	12.7	-242.7
Cash Flow From Operations	3,716.0	1,100.3	-396.1	-396.1
Balance Sheet (000's)				
Cash & Equivalents	23,688.0	1,955.6	854.5	n.a.
Total Current Assets	58,752.0	15,949.9	2,055.1	n.a.
Fixed Assets, Net	3,468.0	603.8	124.0	n.a.
Total Assets	96,906.0	17,360.1	2,558.7	n.a.
Total Current Liabilities	5,745.0	9,034.8	580.4	n.a.
Long-Term Debt	0.0	0.0	0.0	n.a.
Stockholders' Equity	88,190.0	8,325.3	1,978.4	n.a.
Performance & Financial Condition				
Return on Total Revenues %	14.55	-12.68	0.36	-21.54
Return on Avg Stockholders' Equity %	25.92	-90.34	0.98	-80.89
Return on Average Assets %	21.90	-46.73	0.79	-69.33
Current Ratio	10.23	1.77	3.54	n.a.
Debt / Equity %	n.a.	n.a.	n.a.	n.a.

Compound Growth %'s	EPS % n.a.	Net Income % n.a.	Total Revenues % 324.20

Comments

Net sales increased 131% in 1998 primarily due to the continued market acceptance of the Company's Tight Lies Line of fairway woods and, to a lesser extent, the introduction of new products. The Company introduced the SC Series Titanium drivers and the Faldo Series wedges in January 1999. Accordingly, no sales for these products are reflected above. Despite declining sales in the industry as a whole, 1998 was a great year for the Company with an impressive bottom line. Proceeds of the public offering were used for working capital and general corporate purposes, including capital expenditures, expansion of the Company's product development efforts, additional advertising and expansion of the Company's international sales efforts. The December 31, 1998 balance sheet is flush with cash and marketable securities which totalled $58.1 million ($2.58 per share).

Officers	Position	Ownership Information	
B.H. (Barney) Adams	President, CEO	Number of Shares Outstanding	22,479,282
Darl P. Hatfield	Senior VP, CFO	Market Capitalization	$ 91,265,885
James E. Farrell	VP - Finance	Number of Shareholders	7,000
Richard H. Murtland	Vice President, Secretary	Where Listed / Symbol	NASDAQ / ADGO

Other Information			
Transfer Agent	American Stock Transfer & Trust Co. New York, NY	SIC Code	3949
Auditor	KPMG LLP	Employees	248
		Web Site	adamsgolf.com

Advanced Deposition Technologies, Inc.

580 Myles Standish Industrial Park   Taunton, MA 02780   Telephone (508)823-0707   Fax (508)823-4434

Company Description

Advanced Deposition Technologies, Inc., founded in 1985, develops, manufactures, markets and sells standard and proprietary metallized films for energy management applications. The Company's primary markets are the electronic capacitor market and the microwave food packaging market. The Company produces metallized films by applying an ultra-thin layer or layers of vaporized metal onto different types of polymer films. These thin films are then incorporated into a wide variety of end-use applications such as capacitors for florescent lighting, motors, power factor correction systems and microwave food packaging for pizza, popcorn, pastries and other foods. The Company acquired operations in Madrid, Spain in December 1997, and Kuala Lumpur, Malaysia in October 1998.

	12/31/98	12/31/97	12/31/96	12/31/95
Per Share Information				
Stock Price	1.22	4.06	3.62	2.37
Earnings Per Share	-0.63	-0.09	0.35	0.0
Price / Earnings Ratio	n.a.	n.a.	10.34	n.a.
Book Value Per Share	1.74	2.35	2.52	1.29
Price / Book Value %	70.11	172.77	143.65	183.72
Dividends Per Share	0.0	0.0	0.0	0.0
Annual Financial Data				
Operating Results (000's)				
Total Revenues	23,853.0	12,341.0	10,595.0	9,555.0
Costs & Expenses	-25,073.0	-12,699.0	-9,295.0	-9,549.0
Income Before Taxes and Other	-1,220.0	-358.0	1,300.0	6.0
Other Items	-1,377.0	0.0	0.0	0.0
Income Tax	-98.0	-4.0	0.0	0.0
Net Income	-2,695.0	-362.0	1,300.0	6.0
Cash Flow From Operations	97.0	177.0	-1,421.0	-224.0
Balance Sheet (000's)				
Cash & Equivalents	411.0	919.0	1,170.0	598.0
Total Current Assets	10,848.0	11,574.0	5,653.0	4,878.0
Fixed Assets, Net	7,676.0	6,331.0	5,189.0	5,456.0
Total Assets	23,950.0	23,943.0	12,582.0	10,334.0
Total Current Liabilities	10,343.0	9,869.0	1,441.0	6,258.0
Long-Term Debt	4,010.0	3,298.0	2,034.0	0.0
Stockholders' Equity	7,383.0	9,981.0	9,107.0	4,059.0
Performance & Financial Condition				
Return on Total Revenues %	-11.30	-2.93	12.27	0.06
Return on Avg Stockholders' Equity %	-31.04	-3.79	19.75	0.09
Return on Average Assets %	-11.25	-1.98	11.35	0.05
Current Ratio	1.05	1.17	3.92	0.78
Debt / Equity %	54.31	33.04	22.33	n.a.

Compound Growth %'s	EPS % n.a.	Net Income % n.a.	Total Revenues % 35.66

Comments

Acquisitions accounted for the entire increase in revenues recorded for 1998 and offset $4.3 million of sales declines related to a line of "home use" food reheating bags. The Company also wrote off $1,108,000 of assets associated with this product. Organizational restructuring was planned for the second quarter of 1999 as we went to press. Part of what must be addressed is dwindling working capital. At December 31, 1998, the Company had $3.9 million of goodwill reflected as assets which equated to approximately 53% of stockholders' equity and book value per share. At that date the Company also had $4.8 million of tax loss carryovers available to offset future income.

Officers	Position	Ownership Information	
Glenn J. Walters	President, CEO	Number of Shares Outstanding	4,253,950
John J. Moroney	COO	Market Capitalization	$ 5,189,819
Mark R. Thomas	CFO	Number of Shareholders	1,986
Richard W. Cowen	Vice President	Where Listed / Symbol	NASDAQ / ADTC

Other Information			
Transfer Agent	American Securities Transfer, Inc. Denver, CO	SIC Code	3490
Auditor	BDO Seidman LLP	Employees	242
		Web Site	adv-dep.com

Advanced Photonix, Inc.

1240 Avenida Acaso   Camarillo, CA 93012   Telephone (805)987-0146   Fax (805)484-9935

Company Description

Advanced Photonix, Inc. is engaged in the development and manufacture of proprietary and other solid state light and radiation detection devices. The Company believes that its technology represents a leading-edge advancement in photodetection and imaging and is an alternative to photomultiplier vacuum tubes which have been used for many years as the primary technological solution for highly sensitive light detection in certain measurement, control and monitoring applications used in industrial, medical, military, scientific and commercial settings. The Company was founded in 1988.

	03/29/98	03/30/97	03/31/96	04/02/95
Per Share Information				
Stock Price as of 12/31	0.69	2.00	2.75	1.25
Earnings Per Share	0.0	-0.17	-0.28	-0.28
Price / Earnings Ratio	n.a.	n.a.	n.a.	n.a.
Book Value Per Share	0.47	0.47	0.64	0.41
Price / Book Value %	146.81	425.53	429.69	304.88
Dividends Per Share	0.0	0.0	0.0	0.0
Annual Financial Data				
Operating Results (000's)				
Total Revenues	7,133.0	6,550.0	8,019.0	6,877.0
Costs & Expenses	-7,123.0	-8,436.0	-8,673.0	-9,227.0
Income Before Taxes and Other	10.0	-1,886.0	-654.0	-2,368.0
Other Items	0.0	0.0	0.0	0.0
Income Tax	0.0	0.0	0.0	0.0
Net Income	10.0	-1,886.0	-654.0	-2,368.0
Cash Flow From Operations	271.0	-2,522.0	241.0	-1,618.0
Balance Sheet (000's)				
Cash & Equivalents	1,386.0	1,217.0	4,042.0	903.0
Total Current Assets	4,986.0	4,453.0	5,733.0	3,101.0
Fixed Assets, Net	698.0	967.0	1,160.0	1,679.0
Total Assets	6,366.0	6,165.0	7,706.0	5,580.0
Total Current Liabilities	1,249.0	1,119.0	802.0	1,018.0
Long-Term Debt	0.0	0.0	0.0	26.0
Stockholders' Equity	5,117.0	5,046.0	6,806.0	4,438.0
Performance & Financial Condition				
Return on Total Revenues %	0.14	-28.79	-8.16	-34.43
Return on Avg Stockholders' Equity %	0.20	-31.83	-11.63	-47.36
Return on Average Assets %	0.16	-27.19	-9.84	-39.47
Current Ratio	3.99	3.98	7.15	3.05
Debt / Equity %	n.a.	n.a.	n.a.	0.59

Compound Growth %'s	EPS % n.a.	Net Income % n.a.	Total Revenues % 1.23

Comments

With an increase in revenues, due to higher shipments of military aerospace products, and a reduction in research and development costs, the Company has turned its first net profit in many years. New technology remains early in its commercialization stage and represents only 3% of revenue. A private placement of shares in 1995 contributed to a strong balance sheet despite ongoing losses. But now is the time to see if all these past efforts will produce meaningful earnings on a per share basis. For the nine months ended December 31, 1998, the Company reported revenues and net income of $5.8 million and $400,000 ($.04 per share) as compared to $5.0 million and a net loss of $92,000 ($.01 per share) for the same period of the preceding year.

Officers	Position	Ownership Information	
Harry Melkonian	President, CEO	Number of Shares Outstanding	10,838,260
Patrick J. Holmes	Exec VP, CFO	Market Capitalization	$ 7,478,399
Robert G. Allison	Director	Number of Shareholders	1,300
James A. Gordon	Director	Where Listed / Symbol	AMEX / API

Other Information			
Transfer Agent	Continental Stock Transfer & Trust Co. New York, NY	SIC Code	3674
Auditor	Arthur Andersen LLP	Employees	61

Advanced Tobacco Products, Inc.

16607 Blanco Road, Suite 1504   San Antonio, TX 78232   Telephone (210)408-7077   Fax (210)408-7077

Company Description

Advanced Tobacco Products, Inc., doing business as Advanced Therapeutic Products, Inc. was organized to develop and market a product based on nicotine technology. In 1987, the Company sold its nicotine technology and related assets to Pharmacia & Upjohn, Inc., a worldwide pharmaceutical company, under royalty payment agreements. Based on the transferred technology, Pharmacia & Upjohn developed the Nicotrol/Nicorette Inhaler for use in nicotine replacement therapy. In early September 1998, McNeil Consumer Products Company, a Johnson & Johnson Company and sub-licensee of the technology, launched the Inhaler nationwide in the United States as a prescription product.

	06/30/98	06/30/97	06/30/96	06/30/95
Per Share Information				
Stock Price as of 12/31	0.84	0.84	0.82	0.12
Earnings Per Share	0.06	0.01	0.0	0.0
Price / Earnings Ratio	14.00	84.00	n.a.	n.a.
Book Value Per Share	0.25	0.20	0.19	0.19
Price / Book Value %	336.00	420.00	431.58	63.16
Dividends Per Share	0.0	0.0	0.0	0.0
Annual Financial Data				
Operating Results (000's)				
Total Revenues	593.9	235.9	76.9	100.3
Costs & Expenses	-126.8	-141.2	-91.8	-103.4
Income Before Taxes and Other	467.1	94.8	-15.0	-3.1
Other Items	0.0	0.0	0.0	0.0
Income Tax	0.0	0.0	0.0	0.0
Net Income	467.1	94.8	-15.0	-3.1
Cash Flow From Operations	93.0	-51.2	-98.7	-62.0
Balance Sheet (000's)				
Cash & Equivalents	91.4	38.9	84.9	86.4
Total Current Assets	942.7	572.8	322.4	403.2
Fixed Assets, Net	0.0	0.0	0.0	0.0
Total Assets	2,063.7	1,600.5	1,485.0	1,495.3
Total Current Liabilities	2.8	6.8	3.5	18.8
Long-Term Debt	0.0	0.0	0.0	0.0
Stockholders' Equity	2,060.8	1,593.7	1,481.5	1,476.4
Performance & Financial Condition				
Return on Total Revenues %	78.65	40.16	-19.45	-3.05
Return on Avg Stockholders' Equity %	25.56	6.16	-1.01	-0.22
Return on Average Assets %	25.50	6.14	-1.00	-0.22
Current Ratio	336.43	84.74	91.37	21.40
Debt / Equity %	n.a.	n.a.	n.a.	n.a.

Compound Growth %'s	EPS %	500.00	Net Income %	392.96	Total Revenues %	80.89

Comments

Royalty payments totaled $516,600 and $157,200 in fiscal 1998 and 1997, respectively. An initial dividend of $.07 per share was declared in September 1998. Management anticipates paying additional dividends from future royalty revenues. As of June 30, 1998, the Company has tax loss carryovers of approximately $10 million. For the six months ended December 31, 1998, the Company reported royalty payments and net income of $317,900 and $299,080 ($.04 per share) as compared to $102,500 and $95,029 ($.01 per share) for the same period of the preceding year.

Officers	Position	Ownership Information	
J. W. Linehan	President, CEO	Number of Shares Outstanding	8,092,136
James E. Turner	Director	Market Capitalization	$ 6,797,394
J. H. Uptmore	Director	Number of Shareholders	1,875
Brenda Ray	Director	Where Listed / Symbol	OTC-BB / AVTH

Other Information			
Transfer Agent	Bank of New York Houston, TX	SIC Code	6794
Auditor	Arthur Andersen LLP	Employees	n.a.
Market Maker	M.H. Meyerson & Co., Inc. (800)333-3113		
	Fahnestock & Co., Inc. (800)223-3012		

Advantage Marketing Systems, Inc.

2601 N.W. Expressway, Suite 1210W   Oklahoma City, OK 73112-7293   Telephone (405)842-0131   Fax (405)843-4935

Company Description

Advantage Marketing Systems, Inc., as reorganized in 1995, is a marketer of consumer oriented services and products which are packaged together in special programs and sold to independent sales associates who use the products and services themselves and also sell them to others. The Company also produces nutritional supplements, cosmetics and skin care products. Approximately 50% of total Company sales are from the AM-300 weight management product which contains ephedra concentrate. Ephedra products are under scrutiny and may possibly be restricted by the Food and Drug Administration (FDA). The Company was formed in 1988.

	12/31/98	12/31/97	12/31/96	12/31/95
Per Share Information				
Stock Price	2.06	2.75	5.50	6.00
Earnings Per Share	0.09	0.04	0.29	0.09
Price / Earnings Ratio	22.89	68.75	18.97	66.67
Book Value Per Share	2.23	2.16	0.43	-0.01
Price / Book Value %	92.38	127.31	1,279.07	n.a.
Dividends Per Share	0.0	0.0	0.0	0.0
Annual Financial Data				
Operating Results (000's)				
Total Revenues	13,637.0	10,254.3	6,163.7	4,518.2
Costs & Expenses	-12,548.0	-10,064.5	-5,838.2	-4,268.5
Income Before Taxes and Other	1,089.0	189.7	325.5	249.7
Other Items	-421.6	0.0	0.0	0.0
Income Tax	-253.3	-59.7	499.6	0.0
Net Income	414.0	130.0	825.2	249.7
Cash Flow From Operations	1,242.3	-118.6	426.4	360.8
Balance Sheet (000's)				
Cash & Equivalents	5,289.2	5,775.3	169.6	112.1
Total Current Assets	7,050.5	6,999.4	655.2	283.3
Fixed Assets, Net	1,090.3	695.9	377.2	159.8
Total Assets	10,717.5	10,336.3	1,790.3	533.0
Total Current Liabilities	1,227.3	856.3	638.9	454.1
Long-Term Debt	94.3	82.4	19.0	28.5
Stockholders' Equity	9,222.6	9,176.4	921.4	-25.2
Performance & Financial Condition				
Return on Total Revenues %	3.04	1.27	13.39	5.53
Return on Avg Stockholders' Equity %	4.50	2.58	184.15	n.a.
Return on Average Assets %	3.93	2.14	71.03	70.34
Current Ratio	5.74	8.17	1.03	0.62
Debt / Equity %	1.02	0.90	2.07	n.a.

Compound Growth %'s	EPS %	0.00	Net Income %	18.36	Total Revenues %	44.52

Comments

The Company executed a 1 for 8 reverse split in 1996. All per share amounts have been restated accordingly. Several acquisitions over the last two years have resulted in the Company acquiring 6,790 distributors and adding 115 products to its product line. The Company currently markets approximately 100 products. Revenues increased 30.4% during 1998, largely as a result of increased sales volume of dietary and nutritional supplements and the expansion of the Company's network of independent sales representatives. 1998 results include a nonrecurring expense of $421,623 related to the settlement of tax liabilities. Management cautions investors that the loss of its AM-300 product line, if restricted by the FDA, could result in a material loss to the Company. 1996 results include a nonrecurring benefit from the utilization of tax loss carryforwards of $499,613 ($.18 per share).

Officers	Position	Ownership Information	
John W. Hail	Chairman, CEO	Number of Shares Outstanding	4,141,014
Roger P. Baresel	President, CFO	Market Capitalization	$ 8,530,489
Curtis H. Wilson, Sr.	Director	Number of Shareholders	1,874
R. Terren Dunlap	Director	Where Listed / Symbol	NASDAQ / AMSO

Other Information			
Transfer Agent	U.S. Stock Transfer Corp. Glendale, CA	SIC Code	5120
Auditor	Deloitte & Touche LLP	Employees	46

Aero Systems Engineering, Inc.

358 East Fillmore Avenue   St. Paul, MN 55107-1289   Telephone (651)227-7515   Fax (651)227-0519

Company Description

Aero Systems Engineering, Inc., founded in 1967, is engaged in the design and manufacture of electronic, mechanical, and computerized engine and engine accessory test equipment as well as the design, equipping, and construction of engine test facilities, wind tunnels and other aerodynamic test facilities. In addition, the Company provides aeropropulsion component testing and vehicle aerodynamic testing services. The Company is an 80% owned subsidiary of Celsius AB, a Swedish company.

	12/31/98	12/31/97	12/31/96	12/31/95
Per Share Information				
Stock Price	1.44	0.95	0.65	0.80
Earnings Per Share	0.15	-0.09	-0.57	0.04
Price / Earnings Ratio	9.60	n.a.	n.a.	20.00
Book Value Per Share	1.12	0.97	1.06	1.63
Price / Book Value %	128.57	97.94	61.32	49.08
Dividends Per Share	0.0	0.0	0.0	0.0
Annual Financial Data				
Operating Results (000's)				
Total Revenues	27,181.5	25,039.9	20,388.6	26,088.2
Costs & Expenses	-26,516.3	-25,382.3	-22,857.9	-25,872.1
Income Before Taxes and Other	665.2	-393.2	-2,522.8	212.1
Other Items	0.0	0.0	0.0	0.0
Income Tax	0.0	-7.5	-5.0	-22.6
Net Income	665.2	-400.7	-2,527.8	189.5
Cash Flow From Operations	1,008.4	522.5	1,017.3	-1,421.1
Balance Sheet (000's)				
Cash & Equivalents	16.1	117.0	135.1	140.6
Total Current Assets	16,004.5	14,936.6	11,006.6	17,391.4
Fixed Assets, Net	5,475.6	5,607.2	6,167.9	6,182.9
Total Assets	21,480.1	20,574.7	17,754.4	24,176.1
Total Current Liabilities	15,850.4	15,107.4	10,469.6	13,776.0
Long-Term Debt	0.0	400.0	1,200.0	1,200.0
Stockholders' Equity	4,915.1	4,249.9	4,650.6	7,178.4
Performance & Financial Condition				
Return on Total Revenues %	2.45	-1.60	-12.40	0.73
Return on Avg Stockholders' Equity %	14.52	-9.00	-42.74	2.68
Return on Average Assets %	3.16	-2.09	-12.06	1.21
Current Ratio	1.01	0.99	1.05	1.26
Debt / Equity %	n.a.	9.41	25.80	16.72

Compound Growth %'s	EPS %	55.36	Net Income %	51.98	Total Revenues %	1.38

Comments

The Company declared a 3 for 2 stock split in 1998 and a 15% stock dividend in February 1999. All per share amounts have been restated for consistency. A large operating loss in 1996 caused management to make significant changes to marketing and project management in late 1996. Although the Company was not profitable in 1997, as predicted by management, the rebound was strong. A profitable 1998 was credited to the early organizational changes. No income tax expense was required in 1998 and the Company still has $3.6 million of tax loss carryovers to offset future income. The order backlog increased from $14.3 million at the end to 1997 to $26.5 million at the end of 1998.

Officers	Position	Ownership Information	
Christer Persson	Chairman	Number of Shares Outstanding	4,401,708
Leon Ring	President, CEO	Market Capitalization	$ 6,338,460
Steven R. Hedberg	CFO, Secretary	Number of Shareholders	800
Lennart Hednert	Director	Where Listed / Symbol	NASDAQ / AERS

Other Information			
Transfer Agent	Norwest Capital Resources South St. Paul, MN	SIC Code	3823
Auditor	Ernst & Young LLP	Employees	171
Market Maker	Carr Securities Corporation (800)221-2243	Web Site	aerosysengr.com

Aerovox Incorporated

740 Belleville Avenue New Bedford, MA 02745-6194 Telephone (508)994-9661 Fax (508)995-3000

Company Description

Aerovox Incorporated is a leading manufacturer of film, paper, and aluminum electrolytic capacitors. The Company sells its products worldwide, principally to original equipment manufacturers of electrical and electronic products. Applications include air conditioners, fluorescent and high intensity discharge lighting fixtures, a variety of appliances including microwave ovens, motors, power supplies, photocopiers, telecommunication, computer and medical equipment, and industrial electrical systems. The Company's predecessor, Aerovox Corporation, began business in 1922 producing crystal wireless radios.

	01/02/99	12/27/97	12/28/96	12/30/95
Per Share Information				
Stock Price as of 12/31	2.06	4.12	4.75	5.87
Earnings Per Share	0.33	-2.15	-0.25	0.30
Price / Earnings Ratio	6.24	n.a.	n.a.	19.57
Book Value Per Share	4.69	4.41	6.60	6.68
Price / Book Value %	43.92	93.42	71.97	87.87
Dividends Per Share	0.0	0.0	0.0	0.0
Annual Financial Data				
Operating Results (000's)				
Total Revenues	117,714.0	119,981.0	125,975.0	129,593.0
Costs & Expenses	-115,076.0	-120,973.0	-128,095.0	-126,941.0
Income Before Taxes and Other	2,638.0	-992.0	-2,451.0	2,652.0
Other Items	0.0	-13,000.0	0.0	0.0
Income Tax	-852.0	2,493.0	1,104.0	-1,051.0
Net Income	1,786.0	-11,499.0	-1,347.0	1,601.0
Cash Flow From Operations	1,731.0	9,361.0	8,317.0	1,529.0
Balance Sheet (000's)				
Cash & Equivalents	1,149.0	693.0	864.0	573.0
Total Current Assets	35,841.0	33,755.0	38,914.0	45,773.0
Fixed Assets, Net	30,500.0	32,263.0	40,530.0	41,251.0
Total Assets	70,571.0	71,559.0	84,976.0	89,331.0
Total Current Liabilities	22,372.0	18,539.0	17,946.0	18,322.0
Long-Term Debt	11,208.0	16,723.0	22,510.0	27,705.0
Stockholders' Equity	25,289.0	23,766.0	35,073.0	35,505.0
Performance & Financial Condition				
Return on Total Revenues %	1.52	-9.58	-1.07	1.24
Return on Avg Stockholders' Equity %	7.28	-39.09	-3.82	4.60
Return on Average Assets %	2.51	-14.69	-1.55	1.91
Current Ratio	1.60	1.82	2.17	2.50
Debt / Equity %	44.32	70.37	64.18	78.03

Compound Growth %'s	EPS %	3.23	Net Income %	3.71	Total Revenues %	-3.15

Comments

At December 31, 1996, the Company's on-time delivery level sat at an unacceptable 62%. Management targeted 90% as achievable. It increased to 83% in 1997, 90% in 1998 and, according to management, is still rising. 1998 was also a pivotal year for the Company in terms of expense controls and profitability. Gross margins improved to 17.3% from 14.1% in 1997. Net earnings were impressive. Included in 1997 results is a provision of $13 million for environmental costs, and plant remediation and impairment of assets related to the identification of PCB contamination at the New Bedford plant and the Company's consequent decision to vacate that facility. A new state-of-the-art facility should be operational by mid-2000.

Officers	Position	Ownership Information	
Sherel D. Horsley	Chairman	Number of Shares Outstanding	5,393,221
Robert D. Elliott	President, CEO	Market Capitalization	$ 11,110,035
Jeffrey A. Templer	Senior VP, CFO	Number of Shareholders	8,738
Timothy J. Brown	Senior VP	Where Listed / Symbol	NASDAQ / ARVX

Other Information			
Transfer Agent	American Stock Transfer & Trust Company New York, NY	SIC Code	3620
Auditor	PricewaterhouseCoopers LLP	Employees	1,428
		Web Site	aerovox.com

Ag-Bag International Limited

2320 S E Ag-Bag Lane   Warrenton, OR 97146   Telephone (503)861-1644   Fax (503)861-2527

Company Description

Ag-Bag International, founded in 1978, has pioneered an alternate method of storing feed for livestock. Traditional methods of storing feed have included placing it in bunkers, pits, and silos or bailing and stacking it. The Company's method is to store the feed in huge plastic bags of up to 250 feet in length and up to 12 feet in diameter by tightly stuffing the feed into the bag. The Company assembles the machines for stuffing the feed into the bags. It has the bags manufactured to its specifications and then folds and distributes the bags through its dealer network. The benefits of bagging the feed include reduced cost, additional flexibility in harvesting and storing the feed, enhanced feed quality, and relatively small capital requirements. The Company also sells ancillary products which complement the Company's main line of bagging machines and bags as well as machines and bags for composting.

	12/31/98	12/31/97	12/31/96	12/31/95
Per Share Information				
Stock Price	0.41	0.53	1.03	1.37
Earnings Per Share	0.06	-0.32	0.03	0.01
Price / Earnings Ratio	6.83	n.a.	34.33	137.00
Book Value Per Share	0.69	0.63	0.95	0.92
Price / Book Value %	59.42	84.13	108.42	148.91
Dividends Per Share	0.0	0.0	0.0	0.0
Annual Financial Data				
Operating Results (000's)				
Total Revenues	28,084.4	20,332.3	23,358.6	17,502.0
Costs & Expenses	-26,858.0	-19,164.0	-20,514.8	-16,839.0
Income Before Taxes and Other	1,226.4	-1,193.7	570.2	479.0
Other Items	0.0	-4,271.4	50.5	-86.0
Income Tax	-422.0	1,650.0	-257.3	-286.0
Net Income	804.4	-3,815.1	363.5	107.0
Cash Flow From Operations	2,971.6	-1,890.0	1,502.9	-1,250.6
Balance Sheet (000's)				
Cash & Equivalents	361.6	0.7	0.7	0.7
Total Current Assets	9,390.5	9,888.7	8,745.7	9,378.8
Fixed Assets, Net	3,934.4	4,378.4	4,848.1	3,520.3
Total Assets	13,820.3	15,190.3	16,903.1	16,297.5
Total Current Liabilities	2,573.1	4,207.6	2,656.1	3,300.8
Long-Term Debt	2,209.6	2,666.6	2,020.9	1,237.5
Stockholders' Equity	9,037.5	8,292.3	12,186.4	11,759.1
Performance & Financial Condition				
Return on Total Revenues %	2.86	-18.76	1.56	0.61
Return on Avg Stockholders' Equity %	9.28	-37.26	3.04	0.92
Return on Average Assets %	5.55	-23.78	2.19	0.67
Current Ratio	3.65	2.35	3.29	2.84
Debt / Equity %	24.45	32.16	16.58	10.52

Compound Growth %'s	EPS %	81.71	Net Income %	95.90	Total Revenues %	17.07

Comments

Sales increased 35.5% in 1998 as a result of continued improving milk prices and lower feed costs which spurred capital expenditures for machinery and equipment. Recent university research articles published on the benefits of bagging over the use of bunkers also helped increase sales. International sales declined due to weak conditions abroad. Net income for 1998 reflected an impressive turnaround. During 1997, the Company discontinued its European operations by selling a subsidiary resulting in a loss of $872,000. The Company also recognized an unusual charge of $3.4 million related to obsolescent inventory and other assets. The Company's financial condition is excellent and intangible assets are immaterial to stockholders' equity.

Officers	Position	Ownership Information	
Larry R. Inman	President, CEO	Number of Shares Outstanding	12,061,991
Michael R. Wallis	VP - Finance, CFO	Market Capitalization	$ 4,945,416
Lou Ann Tucker	Vice President, Secretary	Number of Shareholders	2,400
Walter L. Jay	VP - Manufacturing	Where Listed / Symbol	NASDAQ / AGBG

Other Information			
Transfer Agent	Corporate Stock Transfer, Inc. Denver, CO	SIC Code	3089
Auditor	Yergen & Meyer LLP	Employees	110
		Web Site	ag-bag.com

Aldila, Inc.

15822 Bernardo Center Drive   San Diego, CA 92127   Telephone (619)513-1801   Fax (619)513-1970

Company Description

Aldila, Inc. is a leading designer and manufacturer of high quality innovative graphite golf shafts in the United States. The Company manufactures shafts for most major domestic and many foreign golf club manufacturers including Calloway Golf Company, Karsten Manufacturing (Ping), Titleist and Taylor Made. The current product line consists of Aldila and G. Loomis branded products designed for custom club makers as well as hundreds of custom shafts developed in conjunction with its major customers. Aldila was founded in 1972 and in 1994 started to manufacture its own raw materials. A new state of the art facility for the manufacture of graphite became operational in 1998.

	12/31/98	12/31/97	12/31/96	12/31/95
Per Share Information				
Stock Price	2.41	4.31	4.69	4.25
Earnings Per Share	0.18	0.10	0.35	0.37
Price / Earnings Ratio	13.39	43.10	13.40	11.49
Book Value Per Share	5.19	5.01	4.92	4.55
Price / Book Value %	46.44	86.03	95.33	93.41
Dividends Per Share	0.0	0.0	0.0	0.0
Annual Financial Data				
Operating Results (000's)				
Total Revenues	62,705.0	56,054.0	59,121.0	57,402.0
Costs & Expenses	-56,406.0	-51,465.0	-49,039.0	-46,362.0
Income Before Taxes and Other	6,299.0	4,589.0	10,082.0	11,040.0
Other Items	-1,200.0	-1,500.0	0.0	0.0
Income Tax	-2,300.0	-1,550.0	-4,400.0	-4,770.0
Net Income	2,799.0	1,539.0	5,682.0	6,270.0
Cash Flow From Operations	4,585.0	1,210.0	7,192.0	9,757.0
Balance Sheet (000's)				
Cash & Equivalents	1,972.0	3,046.0	19,676.0	19,345.0
Total Current Assets	28,851.0	24,522.0	32,714.0	32,225.0
Fixed Assets, Net	27,649.0	26,170.0	14,883.0	13,545.0
Total Assets	117,034.0	113,128.0	111,935.0	111,853.0
Total Current Liabilities	13,120.0	7,747.0	4,440.0	7,455.0
Long-Term Debt	16,000.0	20,000.0	20,000.0	20,000.0
Stockholders' Equity	80,254.0	77,283.0	78,826.0	75,481.0
Performance & Financial Condition				
Return on Total Revenues %	4.46	2.75	9.61	10.92
Return on Avg Stockholders' Equity %	3.55	1.97	7.36	8.63
Return on Average Assets %	2.43	1.37	5.08	5.66
Current Ratio	2.20	3.17	7.37	4.32
Debt / Equity %	19.94	25.88	25.37	26.50

Compound Growth %'s	EPS %	-21.35	Net Income %	-23.57	Total Revenues %	2.99

Comments

In November 1997, the Company announced plans to consolidate its U.S. graphite golf club shaft manufacturing operations into one facility in Poway, California. In connection with this decision, expenses of $1,200,000 and $1,500,000 were recorded in 1998 and 1997, respectively. After years of sluggish growth, unit sales increased 22% in 1998 which was partially offset by a 12% decrease in the average unit price. The Company also had $1.5 million in new revenue from the sale of carbon fiber products. Based on an overall weak demand for golf clubs, management predicted a weak first half of 1999. Sales to two major customers dropped from 54% in 1997 to 41% in 1998. At December 31, 1998, the Company had $46.2 million of goodwill reflected as assets which equates to approximately 58% of stockholders' equity and book value per share.

Officers	Position	Ownership Information	
Gary T. Barbera	Chairman, CEO	Number of Shares Outstanding	15,462,204
Robert J. Cierzan	VP - Finance, CFO	Market Capitalization	$ 37,263,912
Peter R. Mathewson	Vice President, COO	Number of Shareholders	2,000
Jon B. DeVault	Vice President	Where Listed / Symbol	NASDAQ / ALDA

Other Information			
Transfer Agent	ChaseMellon Shareholder Services Ridgefield Park, NJ	SIC Code	3949
Auditor	Deloitte & Touche LLP	Employees	1,000

Alfa Leisure, Inc.

13501 5th Street   Chino, CA 91710   Telephone (909)628-5574   Fax (909)591-7902

Company Description

Alfa Leisure, Inc. manufactures and sells recreational vehicles designed as short-period accommodations for vacationers or long-period accommodations for travelers who live full-time in their vehicles. These products are fifth wheel travel trailers designed to be towed behind and attached to special couplers in the bed of pickup trucks. The Company's products are marketed under the brand names Gold, Toyhouse, See Ya and Ideal. They are distributed by approximately 47 independent dealers located throughout the United States. The Company was founded in 1969 under the name Brougham Coach, Inc. which subsequently hit bad times and filed for bankruptcy protection in 1985. But the Company has found better times more recently.

	04/30/98	04/30/97	04/30/96	04/30/95
Per Share Information				
Stock Price as of 12/31	1.25	0.16	0.12	0.12
Earnings Per Share	0.44	0.11	0.22	0.27
Price / Earnings Ratio	2.84	1.45	0.55	0.44
Book Value Per Share	1.02	0.55	0.45	0.25
Price / Book Value %	122.55	29.09	26.67	48.00
Dividends Per Share	0.0	0.0	0.0	0.0
Annual Financial Data				
Operating Results (000's)				
Total Revenues	36,025.6	28,590.3	25,749.6	27,348.9
Costs & Expenses	-34,515.6	-28,151.7	-25,605.4	-26,414.0
Income Before Taxes and Other	1,510.0	438.6	144.3	934.9
Other Items	0.0	0.0	0.0	0.0
Income Tax	-165.3	-109.0	520.4	-111.0
Net Income	1,344.6	329.5	664.7	823.9
Cash Flow From Operations	1,285.8	996.1	45.6	207.9
Balance Sheet (000's)				
Cash & Equivalents	410.7	393.2	505.0	332.5
Total Current Assets	3,738.0	3,767.0	4,311.2	4,569.9
Fixed Assets, Net	1,300.4	1,103.2	1,136.7	1,133.5
Total Assets	5,558.9	5,406.4	5,988.2	5,703.4
Total Current Liabilities	2,454.7	2,750.9	2,599.8	3,240.7
Long-Term Debt	0.0	972.5	1,997.5	1,697.5
Stockholders' Equity	3,096.0	1,674.8	1,382.7	757.0
Performance & Financial Condition				
Return on Total Revenues %	3.73	1.15	2.58	3.01
Return on Avg Stockholders' Equity %	56.37	21.56	62.13	117.70
Return on Average Assets %	24.53	5.78	11.37	14.98
Current Ratio	1.52	1.37	1.66	1.41
Debt / Equity %	n.a.	58.07	144.47	224.24

Compound Growth %'s	EPS %	17.68	Net Income %	17.74	Total Revenues %	9.62

Comments

Revenues increased 26% in 1998 as compared to 1997. This was the result of a 17% increase in units shipped, price increases for 1998 models, and a change in sales mix to a higher ratio of larger trailers in 1998 as compared to 1997. A minor improvement to gross margins and tight control over expenses helped create a record profit for the year. Income taxes have been disproportionately low due to the use of tax loss carryovers. Only $549,000 in losses remains to offset future taxable income as of April 30, 1998. A strong cash flow from operations was used to pay off all long term debt. Also absent from the balance sheet are intangible assets. For the nine months ended January 31, 1999, the Company reported revenues and net income of $27.8 million and $526,887 ($.17 per share) as compared to $24.9 million and $430,187 ($.14 per share) for the same period of the preceding year.

Officers	Position	Ownership Information	
Johnnie R. Crean	President	Number of Shares Outstanding	3,048,137
Mark Schwartz	VP - Finance, CFO	Market Capitalization	$ 3,810,171
Carol Smith	Director	Number of Shareholders	400
Robert A. Rudolph	Director	Where Listed / Symbol	NASDAQ / ALEI

Other Information

Transfer Agent	American Stock Transfer & Trust Co. New York, NY		SIC Code	3790
Auditor	Deloitte & Touche LLP		Employees	333
Market Maker	Carr Securities Corporation	(800)221-2243	Web Site	alfaleisure.com
	Sharpe Capital Inc.	(800)355-5781		

All American Semiconductor, Inc.

16115 N.W. 52nd Avenue   Miami, FL 33014   Telephone (305)621-8282   Fax (305)624-5258

Company Description

All American Semiconductor, Inc. is a national distributor of electronic components manufactured by others including transistors, diodes, memory devices and other integrated circuits; passive components, such as capacitors, resistors, inductors; and electromechanical products, including cable, switches, connectors, filters and sockets. The Company's products are sold primarily to original equipment manufacturers in a diverse and growing range of industries. The Company also designs and has manufactured certain board level products including memory modules and flat panel display driver boards. The Company was founded in 1964.

	12/31/98	12/31/97	12/31/96	12/31/95
Per Share Information				
Stock Price	0.81	1.38	1.00	2.31
Earnings Per Share	0.04	0.16	-0.49	0.12
Price / Earnings Ratio	20.25	8.63	n.a.	19.25
Book Value Per Share	1.33	1.29	1.13	1.62
Price / Book Value %	60.90	106.98	88.50	142.59
Dividends Per Share	0.0	0.0	0.0	0.0
Annual Financial Data				
Operating Results (000's)				
Total Revenues	250,044.0	265,640.0	237,846.0	177,335.0
Costs & Expenses	-245,792.0	-260,227.0	-244,067.0	-173,149.0
Income Before Taxes and Other	4,252.0	5,413.0	-11,163.0	3,088.0
Other Items	-2,860.0	0.0	-1,699.0	79.0
Income Tax	-561.0	-2,163.0	2,942.0	-1,281.0
Net Income	831.0	3,250.0	-9,920.0	1,886.0
Cash Flow From Operations	-2,401.0	11,562.0	-12,606.0	-8,286.0
Balance Sheet (000's)				
Cash & Equivalents	473.0	444.0	525.0	276.0
Total Current Assets	109,931.0	103,324.0	102,561.0	104,799.0
Fixed Assets, Net	4,506.0	4,779.0	5,454.0	3,882.0
Total Assets	118,957.0	112,286.0	112,921.0	114,474.0
Total Current Liabilities	41,739.0	40,016.0	32,738.0	45,447.0
Long-Term Debt	49,493.0	45,377.0	56,551.0	36,415.0
Stockholders' Equity	26,509.0	25,674.0	22,396.0	32,267.0
Performance & Financial Condition				
Return on Total Revenues %	0.33	1.22	-4.17	1.06
Return on Avg Stockholders' Equity %	3.18	13.52	-36.30	7.66
Return on Average Assets %	0.72	2.89	-8.72	2.19
Current Ratio	2.63	2.58	3.13	2.31
Debt / Equity %	186.70	176.74	252.50	112.86

Compound Growth %'s	EPS % -30.66	Net Income % -23.91	Total Revenues % 12.13

Comments

The decrease in sales experienced in 1998 was attributable to price erosion and adverse market conditions within the industry. Sales were also negatively impacted by the distractions resulting from a failed acquisition. 1998 results include nonrecurring expenses of $2,860,000 related to the abandoned acquisition. 1996 results include $4,942,000 of restructuring charges and $1,699,000 of losses from discontinued operations. At December 31, 1998, intangible assets were immaterial. On March 17, 1999, the Company was advised by The Nasdaq Stock Market that it may be delisted because it failed to maintain a stock price in excess of $1.00 per share despite the fact that the Company is profitable and solvent, has positive working capital, has a clean audit opinion, and has been in business for 35 years.

Officers	Position	Ownership Information	
Paul Goldberg	Chairman	Number of Shares Outstanding	19,866,906
Bruce M. Goldberg	President, CEO	Market Capitalization	$ 16,092,194
Howard L. Flanders	Exec VP, CFO	Number of Shareholders	6,300
Rick Gordon	Senior VP	Where Listed / Symbol	NASDAQ / SEMI

Other Information			
Transfer Agent	American Stock Transfer & Trust Company New York, NY	SIC Code	5065
Auditor	Lazar, Levine & Felix LLP	Employees	523
		Web Site	allamerican.com

All Communications Corporation

225 Long Avenue, P.O. Box 794   Hillside, NJ 07205   Telephone (973)282-2000   Fax (973)282-2033

Company Description

All Communications Corporation is engaged in the business of selling, installing and servicing voice and videoconferencing communications systems, concentrating on the commercial and industrial marketplace. The Company's voice communications products are intended principally for small to medium-sized business use; its videoconferencing communications products are intended for use by all business, governmental, educational and medical entities. In January 1999, the Company executed an agreement with Sprint Communications Company to act as an authorized sales agent for Sprint's advanced network and videoconferencing services. The Company was founded in 1991 and had its initial public offering in 1997.

	12/31/98	12/31/97	12/31/96	12/31/95
Per Share Information				
Stock Price	0.69	0.47	7.00	0.03
Earnings Per Share	-0.16	-0.21	0.03	0.01
Price / Earnings Ratio	n.a.	n.a.	233.33	3.00
Book Value Per Share	0.81	0.96	0.18	0.05
Price / Book Value %	85.19	48.96	3,888.89	60.00
Dividends Per Share	0.0	0.0	0.0	0.0
Annual Financial Data				
Operating Results (000's)				
Total Revenues	13,273.5	7,043.4	3,884.7	2,642.0
Costs & Expenses	-14,048.0	-7,988.1	-3,794.5	-2,599.7
Income Before Taxes and Other	-774.4	-944.7	90.2	17.2
Other Items	0.0	0.0	0.0	0.0
Income Tax	-2.9	52.4	-38.6	-8.0
Net Income	-777.3	-892.3	51.6	9.2
Cash Flow From Operations	-3,849.1	-1,974.2	-461.3	70.7
Balance Sheet (000's)				
Cash & Equivalents	325.9	2,175.0	645.6	153.9
Total Current Assets	8,229.6	5,537.0	1,845.1	654.0
Fixed Assets, Net	611.5	438.0	129.0	91.8
Total Assets	8,922.6	6,007.0	2,458.4	754.6
Total Current Liabilities	2,527.8	1,273.0	1,096.8	601.4
Long-Term Debt	2,403.2	0.0	801.4	65.2
Stockholders' Equity	3,968.4	4,734.0	545.4	81.3
Performance & Financial Condition				
Return on Total Revenues %	-5.86	-12.67	1.33	0.35
Return on Avg Stockholders' Equity %	-17.86	-33.80	16.47	4.61
Return on Average Assets %	-10.41	-21.08	3.21	0.92
Current Ratio	3.26	4.35	1.68	1.09
Debt / Equity %	60.56	n.a.	146.93	80.22

Compound Growth %'s	EPS % n.a.	Net Income % n.a.	Total Revenues %	71.27

Comments

Despite substantial increases in revenue, the Company has reported two consecutive losses. Management has been content to plow available funds into expanding operations which has offset the increasing gross margins. Revenue in 1998 benefitted from a significant new customer as well as an expanded sales force. The new customer accounted for 11% of 1998 revenues. Fortunately, the Company is keeping a watchful eye on working capital and is in relatively good financial condition.

Officers	Position	Ownership Information	
Richard Riess	President, CEO	Number of Shares Outstanding	4,910,000
Scott Tansey	VP - Finance	Market Capitalization	$ 3,387,900
Peter Barrett	Vice President	Number of Shareholders	1,000
Joseph Scotti	VP - Sales	Where Listed / Symbol	OTC-BB / ACUC

Other Information			
Transfer Agent	American Stock Transfer & Trust Co. New York, NY	SIC Code	4813
Auditor	BDO Seidman LLP	Employees	54
Market Maker	Olsen Payne & Co. (800)453-5321	Web Site	allcommunications.com
	Sherwood Securities Corp. (800)435-1235		

Allied Devices Corporation

2365 Milburn Avenue   Baldwin, NY 11510   Telephone (516)223-9100   Fax (516)223-9172

Company Description

Allied Devices Corporation, founded in 1981, is a broad-line manufacturer and distributor of high precision mechanical components used in the manufacture and maintenance of industrial and commercial instruments and equipment. The Company has the capability of producing close tolerance parts and intricate assemblies at competitive costs and with short lead times. Allied Devices' major product groups include precision motion control and servo assemblies, instrument related fasteners, gears and gear products, and other components and sub-assemblies built to customer specifications.

	09/30/98	09/30/97	09/30/96	09/30/95
Per Share Information				
Stock Price as of 12/31	1.62	1.87	2.50	3.50
Earnings Per Share	0.22	0.21	0.20	0.15
Price / Earnings Ratio	7.36	8.90	12.50	23.33
Book Value Per Share	1.84	1.52	1.32	1.11
Price / Book Value %	88.04	123.03	189.39	315.32
Dividends Per Share	0.0	0.0	0.0	0.0
Annual Financial Data				
Operating Results (000's)				
Total Revenues	18,448.5	16,215.9	17,793.1	15,521.4
Costs & Expenses	-16,833.8	-14,525.0	-16,199.0	-14,352.5
Income Before Taxes and Other	1,614.7	1,690.9	1,594.1	1,168.9
Other Items	0.0	0.0	0.0	0.0
Income Tax	-584.0	-629.0	-593.1	-381.6
Net Income	1,030.7	1,061.9	1,001.0	787.3
Cash Flow From Operations	599.3	818.3	38.1	910.6
Balance Sheet (000's)				
Cash & Equivalents	275.2	162.1	54.9	198.5
Total Current Assets	12,111.6	8,999.6	8,211.6	7,402.0
Fixed Assets, Net	7,607.2	1,837.2	1,965.7	1,756.4
Total Assets	22,973.6	10,977.0	10,376.7	9,403.5
Total Current Liabilities	2,516.8	1,691.8	1,705.9	3,973.8
Long-Term Debt	11,031.7	2,084.2	2,642.4	497.5
Stockholders' Equity	9,116.1	7,025.9	5,807.4	4,750.0
Performance & Financial Condition				
Return on Total Revenues %	5.59	6.55	5.63	5.07
Return on Avg Stockholders' Equity %	12.77	16.55	18.96	18.29
Return on Average Assets %	6.07	9.95	10.12	8.69
Current Ratio	4.81	5.32	4.81	1.86
Debt / Equity %	121.01	29.66	45.50	10.47

Compound Growth %'s	EPS %	13.62	Net Income %	9.39	Total Revenues %	5.93

Comments

During fiscal 1998, the Company successfully completed two acquisitions as part of its growth strategy which accounted for the increase in revenues. Revenues would have otherwise declined because of the economic and financial turmoil in East Asia. Fiscal 1998 operating results were hindered by a fire which destroyed the central computer, data communications equipment and certain underlying records. The decrease in fiscal 1997 revenue was principally the result of a sharp downturn in the semiconductor equipment sector. The Company accounts for inventory using the last-in, first-out (LIFO) method. Had the Company used the more traditional first-in, first-out (FIFO) method for public companies, inventory would have been $1.5 million higher and stockholders' equity would have been approximately $1.1 million higher. At September 30, 1998, the Company had $2.9 million of goodwill recorded as assets which approximated 32% of stockholders' equity and book value per share.

Officers	Position	Ownership Information	
Mark Hopkinson	Chairman, CEO	Number of Shares Outstanding	4,947,942
P. K. Bartow	President	Market Capitalization	$ 8,015,666
Salvator Baldi	Exec VP	Number of Shareholders	441
Paul M. Cervino	CFO, COO	Where Listed / Symbol	NASDAQ / ALDV

Other Information			
Transfer Agent	American Stock Transfer & Trust Co. New York, NY	SIC Code	3452
Auditor	BDO Seidman LLP	Employees	261
		Web Site	allieddevices.com

Allstar Systems, Inc.

6401 Southwest Freeway   Houston, TX 77074   Telephone (713)795-2000   Fax (713)795-2036

Company Description

Allstar Systems, Inc. is a regional provider of computer and telecommunications hardware and software products and related services. The Company primarily markets its products and services in Texas from five locations in the Houston, Dallas-Fort Worth, El Paso, Austin and San Antonio metropolitan areas. During 1998, the Company's customer base of approximately 2,700 accounts was comprised primarily of mid-sized customers and regional offices of larger customers in commercial, educational and governmental sectors. The Company was founded in 1983 and went public on July 7, 1997.

	12/31/98	12/31/97	12/31/96	12/31/95
Per Share Information				
Stock Price	1.75	3.88	n.a.	n.a.
Earnings Per Share	-0.25	0.52	0.60	0.19
Price / Earnings Ratio	n.a.	7.46	n.a.	n.a.
Book Value Per Share	3.00	3.31	1.62	1.02
Price / Book Value %	58.33	117.22	n.a.	n.a.
Dividends Per Share	0.0	0.0	0.0	0.0
Annual Financial Data				
Operating Results (000's)				
Total Revenues	167,173.0	129,167.0	120,359.0	91,085.0
Costs & Expenses	-168,812.0	-126,197.0	-117,769.0	-90,224.0
Income Before Taxes and Other	-1,639.0	2,970.0	2,590.0	861.0
Other Items	0.0	0.0	0.0	0.0
Income Tax	541.0	-1,126.0	-987.0	-342.0
Net Income	-1,098.0	1,844.0	1,603.0	519.0
Cash Flow From Operations	-10,831.0	2,000.0	89.0	-123.0
Balance Sheet (000's)				
Cash & Equivalents	2,538.0	1,581.0	229.0	1,029.0
Total Current Assets	47,928.0	31,090.0	22,684.0	23,274.0
Fixed Assets, Net	2,902.0	2,013.0	1,644.0	986.0
Total Assets	51,028.0	33,184.0	24,720.0	24,266.0
Total Current Liabilities	38,128.0	18,266.0	20,393.0	21,542.0
Long-Term Debt	0.0	0.0	0.0	0.0
Stockholders' Equity	12,705.0	14,723.0	4,327.0	2,724.0
Performance & Financial Condition				
Return on Total Revenues %	-0.66	1.43	1.33	0.57
Return on Avg Stockholders' Equity %	-8.01	19.36	45.47	21.06
Return on Average Assets %	-2.61	6.37	6.54	2.39
Current Ratio	1.26	1.70	1.11	1.08
Debt / Equity %	n.a.	n.a.	n.a.	n.a.

Compound Growth %'s	EPS % n.a.	Net Income % n.a.	Total Revenues % 22.44

Comments

Revenues increased 29.4% in 1998 which was generally attributable to increased sales of products and services to new and existing customers and to sales generated in the Company's newer branch offices. Operating income was negatively affected by asset valuation markdowns of $2,040,000 related to reducing the carrying value of inventory and certain accounts receivable. The Company decided that the mark-downs in inventory value were necessary based upon an analysis of the impact of changes in product return privileges and price protection policies made available to certain customers. The Company reacquired 271,200 shares of its common stock during 1998 at an average price of $3.07 per share. The price per share was at a substantial discount to book value at year end and the balance sheet is free of intangible assets.

Officers	Position	Ownership Information	
James H. Long	President, CEO	Number of Shares Outstanding	4,232,211
Ronald J. Burger	COO	Market Capitalization	$ 7,406,369
Frank Cano	Senior VP	Number of Shareholders	890
Donald R. Chadwick	CFO, Secretary	Where Listed / Symbol	NASDAQ / ALLS

Other Information			
Transfer Agent	American Stock Transfer & Trust Co. New York, NY	SIC Code	5045
Auditor	Deloitte & Touche LLP	Employees	513
		Web Site	allstar.com

AlphaNet Solutions, Inc.

7 Ridgedale Avenue   Cedar Knolls, NJ 07927   Telephone (973)267-0088   Fax (973)267-8675

Company Description

AlphaNet Solutions, Inc. is a single-source provider of information technology (IT) products, services and support to Fortune 1000 and other large and mid-sized companies located primarily in the New York-to-Philadelphia corridor. The Company is authorized by many industry-leading manufacturers of IT products, including 3Com, Bay Networks, Cisco Systems, Compaq, Hewlett-Packard, IBM, Intel, Lucent Technologies, Microsoft, NEC, Novell and Sun Microsystems to resell their products and provide related services. Such products include workstations, servers, networking and communications equipment, enterprise computing products, and application software. On August 1, 1997, the Company consummated the acquisition of certain assets and assumed certain liabilities of the Lande Group, Inc., a computer equipment reseller and provider of systems integration services, for $1.8 million, including acquisition costs. AlphaNet was originally founded in 1984.

	12/31/98	12/31/97	12/31/96	12/31/95
Per Share Information				
Stock Price	3.00	11.25	16.00	10.00
Earnings Per Share	0.11	0.93	0.82	1.17
Price / Earnings Ratio	27.27	12.10	19.51	8.55
Book Value Per Share	6.68	6.67	3.71	1.93
Price / Book Value %	44.91	168.67	431.27	518.13
Dividends Per Share	0.0	0.0	0.0	0.0
Annual Financial Data				
Operating Results (000's)				
Total Revenues	171,972.0	191,611.0	119,840.0	74,070.0
Costs & Expenses	-170,638.0	-182,246.0	-113,986.0	-69,981.0
Income Before Taxes and Other	1,334.0	9,365.0	5,854.0	4,089.0
Other Items	0.0	0.0	0.0	0.0
Income Tax	-623.0	-3,844.0	-1,970.0	-124.0
Net Income	711.0	5,521.0	3,884.0	3,965.0
Cash Flow From Operations	14,636.0	-11,879.0	-4,620.0	5,924.0
Balance Sheet (000's)				
Cash & Equivalents	13,377.0	2,689.0	1,610.0	1,223.0
Total Current Assets	54,009.0	63,267.0	38,417.0	16,639.0
Fixed Assets, Net	5,491.0	6,386.0	3,856.0	2,131.0
Total Assets	61,894.0	72,541.0	43,647.0	18,770.0
Total Current Liabilities	18,634.0	30,144.0	24,010.0	11,606.0
Long-Term Debt	0.0	0.0	0.0	0.0
Stockholders' Equity	42,536.0	41,722.0	18,921.0	6,574.0
Performance & Financial Condition				
Return on Total Revenues %	0.41	2.88	3.24	5.35
Return on Avg Stockholders' Equity %	1.69	18.21	30.47	75.65
Return on Average Assets %	1.06	9.50	12.45	22.36
Current Ratio	2.90	2.10	1.60	1.43
Debt / Equity %	n.a.	n.a.	n.a.	n.a.

Compound Growth %'s	EPS %	-54.53	Net Income %	-43.61	Total Revenues %	32.42

Comments

The acquisition referred to above was reported under the purchase method of accounting. Therefore operating results have been combined since the date of the acquisition. In 1998, revenue declined for the first time in the Company's history. The decline was primarily attributable to increased competition, reduced unit volume and lower average selling prices. Some customers have begun purchasing directly from equipment manufacturers at discounted prices. The Company also wrote off assets of $2.5 million in the third quarter. Book value is a solid number. It will be important to see if management can overcome the slide in profits experienced during 1998.

Officers	Position	Ownership Information	
Stan Gang	President, CEO	Number of Shares Outstanding	6,366,228
John Centinaro	Senior VP	Market Capitalization	$ 19,098,684
Robert G. Petoia	Vice President, CFO	Number of Shareholders	3,900
Gary T. Gann	Vice President, Secretary	Where Listed / Symbol	NASDAQ / ALPH

Other Information			
Transfer Agent	American Stock Transfer & Trust Co. New York, NY	SIC Code	5045
Auditor	PricewaterhouseCoopers LLP	Employees	694
		Web Site	alphanetcorp.com

American Consumers, Inc.

P.O. Box 2328   Fort Oglethorpe, GA 30742   Telephone (706)861-3347   Fax (706)861-3364

Company Description

The Company, incorporated in Georgia in 1968, operates a chain of six retail grocery stores in Tennessee, Alabama and Georgia. The stores are operated under the name of Shop-Rite Supermarket and are on the average 20,000 square feet in size. The majority of the Company's merchandise is made up of national brands and is purchased from Fleming Co., Inc., a large national distributor.

	05/30/98	05/31/97	06/01/96	06/03/95
Per Share Information				
Stock Price as of 12/31	0.50	0.50	0.50	0.50
Earnings Per Share	0.09	0.12	0.25	0.18
Price / Earnings Ratio	5.56	4.17	2.00	2.78
Book Value Per Share	2.86	2.80	2.74	2.52
Price / Book Value %	17.48	17.86	18.25	19.84
Dividends Per Share	0.0	0.06	0.04	0.08
Annual Financial Data				
Operating Results (000's)				
Total Revenues	26,984.5	28,050.4	29,314.3	28,876.3
Costs & Expenses	-26,861.9	-27,921.7	-28,937.9	-28,589.4
Income Before Taxes and Other	122.5	128.6	376.4	287.0
Other Items	0.0	0.0	0.0	0.0
Income Tax	-37.0	-19.7	-140.5	-114.9
Net Income	85.6	108.9	236.0	172.1
Cash Flow From Operations	306.3	215.1	562.7	22.6
Balance Sheet (000's)				
Cash & Equivalents	945.2	1,234.9	1,333.5	753.5
Total Current Assets	3,359.8	3,221.7	3,242.3	2,859.8
Fixed Assets, Net	893.5	1,069.8	1,241.9	837.4
Total Assets	4,257.2	4,301.5	4,502.7	3,736.6
Total Current Liabilities	1,268.5	1,221.2	1,397.2	1,208.3
Long-Term Debt	0.0	0.0	0.0	0.0
Stockholders' Equity	2,634.8	2,580.2	2,529.8	2,333.8
Performance & Financial Condition				
Return on Total Revenues %	0.32	0.39	0.80	0.60
Return on Avg Stockholders' Equity %	3.28	4.26	9.70	7.51
Return on Average Assets %	2.00	2.47	5.73	4.56
Current Ratio	2.65	2.64	2.32	2.37
Debt / Equity %	n.a.	n.a.	n.a.	n.a.

Compound Growth %'s	EPS % -20.63	Net Income % -20.77	Total Revenues % -2.23

Comments

The Company operates on a 52/53 week year. Entry into the Company's trade area by two large chains, Winn Dixie and Save-A-Lot, and further expansion by another large chain, Food Lion, had a negative impact on sales and profits during each of the last two fiscal years. The Company reported sales of $19.3 million and a net loss of $13,413 ($.015 per share) for the 39 weeks ended February 28, 1999, as compared to $20.3 million and a net profit of $47,892 ($.053 per share) for the same period in 1998. The Company did not declare a dividend in fiscal 1998. During the late fiscal year, the Company repurchased 30,910 shares of its common stock for $1.00 per share. Book value per share at May 31, 1998, was $2.86.

Officers	Position	Ownership Information	
Michael A. Richardson	President, CEO	Number of Shares Outstanding	921,507
Paul R. Cook	Exec VP, Treasurer	Market Capitalization	$ 460,754
Reba S. Southern	Secretary	Number of Shareholders	945
James E. Floyd	Vice President	Where Listed / Symbol	OTC-PS / ANCS

Other Information			
Transfer Agent	Company Office Fort Oglethorpe, GA	SIC Code	5410
Auditor	Hazlett, Lewis & Bieter, PLLC	Employees	190
Market Maker	Paragon Capital Corporation	(800)521-8877	
	The Seidler Companies Inc.	(800)966-7022	

American Dental Technologies, Inc.

18860 West Ten Mile Road   Southfield, MI 48075   Telephone (248)395-3900   Fax (248)395-3901

Company Description

American Dental Technologies, Inc. develops, manufactures and markets high technology dental products designed for general dentistry. The Company's primary products are air abrasive kinetic cavity preparation systems and pulsed dental lasers, primarily the PulseMaster models, which are developed and manufactured at its manufacturing facility in Corpus Christi, Texas. American Dental also develops, manufactures and markets precision air abrasive jet machining systems for industrial applications. The Company was founded in 1989 and had its initial public offering in 1991.

	12/31/98	12/31/97	12/31/96	12/31/95
Per Share Information				
Stock Price	3.62	5.00	7.20	2.80
Earnings Per Share	1.20	0.47	0.90	-0.34
Price / Earnings Ratio	3.02	10.64	8.00	n.a.
Book Value Per Share	4.29	2.92	2.42	0.47
Price / Book Value %	84.38	171.23	297.52	595.74
Dividends Per Share	0.0	0.0	0.0	0.0
Annual Financial Data				
Operating Results (000's)				
Total Revenues	28,426.8	22,026.9	23,210.2	13,617.3
Costs & Expenses	-24,649.6	-18,405.1	-17,021.4	-14,891.5
Income Before Taxes and Other	3,777.2	3,621.8	5,628.8	-1,274.2
Other Items	0.0	0.0	0.0	0.0
Income Tax	5,072.1	0.0	0.0	0.0
Net Income	8,849.3	3,621.8	5,628.8	-1,274.2
Cash Flow From Operations	1,019.1	1,699.4	203.7	124.3
Balance Sheet (000's)				
Cash & Equivalents	1,409.4	1,831.7	1,832.2	1,665.7
Total Current Assets	21,278.5	10,427.2	9,048.0	6,049.9
Fixed Assets, Net	2,462.7	1,199.1	1,192.5	262.0
Total Assets	41,855.2	22,530.3	21,280.9	12,984.7
Total Current Liabilities	3,774.5	2,137.5	3,938.2	7,487.2
Long-Term Debt	5,950.0	0.0	0.0	0.0
Stockholders' Equity	31,809.3	20,257.4	16,765.5	1,832.5
Performance & Financial Condition				
Return on Total Revenues %	31.13	16.44	24.25	-9.36
Return on Avg Stockholders' Equity %	33.99	19.57	60.53	-63.36
Return on Average Assets %	27.49	16.53	32.85	-10.56
Current Ratio	5.64	4.88	2.30	0.81
Debt / Equity %	18.71	n.a.	n.a.	n.a.

Compound Growth %'s	EPS % n.a.	Net Income % n.a.	Total Revenues % 27.80

Comments

The Company executed a 1 for 4 reverse stock split in 1997. All per share amounts have been restated for consistency. Revenues were 31% higher in 1998 than in 1997, part of which was attributable to an acquisition. But also, sales increased 44% in Japan, reversing two years of decreasing sales. An income tax benefit from tax loss carryovers was recorded in 1998, distorting the bottom line. Therefore we did not display compound growth rates in earnings per share or net income. Net income without nonrecurring items increased 16% in 1998. At December 31, 1998 the Company had $14.6 million of intangible assets recorded on its ledgers which equated to approximately 46% of stockholders' equity and book value per share.

Officers	Position	Ownership Information	
Ben J. Gallant	President, CEO	Number of Shares Outstanding	7,419,259
John E. Vickers	Exec VP, Secretary	Market Capitalization	$ 26,857,718
William S. Parker	Senior VP	Number of Shareholders	4,000
Diane M. Miller	CFO	Where Listed / Symbol	NASDAQ / ADLI

Other Information			
Transfer Agent	State Street Bank & Trust Co. Boston, MA	SIC Code	3845
Auditor	Ernst & Young LLP	Employees	111
		Web Site	americandentaltech.com

American Residential Services, Inc.

Post Oak Tower, Suite 725, 5051 Westheimer Road   Houston, TX 77056-5604   Telephone (713)599-0100   Fax (713)599-0200

Company Description

American Residential Services, Inc. is a leading national provider of 1) comprehensive maintenance, repair and replacement services for heating, ventilating and air conditioning (HVAC), plumbing, electrical, indoor air quality and other systems and major home appliances in homes and small commercial buildings and 2) new installations of those systems in homes and small commercial facilities under construction. ARS also provides comprehensive maintenance, repair, replacement, reconfiguration and monitoring services for HVAC, plumbing and electrical systems and controls in existing large commercial, industrial and institutional facilities and retail centers. To achieve its goal of becoming the leading national provider of residential services and commercial maintenance services, the Company has undertaken an aggressive acquisition program and is implementing a national operating strategy designed to increase internal growth and capitalize on cost efficiencies. The Company went public on September 25, 1996.

	12/31/98	12/31/97	12/31/96	12/31/95
Per Share Information				
Stock Price	3.25	15.62	27.12	n.a.
Earnings Per Share	-0.50	-0.33	-0.48	0.77
Price / Earnings Ratio	n.a.	n.a.	n.a.	n.a.
Book Value Per Share	8.61	8.78	8.68	-38.84
Price / Book Value %	37.75	177.90	312.44	n.a.
Dividends Per Share	0.0	0.0	0.0	0.0
Annual Financial Data				
Operating Results (000's)				
Total Revenues	506,439.0	383,591.0	150,939.0	97,895.0
Costs & Expenses	-505,984.0	-365,099.0	-143,997.0	-92,652.0
Income Before Taxes and Other	455.0	18,492.0	6,942.0	5,243.0
Other Items	-8,256.0	-24,194.0	-8,174.0	0.0
Income Tax	-60.0	1,001.0	-1,803.0	-2,088.0
Net Income	-7,861.0	-4,701.0	-3,035.0	3,155.0
Cash Flow From Operations	908.0	-11,514.0	2,949.0	6,513.0
Balance Sheet (000's)				
Cash & Equivalents	4,843.0	5,190.0	9,984.0	2,873.0
Total Current Assets	115,673.0	88,285.0	57,333.0	13,111.0
Fixed Assets, Net	30,117.0	35,528.0	21,660.0	0.0
Total Assets	382,217.0	335,313.0	211,624.0	32,436.0
Total Current Liabilities	76,591.0	65,191.0	38,158.0	191,077.0
Long-Term Debt	173,281.0	135,087.0	53,861.0	0.0
Stockholders' Equity	131,972.0	134,563.0	116,251.0	-158,641.0
Performance & Financial Condition				
Return on Total Revenues %	-1.55	-1.23	-2.01	3.22
Return on Avg Stockholders' Equity %	-5.90	-3.75	n.a.	66.37
Return on Average Assets %	-2.19	-1.72	-2.49	13.40
Current Ratio	1.51	1.35	1.50	0.07
Debt / Equity %	131.30	100.39	46.33	n.a.

Compound Growth %'s	EPS % n.a.	Net Income % n.a.	Total Revenues % 72.95

Comments

Most of the revenue increase reported for 1998 was attributable to acquired businesses. 1998 results include special charges and losses attributable to discontinued businesses of $8,256,000. 1997 results include special charges of $24,4194,000. A New York Stock Exchange listing does not mean that a company is a risk-free investment. At December 31, 1998, the Company had $230 million recorded as goodwill on its books which equated to approximately 174% of stockholders' equity and book value per share. Long term debt was $173 million which is approximately 131% of stockholders' equity including intangible assets.

Officers	Position	Ownership Information	
Thomas N. Amonett	President, CEO	Number of Shares Outstanding	15,321,322
Harry O. Nicodemus, IV	Senior VP, CFO	Market Capitalization	$ 49,794,297
John D. Held	Senior VP, Secretary	Number of Shareholders	2,000
Frank N. Menditch	Senior VP	Where Listed / Symbol	NYSE / ARS

Other Information			
Transfer Agent	ChaseMellon Shareholder Services Ridgefield Park, NJ	SIC Code	1711
Auditor	Arthur Andersen LLP	Employees	5,000
		Web Site	ars.com

Amistar Corporation

237 Via Vera Cruz   San Marcos, CA 92069   Telephone (760)471-1700   Fax (760)471-9065

Company Description

Amistar Corporation designs, develops, manufactures, markets and services a variety of automatic equipment used to assemble electronic components with printed circuit boards. The Company's first product was introduced in 1973. Since that time a number of new products which offer increased capacity, versatility and additional capabilities to enhance the productivity and cost efficiency of the assembly process have been introduced. In addition, the Company is a contract assembler of printed circuit board assemblies. Customers are predominately located in the United States and Europe.

	12/31/98	12/31/97	12/31/96	12/31/95
Per Share Information				
Stock Price	1.97	3.25	3.00	9.25
Earnings Per Share	0.07	0.34	0.53	0.65
Price / Earnings Ratio	28.14	9.56	5.66	14.23
Book Value Per Share	4.92	4.77	4.44	3.91
Price / Book Value %	40.04	68.13	67.57	236.57
Dividends Per Share	0.0	0.0	0.0	0.0
Annual Financial Data				
Operating Results (000's)				
Total Revenues	20,954.1	23,139.0	23,425.0	25,533.7
Costs & Expenses	-20,773.4	-21,541.3	-21,586.3	-23,157.1
Income Before Taxes and Other	180.6	1,597.7	1,838.8	2,376.6
Other Items	0.0	0.0	0.0	0.0
Income Tax	50.0	-505.0	-117.0	-300.0
Net Income	230.6	1,092.7	1,721.8	2,076.6
Cash Flow From Operations	-320.3	1,380.0	665.9	1,730.3
Balance Sheet (000's)				
Cash & Equivalents	1,476.6	2,521.4	1,891.5	1,982.5
Total Current Assets	13,544.5	14,920.3	14,651.4	13,443.6
Fixed Assets, Net	5,768.3	5,146.2	4,949.4	4,491.1
Total Assets	21,758.9	22,236.1	21,550.6	19,742.3
Total Current Liabilities	1,835.3	2,287.9	2,713.0	2,629.1
Long-Term Debt	4,500.0	4,500.0	4,500.0	4,500.0
Stockholders' Equity	15,423.6	15,448.2	14,337.6	12,613.1
Performance & Financial Condition				
Return on Total Revenues %	1.10	4.72	7.35	8.13
Return on Avg Stockholders' Equity %	1.49	7.34	12.78	17.98
Return on Average Assets %	1.05	4.99	8.34	11.17
Current Ratio	7.38	6.52	5.40	5.11
Debt / Equity %	29.18	29.13	31.39	35.68

Compound Growth %'s	EPS % -52.42	Net Income % -51.93	Total Revenues % -6.38

Comments

Sales in 1998 and 1997 were negatively impacted by delays in the delivery of the newest and highest volume private label model from the Company's offshore supplier. After initial deliveries, it was discovered that the early production units required modifications in order to be suitable for applications required by the customer base. But the order backlog is still growing and stood at $6.5 million at the end of 1998 as compared to $4.3 million one year earlier. Research and development expense totalled $1,202,000, $1,461,000, $1,234,000 and $951,000 in 1998, 1997, 1996 and 1995, respectively. Income tax expenses in 1996 and 1995 were disproportionately low due to changes in the valuation of deferred taxes. Book value is real; there are no intangibles.

Officers	Position	Ownership Information	
Stuart Baker	Chairman, President	Number of Shares Outstanding	3,136,500
William W. Holl	VP - Finance, Treasurer	Market Capitalization	$ 6,178,905
Daniel C. Finn	Vice President	Number of Shareholders	1,000
Harry A. Munn	VP - Sales	Where Listed / Symbol	NASDAQ / AMTA

Other Information			
Transfer Agent	U.S. Stock Transfer Corp. Glendale, CA	SIC Code	3559
Auditor	KPMG LLP	Employees	155
		Web Site	amistar.com

Amtech Systems, Inc.

131 South Clark Drive   Tempe, AZ 85281   Telephone (602)967-5146   Fax (602)968-3763

Company Description

Amtech Systems, Inc. designs, assembles, sells and installs capital equipment and related consumables used in the manufacture of various kinds of wafers, primarily silicon wafers used by the semiconductor industry and in certain processes of semiconductor fabrication. These products are sold to manufacturers of silicon wafers and semiconductors world-wide, particularly to the United States, Korea, and northern Europe. During fiscal 1998, the Company began producing and selling conveyor diffusion furnace systems used to produce thick films for the electronics industry. During fiscal 1997, the Company began providing preventative maintenance services to the semiconductor industry in the United States. Amtech Systems began business in 1981.

	09/30/98	09/30/97	09/30/96	09/30/95
Per Share Information				
Stock Price as of 12/31	0.59	2.37	3.12	4.00
Earnings Per Share	-0.14	0.06	0.10	0.06
Price / Earnings Ratio	n.a.	39.50	31.20	66.67
Book Value Per Share	1.53	1.66	1.61	1.63
Price / Book Value %	38.56	142.77	193.79	245.40
Dividends Per Share	0.0	0.0	0.0	0.0
Annual Financial Data				
Operating Results (000's)				
Total Revenues	16,268.4	11,273.4	8,640.8	7,085.5
Costs & Expenses	-17,118.2	-10,895.7	-8,293.2	-6,824.5
Income Before Taxes and Other	-849.9	377.7	347.6	261.1
Other Items	0.0	0.0	311.1	55.5
Income Tax	260.0	-140.0	-150.0	-90.0
Net Income	-589.9	237.7	508.7	226.6
Cash Flow From Operations	-310.1	-46.6	749.0	106.1
Balance Sheet (000's)				
Cash & Equivalents	1,351.5	1,395.8	1,994.2	833.8
Total Current Assets	7,524.2	7,379.5	7,049.4	7,526.6
Fixed Assets, Net	1,243.0	1,360.0	976.3	649.8
Total Assets	9,325.5	9,355.1	8,458.6	8,365.5
Total Current Liabilities	2,530.7	2,108.2	1,569.0	1,363.3
Long-Term Debt	347.7	318.7	265.4	0.0
Stockholders' Equity	6,447.1	6,928.2	6,624.3	7,002.2
Performance & Financial Condition				
Return on Total Revenues %	-3.63	2.11	5.89	3.20
Return on Avg Stockholders' Equity %	-8.82	3.51	7.47	4.48
Return on Average Assets %	-6.32	2.67	6.05	3.67
Current Ratio	2.97	3.50	4.49	5.52
Debt / Equity %	5.39	4.60	4.01	n.a.

Compound Growth %'s	EPS %	n.a.	Net Income %	n.a.	Total Revenues %	31.92

Comments

The Company declared a 2 for 1 stock split in fiscal 1996. All per share amounts have been adjusted for consistency. Fiscal 1998 revenues were sharply higher due to an acquisition and the Company's new preventive maintenance services. The net loss for the year was primarily as result of the cyclical downturn in the semiconductor equipment industry and other costs associated with introducing new products. The Company discontinued the technical contract personnel segment of its business in 1995. The results of these operations are reflected as a discontinued business and are not included in revenues. Discontinued operations contributed $26,757 and $226,568 to net income in fiscal 1996 and 1995, respectively. Fiscal 1996 results also reflect a nonrecurring gain of $284,335.

Officers	Position	Ownership Information	
Jong S. Whang	President, CEO	Number of Shares Outstanding	4,220,606
Robert T. Hass	VP - Finance, CFO	Market Capitalization	$ 2,490,158
Donald F. Johnston	Director	Number of Shareholders	1,479
Alvin Katz	Director	Where Listed / Symbol	NASDAQ / ASYS

Other Information			
Transfer Agent	American Securities Transfer, Inc. Lakewood, CO	SIC Code	7363
Auditor	Arthur Andersen LLP	Employees	89
		Web Site	amtechsystems.com

Apple Orthodontix, Inc.

2777 Allen Parkway, Suite 700 Houston, TX 77019 Telephone (713)852-2500 Fax (713)852-2550

Company Description

Apple Orthodontix, Inc., founded in 1996, provides practice management services (which exclude the management and delivery of orthodontic services) to orthodontic practices in the United States and Canada. In connection with its initial public offering in May 1997, the Company acquired substantially all of the tangible and intangible assets and assumed certain liabilities of, and began providing long-term management services to, 31 orthodontists operating in 58 offices located in 13 states and Canada. As of April 14, 1999, the Company provided services to 62 orthodontic practices representing 88 orthodontists operating in 17 states in the United States and three provinces in Canada.

	12/31/98	12/31/97	12/31/96
Per Share Information			
Stock Price	3.25	11.87	n.a.
Earnings Per Share	-0.75	0.09	-7.24
Price / Earnings Ratio	n.a.	131.89	n.a.
Book Value Per Share	2.09	2.70	-0.26
Price / Book Value %	155.50	439.63	n.a.
Dividends Per Share	0.0	0.0	0.0
Annual Financial Data			
Operating Results (000's)			
Total Revenues	47,517.0	19,392.2	0.0
Costs & Expenses	-42,617.0	-18,236.2	-24,309.4
Income Before Taxes and Other	4,900.0	1,156.0	-24,309.4
Other Items	-21,726.0	0.0	0.0
Income Tax	6,496.0	-439.3	0.0
Net Income	-10,330.0	716.7	-24,309.4
Cash Flow From Operations	-4,320.0	-3,240.7	-475.2
Balance Sheet (000's)			
Cash & Equivalents	755.0	2,114.4	21.3
Total Current Assets	9,335.0	7,511.0	21.3
Fixed Assets, Net	6,649.0	6,025.4	0.0
Total Assets	71,462.0	55,180.3	1,461.3
Total Current Liabilities	6,722.0	4,866.4	2,345.0
Long-Term Debt	23,654.0	247.6	0.0
Stockholders' Equity	29,688.0	35,492.8	-883.7
Performance & Financial Condition			
Return on Total Revenues %	-21.74	3.70	n.a.
Return on Avg Stockholders' Equity %	-31.70	4.14	n.a.
Return on Average Assets %	-16.31	2.53	-3,472.77
Current Ratio	1.39	1.54	0.01
Debt / Equity %	79.68	0.70	n.a.

Compound Growth %'s	EPS % n.a.	Net Income % n.a.	Total Revenues % 145.03

Comments

The increase in revenues recorded in 1998 as compared to 1997 is attributable to a full twelve months of operating revenues as compared to only seven months of revenues in 1997. 1998 results include $21,726,000 of special charges associated primarily with severance agreements and the reevaluation of various assets. 1996 results include $23.4 million in special compensation and consulting expense. At December 31, 1998, the Company had goodwill of $49.3 million recorded as assets which equated to approximately 166% of stockholders' equity and book value per share. All may be well if the Company is really capable of making a profit. But several allegations that the Company has breached its service contracts have to be of concern. Can we make it through a year without those special charges?

Officers	Position	Ownership Information	
John G. Vondrak	Chairman	Number of Shares Outstanding	14,204,000
A. Stone Douglass	President, CEO	Market Capitalization	$ 46,163,000
W. Daniel Cook	Senior VP	Number of Shareholders	2,000
Michael J. Marrone	Vice President, CFO	Where Listed / Symbol	AMEX / AOI

Other Information

Transfer Agent	ChaseMellon Shareholder Services Ridgefield Park, NJ	SIC Code	8000
Auditor	Arthur Andersen LLP	Employees	698
		Web Site	appleorthodontix.com

Applied Cellular Technology, Inc.

400 Royal Palm Way, Suite 410   Palm Beach, FL 33480   Telephone (561)366-4800   Fax (561)366-0002

Company Description

Applied Cellular Technology, Inc. is a diversified technology company that specializes in providing services and solutions to the wireless, telecommunications and digital industry. The Company's overall goal is to acquire the development, manufacturing and delivery capabilities needed to take full advantage of the industry's move from analog to digital and from wireline to wireless systems. The Company currently operates in the United States, Canada and the United Kingdom. The largest part of the Company's current operations are the result of acquisitions completed during the last three years. The Company was formed in 1993.

	12/31/98	12/31/97	12/31/96	12/31/95
Per Share Information				
Stock Price	3.50	4.50	5.00	3.75
Earnings Per Share	0.13	0.15	0.15	0.09
Price / Earnings Ratio	26.92	30.00	33.33	41.67
Book Value Per Share	1.90	1.76	1.42	1.53
Price / Book Value %	184.21	255.68	352.11	245.10
Dividends Per Share	0.0	0.0	0.0	0.0
Annual Financial Data				
Operating Results (000's)				
Total Revenues	207,501.0	103,351.8	20,009.3	2,410.9
Costs & Expenses	-199,799.0	-100,225.2	-18,828.6	-2,182.6
Income Before Taxes and Other	7,702.0	3,126.6	1,180.7	228.3
Other Items	-424.0	982.4	-132.3	-49.0
Income Tax	-2,588.0	-1,768.7	-362.1	0.0
Net Income	4,690.0	2,340.3	686.2	179.4
Cash Flow From Operations	-2,783.0	-4,666.7	-1,441.7	127.0
Balance Sheet (000's)				
Cash & Equivalents	4,555.0	7,656.9	809.7	125.5
Total Current Assets	65,244.0	39,574.6	13,886.7	1,408.9
Fixed Assets, Net	15,627.0	5,338.7	2,915.1	138.5
Total Assets	124,116.0	61,281.6	33,208.1	4,131.5
Total Current Liabilities	50,757.0	20,112.4	12,214.5	1,003.3
Long-Term Debt	2,838.0	2,199.8	1,385.6	0.0
Stockholders' Equity	67,560.0	36,284.6	8,251.8	3,051.9
Performance & Financial Condition				
Return on Total Revenues %	2.26	2.26	3.43	7.44
Return on Avg Stockholders' Equity %	9.03	10.51	12.14	8.60
Return on Average Assets %	5.06	4.95	3.68	6.53
Current Ratio	1.29	1.97	1.14	1.40
Debt / Equity %	4.20	6.06	16.79	n.a.

Compound Growth %'s	EPS %	13.04	Net Income %	196.81	Total Revenues %	341.52

Comments

Revenues in 1998 increased 100.7% over 1997 and 1997 revenues increased 418.8% over 1996. These significant increases are attributable to the Company's growth of existing businesses and to its growth through acquisition. Selling, general and administrative costs as a percentage of sales have been lower for two consecutive years. The decrease is due to economies of scale that the Company was able to recognize as it grew larger. 1997 results include a gain of $1,679,627 from the sale of assets. Common shares issued in connection with acquisitions have diluted compound growth in earnings per share as compared to compound growth of net income. At December 31, 1998, the Company had $33.4 million of goodwill reflected as assets which equated to approximately 50% of stockholders' equity and book value per share.

Officers	Position	Ownership Information	
Richard J. Sullivan	Chairman, CEO	Number of Shares Outstanding	35,577,000
Garrett A. Sullivan	President, COO	Market Capitalization	$ 124,519,500
David A. Loppert	Vice President, CFO	Number of Shareholders	10,000
Andy Hildalgo	Vice President	Where Listed / Symbol	NASDAQ / ACTC

Other Information			
Transfer Agent	Florida Atlantic Stock Transfer, Inc. Tamarac, FL	SIC Code	5045
Auditor	PricewaterhouseCoopers LLP	Employees	1,650
		Web Site	appliedcell.com

Applied Innovation Inc.

5800 Innovation Drive   Dublin, OH 43016   Telephone (614)798-2000   Fax (614)798-1770

Company Description

Applied Innovation Inc. develops, manufactures and markets network mediation and network bridging products and associated services to support the operation, maintenance, administration and provisioning of the internal data network that is used by telecommunications service providers to manage elements in their customer service network systems. The Company is also developing products which will assist telecommunications service providers in handling the rapidly increasing Internet traffic. The Company was founded in 1986.

	12/31/98	12/31/97	12/31/96	12/31/95
Per Share Information				
Stock Price	3.22	5.25	6.12	11.75
Earnings Per Share	0.14	-0.04	0.14	0.38
Price / Earnings Ratio	23.00	n.a.	43.71	30.92
Book Value Per Share	2.00	1.86	1.90	1.74
Price / Book Value %	161.00	282.26	322.11	675.29
Dividends Per Share	0.0	0.0	0.0	0.0
Annual Financial Data				
Operating Results (000's)				
Total Revenues	55,292.6	47,196.5	41,673.8	36,433.0
Costs & Expenses	-48,645.0	-48,079.6	-38,263.3	-26,540.0
Income Before Taxes and Other	6,647.7	-1,017.2	3,410.6	9,883.0
Other Items	-3,800.0	0.0	0.0	0.0
Income Tax	-538.0	380.0	-1,256.0	-3,829.0
Net Income	2,309.7	-637.2	2,154.6	6,054.0
Cash Flow From Operations	10,241.9	308.6	5,211.3	9,734.0
Balance Sheet (000's)				
Cash & Equivalents	17,211.5	8,195.2	12,278.1	9,176.3
Total Current Assets	30,236.3	24,759.5	24,567.2	20,591.7
Fixed Assets, Net	9,426.2	12,833.9	10,977.6	9,872.8
Total Assets	39,769.7	37,707.5	35,662.2	30,531.7
Total Current Liabilities	8,063.0	8,104.6	5,476.4	3,093.0
Long-Term Debt	0.0	0.0	0.0	0.0
Stockholders' Equity	31,642.7	29,403.0	29,941.9	27,314.9
Performance & Financial Condition				
Return on Total Revenues %	4.18	-1.35	5.17	16.62
Return on Avg Stockholders' Equity %	7.57	-2.15	7.53	24.22
Return on Average Assets %	5.96	-1.74	6.51	20.18
Current Ratio	3.75	3.06	4.49	6.66
Debt / Equity %	n.a.	n.a.	n.a.	n.a.

Compound Growth %'s	EPS %	-28.31	Net Income %	-27.47	Total Revenues %	14.92

Comments

The 15% increase in revenue reflected in 1998 resulted from additional unit sales of all core products. Five customers accounted for 75% of total sales in 1998. A nonrecurring expense of $3.8 million was recorded in 1998 due to the termination of certain development activities. The Company spends substantial amounts on research and development activities. These amounts totaled $12.0 million, $12.9 million, $7.6 million and $6.0 million in 1998, 1997, 1996, and 1995, respectively. Of the four years presented above, all years were profitable except 1997. In 1997, expenses outpaced income primarily due to high research and development costs and higher than usual employment and recruiting expenses. The Company's balance sheet is solid with plenty of working capital and no long term debt.

Officers	Position	Ownership Information	
Gerard B. Moersdorf, Jr.	President, CEO	Number of Shares Outstanding	15,786,132
William H. Largent	Senior VP, CFO	Market Capitalization	$ 50,831,345
Lawrence H. Corbett	Senior VP	Number of Shareholders	745
John M. Spiegel	Controller	Where Listed / Symbol	NASDAQ / AINN

Other Information			
Transfer Agent	National City Bank Cleveland, OH	SIC Code	3661
Auditor	KPMG LLP	Employees	220
		Web Site	aiinet.com

Argosy Gaming Company

219 Piasa Street Alton, IL 62002-6232 Telephone (618)474-7500 Fax (618)474-7636

Company Description

Argosy Gaming Company is a multi-jurisdictional developer, owner and operator of riverboat casinos and related entertainment facilities in the midwestern and southern United States. The Company, through its subsidiaries, owns and operates riverboat casinos in Alton, Illinois; Riverside, Missouri; Baton Rouge, Louisiana; Lawrenceburg, Indiana and Sioux City, Iowa. In 1997, the Company implemented a change in operating strategy in an attempt to build strength and gain momentum as a leading riverboat casino operator. This strategy includes assembling a new management team with significant experience and expertise in gaming industry operations and marketing, adopting new marketing strategies with an emphasis on direct marketing, and prudently investing in gaming and gaming-related assets for its properties.

	12/31/98	12/31/97	12/31/96	12/31/95
Per Share Information				
Stock Price	2.75	3.56	4.62	7.38
Earnings Per Share	0.23	-1.65	-1.02	0.29
Price / Earnings Ratio	11.96	n.a.	n.a.	25.45
Book Value Per Share	1.58	1.33	2.99	4.01
Price / Book Value %	174.05	267.67	154.52	184.04
Dividends Per Share	0.0	0.0	0.0	0.0
Annual Financial Data				
Operating Results (000's)				
Total Revenues	510,250.0	350,020.0	249,052.0	253,127.0
Costs & Expenses	-476,344.0	-373,319.0	-290,410.0	-239,737.0
Income Before Taxes and Other	33,906.0	-23,299.0	-41,358.0	13,390.0
Other Items	-26,205.0	-18,266.0	3,989.0	526.0
Income Tax	-1,140.0	1,352.0	12,530.0	-6,963.0
Net Income	6,561.0	-40,213.0	-24,839.0	6,953.0
Cash Flow From Operations	81,663.0	31,628.0	-7,460.0	49,564.0
Balance Sheet (000's)				
Cash & Equivalents	89,857.0	59,354.0	38,284.0	886.0
Total Current Assets	99,256.0	69,983.0	58,841.0	28,492.0
Fixed Assets, Net	395,920.0	390,343.0	314,480.0	239,480.0
Total Assets	562,752.0	559,856.0	530,528.0	309,882.0
Total Current Liabilities	71,385.0	68,999.0	50,135.0	35,329.0
Long-Term Debt	417,700.0	436,442.0	377,308.0	174,470.0
Stockholders' Equity	40,863.0	32,663.0	72,701.0	97,540.0
Performance & Financial Condition				
Return on Total Revenues %	1.29	-11.49	-9.97	2.75
Return on Avg Stockholders' Equity %	17.85	-76.33	-29.18	7.39
Return on Average Assets %	1.17	-7.38	-5.91	2.56
Current Ratio	1.39	1.01	1.17	0.81
Debt / Equity %	1,022.20	1,336.20	518.99	178.87

Compound Growth %'s	EPS % -7.44	Net Income % -1.92	Total Revenues % 26.32

Comments

Revenues increased 47.2% in 1998 much of which was attributable to the opening of a permanent pavilion at Lawrenceburg. Focused marketing efforts and operating efficiencies were reported for all locations which helped stop the flow of operating losses. 1997 results included nonrecurring expenses of $11,350,000. The Company has $42.8 million of tax loss carryforwards to offset future income. At December 31, 1998, the Company had $51.8 million in recorded goodwill reflected as assets which equated to approximately 127% of stockholders' equity and book value per share.

Officers	Position	Ownership Information	
James B. Perry	President, CEO	Number of Shares Outstanding	25,830,313
Patsy S. Hubbard	Secretary	Market Capitalization	$ 71,033,361
Roger L. Archibald	Vice President	Number of Shareholders	5,000
Dale R. Black	Vice President, CFO	Where Listed / Symbol	NYSE / AGY

Other Information			
Transfer Agent	Harris Trust & Savings Bank Chicago, IL	SIC Code	7900
Auditor	Ernst & Young LLP	Employees	3,955
		Web Site	argosycasinos.com

Arizona Instrument Corporation

4114 East Wood Street   Pheonix, AZ 85040-1941   Telephone (602)470-1414   Fax (602)470-1888

Company Description

Arizona Instrument Corporation designs, manufactures and markets the Computrac line of automated microprocessor controlled analytical instruments used to measure the moisture content of various materials. Other products include the ENCOMPASS and Soil Sentry line of computer-based fuel management and compliance leak detection instruments, used for monitoring underground storage tanks, and the Jerome line of toxic gas detection instruments, primarily used to detect mercury and hydrogen sulfide. The Company discontinued tank testing and related services for the underground storage tank market in 1997.

	12/31/98	12/31/97	12/31/96	12/31/95
Per Share Information				
Stock Price	0.81	0.91	2.37	1.94
Earnings Per Share	0.02	-0.19	0.25	0.08
Price / Earnings Ratio	40.50	n.a.	9.48	24.25
Book Value Per Share	1.11	1.09	1.28	1.01
Price / Book Value %	72.97	83.49	185.16	192.08
Dividends Per Share	0.0	0.0	0.0	0.0
Annual Financial Data				
Operating Results (000's)				
Total Revenues	13,809.3	15,247.1	13,727.3	13,227.1
Costs & Expenses	-13,339.8	-16,212.8	-12,471.3	-12,683.5
Income Before Taxes and Other	469.5	-967.7	1,255.9	543.6
Other Items	0.0	-636.8	0.0	0.0
Income Tax	-344.0	366.0	488.0	-11.0
Net Income	125.5	-1,238.5	1,743.9	532.6
Cash Flow From Operations	2,199.6	-283.1	1,231.1	2,241.7
Balance Sheet (000's)				
Cash & Equivalents	1,098.8	143.2	597.9	486.4
Total Current Assets	6,320.5	6,740.3	6,161.7	5,930.2
Fixed Assets, Net	861.8	975.2	846.5	1,083.2
Total Assets	9,779.0	11,591.7	11,024.2	10,600.2
Total Current Liabilities	2,274.6	4,183.3	2,214.4	2,597.7
Long-Term Debt	12.0	93.4	378.0	1,663.1
Stockholders' Equity	7,492.4	7,315.0	8,431.7	6,339.3
Performance & Financial Condition				
Return on Total Revenues %	0.91	-8.12	12.70	4.03
Return on Avg Stockholders' Equity %	1.69	-15.73	23.61	8.82
Return on Average Assets %	1.17	-10.95	16.13	4.72
Current Ratio	2.78	1.61	2.78	2.28
Debt / Equity %	0.16	1.28	4.48	26.23

Compound Growth %'s	EPS %	-37.00	Net Income %	-38.24	Total Revenues %	1.45

Comments

Net sales increased in 1997 primarily due to increased sales of ENCOMPASS installations, ENCOMPASS systems, and Computrac instruments. This trend reversed itself in 1998. A loss from discontinued operations of $636,799 was reported in 1997. 1996 results included $997,096 of nonrecurring income related to the settlement of litigation. Research and development expenses increased from $984,628 in 1997 to $1,324,640 in 1998. At December 31, 1998, the Company had $1.5 million of goodwill recorded as assets which equated to approximately 20% of stockholders' equity and book value per share. On March 9, 1999, BP Oil Company filed suit against the Company, alleging breach of contract and warranty in connection with its purchase of ENCOMPASS systems. BP Oil seeks recovery of $2 million actual damages plus several million dollars for incidental damages. Although the Company intends to vigorously defend this action, an unfavorable outcome could have a material adverse effect on the Company.

Officers	Position	Ownership Information	
George G. Hays	Chairman, President	Number of Shares Outstanding	6,764,027
Susan Berry	Secretary	Market Capitalization	$ 5,478,862
Walfred R. Raisanen	VP - Research, Treasurer	Number of Shareholders	400
Linda Shepherd	Controller	Where Listed / Symbol	NASDAQ / AZIC

Other Information			
Transfer Agent	ChaseMellon Shareholder Services Ridgefield Park, NJ	SIC Code	3823
Auditor	Toback CPA's P.C.	Employees	73
		Web Site	azic.com

Armanino Foods of Distinction, Inc.

30588 San Antonio Street   Hayward, CA 94544   Telephone (510)441-9300   Fax (510)441-0101

Company Description

Armanino Foods of Distinction, Inc. is engaged in the production and marketing of upscale and innovative food products, including frozen pesto and other Italian-style frozen sauces, frozen stuffed and flat pasta products, frozen focaccia and frozen meatballs. In May 1995, the Company acquired the business of Emilia Romagna for the purpose of expanding its product line to include highly specialized upscale pasta products for the foodservice and industrial markets. The Company was founded in 1978.

	12/31/98	12/31/97	12/31/96	12/31/95
Per Share Information				
Stock Price	2.81	4.55	6.55	23.75
Earnings Per Share	0.10	0.31	0.18	0.45
Price / Earnings Ratio	28.10	14.68	36.39	52.78
Book Value Per Share	4.99	4.87	4.58	3.96
Price / Book Value %	56.31	93.43	143.01	599.75
Dividends Per Share	0.0	0.0	0.0	0.0
Annual Financial Data				
Operating Results (000's)				
Total Revenues	13,670.8	15,548.1	15,569.9	13,638.6
Costs & Expenses	-13,114.5	-14,690.4	-13,757.3	-11,918.3
Income Before Taxes and Other	556.3	842.1	1,807.4	1,714.3
Other Items	-119.5	0.0	-608.1	0.0
Income Tax	-218.3	-124.8	-752.3	-621.6
Net Income	218.5	717.3	447.0	1,092.7
Cash Flow From Operations	1,287.6	855.6	896.2	1,911.2
Balance Sheet (000's)				
Cash & Equivalents	633.6	181.0	742.9	734.0
Total Current Assets	5,660.5	7,308.6	8,263.1	6,330.6
Fixed Assets, Net	4,867.7	5,070.6	2,599.9	2,541.0
Total Assets	11,042.6	12,935.6	11,926.1	9,054.3
Total Current Liabilities	677.8	1,583.8	1,132.4	835.7
Long-Term Debt	0.0	203.4	45.9	71.6
Stockholders' Equity	9,901.5	10,945.4	10,621.8	8,037.0
Performance & Financial Condition				
Return on Total Revenues %	1.60	4.61	2.87	8.01
Return on Avg Stockholders' Equity %	2.10	6.65	4.79	14.64
Return on Average Assets %	1.82	5.77	4.26	12.78
Current Ratio	8.35	4.61	7.30	7.58
Debt / Equity %	n.a.	1.86	0.43	0.89

Compound Growth %'s	EPS %	-39.43	Net Income %	-41.53	Total Revenues %	0.08

Comments

The Company executed a 1 for 5 reverse stock split on January 29, 1999. All per share amounts have been restated to be consistent with this reverse split. A sharp drop in meatball sales to a club-store customer could not be offset by increases in other product lines. The implementation of new equipment in late 1997 increased production efficiency but could not overcome the effect of the sales decline in 1998. Included in 1998 results is a nonrecurring loss on the settlement of lawsuit of $119,460 ($.05 per share). 1996 results include losses from discontinued operations of $608,145 ($.25 per share). The Company has been reacquiring shares of its stock at per share prices ranging from $7.50 in 1996 to $3.00 in 1998.

Officers	Position	Ownership Information	
William J. Armanino	President, CEO	Number of Shares Outstanding	1,982,381
Linda A. Armanino	Exec VP, COO	Market Capitalization	$ 5,570,491
Deborah Armanino-LeBlanc	Vice President, Secretary	Number of Shareholders	448
Tino Barzie	Director	Where Listed / Symbol	NASDAQ / ARMF

Other Information			
Transfer Agent	American Securities Transfer, Inc. Denver, CO	SIC Code	2038
Auditor	Pritchett, Siler & Hardy, P.C.	Employees	35
		Web Site	armaninofoods.com

Arrow-Magnolia International, Inc.

2646 Rodney Lane, P.O. Box 59089   Dallas, TX 75229   Telephone (972)247-7111   Fax (972)484-2896

Company Description

Arrow-Magnolia International, Inc. manufactures and distributes approximately 400 specialty chemical products for use in cleaning and maintaining equipment and for general maintenance and sanitation. The Company also distributes certain nonchemical products, such as paper and other janitorial supplies, related to its chemical products. The products are sold throughout the U.S., Canada and other countries to a variety of customers. The Company was founded in 1937.

	12/31/98	12/31/97	12/31/96	12/31/95
Per Share Information				
Stock Price	4.31	6.02	3.51	3.72
Earnings Per Share	0.36	0.39	0.33	0.22
Price / Earnings Ratio	11.97	15.44	10.64	16.91
Book Value Per Share	2.07	1.67	1.16	1.90
Price / Book Value %	208.21	360.48	302.59	195.79
Dividends Per Share	0.0	0.0	0.0	0.0
Annual Financial Data				
Operating Results (000's)				
Total Revenues	13,856.6	12,815.5	10,338.7	8,420.5
Costs & Expenses	-11,977.3	-10,832.7	-8,689.1	-7,353.8
Income Before Taxes and Other	1,879.3	1,982.8	1,649.6	1,066.7
Other Items	0.0	0.0	0.0	0.0
Income Tax	-672.1	-707.0	-607.2	-387.6
Net Income	1,207.3	1,275.8	1,042.5	679.1
Cash Flow From Operations	1,431.5	403.7	1,103.6	427.2
Balance Sheet (000's)				
Cash & Equivalents	2,386.7	1,878.9	1,755.0	761.4
Total Current Assets	5,979.1	5,698.0	4,260.1	3,588.0
Fixed Assets, Net	804.1	738.9	606.0	371.3
Total Assets	6,984.4	6,646.9	5,022.8	4,135.7
Total Current Liabilities	770.7	1,029.4	921.6	892.0
Long-Term Debt	0.0	600.0	650.0	790.0
Stockholders' Equity	6,109.2	4,913.0	3,328.8	2,202.9
Performance & Financial Condition				
Return on Total Revenues %	8.71	9.96	10.08	8.06
Return on Avg Stockholders' Equity %	21.91	30.96	37.69	38.53
Return on Average Assets %	17.71	21.87	22.77	18.94
Current Ratio	7.76	5.54	4.62	4.02
Debt / Equity %	n.a.	12.21	19.53	35.86

Compound Growth %'s	EPS %	17.84	Net Income %	21.14	Total Revenues %	18.06

Comments

The Company declared 10% stock dividends in 1998 and 1997 and a 2 for 1 stock split in 1996. All per share amounts have been adjusted for consistency. In addition to its employees, the Company is represented by 90 sales representatives that act as independent contractors. The 8% increase in 1998 revenues and the 24% increase in 1997 revenues are primarily attributable to the extension of sales coverage through the addition of sales personnel under an ongoing hiring program. 1998 results include an increase in expenses related to the hiring of additional sales personnel. 1997 results include a charge of $129,500 in compensation expense as a result of issuing stock options and warrants to a key employee and a service provider. The Company is in excellent financial condition with excess working capital and no long term debt.

Officers	Position	Ownership Information	
Morris Schwiff	Chairman, President	Number of Shares Outstanding	2,945,490
Mark I. Kenner	Exec VP	Market Capitalization	$ 12,695,062
Fred Kenner	Secretary, Treasurer	Number of Shareholders	350
Robert D. DeRosier	Director	Where Listed / Symbol	NASDAQ / ARWM

Other Information			
Transfer Agent	Harris Trust & Savings Bank Chicago, IL	SIC Code	2890
Auditor	KPMG LLP	Employees	35
		Web Site	arrowmagnolia.com

Arthur Treacher's, Inc.

7400 Baymeadows Way, Suite 300   Jacksonville, FL 32256   Telephone (904)739-1200   Fax (904)739-2500

Company Description

The Company's principal business is the operation of Company-owned stores and the sale of franchises of Arthur Treacher's Fish & Chips fast food restaurants. The Company has 110 restaurants in the Arthur Treacher's system, consisting of 62 Company owned restaurants and 48 independently operated franchised locations. The restaurants are located in 10 states in the mid-western and eastern United States as well as in Washington D.C. and the province of Ontario, Canada. When an individual franchise is sold, the Company assists the franchisee in site selection, training personnel, implementation of an accounting and store management system, and various other services. The Company was founded in 1969.

	06/30/98	06/30/97	06/30/96	06/30/95
Per Share Information				
Stock Price as of 12/31	0.62	3.50	3.00	0.39
Earnings Per Share	-0.19	-0.16	-0.10	-0.05
Price / Earnings Ratio	n.a.	n.a.	n.a.	n.a.
Book Value Per Share	0.05	0.21	n.a.	-0.05
Price / Book Value %	1,240.00	1,666.67	n.a.	n.a.
Dividends Per Share	0.0	0.0	0.0	0.0
Annual Financial Data				
Operating Results (000's)				
Total Revenues	22,986.8	17,784.8	7,873.2	7,317.6
Costs & Expenses	-25,252.4	-19,863.8	-8,624.1	-7,854.2
Income Before Taxes and Other	-2,768.7	-2,079.0	-750.9	-536.6
Other Items	0.0	0.0	-403.4	0.0
Income Tax	-60.1	0.0	329.1	146.6
Net Income	-2,828.8	-2,079.0	-825.2	-390.0
Cash Flow From Operations	-487.0	-1,715.8	734.4	69.3
Balance Sheet (000's)				
Cash & Equivalents	909.6	867.8	985.6	26.1
Total Current Assets	1,448.5	1,475.7	1,241.3	460.3
Fixed Assets, Net	5,073.3	5,670.5	1,390.5	1,381.9
Total Assets	7,312.6	7,622.9	2,999.4	1,874.5
Total Current Liabilities	3,592.3	2,075.3	2,494.1	1,213.8
Long-Term Debt	1,398.8	1,570.3	458.9	970.8
Stockholders' Equity	2,306.1	3,584.5	0.0	-374.8
Performance & Financial Condition				
Return on Total Revenues %	-12.31	-11.69	-10.48	-5.33
Return on Avg Stockholders' Equity %	-96.04	-116.00	n.a.	n.a.
Return on Average Assets %	-37.88	-39.14	-33.86	-19.50
Current Ratio	0.40	0.71	0.50	0.38
Debt / Equity %	60.66	43.81	n.a.	n.a.

Compound Growth %'s	EPS % n.a.	Net Income % n.a.	Total Revenues % 46.45

Comments

During fiscal 1997, the Company acquired 100% of the common stock of its largest franchisee whose operations included 32 restaurants. An additional eight restaurants were acquired in other transactions. These transactions contributed most of the growth to revenues in fiscal 1997 and all of the growth in fiscal 1998. Same store sales declined 6.6% in fiscal 1998. Fiscal 1998 results include $419,417 of professional fee expense related to abandoned acquisitions. The Company has issued stock in each of the last three years to support working capital needs and acquisitions. Can Arthur Treacher's keep its head above water? For the six months ended December 31, 1998, the Company reported revenues and a net loss of $11.3 million and $1,330,375 ($.09 per share) as compared to $12.2 million and $612,359 ($.04 per share) for the same period of the preceding year.

Officers	Position	Ownership Information	
Bruce R. Galloway	Chairman, CEO	Number of Shares Outstanding	14,869,748
William F. Saculla	President, CFO	Market Capitalization	$ 9,219,244
Skuli Thorvaldsson	Director	Number of Shareholders	551
Fred Knoll	Director	Where Listed / Symbol	OTC-BB / ATCH

Other Information			
Transfer Agent	Atlas Stock Transfer Corp. Salt Lake City, UT	SIC Code	5800
Auditor	KPMG LLP	Employees	700
Market Maker	T.R. Winston & Co. Inc. (800)443-9943		
	Sherwood Securities Corp. (800)435-1235		

Astrex, Inc.

205 Express Street   Plainview, NY 11803   Telephone (516)433-1700   Fax (516)433-1796

Company Description

Astrex, Inc. is a value-added distributor of electronic components used to connect, control, regulate and store electricity in equipment. Approximately 80% of the products sold are connectors, which range in price, depending on complexity and application, from $0.25 to $2,500. Most, however, range from $5 to $70. Control, regulation and storage devices make up the remaining product sales. The Company's largest markets include the defense, aerospace, industrial and computer industries. A large majority of the Company's sales are in the northeast and mid-atlantic United States.

	03/31/98	03/31/97	03/31/96	03/31/95
Per Share Information				
Stock Price as of 12/31	0.27	0.31	0.25	0.25
Earnings Per Share	0.06	0.06	0.04	-0.22
Price / Earnings Ratio	4.50	5.17	6.25	n.a.
Book Value Per Share	0.58	0.57	0.53	0.53
Price / Book Value %	46.55	54.39	47.17	47.17
Dividends Per Share	0.0	0.0	0.0	0.0
Annual Financial Data				
Operating Results (000's)				
Total Revenues	14,263.7	14,385.3	13,518.4	12,313.5
Costs & Expenses	-13,930.2	-14,047.3	-13,297.6	-13,252.1
Income Before Taxes and Other	333.5	338.0	220.8	-1,013.2
Other Items	0.0	0.0	0.0	0.0
Income Tax	-11.5	-31.5	-17.9	-10.0
Net Income	322.0	306.5	202.9	-1,023.2
Cash Flow From Operations	415.5	547.4	-187.8	-156.6
Balance Sheet (000's)				
Cash & Equivalents	2.0	2.0	2.1	3.2
Total Current Assets	4,948.4	4,966.9	5,721.8	5,306.7
Fixed Assets, Net	772.3	840.6	691.9	718.1
Total Assets	5,770.7	5,807.5	6,413.7	6,024.8
Total Current Liabilities	1,366.7	1,393.9	3,712.0	3,537.9
Long-Term Debt	1,200.0	1,226.1	0.0	0.0
Stockholders' Equity	3,126.3	3,062.0	2,701.8	2,486.9
Performance & Financial Condition				
Return on Total Revenues %	2.26	2.13	1.50	-8.31
Return on Avg Stockholders' Equity %	10.41	10.64	7.82	-34.12
Return on Average Assets %	5.56	5.02	3.26	-14.99
Current Ratio	3.62	3.56	1.54	1.50
Debt / Equity %	38.38	40.04	n.a.	n.a.

Compound Growth %'s	EPS %	22.47	Net Income %	25.98	Total Revenues %	5.02

Comments

The continuing improvement in net income was primarily the result of lower interest expense and lower general and administrative expenses. Due to price pressure in all connector markets, the Company's gross margins fell from 24.8% in fiscal 1997 to 23.3% in fiscal 1998. For the nine months ended December 31, 1998, the Company reported revenues and a net loss of $10.4 million and $83,000 ($.02 per share) as compared to $11.0 million and net income of $276,000 ($.05 per share) for the same period of the preceding year.

Officers	Position	Ownership Information	
John C. Loring	Chairman	Number of Shares Outstanding	5,372,863
Michael McGuire	President, CEO	Market Capitalization	$ 1,450,673
Nancy Shields	Exec VP	Number of Shareholders	368
Wayne Miller	Exec VP	Where Listed / Symbol	OTC-BB / ASXI

Other Information			
Transfer Agent	Mellon Securities Trust Company New York, NY	SIC Code	5065
Auditor	KPMG LLP	Employees	52
Market Maker	Carr Securities Corporation (800)221-2243		
	Knight Securities L.P. (800)222-4910		

Athanor Group, Inc.

921 East California Avenue   Ontario, CA 91761   Telephone (909)467-1205   Fax (909)467-1208

Company Description

Athanor Group, Inc. is engaged in the manufacture of screw machine products (nonproprietary metal components) produced in large quantities to customer specifications. In meeting customer orders, the Company manufactures a wide range of products. Before placing an order, a customer provides the Company with detailed drawings and specifications for a specific product. During 1997, the Company expanded into secondary operations that had been contracted to outsiders. The ability to perform these operations in-house will afford the Company better control over inventory and quality standards. The Company is also in the process of adopted the internationally recognized ISO 9000 standard. This will support the strategic direction of the Company's internationally-sensitive customer base and enhance the Company's appeal to potential new customers. The Company was founded in 1958.

	10/31/98	10/31/97	10/31/96	10/31/95
Per Share Information				
Stock Price as of 12/31	1.66	2.37	1.87	1.37
Earnings Per Share	0.31	0.33	0.36	0.18
Price / Earnings Ratio	5.35	7.18	5.19	7.61
Book Value Per Share	2.33	2.02	1.70	1.34
Price / Book Value %	71.24	117.33	110.00	102.24
Dividends Per Share	0.0	0.0	0.0	0.0
Annual Financial Data				
Operating Results (000's)				
Total Revenues	23,646.3	25,104.2	23,652.7	19,329.5
Costs & Expenses	-22,872.5	-24,215.0	-22,846.3	-18,844.8
Income Before Taxes and Other	773.9	831.6	806.4	484.7
Other Items	0.0	0.0	0.0	0.0
Income Tax	-319.2	-348.5	-277.2	-220.9
Net Income	454.7	483.1	529.2	263.8
Cash Flow From Operations	799.0	299.0	633.1	219.3
Balance Sheet (000's)				
Cash & Equivalents	236.3	138.0	115.5	62.4
Total Current Assets	6,294.2	6,640.1	6,097.4	5,532.0
Fixed Assets, Net	1,543.9	1,840.5	1,177.5	1,108.5
Total Assets	8,225.9	8,619.1	7,364.9	6,723.2
Total Current Liabilities	4,012.7	4,373.5	3,705.7	3,686.1
Long-Term Debt	679.5	1,193.5	1,095.2	974.1
Stockholders' Equity	3,403.8	2,971.7	2,497.4	1,968.3
Performance & Financial Condition				
Return on Total Revenues %	1.92	1.92	2.24	1.36
Return on Avg Stockholders' Equity %	14.26	17.67	23.70	13.62
Return on Average Assets %	5.40	6.04	7.51	4.04
Current Ratio	1.57	1.52	1.65	1.50
Debt / Equity %	19.96	40.16	43.85	49.49

Compound Growth %'s	EPS %	19.87	Net Income %	19.91	Total Revenues %	6.95

Comments

A general slowdown in business across the Company's customer base was cited for a volatile year and decline in revenue. Management responded quickly by stressing cost cutting and the deferral of optional repairs and maintenance. Sales for the first quarter of fiscal 1999 were expected to be weak. In October 1997, the Company went on-line with a new fully integrated software system, which has the ability to purchase and schedule materials in conjunction with the manufacturing process. Management expects this system to give the Company an effective tool to control in-house inventories and to provide on time deliveries to its customers.

Officers	Position	Ownership Information	
Duane L. Femrite	President, CEO	Number of Shares Outstanding	1,458,854
Richard Krause	Vice President	Market Capitalization	$ 2,421,698
Robert W. Miller	Director	Number of Shareholders	253
Edmund R. Knauf, Jr.	Director	Where Listed / Symbol	OTC-BB / ATHR

Other Information			
Transfer Agent	U.S. Stock Transfer Corp. Glendale, CA	SIC Code	3450
Auditor	KPMG LLP	Employees	166
Market Maker	Paragon Capital Corporation	(800)345-0505	
	Olsen Payne & Co.	(800)453-5321	

Atlantic Premium Brands, Ltd.

650 Dundee Road, Suite 370   Northbrook, IL 60062   Telephone (847)480-4000   Fax (847)480-0199

Company Description

Atlantic Premium Brands, Ltd. manufactures, markets and distributes branded and unbranded food products for customers in a twelve state region and previously, through its operations in Maryland, distributed specialty, non-alcoholic beverages to customers in the Baltimore and Washington, D.C. metropolitan areas through the end of 1998. The beverage distribution business was sold in two stages at the end of 1998 and the beginning of 1999. The Company manufactures a variety of smoked sausage products and fresh pork sausage products under various trade names of its own as well as under the private labels of others. The Company has grown largely by acquisition. Let's check out the fat content of the numbers below.

	12/31/98	12/31/97	12/31/96	12/31/95
Per Share Information				
Stock Price	1.87	4.00	3.75	1.25
Earnings Per Share	0.04	0.05	0.17	-1.22
Price / Earnings Ratio	46.75	80.00	22.06	n.a.
Book Value Per Share	1.33	1.27	1.03	0.10
Price / Book Value %	140.60	314.96	364.08	1,250.00
Dividends Per Share	0.0	0.0	0.0	0.0
Annual Financial Data				
Operating Results (000's)				
Total Revenues	181,138.4	172,579.7	153,756.4	20,608.1
Costs & Expenses	-178,869.0	-172,172.8	-152,838.6	-20,760.0
Income Before Taxes and Other	2,269.4	406.9	917.8	-151.9
Other Items	-1,495.6	0.0	0.0	-2,938.7
Income Tax	-450.0	-50.0	-22.0	0.0
Net Income	323.8	356.9	895.8	-3,090.6
Cash Flow From Operations	3,899.0	3,460.7	-1,588.0	127.1
Balance Sheet (000's)				
Cash & Equivalents	1,773.8	1,262.8	1,249.0	0.0
Total Current Assets	18,687.1	15,596.7	15,834.4	1,600.8
Fixed Assets, Net	12,288.2	4,939.5	4,820.9	706.5
Total Assets	45,665.1	34,953.7	34,653.1	2,921.1
Total Current Liabilities	17,320.2	19,268.0	20,019.5	2,358.8
Long-Term Debt	17,078.6	6,297.3	7,778.9	0.0
Stockholders' Equity	9,831.4	9,388.5	6,603.8	562.4
Performance & Financial Condition				
Return on Total Revenues %	0.18	0.21	0.58	-15.00
Return on Avg Stockholders' Equity %	3.37	4.46	25.00	-133.50
Return on Average Assets %	0.80	1.03	4.77	-76.35
Current Ratio	1.08	0.81	0.79	0.68
Debt / Equity %	173.71	67.07	117.80	n.a.

Compound Growth %'s	EPS %	-51.49	Net Income %	-39.88	Total Revenues %	106.38

Comments

In March 1998, the Company acquired J.C. Potter Sausage Company, a branded food processing company bases in Durant, Oklahoma. The transaction was accounted for as a purchase. Therefore, result of operations have been combined with those of the Company starting with the date of the transaction. Approximately 90% of the 19.7% increase in revenues realized during 1998 was attributable to the acquisition. The balance related to the introduction of new branded product lines. 1998 results include $1,495,591 of losses ($.20 per share) related to the discontinuance of the beverage distribution business. At December 31, 1998, the Company had $13.5 million of goodwill reflected as assets which equated to approximately 137% of stockholders' equity and book value per share. Working capital is lean and long term debt is substantial.

Officers	Position	Ownership Information	
Merrick M. Elfman	Chairman	Number of Shares Outstanding	7,412,583
Alan F. Sussna	President, CEO	Market Capitalization	$ 13,861,530
Thomas Dalton	Senior VP, CFO	Number of Shareholders	2,000
Tom Wippman	Secretary	Where Listed / Symbol	AMEX / ABR

Other Information			
Transfer Agent	Harris Trust & Savings Bank Chicago, IL	SIC Code	5140
Auditor	Arthur Andersen LLP	Employees	465
		Web Site	atlprem.com

Autologic Information International, Inc.

1050 Rancho Conejo Boulevard   Thousand Oaks, CA 91320   Telephone (805)498-9611   Fax (805)499-1167

Company Description

Autologic Information International, Inc. (AII) designs, develops, manufactures, assembles, integrates, markets, sells, and services computerized image-setting, publication systems equipment and software that automate the various prepress production steps in the publishing process. AII's products are primarily marketed and sold to the newspaper publishing industry, the commercial printing industry and other organizations having internal publishing facilities. AII has traditionally focused its efforts on high-volume and deadline-driven customers, although it continues to take steps to expand into niche portions of the lower-volume, less time-sensitive part of the commercial publishing and electronic document transmission markets.

	10/30/98	10/31/97	11/01/96	11/03/95
Per Share Information				
Stock Price as of 12/31	4.25	6.50	4.25	12.00
Earnings Per Share	0.43	0.25	-0.96	-1.49
Price / Earnings Ratio	9.88	26.00	n.a.	n.a.
Book Value Per Share	6.90	6.46	6.22	-20.99
Price / Book Value %	61.59	100.62	68.33	n.a.
Dividends Per Share	0.0	0.0	0.0	0.0
Annual Financial Data				
Operating Results (000's)				
Total Revenues	87,616.0	84,649.0	88,880.0	70,675.0
Costs & Expenses	-82,895.0	-81,519.0	-92,686.0	-74,783.0
Income Before Taxes and Other	4,563.0	3,128.0	-4,438.0	-4,108.0
Other Items	0.0	-203.0	-428.0	0.0
Income Tax	-2,049.0	-1,473.0	-125.0	-877.0
Net Income	2,514.0	1,452.0	-4,991.0	-4,985.0
Cash Flow From Operations	4,897.0	4,502.0	-1,995.0	1,689.0
Balance Sheet (000's)				
Cash & Equivalents	11,871.0	9,452.0	6,133.0	2,542.0
Total Current Assets	46,292.0	41,965.0	47,085.0	28,195.0
Fixed Assets, Net	5,827.0	5,931.0	6,212.0	3,444.0
Total Assets	56,254.0	53,596.0	59,285.0	31,691.0
Total Current Liabilities	16,322.0	16,178.0	23,274.0	101,744.0
Long-Term Debt	0.0	0.0	0.0	0.0
Stockholders' Equity	39,932.0	37,418.0	36,011.0	-70,053.0
Performance & Financial Condition				
Return on Total Revenues %	2.87	1.72	-5.62	-7.05
Return on Avg Stockholders' Equity %	6.50	3.95	n.a.	n.a.
Return on Average Assets %	4.58	2.57	-10.97	-12.46
Current Ratio	2.84	2.59	2.02	0.28
Debt / Equity %	n.a.	n.a.	n.a.	n.a.

Compound Growth %'s	EPS % n.a.	Net Income % n.a.	Total Revenues % 7.43

Comments

After suffering substantial losses in fiscal 1995 and 1996, gross margins improved 9% in fiscal 1997 and held firm in fiscal 1998. The improvement in margins was due primarily to less discounting of imaging systems than in prior years and lower manufacturing costs. However, management cautions that the imaging system segment of the prepress industry continues to be affected by rapid technological change, open systems architecture, increased third party distribution and oversupply, all of which lead to intense price competition and may affect the Company's ability to maintain margins in the future. In the meantime, the Company's overall financial condition is becoming very strong.

Officers	Position	Ownership Information	
William Shaw	Chairman, CEO	Number of Shares Outstanding	5,787,970
Dennis D. Doolittle	President, COO	Market Capitalization	$ 24,598,873
Anthony F. Marrelli	CFO	Number of Shareholders	654
		Where Listed / Symbol	NASDAQ / AIII

Other Information			
Transfer Agent	Boston EquiServe Boston, MA	SIC Code	3579
Auditor	Ernst & Young LLP	Employees	433
		Web Site	autologic.com

Avesis Incorporated

3724 North Third Street, Suite 300   Phoenix, AZ 85012   Telephone (602)241-3400   Fax (602)240-9100

Company Description

Avesis Incorporated markets and administers dental, vision, hearing and chiropractic managed care and discount programs. These programs are designed to enable members, who are enrolled through various sponsoring organizations such as insurance carriers, HMOs, Blue Cross and Blue Shield organizations, corporations, associations and unions, to realize savings on purchases of products and services through Company organized networks of providers. The Company's discount programs are also designed to reduce the cost to sponsors of providing benefits to members. The Company was founded in 1978.

	05/31/98	05/31/97	05/31/96	05/31/95
Per Share Information				
Stock Price as of 12/31	0.29	0.25	0.69	0.75
Earnings Per Share	0.06	-0.13	-0.12	0.02
Price / Earnings Ratio	4.83	n.a.	n.a.	37.50
Book Value Per Share	-0.31	-0.81	-0.76	-0.74
Price / Book Value %	n.a.	n.a.	n.a.	n.a.
Dividends Per Share	0.0	0.0	0.0	0.0
Annual Financial Data				
Operating Results (000's)				
Total Revenues	8,367.6	5,670.6	6,046.4	6,529.1
Costs & Expenses	-8,053.7	-5,769.0	-6,136.5	-6,023.7
Income Before Taxes and Other	313.9	-190.3	-124.9	505.4
Other Items	0.0	0.0	0.0	0.0
Income Tax	0.0	0.0	0.0	0.0
Net Income	313.9	-190.3	-124.9	505.4
Cash Flow From Operations	841.6	492.9	51.7	408.3
Balance Sheet (000's)				
Cash & Equivalents	993.6	817.5	436.1	815.6
Total Current Assets	1,589.0	1,271.5	864.6	1,242.5
Fixed Assets, Net	409.2	181.8	599.3	353.8
Total Assets	2,241.7	1,639.4	1,650.5	1,839.4
Total Current Liabilities	1,238.6	977.9	441.6	495.0
Long-Term Debt	0.0	0.0	160.0	412.3
Stockholders' Equity	912.7	569.4	759.7	859.6
Performance & Financial Condition				
Return on Total Revenues %	3.75	-3.36	-2.07	7.74
Return on Avg Stockholders' Equity %	42.36	-28.63	-15.42	83.28
Return on Average Assets %	16.17	-11.57	-7.16	33.30
Current Ratio	1.28	1.30	1.96	2.51
Debt / Equity %	n.a.	n.a.	21.06	47.96

Compound Growth %'s	EPS %	44.22	Net Income %	-14.68	Total Revenues %	8.62

Comments

Revenues increased 48% in fiscal 1998 primarily due to the growth of the Company's managed care vision products. Operating expenses also decreased as a percentage of sales and management expects that favorable trend to continue. For the nine months ended February 28, 1999, the Company reported revenues and net income of $7.6 million and $607,849 ($.07 per share) as compared to $5.9 million and $178,288 (a loss of $0.02 per share after preferred stock dividends) for the same period of the preceding year. The preferred stock has a liquidation preference of $2.2 million. We deducted the liquidation preference from equity in determining the book value of the common shares and preferred stock dividends from net income in determining earnings per share.

Officers	Position	Ownership Information	
William L. Richter	Chairman	Number of Shares Outstanding	4,271,126
Alan S. Cohn	President, CEO	Market Capitalization	$ 1,238,627
Joel H. Alperstein	CFO	Number of Shareholders	165
Neal Kempler	Vice President, Secretary	Where Listed / Symbol	OTC-BB / AVSS

Other Information			
Transfer Agent	Continental Stock Transfer & Trust Co. New York, NY	SIC Code	8099
Auditor	KPMG LLP	Employees	44
Market Maker	Herzog, Heine, Geduld, Inc. (800)221-3600		
	M.H. Meyerson & Co., Inc. (800)333-3113		

B.B. Walker Company

414 East Dixie Drive Asheboro, NC 27203-1167   Telephone (336)625-1380   Fax (336)625-8258

Company Description

B.B. Walker Company manufacturers and distributes men's and women's footwear. The Company's products consist of high quality, moderately-priced western and work/outdoor boots and shoes. A majority of the Company's sales are under trademarked brands including Abilene Boot™. The Company also operates two retail shoe stores. Footwear manufactured and wholesaled by the Company in fiscal 1998 comprised 91.8% of total sales. A substantial portion of the Company's common stock is owned by an Employee Stock Ownership Plan. The Company was founded in 1947.

	10/31/98	11/01/97	11/02/96	10/28/95
Per Share Information				
Stock Price as of 12/31	3.75	2.00	4.00	2.00
Earnings Per Share	0.04	0.01	-2.34	-0.72
Price / Earnings Ratio	93.75	200.00	n.a.	n.a.
Book Value Per Share	2.70	2.64	2.57	4.91
Price / Book Value %	138.89	75.76	155.64	40.73
Dividends Per Share	0.0	0.0	0.0	0.0
Annual Financial Data				
Operating Results (000's)				
Total Revenues	28,852.0	32,725.0	37,549.0	43,453.0
Costs & Expenses	-29,588.0	-32,779.0	-42,208.0	-45,321.0
Income Before Taxes and Other	-736.0	-54.0	-4,659.0	-1,868.0
Other Items	-2.0	-2.0	-2.0	-2.0
Income Tax	813.0	80.0	620.0	626.0
Net Income	75.0	24.0	-4,041.0	-1,244.0
Cash Flow From Operations	1,041.0	4,347.0	3,309.0	-1,918.0
Balance Sheet (000's)				
Cash & Equivalents	1.0	1.0	1.0	1.0
Total Current Assets	18,314.0	19,268.0	24,953.0	30,898.0
Fixed Assets, Net	1,622.0	1,750.0	2,208.0	2,968.0
Total Assets	20,080.0	21,174.0	27,375.0	34,377.0
Total Current Liabilities	14,102.0	13,368.0	19,534.0	21,533.0
Long-Term Debt	1,303.0	3,216.0	3,286.0	4,257.0
Stockholders' Equity	4,642.0	4,557.0	4,522.0	8,553.0
Performance & Financial Condition				
Return on Total Revenues %	0.26	0.07	-10.76	-2.86
Return on Avg Stockholders' Equity %	1.63	0.53	-61.81	-13.57
Return on Average Assets %	0.36	0.10	-13.09	-3.64
Current Ratio	1.30	1.44	1.28	1.43
Debt / Equity %	28.07	70.57	72.67	49.77

Compound Growth %'s	EPS %	n.a.	Net Income %	n.a.	Total Revenues %	-12.76

Comments

In December 1995, the Company reorganized its internal structure, moving from a functional organization to two vertically-integrated, separate divisions operating independently and supported by a small corporate staff. However, during fiscal 1996, a soft retail environment persisted and sales and profits did not respond as anticipated. During the fourth quarter of 1996, the Company began implementation of a plan to consolidate operations and reduce overhead. A number of product lines, primarily the outdoor styles, were dropped which accounts for some of the reduction in sales. Substantial restructuring cut $3.4 million from overhead expenses. The bottom line was a return to profitability. However, both fiscal 1998 and 1997 benefitted from income tax credits. In January 1999, the Company entered into a contract to sell one of its plants along with adjacent land. The terms were described as "attractive". The plant operations will be relocated.

Officers	Position	Ownership Information	
Kent T. Anderson	President, CEO	Number of Shares Outstanding	1,720,954
French P. Humphries	Exec VP	Market Capitalization	$ 6,453,578
Carey M. Durham	CFO	Number of Shareholders	1,166
Dorothy W. Craven	Secretary	Where Listed / Symbol	OTC-PS / WLKB

Other Information			
Transfer Agent	Company Office Asheboro, NC	SIC Code	3140
Auditor	PricewaterhouseCoopers LLP	Employees	392
Market Maker	Scott & Stringfellow, Inc.	(800)446-7074	
	Paragon Capital Corporation	(800)345-0505	

BAB Holdings, Inc.

8501 W. Higgins Road, Suite 320   Chicago, IL 60631   Telephone (773)380-6100   Fax (773)380-6183

Company Description

BAB Holdings, Inc. operates and franchises bagel, muffin and coffee retail units under the Big Apple Bagels, My Favorite Muffin and Brewster's Coffee trademarks. These units feature daily, baked from scratch bagels, muffins, cream cheeses, coffee and other related products. Additionally, the Company acts as a licensor of Big Apple Bagels, bagel-deli units owned and operated by Host Marriott Services in airport and travel plaza locations. As of November 30, 1998, there were 22 Company owned and 271 franchised and licensed stores in operation. The Company was founded in 1992 and had an initial public offering in 1995.

	11/30/98	11/30/97	11/30/96	11/30/95
Per Share Information				
Stock Price as of 12/31	1.06	0.87	4.87	5.37
Earnings Per Share	0.06	-0.53	-0.04	-0.12
Price / Earnings Ratio	17.67	n.a.	n.a.	n.a.
Book Value Per Share	0.95	0.88	1.23	1.04
Price / Book Value %	111.58	98.86	395.93	516.35
Dividends Per Share	0.0	0.0	0.0	0.0
Annual Financial Data				
Operating Results (000's)				
Total Revenues	14,722.5	14,244.7	6,640.5	2,048.6
Costs & Expenses	-14,239.7	-17,646.7	-6,948.7	-2,484.4
Income Before Taxes and Other	482.8	-3,402.1	-320.8	-435.8
Other Items	0.0	0.0	0.0	0.0
Income Tax	164.0	0.0	0.0	0.0
Net Income	646.8	-3,402.1	-320.8	-435.8
Cash Flow From Operations	303.2	-1,220.4	68.9	406.2
Balance Sheet (000's)				
Cash & Equivalents	700.2	389.9	2,163.3	7,679.0
Total Current Assets	3,591.0	2,979.2	3,686.3	7,895.5
Fixed Assets, Net	4,202.2	5,088.9	3,533.7	348.4
Total Assets	14,445.0	14,627.2	11,148.0	8,491.6
Total Current Liabilities	2,941.4	4,295.6	2,351.2	1,465.0
Long-Term Debt	1,760.0	1,676.9	1.8	236.3
Stockholders' Equity	9,228.0	8,654.8	8,795.0	6,790.3
Performance & Financial Condition				
Return on Total Revenues %	4.39	-23.88	-4.83	-21.27
Return on Avg Stockholders' Equity %	7.23	-38.99	-4.12	-13.30
Return on Average Assets %	4.45	-26.40	-3.27	-10.89
Current Ratio	1.22	0.69	1.57	5.39
Debt / Equity %	19.07	19.38	0.02	3.48

Compound Growth %'s	EPS %	n.a.	Net Income %	n.a.	Total Revenues %	92.98

Comments

The Company has grown rapidly through internal growth and acquisitions. The reduction in the rate of growth in fiscal 1998, which was anticipated, was due to the closing of seven Company-owned stores in the fourth quarter of fiscal 1997 and an additional six units closed in fiscal 1998. Royalty fees from franchised units increased 34% during fiscal 1998 principally due to the addition of sixty new units. Whereas last year we cautioned our readers that there was no assurance that the Company would operate profitably in the future given its historical losses, wouldn't you know it, the first net profit was recorded in fiscal 1998. At November 30, 1998, the Company had $5.6 million of intangible assets on its books which equated to approximately 60% of stockholders' equity and book value per share.

Officers	Position	Ownership Information	
Michael W. Evans	President, CEO	Number of Shares Outstanding	8,068,406
Tom Fletcher	COO, CFO	Market Capitalization	$ 8,552,510
Joseph M. Merkin	CFO, Treasurer	Number of Shareholders	2,800
Michael K. Murtaugh	Vice President	Where Listed / Symbol	NASDAQ / BAGL

Other Information			
Transfer Agent	LaSalle National Trust, N.A. Chicago, IL	SIC Code	5412
Auditor	Blackman Kallick Bartelstein	Employees	307
		Web Site	babholdings.com

BCT International, Inc.

3000 N.E. 30th Place, 5th Floor Fort Lauderdale, FL 33306 Telephone (954)563-1224 Fax (954)565-0742

Company Description

BCT International, Inc. franchises wholesale thermography printing plants under the name Business Cards Tomorrow for which it receives initial franchise fees and continuing royalties. The Company also supplies business card, stationery, rubber stamp and label catalogs to its franchises and sells the paper products featured in the catalogs. Since its founding in 1975, the system has grown to include 88 franchises and is said to be the world's largest wholesale printing chain.

	02/28/98	02/28/97	02/29/96	02/28/95
Per Share Information				
Stock Price as of 12/31	2.81	2.62	4.12	3.62
Earnings Per Share	0.28	-0.08	0.19	0.18
Price / Earnings Ratio	10.04	n.a.	21.68	20.11
Book Value Per Share	2.08	1.80	1.90	1.70
Price / Book Value %	135.10	145.56	216.84	212.94
Dividends Per Share	0.0	0.0	0.0	0.0
Annual Financial Data				
Operating Results (000's)				
Total Revenues	19,405.0	17,745.0	17,590.0	13,573.0
Costs & Expenses	-16,987.0	-17,897.0	-16,664.0	-12,542.0
Income Before Taxes and Other	2,418.0	-425.0	926.0	1,031.0
Other Items	0.0	18.0	20.0	0.0
Income Tax	-853.0	22.0	195.0	124.0
Net Income	1,565.0	-385.0	1,141.0	1,155.0
Cash Flow From Operations	864.0	-448.0	-112.0	1,090.0
Balance Sheet (000's)				
Cash & Equivalents	1,018.0	314.0	923.0	1,299.0
Total Current Assets	7,516.0	5,258.0	5,752.0	6,943.0
Fixed Assets, Net	651.0	762.0	1,014.0	640.0
Total Assets	14,157.0	11,229.0	10,738.0	10,018.0
Total Current Liabilities	2,484.0	1,644.0	1,119.0	1,401.0
Long-Term Debt	541.0	215.0	5.0	48.0
Stockholders' Equity	11,132.0	9,310.0	9,374.0	7,759.0
Performance & Financial Condition				
Return on Total Revenues %	8.06	-2.17	6.49	8.51
Return on Avg Stockholders' Equity %	15.31	-4.12	13.32	19.77
Return on Average Assets %	12.33	-3.51	10.99	12.98
Current Ratio	3.03	3.20	5.14	4.96
Debt / Equity %	4.86	2.31	0.05	0.62

Compound Growth %'s	EPS %	15.87	Net Income %	10.66	Total Revenues %	12.65

Comments

Revenues increased 9% in fiscal 1998 as a result of further market penetration and the introduction of labels to the revenue mix. In fiscal 1997, management focused on the sale of Company owned plants held for sale and cost containment. The benefits of those changes were not realized until fiscal 1998. For the nine months ended November 30, 1998, revenues and net income were $15.8 million and $1,798,000 ($.32 per share) as compared to $14.2 million and $1,161,000 ($.21 per share) for the same period of the preceding year.

Officers	**Position**	**Ownership Information**	
William A. Wilkerson	Chairman	Number of Shares Outstanding	5,322,000
James H. Kaufenberg	President, CEO	Market Capitalization	$ 14,954,820
Michael R. Hull	Secretary, CFO	Number of Shareholders	835
Thomas J. Cassady	Director	Where Listed / Symbol	NASDAQ / BCTI

Other Information			
Transfer Agent	ChaseMellon Shareholder Services Pittsburgh, PA	SIC Code	5110
Auditor	PricewaterhouseCoopers LLP	Employees	90
		Web Site	bct-net.com

BLC Financial Services, Inc.

645 Madison Avenue, 18th floor   New York, NY 10022-1010   Telephone (212)751-5626   Fax (212)751-9345

Company Description

The Company is primarily engaged in the origination, sale and servicing of Small Business Administration (SBA) loans. The Company sells the SBA guaranteed portion of these loans in the secondary market, without recourse and at a premium. Once the loan is sold, the Company continues to service the loan for an annual fee. In addition to the sale of guaranteed loans the Company periodically sells participations in the unguaranteed portions of its loan portfolio. The Company also recently qualified as a participating lender in the United States Department of Agriculture Business and Industry Guaranteed Loan Program.

	06/30/98	06/30/97	06/30/96	06/30/95
Per Share Information				
Stock Price as of 12/31	2.25	1.47	0.53	0.28
Earnings Per Share	0.15	0.11	0.05	0.01
Price / Earnings Ratio	15.00	13.36	10.60	28.00
Book Value Per Share	0.72	0.41	0.27	0.20
Price / Book Value %	312.50	358.54	196.30	140.00
Dividends Per Share	0.0	0.0	0.0	0.0
Annual Financial Data				
Operating Results (000's)				
Total Revenues	15,729.0	7,168.0	4,997.0	2,536.0
Costs & Expenses	-10,392.0	-5,491.0	-4,305.0	-2,163.0
Income Before Taxes and Other	5,337.0	1,677.0	692.0	373.0
Other Items	0.0	243.0	19.0	-75.0
Income Tax	-2,111.0	27.0	-67.0	-156.0
Net Income	3,226.0	1,947.0	644.0	142.0
Cash Flow From Operations	-7,097.0	-150.0	125.0	722.0
Balance Sheet (000's)				
Cash & Equivalents	1,730.0	803.0	363.0	125.0
Total Current Assets	13,058.0	4,332.0	3,076.0	1,196.0
Fixed Assets, Net	742.0	344.0	159.0	48.0
Total Assets	53,281.0	20,086.0	10,983.0	10,535.0
Total Current Liabilities	2,631.0	3,970.0	1,363.0	1,728.0
Long-Term Debt	32,541.0	8,926.0	4,294.0	5,546.0
Stockholders' Equity	14,269.0	7,190.0	4,601.0	2,608.0
Performance & Financial Condition				
Return on Total Revenues %	20.51	27.16	12.89	9.62
Return on Avg Stockholders' Equity %	30.07	33.03	17.87	5.66
Return on Average Assets %	8.79	12.53	5.99	1.65
Current Ratio	4.96	1.09	2.26	0.69
Debt / Equity %	228.05	124.14	93.33	212.65

Compound Growth %'s	EPS % 146.62	Net Income % 183.22	Total Revenues % 83.73

Comments

Gains on the sale of loans moved substantially higher in fiscal 1998 and accounted for approximately 73% of the increase in total revenues. Expenses also increased due to the Company's growth and expansion. Loans originated during fiscal 1998 totaled $93.9 million, up 121% from $42.3 million in fiscal 1997. The Company's serviced loan portfolio grew 79% to approximately $176 million. For the six months ended December 31, 1998, revenues and net income were $11.5 million and $2,332,000 ($.10 per share) as compared to $7.4 million and $1,672,000 ($.09 per share) for the same period of the preceding year.

Officers	Position	Ownership Information	
Robert F. Tannenhauser	Chairman, President	Number of Shares Outstanding	19,778,449
Leonard Rudolph	Exec VP	Market Capitalization	$ 44,501,510
Jennifer M. Goldstein	Treasurer	Number of Shareholders	913
Robert C. McGee	Vice President	Where Listed / Symbol	AMEX / BCL

Other Information			
Transfer Agent	Continental Stock Transfer & Trust Co. New York, NY	SIC Code	6159
Auditor	Richard A. Eisner & Co., LLP	Employees	60

BTU International, Inc.

23 Esquire Road   North Billerica, MA 01862-2596   Telephone (978)667-4111   Fax (978)667-9068

Company Description

BTU International, Inc. designs, manufactures, sells and services thermal processing equipment and related process controls for use in the electronics, power generation, automotive and other industries. The Company is the major supplier of solder reflow systems used for surface mount applications in printed circuit board assembly. The Company is a worldwide supplier of systems used in low temperature curing/encapsulation, hybrid integrated circuit manufacturing, integrated circuit packaging and sealing, and processing multi-chip modules. The Company also supplies systems for sintering nuclear fuel for commercial power generation. In addition, its products are used in other specialty applications such as brazing and the sintering of ceramics and powdered metals, and the deposition of precise thin film coatings.

	12/31/98	12/31/97	12/31/96	12/31/95
Per Share Information				
Stock Price	3.00	5.12	3.00	4.56
Earnings Per Share	0.22	0.17	0.49	0.68
Price / Earnings Ratio	13.64	30.12	6.12	6.71
Book Value Per Share	3.40	3.22	3.05	2.53
Price / Book Value %	88.24	159.01	98.36	180.24
Dividends Per Share	0.0	0.0	0.0	0.0
Annual Financial Data				
Operating Results (000's)				
Total Revenues	56,946.0	52,596.0	46,237.0	58,637.0
Costs & Expenses	-55,032.0	-50,076.0	-45,340.0	-52,434.0
Income Before Taxes and Other	1,914.0	1,649.0	897.0	6,203.0
Other Items	0.0	0.0	3,400.0	0.0
Income Tax	-381.0	-399.0	-737.0	-1,130.0
Net Income	1,533.0	1,250.0	3,560.0	5,073.0
Cash Flow From Operations	2,067.0	3,026.0	-1,472.0	1,022.0
Balance Sheet (000's)				
Cash & Equivalents	10,594.0	11,873.0	10,218.0	6,145.0
Total Current Assets	33,516.0	35,359.0	32,269.0	29,428.0
Fixed Assets, Net	4,740.0	4,614.0	4,265.0	6,406.0
Total Assets	38,615.0	40,379.0	36,763.0	35,834.0
Total Current Liabilities	8,555.0	9,261.0	7,001.0	11,423.0
Long-Term Debt	5,167.0	5,313.0	5,352.0	5,715.0
Stockholders' Equity	23,137.0	23,558.0	22,207.0	18,696.0
Performance & Financial Condition				
Return on Total Revenues %	2.69	2.38	7.70	8.65
Return on Avg Stockholders' Equity %	6.57	5.46	17.41	33.11
Return on Average Assets %	3.88	3.24	9.81	15.19
Current Ratio	3.92	3.82	4.61	2.58
Debt / Equity %	22.33	22.55	24.10	30.57

Compound Growth %'s	EPS %	-31.35	Net Income %	-32.89	Total Revenues %	-0.97

Comments

Disappointed with the direction of the Company, management sought significant redirection in 1997. New key employees were hired and strategic initiatives were implemented. During 1998 a concentrated focus was placed on improving product quality, cost efficiency, and upgrading the production facility. 1998 revenue was strong despite a down turn in the capital equipment sector of the electronics industry which is the Company's key market. Despite industry wide price pressures that forced most competitors into negative or breakeven earnings, the Company's net earnings improved over 1997. Management's outlook is very positive with 12% to 15% growth for the foreseeable future and 30% growth in the contract manufacturing market. 1996 results include a $3.4 million gain from the sale of assets.

Officers	Position	Ownership Information	
Paul J. van der Wansem	President, CEO	Number of Shares Outstanding	6,806,763
Thomas P. Kealy	VP - Finance, Controller	Market Capitalization	$ 20,420,289
John E. Beard	Secretary	Number of Shareholders	521
David H. Barry	Vice President, General Manager	Where Listed / Symbol	NASDAQ / BTUI

Other Information			
Transfer Agent	Boston EquiServe Boston, MA	SIC Code	3559
Auditor	Arthur Andersen LLP	Employees	327
		Web Site	btu.com

Back Yard Burgers, Inc.

2768 Colony Park Drive   Memphis, TN 38118   Telephone (901)367-0888   Fax (901)367-0999

Company Description

Back Yard Burgers, Inc. owns and operates fast-casual, single drive-thru/dine-in restaurants and is engaged in the sale of franchises in Back Yard Burgers and the collection of royalties based upon related franchise sales. The Company grants franchise rights for the use of Back Yard Burgers, BYB, or BY Burgers trade names and other associated trademarks, signs, emblems, logos, slogans and service marks which have or may be developed. At January 2, 1999, the Company operated 33 restaurants in two states (Arkansas and Tennessee) and franchised 48 restaurants in 15 states. As the name implies, Back Yard Burgers strives to offer the same high quality ingredients and special care typified by outdoor grilling in ones back yard. The Company has been grilling since 1986.

	01/02/99	01/03/98	12/28/96	12/30/95
Per Share Information				
Stock Price as of 12/31	1.87	2.87	2.06	1.50
Earnings Per Share	0.25	0.04	0.08	-0.65
Price / Earnings Ratio	7.48	71.75	25.75	n.a.
Book Value Per Share	2.09	1.94	1.91	1.84
Price / Book Value %	89.47	147.94	107.85	81.52
Dividends Per Share	0.0	0.0	0.0	0.0
Annual Financial Data				
Operating Results (000's)				
Total Revenues	27,395.0	26,048.0	24,066.0	22,774.0
Costs & Expenses	-26,575.0	-25,882.0	-23,709.0	-25,834.0
Income Before Taxes and Other	820.0	162.0	357.0	-3,060.0
Other Items	0.0	0.0	0.0	0.0
Income Tax	351.0	0.0	0.0	107.0
Net Income	1,171.0	162.0	357.0	-2,953.0
Cash Flow From Operations	1,978.0	2,003.0	1,596.0	1,044.0
Balance Sheet (000's)				
Cash & Equivalents	815.0	1,328.0	1,101.0	528.0
Total Current Assets	1,417.0	1,961.0	1,645.0	1,150.0
Fixed Assets, Net	13,365.0	9,451.0	8,131.0	8,128.0
Total Assets	16,948.0	13,155.0	11,572.0	11,149.0
Total Current Liabilities	1,883.0	1,656.0	1,399.0	1,070.0
Long-Term Debt	5,097.0	2,864.0	1,831.0	2,066.0
Stockholders' Equity	9,586.0	8,298.0	8,110.0	7,728.0
Performance & Financial Condition				
Return on Total Revenues %	4.27	0.62	1.48	-12.97
Return on Avg Stockholders' Equity %	13.10	1.97	4.51	-32.09
Return on Average Assets %	7.78	1.31	3.14	-24.55
Current Ratio	0.75	1.18	1.18	1.07
Debt / Equity %	53.17	34.51	22.58	26.73

Compound Growth %'s	EPS %	76.78	Net Income %	81.11	Total Revenues %	6.35

Comments

Same-store sales increased 6.3% in 1998 for company-operated restaurants and 5.8% for franchised restaurants. Same-store sales have improved for nine consecutive quarters. After carefully addressing underperforming markets, management has finally rolled out some beefy profits. Even tax loss carryforwards are expected to be utilized resulting in a tax credit for the last year. 1995 results included a charge for the impairment of assets of $2.6 million after it was determined that a number of restaurants in central Arkansas had serious declines in operating performance. Intangible assets of $1.4 million were recorded at January 2, 1999, which equated to only 14.1% of stockholders' equity and book value per share. Also at the last year end, the Company had a deficiency in working capital.

Officers	Position	Ownership Information	
Lattimore M. Michael	Chairman, CEO	Number of Shares Outstanding	4,596,471
Joseph L. Weiss	President, COO	Market Capitalization	$ 8,595,401
William N. Griffith	Exec VP, Secretary	Number of Shareholders	2,500
Michael C. McDermott	Exec VP	Where Listed / Symbol	NASDAQ / BYBI

Other Information			
Transfer Agent	Union Planters Bank Memphis, TN	SIC Code	5812
Auditor	PricewaterhouseCoopers LLP	Employees	1,000
		Web Site	backyardburgers.com

Bayou Steel Corporation

138 Highway 3217, P.O. Box 5000   LaPlace, LA 70069   Telephone (504)652-4900   Fax (504)652-0339

Company Description

Bayou Steel Corporation is a leading producer of light structural shapes and merchant bar steel products. The Company owns and operates a steel minimill and a stocking warehouse located on the Mississippi River in LaPlace, Louisiana, plus three additional stocking locations and a rolling mill in Harriman, Tennessee. All locations are accessible through the Mississippi River waterway system. Strategic locations create a wide geographic market for product distribution. The Company produces light structural steel products ranging in size from three to eight inches and merchant bar products ranging from one-half to four inches. The Company was founded in 1979.

	09/30/98	09/30/97	09/30/96	09/30/95
Per Share Information				
Stock Price as of 12/31	4.12	3.37	2.62	3.87
Earnings Per Share	1.88	0.09	-0.18	0.73
Price / Earnings Ratio	2.19	37.44	n.a.	5.30
Book Value Per Share	7.55	5.55	5.46	5.63
Price / Book Value %	54.57	60.72	47.99	68.74
Dividends Per Share	0.0	0.0	0.0	0.0
Annual Financial Data				
Operating Results (000's)				
Total Revenues	250,880.8	232,161.1	204,425.9	185,772.3
Costs & Expenses	-229,229.1	-228,327.2	-204,111.3	-175,317.3
Income Before Taxes and Other	21,651.7	3,833.9	314.6	10,454.9
Other Items	-2,506.9	0.0	0.0	0.0
Income Tax	10,954.0	-49.8	0.0	-118.2
Net Income	30,098.9	3,784.1	314.6	10,336.8
Cash Flow From Operations	27,311.8	12,761.9	-4,535.5	8,991.9
Balance Sheet (000's)				
Cash & Equivalents	34,028.9	971.5	748.6	10,521.7
Total Current Assets	150,893.5	103,395.2	105,004.7	100,395.2
Fixed Assets, Net	90,115.9	90,138.3	90,334.4	91,650.0
Total Assets	249,497.5	196,465.1	199,271.7	197,076.2
Total Current Liabilities	33,258.9	31,364.2	34,914.7	27,093.9
Long-Term Debt	118,898.9	80,500.1	83,540.3	85,137.7
Stockholders' Equity	97,339.7	71,511.8	70,327.6	72,605.4
Performance & Financial Condition				
Return on Total Revenues %	11.86	1.63	0.15	5.56
Return on Avg Stockholders' Equity %	35.65	5.34	0.44	15.58
Return on Average Assets %	13.50	1.91	0.16	5.85
Current Ratio	4.54	3.30	3.01	3.71
Debt / Equity %	122.15	112.57	118.79	117.26

Compound Growth %'s	EPS %	37.07	Net Income %	42.80	Total Revenues %	10.97

Comments

Fiscal 1998 produced the best earnings in the Company's history. Revenue benefitted from increases in both volume and pricing. Gross margins were further impacted by low prices for scrap steel, the raw ingredient used in production. Fiscal 1998 results include three nonrecurring items: an extraordinary loss of $5.5 million related to the early extinguishment of debt, a $11.0 million tax credit due to the expectation that the Company will utilize a portion of its tax loss carryovers, and a $3 million favorable legal settlement. Earnings per share are calculated after deduction for preferred stock dividends. The preferred stock was redeemed in fiscal 1998. The common shares are priced at a discount to book value but it's not because of intangibles; the Company's financials are clean.

Officers	Position	Ownership Information	
Howard M. Meyers	Chairman, CEO	Number of Shares Outstanding	12,890,507
Jerry M. Pitts	President, COO	Market Capitalization	$ 53,108,889
Richard J. Gonzalez	Vice President, CFO	Number of Shareholders	3,253
Rodger A. Malehorn	Vice President	Where Listed / Symbol	AMEX / BYX

Other Information			
Transfer Agent	American Stock Transfer & Trust Co. New York, NY	SIC Code	3312
Auditor	Arthur Andersen LLP	Employees	580
		Web Site	bayousteel.com

Berger Holdings, Ltd.

805 Pennsylvania Boulevard   Feasterville, PA 19053   Telephone (215)355-1200   Fax (215)953-7750

Company Description

Berger Holdings, Ltd. is principally engaged in the manufacture and distribution of aluminum, galvanized and copper roof drainage products as well as solid vinyl home siding products. Roof drainage products comprise over 90% of Company revenues. Products are sold primarily to wholesale distributors in the northeastern United States, who in turn sell to roofers and contractors for use on residential properties. The Company was incorporated in 1979 and began operating its current business in 1989 with the acquisition of Berger Bros Company. On January 2, 1998, the Company consummated the acquisition of the Roof Drainage Division of its main competitor, Benjamin Obdyke, Inc. On December 7, 1998, the Company acquired certain assets of Sheet Metal Manufacturing Co., Inc., a manufacturer of roof drainage products. Let's check out the financial statements below for any leaks.

	12/31/98	12/31/97	12/31/96	12/31/95
Per Share Information				
Stock Price	3.12	3.69	1.97	0.88
Earnings Per Share	0.24	0.31	0.41	-0.26
Price / Earnings Ratio	13.00	11.90	4.80	n.a.
Book Value Per Share	2.90	2.39	1.58	1.31
Price / Book Value %	107.59	154.39	124.68	67.18
Dividends Per Share	0.0	0.0	0.0	0.0
Annual Financial Data				
Operating Results (000's)				
Total Revenues	35,745.0	20,762.4	19,750.2	15,684.3
Costs & Expenses	-34,701.3	-19,742.0	-18,595.7	-16,534.2
Income Before Taxes and Other	1,043.6	1,020.4	1,154.5	-849.9
Other Items	0.0	0.0	0.0	0.0
Income Tax	647.2	1,000.0	500.0	0.0
Net Income	1,690.8	2,020.4	1,654.5	-849.9
Cash Flow From Operations	2,298.9	-464.9	20.6	465.2
Balance Sheet (000's)				
Cash & Equivalents	149.9	4,411.3	1,236.7	171.4
Total Current Assets	11,398.9	9,891.9	5,344.1	3,103.5
Fixed Assets, Net	9,789.0	6,110.1	6,080.8	5,742.3
Total Assets	34,587.2	19,751.2	12,292.9	9,885.3
Total Current Liabilities	4,165.2	1,235.8	915.8	3,573.3
Long-Term Debt	14,560.3	6,022.1	3,721.7	1,676.7
Stockholders' Equity	15,361.7	12,493.3	7,655.3	4,635.4
Performance & Financial Condition				
Return on Total Revenues %	4.73	9.73	8.38	-5.42
Return on Avg Stockholders' Equity %	12.14	20.05	26.92	-17.33
Return on Average Assets %	6.22	12.61	14.92	-8.40
Current Ratio	2.74	8.00	5.84	0.87
Debt / Equity %	94.78	48.20	48.62	36.17

Compound Growth %'s	EPS %	-23.49	Net Income %	1.09	Total Revenues %	31.60

Comments

The sharp increase in revenues experienced in 1998 was due to the two acquisitions completed that year. 1998 results include expenses for building up an infrastructure to support the acquisitions made in 1998. Income tax benefits were realized in 1998, 1997 and 1996 as a result of the use of tax loss carryforwards. $6 million of carryovers remain available to offset income in future years. The lower pre-tax income in 1997 versus 1996 is due to costs associated with an extensive marketing and advertising campaign designed to promote its products on a national level as well as cost associated with the introduction of an acquired product line. At December 31, 1998, the Company had $7.3 million of goodwill on its books reflected as assets which equated to approximately 48% of stockholders' equity and book value per share.

Officers	Position	Ownership Information	
Theodore A. Schwartz	Chairman, CEO	Number of Shares Outstanding	5,301,330
Joseph F. Weiderman	President, COO	Market Capitalization	$ 16,540,150
Francis E. Wellock, Jr.	CFO	Number of Shareholders	2,200
Paul L. Spiese, III	Vice President	Where Listed / Symbol	NASDAQ / BGRH

Other Information			
Transfer Agent	OTR / Oxford Transfer & Registrar Portland, OR	SIC Code	3444
Auditor	KPMG LLP	Employees	140
		Web Site	bergerbros.com

Bernard Chaus, Inc.

1410 Broadway   New York, NY 10018   Telephone (212)354-1280   Fax (212)863-4269

Company Description

Bernard Chaus, Inc. designs, arranges for the manufacture of and markets an extensive range of women's career and casual sportswear which are marketed principally under the names CHAUS® and NAUTICA®. By August 1997, the Company had successfully repositioned its Chaus product line into the opening price points of the "better" category. In fiscal 1998, the Company completed a restructuring program pursuant to which it raised $20 million of equity through a rights offering, converted $40.6 million of the Company's indebtedness to Josephine Chaus into 10,510,910 shares of common stock of the Company, entered into a new revolving credit facility with BNY Financial Corporation and closed all of its retail outlet stores.

	06/30/98	06/30/97	06/30/96	06/30/95
Per Share Information				
Stock Price as of 12/31	2.25	2.25	1.62	3.62
Earnings Per Share	0.28	-2.46	-3.91	-1.40
Price / Earnings Ratio	8.04	n.a.	n.a.	n.a.
Book Value Per Share	0.26	-8.53	-1.51	-1.54
Price / Book Value %	865.38	n.a.	n.a.	n.a.
Dividends Per Share	0.0	0.0	0.0	0.0
Annual Financial Data				
Operating Results (000's)				
Total Revenues	191,604.0	160,213.0	170,631.0	181,788.0
Costs & Expenses	-187,048.0	-176,626.0	-194,716.0	-209,400.0
Income Before Taxes and Other	4,556.0	-16,413.0	-24,085.0	-27,612.0
Other Items	0.0	0.0	0.0	0.0
Income Tax	-245.0	-50.0	-301.0	-301.0
Net Income	4,311.0	-16,463.0	-24,386.0	-27,913.0
Cash Flow From Operations	-5,767.0	-11,005.0	-22,705.0	-4,781.0
Balance Sheet (000's)				
Cash & Equivalents	2,039.0	330.0	247.0	418.0
Total Current Assets	37,176.0	32,095.0	30,281.0	25,790.0
Fixed Assets, Net	960.0	1,295.0	1,898.0	2,392.0
Total Assets	39,012.0	34,138.0	32,742.0	28,660.0
Total Current Liabilities	18,497.0	64,824.0	49,764.0	39,704.0
Long-Term Debt	13,500.0	26,374.0	23,588.0	21,335.0
Stockholders' Equity	7,015.0	-57,060.0	-40,610.0	-32,379.0
Performance & Financial Condition				
Return on Total Revenues %	2.25	-10.28	-14.29	-15.35
Return on Avg Stockholders' Equity %	n.a.	n.a.	n.a.	n.a.
Return on Average Assets %	11.79	-49.23	-79.43	-103.38
Current Ratio	2.01	0.50	0.61	0.65
Debt / Equity %	192.44	n.a.	n.a.	n.a.

Compound Growth %'s	EPS % n.a.	Net Income % n.a.	Total Revenues % 1.77

Comments

Retail store sales decreased as a result of the liquidation of the Company's retail outlet stores during the second quarter of fiscal 1998. In fiscal 1998, exclusive of sales associated with the retail outlet stores, units shipped increased by 11.6% with a 14.3% increase in average selling prices from the prior year. The bottom line profit was refreshing after years of significant losses. The improved working capital position is partially the result of a high debt to equity ratio. But now there is equity for the first time since 1993. For the six months ended December 31, 1998, the Company reported revenue and net income of $94.3 million and $4,029,000 ($.15 per share) as compared to $106.0 million and $690,000 ($.10 per share) for the same period of the preceding year.

Officers	Position	Ownership Information	
Josephine Chaus	Chairman	Number of Shares Outstanding	27,115,907
Andrew Grossman	CEO	Market Capitalization	$ 61,010,791
Stuart S. Levy	CFO, Secretary	Number of Shareholders	10,000
Barton Heminover	Vice President, Controller	Where Listed / Symbol	NYSE / CHS

Other Information			
Transfer Agent	ChaseMellon Shareholder Services Ridgefield Park, NJ	SIC Code	2330
Auditor	Deloitte & Touche LLP	Employees	334
		Web Site	bernardchaus.com

Big Dog Holdings, Inc.

121 Gray Avenue Santa Barbara, CA 93101   Telephone (805)963-8727   Fax (805)962-9460

Company Description

Big Dog Holdings, Inc. develops, markets and retails a branded, lifestyle collection of unique, high-quality, popular-priced consumer products, including activewear, casual sportswear, accessories and gifts. BIG DOGS® is an All-American, family-oriented brand that the Company believes has established a unique niche in its dedication to providing quality, value and fun. Big Dog's products were first sold in 1983, and operations remained limited until 1992 when the current controlling stockholders acquired the BIG DOGS® brand and related assets. Following the acquisition, Big Dog initiated a strategy of leveraging the brand through dramatic expansion of its product line and rapid growth in its retail stores. The number of the Company's stores has grown from 5 in 1993 to 177 as of December 31, 1998. The Company had its initial public offering in September 1997 at a price of $14 per share.

	12/31/98	12/31/97	12/31/96	12/31/95
Per Share Information				
Stock Price	4.87	5.56	2.76	1.50
Earnings Per Share	0.32	0.24	0.06	0.07
Price / Earnings Ratio	15.22	23.17	46.00	21.43
Book Value Per Share	3.57	3.46	0.60	0.49
Price / Book Value %	136.41	160.69	460.00	306.12
Dividends Per Share	0.0	0.0	0.0	0.0
Annual Financial Data				
Operating Results (000's)				
Total Revenues	100,677.0	86,181.0	68,683.0	51,541.0
Costs & Expenses	-93,971.0	-81,883.0	-67,613.0	-50,741.0
Income Before Taxes and Other	6,706.0	4,298.0	1,070.0	800.0
Other Items	0.0	0.0	0.0	0.0
Income Tax	-2,674.0	-1,633.0	-435.0	-162.0
Net Income	4,032.0	2,665.0	635.0	638.0
Cash Flow From Operations	3,090.0	7,323.0	-1,762.0	-2,219.0
Balance Sheet (000's)				
Cash & Equivalents	13,458.0	23,508.0	723.0	769.0
Total Current Assets	39,392.0	41,861.0	17,718.0	11,572.0
Fixed Assets, Net	12,983.0	10,232.0	7,445.0	7,439.0
Total Assets	52,994.0	52,584.0	25,773.0	19,011.0
Total Current Liabilities	9,043.0	6,393.0	3,976.0	3,542.0
Long-Term Debt	0.0	0.0	14,400.0	10,732.0
Stockholders' Equity	43,187.0	45,541.0	6,142.0	4,737.0
Performance & Financial Condition				
Return on Total Revenues %	4.00	3.09	0.92	1.24
Return on Avg Stockholders' Equity %	9.09	10.31	11.67	16.29
Return on Average Assets %	7.64	6.80	2.84	3.91
Current Ratio	4.36	6.55	4.46	3.27
Debt / Equity %	n.a.	n.a.	234.45	226.56

Compound Growth %'s	EPS %	65.97	Net Income %	84.88	Total Revenues %	25.00

Comments

Sales in 1998 continued to increase at an impressive rate but were mostly attributable to new stores. Gross profit increased to 59.0% in 1998 from 57.8% in 1997. This increase was primarily due to better sourcing of certain key products. Also contributing to the percentage increase were continued improvements in merchandising, planning and allocation, which led to better product sell-throughs and less markdowns. The balance sheet is strong with an excellent current ratio and no long term debt. The excess working capital may be what encouraged the Company to reacquire approximately 1.1 million shares of its common stock during 1998 at an average price of $6.00 per share.

Officers	Position	Ownership Information	
Andrew D. Feshbach	President, CEO	Number of Shares Outstanding	12,100,350
Douglas N. Nilsen	Exec VP	Market Capitalization	$ 58,928,705
Anthony J. Wall	Exec VP, Secretary	Number of Shareholders	2,000
Andrew W. Wadhams	Exec VP	Where Listed / Symbol	NASDAQ / BDOG

Other Information			
Transfer Agent	American Stock Transfer & Trust Co. Glendale, CA	SIC Code	5651
Auditor	Deloitte & Touche LLP	Employees	1,200
		Web Site	bigdog.com

Big Sky Transportation Co.

1601 Aviation Place Billings, MT 59105 Telephone (406)245-9449 Fax (406)259-8750

Company Description

Big Sky Transportation Co., dba Big Sky Airlines, operates as a regional air carrier, providing scheduled passenger, freight, express package and charter services. Most service is provided to thirteen communities in Montana. The Company's present route system is designed around a small regional air service hub in Billings, Montana. Seven of these communities are served under contract with the U.S. Department of Transportation under the Essential Air Service (EAS) program. The Company filed for bankruptcy protection in 1989 and emerged from those proceedings in 1992.

	06/30/98	06/30/97	06/30/96	06/30/95
Per Share Information				
Stock Price as of 12/31	1.94	1.75	1.31	1.10
Earnings Per Share	0.16	0.19	0.0	0.05
Price / Earnings Ratio	12.13	9.21	n.a.	22.00
Book Value Per Share	1.32	1.02	0.74	0.72
Price / Book Value %	146.97	171.57	177.03	152.78
Dividends Per Share	0.0	0.0	0.0	0.0
Annual Financial Data				
Operating Results (000's)				
Total Revenues	7,947.1	4,907.6	5,108.8	5,184.6
Costs & Expenses	-7,809.8	-4,554.3	-5,103.1	-5,109.2
Income Before Taxes and Other	137.3	339.5	5.7	67.7
Other Items	165.5	0.0	0.0	0.0
Income Tax	-120.0	-142.0	-2.2	-30.9
Net Income	182.9	197.5	3.5	36.8
Cash Flow From Operations	68.9	352.5	62.9	112.2
Balance Sheet (000's)				
Cash & Equivalents	512.7	1,144.9	360.7	408.5
Total Current Assets	2,475.7	1,845.3	1,513.0	1,482.3
Fixed Assets, Net	873.6	700.9	774.3	895.4
Total Assets	3,356.5	2,563.5	2,311.4	2,414.6
Total Current Liabilities	1,412.1	952.7	851.8	824.4
Long-Term Debt	219.3	263.8	397.1	518.9
Stockholders' Equity	1,457.9	1,071.6	775.4	768.2
Performance & Financial Condition				
Return on Total Revenues %	2.30	4.03	0.07	0.71
Return on Avg Stockholders' Equity %	14.46	21.39	0.45	4.97
Return on Average Assets %	6.18	8.10	0.15	1.44
Current Ratio	1.75	1.94	1.78	1.80
Debt / Equity %	15.04	24.61	51.21	67.55

Compound Growth %'s	EPS %	47.36	Net Income %	70.61	Total Revenues %	15.30

Comments

The Company executed a 1 for 5 reverse split in fiscal 1997. All per share amounts have been restated for consistency. In October 1997, the Company began scheduled services linking Billings with Helena and Missoula, Montana, after another air transportation company discontinued its local service to these markets. In October 1998, the Company added service to Spokane, Washington into the schedule. The Company has posted profits for all six years since emerging from bankruptcy. For the six months ended December 31, 1998, revenues and earnings were $6.5 million and $229,344 ($.20 per share) as compared to $3.4 million and $160,645 ($.15 per share) for the same period of the preceding year.

Officers	Position	Ownership Information	
Jon Marchi	Chairman	Number of Shares Outstanding	1,107,637
Kim B. Champney	President, CEO	Market Capitalization	$ 2,148,816
Craig Denney	Exec VP, COO	Number of Shareholders	1,200
Stephen D. Huntington	Secretary	Where Listed / Symbol	PSE / BSA

Other Information			
Transfer Agent	Continental Stock Transfer & Trust Co. New York, NY	SIC Code	4510
Auditor	Eide Bailly LLP	Employees	103

Bingo & Gaming International, Inc.

13581 Pond Springs Road, Suite 105 Austin, TX 78279 Telephone (512)335-0065 Fax (512)335-0078

Company Description

Bingo & Gaming International, Inc. is in the business of owning prepaid phone card vending machines for its own distribution as well as offering them for resale. This effort is facilitated by an exclusive agreement with a manufacturer that offers machines with a patented cartridge based technology that offers superior controls over cash collections and the accounting for promotional prizes paid. The Company owned 325 dispensers at December 31, 1998. The Company also operates three bingo halls at leased locations, all in Mississippi. Revenues generated are primarily from the rental of the bingo facilities to charitable organizations. The Company began doing business in its current form in 1994. Public trading in the Company's stock began in 1995.

	12/31/98	12/31/97	12/31/96	12/31/95
Per Share Information				
Stock Price	0.25	0.44	0.88	0.63
Earnings Per Share	0.01	0.01	-0.01	-0.03
Price / Earnings Ratio	25.00	44.00	n.a.	n.a.
Book Value Per Share	0.07	0.02	0.02	0.02
Price / Book Value %	357.14	2,200.00	4,400.00	3,150.00
Dividends Per Share	0.0	0.0	0.0	0.0
Annual Financial Data				
Operating Results (000's)				
Total Revenues	4,207.3	2,212.2	1,151.4	632.7
Costs & Expenses	-3,875.5	-2,168.7	-1,199.6	-850.5
Income Before Taxes and Other	331.8	43.4	-48.2	-217.8
Other Items	-205.2	0.0	0.0	0.0
Income Tax	0.0	0.0	0.0	0.0
Net Income	126.6	43.4	-48.2	-217.8
Cash Flow From Operations	379.7	36.1	-173.9	-113.8
Balance Sheet (000's)				
Cash & Equivalents	133.2	53.9	53.3	74.1
Total Current Assets	674.1	434.7	324.7	146.1
Fixed Assets, Net	1,357.2	456.9	115.5	167.7
Total Assets	2,193.0	961.2	541.2	471.8
Total Current Liabilities	890.8	557.0	233.2	237.2
Long-Term Debt	268.7	227.2	176.0	82.8
Stockholders' Equity	554.5	177.1	132.0	151.8
Performance & Financial Condition				
Return on Total Revenues %	3.01	1.96	-4.18	-34.43
Return on Avg Stockholders' Equity %	34.62	28.10	-33.94	-142.03
Return on Average Assets %	8.03	5.78	-9.51	-56.75
Current Ratio	0.76	0.78	1.39	0.62
Debt / Equity %	48.46	128.26	133.32	54.56

Compound Growth %'s	EPS % n.a.	Net Income % n.a.	Total Revenues % 88.05

Comments

During 1998, phone card sales grew from $1,621,748 in 1997 to $3,444,523. Bingo related revenue was flat. The increase in phone card sales resulted from the placement of an additional 274 machines during the year. 1998 results include a nonrecurring expense of $205,192 related to the impairment of assets. The Company intends to expand and further develop the phone card business. But the Company continues to operate with a deficit in working capital and needs additional funds to meet contractual obligations. An attempt to sell two of the bingo locations was unsuccessful. Management believes it can make ends meet even if some of the Company's accounts payable are delinquent.

Officers	Position	Ownership Information	
Reid Funderburk	Chairman, CEO	Number of Shares Outstanding	8,425,000
George Majewski	President, COO	Market Capitalization	$ 2,106,250
Rhonda McClellan	CFO	Number of Shareholders	315
Robert H. Hughes	Director	Where Listed / Symbol	OTC-BB / BING

Other Information			
Transfer Agent	Fidelity Transfer & Trust Co. Salt Lake City, UT	SIC Code	6519
Auditor	Brown, Graham and Company, PC	Employees	12
Market Maker	Herzog, Heine, Geduld, Inc.	(800)221-3600	Web Site	bgicorp.com
	Paragon Capital Corporation	(800)345-0505		

Bio-Reference Laboratories, Inc.

481 Edward H. Ross Drive   Elmwood Park, NJ 07407   Telephone (201)791-2600   Fax (201)791-1941

Company Description

Bio-Reference Laboratories, Inc. operates a clinical laboratory located in northern New Jersey, principally servicing the greater New York metropolitan area. The Company offers a comprehensive list of chemical diagnostic tests including blood and urine analysis, blood chemistry, hematology services, serology, radioimmuno analysis, toxicology (including drug screening), pap smears, tissue pathology (biopsies) and other tissue analysis. The Company picks up test specimens directly from the physician and test results are generally transmitted by computerized telephone connections or courier. The Company intends to continue expanding and developing its laboratory operations through acquisitions, on-going marketing efforts and expansion of its specialty testing areas. The Company was founded in 1981 and has been in its current primary business since 1987.

	10/31/98	10/31/97	10/31/96	10/31/95
Per Share Information				
Stock Price as of 12/31	1.00	1.41	1.16	3.00
Earnings Per Share	0.07	0.36	0.10	0.23
Price / Earnings Ratio	14.29	3.92	11.60	13.04
Book Value Per Share	2.25	2.17	1.92	1.85
Price / Book Value %	44.44	64.98	60.42	162.16
Dividends Per Share	0.0	0.0	0.0	0.0
Annual Financial Data				
Operating Results (000's)				
Total Revenues	46,993.9	38,935.1	35,414.3	31,795.0
Costs & Expenses	-46,435.6	-36,775.2	-34,770.5	-30,343.6
Income Before Taxes and Other	558.3	1,035.5	643.8	1,451.4
Other Items	0.0	2,025.7	0.0	0.0
Income Tax	38.3	138.7	-51.9	-49.2
Net Income	596.6	3,199.9	592.0	1,402.2
Cash Flow From Operations	-3,227.6	-171.6	-1,895.5	-769.6
Balance Sheet (000's)				
Cash & Equivalents	2,784.1	2,161.8	1,401.5	636.2
Total Current Assets	29,212.1	22,065.3	18,666.8	16,654.4
Fixed Assets, Net	2,220.5	1,287.7	1,311.3	1,000.0
Total Assets	40,778.3	29,095.1	28,230.7	24,201.0
Total Current Liabilities	20,847.8	12,649.8	14,594.3	12,102.6
Long-Term Debt	3,306.6	668.0	1,433.8	0.0
Stockholders' Equity	16,222.9	15,524.6	12,103.0	11,255.8
Performance & Financial Condition				
Return on Total Revenues %	1.27	8.22	1.67	4.41
Return on Avg Stockholders' Equity %	3.76	23.16	5.07	14.38
Return on Average Assets %	1.71	11.16	2.26	6.74
Current Ratio	1.40	1.74	1.28	1.38
Debt / Equity %	20.38	4.30	11.85	n.a.

Compound Growth %'s	EPS % -32.73	Net Income % -24.79	Total Revenues % 13.91

Comments

Most of the increase in revenues during fiscal 1998 was attributable to an acquisition in April 1998. Two-thirds of the decline in net income was related to a reduction in nonrecurring income. Fiscal 1997 results include a nonrecurring gain of $2.0 million ($.23 per share) related to the sale of intangible assets of its GenCare Division. The balance of the decline was due to lower gross margins and increased general expenses. Still the Company is increasing revenue and has produced five consecutive years of profits. At October 31, 1998, the Company had $8.3 million of intangibles assets reflected on its books which equated to approximately 51% of stockholders' equity and book value per share. The stock is trading below its tangible book value.

Officers	Position	Ownership Information	
Marc D. Grodman	President, CEO	Number of Shares Outstanding	7,212,910
Howard Dubinett	Exec VP, COO	Market Capitalization	$ 7,212,910
Sam Singer	Vice President, CFO	Number of Shareholders	2,000
Frank DeVito	Director	Where Listed / Symbol	NASDAQ / BRLI

Other Information			
Transfer Agent	American Stock Transfer & Trust Co. New York, NY	SIC Code	8071
Auditor	Moore Stephens, P.C.	Employees	672
		Web Site	bio-referencelabs.com

BioSpecifics Technologies Corp.

35 Wilbur Street Lynbrook, NY 11563 Telephone (516)593-7000 Fax (516)593-7039

Company Description

BioSpecifics Technologies Corp. engages in the business of producing and licensing for sale by others a Food and Drug Administration approved enzyme derived from collagenase, named Collagenase ABC. The Company also researches, develops and clinically tests additional products derived therefrom for potential use as pharmaceuticals. Collagenase ABC dissolves collagen (the body's principal connective tissue) and is currently used as a topical enzymatic debridement treatment for dermal ulcers, such as bed sores, and second and third degree burns. The Company currently derives substantially all of its revenues through a licensing agreement with Knoll Pharmaceutical Company (KPC), a major pharmaceutical company. BioSpecifics was founded in 1972.

	01/31/98	01/31/97	01/31/96	01/31/95
Per Share Information				
Stock Price as of 12/31	3.75	4.38	4.50	3.62
Earnings Per Share	0.17	0.23	-0.07	n.a.
Price / Earnings Ratio	22.06	19.04	n.a.	n.a.
Book Value Per Share	1.97	1.84	1.61	1.61
Price / Book Value %	190.36	238.04	279.50	224.84
Dividends Per Share	0.0	0.0	0.0	n.a.
Annual Financial Data				
Operating Results (000's)				
Total Revenues	6,338.1	6,263.1	4,977.3	n.a.
Costs & Expenses	-5,104.2	-4,799.3	-5,285.7	n.a.
Income Before Taxes and Other	1,234.0	1,463.9	-308.4	n.a.
Other Items	-34.3	-37.6	-0.2	n.a.
Income Tax	-363.8	-300.4	-39.9	n.a.
Net Income	835.8	1,125.9	-348.5	n.a.
Cash Flow From Operations	1,121.4	1,606.9	458.2	n.a.
Balance Sheet (000's)				
Cash & Equivalents	4,431.1	3,793.6	2,288.3	1,438.4
Total Current Assets	10,018.6	8,250.2	7,646.8	6,903.8
Fixed Assets, Net	873.6	912.9	981.1	1,086.0
Total Assets	11,198.6	9,906.3	9,266.9	9,020.8
Total Current Liabilities	1,558.8	737.8	1,274.2	1,006.0
Long-Term Debt	0.0	0.0	0.0	0.0
Stockholders' Equity	9,419.5	8,982.5	7,844.2	7,866.5
Performance & Financial Condition				
Return on Total Revenues %	13.19	17.98	-7.00	n.a.
Return on Avg Stockholders' Equity %	9.08	13.38	-4.44	n.a.
Return on Average Assets %	7.92	11.74	-3.81	n.a.
Current Ratio	6.43	11.18	6.00	6.86
Debt / Equity %	n.a.	n.a.	n.a.	n.a.

Compound Growth %'s	EPS %	-26.09	Net Income %	-25.76	Total Revenues %	12.85

Comments

Net sales decreased in fiscal 1998 due to lower sales of Collagenase ABC to KPC. Royalties increased, however, and nearly offset the product sales decline. The Company expects higher orders in fiscal 1999 due to order backlogs and a new agreement between KPC and Ortho-McNeil Pharmaceuticals, Inc. (a Johnson & Johnson Company) to promote the use of certain collagenase products. The agreement was reached in February 1998. Research and development expenses increased from $1.6 million in fiscal 1997 to $1.9 million in fiscal 1998. The Company is supported by an excellent financial condition. For the nine months ended October 31, 1998, the Company reported revenues and net income of $5.4 million and $806,147 ($.17 per share) as compared to $4.2 million and $577,567 ($.12 per share) for the same period of the preceding year.

Officers	Position	Ownership Information	
Edwin H. Wegman	President, CEO	Number of Shares Outstanding	4,789,296
Thomas L. Wegman	Exec VP	Market Capitalization	$ 17,959,860
Harold Stern	Exec VP, COO	Number of Shareholders	1,000
Albert Horcher	CFO, Secretary	Where Listed / Symbol	NASDAQ / BSTC

Other Information			
Transfer Agent	OTC Corporate Transfer Service Co. Hicksville, NY	SIC Code	2834
Auditor	KPMG LLP	Employees	46
		Web Site	biospecifics.com

Birner Dental Management Services, Inc.

3801 East Florida Avenue, Suite 508   Denver, CO 80210   Telephone (303)691-0680   Fax (303)691-0889

Company Description

Birner Dental Management Services, Inc. acquires, develops and manages geographically dense dental practice networks in select markets, currently including Colorado and New Mexico. With its 41 offices in Colorado, the Company believes that it is the largest provider of dental management services in that state. The Company and its dental practice management model provide a solution to the needs of dentists, patients and third-party payors by allowing the Company's affiliated dentists to provide high-quality, efficient dental care in patient-friendly, family practice settings. Dentists practicing at the offices provide comprehensive general dentistry services, and the Company increasingly offers specialty dental services through affiliated specialists. The Company manages 51 dental practices, of which 39 were acquired and 12 were developed internally. The success of the Company's dental practice network in Colorado has led to its expansion into New Mexico and its evaluation of additional markets. The Company had its initial public offering on February 12, 1998 at which time it sold 2.1 million shares at $7 per share.

	12/31/98	12/31/97	12/31/96	12/31/95
Per Share Information				
Stock Price	3.44	7.50	3.00	2.18
Earnings Per Share	0.10	0.01	-0.10	-0.06
Price / Earnings Ratio	34.40	750.00	n.a.	n.a.
Book Value Per Share	2.82	0.43	0.51	0.61
Price / Book Value %	121.99	1,744.19	588.24	357.38
Dividends Per Share	0.0	0.0	0.0	0.0
Annual Financial Data				
Operating Results (000's)				
Total Revenues	21,740.7	12,742.3	5,373.2	300.0
Costs & Expenses	-20,897.5	-12,456.2	-5,708.5	-460.2
Income Before Taxes and Other	843.1	33.8	-335.3	-160.3
Other Items	-39.2	0.0	0.0	0.0
Income Tax	-128.5	0.0	0.0	0.0
Net Income	675.5	33.8	-335.3	-160.3
Cash Flow From Operations	1,397.4	2,246.0	-545.6	25.7
Balance Sheet (000's)				
Cash & Equivalents	2,169.7	977.5	1,797.6	1,464.5
Total Current Assets	5,648.4	3,518.7	2,856.3	1,578.3
Fixed Assets, Net	5,613.0	2,630.9	1,809.8	266.3
Total Assets	25,543.4	15,563.8	9,552.8	2,908.5
Total Current Liabilities	3,339.9	3,977.1	1,039.5	880.7
Long-Term Debt	3,234.1	10,172.1	6,763.2	0.0
Stockholders' Equity	18,745.5	1,388.4	1,684.1	2,004.4
Performance & Financial Condition				
Return on Total Revenues %	3.11	0.27	-6.24	-53.43
Return on Avg Stockholders' Equity %	6.71	2.20	-18.18	-17.81
Return on Average Assets %	3.29	0.27	-5.38	-5.34
Current Ratio	1.69	0.88	2.75	1.79
Debt / Equity %	17.25	732.66	401.59	n.a.

Compound Growth %'s	EPS % n.a.	Net Income % n.a.	Total Revenues % 316.94

Comments

Revenues increased 70.6% in 1998 which was attributable to ten practices that were acquired in 1998, the opening of five de novo offices during 1998, and the first full year of offices that were acquired or opened in 1997. Net earnings were more than marginally profitable for the first time. At December 31, 1998, the Company had $13.9 million of intangible assets recorded on its ledgers which equates to approximately 74% of stockholders' equity and book value per share.

Officers	Position	Ownership Information	
Frederic W. J. Birner	Chairman, CEO	Number of Shares Outstanding	6,636,980
Mark A. Birner	President	Market Capitalization	$ 22,831,211
Dennis N. Genty	CFO, Secretary	Number of Shareholders	1,000
Pamela K. Bernardini	Vice President, Controller	Where Listed / Symbol	NASDAQ / BDMS

Other Information			
Transfer Agent	American Securities Transfer, Inc. Denver, CO	SIC Code	8741
Auditor	Arthur Andersen LLP	Employees	447

Blimpie International, Inc.

740 Broadway   New York, NY 10003   Telephone (212)673-5900   Fax (212)995-2560

Company Description

Blimpie International, Inc. franchises and licenses BLIMPIE Subs & Salads, an international chain of quick-service sandwich locations, and a family of complementary trademarks and marketing concepts globally. Since opening the first BLIMPIE restaurant in Hoboken, New Jersey in 1964, Blimpie International has become the franchisor of a chain with almost 2,000 outlets in 46 states and 12 foreign countries. The Company has a 60% interest in the international distribution of BLIMPIE trademarks, which began in 1995. Traditional BLIMPIE restaurants are located in shopping centers, malls, free-standing buildings and downtown markets. New concept locations include convenience stores, gas station food marts, colleges, office complexes, hospitals, and sports arenas. New distribution formats include "Grab 'n Go" refrigeration cases, carts, kiosks, and vending machines.

	06/30/98	06/30/97	06/30/96	06/30/95
Per Share Information				
Stock Price as of 12/31	2.19	3.44	10.12	10.87
Earnings Per Share	0.26	0.34	0.41	0.27
Price / Earnings Ratio	8.42	10.12	24.68	40.26
Book Value Per Share	2.17	1.98	1.65	0.85
Price / Book Value %	100.92	173.74	613.33	1,278.82
Dividends Per Share	0.07	0.07	0.06	0.05
Annual Financial Data				
Operating Results (000's)				
Total Revenues	38,721.0	39,017.0	36,006.0	26,952.0
Costs & Expenses	-34,797.0	-33,724.0	-29,471.0	-23,028.1
Income Before Taxes and Other	3,924.0	5,293.0	6,535.0	3,923.9
Other Items	0.0	0.0	0.0	0.0
Income Tax	-1,480.0	-2,015.0	-2,495.0	-1,584.0
Net Income	2,444.0	3,278.0	4,040.0	2,339.9
Cash Flow From Operations	2,090.0	1,919.0	2,042.0	5,316.5
Balance Sheet (000's)				
Cash & Equivalents	4,021.0	3,532.0	4,328.5	3,922.2
Total Current Assets	12,801.0	11,767.0	12,613.8	8,026.3
Fixed Assets, Net	1,584.0	1,253.0	972.3	692.6
Total Assets	28,323.0	27,704.0	21,822.7	15,251.5
Total Current Liabilities	3,336.0	4,005.0	4,121.0	5,292.8
Long-Term Debt	0.0	0.0	5.2	12.7
Stockholders' Equity	20,625.0	18,865.0	15,674.5	7,308.0
Performance & Financial Condition				
Return on Total Revenues %	6.31	8.40	11.22	8.68
Return on Avg Stockholders' Equity %	12.38	18.98	35.16	37.09
Return on Average Assets %	8.72	13.24	21.79	17.71
Current Ratio	3.84	2.94	3.06	1.52
Debt / Equity %	n.a.	n.a.	0.03	0.17

Compound Growth %'s	EPS %	-1.25	Net Income %	1.46	Total Revenues %	12.84

Comments

The Company's profitability has been on a decline since fiscal 1996. This is due primarily to a decrease in revenues from the sale of subfranchise territories. Management is responding with several new initiatives, the most notable of which is the introduction of three new brands: Maui Tacos™, Pasta Central™, and Smoothie Island™. During fiscal 1998, the Company also restructured its management personnel. For the six months ended December 31, 1998, the Company reported revenue and net income of $17.3 million and $934,000 ($.10 per share) as compared to $19.7 million and $1,564,000 ($.16 per share) for the same period of the preceding year.

Officers	Position	Ownership Information	
Anthony P. Conza	President, CEO	Number of Shares Outstanding	9,508,000
David L. Siegel	COO	Market Capitalization	$ 20,822,520
Patrick J. Pompeo	Exec VP	Number of Shareholders	2,000
Charles G. Leaness	Exec VP, Secretary	Where Listed / Symbol	AMEX / BLM

Other Information			
Transfer Agent	ChaseMellon Shareholder Services Ridgefield Park, NJ	SIC Code	6794
Auditor	PricewaterhouseCoopers LLP	Employees	109
		Web Site	blimpie.com

Boatracs, Inc.

10675 Sorrento Valley Road, Suite 200   San Diego, CA 92121   Telephone (619)657-0100   Fax (619)587-1073

Company Description

Boatracs, Inc. sells satellite-based communications and tracking hardware and software to the commercial marine industry. This includes commercial fishermen, fuel transporters and the workboat industry of the inland waterways. The Company's primary product is the OmniTRACS System which is manufactured by and licensed from Qualcomm Inc. Boatracs was formed in California in 1990. In January 1995, the Company was merged into an existing publicly held shell company and its stock began trading in April of that year. During 1997, Boatracs purchased the assets of MED Associates, Inc.(MED), a provider of software applications for the marine industry. On July 7, 1998, the Company acquired ENERDYNE which develops, builds and sells digital video compression equipment for the aerospace, military, intelligent transportation, government and commercial markets.

	12/31/98	12/31/97	12/31/96	12/31/95
Per Share Information				
Stock Price	1.75	2.06	1.00	0.88
Earnings Per Share	0.02	-0.02	-0.07	-0.06
Price / Earnings Ratio	87.50	n.a.	n.a.	n.a.
Book Value Per Share	0.77	0.09	0.05	0.10
Price / Book Value %	227.27	2,288.89	2,000.00	880.00
Dividends Per Share	0.0	0.0	0.0	0.0
Annual Financial Data				
Operating Results (000's)				
Total Revenues	10,220.7	5,286.8	3,561.3	2,708.0
Costs & Expenses	-10,253.9	-5,541.6	-4,466.7	-3,361.1
Income Before Taxes and Other	-33.1	-254.9	-905.4	-653.1
Other Items	0.0	0.0	0.0	0.0
Income Tax	422.2	0.0	0.0	0.0
Net Income	389.1	-254.9	-905.4	-653.1
Cash Flow From Operations	-101.6	135.0	-1,042.1	-546.6
Balance Sheet (000's)				
Cash & Equivalents	416.4	392.7	103.1	151.7
Total Current Assets	3,680.9	1,671.2	1,252.1	2,073.0
Fixed Assets, Net	738.3	223.9	120.7	72.4
Total Assets	33,070.5	3,036.5	1,581.3	2,360.2
Total Current Liabilities	3,863.7	1,649.3	981.1	693.5
Long-Term Debt	8,094.8	0.0	0.0	0.0
Stockholders' Equity	14,472.4	1,387.2	600.2	1,297.5
Performance & Financial Condition				
Return on Total Revenues %	3.81	-4.82	-25.42	-24.12
Return on Avg Stockholders' Equity %	4.91	-25.65	-95.43	-124.86
Return on Average Assets %	2.16	-11.04	-45.94	-40.77
Current Ratio	0.95	1.01	1.28	2.99
Debt / Equity %	55.93	n.a.	n.a.	n.a.

Compound Growth %'s   EPS % n.a.   Net Income % n.a.   Total Revenues % 55.70

Comments

In the 1998 edition of this manual, we suggested that 1998 might be the Company's first profitable year. With the help of an income tax credit it was. But it isn't just income tax that deserves credit. Revenues increased 95.5% during 1998. Approximately two-thirds of this growth is attributable to acquisitions. The one-third that came from the original core products was up a whopping 67.2% during 1998. At December 31, 1998, the Company had $28.7 million of intangible assets resulting from acquisitions recorded as assets which equated to approximately 198% of stockholders' equity and book value per share. The Company also had its first long term debt since 1994. $413,000 of interest expense was paid in 1998 without creating a loss.

Officers	Position	Ownership Information	
Michael Silverman	Chairman	Number of Shares Outstanding	18,834,032
Jon S. Gilbert	President, CEO	Market Capitalization	$ 32,959,556
Annette Friskopp	COO, Secretary	Number of Shareholders	310
Curt McLeland	CFO	Where Listed / Symbol	OTC-BB / BTRK

Other Information			
Transfer Agent	ChaseMellon Shareholder Services Ridgefield Park, NJ	SIC Code	4899
Auditor	Deloitte & Touche LLP	Employees	60
Market Maker	Herzog, Heine, Geduld, Inc. (800)221-3600	Web Site	boatracs.com
	Sharpe Capital Inc. (800)355-5781		

Bollinger Industries, Inc.

602 Fountain Parkway   Grand Prairie, TX 75050   Telephone (972)343-1000   Fax (972)343-1199

Company Description

Bollinger is a leading domestic supplier of consumer fitness accessory products and safety products. The Company manufactures and distributes, primarily to mass retailers, an extensive consumer fitness line, including barbells and dumbbells, aerobic steps and other aerobics products, weightlifting belts and gloves, exercise mats, ankle and wrist weights, weightlifting bars, waist trimmers, compression shorts, and walking accessories. The Company sold its trampoline product line in November 1997. The Company also had a healthcare division which was sold or otherwise disposed of during fiscal 1997 and 1996.

	03/31/98	03/31/97	03/31/96	03/31/95
Per Share Information				
Stock Price as of 12/31	0.44	0.62	0.56	11.75
Earnings Per Share	1.37	-1.86	-2.22	0.02
Price / Earnings Ratio	0.32	n.a.	n.a.	587.50
Book Value Per Share	2.62	1.26	3.36	5.52
Price / Book Value %	16.79	49.21	16.67	212.86
Dividends Per Share	0.0	0.0	0.0	0.0
Annual Financial Data				
Operating Results (000's)				
Total Revenues	58,793.8	82,648.8	80,404.4	73,159.3
Costs & Expenses	-64,349.5	-90,659.2	-88,400.9	-72,963.2
Income Before Taxes and Other	-5,555.8	-8,010.3	-7,996.5	149.3
Other Items	11,247.5	477.0	-1,362.0	0.0
Income Tax	-225.5	92.0	1,135.1	-80.0
Net Income	5,466.2	-7,441.4	-8,223.4	69.3
Cash Flow From Operations	3,621.0	4,990.8	3,990.2	-19,592.0
Balance Sheet (000's)				
Cash & Equivalents	136.4	3.5	408.9	116.5
Total Current Assets	14,538.2	33,720.6	53,597.1	50,398.0
Fixed Assets, Net	1,865.0	2,083.4	2,015.3	2,365.0
Total Assets	17,001.3	38,389.4	58,380.9	55,422.4
Total Current Liabilities	5,699.1	17,726.5	45,275.3	34,673.0
Long-Term Debt	36.5	15,641.7	576.8	223.3
Stockholders' Equity	10,487.4	5,021.1	12,462.5	20,467.4
Performance & Financial Condition				
Return on Total Revenues %	9.30	-9.00	-10.23	0.09
Return on Avg Stockholders' Equity %	70.49	-85.12	-49.94	0.35
Return on Average Assets %	19.74	-15.38	-14.45	0.17
Current Ratio	2.55	1.90	1.18	1.45
Debt / Equity %	0.35	311.52	4.63	1.09

Compound Growth %'s	EPS % n.a.	Net Income % n.a.	Total Revenues %	-7.03

Comments

During fiscal 1996 and 1997, the Company suffered substantial operating losses as it changed its marketing focus from celebrity-endorsed products to Bollinger branded items and reduced its significant investment in inventory. This restructuring effort was completed in fiscal 1998. The sale of the Company's trampoline product line provided much needed capital and resulted in a nonrecurring gain of $11,247,513 in fiscal 1998. Although the Company has experienced many areas of improvement, there remain a number of areas that management is attempting to address. For the nine months ended December 31, 1998, the Company reported revenues of $25.3 million and a net loss of $2,944,343 ($.72 per share). Investors are not expressing much confidence as the trading range is well under book value.

Officers	Position	Ownership Information	
Glenn D. Bollinger	Chairman, CEO	Number of Shares Outstanding	4,000,210
Bobby D. Bollinger	President	Market Capitalization	$ 1,760,092
Rose Turner	Exec VP, COO	Number of Shareholders	1,000
Floyd DePauw	Controller	Where Listed / Symbol	OTC-BB / BOLL

Other Information			
Transfer Agent	Chemical Mellon Shareholder Services New York, NY	SIC Code	3949
Auditor	King Griffin & Adamson P.C.	Employees	120
Market Maker	Wm. V. Frankel & Co., Inc. (800)631-3091	Web Site	bollingerfitness.com
	M.H. Meyerson & Co., Inc. (800)333-3113		

Bontex, Inc.

One Bontex Drive Buena Vista, VA 24416-1500 Telephone (540)261-2181 Fax (540)261-3784

Company Description

Bontex, Inc. manufactures and distributes uncoated and coated elastomeric wet web impregnated fiberboard products, generally described by the trademark BONTEX®. BONTEX is primarily used as an insole material in footwear. It is also used as visorboard in headwear, dielectric sealing base in automobile door panels, backing substrate, stiffener and laminating base in luggage, leathergoods, and allied products. All BONTEX fiberboard products are designed to be "environmentally-friendly" because the Company uses recycled and primary cellulose fibers originally derived from trees, a renewable source. International sales account for approximately two-thirds of Company revenue. The Company was founded in 1946 as a leather processing operation and went public in 1959.

	06/30/98	06/30/97	06/30/96	06/30/95
Per Share Information				
Stock Price as of 12/31	1.62	4.62	4.25	2.37
Earnings Per Share	-0.28	1.10	-0.38	-0.93
Price / Earnings Ratio	n.a.	4.20	n.a.	n.a.
Book Value Per Share	6.92	7.32	6.55	7.11
Price / Book Value %	23.41	63.11	64.89	33.33
Dividends Per Share	0.0	0.0	0.0	0.0
Annual Financial Data				
Operating Results (000's)				
Total Revenues	43,571.0	50,417.0	48,221.0	51,426.0
Costs & Expenses	-44,039.0	-47,571.0	-49,003.0	-52,295.0
Income Before Taxes and Other	-583.0	2,846.0	-782.0	-2,346.0
Other Items	-178.0	0.0	0.0	0.0
Income Tax	137.0	-1,113.0	180.0	888.0
Net Income	-624.0	1,733.0	-602.0	-1,458.0
Cash Flow From Operations	57.0	3,037.0	1,180.0	-2,073.0
Balance Sheet (000's)				
Cash & Equivalents	517.0	1,373.0	715.0	4,379.0
Total Current Assets	19,729.0	21,350.0	21,621.0	28,865.0
Fixed Assets, Net	12,042.0	11,032.0	10,455.0	10,662.0
Total Assets	32,513.0	32,906.0	33,181.0	39,527.0
Total Current Liabilities	18,722.0	18,336.0	20,362.0	26,977.0
Long-Term Debt	2,256.0	2,761.0	2,330.0	1,364.0
Stockholders' Equity	10,891.0	11,515.0	10,308.0	11,186.0
Performance & Financial Condition				
Return on Total Revenues %	-1.43	3.44	-1.25	-2.84
Return on Avg Stockholders' Equity %	-5.57	15.88	-5.60	-12.53
Return on Average Assets %	-1.91	5.24	-1.66	-4.13
Current Ratio	1.05	1.16	1.06	1.07
Debt / Equity %	20.71	23.98	22.60	12.19

Compound Growth %'s	EPS %	n.a.	Net Income %	n.a.	Total Revenues %	-5.38

Comments

After management successfully began implementation of a reorganization plan that contributed to an outstanding year in 1997, fiscal 1998 was overshadowed by unprecedented challenges. The largest issues affecting the Company were the financial situation in Asia which markets account for a third of Company revenue, a slow-down in athletic footwear sales, and higher operating costs. Also contributing to a decline in sales were the unfavorable currency translation adjustments amounting to $178,000. For the six months ended December 31, 1998, the Company reported revenues and a net loss of $18.4 million and $548,000 ($.56 per share) as compared to $21.6 million and net income of $40,000 ($.03 per share) in the same period of the preceding year.

Officers	Position	Ownership Information	
James C. Kostelni	President, CEO	Number of Shares Outstanding	1,572,824
Jeffrey C. Kostelni	Treasurer, CFO	Market Capitalization	$ 2,547,975
David A. Dugan	Controller, Secretary	Number of Shareholders	429
Charles W. J. Kostelni	Controller	Where Listed / Symbol	NASDAQ / BOTX

Other Information			
Transfer Agent	Registrar & Transfer Co. Cranford, NJ	SIC Code	2670
Auditor	KPMG LLP	Employees	192
		Web Site	bontex.com

Boonton Electronics Corporation

25 Eastmans Road   Parsippany, NJ 07054-0465   Telephone (973)386-9696   Fax (973)386-9191

Company Description

Boonton Electronics Corporation designs and produces electronic testing and measuring instruments including power meters, voltmeters and modulation meters. Recent models are microprocessor controlled and are often used in computerized automatic testing systems. The equipment is marketed throughout the world to commercial and governmental customers in the electronics industry. During September 1993, the Company and its subsidiaries filed petitions in bankruptcy court for court approved reorganizations. During November 1994, the plans of reorganization were approved. The success of the reorganization was due, in part, to the sale of an appreciated piece of real estate and the termination of an overfunded employee pension plan. The Company was founded in 1947.

	09/30/98	09/30/97	09/30/96	09/30/95
Per Share Information				
Stock Price as of 12/31	0.51	0.97	2.37	2.59
Earnings Per Share	0.09	0.02	-0.72	0.17
Price / Earnings Ratio	5.67	48.50	n.a.	15.24
Book Value Per Share	1.59	1.50	1.42	1.99
Price / Book Value %	32.08	64.67	166.90	130.15
Dividends Per Share	0.0	0.0	0.0	0.0
Annual Financial Data				
Operating Results (000's)				
Total Revenues	6,872.6	7,265.0	6,092.0	6,859.0
Costs & Expenses	-6,615.9	-7,185.0	-6,514.4	-6,718.4
Income Before Taxes and Other	199.5	31.3	-474.2	-82.5
Other Items	0.0	0.0	-350.4	0.0
Income Tax	-56.6	0.0	-225.1	316.3
Net Income	143.0	31.3	-1,049.7	233.8
Cash Flow From Operations	236.0	-161.4	-483.9	35.7
Balance Sheet (000's)				
Cash & Equivalents	113.8	121.6	113.0	146.6
Total Current Assets	3,261.8	2,894.0	2,606.7	2,732.9
Fixed Assets, Net	457.2	534.0	163.9	102.2
Total Assets	4,716.2	4,487.8	3,827.0	4,089.0
Total Current Liabilities	1,572.5	1,290.9	1,110.7	905.2
Long-Term Debt	307.5	375.4	77.8	516.3
Stockholders' Equity	2,617.3	2,449.3	2,218.0	2,667.5
Performance & Financial Condition				
Return on Total Revenues %	2.08	0.43	-17.23	3.41
Return on Avg Stockholders' Equity %	5.64	1.34	-42.97	9.25
Return on Average Assets %	3.11	0.75	-26.52	5.97
Current Ratio	2.07	2.24	2.35	3.02
Debt / Equity %	11.75	15.32	3.51	19.35

Compound Growth %'s	EPS %	-19.10	Net Income %	-15.13	Total Revenues %	0.07

Comments

Fiscal 1996 results include special charges of $350,405 in connection with environmental clean-up matters at a site the Company formerly leased. Sales declined in fiscal 1998 as a result of lower sales to the military. Since such sales carry lower margins, net income actually increased. Fiscal 1997 revenue was up 19.4%, representing a substantial reversal of an industry-wide decline reflected in the preceding year. Management was quite pleased with a second consecutive year of profits and predicted higher revenues and higher net income in fiscal 1999.

Officers	Position	Ownership Information	
Yves Guyomar	President, CEO	Number of Shares Outstanding	1,644,301
John E. Titterton	VP - Finance, Secretary	Market Capitalization	$ 838,594
Ronald T. Deblis	Director	Number of Shareholders	659
Jack Frucht	Director	Where Listed / Symbol	OTC-BB / BOON

Other Information			
Transfer Agent	First Fidelity Bancorporation New York, NY	SIC Code	3825
Auditor	I. Weismann Associates	Employees	48
Market Maker	Carr Securities Corporation	(800)221-2243	Web Site	boonton.com
	M.H. Meyerson & Co., Inc.	(800)333-3113		

Boundless Corporation

100 Marcus Boulevard   Hauppauge, NY 11788   Telephone (516)342-7400   Fax (516)342-7420

Company Description

Boundless Corporation, formerly known as SunRiver Corporation, is engaged in designing and manufacturing computer terminals for business use. The Company's general strategy is to provide highly efficient, low cost access to corporate computing environments, including client/server, mainframes, LANS, WANS, intranets and the Internet. The 1997 fiscal year was one of turnaround for the Company. Leveraging the changes and internal restructuring undertaken in 1996, the Company recorded quarterly and full-year profits in both 1997 and 1998. Join us for a look at the numbers below.

	12/31/98	12/31/97	12/31/96	12/31/95
Per Share Information				
Stock Price	4.87	6.60	15.00	28.75
Earnings Per Share	0.90	0.86	-2.50	0.40
Price / Earnings Ratio	5.41	7.67	n.a.	71.88
Book Value Per Share	3.76	3.00	1.81	2.82
Price / Book Value %	129.52	220.00	828.73	1,019.50
Dividends Per Share	0.0	0.0	0.0	0.0
Annual Financial Data				
Operating Results (000's)				
Total Revenues	90,202.0	98,271.0	138,225.0	94,957.0
Costs & Expenses	-84,545.0	-93,522.0	-138,850.0	-89,565.0
Income Before Taxes and Other	5,657.0	4,749.0	-625.0	5,392.0
Other Items	0.0	0.0	-9,652.0	-1,459.0
Income Tax	-749.0	134.0	-962.0	-1,323.0
Net Income	4,908.0	4,883.0	-11,239.0	2,610.0
Cash Flow From Operations	7,954.0	13,196.0	1,435.0	-9,852.0
Balance Sheet (000's)				
Cash & Equivalents	732.0	2,929.0	5,213.0	369.0
Total Current Assets	31,408.0	34,078.0	46,040.0	41,388.0
Fixed Assets, Net	10,251.0	10,614.0	11,474.0	12,000.0
Total Assets	49,348.0	54,548.0	69,525.0	75,856.0
Total Current Liabilities	22,007.0	25,298.0	42,868.0	25,972.0
Long-Term Debt	5,500.0	8,000.0	13,382.0	33,492.0
Stockholders' Equity	16,657.0	15,407.0	8,802.0	12,837.0
Performance & Financial Condition				
Return on Total Revenues %	5.44	4.97	-8.13	2.75
Return on Avg Stockholders' Equity %	30.61	40.34	-103.88	34.29
Return on Average Assets %	9.45	7.87	-15.46	4.62
Current Ratio	1.43	1.35	1.07	1.59
Debt / Equity %	33.02	51.92	152.03	260.90

Compound Growth %'s	EPS %	31.04	Net Income %	23.43	Total Revenues %	-1.70

Comments

The Company executed a 1 for 10 reverse stock split in 1998. All per share amounts have been restated for consistency. Revenue declined in 1998 due to lower demand for general display terminals. Management believes that this slide will continue because competing technologies are gaining market share. Accordingly, the Company's strategy has been shifted to a greater focus on Windows®-based terminals. 1996 results include $9,652,000 of losses ($2.06 per share) from discontinued operations. At December 31, 1998, the Company had $7.4 million of goodwill recorded as assets which equated to approximately 44% of stockholders' equity and book value per share.

Officers	Position	Ownership Information	
J. Gerald Combs	Chairman, CEO	Number of Shares Outstanding	4,429,000
Joseph Gardner	VP - Finance, CFO	Market Capitalization	$ 21,569,230
Jeffrey K. Moore	Vice President	Number of Shareholders	959
Gary Wood	Director	Where Listed / Symbol	NASDAQ / BDLS

Other Information			
Transfer Agent	American Stock Transfer & Trust Co. New York, NY	SIC Code	7370
Auditor	BDO Seidman LLP	Employees	297
		Web Site	boundless.com

Bradley Pharmaceuticals, Inc.

383 Route 46 West   Fairfield, NJ 07004-2402   Telephone (973)882-1505   Fax (973)575-5366

Company Description

Bradley Pharmaceuticals, Inc. manufactures and markets various brand name prescription and over-the-counter pharmaceutical and health related products which have been acquired through the purchase of trademark rights and patents. The Company has approximately 40 products which are marketed throughout the United States and internationally. Bradley's growth strategy has been to make acquisitions of established products from major pharmaceutical organizations which the Company believes require intensified marketing and promotional attention. The Company was founded in 1985.

	12/31/98	12/31/97	12/31/96	12/31/95
Per Share Information				
Stock Price	1.19	2.00	1.31	1.09
Earnings Per Share	0.10	0.11	0.22	-0.94
Price / Earnings Ratio	11.90	18.18	5.95	n.a.
Book Value Per Share	1.82	1.56	1.45	1.22
Price / Book Value %	65.38	128.21	90.34	89.34
Dividends Per Share	0.0	0.0	0.0	0.0
Annual Financial Data				
Operating Results (000's)				
Total Revenues	15,900.7	15,023.8	14,414.4	10,621.1
Costs & Expenses	-14,861.7	-14,058.9	-12,665.9	-19,038.3
Income Before Taxes and Other	1,039.0	964.9	1,748.5	-8,417.3
Other Items	0.0	0.0	0.0	0.0
Income Tax	-120.0	-58.5	-150.0	1,496.0
Net Income	919.0	906.4	1,598.5	-6,921.2
Cash Flow From Operations	993.4	1,881.9	2,833.1	-1,736.4
Balance Sheet (000's)				
Cash & Equivalents	1,417.7	514.0	0.0	556.1
Total Current Assets	8,317.9	4,770.6	5,528.2	8,614.0
Fixed Assets, Net	357.0	277.8	343.4	570.2
Total Assets	22,564.3	18,181.9	20,703.2	26,899.9
Total Current Liabilities	7,446.9	4,743.4	8,357.0	13,542.1
Long-Term Debt	1,245.9	264.4	531.0	4,491.1
Stockholders' Equity	13,871.4	13,174.1	11,815.2	8,866.8
Performance & Financial Condition				
Return on Total Revenues %	5.78	6.03	11.09	-65.17
Return on Avg Stockholders' Equity %	6.80	7.25	15.46	-59.63
Return on Average Assets %	4.51	4.66	6.72	-25.10
Current Ratio	1.12	1.01	0.66	0.64
Debt / Equity %	8.98	2.01	4.49	50.65

Compound Growth %'s	EPS %	-32.58	Net Income %	-24.18	Total Revenues %	14.40

Comments

The positive trend in stable profitability that began in 1997 continued into 1998. 1996 results included a nonrecurring gain of $1.6 million related to a legal settlement. Without the gain, 1996 would have been marginally profitable. Income tax expense has been minimal because of the utilization of tax loss carryforwards. 1995 results reflect a reorganization of the Company in response to changing trade practices in the health care industry. Intangible assets of $13.8 million were recorded as assets as of December 31, 1998, which equated to approximately 100% of stockholders' equity and book value per share.

Officers	Position	Ownership Information	
Daniel Glassman	President, CEO	Number of Shares Outstanding	7,628,432
Gene L. Goldberg	Senior VP	Market Capitalization	$ 9,077,834
R. Brent Lenczycki	CFO	Number of Shareholders	2,700
David H. Hillman	Secretary	Where Listed / Symbol	NASDAQ / BPRX

Other Information			
Transfer Agent	American Stock Transfer & Trust Co. New York, NY	SIC Code	2834
Auditor	Grant Thornton LLP	Employees	67
		Web Site	bradpharm.com

BridgeStreet Accomodations, Inc.

30670 Bainbridge Road   Solon, OH 44139   Telephone (440)248-3005   Fax (440)542-0317

Company Description

BridgeStreet Accommodations, Inc. is a provider of flexible accommodation services in metropolitan markets located domestically in the Midwest, Mid-Atlantic and Southwest regions of the United States, and internationally in London, England and Toronto, Canada. The Company offers high-quality, fully-furnished apartments, townhouses, condominiums and, to a lesser extent, houses, primarily for individuals traveling on business and company executives relocating to new communities who require lodging for one week to several months. BridgeStreet, founded in August 1996, combined by merger five regional providers of flexible accommodation services in the first quarter of 1997 and subsequently acquired nine additional providers during 1997 and one in 1998.

	12/31/98	12/31/97	12/31/96	12/31/95
Per Share Information				
Stock Price	3.19	10.00	n.a.	n.a.
Earnings Per Share	0.18	0.08	0.42	0.13
Price / Earnings Ratio	17.72	125.00	n.a.	n.a.
Book Value Per Share	5.26	4.82	0.74	0.54
Price / Book Value %	60.65	207.47	n.a.	n.a.
Dividends Per Share	0.0	0.0	0.0	0.0
Annual Financial Data				
Operating Results (000's)				
Total Revenues	96,941.7	51,268.9	12,555.4	9,804.9
Costs & Expenses	-92,885.2	-49,443.4	-11,379.0	-9,415.5
Income Before Taxes and Other	3,756.4	1,825.4	1,176.4	389.4
Other Items	-1,330.0	0.0	0.0	0.0
Income Tax	-1,267.4	-1,371.3	-512.6	-178.3
Net Income	1,159.0	454.1	663.7	211.2
Cash Flow From Operations	561.1	1,333.1	67.5	620.2
Balance Sheet (000's)				
Cash & Equivalents	1,652.0	8,922.2	597.9	834.6
Total Current Assets	11,940.6	13,455.9	1,707.8	2,101.7
Fixed Assets, Net	5,379.0	4,217.7	295.0	253.7
Total Assets	60,123.9	42,563.0	2,013.4	2,510.0
Total Current Liabilities	8,589.8	4,283.5	722.0	1,538.4
Long-Term Debt	7,608.5	25.8	0.0	0.0
Stockholders' Equity	42,986.3	37,578.2	1,183.6	869.1
Performance & Financial Condition				
Return on Total Revenues %	1.20	0.89	5.29	2.15
Return on Avg Stockholders' Equity %	2.88	2.34	64.67	21.12
Return on Average Assets %	2.26	2.04	29.35	10.56
Current Ratio	1.39	3.14	2.37	1.37
Debt / Equity %	17.70	0.07	n.a.	n.a.

Compound Growth %'s	EPS %	11.46	Net Income %	76.40	Total Revenues %	114.63

Comments

Results prior to 1997 are not comparable as they represent operations of only one company that became part of the larger merged entity. 1998 results are the first real look at what the new combined entity can produce. But the increase in revenues reflects the inclusion of 1997 acquisitions for a full year. 1998 expenses include a nonrecurring restructuring charge of $1,330,000 and $300,000 in foreign currency translation losses. At December 31, 1998, $40.6 million of goodwill was reflected on the books as assets and equated to approximately 94% of stockholders' equity and book value per share.

Officers	Position	Ownership Information	
Paul M. Verrochi	Chairman	Number of Shares Outstanding	8,169,835
John E. Danneberg	President, CEO	Market Capitalization	$ 26,061,774
Mark D. Gagne	CFO, Treasurer	Number of Shareholders	1,000
Rocco A. Di Lillo	Vice President, COO	Where Listed / Symbol	AMEX / BDS

Other Information			
Transfer Agent	American Securities Transfer, Inc. Lakewood, CO	SIC Code	7011
Auditor	Arthur Andersen LLP	Employees	450
		Web Site	bridgestreet.com

Bristol Retail Solutions, Inc.

5000 Birch Street, Suite 205   Newport Beach, CA 92660   Telephone (949)475-0800   Fax (949)475-0808

Company Description

Bristol Retail Solutions, Inc. is engaged in key segments of the retail automation industry, including point-of-sale (POS) systems installation and service and systems integration, which provides retailers with turnkey operating solutions. The Company is building an integrated retail automation company through a series of targeted acquisitions and internal development. It plans to build a national network of POS dealers and a group of solution-oriented systems integrators, which together can produce synergistic results. The Company's aim is to serve a broad range of retailers including national and regional chains as well as major single unit operations in selected vertical market segments. The Company has acquired seven dealers since its establishment in April 1996 and now operates in 17 cities in eight states.

	12/31/98	12/31/97	12/31/96
Per Share Information			
Stock Price	0.47	0.56	9.82
Earnings Per Share	-0.38	-0.96	-0.03
Price / Earnings Ratio	n.a.	n.a.	n.a.
Book Value Per Share	0.85	1.31	1.72
Price / Book Value %	55.29	42.75	570.93
Dividends Per Share	0.0	0.0	0.0
Annual Financial Data			
Operating Results (000's)			
Total Revenues	32,297.2	21,108.7	4,196.2
Costs & Expenses	-34,009.7	-26,074.8	-4,298.2
Income Before Taxes and Other	-1,712.4	-4,966.1	-104.8
Other Items	0.0	0.0	0.0
Income Tax	-19.3	-2.5	-1.8
Net Income	-1,731.8	-4,968.6	-106.6
Cash Flow From Operations	-1,790.5	-2,191.8	-43.5
Balance Sheet (000's)			
Cash & Equivalents	146.2	715.9	5,475.7
Total Current Assets	10,982.9	7,800.0	9,097.8
Fixed Assets, Net	844.6	759.7	250.8
Total Assets	17,284.6	13,811.6	11,169.7
Total Current Liabilities	11,158.7	7,536.4	2,933.3
Long-Term Debt	53.6	0.0	0.0
Stockholders' Equity	5,857.3	6,193.4	8,175.0
Performance & Financial Condition			
Return on Total Revenues %	-5.36	-23.54	-2.54
Return on Avg Stockholders' Equity %	-28.74	-69.16	-2.67
Return on Average Assets %	-11.14	-39.78	-1.78
Current Ratio	0.98	1.03	3.10
Debt / Equity %	0.92	n.a.	n.a.

Compound Growth %'s	EPS %	n.a.	Net Income %	n.a.	Total Revenues %	177.43

Comments

Revenue growth totalled 53% in 1998, however all but 2% was entirely attributable to acquisitions. The Company has not yet achieved profitability. 1997 results include a write-down of goodwill amounting to $1,871,000. 1996 results represent a short period beginning on April 3, 1996, with the transaction mentioned above. At December 31, 1998, the Company had $4.5 million of intangible assets recorded on its books which equated to approximately 78% of stockholders' equity and book value per share. The Company also had a small deficiency in working capital. Tax loss carryovers of $3.8 million are available to offset future income. On March 19, 1999, despite its unproven ability, the Company entered into a letter of intent to acquire an additional two companies.

Officers	Position	Ownership Information	
Paul Spindler	Chairman, Exec VP	Number of Shares Outstanding	6,910,519
Richard H. Walker	President, CEO	Market Capitalization	$ 3,247,944
N. Douglas Mazza	Senior VP, COO	Number of Shareholders	714
Michael S. Shimada	CFO	Where Listed / Symbol	NASDAQ / BRTL

Other Information			
Transfer Agent	American Stock Transfer & Trust Company New York, NY	SIC Code	5044
Auditor	Deloitte & Touche LLP	Employees	257

Bull Run Corporation

4370 Peachtree Road, N.E.   Atlanta, GA 30319   Telephone (404)266-8333   Fax (404)261-9607

Company Description

Bull Run Corporation owns a number of business interests including 100% of Datasouth Computer Corporation. Datasouth designs, manufactures and markets heavy-duty dot matrix and thermal printers for vertical markets including transportation, distribution, manufacturing and health care. The Company also owns a 16.9% interest in Gray Communications Systems (NYSE), a communications company; a 30.2% interest in Host Communications, Inc., a multimedia, promotional marketing and event management service company; a 10.4% interest in Rawlings Sporting Goods Company, Inc., a leading manufacturer of sporting equipment, and a 9% interest in Total Sports, Inc., a sports content Internet company. Prior to 1990, Bull Run was engaged in the business of mineral exploration and mining.

	12/31/98	12/31/97	12/31/96	12/31/95
Per Share Information				
Stock Price	3.00	3.50	2.12	2.82
Earnings Per Share	0.11	-0.08	0.23	0.03
Price / Earnings Ratio	27.27	n.a.	9.22	94.00
Book Value Per Share	1.34	1.18	1.30	1.09
Price / Book Value %	223.88	296.61	163.08	258.72
Dividends Per Share	0.0	0.0	0.0	0.0
Annual Financial Data				
Operating Results (000's)				
Total Revenues	39,285.0	23,422.0	27,259.0	27,300.0
Costs & Expenses	-35,071.0	-25,535.0	-25,549.0	-26,397.0
Income Before Taxes and Other	4,214.0	-2,712.0	1,710.0	903.0
Other Items	0.0	0.0	7,610.0	0.0
Income Tax	-1,854.0	939.0	-4,012.0	-180.0
Net Income	2,360.0	-1,773.0	5,308.0	723.0
Cash Flow From Operations	-2,624.0	-1,827.0	1,267.0	410.0
Balance Sheet (000's)				
Cash & Equivalents	58.0	142.0	81.0	146.0
Total Current Assets	11,436.0	8,692.0	7,668.0	7,995.0
Fixed Assets, Net	2,623.0	2,638.0	2,251.0	2,512.0
Total Assets	95,172.0	76,832.0	67,851.0	44,300.0
Total Current Liabilities	8,124.0	6,179.0	3,678.0	4,256.0
Long-Term Debt	51,848.0	41,998.0	31,364.0	14,896.0
Stockholders' Equity	29,791.0	25,056.0	28,318.0	24,079.0
Performance & Financial Condition				
Return on Total Revenues %	6.01	-7.57	19.47	2.65
Return on Avg Stockholders' Equity %	8.61	-6.64	20.26	3.03
Return on Average Assets %	2.74	-2.45	9.47	1.93
Current Ratio	1.41	1.41	2.08	1.88
Debt / Equity %	174.04	167.62	110.76	61.86

Compound Growth %'s	EPS %	54.20	Net Income %	48.34	Total Revenues %	12.90

Comments

Equity in earnings of affiliated companies totalled $6,734,000 in 1998 as compared to a net loss of $599,000 in 1997. Approximately $6.9 million of income was attributable to Gray Communications System's disposal of a television station. 1996 results include a gain of $8.2 million resulting from the initial public offering of Gray Communications. The Company's interest in Gray was reduced from 27.1% to 15.2% at that time. At December 31, 1998, the Company had $7.6 million of goodwill recorded as assets which equated to approximately 25% of stockholders' equity and book value per share. The Company acquired interests in an additional four companies in the first two months of 1999.

Officers	Position	Ownership Information	
J. Mack Robinson	Chairman	Number of Shares Outstanding	22,243,000
Robert S. Prather, Jr.	President, CEO	Market Capitalization	$ 66,729,000
Frederick J. Erickson	VP - Finance, CFO	Number of Shareholders	2,592
Hilton H. Howell, Jr.	Vice President, Secretary	Where Listed / Symbol	NASDAQ / BULL

Other Information			
Transfer Agent	TranSecurities International, Inc. Spokane, WA	SIC Code	3577
Auditor	Ernst & Young LLP	Employees	134
		Web Site	bullruncorp.com

Burke Mills, Inc.

191 Sterling Street N W   Valdese, NC 28690   Telephone (828)874-6341   Fax (828)879-7188

Company Description

Burke Mills, Inc. is engaged in the twisting, texturing, winding, dyeing, processing and selling of filament, novelty and spun yarns and in the dying and processing of these yarns for others on a commission basis. The Company principally serves the upholstery, apparel and industrial markets through the knitting and weaving industry. In 1997 the Company entered into a joint venture with Fibras Quimicas, S.A., a Mexican corporation. The purpose of the joint venture, named Fytek, is the manufacture and marketing of yarns. The Company acquires yarn from Fytek and uses Fytek to market and distribute its dyed yarn in Mexico, Central America and South America. Fytek began production in the fourth quarter of 1997.

	01/02/99	01/03/98	12/28/96	12/30/95
Per Share Information				
Stock Price as of 12/31	2.25	2.87	3.06	2.88
Earnings Per Share	0.29	0.23	0.21	0.34
Price / Earnings Ratio	7.76	12.48	14.57	8.47
Book Value Per Share	5.19	4.90	4.67	4.46
Price / Book Value %	43.35	58.57	65.52	64.57
Dividends Per Share	0.0	0.0	0.0	0.0
Annual Financial Data				
Operating Results (000's)				
Total Revenues	42,335.8	41,311.7	40,783.3	34,228.7
Costs & Expenses	-41,391.3	-40,102.3	-39,914.0	-33,072.2
Income Before Taxes and Other	944.5	1,032.1	869.4	1,156.5
Other Items	227.9	26.5	0.0	0.0
Income Tax	-383.1	-432.5	-284.0	-212.2
Net Income	789.2	626.1	585.4	944.2
Cash Flow From Operations	1,926.1	3,646.3	1,526.9	2,003.9
Balance Sheet (000's)				
Cash & Equivalents	3,384.4	4,306.5	2,157.4	834.8
Total Current Assets	11,213.5	11,784.7	9,904.6	7,641.0
Fixed Assets, Net	12,609.4	12,192.3	12,643.8	13,127.6
Total Assets	24,395.6	24,348.1	22,554.4	20,768.6
Total Current Liabilities	3,383.4	3,377.7	1,737.6	2,171.2
Long-Term Debt	4,562.5	5,312.5	6,000.0	4,963.7
Stockholders' Equity	14,228.8	13,439.6	12,813.5	12,228.1
Performance & Financial Condition				
Return on Total Revenues %	1.86	1.52	1.44	2.76
Return on Avg Stockholders' Equity %	5.71	4.77	4.68	8.03
Return on Average Assets %	3.24	2.67	2.70	5.05
Current Ratio	3.31	3.49	5.70	3.52
Debt / Equity %	32.07	39.53	46.83	40.59

Compound Growth %'s	EPS %	-5.16	Net Income %	-5.80	Total Revenues %	7.34

Comments

Revenues rose slightly in 1998 due to the introduction of new products. But in the fourth quarter of 1998, the Company experienced a weakening market and pricing pressures. These conditions forced reductions in prices to retain customers and resulted in lower gross profits. Management expected these conditions to continue into the first quarter of 1999. Manufacturing overhead declined as a result of cost controls. The good news is that Fytek, the joint venture, contributed $228,000 of earnings in 1998 as compared to $27,000 for the short period of operations in 1997. In 1997, the Company incurred a loss of $177,000 on the disposal of assets as compared to a gain on disposal of assets of $94,000 in 1996. Without these items, 1997 results would have been substantially improved.

Officers	Position	Ownership Information	
Humayun N. Shaikh	Chairman, CEO	Number of Shares Outstanding	2,741,168
Charles P. McCamy	President	Market Capitalization	$ 6,167,628
Thomas I. Nail	VP - Finance, CFO	Number of Shareholders	428
Pender R. McElroy	Secretary	Where Listed / Symbol	NASDAQ / BMLS

Other Information			
Transfer Agent	First Union National Bank of N.C. Charlotte, NC	SIC Code	2200
Auditor	Cole, Samsel & Bernstein LLC	Employees	307

Business Resource Group

2150 North First Street, Suite 101   San Jose, CA 95131   Telephone (408)325-3200   Fax (408)325-3285

Company Description

Business Resource Group is a provider of workspace services and products to businesses, primarily in the western United States. Since commencement of operations in 1986 as an office furniture dealer, the Company has added related services such as computerized space planning and design, project management, product specification, order management, move management, installation, computer-aided facilities management services and ongoing facilities management outsourcing services. The Company markets its services and products through a direct sales force, focusing primarily on rapidly growing companies.

	10/31/98	10/31/97	10/31/96	10/31/95
Per Share Information				
Stock Price as of 12/31	3.00	3.06	5.25	3.63
Earnings Per Share	0.30	-0.16	0.38	0.26
Price / Earnings Ratio	10.00	n.a.	13.82	13.96
Book Value Per Share	2.87	2.53	2.68	2.29
Price / Book Value %	104.53	120.95	195.90	158.52
Dividends Per Share	0.0	0.0	0.0	0.0
Annual Financial Data				
Operating Results (000's)				
Total Revenues	93,565.0	72,767.0	78,404.0	40,635.0
Costs & Expenses	-90,996.0	-74,052.0	-75,241.0	-38,927.0
Income Before Taxes and Other	2,569.0	-1,285.0	3,163.0	1,708.0
Other Items	0.0	0.0	0.0	0.0
Income Tax	-1,066.0	523.0	-1,309.0	-709.0
Net Income	1,503.0	-762.0	1,854.0	999.0
Cash Flow From Operations	-313.0	476.0	-2,068.0	770.0
Balance Sheet (000's)				
Cash & Equivalents	412.0	274.0	1,011.0	5,326.0
Total Current Assets	21,764.0	17,512.0	19,494.0	14,364.0
Fixed Assets, Net	3,107.0	2,346.0	2,017.0	733.0
Total Assets	27,978.0	20,760.0	22,560.0	16,053.0
Total Current Liabilities	12,689.0	8,233.0	9,431.0	4,894.0
Long-Term Debt	733.0	0.0	0.0	0.0
Stockholders' Equity	14,396.0	12,452.0	13,002.0	11,020.0
Performance & Financial Condition				
Return on Total Revenues %	1.61	-1.05	2.36	2.46
Return on Avg Stockholders' Equity %	11.20	-5.99	15.44	13.96
Return on Average Assets %	6.17	-3.52	9.60	8.43
Current Ratio	1.72	2.13	2.07	2.94
Debt / Equity %	5.09	n.a.	n.a.	n.a.

Compound Growth %'s	EPS %	4.89	Net Income %	14.59	Total Revenues %	32.05

Comments

The decline in fiscal 1997 revenues was caused by a significant slowdown in business from Cisco Systems, the Company's largest customer. Operating expenses were higher as management was gearing up for a higher level of revenue. This combination produced a net loss. Fortunately, Cisco ordered $18.6 million more in product during fiscal 1998, accounting for most of the large increase in revenue. Cisco accounted for approximately 44%, 30% and 37% of revenues during fiscal 1998, 1997 and 1996, respectively.

Officers	Position	Ownership Information	
John W. Peth	President, CEO	Number of Shares Outstanding	5,023,778
Brian D. McNay	Exec VP	Market Capitalization	$ 15,071,334
Jeffrey Tuttle	Exec VP	Number of Shareholders	461
John M. Palmer	Vice President, CFO	Where Listed / Symbol	NASDAQ / BRGP

Other Information			
Transfer Agent	American Stock Transfer & Trust Co. New York, NY	SIC Code	5021
Auditor	Deloitte & Touche LLP	Employees	300
		Web Site	brg.com

Butler National Corporation

19920 West 161st Street   Olathe, KS 66062   Telephone (913)780-9595   Fax (913)780-5088

Company Description

Butler National Corporation has a number of businesses remaining after the liquidation of its largest business segment, food distribution, which accounted for 81% of revenue and 24% of assets in fiscal 1997. Aircraft modification, including modification of business-size aircraft from passenger to freighter configuration, conversion to air ambulance, addition of aerial photography capability, and stability enhancing modifications, now comprises approximately 71% of revenue and 53% of total assets. The Company also has business units engaged in environmental monitoring and Native American gaming. The Company was formed in 1960.

	04/30/98	04/30/97	04/30/96	04/30/95
Per Share Information				
Stock Price as of 12/31	0.38	0.87	1.91	2.31
Earnings Per Share	0.01	0.02	0.02	-0.11
Price / Earnings Ratio	38.00	43.50	95.50	n.a.
Book Value Per Share	0.40	0.30	0.23	0.07
Price / Book Value %	95.00	290.00	830.43	3,300.00
Dividends Per Share	0.0	0.0	0.0	0.0
Annual Financial Data				
Operating Results (000's)				
Total Revenues	5,475.2	21,577.9	17,407.8	13,259.6
Costs & Expenses	-5,060.8	-21,059.0	-17,240.6	-13,935.6
Income Before Taxes and Other	414.4	286.0	167.2	-894.9
Other Items	-172.3	0.0	0.0	0.0
Income Tax	-164.4	-120.4	-22.8	0.0
Net Income	77.7	165.7	144.4	-894.9
Cash Flow From Operations	-538.0	-1,275.2	-411.4	-515.5
Balance Sheet (000's)				
Cash & Equivalents	160.6	256.4	745.6	212.8
Total Current Assets	2,896.0	4,221.7	4,070.7	2,169.6
Fixed Assets, Net	1,218.5	866.7	322.2	284.6
Total Assets	10,799.7	11,124.0	8,261.1	4,193.5
Total Current Liabilities	2,276.5	3,539.0	4,092.1	1,539.9
Long-Term Debt	2,622.3	2,640.7	57.1	81.3
Stockholders' Equity	5,861.9	4,872.3	4,112.0	2,572.3
Performance & Financial Condition				
Return on Total Revenues %	1.42	0.77	0.83	-6.75
Return on Avg Stockholders' Equity %	1.45	3.69	4.32	-32.70
Return on Average Assets %	0.71	1.71	2.32	-19.42
Current Ratio	1.27	1.19	0.99	1.41
Debt / Equity %	44.73	54.20	1.39	3.16

Compound Growth %'s	EPS %	-29.29	Net Income %	-26.63	Total Revenues %	-25.53

Comments

Fiscal 1998 results include a loss of $172,000 from discontinued operations. Although revenue declined because of the liquidation of food distribution as a business, revenue from remaining segments grew 34.3% during fiscal 1998. During fiscal 1997, the Company issued convertible debentures which raised $1.1 million in capital. $450,000 of these debentures were converted to stock in fiscal 1998. The Company still needs to improve its working capital structure. For the nine months ended January 31, 1999, revenues and a net loss from continuing operations were $4.9 million and $220,014 ($.02 per share) as compared to $3.7 million and a net profit of $502,952 ($.05 per share) for the same period of the preceding year.

Officers	Position	Ownership Information	
Clark D. Stewart	President, CEO	Number of Shares Outstanding	10,898,069
Edward J. Matukewicz	CFO, Treasurer	Market Capitalization	$ 4,141,266
William A. Griffith	Secretary	Number of Shareholders	3,105
Larry W. Franke	Vice President	Where Listed / Symbol	NASDAQ / BUKS

Other Information			
Transfer Agent	Norwest Bank Minnesota, N.A. South St. Paul, MN	SIC Code	5141
Auditor	Arthur Andersen LLP	Employees	66

CAS Medical Systems, Inc.

44 East Industrial Road   Branford, CT 06405   Telephone (203)488-6056   Fax (203)488-9438

Company Description

CAS Medical Systems, Inc. develops, manufactures, and distributes medical diagnostic and other medical products for use by adults and children. Products include a full line of non-invasive blood pressure monitors, disposable and multi-use blood pressure cuffs, electrocardiograph electrodes, temperature probes and arm boards. The products are sold both in domestic and international markets. The Company was organized in 1984.

	12/31/98	12/31/97	12/31/96	12/31/95
Per Share Information				
Stock Price	0.50	0.66	0.62	0.94
Earnings Per Share	0.08	0.07	0.09	0.08
Price / Earnings Ratio	6.25	9.43	6.89	11.75
Book Value Per Share	0.47	0.38	0.31	0.21
Price / Book Value %	106.38	173.68	200.00	447.62
Dividends Per Share	0.0	0.0	0.0	0.0
Annual Financial Data				
Operating Results (000's)				
Total Revenues	7,851.4	6,976.9	7,223.8	6,442.6
Costs & Expenses	-6,492.1	-5,847.8	-5,688.1	-5,508.7
Income Before Taxes and Other	1,359.3	1,129.0	1,535.7	933.9
Other Items	0.0	0.0	0.0	0.0
Income Tax	-543.0	-464.0	-630.0	-85.0
Net Income	816.3	665.0	905.7	848.9
Cash Flow From Operations	1,506.1	721.2	887.2	1,223.8
Balance Sheet (000's)				
Cash & Equivalents	1,442.3	2,190.3	1,607.0	1,082.0
Total Current Assets	3,460.5	4,153.7	3,669.5	2,733.6
Fixed Assets, Net	2,361.7	231.7	186.0	178.6
Total Assets	5,825.1	4,393.5	3,863.7	2,920.5
Total Current Liabilities	1,485.9	807.6	1,005.8	645.9
Long-Term Debt	0.0	0.0	0.0	0.0
Stockholders' Equity	4,339.2	3,522.9	2,857.9	2,230.1
Performance & Financial Condition				
Return on Total Revenues %	10.40	9.53	12.54	13.18
Return on Avg Stockholders' Equity %	20.76	20.85	35.60	44.21
Return on Average Assets %	15.98	16.11	26.70	33.30
Current Ratio	2.33	5.14	3.65	4.23
Debt / Equity %	n.a.	n.a.	n.a.	n.a.

Compound Growth %'s	EPS %	0.00	Net Income %	-1.30	Total Revenues %	6.81

Comments

1998 results were favorably impacted by a $725,000 one-time contract settlement which was included in income. Sales revenues for 1998 reflect a 22% increase in disposable products offset largely by a 21% decrease in diagnostic equipment sales. Research and development expense rose by 6%, to $548,000 for the year. During November 1998, the Company relocated to a 24,000 square foot office, laboratory and manufacturing facility owned by the Company. The cost of the new facility was approximately $1,933,000. In January 1999, and not reflected in the above numbers, the Company obtained a $1,310,000 mortgage on the property. Although a small company by most standards, CAS maintains a solid financial footing with an excellent working capital and consistent profitability. The Company invests its excess cash in low-risk, short-term interest bearing instruments.

Officers	Position	Ownership Information	
Myron L. Cohen	Chairman, Exec VP	Number of Shares Outstanding	9,329,277
Louis P. Scheps	President, CEO	Market Capitalization	$ 4,664,639
Stanley D. Josephson	Secretary	Number of Shareholders	400
Saul Milles	Director	Where Listed / Symbol	OTC-BB / CMRX

Other Information			
Transfer Agent	American Stock Transfer & Trust Co. New York, NY	SIC Code	3841
Auditor	Arthur Andersen LLP	Employees	58
Market Maker	Herzog, Heine, Geduld, Inc. (800)221-3600	Web Site	casmed.com
	Wien Securities Corp. (800)624-0050		

© 1999 Walker's Manual, LLC   All rights reserved.   (925) 283-9993

CCA Industries, Inc.

200 Murray Hill Parkway   E. Rutherford, NJ 07073   Telephone (201)330-1400   Fax (201)935-0675

Company Description

CCA Industries, Inc. operates in one industry segment, which may be described generally as the health-and-beauty aids business, and sells numerous products in several health-and-beauty categories. Substantially all products are manufactured by contract manufacturers, pursuant to the Company's specifications and formulations. The Company owns (or owns licenses to use) registered trademarks for all of its brand-name products. A sampling of the products would include Nutra Nail, Pro Perm, Wash 'n Curl, Wash 'n Tint, Hair Off, Eat 'n Lose, Hungrex Plus, and Permathene. In May 1998, the Company entered into a license agreement for the marketing of sun care products under various trade names. The Company was founded in 1983.

	11/30/98	11/30/97	11/30/96	11/30/95
Per Share Information				
Stock Price as of 12/31	1.22	2.19	2.31	1.12
Earnings Per Share	0.21	0.25	0.14	-0.23
Price / Earnings Ratio	5.81	8.76	16.50	n.a.
Book Value Per Share	2.15	1.91	1.64	1.54
Price / Book Value %	56.74	114.66	140.85	72.73
Dividends Per Share	0.0	0.0	0.0	0.0
Annual Financial Data				
Operating Results (000's)				
Total Revenues	41,402.3	38,002.9	39,705.0	37,166.7
Costs & Expenses	-38,570.1	-34,730.1	-37,790.4	-39,397.3
Income Before Taxes and Other	2,832.2	3,272.8	1,914.6	-2,230.5
Other Items	-7.6	0.0	0.0	0.0
Income Tax	-1,164.2	-1,267.2	-799.7	664.0
Net Income	1,660.4	2,005.6	1,114.9	-1,566.6
Cash Flow From Operations	-3,686.4	3,194.0	484.6	-362.6
Balance Sheet (000's)				
Cash & Equivalents	542.3	3,649.8	1,422.8	312.2
Total Current Assets	20,478.0	16,163.9	14,054.0	14,992.3
Fixed Assets, Net	866.7	486.0	729.7	713.1
Total Assets	24,010.1	18,867.8	16,708.1	17,744.1
Total Current Liabilities	8,410.7	5,139.8	4,983.9	7,176.5
Long-Term Debt	0.0	0.0	0.0	111.1
Stockholders' Equity	15,591.7	13,728.0	11,724.2	10,456.5
Performance & Financial Condition				
Return on Total Revenues %	4.01	5.28	2.81	-4.21
Return on Avg Stockholders' Equity %	11.33	15.76	10.05	-14.10
Return on Average Assets %	7.74	11.28	6.47	-8.29
Current Ratio	2.43	3.14	2.82	2.09
Debt / Equity %	n.a.	n.a.	n.a.	1.06

Compound Growth %'s	EPS %	22.47	Net Income %	22.03	Total Revenues %	3.66

Comments

Revenue growth was nearly 9% in fiscal 1998 but was all attributable to newly acquired licenses. The Company's pre-existing product lines were down slightly due to lower international sales as well as a small drop in sales of a few of its core products. An unfavorable swing of $219,000 in bad debt expense was a major factor in reducing profits from the 1997 level. The loss in fiscal 1995 was largely attributable to a large decrease in sales of the Company's shampoo products. Since that year, the Company has produced three consecutive profitable years. The balance sheet is very strong with no long term debt.

Officers	Position	Ownership Information	
David Edell	President, CEO	Number of Shares Outstanding	7,259,581
Ira W. Berman	Exec VP, Secretary	Market Capitalization	$ 8,856,689
Dunnan Edell	Exec VP	Number of Shareholders	1,290
Drew Edell	Exec VP	Where Listed / Symbol	NASDAQ / CCAM

Other Information			
Transfer Agent	American Stock Transfer & Trust Co. New York, NY	SIC Code	2844
Auditor	Sheft, Kahn & Company LLP	Employees	139

CPT Holdings, Inc.

1430 Broadway, 13th Floor   New York, NY 10018-3308   Telephone (212)382-1313   Fax (212)391-1393

Company Description

On April 6, 1995, CPT Holdings, Inc. acquired substantially all assets of J&L Structural, Inc. and Trailer Components, Inc. which now comprises most of the Company's business activities. The Company is a nationwide independent producer of high quality lightweight structural steel shapes, with a leading market share in the Northeast, Southeast and Mid-Atlantic regions. The Company's products are used primarily in the manufactured housing, truck trailer, construction, shipbuilding and the oil field service and petrochemical industries. CPT was originally founded in 1971 and reorganized under the U.S. Bankruptcy Act in 1991.

	06/30/98	06/30/97	06/30/96	06/30/95
Per Share Information				
Stock Price as of 12/31	0.31	1.75	0.75	3.50
Earnings Per Share	0.10	-1.76	0.11	2.86
Price / Earnings Ratio	3.10	n.a.	6.82	1.22
Book Value Per Share	-7.34	-7.71	-5.95	-6.40
Price / Book Value %	n.a.	n.a.	n.a.	n.a.
Dividends Per Share	0.0	0.0	0.0	0.0
Annual Financial Data				
Operating Results (000's)				
Total Revenues	110,830.0	98,199.0	101,011.0	31,215.0
Costs & Expenses	-109,771.0	-100,340.0	-102,284.0	-31,168.0
Income Before Taxes and Other	750.0	-2,317.0	-2,009.0	47.0
Other Items	-529.0	0.0	2,220.0	5,077.0
Income Tax	337.0	-337.0	100.0	389.0
Net Income	558.0	-2,654.0	311.0	5,513.0
Cash Flow From Operations	4,241.0	4,646.0	1,866.0	3,056.0
Balance Sheet (000's)				
Cash & Equivalents	37.0	61.0	174.0	972.0
Total Current Assets	21,899.0	19,756.0	19,623.0	19,951.0
Fixed Assets, Net	41,364.0	43,749.0	44,500.0	36,860.0
Total Assets	66,405.0	67,170.0	68,584.0	61,203.0
Total Current Liabilities	21,058.0	18,686.0	15,709.0	16,041.0
Long-Term Debt	53,371.0	56,955.0	58,888.0	52,339.0
Stockholders' Equity	-11,080.0	-11,638.0	-8,984.0	-9,671.0
Performance & Financial Condition				
Return on Total Revenues %	0.50	-2.70	0.31	17.66
Return on Avg Stockholders' Equity %	n.a.	n.a.	n.a.	n.a.
Return on Average Assets %	0.84	-3.91	0.48	15.83
Current Ratio	1.04	1.06	1.25	1.24
Debt / Equity %	n.a.	n.a.	n.a.	n.a.

Compound Growth %'s	EPS %	-67.30	Net Income %	-53.40	Total Revenues %	n.a.

Comments

The increase in fiscal 1998 revenue was due primarily to the continued growth of the manufactured housing segment of the Company's business as well as a significant increase in sales volume of steel service center products. The Company remains with a significant debt and limited working capital. Fiscal 1998 results include a tax benefit rather than an expense. At June 30, 1998, the Company had tax loss carryovers of approximately $100 million to offset future income. For the six months ended December 31, 1998, the Company reported revenues and a net loss of $51.0 million and $591,000 ($.39 per share) as compared to $53.6 million and $54,000 (a loss of $.04 per share on a fully diluted basis) in the same period of the preceding year.

Officers	Position	Ownership Information	
Richard L. Kramer	Chairman, Secretary	Number of Shares Outstanding	1,510,084
William L. Remley	President, Treasurer	Market Capitalization	$ 468,126
Richard C. Hoffman	Director	Number of Shareholders	1,756
		Where Listed / Symbol	OTC-BB / CPTH

Other Information

Transfer Agent	Marquette National Bank Minneapolis, MN		SIC Code	3440
Auditor	Deloitte & Touche LLP		Employees	274
Market Maker	Paragon Capital Corporation	(800)345-0505		
	Sharpe Capital Inc.	(800)355-5781		

CREDO Petroleum Corporation

1801 Broadway, Suite 900   Denver, CO 80202-3837   Telephone (303)297-2200   Fax (303)297-2204

Company Description

CREDO Petroleum Corporation is an independent oil and gas company engaged in oil and gas acquisition, exploration, development and production activities mostly in the Mid-Continent and Rocky Mountain regions of the United States. Operations are concentrated on shallow to medium depth properties generally ranging from 7,000 to 10,000 feet deep The Company's staff oversees the operations of existing properties, evaluates property acquisition opportunities and drilling prospects, and oversees drilling and completion of new wells. The Company was formed in 1978.

	10/31/98	10/31/97	10/31/96	10/31/95
Per Share Information				
Stock Price as of 12/31	1.75	3.00	1.94	1.62
Earnings Per Share	0.11	0.14	0.08	0.08
Price / Earnings Ratio	15.91	21.43	24.25	20.25
Book Value Per Share	2.79	2.69	2.47	2.43
Price / Book Value %	62.72	111.52	78.54	66.67
Dividends Per Share	0.0	0.0	0.0	0.0
Annual Financial Data				
Operating Results (000's)				
Total Revenues	2,835.0	2,690.0	2,287.0	2,129.0
Costs & Expenses	-2,329.0	-2,014.0	-1,886.0	-1,751.0
Income Before Taxes and Other	506.0	676.0	401.0	378.0
Other Items	0.0	0.0	0.0	0.0
Income Tax	-178.0	-237.0	-141.0	-127.0
Net Income	328.0	439.0	260.0	251.0
Cash Flow From Operations	641.0	1,743.0	1,143.0	827.0
Balance Sheet (000's)				
Cash & Equivalents	349.0	3,333.0	344.0	130.0
Total Current Assets	3,620.0	4,033.0	3,287.0	3,048.0
Fixed Assets, Net	6,501.0	6,344.0	5,636.0	5,310.0
Total Assets	10,206.0	10,546.0	9,187.0	8,718.0
Total Current Liabilities	713.0	1,458.0	717.0	473.0
Long-Term Debt	0.0	0.0	0.0	0.0
Stockholders' Equity	8,449.0	8,185.0	7,789.0	7,688.0
Performance & Financial Condition				
Return on Total Revenues %	11.57	16.32	11.37	11.79
Return on Avg Stockholders' Equity %	3.94	5.50	3.36	3.28
Return on Average Assets %	3.16	4.45	2.90	2.81
Current Ratio	5.08	2.77	4.58	6.44
Debt / Equity %	n.a.	n.a.	n.a.	n.a.

Compound Growth %'s	EPS %	11.20	Net Income %	9.33	Total Revenues %	10.02

Comments

1998 was not a good year for most oil and gas companies. Gas prices decreased 10% and oil prices dropped a whopping 31%. But CREDO made up for it by increasing gas volumes by 43% and oil volumes by 2%. Although expenses increased by 15.6%, the Company still produced a reasonable profit. Much effort is being directed to fluid lift technology designed to efficiently lift fluids from wellbores using down-hole pressure differentials. At October 31, 1998, the Company had installed the technology on three of its gas wells. All of the applications have initially resulted in gas production rates which have equaled or exceeded the Company's expectations. Information on proven reserves is available in the annual report to shareholders. The Company maintains an excellent financial condition with no long term debt.

Officers	Position	Ownership Information	
James T. Huffman	President, CEO	Number of Shares Outstanding	3,030,000
William F. Skewes	Secretary	Market Capitalization	$ 5,302,500
Alford B. Neely	Vice President, CFO	Number of Shareholders	4,369
William N. Beach	Director	Where Listed / Symbol	NASDAQ / CRED

Other Information			
Transfer Agent	American Securities Transfer, Inc. Lakewood, CO	SIC Code	1311
Auditor	Hein & Associates LLP	Employees	9

Cable Link, Inc.

280 Cozzins Street Columbus, OH 43215-2379 Telephone (614)221-3131 Fax (614)222-0581

Company Description

Cable Link, Inc. sells new and refurbished cable television equipment in addition to repairing equipment for cable companies within the United States and various international markets. The Company purchases the equipment from cable operators who have surplus due to either an upgrade in their system or an overstock in their warehouse. In 1998, the Company purchased PC & Parts, Inc., dba Auro Computer Systems, which resells computer hardware and assembles computer hardware components into personal computers. Cable Link began business in 1983.

	12/31/98	12/31/97	12/31/96	12/31/95
Per Share Information				
Stock Price	2.00	3.44	1.50	1.62
Earnings Per Share	0.11	0.45	0.02	-0.43
Price / Earnings Ratio	18.18	7.64	75.00	n.a.
Book Value Per Share	1.25	1.13	0.79	0.86
Price / Book Value %	160.00	304.42	189.87	188.37
Dividends Per Share	0.0	0.0	0.0	0.0
Annual Financial Data				
Operating Results (000's)				
Total Revenues	20,570.8	10,097.0	8,253.5	7,650.4
Costs & Expenses	-20,209.6	-8,972.1	-8,252.9	-7,999.3
Income Before Taxes and Other	361.2	1,124.9	0.6	-360.1
Other Items	0.0	0.0	0.0	0.0
Income Tax	-154.2	-257.5	17.6	68.9
Net Income	207.0	867.3	18.2	-291.2
Cash Flow From Operations	-993.7	265.3	330.1	-198.1
Balance Sheet (000's)				
Cash & Equivalents	61.4	205.0	115.8	149.8
Total Current Assets	6,512.0	2,871.2	2,218.7	2,471.6
Fixed Assets, Net	935.0	692.6	719.1	539.0
Total Assets	8,164.3	3,597.9	2,979.8	3,053.6
Total Current Liabilities	5,878.1	1,607.3	2,207.2	2,365.2
Long-Term Debt	0.0	53.4	106.8	2.0
Stockholders' Equity	2,109.9	1,889.2	665.8	586.0
Performance & Financial Condition				
Return on Total Revenues %	1.01	8.59	0.22	-3.81
Return on Avg Stockholders' Equity %	10.35	67.89	2.91	-39.80
Return on Average Assets %	3.52	26.37	0.60	-10.21
Current Ratio	1.11	1.79	1.01	1.04
Debt / Equity %	n.a.	2.83	16.03	0.34

Compound Growth %'s	EPS % n.a.	Net Income % n.a.	Total Revenues % 39.06

Comments

The Company replaced and added senior management in 1994 and 1995, but then had a major upheaval in 1996 with the departure of several key personnel who opened a business in direct competition with Cable Link. A new management team was again in place by the beginning of 1997. Sales of Auro Computer Systems are included in the above numbers since May 5, 1998. The acquisition resulted in losses for 1998 in excess of $450,000 due to extraordinary costs associated with taking control of a new business, and lower than desired margins and sales through the transition period. Management reports that sales and profits are strong on the cable side of the business but may not be enough to offset continuing losses from Auro in the near term.

Officers	Position	Ownership Information	
Bob Binsky	Chairman, CEO	Number of Shares Outstanding	1,689,136
Brenda L. Castle	President	Market Capitalization	$ 3,378,272
Richard M. Rozic	Exec VP, COO	Number of Shareholders	800
Richard L. Baker	VP - Manufacturing	Where Listed / Symbol	OTC-BB / CBLK

Other Information			
Transfer Agent	Fifth Third Bank Cincinnati, OH	SIC Code	4840
Auditor	Groner, Boyle & Quillin, LLP	Employees	100
Market Maker	Wien Securities Corp.	(800)624-0050	Web Site	cable-link.com
	Paragon Capital Corporation	(800)345-0505		

Cache, Inc.

1460 Broadway   New York, NY 10036   Telephone (212)575-3200   Fax (212)840-4225

Company Description

Cache, Inc. owns and operates 184 women's apparel specialty stores, all of which are operated under the trade name Cache. The Company specializes in the sale of high fashion women's apparel and accessories in the better to expensive price range, focusing on social occasion dressing ranging from informal get-togethers to formal black-tie affairs. The typical store averages 2,000 square feet and sells better sportswear, evening wear and upscale accessories. The Company's stores operate in 37 states, as well as in Puerto Rico and the District of Columbia. Stores are concentrated in large metropolitan and suburban areas and are located in the finest shopping malls in the country. The Company was founded in 1975.

	01/02/99	12/27/97	12/28/96	12/30/95
Per Share Information				
Stock Price as of 12/31	3.87	3.03	3.37	3.37
Earnings Per Share	0.43	0.26	0.22	0.21
Price / Earnings Ratio	9.00	11.65	15.32	16.05
Book Value Per Share	3.07	2.64	2.38	2.16
Price / Book Value %	126.06	114.77	141.60	156.02
Dividends Per Share	0.0	0.0	0.0	0.0
Annual Financial Data				
Operating Results (000's)				
Total Revenues	147,058.0	135,833.0	128,993.0	120,640.0
Costs & Expenses	-140,388.0	-131,823.0	-125,846.0	-117,591.0
Income Before Taxes and Other	6,670.0	4,010.0	3,147.0	3,032.0
Other Items	0.0	0.0	0.0	0.0
Income Tax	-2,735.0	-1,645.0	-1,181.0	-1,120.0
Net Income	3,935.0	2,365.0	1,966.0	1,912.0
Cash Flow From Operations	11,093.0	7,274.0	5,856.0	5,338.0
Balance Sheet (000's)				
Cash & Equivalents	13,720.0	5,892.0	2,160.0	1,025.0
Total Current Assets	35,273.0	26,682.0	23,110.0	20,381.0
Fixed Assets, Net	14,776.0	15,869.0	16,385.0	16,577.0
Total Assets	51,558.0	43,508.0	40,610.0	38,047.0
Total Current Liabilities	19,899.0	15,700.0	14,906.0	13,014.0
Long-Term Debt	2,000.0	0.0	0.0	1,300.0
Stockholders' Equity	27,896.0	23,961.0	21,596.0	19,630.0
Performance & Financial Condition				
Return on Total Revenues %	2.68	1.74	1.52	1.58
Return on Avg Stockholders' Equity %	15.18	10.38	9.54	10.60
Return on Average Assets %	8.28	5.62	5.00	5.25
Current Ratio	1.77	1.70	1.55	1.57
Debt / Equity %	7.17	n.a.	n.a.	6.62

Compound Growth %'s	EPS %	26.98	Net Income %	27.20	Total Revenues %	6.82

Comments

The improvement in 1998 net income as compared to 1997 was attributable to an improvement in sales and gross margins at existing stores together with the increase in operating income due to the 16 new stores that were added during the year. Comparable store sales increased 2% during 1998. Management has been focused on keeping a lid on general and administrative expenses which declined as a percentage of sales for each of the last three years. The Company maintains a conservative balance sheet. The only debt that comes close to long term status is $2 million of subordinated debt to a major stockholder.

Officers	Position	Ownership Information	
Andrew Saul	Chairman, CEO	Number of Shares Outstanding	9,091,338
Roy Smith	Exec VP	Market Capitalization	$ 35,183,478
Thomas Reinckens	Exec VP, CFO	Number of Shareholders	700
Mae Soo Hoo	Exec VP, General Manager	Where Listed / Symbol	NASDAQ / CACH

Other Information			
Transfer Agent	Continental Stock Transfer & Trust Co. New York, NY	SIC Code	5621
Auditor	Arthur Andersen LLP	Employees	1,500
		Web Site	cache-inc.com

Cade Industries, Inc.

2365 Woodlake Drive, Suite 120   Okemos, MI 48864   Telephone (517)347-1333   Fax (517)347-6185

Company Description

Cade Industries, Inc. is engaged worldwide in the design, manufacture, and repair and overhaul of high technology composite components for the aerospace, air transport and specialty industries. The Company's core products consist of original equipment components for gas turbine engines, airframe, and auxiliary power units. Its specialty niche products include ground-based test nacelle systems and the repair and overhaul of commercial gas turbine engine components for both commercial and military airframe applications. The Company was founded in 1981. In December 1994, it acquired Pollux Corporation which was in the business of overhauling, repairing and manufacturing flight control surfaces for both commercial and military aircraft. In October 1997, it acquired Central Engineering Company which is engaged in the engine design and testing business.

	12/31/98	12/31/97	12/31/96	12/31/95
Per Share Information				
Stock Price	2.16	2.34	1.22	0.53
Earnings Per Share	0.19	0.11	0.05	-0.02
Price / Earnings Ratio	11.37	21.27	24.40	n.a.
Book Value Per Share	1.24	1.07	0.95	0.91
Price / Book Value %	174.19	218.69	128.42	58.24
Dividends Per Share	0.0	0.0	0.0	0.0
Annual Financial Data				
Operating Results (000's)				
Total Revenues	95,792.4	55,803.8	34,899.4	30,458.6
Costs & Expenses	-89,644.6	-52,413.5	-33,563.9	-31,237.7
Income Before Taxes and Other	6,147.9	3,390.3	1,335.5	-779.0
Other Items	0.0	0.0	0.0	0.0
Income Tax	-1,906.0	-1,037.0	-277.0	397.0
Net Income	4,241.9	2,353.3	1,058.5	-382.0
Cash Flow From Operations	7,952.2	3,396.2	1,249.2	2,300.3
Balance Sheet (000's)				
Cash & Equivalents	274.8	1,093.2	21.6	187.5
Total Current Assets	37,729.0	31,201.2	17,146.6	13,653.4
Fixed Assets, Net	19,196.7	17,662.2	15,006.1	15,759.0
Total Assets	62,274.8	54,569.9	35,304.4	32,684.5
Total Current Liabilities	26,241.5	19,766.5	9,147.9	6,591.8
Long-Term Debt	8,313.3	10,682.6	4,839.2	5,955.9
Stockholders' Equity	27,054.0	23,332.8	20,683.3	19,659.8
Performance & Financial Condition				
Return on Total Revenues %	4.43	4.22	3.03	-1.25
Return on Avg Stockholders' Equity %	16.84	10.69	5.25	-1.92
Return on Average Assets %	7.26	5.24	3.11	-1.16
Current Ratio	1.44	1.58	1.87	2.07
Debt / Equity %	30.73	45.78	23.40	30.29

Compound Growth %'s	EPS %	94.94	Net Income %	100.19	Total Revenues %	46.51

Comments

The acquisitions referred to above were accounted for as purchases. Therefore, results of operations have been combined from the dates of the transactions. 1998 results reflect strong performance throughout the Company, highlighted by improving margins, significant gains in revenue from overhaul and repair services, and more than a three-fold increase in revenues from the sale of test facilities and equipment. At December 31, 1998, the Company had $5.1 million of goodwill reflected as assets which equated to approximately 19% of stockholders' equity and book value per share; that's not much at all after completing two acquisitions. Management was so surprised by the cheap stock price that it could not resist buying back 250,000 shares at an average price of $2.72. Another one million shares has been authorized for repurchase.

Officers	Position	Ownership Information	
John W. Sandford	Chairman, CEO	Number of Shares Outstanding	21,798,627
Richard A. Lund	President, COO	Market Capitalization	$ 47,085,034
Conrad G. Goodkind	Secretary	Number of Shareholders	1,592
Edward B. Stephens	Vice President, CFO	Where Listed / Symbol	NASDAQ / CADE

Other Information			
Transfer Agent	Firstar Trust Company Milwaukee, WI	SIC Code	3724
Auditor	Deloitte & Touche LLP	Employees	690
		Web Site	cade-industries.com

Calloway's Nursery, Inc.

4200 Airport Freeway   Fort Worth, TX 76117-6200   Telephone (817)222-1122   Fax (817)654-2662

Company Description

Calloway's Nursery, Inc. is a specialty retailer of lawn and garden products. The Company presently operates sixteen store locations in the Dallas-Fort Worth Metroplex market. Each retail store has a similar floorplan and design providing over 60,000 square feet of selling space, approximately one-third of which is covered on a year-round basis. In 1997, the Company acquired an established facility for the production of living plants to enhance its ability to provide customers with a selection of top-quality plants at the least comparable cost. The Company was founded in 1987.

	09/30/98	09/30/97	09/30/96	09/30/95
Per Share Information				
Stock Price as of 12/31	1.12	1.37	0.75	0.75
Earnings Per Share	-0.05	0.33	0.04	0.03
Price / Earnings Ratio	n.a.	4.15	18.75	25.00
Book Value Per Share	1.36	1.40	1.09	1.06
Price / Book Value %	82.35	97.86	68.81	70.75
Dividends Per Share	0.0	0.0	0.0	0.0
Annual Financial Data				
Operating Results (000's)				
Total Revenues	27,069.0	26,245.0	23,959.0	22,527.0
Costs & Expenses	-27,396.0	-25,478.0	-23,731.0	-22,343.0
Income Before Taxes and Other	-327.0	767.0	228.0	184.0
Other Items	0.0	0.0	0.0	0.0
Income Tax	43.0	960.0	-27.0	-28.0
Net Income	-284.0	1,727.0	201.0	156.0
Cash Flow From Operations	-617.0	1,320.0	575.0	-812.0
Balance Sheet (000's)				
Cash & Equivalents	1,649.0	3,688.0	2,358.0	1,046.0
Total Current Assets	5,194.0	5,841.0	3,561.0	5,302.0
Fixed Assets, Net	7,815.0	5,466.0	3,947.0	1,630.0
Total Assets	14,685.0	13,111.0	8,863.0	8,417.0
Total Current Liabilities	3,082.0	2,722.0	2,088.0	2,028.0
Long-Term Debt	3,044.0	1,803.0	0.0	0.0
Stockholders' Equity	7,466.0	7,488.0	5,606.0	5,258.0
Performance & Financial Condition				
Return on Total Revenues %	-1.05	6.58	0.84	0.69
Return on Avg Stockholders' Equity %	-3.80	26.38	3.70	3.06
Return on Average Assets %	-2.04	15.72	2.33	1.56
Current Ratio	1.69	2.15	1.71	2.61
Debt / Equity %	40.77	24.08	n.a.	n.a.

Compound Growth %'s	EPS % n.a.	Net Income % n.a.	Total Revenues % 6.31

Comments

A summer heat wave of record proportions reduced consumer demand for living plants and related garden products in the Metroplex. Although sales increased 3.1% (5.0% for the comparable stores), gross margins were lower and operating expenses and advertising expenses were higher. The 1997 net income included a tax benefit of $960,000 ($.18 per share) from the realization of tax loss carryovers. There is still $1.2 million left to offset future income.

Officers	Position	Ownership Information	
James C. Estill	President, CEO	Number of Shares Outstanding	5,485,695
John T. Cosby	Vice President, Secretary	Market Capitalization	$ 6,143,978
John S. Peters	Vice President	Number of Shareholders	1,100
David S. Weger	Vice President	Where Listed / Symbol	NASDAQ / CLWY

Other Information			
Transfer Agent	Harris Trust & Savings Bank Chicago, IL	SIC Code	5261
Auditor	KPMG LLP	Employees	200
		Web Site	calloways.com

Calprop Corporation

13160 Mindanao Way, Suite 180   Marina Del Rey, CA 90292   Telephone (310)306-4314   Fax (310)301-0435

Company Description

Calprop Corporation designs, constructs and sells single-family detached and attached homes and townhouses as part of condominiums or planned unit developments in California and Colorado. The Company selects and acquires a site, secures construction financing and constructs and sells homes. The Company's products range from less expensive homes for first-time buyers to more expensive near custom homes. In recent years, the Company's strategy has been to acquire land in or near major urban centers to construct single-family housing for resale. The Company also sells improved lots in California.

	12/31/98	12/31/97	12/31/96	12/31/95
Per Share Information				
Stock Price	1.44	0.69	0.50	0.81
Earnings Per Share	0.52	-0.18	-1.28	0.01
Price / Earnings Ratio	2.77	n.a.	n.a.	81.00
Book Value Per Share	0.82	0.30	0.47	2.87
Price / Book Value %	175.61	230.00	106.38	28.22
Dividends Per Share	0.0	0.0	0.0	0.0
Annual Financial Data				
Operating Results (000's)				
Total Revenues	33,071.7	22,908.6	13,717.1	17,066.4
Costs & Expenses	-32,332.2	-24,823.6	-17,005.8	-18,954.2
Income Before Taxes and Other	826.9	-1,823.3	-3,106.9	513.4
Other Items	-232.6	17.2	-6,093.5	0.0
Income Tax	4,773.7	185.9	0.0	0.0
Net Income	5,368.0	-1,620.2	-9,200.3	513.4
Cash Flow From Operations	-36,607.3	-4,190.9	-4,432.7	-2,440.8
Balance Sheet (000's)				
Cash & Equivalents	1,590.4	1,100.0	1,224.8	758.3
Total Current Assets	1,679.2	1,123.2	1,254.4	1,087.6
Fixed Assets, Net	65,282.2	29,302.0	25,945.4	30,517.3
Total Assets	72,521.9	30,956.8	27,533.4	31,893.2
Total Current Liabilities	5,056.0	3,954.9	3,025.8	3,224.0
Long-Term Debt	37,524.5	21,769.2	19,877.0	12,257.9
Stockholders' Equity	8,459.5	2,756.6	4,359.2	14,074.7
Performance & Financial Condition				
Return on Total Revenues %	16.19	-7.04	-66.19	2.64
Return on Avg Stockholders' Equity %	95.72	-45.54	-99.82	3.67
Return on Average Assets %	10.38	-5.54	-30.96	1.65
Current Ratio	0.33	0.28	0.41	0.34
Debt / Equity %	443.58	789.71	455.97	87.09

Compound Growth %'s	EPS %	n.a.	Net Income %	n.a.	Total Revenues %	24.67

Comments

The Company's results are somewhat reflective of the California real estate market which experienced a downturn from 1990 through 1996. During 1997, however, real estate began to recover. Unit sales are now on the rise which accounts for the increased revenue recorded in 1997 and 1998. Although 1998 was profitable, $4.8 million of income was a tax benefit recorded in expectation of utilizing $12 million of tax loss carryforwards in future years. The construction backlog was 123 units at the end of 1998 compared to 114 units one year earlier. 1996 results include the recognition of $6.1 million of losses in connection with the impairment of real estate.

Officers	Position	Ownership Information	
Victor Zaccaglin	Chairman, CEO	Number of Shares Outstanding	10,284,135
Ronald S. Petch	President	Market Capitalization	$ 14,809,154
Mark F. Spiro	Vice President, CFO	Number of Shareholders	549
George R. Bravante, Jr.	Director	Where Listed / Symbol	OTC-BB / CLPO

Other Information			
Transfer Agent	ChaseMellon Shareholder Services Ridgefield Park, NJ	SIC Code	1531
Auditor	Deloitte & Touche LLP	Employees	29
Market Maker	Wien Securities Corp.	(800)624-0050	
	Sharpe Capitla Inc.	(800)355-5781	

Cambridge Holdings, Ltd.

1722 Buffehr Creek Road   Vail, CO 81657   Telephone (970)479-2800   Fax (970)479-2822

Company Description

Cambridge Holdings, Ltd., formed in 1980, acquired two parcels of real estate which were sold in fiscal 1996. During fiscal 1997, two undeveloped lots in the Vail, Colorado area were acquired and conveyed to separate limited liability companies, each of which has since developed a luxury residence for sale. The Company has a 50% profit and loss interest in the ventures. The other partner in the ventures is an experienced real estate developer located in Vail. The Company also purchased land in Glenwood Springs, Colorado for potential development. During the quarter ended December 1998, the Company commenced a tender offer for its shares at $.45 per share. The offering was completed in January 1999 with 361,370 shares tendered.

	06/30/98	06/30/97	06/30/96	06/30/95
Per Share Information				
Stock Price as of 12/31	0.45	0.28	0.62	0.34
Earnings Per Share	-0.04	0.03	0.52	0.07
Price / Earnings Ratio	n.a.	9.33	1.19	4.86
Book Value Per Share	1.03	1.09	1.19	0.55
Price / Book Value %	43.69	25.69	52.10	61.82
Dividends Per Share	0.0	0.0	0.0	0.0
Annual Financial Data				
Operating Results (000's)				
Total Revenues	178.1	328.4	2,287.9	763.5
Costs & Expenses	-324.6	-176.2	-451.6	-531.1
Income Before Taxes and Other	-146.5	152.2	1,836.3	232.5
Other Items	0.0	0.0	0.0	0.0
Income Tax	10.0	-49.0	-162.0	0.0
Net Income	-136.5	103.2	1,674.3	232.5
Cash Flow From Operations	21.8	-170.9	-69.0	223.5
Balance Sheet (000's)				
Cash & Equivalents	1,674.5	1,640.2	1,304.3	698.6
Total Current Assets	4,145.9	3,753.5	4,245.8	1,039.1
Fixed Assets, Net	38.6	0.0	0.0	1,552.7
Total Assets	4,184.5	3,756.5	4,249.0	2,591.8
Total Current Liabilities	689.2	63.2	278.1	79.5
Long-Term Debt	0.0	0.0	0.0	0.0
Stockholders' Equity	3,495.2	3,693.3	3,970.9	1,709.4
Performance & Financial Condition				
Return on Total Revenues %	-76.67	31.43	73.18	30.45
Return on Avg Stockholders' Equity %	-3.80	2.69	58.95	14.46
Return on Average Assets %	-3.44	2.58	48.95	9.34
Current Ratio	6.02	59.37	15.26	13.07
Debt / Equity %	n.a.	n.a.	n.a.	n.a.

Compound Growth %'s	EPS % n.a.	Net Income % n.a.	Total Revenues % n.a.

Comments

Since 1996, operating results have been unexciting simply because not much is happening from an accounting standpoint. 1996 results include recognition of a $1,759,368 gain on the sale of property. The activities of the limited liability companies are expected to be of short duration. If management is successful in accumulating a string of profitable ventures, acquiring shares of the Company below book value may become attractive. This may be what management has in mind with its recent tender offer. For the six months ended December 31, 1998, the Company reported a loss of $313,628 ($.09 per share) which included a $101,000 write down on one of the partnership investments.

Officers	Position	Ownership Information	
Gregory Pusey	President, Treasurer	Number of Shares Outstanding	3,398,400
Donald E. Yager	Secretary	Market Capitalization	$ 1,529,280
John H. Altshuler	Director	Number of Shareholders	1,064
Scott Menefee	Director	Where Listed / Symbol	OTC-BB / CDGD

Other Information			
Transfer Agent	Corporate Stock Transfer, Inc. Denver, CO	SIC Code	6500
Auditor	BDO Seidman LLP	Employees	1
Market Maker	Carr Securities Corporation	(800)221-2243	
	Paragon Capital Corporation	(800)345-0505	

Candie's, Inc.

2975 Westchester Avenue   Purchase, NY 10577   Telephone (914)694-8600   Fax (914)694-8608

Company Description

Candie's, Inc. is engaged primarily in the design, marketing and importation of a variety of moderately-priced women's and girls' casual and fashion footwear and handbags under the CANDIE'S® and BONGO® trademarks for distribution to better department and specialty stores worldwide. The Company also markets and distributes, under the CANDIE'S® and BONGO® trademarks, children's footwear designed by it. Additionally, the Company arranges for the manufacture of footwear products, similar to those produced under the CANDIE'S® trademark, for mass market and discount retailers, under one of the Company's other trademarks or under the private label brand of the retailer. Moreover, the Company distributes a variety of men's workboots, hiking boots, winter boots and outdoor casual shoes. The Company was founded in 1978.

	01/31/98	01/31/97	01/31/96	01/31/95
Per Share Information				
Stock Price as of 12/31	3.44	5.81	2.47	2.37
Earnings Per Share	0.33	0.11	0.11	0.0
Price / Earnings Ratio	10.42	52.82	22.45	n.a.
Book Value Per Share	1.99	0.89	0.65	0.50
Price / Book Value %	172.86	652.81	380.00	474.00
Dividends Per Share	0.0	0.0	0.0	0.0
Annual Financial Data				
Operating Results (000's)				
Total Revenues	92,976.4	45,005.4	37,914.1	24,192.0
Costs & Expenses	-87,145.5	-44,795.1	-36,583.9	-24,165.0
Income Before Taxes and Other	5,732.9	135.3	1,217.3	27.0
Other Items	0.0	0.0	0.0	0.0
Income Tax	-1,197.0	1,010.0	-163.3	0.0
Net Income	4,535.9	1,145.3	1,054.0	27.0
Cash Flow From Operations	-8,830.1	662.5	225.3	50.0
Balance Sheet (000's)				
Cash & Equivalents	367.1	389.5	205.0	0.0
Total Current Assets	23,407.7	9,039.2	5,969.0	4,104.0
Fixed Assets, Net	851.3	377.1	121.1	143.0
Total Assets	30,880.9	14,709.3	11,745.8	10,290.0
Total Current Liabilities	6,139.2	5,993.4	6,037.0	5,646.2
Long-Term Debt	61.2	108.0	0.0	252.0
Stockholders' Equity	24,680.5	8,607.9	5,708.8	4,391.9
Performance & Financial Condition				
Return on Total Revenues %	4.88	2.54	2.78	0.11
Return on Avg Stockholders' Equity %	27.25	16.00	20.87	0.60
Return on Average Assets %	19.90	8.66	9.57	0.27
Current Ratio	3.81	1.51	0.99	0.73
Debt / Equity %	0.25	1.25	n.a.	5.74

Compound Growth %'s	EPS %	73.21	Net Income %	451.78	Total Revenues %	56.64

Comments

The sharp increase in revenues resulted from increased brand awareness and consumer acceptance due to increased sales and marketing efforts coupled with increased sales in all product categories, the successful introduction of children's footwear products and increased selling prices. Fiscal 1997 results include the recognition of a $1 million income tax benefit for the expected use of tax loss carryovers. Not reflected in the numbers above is the April 1998, acquisition of NRC Corporation, a related public company. For the nine months ended October 31, 1998, the Company reported revenues and net income of $97.5 million and $5.2 million ($.31 per share) as compared to $70.4 million and $3.8 million ($.28 per share) for the same period of the preceding year.

Officers	Position	Ownership Information	
Neil Cole	President, CEO	Number of Shares Outstanding	12,425,014
Lawrence O'Shaughnessy	Exec VP, COO	Market Capitalization	$ 42,742,048
David Golden	Senior VP, CFO	Number of Shareholders	1,000
Gary Klein	VP - Finance	Where Listed / Symbol	NASDAQ / CAND

Other Information			
Transfer Agent	Continental Stock Transfer & Trust Co. New York, NY	SIC Code	3140
Auditor	Ernst & Young LLP	Employees	93

Canisco Resources, Inc.

300 Delaware Avenue, Suite 714 Wilmington, DE 19801 Telephone (302)777-5050 Fax (302)777-5409

Company Description

Canisco Resources, Inc., formerly Nuclear Support Services, Inc., is an integrated service company which provides a range of maintenance services on an as-needed basis to power generation and process industries, government facilities and major industries in the United States. Approximately one-third of revenues is attributable to nuclear, fossil fuel, hydro-electric and other customers whose operations involve the production of electricity. Contract services involve contracting for the accomplishment of defined tasks for the customer with supervision retained by the Company. Staff augmentation services entail providing qualified manpower to work under the direction of the customer. The Company filed for Chapter 11 voluntary bankruptcy in September 1995 and exited from bankruptcy on July 1, 1996. The Company was founded in 1973.

	03/31/98	03/31/97	09/30/95	09/30/94
Per Share Information				
Stock Price as of 12/31	1.62	2.00	1.25	2.25
Earnings Per Share	0.20	0.21	-1.31	-0.30
Price / Earnings Ratio	8.10	9.52	n.a.	n.a.
Book Value Per Share	1.43	1.20	1.69	3.00
Price / Book Value %	113.29	166.67	73.96	n.a.
Dividends Per Share	0.0	0.0	0.0	0.0
Annual Financial Data				
Operating Results (000's)				
Total Revenues	52,304.3	51,022.4	83,115.9	83,825.2
Costs & Expenses	-51,645.4	-49,449.3	-83,945.9	-84,060.7
Income Before Taxes and Other	658.9	576.8	-1,015.2	-235.5
Other Items	0.0	-72.7	-2,004.8	-517.8
Income Tax	-168.5	-51.7	171.0	111.0
Net Income	490.4	452.4	-2,849.0	-642.3
Cash Flow From Operations	955.9	2,092.4	717.6	2,815.3
Balance Sheet (000's)				
Cash & Equivalents	1,188.4	1,308.2	1,849.3	1,911.0
Total Current Assets	13,512.4	13,690.7	30,838.7	22,404.0
Fixed Assets, Net	3,493.2	3,670.1	6,673.1	13,085.0
Total Assets	20,633.3	21,301.0	39,389.3	35,489.0
Total Current Liabilities	8,219.1	8,422.0	23,403.8	14,275.0
Long-Term Debt	8,281.4	9,220.3	4,184.0	14,710.0
Stockholders' Equity	3,169.9	2,606.4	3,655.7	6,504.0
Performance & Financial Condition				
Return on Total Revenues %	0.94	0.89	-3.43	-0.77
Return on Avg Stockholders' Equity %	16.98	14.45	-56.08	-11.66
Return on Average Assets %	2.34	1.49	-7.61	-2.76
Current Ratio	1.64	1.63	1.32	1.57
Debt / Equity %	261.25	353.76	114.45	226.17

Compound Growth %'s	EPS % n.a.	Net Income % n.a.	Total Revenues %	-12.66

Comments

The Company changed its year end from September to March in 1996. Only full years are presented above. The six months ended March 31, 1996, are not presented but showed total revenue and a net loss of $32.9 million and $1.5 million ($.69 per share), respectively. Revenues are not comparable because of the sale of certain divisions in connection with the plan of reorganization. What may be most important is the return to profitability demonstrated in the last two fiscal years. For the nine months ended December 31, 1998, revenues and net income were $54.1 million and $836,689 ($.32 per share) as compared to $41.7 million and $711,907 ($.30 per share) for the same period of the preceding year.

Officers	Position	Ownership Information	
Donald E. Lyons	Chairman	Number of Shares Outstanding	2,215,540
Ralph A. Trallo	President, CEO	Market Capitalization	$ 3,589,175
Michael J. Olson	CFO	Number of Shareholders	374
Thomas P. McShane	Director	Where Listed / Symbol	NASDAQ / CANRC

Other Information			
Transfer Agent	ChaseMellon Shareholder Services Ridgefield Park, NJ	SIC Code	1700
Auditor	KPMG LLP	Employees	600

Canterbury Park Holding Corporation

1100 Canterbury Road Shakopee, MN 55379 Telephone (612)445-7223 Fax (612)496-6400

Company Description

Canterbury Park Holding Corporation is engaged in the business of conducting live thoroughbred and quarter horse racing and pari-mutuel wagering operations related thereto at its facilities in Shakopee, Minnesota. The Company also conducts "simulcasting", which is pari-mutuel wagering on races held at out-of-state racetracks that are televised simultaneously at the Racetrack. Additionally, the Company derives revenues from related services and activities, such as concessions, parking, admissions and programs, and from other entertainment events held at the Racetrack. The Racetrack was constructed in 1984 but the prior owner ceased all operations in 1992. The Company was formed in 1994 and acquired the Racetrack at that time.

	12/31/98	12/31/97	12/31/96	12/31/95
Per Share Information				
Stock Price	4.12	2.81	2.00	1.62
Earnings Per Share	0.14	0.04	0.02	-0.30
Price / Earnings Ratio	29.43	70.25	100.00	n.a.
Book Value Per Share	2.20	2.04	1.97	1.94
Price / Book Value %	187.27	137.75	101.52	83.51
Dividends Per Share	0.0	0.0	0.0	0.0
Annual Financial Data				
Operating Results (000's)				
Total Revenues	19,203.2	18,208.5	17,383.5	17,665.3
Costs & Expenses	-18,816.5	-18,064.3	-17,312.4	-18,554.4
Income Before Taxes and Other	386.6	144.2	71.1	-889.1
Other Items	0.0	0.0	0.0	0.0
Income Tax	47.1	-8.4	0.0	0.0
Net Income	433.7	135.8	71.1	-889.1
Cash Flow From Operations	1,383.7	1,223.9	977.9	-401.5
Balance Sheet (000's)				
Cash & Equivalents	372.2	364.2	296.7	388.6
Total Current Assets	819.0	752.7	657.6	824.8
Fixed Assets, Net	8,386.4	9,061.2	8,631.8	9,143.7
Total Assets	9,417.7	9,823.4	9,302.1	9,985.7
Total Current Liabilities	2,768.0	3,700.7	3,475.8	4,273.3
Long-Term Debt	0.0	0.0	0.0	0.0
Stockholders' Equity	6,649.7	6,122.8	5,826.3	5,712.4
Performance & Financial Condition				
Return on Total Revenues %	2.26	0.75	0.41	-5.03
Return on Avg Stockholders' Equity %	6.79	2.27	1.23	-14.44
Return on Average Assets %	4.51	1.42	0.74	-9.08
Current Ratio	0.30	0.20	0.19	0.19
Debt / Equity %	n.a.	n.a.	n.a.	n.a.

Compound Growth %'s	EPS %	164.58	Net Income %	146.91	Total Revenues %	2.82

Comments

From 1996 through 1998, the Company held a number of non-horseracing events including snowmobile races, arts and crafts shows, trade shows, concerts, motorcycle races, fund raisers, automobile shows, and private parties. Live racing was resumed at the Track in 1997. On April 11, 1996, legislation became effective that exempted the first $12 million of pari-mutuel revenue from the 6% pari-mutuel tax. The improvement in 1997 results is primarily attributable to the exemption being in effect for the entire year. Operating results continued to improve in 1998. Cash flow from operations has been good for three consecutive years. Depreciation has been a major non-cash expense. The Company appears to handle a deficit in working capital with occasional borrowings from related parties.

Officers	Position	Ownership Information	
Randall D. Sampson	President, CEO	Number of Shares Outstanding	3,020,167
Michael J. Garin	Vice President	Market Capitalization	$ 12,443,088
Troy J. Mertens	Vice President	Number of Shareholders	349
Mark A. Erickson	Vice President	Where Listed / Symbol	NASDAQ / TRAK

Other Information			
Transfer Agent	Norwest Bank Minnesota, N.A. South St. Paul, MN	SIC Code	7948
Auditor	Deloitte & Touche LLP	Employees	215
		Web Site	canterburypark.com

Canyon Resources Corporation

14142 Denver West Parkway, Suite 250   Golden, CO 80401   Telephone (303)278-8464   Fax (303)279-3772

Company Description

Canyon Resources Corporation was organized in 1979 to explore, acquire, develop, and mine precious metal and other mineral properties. The Company is involved in all phases of the mining business from early stage exploration, exploration drilling, development drilling, feasibility studies and permitting through construction, operation and final closure of mining projects. Canyon has gold and industrial mineral production operations in the western United States and conducts exploration activities in search for additional valuable mineral properties in that area as well as in a number of areas throughout Latin America and Africa. During 1998 and 1997, all of the Company's revenues were generated by its production facilities in the United States.

	12/31/98	12/31/97	12/31/96	12/31/95
Per Share Information				
Stock Price	0.25	1.12	2.63	2.37
Earnings Per Share	-0.26	-0.13	-0.21	-0.24
Price / Earnings Ratio	n.a.	n.a.	n.a.	n.a.
Book Value Per Share	0.98	1.26	1.29	0.78
Price / Book Value %	25.51	88.89	203.88	n.a.
Dividends Per Share	0.0	0.0	0.0	0.0
Annual Financial Data				
Operating Results (000's)				
Total Revenues	36,363.2	29,618.8	5,952.5	9,707.7
Costs & Expenses	-39,212.5	-34,641.1	-13,023.6	-15,850.9
Income Before Taxes and Other	-2,849.3	-5,022.3	-7,114.9	-6,143.2
Other Items	-9,209.6	0.0	0.0	0.0
Income Tax	0.0	0.0	0.0	0.0
Net Income	-12,058.9	-5,022.3	-7,114.9	-6,143.2
Cash Flow From Operations	11,217.3	707.7	-8,120.5	-2,356.1
Balance Sheet (000's)				
Cash & Equivalents	1,985.7	3,111.0	4,181.1	27,106.4
Total Current Assets	13,583.9	13,514.3	12,286.5	28,654.8
Fixed Assets, Net	64,987.5	80,956.0	70,339.6	38,524.4
Total Assets	81,871.7	97,282.1	84,384.3	72,424.2
Total Current Liabilities	27,919.9	10,933.1	5,825.9	2,867.4
Long-Term Debt	0.0	28,055.0	28,125.0	47,371.8
Stockholders' Equity	45,298.9	55,038.5	48,440.6	20,070.5
Performance & Financial Condition				
Return on Total Revenues %	-33.16	-16.96	-119.53	-63.28
Return on Avg Stockholders' Equity %	-24.04	-9.71	-20.77	-27.05
Return on Average Assets %	-13.46	-5.53	-9.07	-9.86
Current Ratio	0.49	1.24	2.11	9.99
Debt / Equity %	n.a.	50.97	58.06	236.03

Compound Growth %'s	EPS % n.a.	Net Income % n.a.	Total Revenues %	55.30

Comments

In 1998, the Company changed its method of accounting for exploration costs on unproven properties from capitalizing all expenditures to expensing all costs, other than acquisition costs, prior to the establishment of proven and probable reserves. This resulted in a nonrecurring $8.9 million charge ($.19 per share) in the income statement. Revenues increased in 1998 due to a full year of mining at the Briggs Mine located in southeastern California. Net results for 1997 were impacted by a $2.6 million provision for site restoration at the Kendall Mine. On January 30, 1998, the Company completed an equity financing which raised $2.3 million, net of expenses. But by year end, the Company had a substantial deficiency in working capital and was in default on certain loan covenants. The auditors issued a going concern qualification in their report on the Company's financial statements.

Officers	Position	Ownership Information	
Richard H. De Voto	Chairman, President	Number of Shares Outstanding	46,137,100
Gary C. Huper	VP - Finance, CFO	Market Capitalization	$ 11,534,275
Cheryl A. Martin	Secretary	Number of Shareholders	6,500
John R. Danio	Vice President	Where Listed / Symbol	AMEX / CAU

Other Information			
Transfer Agent	American Securities Transfer, Inc. Denver, CO	SIC Code	1040
Auditor	PricewaterhouseCoopers LLP	Employees	150

Capital Associates, Inc.

7175 West Jefferson Avenue, Suite 4000   Lakewood, CO 80235   Telephone (303)980-1000   Fax (303)980-7017

Company Description

Capital Associates, Inc. is a commercial finance company engaged in the leasing of a variety of equipment. The Company is principally engaged in 1) the origination of equipment leases with equipment users, including the acquisition of leases initially originated by other lessors, 2) the sale of equipment leases to third parties, 3) the management and servicing of equipment leases retained by the Company or sold to private investors or other lessors, 4) the sale and remarketing of equipment as it comes off lease and 5) the sale and servicing of new information technology equipment. All leases and financings are subject to review under the Company's underwriting standards. Each potential lessee or borrower is assigned a credit risk rating based on the application of specific criteria during the credit review process. The Company was founded in 1986.

	05/31/98	05/31/97	05/31/96	05/31/95
Per Share Information				
Stock Price as of 12/31	3.25	3.00	3.50	1.69
Earnings Per Share	0.28	0.14	0.11	0.21
Price / Earnings Ratio	11.61	21.43	31.82	8.05
Book Value Per Share	4.92	4.68	4.58	4.42
Price / Book Value %	66.06	64.10	76.42	n.a.
Dividends Per Share	0.0	0.0	0.0	0.0
Annual Financial Data				
Operating Results (000's)				
Total Revenues	281,074.0	227,534.0	186,681.0	104,944.0
Costs & Expenses	-279,554.0	-226,791.0	-185,875.0	-103,468.0
Income Before Taxes and Other	1,520.0	743.0	806.0	1,476.0
Other Items	0.0	0.0	0.0	0.0
Income Tax	0.0	-10.0	-202.0	-360.0
Net Income	1,520.0	733.0	604.0	1,116.0
Cash Flow From Operations	46,900.0	33,172.0	29,590.0	14,334.0
Balance Sheet (000's)				
Cash & Equivalents	17,684.0	6,194.0	2,851.0	923.0
Total Current Assets	24,660.0	7,337.0	5,645.0	33,323.0
Fixed Assets, Net	0.0	114,530.0	89,369.0	20,053.0
Total Assets	214,993.0	146,517.0	127,511.0	158,672.0
Total Current Liabilities	36,408.0	40,838.0	23,343.0	25,810.0
Long-Term Debt	49,088.0	20,712.0	17,538.0	0.0
Stockholders' Equity	25,186.0	23,501.0	22,881.0	22,490.0
Performance & Financial Condition				
Return on Total Revenues %	0.54	0.32	0.32	1.06
Return on Avg Stockholders' Equity %	6.24	3.16	2.66	5.12
Return on Average Assets %	0.84	0.53	0.42	0.61
Current Ratio	0.68	0.18	0.24	1.29
Debt / Equity %	194.90	88.13	76.65	n.a.

Compound Growth %'s	EPS %	10.06	Net Income %	10.85	Total Revenues %	38.87

Comments

Fiscal 1998 included a number of accomplishments such as six consecutive years and twenty-four consecutive quarters of profitability. The Company originated leases exceeding $300 million in fiscal 1998, the highest level during the last five years. Acquisitions also played a role in the growth of the Company. Tax loss and credit carryovers have enabled the Company to avoid income tax expense but those carryovers are starting to run low. Income tax may be incurred in fiscal 1999. For the nine months ended February 28, 1999, the Company reported revenues and net income of $179.5 million and $664,000 ($.13 per share) as compared to $197.6 million and $1,391,000 ($.27 per share) for the same period of the preceding year.

Officers	Position	Ownership Information	
James D. Walker	President, CEO	Number of Shares Outstanding	5,123,000
Anthony M. DiPaolo	Senior VP, CFO	Market Capitalization	$ 16,649,750
Philip J. Teigen	Vice President, Secretary	Number of Shareholders	490
John Gordon	Controller	Where Listed / Symbol	NASDAQ / CAII

Other Information			
Transfer Agent	Mellon Bank, N.A. Pittsburgh, PA	SIC Code	6159
Auditor	KPMG LLP	Employees	170
		Web Site	cai-lease.com

Capital Pacific Holdings, Inc.

4100 MacArthur Boulevard, Suite 200   Newport Beach, CA 92660   Telephone (714)622-8400   Fax (714)622-8404

Company Description

Capital Pacific Holdings, Inc., successor to the business of J.M. Peters Company, Inc., is a regional builder of single-family homes with operations throughout selected metropolitan areas of California, Nevada, Texas and Arizona. J.M. Peters Company has built and sold in excess of 10,000 homes in California, principally Orange County, since 1975. Ownership of J.M. Peters was acquired for $47.25 million from the Resolution Trust Corporation in August 1992. The Company has recently expanded its operating strategy to encompass the development of commercial and mixed-use projects, as well as ownership of existing commercial properties.

	02/28/98	02/28/97	02/29/96	02/28/95
Per Share Information				
Stock Price as of 12/31	2.56	2.87	3.12	3.19
Earnings Per Share	-0.15	0.23	0.17	0.24
Price / Earnings Ratio	n.a.	12.48	18.35	13.29
Book Value Per Share	4.41	4.46	4.22	4.05
Price / Book Value %	58.05	64.35	73.93	78.77
Dividends Per Share	0.0	0.0	0.0	0.0
Annual Financial Data				
Operating Results (000's)				
Total Revenues	193,253.0	212,415.0	169,018.0	143,089.0
Costs & Expenses	-187,710.0	-208,546.0	-164,833.0	-136,416.0
Income Before Taxes and Other	5,543.0	3,869.0	4,185.0	6,673.0
Other Items	-8,469.0	192.0	-1,080.0	-2,808.0
Income Tax	735.0	-539.0	-503.0	-216.0
Net Income	-2,191.0	3,522.0	2,602.0	3,649.0
Cash Flow From Operations	8,255.0	-7,604.0	-40,910.0	-57,418.0
Balance Sheet (000's)				
Cash & Equivalents	4,328.0	11,434.0	13,850.0	22,401.0
Total Current Assets	243,798.0	264,172.0	259,823.0	195,447.0
Fixed Assets, Net	7,857.0	7,746.0	6,685.0	0.0
Total Assets	251,655.0	271,918.0	266,508.0	215,175.0
Total Current Liabilities	158,544.0	204,690.0	200,268.0	50,907.0
Long-Term Debt	0.0	0.0	0.0	100,000.0
Stockholders' Equity	63,050.0	66,868.0	63,346.0	60,744.0
Performance & Financial Condition				
Return on Total Revenues %	-1.13	1.66	1.54	2.55
Return on Avg Stockholders' Equity %	-3.37	5.41	4.19	6.27
Return on Average Assets %	-0.84	1.31	1.08	2.16
Current Ratio	1.54	1.29	1.30	3.84
Debt / Equity %	n.a.	n.a.	n.a.	164.63

Compound Growth %'s	EPS %	n.a.	Net Income %	n.a.	Total Revenues %	10.54

Comments

Fiscal 1998 results include a non-cash charge of $8 million related to the impaired value of assets. The level of units sold was negatively impacted by the unusually wet winter in California precipitated by the El Nino weather phenomenon. On October 1, 1997, Farallon Capital Management, a San Francisco based investment fund, invested $30 million into the Company for a 32% interest. Subsequent to February 28, 1998, the Company invested in four new residential real estate projects. For the nine months ended November 30, 1998, the Company reported net profits of $1.4 million ($.10 per share) as compared to a net loss of $2.7 million ($.18 per share), which was attributable to the $8 million non-cash charge mentioned above, for the comparable period of fiscal 1998.

Officers	Position	Ownership Information	
Hadi Makarechian	Chairman, CEO	Number of Shares Outstanding	14,305,511
Dale Dowers	President, COO	Market Capitalization	$ 36,622,108
Steven O. Spelman, Jr.	Vice President, CFO	Number of Shareholders	1,000
Marquis L. Cummings	Vice President, Treasurer	Where Listed / Symbol	AMEX / CPH

Other Information			
Transfer Agent	American Stock Transfer & Trust Co. New York, NY	SIC Code	1531
Auditor	Arthur Andersen LLP	Employees	229
		Web Site	cph-inc.com

Capital Title Group, Inc.

14555 North Scottsdale Road, Suite 320   Scottsdale, AZ 85254   Telephone (602)483-8868   Fax (602)483-8968

Company Description

Capital Title Group, Inc. operates an independent title agency and escrow business through its wholly owned subsidiary, Capital Title Agency, Inc. The current structure was created in May 1996 when Capital Title Group acquired the Capital Title Agency. Capital Title Group had no significant business prior to the acquisition. Since 1981, Capital Title Agency has provided continuous services to the real estate industry in Yavapai County, Arizona. In July 1996, Capital Title expanded its operations into metropolitan Phoenix and Maricopa County in general. In 1998, the Company expanded into the California marketplace with the acquisitions of New Century Title Company of Northern California and Northwestern Consolidated Corporation. As of the end of 1998, the Company had 41 branch offices.

	12/31/98	12/31/97	10/31/96
Per Share Information			
Stock Price	3.37	1.56	2.50
Earnings Per Share	0.11	-0.02	-0.11
Price / Earnings Ratio	30.64	n.a.	n.a.
Book Value Per Share	0.64	0.07	0.02
Price / Book Value %	526.56	2,228.57	n.a.
Dividends Per Share	0.0	0.0	0.0
Annual Financial Data			
Operating Results (000's)			
Total Revenues	23,206.2	8,348.5	2,582.7
Costs & Expenses	-21,370.7	-8,635.7	-3,630.6
Income Before Taxes and Other	1,835.5	-287.2	-1,048.0
Other Items	0.0	0.0	0.0
Income Tax	-159.4	42.4	0.0
Net Income	1,676.0	-244.7	-1,048.0
Cash Flow From Operations	2,471.8	-198.5	-678.3
Balance Sheet (000's)			
Cash & Equivalents	4,833.8	198.9	76.4
Total Current Assets	6,180.5	361.7	177.4
Fixed Assets, Net	8,863.1	1,560.7	953.4
Total Assets	16,528.4	2,253.8	1,364.5
Total Current Liabilities	3,853.7	1,020.8	794.7
Long-Term Debt	1,766.8	415.4	404.7
Stockholders' Equity	10,790.0	817.7	165.1
Performance & Financial Condition			
Return on Total Revenues %	7.22	-2.93	-40.58
Return on Avg Stockholders' Equity %	28.88	-49.80	n.a.
Return on Average Assets %	17.85	-13.53	-174.67
Current Ratio	1.60	0.35	0.22
Debt / Equity %	16.37	50.80	245.08

Compound Growth %'s	EPS % n.a.	Net Income % n.a.	Total Revenues % 199.76

Comments

The Company changed to calendar year reporting in 1997. All period presented are for a full twelve months. For the two months ended December 31, 1996, not included above, the Company reported revenues of $769,516 and a loss of $271,356 ($.03 per share). During 1998, there was a significant increase in the refinance market as a result of the low mortgage interest rates. Low mortgage interest rates coupled with a strong economy also had a positive impact on the volume of residential home sales. The 178% increase in revenues experienced in 1998 is mostly attributable to expansion and increased market share with only a quarter of the increase attributable to acquisitions. Tax loss carryovers, which kept 1998 income tax to a minimum, have now been fully utilized.

Officers	Position	Ownership Information	
Donald R. Head	Chairman, CEO	Number of Shares Outstanding	16,926,791
Andrew A. Johns	President	Market Capitalization	$ 57,043,286
Milt Ferrantelli	Exec VP	Number of Shareholders	2,000
Mark C. Walker	VP - Finance, CFO	Where Listed / Symbol	NASDAQ / CTGI

Other Information			
Transfer Agent	Western States Transfer & Registrar Salt Lake City, UT	SIC Code	6360
Auditor	Ernst & Young LLP	Employees	477
		Web Site	capitaltitlegroup.com

CareAdvantage, Inc.

485-C Route 1 South, 4th Floor   Inselin, NJ 08830   Telephone (732)602-7000   Fax (732)602-7027

Company Description

CareAdvantage, Inc. is in the business of providing health care cost containment services designed to enable health care insurers and other health service organizations to reduce the costs of medical services provided to their subscribers. The services provided include utilization review in medical/surgical cases where pre-authorization is required for hospitalization and for certain in-patient and outpatient procedures, case management and disease management. The Company's services have been principally provided to the statewide Blue Cross/Blue Shield health service organizations in the northeastern United States. The Company was founded in 1994.

	10/31/98	10/31/97	10/31/96	10/31/95
Per Share Information				
Stock Price as of 12/31	0.03	0.23	0.31	1.50
Earnings Per Share	0.04	0.0	-0.23	0.95
Price / Earnings Ratio	0.75	n.a.	n.a.	1.58
Book Value Per Share	0.04	-0.03	-0.08	-0.10
Price / Book Value %	75.00	n.a.	n.a.	n.a.
Dividends Per Share	0.0	0.0	0.0	0.0
Annual Financial Data				
Operating Results (000's)				
Total Revenues	18,903.0	14,076.6	11,792.2	8,971.0
Costs & Expenses	-15,655.0	-14,069.4	-17,127.1	-21,962.9
Income Before Taxes and Other	3,248.0	7.2	-5,334.9	-12,991.9
Other Items	0.0	0.0	0.0	0.0
Income Tax	-165.0	0.0	0.0	0.0
Net Income	3,083.0	7.2	-5,334.9	-12,991.9
Cash Flow From Operations	4,415.0	1,117.3	-2,569.1	-3,978.0
Balance Sheet (000's)				
Cash & Equivalents	3,745.0	1,038.2	1,167.1	536.5
Total Current Assets	5,567.0	2,748.4	2,220.3	692.0
Fixed Assets, Net	1,374.0	1,502.7	1,480.7	2,077.3
Total Assets	8,800.0	5,981.2	5,861.0	4,432.6
Total Current Liabilities	4,490.0	5,235.2	6,411.6	3,602.1
Long-Term Debt	0.0	0.0	996.6	1,493.1
Stockholders' Equity	3,484.0	-1,975.9	-1,983.1	-662.6
Performance & Financial Condition				
Return on Total Revenues %	16.31	0.05	-45.24	-144.82
Return on Avg Stockholders' Equity %	408.86	n.a.	n.a.	-296.28
Return on Average Assets %	41.72	0.12	-103.65	-180.23
Current Ratio	1.24	0.52	0.35	0.19
Debt / Equity %	n.a.	n.a.	n.a.	n.a.

Compound Growth %'s	EPS % n.a.	Net Income % n.a.	Total Revenues % 28.20

Comments

During fiscal 1996, the Company executed a 1 for 6 reverse stock split. All per share amounts have been adjusted for consistency. The Company had a positive working capital at the end of fiscal 1998. This was achieved by converting a note payable to stock and generating cash flow from operations. Approximately one-half of the increase in revenues was attributable to a re-negotiation of the Company's existing contracts. The loss of two key contracts may have been the culprit in hammering the stock price down to $.03 per share at December 31, 1998. As we went to press a strong recovery was in process. Any valuation will obviously be reflective of the 82 million shares of common stock outstanding.

Officers	Position	Ownership Information	
William J. Marino	Chairman	Number of Shares Outstanding	82,189,883
Richard W. Freeman	President, COO	Market Capitalization	$ 2,465,696
David Noone	CEO	Number of Shareholders	2,892
Stephan D. Deutsch	Senior VP	Where Listed / Symbol	OTC-BB / CADV

Other Information			
Transfer Agent	American Stock Transfer & Trust Co. New York, NY	SIC Code	8741
Auditor	Richard A. Eisner & Co., LLP	Employees	142
Market Maker	Carr Securities Corporation (800)221-2243		
	Furman Selz LLC (800)448-3223		

Carlyle Industries, Inc.

One Palmer Terrace   Carlstadt, NJ 07072   Telephone (201)935-6220   Fax (212)239-8696

Company Description

Carlyle Industries, Inc., formerly Belding Heminway Company, distributes a line of home sewing and craft products, principally buttons. The Company packages and distributes an extensive variety of buttons and embellishments for home sewing and crafts to mass merchandisers, specialty chains and independent retailers and wholesalers throughout the United States. The Company also produces and distributes a private-label line for one of the nation's best-known retailers. Additionally, the Company markets complimentary product lines, including appliques, craft kits and fashion and jewelry accessories to its home sewing and craft customers.

	12/31/98	12/31/97	12/31/96	12/31/95
Per Share Information				
Stock Price	1.06	1.50	2.37	3.12
Earnings Per Share	0.27	-1.06	0.43	-5.51
Price / Earnings Ratio	3.93	n.a.	5.51	n.a.
Book Value Per Share	-2.34	-2.62	-1.55	-1.98
Price / Book Value %	n.a.	n.a.	n.a.	n.a.
Dividends Per Share	0.0	0.0	0.0	0.0
Annual Financial Data				
Operating Results (000's)				
Total Revenues	23,801.0	19,641.0	22,162.0	20,352.0
Costs & Expenses	-18,774.0	-13,793.0	-17,660.0	-18,792.0
Income Before Taxes and Other	5,027.0	5,848.0	4,502.0	1,560.0
Other Items	0.0	-10,117.0	1,814.0	-40,485.0
Income Tax	-1,867.0	-2,121.0	-1,744.0	-628.0
Net Income	3,160.0	-6,390.0	4,572.0	-39,553.0
Cash Flow From Operations	-4,897.0	-2,237.0	2,460.0	102.0
Balance Sheet (000's)				
Cash & Equivalents	55.0	12,475.0	131.0	629.0
Total Current Assets	12,213.0	20,914.0	62,273.0	32,356.0
Fixed Assets, Net	1,829.0	1,770.0	2,650.0	29,475.0
Total Assets	17,824.0	25,062.0	67,169.0	94,124.0
Total Current Liabilities	3,025.0	10,268.0	10,346.0	22,570.0
Long-Term Debt	10,421.0	78.0	33,058.0	44,666.0
Stockholders' Equity	-17,285.0	-19,306.0	-11,471.0	-14,677.0
Performance & Financial Condition				
Return on Total Revenues %	13.28	-32.53	20.63	-194.34
Return on Avg Stockholders' Equity %	n.a.	n.a.	n.a.	-688.78
Return on Average Assets %	14.74	-13.86	5.67	-41.81
Current Ratio	4.04	2.04	6.02	1.43
Debt / Equity %	n.a.	n.a.	n.a.	n.a.

Compound Growth %'s	EPS %	-20.76	Net Income %	-16.86	Total Revenues %	5.36

Comments

The Company acquired Westwater Industries, Inc. in June 1998. The transaction was recorded using the purchase method of accounting. Westwater has contributed $4.7 million in incremental sales since the date of the acquisition which has more than offset a small decline in recurring operations. 1998 demonstrated a return to profitability and an improving financial condition. 1997 and 1995 results include losses from discontinued operations of $10.1 million ($1.37 per share) and $40.5 million ($5.46 per share), respectively. 1996 results include nonrecurring gains of $1.8 million ($.24 per share). Dividends on preferred stock have been deducted in determining earnings per common share. Approximately one-half of the preferred shares were redeemed in 1998.

Officers	**Position**	**Ownership Information**	
Robert A. Levinson	President, CEO	Number of Shares Outstanding	7,382,782
Edward F. Cooke	Vice President, CFO	Market Capitalization	$ 7,825,749
Robin R. Hoy	Vice President, Controller	Number of Shareholders	2,148
		Where Listed / Symbol	OTC-BB / CRLH

Other Information			
Transfer Agent	Bank of New York New York, NY	SIC Code	2200
Auditor	Arthur Andersen LLP	Employees	170
Market Maker	Herzog, Heine, Geduld, Inc. (800)221-3600		
	Wien Securities Corp. (800)624-0050		

Casa Olé Restaurants, Inc.

1135 Edgebrook Houston, TX 77034-1899   Telephone (713)943-7574   Fax (713)943-9554

Company Description

Casa Olé Restaurants, Inc., soon to become Mexican Restaurants Inc., operates and franchises Mexican-theme, neighborhood family dining restaurants featuring traditional Mexican and Tex-Mex selections, under the name Casa Olé. The first Casa Olé restaurant was opened in 1973 in Pasadena, Texas. The Company now operates 47 restaurants and franchises 32 restaurants in various communities across Texas, Louisiana, Oklahoma, Idaho, West Virginia and Tennessee. The restaurants are designed to appeal to a broad range of middle-income customers and are located primarily in small and medium-sized communities. The restaurants offer fresh, quality food, affordable prices, friendly service and comfortable surroundings. The Company had its initial public offering in April 1996. There was no public market for the Company's stock prior to that date.

	01/03/99	12/28/97	12/27/96	12/29/95
Per Share Information				
Stock Price as of 12/31	4.00	3.50	8.75	n.a.
Earnings Per Share	0.54	0.28	0.53	n.a.
Price / Earnings Ratio	7.41	12.50	16.51	n.a.
Book Value Per Share	3.77	3.26	2.98	n.a.
Price / Book Value %	106.10	107.36	293.62	n.a.
Dividends Per Share	0.0	0.0	0.0	n.a.
Annual Financial Data				
Operating Results (000's)				
Total Revenues	47,139.4	35,751.3	19,029.8	17,760.7
Costs & Expenses	-43,997.0	-33,652.9	-16,303.5	-16,281.3
Income Before Taxes and Other	3,142.4	2,098.4	2,726.3	1,479.5
Other Items	40.0	-433.2	-48.7	44.2
Income Tax	-1,209.8	-650.4	-858.2	-75.0
Net Income	1,972.6	1,014.8	1,819.5	1,448.7
Cash Flow From Operations	2,083.6	2,583.5	2,381.2	1,665.6
Balance Sheet (000's)				
Cash & Equivalents	462.8	986.0	6,419.3	1,003.6
Total Current Assets	2,203.8	2,521.5	8,204.0	1,479.6
Fixed Assets, Net	14,042.6	17,298.5	3,855.8	1,378.8
Total Assets	23,421.0	26,508.1	12,145.8	2,858.3
Total Current Liabilities	3,251.2	4,545.0	1,347.3	861.6
Long-Term Debt	2,870.0	121.1	0.0	62.5
Stockholders' Equity	13,559.2	11,735.2	10,720.4	1,934.2
Performance & Financial Condition				
Return on Total Revenues %	4.18	2.84	9.56	8.16
Return on Avg Stockholders' Equity %	15.60	9.04	28.76	81.66
Return on Average Assets %	7.90	5.25	24.25	50.40
Current Ratio	0.68	0.55	6.09	1.72
Debt / Equity %	21.17	1.03	n.a.	3.23

Compound Growth %'s	EPS %	0.94	Net Income %	10.84	Total Revenues %	38.45

Comments

Revenue increased substantially in 1998 as the result of the inclusion of restaurants that were acquired in 1997 for a full twelve months in 1998. Same-store sales rose 2.44% and franchise-owned same-store sales rose 4.76%. Net income rebounded to a record level. In 1997, management experienced operational and concept difficulties which necessitated the closing of one restaurant, a few other asset write-downs, and certain restructuring costs which totalled $433,173. There remains a huge deficit in working capital and $10 million of long term debt. Furthermore, approximately 46% of stockholders' equity and book value per share is represented by goodwill of $6.3 million. An acquisition of La Señorita Restaurants in Michigan is expected to close in the second quarter of 1999.

Officers	Position	Ownership Information	
Louis P. Neeb	Chairman, CEO	Number of Shares Outstanding	3,597,705
Curt Glowacki	President, COO	Market Capitalization	$ 14,390,820
Charles T. Badrick	Secretary	Number of Shareholders	600
Andrew J. Dennard	Vice President, Controller	Where Listed / Symbol	NASDAQ / CASA

Other Information			
Transfer Agent	Harris Trust & Savings Bank Chicago, IL	SIC Code	5812
Auditor	KPMG LLP	Employees	1,900
		Web Site	casaole.com

Cell Robotics International, Inc.

2715 Broadbent Parkway N.E. Albuquerque, NM 87107 Telephone (505)343-1131 Fax (505)344-8112

Company Description

Cell Robotics International develops, manufactures and markets a series of laser-based medical devices with applications in the blood sample collection, skin resurfacing, and in vitro fertilization markets. The Lasette™ is a compact, lightweight, portable skin perforator which has been designed to permit nearly painless sampling of the capillary blood in both clinical and home settings for the purpose of subsequent glucose or hematocrit testing. The Company also develops, produces and markets a line of advanced scientific instruments which increase the usefulness and importance of the conventional laboratory microscope. All products are marketed in both domestic and international markets. The Company was founded in 1988.

	12/31/98	12/31/97	12/31/96	12/31/95
Per Share Information				
Stock Price	2.56	2.81	2.00	2.75
Earnings Per Share	-0.39	-0.48	-0.37	-0.66
Price / Earnings Ratio	n.a.	n.a.	n.a.	n.a.
Book Value Per Share	-0.27	0.08	0.44	0.44
Price / Book Value %	n.a.	3,512.50	454.55	625.00
Dividends Per Share	0.0	0.0	0.0	0.0
Annual Financial Data				
Operating Results (000's)				
Total Revenues	1,514.4	1,081.5	725.0	959.8
Costs & Expenses	-3,297.8	-3,554.4	-2,269.0	-2,267.0
Income Before Taxes and Other	-1,783.3	-2,472.9	-1,544.1	-1,351.2
Other Items	0.0	0.0	0.0	0.0
Income Tax	0.0	0.0	0.0	0.0
Net Income	-1,783.3	-2,472.9	-1,544.1	-1,351.2
Cash Flow From Operations	-1,935.8	-2,253.9	-1,315.9	-1,267.9
Balance Sheet (000's)				
Cash & Equivalents	1,375.6	623.6	1,724.7	740.0
Total Current Assets	2,271.7	1,469.6	2,221.8	1,752.7
Fixed Assets, Net	272.9	194.7	256.6	213.4
Total Assets	2,583.1	1,979.8	2,571.0	2,000.1
Total Current Liabilities	533.3	1,035.0	363.7	310.2
Long-Term Debt	0.0	0.0	0.0	0.0
Stockholders' Equity	2,049.7	444.9	2,207.2	1,689.9
Performance & Financial Condition				
Return on Total Revenues %	-117.76	-228.65	-212.99	-140.77
Return on Avg Stockholders' Equity %	-142.98	-186.49	-79.24	n.a.
Return on Average Assets %	-78.17	-108.68	-67.56	-100.71
Current Ratio	4.26	1.42	6.11	5.65
Debt / Equity %	n.a.	n.a.	n.a.	n.a.

Compound Growth %'s	EPS %	n.a.	Net Income %	n.a.	Total Revenues %	16.42

Comments

In 1998, the Company introduced to market three of its laser-based product lines, achieved major regulatory breakthroughs with both the federal Food and Drug Administration and the European Community, and greatly enhanced its marketing and sales base through the execution of key distribution and manufacturer's representatives agreements. But the Company's operating activities were still limited to continuing efforts to complete the development of its laser-based medical devices and make their initial introduction. Product sales were generated only from sales of scientific research instruments. Since its inception, the Company has relied principally upon the proceeds of both debt and equity financings to provide working capital. $3.8 million of working capital was generated during 1998 by issuing preferred stock. Tax loss carryforwards of approximately $14 million are available to offset future income.

Officers	Position	Ownership Information	
Ronald K. Lohrding	President, CEO	Number of Shares Outstanding	6,739,248
Jean Scharf	CFO	Market Capitalization	$ 17,252,475
Craig T. Rogers	Secretary, Treasurer	Number of Shareholders	1,000
Raymond Radosevich	Director	Where Listed / Symbol	OTC-BB / CRII

Other Information			
Transfer Agent	Corporate Stock Transfer, Inc. Denver, CO	SIC Code	3826
Auditor	KPMG LLP	Employees	18
Market Maker	Paragon Capital Corporation (800)345-0505	Web Site	cellrobotics.com
	Mayer & Schweitzer, Inc. (800)631-3094		

Celox Laboratories, Inc.

1311 Helmo Avenue   St. Paul, MN 55128   Telephone (651)730-1500   Fax (651)730-8900

Company Description

Celox Laboratories, Inc. is a biotechnology company formed in 1985 that researches, develops, manufactures, and markets cell biology products which are used in the propagation of cells derived from mammals, including humans. These specialized cell growth products are used primarily in academic, pharmaceutical and other commercial laboratories to improve the growth, productivity and quality of cell-derived medical and other biological products such as vaccines, monoclonal antibodies, interferons, and human growth factor. Since its inception, the Company has pursued a strategy of developing non-serum-based products for the growth of human and other mammalian cells. The development of genetic engineering and the use of mammalian cells for the production of biological products has advanced cell culturing to new levels. Management believes this has significant commercial potential.

	08/31/98	08/31/97	08/31/96	08/31/95
Per Share Information				
Stock Price as of 12/31	0.09	0.62	0.56	0.69
Earnings Per Share	-0.11	-0.14	-0.14	-0.13
Price / Earnings Ratio	n.a.	n.a.	n.a.	n.a.
Book Value Per Share	0.36	0.47	0.61	0.77
Price / Book Value %	25.00	131.91	91.80	89.61
Dividends Per Share	0.0	0.0	0.0	0.0
Annual Financial Data				
Operating Results (000's)				
Total Revenues	335.6	289.2	507.6	291.8
Costs & Expenses	-638.2	-648.6	-891.7	-892.0
Income Before Taxes and Other	-302.6	-388.5	-384.0	-600.2
Other Items	0.0	0.0	0.0	253.6
Income Tax	0.0	0.0	0.0	0.0
Net Income	-302.6	-388.5	-384.0	-346.6
Cash Flow From Operations	-258.8	-261.4	-391.1	-420.0
Balance Sheet (000's)				
Cash & Equivalents	809.6	1,145.4	420.2	919.4
Total Current Assets	885.9	1,259.3	1,632.2	1,906.3
Fixed Assets, Net	171.7	170.2	93.6	126.1
Total Assets	1,116.4	1,448.3	1,748.3	2,165.4
Total Current Liabilities	120.2	152.4	63.2	52.9
Long-Term Debt	0.0	0.0	0.0	0.0
Stockholders' Equity	996.2	1,295.8	1,684.3	2,107.1
Performance & Financial Condition				
Return on Total Revenues %	-90.18	-134.31	-75.65	-118.79
Return on Avg Stockholders' Equity %	-26.41	-26.07	-20.26	-15.27
Return on Average Assets %	-23.60	-24.31	-19.62	-14.72
Current Ratio	7.37	8.26	25.83	36.02
Debt / Equity %	n.a.	n.a.	n.a.	n.a.

Compound Growth %'s	EPS % n.a.	Net Income % n.a.	Total Revenues % 4.77

Comments

Research and development expenses increased by 119% to $104,309 in fiscal 1998. The increase between years results from the timing and amount of professional fees and other costs associated with patent applications. Although the Company has completed the research and development of most of its current products, it intends to refine these products, as necessary, to meet customer requirements and to take advantage of technological changes. The issue remains as to the prospect of increased revenue. Management intends to focus attention to just that, but does not expect that fiscal 1999 will be the first profitable year. For the six months ended February 28, 1999, revenues and the net loss were $92,350 and $181,180 ($.07 per share).

Officers	Position	Ownership Information	
Milo R. Polovina	President, CEO	Number of Shares Outstanding	2,744,169
		Market Capitalization	$ 246,975
		Number of Shareholders	900
		Where Listed / Symbol	OTC-BB / CELX

Other Information

Transfer Agent	Norwest Bank Minnesota, N.A. Minneapolis, MN		SIC Code	2836
Auditor	Boulay, Heutmaker, Zibell		Employees	4
Market Maker	Herzog, Heine, Geduld, Inc.	(800)221-3600		
	Wien Securities Corp.	(800)624-0050		

Central Financial Acceptance Corporation

5480 East Ferguson Drive   Commerce, CA 90022   Telephone (323)720-8600   Fax (323)720-8647

Company Description

Central Financial Acceptance Corporation is a specialized consumer finance company that primarily serves the financing needs of the rapidly growing low income Hispanic population. The Company does the following: provides small, unsecured personal loans; purchases and services consumer finance receivables that customers generate for purchases of high quality brand name consumer products, appliances and furniture sold by Banner's Central Electric, Inc., an affiliate of the Company, and by independent retailers; sells airline tickets and originates and services travel-related finance receivables; and provides insurance products and insurance premium financing to customers. The Company has been operated under varying ownership since 1956 and had its initial public offering on June 26, 1996, with the issuance of 2,127,000 shares at $15 per share.

	12/31/98	12/31/97	12/31/96	12/31/95
Per Share Information				
Stock Price	3.87	9.25	19.00	15.00
Earnings Per Share	0.60	0.60	0.95	0.61
Price / Earnings Ratio	6.45	15.42	20.00	24.59
Book Value Per Share	9.64	9.03	8.43	6.53
Price / Book Value %	40.15	102.44	225.39	229.71
Dividends Per Share	0.0	0.0	0.0	0.0
Annual Financial Data				
Operating Results (000's)				
Total Revenues	46,888.0	52,040.0	36,427.0	22,163.0
Costs & Expenses	-39,554.0	-44,827.0	-26,478.0	-17,015.0
Income Before Taxes and Other	7,334.0	7,213.0	9,949.0	5,148.0
Other Items	0.0	0.0	-91.0	50.0
Income Tax	-2,933.0	-2,823.0	-3,979.0	-2,079.0
Net Income	4,401.0	4,390.0	5,879.0	3,119.0
Cash Flow From Operations	19,719.0	9,610.0	16,312.0	9,227.0
Balance Sheet (000's)				
Cash & Equivalents	8,295.0	4,794.0	5,848.0	57.0
Total Current Assets	12,634.0	111,087.0	128,884.0	94,731.0
Fixed Assets, Net	6,677.0	5,880.0	3,425.0	3,000.0
Total Assets	129,085.0	135,149.0	145,357.0	101,730.0
Total Current Liabilities	6,941.0	6,556.0	8,178.0	4,131.0
Long-Term Debt	52,000.0	62,850.0	74,874.0	63,967.0
Stockholders' Equity	70,144.0	65,743.0	61,353.0	33,632.0
Performance & Financial Condition				
Return on Total Revenues %	9.39	8.44	16.14	14.07
Return on Avg Stockholders' Equity %	6.48	6.91	12.38	10.83
Return on Average Assets %	3.33	3.13	4.76	3.55
Current Ratio	1.82	16.94	15.76	22.93
Debt / Equity %	74.13	95.60	122.04	190.20

Compound Growth %'s	EPS %	-0.55	Net Income %	12.16	Total Revenues %	28.37

Comments

In February 1998, the Company entered into a definitive agreement to acquire Mission Savings and Loan Association of Riverside, California. The transaction was awaiting regulatory approval as we went to press. The provision for loan losses in 1998 decreased to $8.8 million from the $12.3 million that was expensed in 1997. The decrease results from the Company's decision in 1997 to phase out its relationship with approximately 100 small retailers regarded as high credit risks. At December 31, 1998, the Company had $8.7 million of intangible assets recorded on its books which equated to only 12.3% of stockholders' equity and book value per share.

Officers	Position	Ownership Information	
Gary M. Cypres	Chairman, CEO	Number of Shares Outstanding	7,277,000
Anthony S. Fortunato	President	Market Capitalization	$ 28,161,990
Russell J. Grisanti	Senior VP	Number of Shareholders	1,000
A. Keith Wall	CFO	Where Listed / Symbol	NASDAQ / CFAC

Other Information			
Transfer Agent	U.S. Stock Transfer Corp. Glendale, CA	SIC Code	6141
Auditor	Arthur Andersen LLP	Employees	528

Centrum Industries, Inc.

6135 Trust Drive, Suite 104A   Holland, OH 43528   Telephone (419)838-3441   Fax (419)838-3490

Company Description

Centrum Industries, Inc. has three distinct business segments: metal forming operations produces specialty steel forgings, steel seamless rolled rings, and nonferrous castings; material handling systems offers material handling systems and components to companies with warehouse and distribution facilities; and, motor production systems designs and manufactures armature and stator winding machines and complete production systems for small fractional horsepower electric motors used primarily in the automotive and consumer durable goods markets. All of these businesses have been acquired since 1993.

	03/31/98	03/31/97	03/31/96	03/31/95
Per Share Information				
Stock Price as of 12/31	1.44	1.87	2.12	0.62
Earnings Per Share	0.15	0.28	0.13	0.03
Price / Earnings Ratio	9.60	6.68	16.31	20.67
Book Value Per Share	1.12	1.04	0.58	0.26
Price / Book Value %	128.57	179.81	365.52	238.46
Dividends Per Share	0.0	0.0	0.0	0.0
Annual Financial Data				
Operating Results (000's)				
Total Revenues	79,793.7	71,429.5	27,638.7	18,353.1
Costs & Expenses	-77,848.9	-69,752.9	-26,575.7	-17,966.1
Income Before Taxes and Other	1,944.8	1,676.6	1,063.1	386.9
Other Items	0.0	0.0	0.0	0.0
Income Tax	-639.5	773.7	-257.8	-223.7
Net Income	1,305.3	2,450.3	805.2	163.2
Cash Flow From Operations	3,711.3	-1,579.3	509.9	-131.2
Balance Sheet (000's)				
Cash & Equivalents	1,297.7	2,758.2	2,100.7	473.0
Total Current Assets	30,394.1	25,768.4	23,195.2	5,393.0
Fixed Assets, Net	17,204.1	10,627.8	11,062.2	4,000.0
Total Assets	53,171.7	43,000.6	40,611.7	9,547.0
Total Current Liabilities	31,288.9	22,640.4	24,028.7	4,432.0
Long-Term Debt	11,180.9	11,021.9	12,173.4	3,609.0
Stockholders' Equity	10,124.3	8,742.6	3,583.0	1,506.0
Performance & Financial Condition				
Return on Total Revenues %	1.64	3.43	2.91	0.89
Return on Avg Stockholders' Equity %	13.84	39.76	31.65	12.55
Return on Average Assets %	2.71	5.86	3.21	1.87
Current Ratio	0.97	1.14	0.97	1.22
Debt / Equity %	110.44	126.07	339.76	239.64

Compound Growth %'s	EPS %	71.00	Net Income %	99.97	Total Revenues %	63.21

Comments

The increase in fiscal 1998 revenues is attributable to an acquisition. Excluding the current year acquisition, revenues declined 7.1% primarily as a result of a shift in product mix in the motor production business. Income also included a one-time gain of $745,000 related to the relinquishment of a contractual right to purchase a property. Fiscal 1997 results include an income tax benefit of $773,675 due to an adjustment in the accrual of deferred income taxes. The increase in fiscal 1997 revenues as compared to fiscal 1996 is attributable to the inclusion of the metal forming business, which was acquired in March 1996, for a full year. For the nine months ended December 31, 1998, revenues and a net loss were $59.5 million and $651,000 ($.07 per share) as compared to $56.8 million and a net profit of $1,009,633 ($.12 per share) for the same period of the preceding year.

Officers	Position	Ownership Information	
George H. Wells	CEO	Number of Shares Outstanding	8,403,501
Anthony A. Montani	COO	Market Capitalization	$ 12,101,041
Timothy M. Hunter	CFO	Number of Shareholders	1,000
		Where Listed / Symbol	OTC-BB / CIII

Other Information

Transfer Agent	KeyCorp Shareholder Services, Inc. Brooklyn, OH		SIC Code	3537
Auditor	PricewaterhouseCoopers LLP		Employees	515
Market Maker	Troster Singer Corporation	(800)526-3160		
	Paragon Capital Corporation	(800)345-0505		

Ceramics Process Systems Corporation

111 South Worcester Steet, P.O. Box 338   Chartley, MA 02712   Telephone (508)222-0614   Fax (508)222-0220

Company Description

Ceramics Process Systems Corporation serves the wireless communications, satellite communications, motor controller and other microelectronic markets. The Company develops, manufactures, and markets advanced metal-matrix composite and ceramic components to house, interconnect and thermally manage microelectronic devices. The Company's products are typically in the form of housings, packages, lids, substrates, thermal planes, or heat sinks, and are used in applications where thermal management and/or weight are important considerations. Although the Company's focus is in microelectronics markets, it participates in other markets by licensing its technology to companies who manufacture and sell products in those other markets. The Company was founded in 1984.

	12/26/98	12/27/97	12/28/96	12/27/95
Per Share Information				
Stock Price as of 12/31	1.25	2.25	0.31	0.34
Earnings Per Share	0.14	0.18	-0.05	-0.14
Price / Earnings Ratio	8.93	12.50	n.a.	n.a.
Book Value Per Share	0.19	-0.19	-0.37	-0.19
Price / Book Value %	657.89	n.a.	n.a.	n.a.
Dividends Per Share	0.0	0.0	0.0	0.0
Annual Financial Data				
Operating Results (000's)				
Total Revenues	5,657.5	4,607.6	2,038.7	1,388.3
Costs & Expenses	-3,854.2	-3,230.5	-2,450.0	-2,437.1
Income Before Taxes and Other	1,803.3	1,377.1	-411.3	-1,107.5
Other Items	0.0	0.0	0.0	0.0
Income Tax	-130.9	0.0	0.0	0.0
Net Income	1,672.4	1,377.1	-411.3	-1,107.5
Cash Flow From Operations	1,603.1	784.2	202.9	-565.3
Balance Sheet (000's)				
Cash & Equivalents	1,498.8	561.2	113.3	32.1
Total Current Assets	2,251.9	1,326.1	412.2	604.4
Fixed Assets, Net	723.6	573.5	380.7	327.5
Total Assets	2,984.3	1,904.7	795.2	931.9
Total Current Liabilities	470.0	3,114.4	3,611.9	769.6
Long-Term Debt	0.0	137.9	0.0	0.0
Stockholders' Equity	2,389.2	-1,519.6	-2,904.7	-1,457.8
Performance & Financial Condition				
Return on Total Revenues %	29.56	29.89	-20.17	-79.77
Return on Avg Stockholders' Equity %	384.68	n.a.	n.a.	n.a.
Return on Average Assets %	68.42	102.01	-47.63	-108.35
Current Ratio	4.79	0.43	0.11	0.79
Debt / Equity %	n.a.	n.a.	n.a.	n.a.

Compound Growth %'s	EPS % n.a.	Net Income % n.a.	Total Revenues %	59.73

Comments

Revenue increased 128% during 1997, due primarily to a shift in mix from small prototyping runs to recurring production of several products. Because metal-matrix composites are relatively new materials, the Company's customers often take one to three years to evaluate prototypes and modify designs to take advantage of the benefits that metal-matrix composites offer. It is only then that they begin to purchase production quantities. Revenues advanced another 20.4% in 1998, benefiting from the same trend started in 1997. In 1998, the Company's three largest customers accounted for 72%, 13% and 6% of total revenues, respectively. The Company also substantially improved its financial condition by issuing new common shares in satisfaction of debt.

Officers	Position	Ownership Information	
Grant C. Bennett	President, CEO	Number of Shares Outstanding	12,285,969
H. Kent Bowen	Director	Market Capitalization	$ 15,357,461
Francis J. Hughes, Jr.	Director	Number of Shareholders	836
Michael Bernique	Director	Where Listed / Symbol	OTC-BB / CPSX

Other Information			
Transfer Agent	Registrar & Transfer Co. Cranford, NJ	SIC Code	3260
Auditor	PricewaterhouseCoopers LLP	Employees	40
Market Maker	Wm. V. Frankel & Co., Inc.	(800)631-3091	
	M.H. Meyerson & Co., Inc.	(800)333-3113	

Champion Parts, Inc.

751 Roosevelt Road, Building 7, Suite 110   Glen Ellyn, IL 60137   Telephone (630)942-8317   Fax (630)573-0348

Company Description

Champion Parts, Inc. remanufactures and sells replacement fuel system components (carburetors and diesel fuel injection components) and constant velocity drive assemblies for substantially all makes and models of domestic and foreign automobiles and trucks. It also remanufactures and sells replacement electrical and mechanical products for certain passenger car, agricultural and heavy duty truck original equipment applications. In 1995, the Company exited the manufacture and sale of passenger car electrical and mechanical products sold to traditional warehouse distributors and retailers which accounted for approximately 56% of the Company's 1995 revenues.

	12/27/98	12/28/97	12/29/96	12/31/95
Per Share Information				
Stock Price as of 12/31	0.55	0.22	0.39	0.39
Earnings Per Share	0.41	-0.05	-0.40	-5.15
Price / Earnings Ratio	1.34	n.a.	n.a.	n.a.
Book Value Per Share	-0.78	-1.25	-1.23	-0.80
Price / Book Value %	n.a.	n.a.	n.a.	n.a.
Dividends Per Share	0.0	0.0	0.0	0.0
Annual Financial Data				
Operating Results (000's)				
Total Revenues	26,798.0	24,165.0	27,556.0	52,954.0
Costs & Expenses	-25,532.0	-24,921.0	-29,016.0	-71,793.0
Income Before Taxes and Other	1,266.0	-756.0	-1,460.0	-18,839.0
Other Items	279.0	596.0	0.0	0.0
Income Tax	-42.0	0.0	-7.0	-1.0
Net Income	1,503.0	-160.0	-1,467.0	-18,840.0
Cash Flow From Operations	1,621.0	1,084.0	3,142.0	7,380.0
Balance Sheet (000's)				
Cash & Equivalents	784.0	488.0	707.0	874.0
Total Current Assets	12,667.0	11,936.0	13,689.0	18,141.0
Fixed Assets, Net	4,613.0	5,282.0	5,509.0	9,834.0
Total Assets	17,319.0	17,276.0	19,666.0	28,565.0
Total Current Liabilities	13,563.0	19,120.0	23,630.0	29,370.0
Long-Term Debt	6,263.0	2,377.0	43.0	701.0
Stockholders' Equity	-2,858.0	-4,572.0	-4,485.0	-2,909.0
Performance & Financial Condition				
Return on Total Revenues %	5.61	-0.66	-5.32	-35.58
Return on Avg Stockholders' Equity %	n.a.	n.a.	n.a.	n.a.
Return on Average Assets %	8.69	-0.87	-6.08	-44.92
Current Ratio	0.93	0.62	0.58	0.62
Debt / Equity %	n.a.	n.a.	n.a.	n.a.

Compound Growth %'s	EPS % n.a.	Net Income % n.a.	Total Revenues % -20.31

Comments

Included in 1998 and 1997 results are extraordinary gains of $279,000 ($.08 per share) and $596,000 ($.16 per share), respectively. 1995 results include a $6.1 million charge to reflect the Company's decision to exit the manufacturing and sale of automotive electrical and mechanical products as referred to above. The decline in revenues is also reflective of that decision. The auditors issued a going concern qualification in the 1997 report but changed the qualification to one of customer concentration in 1998. 82% of the Company's sales are concentrated in three customers. It appears that the worst is over as to the Company's restructuring. 1998 profits were impressive.

Officers	Position	Ownership Information	
Jerry A. Bragiel	President, CEO	Number of Shares Outstanding	3,655,266
Roland H. Millington	Treasurer	Market Capitalization	$ 2,010,396
Richard W. Simmons	Controller, Secretary	Number of Shareholders	776
Gary S. Hopmayer	Director	Where Listed / Symbol	OTC-BB / CREB

Other Information			
Transfer Agent	Exchange National Bank of Chicago Chicago, IL	SIC Code	3714
Auditor	BDO Seidman LLP	Employees	495
Market Maker	Troster Singer Corporation	(800)526-3160	Web Site	championauto.com
	M.H. Meyerson & Co., Inc.	(800)333-3113		

Charming Shoppes, Inc.

450 Winks Lane   Bensalem, PA 19020   Telephone (215)245-9100   Fax (215)638-6759

Company Description

Charming Shoppes, Inc. operates 1,135 women's specialty apparel stores in 42 states, the substantial majority of which are located in the northeast quadrant of the United States. The Company's 1,077 Fashion Bug stores specialize in selling, at moderate and popular prices, a wide variety of junior, misses, large-size and girls-size sportswear, dresses, coats, lingerie, accessories and casual footwear. The Company's stores sell both brand-name merchandise and specially manufactured garments under one of the Company's private labels. The Company was founded in 1969. On March 5, 1998, the Company announced plans to downsize approximately 100 stores and close approximately 65 underperforming stores.

	01/31/98	02/01/97	02/03/96	01/28/95
Per Share Information				
Stock Price as of 12/31	4.19	4.62	5.00	2.81
Earnings Per Share	0.18	-0.07	-1.35	0.42
Price / Earnings Ratio	23.28	n.a.	n.a.	6.69
Book Value Per Share	4.14	3.99	4.06	5.43
Price / Book Value %	101.21	115.79	123.15	51.75
Dividends Per Share	0.0	0.0	0.05	0.09
Annual Financial Data				
Operating Results (000's)				
Total Revenues	1,032,523.0	1,023,761.0	1,108,039.0	1,282,051.0
Costs & Expenses	-1,016,119.0	-1,033,681.0	-1,220,027.0	-1,219,532.0
Income Before Taxes and Other	16,404.0	-9,920.0	-214,988.0	62,519.0
Other Items	13,018.0	0.0	0.0	0.0
Income Tax	-10,088.0	2,683.0	75,747.0	-17,830.0
Net Income	19,334.0	-7,237.0	-139,241.0	44,689.0
Cash Flow From Operations	83,484.0	131,399.0	-55,434.0	70,700.0
Balance Sheet (000's)				
Cash & Equivalents	12,349.0	78,979.0	25,117.0	43,923.0
Total Current Assets	305,881.0	366,226.0	405,561.0	431,715.0
Fixed Assets, Net	186,004.0	200,394.0	234,588.0	325,000.0
Total Assets	709,738.0	710,397.0	681,746.0	840,809.0
Total Current Liabilities	142,673.0	142,082.0	206,104.0	239,900.0
Long-Term Debt	138,116.0	138,128.0	38,102.0	17,298.0
Stockholders' Equity	416,810.0	421,035.0	419,029.0	558,822.0
Performance & Financial Condition				
Return on Total Revenues %	1.87	-0.71	-12.57	3.49
Return on Avg Stockholders' Equity %	4.62	-1.72	-28.48	8.27
Return on Average Assets %	2.72	-1.04	-18.29	5.35
Current Ratio	2.14	2.58	1.97	1.80
Debt / Equity %	33.14	32.81	9.09	3.10

Compound Growth %'s	EPS %	-24.61	Net Income %	-24.37	Total Revenues %	-6.96

Comments

After a significant management and financial restructuring in the fall of 1995, the Company now focuses efforts on providing fashion apparel and related merchandise which meet the demands of its primary customers. Such customers are generally in the 20 to 45 year old age group, in the lower-middle to middle income range, and tend to follow, rather than set, fashion trends. Fiscal 1998 results include a nonrecurring gain of $13 million from asset restructuring. Fiscal 1996 results include a nonrecurring (so we hope) restructuring expense of $103 million. On November 2, 1997, the Board of Directors authorized the repurchase of 10 million shares of stock, approximately 10% of outstanding shares. By year end, 5,580,000 shares were acquired. For the year ended January 30, 1999, the Company reported revenues of $1.05 billion and a net loss of $20.1 million ($.20 per share), which included restructuring charges of $54.2 million. The full financials were not yet released when we went to press.

Officers	Position	Ownership Information	
Dorrit J. Bern	President, CEO	Number of Shares Outstanding	100,669,385
Eric M. Specter	Exec VP, CFO	Market Capitalization	$ 421,804,723
Colin D. Stern	Exec VP, Secretary	Number of Shareholders	2,839
Elizabeth Williams	Exec VP	Where Listed / Symbol	NASDAQ / CHRS

Other Information			
Transfer Agent	American Stock Transfer & Trust Co. New York, NY	SIC Code	5621
Auditor	Ernst & Young LLP	Employees	12,600

Chicago Pizza & Brewery, Inc.

26131 Marguerite Parkway, Suite A   Mission Viejo, CA 92692   Telephone (949)367-8616   Fax (949)367-8623

Company Description

Chicago Pizza & Brewery, Inc. owns and operates 26 restaurants in Southern California, Oregon, Washington and Colorado. It also has an interest in one restaurant in Lahaina, Maui. All units are operating under the names, BJ's Pizza, Grill & Brewery; BJ's Pizza & Grill; or Pietro's Pizza. The names identify the style of restaurant: brewery facilities on site, extensive menu and selection of foods and microbrewed beers, or limited dining service featuring pizza, pasta, sandwiches and salads. The Company was formed in 1991 and received $6.8 million in 1996 from an initial public offering. There was no public trading in the Company's stock prior to 1996.

	12/31/98	12/31/97	12/31/96	12/31/95
Per Share Information				
Stock Price	1.44	1.50	5.00	n.a.
Earnings Per Share	0.01	-0.05	-0.52	-0.55
Price / Earnings Ratio	144.00	n.a.	n.a.	n.a.
Book Value Per Share	1.86	1.84	1.89	1.06
Price / Book Value %	77.42	81.52	264.55	n.a.
Dividends Per Share	0.0	0.0	0.0	0.0
Annual Financial Data				
Operating Results (000's)				
Total Revenues	30,051.5	26,413.0	19,865.4	6,586.2
Costs & Expenses	-29,909.1	-26,716.1	-21,792.6	-8,108.5
Income Before Taxes and Other	142.4	-303.1	-2,307.3	-1,626.3
Other Items	-56.3	-11.1	27.2	26.8
Income Tax	-1.6	-0.8	-8.6	-6.4
Net Income	84.6	-314.9	-2,288.6	-1,605.9
Cash Flow From Operations	2,070.4	-147.0	-113.8	-973.3
Balance Sheet (000's)				
Cash & Equivalents	1,490.7	1,705.3	5,485.8	1,791.8
Total Current Assets	2,307.5	3,075.0	6,443.1	2,350.8
Fixed Assets, Net	9,567.6	8,673.8	6,234.1	1,870.5
Total Assets	17,594.7	17,841.8	18,913.7	9,943.2
Total Current Liabilities	3,103.1	2,843.3	3,114.5	2,329.1
Long-Term Debt	355.3	2,644.4	3,202.7	3,122.8
Stockholders' Equity	11,893.0	11,808.4	12,123.3	4,023.4
Performance & Financial Condition				
Return on Total Revenues %	0.28	-1.19	-11.52	-24.38
Return on Avg Stockholders' Equity %	0.71	-2.63	-28.35	-40.15
Return on Average Assets %	0.48	-1.71	-15.86	-20.07
Current Ratio	0.74	1.08	2.07	1.01
Debt / Equity %	2.99	22.39	26.42	77.61

Compound Growth %'s	EPS % n.a.	Net Income % n.a.	Total Revenues % 65.86

Comments

The Company experienced handsome same store sales increases in 1998, up 15.7% for the year. Higher customer counts, price increases, and better selling techniques all contributed to the rise. Revenues increased 31.8% during 1997, mostly as the result of new restaurants coming into operation. Same store sales increased 8.7% in 1997 for the restaurants that were open for a full year in 1996. The recent momentum allowed the Company to report its first year of net earnings. During 1995 and 1996, the Company incurred a number of nonrecurring charges in connection with the development and implementation of its extended menu, and a change in both restaurant concept and brewery concept. At December 31, 1998, the Company had $5.4 million of goodwill on the books which equated to approximately 45% of stockholders' equity and book value per share. The Company also had a deficit in working capital as of the last year end.

Officers	Position	Ownership Information	
Paul A. Motenko	Chairman, CEO	Number of Shares Outstanding	6,408,321
Jerry J. Hennessy	President, COO	Market Capitalization	$ 9,227,982
Alexander M. Puchner	Vice President	Number of Shareholders	1,000
Barry J. Grumman	Director	Where Listed / Symbol	NASDAQ / CHGO

Other Information			
Transfer Agent	U.S. Stock Transfer Corp. Glendale, CA	SIC Code	5812
Auditor	PricewaterhouseCoopers LLP	Employees	1,409
		Web Site	bjsbrewhouse.com

ChoiceTel Communications, Inc.

9724 10th Avenue North   Plymouth, MN 55441   Telephone (612)544-1260   Fax (612)544-1281

Company Description

ChoiceTel Communications, Inc. is the largest independent payphone service provider in Minnesota. The Company installed its first payphones in early 1990 and as of December 31, 1998, had an installed phone base of approximately 4,500 payphones in 14 states and Puerto Rico. The Company has grown its business through the installation of pay telephones in new areas and through strategic asset acquisitions of payphone routes and related assets. The Company was founded in 1989 and had its initial public offering in 1997. Most of the proceeds were used to pay down short term and acquisition related debt.

	12/31/98	12/31/97	12/31/96	12/31/95
Per Share Information				
Stock Price	2.50	4.50	7.00	n.a.
Earnings Per Share	0.04	-0.06	-0.31	0.04
Price / Earnings Ratio	62.50	n.a.	n.a.	n.a.
Book Value Per Share	2.05	2.00	0.35	0.30
Price / Book Value %	121.95	225.00	2,000.00	n.a.
Dividends Per Share	0.0	0.0	0.0	0.0
Annual Financial Data				
Operating Results (000's)				
Total Revenues	9,344.2	7,081.2	3,561.9	2,817.0
Costs & Expenses	-9,134.2	-7,365.4	-4,166.8	-2,695.0
Income Before Taxes and Other	210.1	-284.2	-604.9	122.0
Other Items	0.0	0.0	0.0	0.0
Income Tax	-95.0	150.0	0.0	-43.0
Net Income	115.1	-134.2	-604.9	79.0
Cash Flow From Operations	1,307.5	1,261.8	677.8	160.6
Balance Sheet (000's)				
Cash & Equivalents	363.2	343.7	952.5	29.1
Total Current Assets	2,817.6	3,223.1	1,270.8	217.6
Fixed Assets, Net	6,336.4	4,521.0	1,558.3	1,405.8
Total Assets	14,756.8	11,048.7	3,030.6	1,942.8
Total Current Liabilities	4,225.9	3,496.7	1,796.8	621.5
Long-Term Debt	3,891.7	1,270.0	569.7	828.5
Stockholders' Equity	5,986.1	5,833.1	664.1	492.7
Performance & Financial Condition				
Return on Total Revenues %	1.23	-1.89	-16.98	2.80
Return on Avg Stockholders' Equity %	1.95	-4.13	-104.59	15.80
Return on Average Assets %	0.89	-1.91	-24.33	3.95
Current Ratio	0.67	0.92	0.71	0.35
Debt / Equity %	65.01	21.77	85.79	168.15

Compound Growth %'s	EPS %	0.00	Net Income %	13.36	Total Revenues %	49.14

Comments

Revenues climbed 32% during 1998 due to a higher number of pay telephones in operation. Commencing in the fourth quarter of 1998, the Company experienced a significant decrease in coin revenues in the Midwest region. Management attributes the reduction to increased competition from wireless communication devices. At December 31, 1998, the Company had rental contracts of $5.5 million recorded as assets. This amount represents the purchase price paid for phone location agreements in excess of the purchase price of the related equipment on site and is therefore an intangible asset. This asset equates to approximately 92% of shareholders' equity and book value per share.

Officers	Position	Ownership Information	
Jeffrey R. Paletz	President	Number of Shares Outstanding	2,915,006
Melvin Graf	Exec VP, Secretary	Market Capitalization	$ 7,287,515
Jack S. Kohler	Vice President, CFO	Number of Shareholders	300
Dustin Elder	Vice President	Where Listed / Symbol	NASDAQ / PHON

Other Information			
Transfer Agent	American Stock Transfer & Trust Co. New York, NY	SIC Code	4813
Auditor	Schechter Dokken Kanter et al	Employees	65
		Web Site	choicetel.com

Circuit Systems, Inc.

2350 E. Lunt Avenue   Elk Grove Village, IL 60007   Telephone (847)439-1999   Fax (847)437-5910

Company Description

Circuit Systems, Inc. manufactures and sells single-sided, double-sided and multilayer printed circuit boards. All of the Company's printed circuit boards are specially designed by the customer and are manufactured to exacting customer specifications. The boards are sold primarily to original equipment and contract manufacturers of computers and peripherals, consumer and industrial electronic equipment and telecommunications equipment, primarily by independent sales representative companies. The Company also owns 488,413 shares of SigmaTron International, Inc., an electronics contract manufacturer, representing an approximate 17% interest. SigmaTron's common stock trades on the NASDAQ national market system under the symbol SGMA. The Company was founded in 1967.

	04/30/98	04/30/97	04/30/96	04/30/95
Per Share Information				
Stock Price as of 12/31	3.12	4.31	3.75	6.12
Earnings Per Share	-0.20	0.40	0.58	0.42
Price / Earnings Ratio	n.a.	10.78	6.47	14.57
Book Value Per Share	4.05	4.35	3.98	3.40
Price / Book Value %	77.04	99.08	94.22	180.00
Dividends Per Share	0.0	0.0	0.0	0.0
Annual Financial Data				
Operating Results (000's)				
Total Revenues	75,618.1	65,579.1	66,249.7	60,401.7
Costs & Expenses	-77,232.3	-62,243.1	-61,247.8	-56,713.2
Income Before Taxes and Other	-1,614.2	3,336.0	5,001.9	3,664.0
Other Items	0.0	0.0	0.0	0.0
Income Tax	631.0	-1,217.0	-1,918.0	-1,422.0
Net Income	-983.2	2,119.0	3,083.9	2,242.0
Cash Flow From Operations	-916.4	7,553.3	3,247.2	1,855.6
Balance Sheet (000's)				
Cash & Equivalents	1,531.5	294.2	243.3	127.9
Total Current Assets	26,384.8	14,071.5	16,564.2	14,846.1
Fixed Assets, Net	36,811.4	27,773.9	24,890.4	20,240.4
Total Assets	67,606.7	45,758.1	45,816.3	39,411.1
Total Current Liabilities	19,173.4	10,336.8	8,518.0	8,411.1
Long-Term Debt	27,380.1	10,640.4	14,535.8	11,622.4
Stockholders' Equity	18,527.4	22,461.7	21,202.4	18,118.5
Performance & Financial Condition				
Return on Total Revenues %	-1.30	3.23	4.65	3.71
Return on Avg Stockholders' Equity %	-4.80	9.71	15.69	11.80
Return on Average Assets %	-1.73	4.63	7.24	5.60
Current Ratio	1.38	1.36	1.94	1.77
Debt / Equity %	147.78	47.37	68.56	64.15

Compound Growth %'s	EPS % n.a.	Net Income % n.a.	Total Revenues % 7.78

Comments

The increase in fiscal 1998 revenues is attributable to acquisitions. A lower gross margin was the result of competitive pricing (partially stemming from the Asian economic crisis), operating inefficiencies during facility realignments, and sales volume that was well below the potential capacity. The Company reacquired 580,900 shares of its stock during fiscal 1998 at an average price of $4.88. For the nine months ended January 31, 1999, the Company reported revenues and net income of $68.4 million and $421,055 ($.10 per share) as compared to $52.2 million and a net loss of $534,671 ($.11 per share) for the same period of fiscal 1998.

Officers	**Position**	**Ownership Information**	
D. S. Patel	President, CEO	Number of Shares Outstanding	4,577,173
Magan H. Patel	Exec VP	Market Capitalization	$ 14,280,780
James E. Robbs	VP - Finance, CFO	Number of Shareholders	650
Thomas W. Rieck	Secretary	Where Listed / Symbol	NASDAQ / CSYI

Other Information			
Transfer Agent	American Stock Transfer & Trust Co. New York, NY	SIC Code	3672
Auditor	Grant Thornton LLP	Employees	625
		Web Site	cirsys.com

Cistron Biotechnology, Inc.

10 Bloomfield Avenue, Box 2004   Pine Brook, NJ 07058   Telephone (973)575-1700   Fax (973)575-4854

Company Description

Cistron Biotechnology, Inc. uses recombinant DNA and immunological techniques to manufacture a line of cytokine products which it sells to the research market worldwide. Cytokines, consisting of lymphokines and monokines, are proteins that are regulators of the human immune response system released in the body by white blood cells. The Company has also initiated development of immune system related products which may have applications in the diagnostic markets. The Company was formed in 1983.

	06/30/98	06/30/97	06/30/96	06/30/95
Per Share Information				
Stock Price as of 12/31	0.20	0.21	0.29	0.05
Earnings Per Share	-0.02	0.42	-0.04	0.01
Price / Earnings Ratio	n.a.	0.50	n.a.	5.00
Book Value Per Share	0.48	0.44	-0.02	0.02
Price / Book Value %	41.67	47.73	n.a.	250.00
Dividends Per Share	0.0	0.0	0.0	0.0
Annual Financial Data				
Operating Results (000's)				
Total Revenues	760.2	15,940.5	994.1	1,643.5
Costs & Expenses	-1,528.7	-2,103.3	-2,100.2	-1,358.5
Income Before Taxes and Other	-768.5	13,837.2	-1,106.2	285.0
Other Items	0.0	0.0	0.0	0.0
Income Tax	292.0	-1,491.3	0.0	-5.7
Net Income	-476.5	12,346.0	-1,106.2	279.3
Cash Flow From Operations	-140.5	6,267.4	-526.0	736.9
Balance Sheet (000's)				
Cash & Equivalents	5,832.0	6,368.2	359.6	891.2
Total Current Assets	9,207.2	9,428.3	602.0	1,050.9
Fixed Assets, Net	26.2	31.3	6.0	10.6
Total Assets	12,999.5	15,757.9	659.8	1,115.9
Total Current Liabilities	1,154.9	1,621.1	512.8	342.3
Long-Term Debt	0.0	0.0	747.6	0.0
Stockholders' Equity	10,942.5	11,745.7	-600.6	505.6
Performance & Financial Condition				
Return on Total Revenues %	-62.68	77.45	-111.28	16.99
Return on Avg Stockholders' Equity %	-4.20	221.55	n.a.	76.32
Return on Average Assets %	-3.31	150.40	-124.59	36.67
Current Ratio	7.97	5.82	1.17	3.07
Debt / Equity %	n.a.	n.a.	n.a.	n.a.

Compound Growth %'s	EPS % n.a.	Net Income % n.a.	Total Revenues % n.a.

Comments

In fiscal 1997, the Company settled certain litigation with Immunex Corporation whereby Immunex agreed to pay the Company $21 million over a number of years. $14.7 million of income was recognized as income after the deduction of legal fees. This left the Company with a substantial amount of cash in excess of normal business needs. In September 1997, the Company engaged the services of BlueStone Capital Partners to act as Cistron's financial advisor as to corporate strategic and financial initiatives. That engagement was apparently not successful as the Company has announced that it is looking for a new advisor. Book value per share, which is twice the trading price, is comprised largely of cash and amounts due from Immunex. For the six months ended December 31, 1998, the Company reported a net loss of $311,280 ($.01 per share) as compared to a net loss of $252,621 ($.01 per share) for the same period of fiscal 1998.

Officers	Position	Ownership Information	
Bruce C. Galton	President, CEO	Number of Shares Outstanding	22,983,687
Richard S. Dondero	Vice President	Market Capitalization	$ 4,596,737
Thomas P. Carney	Director	Number of Shareholders	735
Robert W. Naismith	Director	Where Listed / Symbol	OTC-BB / CIST

Other Information			
Transfer Agent	Continental Stock Transfer & Trust Co. New York, NY	SIC Code	2835
Auditor	Deloitte & Touche LLP	Employees	6
Market Maker	Herzog, Heine, Geduld, Inc. (800)221-3600	Web Site	cistronbio.com
	Paragon Capital Corporation (800)345-0505		

Coast Distribution System (The)

1982 Zanker Road   San Jose, CA 95112   Telephone (408)436-8611   Fax (408)436-0670

Company Description

The Coast Distribution System is the largest supplier of replacement parts, supplies and accessories for recreational vehicles, and one of the largest suppliers of replacement parts, supplies and accessories for boats, in North America. The Company supplies more than 25,000 products and serves more than 15,000 customers throughout the United States and Canada from 14 regional distribution centers in the United States and 4 regional distribution centers in Canada.

	12/31/98	12/31/97	12/31/96	12/31/95
Per Share Information				
Stock Price	2.87	3.12	3.62	6.00
Earnings Per Share	0.02	-1.01	-0.03	0.64
Price / Earnings Ratio	143.50	n.a.	n.a.	9.38
Book Value Per Share	6.41	6.48	7.57	7.58
Price / Book Value %	44.77	48.15	47.82	79.16
Dividends Per Share	0.0	0.0	0.0	0.0
Annual Financial Data				
Operating Results (000's)				
Total Revenues	148,680.0	136,625.0	143,169.0	170,763.0
Costs & Expenses	-147,627.0	-141,001.0	-143,486.0	-165,337.0
Income Before Taxes and Other	1,053.0	-4,376.0	-317.0	5,426.0
Other Items	0.0	-2,193.0	0.0	0.0
Income Tax	-927.0	1,303.0	194.0	-2,082.0
Net Income	126.0	-5,266.0	-123.0	3,344.0
Cash Flow From Operations	5,194.0	1,544.0	4,182.0	184.0
Balance Sheet (000's)				
Cash & Equivalents	435.0	308.0	214.0	501.0
Total Current Assets	52,351.0	57,404.0	60,039.0	63,473.0
Fixed Assets, Net	3,904.0	4,709.0	5,355.0	6,133.0
Total Assets	66,813.0	72,663.0	88,442.0	92,136.0
Total Current Liabilities	9,414.0	8,405.0	14,400.0	13,469.0
Long-Term Debt	23,175.0	29,726.0	33,771.0	38,691.0
Stockholders' Equity	33,831.0	33,996.0	39,450.0	39,392.0
Performance & Financial Condition				
Return on Total Revenues %	0.08	-3.85	-0.09	1.96
Return on Avg Stockholders' Equity %	0.37	-14.34	-0.31	8.90
Return on Average Assets %	0.18	-6.54	-0.14	3.76
Current Ratio	5.56	6.83	4.17	4.71
Debt / Equity %	68.50	87.44	85.60	98.22

Compound Growth %'s	EPS %	-68.50	Net Income %	-66.48	Total Revenues %	-4.51

Comments

The Company's major supplier decided to vertically integrate in early 1996. As a result, the Company encountered difficulties in meeting customer demand for its products in the spring and summer months of 1996, when demand is the highest. Although the supply problems were largely remedied by 1997, operating results were adversely affected as the Company was unable to recapture market share for the higher margin products that were affected by those problems. Also, 1997 results include a loss on the sale of investments of $2,193,000. Higher sales, partly from an acquisition, and improved gross margins helped pull the Company back to profitable results in 1998. At December 31, 1998, the Company had $8.1 million of goodwill recorded as assets which equated to approximately 24% of stockholders' equity and book value per share.

Officers	Position	Ownership Information	
Thomas R. McGuire	President, CEO	Number of Shares Outstanding	5,279,854
Sandra A. Knell	Exec VP, CFO	Market Capitalization	$ 15,153,181
Jeffrey R. Wannamaker	Exec VP	Number of Shareholders	1,265
David A. Berger	Exec VP	Where Listed / Symbol	AMEX / CRV

Other Information

Transfer Agent	ChaseMellon Shareholder Services Ridgefield Park, NJ	SIC Code	5013
Auditor	Grant Thornton LLP	Employees	360
		Web Site	rvamerica.com

Coda Music Technology, Inc.

6210 Bury Drive   Eden Prairie, MN 55346-1718   Telephone (612)937-9611   Fax (612)937-9760

Company Description

Coda Music Technology, Inc. develops and markets proprietary music technology products designed to enhance music learning and composition, increase productivity and make practicing and performing music fun. Since 1988, the Company and its predecessor have marketed the award-winning Finale® music notation software products which eliminate the restrictiveness and tedium of music notation and have established the Company as a leader in this market. In June 1994, the Company introduced the Vivace® system, an innovative musical accompaniment system that responds to the musician in real-time.

	12/31/98	12/31/97	12/31/96	12/31/95
Per Share Information				
Stock Price	1.25	0.94	1.75	4.37
Earnings Per Share	-0.13	-0.28	-0.41	-0.44
Price / Earnings Ratio	n.a.	n.a.	n.a.	n.a.
Book Value Per Share	0.48	0.60	0.69	1.09
Price / Book Value %	260.42	156.67	253.62	400.92
Dividends Per Share	0.0	0.0	0.0	0.0
Annual Financial Data				
Operating Results (000's)				
Total Revenues	6,501.7	5,661.5	5,611.0	4,989.3
Costs & Expenses	-7,306.2	-7,173.8	-7,382.0	-6,639.8
Income Before Taxes and Other	-804.5	-1,512.2	-1,771.0	-1,650.4
Other Items	0.0	0.0	0.0	0.0
Income Tax	0.0	0.0	0.0	0.0
Net Income	-804.5	-1,512.2	-1,771.0	-1,650.4
Cash Flow From Operations	296.7	-742.6	-1,925.4	-1,516.4
Balance Sheet (000's)				
Cash & Equivalents	563.7	1,233.5	1,174.3	2,499.5
Total Current Assets	2,618.9	3,400.3	2,807.7	5,145.3
Fixed Assets, Net	273.4	370.1	494.8	560.1
Total Assets	3,808.6	4,631.2	4,081.8	5,705.5
Total Current Liabilities	854.0	886.9	1,084.3	1,048.5
Long-Term Debt	0.0	0.0	0.0	0.0
Stockholders' Equity	2,954.6	3,744.4	2,997.5	4,657.0
Performance & Financial Condition				
Return on Total Revenues %	-12.37	-26.71	-31.56	-33.08
Return on Avg Stockholders' Equity %	-24.02	-44.86	-46.27	-43.41
Return on Average Assets %	-19.06	-34.71	-36.19	-34.38
Current Ratio	3.07	3.83	2.59	4.91
Debt / Equity %	n.a.	n.a.	n.a.	n.a.

Compound Growth %'s	EPS % n.a.	Net Income % n.a.	Total Revenues % 9.23

Comments

During 1998, the Company achieved a 37% increase in gross profit dollars as a result of an increase in sales, reduction in product costs for all product lines, and a reduction in licensing fees as the result of a contract re-negotiation. Some of the best bargains can be found when a Company is becoming profitable for the first time. Although the numbers above are losses and are only trending towards profitability, it may be more important to note two consecutive quarters of profits in the third and fourth quarters of 1998. If the trend continues, the Company will also benefit from $9.3 million of tax loss carryovers at December 31, 1998.

Officers	Position	Ownership Information	
John W. Paulson	Chairman, CEO	Number of Shares Outstanding	6,194,732
Ronald B. Raup	President, COO	Market Capitalization	$ 7,743,415
Mark E. Dunn	Senior VP	Number of Shareholders	1,650
Barbara S. Remley	CFO, Secretary	Where Listed / Symbol	NASDAQ / COMT

Other Information			
Transfer Agent	Norwest Bank Minnesota, N.A. South St. Paul, MN	SIC Code	7372
Auditor	McGladrey & Pullen, LLP	Employees	43
		Web Site	codamusic.com

Coeur d'Alenes Company (The)

3900 E. Broadway   Spokane, WA 99220-2610   Telephone (509)924-6363   Fax (509)924-6924

Company Description

The Coeur d'Alenes Company is engaged in the distribution, processing and fabrication of steel and related products to customer specifications. Operations include activities such as bending, drilling, riveting, welding and assembling. The Company was first established as J.R. Marks & Co. during the Idaho gold rush of 1884 as a supply house for miners. By 1886, there were five stores in northern Idaho that became The Coeur d'Alene Hardware Co. in 1892. In 1913, the Company was merged with Coeur d'Alene Ironworks.

	09/26/98	09/27/97	09/28/96	09/30/95
Per Share Information				
Stock Price as of 12/31	0.26	0.20	0.17	0.15
Earnings Per Share	0.04	0.02	0.05	0.04
Price / Earnings Ratio	6.50	10.00	3.40	3.75
Book Value Per Share	0.55	0.51	0.48	0.50
Price / Book Value %	47.27	39.22	35.42	30.00
Dividends Per Share	0.0	0.0	0.0	0.0
Annual Financial Data				
Operating Results (000's)				
Total Revenues	14,430.4	12,992.3	12,667.0	12,240.4
Costs & Expenses	-14,068.9	-12,812.1	-12,244.1	-11,851.6
Income Before Taxes and Other	361.5	180.2	422.9	388.8
Other Items	0.0	0.0	0.0	0.0
Income Tax	-110.5	-54.9	-132.7	-132.2
Net Income	251.0	125.3	290.2	256.6
Cash Flow From Operations	220.2	45.4	198.0	351.7
Balance Sheet (000's)				
Cash & Equivalents	39.5	89.5	68.6	128.1
Total Current Assets	4,066.1	3,743.2	4,109.3	3,560.8
Fixed Assets, Net	3,357.0	3,335.4	3,097.5	1,874.7
Total Assets	7,495.2	7,152.0	7,257.6	5,491.0
Total Current Liabilities	1,963.9	1,858.4	2,472.4	1,995.0
Long-Term Debt	2,328.2	2,521.8	2,159.4	1,280.1
Stockholders' Equity	2,955.2	2,706.7	2,581.4	2,169.2
Performance & Financial Condition				
Return on Total Revenues %	1.74	0.96	2.29	2.10
Return on Avg Stockholders' Equity %	8.87	4.74	12.22	12.57
Return on Average Assets %	3.43	1.74	4.55	4.77
Current Ratio	2.07	2.01	1.66	1.78
Debt / Equity %	78.78	93.17	83.65	59.02

Compound Growth %'s	EPS %	0.00	Net Income %	-0.73	Total Revenues %	5.64

Comments

During fiscal 1998, fabrication business sales represented 16% of total Company's sales and the distribution sales represented the remaining 84%. Both segments grew at a 12% rate during the year. During the past several years, the Company has made significant changes in the structure of its operations in response to changing market conditions. Management believes that the distribution business in fiscal 1999 will be significantly weaker than it was for fiscal 1998. The fabrication business is expected to be stronger. Despite the fact that this company is very small, annual results have been relatively consistent and working capital is maintained at adequate levels.

Officers	Position	Ownership Information	
Jimmie T. G. Coulson	President, CEO	Number of Shares Outstanding	5,350,338
Marilyn A. Schroeder	CFO, Secretary	Market Capitalization	$ 1,391,088
Lawrence A. Coulson	Vice President	Number of Shareholders	996
Joel E. Simpson	Vice President	Where Listed / Symbol	OTC-BB / CDAL

Other Information			
Transfer Agent	Company Office Spokane, WA	SIC Code	3440
Auditor	BDO Seidman LLP	Employees	72
Market Maker	Empire Securities Inc. of WA (800)541-5558	Web Site	coeurdal.com
	Sharpe Capital Inc. (800)355-5781		

Cohesant Technologies Inc.

5845 West 82nd Street, Suite 102 Indianapolis, IN 46278 Telephone (317)875-5592 Fax (317)875-5456

Company Description

Cohesant Technologies Inc. is engaged in the design, development, manufacture and sale of specialized two component spray finishing and coating application equipment, replacement parts and supplies used in the operation of this equipment and specialty two component epoxy coating and grout products. The Company's spray finishing and coating application equipment systems are designed specifically for use with multiple component formulations such as fiberglass reinforced plastics and polyurethane foam. These equipment systems are commonly employed in the construction, transportation and marine industries to apply insulation, protective coating, sealant and anti-corrosive products as well as to fill molds for diverse products such as recreational boat hulls and plumbing fixtures. The Company was founded in 1994.

	11/30/98	11/30/97	11/30/96	11/30/95
Per Share Information				
Stock Price as of 12/31	1.62	1.06	1.19	2.37
Earnings Per Share	0.26	-0.54	-0.32	0.16
Price / Earnings Ratio	6.23	n.a.	n.a.	14.81
Book Value Per Share	1.97	1.69	2.23	2.55
Price / Book Value %	82.23	62.72	53.36	92.94
Dividends Per Share	0.0	0.0	0.0	0.0
Annual Financial Data				
Operating Results (000's)				
Total Revenues	11,896.4	9,890.6	13,704.7	14,156.3
Costs & Expenses	-11,200.1	-9,656.4	-14,622.8	-13,464.7
Income Before Taxes and Other	696.3	234.2	-918.1	691.5
Other Items	0.0	-1,712.1	0.0	-14.9
Income Tax	0.0	20.1	47.7	-251.3
Net Income	696.3	-1,457.9	-870.4	425.3
Cash Flow From Operations	1,205.5	-1,538.8	-684.2	223.4
Balance Sheet (000's)				
Cash & Equivalents	120.0	59.9	500.8	1,247.1
Total Current Assets	5,807.1	6,764.2	6,014.9	7,246.5
Fixed Assets, Net	605.7	627.9	937.2	780.5
Total Assets	7,571.5	8,876.8	8,196.6	8,764.8
Total Current Liabilities	2,679.1	4,264.1	2,100.7	1,930.6
Long-Term Debt	0.0	0.0	0.0	0.0
Stockholders' Equity	4,740.7	4,550.1	6,007.9	6,713.3
Performance & Financial Condition				
Return on Total Revenues %	5.85	-14.74	-6.35	3.00
Return on Avg Stockholders' Equity %	14.99	-27.62	-13.68	6.86
Return on Average Assets %	8.47	-17.08	-10.26	5.06
Current Ratio	2.17	1.59	2.86	3.75
Debt / Equity %	n.a.	n.a.	n.a.	n.a.

Compound Growth %'s	EPS %	17.57	Net Income %	17.87	Total Revenues %	-5.63

Comments

Despite weak product sales to the Asian/Pacific region, the Company posted a 19.4% increase in revenues in fiscal 1998. This was spurred by an 89.3% increase in coating and grout products and a 22% increase in domestic equipment sales. The negative compound growth rate in revenue is reflective of discontinued operations that were included in base year revenue. Fiscal 1997 results include a loss from discontinued operations of $1,712,136 ($.64 per share). At November 30, 1998, the Company still had approximately $2 million in tax loss carryovers available to offset future taxable income. The Company maintains a strong financial condition and invests in research and development for new products.

Officers	Position	Ownership Information	
Morton A. Cohen	Chairman, CEO	Number of Shares Outstanding	2,407,743
Dwight D. Goodman	President, CEO	Market Capitalization	$ 3,900,544
Michael L. Boeckman	Director	Number of Shareholders	490
Richard L. Immerman	Director	Where Listed / Symbol	NASDAQ / COHT

Other Information			
Transfer Agent	Continental Stock Transfer & Trust Co. New York, NY	SIC Code	3560
Auditor	Arthur Andersen LLP	Employees	70
		Web Site	cohesant.com

Collins Industries, Inc.

15 Compound Drive Hutchinson, KS 67502-4349 Telephone (316)663-5551 Fax (316)663-1630

Company Description

Collins Industries, Inc. was founded in 1971 as a manufacturer of small school buses and ambulances built from modified cargo vans. The Company's initial product was the first "Type A" school bus, designed to carry 16 to 20 passengers. Today the Company manufactures specialty vehicles and accessories for various basic service niches of the transportation industry. The Company's products include ambulances, small school buses, shuttle and mid-size commercial buses, terminal trucks, and commercial bus chassis. From its inception, Collins' stated goal has been to become the largest manufacturer of specialty vehicles in the United States. The Company has grown primarily through the internal development of new products and the acquisition of complementary product lines.

	10/31/98	10/31/97	10/31/96	10/31/95
Per Share Information				
Stock Price as of 12/31	3.94	6.50	5.87	1.50
Earnings Per Share	0.39	0.94	0.66	-0.05
Price / Earnings Ratio	10.10	6.91	8.89	n.a.
Book Value Per Share	2.73	2.69	1.91	1.21
Price / Book Value %	144.32	241.64	307.33	123.97
Dividends Per Share	0.23	0.07	0.0	0.0
Annual Financial Data				
Operating Results (000's)				
Total Revenues	156,805.2	157,784.3	152,141.3	140,725.1
Costs & Expenses	-152,068.1	-148,941.1	-147,129.2	-140,618.7
Income Before Taxes and Other	4,737.1	8,843.2	5,012.1	79.7
Other Items	0.0	0.0	0.0	-420.4
Income Tax	-1,710.0	-1,600.0	0.0	0.0
Net Income	3,027.1	7,243.2	5,012.1	-340.8
Cash Flow From Operations	4,062.9	8,141.7	5,759.9	5,260.0
Balance Sheet (000's)				
Cash & Equivalents	144.0	189.2	255.4	843.0
Total Current Assets	31,746.7	34,002.1	32,639.8	32,085.9
Fixed Assets, Net	16,745.2	12,431.8	12,037.2	13,422.1
Total Assets	49,076.0	47,163.1	45,744.5	46,881.1
Total Current Liabilities	16,072.4	18,959.3	18,435.6	18,670.2
Long-Term Debt	12,733.1	8,361.9	12,827.4	17,659.9
Stockholders' Equity	20,270.6	19,841.9	13,890.8	8,805.2
Performance & Financial Condition				
Return on Total Revenues %	1.93	4.59	3.29	-0.24
Return on Avg Stockholders' Equity %	15.09	42.94	44.17	-3.10
Return on Average Assets %	6.29	15.59	10.82	-0.74
Current Ratio	1.98	1.79	1.77	1.72
Debt / Equity %	62.82	42.14	92.34	200.56

Compound Growth %'s	EPS %	-23.13	Net Income %	-22.28	Total Revenues %	3.67

Comments

A softness in the ambulance and terminal truck market resulted in lower fiscal 1998 revenues. Income tax expense as a percent of pretax income increased in fiscal 1998 as a result of the complete utilization of net operating loss carryforwards and general business tax credits in fiscal 1997. Fiscal 1995 results include a nonrecurring expense of $420,444 related to the early retirement of debt. On December 1, 1998, the Company completed the acquisition of Mid Bus, Inc., a manufacturer of school buses. The acquisition, which was financed through borrowings on the Company's revolving credit facility, will be accounted for as a purchase.

Officers	Position	Ownership Information	
Donald Lynn Collins	President, CEO	Number of Shares Outstanding	7,430,881
Larry W. Sayre	VP - Finance, CFO	Market Capitalization	$ 29,277,671
Don L. Collins	Director	Number of Shareholders	650
Lewis W. Ediger	Director	Where Listed / Symbol	NASDAQ / COLL

Other Information

Transfer Agent	ChaseMellon Shareholder Services Ridgefield Park, NJ	SIC Code	3711
Auditor	Arthur Andersen LLP	Employees	900

Colonial Commercial Corp.

3601 Hempstead Turnpike, Suite 121-I Levittown, NY 11756-1315 Telephone (516)796-8400 Fax (516)796-8696

Company Description

As the result of an acquisition in 1995, Colonial Commercial Corp. is principally a distributor of door hardware, doors and door frames used in new building construction, buildings under rehabilitation, interior tenant buildouts and building maintenance. The Company services the contract hardware market, usually as a material supplier only, on a wide range of commercial, residential and institutional construction projects. Customers are located primarily in New York, New Jersey, Pennsylvania, Georgia and Illinois. On March 25, 1999, the Company announced a definitive agreement to acquire Universal Supply Group, Inc., a leading distributor of heating and air conditioning equipment and climate controls.

	12/31/98	12/31/97	12/31/96	12/31/95
Per Share Information				
Stock Price	2.28	1.85	3.10	1.55
Earnings Per Share	1.23	0.21	0.17	0.28
Price / Earnings Ratio	1.85	8.81	18.24	5.54
Book Value Per Share	1.95	0.43	-1.14	-1.84
Price / Book Value %	116.92	430.23	n.a.	n.a.
Dividends Per Share	0.0	0.0	0.0	0.0
Annual Financial Data				
Operating Results (000's)				
Total Revenues	28,458.7	23,446.6	25,453.0	14,702.2
Costs & Expenses	-24,527.6	-22,929.9	-24,718.9	-13,722.7
Income Before Taxes and Other	3,931.1	516.7	734.0	979.5
Other Items	0.0	0.0	0.0	0.0
Income Tax	-79.4	155.7	-186.4	-104.3
Net Income	3,851.8	672.4	547.7	875.3
Cash Flow From Operations	-539.6	47.5	-864.6	82.0
Balance Sheet (000's)				
Cash & Equivalents	5,001.9	1,241.0	1,322.5	1,856.0
Total Current Assets	15,171.9	14,162.9	11,520.8	10,788.7
Fixed Assets, Net	502.3	344.7	127.0	109.3
Total Assets	16,325.3	15,160.5	15,695.9	14,609.3
Total Current Liabilities	4,753.8	5,373.8	7,151.1	6,405.4
Long-Term Debt	0.0	0.0	447.4	916.4
Stockholders' Equity	10,807.1	8,949.1	7,146.9	6,221.2
Performance & Financial Condition				
Return on Total Revenues %	13.53	2.87	2.15	5.95
Return on Avg Stockholders' Equity %	38.99	8.35	8.19	15.65
Return on Average Assets %	24.47	4.36	3.61	7.98
Current Ratio	3.19	2.64	1.61	1.68
Debt / Equity %	n.a.	n.a.	6.26	14.73

Compound Growth %'s	EPS %	63.78	Net Income %	63.87	Total Revenues %	24.63

Comments

The Company effected a 1 for 5 reverse stock split on January 30, 1998. All per share amounts have been restated for consistency. 1998 was a banner year for the Company. Net income from core operations increased from $727,448 in 1997 to $1,291,552 in 1998. The Company also realized $2.9 million of nonrecurring gains on the sale of an investment and land. Income tax expense has been light with $32 million of tax loss carryovers still available at December 31, 1998. A change in accounting method for reporting income taxes created an income tax credit in 1997. Included in 1997 results was a write-off of costs associated with an abandoned acquisition, amounting to $385,705, and gains on the sale of land and investments of $434,099. Book value is calculated after deducting the liquidation preference of preferred shares. Assuming conversion of the preferred, book value would be $3.54 per share.

Officers	Position	Ownership Information	
Bernard Korn	Chairman, President	Number of Shares Outstanding	1,463,052
James W. Stewart	Exec VP, Secretary	Market Capitalization	$ 3,335,759
Gerald S. Deutsch	Director	Number of Shareholders	1,077
Donald K. MacNeill	Director	Where Listed / Symbol	NASDAQ / CCOM

Other Information			
Transfer Agent	American Stock Transfer & Trust Company New York, NY	SIC Code	6141
Auditor	KPMG LLP	Employees	64

Command Security Corporation

Lexington Park, P.O. Box 340   Lagrangeville, NY 12540   Telephone (914)454-3703   Fax (914)454-0075

Company Description

Command Security Corporation principally provides uniformed security services from its eighteen operating offices in New York, New Jersey, Illinois, California, Pennsylvania, Connecticut, Florida and Georgia to commercial, financial, industrial, aviation and governmental clients in the United States. Security services include providing uniformed guards for access control, theft prevention, surveillance, vehicular and foot patrol and crowd control. The Company was founded in 1980.

	03/31/98	03/31/97	03/31/96	03/31/95
Per Share Information				
Stock Price as of 12/31	1.16	1.00	1.25	1.18
Earnings Per Share	-0.62	0.05	0.06	-0.70
Price / Earnings Ratio	n.a.	20.00	20.83	n.a.
Book Value Per Share	0.15	0.68	0.64	0.63
Price / Book Value %	773.33	147.06	195.31	187.30
Dividends Per Share	0.0	0.0	0.0	0.0
Annual Financial Data				
Operating Results (000's)				
Total Revenues	52,061.4	49,417.0	55,167.6	39,693.1
Costs & Expenses	-55,815.4	-49,107.3	-54,956.5	-42,730.4
Income Before Taxes and Other	-3,754.1	309.7	211.1	-3,037.3
Other Items	0.0	0.0	0.0	0.0
Income Tax	-259.8	140.4	300.5	53.4
Net Income	-4,013.9	450.0	511.7	-2,983.8
Cash Flow From Operations	2,897.5	1,105.2	-553.1	483.4
Balance Sheet (000's)				
Cash & Equivalents	0.0	0.0	0.0	0.0
Total Current Assets	12,104.8	15,010.0	14,043.4	11,254.9
Fixed Assets, Net	1,176.2	1,100.0	975.8	953.2
Total Assets	17,697.3	23,180.0	22,384.4	20,267.1
Total Current Liabilities	13,227.7	13,590.0	13,824.4	11,786.5
Long-Term Debt	459.0	1,190.0	1,179.0	1,187.3
Stockholders' Equity	3,134.5	5,730.0	5,189.2	4,993.9
Performance & Financial Condition				
Return on Total Revenues %	-7.71	0.91	0.93	-7.52
Return on Avg Stockholders' Equity %	-90.56	8.24	10.05	-58.92
Return on Average Assets %	-19.64	1.98	2.40	-15.70
Current Ratio	0.92	1.10	1.02	0.95
Debt / Equity %	14.64	20.77	22.72	23.78

Compound Growth %'s	EPS % n.a.	Net Income % n.a.	Total Revenues % 9.46

Comments

The increase in revenues in fiscal 1998 was primarily due to an acquisition. Gross margins decreased due to lower pricing on new contracts and higher payroll costs. The latter is due to a current shortage of qualified personnel and increases in overtime pay. Management expects the trend of increasing pressures on margins to continue. The Company's auditor issued a going concern qualification in its annual report because of the deficiency in working capital. For the nine months ended December 31, 1998, the Company reported revenues and net income of $44.5 million and $36,311 ($.01 per share) as compared to $38.3 million and a net loss of $2,433,605 ($.36 per share) for the same period of the preceding year. Could this be a turnaround? We have noted small profits in 1996 and 1997 surrounded by larger losses.

Officers	Position	Ownership Information	
William C. Vassell	Chairman	Number of Shares Outstanding	8,013,543
Franklyn H. Snitow	President, CEO	Market Capitalization	$ 9,295,710
Eugene U. McDonald	Senior VP	Number of Shareholders	1,500
Debra M. Miller	Secretary	Where Listed / Symbol	NASDAQ / CMMD

Other Information			
Transfer Agent	American Securities Transfer, Inc. Denver, CO	SIC Code	7381
Auditor	D'Arcangelo & Co., LLP	Employees	3,765
		Web Site	commandsecurity.com

Command Systems, Inc.

Pond View Corporate Center, 76 Batterson Park Road Farmington, CT 06032   Telephone (860)409-2000 Fax (860)409-2099

Company Description

Command Systems, Inc. provides a wide range of information technology (IT) solutions and services to financial services organizations to support their evolving business processes. The Company utilizes leading technologies to offer its customers a comprehensive range of IT services, including technology services, management consulting, and product procurement and education services. In anticipation of the growing demand for IT services, including Year 2000 solutions services, and the shortage of skilled IT professionals in the United States, in 1996 the Company established a software development facility in Bangalore, India which today provides its customers with increased access to skilled IT professionals on a cost-effective basis. The Company had its initial public offering in January 1998 at which time it issued 2,760,000 shares for $12 per share.

	12/31/98	12/31/97	12/31/96	12/31/95
Per Share Information				
Stock Price	3.25	12.00	n.a.	n.a.
Earnings Per Share	-0.29	0.01	-0.09	0.05
Price / Earnings Ratio	n.a.	1,200.00	n.a.	n.a.
Book Value Per Share	3.98	-0.17	-0.01	0.09
Price / Book Value %	81.66	n.a.	n.a.	n.a.
Dividends Per Share	0.0	0.0	0.0	0.0
Annual Financial Data				
Operating Results (000's)				
Total Revenues	36,208.9	25,090.0	17,126.3	12,438.7
Costs & Expenses	-36,493.7	-24,537.5	-17,798.8	-12,173.7
Income Before Taxes and Other	-284.8	552.5	-672.5	265.0
Other Items	-1,800.0	-451.4	241.4	0.0
Income Tax	317.6	-597.8	8.1	-43.6
Net Income	-1,767.3	-496.7	-423.0	221.4
Cash Flow From Operations	-1,635.5	290.5	-1,072.3	-108.2
Balance Sheet (000's)				
Cash & Equivalents	16,169.7	391.7	443.5	222.9
Total Current Assets	26,364.2	5,001.9	3,234.7	2,014.8
Fixed Assets, Net	2,282.8	2,034.2	1,072.5	259.5
Total Assets	35,647.7	14,425.1	4,816.3	2,294.1
Total Current Liabilities	5,192.3	4,542.0	3,333.7	1,929.6
Long-Term Debt	0.0	0.0	1,145.5	0.0
Stockholders' Equity	30,455.3	-722.4	-58.5	364.5
Performance & Financial Condition				
Return on Total Revenues %	-4.88	-1.98	-2.47	1.78
Return on Avg Stockholders' Equity %	-11.89	n.a.	-276.41	221.44
Return on Average Assets %	-7.06	-5.16	-11.90	11.07
Current Ratio	5.08	1.10	0.97	1.04
Debt / Equity %	n.a.	n.a.	n.a.	n.a.

Compound Growth %'s	EPS % n.a.	Net Income % n.a.	Total Revenues % 42.78

Comments

Revenues skyrocketed 41% in 1998, largely resulting from Year 2000 compliance services. Operating expenses increased more than the increase in income creating a loss for the year. A class action lawsuit has been filed in connection with the Company's initial public offering. In late 1998, a memorandum of understanding outlined a proposed settlement. The memorandum is not yet a definitive agreement. 1998 results include $1.8 million of shareholder litigation costs which represents the Company's share of the proposed settlement and legal fees. At December 31, 1998, the Company had $6.4 million of goodwill recorded as assets which equated to approximately 21% of stockholders' equity and book value per share. This will remain a highly speculative investment until management demonstrates an ability to record consistent profits.

Officers	Position	Ownership Information	
Edward G. Caputo	President, CEO	Number of Shares Outstanding	7,656,750
Stephen L. Willcox	Exec VP, COO	Market Capitalization	$ 24,884,438
Robert B. Dixon	VP - Finance	Number of Shareholders	1,000
Glenn M. King	Secretary	Where Listed / Symbol	NASDAQ / CMND

Other Information			
Transfer Agent	Boston EquiServe Boston, MA	SIC Code	7371
Auditor	Ernst & Young LLP	Employees	408
		Web Site	commandsys.com

Compare Generiks, Inc.

300 Oser Avenue Hauppauge, NY 11788 Telephone (800)342-6555 Fax (516)273-2687

Company Description

Compare Generiks, Inc. is engaged in the distribution, marketing and sale of dietary supplements and over-the-counter non-prescription pharmaceuticals. The Company distributes its products under Company owned trademarks through direct sales to major wholesalers, particularly those that service convenience stores, drug stores, discount department stores, wholesale clubs, petroleum marketers, hospital gift shops and airport gift. Distribution is supported by a sophisticated broker network. The Company commenced business on April 25, 1995.

	03/31/98	03/31/97	03/31/96
Per Share Information			
Stock Price as of 12/31	0.12	3.62	5.75
Earnings Per Share	-0.12	-0.32	-0.07
Price / Earnings Ratio	n.a.	n.a.	n.a.
Book Value Per Share	0.71	0.85	0.92
Price / Book Value %	16.90	425.88	625.00
Dividends Per Share	0.0	0.0	0.0
Annual Financial Data			
Operating Results (000's)			
Total Revenues	9,160.1	2,345.8	545.7
Costs & Expenses	-8,923.0	-3,553.5	-759.8
Income Before Taxes and Other	-496.8	-1,207.6	-214.2
Other Items	0.0	0.0	0.0
Income Tax	87.0	43.0	0.0
Net Income	-409.8	-1,164.6	-214.2
Cash Flow From Operations	-675.5	-967.2	-280.2
Balance Sheet (000's)			
Cash & Equivalents	107.3	890.5	2,047.5
Total Current Assets	3,307.9	2,305.5	2,603.1
Fixed Assets, Net	65.1	52.2	3.7
Total Assets	4,970.2	5,130.1	4,325.5
Total Current Liabilities	1,109.5	1,236.6	320.4
Long-Term Debt	0.0	0.0	0.0
Stockholders' Equity	3,360.7	3,893.5	4,005.1
Performance & Financial Condition			
Return on Total Revenues %	-4.47	-49.65	-39.25
Return on Avg Stockholders' Equity %	-11.30	-29.49	-5.35
Return on Average Assets %	-8.12	-24.63	-4.76
Current Ratio	2.98	1.86	8.13
Debt / Equity %	n.a.	n.a.	n.a.

Compound Growth %'s	EPS % n.a.	Net Income % n.a.	Total Revenues % 309.72

Comments

Fiscal 1996 includes approximately eleven months of operations. The Company purchases all of its products and product supplies from PDK Labs., Inc. a company that is also presented in this manual. PDK also provides certain management, administrative facilities and personnel and owns an interest in the Company. The increase in fiscal 1998 revenues is attributable to an exclusive supply and licensing agreement with PDK whereby the Company has the exclusive right to distribute products bearing the Max Brand and Heads UP trademarks. Fiscal 1998 results include a $734,000 loss from an investment in marketable securities. For the nine months ended December 31, 1998, revenues and a net loss were $22.7 million and $112,785 ($.04 per share) as compared to $6.5 million and a net profit of $263,433 ($.06 per share) for the same period of the preceding year. Untangling the possible web of operations that revolve around PDK Labs may be the secret in determining the possible value of this enterprise.

Officers	Position	Ownership Information	
Thomas A. Keith	President, CEO	Number of Shares Outstanding	3,890,000
Daniel Durchslag	Director	Market Capitalization	$ 466,800
Theresa Giove	Director	Number of Shareholders	500
		Where Listed / Symbol	NASDAQ / COGE

Other Information			
Transfer Agent	American Stock Transfer & Trust Co. New York, NY	SIC Code	2834
Auditor	Holtz Rubenstein & Co., LLP	Employees	4

Comprehensive Care Corporation

4200 West Cypress Street, Suite 300   Tampa, FL 33607   Telephone (813)876-5036   Fax (813)872-1561

Company Description

Comprehensive Care Corporation provides managed care services in the behavioral health and psychiatric fields which represented approximately 83% of its revenue in fiscal 1998. The managed care operations include administrative service contracts, fee-for-service agreements, and capitation contracts. The customer base for its services includes both corporate and governmental entities. During the past several years, the Company has transitioned from its ownership, operation and management of psychiatric hospitals, substance abuse facilities, and the management of similar programs located in unaffiliated hospitals. The Company was founded in 1969.

	05/31/98	05/31/97	05/31/96	05/31/95
Per Share Information				
Stock Price as of 12/31	3.94	6.87	12.12	8.62
Earnings Per Share	0.51	-0.92	-1.60	-5.09
Price / Earnings Ratio	7.73	n.a.	n.a.	n.a.
Book Value Per Share	-1.01	-1.65	-2.64	-2.41
Price / Book Value %	n.a.	n.a.	n.a.	n.a.
Dividends Per Share	0.0	0.0	0.0	0.0
Annual Financial Data				
Operating Results (000's)				
Total Revenues	46,833.0	39,810.0	34,894.0	30,156.0
Costs & Expenses	-44,790.0	-44,697.0	-41,532.0	-41,155.0
Income Before Taxes and Other	2,034.0	-5,310.0	-6,720.0	-11,353.0
Other Items	0.0	2,172.0	0.0	0.0
Income Tax	-63.0	341.0	2,478.0	-180.0
Net Income	1,971.0	-2,797.0	-4,242.0	-11,533.0
Cash Flow From Operations	-1,867.0	1,145.0	4,431.0	n.a.
Balance Sheet (000's)				
Cash & Equivalents	6,016.0	3,991.0	4,433.0	1,542.0
Total Current Assets	17,921.0	12,251.0	9,972.0	8,012.0
Fixed Assets, Net	7,043.0	6,318.0	5,500.0	10,000.0
Total Assets	30,405.0	24,746.0	25,119.0	26,001.0
Total Current Liabilities	28,690.0	24,908.0	31,143.0	24,354.0
Long-Term Debt	2,704.0	2,712.0	24.0	5,077.0
Stockholders' Equity	-1,286.0	-3,570.0	-7,798.0	-5,933.0
Performance & Financial Condition				
Return on Total Revenues %	4.21	-7.03	-12.16	-38.24
Return on Avg Stockholders' Equity %	n.a.	n.a.	n.a.	n.a.
Return on Average Assets %	7.15	-11.22	-16.60	-48.05
Current Ratio	0.62	0.49	0.32	0.33
Debt / Equity %	n.a.	n.a.	n.a.	n.a.

Compound Growth %'s	EPS % n.a.	Net Income % n.a.	Total Revenues % 15.80

Comments

The restructuring referred to above took many years with substantial losses. Working capital has been depleted to the point that the auditors issued a going concern qualification on the financial statements of this New York Stock Exchange company. But the Company is shedding its two hospitals and staunchly defending itself against the Internal Revenue Service for past refunds the government wants back. A careful review is in order but may be worth the effort. The Company reported a solid profit in fiscal 1998. But for the nine months ended February 28, 1999, the Company reported revenues and a net loss of $30.6 million and $1,866,000 ($.55 per share) as compared to $29.6 million and a net profit of $822,000 ($.23 per share) for the same period of the preceding year.

Officers	Position	Ownership Information	
Chriss W. Street	President, CEO	Number of Shares Outstanding	3,415,402
Robert J. Landis	Exec VP, CFO	Market Capitalization	$ 13,456,684
Mary Jane Johnson	Exec VP	Number of Shareholders	1,567
Joni Cummings	Exec VP	Where Listed / Symbol	OTC-BB / CHCR

Other Information			
Transfer Agent	Continental Stock Transfer & Trust Co. New York, NY	SIC Code	8093
Auditor	Ernst & Young LLP	Employees	347

CompuCom Systems, Inc.

7171 Forest Lane   Dallas, TX 75230   Telephone (972)856-3600   Fax (972)856-3200

Company Description

CompuCom Systems, Inc. is a provider of network integration services to large and medium-sized businesses throughout the United States. CompuCom helps Fortune 1000 companies manage information technology and achieve their business goals by providing a wide range of services in provisioning, support and technology management. The Company is an authorized dealer of major distributed desktop computer products, networking and related products, computer-related peripheral equipment and software for a number of manufacturers, including Compaq, IBM, Hewlett-Packard, Toshiba, Intel and Microsoft. The Company was founded in 1987.

	12/31/98	12/31/97	12/31/96	12/31/95
Per Share Information				
Stock Price	3.28	8.25	10.62	9.50
Earnings Per Share	-0.01	0.71	0.61	0.45
Price / Earnings Ratio	n.a.	11.62	17.41	21.11
Book Value Per Share	4.10	4.23	3.48	2.80
Price / Book Value %	74.04	195.04	305.17	339.29
Dividends Per Share	0.0	0.0	0.0	0.0
Annual Financial Data				
Operating Results (000's)				
Total Revenues	2,254,465.0	1,949,802.0	1,995,191.0	1,441,597.0
Costs & Expenses	-2,237,360.0	-1,896,768.0	-1,953,313.0	-1,407,262.0
Income Before Taxes and Other	17,105.0	53,034.0	41,878.0	34,335.0
Other Items	-16,437.0	5,624.0	8,738.0	0.0
Income Tax	-267.0	-23,464.0	-20,145.0	-13,665.0
Net Income	401.0	35,194.0	30,471.0	20,670.0
Cash Flow From Operations	99,383.0	153,923.0	-81,055.0	6,597.0
Balance Sheet (000's)				
Cash & Equivalents	4,526.0	4,456.0	4,320.0	4,249.0
Total Current Assets	415,422.0	382,435.0	618,890.0	468,002.0
Fixed Assets, Net	72,004.0	63,359.0	54,308.0	29,900.0
Total Assets	545,489.0	462,590.0	692,985.0	508,704.0
Total Current Liabilities	251,242.0	147,266.0	276,428.0	243,047.0
Long-Term Debt	81,929.0	97,400.0	236,450.0	120,364.0
Stockholders' Equity	210,281.0	210,200.0	171,098.0	138,341.0
Performance & Financial Condition				
Return on Total Revenues %	0.02	1.81	1.53	1.43
Return on Avg Stockholders' Equity %	0.19	18.46	19.69	17.76
Return on Average Assets %	0.08	6.09	5.07	8.88
Current Ratio	1.65	2.60	2.24	1.93
Debt / Equity %	38.96	46.34	138.20	87.01

Compound Growth %'s	EPS % n.a.	Net Income % -73.13	Total Revenues % 16.07

Comments

The majority of the 1998 increase in revenues was attributable to acquisitions. On October 22, 1998, the Company approved a restructuring plan designed to reduce the Company's cost structure by closing branch facilities and reducing its workforce by about 10%. A restructuring charge of $16,437,000 is reflected in 1998 results. Results for 1997 and 1996 include $5,624,000 and $8,738,000 of nonrecurring gains, respectively. At December 31, 1998, the Company had $54.8 million of goodwill recorded as assets which equated to approximately 26% of stockholders' equity and book value per share.

Officers	Position	Ownership Information	
Charles A. Root	Chairman	Number of Shares Outstanding	47,441,820
Edward Anderson	President, CEO	Market Capitalization	$ 155,609,170
William D. Barry	Exec VP, COO	Number of Shareholders	10,000
M. Lazane Smith	Senior VP, CFO	Where Listed / Symbol	NASDAQ / CMPC

Other Information

Transfer Agent	ChaseMellon Shareholder Services Ridgefield Park, NJ	SIC Code	5045
Auditor	KPMG LLP	Employees	4,800
		Web Site	compucom.com

Computer Research, Inc.

Southpoint Plaza 1, Ste. 300, 400 Southpointe Blvd   Canonsburg, PA 15317   Telephone (724)745-0600   Fax (724)745-8200

Company Description

Computer Research, Inc. provides a computerized Accounting and Recordkeeping System that is utilized by stock and bond brokerage clients, as well as by brokerage subsidiaries and the capital market divisions of banks. A fully integrated subsystem of software modules, when operated on electronic computing equipment, offers a comprehensive on-line automated system for serving financial institutions with brokerage accounting, institutional safekeeping, capital markets and portfolio accounting. The Company was formed in 1969.

	08/31/98	08/31/97	08/31/96	08/31/95
Per Share Information				
Stock Price as of 12/31	0.81	1.37	2.12	0.69
Earnings Per Share	0.06	0.23	0.26	0.10
Price / Earnings Ratio	13.50	5.96	8.15	6.90
Book Value Per Share	0.85	0.79	0.56	0.31
Price / Book Value %	95.29	173.42	378.57	222.58
Dividends Per Share	0.0	0.0	0.0	0.0
Annual Financial Data				
Operating Results (000's)				
Total Revenues	6,778.5	7,767.6	7,385.4	6,217.8
Costs & Expenses	-6,370.7	-6,392.9	-6,091.9	-5,792.8
Income Before Taxes and Other	407.8	1,374.7	1,293.5	424.9
Other Items	0.0	0.0	0.0	0.0
Income Tax	-146.0	-458.0	-265.0	-26.8
Net Income	261.8	916.7	1,028.5	398.1
Cash Flow From Operations	362.7	700.1	1,509.2	281.1
Balance Sheet (000's)				
Cash & Equivalents	766.8	336.3	1,486.9	873.5
Total Current Assets	3,608.6	3,678.2	3,165.9	1,806.0
Fixed Assets, Net	554.4	424.7	292.7	279.5
Total Assets	4,202.9	4,102.9	3,458.5	2,086.9
Total Current Liabilities	655.5	801.5	1,170.6	818.3
Long-Term Debt	97.1	108.9	12.0	35.9
Stockholders' Equity	3,450.4	3,188.6	2,271.9	1,214.8
Performance & Financial Condition				
Return on Total Revenues %	3.86	11.80	13.93	6.40
Return on Avg Stockholders' Equity %	7.89	33.57	58.99	39.28
Return on Average Assets %	6.30	24.25	37.09	21.25
Current Ratio	5.51	4.59	2.70	2.21
Debt / Equity %	2.81	3.41	0.53	2.95

Compound Growth %'s	EPS %	-15.66	Net Income %	-13.04	Total Revenues %	2.92

Comments

Approximately 20% of revenue had been derived from Wachovia Operational Services Corporation in years prior to fiscal 1998. As the result of the loss of Wachovia as a customer, which had been anticipated, revenues declined $1 million. Management believes that its ability to generate new software license revenues from existing clients and new clients will replace the lost revenue by fiscal 1999. If so, the Company will have handled this major transition with an excellent financial condition. For the six months ended February 28, 1999, revenue and net income were $3.7 million and $135,413 ($.03 per share) as compared to $3.5 million and $223,401 ($.06 per share) in the same period of the preceding year.

Officers	Position	Ownership Information	
James L. Schultz	President, CEO	Number of Shares Outstanding	4,037,255
David J. Vagnoni	Exec VP	Market Capitalization	$ 3,270,177
Kenneth C. Ebbitt	Director	Number of Shareholders	900
David K. Klotz	Director	Where Listed / Symbol	OTC-BB / CRIX

Other Information			
Transfer Agent	Registrar & Transfer Co. Cranford, NJ	SIC Code	7374
Auditor	Arthur Andersen LLP	Employees	50
Market Maker	Legg Mason Wood Walker, Inc. (800)346-5075		
	Paragon Capital Corporation (800)521-8877		

Comstock Resources, Inc.

5005 LBJ Freeway, Suite 1000   Dallas, TX 75244   Telephone (972)701-2000   Fax (972)701-2111

Company Description

Comstock Resources, Inc. is an independent energy company engaged in the acquisition, development, production and exploration of oil and natural gas properties. The Company has an oil and gas reserve base which is entirely focused in the Gulf of Mexico, Southeast Texas and East Texas/North Louisiana regions. The Company prefers to operate the properties it acquires, allowing it to exercise greater control over the timing and plans for future development, the level of drilling and lifting costs, and the marketing of production. The Company operates 366 of the 580 wells in which it owns an interest which comprise approximately 83% of its present value of proved reserves as of December 31, 1998.

	12/31/98	12/31/97	12/31/96	12/31/95
Per Share Information				
Stock Price	3.12	11.94	13.00	5.37
Earnings Per Share	-0.71	0.85	1.32	2.24
Price / Earnings Ratio	n.a.	14.05	9.85	2.40
Book Value Per Share	4.50	5.15	4.90	1.71
Price / Book Value %	69.33	231.84	265.31	314.04
Dividends Per Share	0.0	0.0	0.0	0.0
Annual Financial Data				
Operating Results (000's)				
Total Revenues	93,235.0	89,344.0	70,955.0	22,374.0
Costs & Expenses	-119,647.0	-55,566.0	-44,868.0	-51,799.0
Income Before Taxes and Other	-26,412.0	33,778.0	26,087.0	-29,425.0
Other Items	0.0	0.0	1,866.0	3,264.0
Income Tax	9,244.0	-11,622.0	0.0	0.0
Net Income	-17,168.0	22,156.0	27,953.0	-26,161.0
Cash Flow From Operations	40,726.0	84,277.0	45,919.0	8,407.0
Balance Sheet (000's)				
Cash & Equivalents	5,176.0	14,504.0	16,162.0	1,917.0
Total Current Assets	24,494.0	45,917.0	35,833.0	17,247.1
Fixed Assets, Net	404,017.0	410,781.0	185,928.0	102,851.6
Total Assets	429,672.0	456,800.0	222,002.0	120,098.7
Total Current Liabilities	72,756.0	56,184.0	22,881.0	35,188.4
Long-Term Debt	240,000.0	260,000.0	80,000.0	54,782.5
Stockholders' Equity	109,663.0	124,594.0	118,216.0	30,127.8
Performance & Financial Condition				
Return on Total Revenues %	-18.41	24.80	39.40	-116.93
Return on Avg Stockholders' Equity %	-14.66	18.25	37.69	-73.35
Return on Average Assets %	-3.87	6.53	16.34	-24.72
Current Ratio	0.34	0.82	1.57	0.49
Debt / Equity %	218.85	208.68	67.67	181.83

Compound Growth %'s	EPS %	n.a.	Net Income %	n.a.	Total Revenues %	60.92

Comments

The Company has achieved substantial growth in reserves, production and revenues since 1993. Management has focused on a strict control over operations and costs thereby lowering general and administration expenses per unit of production. The increase in 1998 revenue is attributable to a 17% increase in natural gas production and a 92% increase in oil production, offset by 18% lower realized natural gas prices and 35% lower realized oil prices. Due to the substantial drop in oil and gas prices during 1998, the Company provided an impairment of $17 million in 1998 of its oil and gas properties. The Company's stock price has dropped to less than one-quarter of its 1996 level which makes this NYSE company one to watch.

Officers	Position	Ownership Information	
M. Jay Allison	President, CEO	Number of Shares Outstanding	24,350,452
Roland O. Burns	Senior VP, CFO	Market Capitalization	$ 75,973,410
Michael W. Taylor	Vice President	Number of Shareholders	8,500
Daniel K. Presley	Vice President, Controller	Where Listed / Symbol	NYSE / CRK

Other Information			
Transfer Agent	American Stock Transfer & Trust Co. New York, NY	SIC Code	1311
Auditor	Arthur Andersen LLP	Employees	47

Comtrex Systems Corporation

102 Executive Drive   Moorestown, NJ 08057-4224   Telephone (609)778-0090   Fax (609)778-9322

Company Description

Comtrex Systems Corporation designs, develops, assembles and markets electronic terminals and computer software which provide target retailers with transaction processing, in-store controls and management information. Between March 1992 and February 1995, the Company's products were marketed in the United States by Sharp Electronics Corporation, under the Sharp brand name, under an exclusive licensing agreement. The Company began selling products in the United States through its own distribution network in March 1995. Comtrex was founded in 1981.

	03/31/98	03/31/97	03/31/96	03/31/95
Per Share Information				
Stock Price as of 12/31	0.81	0.81	0.59	0.75
Earnings Per Share	-0.07	-0.03	-0.07	0.08
Price / Earnings Ratio	n.a.	n.a.	n.a.	9.38
Book Value Per Share	0.77	0.71	0.74	0.81
Price / Book Value %	105.19	114.08	79.73	92.59
Dividends Per Share	0.0	0.0	0.0	0.0
Annual Financial Data				
Operating Results (000's)				
Total Revenues	6,382.9	5,430.2	5,033.7	5,689.9
Costs & Expenses	-6,131.9	-5,519.2	-5,267.5	-5,451.5
Income Before Taxes and Other	251.1	-89.0	-233.7	238.4
Other Items	84.4	0.0	0.0	96.0
Income Tax	-94.1	0.0	0.0	-96.0
Net Income	241.4	-89.0	-233.7	238.4
Cash Flow From Operations	442.4	156.3	-324.0	175.2
Balance Sheet (000's)				
Cash & Equivalents	313.6	142.9	218.2	750.7
Total Current Assets	3,311.9	2,457.9	2,475.3	2,834.5
Fixed Assets, Net	753.1	147.5	142.5	150.0
Total Assets	4,803.5	2,943.2	2,868.8	3,120.7
Total Current Liabilities	1,441.5	706.0	542.6	563.4
Long-Term Debt	596.6	0.0	0.0	0.0
Stockholders' Equity	2,755.0	2,237.2	2,326.2	2,557.3
Performance & Financial Condition				
Return on Total Revenues %	3.78	-1.64	-4.64	4.19
Return on Avg Stockholders' Equity %	9.67	-3.90	-9.57	9.93
Return on Average Assets %	6.23	-3.06	-7.81	8.22
Current Ratio	2.30	3.48	4.56	5.03
Debt / Equity %	21.65	n.a.	n.a.	n.a.

Compound Growth %'s	EPS % n.a.	Net Income % n.a.	Total Revenues % 3.91

Comments

The increase in fiscal 1998 revenue was largely due to the acquisition of the Company's distributor in the United Kingdom and the resulting consolidation of sales. Fiscal 1998 results include an extraordinary credit of $84,416 ($.02 per share) from the use of tax loss carryovers. Fiscal 1995 results include a similar credit of $96,000 ($.03 per share). $3.1 million of tax loss carryovers remain available to offset future income. Operating results have been lackluster if not outright boring. Can the Company break out? For the nine months ended December 31, 1998, the Company reported revenues and net income of $6.3 million and $269,451 ($.08 per share) as compared to $4.4 million and $196,072 ($.06 per share) for the same period of the preceding year.

Officers	Position	Ownership Information	
Jeffrey C. Rice	President, CEO	Number of Shares Outstanding	3,583,572
Lisa J. Mudrick	Treasurer, CFO	Market Capitalization	$ 2,902,693
Brian C. Moseley	Vice President	Number of Shareholders	400
Alan G. Schwartz	Director	Where Listed / Symbol	NASDAQ / COMX

Other Information			
Transfer Agent	American Stock Transfer & Trust Company New York, NY	SIC Code	3578
Auditor	Drucker, Math & Whitman, P.C.	Employees	35
		Web Site	comtrex.com

Conrad Industries, Inc.

1501 Front Street, P.O. Box 790   Morgan City, LA 70381   Telephone (504)384-3060   Fax (504)385-4090

Company Description

Conrad Industries, Inc. specializes in the construction, conversion and repair of a wide variety of marine vessels for commercial and government customers and the fabrication of modular components of offshore drilling rigs and of floating production, storage and offloading vessels. The Company constructs a variety of marine vessels, including large and small deck barges, single and double hull tank barges, lift boats, push boats, tow boats and offshore tug boats. The Company serves a variety of customers and markets, including the offshore oil and gas industry, other commercial markets and the U.S. government. The Company acquired Orange Shipbuilding in December 1997 for $25.8 million. Conrad followed the acquisition with its initial public offering in June 1998, placing 2.25 million shares at $12 per share.

	12/31/98	12/31/97	12/31/96	12/31/95
Per Share Information				
Stock Price	4.62	n.a.	n.a.	n.a.
Earnings Per Share	0.04	1.05	0.92	0.57
Price / Earnings Ratio	115.50	n.a.	n.a.	n.a.
Book Value Per Share	4.31	3.28	2.66	2.15
Price / Book Value %	107.19	n.a.	n.a.	n.a.
Dividends Per Share	0.0	0.0	0.0	0.0
Annual Financial Data				
Operating Results (000's)				
Total Revenues	46,597.0	22,305.0	23,244.0	20,954.0
Costs & Expenses	-39,060.0	-17,400.0	-18,946.0	-18,309.0
Income Before Taxes and Other	7,537.0	4,905.0	4,298.0	2,645.0
Other Items	-4,676.0	0.0	0.0	0.0
Income Tax	-2,607.0	0.0	0.0	0.0
Net Income	254.0	4,905.0	4,298.0	2,645.0
Cash Flow From Operations	1,988.0	6,114.0	5,313.0	3,604.0
Balance Sheet (000's)				
Cash & Equivalents	3,074.0	7,551.0	3,209.0	2,476.0
Total Current Assets	14,240.0	15,294.0	6,687.0	5,696.0
Fixed Assets, Net	18,104.0	18,304.0	8,514.0	7,465.0
Total Assets	47,519.0	48,945.0	15,236.0	13,895.0
Total Current Liabilities	6,562.0	7,534.0	2,285.0	1,963.0
Long-Term Debt	7,318.0	23,537.0	572.0	1,900.0
Stockholders' Equity	30,482.0	15,279.0	12,379.0	10,032.0
Performance & Financial Condition				
Return on Total Revenues %	0.55	21.99	18.49	12.62
Return on Avg Stockholders' Equity %	1.11	35.47	38.36	29.42
Return on Average Assets %	0.53	15.28	29.51	21.78
Current Ratio	2.17	2.03	2.93	2.90
Debt / Equity %	24.01	154.05	4.62	18.94

Compound Growth %'s	EPS %	-58.75	Net Income %	-54.21	Total Revenues %	30.53

Comments

The Company was under Subchapter S status prior to the public offering. Accordingly, no income tax expense was incurred in years prior to 1998. The proceeds of the offering were used to repay debt incurred in the acquisition mentioned above. In 1998, the Company recognized $4,676,000 of executive compensation expense due to stock options granted to two key executive officers of the Company. Approximately 70% of increased revenues in 1998, as compared to 1997, was attributable to the acquired Company. But this leaves Conrad with a healthy $7.2 million of increased revenues for the same period. At December 31, 1998, the Company had $15 million of goodwill recorded as assets which equated to approximately 49% of stockholders' equity and book value per share.

Officers	Position	Ownership Information	
J. Parker Conrad	Chairman	Number of Shares Outstanding	7,077,723
John P. Conrad, Jr.	Chairman	Market Capitalization	$ 32,699,080
William H. Hildalgo	President, CEO	Number of Shareholders	1,000
Cecil A. Hernandez	VP - Finance, CFO	Where Listed / Symbol	NASDAQ / CNRD

Other Information			
Transfer Agent	American Stock Transfer & Trust Company New York, NY	SIC Code	3730
Auditor	Deloitte & Touche LLP	Employees	285
		Web Site	conradindustries.com

Consolidated Delivery & Logistics, Inc.

380 Allwood Road   Clifton, NJ 07012   Telephone (973)471-1005   Fax (973)471-5519

Company Description

Consolidated Delivery & Logistics, Inc. provides an extensive network of same-day ground and air delivery and logistics services to a wide range of commercial, industrial and retail customers. The Company's ground delivery operations currently are concentrated on the East Coast and in the Midwest, with a strategic presence on the West Coast. The Company's logistics services are provided on a national basis and its air delivery services are provided throughout the United States and to major cities around the world. The Company was formed in 1994. However, it wasn't until November 1995, with the closing of the Company's initial public offering and a merger with eleven other companies, that it began doing business.

	12/31/98	12/31/97	12/31/96	12/31/95
Per Share Information				
Stock Price	3.12	2.50	4.38	10.38
Earnings Per Share	0.34	0.07	-0.10	-0.10
Price / Earnings Ratio	9.18	35.71	n.a.	n.a.
Book Value Per Share	1.67	1.29	1.28	1.25
Price / Book Value %	186.83	193.80	342.19	830.40
Dividends Per Share	0.0	0.0	0.0	0.0
Annual Financial Data				
Operating Results (000's)				
Total Revenues	185,865.0	172,489.0	171,510.0	39,401.0
Costs & Expenses	-182,138.0	-169,944.0	-173,037.0	-39,014.0
Income Before Taxes and Other	3,727.0	2,545.0	-1,527.0	387.0
Other Items	0.0	-1,198.0	0.0	0.0
Income Tax	-1,416.0	-888.0	844.0	-582.0
Net Income	2,311.0	459.0	-683.0	-195.0
Cash Flow From Operations	4,978.0	2,572.0	-3,573.0	2,573.0
Balance Sheet (000's)				
Cash & Equivalents	295.0	1,812.0	1,725.0	6,589.0
Total Current Assets	27,346.0	26,079.0	27,059.0	26,886.0
Fixed Assets, Net	6,630.0	5,667.0	4,316.0	3,925.0
Total Assets	52,088.0	36,159.0	35,690.0	32,270.0
Total Current Liabilities	31,542.0	23,560.0	21,587.0	19,344.0
Long-Term Debt	6,383.0	2,240.0	3,415.0	3,027.0
Stockholders' Equity	11,407.0	8,614.0	8,730.0	8,311.0
Performance & Financial Condition				
Return on Total Revenues %	1.24	0.27	-0.40	-0.49
Return on Avg Stockholders' Equity %	23.09	5.29	-8.02	-4.33
Return on Average Assets %	5.24	1.28	-2.01	-1.22
Current Ratio	0.87	1.11	1.25	1.39
Debt / Equity %	55.96	26.00	39.12	36.42

Compound Growth %'s	EPS % n.a.	Net Income % n.a.	Total Revenues % 67.71

Comments

In 1997 steps were taken to focus the business, improve administrative and operational efficiencies, eliminate underperforming subsidiaries and products, and establish a management incentive system. A loss of $1.2 million was recorded from discontinued operations. Included in 1997 income from continuing operations is a $816,000 gain from the sale of a subsidiary. In 1998 the Company produced solid profits without the aid of unusual items. At December 31, 1998, the Company had recorded $16.5 million of intangibles as assets which approximated 145% of stockholders' equity and book value per share. The Company also had a deficiency in working capital as it used its line of credit to finance business acquisitions. On January 29, 1999, the Company completed a private placement of senior subordinated notes to raise $15 million used to repay other debt and provide working capital.

Officers	Position	Ownership Information	
Albert W. Van Ness, Jr.	Chairman, CEO	Number of Shares Outstanding	6,814,335
William T. Brannan	President, COO	Market Capitalization	$ 21,260,725
Joseph G. Wojak	Exec VP, CFO	Number of Shareholders	1,600
Joseph J. Leonhard	Vice President, Controller	Where Listed / Symbol	AMEX / CDV

Other Information			
Transfer Agent	American Stock Transfer & Trust Co. New York, NY	SIC Code	4213
Auditor	Arthur Andersen LLP	Employees	3,500
		Web Site	cdl.net

Consumer Portfolio Services, Inc.

16355 Laguna Canyon Road   Irvine, CA 92618   Telephone (949)753-6800   Fax (949)753-6860

Company Description

Consumer Portfolio Services, Inc. is a consumer finance company specializing in the business of purchasing, selling and servicing retail automobile installment contracts originated by dealers in the sale of new and used automobiles, light trucks and passenger vans. Through its purchases, the Company provides indirect financing to borrowers with limited credit histories, low incomes or past credit problems. The Company serves as an alternative source of financing for dealers, allowing sales to customers who otherwise might not be able to obtain financing from more traditional sources of automobile financing such as banks, credit unions or finance companies affiliated with major automobile manufacturers. The Company was formed in 1991 and had its initial public offering in 1995 by issuing one million common shares at $14.75 per share.

	12/31/98	12/31/97	12/31/96	12/31/95
Per Share Information				
Stock Price	3.31	9.56	11.12	9.12
Earnings Per Share	1.50	1.17	0.93	0.52
Price / Earnings Ratio	2.21	8.17	11.96	17.54
Book Value Per Share	7.60	5.43	4.13	3.12
Price / Book Value %	43.55	176.06	269.25	292.31
Dividends Per Share	0.0	0.0	0.0	0.0
Annual Financial Data				
Operating Results (000's)				
Total Revenues	126,280.0	79,339.6	51,193.8	24,254.7
Costs & Expenses	-81,960.0	-47,380.7	-27,501.4	-11,597.4
Income Before Taxes and Other	44,320.0	31,958.9	23,692.4	12,657.3
Other Items	0.0	0.0	0.0	0.0
Income Tax	-18,617.0	-13,426.7	-9,595.0	-5,082.2
Net Income	25,703.0	18,532.2	14,097.4	7,575.1
Cash Flow From Operations	-71,135.0	-26,131.8	-8,352.8	-18,533.4
Balance Sheet (000's)				
Cash & Equivalents	1,940.0	1,745.2	154.0	10,895.0
Total Current Assets	14,707.0	10,537.7	4,794.3	13,895.0
Fixed Assets, Net	4,272.0	3,128.1	629.8	549.0
Total Assets	431,962.0	225,895.2	101,946.4	77,878.0
Total Current Liabilities	11,088.0	10,426.9	1,697.1	5,897.0
Long-Term Debt	252,414.0	103,171.2	36,264.6	30,500.0
Stockholders' Equity	119,081.0	82,606.8	56,957.5	41,481.0
Performance & Financial Condition				
Return on Total Revenues %	20.35	23.36	27.54	31.23
Return on Avg Stockholders' Equity %	25.49	26.56	28.64	30.30
Return on Average Assets %	7.81	11.31	15.68	16.29
Current Ratio	1.33	1.01	2.83	2.36
Debt / Equity %	211.97	124.89	63.67	73.53

Compound Growth %'s	EPS %	42.35	Net Income %	50.27	Total Revenues %	73.32

Comments

The Company declared a 2 for 1 stock split in 1996. All per share amounts have been adjusted for consistency. The Company changed its reporting period in 1995. Results of operations displayed above for 1995 are for the nine months ended December 31, 1995. Accordingly, compound growth rates are slightly distorted. Revenues have been rising rapidly as the Company is processing an ever increasing number of contracts. Gains in 1998 from the sale of contracts and fees from servicing contracts were higher by 67.8% and 77.8%, respectively. Due to the inherent uncertainty of the future performance of the underlying contracts, the Company established a provision for future losses on residual interests in the amount of $7.8 million during 1998. The Company also provides reserves for credit losses. The adequacy of reserves should be studied by the interested investor.

Officers	Position	Ownership Information	
Charles E. Bradley, Jr.	President, CEO	Number of Shares Outstanding	15,658,501
Jeffrey P. Fritz	Senior VP, CFO	Market Capitalization	$ 51,829,638
William L. Brummund, Jr.	Senior VP	Number of Shareholders	2,000
Nicholas P. Brockman	Senior VP	Where Listed / Symbol	NASDAQ / CPSS

Other Information			
Transfer Agent	American Stock Transfer & Trust Co. New York, NY	SIC Code	6189
Auditor	KPMG LLP	Employees	666
		Web Site	consumerportfolio.com

Continental Information Systems Corporation

45 Broadway Atrium, Suite 1105   New York, NY 10006   Telephone (212)771-1000   Fax (212)771-1100

Company Description

The Company is engaged in the leasing, sales and management of commercial aircraft and aircraft engines, equipment leasing and other financing activities, including commercial real estate financing. In fiscal 1998, the Company discontinued a telecommunications equipment resale business and a laser printing business. At the time of its formation in 1968 and in its early years, the Company was primarily involved with the sale and marketing of mainframe and peripheral computer equipment. In 1989, the Company filed voluntary petitions for reorganization under Chapter 11 of the United States Bankruptcy Code. The plan of reorganization was confirmed on December 21, 1994.

	05/31/98	05/31/97	05/31/96	05/31/95
Per Share Information				
Stock Price as of 12/31	1.47	2.50	2.00	2.12
Earnings Per Share	-0.77	0.15	0.01	-0.23
Price / Earnings Ratio	n.a.	16.67	200.00	n.a.
Book Value Per Share	4.17	4.92	4.78	4.77
Price / Book Value %	35.25	50.81	41.84	44.44
Dividends Per Share	0.0	0.0	0.0	0.0
Annual Financial Data				
Operating Results (000's)				
Total Revenues	18,419.0	31,301.0	26,822.0	11,762.0
Costs & Expenses	-17,563.0	-29,662.0	-25,211.0	-9,529.0
Income Before Taxes and Other	856.0	1,639.0	1,611.0	2,233.0
Other Items	-5,904.0	70.0	-934.0	-2,997.0
Income Tax	-325.0	-623.0	-611.0	-849.0
Net Income	-5,373.0	1,086.0	66.0	-1,613.0
Cash Flow From Operations	15,406.0	11,739.0	6.8	12,345.0
Balance Sheet (000's)				
Cash & Equivalents	3,211.0	9,005.0	5,382.0	13,015.0
Total Current Assets	7,602.0	23,416.0	14,009.0	18,970.0
Fixed Assets, Net	398.0	218.0	625.0	1,059.0
Total Assets	45,202.0	44,077.0	53,550.0	41,130.0
Total Current Liabilities	2,377.0	1,302.0	2,949.0	2,076.0
Long-Term Debt	4,429.0	0.0	0.0	0.0
Stockholders' Equity	28,960.0	34,601.0	33,453.0	33,387.0
Performance & Financial Condition				
Return on Total Revenues %	-29.17	3.47	0.25	-13.71
Return on Avg Stockholders' Equity %	-16.91	3.19	0.20	-4.72
Return on Average Assets %	-12.04	2.22	0.14	-3.58
Current Ratio	3.20	17.98	4.75	9.14
Debt / Equity %	15.29	n.a.	n.a.	n.a.

Compound Growth %'s	EPS % n.a.	Net Income % n.a.	Total Revenues % 16.13

Comments

Fiscal 1998 results include a loss from discontinued operations of $.85 per share. The significant decline in revenues is in part due to discontinued operations. Fiscal 1995 results are for the six month period following the bankruptcy reorganization. Accordingly, compound growth rates were not displayed. For the nine months ended February 28, 1999, revenues and a net loss totalled $12.9 million and $183,000 ($.03 per share) as compared to $12.8 million and a net loss of $135,000 ($.02 per share) for the same period ended of the preceding year.

Officers	Position	Ownership Information	
James P. Hassett	Chairman	Number of Shares Outstanding	6,939,060
Michael L. Rosen	President, CEO	Market Capitalization	$ 10,200,418
Jonah M. Meer	Senior VP, COO	Number of Shareholders	1,236
James J. Mosher	Secretary	Where Listed / Symbol	NASDAQ / CISC

Other Information

Transfer Agent	ChaseMellon Shareholder Services Ridgefield Park, NJ		SIC Code	5045
Auditor	PricewaterhouseCoopers LLP		Employees	25
Market Maker	Carr Securities Corporation	(800)221-2243	Web Site	ciscorporation.com
	Herzog, Heine, Geduld, Inc.	(800)221-3600		

Creative Host Services, Inc.

6335 Ferris Square, Suites G-H   San Diego, CA 92126   Telephone (619)587-7300   Fax (619)587-7309

Company Description

Creative Host Services, Inc. is primarily engaged in the business of acquiring and operating food, beverage and other concessions at airports throughout the United States. The Company currently has 35 operating concession facilities at 18 airports, 34 of which are Company owned and one of which is franchised. The Company's strategy is to expand its concession business to more airports in the United States, and eventually to other public venues. The Company also intends to seek to expand the types of concession services which it provides, and to be awarded more multiple master concession contracts. The Company completed its initial public offering in July 1997.

	12/31/98	12/31/97	12/31/96	12/31/95
Per Share Information				
Stock Price	1.62	2.12	n.a.	n.a.
Earnings Per Share	0.15	-0.02	0.10	-0.53
Price / Earnings Ratio	10.80	n.a.	n.a.	n.a.
Book Value Per Share	1.62	1.45	0.05	-0.11
Price / Book Value %	100.00	146.21	n.a.	n.a.
Dividends Per Share	0.0	0.0	0.0	0.0
Annual Financial Data				
Operating Results (000's)				
Total Revenues	14,720.4	9,809.2	5,691.6	2,059.6
Costs & Expenses	-14,223.5	-9,771.5	-5,504.1	-2,638.6
Income Before Taxes and Other	496.8	37.6	187.6	-579.0
Other Items	0.0	0.0	0.0	0.0
Income Tax	-16.3	0.0	0.0	0.0
Net Income	480.5	37.6	187.6	-579.0
Cash Flow From Operations	961.8	755.0	281.8	-600.0
Balance Sheet (000's)				
Cash & Equivalents	139.7	1,109.2	1.0	131.1
Total Current Assets	1,151.6	1,890.3	582.8	331.1
Fixed Assets, Net	9,582.7	5,056.1	1,984.8	1,800.0
Total Assets	11,271.4	7,109.8	2,831.5	2,131.1
Total Current Liabilities	2,186.2	1,712.0	1,521.1	1,500.0
Long-Term Debt	2,952.8	144.3	0.0	0.0
Stockholders' Equity	5,201.7	4,489.8	55.7	-131.9
Performance & Financial Condition				
Return on Total Revenues %	3.26	0.38	3.30	-28.11
Return on Avg Stockholders' Equity %	9.92	1.66	n.a.	n.a.
Return on Average Assets %	5.23	0.76	7.56	-26.32
Current Ratio	0.53	1.10	0.38	0.22
Debt / Equity %	56.77	3.21	n.a.	n.a.

Compound Growth %'s	EPS %	22.47	Net Income %	60.06	Total Revenues %	92.62

Comments

Most of the increase in revenues realized during 1998 is attributable to full year operations for the concession locations opened during 1997 and partial year operations for an additional two concession locations which opened during 1998. However, for the ten locations that were opened a full twelve months in both 1997 and 1998, revenues increased 8.3%. Cost of goods sold and salary costs are higher as a percentage of sales for newly added stores due to training and the absence of operating data for inventory stocking purposes. The improvement in operating results in 1998 reflects fewer new openings than in 1997. The Company had a deficiency in working capital at the end of 1998 and capital requirements of approximately $3.5 million in 1999 to complete the construction of new concession facilities. Management believes it has several financing alternatives available.

Officers	Position	Ownership Information	
Sayed Ali	Chairman, President	Number of Shares Outstanding	3,211,033
Tasneem Vakharia	Secretary	Market Capitalization	$ 5,201,873
Booker T. Graves	Director	Number of Shareholders	1,000
John P. Donohue, Jr.	Director	Where Listed / Symbol	NASDAQ / CHST

Other Information			
Transfer Agent	American Securities Transfer, Inc. Denver, CO	SIC Code	5812
Auditor	Stonefield Josephson, Inc.	Employees	546

Creative Technologies Corp.

170 53rd Street   Brooklyn, NY 11232   Telephone (718)492-8400   Fax (718)492-3878

Company Description

Creative Technologies Corp. is the exclusive distributor in the United States and Canada of products manufactured by Brabantia International and Soehnle-Waagen GmbH & Co. Brabantia, headquartered in the Netherlands, is a leading manufacturer of top of the line non-electric houseware products in Europe. Soehnle-Waagen, headquartered in Germany, manufactures a full line of bathroom scales. In October 1997, the Company acquired Ace Surgical Supply Co., Inc., a company which distributes medical, janitorial and dietary products to hospitals, nursing homes and medical care facilities. Prior to June 30, 1997, the Company was a manufacturer of electric motor driven pasta machines and electric grillers. These manufacturing activities were discontinued in 1997.

	12/31/98	12/31/97	12/31/96	12/31/95
Per Share Information				
Stock Price	0.28	0.47	1.31	1.31
Earnings Per Share	-0.09	-0.90	-2.90	-1.33
Price / Earnings Ratio	n.a.	n.a.	n.a.	n.a.
Book Value Per Share	-2.86	-2.88	-2.29	0.14
Price / Book Value %	n.a.	n.a.	n.a.	935.71
Dividends Per Share	0.0	0.0	0.0	0.0
Annual Financial Data				
Operating Results (000's)				
Total Revenues	15,263.0	10,862.0	4,986.0	14,142.0
Costs & Expenses	-15,170.0	-13,216.0	-13,495.0	-21,635.0
Income Before Taxes and Other	93.0	-2,354.0	-8,509.0	-7,493.0
Other Items	188.0	0.0	0.0	0.0
Income Tax	0.0	0.0	-481.0	242.0
Net Income	281.0	-2,354.0	-8,990.0	-7,251.0
Cash Flow From Operations	-214.0	-286.0	-575.0	-7,651.0
Balance Sheet (000's)				
Cash & Equivalents	1.0	16.0	100.0	771.0
Total Current Assets	4,419.0	5,587.0	2,541.0	8,112.0
Fixed Assets, Net	188.0	264.0	781.0	2,191.0
Total Assets	5,441.0	6,718.0	3,376.0	10,544.0
Total Current Liabilities	11,088.0	12,282.0	7,387.0	9,468.0
Long-Term Debt	0.0	400.0	200.0	0.0
Stockholders' Equity	-6,355.0	-6,237.0	-4,211.0	1,076.0
Performance & Financial Condition				
Return on Total Revenues %	1.84	-21.67	-180.30	-51.27
Return on Avg Stockholders' Equity %	n.a.	n.a.	n.a.	n.a.
Return on Average Assets %	4.62	-46.64	-129.17	-111.55
Current Ratio	0.40	0.45	0.34	0.86
Debt / Equity %	n.a.	n.a.	n.a.	n.a.

Compound Growth %'s	EPS %	n.a.	Net Income %	n.a.	Total Revenues %	2.58

Comments

The Company had an operating profit in 1998 after a substantial loss in 1997. The increase in revenue reported in 1998 was primarily the result of greater sales of Brabantia and the inclusion of Ace for a full year. 1998 results included a $188,000 gain on the settlement of debt. Earnings per share are calculated after deducting preferred stock dividends. The liquidation preferences on preferred shares were deducted in arriving at book value per common share. At December 31, 1998, the Company had $7.6 million of tax loss carryovers available to offset future taxable income. Because of a substantial working capital deficiency, the Company received a going concern qualification in the auditors report on the Company's last financial statements.

Officers	Position	Ownership Information	
David Guttmann	Chairman, CEO	Number of Shares Outstanding	4,127,000
Richard Helfman	President, CFO	Market Capitalization	$ 1,155,560
David Selengut	Secretary	Number of Shareholders	750
David Refson	Director	Where Listed / Symbol	OTC-BB / CRTV

Other Information			
Transfer Agent	American Transfer Company New York, NY	SIC Code	3634
Auditor	Goldstein Golub Kessler & Co.	Employees	33
Market Maker	Mayer & Schweitzer, Inc. (800)631-3094	Web Site	ctny.com
	Fahnestock & Co., Inc. (800)223-3012		

Cumberland Technologies, Inc.

4311 West Waters Avenue, Suite 501   Tampa, FL 33614   Telephone (813)885-2112   Fax (813)885-6734

Company Description

Cumberland Technologies, Inc. conducts its business through five subsidiaries and a number of independent agencies which focus on selling and delivering surety insurance products to consumers including performance and payment bonds for contractors and miscellaneous surety bonds to federal and local government agencies. The Company also has general insurance line agencies and a claim and contracting consulting services business. The Company was formed in 1992 when Kimmins Corp. spun off these businesses and distributed the shares in Cumberland to its then existing shareholders.

	12/31/98	12/31/97	12/31/96	12/31/95
Per Share Information				
Stock Price	2.00	2.75	3.00	0.37
Earnings Per Share	-0.06	0.03	-0.14	-0.06
Price / Earnings Ratio	n.a.	91.67	n.a.	n.a.
Book Value Per Share	0.98	1.10	1.07	0.34
Price / Book Value %	204.08	250.00	280.37	108.82
Dividends Per Share	0.0	0.0	0.0	0.0
Annual Financial Data				
Operating Results (000's)				
Total Revenues	9,010.4	7,769.8	6,369.4	6,787.9
Costs & Expenses	-9,331.8	-7,599.3	-6,952.1	-7,016.2
Income Before Taxes and Other	-321.4	170.5	-582.7	-228.2
Other Items	0.0	0.0	0.0	0.0
Income Tax	0.0	0.0	0.0	0.0
Net Income	-321.4	170.5	-582.7	-228.2
Cash Flow From Operations	-193.7	1,925.9	-17.0	-375.7
Balance Sheet (000's)				
Cash & Equivalents	4,202.4	1,803.5	669.1	1,235.9
Total Current Assets	12,361.1	12,828.0	9,780.4	10,110.7
Fixed Assets, Net	0.0	0.0	0.0	0.0
Total Assets	16,345.1	15,321.4	12,372.3	12,709.0
Total Current Liabilities	8,665.2	7,893.6	5,025.4	5,057.5
Long-Term Debt	2,330.6	1,418.5	1,533.3	6,361.7
Stockholders' Equity	5,349.2	6,009.3	5,813.7	1,289.8
Performance & Financial Condition				
Return on Total Revenues %	-3.57	2.19	-9.15	-3.36
Return on Avg Stockholders' Equity %	-5.66	2.88	-16.41	-17.51
Return on Average Assets %	-2.03	1.23	-4.65	-1.79
Current Ratio	1.43	1.63	1.95	2.00
Debt / Equity %	43.57	23.61	26.37	493.24

Compound Growth %'s	EPS %	n.a.	Net Income %	n.a.	Total Revenues %	9.90

Comments

During 1998, premiums written increased as a result of the marketing direction of the Company, which is to penetrate the direct market while decreasing the volume of reinsurance premiums assumed through pooling agreements. Direct written premiums increased 39.1% in 1998. A higher than usual loss under pooling agreements produced a negative bottom line for 1998. Management anticipates a decline in 1999 for claims attributable to pooling agreements. At December 31, 1998, the Company had $1.5 million of intangible assets on its books which equated to approximately 27% of stockholders' equity and book value per share.

Officers	Position	Ownership Information	
Francis M. Williams	Chairman	Number of Shares Outstanding	5,444,958
Joseph M. Williams	President, Treasurer	Market Capitalization	$ 10,889,916
Carol S. Black	CFO, Secretary	Number of Shareholders	903
George A. Chandler	Director	Where Listed / Symbol	NASDAQ / CUMB

Other Information			
Transfer Agent	Continental Stock Transfer & Trust Co. New York, NY	SIC Code	6331
Auditor	Ernst & Young LLP	Employees	37

Cylink Corporation

910 Hermosa Court, P.O. Box 3759 Sunnyvale, CA 94086 Telephone (408)735-5800 Fax (408)735-6614

Company Description

Cylink Corporation develops, markets and supports network security products that enable and manage the secure transmission and authentication of information over local area networks, wide area networks, public packet switched networks, such as the Internet, and broadcast networks. The Company's products offer an integrated, flexible solution for transforming any portion of an enterprise's network into a virtual private network by utilizing public key encryption technologies to create and manage an enterprise's security infrastructure. Secure access for local and remote authorized users of its proprietary information and services is also provided. Additionally, the Company conducts advanced research and development in the field of digital water marking for protection of intellectual property. The Company was founded in 1984 and had its initial public offering in 1996.

	12/31/98	12/31/97	12/31/96	12/31/95
Per Share Information				
Stock Price	3.75	9.75	12.87	15.00
Earnings Per Share	0.18	-2.37	0.23	-0.24
Price / Earnings Ratio	20.83	n.a.	55.96	n.a.
Book Value Per Share	2.58	2.41	3.80	0.77
Price / Book Value %	145.35	404.56	338.68	1,948.05
Dividends Per Share	0.0	0.0	0.0	0.0
Annual Financial Data				
Operating Results (000's)				
Total Revenues	45,107.0	52,347.0	29,096.0	21,584.0
Costs & Expenses	-71,618.0	-115,659.0	-34,001.0	-25,667.0
Income Before Taxes and Other	-26,511.0	-63,312.0	-5,522.0	-4,260.0
Other Items	22,517.0	4,535.0	6,719.0	3,181.0
Income Tax	9,155.0	0.0	0.0	0.0
Net Income	5,161.0	-58,777.0	1,197.0	-1,079.0
Cash Flow From Operations	-25,733.0	-4,612.0	-4,301.0	-2,400.0
Balance Sheet (000's)				
Cash & Equivalents	46,575.0	22,977.0	78,849.0	3,240.0
Total Current Assets	79,537.0	63,472.0	103,142.0	20,246.0
Fixed Assets, Net	5,731.0	6,699.0	3,760.0	2,295.0
Total Assets	94,318.0	82,593.0	107,088.0	22,725.0
Total Current Liabilities	18,950.0	13,222.0	9,624.0	7,642.0
Long-Term Debt	0.0	0.0	0.0	478.0
Stockholders' Equity	75,221.0	69,102.0	97,211.0	14,605.0
Performance & Financial Condition				
Return on Total Revenues %	11.44	-112.28	4.11	-5.00
Return on Avg Stockholders' Equity %	7.15	-70.68	2.14	-7.49
Return on Average Assets %	5.83	-61.97	1.84	-4.97
Current Ratio	4.20	4.80	10.72	2.65
Debt / Equity %	n.a.	n.a.	n.a.	3.27

Compound Growth %'s	EPS % n.a.	Net Income % n.a.	Total Revenues % 27.85

Comments

On March 28, 1998, the Company sold its Wireless Communications Group for $58.4 million resulting in a nonrecurring gain of $22,517,000. Results from continuing operations were severely negative. 1997 results include a $63.9 million expense related to purchased in-process technology in connection with the acquisition of Algorithmic Research Ltd. Income and expense from discontinued operations are displayed as Other Items in the above section on operating results. A management shake out, the loss of other key personnel, and class action lawsuits have dampened investor enthusiasm. Although the balance sheet is strong at December 31, 1998, the Company must demonstrate profitability with its downsized business.

Officers	Position	Ownership Information	
Leo A. Guthart	Chairman	Number of Shares Outstanding	29,115,000
William Cromwell	President, CEO	Market Capitalization	$ 109,181,250
Roger A. Barnes	VP - Finance, CFO	Number of Shareholders	5,000
Robert B. Fougner	Secretary	Where Listed / Symbol	NASDAQ / CYLK

Other Information			
Transfer Agent	Boston EquiServe Boston, MA	SIC Code	3577
Auditor	PricewaterhouseCoopers LLP	Employees	325
		Web Site	cylink.com

DCI Telecommunications, Inc.

611 Access Road   Stratford, CT 06497   Telephone (203)380-0910   Fax (203)380-0915

Company Description

DCI Telecommunications, Inc. has been involved in numerous acquisition and merger activities resulting in a telecommunications company with several different business units including long distance telecommunications, prepaid cellular and Internet related products and services. The Company's growth plan is based on internal product development supported by strategic acquisitions and joint ventures in the telecommunications area which will immediately and significantly enhance its product offerings, distribution channels, market penetration and earnings. The Company was founded in 1985.

	03/31/98	03/31/97	03/31/96	03/31/95
Per Share Information				
Stock Price as of 12/31	2.69	1.81	1.56	n.a.
Earnings Per Share	0.02	-0.07	-0.36	n.a.
Price / Earnings Ratio	134.50	n.a.	n.a.	n.a.
Book Value Per Share	0.77	0.70	0.67	n.a.
Price / Book Value %	349.35	258.57	232.84	n.a.
Dividends Per Share	0.0	0.0	0.0	n.a.
Annual Financial Data				
Operating Results (000's)				
Total Revenues	8,183.8	2,813.5	1,842.3	110.4
Costs & Expenses	-10,592.1	-3,186.8	-2,554.2	-1,205.9
Income Before Taxes and Other	-2,408.3	-373.3	-711.9	-1,095.5
Other Items	3,547.7	0.0	0.0	0.0
Income Tax	-201.0	0.0	0.0	0.0
Net Income	938.4	-373.3	-711.9	-1,095.5
Cash Flow From Operations	-2,053.5	-744.8	-311.2	-1,095.5
Balance Sheet (000's)				
Cash & Equivalents	1,837.0	1,314.1	42.2	n.a.
Total Current Assets	13,166.0	3,729.0	309.4	n.a.
Fixed Assets, Net	433.3	306.1	129.9	n.a.
Total Assets	21,671.1	10,734.0	2,606.5	n.a.
Total Current Liabilities	8,902.5	1,960.1	597.1	n.a.
Long-Term Debt	35.2	180.0	83.7	n.a.
Stockholders' Equity	11,151.2	5,931.3	1,925.8	n.a.
Performance & Financial Condition				
Return on Total Revenues %	11.47	-13.27	-38.64	-992.42
Return on Avg Stockholders' Equity %	10.99	-9.50	-29.86	-89.64
Return on Average Assets %	5.79	-5.60	-23.85	-65.09
Current Ratio	1.48	1.90	0.52	n.a.
Debt / Equity %	0.32	3.04	4.34	n.a.

Compound Growth %'s	EPS % n.a.	Net Income % n.a.	Total Revenues % 320.10

Comments

The Company discontinued certain operations in fiscal 1998 resulting in $3.5 million of nonrecurring gains from the disposal of assets. A loss from continuing operations totaled $2.6 million ($.30 per share). Preferred stock dividends were deducted from income in calculating earnings per share. The substantial increase in revenues was attributable to companies that had been acquired and included in consolidated numbers for a full year. At March 31, 1998, the Company had approximately $6.6 million recorded as intangible assets, which equated to 60% of stockholders' equity and book value per share. For the nine months ended December 31, 1998, the Company reported revenue and a net loss of $28.1 million and $1.9 million ($.13 per share) as compared to $8.0 million and $879,160 ($.04 per share) for the same period of the preceding year.

Officers	Position	Ownership Information	
Joseph J. Murphy	President, CEO	Number of Shares Outstanding	14,092,625
Larry Shatsoff	Vice President, COO	Market Capitalization	$ 37,909,161
John J. Adams	Vice President	Number of Shareholders	2,300
Carter Hills	Director	Where Listed / Symbol	OTC-BB / DCTC

Other Information			
Transfer Agent	Nevada Agency & Trust Co. Reno, NV	SIC Code	4813
Auditor	Schnitzer & Kondub, P.C.	Employees	43
Market Maker	Olsen Payne & Co. (800)453-5321	Web Site	dcic.com
	Wilson-Davis & Co., Inc. (800)453-5735		

DMI Furniture, Inc.

One Oxmoor Place, 101 Bullitt Lane   Louisville, KY 40222   Telephone (502)426-4351   Fax (502)429-6285

Company Description

DMI Furniture, Inc. manufactures, imports, and sells low to medium-priced bedroom furniture, dining furniture, occasional and accent furniture, commercial and home office furniture, conference tables and chairs. Its principal distribution channels are multi-market furniture retailers, distributors, independent retailers, catalogers, and warehouse clubs. DMI Furniture owns three furniture manufacturing plants, a saw mill, a dimension parts plant, and a fabrication plant. The Company's six largest customers accounted for 51% of the Company's total sales in fiscal 1998.

	08/29/98	08/30/97	08/31/96	09/02/95
Per Share Information				
Stock Price as of 12/31	3.31	2.69	2.62	1.25
Earnings Per Share	0.07	0.40	0.07	0.14
Price / Earnings Ratio	47.29	6.73	37.43	8.93
Book Value Per Share	2.64	2.94	2.31	2.22
Price / Book Value %	125.38	91.50	113.42	56.31
Dividends Per Share	0.0	0.0	0.0	0.0
Annual Financial Data				
Operating Results (000's)				
Total Revenues	64,841.9	56,697.0	55,649.8	67,792.4
Costs & Expenses	-61,710.7	-52,937.0	-54,995.8	-66,498.8
Income Before Taxes and Other	3,131.2	3,878.9	608.8	1,289.9
Other Items	0.0	0.0	0.0	0.0
Income Tax	-1,156.3	-1,463.0	-233.2	-485.4
Net Income	1,974.9	2,415.8	375.7	804.5
Cash Flow From Operations	-1,211.2	23.4	8,504.4	207.3
Balance Sheet (000's)				
Cash & Equivalents	1,092.5	1,592.6	96.5	68.7
Total Current Assets	28,916.2	24,158.1	19,511.3	25,570.7
Fixed Assets, Net	11,937.1	10,957.3	10,913.0	12,020.7
Total Assets	41,329.3	35,551.4	31,177.8	38,512.0
Total Current Liabilities	8,173.6	8,020.5	7,185.1	6,413.7
Long-Term Debt	21,392.9	12,845.6	11,631.5	20,030.6
Stockholders' Equity	10,257.1	13,261.0	11,054.0	10,657.1
Performance & Financial Condition				
Return on Total Revenues %	3.05	4.26	0.68	1.19
Return on Avg Stockholders' Equity %	16.80	19.87	3.46	7.78
Return on Average Assets %	5.14	7.24	1.08	2.05
Current Ratio	3.54	3.01	2.72	3.99
Debt / Equity %	208.57	96.87	105.22	187.96

Compound Growth %'s	EPS %	-20.63	Net Income %	34.90	Total Revenues %	-1.47

Comments

Revenue increased 15% in fiscal 1998 due to increased home office furniture sales and a new division. The Company permanently closed a plant and warehouse resulting in a net charge of $868,000 in fiscal 1998. Also, 740,000 shares of common stock were issued in connection with the redemption of preferred shares which diluted earnings per share as compared to earlier years. The Company had plant closing costs of $868,000 in fiscal 1996 with a recovery of $118,912 of such costs in fiscal 1997. For the six months ended February 28, 1999, the Company reported revenues and net income of $43.3 million and $1,259,000 ($.29 per share) as compared to $30.2 million and $773,000 ($.15 per share) for the same period of the preceding year.

Officers	Position	Ownership Information	
Donald D. Dreher	President, CEO	Number of Shares Outstanding	3,892,013
Joseph G. Hill	VP - Finance, Secretary	Market Capitalization	$ 12,882,563
Richard L. Rosbottom	Vice President	Number of Shareholders	1,594
Robert N. Benton	Vice President	Where Listed / Symbol	NASDAQ / DMIF

Other Information			
Transfer Agent	American Stock Transfer & Trust Co. New York, NY	SIC Code	2511
Auditor	Arthur Andersen LLP	Employees	441

DeVlieg-Bullard, Inc.

One Gorham Island   Westport, CT 06880   Telephone (203)221-8201   Fax (203)221-0780

Company Description

DeVlieg-Bullard, Inc. is a diversified industrial concern specializing in manufacturing, servicing, upgrading, automating and remanufacturing precision engineered machine tools. The Company also manufactures sophisticated original and replacement tooling products used in industrial machine tools. In addition, the Company produces high quality stationary power tools for use in the woodworking and metalworking industries as well as producing a variety of power tools for niche industrial markets. The Company was founded in 1986.

	07/31/98	07/31/97	07/31/96	07/31/95
Per Share Information				
Stock Price as of 12/31	0.59	3.81	2.69	2.25
Earnings Per Share	-0.45	0.26	-0.06	0.11
Price / Earnings Ratio	n.a.	14.65	n.a.	20.45
Book Value Per Share	1.57	2.09	1.76	1.68
Price / Book Value %	37.58	182.30	152.84	133.93
Dividends Per Share	0.0	0.0	0.0	0.0
Annual Financial Data				
Operating Results (000's)				
Total Revenues	116,767.0	130,623.0	113,363.0	78,484.0
Costs & Expenses	-119,972.0	-123,950.0	-109,532.0	-76,173.0
Income Before Taxes and Other	-3,205.0	6,673.0	-769.0	811.0
Other Items	-5,564.0	0.0	0.0	0.0
Income Tax	2,363.0	-2,775.0	52.0	582.0
Net Income	-6,406.0	3,898.0	-717.0	1,393.0
Cash Flow From Operations	-2,049.0	3,148.0	3,494.0	1,363.0
Balance Sheet (000's)				
Cash & Equivalents	365.0	637.0	768.0	415.0
Total Current Assets	72,137.0	66,149.0	61,509.0	36,321.0
Fixed Assets, Net	8,781.0	12,657.0	13,306.0	6,876.0
Total Assets	123,915.0	121,444.0	119,803.0	66,232.0
Total Current Liabilities	58,503.0	47,876.0	48,515.0	25,490.0
Long-Term Debt	13,528.0	14,179.0	15,175.0	13,639.0
Stockholders' Equity	19,406.0	25,713.0	21,584.0	20,570.0
Performance & Financial Condition				
Return on Total Revenues %	-5.49	2.98	-0.63	1.77
Return on Avg Stockholders' Equity %	-28.40	16.48	-3.40	7.34
Return on Average Assets %	-5.22	3.23	-0.77	2.37
Current Ratio	1.23	1.38	1.27	1.42
Debt / Equity %	69.71	55.14	70.31	66.31

Compound Growth %'s	EPS %	n.a.	Net Income %	n.a.	Total Revenues %	14.16

Comments

After years of impressive growth, fiscal 1998 was a year of transition as the Company made further strides for long term efficiency. The Company moved to outsource parts for the aftermarket and new machine businesses as part of an effort to streamline operations by eliminating redundancies in manufacturing. Two facilities were closed. The decline in revenue was the result of inadequate inventory levels to support the Company during the transition. The write off of goodwill and accrued expenses related to the plant closings amounted to $5,883,000 or $.34 per share. Fiscal 1996 results include a nonrecurring litigation expense of $4.6 million which was the reason a net loss was reported for the year. For the six months ended January 31, 1999, the Company reported revenue of $51.0 million and a net loss of $6,369,000 ($.45 per share) as compared to $54.5 million and a net loss of $2,164,000 ($.15 per share) for the same period of the preceding year.

Officers	Position	Ownership Information	
Charles E. Bradley	Chairman	Number of Shares Outstanding	12,334,900
William O. Thomas	President, CEO	Market Capitalization	$ 7,277,591
George W. Delaney	Vice President	Number of Shareholders	1,000
Joe L. Menger	Vice President	Where Listed / Symbol	NASDAQ / DVLG

Other Information			
Transfer Agent	Boston EquiServe Boston, MA	SIC Code	3540
Auditor	PricewaterhouseCoopers LLP	Employees	810

DenAmerica Corp.

7373 North Scottsdale Road, Suite D-120   Scottsdale, AZ 85253   Telephone (602)483-7055   Fax (602)483-9592

Company Description

DenAmerica Corp. currently operates 201 family-oriented, full service restaurants in 25 states, primarily in the southeastern, midwestern, western and southwestern United States. Of the Company's 201 restaurants, 100 are Denny's restaurants which represents approximately 5.8% of the Denny's system and makes the Company the largest Denny's franchisee in terms of revenue and the number of restaurants operated. The Company also owns and operates 101 Black-eyed Pea restaurants in six states. In March 1998, the Company completed the sale of 63 Denny's restaurants and eight non-branded restaurants to an existing Denny's franchisee for gross proceeds of $28.7 million. DenAmerica was founded in 1986.

	12/31/98	12/31/97	12/31/96	12/27/95
Per Share Information				
Stock Price	1.19	1.94	3.13	5.75
Earnings Per Share	-0.35	-1.56	0.08	-0.06
Price / Earnings Ratio	n.a.	n.a.	39.13	n.a.
Book Value Per Share	-0.25	0.09	1.65	0.08
Price / Book Value %	n.a.	2,155.56	189.70	7,187.50
Dividends Per Share	0.0	0.0	0.0	0.0
Annual Financial Data				
Operating Results (000's)				
Total Revenues	255,956.0	300,579.0	241,480.0	74,683.0
Costs & Expenses	-262,898.0	-318,817.0	-239,251.0	-73,887.0
Income Before Taxes and Other	-6,942.0	-18,238.0	2,229.0	796.0
Other Items	1,371.0	519.0	-390.0	-884.0
Income Tax	914.0	-3,258.0	-870.0	-305.0
Net Income	-4,657.0	-20,977.0	969.0	-393.0
Cash Flow From Operations	-1,357.0	-1,458.0	9,664.0	7,486.0
Balance Sheet (000's)				
Cash & Equivalents	2,330.0	1,267.0	2,609.0	1,181.0
Total Current Assets	13,416.0	41,967.0	14,382.0	3,834.0
Fixed Assets, Net	55,648.0	61,328.0	73,724.0	33,817.0
Total Assets	134,507.0	170,264.0	179,189.0	54,966.0
Total Current Liabilities	58,254.0	78,384.0	47,411.0	13,240.0
Long-Term Debt	72,494.0	78,418.0	94,132.0	30,252.0
Stockholders' Equity	-3,334.0	1,248.0	22,128.0	564.0
Performance & Financial Condition				
Return on Total Revenues %	-1.82	-6.98	0.40	-0.53
Return on Avg Stockholders' Equity %	n.a.	-179.47	8.54	-51.68
Return on Average Assets %	-3.06	-12.01	0.83	-0.87
Current Ratio	0.23	0.54	0.30	0.29
Debt / Equity %	n.a.	6,283.49	425.40	5,363.83

Compound Growth %'s	EPS %	n.a.	Net Income %	n.a.	Total Revenues %	50.77

Comments

Cash proceeds from the transaction mentioned above were used to pay debt, cancel outstanding warrants to purchase common shares, and repay certain equipment operating leases. The decline in 1998 revenue as compared to 1997 was attributable to the sale of restaurants. Despite a nonrecurring gain of $1,371,000 on the repayment of debt, the Company registered another year of losses. 1997 results included a charge for impaired assets associated with the restaurants sold of approximately $14.1 million, due primarily to the reduction of the value of intangible assets. Approximately $50.1 million of intangibles remain on the books as of December 31, 1998, and the Company is highly leveraged. The auditors issued a going concern qualification in their report on the Company's most recent financial statement. But in April 1999, the Company obtained a loan commitment for new borrowings and intends to pursue various alternatives to further match its cash flows with its debt service obligations.

Officers	Position	Ownership Information	
Jack M. Lloyd	President, CEO	Number of Shares Outstanding	13,485,277
William G. Cox	COO	Market Capitalization	$ 16,047,480
William J. Howard	Exec VP, Secretary	Number of Shareholders	1,200
Todd S. Brown	Senior VP, CFO	Where Listed / Symbol	AMEX / DEN

Other Information			
Transfer Agent	American Stock Transfer & Trust Co. New York, NY	SIC Code	5812
Auditor	Deloitte & Touche LLP	Employees	10,000
		Web Site	denamerica.com

Diagnostic Health Services, Inc.

2777 Stemmons Freeway, Suite 1525   Dallas, TX 75207   Telephone (214)634-0403   Fax (214)631-8531

Company Description

Diagnostic Health Services, Inc. (DHS) is an outsource provider of medical services to hospitals, physicians' offices and other healthcare facilities in the Midwest, West and South Central United States. DHS primarily provides radiology and cardiology diagnostic services and equipment as well as departmental management services, to healthcare facilities on an in-house and shared basis. In addition to significant internal growth, the Company has expanded its business through numerous acquisitions. At year-end 1998, the Company provided shared services to 290 of its approximately 394 hospital customers and approximately 844 additional clients across the healthcare spectrum. The Company was founded in 1983.

	12/31/98	12/31/97	12/31/96	12/31/95
Per Share Information				
Stock Price	2.16	11.50	7.87	5.06
Earnings Per Share	-3.73	0.48	0.29	0.21
Price / Earnings Ratio	n.a.	23.96	27.14	24.10
Book Value Per Share	0.81	4.33	3.24	1.79
Price / Book Value %	266.67	265.59	242.90	282.68
Dividends Per Share	0.0	0.0	0.0	0.0
Annual Financial Data				
Operating Results (000's)				
Total Revenues	44,928.2	53,290.2	24,658.0	17,181.0
Costs & Expenses	-75,387.4	-45,314.0	-21,137.3	-15,778.3
Income Before Taxes and Other	-30,459.2	7,976.3	3,520.6	1,402.6
Other Items	-10,833.2	-326.9	0.0	0.0
Income Tax	0.0	-2,215.7	-1,061.6	-174.9
Net Income	-41,292.4	5,433.6	2,459.1	1,227.7
Cash Flow From Operations	124.5	-718.9	593.3	757.3
Balance Sheet (000's)				
Cash & Equivalents	1,087.3	5,126.1	229.5	705.2
Total Current Assets	13,713.7	26,997.7	19,422.8	4,671.0
Fixed Assets, Net	24,209.8	28,699.7	15,849.2	10,201.2
Total Assets	67,866.7	107,854.2	53,320.4	19,291.5
Total Current Liabilities	11,079.5	17,776.4	9,405.2	4,164.6
Long-Term Debt	27,190.0	24,961.6	7,081.7	5,000.0
Stockholders' Equity	15,081.3	49,952.7	29,976.6	8,906.2
Performance & Financial Condition				
Return on Total Revenues %	-91.91	10.20	9.97	7.15
Return on Avg Stockholders' Equity %	-126.99	13.60	12.65	6.82
Return on Average Assets %	-47.00	6.74	6.77	3.61
Current Ratio	1.24	1.52	2.07	1.12
Debt / Equity %	180.29	49.97	23.62	56.14

Compound Growth %'s	EPS % n.a.	Net Income % n.a.	Total Revenues %	37.77

Comments

In 1998, the Company's financial performance declined dramatically as a result of the need to restructure acquired businesses. The Company went through a period in which liquid resources were depleted and the balance sheet became overleveraged. The restructuring was substantially completed by the end of 1998. Still, care should be exercised by potential investors. At December 31, 1998, intangible assets of $18.6 million were reflected on the Company's records which equates to approximately 123% of stockholders' equity and book value on a per share basis. Long term debt remained substantial at $27.2 million.

Officers	Position	Ownership Information	
Max W. Batzer	Chairman, CEO	Number of Shares Outstanding	11,480,636
Brad A. Hummel	President, COO	Market Capitalization	$ 24,798,174
Don W. Caughron	Senior VP	Number of Shareholders	1,300
Christopher L. Turner	CFO	Where Listed / Symbol	NASDAQ / DHSM

Other Information			
Transfer Agent	American Stock Transfer & Trust Co. New York, NY	SIC Code	8071
Auditor	Simonton, Kutac & Barnidge	Employees	385
		Web Site	dhsinc.com

Diamond Home Services, Inc.

222 Church Street   Woodstock, IL 60098   Telephone (815)334-1414   Fax (815)334-1421

Company Description

Diamond Home Services, founded in 1993, is a marketer and contractor of installed home improvement products, including roofing, gutters, doors and fencing. The Company markets its home improvement products and services directly to consumers primarily under the Sears name pursuant to a three-year non-exclusive license agreement with Sears, Roebuck and Co. which expires June 30, 1999. The Company currently markets its products directly to residential customers in 44 states through a combination of national and local advertising and its sales associates. The Company has approximately 70 sales offices located in major cities across the U.S. The Company installs its products through a network of qualified independent installers and purchases its products through local and regional independent distributors.

	12/31/98	12/31/97	12/31/96	12/31/95
Per Share Information				
Stock Price	3.66	7.12	26.25	2.71
Earnings Per Share	0.01	0.26	0.88	0.60
Price / Earnings Ratio	366.00	27.38	29.83	4.52
Book Value Per Share	4.04	4.02	3.99	2.08
Price / Book Value %	90.59	177.11	657.89	130.29
Dividends Per Share	0.0	0.0	0.0	0.0
Annual Financial Data				
Operating Results (000's)				
Total Revenues	245,393.0	161,834.0	157,251.0	124,848.0
Costs & Expenses	-243,070.0	-157,847.0	-146,079.0	-118,463.0
Income Before Taxes and Other	2,323.0	3,987.0	11,172.0	6,385.0
Other Items	-1,540.0	0.0	0.0	0.0
Income Tax	-698.0	-1,683.0	-4,357.0	-2,650.0
Net Income	85.0	2,304.0	6,815.0	3,735.0
Cash Flow From Operations	3,681.0	3,784.0	2,159.0	10,448.0
Balance Sheet (000's)				
Cash & Equivalents	5,104.0	9,966.0	18,982.0	4,715.0
Total Current Assets	49,804.0	20,413.0	31,499.0	9,617.0
Fixed Assets, Net	20,812.0	5,546.0	1,607.0	1,732.0
Total Assets	126,129.0	56,589.0	58,793.0	30,143.0
Total Current Liabilities	34,027.0	12,674.0	14,321.0	14,431.0
Long-Term Debt	44,705.0	0.0	0.0	6,216.0
Stockholders' Equity	34,412.0	34,210.0	36,236.0	6,233.0
Performance & Financial Condition				
Return on Total Revenues %	0.03	1.42	4.33	2.99
Return on Avg Stockholders' Equity %	0.25	6.54	32.09	19.66
Return on Average Assets %	0.09	3.99	15.33	9.34
Current Ratio	1.46	1.61	2.20	0.67
Debt / Equity %	129.91	n.a.	n.a.	99.73

Compound Growth %'s	EPS %	-74.46	Net Income %	-71.66	Total Revenues %	25.26

Comments

The increase in revenues in 1998 was attributable to the acquisition of Reeves Southeastern Corporation on April 20, 1998. The transaction was accounted for as a purchase. 1998 results include a restructuring expense amounting to $1,540,000. The decline in profits over the last two years was traced primarily to a large increase in general, sales and administration expenses which management said was due to expansion of the overall infrastructure to accomodate additional growth. At December 31, 1998, the Company had $39 million of intangible assets recorded on its books which equated to approximately 113% of stockholders' equity and book value per share.

Officers	Position	Ownership Information	
C. Stephen Clegg	Chairman, CEO	Number of Shares Outstanding	8,507,375
Geoffrey Foreman	President, COO	Market Capitalization	$ 31,136,993
Richard G. Reece	Vice President, CFO	Number of Shareholders	2,000
Joseph U. Schorer	Vice President, Secretary	Where Listed / Symbol	NASDAQ / DHMS

Other Information			
Transfer Agent	Harris Trust & Savings Bank Chicago, IL	SIC Code	1520
Auditor	Ernst & Young LLP	Employees	1,170

Diehl Graphsoft, Inc.

10270 Old Columbia Road   Columbia, MD 21046-1751   Telephone (410)290-5114   Fax (410)290-8050

Company Description

Diehl Graphsoft, Inc. is a computer software developer. The Company publishes computer aided design (CAD) and computer aided engineering (CAE) software which enables sophisticated design, architectural, and engineering projects to be successfully undertaken with relatively inexpensive computer hardware. The Company's strategy also includes offering integrated industry-specific software tools based on the Company's CAD technology. Its aim is to serve the needs of design, engineering, and architectural professionals in a cost effective manner. The Company has also developed a related set of CAD software packages for the Apple Macintosh microcomputer and for the IBM compatible microcomputers using the Microsoft Windows operating systems. The Company was founded in 1985.

	05/31/98	05/31/97	05/31/96	05/31/95
Per Share Information				
Stock Price as of 12/31	2.69	3.12	6.37	6.00
Earnings Per Share	0.32	0.17	0.22	0.50
Price / Earnings Ratio	8.41	18.35	28.95	12.00
Book Value Per Share	2.95	2.63	2.46	1.86
Price / Book Value %	91.19	118.63	258.94	322.58
Dividends Per Share	0.0	0.0	0.0	0.0
Annual Financial Data				
Operating Results (000's)				
Total Revenues	7,767.6	6,402.8	5,265.4	5,248.3
Costs & Expenses	-6,306.9	-5,562.1	-4,178.5	-3,243.6
Income Before Taxes and Other	1,460.7	840.7	1,086.8	2,004.7
Other Items	0.0	0.0	0.0	0.0
Income Tax	-467.8	-294.7	-417.8	-778.7
Net Income	992.9	546.0	669.0	1,226.0
Cash Flow From Operations	2,278.6	977.4	843.1	-1,145.0
Balance Sheet (000's)				
Cash & Equivalents	376.8	247.4	375.3	722.1
Total Current Assets	8,986.1	7,729.0	7,356.6	4,270.2
Fixed Assets, Net	335.4	319.2	278.6	205.3
Total Assets	10,253.0	8,857.0	8,357.2	6,139.1
Total Current Liabilities	621.5	309.5	359.5	600.3
Long-Term Debt	0.0	0.0	0.0	0.0
Stockholders' Equity	9,296.8	8,268.6	7,722.6	5,382.2
Performance & Financial Condition				
Return on Total Revenues %	12.78	8.53	12.71	23.36
Return on Avg Stockholders' Equity %	11.30	6.83	10.21	34.66
Return on Average Assets %	10.39	6.34	9.23	29.40
Current Ratio	14.46	24.97	20.47	7.11
Debt / Equity %	n.a.	n.a.	n.a.	n.a.

Compound Growth %'s	EPS % -13.82	Net Income % -6.79	Total Revenues % 13.96

Comments

Despite troubles at Apple Computer that reduced demand for some Company products, revenues posted a strong 22.3% increase in the last fiscal year and the balance sheet remained excessively strong. This followed the 21.6% increase experienced in fiscal 1997. A major percentage of book value is comprised of marketable securities. New products are under development and the technical staff has been increased from 15 to 30 people over the course of the last two years. For the nine months ended February 28, 1999, revenues and net income were $5.5 million and $634,840 ($.20 per share) as compared to $5.1 million and $542,867 ($.17 per share) for the same period of the preceding year.

Officers	Position	Ownership Information	
Richard Diehl	President, CEO	Number of Shares Outstanding	3,147,637
Don Webster	Exec VP, COO	Market Capitalization	$ 8,467,144
Joseph Schmelzle	VP - Finance, CFO	Number of Shareholders	1,000
Sean Flaherty	Vice President	Where Listed / Symbol	NASDAQ / DIEG

Other Information			
Transfer Agent	Liberty Transfer Co. Huntington, NY	SIC Code	7372
Auditor	Ernst & Young LLP	Employees	60
		Web Site	diehlgraphsoft.com

Digital Solutions, Inc.

300 Atrium Drive Somerset, NJ 08873 Telephone (732)748-1700 Fax (732)748-3206

Company Description

Digital Solutions, Inc. (DSI) provides a broad spectrum of human resource services including professional employer services, payroll processing, human resource administration and placement of temporary and permanent employees. Essentially, the Company provides services that function as the personnel department for small to medium sized companies. Sales/service centers are located in New York, New Jersey, Florida, and Texas. DSI currently services over 1,200 client organizations with approximately 4,350 worksites and believes it currently ranks, in terms of revenues and worksite employee base, as one of the largest professional employer organizations in the United States. The Company was founded in 1969.

	09/30/98	09/30/97	09/30/96	09/30/95
Per Share Information				
Stock Price as of 12/31	1.12	1.87	3.31	1.50
Earnings Per Share	0.14	-0.15	-0.04	-0.24
Price / Earnings Ratio	8.00	n.a.	n.a.	n.a.
Book Value Per Share	0.41	0.25	0.38	0.20
Price / Book Value %	273.17	748.00	871.05	750.00
Dividends Per Share	0.0	0.0	0.0	0.0
Annual Financial Data				
Operating Results (000's)				
Total Revenues	139,758.0	122,755.0	101,150.0	73,945.0
Costs & Expenses	-138,351.0	-125,587.0	-101,713.0	-77,012.0
Income Before Taxes and Other	1,407.0	-2,832.0	-563.0	-3,453.0
Other Items	0.0	0.0	0.0	0.0
Income Tax	1,296.0	0.0	-34.0	137.0
Net Income	2,703.0	-2,832.0	-597.0	-3,316.0
Cash Flow From Operations	-48.0	962.0	-2,361.0	-3,098.0
Balance Sheet (000's)				
Cash & Equivalents	1,530.0	841.0	0.0	20.0
Total Current Assets	9,112.0	7,801.0	7,818.0	6,196.0
Fixed Assets, Net	792.0	907.0	837.0	817.0
Total Assets	16,648.0	14,163.0	14,800.0	13,816.0
Total Current Liabilities	5,793.0	9,202.0	7,532.0	10,792.0
Long-Term Debt	2,981.0	89.0	100.0	133.0
Stockholders' Equity	7,874.0	4,872.0	7,168.0	2,849.0
Performance & Financial Condition				
Return on Total Revenues %	1.93	-2.31	-0.59	-4.48
Return on Avg Stockholders' Equity %	42.41	-47.04	-11.92	-83.90
Return on Average Assets %	17.55	-19.56	-4.17	-30.78
Current Ratio	1.57	0.85	1.04	0.57
Debt / Equity %	37.86	1.83	1.40	4.67

Compound Growth %'s	EPS % n.a.	Net Income % n.a.	Total Revenues % 23.64

Comments

The 13.8% and 21.6% increases in revenue for fiscal 1998 and 1997, respectively, are entirely attributable to internal growth. Management credits its internal sales force for a job well done. During years of rapid expansion, the Company has had to reorganize and discontinue certain operations. These actions resulted in a number of nonrecurring expenses spread among the years. However, fiscal 1998 witnessed a return to profitability and a greatly improved financial condition. The placement of a long term credit facility allowed the Company to have a positive working capital. Despite being on firmer ground, the Company's stock lost approximately one-third of its value during 1998.

Officers	Position	Ownership Information	
Karl E. Dieckmann	Chairman	Number of Shares Outstanding	19,356,833
Donald W. Kappauf	President, CEO	Market Capitalization	$ 21,679,653
Donald T. Kelly	Vice President, CFO	Number of Shareholders	4,000
George J. Eklund	Director	Where Listed / Symbol	NASDAQ / DGSI

Other Information			
Transfer Agent	Continental Stock Transfer & Trust Co. New York, NY	SIC Code	7363
Auditor	Arthur Andersen LLP	Employees	122
		Web Site	digitalsolutions.com

Diodes Incorporated

3050 East Hillcrest Drive   Westlake Village, CA 91362   Telephone (805)446-4800   Fax (805)446-4850

Company Description

Diodes Incorporated is engaged in the manufacture, sale, and distribution of discrete semiconductors worldwide, primarily to manufacturers of automotive, computer and telecommunication products and to distributors of electronic components. In addition to the Company's corporate headquarters in Westlake Village, California, which provides sales, marketing and engineering functions, the Company maintains a sales, manufacturing, engineering and purchasing facility in Taipei, Taiwan and a manufacturing facility in Shanghai, China. The Company, following a restructuring in 1990, has grown rapidly as a supplier of discrete semiconductors.

	12/31/98	12/31/97	12/31/96	12/31/95
Per Share Information				
Stock Price	4.87	9.75	7.25	10.50
Earnings Per Share	0.50	0.93	0.55	0.90
Price / Earnings Ratio	9.74	10.48	13.18	11.67
Book Value Per Share	5.44	4.91	3.93	3.33
Price / Book Value %	89.52	198.57	184.48	315.32
Dividends Per Share	0.0	0.0	0.0	0.0
Annual Financial Data				
Operating Results (000's)				
Total Revenues	61,116.0	66,669.0	56,739.0	58,749.0
Costs & Expenses	-56,932.0	-58,913.0	-52,101.0	-51,439.0
Income Before Taxes and Other	4,184.0	7,756.0	4,638.0	7,310.0
Other Items	0.0	0.0	0.0	0.0
Income Tax	-1,511.0	-2,631.0	-1,673.0	-2,610.0
Net Income	2,673.0	5,125.0	2,965.0	4,700.0
Cash Flow From Operations	5,529.0	3,972.0	3,567.0	4,550.0
Balance Sheet (000's)				
Cash & Equivalents	2,415.0	2,325.0	1,820.0	478.0
Total Current Assets	27,356.0	29,149.0	25,235.0	25,883.0
Fixed Assets, Net	13,750.0	5,165.0	4,628.0	1,527.0
Total Assets	45,389.0	38,354.0	32,546.0	29,363.0
Total Current Liabilities	10,717.0	10,450.0	7,832.0	12,620.0
Long-Term Debt	5,991.0	3,226.0	4,288.0	244.0
Stockholders' Equity	27,460.0	24,453.0	19,464.0	16,499.0
Performance & Financial Condition				
Return on Total Revenues %	4.37	7.69	5.23	8.00
Return on Avg Stockholders' Equity %	10.30	23.34	16.49	34.47
Return on Average Assets %	6.38	14.46	9.58	20.04
Current Ratio	2.55	2.79	3.22	2.05
Debt / Equity %	21.82	13.19	22.03	1.48

Compound Growth %'s	EPS %	-17.79	Net Income %	-17.15	Total Revenues %	1.33

Comments

Net sales for 1998 compared to 1997 decreased $5,438,000, or approximately 8.3%. The decrease in net sales was due primarily to industry-wide pricing pressures that offset increased unit sales of approximately 3.3%. Pricing pressures within the industry resulted from decreased demand and excess on-hand inventories. The decline in gross margin and net income were also attributable to the lower sales level. Despite a clean balance sheet and good financial condition, the Company's stock is trading for approximately one-half of its traditional level and less than its book value.

Officers	Position	Ownership Information	
Raymond Soong	Chairman	Number of Shares Outstanding	5,047,237
Michael A. Rosenberg	President, CEO	Market Capitalization	$ 24,580,044
Carl Wertz	VP - Finance, CFO	Number of Shareholders	1,000
Leonard M. Silverman	Director	Where Listed / Symbol	AMEX / DIO

Other Information

Transfer Agent	Continental Stock Transfer & Trust Co. New York, NY	SIC Code	3674
Auditor	Moss Adams LLP	Employees	67
		Web Site	diodes.com

Disc Graphics, Inc.

10 Gilpin Avenue Hauppauge, NY 11788 Telephone (516)234-1400 Fax (516)234-1460

Company Description

Disc Graphics, Inc. is a diversified manufacturer and printer of specialty packaging focused on the home video, pharmaceutical, music, entertainment software, publishing and cosmetics markets. Products include: pre-recorded video, CD-ROM and audio cassette packaging; folding cartons for pharmaceuticals and cosmetics; and book jacket, poster, pressure sensitive label and general commercial printing. The Company was formed in 1992 and went public in 1993 to raise money for a future but unidentified acquisition. It acquired its existing business on October 30, 1995. On May 18, 1996, the Company acquired Pointville, Inc. in order to gain a foothold in the California market. On October 24, 1997, the Company acquired Benham Press, Inc., an Indiana based printing company.

	12/31/98	12/31/97	12/31/96	12/31/95
Per Share Information				
Stock Price	4.25	4.37	2.06	3.25
Earnings Per Share	0.52	0.40	0.29	0.18
Price / Earnings Ratio	8.17	10.93	7.10	18.06
Book Value Per Share	2.53	2.05	1.67	1.50
Price / Book Value %	167.98	213.17	123.35	216.67
Dividends Per Share	0.0	0.0	0.0	0.0
Annual Financial Data				
Operating Results (000's)				
Total Revenues	59,031.2	48,444.9	42,575.1	36,149.1
Costs & Expenses	-54,265.8	-44,847.1	-40,040.1	-35,239.8
Income Before Taxes and Other	4,765.4	3,597.8	2,535.0	868.5
Other Items	0.0	0.0	0.0	0.0
Income Tax	-1,901.0	-1,439.0	-1,081.0	-368.0
Net Income	2,864.4	2,158.8	1,454.0	500.5
Cash Flow From Operations	3,691.3	1,854.0	5,308.9	102.3
Balance Sheet (000's)				
Cash & Equivalents	43.3	31.8	30.9	1,309.7
Total Current Assets	16,378.5	14,575.5	12,485.1	11,470.0
Fixed Assets, Net	9,997.7	10,510.3	8,254.9	6,776.4
Total Assets	28,371.5	26,746.6	22,045.7	18,603.5
Total Current Liabilities	7,694.3	7,141.1	7,483.3	3,933.6
Long-Term Debt	1,415.6	4,253.0	515.2	3,000.0
Stockholders' Equity	13,940.4	11,111.7	8,964.0	7,427.1
Performance & Financial Condition				
Return on Total Revenues %	4.85	4.46	3.42	1.38
Return on Avg Stockholders' Equity %	22.87	21.51	17.74	10.31
Return on Average Assets %	10.39	8.85	7.15	3.07
Current Ratio	2.13	2.04	1.67	2.92
Debt / Equity %	10.15	38.27	5.75	40.39

Compound Growth %'s	EPS %	42.42	Net Income %	78.87	Total Revenues %	17.76

Comments

Revenues increased 22% in 1998 of which 14.3% was attributable to internal growth and 7.7% was attributable to the Benham acquisition. The increase in revenue experienced during 1998 was largely attributable to significant growth in video and entertainment software packaging and music and audio packaging. Improved manufacturing efficiencies through improved processes, competitive purchasing practices, and capital investment has enabled the Company to remain competitive and increase profitability despite an environment of downward price pressure. At December 31, 1998, goodwill was only 9% of stockholders' equity and book value per share.

Officers	Position	Ownership Information	
Donald Sinkin	President, CEO	Number of Shares Outstanding	5,518,412
Margaret Krumholz	CFO	Market Capitalization	$ 23,453,251
Stephen Frey	Vice President	Number of Shareholders	500
John Rebecchi	VP - Sales	Where Listed / Symbol	NASDAQ / DSGR

Other Information			
Transfer Agent	American Stock Transfer & Trust Co. New York, NY	SIC Code	2679
Auditor	KPMG LLP	Employees	455
		Web Site	discgraphics.com

Drypers Corporation

5300 Memorial, Suite 900   Houston, TX 77007   Telephone (713)869-8693   Fax (713)682-3104

Company Description

Drypers is a leading manufacturer and marketer of premium quality, value-priced disposable baby diapers and training pants sold under the Drypers brand name in the United States and under the Drypers and other brand names internationally. The Company also manufactures and sells lower-priced diapers under other brand names in the United States and internationally, as well as private label diapers and training pants and pre-moistened baby wipes. The Company's Drypers brand is the fourth largest selling diaper brand in the United States, and the second largest selling training pant brand in U.S. grocery stores.

	12/31/98	12/31/97	12/31/96	12/31/95
Per Share Information				
Stock Price	2.87	5.62	3.62	2.87
Earnings Per Share	-0.51	0.09	0.09	-2.35
Price / Earnings Ratio	n.a.	62.44	40.22	n.a.
Book Value Per Share	2.85	4.43	6.62	5.50
Price / Book Value %	100.70	126.86	54.68	52.18
Dividends Per Share	0.0	0.0	0.0	0.0
Annual Financial Data				
Operating Results (000's)				
Total Revenues	337,106.0	287,263.0	207,014.0	163,947.0
Costs & Expenses	-337,195.0	-275,276.0	-205,392.0	-175,801.0
Income Before Taxes and Other	-89.0	11,788.0	1,622.0	-11,854.0
Other Items	-6,471.0	-7,769.0	0.0	-7,440.0
Income Tax	-1,565.0	-2,344.0	-309.0	3,829.0
Net Income	-8,125.0	1,675.0	1,313.0	-15,465.0
Cash Flow From Operations	-17,520.0	-6,948.0	-4,291.0	6,255.0
Balance Sheet (000's)				
Cash & Equivalents	12,309.0	9,269.0	4,923.0	2,236.0
Total Current Assets	119,548.0	77,030.0	51,580.0	40,625.0
Fixed Assets, Net	81,903.0	53,270.0	35,154.0	34,208.0
Total Assets	300,172.0	205,232.0	150,555.0	137,420.0
Total Current Liabilities	93,316.0	28,302.0	42,873.0	44,222.0
Long-Term Debt	148,964.0	116,755.0	46,247.0	44,950.0
Stockholders' Equity	50,528.0	55,580.0	53,608.0	41,822.0
Performance & Financial Condition				
Return on Total Revenues %	-2.41	0.58	0.63	-9.43
Return on Avg Stockholders' Equity %	-15.31	3.07	2.75	-31.37
Return on Average Assets %	-3.22	0.94	0.91	-11.49
Current Ratio	1.28	2.72	1.20	0.92
Debt / Equity %	294.81	210.07	86.27	107.48

Compound Growth %'s	EPS % n.a.	Net Income % n.a.	Total Revenues % 27.16

Comments

1998 results include a $6,471,000 loss ($.40 per share) from the discontinuance of the laundry detergent business. On August 8, 1998, the Company's manufacturing facility in Argentina was extensively damaged as the result of a fire. Included in 1998 results is approximately $4 million of income related to fire insurance claims. 1998 revenues continued to grow, particularly in foreign markets. 1997 results include a nonrecurring expense related to the extinguishment of debt of $7,769,000 ($.42 per share). 1995 results also included unusual expenses and a restructuring charge totalling $7.4 million, approximately 38% of the reported pre-tax loss for the year. At December 31, 1998, the Company had $98.7 million of intangible assets recorded on its books which equates to approximately 195% of stockholders' equity and book value per share. Also at year end, the Company was in default under certain of the financial covenants contained in its revolving credit facility. Yes, diapers can be a dirty business.

Officers	Position	Ownership Information	
Walter V. Klemp	Chairman, CEO	Number of Shares Outstanding	17,706,660
Raymond M. Chambers	Chairman, CEO	Market Capitalization	$ 50,818,114
Terry A. Tognietti	President, CEO	Number of Shareholders	2,000
Jonathan P. Foster	Exec VP, CFO	Where Listed / Symbol	NASDAQ / DYPR

Other Information			
Transfer Agent	ChaseMellon Shareholder Services Dallas, TX	SIC Code	2676
Auditor	Arthur Andersen LLP	Employees	1,491
		Web Site	drypers.com

Dynamex Inc.

1431 Greenway Drive, Suite 345   Irving, TX 75038   Telephone (972)756-8180   Fax (972)756-8199

Company Description

Dynamex Inc. is a leading provider of same-day delivery and logistics services in the United States and Canada. From its base as the largest nationwide same-day transportation company in Canada, over the last three years Dynamex has established a presence in 21 metropolitan markets in the United States and has continued to expand its system in Canada. Through its network of branch offices, the Company provides same-day, door-to-door delivery services utilizing its ground couriers. In addition to traditional on-demand delivery services, the Company offers scheduled distribution services which encompass recurring, often daily, point-to-point deliveries or multiple destination deliveries that often require intermediate handling. The Company was founded in 1992 and had its initial public offering in August 1996 at which time it issued 2.6 million shares at $8 per share.

	07/31/98	07/31/97	07/31/96	07/31/95
Per Share Information				
Stock Price as of 12/31	4.00	11.00	9.62	8.00
Earnings Per Share	0.42	0.51	0.23	-0.81
Price / Earnings Ratio	9.52	21.57	41.83	n.a.
Book Value Per Share	7.44	5.60	2.42	1.83
Price / Book Value %	53.76	196.43	397.52	437.16
Dividends Per Share	0.0	0.0	0.0	0.0
Annual Financial Data				
Operating Results (000's)				
Total Revenues	207,746.0	131,867.0	71,812.0	21,032.0
Costs & Expenses	-202,216.0	-125,535.0	-70,760.0	-22,497.0
Income Before Taxes and Other	5,530.0	6,332.0	1,052.0	-1,622.0
Other Items	0.0	-335.0	0.0	0.0
Income Tax	-2,152.0	-2,485.0	-176.0	-3.0
Net Income	3,378.0	3,512.0	876.0	-1,625.0
Cash Flow From Operations	6,953.0	4,926.0	2,380.0	-944.0
Balance Sheet (000's)				
Cash & Equivalents	1,361.0	1,326.0	894.0	506.0
Total Current Assets	35,352.0	26,091.0	12,891.0	8,104.0
Fixed Assets, Net	9,890.0	5,787.0	2,047.0	1,519.0
Total Assets	128,554.0	88,151.0	34,999.0	17,194.0
Total Current Liabilities	17,325.0	14,663.0	8,805.0	6,620.0
Long-Term Debt	36,287.0	32,388.0	20,036.0	5,924.0
Stockholders' Equity	74,942.0	41,100.0	6,158.0	4,650.0
Performance & Financial Condition				
Return on Total Revenues %	1.63	2.66	1.22	-7.73
Return on Avg Stockholders' Equity %	5.82	14.86	16.21	-32.50
Return on Average Assets %	3.12	5.70	3.36	-8.13
Current Ratio	2.04	1.78	1.46	1.22
Debt / Equity %	48.42	78.80	325.37	127.40

Compound Growth %'s	EPS %	35.13	Net Income %	96.37	Total Revenues %	114.56

Comments

The substantial increase in revenues during fiscal 1998 was primarily attributable to acquisitions that occurred in fiscal 1998 and fiscal 1997. In the fourth quarter of fiscal 1998, the Company recorded unusual expenses of $2.1 million in connection with settlements and bad debts. At July 31, 1998, the Company had $82 million of intangible assets recorded on its books which equated to approximately 109% of stockholders' equity and book value per share. For the six months ended January 31, 1999, the Company reported revenues of $117.2 million and a net loss of $1,354,000 ($.13 per share) as compared to $95.3 million and a net profit of $2,007,000 ($.27 per share) for the same period of the preceding year.

Officers	Position	Ownership Information	
Richard K. McClelland	President, CEO	Number of Shares Outstanding	10,069,000
Robert P. Capps	Exec VP, CFO	Market Capitalization	$ 40,276,000
John J. Wellik	Vice President, Controller	Number of Shareholders	500
James M. Hoak	Director	Where Listed / Symbol	NASDAQ / DYMX

Other Information			
Transfer Agent	Harris Trust & Savings Bank Chicago, IL	SIC Code	4210
Auditor	Deloitte & Touche LLP	Employees	2,750
		Web Site	dynamex.com

Dynamic Homes, Inc.

525 Roosevelt Avenue Detroit Lakes, MN 56501 Telephone (218)847-2611 Fax (218)847-2617

Company Description

Dynamic Homes, Inc. manufactures and markets modular, preconstructed single-family and multi-family homes and light commercial buildings in the upper midwest region of the United States. The Company's principal product, the single-family modular home, is offered in 60 basic designs with various options and floor plan variations. Auxiliary products include garages, wood basements and retail sales. During 1995, the Company acquired a hotel/resort located in Ely, Minnesota which is managed by an unrelated party in accordance with a management agreement. The Company was founded in 1970.

	12/26/98	12/27/97	12/28/96	12/30/95
Per Share Information				
Stock Price as of 12/31	1.50	2.19	2.25	1.87
Earnings Per Share	0.17	0.15	0.38	0.37
Price / Earnings Ratio	8.82	14.60	5.92	5.05
Book Value Per Share	2.28	2.11	1.93	1.54
Price / Book Value %	65.79	103.79	116.58	121.43
Dividends Per Share	0.0	0.0	0.0	0.0
Annual Financial Data				
Operating Results (000's)				
Total Revenues	14,003.6	12,946.6	12,197.6	10,913.4
Costs & Expenses	-13,267.7	-12,381.8	-10,692.0	-9,559.3
Income Before Taxes and Other	735.9	556.1	1,502.1	1,354.1
Other Items	-93.6	0.0	0.0	0.0
Income Tax	-268.0	-227.0	-594.0	-545.0
Net Income	374.3	329.1	908.1	809.1
Cash Flow From Operations	-511.6	813.5	1,000.4	442.6
Balance Sheet (000's)				
Cash & Equivalents	312.3	1,329.5	554.1	543.0
Total Current Assets	4,425.6	3,748.1	3,001.2	3,009.3
Fixed Assets, Net	4,578.3	4,603.7	4,216.8	2,786.0
Total Assets	9,425.2	8,881.5	7,619.9	5,833.2
Total Current Liabilities	1,390.2	1,117.9	1,105.4	1,262.6
Long-Term Debt	2,852.5	2,951.4	2,077.4	1,066.3
Stockholders' Equity	5,106.5	4,732.2	4,403.1	3,479.3
Performance & Financial Condition				
Return on Total Revenues %	2.67	2.54	7.44	7.41
Return on Avg Stockholders' Equity %	7.61	7.21	23.04	25.79
Return on Average Assets %	4.09	3.99	13.50	16.32
Current Ratio	3.18	3.35	2.72	2.38
Debt / Equity %	55.86	62.37	47.18	30.65

Compound Growth %'s	EPS %	-22.84	Net Income %	-22.66	Total Revenues %	8.67

Comments

The Company completed the final phase of several large single-family housing contracts during 1997. The Company managed to replace the revenues generated by the contracts with a promotional sale in 1998. Last year's results also include a nonrecurring expense of $93,600 ($.04 per share) related to the change of an accounting method. The order backlog was $5.0 million as of March 15, 1999, as compared with $5.7 million one year earlier. The resort business has yet to become profitable with losses of $47,500 and $128,500 in 1998 and 1997, respectively. The lack of glamour has this Company's stock priced at a hefty discount to book value.

Officers	Position	Ownership Information	
D. Raymond Madison	Chairman, CEO	Number of Shares Outstanding	2,240,920
Glenn R. Anderson	President	Market Capitalization	$ 3,361,380
Clyde R. Lund, Jr.	Secretary	Number of Shareholders	390
Eldon R. Matz	Controller	Where Listed / Symbol	NASDAQ / DYHM

Other Information

Transfer Agent	Norwest Bank Minnesota, N.A. South St. Paul, MN	SIC Code	2452
Auditor	Eide Bailly, L.L.P.	Employees	131
		Web Site	dynamichomes.com

Dynamic International, Ltd.

58 Second Avenue   Brooklyn, NY 11215   Telephone (718)369-4160   Fax (718)369-2210

Company Description

The Company is engaged in the design, marketing and sale of a diverse line of hand exercise and light exercise equipment. Products include hand grips, running weights, jump ropes, aerobic steps and slides. These items are marketed under the trademarked names, Spaulding, Kathy Ireland and Shape Shop. In addition, the Company designs and markets sports bags and luggage under the names Jeep, Santa Fe, Polaris Expedition and Sports Gear. As a result of an unsuccessful venture into a new product line during 1994 and 1995, the Company incurred significant operating losses and filed for bankruptcy protection in August 1995. In May 1996, the bankruptcy court approved a plan of reorganization. In late 1997, a public offering of units consisting of one share of stock and two warrants created a public market for the Company's shares.

	04/30/98	04/30/97	04/30/96	04/30/95
Per Share Information				
Stock Price as of 12/31	0.30	5.38	n.a.	n.a.
Earnings Per Share	0.03	0.0	0.0	n.a.
Price / Earnings Ratio	10.00	n.a.	n.a.	n.a.
Book Value Per Share	1.17	0.05	-0.03	n.a.
Price / Book Value %	25.64	10,760.00	n.a.	n.a.
Dividends Per Share	0.0	0.0	0.0	n.a.
Annual Financial Data				
Operating Results (000's)				
Total Revenues	8,043.1	9,540.7	7,250.0	32,603.7
Costs & Expenses	-7,774.9	-9,343.8	-16,547.2	-43,913.2
Income Before Taxes and Other	268.2	146.7	-9,746.9	-11,309.4
Other Items	0.0	0.0	9,181.2	0.0
Income Tax	-139.3	-103.7	7,511.0	82.1
Net Income	129.0	43.0	6,945.3	-11,227.3
Cash Flow From Operations	-2,089.8	-359.1	-1,145.6	799.2
Balance Sheet (000's)				
Cash & Equivalents	1,575.2	43.5	26.5	n.a.
Total Current Assets	5,476.2	4,400.5	3,982.5	n.a.
Fixed Assets, Net	124.8	125.3	230.1	n.a.
Total Assets	5,715.4	4,807.1	4,253.4	n.a.
Total Current Liabilities	557.0	4,446.3	4,276.4	n.a.
Long-Term Debt	0.0	215.3	0.0	n.a.
Stockholders' Equity	5,158.5	145.5	-47.0	n.a.
Performance & Financial Condition				
Return on Total Revenues %	1.60	0.45	95.80	n.a.
Return on Avg Stockholders' Equity %	4.86	87.35	n.a.	n.a.
Return on Average Assets %	2.45	0.95	n.a.	n.a.
Current Ratio	9.83	0.99	0.93	n.a.
Debt / Equity %	n.a.	147.91	n.a.	n.a.

Compound Growth %'s	EPS %	n.a.	Net Income %	n.a.	Total Revenues %	n.a.

Comments

The financial information above reflects the financial position of the reorganized Company as of April 30, 1998 and 1997. Operating information for the year ended April 30, 1997 consists of nine months of the reorganized company and three months of the predecessor company. For the nine months ended January 31, 1999, the Company had revenues and a net loss of $4.8 million and $309,314 ($.07 per share), as compared to $6.1 million and net income of $179,313 ($.05 per share), for the same period of the prior year. Earnings per share prior to the reorganization are not presented as they are not meaningful.

Officers	Position	Ownership Information	
Marton Grossman	Chairman, President	Number of Shares Outstanding	4,418,258
Gordon Sulltrop	Exec VP	Market Capitalization	$ 1,325,477
William P. Dolan	VP - Finance	Number of Shareholders	700
Isaac Grossman	Treasurer, Secretary	Where Listed / Symbol	OTC-BB / DYNI

Other Information			
Transfer Agent	American Stock Transfer & Trust Co. New York, NY	SIC Code	5090
Auditor	Moore Stephens, P.C.	Employees	11
Market Maker	Knight Securities L.P. (800)222-4910		
	M.H. Meyerson & Co., Inc. (800)333-3113		

Dynatronics Corporation

7030 Park Centre Drive   Salt Lake City, UT 84121   Telephone (801)568-7000   Fax (801)568-7711

Company Description

Dynatronics Corporation designs, manufactures and sells medical devices for therapeutic use by medical practitioners. The principal products of the Company are: 1) medical devices for therapeutic and aesthetic applications, 2) medical supplies and soft goods, 3) treatment tables and rehabilitation products, and 4) nutritional supplements. These products are used primarily by physical therapists, chiropractors, sports medicine doctors and other physical medicine practitioners. The Company distributes its products through independent dealers nationwide and internationally as well as through its own full-line catalog. Dynatronics was organized in 1983 as a successor to two business units that commenced operating in 1979 and 1980.

	06/30/98	06/30/97	06/30/96	06/30/95
Per Share Information				
Stock Price as of 12/31	2.50	1.00	0.94	1.25
Earnings Per Share	0.07	0.07	-0.02	0.03
Price / Earnings Ratio	35.71	14.29	n.a.	41.67
Book Value Per Share	0.67	0.59	0.52	0.54
Price / Book Value %	373.13	169.49	180.77	231.48
Dividends Per Share	0.0	0.0	0.0	0.0
Annual Financial Data				
Operating Results (000's)				
Total Revenues	12,359.9	10,612.2	6,978.3	6,314.2
Costs & Expenses	-11,438.8	-9,672.2	-6,685.0	-5,954.6
Income Before Taxes and Other	921.1	940.0	-426.9	359.6
Other Items	0.0	0.0	0.0	0.0
Income Tax	-256.3	-327.5	233.0	-142.5
Net Income	664.8	612.5	-193.9	217.1
Cash Flow From Operations	-41.1	665.4	782.2	348.8
Balance Sheet (000's)				
Cash & Equivalents	748.1	544.6	416.9	779.1
Total Current Assets	6,075.2	5,122.5	3,871.6	3,843.5
Fixed Assets, Net	3,583.8	2,605.9	2,635.8	2,663.2
Total Assets	11,641.9	9,642.5	8,508.6	7,187.3
Total Current Liabilities	2,572.4	2,095.4	1,255.1	524.3
Long-Term Debt	2,844.9	2,087.5	2,484.5	2,086.4
Stockholders' Equity	5,693.5	5,012.6	4,397.2	4,263.7
Performance & Financial Condition				
Return on Total Revenues %	5.38	5.77	-2.78	3.44
Return on Avg Stockholders' Equity %	12.42	13.02	-4.48	5.29
Return on Average Assets %	6.25	6.75	-2.47	3.02
Current Ratio	2.36	2.44	3.08	7.33
Debt / Equity %	49.97	41.65	56.50	48.93

Compound Growth %'s	EPS %	32.64	Net Income %	45.22	Total Revenues %	25.09

Comments

Fiscal 1996 results include a nonrecurring loss on the write off of a related party note receivable of $720,000. The Company would otherwise have been profitable that year. Management characterized 1997 as a breakthrough year with a 50 percent increase in revenue and operating profits and predicted continued growth and expansion. A 21% revenue growth in fiscal 1998 was solid but below expectations. But fiscal 1999 is off to a record start. For the six months ended December 31, 1998, the Company reported revenues and net income of $8.9 million and $600,981 ($.07 per share) as compared to $6.0 million and $326,503 ($.04 per share) for the same period of the preceding year.

Officers	Position	Ownership Information	
Kelvyn H. Cullimore, Jr.	President, CEO	Number of Shares Outstanding	8,447,343
Larry K. Beardall	Exec VP	Market Capitalization	$ 21,118,358
John S. Ramey	Senior VP	Number of Shareholders	2,000
Robert J. Cardon	Secretary	Where Listed / Symbol	NASDAQ / DYNT

Other Information

Transfer Agent	Interwest Transfer Co., Inc. Salt Lake City, UT	SIC Code	3845
Auditor	KPMG LLP	Employees	124
		Web Site	dynatronics.com

EA Engineering, Science, and Technology, Inc.

11019 McCormick Road   Hunt Valley, MD 21031   Telephone (410)584-7000   Fax (410)771-1625

Company Description

EA Engineering, Science, and Technology, Inc. is an international consulting firm specializing in the fields of energy, the environment, and health and safety. Through its network of more than 20 branch and satellite offices and its analytical and international operations, EA provides scientific, engineering, economic, analytical, and management solutions to government, industrial and utility clients. The goal of the Company is to help management in industry and government improve their performance and achieve their business and organizational objectives. The Company was founded in 1973.

	08/31/98	08/31/97	08/31/96	08/31/95
Per Share Information				
Stock Price as of 12/31	1.25	2.00	2.38	3.88
Earnings Per Share	0.10	-0.87	-0.09	0.36
Price / Earnings Ratio	12.50	n.a.	n.a.	10.78
Book Value Per Share	2.23	2.13	3.01	3.06
Price / Book Value %	56.05	93.90	79.07	126.80
Dividends Per Share	0.0	0.0	0.0	0.0
Annual Financial Data				
Operating Results (000's)				
Total Revenues	60,086.0	73,982.5	88,415.2	92,459.5
Costs & Expenses	-59,122.0	-82,359.4	-89,216.3	-88,747.0
Income Before Taxes and Other	964.0	-8,376.9	-801.1	3,712.5
Other Items	0.0	0.0	0.0	0.0
Income Tax	-359.2	2,969.3	221.0	-1,485.1
Net Income	604.8	-5,407.6	-580.1	2,227.4
Cash Flow From Operations	1,109.6	1,946.3	-241.6	907.6
Balance Sheet (000's)				
Cash & Equivalents	1,782.6	2,333.3	1,308.6	3,813.9
Total Current Assets	18,117.6	21,235.3	28,060.4	31,118.3
Fixed Assets, Net	1,781.1	2,396.8	3,124.9	3,300.0
Total Assets	23,474.9	26,641.9	33,328.5	36,367.8
Total Current Liabilities	8,185.7	11,053.2	12,105.9	13,455.4
Long-Term Debt	1,279.8	2,331.7	2,664.5	4,032.7
Stockholders' Equity	14,009.4	13,257.0	18,558.1	18,879.7
Performance & Financial Condition				
Return on Total Revenues %	1.01	-7.31	-0.66	2.41
Return on Avg Stockholders' Equity %	4.44	-33.99	-3.10	13.08
Return on Average Assets %	2.41	-18.03	-1.66	6.96
Current Ratio	2.21	1.92	2.32	2.31
Debt / Equity %	9.14	17.59	14.36	21.36

Compound Growth %'s	EPS %	-34.75	Net Income %	-35.25	Total Revenues %	-13.38

Comments

During the past several years the regulatory pace has slowed, resulting in an increasingly competitive environment and a decline in total revenues. Management was able to recognize the need for reorganization and returned the Company to profitability in fiscal 1998. Fiscal 1997 results include $3 million of restructuring expense. Although the year end stock price is a bargain at a fraction of book value, investors still have to question how shareholders will benefit from a professional service organization that has no dividend history. A lot will depend on the Company's ability to record a string of profitable years. For the six months ended February 28, 1999, the Company reported revenues of $26.0 million and a net loss of $2,077,800 ($.33 per share) as compared to $30.6 million and net income of $405,600 ($.06 per share) for the same period of the preceding year.

Officers	Position	Ownership Information	
Loren D. Jensen	Chairman	Number of Shares Outstanding	6,285,000
Donald A. Deieso	President, CEO	Market Capitalization	$ 7,856,250
Bijan S. Saless	Exec VP	Number of Shareholders	1,001
Jack P. Adler	Senior VP, Secretary	Where Listed / Symbol	NASDAQ / EACO

Other Information			
Transfer Agent	ChaseMellon Shareholder Services Pittsburgh, PA	SIC Code	8711
Auditor	Arthur Andersen LLP	Employees	400
		Web Site	eaest.com

EFI Electronics Corporation

1751 South 4800 West   Salt Lake City, UT 84104   Telephone (801)977-9009   Fax (801)877-0200

Company Description

EFI Electronics Corporation is primarily engaged in the manufacture and marketing of transient voltage surge suppression (TVSS) devices. TVSS devices protect electronic equipment from electrical disturbances such as lightning, grid switching, switching of air conditioners, power tools, elevators, welding units and electrical accidents. These disturbances can cause hardware failure, data/communication disruptions and transient induced software "bugs" resulting in equipment damage and/or down time. The Company began business in 1979.

	03/31/98	03/31/97	03/31/96	03/31/95
Per Share Information				
Stock Price as of 12/31	0.87	2.00	1.31	1.56
Earnings Per Share	0.01	-0.13	-0.58	-1.04
Price / Earnings Ratio	87.00	n.a.	n.a.	n.a.
Book Value Per Share	0.56	0.24	0.15	0.72
Price / Book Value %	155.36	833.33	873.33	216.67
Dividends Per Share	0.0	0.0	0.0	0.0
Annual Financial Data				
Operating Results (000's)				
Total Revenues	16,377.2	13,911.7	12,053.1	12,992.4
Costs & Expenses	-16,269.5	-14,375.2	-13,725.3	-16,163.1
Income Before Taxes and Other	103.8	-463.4	-1,745.7	-3,245.7
Other Items	0.0	0.0	0.0	0.0
Income Tax	-29.4	-33.9	-75.0	445.1
Net Income	74.4	-497.3	-1,820.7	-2,800.6
Cash Flow From Operations	-614.3	-883.7	-1,400.6	31.3
Balance Sheet (000's)				
Cash & Equivalents	9.6	10.1	8.5	96.3
Total Current Assets	7,441.2	5,737.8	5,005.0	5,885.0
Fixed Assets, Net	2,539.3	1,658.9	1,896.5	2,423.4
Total Assets	10,794.9	7,694.8	7,304.3	8,608.3
Total Current Liabilities	6,462.0	5,635.0	3,042.1	3,348.3
Long-Term Debt	895.1	1,048.0	3,776.1	3,068.7
Stockholders' Equity	3,084.3	1,011.8	486.1	2,191.3
Performance & Financial Condition				
Return on Total Revenues %	0.45	-3.57	-15.11	-21.56
Return on Avg Stockholders' Equity %	3.63	-66.40	-136.00	-81.80
Return on Average Assets %	0.80	-6.63	-22.88	-31.50
Current Ratio	1.15	1.02	1.65	1.76
Debt / Equity %	29.02	103.58	776.76	140.04

Compound Growth %'s	EPS % n.a.	Net Income % n.a.	Total Revenues % 8.02

Comments

The impressive 19% increase in revenue is a result of the Company's focus on expanding its international and utility markets. In addition, management reports strong growth in government business. Tight expense controls and concentration on the TVSS segment of the business has also contributed in returning the Company to profitability after four years of operating losses. Research and development expense increased from $552,000 in fiscal 1997 to $918,000 in fiscal 1998. At the end of the last fiscal year, the Company had $3.6 million of tax loss carryforwards available to offset future income. For the nine months ended December 31, 1998, revenue and net income were $11.3 million and $203,201 ($.04 per share) as compared to $12.1 million and $165,994 ($.03 per share) for the same period of the preceding year.

Officers	Position	Ownership Information	
Gaylor K. Swim	Chairman	Number of Shares Outstanding	5,504,644
Richard D. Clasen	President, CEO	Market Capitalization	$ 4,789,040
David G. Bevan	Exec VP, CFO	Number of Shareholders	277
John R. Worden	Exec VP	Where Listed / Symbol	NASDAQ / EFIC

Other Information			
Transfer Agent	First Security Bank of Utah Salt Lake City, UT	SIC Code	3620
Auditor	Grant Thornton LLP	Employees	122
		Web Site	efinet.com

EKCO Group, Inc.

98 Spit Brook Road, Suite 102   Nashua, NH 03062   Telephone (603)888-1212   Fax (603)888-1427

Company Description

EKCO Group, Inc. is a leading United States developer, manufacturer and marketer of multiple categories of branded houseware products for everyday home use. The Company believes that it is the leading United States supplier of metal bakeware, kitchen tools and gadgets and non-toxic pest control products. In addition, the Company believes that it is a leading United States supplier of cleaning products (primarily brushes, brooms and mops), small animal care and control products and dog and cat supplies and accessories. The Company was founded in 1968.

	01/03/99	12/28/97	12/29/96	12/31/95
Per Share Information				
Stock Price as of 12/31	3.75	7.75	4.37	5.87
Earnings Per Share	-0.20	0.29	-1.85	0.40
Price / Earnings Ratio	n.a.	26.72	n.a.	14.68
Book Value Per Share	5.68	5.77	5.52	7.57
Price / Book Value %	66.02	134.32	79.17	77.54
Dividends Per Share	0.0	0.0	0.04	0.08
Annual Financial Data				
Operating Results (000's)				
Total Revenues	329,235.0	271,346.0	250,019.0	247,101.0
Costs & Expenses	-330,140.0	-259,082.0	-250,320.0	-227,311.0
Income Before Taxes and Other	-905.0	12,264.0	-301.0	19,790.0
Other Items	3,500.0	0.0	-31,503.0	-1,917.0
Income Tax	-6,527.0	-6,247.0	-2,370.0	-9,828.0
Net Income	-3,932.0	6,017.0	-34,174.0	8,045.0
Cash Flow From Operations	18,975.0	-11,357.0	20,183.0	21,720.0
Balance Sheet (000's)				
Cash & Equivalents	1,179.0	14,565.0	15,706.0	142.0
Total Current Assets	157,126.0	150,142.0	139,377.0	102,610.0
Fixed Assets, Net	38,887.0	35,678.0	34,998.0	30,000.0
Total Assets	318,240.0	300,805.0	292,076.0	304,375.0
Total Current Liabilities	59,089.0	49,674.0	49,734.0	57,935.0
Long-Term Debt	136,136.0	124,270.0	124,182.0	106,559.0
Stockholders' Equity	108,324.0	109,994.0	102,515.0	139,383.0
Performance & Financial Condition				
Return on Total Revenues %	-1.19	2.22	-13.67	3.26
Return on Avg Stockholders' Equity %	-3.60	5.66	-28.25	6.07
Return on Average Assets %	-1.27	2.03	-11.46	2.62
Current Ratio	2.66	3.02	2.80	1.77
Debt / Equity %	125.67	112.98	121.14	76.45

Compound Growth %'s	EPS % n.a.	Net Income % n.a.	Total Revenues % 10.04

Comments

In 1998, the Company continued a repositioning program, initiated two years earlier, by selling two businesses and acquiring two others. A $3.5 million gain was recorded on the sales. Sales of the Company's kitchenware products increased revenue 9.5% from the prior year. Acquisitions were responsible for the balance of the increase. During 1998, the Company wrote off goodwill and other assets as a special charge which amounted to $16.2 million. As most of the charge was not deductible for income tax purposes, the income tax expense appears disproportionate to net income. 1996 results included losses of $28.3 million from discontinued operations and $3.2 million of nonrecurring expense in connection with the early extinguishment of debt. These items amounted to $1.71 per share. At December 31, 1998, the Company had $114.3 million of goodwill on its books which equated to approximately 105% of stockholders' equity and book value per share.

Officers	Position	Ownership Information	
Malcolm L. Sherman	Chairman, CEO	Number of Shares Outstanding	19,065,000
Jeffrey Weinstein	Exec VP	Market Capitalization	$ 71,493,750
Donato DeNovellis	Exec VP, CFO	Number of Shareholders	2,000
Stuart Cohen	Vice President	Where Listed / Symbol	NYSE / EKO

Other Information			
Transfer Agent	American Stock Transfer & Trust Co. New York, NY	SIC Code	3460
Auditor	KPMG LLP	Employees	1,067
		Web Site	ekco.com

EMCON

400 South El Camino Real, Suite 1200 San Mateo, CA 94402 Telephone (650)375-1522 Fax (650)375-0763

Company Description

EMCON provides comprehensive environmental engineering, design, construction, operations and maintenance, and equipment fabrication services to a variety of public and private industrial and solid waste clients. The Company is a leader in the design, construction and remediation of solid and hazardous waste facilities, having participated in the design, construction and remediation of several hundred transfer, storage and disposal facilities in the United States and abroad. The Company's professional staff includes chemical, civil, geotechnical, mechanical, electrical and environmental engineers; marine and terrestrial biologists; oceanographers; plant ecologists; chemists; geologists; hydrogeologists; hydrologists and toxicologists. The Company was founded in 1971.

	12/31/98	12/31/97	12/31/96	12/31/95
Per Share Information				
Stock Price	3.19	4.87	3.50	3.75
Earnings Per Share	0.19	0.25	-1.19	0.21
Price / Earnings Ratio	16.79	19.48	n.a.	17.86
Book Value Per Share	7.11	6.78	6.56	7.84
Price / Book Value %	44.87	71.83	53.35	47.83
Dividends Per Share	0.0	0.0	0.0	0.0
Annual Financial Data				
Operating Results (000's)				
Total Revenues	130,508.0	110,018.0	118,249.0	103,811.0
Costs & Expenses	-127,367.0	-105,888.0	-131,088.0	-101,168.0
Income Before Taxes and Other	3,141.0	4,128.0	-12,839.0	2,569.0
Other Items	0.0	-810.0	-188.0	0.0
Income Tax	-1,508.0	-1,161.0	2,936.0	-783.0
Net Income	1,633.0	2,157.0	-10,091.0	1,786.0
Cash Flow From Operations	4,741.0	6,189.0	1,583.0	2,400.0
Balance Sheet (000's)				
Cash & Equivalents	2,677.0	6,106.0	5,331.0	9,451.0
Total Current Assets	53,475.0	53,381.0	52,901.0	47,943.0
Fixed Assets, Net	16,519.0	16,182.0	14,700.0	16,690.0
Total Assets	95,889.0	93,075.0	90,912.0	78,636.0
Total Current Liabilities	25,168.0	20,798.0	18,300.0	11,630.0
Long-Term Debt	9,400.0	11,441.0	16,799.0	1,700.0
Stockholders' Equity	59,137.0	58,100.0	55,813.0	65,306.0
Performance & Financial Condition				
Return on Total Revenues %	1.08	1.54	-7.30	1.45
Return on Avg Stockholders' Equity %	2.79	3.79	-16.66	2.98
Return on Average Assets %	1.73	2.34	-11.90	2.23
Current Ratio	2.12	2.57	2.89	4.12
Debt / Equity %	15.90	19.69	30.10	2.60

Compound Growth %'s	EPS %	-3.28	Net Income %	-2.94	Total Revenues %	7.93

Comments

The demand for EMCON's services continued to grow in 1998 as revenues increased 18.7%. By factoring out discontinued operations from 1997, numbers produce a 24.3% revenue growth rate for 1998. 1996 results include $11.5 million of nonrecurring charges related to the disposition of a laboratory and restructuring. At December 31, 1998, the Company had $14.9 million of goodwill recorded as assets which equated to approximately 25% of stockholders' equity and book value per share.

Officers	Position	Ownership Information	
Douglas P. Crane	Chairman	Number of Shares Outstanding	8,315,399
Eugene M. Herson	President, CEO	Market Capitalization	$ 26,526,123
R. Michael Momboisse	CFO, Secretary	Number of Shareholders	1,771
Donald R. Andres	Vice President	Where Listed / Symbol	NASDAQ / MCON

Other Information			
Transfer Agent	ChaseMellon Shareholder Services Ridgefield Park, NJ	SIC Code	8711
Auditor	Ernst & Young LLP	Employees	1,088
		Web Site	emconinc.com

ERC Industries, Inc.

1441 Park Ten Boulevard   Houston, TX 77084   Telephone (281)398-8901   Fax (281)398-8606

Company Description

ERC Industries, Inc. and its subsidiaries manufacture, remanufacture and service oilfield valves and wellhead equipment. To a lesser extent, the Company also serves the geothermal valve market. Products and services are primarily sold to customers in the oil and gas production industry located in the major oil and gas producing regions of the United States and overseas countries. The Company also leases certain oilfield equipment to customers. Approximately 88.5% of the outstanding shares of the Company's common stock are owned by the John Wood Group PLC, a U.K. company located in Scotland. Since January 1997, the Company has been conducting business under the name Wood Group Pressure Control. On July 1, 1997, the Company acquired Church Oil Tools, Inc., a manufacturer of drilling equipment. On February 2, 1998, the Company acquired Bompet, C.A., a Venezuelan manufacturer of drilling and production equipment.

	12/31/98	12/31/97	12/31/96	12/31/95
Per Share Information				
Stock Price	0.56	1.87	1.75	0.88
Earnings Per Share	-0.04	0.05	0.06	-0.06
Price / Earnings Ratio	n.a.	37.40	29.17	n.a.
Book Value Per Share	1.18	1.16	0.83	0.72
Price / Book Value %	47.46	161.21	210.84	122.22
Dividends Per Share	0.0	0.0	0.0	0.0
Annual Financial Data				
Operating Results (000's)				
Total Revenues	107,111.0	80,845.0	51,059.0	34,906.0
Costs & Expenses	-104,529.0	-78,227.0	-49,471.0	-35,954.0
Income Before Taxes and Other	2,582.0	2,618.0	1,588.0	-1,048.0
Other Items	-3,010.0	0.0	0.0	0.0
Income Tax	-803.0	-1,394.0	-573.0	273.0
Net Income	-1,231.0	1,224.0	1,015.0	-775.0
Cash Flow From Operations	-4,712.0	-9,109.0	-1,761.0	-2,128.0
Balance Sheet (000's)				
Cash & Equivalents	2,019.0	0.0	1.0	0.0
Total Current Assets	58,360.0	46,519.0	27,961.0	15,829.0
Fixed Assets, Net	8,914.0	7,743.0	4,932.0	2,860.0
Total Assets	71,433.0	60,383.0	35,309.0	20,879.0
Total Current Liabilities	36,348.0	24,504.0	15,862.0	9,179.0
Long-Term Debt	2,710.0	3,977.0	1,826.0	1,787.0
Stockholders' Equity	32,375.0	31,902.0	17,621.0	9,913.0
Performance & Financial Condition				
Return on Total Revenues %	-1.15	1.51	1.99	-2.22
Return on Avg Stockholders' Equity %	-3.83	4.94	7.37	-7.53
Return on Average Assets %	-1.87	2.56	3.61	-3.88
Current Ratio	1.61	1.90	1.76	1.72
Debt / Equity %	8.37	12.47	10.36	18.03

Compound Growth %'s	EPS % n.a.	Net Income % n.a.	Total Revenues % 45.32

Comments

$7.7 million of the 1998 increase in revenue is attributable to the Bompet acquisition mentioned above. The balance is due to an increase in customer activity, market share gains, and a full year's activity from Church Oil Tools. 1998 results include a $3,010,000 charge for asset impairment as a result of difficult market conditions experienced in the latter part of 1998. The active domestic rig count is a clear indicator of likely product demand and has been dropping. The Company intends to focus on increasing international sales in 1999. At December 31, 1998, the Company had $4.2 million of goodwill recorded as assets which equated to only 12.8% of stockholders' equity and book value per share.

Officers	Position	Ownership Information	
J. Derek P. Jones	Chairman	Number of Shares Outstanding	27,498,272
Wendell R. Brooks	President, CEO	Market Capitalization	$ 15,399,032
James E. Klima	Vice President, CFO	Number of Shareholders	3,000
Carl R. Caldwell	Controller	Where Listed / Symbol	NASDAQ / ERCI

Other Information			
Transfer Agent	American Stock Transfer & Trust Co. New York, NY	SIC Code	3533
Auditor	PricewaterhouseCoopers LLP	Employees	583

EXX INC

Company Description

EXX INC is engaged in the design, production and sale of consumer goods in the form of so-called impulse toys, watches and kites. In addition, it is engaged in the design, production and sale of electric motors geared toward the original equipment market, and the design, production and sale of cable pressurization equipment sold to the telecommunications industry. It formerly manufactured machine tools and machine tool replacement parts. The Company continues to receive royalty income from machine tools and replacement parts as part payment for its sale of a subsidiary's assets.

	12/31/98	12/31/97	12/31/96	12/31/95
Per Share Information				
Stock Price	1.87	3.12	3.87	5.32
Earnings Per Share	0.29	-0.08	-0.60	0.86
Price / Earnings Ratio	6.45	n.a.	n.a.	6.19
Book Value Per Share	3.58	3.31	3.39	4.00
Price / Book Value %	52.23	94.26	114.16	133.00
Dividends Per Share	0.0	0.0	0.0	0.0
Annual Financial Data				
Operating Results (000's)				
Total Revenues	21,454.0	22,880.0	20,096.0	30,946.0
Costs & Expenses	-20,287.0	-23,233.0	-22,527.0	-27,416.0
Income Before Taxes and Other	1,167.0	-353.0	-2,431.0	3,530.0
Other Items	0.0	0.0	0.0	0.0
Income Tax	-406.0	130.0	807.0	-1,200.0
Net Income	761.0	-223.0	-1,624.0	2,330.0
Cash Flow From Operations	1,625.0	1,688.0	450.0	-2,720.0
Balance Sheet (000's)				
Cash & Equivalents	3,383.0	3,654.0	3,092.0	4,723.0
Total Current Assets	13,776.0	12,961.0	12,066.0	13,591.0
Fixed Assets, Net	2,386.0	2,586.0	830.0	998.0
Total Assets	16,440.0	15,851.0	13,419.0	15,418.0
Total Current Liabilities	4,667.0	4,822.0	4,018.0	4,372.0
Long-Term Debt	1,745.0	1,793.0	0.0	0.0
Stockholders' Equity	9,281.0	8,918.0	9,141.0	10,793.0
Performance & Financial Condition				
Return on Total Revenues %	3.55	-0.97	-8.08	7.53
Return on Avg Stockholders' Equity %	8.36	-2.47	-16.29	24.20
Return on Average Assets %	4.71	-1.52	-11.26	14.10
Current Ratio	2.95	2.69	3.00	3.11
Debt / Equity %	18.80	20.11	n.a.	n.a.

Compound Growth %'s	EPS %	-30.40	Net Income %	-31.13	Total Revenues %	-11.49

Comments

The Company's toy division continues to suffer from industry wide pressures. Sales declined another 21% in 1998. However, this drop was mostly offset by increased revenue of the Company's mechanical equipment division. Management's attention to cutting expenses helped engineer a return to profitability. A retrenchment of the toy division in 1996, that was reflective of the industry as a whole, was responsible for the large operating loss. The Company has a liquid financial condition as of December 31, 1998, with cash and short term investments of $6.9 million ($2.66 per share) which approximates 74.2% of stockholders' equity and book value per share. The last trade at December 31, 1998 was at $1.87 per share, less than its share of cash and short term investments.

Officers	Position	Ownership Information	
David A. Segal	CEO, CFO	Number of Shares Outstanding	2,594,012
Frederic Remington	Director	Market Capitalization	$ 4,850,802
Norman H. Perlmutter	Director	Number of Shareholders	1,250
Jerry Fishman	Director	Where Listed / Symbol	AMEX / EXXA

Other Information			
Transfer Agent	First City Transfer Co. Edison, NJ	SIC Code	3621
Auditor	Rothstein, Kass & Company, PC	Employees	145

Eagle Food Centers, Inc.

Route 67 & Knoxville Road   Milan, IL 61264   Telephone (309)787-7700   Fax (309)787-7264

Company Description

Eagle Food Centers, Inc. is a regional supermarket chain operating 90 supermarkets in the Quad Cities area of Illinois and Iowa as well as in much of the remainder of Illinois, eastern Iowa, and northeastern Indiana. Most Eagle supermarkets offer a full line of groceries, meats, fresh produce, dairy products, delicatessen and bakery products, health and beauty aids, and other general merchandise. The Company has a proud history that stretches back to 1893. The most recent ownership change occurred in 1989 when a controlling interest in Lucky Stores, Inc. was redeemed.

	01/31/98	02/02/97	02/03/96	01/28/95
Per Share Information				
Stock Price as of 12/31	3.12	4.00	4.00	3.75
Earnings Per Share	0.45	0.29	-1.68	-1.71
Price / Earnings Ratio	6.93	13.79	n.a.	n.a.
Book Value Per Share	2.94	2.46	2.19	3.84
Price / Book Value %	106.12	162.60	182.65	97.66
Dividends Per Share	0.0	0.0	0.0	0.0
Annual Financial Data				
Operating Results (000's)				
Total Revenues	967,090.0	1,014,889.0	1,023,664.0	1,015,063.0
Costs & Expenses	-962,398.0	-1,011,641.0	-1,042,340.0	-1,039,294.0
Income Before Taxes and Other	4,692.0	3,248.0	-18,676.0	-24,231.0
Other Items	0.0	0.0	-625.0	0.0
Income Tax	400.0	0.0	609.0	5,357.0
Net Income	5,092.0	3,248.0	-18,692.0	-18,874.0
Cash Flow From Operations	8,536.0	24,193.0	14,556.0	4,127.0
Balance Sheet (000's)				
Cash & Equivalents	5,113.0	9,134.0	1,481.0	4,096.0
Total Current Assets	112,717.0	108,922.0	112,117.0	114,185.0
Fixed Assets, Net	113,124.0	118,473.0	136,453.0	167,749.0
Total Assets	261,624.0	254,748.0	265,278.0	311,484.0
Total Current Liabilities	99,769.0	97,192.0	110,547.0	113,385.0
Long-Term Debt	100,000.0	100,000.0	100,000.0	100,000.0
Stockholders' Equity	32,237.0	26,688.0	23,921.0	42,485.0
Performance & Financial Condition				
Return on Total Revenues %	0.53	0.32	-1.83	-1.86
Return on Avg Stockholders' Equity %	17.28	12.84	-56.30	-36.22
Return on Average Assets %	1.97	1.25	-6.48	-5.84
Current Ratio	1.13	1.12	1.01	1.01
Debt / Equity %	310.20	374.70	418.04	235.38

Compound Growth %'s	EPS % n.a.	Net Income % n.a.	Total Revenues % -1.60

Comments

The improved operating performance includes higher margins, an improved sales mix, and reduced selling and administrative expenses which occurred after a major reorganization in fiscal 1996 and 1995 was undertaken to restore profitability. Revenues declined 4.7% in fiscal 1998 due to competitive store openings during the year. The two years prior to fiscal 1998 include expenses for store closings and voluntary severance. Management claims that its financial position is strong. Although it may be better than it was, it is still a highly leveraged company with $100 million in long term debt. For the nine months ended October 31, 1998, the Company reported revenues and net income of $692.6 million and $1,425,000 ($.13 per share) as compared to $719.5 million and $2,703,000 ($.24 per share) for the same period of the preceding year.

Officers	Position	Ownership Information	
Robert J. Kelly	President, CEO	Number of Shares Outstanding	10,946,873
David S. Norton	Senior VP	Market Capitalization	$ 34,154,244
S. Patric Plumley	Vice President, CFO	Number of Shareholders	2,693
Alain Oberrotman	Director	Where Listed / Symbol	NASDAQ / EGLE

Other Information			
Transfer Agent	First Chicago Trust Co. of New York Jersey City, NJ	SIC Code	5411
Auditor	Deloitte & Touche LLP	Employees	6,337
		Web Site	eaglefoods.com

Eagle Geophysical, Inc.

2603 Agusta, Suite 1400   Houston, TX 77057   Telephone (713)243-6100   Fax (713)243-6157

Company Description

Eagle Geophysical, Inc. is a highly focused international oilfield service company engaged in the acquisition of seismic information, with a specialization in the acquisition of high definition three-dimensional seismic data in logistically difficult wetland environments and in congested offshore areas. Seismic data is used by oil and gas companies in the exploration for new oil and gas reserves and the development of existing reserves. The Company was formed in December 1996 from the onshore seismic data acquisition business of Seitel Geophysical Inc., a wholly-owned subsidiary of Seitel, Inc. The Company remained a wholly-owned subsidiary of Seitel until August 11, 1997 when the Company completed an initial public offering of 6,524,000 shares of common stock at $17 per share.

	12/31/98	12/31/97	12/31/96	12/31/95
Per Share Information				
Stock Price	3.37	13.00	n.a.	n.a.
Earnings Per Share	0.46	0.81	1.23	0.47
Price / Earnings Ratio	7.33	16.05	n.a.	n.a.
Book Value Per Share	10.22	9.89	2.29	-1.65
Price / Book Value %	32.97	131.45	n.a.	n.a.
Dividends Per Share	0.0	0.0	0.0	0.0
Annual Financial Data				
Operating Results (000's)				
Total Revenues	123,597.0	79,061.0	48,136.0	29,275.0
Costs & Expenses	-116,541.0	-71,667.0	-41,537.0	-26,739.0
Income Before Taxes and Other	7,056.0	7,394.0	6,599.0	2,536.0
Other Items	0.0	0.0	0.0	0.0
Income Tax	-3,045.0	-2,994.0	-2,420.0	-933.0
Net Income	4,011.0	4,400.0	4,179.0	1,603.0
Cash Flow From Operations	27,546.0	12,889.0	4,640.0	633.0
Balance Sheet (000's)				
Cash & Equivalents	10,331.0	19,482.0	0.0	373.0
Total Current Assets	58,867.0	50,888.0	14,447.0	7,117.0
Fixed Assets, Net	175,238.0	55,197.0	12,205.0	20,923.0
Total Assets	273,195.0	124,305.0	26,721.0	28,040.0
Total Current Liabilities	52,792.0	32,365.0	8,942.0	18,517.0
Long-Term Debt	105,385.0	0.0	6,039.0	2,600.0
Stockholders' Equity	89,800.0	83,996.0	7,789.0	-5,626.0
Performance & Financial Condition				
Return on Total Revenues %	3.25	5.57	8.68	5.48
Return on Avg Stockholders' Equity %	4.62	9.59	386.41	57.08
Return on Average Assets %	2.02	5.83	15.26	9.90
Current Ratio	1.12	1.57	1.62	0.38
Debt / Equity %	117.36	n.a.	77.53	n.a.

Compound Growth %'s	EPS %	-0.71	Net Income %	35.76	Total Revenues %	61.62

Comments

Higher 1998 revenues reflect a full year of revenue of acquired operations and a partial year for operations acquired in 1998. Results of operations prior to December 1996 represent those of the predecessor business. The compound growth of earnings per share is diluted from the growth in net income because of the issuance of new shares. At December 31, 1998, the Company had $19.2 million of goodwill recorded as assets which represents approximately 21.4% of stockholders' equity and book value per share. The Company is highly leveraged as working capital is relatively low and the debt to equity ratio is relatively high.

Officers	Position	Ownership Information	
William L. Lurie	Chairman	Number of Shares Outstanding	8,788,310
Jay N. Silverman	President, CEO	Market Capitalization	$ 29,616,605
Gerald M. Harrison	Exec VP	Number of Shareholders	1,000
George Purdie	Senior VP	Where Listed / Symbol	NASDAQ / EGEO

Other Information			
Transfer Agent	ChaseMellon Shareholder Services Ridgefield Park, NJ	SIC Code	1382
Auditor	Arthur Andersen LLP	Employees	671

Eagle Pacific Industries, Inc.

333 South Seventh Street, 2430 Metropolitan Centre   Minneapolis, MN 55402   Telephone (612)371-9650   Fax (612)371-9651

Company Description

The Company, through its subsidiaries Eagle Plastics, Inc. and Pacific Plastics, Inc., is a leading producer of polyvinyl chloride (PVC) pipe and polyethylene (PH) tubing products. Based on the Company's specific product lines, small and medium diameter pipe and tubing, the Company is believed to be among the top five producers in the United States. The Company produces more than 200 miles of PVC and PE pipe each day. Manufacturing facilities are located in Nebraska, Oregon and Utah. Products are used for turf irrigation, commercial and industrial plumbing, transporting natural gas and water, and many other uses in the agriculture and communications industries. The products are sold in 30 states and three western Canadian provinces. Subsequent to year end, the Company announced a major acquisition of the pipe business of Lamson & Sessions Co.

	12/31/98	12/31/97	12/31/96	12/31/95
Per Share Information				
Stock Price	1.87	2.25	2.63	1.44
Earnings Per Share	0.05	0.06	0.25	-0.27
Price / Earnings Ratio	37.40	37.50	10.52	n.a.
Book Value Per Share	1.18	1.18	1.24	0.43
Price / Book Value %	158.47	190.68	212.10	334.88
Dividends Per Share	0.0	0.0	0.0	0.0
Annual Financial Data				
Operating Results (000's)				
Total Revenues	74,090.2	71,725.9	65,326.7	51,466.7
Costs & Expenses	-72,148.3	-70,966.4	-62,788.6	-52,550.8
Income Before Taxes and Other	1,941.9	759.4	2,538.1	-1,084.1
Other Items	-656.4	-520.4	-1,887.6	-138.4
Income Tax	-154.0	171.3	1,009.7	164.0
Net Income	1,131.4	410.4	1,660.2	-1,058.5
Cash Flow From Operations	5,659.2	819.9	5,757.4	6,199.4
Balance Sheet (000's)				
Cash & Equivalents	6,310.0	0.0	0.0	303.0
Total Current Assets	19,269.1	20,537.7	17,189.6	15,453.5
Fixed Assets, Net	22,634.6	16,854.4	11,486.0	9,354.7
Total Assets	49,618.8	43,829.0	35,426.6	31,917.8
Total Current Liabilities	21,233.2	16,457.4	16,063.4	15,002.6
Long-Term Debt	10,582.6	9,672.5	11,008.0	11,743.5
Stockholders' Equity	7,803.0	7,699.1	8,024.0	4,575.1
Performance & Financial Condition				
Return on Total Revenues %	1.53	0.57	2.54	-2.06
Return on Avg Stockholders' Equity %	14.60	5.22	26.35	-24.60
Return on Average Assets %	2.42	1.04	4.93	-4.14
Current Ratio	0.91	1.25	1.07	1.03
Debt / Equity %	135.62	125.63	137.19	256.68

Compound Growth %'s	EPS %	-55.28	Net Income %	-17.45	Total Revenues %	12.91

Comments

Interest costs and preferred stock dividends have had a significant negative impact on the bottom line. Interests costs have ranged from $2.2 million to $2.9 million during the past four years. Preferred stock dividends totalled $802,000 in 1998. At December 31, 1998, the Company had $10 million of redeemable preferred stock in addition to long-term debt of approximately $10.6 million. Approximately one-half of stockholders' equity and book value per share is comprised of intangible assets. 1998 and 1996 results include nonrecurring losses from the prepayment of debts amounting to $656,419 ($.09 per share) and $1,728,353 ($.24 per share), respectively.

Officers	Position	Ownership Information	
Harry W. Spell	Chairman	Number of Shares Outstanding	6,635,035
G. Peter Konen	President	Market Capitalization	$ 12,407,515
William H. Spell	CEO	Number of Shareholders	3,570
Patrick M. Mertens	CFO	Where Listed / Symbol	NASDAQ / EPII

Other Information			
Transfer Agent	Norwest Bank Minnesota, N.A. Minneapolis, MN	SIC Code	3080
Auditor	Deloitte & Touche LLP	Employees	384

EcoScience Corporation

10 Alvin Court   East Brunswick, NJ 08816   Telephone (732)432-8200   Fax (732)432-0770

Company Description

EcoScience Corporation is a marketing, sales and product development company, servicing the needs of the agriculture specialties markets and professional pest control operators. The Company provides 1) sophisticated growing systems to greenhouse operators, 2) technologically advanced sorting, grading and packing systems to greenhouse operators, 3) equipment, coatings and disease control products, including natural biologicals for protecting fruits, vegetables and ornamentals in storage and transit to market, and 4) biological pest control products to consumers and industry. On September 30, 1998, the Company acquired Agro Power Development, Inc., the largest producer of premium quality, greenhouse grown tomatoes in the United States, in exchange for 9,421,487 shares of common stock.

	06/30/98	06/30/97	06/30/96	06/30/95
Per Share Information				
Stock Price as of 12/31	4.00	1.56	1.00	0.94
Earnings Per Share	-0.09	0.04	-0.06	-1.71
Price / Earnings Ratio	n.a.	39.00	n.a.	n.a.
Book Value Per Share	0.30	0.39	0.26	0.28
Price / Book Value %	1,333.33	400.00	384.62	335.71
Dividends Per Share	0.0	0.0	0.0	0.0
Annual Financial Data				
Operating Results (000's)				
Total Revenues	22,435.0	20,965.0	14,475.0	12,335.0
Costs & Expenses	-23,402.0	-20,580.0	-15,303.0	-27,429.0
Income Before Taxes and Other	-967.0	385.0	-828.0	-15,094.0
Other Items	0.0	0.0	241.0	0.0
Income Tax	0.0	0.0	0.0	0.0
Net Income	-967.0	385.0	-587.0	-15,094.0
Cash Flow From Operations	-1,685.0	184.0	-2,651.0	-10,959.0
Balance Sheet (000's)				
Cash & Equivalents	358.0	1,247.0	734.0	561.0
Total Current Assets	7,112.0	6,345.0	7,019.0	11,199.0
Fixed Assets, Net	895.0	562.0	998.0	4,478.0
Total Assets	9,626.0	8,875.0	10,111.0	18,769.0
Total Current Liabilities	6,333.0	4,710.0	7,327.0	7,852.0
Long-Term Debt	7.0	1.0	11.0	5,693.0
Stockholders' Equity	3,136.0	4,014.0	2,473.0	2,492.0
Performance & Financial Condition				
Return on Total Revenues %	-4.31	1.84	-4.06	-115.40
Return on Avg Stockholders' Equity %	-27.05	11.87	-23.65	-146.53
Return on Average Assets %	-10.45	4.06	-4.07	-57.22
Current Ratio	1.12	1.35	0.96	1.43
Debt / Equity %	0.22	0.02	0.44	228.45

Compound Growth %'s	EPS % n.a.	Net Income % n.a.	Total Revenues % 22.07

Comments

In fiscal 1997, the Company achieved profitability as an operating company for the first time. Lower gross margins caused the Company to return to red ink in fiscal 1998. But the new combined company is 80% owned by the former shareholders of Agro Power Development. For the six months ended December 31, 1998, the Company reported revenues of $26.2 million and a net loss of $8,487,000 ($.73 per share) as compared to $11.9 million and a net loss of $410,000 ($.04 per share) for the same period of the preceding year. The short period results were adversely affected by the costs associated with the merger, the integration of the two companies, the significant increase in interest payments for four new greenhouse projects, and the continued investment in development of biological-based technologies. At December 31, 1998, the Company had a substantial working capital deficiency.

Officers	Position	Ownership Information	
Michael A. DeGiglio	President, CEO	Number of Shares Outstanding	10,488,455
David W. Miller	Senior VP	Market Capitalization	$ 41,953,820
David Suchniak	Senior VP, CFO	Number of Shareholders	1,823
Harold A. Joannidi	Treasurer, Controller	Where Listed / Symbol	NASDAQ / ECSC

Other Information			
Transfer Agent	Boston EquiServe Boston, MA	SIC Code	2870
Auditor	Arthur Andersen LLP	Employees	65
		Web Site	ecosci.com

Edac Technologies Corporation

1806 New Britain Avenue   Farmington, CT 06032   Telephone (860)678-8140   Fax (860)674-2718

Company Description

Edac Technologies Corporation offers design and manufacturing services for the aerospace industry in areas such as special tooling, equipment and gauges, and components used in the manufacture, assembly and inspection of jet engines. Edac also specializes in the design and repair of precision spindles. Spindles are an integral part of numerous machine tools which are found in virtually any type of manufacturing environment. Edac maintains manufacturing facilities with computerized, numerically controlled machining centers, grinding, welding, and sheet metal fabrication, painting and assembly capabilities. The Company was formed in 1985 for the purpose of acquiring Gros-Ite Industries which had been founded in 1946.

	01/02/99	12/31/97	12/31/96	12/31/95
Per Share Information				
Stock Price as of 12/31	4.62	8.62	1.87	1.25
Earnings Per Share	0.50	0.43	0.0	-0.30
Price / Earnings Ratio	9.24	20.05	n.a.	n.a.
Book Value Per Share	2.25	1.80	1.46	1.46
Price / Book Value %	205.33	478.89	128.08	85.62
Dividends Per Share	0.0	0.0	0.0	0.0
Annual Financial Data				
Operating Results (000's)				
Total Revenues	53,253.2	38,310.6	30,300.5	24,608.7
Costs & Expenses	-50,272.1	-36,593.4	-30,293.4	-25,691.9
Income Before Taxes and Other	2,981.1	1,717.1	7.1	-1,083.2
Other Items	0.0	0.0	0.0	0.0
Income Tax	-704.8	-21.0	0.0	0.0
Net Income	2,276.3	1,696.1	7.1	-1,083.2
Cash Flow From Operations	3,199.0	1,676.9	1,765.1	-1,335.9
Balance Sheet (000's)				
Cash & Equivalents	229.5	137.6	195.4	158.1
Total Current Assets	20,881.3	15,195.8	14,058.3	14,115.2
Fixed Assets, Net	19,192.0	7,584.3	5,473.1	5,950.0
Total Assets	52,607.9	23,849.6	19,917.7	20,352.1
Total Current Liabilities	20,245.0	10,694.9	9,401.8	9,166.5
Long-Term Debt	21,606.0	5,368.9	4,510.0	5,854.0
Stockholders' Equity	9,582.8	6,885.8	5,472.9	5,331.6
Performance & Financial Condition				
Return on Total Revenues %	4.27	4.43	0.02	-4.40
Return on Avg Stockholders' Equity %	27.64	27.45	0.13	-18.36
Return on Average Assets %	5.95	7.75	0.04	-5.42
Current Ratio	1.03	1.42	1.50	1.54
Debt / Equity %	225.47	77.97	82.41	109.80

Compound Growth %'s	EPS %	n.a.	Net Income %	n.a.	Total Revenues %	29.35

Comments

Following the substantial operating loss in 1995, the Company reorganized under new management with focused business units based on specific products and markets. Certain assets were disposed of and on June 29, 1998, the Company completed the acquisition of Apex Machine Tool Company. The transaction was accounted for as a purchase. Therefore, results have been combined with that of the Company's since the date of the transaction. Approximately $9.9 million of the advance in 1998 revenues was attributable to the acquisition. Approximately one-third of the increase was internal. At December 31, 1998, the Company had $11.2 million of goodwill recorded as assets which equated to approximately 117% of stockholders' equity and book value per share. The acquisition also had its price with regard to the overall financial condition of the Company as working capital has all but disappeared and long term debt is significant.

Officers	Position	Ownership Information	
John Di Francesco	Chairman	Number of Shares Outstanding	4,261,580
Edward J. McNerney	President, CEO	Market Capitalization	$ 19,688,500
Ronald G. Popolizio	CFO, Secretary	Number of Shareholders	500
Francis W. Moskey	Vice President	Where Listed / Symbol	NASDAQ / EDAC

Other Information			
Transfer Agent	Continental Stock Transfer & Trust Co. New York, NY	SIC Code	3724
Auditor	Arthur Andersen LLP	Employees	387
		Web Site	edactechnologies.com

Educational Insights, Inc.

16941 Keegan Avenue   Carson, CA 90746   Telephone (310)884-2000   Fax (310)884-2013

Company Description

Educational Insights, Inc. designs, develops and markets a variety of supplemental educational materials including electronic learning aids, activity books, science kits, board games and other materials intended for use in both homes and schools. The Company sells its products to school districts, independent toy dealers, and mass merchandisers principally located throughout the United States and Canada. The Company was founded in 1962 to develop and market supplemental educational materials to assist in the teaching of reading. The product line has grown to approximately 750 items and the Company is continuing to develop new products.

	12/31/98	12/31/97	12/31/96	12/31/95
Per Share Information				
Stock Price	1.53	2.16	2.25	2.75
Earnings Per Share	-0.32	0.01	0.12	-0.02
Price / Earnings Ratio	n.a.	216.00	18.75	n.a.
Book Value Per Share	3.02	3.34	3.33	3.21
Price / Book Value %	50.66	64.67	67.57	85.67
Dividends Per Share	0.0	0.0	0.0	0.0
Annual Financial Data				
Operating Results (000's)				
Total Revenues	39,310.0	38,643.0	41,778.0	40,274.0
Costs & Expenses	-43,035.0	-38,481.0	-40,465.0	-40,541.0
Income Before Taxes and Other	-3,725.0	162.0	1,313.0	-267.0
Other Items	0.0	0.0	0.0	0.0
Income Tax	1,445.0	-97.0	-484.0	95.0
Net Income	-2,280.0	65.0	829.0	-172.0
Cash Flow From Operations	-1,638.0	626.0	214.0	-1,215.0
Balance Sheet (000's)				
Cash & Equivalents	748.0	235.0	1,018.0	378.0
Total Current Assets	23,557.0	24,335.0	24,577.0	22,066.0
Fixed Assets, Net	5,088.0	5,218.0	5,446.0	5,844.0
Total Assets	29,279.0	30,130.0	30,904.0	28,254.0
Total Current Liabilities	7,110.0	5,192.0	5,903.0	4,084.0
Long-Term Debt	930.0	1,064.0	1,185.0	1,394.0
Stockholders' Equity	21,239.0	23,519.0	23,464.0	22,584.0
Performance & Financial Condition				
Return on Total Revenues %	-5.80	0.17	1.98	-0.43
Return on Avg Stockholders' Equity %	-10.19	0.28	3.60	-0.76
Return on Average Assets %	-7.68	0.21	2.80	-0.61
Current Ratio	3.31	4.69	4.16	5.40
Debt / Equity %	4.38	4.52	5.05	6.17

Compound Growth %'s	EPS % n.a.	Net Income % n.a.	Total Revenues %	-0.80

Comments

The Company experienced an unusually high level of difficulty in bringing new products to market in 1997. Four products which, on a combined basis, were expected to add significantly to the Company's revenue, were introduced late or with technical difficulties which effectively diminished their contribution to 1997 revenues. This led to a management reorganization in late 1998 as well as to decisions to discontinue certain low volume product lines. Gross margins dropped from 50.2% in 1997 to 42.3% in 1998. This, however, resulted from charges related to excess inventory. The Company has a solid financial condition with little long term debt and no intangible assets on the balance sheet. The price per share is at a substantial discount from book value. Let's watch for profits to return in 1999.

Officers	Position	Ownership Information	
Burton Cutler	Chairman	Number of Shares Outstanding	7,040,000
Theodore Eischeid	President, CEO	Market Capitalization	$ 10,771,200
James B. Whitney	VP - Sales	Number of Shareholders	1,500
Stephen E. Billis	Controller, Secretary	Where Listed / Symbol	NASDAQ / EDIN

Other Information			
Transfer Agent	American Stock Transfer & Trust Company New York, NY	SIC Code	3944
Auditor	Deloitte & Touche LLP	Employees	191
		Web Site	edin.com

Elantec Semiconductor, Inc.

675 Trade Zone Boulevard Milpitas, CA 95035 Telephone (408)945-1323 Fax (408)945-9305

Company Description

Elantec Semiconductor, Inc. designs, manufactures and markets high performance analog integrated circuits primarily for the video/multimedia, data processing, instrumentation and communications markets. The Company targets high growth commercial markets in which advances in digital technology are driving increasing demand for high speed, high precision and low power consumption analog circuits. The Company offers approximately 150 high performance analog products, such as amplifiers, drivers, faders, transceivers and multiplexers, most of which are available in multiple packaging configurations. The Company's products are manufactured at the Company's internal manufacturing facility in Milpitas, California as well as at third party wafer foundries. The Company was founded in 1983.

	09/30/98	09/30/97	09/30/96	09/30/95
Per Share Information				
Stock Price as of 12/31	3.56	6.00	4.37	10.00
Earnings Per Share	0.75	0.06	0.47	0.34
Price / Earnings Ratio	4.75	100.00	9.30	29.41
Book Value Per Share	3.51	2.75	2.75	1.60
Price / Book Value %	101.42	218.18	158.91	625.00
Dividends Per Share	0.0	0.0	0.0	0.0
Annual Financial Data				
Operating Results (000's)				
Total Revenues	46,884.0	36,147.0	37,493.0	27,079.0
Costs & Expenses	-42,362.0	-35,500.0	-32,732.0	-24,128.0
Income Before Taxes and Other	4,522.0	647.0	4,761.0	2,951.0
Other Items	0.0	0.0	0.0	0.0
Income Tax	2,683.0	-81.0	-372.0	-238.0
Net Income	7,205.0	566.0	4,389.0	2,713.0
Cash Flow From Operations	4,691.0	1,464.0	5,106.0	2,844.0
Balance Sheet (000's)				
Cash & Equivalents	5,815.0	9,839.0	9,377.0	6,009.0
Total Current Assets	27,699.0	27,239.0	27,244.0	15,309.0
Fixed Assets, Net	18,625.0	9,230.0	7,360.0	4,721.0
Total Assets	47,544.0	37,091.0	35,246.0	20,910.0
Total Current Liabilities	10,913.0	8,952.0	9,606.0	8,455.0
Long-Term Debt	4,354.0	3,336.0	1,566.0	1,313.0
Stockholders' Equity	32,277.0	24,803.0	24,074.0	11,142.0
Performance & Financial Condition				
Return on Total Revenues %	15.37	1.57	11.71	10.02
Return on Avg Stockholders' Equity %	25.25	2.32	24.93	27.88
Return on Average Assets %	17.03	1.56	15.63	15.14
Current Ratio	2.54	3.04	2.84	1.81
Debt / Equity %	13.49	13.45	6.50	11.78

Compound Growth %'s	EPS %	30.17	Net Income %	38.48	Total Revenues %	20.08

Comments

During fiscal 1998, the Company experienced strong growth in each of its major end markets and particularly in the data processing area. Geographically, the Company experienced a 38% increase in domestic revenues and a 25% increase in international revenues. Substantial amounts continue to be invested in research and development with $7.2 million, $6.2 million and $6.4 million expended during fiscal 1998, 1997 and 1996, respectively. The Company recorded a net tax benefit in fiscal 1998 after making a change in accounting for income taxes which resulted in a $3.1 nonrecurring favorable adjustment. Compound growth rates of earnings per share and net income are therefore distorted. The Company maintains a strong financial condition.

Officers	Position	Ownership Information	
James V. Diller	President, CEO	Number of Shares Outstanding	9,188,000
Ephraim Kwok	VP - Finance, CFO	Market Capitalization	$ 32,709,280
Richard E. Corbin	Vice President	Number of Shareholders	3,400
Ralph S. Granchelli, Jr.	VP - Sales	Where Listed / Symbol	NASDAQ / ELNT

Other Information			
Transfer Agent	ChaseMellon Shareholder Services Ridgefield Park, NJ	SIC Code	3674
Auditor	Deloitte & Touche LLP	Employees	182
		Web Site	elantec.com

Eldorado Artesian Springs, Inc.

P.O. Box 445 Eldorado Springs, CO 80025 Telephone (303)499-1316 Fax (303)499-1339

Company Description

Eldorado Artesian Springs, Inc., founded in 1983, bottles and sells Artesian Spring Water. The Company also owns and operates a resort/spa on its property during the summer months and rents four single-family homes and mobile home spaces on the property. The Company's water bottling operations account for 95.6% of the Company's revenues. Water is produced at two springs and eleven wells on the Company's property. The well heads are in close proximity to the bottling operation. The source water is bacteria-free as it emanates from the earth, and nothing is added to or removed from the water during the bottling process. As a safeguard against any contamination, the water passes through a protective filter and an ultra-violet light. The product is packaged only in glass or high quality plastic bottles.

	03/31/98	03/31/97	03/31/96	03/31/95
Per Share Information				
Stock Price as of 12/31	0.62	0.48	0.12	0.12
Earnings Per Share	0.03	0.05	0.03	0.03
Price / Earnings Ratio	20.67	9.60	4.00	4.00
Book Value Per Share	0.20	0.17	0.13	0.10
Price / Book Value %	310.00	282.35	92.31	120.00
Dividends Per Share	0.0	0.0	0.0	0.0
Annual Financial Data				
Operating Results (000's)				
Total Revenues	3,333.2	2,645.5	2,154.7	1,817.9
Costs & Expenses	-3,212.7	-2,458.3	-2,058.2	-1,700.6
Income Before Taxes and Other	117.6	187.2	96.5	117.3
Other Items	0.0	0.0	0.0	0.0
Income Tax	-34.4	-63.1	-23.2	-29.1
Net Income	83.2	124.2	73.3	88.2
Cash Flow From Operations	126.5	388.5	326.9	225.4
Balance Sheet (000's)				
Cash & Equivalents	70.2	244.8	82.3	44.1
Total Current Assets	761.8	642.4	459.9	373.5
Fixed Assets, Net	1,525.4	1,212.5	1,144.3	918.8
Total Assets	2,456.7	2,024.4	1,781.8	1,571.9
Total Current Liabilities	421.1	292.3	204.9	261.9
Long-Term Debt	1,431.8	1,223.6	1,203.0	1,051.1
Stockholders' Equity	550.9	467.7	343.5	258.9
Performance & Financial Condition				
Return on Total Revenues %	2.50	4.69	3.40	4.85
Return on Avg Stockholders' Equity %	16.34	30.61	24.34	31.51
Return on Average Assets %	3.71	6.52	4.37	5.88
Current Ratio	1.81	2.20	2.24	1.43
Debt / Equity %	259.90	261.62	350.17	405.96

Compound Growth %'s	EPS %	0.00	Net Income %	-1.93	Total Revenues %	22.39

Comments

The Company executed a 1 for 12 reverse split on March 23, 1998. All per share amounts have been restated for consistency. On April 22, 1998, the Company completed a private placement of 300,000 shares of common stock at $2.75 per share. This may be the cause of a huge spread between the bid price of $.62 and the ask price of $3.00 that is posted by market makers. For the nine months ended December 31, 1998, the Company reported revenues and net income of $3.0 million and $111,362 ($.04 per share) as compared to $2.5 million and $158,741 ($.06 per share) for the same period of the fiscal 1998.

Officers	Position	Ownership Information	
Douglas A. Larson	President, CEO	Number of Shares Outstanding	2,695,412
Kevin M. Sipple	Vice President, Secretary	Market Capitalization	$ 1,671,155
Jeremy S. Martin	Vice President	Number of Shareholders	3,000
		Where Listed / Symbol	OTC-BB / ELAR

Other Information			
Transfer Agent	Corporate Stock Transfer, Inc. Denver, CO	SIC Code	5140
Auditor	Ehrhardt Keefe Steiner Hottman	Employees	47
Market Maker	Howe Barnes Investments, Inc. (800)621-2364	Web Site	eldoradosprings.com
	Paragon Capital Corporation (800)345-0505		

Electric & Gas Technology, Inc.

13636 Neutron Road   Dallas, TX 75244-4410   Telephone (972)934-8797   Fax (972)991-3265

Company Description

Electric & Gas Technology, Inc. operates in three distinct business segments: 1) production of atmospheric water, filtration and enhanced water products; 2) the manufacture and sale of natural gas measurement, metering and odorization equipment; and, 3) the manufacture and sale of electric meter enclosures and pole-line hardware for the electricity utility industry and the general public. Two other business segments, the design and manufacture of defense electronic components and the manufacture of vacuum-form and injection-mold products, were discontinued in fiscal 1998. The Company was formed in 1985.

	07/31/98	07/31/97	07/31/96	07/31/95
Per Share Information				
Stock Price as of 12/31	1.19	1.25	0.56	2.87
Earnings Per Share	0.05	1.01	-0.66	0.11
Price / Earnings Ratio	23.80	1.24	n.a.	26.09
Book Value Per Share	1.86	1.88	0.73	1.37
Price / Book Value %	63.98	66.49	76.71	209.49
Dividends Per Share	0.0	0.0	0.0	0.0
Annual Financial Data				
Operating Results (000's)				
Total Revenues	11,375.9	16,340.5	18,294.1	28,489.4
Costs & Expenses	-12,880.9	-21,481.5	-21,085.8	-28,326.3
Income Before Taxes and Other	-1,504.9	-5,143.7	-4,605.6	163.2
Other Items	2,094.5	14,292.7	-427.0	632.5
Income Tax	-160.4	213.4	0.0	54.9
Net Income	429.2	9,362.4	-5,032.6	850.6
Cash Flow From Operations	-2,957.9	-1,527.0	-764.2	-1,131.6
Balance Sheet (000's)				
Cash & Equivalents	542.1	14,529.9	879.1	1,044.9
Total Current Assets	12,483.1	21,008.2	7,722.7	15,331.6
Fixed Assets, Net	1,902.8	3,211.6	3,634.3	9,944.1
Total Assets	21,205.5	25,364.6	15,094.1	28,233.7
Total Current Liabilities	3,393.8	6,318.8	6,023.6	11,426.9
Long-Term Debt	918.9	2,196.8	1,643.9	0.0
Stockholders' Equity	16,137.4	16,041.1	6,720.9	10,427.9
Performance & Financial Condition				
Return on Total Revenues %	3.77	57.30	-27.51	2.99
Return on Avg Stockholders' Equity %	2.67	82.26	-58.69	8.63
Return on Average Assets %	1.84	46.28	-23.23	2.90
Current Ratio	3.68	3.32	1.28	1.34
Debt / Equity %	5.69	13.69	24.46	n.a.

Compound Growth %'s	EPS %	-23.11	Net Income %	-20.39	Total Revenues %	-26.36

Comments

Fiscal 1998 results include an investment gain of $2 million. The loss from continuing operations was $1.9 million. During fiscal 1997, the Company disposed of its metal fabrication business resulting in a nonrecurring gain of $12.6 million. The loss from continuing operations was $1.7 million. Management states that its entrance into the water industry will be a major focus for the future development and growth of the Company. But the balance sheet may be more slippery than it appears. The auditors qualified their fiscal 1998 report because they were not able to satisfy themselves as to the collectibility of a note receivable in the amount of $2.4 million. For the six months ended January 31, 1999, the Company reported revenues and a net loss of $5.6 million and $270,276 ($.03 per share) as compared to $5.5 million and net income of $44,796 ($.01 per share) for the same period of the preceding year.

Officers	Position	Ownership Information	
S. Mort Zimmerman	President, CEO	Number of Shares Outstanding	8,198,224
Daniel A. Zimmerman	Senior VP	Market Capitalization	$ 9,755,887
Marie W. Pazol	Secretary	Number of Shareholders	2,000
Edmund W. Bailey	Vice President, CFO	Where Listed / Symbol	NASDAQ / ELGT

Other Information			
Transfer Agent	Harris Trust Co. of New York New York, NY	SIC Code	3825
Auditor	Jackson & Rhodes P.C.	Employees	75

Electronic Systems Technology, Inc.

415 North Quay Street, Suite 4   Kennewick, WA 99336   Telephone (509)735-9092   Fax (509)735-9196

Company Description

Electronic Systems Technology, Inc. specializes in the manufacture and development of wireless modem products. Products offered provide innovative communication solutions for applications not served by existing conventional systems. The Company's products are offered to commercial, industrial and government customers, both domestically and internationally. The products provide communication links between computers, peripherals, and instrumentation using radio frequency waves. Given the rapidly changing, competitive market in which the Company operates, it is constantly updating, enhancing and creating new products.

	12/31/98	12/31/97	12/31/96	12/31/95
Per Share Information				
Stock Price	0.28	0.26	0.25	0.41
Earnings Per Share	0.03	0.03	0.03	0.05
Price / Earnings Ratio	9.33	8.67	8.33	8.20
Book Value Per Share	0.45	0.43	0.41	0.37
Price / Book Value %	62.22	60.47	60.98	110.81
Dividends Per Share	0.01	0.01	0.0	0.0
Annual Financial Data				
Operating Results (000's)				
Total Revenues	1,564.9	1,408.9	1,333.4	1,617.7
Costs & Expenses	-1,322.1	-1,161.1	-1,099.0	-1,161.7
Income Before Taxes and Other	242.8	247.8	234.5	404.1
Other Items	0.0	0.0	0.0	0.0
Income Tax	-79.9	-81.6	-75.7	-136.4
Net Income	162.9	166.2	158.7	267.7
Cash Flow From Operations	50.5	128.4	80.8	578.2
Balance Sheet (000's)				
Cash & Equivalents	1,213.3	1,060.9	930.3	964.7
Total Current Assets	2,206.7	2,065.5	1,892.3	1,857.4
Fixed Assets, Net	112.3	132.9	141.2	145.2
Total Assets	2,354.1	2,205.8	2,042.7	2,010.8
Total Current Liabilities	87.1	77.2	30.8	133.6
Long-Term Debt	0.0	0.0	0.0	0.0
Stockholders' Equity	2,242.0	2,128.6	2,011.9	1,877.2
Performance & Financial Condition				
Return on Total Revenues %	10.41	11.80	11.90	16.55
Return on Avg Stockholders' Equity %	7.46	8.03	8.16	15.60
Return on Average Assets %	7.15	7.82	7.83	14.84
Current Ratio	25.32	26.75	61.49	13.90
Debt / Equity %	n.a.	n.a.	n.a.	n.a.

Compound Growth %'s	EPS %	-15.66	Net Income %	-15.26	Total Revenues %	-1.10

Comments

Measured by revenue, the Company is one of the smallest and consistently profitable companies that we selected for inclusion in the manual. Total Revenues and Net Income have had only minor changes over the past four years. The 10% increase in 1998 revenue was a surprise to management and resulted from unexpected government contracts. New products were released in the first quarter of 1999. The Company maintains a healthy balance sheet which will be helpful for future product research and development. In fact, at December 31, 1998, cash and securities totaled $1,426,381 ($.29 per share) which equated to approximately 64% of stockholders' equity and book value per share. The last trade in 1998 was at $.28 per share.

Officers	Position	Ownership Information	
T. L. Kirchner	President	Number of Shares Outstanding	4,953,667
Robert Southworth	Secretary, Treasurer	Market Capitalization	$ 1,387,027
John L. Schooley	Director	Number of Shareholders	650
John Rector	Director	Where Listed / Symbol	OTC-BB / ELST

Other Information

Transfer Agent	TranSecurities International, Inc. Spokane, WA		SIC Code	3670
Auditor	Robert Moe & Associates, P.S.		Employees	12
Market Maker	Herzog, Heine, Geduld, Inc.	(800)212-3600	Web Site	esteem.com
	Paragon Capital Corporation	(800)345-0505		

Electronic Tele-Communications, Inc.

1915 MacArthur Road   Waukesha, WI 53188   Telephone (414)542-5600   Fax (414)542-1524

Company Description

Electronic Tele-Communications, Inc. manufactures, markets and leases digital voice information and call processing systems and related software and services. The Company's equipment, compatible with most telephone systems, provides a wide range of audio information and call handling capabilities via the telephone network. The Company's systems interface with customer computer systems to provide voice access to computerized information. Examples of these voice information capabilities include time, temperature, road conditions, stock prices, and repair status. The Company was founded in 1980.

	12/31/98	12/31/97	12/31/96	12/31/95
Per Share Information				
Stock Price	0.62	2.00	1.87	2.75
Earnings Per Share	0.08	-0.25	0.12	-0.08
Price / Earnings Ratio	7.75	n.a.	15.58	n.a.
Book Value Per Share	2.39	2.35	2.72	2.72
Price / Book Value %	25.94	85.11	68.75	101.10
Dividends Per Share	0.04	0.12	0.12	0.12
Annual Financial Data				
Operating Results (000's)				
Total Revenues	13,150.2	11,643.9	12,937.8	12,903.5
Costs & Expenses	-12,756.4	-12,365.9	-12,480.2	-13,179.8
Income Before Taxes and Other	393.8	-761.3	418.0	-307.4
Other Items	0.0	0.0	0.0	0.0
Income Tax	-214.5	84.0	-161.4	76.7
Net Income	179.3	-677.3	256.6	-230.7
Cash Flow From Operations	-389.2	-243.8	916.9	349.5
Balance Sheet (000's)				
Cash & Equivalents	848.1	489.6	1,002.0	498.0
Total Current Assets	5,156.2	3,934.7	5,188.0	4,859.5
Fixed Assets, Net	1,628.4	1,721.0	1,847.3	2,091.5
Total Assets	8,438.8	7,097.5	8,115.1	8,124.3
Total Current Liabilities	2,396.9	1,080.2	1,071.9	979.4
Long-Term Debt	52.4	126.8	0.0	0.0
Stockholders' Equity	5,989.5	5,890.5	6,816.5	6,820.4
Performance & Financial Condition				
Return on Total Revenues %	1.36	-5.82	1.98	-1.79
Return on Avg Stockholders' Equity %	3.02	-10.66	3.76	-3.27
Return on Average Assets %	2.31	-8.90	3.16	-2.66
Current Ratio	2.15	3.64	4.84	4.96
Debt / Equity %	0.87	2.15	n.a.	n.a.

Compound Growth %'s	EPS %	-18.35	Net Income %	-16.40	Total Revenues %	0.63

Comments

The loss and sales decline of 1997 caused management to make a number of organizational changes including hiring a new marketing team. 1998 started slowly but results steadily improved throughout the year. The fourth quarter finished with very strong sales of $4,269,000 and a profit of $351,000 ($.14 per share) part of which was attributable to one very large order. The Company has two classes of common stock. Class A shares have a liquidation and dividend preference. Book value per share disclosed above is based on total shares without regard to the preferences.

Officers	Position	Ownership Information	
Dean W. Danner	President, CEO	Number of Shares Outstanding	2,508,947
Hazel Danner	Secretary	Market Capitalization	$ 1,555,547
Jeffrey M. Nigl	Vice President, CFO	Number of Shareholders	800
Bonita M. Danner	Vice President	Where Listed / Symbol	NASDAQ / ETCIA

Other Information

Transfer Agent	Firstar Trust Company Milwaukee, WI	SIC Code	3661
Auditor	Ernst & Young LLP	Employees	127
		Web Site	etcia.com

Emerson Radio Corp.

9 Entin Road   Parsippany, NJ 07054   Telephone (973)884-5800   Fax (973)428-2033

Company Description

Emerson Radio Corp. designs, sources, imports and markets a variety of televisions and other video products, microwave ovens, audio, home theater, specialty and other consumer electronic products. The Company distributes its products primarily through mass merchants and discount retailers. The trade name Emerson Radio dates back to 1912 and is one of the oldest names in the consumer electronics industry. The Company was founded in 1956 and reorganized under Chapter 11 of the Federal Bankruptcy Code in 1994.

	04/03/98	03/31/97	03/31/96	03/31/95
Per Share Information				
Stock Price as of 12/31	0.56	0.60	1.75	2.12
Earnings Per Share	-0.04	-0.61	-0.35	0.16
Price / Earnings Ratio	n.a.	n.a.	n.a.	13.25
Book Value Per Share	0.18	0.17	0.77	1.11
Price / Book Value %	311.11	352.94	227.27	190.99
Dividends Per Share	0.0	0.0	0.0	0.0
Annual Financial Data				
Operating Results (000's)				
Total Revenues	164,254.0	178,708.0	245,667.0	654,671.0
Costs & Expenses	-164,716.0	-202,446.0	-259,030.0	-647,029.0
Income Before Taxes and Other	-1,176.0	-23,738.0	-13,363.0	7,642.0
Other Items	0.0	0.0	0.0	0.0
Income Tax	-254.0	-230.0	-26.0	-267.0
Net Income	-1,430.0	-23,968.0	-13,389.0	7,375.0
Cash Flow From Operations	6,091.0	16,688.0	-13,197.0	-20,974.0
Balance Sheet (000's)				
Cash & Equivalents	2,608.0	2,640.0	16,133.0	17,020.0
Total Current Assets	28,207.0	34,918.0	83,442.0	102,380.0
Fixed Assets, Net	1,381.0	2,130.0	3,501.0	4,676.0
Total Assets	51,920.0	58,768.0	96,576.0	113,969.0
Total Current Liabilities	17,043.0	21,660.0	35,008.0	59,782.0
Long-Term Debt	20,750.0	20,856.0	20,886.0	536.0
Stockholders' Equity	13,948.0	16,029.0	40,382.0	53,651.0
Performance & Financial Condition				
Return on Total Revenues %	-0.87	-13.41	-5.45	1.13
Return on Avg Stockholders' Equity %	-9.54	-84.98	-28.48	15.69
Return on Average Assets %	-2.58	-30.86	-12.72	7.02
Current Ratio	1.66	1.61	2.38	1.71
Debt / Equity %	148.77	130.11	51.72	1.00

Compound Growth %'s	EPS % n.a.	Net Income % n.a.	Total Revenues %	-36.93

Comments

The Company reported a decline in its net sales for the last three fiscal years due to the licensing of video sales, increased price competition, weak consumer demand, and a soft retail market. Management reported that licensing revenues and commission are likely to increase in future years. Although this may be music to the ears of some shareholders, working capital remains weak and the debt to equity ratio is too high. Management was successful in converting some preferred stock to common in fiscal 1998. For the nine months ended December 31, 1998, the Company reported revenues and net income of $137.5 million and $1,657,000 ($.02 per share) as compared to $123.8 million and a net loss of $210,000 ($.01 per share) for the same period of the preceding year.

Officers	Position	Ownership Information	
Geoffrey P. Jurick	President, CEO	Number of Shares Outstanding	51,044,730
John P. Walker	Exec VP, CFO	Market Capitalization	$ 28,585,049
John J. Raab	Senior VP	Number of Shareholders	511
Elizabeth J. Calianese	Vice President, Secretary	Where Listed / Symbol	NASDAQ / MSN

Other Information			
Transfer Agent	American Stock Transfer & Trust Co. New York, NY	SIC Code	3651
Auditor	Ernst & Young LLP	Employees	108
		Web Site	emersonradio.com

Emons Transportation Group, Inc.

96 South George Street   York, PA 17401-1436   Telephone (717)771-1700   Fax (717)854-6275

Company Description

Emons Transportation Group, Inc. is a freight transportation and distribution services company serving the Mid-Atlantic and Northeast regions of the United States. The Company owns four short line railroads, operates rail/truck transload facilities and a rail intermodal terminal, and provides its customers with logistics services for movement and storage of their freight. The Company was founded in 1955.

	06/30/98	06/30/97	06/30/96	06/30/95
Per Share Information				
Stock Price as of 12/31	2.44	2.94	3.50	1.87
Earnings Per Share	0.63	0.09	0.04	0.09
Price / Earnings Ratio	3.87	32.67	87.50	20.78
Book Value Per Share	1.42	0.54	0.40	0.29
Price / Book Value %	171.83	544.44	875.00	644.83
Dividends Per Share	0.0	0.0	0.0	0.0
Annual Financial Data				
Operating Results (000's)				
Total Revenues	17,787.2	16,311.6	15,073.9	14,061.2
Costs & Expenses	-16,299.6	-15,140.8	-14,314.9	-12,986.8
Income Before Taxes and Other	1,487.6	1,170.8	759.0	1,074.4
Other Items	0.0	0.0	0.0	0.0
Income Tax	3,430.0	-397.0	-289.5	-308.3
Net Income	4,917.6	773.8	469.5	766.1
Cash Flow From Operations	3,097.8	1,764.3	2,430.4	1,896.7
Balance Sheet (000's)				
Cash & Equivalents	2,677.0	1,515.2	1,265.4	1,232.9
Total Current Assets	5,930.8	4,416.2	4,293.3	3,698.4
Fixed Assets, Net	20,659.8	19,392.7	18,252.5	16,684.9
Total Assets	28,673.3	24,301.9	22,789.9	20,745.6
Total Current Liabilities	5,274.3	4,278.3	4,939.3	3,694.3
Long-Term Debt	11,006.8	10,976.3	10,118.2	10,043.3
Stockholders' Equity	11,634.0	6,439.2	5,618.6	5,116.3
Performance & Financial Condition				
Return on Total Revenues %	27.65	4.74	3.11	5.45
Return on Avg Stockholders' Equity %	54.42	12.83	8.75	16.24
Return on Average Assets %	18.57	3.29	2.16	3.77
Current Ratio	1.12	1.03	0.87	1.00
Debt / Equity %	94.61	170.46	180.08	196.30

Compound Growth %'s	EPS %	91.29	Net Income %	85.85	Total Revenues %	8.15

Comments

Based upon the sustained significant increase in taxable income in the current year, new business added to the Company's railroad operations in the current year, and acquisitions completed during the current year, the Company reduced the valuation allowance attributable to the net operating loss deferred tax assets in fiscal 1998. This was because management's reassessment had indicated that it appeared more likely than not that the tax benefits would be realized and in fact, it resulted in a $3,430,000 tax benefit. Preferred stock dividends were deducted in determining earnings per common share. For the six months ended December 31, 1998, revenue and net income were $10.3 million and $721,886 ($.09 per share) as compared to $8.2 million and $650,658 ($.08 per share) for the same period of the preceding year.

Officers	Position	Ownership Information	
Robert Grossman	President, CEO	Number of Shares Outstanding	6,039,811
Scott F. Ziegler	VP - Finance, Controller	Market Capitalization	$ 14,737,139
Phillip A. DuPont	Vice President	Number of Shareholders	1,766
Matthew Jacobson	Vice President	Where Listed / Symbol	NASDAQ / EMON

Other Information			
Transfer Agent	American Stock Transfer & Trust Co. New York, NY	SIC Code	4011
Auditor	Arthur Andersen LLP	Employees	140
		Web Site	emonstransportation.com

Encore Medical Corporation

9800 Metric Boulevard   Austin, TX 78758   Telephone (512)832-9500   Fax (512)834-6300

Company Description

Encore Medical Corporation designs, markets and distributes orthopedic products and supplies. Its products are used primarily by orthopedic medical specialists to treat patients with musculoskeletal conditions resulting from degenerative diseases, deformities, traumatic events and participation in sporting events. Encore's products cover a broad variety of orthopedic needs and include hip, knee and shoulder implants to reconstruct damaged joints and trauma products to reconstruct bone fractures. Encore's first product, the Foundation® Knee System, was introduced in Europe in October 1992 and in the United States in February 1993. The Company was founded in April 1992.

	12/31/98	12/31/97	12/31/96	12/31/95
Per Share Information				
Stock Price	2.75	3.87	4.88	4.50
Earnings Per Share	0.17	0.12	-0.04	0.23
Price / Earnings Ratio	16.18	32.25	n.a.	19.57
Book Value Per Share	2.17	1.99	0.65	0.51
Price / Book Value %	126.73	194.47	750.77	882.35
Dividends Per Share	0.0	0.0	0.0	0.0
Annual Financial Data				
Operating Results (000's)				
Total Revenues	28,990.0	24,517.0	17,670.0	13,877.0
Costs & Expenses	-26,243.0	-22,595.0	-16,446.0	-12,313.0
Income Before Taxes and Other	2,747.0	1,849.0	1,177.0	1,459.0
Other Items	0.0	-598.0	-1,266.0	-35.0
Income Tax	-970.0	8.0	-144.0	-51.0
Net Income	1,777.0	1,259.0	-233.0	1,373.0
Cash Flow From Operations	-158.0	61.0	-4,346.0	-926.0
Balance Sheet (000's)				
Cash & Equivalents	1.0	9.0	472.0	1,200.0
Total Current Assets	23,083.0	19,135.0	15,388.0	10,339.0
Fixed Assets, Net	6,147.0	5,099.0	3,931.0	2,418.0
Total Assets	30,556.0	25,721.0	20,275.0	12,757.0
Total Current Liabilities	5,129.0	4,453.0	5,376.0	3,108.0
Long-Term Debt	5,603.0	2,444.0	4,913.0	4,479.0
Stockholders' Equity	19,824.0	18,024.0	6,589.0	5,170.0
Performance & Financial Condition				
Return on Total Revenues %	6.13	5.14	-1.32	9.89
Return on Avg Stockholders' Equity %	9.39	10.23	-3.96	27.46
Return on Average Assets %	6.32	5.47	-1.41	9.15
Current Ratio	4.50	4.30	2.86	3.33
Debt / Equity %	28.26	13.56	74.56	86.63

Compound Growth %'s	EPS %	-9.59	Net Income %	8.98	Total Revenues %	27.84

Comments

Revenue increased 18.6% in 1998 as the result of an increase in the number of sales agents and more productive sales territories. International sales were weak due to the Asian crisis, but improvement in the Japanese market was noted in the fourth quarter. The Company had its first normal income tax expense in 1998. It should be noted that pre-tax profits actually increased 48.6% in 1998 and were the highest then out of the four years presented. 1997 results include a nonrecurring expense related to the extinguishment of debt of $598,000 ($.06 per share). 1996 results include a nonrecurring charge of $1,266,000, approximately $.21 per share, related to a restructuring of warrants.

Officers	**Position**	**Ownership Information**	
Nick Cindrich	Chairman, CEO	Number of Shares Outstanding	9,138,000
Craig L. Smith	President	Market Capitalization	$ 25,129,500
August Faske	VP - Finance, CFO	Number of Shareholders	1,050
Harry L. Zimmer	Vice President, Secretary	Where Listed / Symbol	NASDAQ / ENMC

Other Information			
Transfer Agent	American Stock Transfer & Trust Co. New York, NY	SIC Code	3800
Auditor	PricewaterhouseCoopers LLP	Employees	95
		Web Site	encoremed.com

Endogen, Inc.

30 Commerce Way   Woburn, MA 01801-1059   Telephone (781)937-0890   Fax (781)937-0891

Company Description

Endogen, Inc. is a supplier of specialty reagents, immuno-assay test kits and molecular research products to customers involved in biomedical research, the biotechnology industry and pharmaceutical drug discovery. Endogen uses monoclonal antibody and recombinant DNA technology to develop and manufacture products in the field of cytokines, chemokines and related immune system factors having to do with the chemical messengers which convey signals within the immune system. Endogen's product lines provide researchers with tools for investigating the basic cellular mechanisms underlying the human immune system and its response to infection, AIDS, cancer and other diseases. The Company commenced commercial operations in 1985.

	05/31/98	05/31/97	05/31/96	05/31/95
Per Share Information				
Stock Price as of 12/31	3.37	3.75	4.00	3.62
Earnings Per Share	0.13	0.29	-0.25	0.01
Price / Earnings Ratio	25.92	12.93	n.a.	362.00
Book Value Per Share	1.87	1.70	0.98	1.17
Price / Book Value %	180.21	220.59	408.16	309.40
Dividends Per Share	0.0	0.0	0.0	0.0
Annual Financial Data				
Operating Results (000's)				
Total Revenues	10,033.5	9,589.3	6,622.2	5,090.4
Costs & Expenses	-9,537.8	-8,994.7	-7,322.7	-5,066.1
Income Before Taxes and Other	495.7	594.6	-700.5	24.3
Other Items	0.0	0.0	0.0	0.0
Income Tax	-38.0	381.0	0.0	0.0
Net Income	457.7	975.6	-700.5	24.3
Cash Flow From Operations	1,071.2	793.6	732.9	-112.5
Balance Sheet (000's)				
Cash & Equivalents	1,175.5	334.1	763.7	1,304.0
Total Current Assets	4,991.7	4,174.3	3,748.6	3,278.0
Fixed Assets, Net	2,020.1	2,327.6	1,895.0	810.3
Total Assets	7,920.3	7,477.8	6,556.4	4,415.2
Total Current Liabilities	1,296.1	1,439.4	1,605.0	899.0
Long-Term Debt	195.1	0.0	0.0	0.0
Stockholders' Equity	6,421.3	5,823.5	2,891.4	3,181.8
Performance & Financial Condition				
Return on Total Revenues %	4.56	10.17	-10.58	0.48
Return on Avg Stockholders' Equity %	7.48	22.39	-23.07	0.78
Return on Average Assets %	5.94	13.90	-12.77	0.60
Current Ratio	3.85	2.90	2.34	3.65
Debt / Equity %	3.04	n.a.	n.a.	n.a.

Compound Growth %'s	EPS %	135.13	Net Income %	166.05	Total Revenues %	25.38

Comments

The loss of one major private label customer dampened the revenue advance in fiscal 1998. Research and development expenses increased $308,828 to $1,688,372 in the same period. The Company plans to continue to spend heavily on product development for new products and to upgrade existing products in fiscal 1999. Approximately 48% of the Company's sales are from foreign countries. For the nine months ended February 28, 1999, revenues and a net loss were $7.5 million and $461,511 ($.13 per share) as compared to $7.4 million and a net profit of $286,467 ($.08 per share) in the same period of the preceding year.

Officers	Position	Ownership Information	
Owen Dempsey	President, CEO	Number of Shares Outstanding	3,442,802
Avery Catlin	VP - Finance, CFO	Market Capitalization	$ 11,602,243
Daniel Burns	Controller	Number of Shareholders	1,200
Irwin J. Gruverman	Director	Where Listed / Symbol	NASDAQ / ENDG

Other Information			
Transfer Agent	American Stock Transfer & Trust Co. New York, NY	SIC Code	2835
Auditor	PricewaterhouseCoopers LLP	Employees	76
		Web Site	endogen.com

Environmental Safeguards, Inc.

2600 South Loop West, Suite 645   Houston, TX 77054   Telephone (713)641-3838   Fax (713)641-0756

Company Description

Environmental Safeguards, Inc. is engaged in the development, production and sale of environmental remediation technologies and services. The services provided by the Company have involved the removal of hydrocarbon contaminants from soil using indirect thermal desorption remediation technology. The Company owned 50% of OnSite Technology, L.L.C., a joint venture with Parker Drilling Company, until 1997 when it acquired the remaining 50%. $8 million was raised through the sale of convertible preferred stock to finance the acquisition and provide working capital. During 1998, OnSite entered into a 50/50 joint venture agreement with an Oman based company to pursue environmental projects in the Arabian Gulf region.

	12/31/98	12/31/97	12/31/96	12/31/95
Per Share Information				
Stock Price	1.25	3.06	3.00	1.00
Earnings Per Share	-0.17	-0.65	-0.10	-0.26
Price / Earnings Ratio	n.a.	n.a.	n.a.	n.a.
Book Value Per Share	0.09	0.13	0.15	-0.06
Price / Book Value %	1,388.89	2,353.85	2,000.00	n.a.
Dividends Per Share	0.0	0.0	0.0	0.0
Annual Financial Data				
Operating Results (000's)				
Total Revenues	11,002.0	6,874.0	21.1	116.4
Costs & Expenses	-10,450.0	-6,554.0	-742.0	-1,332.0
Income Before Taxes and Other	552.0	289.0	-720.9	-1,215.6
Other Items	-595.0	-933.0	74.0	0.0
Income Tax	-756.0	-1,205.0	0.0	0.0
Net Income	-799.0	-1,849.0	-646.9	-1,215.6
Cash Flow From Operations	-1,591.0	-667.0	-297.2	-368.5
Balance Sheet (000's)				
Cash & Equivalents	4,792.0	6,686.0	3,363.3	194.4
Total Current Assets	9,073.0	8,531.0	3,420.6	194.4
Fixed Assets, Net	8,256.0	6,286.0	4.4	18.2
Total Assets	20,164.0	18,298.0	5,481.0	318.1
Total Current Liabilities	3,642.0	3,254.0	72.3	623.9
Long-Term Debt	6,636.0	4,117.0	3,000.0	0.0
Stockholders' Equity	7,813.0	9,206.0	1,055.0	-305.8
Performance & Financial Condition				
Return on Total Revenues %	-7.26	-26.90	-3,063.13	-1,044.37
Return on Avg Stockholders' Equity %	-9.39	-36.04	-172.70	-607.81
Return on Average Assets %	-4.15	-15.55	-22.31	-121.56
Current Ratio	2.49	2.62	47.28	0.31
Debt / Equity %	84.94	44.72	284.37	n.a.

Compound Growth %'s	EPS % n.a.	Net Income % n.a.	Total Revenues % n.a.

Comments

1998 and 1997 revenue primarily resulted from the sale and operation of ITD (indirect thermal desorption) Units. Each unit is an easily transportable, state-of-the-art processing system which produces clean soil from contaminated soil while reclaiming the hydrocarbons. During 1998, an average of 3.6 ITD systems were operating as compared to an average 2.5 systems in 1997. Notwithstanding the challenges posed by cutbacks in oil company budgets in the face of the lowest oil prices in more than a decade, management reported significant progress in assembling the building blocks for future growth and profitability. The 1997 net loss was augmented by a $762,000 write-off on acquired research and development in connection with the acquisition of OnSite. A $352,000 extraordinary charge was also incurred from the extinguishment of debt. The Company has yet to record an annual net profit.

Officers	Position	Ownership Information	
James S. Percell	President, CEO	Number of Shares Outstanding	10,092,444
Ronald L. Bianco	CFO, Treasurer	Market Capitalization	$ 12,615,555
Albert M. Wolford	Secretary	Number of Shareholders	1,000
Douglas A. Schonacher, Jr.	Vice President, COO	Where Listed / Symbol	AMEX / EVV

Other Information			
Transfer Agent	Colonial Stock Transfer Co., Inc. Salt Lake City, UT	SIC Code	4953
Auditor	Ernst & Young, LLP	Employees	20

Equivest Finance, Inc.

2 Clinton Square   Syracuse, NY 13202   Telephone (315)422-9088   Fax (315)422-9477

Company Description

Equivest Finance, Inc. provides financing to resort developers through the purchase of their vacation ownership interests (VOIs or timeshare intervals) and through the direct financing of resort properties to be developed and sold to consumers pursuant to timeshare interval programs. The business was acquired as a result of and in connection with the bankruptcy of an affiliated company, effective February 16, 1996. Prior to that time, the Company operated as an insurance premium finance company, which business was discontinued in 1995. In August 1998, the Company acquired Eastern Resorts Company LLC which operates seven timeshare resorts in the northeastern United States.

	12/31/98	12/31/97	12/31/96	12/31/95
Per Share Information				
Stock Price	4.00	5.06	0.31	4.12
Earnings Per Share	0.20	0.22	0.06	-0.07
Price / Earnings Ratio	20.00	23.00	5.17	n.a.
Book Value Per Share	2.12	1.49	0.43	0.25
Price / Book Value %	188.68	339.60	72.09	1,648.00
Dividends Per Share	0.0	0.0	0.0	0.0
Annual Financial Data				
Operating Results (000's)				
Total Revenues	29,636.5	15,964.5	14,263.4	13,194.6
Costs & Expenses	-21,122.6	-12,540.1	-12,574.1	-11,073.3
Income Before Taxes and Other	8,513.9	3,424.4	1,689.2	2,121.3
Other Items	0.0	0.0	0.0	-2,186.1
Income Tax	-3,270.0	-193.0	-29.0	-595.4
Net Income	5,243.9	3,231.4	1,660.2	-660.1
Cash Flow From Operations	10,093.0	5,184.2	-7,590.9	n.a.
Balance Sheet (000's)				
Cash & Equivalents	3,486.7	4,620.5	4,037.2	1,302.9
Total Current Assets	145,813.1	127,191.0	106,809.4	85,255.8
Fixed Assets, Net	3,048.3	0.0	0.0	0.0
Total Assets	197,384.5	133,484.0	113,203.8	88,600.9
Total Current Liabilities	8,192.8	964.4	2,391.3	7,655.7
Long-Term Debt	133,117.0	99,961.4	106,745.5	78,538.3
Stockholders' Equity	53,506.3	32,528.4	4,037.3	2,377.0
Performance & Financial Condition				
Return on Total Revenues %	17.69	20.24	11.64	-5.00
Return on Avg Stockholders' Equity %	12.19	17.67	51.77	-19.04
Return on Average Assets %	3.17	2.62	1.65	-1.08
Current Ratio	17.80	131.88	44.67	11.14
Debt / Equity %	248.79	307.30	2,643.99	3,304.05

Compound Growth %'s	EPS %	82.57	Net Income %	77.72	Total Revenues %	30.96

Comments

The 1998 acquisition was accounted for as a purchase. Therefore results of operations have been combined since August 28, 1998, the date of the transaction. The 1996 acquisition was accounted for as a pooling of interest. Accordingly the financial statements have been adjusted to include results of operations prior to the transaction. Approximately 60% of the 1998 revenue growth was attributable to the Eastern Resorts acquisition with the balance coming from finance operations. 1995 results include a loss of $2,186,065 from discontinued operations. At December 31, 1998, the Company had $27.2 million of goodwill on the books which equated to approximately 51% of stockholders' equity and book value per share.

Officers	Position	Ownership Information	
Richard C. Breeden	Chairman, CEO	Number of Shares Outstanding	25,198,351
Thomas J. Hamel	President, COO	Market Capitalization	$ 100,793,404
Gerald L. Klaben, Jr.	Senior VP, CFO	Number of Shareholders	10,000
Eric C. Cotton	Secretary	Where Listed / Symbol	NASDAQ / EQUI

Other Information			
Transfer Agent	Continental Stock Transfer & Trust Co. New York, NY	SIC Code	6141
Auditor	Firley, Moran, Freer & Eassa	Employees	285

Esquire Communications Ltd.

750 B Street   San Diego, CA 92101   Telephone (619)515-0811   Fax (619)515-0808

Company Description

Esquire Communications Ltd. is a court reporting firm using state-of-the-art technology to provide printed and computerized transcripts and video recordings of testimony from depositions to the legal profession through offices located in 34 markets in 11 states and the District of Columbia. The Company's strategy is to become a national court reporting firm by acquiring court reporting companies in major business communities around the country. At December 31, 1998, the Company had approximately 1,000 free-lance court reporters in addition to its 700 full-time employees. The Company had its initial public offering in 1993.

	12/31/98	12/31/97	12/31/96	12/31/95
Per Share Information				
Stock Price	4.19	5.12	2.37	2.87
Earnings Per Share	-0.48	-0.56	-0.03	0.06
Price / Earnings Ratio	n.a.	n.a.	n.a.	47.83
Book Value Per Share	3.51	1.28	1.25	1.79
Price / Book Value %	119.37	400.00	189.60	160.34
Dividends Per Share	0.0	0.0	0.0	0.0
Annual Financial Data				
Operating Results (000's)				
Total Revenues	110,586.0	53,219.0	29,510.0	26,793.0
Costs & Expenses	-112,019.0	-55,549.0	-29,670.0	-25,898.0
Income Before Taxes and Other	-1,433.0	-2,330.0	-160.0	895.0
Other Items	0.0	0.0	0.0	0.0
Income Tax	589.0	-125.0	-216.0	-574.0
Net Income	-844.0	-2,455.0	-376.0	321.0
Cash Flow From Operations	-1,560.0	-416.0	-175.0	905.0
Balance Sheet (000's)				
Cash & Equivalents	933.0	116.0	186.0	171.0
Total Current Assets	31,451.0	15,376.0	9,218.0	4,605.3
Fixed Assets, Net	5,937.0	3,056.0	2,041.0	1,025.6
Total Assets	151,256.0	82,851.0	31,834.0	19,073.4
Total Current Liabilities	20,130.0	13,704.0	5,646.0	3,004.5
Long-Term Debt	90,329.0	45,442.0	12,990.0	8,669.4
Stockholders' Equity	40,466.0	23,540.0	12,931.0	7,399.5
Performance & Financial Condition				
Return on Total Revenues %	-0.76	-4.61	-1.27	1.20
Return on Avg Stockholders' Equity %	-2.64	-13.46	-3.70	3.21
Return on Average Assets %	-0.72	-4.28	-1.48	1.40
Current Ratio	1.56	1.12	1.63	1.53
Debt / Equity %	223.22	193.04	100.46	117.16

Compound Growth %'s	EPS % n.a.	Net Income % n.a.	Total Revenues % 60.41

Comments

Revenue increased by approximately $57.4 million, or 108%, in 1998 as compared to 1997. Substantially all of the increase was due to the effect of acquisitions. 1998 results included two nonrecurring expense items that prevented a return to bottom-line profitability: $1.3 million relating to an officer's termination agreement and $839,000 of costs associated with an abandoned secondary offering. Preferred shares have a liquidation preference which has been deducted in computing book value per common share. Preferred stock dividends have been deducted in calculating the loss per common share. At December 31, 1998, the Company had $112.8 million of goodwill recorded on its books which equated to approximately 628% of common stockholders' equity and book value per common share.

Officers	Position	Ownership Information	
David A. White	CEO	Number of Shares Outstanding	5,121,979
David A. Higson	Senior VP, CFO	Market Capitalization	$ 21,461,092
Carole L. Hughes	Senior VP	Number of Shareholders	2,000
Gregory J. Mazares	Senior VP	Where Listed / Symbol	NASDAQ / ESQS

Other Information			
Transfer Agent	Continental Stock Transfer & Trust Co. New York, NY	SIC Code	7338
Auditor	KPMG LLP	Employees	700
		Web Site	esquirecom.com

Everest Medical Corporation

13755 First Avenue North, Suite 500   Minneapolis, MN 55441-5454   Telephone (612)473-6262   Fax (612)473-6465

Company Description

Everest Medical Corporation is engaged primarily in the development, manufacturing and marketing of bipolar electrosurgical devices for use in minimally invasive surgical procedures. Minimally invasive procedures are being utilized for a growing range of surgical specialties such as gynecological, gastroenterological, cardiovascular and general surgery. As minimally invasive surgical techniques have evolved, becoming increasingly complex and involving anatomically crowded areas of the human body, the need for safer instrumentation has become more evident. The Company believes that bipolar electrosurgery is gaining increasing scientific recognition and acceptance in the growing minimally invasive surgery markets. The Company's first commercial sales were in 1991.

	12/31/98	12/31/97	12/31/96	12/31/95
Per Share Information				
Stock Price	1.41	1.75	2.63	2.75
Earnings Per Share	0.04	-0.10	-0.11	-0.18
Price / Earnings Ratio	35.25	n.a.	n.a.	n.a.
Book Value Per Share	-0.37	-0.49	-0.42	-0.86
Price / Book Value %	n.a.	n.a.	n.a.	n.a.
Dividends Per Share	0.0	0.0	0.0	0.0
Annual Financial Data				
Operating Results (000's)				
Total Revenues	10,727.8	7,382.2	6,064.5	4,387.6
Costs & Expenses	-10,057.5	-7,767.0	-6,403.5	-5,160.9
Income Before Taxes and Other	670.3	-384.8	-339.1	-773.3
Other Items	0.0	0.0	0.0	0.0
Income Tax	-10.0	0.0	0.0	0.0
Net Income	660.3	-384.8	-339.1	-773.3
Cash Flow From Operations	404.5	-787.7	-631.0	-782.9
Balance Sheet (000's)				
Cash & Equivalents	217.5	80.4	712.8	1,028.5
Total Current Assets	3,791.6	2,798.8	2,796.2	2,655.1
Fixed Assets, Net	305.5	281.7	249.3	270.2
Total Assets	4,097.4	3,083.1	3,061.0	2,960.1
Total Current Liabilities	1,247.9	677.6	602.6	1,127.7
Long-Term Debt	0.0	600.0	0.0	126.7
Stockholders' Equity	2,849.4	1,805.5	2,439.6	1,696.5
Performance & Financial Condition				
Return on Total Revenues %	6.16	-5.21	-5.59	-17.62
Return on Avg Stockholders' Equity %	28.37	-18.13	-16.39	-48.09
Return on Average Assets %	18.39	-12.53	-11.26	-27.62
Current Ratio	3.04	4.13	4.64	2.35
Debt / Equity %	n.a.	33.23	n.a.	7.47

Compound Growth %'s	EPS %	n.a.	Net Income %	n.a.	Total Revenues %	34.72

Comments

1998 marks the first profitable year for the Company. A strong 46% sales increase pushed gross margins 4.4% higher. There was also effective control of other operating expenses. Research and development expenses did increase 35% to $858,816 as they obtained ISO 9001 certification and continued work on invasive cardiovascular products. Management believes that it will maintain profitability in 1999 as it increases market share in its core businesses. The Company has four classes of preferred stock outstanding. Preferred stock dividends were deducted in calculating earnings per common share and the liquidation value of the preferred stock was deducted in calculating the book value per common share.

Officers	Position	Ownership Information	
John L. Shannon, Jr.	President, CEO	Number of Shares Outstanding	7,465,875
Thomas F. Murphy	VP - Finance	Market Capitalization	$ 10,526,884
Steven M. Blakemore	Vice President	Number of Shareholders	2,600
Michael E. Geraghty	VP - Sales	Where Listed / Symbol	NASDAQ / EVMD

Other Information			
Transfer Agent	Norwest Bank Minnesota, N.A. South St. Paul, MN	SIC Code	3845
Auditor	Ernst & Young LLP	Employees	105
		Web Site	everestmedical.com

Exigent International, Inc.

1225 Evans Road   Melbourne, FL 32904-2314   Telephone (407)952-7550   Fax (407)676-4510

Company Description

Exigent International, Inc. is the parent holding company of Software Technology, Inc., which is the main operating company. The Company provides systems software engineering services, and develops technical solutions for government and industry. The Company's research and development specializes in command, control and data acquisitions systems for spacecraft constellation development and operations. It provides operational systems that support space-based applications, including ground station support, test and integration systems, mission tasking systems, launch support systems and data analysis centers supporting space-based systems. As world-wide demand for satellite-based applications has increased, Exigent has responded by developing a suite of commercial-off-the-shelf products based on the Company's twenty years of experience in building such systems.

	12/31/98	01/31/98	01/31/97	01/31/96
Per Share Information				
Stock Price as of 12/31	2.72	2.87	4.00	14.03
Earnings Per Share	0.08	0.29	-0.13	0.29
Price / Earnings Ratio	34.00	9.90	n.a.	48.38
Book Value Per Share	2.09	1.56	1.20	1.27
Price / Book Value %	130.14	183.97	333.33	1,104.72
Dividends Per Share	0.0	0.0	0.07	0.05
Annual Financial Data				
Operating Results (000's)				
Total Revenues	31,185.2	35,791.8	29,991.6	25,317.1
Costs & Expenses	-30,587.0	-33,611.0	-30,328.2	-23,430.0
Income Before Taxes and Other	598.2	2,176.2	-336.5	1,887.1
Other Items	0.0	0.0	0.0	0.0
Income Tax	-180.0	-830.8	-149.7	-755.4
Net Income	418.2	1,345.4	-486.2	1,131.7
Cash Flow From Operations	-204.9	5,239.8	1,680.0	2,592.9
Balance Sheet (000's)				
Cash & Equivalents	430.0	3,640.5	428.7	270.1
Total Current Assets	8,826.1	10,944.2	8,364.9	6,843.3
Fixed Assets, Net	2,283.4	2,168.7	1,848.0	1,212.3
Total Assets	15,664.4	14,693.0	10,948.7	8,327.7
Total Current Liabilities	5,253.0	5,800.4	4,128.5	3,345.3
Long-Term Debt	427.8	466.7	311.1	4.5
Stockholders' Equity	8,628.6	7,780.8	6,257.6	4,892.5
Performance & Financial Condition				
Return on Total Revenues %	1.34	3.76	-1.62	4.47
Return on Avg Stockholders' Equity %	5.10	19.17	-8.72	25.63
Return on Average Assets %	2.76	10.49	-5.04	15.29
Current Ratio	1.68	1.89	2.03	2.05
Debt / Equity %	4.96	6.00	4.97	0.09

Compound Growth %'s	EPS %	-34.90	Net Income %	-28.24	Total Revenues %	7.20

Comments

All per share information was restated to reflect the 1996 formation of Exigent and the reverse acquisition of Software Technology on a pro forma basis. The Company changed to calendar year reporting in 1998. The operating results for the period ended December 31, 1998, are for eleven months. Therefore, compound growth rates are partially distorted. Management attributes the fiscal 1997 loss to the approximately $1 million of costs incurred in connection with a public offering. Increased revenue and a significant jump in gross margins brought the Company back into profitability in 1997. The increase in gross margins was attributable to higher sales and lower labor costs on programs. 1998 results did not match the preceding year due to the short period, lower margins on a large fixed price development contract, and more conservative accounting for capitalized software costs.

Officers	Position	Ownership Information	
Bernard R. Smedley	President, CEO	Number of Shares Outstanding	4,130,103
Don F. Riordan, Jr.	Exec VP, Treasurer	Market Capitalization	$ 11,233,880
Jeffery B. Weinress	CFO	Number of Shareholders	1,093
Patricia A. Frank	Secretary	Where Listed / Symbol	NASDAQ / XGNT

Other Information			
Transfer Agent	Mid-America Bank of Louisville Louisville, KY	SIC Code	7373
Auditor	Ernst & Young LLP	Employees	303
		Web Site	xgnt.com

FAFCO, Inc.

2690 Middlefield Road   Redwood City, CA 94063-3455   Telephone (650)363-2690   Fax (650)363-2890

Company Description

FAFCO, Inc. designs, manufactures and markets heat exchangers made primarily of polymers for use in solar swimming pool heaters and for thermal energy storage. The Company has manufactured, using proprietary and patented technology, over one million polymer heat exchangers since its incorporation in 1972. FAFCO is the largest manufacturer of solar pool heating systems in the United States. The Company's thermal energy storage products are used commercially by electric utilities to produce ice in off-peak energy hours. The cooling energy stored in the ice is then reclaimed the next day to provide for process cooling. FAFCO has been issued 21 patents and operates worldwide.

	12/31/98	12/31/97	12/31/96	12/31/95
Per Share Information				
Stock Price	0.94	0.75	0.13	0.25
Earnings Per Share	0.20	0.22	0.10	-0.60
Price / Earnings Ratio	4.70	3.41	1.30	n.a.
Book Value Per Share	0.87	0.62	0.36	0.20
Price / Book Value %	108.05	120.97	36.11	125.00
Dividends Per Share	0.0	0.0	0.0	0.0
Annual Financial Data				
Operating Results (000's)				
Total Revenues	11,266.4	10,723.3	8,922.6	7,915.8
Costs & Expenses	-10,532.2	-9,834.1	-8,647.9	-9,772.6
Income Before Taxes and Other	734.2	889.2	274.7	-1,856.8
Other Items	0.0	0.0	0.0	0.0
Income Tax	107.4	-23.2	36.7	-1.6
Net Income	841.6	866.0	311.4	-1,858.4
Cash Flow From Operations	752.1	876.4	-270.2	-867.5
Balance Sheet (000's)				
Cash & Equivalents	477.5	46.3	88.2	126.2
Total Current Assets	4,170.9	3,420.9	3,502.2	2,327.7
Fixed Assets, Net	583.4	378.6	349.6	259.2
Total Assets	5,377.0	4,436.5	4,345.2	3,400.4
Total Current Liabilities	1,533.7	1,414.1	2,217.5	2,105.3
Long-Term Debt	925.0	0.0	0.0	0.0
Stockholders' Equity	2,886.4	2,042.3	1,176.3	614.7
Performance & Financial Condition				
Return on Total Revenues %	7.47	8.08	3.49	-23.48
Return on Avg Stockholders' Equity %	34.15	53.81	34.77	-118.19
Return on Average Assets %	17.15	19.72	8.04	-44.76
Current Ratio	2.72	2.42	1.58	1.11
Debt / Equity %	32.05	n.a.	n.a.	n.a.

Compound Growth %'s	EPS %	41.42	Net Income %	64.40	Total Revenues %	12.49

Comments

The Company's net loss in 1995 was the only interruption in 11 years of profitable operations. 1998 was another profitable year despite record-setting rains in California and adverse weather in Florida. A credit for income tax helped the bottom line as the Company recorded the benefit of utilizing tax loss carryovers. 1996 and 1997 results benefitted from reductions in operating and overhead expenses as well as investments made during 1995 in the Company's core technologies. Management said that early indications point towards a continuation of the upward trend in sales and continued profitability in 1999. At December 31, 1998, FAFCO's bank line of credit was unused and both cash and working capital were higher than the levels of the preceding year.

Officers	Position	Ownership Information	
Freeman A. Ford	President, CEO	Number of Shares Outstanding	3,303,311
Alex N. Watt	VP - Finance, CFO	Market Capitalization	$ 3,105,112
David K. Harris	VP - Sales	Number of Shareholders	706
William A. Berry	Director	Where Listed / Symbol	OTC-BB / FAFO

Other Information			
Transfer Agent	Boston EquiServe Boston, MA	SIC Code	3585
Auditor	Burr, Pilger & Mayer	Employees	61
Market Maker	J. Alexander Securities Inc.	(800)421-0258	Web Site	fafco.com
	Paragon Capital Corporation	(800)521-8877		

FARO Technologies, Inc.

125 Technology Park Lake Mary, FL 32746 Telephone (407)333-9911 Fax (407)333-4181

Company Description

FARO Technologies, Inc. designs, develops, markets and supports portable, software-driven, 3-D measurement systems that are used in a broad range of manufacturing and industrial applications. These systems integrate the measurement and quality inspection function with CAD, CAM and computer-aided engineering technology to improve productivity, enhance product quality and decrease rework and scrap in the manufacturing process. The Company's products have been purchased by more than 1,100 customers worldwide, ranging from small machine shops to such large manufacturing and industrial companies as General Motors, DaimlerChrysler, Ford, Boeing, Lockheed Martin, General Electric, Westinghouse Electric, Caterpillar and Komatsu Dresser. The Company was founded in 1981 and had its initial public offering of 2.9 million shares at $11 per share on September 18, 1997.

	12/31/98	12/31/97	12/31/96	12/31/95
Per Share Information				
Stock Price	3.94	11.62	n.a.	n.a.
Earnings Per Share	-0.46	0.39	0.19	0.22
Price / Earnings Ratio	n.a.	29.79	n.a.	n.a.
Book Value Per Share	4.12	3.93	0.54	0.33
Price / Book Value %	95.63	295.67	n.a.	n.a.
Dividends Per Share	0.0	0.0	0.0	0.0
Annual Financial Data				
Operating Results (000's)				
Total Revenues	28,731.8	24,016.1	14,681.5	9,924.5
Costs & Expenses	-33,212.3	-18,694.9	-12,158.9	-8,666.8
Income Before Taxes and Other	-4,480.6	5,321.3	2,522.6	1,257.7
Other Items	0.0	0.0	0.0	0.0
Income Tax	-450.5	-2,114.6	-1,115.9	342.0
Net Income	-4,931.1	3,206.6	1,406.7	1,599.7
Cash Flow From Operations	-3,066.8	-831.6	1,524.4	935.7
Balance Sheet (000's)				
Cash & Equivalents	1,183.7	28,815.1	263.3	3.9
Total Current Assets	34,595.1	39,485.8	6,698.1	2,257.3
Fixed Assets, Net	1,525.2	827.8	601.4	600.0
Total Assets	49,120.1	41,192.3	7,815.7	5,479.7
Total Current Liabilities	3,597.3	2,208.3	2,865.7	935.8
Long-Term Debt	37.3	0.0	890.2	2,200.0
Stockholders' Equity	45,375.4	38,939.4	3,773.7	2,343.9
Performance & Financial Condition				
Return on Total Revenues %	-17.16	13.35	9.58	16.12
Return on Avg Stockholders' Equity %	-11.70	15.01	45.99	107.32
Return on Average Assets %	-10.92	13.09	21.16	32.96
Current Ratio	9.62	17.88	2.34	2.41
Debt / Equity %	0.08	n.a.	23.59	93.86

Compound Growth %'s	EPS % n.a.	Net Income % n.a.	Total Revenues % 42.52

Comments

In 1998, revenues rose 17% on the strength of activity with European customers, more than offsetting declines in Asia. Gross profit increased due to the higher sales level as the gross margin percentage was maintained at the 1997 level. 1998 results include $3,210,000 of nonrecurring expense related to purchased in-process research and development costs that were expensed immediately upon the acquisition of another company. Normal research and development costs increased from $1.1 million in 1997 to $2.6 million in 1998 as the number of research projects increased from 14 at December 31, 1997, to 43 at December 31, 1998. At December 31, 1998, the Company had $12.8 million of goodwill recorded as assets which equated to approximately 28% of stockholders' equity and book value per share. Also at 1998 year end, the Company had $18.2 million of cash and short-term investments.

Officers	Position	Ownership Information	
Simon Raab	President, CEO	Number of Shares Outstanding	11,008,137
Gregory A. Fraser	Exec VP, CFO	Market Capitalization	$ 43,372,060
Andre Julien	Director	Number of Shareholders	2,000
Ali S. Sajedi	Other	Where Listed / Symbol	NASDAQ / FARO

Other Information

Transfer Agent	Firstar Trust Company Milwaukee, WI	SIC Code	3829
Auditor	Deloitte & Touche LLP	Employees	190
		Web Site	faro.com

FTI Consulting, Inc.

2021 Research Drive Annapolis, MD 21401 Telephone (410)224-8770 Fax (410)244-4849

Company Description

FTI Consulting, Inc., formerly Forensic Technologies International Corporation, is a leading provider of litigation support consulting services, including visual communications, engineering services and trial consulting, that assist attorneys and corporations in developing their trial themes and strategies, assessing the strength of their cases, and creating state-of-the-art courtroom presentations. The Company completed one acquisition in 1997 and three in 1998 to broaden its product and service offerings. The Company believes that continued increases in the volume, risk, complexity and cost of litigation have driven the need for litigation support services that utilize advanced technologies to provide competitive advantages in the courtroom on a cost-effective basis. The Company was founded in 1982 and had its initial public offering in 1996.

	12/31/98	12/31/97	12/31/96	12/31/95
Per Share Information				
Stock Price	3.25	12.12	9.12	8.50
Earnings Per Share	0.51	0.70	0.42	0.27
Price / Earnings Ratio	6.37	17.31	21.71	31.48
Book Value Per Share	5.35	4.62	3.90	0.83
Price / Book Value %	60.75	262.34	233.85	1,024.10
Dividends Per Share	0.0	0.0	0.0	0.0
Annual Financial Data				
Operating Results (000's)				
Total Revenues	58,934.0	44,518.0	30,934.0	23,423.0
Costs & Expenses	-54,412.0	-38,975.0	-27,985.0	-21,517.0
Income Before Taxes and Other	4,522.0	5,543.0	2,949.0	1,906.0
Other Items	0.0	0.0	0.0	-430.0
Income Tax	-1,954.0	-2,250.0	-1,235.0	-779.0
Net Income	2,568.0	3,293.0	1,714.0	697.0
Cash Flow From Operations	5,293.0	3,648.0	-515.0	1,525.0
Balance Sheet (000's)				
Cash & Equivalents	3,223.0	2,456.0	5,894.0	245.0
Total Current Assets	26,221.0	17,689.0	16,246.0	6,701.0
Fixed Assets, Net	8,287.0	6,288.0	4,106.0	2,957.9
Total Assets	79,747.0	29,176.0	20,868.0	9,658.9
Total Current Liabilities	17,150.0	7,055.0	2,935.0	4,574.7
Long-Term Debt	35,630.0	730.0	80.0	2,317.7
Stockholders' Equity	25,594.0	21,019.0	17,628.0	2,766.5
Performance & Financial Condition				
Return on Total Revenues %	4.36	7.40	5.54	2.98
Return on Avg Stockholders' Equity %	11.02	17.04	16.81	42.23
Return on Average Assets %	4.72	13.16	11.23	7.40
Current Ratio	1.53	2.51	5.54	1.46
Debt / Equity %	139.21	3.47	0.45	83.78

Compound Growth %'s	EPS %	23.61	Net Income %	54.45	Total Revenues %	36.01

Comments

1998 revenues rose 32.7% over 1997. Most of the increase was attributable to acquisitions. But income from operations remained about the same. Interest expense rose $1.3 million due to increased debt and effectively reduced net income below the level achieved in 1997. 1995 results included a loss from discontinued operations of $430,000, or $.13 per share. At December 31, 1998, the Company had $45.2 million of goodwill recorded as assets which equated to approximately 176% of stockholders' equity and book value per share. Management expects cash flow from operations to increase in 1999, in part as a result of additional operating cash provided from businesses acquired in late 1998.

Officers	Position	Ownership Information	
Jack B. Dunn, IV	President, CEO	Number of Shares Outstanding	4,781,895
Gary Sindler	Exec VP, CFO	Market Capitalization	$ 15,541,159
Patrick Brady	Exec VP, COO	Number of Shareholders	1,950
Joseph R. Reynolds Jr.	Director	Where Listed / Symbol	AMEX / FCN

Other Information			
Transfer Agent	American Stock Transfer & Trust Co. New York, NY	SIC Code	8742
Auditor	Ernst & Young LLP	Employees	416
		Web Site	fticonsulting.com

Fairmount Chemical Co., Inc.

117 Blanchard Street   Newark, NJ 07105   Telephone (973)344-5790   Fax (973)690-5298

Company Description

Fairmount Chemical Co., Inc. manufactures and sells chemicals. These are principally imaging chemicals, hydrazine-based products, additives used in the manufacture of plastics, and specialty chemicals including pharmaceutical intermediates. Imaging chemicals are used in the manufacture of photographic film and lithographic printing plates. Hydrazine-based products are used as corrosion control chemicals for commercial boiler systems and for a variety of other purposes in different industries. The Company was founded in 1938.

	12/31/98	12/31/97	12/31/96	12/31/95
Per Share Information				
Stock Price	0.18	0.11	0.11	0.23
Earnings Per Share	0.13	-0.04	-0.02	0.03
Price / Earnings Ratio	1.38	n.a.	n.a.	7.67
Book Value Per Share	0.28	0.05	0.12	0.16
Price / Book Value %	64.29	220.00	91.67	143.75
Dividends Per Share	0.0	0.0	0.0	0.0
Annual Financial Data				
Operating Results (000's)				
Total Revenues	12,887.8	12,129.0	12,809.6	12,441.3
Costs & Expenses	-12,170.9	-12,115.2	-13,086.7	-12,060.9
Income Before Taxes and Other	716.9	13.8	-277.1	380.4
Other Items	1,140.1	-310.0	0.0	0.0
Income Tax	0.0	0.0	0.0	0.0
Net Income	1,857.0	-296.2	-277.1	380.4
Cash Flow From Operations	1,304.5	485.0	535.2	407.1
Balance Sheet (000's)				
Cash & Equivalents	2,422.7	711.8	427.9	432.8
Total Current Assets	6,451.9	4,652.4	4,502.9	4,591.4
Fixed Assets, Net	4,185.9	4,504.4	4,775.0	5,163.6
Total Assets	10,638.5	9,201.7	9,333.9	9,755.7
Total Current Liabilities	959.8	1,264.7	940.4	1,161.2
Long-Term Debt	1,571.6	1,605.5	1,191.7	1,156.0
Stockholders' Equity	7,698.1	5,845.2	6,356.8	6,716.0
Performance & Financial Condition				
Return on Total Revenues %	14.41	-2.44	-2.16	3.06
Return on Avg Stockholders' Equity %	27.42	-4.85	-4.24	5.88
Return on Average Assets %	18.72	-3.20	-2.90	4.13
Current Ratio	6.72	3.68	4.79	3.95
Debt / Equity %	20.42	27.47	18.75	17.21

Compound Growth %'s	EPS % n.a.	Net Income % n.a.	Total Revenues % 1.18

Comments

During the second quarter of 1997, management began implementing a restructuring of the organization. This included a reduction of the workforce by 18 employees and a discontinuance of the manufacture of a number of small volume products that were no longer profitable to produce. 1997 results include restructuring charges of $310,000 for severance and early retirement. The restructuring has resulted in the Company operating profitably since the third quarter of 1997. Included in 1998 results are insurance proceeds of $1,140,100 received in connection with a dryer explosion. A final payment of $375,000 was received in February 1999 and is not reflected above. Research and development expenses declined to $359,100 in 1998 from $418,900 in 1997. The Company has tax loss carryforwards of approximately $11.0 million to offset future income and has an excellent financial condition.

Officers	Position	Ownership Information	
Howard R. Leistner	Chairman	Number of Shares Outstanding	8,292,866
Reidar T. Halle	President, CEO	Market Capitalization	$ 1,492,716
James F. Gilday	Secretary, CFO	Number of Shareholders	1,000
William C. Kalnecker	Controller	Where Listed / Symbol	OTC-BB / FMTC

Other Information			
Transfer Agent	Continental Stock Transfer & Trust Co. New York, NY	SIC Code	2860
Auditor	KPMG LLP	Employees	51
Market Maker	Herzog, Heine, Geduld, Inc. (800)221-3600		
	M.H. Meyerson & Co., Inc. (800)333-3113		

Farm Fish, Inc.

100 West Woodrow Wilson Drive   Jackson, MS 39213   Telephone (601)354-3801   Fax (601)355-9134

Company Description

Farm Fish, Inc. is engaged in the hatching and growing of catfish on approximately 1,375 acres of farmland devoted mostly to 20 acre ponds in the state of Mississippi. The catfish are raised until they reach marketable size. They are then harvested and sold to processors for distribution and sale to the public. The Company is one of the largest producers of catfish in a very fragmented industry. Delta Industries, Inc., owns 80% of the Company's common stock. The Company was founded in 1972.

	12/31/98	12/31/97	12/31/96	12/31/95
Per Share Information				
Stock Price	1.25	1.62	1.50	1.00
Earnings Per Share	0.02	0.08	0.20	0.18
Price / Earnings Ratio	62.50	20.25	7.50	5.56
Book Value Per Share	1.60	1.58	1.50	1.29
Price / Book Value %	78.13	102.53	100.00	77.52
Dividends Per Share	0.0	0.0	0.0	0.0
Annual Financial Data				
Operating Results (000's)				
Total Revenues	3,773.7	3,231.1	3,267.9	3,847.2
Costs & Expenses	-3,691.7	-2,952.5	-2,397.1	-2,979.6
Income Before Taxes and Other	81.9	278.6	870.8	763.7
Other Items	0.0	0.0	0.0	0.0
Income Tax	-18.8	-67.3	-324.2	-280.6
Net Income	63.1	211.3	546.6	483.1
Cash Flow From Operations	857.2	179.1	-63.2	853.4
Balance Sheet (000's)				
Cash & Equivalents	25.0	50.1	80.8	22.2
Total Current Assets	4,853.1	5,336.7	4,918.7	3,954.1
Fixed Assets, Net	2,108.3	2,169.5	2,276.0	2,178.4
Total Assets	7,250.3	7,842.5	7,503.4	6,509.8
Total Current Liabilities	2,835.0	3,480.3	3,079.5	2,338.6
Long-Term Debt	0.0	0.0	270.0	570.0
Stockholders' Equity	4,299.4	4,236.2	4,024.9	3,478.3
Performance & Financial Condition				
Return on Total Revenues %	1.67	6.54	16.73	12.56
Return on Avg Stockholders' Equity %	1.48	5.12	14.57	14.93
Return on Average Assets %	0.84	2.75	7.80	7.25
Current Ratio	1.71	1.53	1.60	1.69
Debt / Equity %	n.a.	n.a.	6.71	16.39

Compound Growth %'s	EPS %	-51.93	Net Income %	-49.26	Total Revenues %	-0.64

Comments

The catfish farming industry has grown rapidly since its inception in the late 1960's. In 1969, approximately 3.2 million pounds of catfish were sold to processing plants at an average sales price of $.37 per pound. In 1998, the number of pounds sold to catfish processors had increased to approximately 564 million pounds, at sales prices ranging from $.69 to $.79 per pound. In 1998, two processors represented 85%, and 7% of the Company's sales. Pounds of catfish sold rose 14% in 1998 and prices increased 2% resulting in a 17% increase in revenue for the year. Expenses were higher in 1998 because of an increase in preharvest mortality that was in itself due to extreme temperatures during the summer months. The expense recorded for mortality was $310,000 in 1998 as compared to $200,000 in 1997, but both years were higher than historical levels.

Officers	Position	Ownership Information	
Leland R. Speed	Chairman	Number of Shares Outstanding	2,688,605
Thomas R. Slough, Jr.	President	Market Capitalization	$ 3,360,756
Jayne Dew	Secretary, Treasurer	Number of Shareholders	1,843
David Robison	Vice President	Where Listed / Symbol	OTC-BB / FFIH

Other Information			
Transfer Agent	KeyCorp Shareholder Services, Inc. Brooklyn, OH	SIC Code	0200
Auditor	Ernst & Young LLP	Employees	22
Market Maker	S.J. Wolfe & Co.	(800)262-2244	
	Paragon Capital Corporation	(800)521-8877	

Farmstead Telephone Group, Inc.

22 Prestige Park Circle   East Hartford, CT 06108   Telephone (860)610-6000   Fax (860)610-6001

Company Description

Farmstead Telephone Group, Inc. is presently engaged in the Customer Premise Equipment segment (equipment that resides at the customer's premises) of the telecommunications industry, principally as a secondary market reseller of used, remanufactured and/or refurbished Lucent Technologies, Inc. business telephone parts and systems. In 1998, the Company became an Authorized Remarketing Supplier of Classic Lucent telephone equipment. The Company also provides equipment repair and refurbishing, inventory management, and other related value-added services. The Company was founded in 1986 and went public in 1987.

	12/31/98	12/31/97	12/31/96	12/31/95
Per Share Information				
Stock Price	2.50	1.94	2.94	2.19
Earnings Per Share	0.17	-0.57	0.35	-0.27
Price / Earnings Ratio	14.71	n.a.	8.40	n.a.
Book Value Per Share	1.94	1.77	2.34	1.42
Price / Book Value %	128.87	109.60	125.64	154.23
Dividends Per Share	0.0	0.0	0.0	0.0
Annual Financial Data				
Operating Results (000's)				
Total Revenues	27,810.0	20,659.0	20,333.0	15,331.0
Costs & Expenses	-27,014.0	-20,772.0	-19,308.0	-15,678.0
Income Before Taxes and Other	796.0	-557.0	901.0	-544.0
Other Items	-209.0	-1,266.0	0.0	0.0
Income Tax	-16.0	-43.0	-19.0	-9.0
Net Income	571.0	-1,866.0	882.0	-553.0
Cash Flow From Operations	-2,424.0	-2,199.0	-1,064.0	-1,122.0
Balance Sheet (000's)				
Cash & Equivalents	590.0	1,102.0	3,161.0	622.0
Total Current Assets	12,584.0	9,503.0	11,472.0	5,398.0
Fixed Assets, Net	845.0	935.0	186.0	256.0
Total Assets	13,498.0	10,829.0	12,074.0	5,909.0
Total Current Liabilities	5,185.0	3,063.0	4,439.0	2,903.0
Long-Term Debt	1,916.0	1,997.0	0.0	0.0
Stockholders' Equity	6,344.0	5,769.0	7,635.0	3,006.0
Performance & Financial Condition				
Return on Total Revenues %	2.05	-9.03	4.34	-3.61
Return on Avg Stockholders' Equity %	9.43	-27.84	16.58	-13.83
Return on Average Assets %	4.69	-16.29	9.81	-7.90
Current Ratio	2.43	3.10	2.58	1.86
Debt / Equity %	30.20	34.62	n.a.	n.a.

Compound Growth %'s	EPS %	-30.31	Net Income %	-19.54	Total Revenues %	21.96

Comments

The Company executed a 1 for 10 reverse split in 1996. 1995 per share amounts have been restated for consistency. During 1998, the Company established several new sales offices throughout the country and increased its sales force. This was the main factor in a 34.9% increase in revenue. End user equipment sales accounted for 81% of revenues in 1998. The overall gross profit margin was 25% in each of the last two years. Management expects the same for 1999. 1998 and 1997 results include losses from discontinued operations of $209,000 ($.06 per share) and $1,266,000 ($.39 per share), respectively.

Officers	Position	Ownership Information	
George J. Taylor, Jr.	President, CEO	Number of Shares Outstanding	3,264,579
Robert G. LaVigne	Exec VP, CFO	Market Capitalization	$ 8,161,448
Alexander E. Capo	Vice President	Number of Shareholders	3,900
Joseph A. Novak Jr.	Vice President	Where Listed / Symbol	AMEX / FTG

Other Information

Transfer Agent	American Securities Transfer, Inc. Lakewood, CO	SIC Code	5065
Auditor	Deloitte & Touche LLP	Employees	81
		Web Site	farmstead.com

Farrel Corporation

25 Main Street   Ansonia, CT 06401   Telephone (203)736-5500   Fax (203)735-6267

Company Description

Farrel Corporation designs, manufactures, sells and services machinery and associated equipment for the rubber and plastics industries. The Company's principal products are batch and continuous mixers, single and twin-screw extruders, pelletizers, gear pumps, calenders and mills. In conjunction with sales of capital equipment, the Company provides process engineering, process design and related services for rubber and plastics processing installations. The Company's aftermarket business consists of repair, refurbishment and equipment upgrade services, spare parts sales and field services. The Company also provides laboratory services and facilities for product demonstrations and for the development and testing of rubber and plastics equipment and processes.

	12/31/98	12/31/97	12/31/96	12/31/95
Per Share Information				
Stock Price	2.06	4.81	2.50	4.81
Earnings Per Share	0.38	0.23	0.05	0.15
Price / Earnings Ratio	5.42	20.91	50.00	32.07
Book Value Per Share	4.43	4.34	4.81	4.64
Price / Book Value %	46.50	110.83	51.98	103.66
Dividends Per Share	0.08	0.64	0.06	0.20
Annual Financial Data				
Operating Results (000's)				
Total Revenues	98,580.0	85,902.0	76,039.0	80,412.0
Costs & Expenses	-94,757.0	-83,818.0	-75,327.0	-78,562.0
Income Before Taxes and Other	3,823.0	2,084.0	480.0	1,456.0
Other Items	0.0	0.0	0.0	0.0
Income Tax	-1,546.0	-727.0	-154.0	-554.0
Net Income	2,277.0	1,357.0	326.0	902.0
Cash Flow From Operations	5,457.0	5,681.0	1,782.0	-83.0
Balance Sheet (000's)				
Cash & Equivalents	5,786.0	1,447.0	3,832.0	4,066.0
Total Current Assets	48,273.0	37,104.0	40,187.0	41,991.0
Fixed Assets, Net	11,614.0	12,416.0	9,555.0	9,676.0
Total Assets	62,723.0	56,381.0	50,731.0	53,412.0
Total Current Liabilities	28,351.0	23,286.0	19,841.0	22,878.0
Long-Term Debt	3,983.0	5,283.0	214.0	388.0
Stockholders' Equity	26,301.0	25,782.0	28,553.0	27,814.0
Performance & Financial Condition				
Return on Total Revenues %	2.31	1.58	0.43	1.12
Return on Avg Stockholders' Equity %	8.74	4.99	1.16	3.19
Return on Average Assets %	3.82	2.53	0.63	1.73
Current Ratio	1.70	1.59	2.03	1.84
Debt / Equity %	15.14	20.49	0.75	1.39

Compound Growth %'s	EPS %	36.32	Net Income %	36.16	Total Revenues %	7.03

Comments

Management's focus on growth through acquisitions of technology and product lines led to the December 1997 acquisition of the Francis Shaw Rubber Machinery business in the United Kingdom. The increase in revenue recognized in 1998 was mostly attributable to the acquisition. At December 31, 1998, goodwill of $1.6 million was recorded as assets in connection with the transaction and represented only 6% of stockholders' equity. Gross margins improved in 1998, due to cost reductions and product mix, which caused a significant improvement in net income. Research and development expenses were reduced from $1.6 million in 1997 to $1.5 million in 1998.

Officers	Position	Ownership Information	
Rolf K. Liebergesell	President, CEO	Number of Shares Outstanding	5,939,486
Alberto Shaio	Senior VP	Market Capitalization	$ 12,235,341
Karl N. Svensson	Senior VP	Number of Shareholders	850
Catherine M. Boisvert	Vice President, Controller	Where Listed / Symbol	NASDAQ / FARL

Other Information			
Transfer Agent	State Street Bank & Trust Co. Boston, MA	SIC Code	3559
Auditor	Ernst & Young LLP	Employees	498
		Web Site	farrel.com

FiberCore, Inc.

253 Worcester Road, P.O. Box 180 Charlton, MA 01507 Telephone (508)248-3900 Fax (508)248-5588

Company Description

FiberCore, Inc. is engaged in the business of developing, manufacturing, and marketing single-mode and multi-mode optical fiber and optical fiber preforms for the telecommunications and data communications industry. Preforms are the basic component from which optical fiber is drawn and subsequently cabled. The Company has developed a patented preform production process which management believes to be more cost effective than other production methods in use. The Company also manufactures patented cable monitoring systems, a patented long range fault locator, cable protection devices, and electro-optical talk sets.

	12/31/98	12/31/97	12/31/96	12/31/95
Per Share Information				
Stock Price	0.13	0.31	3.50	2.38
Earnings Per Share	-0.07	-0.09	-0.13	-0.15
Price / Earnings Ratio	n.a.	n.a.	n.a.	n.a.
Book Value Per Share	0.21	0.27	0.28	0.21
Price / Book Value %	61.90	114.81	1,250.00	1,133.33
Dividends Per Share	0.0	0.0	0.0	0.0
Annual Financial Data				
Operating Results (000's)				
Total Revenues	8,459.0	7,104.0	8,204.0	3,242.0
Costs & Expenses	-10,801.0	-9,948.0	-12,337.0	-7,200.0
Income Before Taxes and Other	-2,342.0	-3,078.0	-4,133.0	-4,009.0
Other Items	0.0	0.0	0.0	0.0
Income Tax	0.0	0.0	0.0	0.0
Net Income	-2,342.0	-3,078.0	-4,133.0	-4,009.0
Cash Flow From Operations	-1,697.0	-3,068.0	-1,972.0	-3,232.0
Balance Sheet (000's)				
Cash & Equivalents	150.0	2,128.0	190.0	833.0
Total Current Assets	10,997.0	11,591.0	3,222.0	3,138.0
Fixed Assets, Net	5,230.0	4,808.0	3,771.0	4,119.0
Total Assets	25,768.0	26,107.0	17,642.0	14,783.0
Total Current Liabilities	4,660.0	3,500.0	3,072.0	3,415.0
Long-Term Debt	9,328.0	9,851.0	4,545.0	5,000.0
Stockholders' Equity	7,641.0	9,539.0	10,025.0	6,368.0
Performance & Financial Condition				
Return on Total Revenues %	-27.69	-43.33	-50.38	-123.66
Return on Avg Stockholders' Equity %	-27.26	-31.47	-50.42	-89.58
Return on Average Assets %	-9.03	-14.07	-25.49	-42.08
Current Ratio	2.36	3.31	1.05	0.92
Debt / Equity %	122.08	103.27	45.34	78.52

Compound Growth %'s	EPS % n.a.	Net Income % n.a.	Total Revenues %	37.67

Comments

The 15.9% increase in revenue experienced in 1998 was due to a 20% increase in the number of shipped units offset somewhat by lower average selling prices. This moved the Company one step forward towards achieving profitability. At December 31, 1998, the Company had $9 million of tax loss carryovers available to offset any future taxable income. At the same date, intangible assets amounting to $5.4 million were recorded as assets and equated to approximately 70% of stockholders' equity and book value per share. Working capital appears adequate for the foreseeable future. However, there is a large long term debt relative to capital and there are many common shares outstanding.

Officers	Position	Ownership Information	
Mohd A. Aslami	President, CEO	Number of Shares Outstanding	35,936,463
Charles De Luca	Exec VP, Secretary	Market Capitalization	$ 4,671,740
Michael J. Beecher	CFO, Treasurer	Number of Shareholders	1,500
Steven Phillips	Director	Where Listed / Symbol	OTC-BB / FBCE

Other Information			
Transfer Agent	Interstate Transfer Company Salt Lake City, UT	SIC Code	3231
Auditor	Deloitte & Touche LLP	Employees	80
Market Maker	Herzog, Heine, Geduld, Inc. (800)221-3600	Web Site	fibercoreusa.com
	Fahnestock & Co., Inc. (800)223-3012		

Fiberstars, Inc.

2883 Bayview Drive   Fremont, CA 94538   Telephone (510)490-0719   Fax (510)490-3247

Company Description

Fiberstars, Inc. develops and markets fiber optic lighting systems, which are used in a variety of commercial and residential applications. The Company pioneered the use of fiber optic technology in lighting. The Company's products often have advantages over conventional lighting in areas of efficiency, safety, maintenance and beauty, and thus can be used in place of conventional lighting in a number of applications. By delivering special lighting effects which conventional lighting cannot match, fiber optic lighting systems are especially attractive for a wide range of decorative applications, such as the lighting of swimming pools and spas, signage, "neon" decoration, landscaping, and other segments within the commercial and residential markets. The Company was founded in 1985.

	12/31/98	12/31/97	12/31/96	12/31/95
Per Share Information				
Stock Price	3.75	5.37	4.37	3.87
Earnings Per Share	0.21	0.18	0.14	0.0
Price / Earnings Ratio	17.86	29.83	31.21	n.a.
Book Value Per Share	3.38	3.05	2.91	2.77
Price / Book Value %	110.95	176.07	150.17	139.71
Dividends Per Share	0.0	0.0	0.0	0.0
Annual Financial Data				
Operating Results (000's)				
Total Revenues	23,707.0	18,119.0	15,836.0	12,106.0
Costs & Expenses	-22,498.0	-17,038.0	-14,982.0	-12,132.0
Income Before Taxes and Other	1,209.0	1,081.0	854.0	-26.0
Other Items	0.0	0.0	0.0	0.0
Income Tax	-447.0	-437.0	-343.0	11.0
Net Income	762.0	644.0	511.0	-15.0
Cash Flow From Operations	780.0	818.0	853.0	336.0
Balance Sheet (000's)				
Cash & Equivalents	1,290.0	523.0	1,520.0	1,700.0
Total Current Assets	12,326.0	11,924.0	10,481.0	9,564.0
Fixed Assets, Net	1,522.0	1,003.0	832.0	754.0
Total Assets	18,924.0	13,124.0	12,062.0	11,494.0
Total Current Liabilities	4,903.0	2,399.0	2,102.0	2,088.0
Long-Term Debt	667.0	17.0	28.0	40.0
Stockholders' Equity	13,354.0	10,708.0	9,932.0	9,366.0
Performance & Financial Condition				
Return on Total Revenues %	3.21	3.55	3.23	-0.12
Return on Avg Stockholders' Equity %	6.33	6.24	5.30	-0.16
Return on Average Assets %	4.76	5.11	4.34	-0.14
Current Ratio	2.51	4.97	4.99	4.58
Debt / Equity %	4.99	0.16	0.28	0.43

Compound Growth %'s	EPS %	22.47	Net Income %	22.11	Total Revenues %	25.11

Comments

Product sales increased 27% in 1998 primarily as a result of growth in the commercial lighting products segment. Pool lighting sales also grew for the year after starting the year with a decrease due to adverse weather conditions and product problems with a new line. Additional new products were introduced in 1998 and early 1999. International sales accounted for approximately 17% of 1998 revenue. 1998 results include $801,000 of income generated from the sale of product rights. Research and development expense increased 21% to $1,165,000 in 1998. At December 31, 1998, the Company had $4.4 million of goodwill reflected as assets which equated to approximately 33% of stockholders' equity and book value per share.

Officers	Position	Ownership Information	
David N. Ruckert	President, CEO	Number of Shares Outstanding	3,952,601
Barry R. Greenwald	Senior VP, General Manager	Market Capitalization	$ 14,822,254
Robert A. Connors	Vice President, CFO	Number of Shareholders	1,025
George K. Awai	Vice President	Where Listed / Symbol	NASDAQ / FBST

Other Information			
Transfer Agent	ChaseMellon Shareholder Services Ridgefield Park, NJ	SIC Code	3640
Auditor	PricewaterhouseCoopers LLP	Employees	106
		Web Site	fiberstars.com

Financial Performance Corporation

335 Madison Avenue   New York, NY 10017   Telephone (212)557-0401   Fax (212)557-0490

Company Description

Financial Performance Corporation provides specialized merger communications consulting services and computer software to the financial services industry. The Company's services and software are designed to identify and analyze the financial impact and competitive position of its customer's products and services and assist its customers in developing and analyzing marketing and communications strategies. The Company has developed a particular expertise in providing services to banks with respect to communications concerning mergers and other business combinations as well as marketing and financial information software. Although the Company was formed in 1984, it ceased operations and was inactive from 1990 through 1992. The Company resumed operations after it raised working capital through private debt and equity issuances.

	12/31/98	09/30/97	09/30/96	09/30/95
Per Share Information				
Stock Price	1.69	0.22	1.00	0.50
Earnings Per Share	0.23	-0.07	-0.05	-0.25
Price / Earnings Ratio	7.35	n.a.	n.a.	n.a.
Book Value Per Share	0.44	0.22	0.26	-0.24
Price / Book Value %	384.09	100.00	384.62	n.a.
Dividends Per Share	0.0	0.0	0.0	0.0
Annual Financial Data				
Operating Results (000's)				
Total Revenues	21,572.7	7,834.7	8,797.2	1,442.7
Costs & Expenses	-18,545.9	-8,357.2	-8,595.3	-1,690.8
Income Before Taxes and Other	3,026.8	-522.5	100.9	-248.1
Other Items	-657.0	3.0	-219.9	-553.2
Income Tax	-262.1	-25.4	-116.1	0.0
Net Income	2,107.7	-544.8	-235.0	-801.3
Cash Flow From Operations	4,329.6	-800.4	262.3	-880.2
Balance Sheet (000's)				
Cash & Equivalents	6,287.1	1,140.0	1,972.1	348.8
Total Current Assets	6,661.2	2,855.2	2,931.9	613.4
Fixed Assets, Net	213.7	172.2	111.9	69.4
Total Assets	7,851.1	3,910.1	3,760.4	1,085.6
Total Current Liabilities	2,841.2	1,733.6	1,483.1	489.5
Long-Term Debt	0.0	0.0	168.1	1,291.0
Stockholders' Equity	4,161.8	1,753.4	1,853.2	-849.9
Performance & Financial Condition				
Return on Total Revenues %	9.77	-6.95	-2.67	-55.54
Return on Avg Stockholders' Equity %	71.26	-30.21	-46.86	-200.32
Return on Average Assets %	35.84	-14.21	-9.70	-40.06
Current Ratio	2.34	1.65	1.98	1.25
Debt / Equity %	n.a.	n.a.	9.07	n.a.

Compound Growth %'s	EPS %	n.a.	Net Income %	n.a.	Total Revenues %	146.36

Comments

The Company changed to calendar year reporting in 1998. All years presented are for a full twelve months. The three month period ended December 31, 1997, has been omitted from the presentation. However, for that period the Company reported revenues and net income of $1,970,312 and $10,704 ($.001 per share), respectively. The increase in revenues during 1998 is attributable to the increased size of the merger projects for which the Company has been engaged. Three major customers accounted for 83% of revenues with the largest customer accounting for 55% of revenues. Income taxes are minimized due to the utilization of tax loss carryforwards. $3.6 million of carryforwards remained at December 31, 1998.

Officers	Position	Ownership Information	
William F. Finley	President, CEO	Number of Shares Outstanding	9,471,534
Richard Levy	Secretary	Market Capitalization	$ 16,006,892
Duncan C. Burke	Vice President	Number of Shareholders	2,000
Ottavio Serena	Director	Where Listed / Symbol	OTC-BB / FPCX

Other Information			
Transfer Agent	American Stock Transfer & Trust Co. New York, NY	SIC Code	8742
Auditor	Goldstein and Morris	Employees	16
Market Maker	Herzog, Heine, Geduld, Inc.	(800)221-3600	
	Wilson-Davis & Co., Inc.	(800)453-5735	

Firecom, Inc.

39-27 59th Street   Woodside, NY 11377   Telephone (718)899-6100   Fax (718)899-1932

Company Description

Firecom, Inc. operates in the building products industry including the design, manufacture and service of fire safety systems and products. The Company sells its products and services to a variety of end users (i.e. building owners and managers) and contractors, primarily in the New York metropolitan area. The Company also sells Life Safety and other electronic building systems manufactured by other companies. For the fiscal year ended April 30, 1998, revenues earned from servicing systems constituted approximately 45% of total revenues. The Company was formed in 1978.

	04/30/98	04/30/97	04/30/96	04/30/95
Per Share Information				
Stock Price as of 12/31	0.48	1.19	1.13	0.64
Earnings Per Share	0.05	0.23	0.25	0.30
Price / Earnings Ratio	9.60	5.17	4.52	2.13
Book Value Per Share	0.47	0.77	0.75	0.60
Price / Book Value %	102.13	154.55	150.67	106.67
Dividends Per Share	0.0	0.0	0.0	0.0
Annual Financial Data				
Operating Results (000's)				
Total Revenues	14,275.0	15,410.0	14,914.0	14,089.0
Costs & Expenses	-13,416.0	-12,831.0	-11,948.0	-11,423.0
Income Before Taxes and Other	859.0	2,579.0	2,966.0	2,666.0
Other Items	0.0	0.0	0.0	0.0
Income Tax	-305.0	-1,170.0	-1,404.0	-775.0
Net Income	554.0	1,409.0	1,562.0	1,891.0
Cash Flow From Operations	2,329.0	849.0	1,505.0	2,123.0
Balance Sheet (000's)				
Cash & Equivalents	4,204.0	2,465.0	2,165.0	1,704.0
Total Current Assets	9,262.0	8,557.0	7,483.0	6,551.0
Fixed Assets, Net	665.0	575.0	476.0	460.0
Total Assets	10,049.0	9,289.0	8,116.0	7,231.0
Total Current Liabilities	2,705.0	1,930.0	1,785.0	1,623.0
Long-Term Debt	1,401.0	1,671.0	624.0	1,029.0
Stockholders' Equity	5,533.0	4,842.0	4,950.0	4,444.0
Performance & Financial Condition				
Return on Total Revenues %	3.88	9.14	10.47	13.42
Return on Avg Stockholders' Equity %	10.68	28.78	33.26	54.05
Return on Average Assets %	5.73	16.19	20.36	27.66
Current Ratio	3.42	4.43	4.19	4.04
Debt / Equity %	25.32	34.51	12.61	23.15

Compound Growth %'s	EPS %	-44.97	Net Income %	-33.58	Total Revenues %	0.44

Comments

The decrease in fiscal 1998 revenues was anticipated because of a relatively low level of new construction in New York City. Preferred stock was converted to common shares during fiscal 1998. The order backlog was $2,742,000 at April 30, 1998, up $370,000 over the previous year. Although this is a small company, the price per share is extremely favorable in terms of price/earnings ratio and price to book value. For the nine months ended January 31, 1999, the Company had total revenue and net income of $13.2 million and $642,000 ($.05 per share) as compared to $10.2 million and $307,000 ($.02 per share) for the same period in fiscal year 1997.

Officers	Position	Ownership Information	
Paul Mendez	President, CEO	Number of Shares Outstanding	11,816,388
Howard L. Kogen	Exec VP, COO	Market Capitalization	$ 5,671,866
Antoine P. Sayour	Senior VP	Number of Shareholders	1,000
Jeffrey Cohen	VP - Finance	Where Listed / Symbol	OTC-BB / FRCM

Other Information			
Transfer Agent	American Stock Transfer & Trust Co. New York, NY	SIC Code	3669
Auditor	Rothstein, Kass & Company, PC	Employees	123
Market Maker	Robotti & Co., Inc.	(212)986-0800	
	Carr Securities Corporation	(800)221-2243	

First Alliance Corporation

17305 Von Karman Avenue Irvine, CA 92614 Telephone (949)224-8500 Fax (949)224-8351

Company Description

First Alliance Corporation is a financial services organization principally engaged in mortgage loan origination, purchases, sales and servicing. Loans originated by the Company primarily consist of fixed and adjustable rate loans secured by first mortgages on single family residences. Typically, the Company's borrowers are individuals who do not qualify for conventional loans because of impaired or unsubstantiated credit characteristics and/or unverifiable income, and whose borrowing needs are not met by conventional lending institutions. A significant portion of the mortgages are securitized with the Company retaining the right to service the loans. The Company is currently licensed to engage in the mortgage finance business in 18 states, the District of Columbia and the United Kingdom. The Company was founded in 1988 and had its initial public offering in July, 1996.

	12/31/98	12/31/97	12/31/96	12/31/95
Per Share Information				
Stock Price	3.25	18.37	19.67	8.00
Earnings Per Share	0.73	1.49	1.72	1.91
Price / Earnings Ratio	4.45	12.33	11.44	4.19
Book Value Per Share	4.11	4.34	3.52	2.12
Price / Book Value %	79.08	423.27	558.81	451.98
Dividends Per Share	0.0	0.0	0.0	0.0
Annual Financial Data				
Operating Results (000's)				
Total Revenues	83,808.0	95,649.0	70,871.0	58,880.0
Costs & Expenses	-60,855.0	-43,004.0	-32,632.0	-27,860.0
Income Before Taxes and Other	22,953.0	52,645.0	38,239.0	31,020.0
Other Items	0.0	0.0	0.0	0.0
Income Tax	-8,737.0	-19,873.0	-6,100.0	-478.0
Net Income	14,216.0	32,772.0	32,139.0	30,542.0
Cash Flow From Operations	-6,446.0	-33,537.0	38,742.0	5,980.0
Balance Sheet (000's)				
Cash & Equivalents	18,052.0	14,032.0	27,414.0	4,019.0
Total Current Assets	83,415.0	22,472.0	37,746.0	56,925.0
Fixed Assets, Net	9,733.0	8,587.0	3,410.0	2,141.0
Total Assets	177,603.0	158,147.0	87,457.0	66,987.0
Total Current Liabilities	85,463.0	9,103.0	9,348.0	23,543.0
Long-Term Debt	17,553.0	57,767.0	131.0	1,123.0
Stockholders' Equity	74,587.0	91,277.0	77,978.0	42,321.0
Performance & Financial Condition				
Return on Total Revenues %	16.96	34.26	45.35	51.87
Return on Avg Stockholders' Equity %	17.14	38.73	53.43	61.08
Return on Average Assets %	8.47	26.69	41.62	43.63
Current Ratio	0.98	2.47	4.04	2.42
Debt / Equity %	23.53	63.29	0.17	2.65

Compound Growth %'s	EPS %	-27.43	Net Income %	-22.50	Total Revenues %	12.49

Comments

The Company declared a 3 for 2 stock split in 1997. All per share amounts have been adjusted for consistency. Gain on sale of loans decreased $11.9 million or 53% in 1998 as compared to 1997. This decrease is primarily attributable to a $5.0 million write down of residual interest. The write down during 1998 was the result of an increase in the Company's prepayment rates primarily related to its adjustable rate loans. The Company was exempt from income tax under Subchapter S until it went public. 1995 therefore represents a partial year of regular taxation. The Company reacquired approximately 2.9 million shares of its stock during 1998 at an average price of $10.79 per share.

Officers	Position	Ownership Information	
Brian Chisick	President, CEO	Number of Shares Outstanding	18,139,488
Jeffrey W. Smith	Exec VP, COO	Market Capitalization	$ 58,953,336
Francisco Nbot	Exec VP, CFO	Number of Shareholders	1,900
Sarah Chisick	Vice President	Where Listed / Symbol	NASDAQ / FACO

Other Information			
Transfer Agent	American Stock Transfer & Trust Co. New York, NY	SIC Code	6189
Auditor	Deloitte & Touche LLP	Employees	445
		Web Site	firstalliance.com

First American Health Concepts, Inc.

7776 South Pointe Parkway West, Suite 150   Phoenix, AZ 85044   Telephone (602)414-0300   Fax (602)414-1383

Company Description

First American Health Concepts, Inc. markets and administers vision care programs under the registered trade names of Eye Care Plan of America® and ECPA®. The Company has developed the nation's largest direct access preferred pricing vision care program through a preferred provider network of independent and retail optometrists, opticians and ophthalmologists. In 1993, the Company introduced managed vision care programs. The Company was founded in 1981 and went public in 1985. Management considers itself to be well positioned for growth now that the demand for vision care services is stronger than ever.

	07/31/98	07/31/97	07/31/96	07/31/95
Per Share Information				
Stock Price as of 12/31	3.81	4.50	3.12	5.00
Earnings Per Share	0.14	0.12	0.14	0.25
Price / Earnings Ratio	27.21	37.50	22.29	20.00
Book Value Per Share	2.06	1.90	1.82	1.70
Price / Book Value %	184.95	236.84	171.43	294.12
Dividends Per Share	0.0	0.0	0.0	0.0
Annual Financial Data				
Operating Results (000's)				
Total Revenues	7,972.3	7,366.1	5,921.1	4,656.9
Costs & Expenses	-7,382.5	-6,885.7	-5,332.0	-3,989.1
Income Before Taxes and Other	589.8	480.4	589.1	667.8
Other Items	0.0	0.0	0.0	0.0
Income Tax	-239.0	-184.0	-230.0	0.0
Net Income	350.7	296.4	359.1	667.8
Cash Flow From Operations	-141.4	265.7	723.9	n.a.
Balance Sheet (000's)				
Cash & Equivalents	1,342.8	547.7	1,599.6	2,069.1
Total Current Assets	4,843.2	3,531.3	4,639.1	5,399.2
Fixed Assets, Net	2,000.4	2,089.3	2,000.0	919.2
Total Assets	7,536.4	6,905.0	6,737.5	6,318.4
Total Current Liabilities	2,235.2	1,964.4	1,972.7	1,489.2
Long-Term Debt	21.1	105.5	0.0	0.0
Stockholders' Equity	5,280.1	4,824.6	4,764.7	4,507.7
Performance & Financial Condition				
Return on Total Revenues %	4.40	4.02	6.06	14.34
Return on Avg Stockholders' Equity %	6.94	6.18	7.75	16.15
Return on Average Assets %	4.86	4.34	5.50	11.49
Current Ratio	2.17	1.80	2.35	3.63
Debt / Equity %	0.40	2.19	n.a.	n.a.

Compound Growth %'s	EPS %	-17.57	Net Income %	-19.32	Total Revenues %	19.63

Comments

The Company is in a multi-year transition towards becoming a full-service managed vision care provider. Although revenue growth was 9% in fiscal 1998, it was significantly below the accelerated pace achieved in fiscal 1997. Costs have also risen faster than income in both fiscal 1998 and 1997. For the six months ended January 31, 1999, the Company reported revenues and a net loss of $3.9 million and $13,416 ($.01 per share) as compared to $4.0 million and a net profit of $185,760 ($.07 per share) for the same period of the preceding year. The Company is banking on vision care becoming a mainstream employee benefit. But it will also have to figure out a way to make it more profitable to the provider.

Officers	Position	Ownership Information	
John A. Raycraft	President, CEO	Number of Shares Outstanding	2,564,736
Margaret Eardley	VP - Finance, CFO	Market Capitalization	$ 9,771,644
Carolyn Hall	Secretary, Treasurer	Number of Shareholders	1,000
Laura J. Arnold	Vice President	Where Listed / Symbol	NASDAQ / FAHC

Other Information			
Transfer Agent	OTR / Oxford Transfer & Registrar Portland, OR	SIC Code	7389
Auditor	KPMG LLP	Employees	150
		Web Site	ecpa.com

First Montauk Financial Corp.

328 Newman Springs Road   Red Bank, NJ 07701   Telephone (732)842-4700   Fax (732)842-9047

Company Description

First Montauk Financial Corp. is engaged in securities brokerage, investment banking, and trading. Its principal subsidiary is a broker-dealer registered with the Securities and Exchange Commission. The Company executes principal and agency transactions, makes markets in over-the-counter securities, and performs underwriting and investment banking services. The Company also sells insurance products and investments in equipment leases. First Montauk has 148 affiliate branch and satellite offices in addition to its main office and is licensed in a total of 49 states, the District of Columbia, and the Commonwealth of Puerto Rico.

	12/31/98	12/31/97	12/31/96	12/31/95
Per Share Information				
Stock Price	1.44	2.84	0.96	0.87
Earnings Per Share	-0.28	0.14	0.01	0.09
Price / Earnings Ratio	n.a.	20.29	96.00	9.67
Book Value Per Share	0.63	0.75	0.45	0.45
Price / Book Value %	228.57	378.67	213.33	193.33
Dividends Per Share	0.0	0.0	0.0	0.0
Annual Financial Data				
Operating Results (000's)				
Total Revenues	41,876.4	37,742.6	35,089.7	28,342.2
Costs & Expenses	-43,468.8	-35,297.6	-35,074.6	-27,090.3
Income Before Taxes and Other	-1,592.4	2,445.0	15.0	1,251.9
Other Items	-1,775.0	0.0	0.0	0.0
Income Tax	604.5	-968.2	17.7	-483.8
Net Income	-2,762.8	1,476.8	32.8	768.1
Cash Flow From Operations	-378.3	420.9	1,082.5	999.5
Balance Sheet (000's)				
Cash & Equivalents	613.5	789.9	1,069.5	845.5
Total Current Assets	7,072.0	5,620.8	5,962.4	8,701.4
Fixed Assets, Net	2,074.5	1,357.9	1,200.9	804.7
Total Assets	11,543.7	11,971.9	8,742.0	10,487.0
Total Current Liabilities	3,566.3	4,732.5	4,625.3	6,886.0
Long-Term Debt	918.5	0.0	0.0	0.0
Stockholders' Equity	6,187.1	6,893.0	3,695.3	3,600.9
Performance & Financial Condition				
Return on Total Revenues %	-6.60	3.91	0.09	2.71
Return on Avg Stockholders' Equity %	-42.25	27.90	0.90	23.22
Return on Average Assets %	-23.50	14.26	0.34	8.74
Current Ratio	1.98	1.19	1.29	1.26
Debt / Equity %	14.84	n.a.	n.a.	n.a.

Compound Growth %'s	EPS % n.a.	Net Income % n.a.	Total Revenues % 13.90

Comments

1998 was the Company's tenth consecutive year of record revenues. The Company benefited along with the rest of the brokerage industry from the extremely favorable market trends and record activity in the equity markets. Despite continued strong revenue growth, the bottom line was negatively affected by legal expenses to defend and settle various legal matters. Legal matters and related costs totaled $2.4 million, $1.5 million and $2.7 million in 1998, 1997 and 1996, respectively. The Securities and Exchange Commission has found fault with the supervision, or failure thereof, of some of the Company's affiliate offices and there are also pending customer arbitrations. Management believes it has taken action to assist in the reduction of customer claims. 1998 results were also subject to a $1,775,000 write-down of loans due from a former affiliate.

Officers	Position	Ownership Information	
Herbert Kurinsky	President, CEO	Number of Shares Outstanding	9,801,493
William J. Kurinsky	Exec VP, CFO	Market Capitalization	$ 14,114,150
Brian M. Cohen	Vice President	Number of Shareholders	2,000
David I. Portman	Director	Where Listed / Symbol	OTC-BB / FMFK

Other Information			
Transfer Agent	North American Transfer Co. Freeport, NY	SIC Code	6211
Auditor	Schneider Ehrlich & Associates	Employees	448
Market Maker	M.H. Meyerson & Co., Inc.	(800)333-3113	Web Site	firstmontauk.com
	Herzog, Heine, Geduld, Inc.	(800)221-3600		

Flanders Corporation

531 Flanders Filters Road   Washington, NC 27889   Telephone (919)946-8081   Fax (919)946-3425

Company Description

Flanders Corporation designs, manufactures and markets a broad range of air filtration products, including 1) high efficiency particulate air filters and absolute isolation barriers for the creation of synthesized atmospheres to control manufacturing environments and for the absolute control and containment of contaminants and toxic gases in certain manufacturing processes, 2) mid-range filters for individual and commercial use, and 3) standard-grade, low cost filters typically off-the-shelf for standard residential and commercial furnace and air conditioning applications. In 1996, the Company began diversifying its product line by implementing a strategy of growth by acquisition through the purchase of five other companies over three years. Although ownership changed hands in 1995, the Company has been in business since 1950.

	12/31/98	12/31/97	12/31/96	12/31/95
Per Share Information				
Stock Price	3.87	9.31	9.37	2.50
Earnings Per Share	0.20	0.27	0.23	0.12
Price / Earnings Ratio	19.35	34.48	40.74	20.83
Book Value Per Share	4.28	4.14	1.59	0.61
Price / Book Value %	90.42	224.88	589.31	409.84
Dividends Per Share	0.0	0.0	0.0	0.0
Annual Financial Data				
Operating Results (000's)				
Total Revenues	159,680.6	135,370.0	74,031.9	38,679.7
Costs & Expenses	-150,794.2	-125,826.0	-68,260.6	-36,849.4
Income Before Taxes and Other	8,886.4	9,544.0	5,771.4	1,830.2
Other Items	0.0	0.0	0.0	0.0
Income Tax	-3,597.8	-3,704.7	-2,177.6	-684.6
Net Income	5,288.6	5,839.3	3,593.8	1,145.7
Cash Flow From Operations	-796.8	5,849.6	1,613.2	1,610.5
Balance Sheet (000's)				
Cash & Equivalents	13,672.7	35,454.6	2,390.4	2,973.8
Total Current Assets	70,321.6	76,251.7	41,492.8	13,044.6
Fixed Assets, Net	61,089.4	47,760.4	30,099.6	5,301.1
Total Assets	167,780.2	145,880.5	86,518.4	18,529.2
Total Current Liabilities	22,350.0	21,072.2	18,922.7	9,014.2
Long-Term Debt	30,105.7	13,679.1	29,776.3	1,306.6
Stockholders' Equity	109,602.8	106,206.9	25,352.8	8,208.4
Performance & Financial Condition				
Return on Total Revenues %	3.31	4.31	4.85	2.96
Return on Avg Stockholders' Equity %	4.90	8.88	21.42	18.84
Return on Average Assets %	3.37	5.03	6.84	6.96
Current Ratio	3.15	3.62	2.19	1.45
Debt / Equity %	27.47	12.88	117.45	15.92

Compound Growth %'s	EPS %	18.56	Net Income %	66.51	Total Revenues %	60.42

Comments

Approximately one-half of the 17.7% increase in revenue in 1998 as compared to 1997 was attributable to the Company's success in attracting work and expanding its original core business. The balance was acquisition related. Research and development expenses rose sharply in 1998 and totalled $2,250,000 as compared to $373,000 in 1997. Management has done well in terms of absorbing new operations without great disturbances in bottom line results. At December 31, 1998, the Company had $29.0 million of intangible assets recorded on its ledgers which equated to approximately 26% of stockholders' equity and book value per share. The Company's overall financial condition is very respectable.

Officers	Position	Ownership Information	
Thomas T. Allan	Chairman	Number of Shares Outstanding	25,624,339
Robert R. Amerson	President, CEO	Market Capitalization	$ 99,166,192
Steven K. Clark	VP - Finance, CFO	Number of Shareholders	600
Steven D. Klocke	Vice President	Where Listed / Symbol	NASDAQ / FLDR

Other Information			
Transfer Agent	OTC Stock Transfer, Inc. Salt Lake City, UT	SIC Code	3564
Auditor	McGladrey & Pullen, LLP	Employees	2,152
		Web Site	flanderscorp.com

Flour City International, Inc.

915 Riverview Drive, Suite One   Johnson City, TN 37601   Telephone (423)928-2724   Fax (423)928-0216

Company Description

Flour City International, Inc. is a worldwide leader in the design, fabrication, and installation of curtainwall, nonload bearing exterior wall systems. The Company focuses on custom curtainwall projects, which typically represent as much as 15% of a building's cost structure. Custom projects, as opposed to standard ones, are typically larger projects characterized by higher margins and less competition. Flour City works on many diverse public and private sector projects, including mid- to high-rise commercial offices and governmental and landmark buildings. During 1998, the Company entered into a joint venture with a Mexican company for the construction and operation of a manufacturing facility in Monterrey, Mexico. Also during 1998, the Company entered into a joint venture with a Philippino company for the manufacturing and installation of custom curtainwall units in the Philippines.

	10/31/98	10/31/97	10/31/96	10/31/95
Per Share Information				
Stock Price as of 12/31	3.50	3.50	n.a.	n.a.
Earnings Per Share	0.78	1.21	0.32	0.22
Price / Earnings Ratio	4.49	2.89	n.a.	n.a.
Book Value Per Share	4.17	1.76	0.38	0.08
Price / Book Value %	83.93	198.86	n.a.	n.a.
Dividends Per Share	0.0	0.03	0.03	0.33
Annual Financial Data				
Operating Results (000's)				
Total Revenues	32,965.0	32,245.0	6,684.0	4,806.0
Costs & Expenses	-27,691.0	-23,889.0	-5,018.0	-3,713.0
Income Before Taxes and Other	4,894.0	7,019.0	1,569.0	1,093.0
Other Items	-53.0	6.0	-9.0	0.0
Income Tax	-868.0	-1,752.0	-149.0	0.0
Net Income	3,973.0	5,273.0	1,411.0	1,093.0
Cash Flow From Operations	6,592.0	-785.0	-998.0	1,000.0
Balance Sheet (000's)				
Cash & Equivalents	19,297.0	342.0	1,401.0	2,450.0
Total Current Assets	39,435.0	20,101.0	7,014.0	4,030.0
Fixed Assets, Net	1,454.0	455.0	557.0	320.0
Total Assets	42,251.0	21,083.0	7,571.0	4,350.0
Total Current Liabilities	14,508.0	11,588.0	5,910.0	3,980.0
Long-Term Debt	0.0	0.0	0.0	0.0
Stockholders' Equity	26,152.0	7,674.0	1,661.0	370.0
Performance & Financial Condition				
Return on Total Revenues %	12.05	16.35	21.11	22.74
Return on Avg Stockholders' Equity %	23.49	112.97	138.95	156.14
Return on Average Assets %	12.55	36.80	23.67	27.33
Current Ratio	2.72	1.73	1.19	1.01
Debt / Equity %	n.a.	n.a.	n.a.	n.a.

Compound Growth %'s	EPS %	52.48	Net Income %	53.76	Total Revenues %	90.00

Comments

The Company executed a 1 for 7 reverse stock split in fiscal 1998. All per share amounts have been restated for consistency. The Company's initial public offering was completed in May 1988 and raised approximately $14 million. The proceeds will allow the Company to pursue several capital projects as well as strengthen the balance sheet. As of December 31, 1998, the Company had an order backlog of approximately $100 million, over twice the $45 million that was logged one year earlier. A refreshing change to the days of acquisitions and huge intangible assets, Flour City actually has negative goodwill of $1.4 million recorded on its books. This means that it bought businesses at a net discount to recorded value.

Officers	Position	Ownership Information	
John W. Tang	Chairman, Secretary	Number of Shares Outstanding	6,267,539
Michael J. Russo	President, CEO	Market Capitalization	$ 21,936,387
Robert O. Bruce	CFO, Treasurer	Number of Shareholders	500
Paul D. Lynam	Director	Where Listed / Symbol	NASDAQ / FCIN

Other Information			
Transfer Agent	Jersey Transfer & Trust Co. Verona, NJ	SIC Code	1700
Auditor	Deloitte & Touche LLP	Employees	296
		Web Site	flourcity.com

Foilmark, Inc.

5 Malcolm Hoyt Drive   Newburyport, MA 01950   Telephone (978)462-7300   Fax (978)462-7650

Company Description

Foilmark, Inc. manufactures and markets foils, films and applicating systems and supplies that are used to mark and/or enhance products and packaging. Hot stamping is a dry process for marking, labeling and decorating products that uses heat and pressure to apply a design or lettering to a flat, contoured or cylindrical surface. The Company's products are sold to the appliance, television manufacturing, automotive, pharmaceutical, graphics and general plastics industries. In October 1997, the Company decided to discontinue the manufacture of hot stamping equipment. Foilmark was incorporated as a separate company in 1977 but traces its roots to Kensol-Olsenmark, Inc. which was established in 1924.

	12/31/98	12/31/97	12/31/96	12/31/95
Per Share Information				
Stock Price	1.62	3.09	2.31	6.00
Earnings Per Share	0.09	-0.80	-0.25	0.46
Price / Earnings Ratio	18.00	n.a.	n.a.	13.04
Book Value Per Share	3.68	3.59	4.40	4.65
Price / Book Value %	44.02	86.07	52.50	129.03
Dividends Per Share	0.0	0.0	0.0	0.0
Annual Financial Data				
Operating Results (000's)				
Total Revenues	30,909.5	33,417.6	37,402.3	36,920.8
Costs & Expenses	-30,430.9	-30,958.8	-38,615.4	-33,747.5
Income Before Taxes and Other	478.6	2,458.8	-1,518.1	3,173.3
Other Items	0.0	-4,786.5	0.0	0.0
Income Tax	-121.8	-983.5	478.0	-1,330.0
Net Income	356.7	-3,311.2	-1,040.1	1,843.3
Cash Flow From Operations	2,966.5	1,643.5	62.6	784.1
Balance Sheet (000's)				
Cash & Equivalents	237.6	795.8	199.9	464.3
Total Current Assets	15,047.7	17,225.9	21,300.8	18,578.2
Fixed Assets, Net	9,088.9	9,150.5	12,518.6	11,541.7
Total Assets	29,820.9	32,082.1	40,332.1	37,952.1
Total Current Liabilities	4,656.0	5,468.5	8,518.7	6,811.7
Long-Term Debt	8,571.1	10,750.2	12,165.1	10,732.1
Stockholders' Equity	15,365.6	14,978.5	18,249.8	19,243.3
Performance & Financial Condition				
Return on Total Revenues %	1.15	-9.91	-2.78	4.99
Return on Avg Stockholders' Equity %	2.35	-19.93	-5.55	10.41
Return on Average Assets %	1.15	-9.15	-2.66	5.72
Current Ratio	3.23	3.15	2.50	2.73
Debt / Equity %	55.78	71.77	66.66	55.77

Compound Growth %'s	EPS %	-41.95	Net Income %	-42.16	Total Revenues %	-5.75

Comments

The decision to exit the hot-stamp machine operation business came after very serious ongoing and everlasting losses. The 1997 loss and costs of closing down the machine operation necessitated a $4.8 million nonrecurring charge ($1.15 per share) to operations. Without the discontinued operation, the Company would have had net income of $1,475,179 ($.35 per share). Revenues declined in 1998 largely due to weak export markets, but the Company still managed to return to profitability. At December 31, 1998, the Company had $4.3 million of intangible assets on its books which equated to approximately 28% of stockholders' equity and book value per share. Still, the stock price at that date was only approximately 61% of tangible book value.

Officers	Position	Ownership Information	
Frank J. Olsen, Jr.	Chairman, CEO	Number of Shares Outstanding	4,179,601
Leonard A. Mintz	Senior VP	Market Capitalization	$ 6,770,954
Philip Leibel	VP - Finance, CFO	Number of Shareholders	568
Carol J. Robie	Vice President	Where Listed / Symbol	NASDAQ / FLMK

Other Information			
Transfer Agent	ChaseMellon Shareholder Services Ridgefield Park, NJ	SIC Code	3490
Auditor	KPMG LLP	Employees	211
		Web Site	foilmark.com

Fortress Group, Inc. (The)

1650 Tysons Boulevard, Suite 600   McLean, VA 22102   Telephone (703)442-4545   Fax (703)442-7730

Company Description

The Fortress Group, Inc. was formed in June 1995 to create a national homebuilding company for the acquisition and development of land or improved lots and the construction of residential for-sale housing. Four homebuilding companies were acquired by Fortress simultaneous with the closing of its initial public offering. These companies include Buffington Homes, Inc. (doing business in Austin and San Antonio, Texas), Christopher Homes (doing business in Las Vegas, Nevada), The Genesee Company (doing business in Denver and Fort Collins, Colorado, and Tucson, Arizona) and the Solaris Development Corporation (doing business in Raleigh-Durham, North Carolina). The Company acquired two additional companies in 1996, four in 1997, and three in 1998.

	12/31/98	12/31/97	12/31/96	12/31/95
Per Share Information				
Stock Price	2.25	4.25	6.00	n.a.
Earnings Per Share	0.42	0.63	0.87	0.55
Price / Earnings Ratio	5.36	6.75	6.90	n.a.
Book Value Per Share	3.72	3.72	2.72	0.84
Price / Book Value %	60.48	114.25	220.59	n.a.
Dividends Per Share	0.01	0.01	0.0	0.0
Annual Financial Data				
Operating Results (000's)				
Total Revenues	696,330.0	446,454.0	277,741.0	199,220.0
Costs & Expenses	-674,702.0	-432,537.0	-263,065.0	-192,399.0
Income Before Taxes and Other	21,628.0	13,917.0	14,676.0	6,821.0
Other Items	0.0	6.0	-181.0	-745.0
Income Tax	-8,794.0	-5,463.0	-5,013.0	-21.0
Net Income	12,834.0	8,460.0	9,482.0	6,055.0
Cash Flow From Operations	11,498.0	-1,497.0	-27,004.0	-1,754.0
Balance Sheet (000's)				
Cash & Equivalents	23,102.0	12,406.0	16,212.0	2,735.0
Total Current Assets	347,900.0	256,108.0	176,194.0	113,857.0
Fixed Assets, Net	13,785.0	10,246.0	3,543.0	2,099.0
Total Assets	449,903.0	337,304.0	193,733.0	123,812.0
Total Current Liabilities	62,469.0	45,719.0	21,337.0	25,077.0
Long-Term Debt	292,769.0	228,420.0	140,136.0	87,604.0
Stockholders' Equity	91,193.0	62,897.0	31,986.0	9,836.0
Performance & Financial Condition				
Return on Total Revenues %	1.84	1.89	3.41	3.04
Return on Avg Stockholders' Equity %	16.66	17.83	45.34	76.38
Return on Average Assets %	3.26	3.19	5.97	5.15
Current Ratio	5.57	5.60	8.26	4.54
Debt / Equity %	321.04	363.17	438.12	890.65

Compound Growth %'s	EPS %	-8.60	Net Income %	28.45	Total Revenues %	51.76

Comments

The financial information presented for years prior to 1996 is that of the acquired companies on a combined basis. Each subsequent acquisition has been accounted for under the purchase method of accounting. Therefore results have only been combined since the date of the acquisition. Convertible preferred stock has been issued in connection with certain of the acquisitions. Approximately $7.4 million of 1998 earnings were allocated to the preferred shareholders. Book value per share at December 31, 1998, is the calculated net of preferred stock liquidation preferences. At that date, there was also goodwill on the books of $39.2 million which equated to approximately $3.29 of intangible book value per common share. At December 31, 1998, the Company's backlog totalled $308.8 million as compared to $198.2 million one year earlier.

Officers	Position	Ownership Information	
J. Marshall Coleman	Chairman	Number of Shares Outstanding	11,908,107
George C. Yeonas	President, COO	Market Capitalization	$ 26,793,241
Jeffrey W. Shirley	VP - Finance, CFO	Number of Shareholders	2,000
Mark L. Fine	Director	Where Listed / Symbol	NASDAQ / FRTG

Other Information			
Transfer Agent	American Securities Transfer, Inc. Denver, CO	SIC Code	1520
Auditor	PricewaterhouseCoopers LLP	Employees	1,190
		Web Site	fortressgroup.com

Fotoball USA, Inc.

3738 Ruffin Road   San Diego, CA 92123   Telephone (619)467-9900   Fax (619)467-9947

Company Description

Fotoball USA, Inc. designs, develops and manufactures high quality custom sports and non-sports-related products for promotional purposes. Its custom-imprinted merchandise includes baseballs, footballs, basketballs, hockey pucks, lapel pins, and other items. Additionally, the Company designs and manufactures custom sports products which are sold in the licensed product retail market through independent manufacturers' representatives. It also sells directly to a nationwide network of over 2,000 retailers including Walmart, J.C. Penney, Kmart, Target, Pro Image and The Sports Authority. A major component of the Company's operations is the design, development and manufacture of promotions for major corporations using imprinted sports-related products and non-sports-related products. The Company was founded in 1988.

	12/31/98	12/31/97	12/31/96	12/31/95
Per Share Information				
Stock Price	3.00	1.25	4.50	4.37
Earnings Per Share	0.22	-1.04	0.47	0.0
Price / Earnings Ratio	13.64	n.a.	9.57	n.a.
Book Value Per Share	2.18	1.97	3.01	2.54
Price / Book Value %	137.61	63.45	149.50	172.05
Dividends Per Share	0.0	0.0	0.0	0.0
Annual Financial Data				
Operating Results (000's)				
Total Revenues	19,157.9	12,269.2	26,145.4	7,973.5
Costs & Expenses	-18,127.0	-15,066.1	-24,075.1	-7,940.6
Income Before Taxes and Other	1,030.9	-2,796.9	2,070.4	33.0
Other Items	0.0	0.0	0.0	0.0
Income Tax	-433.0	0.0	-795.0	-31.8
Net Income	597.9	-2,796.9	1,275.4	1.2
Cash Flow From Operations	-939.1	2,128.3	-3,572.9	-954.3
Balance Sheet (000's)				
Cash & Equivalents	8.5	764.9	981.6	2,162.3
Total Current Assets	6,736.3	4,943.1	10,795.7	6,306.3
Fixed Assets, Net	1,126.6	1,217.9	1,039.2	860.1
Total Assets	7,894.6	6,577.4	12,154.3	7,809.4
Total Current Liabilities	1,851.6	1,079.6	3,956.8	904.4
Long-Term Debt	0.0	0.0	0.0	0.0
Stockholders' Equity	5,888.5	5,267.9	8,058.5	6,757.5
Performance & Financial Condition				
Return on Total Revenues %	3.12	-22.80	4.88	0.01
Return on Avg Stockholders' Equity %	10.72	-41.98	17.22	0.02
Return on Average Assets %	8.26	-29.86	12.78	0.02
Current Ratio	3.64	4.58	2.73	6.97
Debt / Equity %	n.a.	n.a.	n.a.	n.a.

Compound Growth %'s	EPS % n.a.	Net Income % n.a.	Total Revenues % 33.94

Comments

Revenues increased 57% in 1998. Approximately one-half of the increase was attributable to retail sales which has consistently grown more than 25% per year over the last several years. Retail sales grew 81% in 1998. The $13.8 million decrease in revenue in 1997 was due to a $14.1 million decrease in toy car promotional sales. Contributing to the 1997 net loss was a $1,175,000 provision for excess inventory. 1998 results demonstrated solid profitability. Management says to expect more of the same in 1999 as continued improvement is expected. The Company has an excellent financial condition with plenty of working capital and no long term debt.

Officers	Position	Ownership Information	
Michael Favish	President, CEO	Number of Shares Outstanding	2,699,242
Carl E. Francis	Senior VP	Market Capitalization	$ 8,097,726
David G. Forster	VP - Finance, CFO	Number of Shareholders	1,286
Karen M. Betro	Vice President	Where Listed / Symbol	NASDAQ / FUSA

Other Information

Transfer Agent	Continental Stock Transfer & Trust Co. New York, NY	SIC Code	3949
Auditor	Hollander, Lumer & Co. LLP	Employees	86
		Web Site	fotoball.com

Friedman Industries, Incorporated

4001 Homestead Road   Houston, TX 77028   Telephone (713)672-9433   Fax (713)672-7043

Company Description

Friedman Industries, Incorporated, founded in 1965, is in the steel processing and distribution business. The Company has two product groups: coil processing (steel sheet and plate) and tubular products. The Company has coil processing plants located at Lone Star, Texas, Houston, Texas and Hickman, Arkansas. Through its Texas Tubular Products operation in Lone Star, Texas, the Company purchases, markets, processes (e.g. sorting, end-beveling, threading, etc.) and manufactures tubular products. Coil processing and tubular products accounted for approximately 59% and 41%, respectively, of fiscal 1998 revenues.

	03/31/98	03/31/97	03/31/96	03/31/95
Per Share Information				
Stock Price as of 12/31	4.81	6.00	5.75	3.94
Earnings Per Share	0.69	0.53	0.46	0.40
Price / Earnings Ratio	6.97	11.32	12.50	9.85
Book Value Per Share	3.96	3.70	3.50	3.37
Price / Book Value %	121.46	162.16	164.29	116.91
Dividends Per Share	0.30	0.22	0.20	0.21
Annual Financial Data				
Operating Results (000's)				
Total Revenues	148,893.8	120,007.5	106,919.2	98,052.6
Costs & Expenses	-141,605.9	-114,507.4	-102,621.1	-94,328.1
Income Before Taxes and Other	7,287.9	5,500.1	4,298.1	3,724.4
Other Items	0.0	0.0	0.0	0.0
Income Tax	-2,477.9	-1,870.0	-1,461.4	-1,266.3
Net Income	4,810.0	3,630.1	2,836.8	2,458.1
Cash Flow From Operations	3,810.7	1,699.0	2,443.0	-1,842.7
Balance Sheet (000's)				
Cash & Equivalents	1,361.7	168.2	595.2	664.5
Total Current Assets	39,347.5	33,357.2	27,524.7	25,956.6
Fixed Assets, Net	6,611.0	4,709.5	5,268.4	5,415.2
Total Assets	46,039.4	38,117.2	32,813.0	32,074.9
Total Current Liabilities	13,437.2	10,172.7	6,410.5	5,816.3
Long-Term Debt	6,366.7	4,600.0	5,400.0	7,000.0
Stockholders' Equity	25,733.0	22,782.0	20,428.9	18,722.8
Performance & Financial Condition				
Return on Total Revenues %	3.23	3.02	2.65	2.51
Return on Avg Stockholders' Equity %	19.83	16.80	14.49	13.60
Return on Average Assets %	11.43	10.24	8.74	8.19
Current Ratio	2.93	3.28	4.29	4.46
Debt / Equity %	24.74	20.19	26.43	37.39

Compound Growth %'s	EPS %	19.93	Net Income %	25.08	Total Revenues %	14.94

Comments

The Company declared 5% stock dividends in each of the last four years. Per share amounts have not been restated for consistency because it would not agree with the Company's presentation. Fiscal 1998 results reflect an aggressive growth program which was set into place in fiscal 1995. Management also attributes the success to strong market conditions. $2.6 million of new equipment was placed into service during fiscal 1998. The Company continues to pay a healthy cash dividend while maintaining a strong financial condition. For the nine months ended December 31, 1998, the Company reported revenues and net income of $98.0 million and $2,719,532 ($.40 per share) as compared to $109.6 million and $3,203,643 ($.46 per share) for the same period of fiscal 1998.

Officers	Position	Ownership Information	
Jack Friedman	Chairman, CEO	Number of Shares Outstanding	6,491,808
William E. Crow	President, COO	Market Capitalization	$ 31,225,596
Benny Harper	Senior VP, CFO	Number of Shareholders	700
Thomas Thompson	Senior VP	Where Listed / Symbol	AMEX / FRD

Other Information			
Transfer Agent	American Stock Transfer & Trust Co. New York, NY	SIC Code	5051
Auditor	Ernst & Young LLP	Employees	170

Frontier Adjusters of America, Inc.

45 East Monterey Way   Phoenix, AZ 85011   Telephone (602)264-1061   Fax (602)279-5813

Company Description

Frontier Adjusters of America, Inc. licenses and franchises independent insurance adjusters throughout the United States and Canada and provides support services to the adjusters. The adjusters are engaged by insurance carriers and self-insured companies to adjust claims made against them by claimants and by policyholders. As of June 30, 1998, the Company had entered into 480 license and franchise agreements with 434 entities; it operated 439 offices with 662 advertised locations in all 50 states, the District of Columbia and Canada. In addition, the Company owns and operates independent insurance adjusting and risk management businesses in Arizona and Nevada. The Company was founded in 1957.

	06/30/98	06/30/97	06/30/96	06/30/95
Per Share Information				
Stock Price as of 12/31	2.50	2.12	3.25	2.56
Earnings Per Share	0.13	0.21	0.25	0.22
Price / Earnings Ratio	19.23	10.10	13.00	11.64
Book Value Per Share	1.40	1.43	1.35	1.26
Price / Book Value %	178.57	148.25	240.74	203.17
Dividends Per Share	0.15	0.15	0.14	0.12
Annual Financial Data				
Operating Results (000's)				
Total Revenues	5,968.8	6,359.8	5,796.2	5,417.2
Costs & Expenses	-4,927.8	-4,686.5	-3,940.3	-3,738.2
Income Before Taxes and Other	1,027.9	1,598.3	1,855.8	1,679.1
Other Items	0.0	0.0	0.0	0.0
Income Tax	-415.4	-619.1	-721.3	-652.2
Net Income	612.5	979.2	1,134.5	1,026.8
Cash Flow From Operations	1,063.8	1,854.2	1,437.2	537.8
Balance Sheet (000's)				
Cash & Equivalents	929.4	1,012.2	534.5	359.0
Total Current Assets	4,558.0	4,615.8	3,781.5	3,620.5
Fixed Assets, Net	1,724.3	1,736.2	1,554.4	1,484.5
Total Assets	7,800.7	7,912.1	6,875.8	6,597.1
Total Current Liabilities	1,343.5	1,314.5	585.0	673.7
Long-Term Debt	5.0	33.5	60.0	84.7
Stockholders' Equity	6,452.2	6,564.2	6,230.8	5,838.7
Performance & Financial Condition				
Return on Total Revenues %	10.26	15.40	19.57	18.96
Return on Avg Stockholders' Equity %	9.41	15.31	18.80	18.13
Return on Average Assets %	7.80	13.24	16.84	15.69
Current Ratio	3.39	3.51	6.46	5.37
Debt / Equity %	0.08	0.51	0.96	1.45

Compound Growth %'s	EPS %	-16.08	Net Income %	-15.82	Total Revenues %	3.28

Comments

In November 1998, the Company entered into a tentative agreement to sell a 52% interest in the Company to United Financial Adjusting Company. Shareholders have the option to retain their shares and receive a cash distribution of $1.60 per share or to surrender their shares for a price of $2.90 per share. The decrease in fiscal 1998 revenue reflects lower demand for adjusting services due to relatively fewer incidents of natural and manmade disasters during the period. The decrease also reflects the loss of a major client that accounted for 9.2% and 18.8% of license fees in fiscal 1998 and 1997, respectively. For the six months ended December 31, 1998, the Company reported revenue and net income of $3.2 million and $435,415 ($.09 per share) as compared to $2.9 million and $493,033 ($.11 per share) for the same period of the preceding year.

Officers	Position	Ownership Information	
William Rocke	Chairman, CEO	Number of Shares Outstanding	4,605,358
Jean E. Ryberg	President	Market Capitalization	$ 11,513,395
Francis J. LaPallo	Exec VP	Number of Shareholders	908
James S. Rocke	Secretary, Treasurer	Where Listed / Symbol	AMEX / FAJ

Other Information			
Transfer Agent	U.S. Stock Transfer Corp. Glendale, CA	SIC Code	6794
Auditor	McGladrey & Pullen, LLP	Employees	n.a.
		Web Site	frontieradjusters.com

Frontier Airlines, Inc.

12015 East 46th Avenue, Suite 200   Denver, CO 80239   Telephone (303)371-7400   Fax (303)371-7007

Company Description

Frontier Airlines, Inc. is a low-fare, full-service airline based in Denver, Colorado. Principally serving markets abandoned by Continental Airlines during that carrier's downsizing of its Denver hub in 1993 and 1994, the Company currently operates routes linking its Denver hub to 14 cities in 12 states spanning the nation coast to coast. At present, the Company utilizes four gates at Denver International Airport for approximately 60 daily flight departures and arrivals. The Company was organized in February, 1994. Its fleet has grown to 14 leased jets, including seven Boeing 737-200s and seven larger Boeing 737-300s.

	03/31/98	03/31/97	03/31/96	03/31/95
Per Share Information				
Stock Price as of 12/31	4.53	1.97	3.25	6.75
Earnings Per Share	-1.95	-1.49	-1.23	-2.56
Price / Earnings Ratio	n.a.	n.a.	n.a.	n.a.
Book Value Per Share	-0.61	1.12	0.87	0.48
Price / Book Value %	n.a.	175.89	373.56	1,406.25
Dividends Per Share	0.0	0.0	0.0	0.0
Annual Financial Data				
Operating Results (000's)				
Total Revenues	147,950.7	117,534.1	70,812.3	24,815.7
Costs & Expenses	-165,697.0	-129,662.1	-76,325.2	-32,692.4
Income Before Taxes and Other	-17,746.4	-12,186.3	-5,581.7	-7,998.6
Other Items	0.0	0.0	0.0	0.0
Income Tax	0.0	0.0	0.0	0.0
Net Income	-17,746.4	-12,186.3	-5,581.7	-7,998.6
Cash Flow From Operations	-8,158.1	-6,468.3	-838.3	-4,226.0
Balance Sheet (000's)				
Cash & Equivalents	3,641.4	10,286.5	6,359.3	3,834.7
Total Current Assets	33,999.4	31,470.0	25,797.0	8,269.9
Fixed Assets, Net	5,579.0	4,341.0	1,983.1	1,598.2
Total Assets	50,598.5	44,092.5	30,990.2	13,746.1
Total Current Liabilities	50,324.4	32,744.8	25,844.4	9,528.8
Long-Term Debt	3,468.1	0.0	0.0	0.0
Stockholders' Equity	-5,673.2	9,882.9	4,701.0	1,642.5
Performance & Financial Condition				
Return on Total Revenues %	-11.99	-10.37	-7.88	-32.23
Return on Avg Stockholders' Equity %	-843.11	-167.12	-175.98	-266.62
Return on Average Assets %	-37.48	-32.46	-24.95	-39.99
Current Ratio	0.68	0.96	1.00	0.87
Debt / Equity %	n.a.	n.a.	n.a.	n.a.

Compound Growth %'s	EPS % n.a.	Net Income % n.a.	Total Revenues % 81.33

Comments

The Company has financed its growth and operating losses with the placement of additional shares since its initial public offering in fiscal 1995. Management believes that the bottom line was adversely affected in fiscal 1998 by costs associated with a failed acquisition of a small airline, costs associated with its newer aircraft, and higher maintenance expenses. But for the nine months ended December 31, 1998, the Company was flying high; revenues and net income were $150.4 million and $12.8 million ($.93 per share) as compared to $105.3 million and a loss of $15.7 million ($1.73 per share) for the same period of the preceding year.

Officers	Position	Ownership Information	
Samuel D. Addoms	President, CEO	Number of Shares Outstanding	9,253,563
Jimmie P. Wyche	Exec VP	Market Capitalization	$ 41,918,640
Arthur T. Voss	Vice President, Secretary	Number of Shareholders	541
Elissa A. Potucek	Vice President, Controller	Where Listed / Symbol	NASDAQ / FRNT

Other Information			
Transfer Agent	American Securities Transfer, Inc. Lakewood, CO	SIC Code	4700
Auditor	KPMG LLP	Employees	942
		Web Site	frontierairlines.com

G-III Apparel Group, Ltd.

345 West 37th Street   New York, NY 10018   Telephone (212)629-8830   Fax (212)719-0921

Company Description

G-III Apparel Group, Ltd. designs, manufactures, imports and markets an extensive range of leather and non-leather apparel including coats, jackets, pants, skirts and other sportswear items under its G-III™, Siena Studio™ and Colebrook and Co.™ labels and under licensed and private retail labels. The Company commenced operations in 1974, initially selling moderately priced women's leather coats and jackets under its G-III label. The Company has continuously expanded its product lines and began selling higher priced, more fashion oriented women's leather apparel in 1981. In 1990, the Company formed a textile division which designs, imports and markets a moderately priced line of women's textile outerwear and sportswear under the J.L. Colebrook label.

	01/31/98	01/31/97	01/31/96	01/31/95
Per Share Information				
Stock Price as of 12/31	4.81	4.94	3.37	3.00
Earnings Per Share	0.40	0.46	-0.06	1.82
Price / Earnings Ratio	12.03	10.74	n.a.	1.65
Book Value Per Share	5.48	5.07	4.59	4.66
Price / Book Value %	87.77	97.44	73.42	64.38
Dividends Per Share	0.0	0.0	0.0	0.0
Annual Financial Data				
Operating Results (000's)				
Total Revenues	120,136.0	117,645.0	121,663.0	171,441.0
Costs & Expenses	-116,880.0	-113,674.0	-121,971.0	-176,266.0
Income Before Taxes and Other	3,256.0	3,971.0	-308.0	-4,825.0
Other Items	449.0	0.0	0.0	-10,996.0
Income Tax	-906.0	-885.0	-89.0	4,087.0
Net Income	2,799.0	3,086.0	-397.0	-11,734.0
Cash Flow From Operations	-7,785.0	2,841.0	17,634.0	927.0
Balance Sheet (000's)				
Cash & Equivalents	5,842.0	13,067.0	7,617.0	1,421.0
Total Current Assets	39,249.0	35,198.0	32,289.0	45,037.0
Fixed Assets, Net	3,431.0	5,030.0	6,324.0	7,015.0
Total Assets	46,746.0	44,555.0	41,257.0	54,572.0
Total Current Liabilities	10,010.0	10,701.0	10,065.0	22,435.0
Long-Term Debt	0.0	0.0	0.0	0.0
Stockholders' Equity	35,686.0	32,825.0	29,716.0	30,101.0
Performance & Financial Condition				
Return on Total Revenues %	2.33	2.62	-0.33	-6.84
Return on Avg Stockholders' Equity %	8.17	9.87	-1.33	-32.62
Return on Average Assets %	6.13	7.19	-0.83	-19.21
Current Ratio	3.92	3.29	3.21	2.01
Debt / Equity %	n.a.	n.a.	n.a.	n.a.

Compound Growth %'s	EPS % n.a.	Net Income % n.a.	Total Revenues % -11.18

Comments

During fiscal 1998, the Company continued its strategy of expanding its product offering of licensed branded apparel. In March 1998, the Company entered into a license agreement with the National Basketball Association to market adult's and children's leather and leather/textile combination outerwear apparel. Operating results were impressive for both fiscal 1998 and 1997. Fiscal 1995 results include $11,320,000 of nonrecurring expense related to the closure of a manufacturing facility. For the nine months ended October 31, 1998, the Company reported revenue and net income of $101.9 million and $1,906,000 ($.27 per share) as compared to $100.8 million and $4,852,000 ($.69 per share) for the same period of the preceding year. The Company maintains a solid financial condition and has no long term debt or intangible assets.

Officers	Position	Ownership Information	
Morris Goldfarb	Chairman, CEO	Number of Shares Outstanding	6,506,276
Aron Goldfarb	Chairman, Director	Market Capitalization	$ 31,295,188
Jeanette Katz-Nostra	President	Number of Shareholders	1,500
Alan Feller	Exec VP, COO	Where Listed / Symbol	NASDAQ / GIII

Other Information

Transfer Agent	Norwest Bank Minnesota, N.A. South St. Paul, MN	SIC Code	2387
Auditor	Grant Thornton LLP	Employees	243
		Web Site	g3leather.com

GZA GeoEnvironmental Technologies, Inc.

320 Needham Street   Newton Upper Falls, MA 02164   Telephone (617)969-0050   Fax (617)965-7769

Company Description

GZA GeoEnvironmental Technologies, Inc. provides geotechnical engineering, environmental consulting, environmental remediation and information systems and management services to industrial, commercial, financial, public service and government clients. Geotechnical services involve the evaluation of soil, rock and groundwater conditions for the design and construction of buildings, highways, tunnels, dams, piers and other structures. Environmental services range from the initial assessment and evaluation of contaminated sites to the design, construction and operation of remediation systems to treat, control or remove contamination. GZA also helps clients to plan, coordinate and implement effective environmental and occupational health and safety management programs.

	02/28/98	02/28/97	02/29/96	02/28/95
Per Share Information				
Stock Price as of 12/31	3.94	4.87	3.00	3.00
Earnings Per Share	0.34	0.13	0.18	-0.37
Price / Earnings Ratio	11.59	37.46	16.67	n.a.
Book Value Per Share	6.31	5.89	5.81	5.67
Price / Book Value %	62.44	82.68	51.64	52.91
Dividends Per Share	0.0	0.0	0.0	0.0
Annual Financial Data				
Operating Results (000's)				
Total Revenues	59,989.0	59,706.0	70,168.0	65,144.0
Costs & Expenses	-57,736.0	-58,885.0	-68,875.0	-63,872.0
Income Before Taxes and Other	2,247.0	821.0	1,283.0	1,272.0
Other Items	0.0	0.0	-99.0	-2,216.0
Income Tax	-877.0	-292.0	-485.0	-450.0
Net Income	1,370.0	529.0	699.0	-1,394.0
Cash Flow From Operations	3,265.0	5,218.0	397.0	1,092.0
Balance Sheet (000's)				
Cash & Equivalents	4,594.0	4,229.0	3,318.0	3,021.0
Total Current Assets	27,959.0	29,125.0	29,832.0	30,820.0
Fixed Assets, Net	5,344.0	5,514.0	5,690.0	5,938.0
Total Assets	34,221.0	35,535.0	36,715.0	39,111.0
Total Current Liabilities	10,593.0	11,948.0	11,657.0	14,238.0
Long-Term Debt	0.0	0.0	1,860.0	2,730.0
Stockholders' Equity	22,886.0	23,257.0	22,465.0	21,685.0
Performance & Financial Condition				
Return on Total Revenues %	2.28	0.89	1.00	-2.14
Return on Avg Stockholders' Equity %	5.94	2.31	3.17	-6.64
Return on Average Assets %	3.93	1.46	1.84	-3.87
Current Ratio	2.64	2.44	2.56	2.16
Debt / Equity %	n.a.	n.a.	8.28	12.59

Compound Growth %'s	EPS %	37.44	Net Income %	40.00	Total Revenues %	-2.71

Comments

Lower revenue in fiscal 1998 was attributable to the closing of the Phoenix office and lower prices due to increasingly competitive market conditions. Fiscal 1995 results include a loss from discontinued operations of $2.2 million which equates to $.59 per share. For the nine months ended November 30, 1998, the Company reported revenues and net income of $46.0 million and $1,454,000 ($.40 per share) as compared to $44.1 million and $1,150,000 ($.28 per share) for the same period of the preceding year. The stock being priced at a substantial discount from book value might explain the Company's repurchase of 400,475 shares during fiscal 1998. The Company's financial condition is very strong.

Officers	Position	Ownership Information	
Donald T. Goldberg	Chairman	Number of Shares Outstanding	3,626,965
Andrew P. Pajak	President, CEO	Market Capitalization	$ 14,290,242
Joseph P. Hehir	Exec VP, CFO	Number of Shareholders	1,000
Joseph D. Guertin	Senior VP	Where Listed / Symbol	NASDAQ / GZEA

Other Information			
Transfer Agent	American Stock Transfer & Trust Co. New York, NY	SIC Code	4955
Auditor	PricewaterhouseCoopers LLP	Employees	442
		Web Site	gza.com

Galaxy Foods Company

2441 Viscount Row   Orlando, FL 32809   Telephone (407)855-5500   Fax (407)855-7485

Company Description

Galaxy Foods Company is principally engaged in the development, manufacturing and marketing of a variety of healthy cheese and dairy-related products, as well as other cheese alternatives including soy-based, rice-based and non-dairy cheese products. These healthy cheese and dairy related products include low or no fat, low or no cholesterol and lactose-free varieties. The Company also manufactures and markets non-branded and private label process and blended cheese products. Galaxy produces all of its products from a high-tech, state-of-the-art 60,000 square foot facility in Orlando, Florida. The Company was originally organized in 1980 under the name Galaxy Cheese Company and went public in 1987.

	03/31/98	03/31/97	03/31/96	03/31/95
Per Share Information				
Stock Price as of 12/31	0.59	0.75	0.84	0.50
Earnings Per Share	0.01	-0.12	-0.25	-0.54
Price / Earnings Ratio	59.00	n.a.	n.a.	n.a.
Book Value Per Share	0.17	0.18	0.14	0.14
Price / Book Value %	347.06	416.67	n.a.	n.a.
Dividends Per Share	0.0	0.0	0.0	0.0
Annual Financial Data				
Operating Results (000's)				
Total Revenues	20,569.2	17,279.2	4,239.7	4,907.9
Costs & Expenses	-20,191.7	-20,002.4	-7,483.3	-9,362.7
Income Before Taxes and Other	377.5	-2,736.7	-3,282.6	-5,013.6
Other Items	0.0	0.0	0.0	0.0
Income Tax	0.0	0.0	0.0	0.0
Net Income	377.5	-2,736.7	-3,282.6	-5,013.6
Cash Flow From Operations	-12.4	-3,569.6	-4,420.6	-2,690.7
Balance Sheet (000's)				
Cash & Equivalents	20.1	16.5	127.9	16.2
Total Current Assets	5,590.2	4,094.8	2,323.4	961.0
Fixed Assets, Net	10,668.2	8,186.0	5,286.5	4,327.4
Total Assets	16,449.1	12,492.4	8,032.0	5,950.0
Total Current Liabilities	4,391.4	2,263.5	727.4	3,886.7
Long-Term Debt	1,276.8	0.0	0.0	0.0
Stockholders' Equity	10,769.7	10,196.2	7,268.7	1,969.2
Performance & Financial Condition				
Return on Total Revenues %	1.84	-15.84	-77.43	-102.15
Return on Avg Stockholders' Equity %	3.60	-31.34	-71.07	-228.13
Return on Average Assets %	2.61	-26.67	-46.95	-77.83
Current Ratio	1.27	1.81	3.19	0.25
Debt / Equity %	11.86	n.a.	n.a.	n.a.

Compound Growth %'s	EPS % n.a.	Net Income % n.a.	Total Revenues % 61.23

Comments

During fiscal 1998, the 19.7% increase in sales was attributable to the introduction of new and improved products to the retail market, as well as increased consumer awareness of the Company's branded products. The new sales level allowed the Company to reach a breakeven level to cover fixed costs of the new manufacturing facility and resulted in the first net profit for a full year. For the nine months ended December 31, 1998, revenues and net income were $21.4 million and $1,236,880 ($.02 per share) as compared to $15.5 million and $347,128 ($.01 per share) for the same period of the preceding year.

Officers	Position	Ownership Information	
Angelo S. Morini	President, CEO	Number of Shares Outstanding	61,706,551
Cynthia L. Hunter	CFO	Market Capitalization	$ 36,406,865
Thomas Perno	Vice President	Number of Shareholders	683
Donald F. Warrick	Vice President	Where Listed / Symbol	NASDAQ / GALX

Other Information			
Transfer Agent	Continental Stock Transfer & Trust Co. New York, NY	SIC Code	2020
Auditor	BDO Seidman LLP	Employees	141
		Web Site	galaxyfoods.com

GameTech International, Inc.

2209 West 1st Street   Tempe, AZ 85281   Telephone (602)804-1101   Fax (602)804-1403

Company Description

GameTech International, Inc. designs develops and markets interactive electronic bingo systems. The Company currently markets a fixed-base system with light pen activated monitors and a portable, hand-held system which can be played anywhere within a bingo hall. The Company's electronic bingo units enable players to play substantially more bingo simultaneously than they can play on paper cards, leading to a greater spend per player and higher profit per bingo session for the bingo hall operator. GameTech installs the electronic bingo systems at no cost to the operator in exchange for a percentage of the sales generated by each unit. The Company was founded in 1994 and on December 1, 1997, completed its initial public offering of its common stock.

	10/31/98	10/31/97	10/31/96	10/31/95
Per Share Information				
Stock Price as of 12/31	2.25	10.62	0.71	n.a.
Earnings Per Share	0.20	0.43	0.13	0.08
Price / Earnings Ratio	11.25	24.70	5.46	n.a.
Book Value Per Share	4.30	0.82	0.34	0.02
Price / Book Value %	52.33	1,295.12	208.82	n.a.
Dividends Per Share	0.0	0.0	0.0	0.0
Annual Financial Data				
Operating Results (000's)				
Total Revenues	17,545.7	12,605.5	5,368.4	3,350.0
Costs & Expenses	-12,175.6	-7,685.6	-4,004.5	-2,480.0
Income Before Taxes and Other	3,370.1	4,741.1	1,363.9	870.0
Other Items	0.0	0.0	0.0	0.0
Income Tax	-1,300.0	-1,880.0	-559.2	-278.0
Net Income	2,070.1	2,861.1	804.7	592.0
Cash Flow From Operations	5,259.3	4,980.1	1,288.6	500.0
Balance Sheet (000's)				
Cash & Equivalents	21,484.6	1,019.5	166.0	37.0
Total Current Assets	28,332.8	3,624.8	366.0	137.0
Fixed Assets, Net	12,495.6	9,024.9	5,428.0	2,646.0
Total Assets	42,477.4	13,250.7	5,794.0	2,783.0
Total Current Liabilities	1,073.4	2,945.9	1,668.0	74.0
Long-Term Debt	514.5	1,599.7	2,341.0	1,729.0
Stockholders' Equity	40,322.1	3,975.7	1,785.0	980.0
Performance & Financial Condition				
Return on Total Revenues %	11.80	22.70	14.99	17.67
Return on Avg Stockholders' Equity %	9.35	99.33	58.21	59.20
Return on Average Assets %	7.43	30.05	18.76	19.73
Current Ratio	26.40	1.23	0.22	1.85
Debt / Equity %	1.28	40.24	131.15	176.43

Compound Growth %'s	EPS %	35.72	Net Income %	51.78	Total Revenues %	73.66

Comments

The 28.6% increase in revenue during fiscal 1998 was due to an increase in the average number of bingo units that were installed and operational. However, a competitive price adjustment was required in mid-year as the electronic bingo industry has been characterized by intense competition. In fiscal 1998, the Company spent $638,000 on research and development activities, as compared to $547,000 and $477,000 in fiscal 1997 and 1996, respectively. Large cash balances and a strong financial condition caused the Company to acquire 755,400 treasury shares in fiscal 1998. Shares that had been sold to the public for $11 each cost the Company an average of only $3.72. Did someone say "BINGO!"?

Officers	Position	Ownership Information	
Todd S. Myhre	CEO	Number of Shares Outstanding	9,370,826
Richard T. Fedor	Chairman	Market Capitalization	$ 21,084,359
John J. Paulson	CFO	Number of Shareholders	1,000
Gary R. Held	Vice President	Where Listed / Symbol	NASDAQ / GMTC

Other Information			
Transfer Agent	ChaseMellon Shareholder Services Los Angeles, CA	SIC Code	7990
Auditor	Ernst & Young LLP	Employees	83
		Web Site	gametechinc.com

Genelabs Technologies, Inc.

505 Penobscot Drive   Redwood City, CA 94063   Telephone (650)369-9500   Fax (650)368-0709

Company Description

Genelabs Technologies, Inc. is a biopharmaceutical company that conducts research focused on the discovery of small molecule drugs that act by binding to DNA to regulate gene expression or inactive pathogens. The lead research program is based on a proprietary enabling technology, MERLIN, for creating gene-specific, small organic, DNA-binding molecules. The Company's development efforts are focused on its lead compound, GL701, which completed Phase III clinical trials as a new therapy for systemic lupus erythematosus. In late March 1999, the FDA designated GL701 for priority treatment as a Fast Track product. The Company also sells diagnostic tests for infectious diseases primarily in Europe and Asia.

	12/31/98	12/31/97	12/31/96	12/31/95
Per Share Information				
Stock Price	2.72	2.75	5.88	4.75
Earnings Per Share	-0.17	-0.33	-0.32	-0.38
Price / Earnings Ratio	n.a.	n.a.	n.a.	n.a.
Book Value Per Share	0.45	0.34	0.70	0.48
Price / Book Value %	604.44	808.82	840.00	989.58
Dividends Per Share	0.0	0.0	0.0	0.0
Annual Financial Data				
Operating Results (000's)				
Total Revenues	10,359.0	14,168.0	14,511.0	19,126.0
Costs & Expenses	-16,964.0	-26,488.0	-25,643.0	-29,584.0
Income Before Taxes and Other	-6,605.0	-12,897.0	-11,397.0	-10,511.0
Other Items	0.0	0.0	0.0	0.0
Income Tax	0.0	0.0	0.0	0.0
Net Income	-6,605.0	-12,897.0	-11,397.0	-10,511.0
Cash Flow From Operations	-7,566.0	-9,583.0	-10,582.0	-6,699.0
Balance Sheet (000's)				
Cash & Equivalents	3,631.0	4,230.0	4,377.0	22,557.0
Total Current Assets	20,684.0	25,948.0	37,896.0	29,098.0
Fixed Assets, Net	1,401.0	1,239.0	1,463.0	1,945.0
Total Assets	26,807.0	31,139.0	44,119.0	36,198.0
Total Current Liabilities	8,374.0	7,233.0	7,672.0	10,322.0
Long-Term Debt	647.0	696.0	523.0	124.0
Stockholders' Equity	17,786.0	23,210.0	35,924.0	25,752.0
Performance & Financial Condition				
Return on Total Revenues %	-63.76	-91.03	-78.54	-54.96
Return on Avg Stockholders' Equity %	-32.22	-43.62	-36.96	-66.75
Return on Average Assets %	-22.80	-34.27	-28.38	-52.56
Current Ratio	2.47	3.59	4.94	2.82
Debt / Equity %	3.64	3.00	1.46	0.48

Compound Growth %'s	EPS % n.a.	Net Income % n.a.	Total Revenues % -18.49

Comments

The red ink on the bottom line almost scared us away. But then we found that management had no intention of showing a profit, at least not yet. A $3.5 million grant from the U.S. Defense Advanced Research Projects Agency was received in 1998 for the development of agents to counteract biological warfare. This helped reduce the loss reported in 1998 as compared to 1997. Research and development costs totaled $12.6 million and $12.4 million in 1998 and 1997, respectively, and amounted to approximately three out of every four dollars spent by the Company. The Company had $20.3 million of cash and short-term investments at the end of 1998 which will finance continuing operations. Tax loss carryovers totalled $104 million at December 31, 1998, should GL701 be the next miracle drug.

Officers	Position	Ownership Information	
Max Wilhelm	Chairman	Number of Shares Outstanding	39,737,000
Irene A. Chow	President, CEO	Market Capitalization	$ 108,084,640
James A. D. Smith	COO, CFO	Number of Shareholders	7,800
Matthew M. Loar	VP - Finance, Controller	Where Listed / Symbol	NASDAQ / GNLB

Other Information			
Transfer Agent	ChaseMellon Shareholder Services Ridgefield Park, NJ	SIC Code	2835
Auditor	Ernst & Young LLP	Employees	91
		Web Site	genelabs.com

Gentner Communications Corporation

1825 Research Way   Salt Lake City, UT 84119   Telephone (801)975-7200   Fax (801)977-0087

Company Description

Gentner Communications Corporation designs and manufactures high-technology electronic equipment for the Teleconferencing, Telephone Interface, and Remote Facilities Management markets. The Company also provides domestic and international conference calling services. The Company was founded in 1981. Beware—Gentner probably sends out more promotional material to hype their stock than any other company we know. We do not consider this a necessary use of corporate funds. Furthermore, most of what we receive is not particularly interesting. But the results from last year and the most recent six months did catch our attention. Join us for an impartial look at the numbers.

	06/30/98	06/30/97	06/30/96	06/30/95
Per Share Information				
Stock Price as of 12/31	3.87	1.16	0.81	1.06
Earnings Per Share	0.18	-0.05	0.04	-0.02
Price / Earnings Ratio	21.50	n.a.	20.25	n.a.
Book Value Per Share	0.68	0.50	0.54	0.50
Price / Book Value %	569.12	232.00	150.00	n.a.
Dividends Per Share	0.0	0.0	0.0	0.0
Annual Financial Data				
Operating Results (000's)				
Total Revenues	17,294.6	13,379.7	11,478.7	11,117.6
Costs & Expenses	-15,851.1	-13,697.4	-11,195.8	-11,227.4
Income Before Taxes and Other	1,443.4	-336.0	282.9	-115.2
Other Items	0.0	0.0	0.0	0.0
Income Tax	-39.0	-36.9	-0.9	-0.9
Net Income	1,404.4	-372.9	282.0	-116.1
Cash Flow From Operations	2,065.9	798.5	529.3	-1,234.8
Balance Sheet (000's)				
Cash & Equivalents	715.3	64.0	213.8	119.0
Total Current Assets	5,828.4	4,551.2	5,111.7	5,229.0
Fixed Assets, Net	2,320.3	2,493.3	1,514.6	1,829.0
Total Assets	8,311.7	7,335.9	6,780.2	7,198.0
Total Current Liabilities	1,919.4	2,062.6	2,016.0	2,972.0
Long-Term Debt	402.6	687.3	427.3	513.0
Stockholders' Equity	5,237.0	3,801.6	4,173.8	3,713.0
Performance & Financial Condition				
Return on Total Revenues %	8.12	-2.79	2.46	-1.04
Return on Avg Stockholders' Equity %	31.08	-9.35	7.15	-3.11
Return on Average Assets %	17.95	-5.28	4.03	-1.73
Current Ratio	3.04	2.21	2.54	1.76
Debt / Equity %	7.69	18.08	10.24	13.82

Compound Growth %'s	EPS % 112.13	Net Income % 123.17	Total Revenues % 15.87

Comments

The 29% increase in revenue in fiscal 1998 was mainly due to the strong growth of sales in the teleconferencing market, but growth in broadcast market revenues also contributed to the increase. Gross profit margins also increased due to price increases at the beginning of the year, aggressive vendor pricing, new products with higher gross margins, and increased efficiencies in the manufacturing process. A hopefully nonrecurring expense of the severance package of the former CEO contributed to an increase in general and administrative expense. Oh yes, there are also all those mailing costs in the investor relations department. For the six months ended December 31, 1998, revenue and net income were $10.8 million and $1,025,879 ($.12 per share) as compared to $7.7 million and $495,701 ($.06 per share) for the same period of the preceding year.

Officers	Position	Ownership Information	
Frances M. Flood	President, CEO	Number of Shares Outstanding	7,698,523
Susie Strohm	VP - Finance, Secretary	Market Capitalization	$ 29,793,284
Edward Dallin Bagley	Director	Number of Shareholders	3,500
		Where Listed / Symbol	NASDAQ / GTNR

Other Information			
Transfer Agent	American Stock Transfer & Trust Co. New York, NY	SIC Code	3663
Auditor	Ernst & Young LLP	Employees	143
		Web Site	gentner.com

George Risk Industries, Inc.

802 South Elm   Kimball, NE 69145-1599   Telephone (308)235-4645   Fax (308)235-2554

Company Description

The Company, which was formed in 1967, is engaged in the design, manufacture, and sale of computer keyboards, push button switches, and burglar alarm components and systems. Security alarm products comprise approximately 89% of revenues. The Company continues to search for a business acquisition that would complement its existing business. It is management's intent that such acquisition would not require outside financing as the Company has accumulated a substantial cash and investment reserve.

	04/30/98	04/30/97	04/30/96	04/30/95
Per Share Information				
Stock Price as of 12/31	1.81	2.16	1.50	0.70
Earnings Per Share	0.30	0.27	0.20	0.18
Price / Earnings Ratio	6.03	8.00	7.50	3.89
Book Value Per Share	1.44	1.14	0.88	0.66
Price / Book Value %	125.69	189.47	170.45	106.06
Dividends Per Share	0.0	0.0	0.0	0.0
Annual Financial Data				
Operating Results (000's)				
Total Revenues	11,799.0	11,259.0	9,813.0	9,769.0
Costs & Expenses	-8,903.0	-8,584.0	-7,636.0	-7,699.0
Income Before Taxes and Other	2,876.0	2,650.0	2,177.0	1,989.0
Other Items	0.0	0.0	0.0	0.0
Income Tax	-1,012.0	-1,001.0	-915.0	-760.0
Net Income	1,864.0	1,649.0	1,262.0	1,229.0
Cash Flow From Operations	464.0	5.0	619.0	1,041.0
Balance Sheet (000's)				
Cash & Equivalents	903.0	653.0	907.0	479.0
Total Current Assets	8,883.0	7,341.0	5,681.0	4,666.0
Fixed Assets, Net	665.0	680.0	567.0	598.0
Total Assets	9,795.0	8,064.0	6,351.0	5,277.0
Total Current Liabilities	619.0	610.0	498.0	493.0
Long-Term Debt	157.0	208.0	248.0	0.0
Stockholders' Equity	8,986.0	7,212.0	5,578.0	4,754.0
Performance & Financial Condition				
Return on Total Revenues %	15.80	14.65	12.86	12.58
Return on Avg Stockholders' Equity %	23.02	25.79	24.43	29.80
Return on Average Assets %	20.87	22.88	21.71	26.16
Current Ratio	14.35	12.03	11.41	9.46
Debt / Equity %	1.75	2.88	4.45	n.a.

Compound Growth %'s	EPS %	18.56	Net Income %	14.89	Total Revenues %	6.50

Comments

Net income continued to advance in fiscal 1998, up 13% over the preceding year. Management predicts continued growth in 1999 through volume increases from present customers and sales to added customers. New products are expected to enhance applications in the area of hydraulics, automotive, machine tools and material handling. For the nine months ended January 31, 1999, the Company had sales and net income of $9.5 million and $1,349,000 ($.22 per share) as compared to $8.4 million and $1,258,000 ($.21 per share) for the same period in the prior year. The Company has a very strong balance sheet.

Officers	Position	Ownership Information	
Ken R. Risk	Chairman, President	Number of Shares Outstanding	6,054,108
Mary Ann Brothers	Exec VP	Market Capitalization	$ 10,957,935
Peggy Dilley	CFO	Number of Shareholders	1,500
Eileen M. Risk	Secretary, Treasurer	Where Listed / Symbol	OTC-BB / RISKA

Other Information			
Transfer Agent	Company Office Kimball, NE	SIC Code	3669
Auditor	Mason Russell West, LLC	Employees	250
Market Maker	Wilson-Davis & Co., Inc.	(800)453-5735	Web Site	grisk.com
	M.H. Meyerson & Co., Inc.	(800)333-3113		

Glassmaster Company

P.O. Box 788   Lexington, SC 29071   Telephone (803)359-2594   Fax (803)359-0897

Company Description

Glassmaster Company is a manufacturer of thermoplastic and thermoset plastic materials that result in a variety of products within a single industry segment and are categorized by product line as follows: extruded (thermoplastic) synthetic monofilament, pultruded (thermoset) fiberglass and composites, and flexible steel wire controls and molded plastic control panels. The Company was founded in 1946 as the Koolvent Awning Company. In 1958 it introduced the Glassmaster line of fiberglass pleasure boats and, because of the cyclical nature of the boat business, later began to diversify into industrial related manufacturing. The metal awning division was sold in 1959.

	08/31/98	08/31/97	08/31/96	08/31/95
Per Share Information				
Stock Price as of 12/31	1.50	3.37	1.12	2.00
Earnings Per Share	0.07	0.14	0.08	0.22
Price / Earnings Ratio	21.43	24.07	14.00	9.09
Book Value Per Share	2.36	2.33	2.18	2.14
Price / Book Value %	63.56	144.64	n.a.	93.46
Dividends Per Share	0.0	0.0	0.03	0.06
Annual Financial Data				
Operating Results (000's)				
Total Revenues	24,548.8	21,321.5	22,323.5	24,087.6
Costs & Expenses	-24,350.3	-21,021.6	-22,121.8	-23,974.2
Income Before Taxes and Other	198.5	299.9	201.7	113.4
Other Items	0.0	0.0	0.0	287.1
Income Tax	-79.1	-65.2	-70.3	-49.1
Net Income	119.4	234.7	131.4	351.4
Cash Flow From Operations	680.2	971.5	1,045.0	-532.7
Balance Sheet (000's)				
Cash & Equivalents	142.8	119.1	129.3	161.8
Total Current Assets	6,753.9	6,247.8	6,011.8	6,655.3
Fixed Assets, Net	6,184.9	5,802.6	5,876.3	5,679.0
Total Assets	13,471.6	12,486.9	12,226.9	12,586.9
Total Current Liabilities	3,759.6	5,083.3	4,514.9	5,359.2
Long-Term Debt	5,272.3	0.0	3,682.8	0.0
Stockholders' Equity	3,848.8	3,766.9	3,529.2	3,427.7
Performance & Financial Condition				
Return on Total Revenues %	0.49	1.10	0.59	1.46
Return on Avg Stockholders' Equity %	3.14	6.43	3.78	10.74
Return on Average Assets %	0.92	1.90	1.06	3.11
Current Ratio	1.80	1.23	1.33	1.24
Debt / Equity %	136.99	n.a.	104.35	n.a.

Compound Growth %'s	EPS % -31.73	Net Income % -30.21	Total Revenues % 0.63

Comments

After years of stagnant revenue growth, new life has appeared in all business lines resulting in a 15% increase in fiscal 1998 revenue. However, a decline in gross profit in its fiberglass and composites division offset the additional profit contributions from the monofilament and controls divisions. For the six months ended February 28, 1999, the Company reported revenue and a net loss of $10.7 million and $381,000 ($.23 per share) as compared to $11.6 million and a net profit of $10,000 ($.01 per share) for the same period of the preceding year. The sales decline was attributed to a decision to discontinue certain low margin products, lower demand, pricing pressures, and a less favorable product mix. Operating costs were higher due to the start up of a new division.

Officers	Position	Ownership Information	
Stephen W. Trewhella	Chairman	Number of Shares Outstanding	1,627,896
Raymond M. Trewhella	President, CEO	Market Capitalization	$ 2,441,844
Steven R. Menchinger	Treasurer, Controller	Number of Shareholders	1,209
Neil A. McLeod, Jr.	Vice President	Where Listed / Symbol	NASDAQ / GLMA

Other Information			
Transfer Agent	Company Office Lexington, SC	SIC Code	2820
Auditor	Brittingham, Dial & Jeffcoat	Employees	218
Market Maker	Koonce Securities, Inc. (800)368-2806	Web Site	glassmasterco.com
	Knight Securities L.P. (800)232-3684		

Global Maintech Corporation

7578 Market Place Drive   Eden Prairie, MN 55344   Telephone (612)944-0400   Fax (612)944-3311

Company Description

Global Maintenance Corporation designs, develops and markets a computer system, consisting of hardware and software, which monitors and controls diverse computers in a data center from a single, master console. The Virtual Command Center (VCC) can simultaneously manage mainframes, mid-range computers and networks. The VCC is designed to consolidate consoles into one monitor which functions as a single point of control, monitor and control the computers connected to the VCC, and automate the routine processes performed by computer platforms and operating systems. In 1995, the Company installed its first three VCC units in the data centers of a large industrial and financial company. In 1996, the Company sold or leased seven additional VCC units. As of December 31, 1997 and 1998, the Company had sold or leased a cumulative total of twenty-one and thirty-eight VCC units, respectively.

	12/31/98	12/31/97	12/31/96	12/31/95
Per Share Information				
Stock Price	1.40	2.44	1.00	0.07
Earnings Per Share	-0.11	0.01	0.02	-0.16
Price / Earnings Ratio	n.a.	244.00	50.00	n.a.
Book Value Per Share	0.18	0.17	-0.01	-0.05
Price / Book Value %	777.78	1,435.29	n.a.	n.a.
Dividends Per Share	0.0	0.0	0.0	0.0
Annual Financial Data				
Operating Results (000's)				
Total Revenues	6,356.1	3,094.9	2,129.5	1,181.1
Costs & Expenses	-8,359.3	-2,914.3	-1,798.9	-1,362.1
Income Before Taxes and Other	-2,003.2	158.5	328.1	-188.8
Other Items	0.0	70.0	0.0	-595.2
Income Tax	0.0	0.0	-18.5	-5.9
Net Income	-2,003.2	228.5	309.6	-789.9
Cash Flow From Operations	-1,282.8	-302.1	163.1	-651.3
Balance Sheet (000's)				
Cash & Equivalents	664.1	1,726.9	32.9	39.4
Total Current Assets	4,057.4	3,566.3	750.7	608.5
Fixed Assets, Net	1,042.4	308.3	31.2	16.3
Total Assets	9,132.9	5,863.4	1,351.6	624.8
Total Current Liabilities	1,989.7	682.8	1,151.1	1,627.5
Long-Term Debt	1,700.0	0.0	0.0	58.0
Stockholders' Equity	5,443.3	3,280.7	183.9	-1,060.8
Performance & Financial Condition				
Return on Total Revenues %	-31.52	7.38	14.54	-66.88
Return on Avg Stockholders' Equity %	-45.92	13.19	n.a.	n.a.
Return on Average Assets %	-26.72	6.33	31.33	-67.40
Current Ratio	2.04	5.22	0.65	0.37
Debt / Equity %	31.23	n.a.	n.a.	n.a.

Compound Growth %'s	EPS %	n.a.	Net Income %	n.a.	Total Revenues %	75.24

Comments

The increase in revenues in 1998 is directly related to the installation of an additional seventeen VCC units and the cumulative total of units in operation rising to thirty-eight. But after two consecutive years of profits, lower margins and a big increase in staff punctured a hole in the bottom line of the financial statements. Although working capital looks adequate, management will need to pay close attention to its burn rate while it attempts to regain a profitable momentum.

Officers	Position	Ownership Information	
Robert E. Donaldson	President	Number of Shares Outstanding	18,409,397
David McCaffrey	CEO	Market Capitalization	$ 25,773,156
James Geiser	CFO, Secretary	Number of Shareholders	3,100
John E. Haugo	Director	Where Listed / Symbol	OTC-BB / GLBM

Other Information			
Transfer Agent	Norwest Bank Minnesota, N.A. South St. Paul, MN	SIC Code	3571
Auditor	KPMG LLP	Employees	87
Market Maker	R.J. Steichen and Co.	(800)328-8217	Web Site	globalmt.com
	Sherwood Securities Corp.	(800)435-1235		

GlobeNet International I, Inc.

10575 Newkirk, Suite 780   Dallas, TX 75220   Telephone (972)401-0052   Fax (972)869-1974

Company Description

GlobeNet International I, Inc. is engaged in the marketing of over 200 nutritional supplements and personal care products. Nutritional products include herbs, vitamins and minerals. Personal care products include natural skin, hair and body care products. Marketing and distribution of products is primarily through an independent distributor sales force. Distributors receive sales commissions and rebates based on the amount of purchases by the distributor. At December 31, 1998, the Company had approximately 95,000 independent distributors. Effective April 4, 1997, GlobeNet Inc., a private company, merged into Mighty Power U.S.A., Inc. which subsequently changed its name to GlobeNet International I, Inc. Each Company had existing product lines.

	12/31/98	12/31/97	12/31/96	12/31/95
Per Share Information				
Stock Price	0.94	0.75	0.06	0.10
Earnings Per Share	0.03	-0.05	0.0	-0.25
Price / Earnings Ratio	31.33	n.a.	n.a.	n.a.
Book Value Per Share	0.31	0.26	0.47	0.06
Price / Book Value %	303.23	288.46	12.77	166.67
Dividends Per Share	0.0	0.0	0.0	0.0
Annual Financial Data				
Operating Results (000's)				
Total Revenues	27,188.8	14,050.6	8,638.9	6,082.7
Costs & Expenses	-26,681.6	-14,724.5	-8,646.9	-6,998.0
Income Before Taxes and Other	507.2	-673.9	-8.0	-915.3
Other Items	-84.7	0.0	0.0	18.6
Income Tax	12.3	-13.0	-17.4	-8.8
Net Income	434.9	-686.9	-25.4	-905.5
Cash Flow From Operations	569.2	-1,212.0	-21.8	103.6
Balance Sheet (000's)				
Cash & Equivalents	382.4	166.4	94.6	74.7
Total Current Assets	3,749.7	2,094.9	1,414.9	1,573.4
Fixed Assets, Net	1,275.5	759.2	487.8	400.0
Total Assets	7,923.9	5,983.5	3,967.5	2,470.7
Total Current Liabilities	3,166.6	1,581.9	1,564.1	1,904.5
Long-Term Debt	510.8	818.1	367.6	340.0
Stockholders' Equity	4,246.5	3,583.5	1,984.1	226.2
Performance & Financial Condition				
Return on Total Revenues %	1.60	-4.89	-0.29	-14.89
Return on Avg Stockholders' Equity %	11.11	-24.67	-2.30	n.a.
Return on Average Assets %	6.25	-13.81	-0.79	-33.87
Current Ratio	1.18	1.32	0.90	0.83
Debt / Equity %	12.03	22.83	18.53	150.27

Compound Growth %'s	EPS % n.a.	Net Income % n.a.	Total Revenues % 64.73

Comments

The numbers presented above reflect the combined entities on a pro-forma basis for the period prior to the merger. The 112% increase in revenue experienced in 1998 is primarily the result of growth in the independent distributor base in the United States. This growth in the distributor base was mainly attributable to a successful direct mail campaign that centered on the Company's leading product, Microhydrin®, which is an antioxidant product the Company introduced in September 1997. The product currently accounts for approximately 33% of total sales. Just as management predicted, 1998 was a profitable year. At December 31, 1998, the Company had $2.7 million of goodwill recorded as assets which equated to approximately 63% of stockholders' equity and book value per share.

Officers	Position	Ownership Information	
Clinton H. Howard	Chairman, President	Number of Shares Outstanding	13,862,205
Ken Sabot	Senior VP	Market Capitalization	$ 13,030,473
Steven E. Brown	Vice President, CFO	Number of Shareholders	452
Andrew V. Howard	Vice President	Where Listed / Symbol	OTC-BB / GNII

Other Information			
Transfer Agent	Fidelity Transfer & Trust Co. Salt Lake City, UT	SIC Code	5190
Auditor	Osborn, Swalm, Thomas & Assoc.	Employees	125
Market Maker	Wien Securities Corp. (800)624-0050	Web Site	rbcglobenet.com
	Sharpe Capital Inc. (800)355-5781		

Go-Video, Inc.

7835 East McClain Drive   Scottsdale, AR 85260-1732   Telephone (602)998-3400   Fax (602)951-4404

Company Description

Go-Video, Inc. develops, designs, engineers and markets consumer electronic video products. The Company currently contracts with independent consumer electronics manufacturers to produce products to its specific standards. The Company believes that it and its licensees are the exclusive North American distributors of video cassette player/recorders (VCR) with two decks built into one unit - the Dual-Deck™ VCR. The Company patented the Dual-Deck system which incorporates proprietary circuitry and software to perform duplicating, dual recording, editing, and video view switching functions not available from single deck VCRs. The Dual-Deck VCR has constituted substantially all of the Company's sales over the last five fiscal years. The Company was founded in 1984 and went public in 1986.

	03/31/98	03/31/97	03/31/96	03/31/95
Per Share Information				
Stock Price as of 12/31	2.87	2.25	1.19	1.25
Earnings Per Share	0.23	0.17	-0.25	0.01
Price / Earnings Ratio	12.48	13.24	n.a.	125.00
Book Value Per Share	0.88	0.60	0.41	0.41
Price / Book Value %	326.14	375.00	290.24	304.88
Dividends Per Share	0.0	0.0	0.0	0.0
Annual Financial Data				
Operating Results (000's)				
Total Revenues	48,909.1	40,192.0	34,650.7	27,617.5
Costs & Expenses	-46,244.1	-38,194.2	-37,506.2	-27,499.7
Income Before Taxes and Other	2,656.4	1,924.3	-2,871.2	117.8
Other Items	0.0	0.0	0.0	0.0
Income Tax	427.0	-40.0	0.0	0.0
Net Income	3,083.4	1,884.3	-2,871.2	117.8
Cash Flow From Operations	1,578.6	-535.5	1,078.7	-641.4
Balance Sheet (000's)				
Cash & Equivalents	445.9	302.8	313.9	313.9
Total Current Assets	16,065.2	12,489.7	9,630.2	9,630.2
Fixed Assets, Net	901.0	1,136.7	1,172.6	1,172.6
Total Assets	19,044.6	13,881.3	11,198.0	11,198.0
Total Current Liabilities	7,068.7	5,486.9	6,236.7	6,236.7
Long-Term Debt	740.8	0.0	0.0	262.9
Stockholders' Equity	11,107.2	7,126.3	4,677.9	4,677.9
Performance & Financial Condition				
Return on Total Revenues %	6.30	4.69	-8.29	0.43
Return on Avg Stockholders' Equity %	33.82	31.93	-61.38	2.00
Return on Average Assets %	18.73	15.03	-25.64	1.08
Current Ratio	2.27	2.28	1.54	1.54
Debt / Equity %	6.67	n.a.	n.a.	5.62

Compound Growth %'s	EPS %	n.a.	Net Income %	n.a.	Total Revenues %	n.a.

Comments

The 22% increase in revenue during fiscal 1998 was attributable to a 30% increase in Dual-Deck VCR units sold which was partially offset by a 6.2% decrease in the average selling price per unit. The Company changed its fiscal year end from July to March in 1995. Fiscal 1995 results are for the eight month period ended March 31. Accordingly, compound growth rates in revenues and earnings were not displayed. Increased expenses and discontinuation of a product line were the main factors in the loss recorded in fiscal 1996. For the nine months ended December 31, 1998, the Company reported revenues and net income of $51.3 million and $1,743,147 ($.12 per share) as compared to $36.3 million and $2,084,057 ($.16 per share) for the same period of the preceding year.

Officers	Position	Ownership Information	
Roger B. Hackett	President, CEO	Number of Shares Outstanding	12,643,297
Ralph F. Palaia	Senior VP	Market Capitalization	$ 36,286,262
Steven G. T. Maine	Senior VP	Number of Shareholders	8,000
Douglas P. Klein	Vice President, CFO	Where Listed / Symbol	AMEX / VCR

Other Information			
Transfer Agent	American Securities Transfer, Inc. Denver, CO	SIC Code	3651
Auditor	Deloitte & Touche LLP	Employees	76

Goddard Industries, Inc.

705 Plantation Street   Worcester, MA 01605   Telephone (508)852-2435   Fax (508)852-2443

Company Description

Goddard Industries, Inc. is primarily engaged in the design, manufacture, distribution and sale of cryogenic valves for industrial and commercial use and in the distribution of plumbing goods, valves and fittings for residential and commercial use. The Company's indirect subsidiary (referred to as the Webstone Division) imports brass, stainless steel and plastic plumbing products and valves for the gas industry, all of which are manufactured and packaged to its specifications in the Far East and in Europe. The Company was formed in 1959.

	10/03/98	09/30/97	09/28/96	09/30/95
Per Share Information				
Stock Price as of 12/31	2.31	3.50	1.75	0.44
Earnings Per Share	0.35	0.42	0.32	0.21
Price / Earnings Ratio	6.60	8.33	5.47	2.10
Book Value Per Share	2.34	2.00	1.64	1.30
Price / Book Value %	98.72	175.00	106.71	33.85
Dividends Per Share	0.0	0.0	0.0	0.0
Annual Financial Data				
Operating Results (000's)				
Total Revenues	9,764.7	10,139.6	8,355.8	6,818.1
Costs & Expenses	-8,503.9	-8,624.3	-7,205.7	-6,109.0
Income Before Taxes and Other	1,260.8	1,515.3	685.1	709.1
Other Items	0.0	0.0	0.0	0.0
Income Tax	-514.0	-625.0	0.0	-279.0
Net Income	746.8	890.3	685.1	430.1
Cash Flow From Operations	1,029.7	782.9	417.5	405.9
Balance Sheet (000's)				
Cash & Equivalents	283.5	82.9	66.0	74.9
Total Current Assets	5,100.1	4,992.5	5,434.1	4,038.7
Fixed Assets, Net	1,614.8	1,440.8	1,052.6	950.7
Total Assets	6,856.7	6,612.9	6,672.0	5,150.5
Total Current Liabilities	978.3	1,014.4	1,755.0	894.1
Long-Term Debt	377.5	786.7	1,026.4	1,092.5
Stockholders' Equity	4,992.4	4,260.9	3,339.7	2,650.9
Performance & Financial Condition				
Return on Total Revenues %	7.65	8.78	8.20	6.31
Return on Avg Stockholders' Equity %	16.14	23.43	22.87	17.66
Return on Average Assets %	11.09	13.40	11.59	8.74
Current Ratio	5.21	4.92	3.10	4.52
Debt / Equity %	7.56	18.46	30.73	41.21

Compound Growth %'s	EPS %	18.56	Net Income %	20.19	Total Revenues %	12.72

Comments

In fiscal 1998, one customer accounted for 30% of the Company's cryogenic valve business (approximately 17.7% of total revenues). The 1998 decrease in revenue was attributable to a decline in orders received by the Company's customers in Asia and equated to a 13.2% reduction to valve division income. Webstone division sales increased 15.2% as a result of a broader marketing program. In fiscal 1997, an additional 10,000 square feet of steel structure was added to the existing 27,000 square feet of masonry structure, expanding the operating facility so as to be adequate to meet Company needs for the foreseeable future. We featured this Company in the 1996 edition of Walker's Manual of Unlisted Stocks at which time the stock was trading at $.44 per share.

Officers	Position	Ownership Information	
Saul I. Reck	Chairman	Number of Shares Outstanding	2,129,982
Salvatore J. Vinciguerra	President, CFO	Market Capitalization	$ 4,920,258
Donald R. Nelson	Vice President	Number of Shareholders	860
Robert E. Humphreys	Director	Where Listed / Symbol	OTC-BB / GODD

Other Information			
Transfer Agent	American Stock Transfer & Trust Co. New York, NY	SIC Code	3494
Auditor	Greenberg, Rosenblatt et al.	Employees	38
Market Maker	Howe Barnes Investments, Inc. (800)621-2364		
	Paragon Capital Corporation (800)345-0505		

Golden Genesis Company

4585 McIntyre Street   Golden, CO 80403   Telephone (303)271-7465   Fax (303)271-7193

Company Description

Golden Genesis Company, formerly Photocomm, Inc., is engaged primarily in the development, manufacturing and marketing of photovoltaic (solar electric) power systems and related products. In 1990, the Company entered into an agreement with Westinghouse Electric Corporation that allowed Westinghouse a substantial interest in the Company in exchange for financing. In 1993, the Company entered into an agreement with The New World Power Corporation (NWP) for additional financing in exchange for an equity interest. NWP subsequently acquired Westinghouse's interest. But on November 21, 1996, the Company entered into a new financial and strategic agreement with a subsidiary of ACX Technologies (NYSE).

		12/31/98	12/31/97	08/31/96	08/31/95
Per Share Information					
	Stock Price	1.31	1.53	2.06	3.00
	Earnings Per Share	-0.09	-0.03	0.07	0.06
	Price / Earnings Ratio	n.a.	n.a.	29.43	50.00
	Book Value Per Share	0.64	0.71	0.65	0.47
	Price / Book Value %	204.69	215.49	316.92	638.30
	Dividends Per Share	0.0	0.0	0.0	0.0
Annual Financial Data					
Operating Results (000's)					
	Total Revenues	43,555.0	32,829.4	23,043.4	20,618.2
	Costs & Expenses	-45,037.0	-33,322.0	-22,246.1	-19,714.3
	Income Before Taxes and Other	-1,482.0	-525.3	797.3	904.0
	Other Items	0.0	0.0	0.0	0.0
	Income Tax	0.0	0.0	350.0	0.0
	Net Income	-1,482.0	-525.3	1,147.3	904.0
	Cash Flow From Operations	94.0	-2,805.8	-1,059.1	-426.4
Balance Sheet (000's)					
	Cash & Equivalents	1,259.0	1,182.3	200.1	520.3
	Total Current Assets	19,881.0	15,701.9	10,933.9	6,452.9
	Fixed Assets, Net	2,327.0	1,683.6	2,517.8	2,064.0
	Total Assets	28,025.0	19,504.6	15,586.0	8,825.2
	Total Current Liabilities	11,949.0	3,648.2	5,214.3	1,707.9
	Long-Term Debt	5,155.0	4,150.5	638.4	720.2
	Stockholders' Equity	10,921.0	11,706.0	9,733.3	6,397.1
Performance & Financial Condition					
	Return on Total Revenues %	-3.40	-1.60	4.98	4.38
	Return on Avg Stockholders' Equity %	-13.10	-4.90	14.23	15.92
	Return on Average Assets %	-6.24	-2.99	9.40	11.19
	Current Ratio	1.66	4.30	2.10	3.78
	Debt / Equity %	47.20	35.46	6.56	11.26

Compound Growth %'s	EPS % n.a.	Net Income % n.a.	Total Revenues %	28.31

Comments

The Company changed to calendar year reporting in 1997. Only full reporting years are presented above. For the four months ended December 31, 1996, not shown above, revenues of $9.7 million and a net loss of $1,389,000 ($.10 per share) were reported. In 1998, sales increased in every market in which the Company operates. An acquisition also contributed to the 32% revenue advance. The added revenue only produced a slight increase in gross profit because of lower margins brought on by one time charges of $916,000. The net loss in 1997 was primarily attributable to severance charges and lower gross margins. At December 31, 1998, the Company had $5.3 million of goodwill recorded as assets which equated to approximately 48% of stockholders' equity and book value per share. Also as of that date, the Company had $8 million of tax loss carryovers available to offset future income.

Officers	Position	Ownership Information	
J. Michael Davis	CEO, COO	Number of Shares Outstanding	17,151,948
John K. Coors	President	Market Capitalization	$ 22,469,052
Jeffrey C. Brines	Vice President, CFO	Number of Shareholders	3,700
Myron D. Anduri	Vice President	Where Listed / Symbol	NASDAQ / GGGO

Other Information			
Transfer Agent	Harris Trust & Savings Bank Chicago, IL	SIC Code	3620
Auditor	KPMG LLP	Employees	146
		Web Site	goldengenesis.com

Government Technology Services, Inc.

3901 Stonecroft Boulevard Chantilly, VA 20151-0808 Telephone (703)502-2000 Fax (703)222-5275

Company Description

Government Technology Services, Inc. (GTSI) is a leading dedicated reseller of microcomputer and Unix workstation hardware, software and networking products to the Federal government market. GTSI offers its customers a convenient and cost-effective centralized source for microcomputer and workstation solutions through its broad selection of popular products and services at competitive prices. The Company specializes in understanding both the various information technology needs and the procurement processes of Government customers. On February 12, 1998, the Company acquired certain assets of BTG, Inc. which resells computer hardware, software and integrated systems to the Government.

	12/31/98	12/31/97	12/31/96	12/31/95
Per Share Information				
Stock Price	4.53	5.75	5.62	4.25
Earnings Per Share	0.26	-0.76	-2.67	-1.09
Price / Earnings Ratio	17.42	n.a.	n.a.	n.a.
Book Value Per Share	5.65	5.90	6.64	9.32
Price / Book Value %	80.18	97.46	84.64	45.60
Dividends Per Share	0.0	0.0	0.0	0.0
Annual Financial Data				
Operating Results (000's)				
Total Revenues	605,884.0	486,377.0	491,642.0	526,962.0
Costs & Expenses	-602,568.0	-491,481.0	-511,511.0	-538,574.0
Income Before Taxes and Other	3,316.0	-5,104.0	-19,869.0	-11,612.0
Other Items	0.0	0.0	0.0	0.0
Income Tax	-977.0	0.0	2,031.0	4,435.0
Net Income	2,339.0	-5,104.0	-17,838.0	-7,177.0
Cash Flow From Operations	10,531.0	-3,047.0	45,193.0	16,138.0
Balance Sheet (000's)				
Cash & Equivalents	39.0	856.0	48.0	18.0
Total Current Assets	146,016.0	128,184.0	129,375.0	166,101.0
Fixed Assets, Net	11,381.0	8,217.0	9,146.0	8,065.0
Total Assets	161,090.0	137,464.0	141,001.0	185,340.0
Total Current Liabilities	103,810.0	97,324.0	94,776.0	120,504.0
Long-Term Debt	0.0	0.0	0.0	0.0
Stockholders' Equity	55,324.0	39,874.0	44,848.0	62,477.0
Performance & Financial Condition				
Return on Total Revenues %	0.39	-1.05	-3.63	-1.36
Return on Avg Stockholders' Equity %	4.91	-12.05	-33.24	-12.37
Return on Average Assets %	1.57	-3.67	-10.93	-4.35
Current Ratio	1.41	1.32	1.37	1.38
Debt / Equity %	n.a.	n.a.	n.a.	n.a.

Compound Growth %'s	EPS %	n.a.	Net Income %	n.a.	Total Revenues %	4.76

Comments

The Company reversed three years of declining sales revenues in 1998. The primary reasons for the 24.6% increase as compared to 1997 was higher sales under the Company's indefinite-delivery/indefinite-quantity contracts, revenues generated in connection with the BTG asset acquisition, and deliveries under a large contract that was awarded in November 1997. The Company also turned a profit for the first time since 1994. Results were helped by a positive inventory adjustment of $2.2 million based on a physical inventory count. The magnitude of the losses posted in 1995, 1996 and 1997 have to be a concern to potential investors. Management will have to string a number of profitable years together if it wishes to restore investor confidence. The discount of the stock price to book value is not worth much without profits.

Officers	Position	Ownership Information	
M. Dendy Young	President, CEO	Number of Shares Outstanding	9,799,490
Robert Russell	VP - Finance, CFO	Market Capitalization	$ 44,391,690
Judith B. Kassel	Vice President, Secretary	Number of Shareholders	1,500
Charles A. Hasper	Vice President, Controller	Where Listed / Symbol	NASDAQ / GTSI

Other Information			
Transfer Agent	First Union National Bank of N.C. Charlotte, NC	SIC Code	5045
Auditor	Arthur Andersen LLP	Employees	505
		Web Site	gtsi.com

Great Lakes Aviation, Ltd.

1965-330th Street   Spencer, IA 51301   Telephone (712)262-1000   Fax (712)264-9160

Company Description

Great Lakes Aviation, Ltd. is a regional airline which operates under two marketing identities: United Express and Great Lakes Airlines. The Company is one of several companies operating as United Express under code sharing agreements with United Air Lines, Inc. Under the agreement, approximately 50 destinations are served for United in the Upper Midwest region of the United States. A similar arrangement with Midway Airlines Corporation was terminated in 1997. As of December 31, 1998, the Company's fleet consisted of 40 Beechcraft Model 1900 19-passenger aircraft and 8 Embraer Brasilia 30-passenger aircraft. The Company also has four Beechcraft Model 1900C aircraft being used exclusively for freight operations.

	12/31/98	12/31/97	12/31/96	12/31/95
Per Share Information				
Stock Price	2.56	1.75	2.37	3.37
Earnings Per Share	0.31	-2.41	-1.69	-0.35
Price / Earnings Ratio	8.26	n.a.	n.a.	n.a.
Book Value Per Share	0.68	0.15	2.47	4.16
Price / Book Value %	376.47	1,166.67	95.95	81.01
Dividends Per Share	0.0	0.0	0.0	0.0
Annual Financial Data				
Operating Results (000's)				
Total Revenues	114,032.0	83,790.0	109,669.7	88,046.1
Costs & Expenses	-111,004.6	-92,826.8	-123,946.5	-92,236.7
Income Before Taxes and Other	2,836.8	-9,036.8	-14,276.8	-4,190.6
Other Items	0.0	-9,233.8	0.0	0.0
Income Tax	-115.0	0.0	1,453.6	1,503.0
Net Income	2,721.8	-18,270.7	-12,823.2	-2,687.6
Cash Flow From Operations	-1,805.8	-6,837.2	-3,559.0	4,109.8
Balance Sheet (000's)				
Cash & Equivalents	189.0	5.8	6,676.3	6,784.5
Total Current Assets	27,644.4	20,831.6	28,872.4	27,039.5
Fixed Assets, Net	42,118.3	41,310.4	87,243.1	112,030.7
Total Assets	72,781.3	63,758.4	118,609.3	140,714.7
Total Current Liabilities	30,669.3	26,426.5	28,269.6	14,901.3
Long-Term Debt	28,471.1	28,471.5	65,985.7	87,477.7
Stockholders' Equity	5,849.9	1,126.6	18,739.7	31,540.2
Performance & Financial Condition				
Return on Total Revenues %	2.39	-21.81	-11.69	-3.05
Return on Avg Stockholders' Equity %	78.03	-183.94	-51.01	-8.18
Return on Average Assets %	3.99	-20.04	-9.89	-1.90
Current Ratio	0.90	0.79	1.02	1.81
Debt / Equity %	486.69	2,527.12	352.12	277.35

Compound Growth %'s	EPS % n.a.	Net Income % n.a.	Total Revenues %	9.00

Comments

On May 16, 1997, following inspections of the Company's operations by the Federal Aviation Administration (FAA), the Company voluntarily suspended flight operations pending a more detailed examination by the FAA. The Company was imposed with a $1 million penalty for a number of violations of FAA standards. Most planes were returned to service by the end of 1997. This action and the termination of the Midway arrangement, referred to above, resulted in a shutdown and other nonrecurring expense of $9,233,839 during 1997. Despite the profits posted for 1998, the auditors have still issued a going concern qualification in their report. Accumulated losses, a deficiency in working capital, and the need to renew debt agreements were all cited. However, management was more optimistic as to the state of affairs.

Officers	Position	Ownership Information	
Douglas G. Voss	President, CEO	Number of Shares Outstanding	8,590,843
Richard H. Fontaine	Senior VP	Market Capitalization	$ 21,992,558
Richard A. Hanson	Vice President, Controller	Number of Shareholders	1,800
Jeffrey Davis	Vice President	Where Listed / Symbol	NASDAQ / GLUX

Other Information			
Transfer Agent	Norwest Bank Minnesota, N.A. South St. Paul, MN	SIC Code	4512
Auditor	KPMG LLP	Employees	1,120
		Web Site	greatlakesav.com

Grill Concepts, Inc.

11661 San Vicente Boulevard, Suite 404 Los Angeles, CA 90049 Telephone (310)820-5559 Fax (310)820-6530

Company Description

Founded in 1988, Grill Concepts currently operates eight Daily Grill restaurants in southern California, a Daily Grill in Washington, D.C., three Pizzeria Uno restaurants on the East Coast, and two The Grill on the Alley restaurants. Daily Grill represents a modern approach to the traditional American grills of the 1920's that were the landmark restaurants of their day. Using home-cooking techniques, they served straight-forward food made from fresh ingredients purchased daily, soups and sauces slow simmered from fresh stock, with meats and fish prepared and served any way you wanted. During 1998, the Company initiated a strategic growth plan whereby it plans to open and operate Daily Grill and The Grill on the Alley restaurants in hotel properties in strategic markets throughout the united States.

	12/27/98	12/28/97	12/29/96	12/31/95
Per Share Information				
Stock Price as of 12/31	0.87	1.00	1.31	1.25
Earnings Per Share	-0.09	-0.05	-0.21	0.01
Price / Earnings Ratio	n.a.	n.a.	n.a.	125.00
Book Value Per Share	0.24	0.33	0.30	0.33
Price / Book Value %	362.50	303.03	436.67	378.79
Dividends Per Share	0.0	0.0	0.0	0.0
Annual Financial Data				
Operating Results (000's)				
Total Revenues	34,908.1	28,993.7	22,743.9	20,253.2
Costs & Expenses	-36,256.6	-29,465.9	-25,358.1	-20,182.4
Income Before Taxes and Other	-1,348.5	-472.3	-2,844.9	70.8
Other Items	0.0	0.0	0.0	0.0
Income Tax	-9.5	-5.0	-7.8	-7.6
Net Income	-1,358.0	-477.3	-2,852.7	63.2
Cash Flow From Operations	696.9	49.1	-144.9	191.2
Balance Sheet (000's)				
Cash & Equivalents	438.2	272.6	372.3	631.1
Total Current Assets	2,064.3	1,905.6	1,649.6	1,528.4
Fixed Assets, Net	8,342.3	6,063.1	5,225.1	3,737.5
Total Assets	11,387.0	9,010.9	8,082.0	8,031.8
Total Current Liabilities	4,364.3	3,128.3	2,848.6	2,477.1
Long-Term Debt	2,001.8	699.4	1,030.9	1,325.9
Stockholders' Equity	3,866.9	5,183.2	4,202.5	4,228.8
Performance & Financial Condition				
Return on Total Revenues %	-3.89	-1.65	-12.54	0.31
Return on Avg Stockholders' Equity %	-30.01	-10.17	-67.67	4.00
Return on Average Assets %	-13.32	-5.58	-35.41	1.06
Current Ratio	0.47	0.61	0.58	0.62
Debt / Equity %	51.77	13.49	24.53	31.35

Compound Growth %'s	EPS % n.a.	Net Income % n.a.	Total Revenues % 19.90

Comments

Revenues increased in 1998 primarily as the result of new locations placed in service in both 1998 and 1997. Same store sales for locations that were opened for a full twelve months in the prior year increased 5.8%. 1998 results include a $964,000 expense related to the write off of assets and a change in accounting method. At December 31, 1998, the Company had a working capital deficiency of $2.3 million. Six new restaurant locations are expected to open during 1999. Management believes that operating cash flow will be adequate to fund current operations but that the Company will require, and intends to raise, additional capital through additional bank borrowings or the issuance of debt or equity securities.

Officers	Position	Ownership Information	
Robert Wechsler	Chairman	Number of Shares Outstanding	16,015,553
Robert Spivak	President, CEO	Market Capitalization	$ 13,933,531
Michael Weinstock	Exec VP, Secretary	Number of Shareholders	426
Ben Sumner	Treasurer, CFO	Where Listed / Symbol	NASDAQ / GRIL

Other Information			
Transfer Agent	Securities Transfer Corp. Dallas, TX	SIC Code	5812
Auditor	PricewaterhouseCoopers LLP	Employees	1,000
		Web Site	dailygrill.com

Gristede's Sloan's, Inc.

823 Eleventh Avenue   New York, NY 10019-3535   Telephone (212)956-5803   Fax (212)247-4509

Company Description

Gristede's Sloan's, Inc. owns and operates 40 supermarkets: 35 in Manhattan, three in Westchester County, one in Brooklyn, and one in Long Island. Eleven of the supermarkets use the Sloan's name and 29 of them use the Gristede's name. The Company was formed in 1956 as Designcraft Industries, Inc. Up until 1993, its main business was the manufacture of cast component parts for the fine jewelry industry. The Company sold the assets of the jewelry business and acquired eleven supermarkets in 1993. The name Gristede's can be traced back to 1888 when two teenaged boys used all of their savings to open a little grocery store. The boys did well and by 1938 there were 161 stores. Gristede's was sold to Southland Corporation in 1969 which, in turn, sold it to the Red Apple Group in 1986. Mr. Catsimatidis, chairman and CEO of the Company, owns Red Apple Group and is under contract with the Company to operate the supermarkets.

	11/29/98	03/02/97	03/03/96	02/26/95
Per Share Information				
Stock Price as of 12/31	2.00	1.87	2.12	3.50
Earnings Per Share	-0.01	0.37	0.55	0.12
Price / Earnings Ratio	n.a.	5.05	3.85	29.17
Book Value Per Share	0.73	2.60	2.23	1.68
Price / Book Value %	273.97	71.92	95.07	n.a.
Dividends Per Share	0.0	0.0	0.0	0.0
Annual Financial Data				
Operating Results (000's)				
Total Revenues	158,024.8	51,815.1	51,334.5	48,408.2
Costs & Expenses	-158,296.0	-50,278.1	-49,027.4	-47,553.2
Income Before Taxes and Other	-271.1	1,208.0	1,892.9	459.6
Other Items	0.0	0.0	-88.7	-17.5
Income Tax	-17.2	-48.3	-62.0	-80.1
Net Income	-288.3	1,159.7	1,742.3	362.1
Cash Flow From Operations	-1,311.8	1,522.7	1,146.3	1,378.0
Balance Sheet (000's)				
Cash & Equivalents	53.8	70.2	71.2	75.5
Total Current Assets	25,923.9	8,576.2	6,509.9	4,674.6
Fixed Assets, Net	31,550.5	12,643.4	14,171.2	11,716.1
Total Assets	60,706.5	22,815.5	22,093.5	16,390.7
Total Current Liabilities	18,721.0	9,662.7	8,969.2	7,699.9
Long-Term Debt	18,663.9	4,200.0	5,400.0	3,434.6
Stockholders' Equity	14,381.7	8,158.1	6,998.4	5,256.2
Performance & Financial Condition				
Return on Total Revenues %	-0.18	2.24	3.39	0.75
Return on Avg Stockholders' Equity %	-2.56	15.30	28.43	7.72
Return on Average Assets %	-0.69	5.16	9.05	2.13
Current Ratio	1.38	0.89	0.73	0.61
Debt / Equity %	129.78	51.48	77.16	65.34

Compound Growth %'s	EPS % n.a.	Net Income % n.a.	Total Revenues % 48.34

Comments

On November 10, 1997, 29 supermarkets were merged into the Company making the Company one of the largest supermarket chains in New York City. This transaction is the primary reason for the increase in reported revenues. The Company also changed its annual year to a November year end. We only presented full years above. For the 36 weeks ended November 9, 1997, the Company reported revenues of $68.7 million and a loss of $4.0 million. The short period loss was attributable to the absence of the peak holiday season as well as unusually beautiful weather during the summer months which encouraged New Yorkers to take prolonged vacations elsewhere.

Officers	Position	Ownership Information	
John A. Catsimatidis	Chairman, CEO	Number of Shares Outstanding	19,636,574
Stuart Spivak	Exec VP, CFO	Market Capitalization	$ 39,273,148
Franklin Georges	Treasurer	Number of Shareholders	3,000
Michael Seltzer	Vice President, Secretary	Where Listed / Symbol	AMEX / GRI

Other Information			
Transfer Agent	American Stock Transfer & Trust Co. New York, NY	SIC Code	5411
Auditor	BDO Seidman LLP	Employees	1,323

Guardian International, Inc.

3880 N. 28 Terrace   Hollywood, FL 33020   Telephone (954)926-5200   Fax (954)926-1809

Company Description

Guardian International, Inc. is a supplier of security monitoring and high grade monitored security systems in Florida and New York City. The Company's principal activities include monitoring services provided pursuant to alarm contracts owned by the Company; monitoring services provided pursuant to alarm contracts owned by other alarm companies (wholesale monitoring); the sales and installation of electronic security systems including alarm, CCTV and access control systems; maintenance of electronic security systems; and acquisition of alarm contracts in connection with the acquisition of other alarm companies. The Company was founded in 1986.

	12/31/98	12/31/97	12/31/96	12/31/95
Per Share Information				
Stock Price	0.84	2.31	1.75	2.50
Earnings Per Share	-0.28	-0.21	-0.13	-0.08
Price / Earnings Ratio	n.a.	n.a.	n.a.	n.a.
Book Value Per Share	0.99	0.03	0.48	0.06
Price / Book Value %	84.85	7,700.00	364.58	4,166.67
Dividends Per Share	0.0	0.0	0.0	0.0
Annual Financial Data				
Operating Results (000's)				
Total Revenues	15,165.8	5,624.8	3,621.0	1,092.0
Costs & Expenses	-17,354.1	-7,198.9	-3,633.7	-1,275.0
Income Before Taxes and Other	-2,188.3	-1,574.1	-590.3	-270.0
Other Items	0.0	0.0	0.0	0.0
Income Tax	0.0	0.0	0.0	0.0
Net Income	-2,188.3	-1,574.1	-590.3	-270.0
Cash Flow From Operations	3,531.0	427.5	212.6	n.a.
Balance Sheet (000's)				
Cash & Equivalents	865.9	94.3	1,037.9	14.0
Total Current Assets	3,573.9	755.0	1,627.8	172.0
Fixed Assets, Net	2,438.9	729.1	484.9	210.0
Total Assets	39,779.0	11,075.1	8,982.0	2,633.0
Total Current Liabilities	6,155.4	1,097.2	786.6	309.0
Long-Term Debt	6,799.7	961.6	5,079.8	2,138.0
Stockholders' Equity	9,115.5	9,016.2	3,115.6	186.0
Performance & Financial Condition				
Return on Total Revenues %	-14.43	-27.98	-16.30	-24.73
Return on Avg Stockholders' Equity %	-24.14	-25.95	-35.76	-27.00
Return on Average Assets %	-8.61	-15.70	-10.17	-6.75
Current Ratio	0.58	0.69	2.07	0.56
Debt / Equity %	74.59	10.67	163.05	1,149.46

Compound Growth %'s	EPS % n.a.	Net Income % n.a.	Total Revenues %	140.37

Comments

Revenues rose 170% during 1998 which is primarily attributable to acquisitions which added approximately 11,700 retail customers. The Company had a total of 23,400 customers at December 31, 1998. The bottom line might be red but management has a different way of looking at things. Its key measure of performance is EBITDA (earnings before interest, taxes, depreciation and amortization). EBITDA was $3.7 million in 1998, up from just $900,000 in 1997. That is not to say we should ignore those other numbers. At December 31, 1998, the Company had intangible assets of $33.6 million reflected as assets which equated to approximately 369% of stockholders' equity and book value per share. Most of the intangibles relate to the purchase price of customer accounts. Tax loss carryovers of $4.6 million are available to offset future profits.

Officers	Position	Ownership Information	
Harold Ginsburg	Chairman	Number of Shares Outstanding	9,216,276
Richard Ginsburg	President, CEO	Market Capitalization	$ 7,741,672
Darius G. Nevin	Vice President, CFO	Number of Shareholders	2,000
Terry E. Atkins	Vice President, COO	Where Listed / Symbol	OTC-BB / GIIS

Other Information			
Transfer Agent	Interwest Transfer Co., Inc. Salt Lake City, UT	SIC Code	7381
Auditor	McKean, Paul, Chrycy et al	Employees	194
Market Maker	Sharpe Capital Inc. (800)355-5781	Web Site	4guardian.com
	Knight Securities L.P. (800)222-4910		

Guess ?, Inc.

1444 South Alameda Street   Los Angeles, CA 90021   Telephone (213)765-3100   Fax (213)765-3170

Company Description

Guess ?, Inc., founded in 1981, designs, markets, distributes and licenses one of the world's leading lifestyle collections of casual apparel, accessories and related consumer products. The Company's apparel for men and women is marketed under numerous trademarks including Guess, Guess ?, Guess U.S.A., Guess Collection and Triangle Design. The lines include full collections of denim and cotton clothing, including jeans, pants, overalls, skirts, dresses, shorts, blouses, shirts, jackets and knitwear. In addition, the Company has granted licenses to manufacture and distribute a broad range of products that complement the Company's apparel lines, including clothing for infants and children, activewear, footwear, eyewear, watches, home products and other fashion accessories. The Company went public on August 7, 1996, by the issuance of seven million common shares at $18 per share.

	12/31/98	12/31/97	12/31/96	12/31/95
Per Share Information				
Stock Price	4.81	6.88	14.37	18.00
Earnings Per Share	0.59	0.87	1.18	0.96
Price / Earnings Ratio	8.15	7.91	12.18	18.75
Book Value Per Share	2.34	1.76	0.82	0.26
Price / Book Value %	205.56	390.91	1,752.44	6,923.08
Dividends Per Share	0.0	0.0	0.0	0.0
Annual Financial Data				
Operating Results (000's)				
Total Revenues	435,128.0	515,372.0	551,162.0	486,733.0
Costs & Expenses	-391,837.0	-460,485.0	-465,036.0	-419,919.0
Income Before Taxes and Other	43,291.0	54,887.0	82,567.0	66,814.0
Other Items	0.0	3,961.0	0.0	0.0
Income Tax	-18,180.0	-21,337.0	-33,241.0	-26,726.0
Net Income	25,111.0	37,511.0	49,326.0	40,088.0
Cash Flow From Operations	65,200.0	30,242.0	76,835.0	108,436.0
Balance Sheet (000's)				
Cash & Equivalents	5,853.0	8,204.0	8,800.0	6,417.0
Total Current Assets	156,092.0	167,622.0	151,315.0	121,764.0
Fixed Assets, Net	86,453.0	98,170.0	64,302.0	68,199.0
Total Assets	263,772.0	287,814.0	239,306.0	202,635.0
Total Current Liabilities	54,782.0	60,952.0	74,494.0	64,192.0
Long-Term Debt	99,000.0	141,300.0	121,217.0	127,371.0
Stockholders' Equity	100,409.0	75,330.0	34,928.0	10,997.0
Performance & Financial Condition				
Return on Total Revenues %	5.77	7.28	8.95	8.24
Return on Avg Stockholders' Equity %	28.58	68.04	214.81	705.15
Return on Average Assets %	9.11	14.23	22.32	19.54
Current Ratio	2.85	2.75	2.03	1.90
Debt / Equity %	98.60	187.57	347.05	1,158.23

Compound Growth %'s	EPS %	-14.98	Net Income %	-14.44	Total Revenues %	-3.67

Comments

In 1998, the Company's domestic wholesale revenue declined primarily as a result of increased competition in branded denim apparel. International revenues decreased due to the sale in June 1997 of Guess? Italia which had contributed $13.5 million during the first five months of 1997, as well as to soft performance in Asian and South American markets. 1997 results include a net benefit from an accounting change of $3,961,000 ($.09 per share). The Company was not subject to income tax during 1995 and part of 1996 because of its status as an S corporation. Income taxes for those years are reflected above on a pro forma basis as if the Company had been subject to regular corporate income tax. Intangible assets comprise approximately 20% of stockholders' equity and book value per share as of December 31, 1998.

Officers	Position	Ownership Information	
Maurice Marciano	Chairman, CEO	Number of Shares Outstanding	42,906,535
Paul Marciano	President, COO	Market Capitalization	$ 206,380,433
Armand Marciano	Senior VP, Secretary	Number of Shareholders	5,000
Terence Tsang	VP - Finance, CFO	Where Listed / Symbol	NYSE / GES

Other Information			
Transfer Agent	Boston EquiServe Boston, MA	SIC Code	2340
Auditor	KPMG LLP	Employees	3,200
		Web Site	guess.com

Gundle/SLT Environmental, Inc.

19103 Gundle Road   Houston, TX 77073   Telephone (281)443-8564   Fax (281)875-6010

Company Description

Gundle/SLT Environmental, Inc. is the world leader in the manufacture and installation of geosynthetic lining products and services for environmental protection and other uses. The Company manufactures, sells, and installs flexible geomembrane liners, geonets, geosynthetic clay liners, concrete protection liners, and geocomposite products made from specially formulated polyethylene resins. Its fabrication department offers a variety of specialty products, such as manholes, sumps, pipe penetration boots, floats, floating covers, and vertical membrane barrier wall panels. The Company's products are used in containment systems for the prevention of groundwater contaminations, and for the confinement of water, industrial liquids and solids.

	12/31/98	12/31/97	12/31/96	12/31/95
Per Share Information				
Stock Price	4.00	5.25	6.62	5.56
Earnings Per Share	0.30	0.29	0.67	-0.13
Price / Earnings Ratio	13.33	18.10	9.88	n.a.
Book Value Per Share	6.84	6.48	6.30	5.67
Price / Book Value %	58.48	81.02	105.08	98.06
Dividends Per Share	0.0	0.0	0.0	0.0
Annual Financial Data				
Operating Results (000's)				
Total Revenues	180,822.0	201,114.0	211,640.0	249,116.0
Costs & Expenses	-173,890.0	-193,268.0	-191,560.0	-235,142.0
Income Before Taxes and Other	6,932.0	7,846.0	20,080.0	13,974.0
Other Items	0.0	0.0	0.0	-15,270.0
Income Tax	-2,912.0	-3,296.0	-8,434.0	-935.0
Net Income	4,020.0	4,550.0	11,646.0	-2,231.0
Cash Flow From Operations	17,272.0	17,227.0	42,098.0	14,196.0
Balance Sheet (000's)				
Cash & Equivalents	29,399.0	24,844.0	43,122.0	16,057.0
Total Current Assets	103,010.0	109,960.0	131,151.0	121,928.0
Fixed Assets, Net	34,838.0	35,283.0	40,282.0	43,940.0
Total Assets	169,320.0	177,961.0	204,046.0	196,021.0
Total Current Liabilities	43,441.0	49,499.0	44,566.0	42,382.0
Long-Term Debt	32,048.0	37,628.0	44,092.0	50,147.0
Stockholders' Equity	89,793.0	86,110.0	109,513.0	97,550.0
Performance & Financial Condition				
Return on Total Revenues %	2.22	2.26	5.50	-0.90
Return on Avg Stockholders' Equity %	4.57	4.65	11.25	-2.28
Return on Average Assets %	2.32	2.38	5.82	-1.10
Current Ratio	2.37	2.22	2.94	2.88
Debt / Equity %	35.69	43.70	40.26	51.41

Compound Growth %'s EPS % -33.09   Net Income % -41.25   Total Revenues % -10.13

Comments

Revenues have declined for three consecutive years. Most of the decrease reflects increased price competition because of excess liner manufacturing capacity in the marketplace. This had led to lower unit pricing and lower margins. Some of the decline is also reflective of currency fluctuations. 1995 results include $15,270,000 of nonrecurring restructuring charges related to manufacturing operations. At December 31, 1998, the Company had $26.9 million of goodwill recorded as assets which equated to approximately 30% of stockholders' equity and book value per share. But the trading price per share is still less than the tangible book value per share. Management finds these prices attractive and the Company bought back over 4 million shares of its stock in 1997 at an average price of $6.12 per share.

Officers	Position	Ownership Information	
Simar T. Badawi	President, CEO	Number of Shares Outstanding	13,127,647
Roger Klatt	CFO, Secretary	Market Capitalization	$ 52,510,588
Friedrich Struve	Vice President	Number of Shareholders	3,000
E. C. English	Vice President, Controller	Where Listed / Symbol	NYSE / GSE

Other Information			
Transfer Agent	ChaseMellon Shareholder Services Ridgefield Park, NJ	SIC Code	3081
Auditor	Ernst & Young LLP	Employees	581
		Web Site	gseworld.com

HEARx Ltd.

1250 Northpoint Parkway   West Palm Beach, FL 33407   Telephone (561)478-8770   Fax (561)478-9603

Company Description

HEARx Ltd. operates a network of hearing care centers which provide a full range of audiological products and services for the hearing impaired. The Company's strategy focuses on contracting with managed care and health insurance companies to provide to their members and beneficiaries with high quality hearing care. The Company utilizes state-of-the-art facilities with a full range of diagnostic and rehabilitative services, qualified professional staff and hearing education learning programs. The Company was founded in 1986.

	12/25/98	12/31/97	12/27/96	12/29/95
Per Share Information				
Stock Price as of 12/31	0.50	1.56	2.81	1.31
Earnings Per Share	-0.13	-0.12	-0.25	-0.05
Price / Earnings Ratio	n.a.	n.a.	n.a.	n.a.
Book Value Per Share	0.17	0.16	0.20	-0.12
Price / Book Value %	294.12	975.00	1,405.00	n.a.
Dividends Per Share	0.0	0.0	0.0	0.0
Annual Financial Data				
Operating Results (000's)				
Total Revenues	27,493.8	24,213.9	18,490.6	11,170.1
Costs & Expenses	-39,222.1	-33,417.9	-26,349.5	-13,383.5
Income Before Taxes and Other	-12,343.7	-9,204.0	-7,859.0	-2,213.5
Other Items	0.0	0.0	0.0	0.0
Income Tax	0.0	0.0	0.0	0.0
Net Income	-12,343.7	-9,204.0	-7,859.0	-2,213.5
Cash Flow From Operations	-9,119.9	-8,054.5	-6,431.1	-1,486.5
Balance Sheet (000's)				
Cash & Equivalents	2,650.1	3,644.8	1,811.4	933.5
Total Current Assets	15,278.0	18,019.7	17,378.4	3,086.9
Fixed Assets, Net	7,100.5	9,014.2	8,068.7	2,523.9
Total Assets	25,208.3	28,216.2	26,627.5	6,450.6
Total Current Liabilities	7,663.9	4,883.5	4,922.0	4,404.1
Long-Term Debt	123.3	177.9	230.3	2,316.3
Stockholders' Equity	17,421.1	23,154.7	21,475.2	-269.8
Performance & Financial Condition				
Return on Total Revenues %	-44.90	-38.01	-42.50	-19.82
Return on Avg Stockholders' Equity %	-60.84	-41.25	-74.12	n.a.
Return on Average Assets %	-46.21	-33.56	-47.52	-44.47
Current Ratio	1.99	3.69	3.53	0.70
Debt / Equity %	0.71	0.77	1.07	n.a.

Compound Growth %'s	EPS % n.a.	Net Income % n.a.	Total Revenues % 35.02

Comments

The Company continues to increase market share but operating losses remain substantial. Difficulties were experienced in the Northeast as a number of managed care companies decided to withdraw from that market. In order to reduce losses from this region, the Company closed 12 of its most severely impacted centers. On a positive note, sales were 35% higher in Florida and management claims that it is profitable at the center level. With a continual issuance of new shares, the balance sheet has remained strong. But after awhile, this becomes like printing money with no sound financial support. With over 100 million shares outstanding, HEARx will likely be a penny stock by this same time next year even if the Company makes a profit.

Officers	Position	Ownership Information	
Paul A. Brown	Chairman, CEO	Number of Shares Outstanding	103,618,332
Stephen J. Hansbrough	President, COO	Market Capitalization	$ 51,809,166
James W. Peklenk	Vice President, CFO	Number of Shareholders	28,926
Tommy E. Lee	Vice President, Secretary	Where Listed / Symbol	AMEX / EAR

Other Information			
Transfer Agent	Bank of New York New York, NY	SIC Code	8049
Auditor	BDO Seidman LLP	Employees	300
		Web Site	hearx.com

HIA, Inc.

4275 Forest Street   Denver, CO 80216   Telephone (303)394-6040   Fax (303)394-2667

Company Description

HIA, Inc. is a holding company which conducts all of its business conducted through its wholly-owned subsidiary, CPS Distributors, Inc.(CPS). The Company distributes turf irrigation equipment and commercial, industrial and residential well pumps and related equipment on a wholesale basis. CPS is a 90-year-old company based in Denver, Colorado, serving five states in the Rocky Mountain region. CPS carries a variety of brand name products, including pumps and water systems, water conditioning equipment, pump and well accessories, pipe valves and fittings and sprinkler system equipment.

	11/30/98	11/30/97	11/30/96	11/30/95
Per Share Information				
Stock Price as of 12/31	0.16	0.16	0.17	0.06
Earnings Per Share	0.04	0.04	0.05	0.03
Price / Earnings Ratio	4.00	4.00	3.40	2.00
Book Value Per Share	0.56	0.29	0.25	0.19
Price / Book Value %	28.57	55.17	68.00	31.58
Dividends Per Share	0.0	0.0	0.0	0.0
Annual Financial Data				
Operating Results (000's)				
Total Revenues	18,830.3	17,049.7	16,517.9	14,472.6
Costs & Expenses	-18,166.2	-16,444.8	-15,712.1	-13,834.0
Income Before Taxes and Other	664.2	604.9	805.8	638.6
Other Items	0.0	0.0	0.0	0.0
Income Tax	-246.2	-187.4	-268.1	-285.1
Net Income	417.9	417.6	537.7	353.5
Cash Flow From Operations	1,183.0	-502.3	258.0	-182.2
Balance Sheet (000's)				
Cash & Equivalents	29.9	15.3	141.6	115.1
Total Current Assets	3,955.6	4,338.5	3,864.9	3,426.8
Fixed Assets, Net	529.1	567.4	164.1	128.7
Total Assets	4,609.3	5,032.9	4,104.6	3,627.9
Total Current Liabilities	1,162.0	2,348.0	1,837.3	1,589.4
Long-Term Debt	0.0	0.0	0.0	0.0
Stockholders' Equity	3,160.1	2,684.9	2,267.4	2,038.5
Performance & Financial Condition				
Return on Total Revenues %	2.22	2.45	3.26	2.44
Return on Avg Stockholders' Equity %	14.30	16.86	24.97	17.89
Return on Average Assets %	8.67	9.14	13.91	10.73
Current Ratio	3.40	1.85	2.10	2.16
Debt / Equity %	n.a.	n.a.	n.a.	n.a.

Compound Growth %'s	EPS %	10.06	Net Income %	5.74	Total Revenues %	9.17

Comments

Fiscal 1998 was another year of record sales. Establishing a separate commercial division at the Denver administrative offices increased commercial irrigation sales by approximately $750,000. The remaining increase related to an across-the-board price increase of approximately 5%. Due to a very competitive labor market in the Rocky Mountain region, pay rate increases were higher than normal in order to attract and keep valuable employees. The end result was that profits were very similar to fiscal 1997. The Company is currently converting its computer systems to be year 2000 compliant, a project which it estimates will cost a total of $654,000. The Company's overall financial condition is excellent with plentiful working capital and no long term debt.

Officers	Position	Ownership Information	
Carl J. Bentley	Chairman	Number of Shares Outstanding	5,680,470
Alan C. Bergold	President, Treasurer	Market Capitalization	$ 908,875
Donald L. Champlin	Exec VP, Secretary	Number of Shareholders	2,000
		Where Listed / Symbol	OTC-BB / HIAI

Other Information			
Transfer Agent	American Securities Transfer, Inc. Denver, CO	SIC Code	5083
Auditor	BDO Seidman LLP	Employees	66
Market Maker	Paragon Capital Corporation	(212)785-4700	
	Herzog, Heine, Geduld, Inc.	(800)221-3600	

HMG Worldwide Corporation

475 Tenth Avenue New York, NY 10018 Telephone (212)736-2300 Fax (212)564-3395

Company Description

HMG Worldwide Corporation is one of the leading companies in the in-store marketing industry. The Company identifies the in-store marketing objectives of its clients and integrates research, creative design, engineering, production, package design and related services to provide point-of-purchase merchandising fixture and display systems intended to meet such objectives. The Company's merchandising systems are designed to increase retail sales by attracting and influencing consumers at the point of sale. The Company's merchandising systems are also designed to improve retail space utilization and product organization, facilitate retail inventory management and reduce retail labor costs. The Company was founded in 1984.

	12/31/98	12/31/97	12/31/96	12/31/95
Per Share Information				
Stock Price	1.97	1.25	1.06	2.75
Earnings Per Share	0.19	0.05	-0.73	-1.34
Price / Earnings Ratio	10.37	25.00	n.a.	n.a.
Book Value Per Share	0.97	0.73	0.64	1.33
Price / Book Value %	203.09	171.23	165.63	206.77
Dividends Per Share	0.0	0.0	0.0	0.0
Annual Financial Data				
Operating Results (000's)				
Total Revenues	68,744.0	46,634.0	45,903.0	48,219.0
Costs & Expenses	-66,809.0	-46,063.0	-51,426.0	-58,323.0
Income Before Taxes and Other	1,935.0	571.0	-5,523.0	-10,104.0
Other Items	0.0	0.0	0.0	0.0
Income Tax	-31.0	-42.0	-12.0	-14.0
Net Income	1,904.0	529.0	-5,535.0	-10,118.0
Cash Flow From Operations	-3,172.0	-3,309.0	-1,957.0	-7,680.0
Balance Sheet (000's)				
Cash & Equivalents	5,730.0	6,439.0	6,950.0	8,139.0
Total Current Assets	37,649.0	22,286.0	17,953.0	22,739.0
Fixed Assets, Net	6,319.0	4,682.0	3,349.0	2,143.0
Total Assets	51,729.0	33,645.0	28,755.0	32,648.0
Total Current Liabilities	36,845.0	22,712.0	21,189.0	20,115.0
Long-Term Debt	3,760.0	2,878.0	266.0	2,457.0
Stockholders' Equity	9,068.0	6,470.0	5,191.0	10,076.0
Performance & Financial Condition				
Return on Total Revenues %	2.77	1.13	-12.06	-20.98
Return on Avg Stockholders' Equity %	24.51	9.07	-72.51	-66.79
Return on Average Assets %	4.46	1.70	-18.03	-29.17
Current Ratio	1.02	0.98	0.85	1.13
Debt / Equity %	41.46	44.48	5.12	24.38

Compound Growth %'s	EPS % n.a.	Net Income % n.a.	Total Revenues % 12.55

Comments

The Company experienced a 47.8% increase in revenues during 1998. Approximately 54% of the increase was attributable to acquisitions and approximately 46% was the result of a more diversified client base along with the national roll out of several new retailer sponsored merchandising programs. Gross margins have significantly improved since 1996, reflecting the Company's efforts towards more direct, internal production of its merchandising systems, lower labor costs and the elimination of the Company's high cost New Jersey plant. At December 31, 1998, the Company had $7.5 million of goodwill recorded as assets which equated to approximately 83% of stockholders' equity and book value per share. Also at that date, the Company also had $34.6 million of tax loss carryovers available to offset future taxable income.

Officers	Position	Ownership Information	
Michael Wahl	Chairman, CEO	Number of Shares Outstanding	9,329,205
Andrew Wahl	President	Market Capitalization	$ 18,378,534
Robert V. Cuddihy, Jr.	COO, CFO	Number of Shareholders	1,325
L. Randy Riley	Exec VP	Where Listed / Symbol	NASDAQ / HMGC

Other Information			
Transfer Agent	American Stock Transfer & Trust Co. New York, NY	SIC Code	3990
Auditor	Friedman Alpren & Green LLP	Employees	425

Hadron, Inc.

4900 Seminary Road, Suite 800   Alexandria, VA 22311   Telephone (703)824-0400   Fax (703)824-8750

Company Description

Hadron, Inc., founded in 1966, provides a broad range of information, management and technical services to businesses and federal government agencies. The Company specializes in the fields of trusted/secure computer systems and intelligent weapons systems product development. During the last few years, the Company has implemented a turnaround program, including cost reductions and aggressive new business development, intended to increase profitability. Let's take a look at the numbers below:

	06/30/98	06/30/97	06/30/96	06/30/95
Per Share Information				
Stock Price as of 12/31	1.62	1.88	0.66	0.56
Earnings Per Share	0.26	0.01	0.11	1.51
Price / Earnings Ratio	6.23	188.00	6.00	0.37
Book Value Per Share	0.01	-0.48	-0.58	-0.70
Price / Book Value %	16,200.00	n.a.	n.a.	n.a.
Dividends Per Share	0.0	0.0	0.0	0.0
Annual Financial Data				
Operating Results (000's)				
Total Revenues	21,139.4	16,987.7	18,440.0	20,555.0
Costs & Expenses	-20,307.3	-16,260.9	-18,246.4	-20,933.6
Income Before Taxes and Other	819.1	56.9	193.6	-436.3
Other Items	0.0	0.0	0.0	2,718.4
Income Tax	-58.5	-44.0	-31.9	-23.7
Net Income	760.6	12.9	161.7	2,258.4
Cash Flow From Operations	-53.6	166.8	214.4	306.9
Balance Sheet (000's)				
Cash & Equivalents	60.5	24.7	43.9	640.6
Total Current Assets	3,245.5	2,447.6	2,769.5	4,100.2
Fixed Assets, Net	116.3	82.8	96.8	181.0
Total Assets	3,507.0	2,711.9	2,874.4	4,372.6
Total Current Liabilities	3,431.6	3,353.4	3,423.6	5,078.9
Long-Term Debt	53.4	120.0	275.0	341.2
Stockholders' Equity	22.0	-810.8	-869.5	-1,047.5
Performance & Financial Condition				
Return on Total Revenues %	3.60	0.08	0.88	10.99
Return on Avg Stockholders' Equity %	n.a.	n.a.	n.a.	n.a.
Return on Average Assets %	24.46	0.46	4.46	47.75
Current Ratio	0.95	0.73	0.81	0.81
Debt / Equity %	242.73	n.a.	n.a.	n.a.

Compound Growth %'s	EPS % n.a.	Net Income % n.a.	Total Revenues % 0.94

Comments

The increase in 1998 revenues was attributable to growth on existing contracts. The healthy profit eliminated the net capital deficiency, allowing the auditors to give an unqualified opinion for the first time in years. Fiscal 1995 results included a nonrecurring gain of $2.7 million, ($1.82 per share) resulting from the retirement of debt. Accordingly, compound growth rates in earnings and earnings per share were not displayed. For the six months ended December 31, 1998, revenues and net income were $9.8 million and $143,200 ($.05 per share) as compared to $10.1 million and $274,200 ($.10 per share) for the same period of the preceding year.

Officers	Position	Ownership Information	
C. W. Gilluly	Chairman, CEO	Number of Shares Outstanding	1,731,956
Donald E. Ziegler	CFO	Market Capitalization	$ 2,805,769
William J. Howard	Director	Number of Shareholders	3,842
Robert J. Lynch, Jr.	Director	Where Listed / Symbol	OTC-BB / HDRN

Other Information			
Transfer Agent	American Stock Transfer & Trust Co. New York, NY	SIC Code	7370
Auditor	Ernst & Young LLP	Employees	240
Market Maker	Carr Securities Corporation (800)221-2243	Web Site	hadron.com
	Pennsylvania Merchant Group (800)762-8624		

Hahn Automotive Warehouse, Inc.

415 West Main Street   Rochester, NY 14608   Telephone (716)235-1595   Fax (716)235-3286

Company Description

Hahn Automotive Warehouse, Inc. is engaged in the sale of automotive aftermarket products to commercial service establishments on a regional basis. The Company's business is conducted through ten full-service distribution centers, nine direct distribution centers and 82 jobber stores that operate in the same areas as the Company's full-service distribution centers, generally under the name Advantage Auto Stores. The Company's operations are located along the Eastern Seaboard and in the Midwest. Until the third quarter of fiscal 1997, the Company's AUTOWORKS, Inc. subsidiary was also engaged in the retail sale of automotive aftermarket products. The Company decided to exit the retail business due to negative cash flow and ongoing losses in that business. Hahn Automotive was founded in 1958.

	09/30/98	09/30/97	09/30/96	09/30/95
Per Share Information				
Stock Price as of 12/31	2.12	5.87	8.00	5.75
Earnings Per Share	0.22	-4.45	0.39	-0.30
Price / Earnings Ratio	9.64	n.a.	20.51	n.a.
Book Value Per Share	2.86	2.61	7.34	7.21
Price / Book Value %	74.13	224.90	108.99	79.75
Dividends Per Share	0.0	0.0	0.0	0.0
Annual Financial Data				
Operating Results (000's)				
Total Revenues	133,914.0	142,961.0	138,995.0	224,898.0
Costs & Expenses	-132,210.0	-140,359.0	-133,892.0	-226,645.0
Income Before Taxes and Other	1,704.0	2,602.0	5,103.0	-1,747.0
Other Items	0.0	-22,726.0	-1,294.0	0.0
Income Tax	-665.0	-1,011.0	-1,950.0	370.0
Net Income	1,039.0	-21,135.0	1,859.0	-1,377.0
Cash Flow From Operations	2,445.0	7,144.0	3,084.0	-2,548.0
Balance Sheet (000's)				
Cash & Equivalents	329.0	632.0	199.0	205.0
Total Current Assets	63,317.0	65,005.0	91,296.0	93,201.0
Fixed Assets, Net	7,613.0	5,062.0	13,362.0	15,269.0
Total Assets	78,311.0	77,792.0	108,958.0	110,480.0
Total Current Liabilities	20,819.0	19,520.0	34,566.0	37,472.0
Long-Term Debt	35,190.0	37,455.0	40,443.0	40,476.0
Stockholders' Equity	13,561.0	12,364.0	33,499.0	31,640.0
Performance & Financial Condition				
Return on Total Revenues %	0.78	-14.78	1.34	-0.61
Return on Avg Stockholders' Equity %	8.02	-92.17	5.71	-4.17
Return on Average Assets %	1.33	-22.63	1.69	-1.25
Current Ratio	3.04	3.33	2.64	2.49
Debt / Equity %	259.49	302.94	120.73	127.93

Compound Growth %'s	EPS %	-24.89	Net Income %	-25.24	Total Revenues %	n.a.

Comments

Fiscal 1997 and 1996 results include losses related to discontinued operations of $22.7 million ($4.45 per share) and $1.3 million ($.27 per share), respectively. Fiscal 1995 revenues include sales from discontinued operations. Accordingly, the compound growth in revenues was not presented. Earnings from ongoing operations declined to $.22 per share, down from $.34 per share and $.66 per share in fiscal 1997 and 1996, respectively. The decreases are generally attributable to softness in the auto parts industry. The reorganization and large loss in fiscal 1997 has brought the stock price to a number below book value. However, continuing profitability will be the key to the franchise value of the Company. Although working capital is plentiful, there remains a large long term debt.

Officers	Position	Ownership Information	
Michael Futerman	President, CEO	Number of Shares Outstanding	4,745,014
Eli N. Futerman	Exec VP	Market Capitalization	$ 10,059,430
Peter J. Adamski	VP - Finance, CFO	Number of Shareholders	1,000
Daniel J. Chessin	Director	Where Listed / Symbol	NASDAQ / HAHN

Other Information			
Transfer Agent	American Stock Transfer & Trust Co. New York, NY	SIC Code	5013
Auditor	PricewaterhouseCoopers LLP	Employees	1,216

Halter Marine Group, Inc.

13085 Seaway Road   Gulfport, MS 39503   Telephone (228)896-0029   Fax (228)897-4828

Company Description

Halter Marine Group, Inc. is a provider of design, construction, conversion, and repair services for offshore drilling rigs, vessels, and engineered products servicing the offshore energy, government and commercial markets. The Company, which conducts its operations in three business segments (Vessels, Rigs, and Engineered Products), meets its customer requirements through multiple production facilities and a current workforce of more than 7,400 skilled employees. The Company is the fourth largest shipbuilder and the largest builder of small to medium sized ocean-going vessels in the United States. The Company was founded in 1958 and had its initial public offering in fiscal 1996.

	03/31/98	03/31/97	03/31/96	03/31/95
Per Share Information				
Stock Price as of 12/31	4.87	28.87	8.00	n.a.
Earnings Per Share	0.78	0.59	0.46	0.58
Price / Earnings Ratio	6.24	48.93	17.39	n.a.
Book Value Per Share	5.24	3.37	2.47	2.01
Price / Book Value %	92.94	856.68	323.89	n.a.
Dividends Per Share	0.0	0.0	0.0	0.0
Annual Financial Data				
Operating Results (000's)				
Total Revenues	670,238.0	406,797.0	254,294.0	250,586.0
Costs & Expenses	-638,525.0	-379,794.0	-233,727.0	-224,708.0
Income Before Taxes and Other	31,713.0	27,003.0	20,567.0	25,878.0
Other Items	0.0	0.0	0.0	0.0
Income Tax	-9,197.0	-10,887.0	-8,102.0	-10,170.0
Net Income	22,516.0	16,116.0	12,465.0	15,708.0
Cash Flow From Operations	38,324.0	12,488.0	23,742.0	16,000.0
Balance Sheet (000's)				
Cash & Equivalents	51,146.0	7,079.0	672.0	524.0
Total Current Assets	272,580.0	147,677.0	86,232.0	85,848.0
Fixed Assets, Net	125,962.0	61,449.0	55,142.0	38,423.0
Total Assets	499,601.0	209,411.0	141,374.0	124,271.0
Total Current Liabilities	121,523.0	59,246.0	49,631.0	44,993.0
Long-Term Debt	218,215.0	52,000.0	25,000.0	25,000.0
Stockholders' Equity	151,103.0	93,301.0	66,743.0	54,278.0
Performance & Financial Condition				
Return on Total Revenues %	3.36	3.96	4.90	6.27
Return on Avg Stockholders' Equity %	18.43	20.14	20.60	33.84
Return on Average Assets %	6.35	9.19	9.38	12.82
Current Ratio	2.24	2.49	1.74	1.91
Debt / Equity %	144.41	55.73	37.46	46.06

Compound Growth %'s	EPS %	10.38	Net Income %	12.75	Total Revenues %	38.81

Comments

The Company declared a 3 for 2 stock split in October 1997. All per share amounts have been restated for consistency. Since fiscal 1995, the Company has acquired ten different companies for an aggregate purchase price of approximately $152 million. Acquisitions have accounted for most of the revenue growth. At March 31, 1998, the Company had $92.1 million of intangible assets on its books which equated to approximately 61% of stockholders' equity and book value per share. For the nine months ended December 31, 1998, the Company reported revenues and net income of $759.8 million and $11.8 million ($.41 per share) as compared to $480.8 million and $22.0 million ($.76 per share) for the same period of fiscal 1998.

Officers	Position	Ownership Information	
John Dane III	President, CEO	Number of Shares Outstanding	28,822,000
Daniel J. Mortimer	Exec VP, COO	Market Capitalization	$ 140,363,140
Rick S. Rees	Exec VP, CFO	Number of Shareholders	10,000
Richard T. McCreary	Senior VP	Where Listed / Symbol	AMEX / HLX

Other Information			
Transfer Agent	Bank of New York New York, NY	SIC Code	3730
Auditor	Ernst & Young LLP	Employees	6,744
		Web Site	haltermarine.com

Hawaiian Airlines, Inc.

3375 Koapaka Street, Suite G-350   Honolulu, HI 96819   Telephone (808)835-3700   Fax (808)835-3690

Company Description

Aloha! Hawaiian Airlines, Inc., founded in 1929, is the largest airline headquartered in Hawaii and is engaged primarily in the scheduled transportation of passengers, cargo and mail. The Company's passenger airline business is its chief source of revenue. Scheduled passenger service consists of, on average and depending on seasonality, approximately 130 to 150 flights per day among the six major islands of Hawaii, daily service to Las Vegas and four key West Coast gateway cities, twice weekly service to Pago Pago, and weekly service to Tahiti. The Company operates a fleet of 14 DC-9 aircraft and 11 DC-10 aircraft.

	12/31/98	12/31/97	12/31/96	12/31/95
Per Share Information				
Stock Price	3.25	3.81	3.38	2.31
Earnings Per Share	0.19	-0.03	-0.05	-0.59
Price / Earnings Ratio	17.11	n.a.	n.a.	n.a.
Book Value Per Share	2.22	2.14	2.13	1.55
Price / Book Value %	146.40	178.04	158.69	149.03
Dividends Per Share	0.0	0.0	0.0	0.0
Annual Financial Data				
Operating Results (000's)				
Total Revenues	428,054.0	404,216.0	384,473.0	346,904.0
Costs & Expenses	-412,046.0	-403,068.0	-385,904.0	-352,410.0
Income Before Taxes and Other	16,008.0	1,148.0	-1,431.0	-5,506.0
Other Items	0.0	-450.0	766.0	0.0
Income Tax	-7,803.0	-1,720.0	-868.0	0.0
Net Income	8,205.0	-1,022.0	-1,533.0	-5,506.0
Cash Flow From Operations	30,193.0	4,087.0	999.0	18,788.0
Balance Sheet (000's)				
Cash & Equivalents	31,011.0	15,713.0	37,237.0	5,389.0
Total Current Assets	81,907.0	66,141.0	78,498.0	38,363.0
Fixed Assets, Net	84,922.0	66,243.0	45,794.0	46,434.0
Total Assets	221,911.0	200,824.0	196,289.0	161,640.0
Total Current Liabilities	75,677.0	70,194.0	70,105.0	90,062.0
Long-Term Debt	14,454.0	3,991.0	6,353.0	6,000.0
Stockholders' Equity	90,887.0	86,873.0	82,873.0	29,178.0
Performance & Financial Condition				
Return on Total Revenues %	1.92	-0.25	-0.40	-1.59
Return on Avg Stockholders' Equity %	9.23	-1.20	-2.74	n.a.
Return on Average Assets %	3.88	-0.51	-0.86	-3.24
Current Ratio	1.08	0.94	1.12	0.43
Debt / Equity %	15.90	4.59	7.67	20.56

Compound Growth %'s	EPS % n.a.	Net Income % n.a.	Total Revenues % 7.26

Comments

The Company emerged from Chapter 11 bankruptcy on September 12, 1994. Under fresh start reporting, the reorganization value of the entity was allocated to identifiable assets and liabilities. The reorganization value in excess of identifiable assets is an intangible asset and totalled $46.9 million on December 31, 1998, which equates to approximately 52% of stockholders' equity and book value per share. Management attributes the improvement in net earnings to the increase in operating revenues while overall costs were kept to a 2% increase. Ever wonder what all those bonus miles are worth? The Company booked a $1.1 million accrued expense to satisfy 3.7 billion accumulated miles. Therefore, the Company values 10,000 miles at $30.

Officers	Position	Ownership Information	
Paul J. Casey	President, CEO	Number of Shares Outstanding	40,997,335
John L. Garibaldi	Exec VP, CFO	Market Capitalization	$ 133,241,339
John B. Happ	Senior VP	Number of Shareholders	10,000
Ruthann S. Yamanaka	Senior VP	Where Listed / Symbol	AMEX / HA

Other Information			
Transfer Agent	ChaseMellon Shareholder Services Los Angeles, CA	SIC Code	4700
Auditor	KPMG LLP	Employees	2,577
		Web Site	hawaiianair.com

Hawker Pacific Aerospace

11240 Sherman Way   Sun Valley, CA 91352   Telephone (818)765-6201   Fax (818)765-8073

Company Description

Hawker Pacific Aerospace repairs and overhauls aircraft and helicopter landing gear, hydromechanical components and wells, brakes and braking system components for a diverse international customer base, including commercial airlines, air cargo operators, domestic government agencies, aircraft leasing companies, aircraft parts distributors and original equipment manufacturers. In addition, the Company distributes and sells new and overhauled spare parts and components for both fixed wing aircraft and helicopters. During the year ended December 31, 1998, the Company had in excess of 500 customers, several of which have entered into long-term service contracts with the Company, including Federal Express Corporation, American Airlines, Inc., the United States Coast Guard, and US Airways, Inc. On February 4, 1998, the Company completed its acquisition of substantially all of the assets of the landing gear repair and overhaul operations of British Airways plc. The Company had its initial public offering in February 1998.

	12/31/98	12/31/97	12/31/96	12/31/95
Per Share Information				
Stock Price	3.62	8.00	n.a.	n.a.
Earnings Per Share	-0.39	0.25	0.15	0.09
Price / Earnings Ratio	n.a.	32.00	n.a.	n.a.
Book Value Per Share	3.50	1.45	0.87	-0.32
Price / Book Value %	103.43	551.72	n.a.	n.a.
Dividends Per Share	0.0	0.0	0.0	0.0
Annual Financial Data				
Operating Results (000's)				
Total Revenues	65,225.0	41,045.0	39,011.0	35,012.0
Costs & Expenses	-68,225.0	-39,758.0	-40,737.0	-35,428.0
Income Before Taxes and Other	-3,000.0	1,255.0	-1,726.0	-416.0
Other Items	-600.0	0.0	0.0	0.0
Income Tax	1,402.0	-467.0	589.0	680.0
Net Income	-2,198.0	788.0	-1,137.0	264.0
Cash Flow From Operations	-3,095.0	3,000.0	2,049.0	-4,223.0
Balance Sheet (000's)				
Cash & Equivalents	560.0	160.0	1,055.0	399.0
Total Current Assets	35,239.0	22,645.0	20,744.0	22,351.0
Fixed Assets, Net	9,298.0	16,150.0	13,373.0	12,350.0
Total Assets	87,237.0	40,898.0	35,178.0	35,455.0
Total Current Liabilities	64,334.0	18,901.0	13,519.0	9,062.0
Long-Term Debt	0.0	11,200.0	12,650.0	0.0
Stockholders' Equity	20,403.0	4,297.0	2,509.0	-917.0
Performance & Financial Condition				
Return on Total Revenues %	-3.37	1.92	-2.91	0.75
Return on Avg Stockholders' Equity %	-17.80	23.16	-142.84	37.71
Return on Average Assets %	-3.43	2.07	-3.22	0.75
Current Ratio	0.55	1.20	1.53	2.47
Debt / Equity %	n.a.	260.65	504.18	n.a.

Compound Growth %'s	EPS %	n.a.	Net Income %	n.a.	Total Revenues %	23.05

Comments

Revenue increased 59% in 1998. The 1998 acquisition was credited with 60% of the increase while the remaining 40% was internal growth. The 1998 net loss was blamed on higher costs of the acquired company which had not yet been reorganized more efficiently. Included in 1998 results is a nonrecurring $600,000 expense related to the early extinguishment of debt. Through October 1996, the Company was a subsidiary of BTR Dunlop Holdings. Earnings per share reflected above for 1996 are for the two months ended December 31, 1996. At December 31, 1998, the Company had a substantial deficit in working capital and was in default of certain loan covenants. The primary lender has since placed additional controls on the Company.

Officers	Position	Ownership Information	
Scott W. Hartman	Chairman	Number of Shares Outstanding	5,822,222
David L. Lokken	President, CEO	Market Capitalization	$ 21,076,444
Daniel J. Lubeck	Secretary, Director	Number of Shareholders	1,371
Brian S. Aune	Vice President, CFO	Where Listed / Symbol	NASDAQ / HPAC

Other Information			
Transfer Agent	U.S. Stock Transfer Corp. Glendale, CA	SIC Code	3728
Auditor	Ernst & Young LLP	Employees	453
		Web Site	hawker.com

Health Fitness Corporation

3500 West 80th Street, Suite 130 Minneapolis, MN 55431 Telephone (612)831-6830 Fax (612)831-7264

Company Description

Health Fitness Corporation has been engaged in two principal lines of business: preventive and rehabilitative healthcare. Preventative healthcare includes the development, marketing, and management of corporate and hospital-based fitness centers, and the selling of fitness equipment, services and fitness related-soft goods such as shirts, hats, and other items. Rehabilitative healthcare relates to the operation of physical therapy clinics that provide a full range of rehabilitation services and the operation of a national network of independent physical therapy clinics. The Company decided to discontinue its involvement in the operation of the physical therapy clinics and has placed them for sale. The original predecessor business of the Company was founded in 1981.

	12/31/98	12/31/97	12/31/96	12/31/95
Per Share Information				
Stock Price	0.62	1.50	2.87	2.25
Earnings Per Share	-0.72	-0.13	0.14	-0.04
Price / Earnings Ratio	n.a.	n.a.	20.50	n.a.
Book Value Per Share	0.49	1.25	1.38	1.15
Price / Book Value %	126.53	120.00	207.97	195.65
Dividends Per Share	0.0	0.0	0.0	0.0
Annual Financial Data				
Operating Results (000's)				
Total Revenues	25,752.9	33,693.0	28,540.6	17,943.1
Costs & Expenses	-26,644.2	-34,739.7	-27,535.0	-18,155.1
Income Before Taxes and Other	-891.3	-1,046.7	1,005.6	-212.0
Other Items	-7,167.8	0.0	0.0	0.0
Income Tax	-50.0	0.0	0.0	0.0
Net Income	-8,109.1	-1,046.7	1,005.6	-212.0
Cash Flow From Operations	-1,667.4	-838.0	1,194.8	-163.3
Balance Sheet (000's)				
Cash & Equivalents	29.6	81.6	0.0	506.7
Total Current Assets	5,474.1	7,928.7	5,544.5	4,890.6
Fixed Assets, Net	1,049.6	3,598.2	2,185.3	807.4
Total Assets	20,614.8	23,732.3	18,178.9	14,283.6
Total Current Liabilities	13,870.6	7,767.7	7,630.1	6,286.5
Long-Term Debt	900.1	5,785.0	576.5	474.1
Stockholders' Equity	5,844.1	10,148.4	9,892.1	7,398.9
Performance & Financial Condition				
Return on Total Revenues %	-31.49	-3.11	3.52	-1.18
Return on Avg Stockholders' Equity %	-101.41	-10.45	11.63	-3.69
Return on Average Assets %	-36.57	-4.99	6.20	-2.03
Current Ratio	0.39	1.02	0.73	0.78
Debt / Equity %	15.40	57.00	5.83	6.41

Compound Growth %'s	EPS % n.a.	Net Income % n.a.	Total Revenues % 12.80

Comments

The operations of the physical therapy clinics have been reported as a discontinued operation since September 1998. 1998 results include a $7.2 million charge ($.63 per share) for discontinued operations including $5.3 million in asset write downs. The fitness center business continues to grow with 20 new corporate and hospital sites added during 1998. But management is going to have to scramble as 1998 closed with a significant working capital deficiency. At December 31, 1998, the Company also had $9.0 million of intangible assets on its books which equated to approximately 154% of stockholders' equity and book value per share. On April 8, 1999, the Company announced that it had engaged a management advisory firm to assist the Company in its restructuring efforts.

Officers	Position	Ownership Information	
Loren S. Brink	President, CEO	Number of Shares Outstanding	11,884,413
Dennis Colacino	Exec VP	Market Capitalization	$ 7,368,336
Charles E. Bidwell	CFO, Treasurer	Number of Shareholders	472
Michael P. Wise	Vice President, Controller	Where Listed / Symbol	NASDAQ / HFIT

Other Information			
Transfer Agent	American Securities Transfer, Inc. Lakewood, CO	SIC Code	8090
Auditor	Grant Thornton LLP	Employees	592

HealthStar Corp.

8745 West Higgins, Suite 300   Chicago, IL 60631   Telephone (773)693-7827   Fax (773)693-7828

Company Description

HealthStar Corp., formerly Champion Financial Corporation (Champion), is a health care management company dedicated to controlling the costs, improving the quality and enhancing the delivery of health care services. The Company also provides related products and services designed to reduce health care costs. The Company markets and provides programs and services to insurance companies, self-insured businesses for their medical plans, health and welfare funds and third parties who administer employee medical plans. Prior to 1997, the Champion was primarily an inactive corporation. On December 15, 1997, Champion acquired all of the outstanding stock of HealthStar, Inc. for $13.7 million. HealthStar, Inc. is a diversified healthcare and financial services company with over 14 years experience in the formulation and management of preferred provider organizations.

	03/31/98	03/31/97	03/31/96
Per Share Information			
Stock Price as of 12/31	3.12	20.50	10.74
Earnings Per Share	0.10	0.06	0.14
Price / Earnings Ratio	31.20	341.67	76.71
Book Value Per Share	1.71	0.04	0.01
Price / Book Value %	182.46	51,250.00	107,400.00
Dividends Per Share	0.0	0.0	0.0
Annual Financial Data			
Operating Results (000's)			
Total Revenues	7,854.0	2,286.2	1,286.0
Costs & Expenses	-7,365.6	-2,167.8	-1,136.5
Income Before Taxes and Other	488.4	118.4	149.5
Other Items	0.0	0.0	0.0
Income Tax	-184.3	-15.0	0.0
Net Income	304.1	103.4	149.5
Cash Flow From Operations	-583.3	334.3	117.7
Balance Sheet (000's)			
Cash & Equivalents	199.5	896.1	0.5
Total Current Assets	2,781.0	1,161.3	0.8
Fixed Assets, Net	2,852.0	158.1	71.5
Total Assets	15,448.7	1,409.2	76.7
Total Current Liabilities	4,033.4	440.6	47.7
Long-Term Debt	6,100.0	0.0	19.5
Stockholders' Equity	5,015.2	968.6	9.5
Performance & Financial Condition			
Return on Total Revenues %	3.87	4.52	11.63
Return on Avg Stockholders' Equity %	10.16	21.13	149.54
Return on Average Assets %	3.61	13.91	74.77
Current Ratio	0.69	2.64	0.02
Debt / Equity %	121.63	n.a.	205.01

Compound Growth %'s	EPS %	-15.48	Net Income %	42.61	Total Revenues %	147.13

Comments

The Company executed a 1 for 2 reverse split in 1998. All per share amounts have been restated for consistency. The increase in the level of revenues and expenses is due primarily to the acquisition of HealthStar. The transaction was accounted for as a purchase. The financial results of HealthStar for 15 weeks are included in fiscal 1998 results. Approximately $9 million of goodwill was recorded on the transaction which equates to approximately 180% of the Company's stockholders' equity and book value per share. For the nine months ended December 31, 1998, revenues and net income were $13.6 million and $99,420 ($.03 per share) as compared to $2.1 million and a loss of $37,555 ($.01 per share) in the same period of the prior year.

Officers	Position	Ownership Information	
Gerald E. Finnell	Chairman, Director	Number of Shares Outstanding	2,927,901
Stephen J. Carder	President, CEO	Market Capitalization	$ 9,135,051
Darren Horndash	Vice President, COO	Number of Shareholders	1,750
Denise Nedza	Vice President, CFO	Where Listed / Symbol	OTC-BB / CPFC

Other Information			
Transfer Agent	Atlas Stock Transfer Corp. Salt Lake City, UT	SIC Code	8090
Auditor	KPMG LLP	Employees	257
Market Maker	Comprehensive Capital Corp.	(800)338-3014	Web Site	healthstarinc.com
	Paragon Capital Corporation	(800)345-0505		

Healthcare Imaging Services, Inc.

200 Schulz Drive   Red Bank, NJ 07701   Telephone (732)224-9292   Fax (732)224-9329

Company Description

HealthCare Imaging Services, Inc. is engaged in the business of establishing and operating fixed-site magnetic resonance imaging (MRI) centers. MRI involves the utilization of high strength magnetic fields and applied radio waves to provide cross sectional images of the anatomy. MRI has become a preferred diagnostic tool of the medical profession because its images are generally better defined and more precise than those produced by other diagnostic tests, without the use of harmful ionizing radiation. In 1998, the Company also expanded into the field of physician practice management. The Company was founded in 1991.

	12/31/98	12/31/97	12/31/96	12/31/95
Per Share Information				
Stock Price	1.16	1.00	0.88	1.18
Earnings Per Share	0.10	-0.13	-0.18	-0.03
Price / Earnings Ratio	11.60	n.a.	n.a.	n.a.
Book Value Per Share	1.48	0.51	0.52	0.35
Price / Book Value %	78.38	196.08	169.23	337.14
Dividends Per Share	0.0	0.0	0.0	0.0
Annual Financial Data				
Operating Results (000's)				
Total Revenues	16,451.1	10,247.9	9,787.6	9,249.3
Costs & Expenses	-13,712.5	-10,579.0	-10,183.8	-9,216.1
Income Before Taxes and Other	2,738.6	-331.1	-396.3	33.2
Other Items	-479.2	-430.2	-416.2	-293.9
Income Tax	-97.7	-43.0	-49.3	142.3
Net Income	2,161.8	-804.3	-861.8	-118.4
Cash Flow From Operations	1,457.6	1,045.9	1,761.9	3,257.8
Balance Sheet (000's)				
Cash & Equivalents	1,506.1	70.6	173.9	281.0
Total Current Assets	18,808.4	5,632.1	5,287.5	4,212.0
Fixed Assets, Net	9,578.8	5,518.8	4,347.7	5,272.0
Total Assets	42,954.7	13,540.6	10,566.7	10,006.0
Total Current Liabilities	20,868.1	4,479.4	2,344.1	3,053.0
Long-Term Debt	0.0	0.0	2,141.6	2,974.0
Stockholders' Equity	17,749.3	5,412.9	5,004.8	3,222.0
Performance & Financial Condition				
Return on Total Revenues %	13.14	-7.85	-8.80	-1.28
Return on Avg Stockholders' Equity %	18.67	-15.44	-20.95	-3.61
Return on Average Assets %	7.65	-6.67	-8.38	-0.99
Current Ratio	0.90	1.26	2.26	1.38
Debt / Equity %	n.a.	n.a.	42.79	92.30

Compound Growth %'s	EPS % n.a.	Net Income % n.a.	Total Revenues % 21.16

Comments

Approximately two-thirds of the 61% increase in revenues recorded in 1998 was attributable to acquisitions with the remaining one-third coming from an increase in same facility revenue. Management was pleased to report its first net earnings for an entire year. At December 31, 1998, the Company had $12.9 million of goodwill recorded as assets which equated to approximately 72% of stockholders' equity and book value per share. The Company also had $4.4 million of tax loss carryovers available to offset future taxable income. But first it will have to deal with a $2 million working capital deficiency as of the last year end. Management believes that refinancing corporate debt will solve the problem.

Officers	Position	Ownership Information	
Elliott H. Vernon	President, CEO	Number of Shares Outstanding	11,356,974
Michael J. Rutkin	COO, Secretary	Market Capitalization	$ 13,174,090
Scott P. McGrory	Vice President, Controller	Number of Shareholders	1,200
Lee H. Turner	Vice President	Where Listed / Symbol	NASDAQ / HISS

Other Information			
Transfer Agent	American Stock Transfer & Trust Co. New York, NY	SIC Code	8071
Auditor	Deloitte & Touche LLP	Employees	136
Market Maker	Sharpe Capital Inc. (800)355-5781		

HemaCare Corporation

4954 Van Nuys Boulevard   Sherman Oaks, CA 91403   Telephone (818)986-3883   Fax (818)986-1417

Company Description

HemaCare Corporation, founded in 1978, provides blood products and services, including apheresis platelet and whole blood component products, therapeutic apheresis and donor testing services, to healthcare institutions in southern California. Operations in Missouri and Illinois were discontinued in 1997. HemaCare was the first publicly traded company in the $2 billion U.S. blood industry to be licensed by the Food and Drug Administration and accredited by the American Association of Blood Banks.

	12/31/98	12/31/97	12/31/96	12/31/95
Per Share Information				
Stock Price	0.46	0.44	2.88	3.50
Earnings Per Share	0.10	0.05	-0.08	-0.60
Price / Earnings Ratio	4.60	8.80	n.a.	n.a.
Book Value Per Share	0.45	0.33	0.28	0.21
Price / Book Value %	102.22	133.33	1,028.57	1,666.67
Dividends Per Share	0.0	0.0	0.0	0.0
Annual Financial Data				
Operating Results (000's)				
Total Revenues	13,124.0	11,229.0	10,921.0	10,783.0
Costs & Expenses	-12,356.0	-11,192.0	-12,011.0	-10,303.0
Income Before Taxes and Other	768.0	37.0	-1,090.0	480.0
Other Items	0.0	293.0	600.0	-4,016.0
Income Tax	-23.0	0.0	0.0	0.0
Net Income	745.0	330.0	-490.0	-3,536.0
Cash Flow From Operations	158.0	240.0	-458.0	-342.0
Balance Sheet (000's)				
Cash & Equivalents	1,372.0	1,249.0	1,136.0	997.0
Total Current Assets	5,573.0	3,724.0	3,814.0	3,224.0
Fixed Assets, Net	1,289.0	585.0	823.0	1,051.0
Total Assets	7,662.0	4,384.0	4,776.0	4,456.0
Total Current Liabilities	3,229.0	1,773.0	2,250.0	1,981.0
Long-Term Debt	491.0	0.0	0.0	0.0
Stockholders' Equity	3,291.0	2,402.0	2,023.0	1,226.0
Performance & Financial Condition				
Return on Total Revenues %	5.68	2.94	-4.49	-32.79
Return on Avg Stockholders' Equity %	26.17	14.92	-30.16	-137.96
Return on Average Assets %	12.37	7.21	-10.62	-88.40
Current Ratio	1.73	2.10	1.70	1.63
Debt / Equity %	14.92	n.a.	n.a.	n.a.

Compound Growth %'s	EPS % n.a.	Net Income % n.a.	Total Revenues % 6.77

Comments

Approximately 65% of the 18% increase in 1998 revenues resulted from acquisitions with the balance coming from internal growth. Operating results improved for two consecutive years which was attributable to improved performance of blood management programs and decreased sales of low profit margin whole blood components. 1997 and 1996 results include $293,000 and $600,000 in gains from discontinued operations which equates to $.04 per share and $.09 per share, respectively. 1995 results include losses of $4,016,000 from discontinued operations which equates to $.68 per share. At December 31, 1998, the Company had only $742,000 of intangible assets on its books but this did equate to 22.5% of stockholders' equity and book value per share.

Officers	Position	Ownership Information	
Alan C. Darlington	Chairman	Number of Shares Outstanding	7,281,120
Hal I. Lieberman	President, CEO	Market Capitalization	$ 3,349,315
Sharon C. Kaiser	Senior VP, CFO	Number of Shareholders	1,000
Charles R. Schwab, Jr.	Director	Where Listed / Symbol	OTC-BB / HEMA

Other Information			
Transfer Agent	U.S. Stock Transfer Corp. Glendale, CA	SIC Code	8090
Auditor	Arthur Andersen LLP	Employees	81
Market Maker	Gruntal & Co. Inc. (800)223-7632	Web Site	hemacare.com
	Fahnestock & Co., Inc. (800)223-3012		

Hemagen Diagnostics, Inc.

34-40 Bear Hill Road   Waltham, MA 02154   Telephone (781)890-3766   Fax (781)890-3748

Company Description

Hemagen Diagnostics, Inc. develops, manufactures and markets proprietary medical diagnostic test kits, or assays, used to aid in the diagnosis of autoimmune and infectious diseases, in general health assessment, and for research purposes. The Company also develops, manufactures and markets materials for the manufacture of such diagnostic test kits. Autoimmune diseases are diseases in which the immune system mistakenly identifies the body's cells and tissues as foreign and attempts to destroy them. Rheumatoid arthritis is an example of an autoimmune disease. The Company offers approximately 135 test kits that have been cleared by the Food and Drug Administration for sale in the United States.

	09/30/98	09/30/97	09/30/96	09/30/95
Per Share Information				
Stock Price as of 12/31	0.71	2.00	2.44	2.50
Earnings Per Share	0.0	0.05	-0.08	-0.31
Price / Earnings Ratio	n.a.	40.00	n.a.	n.a.
Book Value Per Share	1.29	1.29	1.24	0.59
Price / Book Value %	55.04	155.04	196.77	423.73
Dividends Per Share	0.0	0.0	0.0	0.0
Annual Financial Data				
Operating Results (000's)				
Total Revenues	12,408.1	13,036.5	10,317.3	4,082.1
Costs & Expenses	-12,329.1	-12,615.9	-10,781.3	-5,067.0
Income Before Taxes and Other	10.4	405.1	-464.0	-984.9
Other Items	0.0	0.0	0.0	0.0
Income Tax	0.0	0.0	0.0	0.0
Net Income	10.4	405.1	-464.0	-984.9
Cash Flow From Operations	411.6	-159.7	532.1	-601.6
Balance Sheet (000's)				
Cash & Equivalents	412.2	294.1	756.9	1,333.1
Total Current Assets	10,193.0	7,489.0	7,240.9	4,365.4
Fixed Assets, Net	4,367.2	2,545.5	2,931.9	2,538.3
Total Assets	15,963.6	11,546.7	11,809.2	7,305.1
Total Current Liabilities	4,746.5	1,331.5	1,823.8	1,847.2
Long-Term Debt	1,068.4	189.3	562.7	3,593.6
Stockholders' Equity	10,148.8	10,025.9	9,422.7	1,864.3
Performance & Financial Condition				
Return on Total Revenues %	0.08	3.11	-4.50	-24.13
Return on Avg Stockholders' Equity %	0.10	4.17	-8.22	-43.60
Return on Average Assets %	0.08	3.47	-4.85	-16.20
Current Ratio	2.15	5.62	3.97	2.36
Debt / Equity %	10.53	1.89	5.97	192.76

Compound Growth %'s	EPS %	n.a.	Net Income %	n.a.	Total Revenues %	44.86

Comments

Acquisitions contributed significantly to growth in years prior to fiscal 1998. Management is betting that the introduction of a sales force within the United States will reverse the recent decline in business. Research and development expense totaled $1,073,000 and $1,072,000 in fiscal 1998 and 1997, respectively. Has the market overreacted to a flat year? Maybe so, but the Company still has to demonstrate that it can sustain a profitable growth rate without acquisitions.

Officers	Position	Ownership Information	
Carl Franzblau	President, CEO	Number of Shares Outstanding	7,851,890
William Franzblau	CFO	Market Capitalization	$ 5,574,842
Myrna Franzblau	Treasurer	Number of Shareholders	1,000
Alan S. Cohen	Director	Where Listed / Symbol	NASDAQ / HMGN

Other Information			
Transfer Agent	Continental Stock Transfer & Trust Co. New York, NY	SIC Code	2835
Auditor	BDO Seidman LLP	Employees	114
		Web Site	hemagen.com

Hi-Rise Recycling Systems, Inc.

8505 NW 74 Street   Miami, FL 33166   Telephone (305)597-0243   Fax (305)625-4666

Company Description

Hi-Rise Recycling Systems, Inc., founded in 1990, is engaged in manufacturing, distributing, marketing and selling solid waste handling equipment. Until February, 1997, the Company was primarily engaged in distributing, marketing and selling a proprietary automated system known as the hi-rise system designed to collect source-separated recyclables and other solid waste in multi-story residential buildings. In February 1997, the Company expanded its product lines to include sheet metal fabrication products consisting primarily of rubbish and laundry chutes. In 1998 the Company acquired both Hesco Sales, Inc. and Bes-Pac, Inc. and in February 1999, the Company acquired DeVivo Industries, Inc. All three of these companies are in the business of manufacturing and selling solid waste handling equipment products.

	12/31/98	12/31/97	12/31/96	12/31/95
Per Share Information				
Stock Price	2.37	2.16	3.88	8.75
Earnings Per Share	0.27	0.0	-0.47	-0.70
Price / Earnings Ratio	8.78	n.a.	n.a.	n.a.
Book Value Per Share	2.24	1.34	1.26	2.92
Price / Book Value %	105.80	161.19	307.94	299.66
Dividends Per Share	0.0	0.0	0.0	0.0
Annual Financial Data				
Operating Results (000's)				
Total Revenues	31,956.4	11,042.3	3,623.7	3,403.1
Costs & Expenses	-28,878.3	-10,911.1	-6,178.1	-5,722.2
Income Before Taxes and Other	3,078.1	31.2	-2,639.2	-2,319.1
Other Items	0.0	0.0	0.0	0.0
Income Tax	-75.0	-11.0	0.0	0.0
Net Income	3,003.1	20.2	-2,639.2	-2,319.1
Cash Flow From Operations	-1,339.4	-2,864.1	-3,940.7	-3,152.8
Balance Sheet (000's)				
Cash & Equivalents	324.4	1,134.1	1,711.8	5,717.5
Total Current Assets	17,867.2	9,842.7	4,522.4	8,046.4
Fixed Assets, Net	3,430.2	1,172.7	757.4	411.0
Total Assets	53,814.2	19,184.9	9,981.3	12,083.9
Total Current Liabilities	12,498.3	5,354.2	1,950.9	1,740.4
Long-Term Debt	15,776.5	3,195.0	150.0	300.0
Stockholders' Equity	25,539.4	10,635.6	7,880.4	10,043.5
Performance & Financial Condition				
Return on Total Revenues %	9.40	0.18	-72.83	-68.14
Return on Avg Stockholders' Equity %	16.60	0.22	-29.45	-31.19
Return on Average Assets %	8.23	0.14	-23.92	-23.19
Current Ratio	1.43	1.84	2.32	4.62
Debt / Equity %	61.77	30.04	1.90	2.99

Compound Growth %'s	EPS % n.a.	Net Income % n.a.	Total Revenues %	110.97

Comments

Sales of Hi-Rise Systems and trash compaction systems increased by $3.1 million to $7.0 million in 1998. This sparkling growth is all but lost in the $20.7 million revenue growth that mostly came by way of acquisitions. The fact that management was able to produce pre-tax income equal to 10% of gross revenues is a sign of excellent operating controls. At December 31, 1998, the Company had $22.1 million of goodwill recorded as assets which equated to approximately 86% of stockholders' equity and book value per share. At that date the Company also had $800,000 of tax loss carryovers remaining available to offset future taxable income.

Officers	Position	Ownership Information	
Donald Engel	Chairman, CEO	Number of Shares Outstanding	11,413,352
J. Gary McAlpin	COO	Market Capitalization	$ 27,049,644
Bradley Hacker	CFO	Number of Shareholders	1,000
Seymour Oestreicher	Vice President	Where Listed / Symbol	NASDAQ / HIRI

Other Information			
Transfer Agent	American Stock Transfer & Trust Co. New York, NY	SIC Code	3559
Auditor	PricewaterhouseCoopers LLP	Employees	375
		Web Site	hiri.com

Hi-Tech Pharmacal Co., Inc.

369 Bayview Avenue   Amityville, NY 11701   Telephone (516)789-8228   Fax (516)789-1240

Company Description

Hi-Tech Pharmacal Co., Inc. develops, manufactures and markets over 100 pharmaceutical products in liquid and semi-solid form, comprised of over-the-counter (non-prescription) pharmaceuticals, prescription drug products and nutritional preparations, primarily for the generic drug industry. The Company's Health Care Products Division develops, manufactures and markets brand name products. Diabetic Tussin®, its flagship brand, is now ranked the number one selling sugar free cough syrup. The Company also is a leading manufacturer of sterile ophthalmic, otic and inhalation products and provides sterile manufacturing contract services. The Company's customers are generic distributors, drug wholesalers, chain drug stores, mass merchandise chains and mail order companies. The Company was founded in 1983.

	04/30/98	04/30/97	04/30/96	04/30/95
Per Share Information				
Stock Price as of 12/31	3.75	4.75	3.87	7.50
Earnings Per Share	0.38	0.18	0.29	0.38
Price / Earnings Ratio	9.87	26.39	13.34	19.74
Book Value Per Share	3.48	3.09	2.95	2.59
Price / Book Value %	107.76	153.72	131.19	289.58
Dividends Per Share	0.0	0.0	0.0	0.0
Annual Financial Data				
Operating Results (000's)				
Total Revenues	22,366.0	20,767.0	19,674.0	16,781.0
Costs & Expenses	-19,531.0	-19,440.0	-17,468.0	-13,978.0
Income Before Taxes and Other	2,835.0	1,327.0	2,206.0	2,803.0
Other Items	0.0	0.0	0.0	0.0
Income Tax	-1,100.0	-510.0	-871.0	-1,072.0
Net Income	1,735.0	817.0	1,335.0	1,731.0
Cash Flow From Operations	2,706.0	1,409.0	1,099.0	n.a.
Balance Sheet (000's)				
Cash & Equivalents	2,604.0	1,985.0	1,746.0	1,781.0
Total Current Assets	11,878.0	10,581.0	9,570.0	8,229.0
Fixed Assets, Net	9,537.0	10,106.0	10,598.0	10,113.0
Total Assets	21,622.0	20,806.0	20,234.0	18,404.0
Total Current Liabilities	3,557.0	4,669.0	4,406.0	3,988.0
Long-Term Debt	1,450.0	1,896.0	2,427.0	3,150.0
Stockholders' Equity	15,685.0	14,001.0	13,171.0	11,266.0
Performance & Financial Condition				
Return on Total Revenues %	7.76	3.93	6.79	10.32
Return on Avg Stockholders' Equity %	11.69	6.01	10.93	16.25
Return on Average Assets %	8.18	3.98	6.91	10.29
Current Ratio	3.34	2.27	2.17	2.06
Debt / Equity %	9.24	13.54	18.43	27.96

Compound Growth %'s	EPS %	0.00	Net Income %	0.08	Total Revenues %	10.05

Comments

The fiscal 1998 increase in revenues was primarily the result of the introduction of new products. Gross margins also returned to more favorable levels, restoring net earnings after a decrease in fiscal 1997. The latter was primarily the result of dramatic changes in the healthcare industry. A number of mergers and acquisitions among drug distributors and retail stores has created a price competitive environment for generic manufacturers with decreased generic prices and lower margins. For the nine months ended January 31, 1999, the Company reported revenues and net income of $17.0 million and $1,229,000 ($.27 per share) as compared to $16.6 million and $1,057,000 ($.23 per share) for the same period of the preceding year.

Officers	Position	Ownership Information	
Bernard Seltzer	Chairman	Number of Shares Outstanding	4,512,500
David S. Seltzer	President, CEO	Market Capitalization	$ 16,921,875
Elan Bar-Giora	Exec VP	Number of Shareholders	1,119
Arthur S. Goldberg	VP - Finance, CFO	Where Listed / Symbol	NASDAQ / HITK

Other Information			
Transfer Agent	Continental Stock Transfer & Trust Co. New York, NY	SIC Code	2834
Auditor	Richard A. Eisner & Co., LLP	Employees	124
		Web Site	diabeticproducts.com

Hitox Corporation of America

722 Burleson Street   Corpus Christi, TX 78402   Telephone (512)882-5175   Fax (512)882-6948

Company Description

Hitox Corporation of America is a specialty chemical company engaged in the business of manufacturing and marketing mineral products for use as pigments and pigment extenders used in the manufacture of paints, industrial coatings and plastics. The Company's principal product, HITOX® is a unique color pigment with a high titanium dioxide content. Titanium dioxide is the primary pigment used by manufacturers of paints, plastics and paper to impart opacity and durability to the finished product. The Company's business was developed by Benilite Corporation and spun off by Benilite to its shareholders in 1980. Hitox subsequently went public in 1988.

	12/31/98	12/31/97	12/31/96	12/31/95
Per Share Information				
Stock Price	1.69	1.75	2.50	3.37
Earnings Per Share	0.21	0.20	0.17	0.16
Price / Earnings Ratio	8.05	8.75	14.71	21.06
Book Value Per Share	2.16	1.95	1.75	0.94
Price / Book Value %	78.24	89.74	142.86	358.51
Dividends Per Share	0.0	0.0	0.0	0.0
Annual Financial Data				
Operating Results (000's)				
Total Revenues	11,833.7	11,322.4	11,327.4	10,954.0
Costs & Expenses	-10,850.5	-10,364.3	-10,472.4	-10,306.1
Income Before Taxes and Other	983.1	958.2	834.2	604.8
Other Items	0.0	0.0	-112.3	0.0
Income Tax	-13.0	-13.0	-9.0	-4.6
Net Income	970.1	945.2	712.9	600.2
Cash Flow From Operations	990.1	810.5	923.9	887.7
Balance Sheet (000's)				
Cash & Equivalents	1,737.4	1,719.6	1,509.0	828.0
Total Current Assets	8,437.5	7,755.5	6,429.7	6,175.8
Fixed Assets, Net	2,502.7	2,693.3	3,918.5	4,337.8
Total Assets	11,616.5	11,247.5	10,373.5	10,684.9
Total Current Liabilities	1,572.0	1,546.8	1,212.5	1,850.6
Long-Term Debt	0.0	626.2	1,031.8	5,405.7
Stockholders' Equity	10,044.5	9,074.4	8,129.3	3,428.6
Performance & Financial Condition				
Return on Total Revenues %	8.20	8.35	6.29	5.48
Return on Avg Stockholders' Equity %	10.15	10.99	12.34	19.21
Return on Average Assets %	8.49	8.74	6.77	5.36
Current Ratio	5.37	5.01	5.30	3.34
Debt / Equity %	n.a.	6.90	12.69	157.66

Compound Growth %'s	EPS %	9.49	Net Income %	17.36	Total Revenues %	2.61

Comments

Revenues have been relatively flat for several years. Management reports that it has made changes in an effort to improve customer awareness of the benefits of its products and has increased support in a renewed effort to increase sales. During 1997, all personnel were consolidated into one site and the corporate headquarters building was put up for sale. But at the end of 1998, no sale was imminent. What was in the works, however, was an offer from Zemex Corporation (NYSE) to buy the whole Company at $3.00 per share. Management retained an investment banking firm to assist in determining the fairness of the proposal. Meanwhile, the Company remains very solvent and reasonably profitable. At December 31, 1998, the Company also had $11.0 million of tax loss carryovers available to offset future income. The tax benefit of the carryovers is not reflected as an asset.

Officers	Position	Ownership Information	
William B. Hayes	Chairman	Number of Shares Outstanding	4,657,487
Bernard A. Paulson	CEO	Market Capitalization	$ 7,871,153
Kelso C. Brooks, Jr.	Senior VP	Number of Shareholders	800
Elizabeth K. Morgan	Secretary	Where Listed / Symbol	NASDAQ / HTXA

Other Information			
Transfer Agent	Registrar & Transfer Co. Cranford, NJ	SIC Code	2810
Auditor	Ernst & Young LLP	Employees	45
		Web Site	hitox.com

Holiday RV Superstores, Incorporated

7851 Greenbriar Parkway   Orlando, FL 32819   Telephone (407)363-9211   Fax (407)363-2065

Company Description

Holiday RV Superstores, Incorporated is a multi-store retail chain engaged in the retail sales and service of recreational vehicles (RVs) and, at some locations, recreational boats. The Company currently operates seven sales and service retail centers: one in the heart of the Walt Disney World tourist area in Orlando, Florida; two in the Gulf Coast tourist areas of Tampa and Ft. Myers, Florida; one in Atlanta, Georgia; one in Greer, South Carolina; two in California's central valley cities of Sacramento and Bakersfield, and one in Las Cruces, New Mexico. All centers offer a full line of both new and used RVs. The Greer, Las Cruces and Atlanta centers also sell boats. The Company was founded in 1978.

	10/31/98	10/31/97	10/31/96	10/31/95
Per Share Information				
Stock Price as of 12/31	2.22	1.69	1.66	2.19
Earnings Per Share	0.23	0.19	0.18	0.20
Price / Earnings Ratio	9.65	8.89	9.22	10.95
Book Value Per Share	2.43	2.18	1.99	1.80
Price / Book Value %	91.36	77.52	83.42	121.67
Dividends Per Share	0.0	0.0	0.0	0.0
Annual Financial Data				
Operating Results (000's)				
Total Revenues	74,809.8	68,467.9	75,156.6	70,405.2
Costs & Expenses	-72,072.7	-66,189.3	-72,995.7	-67,966.2
Income Before Taxes and Other	2,737.1	2,278.6	2,160.9	2,439.0
Other Items	0.0	0.0	0.0	0.0
Income Tax	-1,044.0	-892.0	-829.0	-980.0
Net Income	1,693.1	1,386.6	1,331.9	1,459.0
Cash Flow From Operations	565.0	2,108.5	2,296.1	116.4
Balance Sheet (000's)				
Cash & Equivalents	7,441.8	7,431.3	5,617.7	4,013.0
Total Current Assets	33,369.5	29,441.8	29,730.3	25,361.0
Fixed Assets, Net	4,038.4	4,209.4	4,350.6	3,947.0
Total Assets	37,717.1	33,979.3	34,411.1	29,717.0
Total Current Liabilities	19,988.7	17,510.2	19,281.5	15,953.0
Long-Term Debt	0.0	0.0	0.0	0.0
Stockholders' Equity	17,507.7	16,183.0	14,772.6	13,416.0
Performance & Financial Condition				
Return on Total Revenues %	2.26	2.03	1.77	2.07
Return on Avg Stockholders' Equity %	10.05	8.96	9.45	11.50
Return on Average Assets %	4.72	4.05	4.15	5.15
Current Ratio	1.67	1.68	1.54	1.59
Debt / Equity %	n.a.	n.a.	n.a.	n.a.

Compound Growth %'s	EPS %	4.77	Net Income %	5.09	Total Revenues %	2.04

Comments

Revenues increased 9.3% during fiscal 1998 primarily due to a 22% increase in the average selling price of new vehicles. Management focused on increasing the sales of higher priced motorhomes and diesel motorhomes since these sales have greater potential for higher gross margins. The majority of the unit sales decrease was in the low priced folding tent trailers that carry low gross margins. With a sharp eye towards controlling expenses, the Company produced the best bottom line in years. The Company's overall financial condition is free from long term debt.

Officers	Position	Ownership Information	
Newton C. Kindlund	President, CEO	Number of Shares Outstanding	7,213,300
Joanne M. Kindlund	Exec VP, Secretary	Market Capitalization	$ 16,013,526
W. Hardee McAlhaney	Vice President, CFO	Number of Shareholders	2,700
James P. Williams	Director	Where Listed / Symbol	NASDAQ / RVEE

Other Information			
Transfer Agent	American Stock Transfer & Trust Co. New York, NY	SIC Code	5561
Auditor	PricewaterhouseCoopers LLP	Employees	193
		Web Site	holidayrv.com

Horizon Medical Products, Inc.

One Horizon Way, P.O. Box 627   Manchester, GA 31816   Telephone (706)846-3126   Fax (706)846-3146

Company Description

Horizon Medical Products, Inc. is a rapidly growing specialty medical device company focused on manufacturing and marketing vascular access products. The Company's vascular access product lines include implantable ports, which are used primarily in cancer treatment protocols, and specialty catheters, which are used in hemodialysis and stem cell apheresis procedures. The Company believes it offers the broadest available product lines in each of these product categories and that it has the largest direct sales force focused exclusively on vascular access products. The Company was founded in 1990 and had its initial public offering in 1998. It issued 3.5 million shares to the public at $14.50 per share.

	12/31/98	12/31/97	12/31/96	12/31/95
Per Share Information				
Stock Price	3.87	13.00	n.a.	n.a.
Earnings Per Share	0.17	-0.97	-0.13	-0.05
Price / Earnings Ratio	22.76	n.a.	n.a.	n.a.
Book Value Per Share	3.10	-1.18	-0.20	-0.11
Price / Book Value %	124.84	n.a.	n.a.	n.a.
Dividends Per Share	0.0	0.0	0.0	0.0
Annual Financial Data				
Operating Results (000's)				
Total Revenues	39,445.6	15,867.9	7,106.2	5,003.6
Costs & Expenses	-36,633.3	-16,720.0	-8,290.4	-5,390.7
Income Before Taxes and Other	2,812.4	-852.1	-1,184.2	-387.1
Other Items	1,016.6	-8,000.0	0.0	-70.0
Income Tax	-1,780.6	-319.8	0.0	0.0
Net Income	2,048.3	-9,172.0	-1,184.2	-457.1
Cash Flow From Operations	-706.3	2,721.3	111.5	-463.2
Balance Sheet (000's)				
Cash & Equivalents	6,232.2	2,893.9	217.8	394.0
Total Current Assets	44,735.3	12,956.2	2,499.7	2,463.0
Fixed Assets, Net	4,043.2	2,341.5	769.9	700.0
Total Assets	104,637.1	31,576.9	6,175.5	6,894.0
Total Current Liabilities	15,968.4	6,113.6	1,481.9	963.0
Long-Term Debt	47,073.7	23,970.8	5,052.8	4,907.0
Stockholders' Equity	41,430.8	-11,149.8	-1,915.8	-1,024.0
Performance & Financial Condition				
Return on Total Revenues %	5.19	-57.80	-16.66	-9.14
Return on Avg Stockholders' Equity %	13.53	n.a.	n.a.	n.a.
Return on Average Assets %	3.01	-48.59	-18.12	-10.03
Current Ratio	2.80	2.12	1.69	2.56
Debt / Equity %	113.62	n.a.	n.a.	n.a.

Compound Growth %'s	EPS %	n.a.	Net Income %	n.a.	Total Revenues %	99.02

Comments

Most of the 149.4% increase in 1998 revenues was attributable to acquisitions. Without the acquisitions, revenue rose 12% in 1998. Higher revenues and gross profit margins produced a net operating profit for the year. 1998 results also include net nonrecurring income of $1,016,584 related to the early extinguishment of a contractual obligation. 1997 results include a nonrecurring expense of $8 million related to a put warrant purchase obligation. At December 31, 1998, the Company had $55.5 million recorded as intangible assets which equated to approximately 134% of stockholders' equity and book value per share.

Officers	Position	Ownership Information	
Marshall B. Hunt	Chairman, CEO	Number of Shares Outstanding	13,366,278
William E. Peterson, Jr.	President	Market Capitalization	$ 51,727,496
Mark A. Jewett	VP - Finance	Number of Shareholders	2,000
J. Ronald Hager	Vice President	Where Listed / Symbol	NASDAQ / HMPS

Other Information			
Transfer Agent	SunTrust Bank Atlanta, GA	SIC Code	5047
Auditor	PricewaterhouseCoopers LLP	Employees	200
		Web Site	hmpvascular.com

Horizon Offshore, Inc.

2500 CityWest Boulevard, Suite 2200   Houston, TX 77042   Telephone (713)361-2600   Fax (713)361-2690

Company Description

Horizon provides marine construction services to the offshore oil and gas industry primarily in the United States Gulf of Mexico. The Company's marine fleet is used primarily to install marine pipelines to transport oil and gas from newly installed production platforms and other subsea production systems. In just a few years, the Company has assembled a fleet of ten vessels which are capable of a wide range of marine construction activities. Founded in 1996, the Company had its initial public offering in 1998.

	12/31/98	12/31/97	12/31/96
Per Share Information			
Stock Price	4.62	2.91	0.28
Earnings Per Share	0.69	0.17	-0.70
Price / Earnings Ratio	6.70	17.12	n.a.
Book Value Per Share	4.76	1.43	-0.47
Price / Book Value %	97.06	203.50	n.a.
Dividends Per Share	0.0	0.0	0.0
Annual Financial Data			
Operating Results (000's)			
Total Revenues	119,840.0	36,787.0	14,128.0
Costs & Expenses	-102,895.0	-34,511.0	-25,325.0
Income Before Taxes and Other	16,945.0	2,276.0	-11,197.0
Other Items	0.0	0.0	0.0
Income Tax	-4,485.0	0.0	1,617.0
Net Income	12,460.0	2,276.0	-9,580.0
Cash Flow From Operations	10,481.0	3,491.0	-9,568.0
Balance Sheet (000's)			
Cash & Equivalents	9,649.0	2,846.0	2,650.0
Total Current Assets	45,949.0	16,088.0	8,670.0
Fixed Assets, Net	145,680.0	55,040.0	29,284.0
Total Assets	193,669.0	72,989.0	39,690.0
Total Current Liabilities	33,288.0	18,201.0	8,136.0
Long-Term Debt	62,268.0	34,729.0	38,104.0
Stockholders' Equity	94,460.0	20,059.0	-6,550.0
Performance & Financial Condition			
Return on Total Revenues %	10.40	6.19	-67.81
Return on Avg Stockholders' Equity %	21.76	33.70	-290.30
Return on Average Assets %	9.35	4.04	-34.21
Current Ratio	1.38	0.88	1.07
Debt / Equity %	65.92	173.13	n.a.

Compound Growth %'s	EPS %	305.88	Net Income %	447.45	Total Revenues %	191.25

Comments

Revenues increased dramatically in 1998 as the Company expanded its fleet to offer an extensive range of pipeline and derrick services. Severe weather conditions in the Gulf in the third quarter of 1998 reduced profit margins and caused delays. Management believes that 1998 results reflect the extensive capabilities of the Company's expanded fleet and its own ability to competitively bid, win and successfully manage projects. Proceeds of the public offering amounted to $68.6 million. Approximately $31.0 million was used to acquire two new ships and approximately $18.3 million was used to repay debt.

Officers	Position	Ownership Information	
Jonathan D. Pollock	Chairman	Number of Shares Outstanding	19,826,480
Bill J. Lam	President, CEO	Market Capitalization	$ 91,598,338
David W. Sharp	Exec VP, CFO	Number of Shareholders	4,000
James K. Cole	Senior VP	Where Listed / Symbol	NASDAQ / HOFF

Other Information			
Transfer Agent	ChaseMellon Shareholder Services Ridgefield Park, NJ	SIC Code	3533
Auditor	Arthur Andersen LLP	Employees	412
		Web Site	horizonoffshore.com

Hydromer, Inc.

35 Columbia Road   Branchburg, NJ 08876-3518   Telephone (908)526-2828   Fax (908)526-3633

Company Description

Hydromer, Inc. is a polymer research and development company organized for the purpose of developing polymeric complexes for commercial markets in the medical and industrial fields. The Company owns several process and applications patents for Hydromer® which is both a polymeric substance that becomes extremely lubricious (slippery) when contacted by water and a technique of grafting or applying this substance onto surfaces which may consist of a wide range of materials, including polyurethane, polyvinyl chloride, and metals. The Company has also been issued patents for a number of other products and additional patent applications are pending. Hydromer, Inc. was formed in 1980.

	06/30/98	06/30/97	06/30/96	06/30/95
Per Share Information				
Stock Price as of 12/31	0.69	0.81	0.28	0.06
Earnings Per Share	0.09	0.08	0.09	-0.04
Price / Earnings Ratio	7.67	10.13	3.11	n.a.
Book Value Per Share	0.46	0.41	0.33	0.20
Price / Book Value %	150.00	197.56	84.85	n.a.
Dividends Per Share	0.0	0.0	0.0	0.0
Annual Financial Data				
Operating Results (000's)				
Total Revenues	2,394.1	2,076.1	1,797.0	1,214.4
Costs & Expenses	-1,860.1	-1,668.2	-1,574.9	-1,523.7
Income Before Taxes and Other	534.0	312.8	222.1	-309.3
Other Items	0.0	0.0	0.0	0.0
Income Tax	-158.5	31.6	167.5	122.4
Net Income	375.5	344.4	389.6	-186.9
Cash Flow From Operations	399.8	640.7	-71.3	-591.3
Balance Sheet (000's)				
Cash & Equivalents	783.5	716.0	167.9	41.0
Total Current Assets	1,807.2	1,473.5	1,070.8	731.0
Fixed Assets, Net	1,585.2	271.7	222.5	183.0
Total Assets	3,492.5	2,020.1	1,534.7	986.0
Total Current Liabilities	447.2	237.1	96.1	98.0
Long-Term Debt	793.3	0.0	0.0	0.0
Stockholders' Equity	2,027.1	1,783.0	1,438.6	888.0
Performance & Financial Condition				
Return on Total Revenues %	15.69	16.59	21.68	-15.39
Return on Avg Stockholders' Equity %	19.71	21.38	33.49	-18.69
Return on Average Assets %	13.62	19.38	30.91	-18.69
Current Ratio	4.04	6.21	11.14	7.46
Debt / Equity %	39.14	n.a.	n.a.	n.a.

Compound Growth %'s	EPS %	0.00	Net Income %	-1.82	Total Revenues %	25.39

Comments

Approximately 58% of revenues are derived from royalties, options and licenses. The Company has nine patents in the United States and various foreign counter parts. Although two patents expired during 1998, management believes that new patents and an increased stream of royalty income will mitigate any lasting negative effects. In fact, the increase in earnings during fiscal 1998 was due to the $372,000 increase in license revenue. The Company incurred an income tax expense in fiscal 1998 as all tax carryforwards were used in fiscal 1997. Pre-tax income increased 70.7%. For the six months ended December 31, 1998, the Company reported revenues and net income of $1.4 million and $188,077 ($.04 per share) as compared to $1.2 million and $239,059 ($.05 per share) for the same period of the preceding year.

Officers	Position	Ownership Information	
Manfred F. Dyck	President, CEO	Number of Shares Outstanding	4,367,987
Robert D. Frawley	Secretary	Market Capitalization	$ 3,013,911
Kenneth P. Brice	Vice President, CFO	Number of Shareholders	723
Joseph A. Ehrhard, Jr.	Vice President	Where Listed / Symbol	OTC-BB / HYDI

Other Information			
Transfer Agent	First City Transfer Co. Iselin, NJ	SIC Code	6794
Auditor	Rosenberg Rich Baker Berman	Employees	14
Market Maker	Carr Securities Corporation	(800)221-2243	Web Site	hydromer.com
	Paragon Capital Corporation	(800)345-0505		

Hytek Microsystems, Inc.

400 Hot Springs Road   Carson City, NV 89703   Telephone (702)883-0820   Fax (702)883-0827

Company Description

Hytek Microsystems, Inc. designs, manufactures and sells custom and standard thick film hybrid microcircuits. Products manufactured by the Company are sold primarily to original equipment manufacturers serving the computer, telecommunications, military, medical, industrial electronics, and automatic test equipment markets. Approximately 96% of the Company's revenues are derived from products designed to meet a particular customer's need. One customer, Chesapeake Sciences, accounted for 64% of net revenues. The products sold to Chesapeake are used in the eventual production of offshore geophysical oil exploration equipment. The Company was formed in 1974.

	01/02/99	01/03/98	12/30/96	12/31/95
Per Share Information				
Stock Price as of 12/31	2.50	2.19	2.50	2.38
Earnings Per Share	0.66	0.54	0.62	0.18
Price / Earnings Ratio	3.79	4.06	4.03	13.22
Book Value Per Share	2.36	1.72	1.15	0.50
Price / Book Value %	105.93	127.33	217.39	476.00
Dividends Per Share	0.0	0.0	0.0	0.0
Annual Financial Data				
Operating Results (000's)				
Total Revenues	12,533.0	9,052.3	8,651.0	5,412.3
Costs & Expenses	-10,374.3	-7,335.7	-6,924.3	-4,891.2
Income Before Taxes and Other	2,158.7	1,716.7	1,726.6	521.0
Other Items	0.0	0.0	0.0	0.0
Income Tax	-66.4	-55.0	200.0	0.0
Net Income	2,092.3	1,661.7	1,926.6	521.0
Cash Flow From Operations	2,088.8	22.7	1,510.1	-250.9
Balance Sheet (000's)				
Cash & Equivalents	2,637.2	1,189.5	1,426.7	93.0
Total Current Assets	7,076.1	6,334.6	3,863.9	2,544.2
Fixed Assets, Net	999.0	755.8	370.4	101.4
Total Assets	8,275.1	7,290.5	4,434.3	2,645.6
Total Current Liabilities	1,012.4	2,019.8	993.4	1,248.2
Long-Term Debt	52.7	101.0	68.0	0.0
Stockholders' Equity	7,171.3	5,046.6	3,372.9	1,397.4
Performance & Financial Condition				
Return on Total Revenues %	16.69	18.36	22.27	9.63
Return on Avg Stockholders' Equity %	34.25	39.47	80.78	46.39
Return on Average Assets %	26.88	28.34	54.43	25.40
Current Ratio	6.99	3.14	3.89	2.04
Debt / Equity %	0.74	2.00	2.02	n.a.

Compound Growth %'s	EPS %	54.20	Net Income %	58.95	Total Revenues %	32.30

Comments

The 39% increase in 1998 revenues, which drove net income higher, was attributable to increased shipments to Chesapeake. The growth compound percentages are impressive and the balance sheet is strong. But there are dangers in being dependent on a major customer. As a result of current low market prices for crude oil combined with a market glut on the crude oil supply side, Chesapeake announced that it has placed its current orders with the Company, valued at approximately $5 million, on an indefinite hold status. This change will have a large negative impact on revenues and operating results in 1999. The Company estimates that 1999 revenues will be in the $6 to $7 million range. By March 1999, the stock price had dropped to approximately one-half of its year end level and approximately one-half of book value.

Officers	Position	Ownership Information	
Shou-Chen Yih	Chairman	Number of Shares Outstanding	3,039,758
Charles S. Byrne	President, CEO	Market Capitalization	$ 7,599,395
Sally B. Chapman	CFO, Controller	Number of Shareholders	500
Jonathan B. Presnell	Vice President, General Manager	Where Listed / Symbol	NASDAQ / HTEK

Other Information			
Transfer Agent	U.S. Stock Transfer Corp. Glendale, CA	SIC Code	3674
Auditor	Ernst & Young LLP	Employees	123
		Web Site	hytek.com

I.C.H. Corporation

9255 Towne Ceentre Drive, Suite 600   San Diego, CA 92121   Telephone (619)587-8533   Fax (619)535-1634

Company Description

I.C.H. Corporation is the post-reorganization successor to ICH Corporation which filed voluntary petitions for bankruptcy relief under Chapter 11 on October 10, 1995. The new Company had no significant operations prior to the acquisition of Sybra, Inc. on April 30, 1997. The Company is the second largest operator of Arby's restaurants, currently operating 181 restaurants in six states. Arby's restaurants are generally known for their roast beef sandwiches, which are made from thinly-sliced beef which is freshly-roasted at each restaurant. On December 14, 1998, the Company acquired Lyon's Restaurants, a chain of 73 full-service family dining restaurants located in northern California and Oregon.

	12/31/98	12/31/97	12/28/96	12/30/95
Per Share Information				
Stock Price	3.62	3.00	n.a.	n.a.
Earnings Per Share	1.14	-0.31	n.a.	n.a.
Price / Earnings Ratio	3.18	n.a.	n.a.	n.a.
Book Value Per Share	5.63	4.63	n.a.	n.a.
Price / Book Value %	64.30	64.79	n.a.	n.a.
Dividends Per Share	0.0	0.0	n.a.	n.a.
Annual Financial Data				
Operating Results (000's)				
Total Revenues	140,032.0	112,922.0	116,124.0	115,531.0
Costs & Expenses	-134,973.0	-112,985.0	-109,564.0	-110,603.0
Income Before Taxes and Other	5,059.0	-63.0	6,560.0	4,928.0
Other Items	388.0	0.0	0.0	0.0
Income Tax	-2,143.0	-181.0	-2,398.0	-1,913.0
Net Income	3,304.0	-244.0	4,162.0	3,015.0
Cash Flow From Operations	14,800.0	1,692.0	12,902.0	8,450.0
Balance Sheet (000's)				
Cash & Equivalents	9,235.0	4,418.0	2,294.0	1,108.0
Total Current Assets	18,966.0	9,142.0	5,972.0	5,108.0
Fixed Assets, Net	40,141.0	24,696.0	53,582.0	50,000.0
Total Assets	113,466.0	75,264.0	75,601.0	74,373.0
Total Current Liabilities	26,425.0	14,148.0	14,427.0	12,220.0
Long-Term Debt	63,193.0	44,718.0	21,081.0	31,152.0
Stockholders' Equity	15,026.0	11,185.0	35,142.0	30,980.0
Performance & Financial Condition				
Return on Total Revenues %	2.36	-0.22	n.a.	n.a.
Return on Avg Stockholders' Equity %	25.21	-1.05	12.59	10.23
Return on Average Assets %	3.50	-0.32	5.55	4.21
Current Ratio	0.72	0.65	n.a.	n.a.
Debt / Equity %	420.56	399.80	n.a.	n.a.

Compound Growth %'s	EPS %	n.a.	Net Income %	3.10	Total Revenues %	6.62

Comments

The Lyon's transaction was accounted for as a purchase. Therefore, results of operations are combined with those of the Company starting with the date of the transaction. Revenue from Lyon's totalled $7.0 million for the short period. Without Lyon's, Company revenue grew 17.6% in 1998. Same store sales increased 4.8%. The Company sliced fat and juicy profits to the bottom line of the income statement. 1998 results include a $388,000 gain ($.13 per share) from a discontinued operation. Per share information is not available prior to 1997 because of the bankruptcy reorganization. The 1997 loss per share represents the eight months ended December 31, 1997. Intangible assets recorded on the books totalled $47.5 million at December 31, 1998, which equated to approximately 316% of stockholders' equity and book value per share.

Officers	Position	Ownership Information	
James R. Arabia	President, CEO	Number of Shares Outstanding	2,666,615
David A. Brainard	Senior VP, CFO	Market Capitalization	$ 9,653,146
John A. Bicks	Senior VP, Secretary	Number of Shareholders	3,402
Kenneth E. Giddens	Controller	Where Listed / Symbol	AMEX / IH

Other Information			
Transfer Agent	Bank of Louisville & Trust Company Louisville, KY	SIC Code	5812
Auditor	PricewaterhouseCoopers LLP	Employees	7,200

ICT Group, Inc.

800 Town Center Drive   Langhorne, PA 19047-1748   Telephone (215)757-0200   Fax (215)757-7877

Company Description

ICT Group, Inc. is an independent provider of call center teleservices, which consist of outbound and inbound telemarketing and customer support services, together with related value-added services such as marketing, research, management and consulting services, to businesses domestically and internationally. The Company provides these services to customers in an increasing array of industries including but not limited to insurance and financial services, publishing, telecommunications, consumer products and services, pharmaceuticals, health care services and computer software and hardware. The Company went public on June 14, 1996 with an initial offering price of $16 per share.

	12/31/98	12/31/97	12/31/96	12/31/95
Per Share Information				
Stock Price	2.50	4.38	4.75	16.00
Earnings Per Share	0.20	0.22	-0.65	0.10
Price / Earnings Ratio	12.50	19.91	n.a.	160.00
Book Value Per Share	3.93	3.76	3.56	0.43
Price / Book Value %	63.61	116.49	133.43	3,720.93
Dividends Per Share	0.0	0.0	0.0	0.0
Annual Financial Data				
Operating Results (000's)				
Total Revenues	121,595.6	92,529.6	72,074.8	52,115.8
Costs & Expenses	-117,619.4	-88,149.6	-69,899.6	-50,545.8
Income Before Taxes and Other	3,976.1	4,380.0	2,175.2	1,570.1
Other Items	0.0	0.0	-12,689.7	0.0
Income Tax	-1,549.3	-1,708.2	2,997.7	-667.3
Net Income	2,426.8	2,671.8	-7,516.7	902.8
Cash Flow From Operations	292.3	6,172.9	443.8	1,089.1
Balance Sheet (000's)				
Cash & Equivalents	14,255.3	17,711.0	18,298.0	447.2
Total Current Assets	42,351.6	37,441.5	32,804.5	10,431.8
Fixed Assets, Net	28,634.3	19,443.6	11,631.9	6,862.6
Total Assets	75,876.3	61,577.8	49,111.8	18,480.7
Total Current Liabilities	15,258.3	11,911.9	5,738.4	12,032.7
Long-Term Debt	14,000.0	4,799.3	1,057.5	761.3
Stockholders' Equity	45,785.1	43,368.2	41,020.3	3,843.0
Performance & Financial Condition				
Return on Total Revenues %	2.00	2.89	-10.43	1.73
Return on Avg Stockholders' Equity %	5.44	6.33	-33.51	29.54
Return on Average Assets %	3.53	4.83	-22.24	5.92
Current Ratio	2.78	3.14	5.72	0.87
Debt / Equity %	30.58	11.07	2.58	19.81

Compound Growth %'s	EPS %	25.99	Net Income %	39.04	Total Revenues %	32.63

Comments

Revenues increased 32% in 1998. Large increases were realized in call center teleservices to the financial services and telecommunications industries and management services. As a percentage of revenues, cost of services increased to 57.5% in 1998 from 55.3% in 1997 primarily due to lower average prices and increased labor costs the Company incurred as a result of the favorable economic climate and historically low employment levels. These conditions made it more difficult for the Company to attract sufficient call center staff. In 1998, one customer accounted for 22% of total revenue, down from 31% in 1997. 1996 results include nonrecurring compensation expense of $12.7 million which caused a net loss for the year. The price of the stock is discounted from book value and there are no intangible assets on the Company's balance sheet.

Officers	Position	Ownership Information	
John J. Brennan	President, CEO	Number of Shares Outstanding	11,642,475
Vincent A. Paccapaniccia	Senior VP, CFO	Market Capitalization	$ 29,106,188
Timothy F. Kowalski	Senior VP	Number of Shareholders	1,000
John Stoops	Director	Where Listed / Symbol	NASDAQ / ICTG

Other Information			
Transfer Agent	American Stock Transfer & Trust Company New York, NY	SIC Code	7389
Auditor	Arthur Andersen LLP	Employees	5,346
		Web Site	ictgroup.com

ILX Resorts Incorporated

2111 East Highland Avenue, Suite 210   Phoenix, AZ 85016   Telephone (602)957-2777   Fax (602)957-2780

Company Description

ILX Resorts Incorporated sells timeshare interests in resorts located in Arizona, Colorado, Florida, Hawaii, Indiana and Mexico. Generally, the Company either owns all of or a controlling interest in the resort itself, or owns a designated number of timeshare interests in a resort and has a corresponding right to sell those timeshare interests to third parties. The properties owned or controlled by the Company are operated as hotels to the extent of unused or unsold timeshare inventory. Except for the resort in Mexico, purchasers of timeshare interests acquire title to an undivided fraction of the entire resort entitling them to use a particular unit for a certain time period each year. The Company was founded in 1986.

	12/31/98	12/31/97	12/31/96	12/31/95
Per Share Information				
Stock Price	2.12	5.30	5.00	6.85
Earnings Per Share	0.0	0.59	0.37	0.59
Price / Earnings Ratio	n.a.	8.98	13.51	11.61
Book Value Per Share	5.50	4.76	4.33	3.83
Price / Book Value %	38.55	111.34	115.47	178.85
Dividends Per Share	0.0	0.0	0.0	0.0
Annual Financial Data				
Operating Results (000's)				
Total Revenues	36,871.6	36,795.3	32,150.8	32,706.1
Costs & Expenses	-36,767.1	-33,804.1	-29,859.4	-32,127.4
Income Before Taxes and Other	104.5	2,991.2	2,291.4	578.7
Other Items	3.3	0.0	-561.4	-501.2
Income Tax	-45.5	-1,145.0	-678.8	547.2
Net Income	62.3	1,846.2	1,051.1	624.7
Cash Flow From Operations	-4,602.0	2,808.9	3,975.8	-3,972.8
Balance Sheet (000's)				
Cash & Equivalents	3,196.7	3,226.0	3,523.0	3,746.5
Total Current Assets	3,196.7	3,226.0	3,523.0	3,746.5
Fixed Assets, Net	4,007.0	3,472.9	4,877.5	3,175.4
Total Assets	51,997.3	43,722.3	41,274.9	37,752.5
Total Current Liabilities	3,234.7	4,993.3	5,786.7	5,609.7
Long-Term Debt	22,107.4	19,884.5	16,434.4	13,527.9
Stockholders' Equity	25,764.3	16,620.8	15,175.1	13,775.1
Performance & Financial Condition				
Return on Total Revenues %	0.17	5.02	3.27	1.91
Return on Avg Stockholders' Equity %	0.29	11.61	7.26	4.67
Return on Average Assets %	0.13	4.34	2.66	1.89
Current Ratio	0.99	0.65	0.61	0.67
Debt / Equity %	85.81	119.64	108.30	98.21

Compound Growth %'s	EPS % n.a.	Net Income % -53.63	Total Revenues % 4.08

Comments

The Company executed a 1 for 5 reverse split in January 1998. All per share amounts have been restated for consistency. As of December 31, 1998, the Company operated six resorts consisting of 392 units and held 8,500 unsold vacation ownership interests in those resorts. 1998 results reflect a decline of 10.5% in the number of vacation ownership interests sold, from 1,660 in 1997 to 1,485 in 1998. Resort operating revenues were up 11.9% as a new property was opened in July 1998. Net resort profits declined, however, because of start-up costs of the new property and an initial lower occupancy rate for the new property. 1998 was narrowly profitable.

Officers	Position	Ownership Information	
Joseph P. Martori	Chairman, CEO	Number of Shares Outstanding	3,992,893
Nancy J. Stone	President, COO	Market Capitalization	$ 8,464,933
Stephen W. Morgan	Senior VP, CFO	Number of Shareholders	1,075
Denise L. Janda	Vice President, Controller	Where Listed / Symbol	AMEX / ILX

Other Information			
Transfer Agent	Harris Trust & Savings Bank Chicago, IL	SIC Code	6532
Auditor	Hansen, Barnett & Maxwell	Employees	790
		Web Site	ilxinc.com

IRI International Corporation

1000 Louisiana, Suite 5900   Houston, TX 77002   Telephone (713)651-8002   Fax (713)659-1526

Company Description

IRI International Corporation is one of the world's largest manufacturers of land-based drilling and well-servicing rigs and rig component parts for use in the global oil and gas industry and is principally engaged in the design, manufacture, service, sale and rental of onshore and offshore oilfield equipment for the domestic and international markets. The Company designs and produces rigs to meet the special requirements of its clientele for service in remote areas and harsh climatic conditions. The Company acquired the business and operations of Bowen Tools on March 31, 1997 and Cardwell International, Ltd. on April 17, 1997. On November 19, 1997, the Company sold 9.9 million shares of common stock in its initial public offering. Net proceeds of $163.9 million were used partially to repay debt in connection with the acquisitions.

	12/31/98	12/31/97	12/31/96	03/31/96
Per Share Information				
Stock Price	4.19	14.00	n.a.	n.a.
Earnings Per Share	0.31	0.35	0.28	0.27
Price / Earnings Ratio	13.52	40.00	n.a.	n.a.
Book Value Per Share	5.27	4.97	0.83	0.29
Price / Book Value %	79.51	281.69	n.a.	n.a.
Dividends Per Share	0.0	0.0	0.0	0.0
Annual Financial Data				
Operating Results (000's)				
Total Revenues	177,258.0	186,830.0	66,388.0	52,877.0
Costs & Expenses	-161,593.0	-171,509.0	-57,913.0	-44,914.0
Income Before Taxes and Other	15,665.0	15,321.0	8,475.0	7,963.0
Other Items	0.0	-1,512.0	0.0	0.0
Income Tax	-3,283.0	-2,786.0	-98.0	0.0
Net Income	12,382.0	11,023.0	8,377.0	7,963.0
Cash Flow From Operations	-1,658.0	-20,128.0	-1,171.0	4,179.0
Balance Sheet (000's)				
Cash & Equivalents	37,475.0	49,473.0	8,635.0	4,242.0
Total Current Assets	185,583.0	202,019.0	55,646.0	33,767.0
Fixed Assets, Net	49,192.0	43,219.0	2,398.0	0.0
Total Assets	239,166.0	251,074.0	58,671.0	40,130.0
Total Current Liabilities	21,337.0	40,129.0	16,988.0	0.0
Long-Term Debt	0.0	0.0	16,780.0	0.0
Stockholders' Equity	210,259.0	198,406.0	24,903.0	8,563.0
Performance & Financial Condition				
Return on Total Revenues %	6.99	5.90	12.62	15.06
Return on Avg Stockholders' Equity %	6.06	9.87	50.06	99.54
Return on Average Assets %	5.05	7.12	16.96	19.91
Current Ratio	8.70	5.03	3.28	n.a.
Debt / Equity %	n.a.	n.a.	67.38	n.a.

Compound Growth %'s	EPS %	4.71	Net Income %	15.85	Total Revenues %	49.66

Comments

In 1998, the Company experienced decreased revenues due to economic and financial turmoil in Russia and the Asia-Pacific region and the downward turn in oil prices, both of which resulted in a decreased demand for the Company's products. Management was quick to respond with an extensive cost restructuring program to preserve net income at the same level as the preceding year. Operating results prior to the acquisitions, referred to above, are stated on a pro forma basis. The period presented ending March 31, 1996, includes a full twelve months, three months of which are also included in calendar 1996 results. The acquisitions resulted in negative goodwill, $4.0 million of which remained on the books at December 31, 1998. The compound growth of earnings per share is diluted from the compound growth of net income because of the additional shares issued in the public offering.

Officers	Position	Ownership Information	
Hushang Ansary	Chairman, CEO	Number of Shares Outstanding	39,900,000
Gary W. Stratulate	President, COO	Market Capitalization	$ 167,181,000
Jeffrey M. Johanson	Exec VP, CFO	Number of Shareholders	5,000
Abdallah Andrawos	Secretary	Where Listed / Symbol	NYSE / IIR

Other Information			
Transfer Agent	Continental Stock Transfer & Trust Co. New York, NY	SIC Code	3533
Auditor	KPMG LLP	Employees	1,203

IRIDEX Corporation

1212 Terra Bella Avenue   Mountain View, CA 94043-1824   Telephone (650)940-4700   Fax (650)940-4710

Company Description

IRIDEX Corporation is the leading worldwide provider of semiconductor-based laser systems used to treat eye diseases in ophthalmology and skin lesions in dermatology. IRIDEX products are sold in the United States predominantly through a direct sales force and internationally through 53 independent distributors into 72 countries. The Company markets its products using three brand names: IRIS Medical to the ophthalmic market, IRIDERM to the dermatological market, and Light Solutions to the research market. The Company was founded in 1989 and had its initial public offering of 1.6 million shares in February 1996, at $9 per share. Existing shareholders tagged onto the offering with an additional 950,000 shares sold to the public.

	01/02/99	12/31/97	12/31/96	12/31/95
Per Share Information				
Stock Price as of 12/31	3.62	7.62	7.25	9.00
Earnings Per Share	0.26	0.31	0.16	0.23
Price / Earnings Ratio	13.92	24.58	45.31	39.13
Book Value Per Share	3.98	3.70	3.38	1.08
Price / Book Value %	90.95	205.95	214.50	833.33
Dividends Per Share	0.0	0.0	0.0	0.0
Annual Financial Data				
Operating Results (000's)				
Total Revenues	24,096.0	18,696.0	13,063.0	8,875.0
Costs & Expenses	-21,765.0	-15,402.0	-11,382.0	-7,423.0
Income Before Taxes and Other	2,331.0	3,278.0	1,681.0	1,452.0
Other Items	0.0	0.0	0.0	0.0
Income Tax	-583.0	-1,180.0	-676.0	-452.0
Net Income	1,748.0	2,098.0	1,005.0	1,000.0
Cash Flow From Operations	-1,976.0	-88.0	-1,256.0	800.0
Balance Sheet (000's)				
Cash & Equivalents	5,791.0	9,900.0	14,107.0	1,227.0
Total Current Assets	25,942.0	24,522.0	23,004.0	6,041.0
Fixed Assets, Net	2,274.0	2,133.0	655.0	254.0
Total Assets	28,377.0	26,686.0	23,707.0	6,395.0
Total Current Liabilities	2,492.0	2,806.0	2,227.0	1,702.0
Long-Term Debt	0.0	0.0	0.0	0.0
Stockholders' Equity	25,885.0	23,880.0	21,478.0	4,685.0
Performance & Financial Condition				
Return on Total Revenues %	7.25	11.22	7.69	11.27
Return on Avg Stockholders' Equity %	7.03	9.25	7.68	24.63
Return on Average Assets %	6.35	8.33	6.68	18.47
Current Ratio	10.41	8.74	10.33	3.55
Debt / Equity %	n.a.	n.a.	n.a.	n.a.

Compound Growth %'s	EPS %	4.17	Net Income %	20.46	Total Revenues %	39.51

Comments

Revenue increases of 30.5% and 46.2% were posted in 1998 and 1997, respectively. The increases were the result of increased unit volumes offset in part by decreasing average selling prices, particularly with respect to the Company's more mature products. International sales declined from 51.8% of total sales in 1997 to 36.6% of sales in 1998. The decrease is primarily due to lower sales from the economically weakened Asian region. Research and development expenses increased to $3.1 million in 1998 as compared to $1.7 million in 1997. The Company's balance sheet is clean with excess working capital, no long term debt, and only an immaterial amount of intangible assets.

Officers	Position	Ownership Information	
Theodore A. Boutacoff	President, CEO	Number of Shares Outstanding	6,506,010
Eduardo Arias	Senior VP	Market Capitalization	$ 23,551,756
Robert Kamenski	Vice President, CFO	Number of Shareholders	1,000
David M. Buzawa	Vice President	Where Listed / Symbol	NASDAQ / IRIX

Other Information			
Transfer Agent	First National Bank of Boston New York, NY	SIC Code	3845
Auditor	PricewaterhouseCoopers LLP	Employees	91
		Web Site	iridex.com

Image Systems Corporation

6103 Blue Circle Drive   Minnetonka, MN 55343   Telephone (612)935-1171   Fax (612)935-1386

Company Description

Image Systems Corporation designs, develops, manufactures and markets large, high resolution computer monitors. The Company's monitors provide high brightness and high resolution which are needed in applications such as medical imaging, scientific analysis, image processing and electronic and mechanical design. The Company's primary market is the medical field, particularly radiology. The Company's secondary market is Air Traffic Control which requires many of the same monitor attributes as the medical marketplace. All production and subassembly work is performed by subcontractors. Final assembly and quality assurance are performed by the Company. The Company was formed in 1988.

	04/30/98	04/30/97	04/30/96	04/30/95
Per Share Information				
Stock Price as of 12/31	1.03	2.37	3.75	2.81
Earnings Per Share	0.05	0.19	0.21	0.08
Price / Earnings Ratio	20.60	12.47	17.86	35.13
Book Value Per Share	0.83	0.77	0.57	0.36
Price / Book Value %	124.10	307.79	657.89	780.56
Dividends Per Share	0.0	0.0	0.0	0.0
Annual Financial Data				
Operating Results (000's)				
Total Revenues	8,201.1	8,135.1	7,940.0	5,026.9
Costs & Expenses	-7,829.2	-6,865.5	-6,458.2	-4,456.7
Income Before Taxes and Other	371.9	1,269.6	1,481.8	570.2
Other Items	0.0	0.0	0.0	0.0
Income Tax	-123.0	-443.0	-572.0	-208.0
Net Income	248.9	826.6	909.8	362.2
Cash Flow From Operations	-613.2	518.2	708.9	74.3
Balance Sheet (000's)				
Cash & Equivalents	57.6	486.5	686.4	46.1
Total Current Assets	3,791.7	3,380.5	3,330.0	2,150.5
Fixed Assets, Net	1,923.1	1,880.5	148.2	146.8
Total Assets	5,714.8	5,261.1	3,478.2	2,297.2
Total Current Liabilities	1,079.7	884.5	1,000.2	719.9
Long-Term Debt	941.3	933.5	0.0	9.2
Stockholders' Equity	3,693.8	3,443.1	2,478.0	1,568.2
Performance & Financial Condition				
Return on Total Revenues %	3.03	10.16	11.46	7.21
Return on Avg Stockholders' Equity %	6.98	27.92	44.97	26.19
Return on Average Assets %	4.54	18.92	31.51	17.84
Current Ratio	3.51	3.82	3.33	2.99
Debt / Equity %	25.48	27.11	n.a.	0.59

Compound Growth %'s	EPS %	-14.50	Net Income %	-11.76	Total Revenues %	17.72

Comments

Revenues in the last fiscal year were well below expectations as revenue growth in the air traffic control area had not yet materialize as planned and the Asian market had its many problems. The Company had geared itself for substantially more production which resulted in a number of nonrecurring costs. Revenue weakness was most evident in the second half of fiscal 1998 and continued into fiscal 1999. Although fiscal 1998 was profitable, management classified fiscal 1999 as a year of rebuilding. For the nine months ended February 28, 1999, the Company reported revenues of $5.1 million and a net loss of $9,092 ($.00 per share) as compared to $6.7 million and net income of $459,679 ($.10 per share) for the same period of the preceding year.

Officers	Position	Ownership Information	
Dean Scheff	President, CEO	Number of Shares Outstanding	4,452,597
Diana Scheff	Secretary	Market Capitalization	$ 4,586,175
David Sorensen	Vice President	Number of Shareholders	1,000
Marta Scheff Volbrecht	VP - Sales	Where Listed / Symbol	NASDAQ / IMSG

Other Information			
Transfer Agent	Securities Transfer Corp. Dallas, TX	SIC Code	3861
Auditor	Arthur Andersen LLP	Employees	37
		Web Site	imagesystemscorp.com

Impac Mortgage Holdings, Inc.

20371 Irvine Avenue   Santa Ana Heights, CA 92707   Telephone (714)556-0122   Fax (714)438-2150

Company Description

Impac Mortgage Holdings, Inc. (IMH) is a specialty finance company which operates three businesses: 1) Long-Term Investment Operations, 2) Conduit Operations, and 3) Warehouse Lending Operations. The Long-Term Investment Operations invests primarily in non-conforming residential mortgage loans and securities backed by such loans. The Conduit Operations purchases and sells or securitizes primarily non-conforming mortgage loans. The Warehouse Lending Operations provides warehouse and repurchase financing to originators of mortgage loans. IMH is organized as a real estate investment trust (REIT) for federal income tax purposes, which generally allows it to pass through qualified income to stockholders without federal income tax at the corporate level.

	12/31/98	12/31/97	12/31/96	12/31/95
Per Share Information				
Stock Price	4.69	17.88	15.83	10.00
Earnings Per Share	-0.25	-0.99	1.32	0.05
Price / Earnings Ratio	n.a.	n.a.	11.99	200.00
Book Value Per Share	9.03	10.16	13.74	10.64
Price / Book Value %	51.94	175.98	115.21	93.98
Dividends Per Share	1.46	1.68	1.56	0.0
Annual Financial Data				
Operating Results (000's)				
Total Revenues	168,104.0	119,859.0	65,169.0	4,584.0
Costs & Expenses	-170,657.0	-135,888.0	-53,290.0	-2,450.0
Income Before Taxes and Other	-2,553.0	-16,029.0	11,879.0	2,134.0
Other Items	0.0	0.0	0.0	0.0
Income Tax	0.0	0.0	0.0	-76.0
Net Income	-2,553.0	-16,029.0	11,879.0	2,058.0
Cash Flow From Operations	42,809.0	9,164.0	6,409.0	-72.0
Balance Sheet (000's)				
Cash & Equivalents	33,876.0	16,214.0	22,610.0	2,284.0
Total Current Assets	43,915.0	31,226.0	29,873.0	12,284.0
Fixed Assets, Net	0.0	3,866.0	0.0	0.0
Total Assets	1,665,504.0	1,752,812.0	972,355.0	613,688.0
Total Current Liabilities	15,287.0	13,895.0	10,909.0	6,000.0
Long-Term Debt	1,395,941.0	1,497,466.0	832,229.0	562,452.0
Stockholders' Equity	251,606.0	229,030.0	129,190.0	45,236.0
Performance & Financial Condition				
Return on Total Revenues %	-1.52	-13.37	18.23	44.90
Return on Avg Stockholders' Equity %	-1.06	-8.95	13.62	7.90
Return on Average Assets %	-0.15	-1.18	1.50	0.66
Current Ratio	2.87	2.25	2.74	2.05
Debt / Equity %	554.81	653.83	644.19	1,243.37

Compound Growth %'s	EPS % n.a.	Net Income % n.a.	Total Revenues % 232.23

Comments

The Company declared a 3 for 2 stock split on November 24, 1997. All per share amounts have been adjusted for consistency. Due to a deterioration of the mortgage-backed securitization market during the third and fourth quarters of 1998, the Company's lenders made margin calls on their reverse repurchase agreements. To provide the necessary liquidity to meet those margin calls, the Company sold mortgage loans and mortgage-backed securities at losses in order to reduce outstanding borrowings on its reverse mortgage agreements. The sharp decline in 1997 net income is due to a $44.4 million expense related to the termination of a management agreement. Excluding this expense, income would have increased to $1.72 per share. The Company has paid an attractive dividend for three consecutive years.

Officers	Position	Ownership Information	
Joseph R. Tomkinson	Chairman, CEO	Number of Shares Outstanding	24,557,657
William S. Ashmore	President	Market Capitalization	$ 115,175,411
Richard J. Johnson	Exec VP, CFO	Number of Shareholders	10,000
Mary C. Glass-Schannault	Senior VP	Where Listed / Symbol	AMEX / IMH

Other Information			
Transfer Agent	Boston EquiServe Boston, MA	SIC Code	6162
Auditor	KPMG LLP	Employees	145
		Web Site	icifc.com

Industrial Services of America, Inc.

7100 Grade Lane, Building 4   Louisville, KY 40232   Telephone (502)368-1661   Fax (502)363-1440

Company Description

Industrial Services of America, Inc. is a ferrous, non-ferrous and fiber recycling as well as an integrated solid waste management company. The ferrous division's major products include recycling of steel and iron products, whereas the non-ferrous division recycles copper, aluminum and brass. The management division is engaged in the business of commercial, retail and industrial waste management and waste handling equipment sales and service. The Company was founded in 1984.

	12/31/98	12/31/97	12/31/96	12/31/95
Per Share Information				
Stock Price	2.25	4.50	11.12	6.00
Earnings Per Share	-0.26	0.07	0.24	0.40
Price / Earnings Ratio	n.a.	64.29	46.33	15.00
Book Value Per Share	1.77	2.02	1.87	1.02
Price / Book Value %	127.12	222.77	594.65	588.24
Dividends Per Share	0.0	0.0	0.0	0.0
Annual Financial Data				
Operating Results (000's)				
Total Revenues	65,273.0	45,298.0	34,351.8	30,604.1
Costs & Expenses	-65,969.4	-45,075.5	-33,588.9	-29,266.4
Income Before Taxes and Other	-696.4	222.4	739.4	1,221.2
Other Items	0.0	0.0	0.0	0.0
Income Tax	189.4	-85.3	-278.6	-517.0
Net Income	-507.0	137.1	460.8	704.2
Cash Flow From Operations	1,590.9	-468.6	1,496.2	1,351.0
Balance Sheet (000's)				
Cash & Equivalents	1,014.1	495.8	1,371.4	507.9
Total Current Assets	11,540.1	8,490.2	6,632.3	4,092.1
Fixed Assets, Net	5,063.6	3,642.7	2,704.2	1,961.4
Total Assets	18,647.5	13,893.0	9,439.5	6,209.4
Total Current Liabilities	12,200.1	8,985.7	5,664.3	4,007.3
Long-Term Debt	2,612.5	759.9	5.4	367.4
Stockholders' Equity	3,423.1	3,889.7	3,608.8	1,768.0
Performance & Financial Condition				
Return on Total Revenues %	-0.78	0.30	1.34	2.30
Return on Avg Stockholders' Equity %	-13.87	3.66	17.14	49.73
Return on Average Assets %	-3.12	1.18	5.89	13.67
Current Ratio	0.95	0.94	1.17	1.02
Debt / Equity %	76.32	19.54	0.15	20.78

Compound Growth %'s	EPS % n.a.	Net Income % n.a.	Total Revenues % 28.72

Comments

Revenue rose 44.2% in 1998 as compared to 1997. The management service business grew 36.7% to $44.1 million while recycling revenues jumped 66.5% to $19.2 million. The influx of foreign steel due to the depressed Asian market caused domestic commodity pricing to plummet. Due to a lack of domestic steel production, demand for the Company's ferrous product declined. Management estimates that the decline in commodity values had a $370,000 negative impact on 1998 results. At December 31, 1998, the Company had $1.5 million of intangible assets recorded on the books which equated to approximately 45% off stockholders' equity and book value per share. At that date, the Company also had a working capital deficiency of $660,000.

Officers	Position	Ownership Information	
Harry Kletter	Chairman, CEO	Number of Shares Outstanding	1,929,600
Sean M. Garber	President, Treasurer	Market Capitalization	$ 4,341,600
Timothy W. Myres	Senior VP	Number of Shareholders	418
Matthew L. Kletter	Vice President, Secretary	Where Listed / Symbol	NASDAQ / IDSA

Other Information

Transfer Agent	American Securities Transfer, Inc. Denver, CO	SIC Code	3670
Auditor	Crowe, Chizek and Company LLP	Employees	127
		Web Site	isa-inc.com

InnerDyne, Inc.

1244 Reamwood Avenue   Sunnyvale, CA 94089   Telephone (408)745-6010   Fax (408)745-6570

Company Description

InnerDyne, Inc. has developed and commercialized a minimally invasive, surgical access family of products based on its proprietary radial dilation technology. It has been recognized as one of the most technologically advanced surgical access systems available. According to management, this family of products has been proven as being a safer, more effective and less costly alternative to traditional access devices. The Company has also developed biocompatible coating technologies utilized for increasing the efficiency of membrane oxygenator fibers and for the application of specialized drugs to the surface of implantable medical devices. InnerDyne's products are marketed primarily to general surgeons and gynecologists both domestically and internationally. The Company was founded in 1985.

	12/31/98	12/31/97	12/31/96	12/31/95
Per Share Information				
Stock Price	1.31	2.69	3.13	2.63
Earnings Per Share	0.02	-0.04	-0.23	-0.32
Price / Earnings Ratio	65.50	n.a.	n.a.	n.a.
Book Value Per Share	0.40	0.37	0.41	0.22
Price / Book Value %	327.50	727.03	763.41	1,195.45
Dividends Per Share	0.0	0.0	0.0	0.0
Annual Financial Data				
Operating Results (000's)				
Total Revenues	16,561.6	15,998.9	9,349.8	5,525.7
Costs & Expenses	-16,136.6	-16,906.4	-14,008.9	-11,151.7
Income Before Taxes and Other	425.0	-907.5	-4,659.1	-5,627.1
Other Items	0.0	0.0	0.0	0.0
Income Tax	0.0	0.0	0.0	0.0
Net Income	425.0	-907.5	-4,659.1	-5,627.1
Cash Flow From Operations	85.2	-1,065.9	-4,916.8	-5,892.6
Balance Sheet (000's)				
Cash & Equivalents	5,757.5	6,091.5	7,270.3	1,720.8
Total Current Assets	10,228.9	10,286.2	10,155.3	4,314.1
Fixed Assets, Net	814.1	987.2	1,159.3	948.3
Total Assets	11,088.7	11,319.1	11,361.6	5,369.6
Total Current Liabilities	2,071.2	2,634.5	1,972.7	1,173.1
Long-Term Debt	348.7	649.1	629.6	186.7
Stockholders' Equity	8,668.8	8,035.6	8,759.3	4,009.8
Performance & Financial Condition				
Return on Total Revenues %	2.57	-5.67	-49.83	-101.84
Return on Avg Stockholders' Equity %	5.09	-10.81	-72.97	-109.25
Return on Average Assets %	3.79	-8.00	-55.69	-85.15
Current Ratio	4.94	3.90	5.15	3.68
Debt / Equity %	4.02	8.08	7.19	4.66

Compound Growth %'s	EPS %	n.a.	Net Income %	n.a.	Total Revenues %	44.18

Comments

Revenues from product sales increased from $4.2 million (33.9%) in 1998, reflecting greater sales of the "Step" device. This device incorporates the Company's proprietary radial dilation technology and was InnerDyne's first product to be launched on a commercial basis. Licensing, contract and grant revenues decreased to $1.3 million from $3.5 million in 1997. These revenues relate to the Company's proprietary thermal ablation technology and licensing of the Company's proprietary biocompatible coating and radial dilation technology. Overall, revenues were 12.4% higher in 1998. That was enough to turn the Company profitable for the first time. At December 31, 1998, the Company had $41.6 million of tax loss carryforwards available to offset future income.

Officers	Position	Ownership Information	
William G. Mavity	President, CEO	Number of Shares Outstanding	21,891,388
Daniel J. Genter	Senior VP	Market Capitalization	$ 28,677,718
Robert A. Stern	Vice President, CFO	Number of Shareholders	4,000
Michael J. Orth	VP - Research	Where Listed / Symbol	NASDAQ / IDYN

Other Information			
Transfer Agent	American Stock Transfer & Trust Co. New York, NY	SIC Code	3841
Auditor	KPMG LLP	Employees	121
		Web Site	innerdyne.com

Innovative Valve Technologies, Inc.

2 Northpoint Drive, Suite 300   Houston, TX 77060   Telephone (281)925-0300   Fax (281)925-0361

Company Description

Innovative Valve Technologies, Inc. (Invatec) was formed in March 1997 to create a single-source provider of comprehensive maintenance, repair, replacement and value-added distribution services for industrial valves, piping systems and other process-system components throughout North America. On October 28, 1997, Invatec closed its initial public offering of its common stock and consolidated seven established businesses providing various repair and distribution services by means of two purchase transactions and a merger in which its affiliate, The Safe Seal Company, Inc. (SSI), became its subsidiary. Prior to those transactions, SSI had purchased three businesses in the first half of 1997 and Invatec had purchased one business in July 1997.

		12/31/98	12/31/97	12/31/96	12/31/95
Per Share Information					
	Stock Price	2.03	20.00	11.73	5.88
	Earnings Per Share	-0.16	-2.16	-0.15	-1.11
	Price / Earnings Ratio	n.a.	n.a.	n.a.	n.a.
	Book Value Per Share	8.20	7.59	-0.94	-0.75
	Price / Book Value %	24.76	263.50	n.a.	n.a.
	Dividends Per Share	0.0	0.0	0.0	0.0
Annual Financial Data					
Operating Results (000's)					
	Total Revenues	154,864.0	58,620.9	3,915.9	2,862.5
	Costs & Expenses	-155,860.0	-59,527.3	-4,292.3	-3,436.8
	Income Before Taxes and Other	-996.0	-909.3	-414.5	-624.4
	Other Items	0.0	-7,613.4	0.0	-880.1
	Income Tax	-420.0	1,022.7	0.0	0.0
	Net Income	-1,416.0	-7,500.0	-414.5	-1,504.5
	Cash Flow From Operations	-12,380.6	-315.2	-890.3	-1,095.2
Balance Sheet (000's)					
	Cash & Equivalents	0.0	2,544.5	396.6	1,458.0
	Total Current Assets	62,490.1	41,107.5	1,080.1	23,009.0
	Fixed Assets, Net	19,469.8	11,474.7	140.4	100.0
	Total Assets	183,699.8	105,432.7	2,288.1	23,109.0
	Total Current Liabilities	19,944.7	19,875.9	1,092.9	22,286.0
	Long-Term Debt	82,640.3	24,562.1	589.0	0.0
	Stockholders' Equity	79,205.0	59,869.3	-1,393.7	-1,075.0
Performance & Financial Condition					
	Return on Total Revenues %	-0.91	-12.79	-10.59	-52.56
	Return on Avg Stockholders' Equity %	-2.04	-25.65	n.a.	n.a.
	Return on Average Assets %	-0.98	-13.92	-3.26	-12.66
	Current Ratio	3.13	2.07	0.99	1.03
	Debt / Equity %	104.34	41.03	n.a.	n.a.

Compound Growth %'s	EPS % n.a.	Net Income % n.a.	Total Revenues %	278.21

Comments

Financial information prior to 1997 represents SSI and is not comparable to the new entity on a proforma basis. Commencing with the second quarter of 1998 and continuing into 1999, the Company's business was negatively impacted by significant slowdowns experienced by its customers in the petroleum refining, petrochemical, chemical, and pulp and paper industries. Declining earnings also caused the Company to default on a credit facility. The Company's acquisition program was suspended in July 1998 as a result of the low price of the Company's common stock and its inability to borrow funds. The increase in revenues reflected in both 1998 and 1997 over the preceding years is attributable to acquisitions. At December 31, 1998, the Company had $96.2 million of goodwill recorded as assets which equated to approximately 121% of stockholders' equity and book value per share.

Officers	Position	Ownership Information	
William E. Haynes	Chairman, CEO	Number of Shares Outstanding	9,664,562
Charles F. Schugart	President	Market Capitalization	$ 19,619,061
Denny A. Rigas	Senior VP	Number of Shareholders	2,000
Douglas R. Harrington, Jr.	Vice President, Controller	Where Listed / Symbol	NASDAQ / IVTC

Other Information			
Transfer Agent	ChaseMellon Shareholder Services Ridgefield Park, NJ	SIC Code	7600
Auditor	Arthur Andersen LLP	Employees	1,200
		Web Site	invatec.com

Integrity Incorporated

1000 Cody Road   Mobile, AL 36695   Telephone (334)633-9000   Fax (334)633-5202

Company Description

Integrity Incorporated is a producer and publisher of Christian lifestyle products developed to facilitate worship, entertainment and education. Product formats include cassettes, compact discs, videos and songbooks. The Company produces Christian music ranging from praise and worship music, its largest category, to other styles of adult contemporary Christian music and children's music. Integrity's products are sold primarily through retail stores and directly to consumers throughout the United States and in over 140 other countries worldwide. The Company was founded in 1987.

	12/31/98	12/31/97	12/31/96	12/31/95
Per Share Information				
Stock Price	4.03	1.25	1.50	2.12
Earnings Per Share	0.32	0.12	-0.67	-0.37
Price / Earnings Ratio	12.59	10.42	n.a.	n.a.
Book Value Per Share	2.35	2.03	1.90	2.30
Price / Book Value %	171.49	61.58	78.95	92.17
Dividends Per Share	0.0	0.0	0.0	0.0
Annual Financial Data				
Operating Results (000's)				
Total Revenues	38,847.0	32,428.0	30,548.0	36,277.0
Costs & Expenses	-37,094.0	-31,725.0	-34,661.0	-39,447.0
Income Before Taxes and Other	1,753.0	642.0	-4,113.0	-3,235.0
Other Items	-268.0	0.0	-248.0	0.0
Income Tax	369.0	0.0	654.0	1,183.0
Net Income	1,854.0	642.0	-3,707.0	-2,052.0
Cash Flow From Operations	7,298.0	5,883.0	3,530.0	433.0
Balance Sheet (000's)				
Cash & Equivalents	989.0	523.0	1,131.0	1,045.0
Total Current Assets	15,898.0	15,044.0	14,050.0	15,705.0
Fixed Assets, Net	3,473.0	3,499.0	3,709.0	4,936.0
Total Assets	31,617.0	30,775.0	31,058.0	34,659.0
Total Current Liabilities	6,071.0	6,093.0	3,583.0	21,757.0
Long-Term Debt	11,121.0	13,279.0	16,834.0	0.0
Stockholders' Equity	12,981.0	11,196.0	10,487.0	12,693.0
Performance & Financial Condition				
Return on Total Revenues %	4.77	1.98	-12.14	-5.66
Return on Avg Stockholders' Equity %	15.34	5.92	-31.98	-14.93
Return on Average Assets %	5.94	2.08	-11.28	-6.76
Current Ratio	2.62	2.47	3.92	0.72
Debt / Equity %	85.67	118.60	160.52	n.a.

Compound Growth %'s	EPS % n.a.	Net Income % n.a.	Total Revenues % 2.31

Comments

After solid profits in the early 1990s, growing pains caused substantial losses in 1995 and 1996. A strategic reevaluation of the direction of the business occurred in late 1995. Management was pleased to report a return to profitability in 1997. With strong unit sales driven by 54 new song releases, 1998 results were even better. Copyright and royalty income also increased to $4.3 million, a 16.9% advance. Two consecutive years of profit permitted the Company to book the benefits of a tax loss carryover which resulted in a net tax benefit for 1998.

Officers	Position	Ownership Information	
P. Michael Coleman	President, CEO	Number of Shares Outstanding	5,514,000
Jerry W. Weimer	Exec VP, COO	Market Capitalization	$ 22,221,420
Donald J. Moen	Exec VP	Number of Shareholders	1,800
Alison S. Richardson	Senior VP, CFO	Where Listed / Symbol	NASDAQ / ITGR

Other Information			
Transfer Agent	First Union National Bank of N.C. Charlotte, NC	SIC Code	2741
Auditor	PricewaterhouseCoopers LLP	Employees	149
		Web Site	integritymusic.com

Intellectual Technology, Inc.

10639 Roselle Street, Suite B   San Diego, CA 92121   Telephone (760)929-9789   Fax (760)929-9764

Company Description

Intellectual Technology, Inc. is engaged in the design, manufacture and sale or lease of equipment for the automated preparation and dispensing of motor vehicle registration forms and license plate decals. At December 31, 1998, the Company's printing systems were installed in the states of Indiana and Maryland. The printing system is designed as a stand-alone unit, which is used as such in individual motor vehicle registration offices and mailrooms, and has also been incorporated into a self-service terminal assembly. Beginning April 1, 1999, the Company began processing all of the approximately 950,000 annual registrations in South Dakota.

	12/31/98	12/31/97	12/31/96
Per Share Information			
Stock Price	0.62	0.13	0.01
Earnings Per Share	-0.01	-0.09	-0.11
Price / Earnings Ratio	n.a.	n.a.	n.a.
Book Value Per Share	-0.15	-0.13	0.01
Price / Book Value %	n.a.	n.a.	100.00
Dividends Per Share	0.0	0.0	0.0
Annual Financial Data			
Operating Results (000's)			
Total Revenues	5,525.3	3,016.2	71.2
Costs & Expenses	-5,665.9	-3,883.4	-1,037.2
Income Before Taxes and Other	-140.5	-867.2	-966.0
Other Items	0.0	0.0	0.0
Income Tax	0.0	0.0	0.0
Net Income	-140.5	-867.2	-966.0
Cash Flow From Operations	2,710.9	-891.5	1,244.9
Balance Sheet (000's)			
Cash & Equivalents	184.8	404.2	54.9
Total Current Assets	622.6	910.1	54.9
Fixed Assets, Net	2,614.3	3,526.7	0.0
Total Assets	6,641.6	8,193.2	55.4
Total Current Liabilities	6,587.4	3,256.6	0.1
Long-Term Debt	1,543.2	2,287.0	0.0
Stockholders' Equity	-1,488.9	-1,348.4	55.3
Performance & Financial Condition			
Return on Total Revenues %	-2.54	-28.75	-1,356.34
Return on Avg Stockholders' Equity %	n.a.	n.a.	-709.33
Return on Average Assets %	-1.89	-21.03	-24.15
Current Ratio	0.09	0.28	616.99
Debt / Equity %	n.a.	n.a.	n.a.

Compound Growth %'s	EPS % n.a.	Net Income % n.a.	Total Revenues % 780.79

Comments

Revenues increased 83% in 1998. The increase is primarily due to a proportional increase in the number of vehicle registrations processed by the Company. Although expenses also increased, the net loss was substantially lower than in prior years. Furthermore, the Company had nearly $2 million of non-cash depreciation expense which explains the positive cash flow from operations. The Company has a substantial deficit in working capital. However, $4 million of current liabilities is due to a related party.

Officers	Position	Ownership Information	
Nicholas Litchin	Chairman	Number of Shares Outstanding	10,000,001
Walter G. Fuller	President	Market Capitalization	$ 6,200,001
Janice L. Welch	Secretary, CFO	Number of Shareholders	1,000
John F. Grim	VP - Sales	Where Listed / Symbol	OTC-BB / ITTI

Other Information

Transfer Agent	Corporate Stock Transfer, Inc. Denver, CO		SIC Code	6770
Auditor	Comiskey & Company		Employees	14
Market Maker	Herzog, Heine, Geduld, Inc.	(800)221-3600		
	Wien Securities Corp.	(800)624-0050		

Intelligent Controls, Inc.

74 Industrial Park Road   Saco, ME 04072   Telephone (207)283-0156   Fax (207)286-1439

Company Description

Intelligent Controls, Inc., founded in 1978, develops, manufactures, and sells electronic measurement systems to the petroleum and power utility industries and for general level measurement and predictive maintenance applications. The Company's products, including related applications and communication software, enable the users to detect leaks, measure liquid levels, and to perform predictive maintenance monitoring of equipment as an early indicator of wear and potential failure. In April 1998, the Company tendered up to 475,000 of its shares at $3.25 per share but only 115,951 shares came in. Then it tendered again at $2.36 per share after the stock price dropped. The numbers deserve close scrutiny.

	12/26/98	12/27/97	12/31/96	12/31/95
Per Share Information				
Stock Price as of 12/31	2.37	2.37	1.87	4.00
Earnings Per Share	0.15	0.13	-0.13	0.05
Price / Earnings Ratio	15.80	18.23	n.a.	80.00
Book Value Per Share	1.48	0.84	0.70	0.83
Price / Book Value %	160.14	282.14	267.14	481.93
Dividends Per Share	0.0	0.0	0.0	0.0
Annual Financial Data				
Operating Results (000's)				
Total Revenues	16,280.9	13,005.2	9,890.7	9,307.9
Costs & Expenses	-14,295.1	-12,136.8	-10,331.3	-9,028.7
Income Before Taxes and Other	1,985.8	681.0	-651.1	279.2
Other Items	-747.7	0.0	0.0	0.0
Income Tax	-567.0	-246.0	231.0	-98.7
Net Income	671.2	435.0	-420.1	180.5
Cash Flow From Operations	1,697.1	1,297.2	-476.8	-1,034.2
Balance Sheet (000's)				
Cash & Equivalents	4,202.1	0.3	133.7	3,225.5
Total Current Assets	9,247.4	4,624.0	5,640.8	4,843.5
Fixed Assets, Net	889.7	856.6	851.1	858.8
Total Assets	10,168.8	5,507.7	6,711.0	5,716.1
Total Current Liabilities	2,645.4	2,306.1	3,762.7	2,464.4
Long-Term Debt	140.3	372.4	410.0	535.7
Stockholders' Equity	7,306.4	2,761.9	2,280.8	2,670.2
Performance & Financial Condition				
Return on Total Revenues %	4.12	3.34	-4.25	1.94
Return on Avg Stockholders' Equity %	13.33	17.25	-16.97	7.04
Return on Average Assets %	8.56	7.12	-6.76	2.82
Current Ratio	3.50	2.01	1.50	1.97
Debt / Equity %	1.92	13.48	17.97	20.06

Compound Growth %'s	EPS %	44.22	Net Income %	54.92	Total Revenues %	20.49

Comments

Revenues increased 24.5% during 1998. The increase was primarily due to a strong petroleum market segment fueled by new construction and compliance deadlines for leak detection mandated by the EPA. Net earnings were disadvantaged with $747,660 of legal settlement costs. There were additional one-time charges incurred in completing an investment transaction with an outside venture capital firm. The details are not disclosed but the Company issued over two million new shares and netted $3.20 per share. The secret investor appears to be Ampersand Specialty Materials out of Wellesley, Massachusetts, with 1.6 million shares, or 32.6% of the Company.

Officers	Position	Ownership Information	
Roger E. Brooks	President, CEO	Number of Shares Outstanding	4,944,809
Alan Lukas	Vice President	Market Capitalization	$ 11,719,197
Enrique Sales	Vice President	Number of Shareholders	440
Andrew B. Clement	Controller, CFO	Where Listed / Symbol	AMEX / ITC

Other Information			
Transfer Agent	American Stock Transfer & Trust Co. New York, NY	SIC Code	3824
Auditor	PricewaterhouseCoopers LLP	Employees	95
		Web Site	intelcon.com

InterDigital Communications Corporation

781 Third Avenue   King of Prussia, PA 19406   Telephone (610)878-7800   Fax (610)278-6801

Company Description

InterDigital Communications Corporation develops and markets advanced digital wireless telecommunications systems using proprietary technologies for voice and data communications. In conjunction with its technology development, InterDigital has developed an extensive body of technical know-how and a broad patent portfolio related to those technologies and related product embodiments. InterDigital offers its customers, licensees and alliance partners what it believes is unique access to both time division multiple access and Broadband Code Division Multiple Access™ proprietary digital wireless technology. The Company was founded in 1972.

	12/31/98	12/31/97	12/31/96	12/31/95
Per Share Information				
Stock Price	4.56	3.06	5.94	7.37
Earnings Per Share	0.75	-0.72	-0.26	0.78
Price / Earnings Ratio	6.08	n.a.	n.a.	9.45
Book Value Per Share	1.57	0.80	1.51	1.34
Price / Book Value %	290.45	382.50	393.38	550.00
Dividends Per Share	0.0	0.0	0.0	0.0
Annual Financial Data				
Operating Results (000's)				
Total Revenues	101,675.0	51,906.0	57,844.0	88,028.0
Costs & Expenses	-55,446.0	-86,139.0	-65,044.0	-47,591.0
Income Before Taxes and Other	46,229.0	-34,233.0	-7,200.0	40,437.0
Other Items	0.0	0.0	-890.0	-2,514.0
Income Tax	-9,261.0	-34.0	-3,554.0	-3,318.0
Net Income	36,968.0	-34,267.0	-11,644.0	34,605.0
Cash Flow From Operations	30,121.0	-23,800.0	-13,295.0	49,420.0
Balance Sheet (000's)				
Cash & Equivalents	20,059.0	17,828.0	11,954.0	9,427.0
Total Current Assets	75,418.0	46,574.0	86,714.0	73,971.0
Fixed Assets, Net	9,697.0	11,373.0	10,517.0	8,000.0
Total Assets	99,523.0	69,363.0	112,636.0	83,167.0
Total Current Liabilities	20,666.0	23,671.0	29,638.0	14,963.0
Long-Term Debt	3,049.0	3,591.0	4,221.0	1,954.0
Stockholders' Equity	75,808.0	38,505.0	72,507.0	62,440.0
Performance & Financial Condition				
Return on Total Revenues %	36.36	-66.02	-20.13	39.31
Return on Avg Stockholders' Equity %	64.68	-61.74	-17.26	89.52
Return on Average Assets %	43.78	-37.66	-11.89	54.50
Current Ratio	3.65	1.97	2.93	4.94
Debt / Equity %	4.02	9.33	5.82	3.13

Compound Growth %'s	EPS %	-1.30	Net Income %	2.23	Total Revenues %	4.92

Comments

During 1995, the Company recognized $67.7 million of licensing and alliance revenue enabling it to report its first profitable year since its inception. Both 1996 and 1997 were loss years as licensing and alliance revenues declined and development costs increased. In 1998, the Company recognized $92.5 million of licensing and alliance revenues and reported record earnings. Management expects that it may continue to experience significant fluctuations in the amount and timing of license and alliance revenues. Included in working capital at December 31, 1998, is $52.3 million of cash and short term investments.

Officers	Position	Ownership Information	
William A. Doyle	President	Number of Shares Outstanding	48,427,000
Howard E. Goldberg	Exec VP	Market Capitalization	$ 220,827,120
Mark Lemmo	Exec VP	Number of Shareholders	2,298
Charles "Rip" Tilden	Exec VP	Where Listed / Symbol	AMEX / IDC

Other Information			
Transfer Agent	ChaseMellon Shareholder Services Ridgefield Park, NJ	SIC Code	6794
Auditor	Arthur Andersen LLP	Employees	215
		Web Site	interdigital.com

Interfoods of America, Inc.

9400 South Dadeland Boulevard, Suite 720   Miami, FL 33156   Telephone (305)670-0746   Fax (305)670-0767

Company Description

Interfoods of America, Inc. is a growth oriented company which is presently engaged in the business of operating 30 Popeyes® chicken franchises in Florida, Alabama and Louisiana. It previously owned and operated franchising rights for restaurants under the SOBIK'S® SUBS name which were sold in December 1997. Management believes that the Company has a competitive advantage over other operators because of its successful track record in site selection and its high retention rate of the managers of its units. Subsequent to the last year end, the Company entered into an agreement to acquire eight Popeyes locations in Missouri. The Company was founded in 1993.

	09/30/98	09/30/97	09/30/96	09/30/95
Per Share Information				
Stock Price as of 12/31	0.87	0.63	0.91	6.00
Earnings Per Share	-0.03	0.05	-0.09	0.0
Price / Earnings Ratio	n.a.	12.60	n.a.	n.a.
Book Value Per Share	0.59	0.61	0.45	0.02
Price / Book Value %	147.46	103.28	202.22	30,000.00
Dividends Per Share	0.0	0.0	0.0	0.0
Annual Financial Data				
Operating Results (000's)				
Total Revenues	24,219.6	14,155.0	6,350.3	279.5
Costs & Expenses	-24,262.2	-14,001.0	-6,759.7	-265.0
Income Before Taxes and Other	-42.6	154.0	-409.4	10.5
Other Items	0.0	0.0	0.0	0.0
Income Tax	-114.1	164.9	0.0	0.0
Net Income	-156.7	318.9	-409.4	10.5
Cash Flow From Operations	1,152.9	135.6	-681.8	0.0
Balance Sheet (000's)				
Cash & Equivalents	1,523.9	0.0	0.0	5.6
Total Current Assets	1,785.8	458.9	162.8	21.2
Fixed Assets, Net	6,077.3	3,699.0	2,573.7	74.3
Total Assets	11,357.5	7,138.7	5,278.0	126.7
Total Current Liabilities	3,098.1	1,406.1	1,400.8	77.1
Long-Term Debt	3,712.7	1,299.1	204.2	0.0
Stockholders' Equity	3,355.8	4,056.4	3,363.3	49.6
Performance & Financial Condition				
Return on Total Revenues %	-0.65	2.25	-6.45	3.74
Return on Avg Stockholders' Equity %	-4.23	8.60	-23.99	0.70
Return on Average Assets %	-1.69	5.14	-15.15	0.42
Current Ratio	0.58	0.33	0.12	0.27
Debt / Equity %	110.64	32.03	6.07	n.a.

Compound Growth %'s	EPS %	n.a.	Net Income %	n.a.	Total Revenues %	342.52

Comments

Revenues increased 68% during fiscal 1998 as the result of acquisitions of additional locations. Expenses increased due to the number of stores and the associated costs of supervisors training and assimilating the Company's procedures and systems into the acquired stores. The Company plans on continuing its policy of locating and acquiring existing Popeyes franchises which it believes are underperforming. At September 30, 1998, the Company had $2.6 million of intangibles recorded as assets which equated to approximately 78% of stockholders' equity and book value per share. Is the Company being acquired by Tubby's? At least Tubby's reports so, subject to shareholder approvals, of course.

Officers	Position	Ownership Information	
Robert S. Berg	Chairman, CEO	Number of Shares Outstanding	5,709,072
Steven M. Wemple	President, COO	Market Capitalization	$ 4,966,893
		Number of Shareholders	1,200
		Where Listed / Symbol	OTC-BB / IFDA

Other Information			
Transfer Agent	Pacific Stock Transfer Co. Las Vegas, NV	SIC Code	5812
Auditor	Arthur Andersen LLP	Employees	592
Market Maker	Wm. V. Frankel & Co., Inc.	(800)631-3091	
	Herzog, Heine, Geduld, Inc.	(800)221-3600	

Interlink Electronics, Inc.

546 Flynn Road   Camarillo, CA 93012   Telephone (805)484-8855   Fax (805)484-8989

Company Description

Interlink Electronics, Inc. designs, manufactures and sells input devices for computers and other electronic products based on the Company's portfolio of proprietary technologies, including its Force Sensing Resistor (FSR) technology. The Company sells a full spectrum of value-added products and components ranging from FSR sensors, to modules incorporating one or more FSR sensors and related electronics mounted on a printed circuit board, to complete products such as remote controls ready for use by an end-user, which Interlink offers on a branded or generic basis. Interlink also designs, manufactures and sells a broad variety of non-computer products based on its FSR technology. Interlink's customers include the leading computer, computer peripheral and presentation device manufacturers, such as NEC, Sharp, Toshiba, In Focus Systems, IBM, Sony and Logitech.

	12/31/98	12/31/97	12/31/96	12/31/95
Per Share Information				
Stock Price	4.50	4.50	6.00	6.50
Earnings Per Share	0.08	0.01	0.11	0.01
Price / Earnings Ratio	56.25	450.00	54.55	650.00
Book Value Per Share	2.81	2.59	2.21	1.78
Price / Book Value %	160.14	173.75	271.49	365.17
Dividends Per Share	0.0	0.0	0.0	0.0
Annual Financial Data				
Operating Results (000's)				
Total Revenues	22,095.0	19,166.0	13,512.0	10,883.0
Costs & Expenses	-21,693.0	-19,136.0	-12,997.0	-10,733.0
Income Before Taxes and Other	402.0	30.0	515.0	150.0
Other Items	0.0	0.0	0.0	0.0
Income Tax	0.0	0.0	0.0	0.0
Net Income	402.0	30.0	515.0	150.0
Cash Flow From Operations	-479.0	-3,026.0	-1,339.0	-1,316.0
Balance Sheet (000's)				
Cash & Equivalents	3,900.0	4,176.0	3,767.0	3,496.0
Total Current Assets	17,628.0	15,839.0	11,335.0	8,279.0
Fixed Assets, Net	1,561.0	1,150.0	1,143.0	1,160.0
Total Assets	19,577.0	17,555.0	13,185.0	10,187.0
Total Current Liabilities	3,489.0	3,378.0	2,366.0	1,926.0
Long-Term Debt	1,074.0	337.0	235.0	159.0
Stockholders' Equity	14,665.0	13,453.0	9,969.0	7,589.0
Performance & Financial Condition				
Return on Total Revenues %	1.82	0.16	3.81	1.38
Return on Avg Stockholders' Equity %	2.86	0.26	5.87	2.67
Return on Average Assets %	2.17	0.20	4.41	1.95
Current Ratio	5.05	4.69	4.79	4.30
Debt / Equity %	7.32	2.51	2.36	2.10

Compound Growth %'s	EPS %	100.00	Net Income %	38.90	Total Revenues %	26.62

Comments

In 1998, revenues grew 15%, following a 42% increase in 1997. This revenue growth is a result of the Company's focus on developing and marketing the computer pointing device product line based on the Company's patented technologies. Because many of the original equipment manufacturers in this market reside in Japan, about 50% of the Company's revenue comes from Japanese customers. Despite growing price competition, gross margins held relatively stable in 1998. However, 1998 results were negatively impacted by a one-time charge of $355,000 related to a legal settlement. The Company maintains a strong financial condition and intangible assets were immaterial at December 31, 1998. Also at that date, the Company had $11.7 million of tax loss carryovers to offset future taxable income.

Officers	Position	Ownership Information	
E. Michael Thoben III	President, CEO	Number of Shares Outstanding	5,216,000
William A. Yates	Senior VP	Market Capitalization	$ 23,472,000
David J. Arthur	Senior VP	Number of Shareholders	1,600
Paul D. Meyer	CFO, Secretary	Where Listed / Symbol	NASDAQ / LINK

Other Information			
Transfer Agent	Boston EquiServe Boston, MA	SIC Code	3577
Auditor	Arthur Andersen LLP	Employees	120
		Web Site	interlinkelec.com

International Airline Support Group, Inc.

1954 Airport Road, Suite 200   Atlanta, GA 30341   Telephone (770)455-7575   Fax (770)455-7550

Company Description

International Airline Support Group, Inc. is a leading redistributor of aftermarket aircraft spare parts used primarily for McDonnell Douglas MD-80 and DC-9 aircraft. Management believes that the Company has one of the most extensive inventories of aftermarket MD-80 and DC-9 parts in the industry. In addition, the Company provides aircraft spare parts for Boeing, Lockheed, Airbus and commuter aircraft. The aircraft spare parts distributed by the Company, including avionics, rotable and expendable airframe and engine parts, are sold to a wide variety of domestic and international air cargo carriers, major commercial and regional passenger airlines, maintenance and repair facilities and other redistributors. The Company was founded in 1982.

	05/31/98	05/31/97	05/31/96	05/31/95
Per Share Information				
Stock Price as of 12/31	4.62	7.00	3.00	4.20
Earnings Per Share	2.03	0.96	12.69	-4.10
Price / Earnings Ratio	2.28	7.29	0.24	n.a.
Book Value Per Share	4.22	1.95	-49.54	-64.81
Price / Book Value %	109.48	358.97	n.a.	n.a.
Dividends Per Share	0.0	0.0	0.0	0.0
Annual Financial Data				
Operating Results (000's)				
Total Revenues	27,963.0	21,232.0	23,205.0	24,983.0
Costs & Expenses	-25,120.0	-18,973.0	-20,905.0	-25,597.0
Income Before Taxes and Other	2,843.0	2,259.0	2,300.0	-614.0
Other Items	0.0	0.0	0.0	0.0
Income Tax	2,820.0	-531.0	-14.0	0.0
Net Income	5,663.0	1,728.0	2,286.0	-614.0
Cash Flow From Operations	4,169.0	582.2	2,094.3	-500.0
Balance Sheet (000's)				
Cash & Equivalents	438.4	465.7	940.3	848.3
Total Current Assets	14,760.1	13,563.3	12,301.1	10,283.0
Fixed Assets, Net	6,375.8	6,658.2	3,831.3	4,227.8
Total Assets	23,636.4	21,287.2	16,132.3	14,510.8
Total Current Liabilities	4,531.8	4,422.3	23,141.5	23,772.4
Long-Term Debt	8,296.1	12,204.6	0.0	0.0
Stockholders' Equity	10,808.5	4,660.3	-7,415.9	-9,701.9
Performance & Financial Condition				
Return on Total Revenues %	20.25	8.14	9.85	-2.46
Return on Avg Stockholders' Equity %	73.22	n.a.	n.a.	n.a.
Return on Average Assets %	25.21	9.24	14.92	-3.07
Current Ratio	3.26	3.07	0.53	0.43
Debt / Equity %	76.76	261.89	n.a.	n.a.

Compound Growth %'s	EPS % -60.00	Net Income % 57.39	Total Revenues % 3.83

Comments

On October 3, 1996, the Company completed a restructuring whereby it effected a 1 for 27 reverse split and issued approximately 2.2 million new shares in exchange for $10 million of debt. Per share amounts have been adjusted for consistency. The compound negative growth in earnings per share is reflective of the new shares. In fiscal 1998, the Company recognized a tax benefit from the probable use of tax loss carryovers, which totalled $5.3 million at year end. This significantly inflates earnings per share from what it would be with a normal tax expense. For the nine months ended February 28, 1999, the Company reported revenues and net income of $16.3 million and $3,610,336 ($1.27 per share) as compared to $14.3 million and $1,536,422 ($.56 per share) for the same period of the preceding year.

Officers	Position	Ownership Information	
Alexius A. Dyer III	President, CEO	Number of Shares Outstanding	2,562,667
George Murnane III	Exec VP, CFO	Market Capitalization	$ 11,839,522
James M. Isaacson	VP - Finance, Secretary	Number of Shareholders	750
Kyle R. Kirkland	Director	Where Listed / Symbol	AMEX / YLF

Other Information			
Transfer Agent	American Stock Transfer & Trust Co. New York, NY	SIC Code	5080
Auditor	Grant Thornton LLP	Employees	28
		Web Site	iasgroup.com

International Electronics, Inc.

427 Turnpike Street   Canton, MA 02021   Telephone (781)821-5566   Fax (781)821-4443

Company Description

International Electronics, Inc. designs, manufactures, markets and sells electronic products for the security industry and for other commercial applications including the following: a line of access control and digital keypad products, electronic glassbreak protectors and voice verification systems. Various trade names include Door-Guard™, Secured Series™, Tri-Guard™ and Glass-Guard™. The Company was formed in 1977.

	08/31/98	08/31/97	08/31/96	08/31/95
Per Share Information				
Stock Price as of 12/31	1.25	1.25	2.62	1.25
Earnings Per Share	0.34	0.04	0.10	-0.16
Price / Earnings Ratio	3.68	31.25	26.20	n.a.
Book Value Per Share	1.27	0.88	0.84	0.69
Price / Book Value %	98.43	142.05	311.90	181.16
Dividends Per Share	0.0	0.0	0.0	0.0
Annual Financial Data				
Operating Results (000's)				
Total Revenues	9,689.5	9,195.0	8,638.7	6,473.7
Costs & Expenses	-9,038.4	-9,097.3	-8,436.8	-6,704.7
Income Before Taxes and Other	651.1	97.7	202.0	-231.0
Other Items	0.0	10.4	0.0	0.0
Income Tax	-121.0	-38.0	-40.0	0.0
Net Income	530.1	70.1	162.0	-231.0
Cash Flow From Operations	893.3	247.7	336.1	24.1
Balance Sheet (000's)				
Cash & Equivalents	895.9	160.1	556.7	327.8
Total Current Assets	2,782.7	2,407.5	2,459.3	1,892.9
Fixed Assets, Net	369.0	357.3	301.3	280.3
Total Assets	3,312.0	3,026.2	3,100.2	2,606.1
Total Current Liabilities	1,336.2	1,606.9	1,414.8	1,151.7
Long-Term Debt	82.9	0.0	0.0	0.0
Stockholders' Equity	1,893.0	1,351.0	1,275.9	1,001.7
Performance & Financial Condition				
Return on Total Revenues %	5.47	0.76	1.88	-3.57
Return on Avg Stockholders' Equity %	32.68	5.34	14.22	-20.50
Return on Average Assets %	16.73	2.29	5.68	-8.75
Current Ratio	2.08	1.50	1.74	1.64
Debt / Equity %	4.38	n.a.	n.a.	n.a.

Compound Growth %'s	EPS %	84.39	Net Income %	80.90	Total Revenues %	14.39

Comments

The increases in revenue in each of the last four fiscal years is primarily attributable to an increase in access control and keypad product sales, offset in part by reductions in glassbreak detector sales. Research and development expenditures increased each year as well, totalling $537,426 in fiscal 1998 as compared to $308,162 in fiscal 1995. Recent efforts include enhancing the Company's voice verification technology. For the six months ended   February 28, 1999, the Company reported revenue and net income of $4.5 million and $175,804 ($.11 per share) as compared to $4.6 million and $217,702 ($.14 per share) for the same period of the preceding year.

Officers	Position	Ownership Information	
John Waldstein	President, CEO	Number of Shares Outstanding	1,493,301
Christopher Hentschel	Vice President	Market Capitalization	$ 1,866,626
James C. Brierley, Jr.	VP - Sales	Number of Shareholders	1,700
Heath Paley	Director	Where Listed / Symbol	NASDAQ / IEIBC

Other Information			
Transfer Agent	American Stock Transfer & Trust Co. New York, NY	SIC Code	3669
Auditor	Deloitte & Touche LLP	Employees	69
		Web Site	ieib.com

International Total Services, Inc.

Crowne Centre, 5005 Rockside Road   Independence, OH 44131   Telephone (216)642-4522   Fax (216)642-4539

Company Description

International Total Services, Inc. is a leading provider of aviation contract support services and is establishing a growing presence in the security services market. Aviation services offered by the Company include skycap, baggage handling and aircraft appearance services, and wheelchair and electric cart operations. The Company's security services extend beyond aviation security, and include the provision of commercial security services to government and business clients, hospitals, arenas and museums. The Company has completed five acquisitions since the end of fiscal 1998. The Company was founded in 1978 and had its initial public offering in fiscal 1998.

	03/31/98	03/31/97	03/31/96	03/31/95
Per Share Information				
Stock Price as of 12/31	4.53	10.00	8.00	3.00
Earnings Per Share	1.00	0.33	0.18	-0.11
Price / Earnings Ratio	4.53	30.30	44.44	n.a.
Book Value Per Share	5.87	0.87	0.66	0.50
Price / Book Value %	77.17	1,149.43	1,212.12	600.00
Dividends Per Share	0.0	0.0	0.0	0.0
Annual Financial Data				
Operating Results (000's)				
Total Revenues	173,235.0	115,745.0	95,900.0	92,654.0
Costs & Expenses	-163,364.0	-112,309.0	-93,467.0	-92,824.0
Income Before Taxes and Other	9,003.0	2,933.0	1,996.0	-170.0
Other Items	0.0	0.0	0.0	0.0
Income Tax	-3,758.0	-1,237.0	-958.0	-548.0
Net Income	5,245.0	1,696.0	1,038.0	-718.0
Cash Flow From Operations	1,502.0	1,943.0	1,964.0	-1,000.0
Balance Sheet (000's)				
Cash & Equivalents	1,032.0	1,452.0	1,873.0	1,267.0
Total Current Assets	27,623.0	16,286.0	13,799.0	12,757.0
Fixed Assets, Net	5,495.0	3,254.0	3,200.0	2,178.0
Total Assets	58,567.0	27,001.0	20,892.0	20,473.0
Total Current Liabilities	18,486.0	15,962.0	16,750.0	17,182.0
Long-Term Debt	544.0	7,555.0	164.0	152.0
Stockholders' Equity	39,103.0	3,195.0	3,978.0	3,139.0
Performance & Financial Condition				
Return on Total Revenues %	3.03	1.47	1.08	-0.77
Return on Avg Stockholders' Equity %	24.80	47.29	29.17	-20.51
Return on Average Assets %	12.26	7.08	5.02	-3.78
Current Ratio	1.49	1.02	0.82	0.74
Debt / Equity %	1.39	236.46	4.12	4.84

Compound Growth %'s	EPS % 135.70	Net Income % 124.79	Total Revenues % 23.19

Comments

The increase in revenues in fiscal 1998 is attributable to acquisitions and internal growth. The current strength of the United States economy, which has driven unemployment to low levels, has adversely impacted the Company's ability to attract and retain the workforce needed to provide the services required under its service contracts. This has resulted in increased overtime pay and a reduction in margins. At March 31, 1998, the Company has $25.3 million of intangible assets on its books which equated to approximately 65% of stockholders' equity and book value per share. For the nine months ended December 31, 1998, the Company reported revenues and net income of $174.9 million and $2.7 million ($.41 per share) as compared to $123.2 million and $3.8 million ($.79 per share) for the same period of the preceding year.

Officers	Position	Ownership Information	
Robert A. Weitzel	Chairman, CEO	Number of Shares Outstanding	6,662,000
James O. Singer	President, COO	Market Capitalization	$ 30,178,860
Brian S. Kenyon	VP - Finance	Number of Shareholders	650
Scott E. Brewer	Vice President	Where Listed / Symbol	NASDAQ / ITSW

Other Information			
Transfer Agent	New York Drop-First Chicago Trust Co. New York, NY	SIC Code	7389
Auditor	Grant Thornton LLP	Employees	15,000
		Web Site	itsw.com

InterSystems, Inc.

7115 Clinton Drive   Houston, TX 77020   Telephone (713)622-7710   Fax (713)675-8479

Company Description

InterSystems, Inc.'s two principal lines of business consist of the operations of its wholly-owned subsidiary, INTERSYSTEMS, INC., which designs, manufactures and sells specialized materials handling equipment, and its wholly-owned subsidiary, CHEMTRUSION, INC., which conducts custom resin compounding operations. Custom resin compounding involves the combining of a resin with various additives such as pigments, impact modifiers, mineral fillers or stabilizers to customize the product to a particular end use. The Company was founded in 1984.

	12/31/98	12/31/97	12/31/96	12/31/95
Per Share Information				
Stock Price	1.00	1.87	1.06	2.12
Earnings Per Share	0.05	0.08	-0.37	-0.16
Price / Earnings Ratio	20.00	23.38	n.a.	n.a.
Book Value Per Share	0.50	0.45	-0.19	0.16
Price / Book Value %	200.00	415.56	n.a.	1,325.00
Dividends Per Share	0.0	0.0	0.0	0.0
Annual Financial Data				
Operating Results (000's)				
Total Revenues	33,345.0	27,025.0	20,508.0	16,622.0
Costs & Expenses	-32,902.0	-26,606.0	-20,907.0	-17,317.0
Income Before Taxes and Other	443.0	419.0	-399.0	-695.0
Other Items	0.0	150.0	-1,920.0	0.0
Income Tax	0.0	0.0	0.0	0.0
Net Income	443.0	569.0	-2,319.0	-695.0
Cash Flow From Operations	1,701.0	1,242.0	33.0	-396.0
Balance Sheet (000's)				
Cash & Equivalents	133.0	802.0	1,374.0	6.0
Total Current Assets	6,312.0	6,729.0	6,046.0	5,320.0
Fixed Assets, Net	23,479.0	21,131.0	18,810.0	5,388.0
Total Assets	30,053.0	28,124.0	25,216.0	11,327.0
Total Current Liabilities	7,724.0	7,194.0	5,629.0	5,947.0
Long-Term Debt	17,806.0	17,458.0	18,697.0	4,675.0
Stockholders' Equity	3,881.0	3,472.0	-1,187.0	705.0
Performance & Financial Condition				
Return on Total Revenues %	1.33	2.11	-11.31	-4.18
Return on Avg Stockholders' Equity %	12.05	49.80	n.a.	-83.13
Return on Average Assets %	1.52	2.13	-12.69	-3.86
Current Ratio	0.82	0.94	1.07	0.89
Debt / Equity %	458.80	502.82	n.a.	663.12

Compound Growth %'s	EPS % n.a.	Net Income % n.a.	Total Revenues % 26.12

Comments

Revenue increased 23.4% during 1998 mostly due to continued demand for equipment manufactured at INTERSYSTEMS. A large overseas order accounted for approximately 70% of the increase. Management is continuing its program of investing significant resources in equipment and personnel to achieve the Company's next level of growth. In January 1999, both Companies completed expansion of their production capabilities. Despite being hampered by a significant amount of debt and a deficiency of working capital, the Company has continued to record an impressive growth rate.

Officers	Position	Ownership Information	
Herbert M. Pearlman	Chairman	Number of Shares Outstanding	7,828,000
Fred S. Zeidman	President, CEO	Market Capitalization	$ 7,828,000
Wm. Chris Mathers	CFO	Number of Shareholders	2,000
David S. Lawi	Secretary	Where Listed / Symbol	AMEX / II

Other Information			
Transfer Agent	American Stock Transfer & Trust Co. New York, NY	SIC Code	3523
Auditor	BDO Seidman LLP	Employees	276
		Web Site	intersystems-inc.com

Interwest Home Medical, Inc.

235 East 6100 South   Salt Lake City, UT 84107-7349   Telephone (801)261-5100   Fax (801)262-5345

Company Description

Interwest Home Medical, Inc. provides a diversified range of home health care services and products. The Company currently conducts its business from twenty-eight locations in the western United States and serves over 20,000 customers. The Company divides its products and services into three general categories: 1) Home Oxygen and Respiratory Care Services, 2) Home Medical Equipment and Supplies, and 3) Rehabilitation Services. Many of Interwest's customers suffer from chronic obstructive pulmonary disease such as emphysema, and require supplemental oxygen or other respiratory therapy services in order to alleviate the symptoms and discomfort of respiratory dysfunction.

	09/30/98	09/30/97	09/30/96	09/30/95
Per Share Information				
Stock Price as of 12/31	3.12	2.75	3.75	5.00
Earnings Per Share	0.35	0.17	0.18	0.42
Price / Earnings Ratio	8.91	16.18	20.83	11.90
Book Value Per Share	2.28	1.93	1.81	1.63
Price / Book Value %	136.84	142.49	207.18	306.75
Dividends Per Share	0.0	0.0	0.0	0.0
Annual Financial Data				
Operating Results (000's)				
Total Revenues	28,842.0	24,946.0	19,937.4	15,544.2
Costs & Expenses	-26,881.0	-24,733.0	-19,267.0	-14,819.5
Income Before Taxes and Other	1,961.0	213.0	670.4	724.7
Other Items	0.0	516.0	0.0	633.3
Income Tax	-535.0	-73.0	-62.0	-130.0
Net Income	1,426.0	656.0	608.4	1,228.0
Cash Flow From Operations	2,854.0	817.0	1,132.5	381.1
Balance Sheet (000's)				
Cash & Equivalents	253.0	901.0	539.3	578.4
Total Current Assets	15,572.0	12,225.0	8,608.0	7,078.2
Fixed Assets, Net	6,745.0	5,006.0	3,166.5	2,454.0
Total Assets	28,381.0	22,541.0	15,789.0	12,577.4
Total Current Liabilities	12,959.0	9,580.0	6,155.0	5,036.7
Long-Term Debt	5,674.0	4,848.0	3,427.3	1,911.4
Stockholders' Equity	9,332.0	7,846.0	5,947.7	5,339.3
Performance & Financial Condition				
Return on Total Revenues %	4.94	2.58	3.05	7.90
Return on Avg Stockholders' Equity %	16.60	9.51	10.78	33.98
Return on Average Assets %	5.60	3.42	4.29	15.35
Current Ratio	1.20	1.28	1.40	1.41
Debt / Equity %	60.80	61.79	57.62	35.80

Compound Growth %'s	EPS %	-5.90	Net Income %	5.11	Total Revenues %	22.88

Comments

The Company completed 17 acquisitions and one merger in both existing and new markets between fiscal 1996 and 1998. Despite the positive impact on revenue from these acquisitions, same store growth was an impressive 13% in fiscal 1998. Fiscal 1997 and 1995 results included gains from the sale of undeveloped real estate of $516,000 and $633,321, respectively. At September 30, 1998, the Company had $5.0 million recorded as goodwill on its books which equated to approximately 53% of stockholders' equity and book value per share. Management has demonstrated its ability to ring up consistent profits while executing its growth strategies.

Officers	Position	Ownership Information	
James E. Robinson	President, CEO	Number of Shares Outstanding	4,089,029
Bret A. Hardy	Controller, CFO	Market Capitalization	$ 12,757,770
James U. Jensen	Director	Number of Shareholders	850
Jeffrey F. Poore	Director	Where Listed / Symbol	NASDAQ / IWHM

Other Information			
Transfer Agent	American Stock Transfer & Trust Co. New York, NY	SIC Code	8082
Auditor	Tanner & Co.	Employees	300

InterWest Medical Corporation

3221 Hulen Street, Suite C   Fort Worth, TX 76107-6193   Telephone (817)731-2743   Fax (817)731-2768

Company Description

InterWest Medical Corporation owns and operates a 156-bed skilled nursing home located on a 9 acre parcel of land in Colton, California. Since its formation in 1983, the Company has also dabbled with construction and real estate development. Uncharacteristic of a focused company, InterWest has acquired oil and gas leases and properties in Texas, Oklahoma, Mississippi and Louisiana. We selected this Company for the second edition because of its low market capitalization relative to income producing properties and a substantial cash flow from operations. Please join us for a look at the numbers.

	12/31/98	12/31/97	12/31/96	12/31/95
Per Share Information				
Stock Price	0.15	0.12	0.12	0.11
Earnings Per Share	0.08	0.04	0.0	0.0
Price / Earnings Ratio	1.88	3.00	n.a.	n.a.
Book Value Per Share	0.24	0.18	0.15	0.15
Price / Book Value %	62.50	66.67	80.00	73.33
Dividends Per Share	0.0	0.0	0.0	0.0
Annual Financial Data				
Operating Results (000's)				
Total Revenues	11,353.8	10,245.2	9,376.7	9,204.6
Costs & Expenses	-10,600.2	-9,636.1	-9,426.0	-8,515.1
Income Before Taxes and Other	753.6	609.1	-49.3	-47.9
Other Items	603.8	0.0	0.0	0.0
Income Tax	-51.8	0.0	0.0	0.0
Net Income	1,305.6	609.1	-49.3	-47.9
Cash Flow From Operations	1,170.6	1,155.1	402.5	839.7
Balance Sheet (000's)				
Cash & Equivalents	282.9	1,090.7	1,954.5	2,096.9
Total Current Assets	5,962.5	5,699.6	3,799.3	3,576.0
Fixed Assets, Net	3,763.3	3,506.2	4,104.0	5,004.9
Total Assets	10,164.6	9,522.2	8,333.6	8,580.9
Total Current Liabilities	2,133.2	1,986.9	1,208.2	1,237.9
Long-Term Debt	4,558.3	4,530.2	4,545.7	4,559.5
Stockholders' Equity	3,473.2	3,005.1	2,579.8	2,783.5
Performance & Financial Condition				
Return on Total Revenues %	10.92	5.95	-0.53	-0.52
Return on Avg Stockholders' Equity %	40.31	21.81	-1.84	-1.84
Return on Average Assets %	13.26	6.82	-0.58	-0.57
Current Ratio	2.80	2.87	3.14	2.89
Debt / Equity %	131.24	150.75	176.20	163.80

Compound Growth %'s	EPS % n.a.	Net Income % n.a.	Total Revenues % 9.11

Comments

In 1998, the Company continued to experience a rise in net patient revenue in the Company's long-term health care facility. Net patient revenue grew 13.4% in 1998 as compared to 1997. 1998 results were also favorably impacted by a gain of $603,753 on the sale of assets. The Company has been reacquiring its shares in recent years and gathered another 2.6 million shares in 1998 at an average price of $.186 per share. Although it may be hard to believe that one could find anything good for $.15 per share, this may be one of the more interesting stocks in that category.

Officers	Position	Ownership Information	
Arch B. Gilbert	President, CEO	Number of Shares Outstanding	14,195,661
Terry M. Gallagher	Director	Market Capitalization	$ 2,129,349
		Number of Shareholders	1,991
		Where Listed / Symbol	OTC-BB / IWMC

Other Information			
Transfer Agent	American Stock Transfer & Trust Co. New York, NY	SIC Code	8051
Auditor	Weaver and Tidwell, L.L.P.	Employees	3
Market Maker	Fahnestock & Co., Inc. (800)223-3012		
	Herzog, Heine, Geduld, Inc. (800)221-3600		

Isomet Corporation

5263 Port Royal Road   Springfield, VA 22151   Telephone (703)321-8301   Fax (703)321-8546

Company Description

Isomet Corporation is a manufacturer of laser control devices, systems and equipment for color image reproduction applications. Isomet's acousto-optic line is comprised of laser control devices and systems for applications that make use of lasers to process or communicate information through various forms of recorded images. Acousto-optic technology is an essential element of image processing systems such as laser printers, laser film recorders, phototypesetters and laser-based inspection systems. Isomet's graphic arts systems product line consists of high resolution digital color scanners, laser film recorders, laser plotters and specialized interface software and electronics packages.

	12/31/98	12/31/97	12/31/96	12/31/95
Per Share Information				
Stock Price	3.00	4.50	1.41	2.62
Earnings Per Share	0.61	0.68	0.35	-0.02
Price / Earnings Ratio	4.92	6.62	4.03	n.a.
Book Value Per Share	3.22	2.60	1.88	1.52
Price / Book Value %	93.17	173.08	75.00	172.37
Dividends Per Share	0.0	0.0	0.0	0.0
Annual Financial Data				
Operating Results (000's)				
Total Revenues	9,412.5	8,653.0	5,804.0	4,799.6
Costs & Expenses	-7,618.8	-6,659.1	-5,186.7	-4,896.2
Income Before Taxes and Other	1,793.7	1,993.9	617.4	-96.6
Other Items	0.0	0.0	-3.8	-0.6
Income Tax	-594.4	-663.2	68.1	53.1
Net Income	1,199.3	1,330.7	681.7	-44.1
Cash Flow From Operations	234.6	1,578.6	478.3	127.9
Balance Sheet (000's)				
Cash & Equivalents	1,426.8	1,534.4	200.9	85.5
Total Current Assets	7,721.9	6,858.9	5,833.2	4,558.8
Fixed Assets, Net	284.8	277.4	315.8	345.0
Total Assets	8,014.1	7,188.6	6,201.3	4,991.0
Total Current Liabilities	1,414.2	1,595.9	1,738.1	963.9
Long-Term Debt	387.5	633.1	864.7	1,122.2
Stockholders' Equity	6,212.4	4,955.1	3,587.6	2,901.0
Performance & Financial Condition				
Return on Total Revenues %	12.74	15.38	11.75	-0.92
Return on Avg Stockholders' Equity %	21.48	31.15	21.01	-1.47
Return on Average Assets %	15.78	19.88	12.18	-0.88
Current Ratio	5.46	4.30	3.36	4.73
Debt / Equity %	6.24	12.78	24.10	38.68

Compound Growth %'s	EPS %	32.02	Net Income %	32.64	Total Revenues %	25.17

Comments

Growth slowed to a moderate 8% in 1998. Management did not comment on this or any other aspect of operations. The balance sheet keeps getting better defying all notions that small companies cannot be on as solid ground as their large competitors. One customer, Polaroid, accounted for 51% of sales in 1998, up from 36% of sales in 1997. This may give some investors the jitters as Polaroid has had troubles of its own. Still the order backlog at December 31, 1998 was $3.3 million, down only slightly from the previous year.

Officers	Position	Ownership Information	
Henry Zenzie	President, CEO	Number of Shares Outstanding	1,927,590
Jerry W. Rayburn	Exec VP, CFO	Market Capitalization	$ 5,782,770
Leon Bademian	Exec VP	Number of Shareholders	500
Vanda Gallagher	Controller	Where Listed / Symbol	NASDAQ / IOMT

Other Information			
Transfer Agent	ChaseMellon Shareholder Services Ridgefield Park, NJ	SIC Code	3577
Auditor	Aronson, Fetridge & Weigle	Employees	49
		Web Site	isomet.com

Ithaca Industries, Inc.

Highway 268 West, P.O. Box 620   Wilkesboro, NC 28697   Telephone (336)667-5231   Fax (336)667-2979

Company Description

Ithaca Industries, Inc. is a leading designer, marketer and manufacturer of private brand men's and boys' underwear and outerwear T-shirt products, women's and girls' underwear and women's hosiery. The Company operates distribution and manufacturing facilities in the southeastern United States and off-shore manufacturing facilities in Central America. On December 16, 1996, the Company emerged from bankruptcy. Pursuant to the plan of reorganization, prior equity interests in the Company were canceled, 10 million shares of common stock were distributed to the holders of subordinated debt, and unsecured claims were paid in full.

	01/31/98	02/01/97	02/02/96	01/27/95
Per Share Information				
Stock Price as of 12/31	1.75	2.62	n.a.	n.a.
Earnings Per Share	0.15	6.26	-4.96	0.75
Price / Earnings Ratio	11.67	0.42	n.a.	n.a.
Book Value Per Share	2.09	1.94	-9.36	-4.39
Price / Book Value %	83.73	135.05	n.a.	n.a.
Dividends Per Share	0.0	0.0	0.0	0.0
Annual Financial Data				
Operating Results (000's)				
Total Revenues	237,021.0	340,311.0	398,819.0	414,800.0
Costs & Expenses	-234,682.0	-346,942.0	-424,029.0	-401,634.0
Income Before Taxes and Other	2,339.0	-6,631.0	-25,210.0	13,166.0
Other Items	0.0	72,064.0	-51,591.0	0.0
Income Tax	-803.0	-2,818.0	27,157.0	-5,653.0
Net Income	1,536.0	62,615.0	-49,644.0	7,513.0
Cash Flow From Operations	16,690.0	42,080.0	-2,283.0	-3,471.0
Balance Sheet (000's)				
Cash & Equivalents	680.0	66.0	10,369.0	7,531.0
Total Current Assets	79,944.0	96,863.0	149,087.0	152,180.0
Fixed Assets, Net	34,115.0	35,531.0	54,295.0	55,389.0
Total Assets	115,990.0	133,687.0	208,642.0	224,471.0
Total Current Liabilities	28,448.0	33,340.0	294,996.0	39,152.0
Long-Term Debt	53,519.0	66,069.0	0.0	229,233.0
Stockholders' Equity	20,895.0	19,359.0	-93,558.0	-43,914.0
Performance & Financial Condition				
Return on Total Revenues %	0.65	18.40	-12.45	1.81
Return on Avg Stockholders' Equity %	7.63	n.a.	n.a.	n.a.
Return on Average Assets %	1.23	36.58	-22.92	3.76
Current Ratio	2.81	2.91	0.51	3.89
Debt / Equity %	256.13	341.28	n.a.	n.a.

Compound Growth %'s	EPS %	-41.52	Net Income %	-41.09	Total Revenues %	-17.02

Comments

In the third and fourth quarter of fiscal 1996 the Company undertook an extensive review of its entire business which led to a consolidation of plants and the moving of sewing operations off-shore. Fiscal 1996 results include nonrecurring write-offs of $51,591,000 in connection with those actions. Fiscal 1997 results include $72,064,000 of nonrecurring income primarily related to the cancellation of debt in the bankruptcy proceedings as discussed above. For the nine months ended October 31, 1998, the Company reported revenues and net income of $205.6 million and $992,000 ($.10 per share) as compared to $182.9 million and $1,649,000 ($.16 per share) for the same period of the preceding year. Although the Company has reported profits, it remains highly leveraged.

Officers	Position	Ownership Information	
Jim D. Waller	President, CEO	Number of Shares Outstanding	10,000,000
David H. Jones	Exec VP	Market Capitalization	$ 17,500,000
Richard P. Thrush	Senior VP, CFO	Number of Shareholders	2,000
		Where Listed / Symbol	OTC-BB / ITHI

Other Information			
Transfer Agent	American Stock Transfer & Trust Co. New York, NY	SIC Code	2250
Auditor	KPMG LLP	Employees	5,500
Market Maker	Mesirow Financial, Inc. (800)545-5428		
	Credit Research & Trading LLC (203)629-6436		

JB Oxford Holdings, Inc.

9665 Wilshire Boulevard, Suite 300   Beverly Hills, CA 90212   Telephone (310)777-8888   Fax (310)385-2236

Company Description

JB Oxford Holdings, Inc., founded in 1987, is a registered securities broker/dealer offering clearing, settlement, execution, safekeeping, cash and margin account services to regional broker/dealers. The Company also provides discount brokerage services to the investing public through its registered representatives as well as electronic and telephone trading services. Retail operations are conducted from offices in Los Angeles, New York, and Miami. The Company's online trading, quotes and research are available on its Internet site. In May 1998, the Company entered into a transaction with Third Capital Partners, LLC and other investors which resulted in a change of control of the Company. The Company's new Board of Directors appointed new management to the Company in June 1998.

	12/31/98	12/31/97	12/31/96	12/31/95
Per Share Information				
Stock Price	2.12	0.69	1.34	2.69
Earnings Per Share	-0.13	0.09	0.23	0.40
Price / Earnings Ratio	n.a.	7.67	5.83	6.73
Book Value Per Share	1.12	1.07	1.18	0.75
Price / Book Value %	189.29	64.49	113.56	358.67
Dividends Per Share	0.0	0.0	0.0	0.0
Annual Financial Data				
Operating Results (000's)				
Total Revenues	67,268.3	69,961.6	57,599.4	39,605.4
Costs & Expenses	-66,055.7	-67,339.1	-51,391.5	-32,864.0
Income Before Taxes and Other	1,212.6	2,622.6	6,207.9	6,741.3
Other Items	-2,530.0	0.0	0.0	0.0
Income Tax	-521.3	-1,099.9	-2,168.3	-1,516.8
Net Income	-1,838.6	1,522.7	4,039.6	5,224.5
Cash Flow From Operations	-136.3	5,848.1	-18,492.4	24,312.1
Balance Sheet (000's)				
Cash & Equivalents	2,496.6	2,598.1	969.9	15,949.6
Total Current Assets	393,095.4	328,442.9	325,714.3	171,659.3
Fixed Assets, Net	2,860.1	3,460.5	2,987.2	2,043.8
Total Assets	405,990.4	342,312.3	330,336.1	175,764.3
Total Current Liabilities	379,901.3	318,377.6	305,436.6	160,448.0
Long-Term Debt	1,381.0	8,811.7	12,541.4	6,872.4
Stockholders' Equity	15,616.6	15,123.0	12,358.2	8,443.9
Performance & Financial Condition				
Return on Total Revenues %	-2.73	2.18	7.01	13.19
Return on Avg Stockholders' Equity %	-11.96	11.08	38.84	133.20
Return on Average Assets %	-0.49	0.45	1.60	3.97
Current Ratio	1.03	1.03	1.07	1.07
Debt / Equity %	8.84	58.27	101.48	81.39

Compound Growth %'s	EPS % n.a.	Net Income % n.a.	Total Revenues % 19.31

Comments

New management's cost containment strategy, combined with an overall increase in market volumes, had a positive effect on the Company's financial results as the Company returned to profitability in the fourth quarter of 1998. 1998 results included a $2,530,000 non-cash expense related to a change in the conversion feature of convertible debt. In 1997, net income decreased substantially from 1997 levels due to several different factors. Legal and other costs associated with the settlement of a legal matter were approximately $1.2 million. The litigation arose from corporate finance activities performed in 1994. The Company has since ceased performing such activities. Trading losses and related write downs also had a negative after tax impact on 1997 earnings of approximately $1.4 million.

Officers	Position	Ownership Information	
Christopher Jarret	Chairman, CEO	Number of Shares Outstanding	13,906,705
James Lewis	President, COO	Market Capitalization	$ 29,482,215
Michael J. Chiodo	CFO, Treasurer	Number of Shareholders	23,900
Scott G. Monson	Director	Where Listed / Symbol	NASDAQ / JBOH

Other Information			
Transfer Agent	Oxford Transfer & Registrar Agency, Inc. Glendale, CA	SIC Code	6210
Auditor	Arthur Andersen LLP	Employees	255
		Web Site	jboxford.com

JLM Couture, Inc.

225 West 37th Street, 5th Floor   New York, NY 10018   Telephone (212)921-7058   Fax (212)921-7608

Company Description

JLM Couture, Inc., whose name was changed from Jim Hjelm's Private Collection, Ltd. in July 1997, was organized in April 1986 to design, manufacture and market high quality bridal wear and related accessories, including bridesmaid gowns. In May 1997, the Company acquired Alvina Valenta Couture Collection, Inc. Alvina designs, manufactures and markets couture-quality bridal wear. The Company's bridal gowns, bridesmaid gowns, veils and related items emphasize contemporary and traditional styles characterized by ankle or floor length gowns, with or without trains, and are principally constructed in satin, silk and lace. The Company also produces a line of less expensive bridal gowns called Visions which is styled similarly to the Company's couture lines, but is constructed from less expensive fabrics.

	10/31/98	10/31/97	10/31/96	10/31/95
Per Share Information				
Stock Price as of 12/31	3.31	5.12	4.50	1.12
Earnings Per Share	0.28	0.41	0.29	0.05
Price / Earnings Ratio	11.82	12.49	15.52	22.40
Book Value Per Share	2.30	2.04	1.43	1.06
Price / Book Value %	143.91	250.98	314.69	105.66
Dividends Per Share	0.0	0.0	0.0	0.0
Annual Financial Data				
Operating Results (000's)				
Total Revenues	15,704.9	14,028.8	12,642.1	7,852.9
Costs & Expenses	-14,790.8	-12,506.7	-11,696.9	-7,748.5
Income Before Taxes and Other	914.1	1,522.0	945.2	104.4
Other Items	0.0	0.0	0.0	0.0
Income Tax	-366.9	-732.1	-474.5	-40.8
Net Income	547.1	789.9	470.7	63.6
Cash Flow From Operations	-280.2	392.4	271.6	-543.9
Balance Sheet (000's)				
Cash & Equivalents	107.7	473.7	83.8	36.6
Total Current Assets	5,795.4	5,293.5	4,698.5	4,200.9
Fixed Assets, Net	275.6	286.4	231.2	196.7
Total Assets	6,911.3	6,223.3	5,124.5	4,526.3
Total Current Liabilities	2,603.1	2,364.2	2,713.4	2,997.2
Long-Term Debt	0.0	64.5	0.0	0.0
Stockholders' Equity	4,260.5	3,733.0	2,339.2	1,455.0
Performance & Financial Condition				
Return on Total Revenues %	3.48	5.63	3.72	0.81
Return on Avg Stockholders' Equity %	13.69	26.02	24.81	4.86
Return on Average Assets %	8.33	13.92	9.75	1.41
Current Ratio	2.23	2.24	1.73	1.40
Debt / Equity %	n.a.	1.73	n.a.	n.a.

Compound Growth %'s	EPS %	77.58	Net Income %	104.91	Total Revenues %	25.99

Comments

The increase in revenue during fiscal 1998 was mostly attributable to a full year of revenues from Alvina which was acquired during fiscal 1997. A decrease in gross profit margins was linked to increased salary costs that were not passed on to customers. Marketing expense also conributed to the decline in profits. As part of an aggressive marketing strategy, the Company opened a European sales office during 1998. The Company maintains a solid balance sheet that is free from long term debt.

Officers	Position	Ownership Information	
Daniel M. Sullivan	Chairman	Number of Shares Outstanding	1,853,181
Joseph L. Murphy	President	Market Capitalization	$ 6,134,029
Frank A. Musto	Vice President, CFO	Number of Shareholders	500
Joseph E. O'Grady	Director	Where Listed / Symbol	NASDAQ / JHPC

Other Information			
Transfer Agent	TranSecurities International, Inc. Spokane, WA	SIC Code	2330
Auditor	Arthur Andersen LLP	Employees	60
		Web Site	jlmcouture.com

JMAR Industries, Inc.

3956 Sorrento Valley Boulevard, Suite D   San Diego, CA 92121   Telephone (619)535-1706   Fax (619)535-1835

Company Description

JMAR Industries, Inc. develops and manufactures a wide range of precision measurement and manufacturing systems based on visible, ultraviolet and infrared light sources, including lasers. The Company also uses customized lasers to manufacture specialty semiconductors and is actively developing advanced semiconductor lithography sources and ultra-precision manufacturing systems based on its patented, diode-pumped, solid state laser technology. The Company was founded in 1987.

	12/31/98	12/31/97	12/31/96	12/31/95
Per Share Information				
Stock Price	2.12	2.50	2.34	0.97
Earnings Per Share	0.04	0.10	0.05	0.01
Price / Earnings Ratio	53.00	25.00	46.80	97.00
Book Value Per Share	0.73	0.70	0.56	0.36
Price / Book Value %	290.41	357.14	425.45	269.44
Dividends Per Share	0.0	0.0	0.0	0.0
Annual Financial Data				
Operating Results (000's)				
Total Revenues	24,622.8	21,566.5	16,431.7	12,210.5
Costs & Expenses	-23,833.8	-20,706.2	-15,827.1	-12,134.2
Income Before Taxes and Other	789.0	860.3	604.6	76.3
Other Items	0.0	590.0	0.0	0.0
Income Tax	-32.2	345.0	175.0	0.0
Net Income	756.8	1,795.3	779.6	76.3
Cash Flow From Operations	-40.6	-1,951.5	-413.7	-1,625.1
Balance Sheet (000's)				
Cash & Equivalents	3,848.2	3,644.1	2,629.3	1,837.6
Total Current Assets	18,359.4	13,508.0	11,103.1	7,282.6
Fixed Assets, Net	2,710.7	2,500.4	2,704.5	571.6
Total Assets	22,874.8	17,268.9	15,395.5	9,249.0
Total Current Liabilities	9,146.3	3,873.4	5,359.3	2,627.5
Long-Term Debt	475.4	907.2	667.3	1,536.3
Stockholders' Equity	13,253.2	12,488.2	9,368.9	5,085.2
Performance & Financial Condition				
Return on Total Revenues %	3.07	8.32	4.74	0.62
Return on Avg Stockholders' Equity %	5.88	16.43	10.79	1.71
Return on Average Assets %	3.77	10.99	6.33	0.83
Current Ratio	2.01	3.49	2.07	2.77
Debt / Equity %	3.59	7.26	7.12	30.21

Compound Growth %'s	EPS %	58.74	Net Income %	114.90	Total Revenues %	26.34

Comments

As a result of the receipt of approximately $26 million in orders during the second half of 1998, sales in the fourth quarter of 1998 rose to $8.4 million, a gain of 66% over revenue in the fourth quarter of 1997 and approximately 35% higher than the sales level in any other quarter in the Company's history. The increase is primarily attributable to the Company's semiconductor-related business. Gross margins decreased in 1998 due to a steep decline in sales of the Company's higher margin precision instruments for the computer industry, expenses related to the rapid build-up of the Company's semiconductor-related business, competitive pricing pressures, and higher engineering costs. Several nonrecurring items net to a $589,969 gain in 1997 as compared to an asset writedown expense of $100,000 in 1998.

Officers	Position	Ownership Information	
John S. Martinez	Chairman, CEO	Number of Shares Outstanding	18,080,853
E. Fred Schiele	President, COO	Market Capitalization	$ 38,331,408
Dennis E. Valentine	VP - Finance, CFO	Number of Shareholders	6,370
John P. Ricardi	Vice President	Where Listed / Symbol	NASDAQ / JMAR

Other Information			
Transfer Agent	American Securities Transfer, Inc. Lakewood, CO	SIC Code	3829
Auditor	Arthur Andersen LLP	Employees	125
		Web Site	jmar.com

Jaco Electronics, Inc.

145 Oser Avenue   Hauppauge, NY 11788   Telephone (516)273-5500   Fax (516)273-5506

Company Description

Jaco Electronics, Inc. markets and distributes passive and active electronic components to original equipment manufacturers (OEMs) throughout the United States and Canada from two distribution centers located on the East and West coasts and 14 sales offices located throughout the United States. The Company distributes products such as semiconductors, capacitors, resistors, electro-mechanical devices, flat panels, computers and computer subsystems, which are used in the manufacture and assembly of electronic products. The Company also provides a variety of value-added services including configuring complete computer systems to customers' specifications, kitting the component requirements of certain customers and furnishing contract manufacturing services. The Company was founded in 1961.

	06/30/98	06/30/97	06/30/96	06/30/95
Per Share Information				
Stock Price as of 12/31	3.69	6.25	8.50	8.62
Earnings Per Share	0.30	0.53	1.08	0.78
Price / Earnings Ratio	12.30	11.79	7.87	11.05
Book Value Per Share	9.47	9.23	8.67	4.03
Price / Book Value %	38.97	67.71	98.04	213.90
Dividends Per Share	0.0	0.0	0.0	0.0
Annual Financial Data				
Operating Results (000's)				
Total Revenues	153,674.2	155,097.7	167,149.4	138,683.0
Costs & Expenses	-151,643.0	-151,604.0	-160,699.6	-135,464.0
Income Before Taxes and Other	2,031.3	3,493.8	6,449.8	3,219.0
Other Items	0.0	0.0	0.0	0.0
Income Tax	-847.0	-1,415.0	-2,600.0	-1,303.0
Net Income	1,184.3	2,078.8	3,849.8	1,916.0
Cash Flow From Operations	1,622.2	1,285.6	-1,682.1	n.a.
Balance Sheet (000's)				
Cash & Equivalents	562.6	463.4	164.2	393.7
Total Current Assets	61,538.1	59,047.8	18,916.0	49,622.3
Fixed Assets, Net	6,102.4	5,009.0	4,500.0	4,106.2
Total Assets	73,419.3	69,995.7	61,143.0	56,323.2
Total Current Liabilities	19,057.4	17,901.4	18,048.0	18,881.1
Long-Term Debt	17,036.6	15,552.5	8,791.0	24,215.6
Stockholders' Equity	36,625.2	35,891.8	34,304.0	13,226.5
Performance & Financial Condition				
Return on Total Revenues %	0.77	1.34	2.30	1.38
Return on Avg Stockholders' Equity %	3.27	5.92	16.20	10.08
Return on Average Assets %	1.65	3.17	6.55	3.83
Current Ratio	3.23	3.30	1.05	2.63
Debt / Equity %	46.52	43.33	25.63	183.08

Compound Growth %'s	EPS %	-27.28	Net Income %	-14.82	Total Revenues %	3.48

Comments

The Company declared a 4 for 3 stock split in fiscal 1996. All per share amounts have been restated for consistency. Fiscal 1998 and 1997 results reflect the continuing industry-wide pressures on pricing, compounded by the softening demand for electronic components. The decrease in fiscal 1998 sales through the Company's distribution operations was partially offset by a $6.8 million, or 68%, increase in sales from contract manufacturing. For the six months ended December 31, 1998, the Company reported revenues and a net loss of $68.2 million and $309,898 ($.08 per share) as compared to $76.7 million and a profit of $861,213 ($.22 per share) for the same period of the preceding year. The Company has significant working capital and only $3.8 million of intangible assets reflected on its ledgers.

Officers	Position	Ownership Information	
Joel H. Girsky	President, CEO	Number of Shares Outstanding	3,866,221
Charles B. Girsky	Exec VP	Market Capitalization	$ 14,266,355
Jeffrey D. Gash	VP - Finance, CFO	Number of Shareholders	1,500
Stephen A. Cohen	Director	Where Listed / Symbol	NASDAQ / JACO

Other Information			
Transfer Agent	American Stock Transfer & Trust Co. New York, NY	SIC Code	5065
Auditor	Grant Thornton LLP	Employees	392
		Web Site	jacoelectronics.com

Janus American Group, Inc.

2300 Corporate Boulevard, N.W., Suite 232   Boca Raton, FL 33431-8596   Telephone (561)994-4800   Fax (561)997-5331

Company Description

Janus American Group, Inc. is the surviving entity of United States Lines, Inc. (United), once one of the largest containerized cargo shipping companies in the world. United filed for bankruptcy protection in 1986 and emerged from bankruptcy in 1990. Armed with a significant tax loss carryforward but no business of its own, the Company set out to find a suitable acquisition. In April 1997, the Company acquired a hospitality business comprised of six hotels, an 85% partnership interest in another hotel, and a hotel management company with 21 hotels under management. Can a company return from the dead? Let's look at the numbers below.

	12/31/98	12/31/97	12/31/96
Per Share Information			
Stock Price	2.50	1.00	1.00
Earnings Per Share	0.13	-0.15	-0.24
Price / Earnings Ratio	19.23	n.a.	n.a.
Book Value Per Share	4.63	3.08	0.99
Price / Book Value %	54.00	32.47	101.01
Dividends Per Share	0.0	0.0	0.0
Annual Financial Data			
Operating Results (000's)			
Total Revenues	30,194.3	11,014.4	247.5
Costs & Expenses	-27,653.5	-10,201.4	-1,121.0
Income Before Taxes and Other	2,540.8	813.0	-873.5
Other Items	51.2	-1,044.8	-320.5
Income Tax	-704.8	-331.0	0.0
Net Income	1,887.2	-562.7	-1,194.0
Cash Flow From Operations	1,904.9	732.3	-1,201.9
Balance Sheet (000's)			
Cash & Equivalents	12,383.7	11,191.5	6,580.8
Total Current Assets	15,170.1	12,636.6	7,521.9
Fixed Assets, Net	74,550.3	34,803.3	582.7
Total Assets	108,683.8	61,404.1	9,047.3
Total Current Liabilities	6,130.4	4,040.4	981.9
Long-Term Debt	60,582.9	17,866.3	0.0
Stockholders' Equity	40,196.6	36,618.4	8,021.6
Performance & Financial Condition			
Return on Total Revenues %	6.25	-5.11	-482.39
Return on Avg Stockholders' Equity %	4.91	-2.52	-29.85
Return on Average Assets %	2.22	-1.60	-26.53
Current Ratio	2.47	3.13	7.66
Debt / Equity %	150.72	48.79	n.a.

Compound Growth %'s	EPS %	n.a.	Net Income %	n.a.	Total Revenues %	n.a.

Comments

Most of the increase in revenue reported in 1998 is due to a full year's operation of the properties. Minor increases in revenue resulted from higher prices. The occupancy rate remained stable at 65%. Management fee income increased from $921,217 in 1997 to $1,754,610 in 1998 as a result of new management contracts. The Company reported net earnings as well as a strong cash flow from operations. 1998 results include 4136,186 gain from discontinued operations. Earnings per share is calculated after deducting the preferred stock dividend requirement. At December 31, 1998, the Company had tax loss carryforwards of $165.4 million subject to certain limitations in the event of a change in ownership. The Company also had $6.5 million of goodwill reflected on its books which equated to only 16% of stockholders' equity and book value per share.

Officers	Position	Ownership Information	
Louis S. Beck	Chairman	Number of Shares Outstanding	8,691,092
James E. Bishop	President, CEO	Market Capitalization	$ 21,727,730
Michael M. Nanosky	COO	Number of Shareholders	3,907
Richard A. Tonges	VP - Finance, CFO	Where Listed / Symbol	NASDAQ / JAGI

Other Information			
Transfer Agent	ChaseMellon Shareholder Services Ridgefield Park, NJ	SIC Code	7900
Auditor	Grant Thornton LLP	Employees	1,120

Jenna Lane, Inc.

1407 Broadway   New York, NY 10018   Telephone (212)704-0002   Fax (212)704-0139

Company Description

Jenna Lane, Inc. designs, manufactures and markets high quality, cut and sewn, popularly priced junior, missy, and large size basic sportswear, basic fashion sportswear, and fashion knit and woven sportswear and other apparel for women and children. The Company was founded by individuals with extensive experience in apparel manufacturing, operations, sales and merchandising. Since its inception, the Company has dedicated its time and resources primarily to the development of three sets of product lines; basic sportswear, basic fashion sportswear and fashion sportswear. The Company was formed on February 14, 1995, and completed its initial public offering in March, 1997.

	03/31/98	03/31/97	03/31/96	03/31/95
Per Share Information				
Stock Price as of 12/31	2.06	13.25	4.50	0.50
Earnings Per Share	0.09	0.03	0.16	-0.03
Price / Earnings Ratio	22.89	441.67	28.13	n.a.
Book Value Per Share	1.71	1.74	0.61	0.33
Price / Book Value %	120.47	761.49	737.70	151.52
Dividends Per Share	0.0	0.0	0.0	0.0
Annual Financial Data				
Operating Results (000's)				
Total Revenues	42,561.8	35,372.4	25,832.3	0.0
Costs & Expenses	-41,642.5	-35,106.2	-24,898.3	-43.9
Income Before Taxes and Other	919.3	208.9	934.0	-43.9
Other Items	0.0	0.0	0.0	0.0
Income Tax	-402.2	-72.7	-432.6	0.0
Net Income	517.2	136.3	501.4	-43.9
Cash Flow From Operations	-24.3	-3,866.3	-1,664.2	-154.4
Balance Sheet (000's)				
Cash & Equivalents	6.6	548.3	1.3	521.4
Total Current Assets	10,757.3	9,698.1	5,051.5	1,367.6
Fixed Assets, Net	501.6	242.8	116.7	9.4
Total Assets	11,537.2	10,034.8	5,209.6	1,409.3
Total Current Liabilities	3,431.0	2,506.3	2,689.2	143.2
Long-Term Debt	3.7	16.8	425.1	0.0
Stockholders' Equity	8,072.6	7,461.8	1,213.6	581.1
Performance & Financial Condition				
Return on Total Revenues %	1.22	0.39	1.94	n.a.
Return on Avg Stockholders' Equity %	6.66	3.14	55.88	-15.15
Return on Average Assets %	4.79	1.79	15.15	-6.28
Current Ratio	3.14	3.87	1.88	9.55
Debt / Equity %	0.05	0.23	35.03	n.a.

Compound Growth %'s	EPS %	-25.00	Net Income %	1.56	Total Revenues %	28.36

Comments

The Company has quite remarkably recorded profits in each of its first three full years of business. Proceeds from the public offering has financed a healthy working capital and allows the Company to operate without the need of long term debt. The Company also factors its receivables to maintain liquidity. Although management is pleased with its success to date in selling basic, basic fashion and fashion sportswear, and believes the Company will continue to benefit from the substantial focus on those areas, a longer-term opportunity for expansion will be the growth and development of sales of imports. For the nine months ended December 31, 1998, the Company reported revenues and net income of $40.2 million and $322,440 ($.07 per share) as compared to $30.8 million and $249,387 ($.04 per share) for the same period of the preceding year.

Officers	Position	Ownership Information	
Gerald L. Kanter	Chairman	Number of Shares Outstanding	4,728,993
Charles Sobel	CEO	Market Capitalization	$ 9,741,726
Mitchell Dobies	CFO	Number of Shareholders	1,000
Gerald Cohen	Director	Where Listed / Symbol	NASDAQ / JLNY

Other Information			
Transfer Agent	American Stock Transfer & Trust Co. New York, NY	SIC Code	2340
Auditor	Edward Isaacs & Company LLP	Employees	88

Jennifer Convertibles, Inc.

419 Crossways Park Drive   Woodbury, NY 11797   Telephone (516)496-1900   Fax (516)496-8380

Company Description

Jennifer Convertibles, Inc. is the owner and licensor of the largest group of sofabed specialty retail stores in the United States, with 121 Jennifer Convertibles® stores located on the Eastern seaboard, in the Midwest, on the West Coast and in the Southwest as of August 29, 1998. The Company also operated 34 Jennifer Leather stores as of that date. Of the Jennifer Convertible® stores, 48 were owned by the Company and 73 were licensed by the Company. The Company grew from 42 stores in 1989 to a high point of 169 stores in 1995. A lack of accounting and internal controls, operating losses and litigation has forced the Company to retrench over the last several years.

	08/29/98	08/30/97	08/31/96	08/26/95
Per Share Information				
Stock Price as of 12/31	2.50	1.94	2.25	2.50
Earnings Per Share	0.02	-0.54	-1.06	-2.12
Price / Earnings Ratio	125.00	n.a.	n.a.	n.a.
Book Value Per Share	-1.48	-2.34	-1.81	-0.75
Price / Book Value %	n.a.	n.a.	n.a.	n.a.
Dividends Per Share	0.0	0.0	0.0	0.0
Annual Financial Data				
Operating Results (000's)				
Total Revenues	112,306.0	98,521.0	107,491.0	128,578.0
Costs & Expenses	-112,096.0	-101,487.0	-113,368.0	-140,486.0
Income Before Taxes and Other	210.0	-2,966.0	-5,877.0	-11,908.0
Other Items	0.0	0.0	0.0	0.0
Income Tax	-120.0	-95.0	-146.0	-160.0
Net Income	90.0	-3,061.0	-6,023.0	-12,068.0
Cash Flow From Operations	-3,607.0	135.0	-3,048.0	-348.0
Balance Sheet (000's)				
Cash & Equivalents	4,384.0	3,405.0	3,600.0	7,729.0
Total Current Assets	15,891.0	12,974.0	13,886.0	20,658.0
Fixed Assets, Net	6,147.0	7,669.0	8,739.0	9,771.0
Total Assets	24,099.0	22,998.0	25,435.0	33,871.0
Total Current Liabilities	27,001.0	30,232.0	29,643.0	31,646.0
Long-Term Debt	0.0	421.0	230.0	337.0
Stockholders' Equity	-8,448.0	-13,367.0	-10,306.0	-4,283.0
Performance & Financial Condition				
Return on Total Revenues %	0.08	-3.11	-5.60	-9.39
Return on Avg Stockholders' Equity %	n.a.	n.a.	n.a.	-689.21
Return on Average Assets %	0.38	-12.64	-20.31	-30.63
Current Ratio	0.59	0.43	0.47	0.65
Debt / Equity %	n.a.	n.a.	n.a.	n.a.

Compound Growth %'s	EPS % n.a.	Net Income % n.a.	Total Revenues % -4.41

Comments

Fiscal 1998 revenue grew 14.1% primarily due to a 37.9% increase of the leather division. Same store sales increased by 15.0%. The primary reason for the significant improvement in the bottom line was due to higher sales which produced greater gross margin dollars and tight control over expenses. Although the financial condition is improving, the Company continues to operate with a substantial working capital deficiency. For the six months ended February 28, 1999, the Company reported revenues and a net loss of $51.6 million and $2,093,000 ($.37 per share) as compared to $53.2 million and $958,000 ($.17 per share) for the same period of the preceding year.

Officers	Position	Ownership Information	
Harley J. Greenfield	Chairman, CEO	Number of Shares Outstanding	5,700,725
Rami Abada	President, COO	Market Capitalization	$ 14,251,813
Edward B. Seidner	Exec VP	Number of Shareholders	1,510
George J. Nadel	Exec VP, CFO	Where Listed / Symbol	OTC-BB / JENN

Other Information			
Transfer Agent	Continental Stock Transfer & Trust Co. Jersey City, NJ	SIC Code	5712
Auditor	Richard A. Eisner & Co., LLP	Employees	452
Market Maker	Knight Securities L.P. (800)222-4910		
	Herzog, Heine, Geduld, Inc. (800)221-3600		

Jerry's Famous Deli, Inc.

12711 Ventura Boulevard, Suite 400 Studio City, CA 91604 Telephone (818)766-8311 Fax (818)766-8315

Company Description

Jerry's Famous Deli, Inc. was established in 1978 to develop the Jerry's Famous Deli restaurant in Studio City, California. Through acquisitions and expansion, the Company now operates 11 restaurants, including nine restaurants located in southern California. Two restaurants operate in southern Florida under the name Wolfie Cohen's Rascal House. The Company also operates The Epicure Market in Miami Beach. Jerry's Famous Deli restaurants have the look and high energy feel of a theme restaurant, with Broadway as the theme, and posters, pictures and colored klieg lighting creating the setting.

	12/31/98	12/31/97	12/31/96	12/31/95
Per Share Information				
Stock Price	1.19	2.25	4.25	8.00
Earnings Per Share	0.02	0.04	-0.44	0.08
Price / Earnings Ratio	59.50	56.25	n.a.	100.00
Book Value Per Share	1.78	1.73	1.33	1.23
Price / Book Value %	66.85	130.06	319.55	650.41
Dividends Per Share	0.0	0.0	0.0	0.0
Annual Financial Data				
Operating Results (000's)				
Total Revenues	66,619.8	56,502.2	40,380.2	28,171.2
Costs & Expenses	-66,649.0	-55,670.8	-39,238.8	-27,022.1
Income Before Taxes and Other	-29.2	829.8	1,141.3	1,149.1
Other Items	-299.6	-132.6	-278.4	-179.8
Income Tax	65.1	-134.0	-284.2	-187.1
Net Income	-263.7	563.2	578.7	782.2
Cash Flow From Operations	4,965.0	1,678.9	3,437.4	141.3
Balance Sheet (000's)				
Cash & Equivalents	985.4	2,264.3	4,145.3	7,214.4
Total Current Assets	3,791.1	4,984.7	6,144.2	7,914.9
Fixed Assets, Net	33,534.8	29,835.5	25,694.5	10,417.6
Total Assets	48,992.7	37,977.6	36,563.0	18,782.3
Total Current Liabilities	6,212.6	4,776.3	6,041.4	4,069.7
Long-Term Debt	15,908.6	7,690.2	5,960.0	1,086.8
Stockholders' Equity	25,859.1	24,575.5	23,624.0	12,766.2
Performance & Financial Condition				
Return on Total Revenues %	-0.40	1.00	1.43	2.78
Return on Avg Stockholders' Equity %	-1.05	2.34	3.18	12.12
Return on Average Assets %	-0.61	1.51	2.09	5.94
Current Ratio	0.61	1.04	1.02	1.94
Debt / Equity %	61.52	31.29	25.23	8.51

Compound Growth %'s   EPS % n.a.   Net Income % n.a.   Total Revenues % 33.23

Comments

The 1998 increase in revenues was attributable to the acquisition of The Epicure Market on April 1, 1998. A 9.3% decline in same store sales was offset by revenue from stores not opened a full year in 1997. In 1998, management hired an outside consultant to investigate the loss of revenue and to make recommendations. Many of the recommendations have already been implemented and management reports favorable customer feedback. 1998 results include $538,000 of preopening expense due to the Company's election to adopt new accounting rules earlier than mandated. This also resulted in a $132,300 ($.01 per share) extraordinary loss. 1996 results include a charge of $5.0 million ($.49 per share) related to the conversion of preferred shares to common shares. This amount represents the discount to market at which the common shares are being issued to the preferred shareholders, called a deemed dividend. At the end of 1998, the Company had $9.7 million in intangible assets which equated to 37% of stockholders' equity and book value per share.

Officers	Position	Ownership Information	
Kenneth J. Abdalla	President	Number of Shares Outstanding	14,508,902
Isaac Starkman	CEO, Chairman	Market Capitalization	$ 17,265,593
Christina Sterling	CFO	Number of Shareholders	2,000
Guy Starkman	Vice President	Where Listed / Symbol	NASDAQ / DELI

Other Information			
Transfer Agent	U.S. Stock Transfer Corp. Glendale, CA	SIC Code	5812
Auditor	PricewaterhouseCoopers LLP	Employees	1,750
		Web Site	jerrysdeli.com

Jetronic Industries, Inc.

4200 Mitchell Street   Philadelphia, PA 19128   Telephone (215)482-7660   Fax (215)482-8530

Company Description

Jetronic Industries, Inc. is a diversified company engaged in the design and manufacture of electronic devices and energy conservation equipment. The Electronics Division designs and manufactures, to customer specification, digital data control terminals. The Transchem Division (energy conservation products group) manufactures and markets precision solid state power supplies, primarily for the aircraft and aerospace industries. During 1996, the Company discontinued its marine electronic and communications business. Jetronic was founded in 1951.

	01/31/98	01/31/97	01/31/96	01/31/95
Per Share Information				
Stock Price as of 12/31	1.00	2.44	1.31	0.56
Earnings Per Share	0.33	0.16	-0.62	0.01
Price / Earnings Ratio	3.03	15.25	n.a.	56.00
Book Value Per Share	0.27	-0.09	-0.25	0.37
Price / Book Value %	370.37	n.a.	n.a.	151.35
Dividends Per Share	0.0	0.0	0.0	0.0
Annual Financial Data				
Operating Results (000's)				
Total Revenues	25,873.0	23,671.0	22,353.0	18,824.0
Costs & Expenses	-24,596.0	-23,095.0	-22,272.0	-18,856.0
Income Before Taxes and Other	1,277.0	576.0	-1,311.0	-32.0
Other Items	0.0	0.0	-938.0	-61.0
Income Tax	-4.0	9.0	26.0	147.0
Net Income	1,273.0	585.0	-2,223.0	54.0
Cash Flow From Operations	-319.0	-700.0	-137.0	-349.0
Balance Sheet (000's)				
Cash & Equivalents	513.0	498.0	652.0	144.0
Total Current Assets	12,101.0	10,106.0	8,251.0	9,746.0
Fixed Assets, Net	418.0	438.0	481.0	500.0
Total Assets	13,486.0	11,381.0	9,407.0	11,565.0
Total Current Liabilities	8,248.0	7,596.0	6,313.0	4,791.0
Long-Term Debt	4,282.0	4,102.0	3,996.0	5,453.0
Stockholders' Equity	956.0	-317.0	-902.0	1,321.0
Performance & Financial Condition				
Return on Total Revenues %	4.92	2.47	-9.94	0.29
Return on Avg Stockholders' Equity %	398.44	n.a.	-1,061.10	4.17
Return on Average Assets %	10.24	5.63	-21.20	0.49
Current Ratio	1.47	1.33	1.31	2.03
Debt / Equity %	447.91	n.a.	n.a.	412.79

Compound Growth %'s	EPS % 220.75	Net Income % 186.73	Total Revenues % 11.18

Comments

Financial results are driven primarily by the energy conversion products group where revenues increased 9.5% to $25.2 million. Part of the increase reflects an acquisition in early fiscal 1998. At January 31, 1998, the Company had $7.3 million of tax loss carryovers available to offset future income. Fiscal 1996 results include a loss from discontinued operations of $938,000 ($.26 per share). For the nine months ended November 30, 1998, the Company reported revenues and net income of $18.1 million and $897,000 ($.22 per share) as compared to $19.4 million and $1,091,000 ($.29 per share) for the same period of the preceding year.

Officers	Position	Ownership Information	
Daniel R. Kursman	Chairman, Treasurer	Number of Shares Outstanding	3,604,499
Peter J. Kursman	President	Market Capitalization	$ 3,604,499
Leonard W. Pietrzak	VP - Finance	Number of Shareholders	1,664
William L. Weiss	Secretary	Where Listed / Symbol	AMEX / JET

Other Information			
Transfer Agent	Continental Stock Transfer & Trust Co. New York, NY	SIC Code	3674
Auditor	Asher & Company, Ltd.	Employees	166

Joulé Inc.

1245 Route 1 South   Edison, NJ 08837   Telephone (732)548-5444   Fax (732)494-6346

Company Description

Joulé Inc. is engaged in the business of personnel outsourcing, as a supplier to industry, of staffing service personnel. These services focus on supplying commercial (skilled office and light industrial) workers, technical professionals, and skilled craft industrial plant and facility maintenance personnel to business and industry on a temporary basis. The Company derived 70%, 71% and 68% of its revenue from services provided to customers in New Jersey in 1998, 1997, and 1996, respectively. In addition to its own employees, the Company has approximately 2,000 persons on assignment in over 400 client organizations. The Company was founded in 1965.

	09/30/98	09/30/97	09/30/96	09/30/95
Per Share Information				
Stock Price as of 12/31	2.25	4.62	3.50	5.00
Earnings Per Share	0.19	0.29	0.28	0.26
Price / Earnings Ratio	11.84	15.93	12.50	19.23
Book Value Per Share	1.88	1.69	1.39	1.08
Price / Book Value %	119.68	273.37	251.80	462.96
Dividends Per Share	0.0	0.0	0.0	0.0
Annual Financial Data				
Operating Results (000's)				
Total Revenues	55,301.0	48,590.0	48,449.0	43,641.0
Costs & Expenses	-54,125.0	-46,814.0	-46,822.0	-42,128.0
Income Before Taxes and Other	1,176.0	1,776.0	1,627.0	1,513.0
Other Items	0.0	0.0	0.0	0.0
Income Tax	-470.0	-710.0	-601.0	-575.0
Net Income	706.0	1,066.0	1,026.0	938.0
Cash Flow From Operations	-1,084.0	1,304.0	2,433.0	-54.0
Balance Sheet (000's)				
Cash & Equivalents	233.0	139.0	175.0	70.0
Total Current Assets	9,125.0	7,105.0	8,623.0	8,902.0
Fixed Assets, Net	3,707.0	3,633.0	2,019.0	1,900.0
Total Assets	12,913.0	10,843.0	10,809.0	10,802.0
Total Current Liabilities	5,640.0	4,251.0	5,279.0	6,427.0
Long-Term Debt	381.0	406.0	431.0	456.0
Stockholders' Equity	6,892.0	6,186.0	5,099.0	3,919.0
Performance & Financial Condition				
Return on Total Revenues %	1.28	2.19	2.12	2.15
Return on Avg Stockholders' Equity %	10.80	18.89	22.75	22.88
Return on Average Assets %	5.94	9.85	9.50	9.38
Current Ratio	1.62	1.67	1.63	1.39
Debt / Equity %	5.53	6.56	8.45	11.64

Compound Growth %'s	EPS %	-9.93	Net Income %	-9.04	Total Revenues %	8.21

Comments

A combination of staff expansion, additional services, and geographic expansion contributed to the seventh consecutive year of sales growth. The 14% increase in the last fiscal year was all attributable to internal growth. New programs related to the aggressive growth strategies negatively affected operating margins in fiscal 1998. Management reported that the impact of these investments on earnings had come to an end by the close of the last year. Fiscal 1998 results also include a nonrecurring provision for legal settlement amounting to $323,000. Management is expecting higher profits in fiscal 1999 as a result of the stronger foundation created in 1998.

Officers	Position	Ownership Information	
Emanuel N. Logothetis	President, CEO	Number of Shares Outstanding	3,670,000
John G. Wellman, Jr.	Exec VP, COO	Market Capitalization	$ 8,257,500
Bernard G. Clarkin	Vice President, CFO	Number of Shareholders	600
John F. Logothetis	Vice President	Where Listed / Symbol	AMEX / JOL

Other Information

Transfer Agent	Continental Stock Transfer & Trust Co. New York, NY	SIC Code	7363
Auditor	Arthur Andersen LLP	Employees	130
		Web Site	jouleinc.com

Judge Group, Inc. (The)

Two Bala Plaza, Suite 800   Bala Cynwyd, PA 19004   Telephone (610)667-7700   Fax (610)668-8622

Company Description

The Judge Group, Inc., founded in 1970, provides 1) information technology (IT) and engineering professionals to its clients on both a temporary basis (through its "Contract Placement" business) and a permanent basis (through its Permanent Placement business), 2) computer network and document management system integration, implementation, maintenance and training (through its Imaging and Network Services business) and 3) information technology training (through its IT Training business) on a range of software and network applications to corporate, governmental and individual clients. In addition to its 467 full time employees, the Company has engaged an additional 865 IT consultants to work on full-time assignments for the Company's clients. The Company was founded in 1970 and had its initial public offering in early 1997 at $7.50 per share.

	12/31/98	12/31/97	12/31/96	12/31/95
Per Share Information				
Stock Price	1.94	4.75	7.50	n.a.
Earnings Per Share	-0.38	0.21	0.10	0.06
Price / Earnings Ratio	n.a.	22.62	75.00	n.a.
Book Value Per Share	1.71	1.97	0.13	0.05
Price / Book Value %	113.45	241.12	5,769.23	n.a.
Dividends Per Share	0.0	0.0	0.0	0.0
Annual Financial Data				
Operating Results (000's)				
Total Revenues	114,498.4	98,627.1	82,371.1	63,299.4
Costs & Expenses	-116,140.3	-93,995.3	-80,511.6	-61,535.5
Income Before Taxes and Other	-1,893.7	4,631.8	986.8	1,066.5
Other Items	-4,021.1	0.0	888.0	7.1
Income Tax	797.8	-1,919.8	-967.9	-588.0
Net Income	-5,117.0	2,711.9	906.9	485.6
Cash Flow From Operations	-6.1	-2,395.5	-4,026.6	-2,289.0
Balance Sheet (000's)				
Cash & Equivalents	43.6	1,684.5	105.1	35.0
Total Current Assets	25,884.1	24,067.7	16,749.5	9,685.0
Fixed Assets, Net	4,945.8	2,886.4	1,923.4	1,000.0
Total Assets	47,885.4	31,933.6	21,969.0	11,632.0
Total Current Liabilities	13,670.3	5,542.4	8,496.9	4,118.0
Long-Term Debt	10,467.1	0.0	12,219.6	5,368.0
Stockholders' Equity	23,081.2	26,274.3	1,122.1	391.0
Performance & Financial Condition				
Return on Total Revenues %	-4.47	2.75	1.10	0.77
Return on Avg Stockholders' Equity %	-20.74	19.80	119.88	69.38
Return on Average Assets %	-12.82	10.06	5.40	3.24
Current Ratio	1.89	4.34	1.97	2.35
Debt / Equity %	45.35	n.a.	1,088.98	1,372.89

Compound Growth %'s	EPS % n.a.	Net Income % n.a.	Total Revenues % 21.84

Comments

In 1998, the Company began to implement a strategy to accelerate its growth through the addition of new services, geographic expansion and strategic acquisitions. Six companies were acquired and three additional branch offices were opened in 1998. The Company's aggressive expansion resulted in additional costs related to a corresponding increase in the infrastructure to adequately manage and service the expanded business. The higher costs produced a net loss for the year. 1998 results include $4,021,099 of nonrecurring charges related to the impairment of purchased goodwill. At December 31, 1998, the Company still had goodwill of $16.3 million recorded as assets which equated to approximately 71% of stockholders' equity and book value per share.

Officers	Position	Ownership Information	
Martin E. Judge, Jr.	Chairman, CEO	Number of Shares Outstanding	13,501,302
Richard T. Furlano	President	Market Capitalization	$ 26,192,526
Michael A. Dunn	Exec VP	Number of Shareholders	2,000
Frank M. Barrett	CFO	Where Listed / Symbol	NASDAQ / JUDG

Other Information			
Transfer Agent	Stocktrans, Inc. Ardmore, PA	SIC Code	7373
Auditor	Rudolph, Palitz LLP	Employees	467
		Web Site	judge.com

K2 Design, Inc.

30 Broad Street, 16th floor   New York, NY 10004   Telephone (212)301-8800   Fax (212)301-8801

Company Description

K2 Design, Inc. primarily provides interactive marketing and communications services to commercial organizations over the Internet and World Wide Web. Commencing after its initial public offering on July 26, 1996, the Company began to develop its vision to become a full-service interactive marketing and communications company, largely in response to and in anticipation of demands from its customers for services complementary to the Company's core Web site design services. Since its inception, the Company, alone and with others, has designed and created more than 80 Web sites, including ones for giant corporations such as MCI, Waterhouse Securities, American Express Company and Bell Communications Research.

	12/31/98	12/31/97	12/31/96	12/31/95
Per Share Information				
Stock Price	2.37	1.75	6.00	1.25
Earnings Per Share	0.35	-0.46	-0.32	0.01
Price / Earnings Ratio	6.77	n.a.	n.a.	125.00
Book Value Per Share	1.37	1.03	1.49	-0.02
Price / Book Value %	172.99	169.90	402.68	n.a.
Dividends Per Share	0.0	0.0	0.0	0.0
Annual Financial Data				
Operating Results (000's)				
Total Revenues	6,580.7	8,434.8	4,167.0	1,196.2
Costs & Expenses	-8,213.4	-10,117.4	-5,062.4	-1,183.3
Income Before Taxes and Other	-1,632.7	-1,682.7	-895.4	12.9
Other Items	2,908.9	0.0	0.0	0.0
Income Tax	-39.1	-20.6	0.0	-1.0
Net Income	1,237.1	-1,703.3	-895.4	11.9
Cash Flow From Operations	473.8	-792.0	-1,925.1	-2.4
Balance Sheet (000's)				
Cash & Equivalents	2,829.6	2,243.0	3,867.4	17.8
Total Current Assets	3,217.1	6,346.2	6,246.6	151.5
Fixed Assets, Net	745.4	930.9	607.4	67.6
Total Assets	6,680.7	7,437.9	6,894.7	223.5
Total Current Liabilities	1,961.4	3,607.0	1,396.0	228.5
Long-Term Debt	0.0	0.0	0.0	0.0
Stockholders' Equity	4,717.5	3,787.1	5,422.2	-31.5
Performance & Financial Condition				
Return on Total Revenues %	18.80	-20.19	-21.49	0.99
Return on Avg Stockholders' Equity %	29.09	-36.99	-33.22	0.50
Return on Average Assets %	17.52	-23.77	-25.16	0.40
Current Ratio	1.64	1.76	4.47	0.66
Debt / Equity %	n.a.	n.a.	n.a.	n.a.

Compound Growth %'s	EPS % n.a.	Net Income % n.a.	Total Revenues % 76.53

Comments

In 1998, the Company sold its CLIQNOW! division, an Internet media selling web site, to 24/7 Media Inc. which went public on August 18, 1998. An investment in 24/7 is reflected on the Company's books at the value assigned to it in the transaction which was $2,558,300, or $13.02 per share. The trading price of 24/7 at March 31, 1999, was $50.00 per share, for an unrecorded unrealized appreciation of $7.3 million, about $2.10 for each share of K2 Design. Included in 1998 results is a net gain from discontinued operations of $2,908,895 ($.82 per share). The loss of two large customers in the third quarter caused a management reorganization. The loss of revenues and a $400,000 severance expense caused a loss from operations for 1998. The Company's financial condition is strong with no long term debt and nearly $10 million of 24/7 stock reflected at cost.

Officers	Position	Ownership Information	
Matthew G. de Ganon	Chairman	Number of Shares Outstanding	3,446,567
Lynn Fantom	President, CEO	Market Capitalization	$ 8,168,364
Douglas E. Cleek	Exec VP	Number of Shareholders	1,000
Seth Bressman	CFO	Where Listed / Symbol	NASDAQ / KTWO

Other Information			
Transfer Agent	Continental Stock Transfer & Trust Co. New York, NY	SIC Code	7389
Auditor	Arthur Andersen LLP	Employees	38
		Web Site	k2design.com

Kaneb Services, Inc.

2435 North Central Expressway   Richardson, TX 75080   Telephone (972)699-4000   Fax (972)699-4025

Company Description

Kaneb Services, Inc. conducts its principal businesses in two industry segments: specialized industrial field services, and pipeline transportation and storage of refined petroleum products. The Company operates its specialized industrial field service business through its wholly-owned subsidiary, Furmanite Worldwide. Furmanite provides underpressure leak sealing, on-site machining, valve testing and repair and other engineering products and services, primarily to electric power generating plants, petroleum refineries and other process industries in Western Europe, North America, Latin America and the Pacific Rim. Kaneb Pipe Line Company operates and manages refined petroleum products pipeline transportation systems and petroleum products and specialty liquids terminal storage and pipeline facilities for the benefit of Kaneb Pipe Line Partners, L.P. (KPP), which owns such systems and facilities. The Company owns a 33% interest in KPP. The Company was founded in 1953.

	12/31/98	12/31/97	12/31/96	12/31/95
Per Share Information				
Stock Price	4.06	5.18	3.25	2.25
Earnings Per Share	0.40	0.30	0.19	1.59
Price / Earnings Ratio	10.15	17.27	17.11	1.42
Book Value Per Share	2.63	2.26	2.05	1.91
Price / Book Value %	154.37	229.20	158.54	117.80
Dividends Per Share	0.0	0.0	0.0	0.0
Annual Financial Data				
Operating Results (000's)				
Total Revenues	376,725.0	237,469.0	229,720.0	212,920.0
Costs & Expenses	-332,207.0	-195,686.0	-192,314.0	-186,371.0
Income Before Taxes and Other	44,518.0	41,087.0	36,574.0	25,512.0
Other Items	-29,174.0	-27,655.0	-26,969.0	36,204.0
Income Tax	-1,768.0	-2,789.0	-2,581.0	-2,535.0
Net Income	13,576.0	10,643.0	7,024.0	59,181.0
Cash Flow From Operations	54,206.0	55,120.0	48,628.0	39,964.0
Balance Sheet (000's)				
Cash & Equivalents	9,134.0	23,025.0	23,693.0	30,389.0
Total Current Assets	76,754.0	71,065.0	69,923.0	76,371.0
Fixed Assets, Net	301,531.0	261,361.0	266,638.0	263,545.0
Total Assets	448,045.0	402,273.0	404,691.0	409,827.0
Total Current Liabilities	71,122.0	50,642.0	49,890.0	60,069.0
Long-Term Debt	196,958.0	181,052.0	186,544.0	190,000.0
Stockholders' Equity	87,445.0	78,447.0	75,366.0	69,022.0
Performance & Financial Condition				
Return on Total Revenues %	3.60	4.48	3.06	27.79
Return on Avg Stockholders' Equity %	16.37	13.84	9.73	134.71
Return on Average Assets %	3.19	2.64	1.72	17.05
Current Ratio	1.08	1.40	1.40	1.27
Debt / Equity %	225.24	230.80	247.52	275.27

Compound Growth %'s	EPS %	n.a.	Net Income %	n.a.	Total Revenues %	20.95

Comments

Revenues increased 59% in 1998, 82% of which directly related to the acquisition of a products marketing business acquired in late March of 1998. The balance of the increase was internally generated. In 1995, the Company recognized a gain of $54.2 million on the transfer of assets to KPP, mentioned above. This distorted compound growth rates in earnings per share and net income which have not been displayed. At the end of 1998, the Company had goodwill of $62.5 million recorded as an asset which equated to approximately 71% of stockholders' equity and book value per share.

Officers	Position	Ownership Information	
John R. Barnes	President, CEO	Number of Shares Outstanding	31,409,622
Edward Doherty II	Senior VP	Market Capitalization	$ 127,523,065
Howard C. Wadsworth	Treasurer, Secretary	Number of Shareholders	10,000
Michael R. Bakke	Controller	Where Listed / Symbol	NYSE / KAB

Other Information			
Transfer Agent	American Stock Transfer & Trust Co. New York, NY	SIC Code	1700
Auditor	PricewaterhouseCoopers LLP	Employees	1,857
		Web Site	kaneb.com

Kentucky Electric Steel, Inc.

P.O. Box 3500   Ashland, KY 41105-3500   Telephone (606)929-1222   Fax (606)929-1261

Company Description

Kentucky Electric Steel, Inc. owns and operates a steel mini-mill near Ashland, Kentucky. The Company recycles steel from scrap, a process designed to result in lower production costs than those of integrated steel mills, which produce steel by processing iron ore and other raw materials in blast furnaces. The Company completed a two-phase capital expenditure program in fiscal 1996. The first phase expanded the Company's casting, rolling and finishing capacity and increased the size range of products the Company can produce. The second phase, installation of a ladle metallurgy facility, removed the refining cycle from the electric arc furnace, thereby increasing total melting capacity. The Company was founded in 1993 as a successor to an existing business.

	09/26/98	09/27/97	09/28/96	09/30/95
Per Share Information				
Stock Price as of 12/31	2.62	5.37	5.50	7.87
Earnings Per Share	0.32	-0.57	0.32	0.95
Price / Earnings Ratio	8.19	n.a.	17.19	8.28
Book Value Per Share	7.89	7.39	7.89	7.82
Price / Book Value %	33.21	72.67	69.71	100.64
Dividends Per Share	0.0	0.0	0.0	0.0
Annual Financial Data				
Operating Results (000's)				
Total Revenues	109,536.0	94,686.0	98,720.0	107,459.0
Costs & Expenses	-107,126.0	-98,917.0	-98,627.0	-99,996.0
Income Before Taxes and Other	2,410.0	-4,231.0	93.0	7,463.0
Other Items	0.0	0.0	0.0	0.0
Income Tax	-916.0	1,599.0	-35.0	-2,812.0
Net Income	1,494.0	-2,632.0	58.0	4,651.0
Cash Flow From Operations	2,325.0	2,450.0	3,948.0	5,000.0
Balance Sheet (000's)				
Cash & Equivalents	150.0	127.0	124.0	327.0
Total Current Assets	38,404.0	35,301.0	35,891.0	37,378.0
Fixed Assets, Net	34,795.0	35,532.0	32,000.0	25,000.0
Total Assets	80,251.0	78,770.0	78,433.0	72,625.0
Total Current Liabilities	24,251.0	23,966.0	20,928.0	27,054.0
Long-Term Debt	20,000.0	20,000.0	20,000.0	7,287.0
Stockholders' Equity	35,192.0	34,211.0	37,110.0	38,097.0
Performance & Financial Condition				
Return on Total Revenues %	1.36	-2.78	0.06	4.33
Return on Avg Stockholders' Equity %	4.31	-7.38	0.15	12.57
Return on Average Assets %	1.88	-3.35	0.08	6.20
Current Ratio	1.58	1.47	1.71	1.38
Debt / Equity %	56.83	58.46	53.89	19.13

Compound Growth %'s	EPS % -30.42	Net Income % -31.51	Total Revenues % 0.64

Comments

The increase in fiscal 1998 revenues is attributable to an increase in shipments and an increase in average selling price. The increase in shipments resulted from a strong demand for the Company's products. Also, shipments in fiscal 1997 were negatively impacted by the effect on production of the melt shop operations being shut down for twelve days in order to decontaminate the baghouse facility, after the detection of a radioactive substance in the baghouse dust. A caster fire caused an interruption to business in fiscal 1996. Management is hopeful that income can be restored to historical levels.

Officers	Position	Ownership Information	
Charles C. Hanebuth	President, CEO	Number of Shares Outstanding	4,458,941
William J. Jessie	Vice President, CFO	Market Capitalization	$ 11,682,425
Clifford R. Borland	Director	Number of Shareholders	1,500
J. Marvin Quin, II	Director	Where Listed / Symbol	NASDAQ / KESI

Other Information			
Transfer Agent	Wachovia Bank, N.A. Winston-Salem, NC	SIC Code	3312
Auditor	Arthur Andersen LLP	Employees	421

Kids Stuff, Inc.

4450 Belden Village Street NW, Suite 406   Canton, OH 44718   Telephone (330)492-8090   Fax (330)492-8290

Company Description

Kids Stuff, Inc. is a specialty direct marketer. The Company publishes catalogs with an emphasis on children's hardgood products (i.e., products not primarily made from fabrics) from prenatal to the age of three. Its three catalogs are: Perfectly Safe—The Catalog For Parents Who Care, Jeannie's Kids Club, and The Natural Baby Catalog. As a result of a reorganization during June 1996, the Company was incorporated and spun off from its parent, Duncan Hill, Inc. The Company acquired the catalog assets of Dunhill in exchange for notes and common and preferred stock. During June 1997, the Company acquired The Natural Baby Catalog. The acquisition was funded with the proceeds of an initial public offering which raised approximately $3.6 million. Duncan Hill, Inc. and its controlling shareholders own 67.8% of the Company's outstanding common stock.

	12/31/98	12/31/97	12/31/96	12/31/95
Per Share Information				
Stock Price	2.69	6.00	n.a.	n.a.
Earnings Per Share	-0.01	0.01	-0.14	-0.15
Price / Earnings Ratio	n.a.	600.00	n.a.	n.a.
Book Value Per Share	0.51	0.52	-0.27	-0.31
Price / Book Value %	527.45	1,153.85	n.a.	n.a.
Dividends Per Share	0.0	0.0	0.0	0.0
Annual Financial Data				
Operating Results (000's)				
Total Revenues	14,172.9	11,016.6	6,644.5	5,732.9
Costs & Expenses	-14,208.7	-9,779.4	-7,166.1	-6,269.9
Income Before Taxes and Other	-35.8	50.1	-521.6	-537.0
Other Items	0.0	0.0	0.0	0.0
Income Tax	0.0	0.0	0.0	0.0
Net Income	-35.8	50.1	-521.6	-537.0
Cash Flow From Operations	120.1	n.a.	-212.6	-540.1
Balance Sheet (000's)				
Cash & Equivalents	25.4	101.9	248.6	37.2
Total Current Assets	2,924.9	2,688.3	1,358.1	1,237.2
Fixed Assets, Net	338.4	265.4	113.6	120.0
Total Assets	5,028.1	4,548.1	1,471.7	1,469.0
Total Current Liabilities	3,241.3	2,525.4	2,161.9	1,800.0
Long-Term Debt	0.0	0.0	300.0	300.0
Stockholders' Equity	1,786.9	1,822.7	-990.2	-631.0
Performance & Financial Condition				
Return on Total Revenues %	-0.25	0.45	-7.85	-9.37
Return on Avg Stockholders' Equity %	-1.98	12.04	n.a.	n.a.
Return on Average Assets %	-0.75	1.66	-35.48	-53.70
Current Ratio	0.90	1.06	0.63	0.69
Debt / Equity %	n.a.	n.a.	n.a.	n.a.

Compound Growth %'s	EPS % n.a.	Net Income % n.a.	Total Revenues % 35.22

Comments

Per Share amounts for 1996 and 1995 are based on pro-forma share amounts as the Company was wholly-owned until its public offering in 1997. The increase in 1998 revenue was attributable to the inclusion of The Natural Baby Catalog for a full year. The net loss in 1998 was due to increased general and administrative expenses, with slightly higher than expected selling expenses. At December 31, 1998, the Company had $1.8 million of intangible assets on its books which equated to approximately 100% of stockholders' equity and book value per share. Also at year end, the Company had a deficiency in working capital. But in March 1999, the Company completed a public offering of preferred stock and raised net proceeds of $1,960,000.

Officers	Position	Ownership Information	
William L. Miller	Chairman, CEO	Number of Shares Outstanding	3,512,856
Jeanne E. Miller	President	Market Capitalization	$ 9,449,583
Clark D. Swisher	Senior VP	Number of Shareholders	1,000
Alfred M. Schmidt	Director	Where Listed / Symbol	OTC-BB / KDST

Other Information

Transfer Agent	American Stock Transfer & Trust Co. New York, NY		SIC Code	5961
Auditor	Hausser & Taylor LLP		Employees	72
Market Maker	S.W. Ryan & Company Inc.	(610)668-8241	Web Site	kidstuff.net
	M.H. Meyerson & Co., Inc.	(800)333-3113		

Kinark Corporation

2250 East 73rd Street, Suite 300   Tulsa, OK 74136-6832   Telephone (918)494-0964   Fax (918)494-3999

Company Description

Kinark Corporation is a diversified holding company with subsidiaries conducting business in hot dip galvanizing, bulk liquid chemical storage and public warehousing. The Company's galvanizing and storage operations provide products and services to more than 2,000 customers nationwide from facilities located in Colorado, Illinois, Kentucky, Missouri, Oklahoma, Tennessee and Texas. Kinark's customers represent a wide range of industries providing basic products and services, such as utilities, petrochemical, transportation, communications, agriculture, recreation, automotive, and construction. Over 80% of the Company's sales are generated from its hot dip galvanizing of fabricated structural steel products. The Company was founded in 1955.

	12/31/98	12/31/97	12/31/96	12/31/95
Per Share Information				
Stock Price	2.19	3.00	3.81	2.94
Earnings Per Share	0.09	0.09	0.21	-0.50
Price / Earnings Ratio	24.33	33.33	18.14	n.a.
Book Value Per Share	2.63	2.53	2.48	2.18
Price / Book Value %	83.27	118.58	153.63	134.86
Dividends Per Share	0.0	0.0	0.0	0.0
Annual Financial Data				
Operating Results (000's)				
Total Revenues	48,313.0	48,556.0	47,697.0	25,246.0
Costs & Expenses	-47,183.0	-47,499.0	-45,365.0	-26,395.0
Income Before Taxes and Other	1,130.0	1,057.0	2,332.0	-1,149.0
Other Items	0.0	0.0	-164.0	-1,176.0
Income Tax	-530.0	-468.0	-894.0	446.0
Net Income	600.0	589.0	1,274.0	-1,879.0
Cash Flow From Operations	3,158.0	2,682.0	3,196.0	89.0
Balance Sheet (000's)				
Cash & Equivalents	189.0	259.0	2,041.0	30.0
Total Current Assets	13,153.0	11,933.0	12,948.0	7,153.0
Fixed Assets, Net	15,607.0	14,890.0	14,305.0	9,007.0
Total Assets	33,108.0	31,955.0	33,439.0	18,375.0
Total Current Liabilities	6,083.0	5,769.0	9,532.0	4,278.0
Long-Term Debt	8,590.0	8,131.0	7,172.0	5,932.0
Stockholders' Equity	17,783.0	17,127.0	16,735.0	8,165.0
Performance & Financial Condition				
Return on Total Revenues %	1.24	1.21	2.67	-7.44
Return on Avg Stockholders' Equity %	3.44	3.48	10.23	-20.64
Return on Average Assets %	1.84	1.80	4.92	-9.56
Current Ratio	2.16	2.07	1.36	1.67
Debt / Equity %	48.30	47.47	42.86	72.65

Compound Growth %'s	EPS %	-34.53	Net Income %	-31.37	Total Revenues %	24.15

Comments

Galvanizing sales were adversely affected in the second half of 1998, compared to the same period of 1997, following the decision by a major customer to galvanize its own product in-house, and to compete directly with the Company by acquiring a galvanizing facility in the Tulsa market. Galvanizing revenue was still up 1.1% for the year. Sales of storage and warehousing services declined 9.8%. Gross margins improved in 1998 due to increased labor productivity in the galvanizing segment and higher sales per square foot in warehousing. At December 31, 1998, the Company had $4.0 million of goodwill recorded as assets which equated to approximately 22% of stockholders' equity and book value per share.

Officers	Position	Ownership Information	
Michael T. Crimmins	Chairman, CEO	Number of Shares Outstanding	6,767,540
Ronald J. Evans	President	Market Capitalization	$ 14,820,913
Carolyn A. Fredrich	Secretary	Number of Shareholders	2,400
Paul R. Chastain	Vice President, CFO	Where Listed / Symbol	AMEX / KIN

Other Information			
Transfer Agent	ChaseMellon Shareholder Services Ridgefield Park, NJ	SIC Code	3470
Auditor	Deloitte & Touche LLP	Employees	416

Kreisler Manufacturing Corporation

5960 Central Avenue, Suite H   St. Petersburg, FL 33707   Telephone (727)347-1144   Fax (727)347-1155

Company Description

Kreisler Manufacturing Corporation fabricates precision metal components and assemblies primarily for aircraft engines with both military and commercial applications. The primary function of the Company's products is to transport substances, including air, to various parts of the aircraft or aircraft engine. The redirection of air is a major element in reducing the high temperatures generated by aerospace propulsion. For the fiscal year ended June 30, 1998, the sales activity was comprised of approximately 35% percent for military aircraft engines and 65% for commercial aircraft engines. The Company was founded in 1956.

	06/30/98	06/30/97	06/30/96	06/30/95
Per Share Information				
Stock Price as of 12/31	4.03	2.34	1.03	1.06
Earnings Per Share	0.76	0.50	-0.48	-0.64
Price / Earnings Ratio	5.30	4.68	n.a.	n.a.
Book Value Per Share	3.10	2.30	1.80	2.28
Price / Book Value %	130.00	101.74	57.22	46.49
Dividends Per Share	0.0	0.0	0.0	0.0
Annual Financial Data				
Operating Results (000's)				
Total Revenues	13,127.6	9,471.9	5,807.7	5,449.1
Costs & Expenses	-11,262.1	-8,796.0	-6,724.2	-6,728.8
Income Before Taxes and Other	1,865.5	675.9	-922.9	-1,279.7
Other Items	0.0	0.0	0.0	0.0
Income Tax	-317.3	295.0	0.0	0.0
Net Income	1,548.2	970.9	-922.9	-1,279.7
Cash Flow From Operations	1,460.4	-113.9	-845.0	-1,046.6
Balance Sheet (000's)				
Cash & Equivalents	1,909.0	691.9	587.1	608.0
Total Current Assets	7,053.0	4,447.4	3,373.9	3,136.2
Fixed Assets, Net	322.9	197.2	204.1	225.4
Total Assets	7,375.9	5,199.6	4,103.3	4,737.2
Total Current Liabilities	1,355.3	727.2	601.8	309.7
Long-Term Debt	0.0	0.0	0.0	0.0
Stockholders' Equity	6,020.5	4,472.4	3,501.5	4,427.5
Performance & Financial Condition				
Return on Total Revenues %	11.79	10.25	-15.89	-23.48
Return on Avg Stockholders' Equity %	29.51	24.35	-23.28	-35.55
Return on Average Assets %	24.62	20.87	-20.88	-29.08
Current Ratio	5.20	6.12	5.61	10.13
Debt / Equity %	n.a.	n.a.	n.a.	n.a.

Compound Growth %'s	EPS %	52.00	Net Income %	59.45	Total Revenues %	34.06

Comments

The Company declared a 4 for 1 stock split in 1997. All per share amounts have been restated for consistency. Over the past two years Kreisler has recovered from five years of losses by changing its operating management, improving manufacturing systems, enhancing product quality, meeting shipping schedules and re-establishing credibility with its customers. The numbers seem to speak for themselves. Tax loss carryovers were completely utilized in fiscal 1997 and 1998. For the six months ended December 31, 1998, the Company reported revenues and net income of $7.1 million and $766,045 ($.37 per share) as compared to $5.7 million and $716,155 ($.36 per share) for the same period of the preceding year. However, these results are better than they look. Pre tax income was $1,276,542 for the last six months as compared to $665,839 for the comparable period one year earlier.

Officers	Position	Ownership Information	
Edward L. Stern	President, CFO	Number of Shares Outstanding	1,942,048
Edward A. Stern	Vice President	Market Capitalization	$ 7,826,453
Michael D. Stern	Vice President	Number of Shareholders	1,000
Robert S. Krupp	Director	Where Listed / Symbol	NASDAQ / KRSL

Other Information			
Transfer Agent	American Stock Transfer & Trust Co. New York, NY	SIC Code	3724
Auditor	Gregory, Sharer & Stuart	Employees	100
		Web Site	kreisler-ind.com

Kyzen Corporation

430 Harding Industrial Drive Nashville, TN 37211 Telephone (615)831-0888 Fax (615)831-0889

Company Description

Kyzen Corporation manufactures or markets 1) environmentally acceptable chemical solutions and processes used in high-technology cleaning applications, including electronic assemblies and precision metal and plastic components, 2) process water reuse machines used in these chemical cleaning applications, 3) specialty cleaning machines, and 4) integrated process support services. These products and services can be sold as a package, as a cleaning process or as separate items that can be integrated into the customer's cleaning process. The Company was formed in 1990.

	12/31/98	12/31/97	12/31/96	12/31/95
Per Share Information				
Stock Price	0.56	1.50	2.06	2.50
Earnings Per Share	0.01	-0.11	-0.15	-0.12
Price / Earnings Ratio	56.00	n.a.	n.a.	n.a.
Book Value Per Share	0.50	0.49	0.60	0.71
Price / Book Value %	112.00	306.12	343.33	352.11
Dividends Per Share	0.0	0.0	0.0	0.0
Annual Financial Data				
Operating Results (000's)				
Total Revenues	5,946.2	5,543.1	5,085.5	4,065.1
Costs & Expenses	-5,878.7	-6,115.1	-5,842.1	-4,194.8
Income Before Taxes and Other	67.5	-572.0	-756.6	-129.8
Other Items	0.0	0.0	0.0	-114.8
Income Tax	0.0	0.0	0.0	0.0
Net Income	67.5	-572.0	-756.6	-244.6
Cash Flow From Operations	48.4	-326.1	-625.1	-668.3
Balance Sheet (000's)				
Cash & Equivalents	523.9	710.8	741.8	1,608.9
Total Current Assets	1,747.6	1,980.8	2,453.6	3,277.6
Fixed Assets, Net	861.5	928.1	786.8	520.0
Total Assets	3,001.8	3,226.3	3,464.5	3,976.2
Total Current Liabilities	505.8	730.2	458.6	482.7
Long-Term Debt	0.0	0.0	6.7	0.0
Stockholders' Equity	2,496.0	2,428.4	2,999.2	3,493.4
Performance & Financial Condition				
Return on Total Revenues %	1.14	-10.32	-14.88	-6.02
Return on Avg Stockholders' Equity %	2.74	-21.08	-23.31	-14.64
Return on Average Assets %	2.17	-17.10	-20.34	-9.13
Current Ratio	3.46	2.71	5.35	6.79
Debt / Equity %	n.a.	n.a.	0.22	n.a.

Compound Growth %'s	EPS % n.a.	Net Income % n.a.	Total Revenues %	13.52

Comments

Revenues were 8% higher in 1998 as compared to 1997. The components vary considerably. Chemical sales increased 13% whereas equipment and systems sales declined 56%, reflecting the Company's focus on more profitable chemical products while downsizing equipment products and peripherals. Gross margins improved dramatically as management executed this strategy. The bottom line was also profitable after years of losses. With all of this good news, someone might wonder what happened to the price per share. The problem appears to be external, namely the lack of investor enthusiasm for small companies. The balance sheet is clean and contains no long term debt.

Officers	Position	Ownership Information	
Michael L. Bixenman	Chairman, Vice President	Number of Shares Outstanding	5,006,781
Kyle J. Doyel	President, CEO	Market Capitalization	$ 2,803,797
Thomas M. Forsythe	Vice President, Treasurer	Number of Shareholders	1,000
Thomas J. Herrmann	Vice President, Secretary	Where Listed / Symbol	NASDAQ / KYZN

Other Information			
Transfer Agent	American Stock Transfer & Trust Co. New York, NY	SIC Code	2842
Auditor	PricewaterhouseCoopers LLP	Employees	34
		Web Site	kyzen.com

L.A. T Sportswear, Inc.

1200 Airport Road Ball Ground, GA 30107 Telephone (770)479-1877 Fax (770)479-4078

Company Description

L.A. T Sportswear, Inc. is a national distributor and manufacturer of quality imprintable and decorative knitted sportswear. Through its distribution operations, the Company is a national distributor of undecorated garments for the imprinted sportswear industry. It carries one of the broadest product lines in the industry, including t-shirts and sweatshirts, golf shirts, baseball and golf caps, athletic jackets, athletic jerseys and shorts, bags and aprons. The Company carries the products and brands of nationally-recognized manufacturers as well as its own line of manufactured apparel. The Company was founded in 1978.

	01/02/99	12/27/97	12/28/96	12/30/95
Per Share Information				
Stock Price as of 12/31	1.12	0.63	0.62	2.12
Earnings Per Share	0.29	-0.18	-0.63	-0.86
Price / Earnings Ratio	3.86	n.a.	n.a.	n.a.
Book Value Per Share	2.72	2.44	2.61	3.25
Price / Book Value %	41.18	25.82	23.75	n.a.
Dividends Per Share	0.0	0.0	0.0	0.0
Annual Financial Data				
Operating Results (000's)				
Total Revenues	81,874.0	72,627.0	94,838.0	124,897.0
Costs & Expenses	-79,354.0	-73,352.0	-97,330.0	-130,011.0
Income Before Taxes and Other	1,285.0	-725.0	-2,492.0	-5,380.0
Other Items	0.0	0.0	0.0	0.0
Income Tax	-76.0	-21.0	-172.0	1,787.0
Net Income	1,209.0	-746.0	-2,664.0	-3,593.0
Cash Flow From Operations	1,878.0	6,476.0	10,525.0	-8,323.0
Balance Sheet (000's)				
Cash & Equivalents	407.0	177.0	938.0	2,784.0
Total Current Assets	31,106.0	24,524.0	31,795.0	50,999.0
Fixed Assets, Net	3,201.0	3,749.0	4,315.0	5,841.0
Total Assets	34,463.0	28,739.0	36,519.0	57,032.0
Total Current Liabilities	12,486.0	6,242.0	6,107.0	41,988.0
Long-Term Debt	10,162.0	11,732.0	18,929.0	821.0
Stockholders' Equity	11,444.0	10,235.0	10,981.0	13,645.0
Performance & Financial Condition				
Return on Total Revenues %	1.48	-1.03	-2.81	-2.88
Return on Avg Stockholders' Equity %	11.15	-7.03	-21.64	-23.27
Return on Average Assets %	3.83	-2.29	-5.70	-7.07
Current Ratio	2.49	3.93	5.21	1.21
Debt / Equity %	88.80	114.63	172.38	6.02

Compound Growth %'s	EPS % n.a.	Net Income % n.a.	Total Revenues % -13.13

Comments

During 1995, the Company achieved a 25% growth in revenues and opened three new distribution facilities. But then the market for Olympic products became saturated and an off-shore manufacturing program was producing defective merchandise. The Company restructured in the fourth quarter of 1995 by closing two distribution centers, consolidating three manufacturing facilities into two, and shutting down its printed operations. The year 1997 came close to a turnaround but a soft market for the Company's products produced a net loss. An intensified sales effort and operational streamlining produced a solid profit in 1998. Income tax was lower than the statutory rate due to tax loss carryovers.

Officers	Position	Ownership Information	
Isador E. Mitzner	Chairman, CEO	Number of Shares Outstanding	4,200,001
J. David Keller	President, Secretary	Market Capitalization	$ 4,704,001
John F. Hankinson	Vice President, CFO	Number of Shareholders	344
Irwin Lowenstein	Director	Where Listed / Symbol	OTC-BB / LATS

Other Information

Transfer Agent	SunTrust Bank Atlanta, GA		SIC Code	5130
Auditor	Deloitte & Touche LLP		Employees	402
Market Maker	Carr Securities Corporation	(800)221-2243		
	Robinson Humphrey Company,Inc.	(800)241-0445		

LaBarge, Inc.

9900A Clayton Road   St. Louis, MO 63178-4499   Telephone (314)997-0800   Fax (314)812-9438

Company Description

LaBarge, Inc. engineers, manufactures, tests and sells sophisticated electronic control systems and devices and complex interconnect assemblies under contract with its customers. Markets for the Company's products are: defense, aerospace, telecommunications, medical equipment, geophysical/energy and various other commercial/industrial markets. The Company was founded in 1968 as the successor by merger with a company founded in 1953.

	06/28/98	06/29/97	06/30/96	07/02/95
Per Share Information				
Stock Price as of 12/31	2.75	4.06	5.87	3.50
Earnings Per Share	0.30	0.50	0.23	0.09
Price / Earnings Ratio	9.17	8.12	25.52	38.89
Book Value Per Share	1.91	1.63	1.14	0.87
Price / Book Value %	143.98	249.08	514.91	402.30
Dividends Per Share	0.0	0.0	0.0	0.0
Annual Financial Data				
Operating Results (000's)				
Total Revenues	99,405.0	96,765.0	75,206.0	61,937.0
Costs & Expenses	-91,824.0	-89,764.0	-71,435.0	-60,935.0
Income Before Taxes and Other	7,461.0	7,001.0	3,771.0	1,002.0
Other Items	89.0	0.0	0.0	0.0
Income Tax	-2,786.0	734.0	-231.0	319.0
Net Income	4,764.0	7,735.0	3,540.0	1,321.0
Cash Flow From Operations	161.0	8,167.0	1,839.0	-198.0
Balance Sheet (000's)				
Cash & Equivalents	540.0	1,467.0	935.0	142.7
Total Current Assets	40,699.0	34,276.0	32,666.0	24,344.3
Fixed Assets, Net	11,254.0	4,090.0	3,194.0	2,676.5
Total Assets	58,992.0	43,459.0	41,550.0	31,608.4
Total Current Liabilities	19,187.0	12,815.0	13,376.0	11,844.5
Long-Term Debt	10,163.0	5,101.0	10,419.0	6,466.7
Stockholders' Equity	29,642.0	25,543.0	17,755.0	13,297.1
Performance & Financial Condition				
Return on Total Revenues %	4.79	7.99	4.71	2.13
Return on Avg Stockholders' Equity %	17.27	35.73	22.80	10.46
Return on Average Assets %	9.30	18.20	9.68	3.47
Current Ratio	2.12	2.67	2.44	2.06
Debt / Equity %	34.29	19.97	58.68	48.63

Compound Growth %'s	EPS %	49.38	Net Income %	53.35	Total Revenues %	17.08

Comments

Two customers, in fiscal 1998, accounted for in excess of 44% of total sales for the year: Lockheed Martin in the aerospace/defense market at 27% of total sales for the year and Schlumberger in the geophysical market at 17% of total sales. The Company lost its largest telecommunications customer, Northern Telecom, in fiscal 1998. Revenue from this customer dropped to 1.1% of total sales as compared to 11.4% of total sales in fiscal 1997. Despite this loss, the Company managed a net advance in revenue of 2.7%. The increase in long term debt relates to the purchase of its headquarters building in St. Louis, Missouri. For the six months ended December 31, 1998, revenues and net income were $48.4 million and $1,443,000 ($.09 per share) as compared to $43.7 million and $1,982,000 ($.13 per share) for the same period of the preceding year.

Officers	Position	Ownership Information	
Pierre Labarge Jr.	Chairman	Number of Shares Outstanding	15,495,280
Craig E. LaBarge	President, CEO	Market Capitalization	$ 42,612,020
William J. Maender	VP - Finance, Treasurer	Number of Shareholders	3,500
Harvey Baker	Vice President	Where Listed / Symbol	AMEX / LB

Other Information			
Transfer Agent	UMB Bank, N.A. Kansas City, MO	SIC Code	3669
Auditor	KPMG LLP	Employees	850
		Web Site	labarge.com

Lannett Company, Inc.

9000 State Road   Philadelphia, PA 19136   Telephone (215)333-9000   Fax (215)333-9004

Company Description

Lannett Company, Inc. manufactures and distributes pharmaceutical products sold under generic names and, historically, has manufactured and distributed pharmaceutical products sold under its trade or brand names. The Company also contract develops and manufactures pharmaceutical products for other companies. In addition to the five products that are currently being manufactured, ten additional products are under development. The Company sells its pharmaceutical products primarily to wholesalers, distributors, warehousing chains, retail chains and other pharmaceutical companies. Lannett Company started business in 1942.

	06/30/98	06/30/97	06/30/96	06/30/95
Per Share Information				
Stock Price as of 12/31	1.12	2.62	2.75	1.94
Earnings Per Share	0.08	-0.15	0.02	0.03
Price / Earnings Ratio	14.00	n.a.	137.50	64.67
Book Value Per Share	-0.70	-0.90	-0.75	-0.78
Price / Book Value %	n.a.	n.a.	n.a.	n.a.
Dividends Per Share	0.0	0.0	0.0	0.0
Annual Financial Data				
Operating Results (000's)				
Total Revenues	9,464.8	3,801.0	3,865.7	4,354.6
Costs & Expenses	-8,589.1	-4,511.3	-3,728.2	-3,859.5
Income Before Taxes and Other	875.7	-789.3	137.1	351.1
Other Items	0.0	0.0	0.0	0.0
Income Tax	150.0	0.0	0.0	-35.0
Net Income	1,025.7	-789.3	137.1	316.1
Cash Flow From Operations	493.1	-342.0	-185.9	-16.1
Balance Sheet (000's)				
Cash & Equivalents	16.7	15.5	25.3	39.0
Total Current Assets	3,513.1	2,488.4	1,838.0	1,113.0
Fixed Assets, Net	4,309.7	2,616.4	1,860.3	1,885.3
Total Assets	8,116.6	5,110.2	3,706.2	3,009.1
Total Current Liabilities	3,674.8	2,393.7	1,332.2	1,093.6
Long-Term Debt	1,357.5	522.4	426.3	5,956.3
Stockholders' Equity	-3,667.3	-4,693.1	-3,903.7	-4,040.8
Performance & Financial Condition				
Return on Total Revenues %	10.84	-20.77	3.55	7.26
Return on Avg Stockholders' Equity %	n.a.	n.a.	n.a.	n.a.
Return on Average Assets %	15.51	-17.91	4.08	11.20
Current Ratio	0.96	1.04	1.38	1.02
Debt / Equity %	n.a.	n.a.	n.a.	n.a.

Compound Growth %'s	EPS %	38.67	Net Income %	48.05	Total Revenues %	29.54

Comments

During fiscal 1997, the Company signed two significant long-term contract manufacturing supply agreements. As a result, fiscal 1998 revenue grew by 149% over the preceding year. Convertible debt and stock options had the result of diluting profits from $.20 per share to $.08 per share. Cash flow from operations and additional borrowings were used to finance the new volume of business and capital improvements. At June 30, 1998, the Company had tax loss carryovers of $5.9 million available to offset future income. For the six months ended December 31, 1998, revenues and net income were $5.1 million and $562,316 ($.04 per share) as compared to $4.9 million and $751,706 ($.05 per share) in the same period of the preceding year.

Officers	Position	Ownership Information	
William Farber	Chairman	Number of Shares Outstanding	5,206,128
Jeffrey Moshal	VP - Finance	Market Capitalization	$ 5,830,863
Audrey Farber	Secretary, Treasurer	Number of Shareholders	506
Vlad Mikijanic	Vice President	Where Listed / Symbol	OTC-BB / LANN

Other Information			
Transfer Agent	Registrar & Transfer Co. Cranford, NJ	SIC Code	2834
Auditor	Deloitte & Touche LLP	Employees	91
Market Maker	Herzog, Heine, Geduld, Inc. (800)221-3600	Web Site	lannett.com
	F.J. Morrissey & Co., Inc. (800)842-8928		

Laser Master International, Inc.

1000 First Street   Harrison, NJ 07029   Telephone (973)482-7200   Fax (973)482-9574

Company Description

Laser Master International, founded in 1981, sells laser printed materials to the textile industry for heat transfer application and also manufactures gift wrap paper for sale to that industry. The Company uses a computerized laser system in its manufacturing process which is faster and more efficient than the traditional press process. Laser master owns a 247,000 square foot building, of which it utilizes approximately 51% for its manufacturing operations. The remainder of the building is leased to two unaffiliated tenants. The Company's President owns 35% of the Company's common stock.

	11/30/98	11/30/97	11/30/96	11/30/95
Per Share Information				
Stock Price as of 12/31	0.18	0.32	0.63	0.88
Earnings Per Share	0.05	-0.06	0.04	-0.03
Price / Earnings Ratio	3.60	n.a.	15.75	n.a.
Book Value Per Share	0.77	0.72	0.78	0.76
Price / Book Value %	23.38	44.44	80.77	115.79
Dividends Per Share	0.0	0.0	0.0	0.0
Annual Financial Data				
Operating Results (000's)				
Total Revenues	14,102.4	12,079.5	11,637.9	8,854.2
Costs & Expenses	-13,538.9	-12,691.0	-11,237.8	-10,405.8
Income Before Taxes and Other	563.4	-611.5	400.1	-1,551.6
Other Items	0.0	0.0	0.0	1,372.7
Income Tax	0.0	38.0	-38.0	0.0
Net Income	563.4	-573.5	362.1	-179.0
Cash Flow From Operations	20.8	818.8	-1,237.4	-579.6
Balance Sheet (000's)				
Cash & Equivalents	239.2	412.4	396.8	808.7
Total Current Assets	6,438.4	5,252.0	5,540.3	4,264.5
Fixed Assets, Net	9,673.6	9,710.8	10,109.7	9,281.0
Total Assets	16,743.6	15,224.1	15,967.2	13,861.2
Total Current Liabilities	4,215.7	2,817.9	2,361.0	3,412.5
Long-Term Debt	4,316.0	4,776.7	5,481.7	5,893.3
Stockholders' Equity	8,171.8	7,629.5	8,043.0	4,501.9
Performance & Financial Condition				
Return on Total Revenues %	4.00	-4.75	3.11	-2.02
Return on Avg Stockholders' Equity %	7.13	-7.32	5.77	-3.90
Return on Average Assets %	3.53	-3.68	2.43	-1.25
Current Ratio	1.53	1.86	2.35	1.25
Debt / Equity %	52.82	62.61	68.15	130.91

Compound Growth %'s	EPS %	11.80	Net Income %	24.74	Total Revenues %	16.78

Comments

The primary reason for the Company's loss in 1997 was the decrease in the gross margin percentage to 22% from 31% in 1996. The decrease was due to disruption in the printing process resulting from repeated problems with the Company's new eight color press. This press, which has been fully operational since January 1998, contributed to both sales and profits in 1998. The press has enabled the Company to enter new markets for its printed paper products such as home furnishings. Management expects to enter additional markets in 1999. At November 30, 1998, the Company had an order backlog of $4.0 million as compared to $2.5 million at November 30, 1997. The Company's production problems appear to be behind them. Does the stock price appear cheap to book value? Yes, and there are no intangibles on the balance sheet.

Officers	Position	Ownership Information	
Mendel Klein	President, Treasurer	Number of Shares Outstanding	10,615,380
Leah Klein	Vice President, Secretary	Market Capitalization	$ 1,910,768
Mirel Spitz	Vice President	Number of Shareholders	525
Muriel Klein	Director	Where Listed / Symbol	OTC-BB / LMTI

Other Information			
Transfer Agent	American Stock Transfer & Trust Co. New York, NY	SIC Code	2750
Auditor	Goldstein and Morris	Employees	78
Market Maker	Paragon Capital Corporation	(800)345-0505	
	Wien Securities Corp.	(800)624-0050	

Laser Technology, Inc.

7070 South Tucson Way   Englewood, CO 80112   Telephone (303)649-1000   Fax (303)649-9710

Company Description

Laser Technology, Inc.'s primary product lines have been its Marksman Laser Speed Detection Systems and Criterion Series of Survey Lasers. Since fiscal 1995, the Company has expanded these product lines through new product development including the introduction of second generation instrumentation. Because of enhancements to the Company's existing products, new product developments and expanding markets for the Company's technology, the Company currently organizes and markets its products in three categories: Traffic Safety products, Survey and Mapping products, and Ship Docking Aid Systems. The Company was founded in 1950.

	09/30/98	09/30/97	09/30/96	09/30/95
Per Share Information				
Stock Price as of 12/31	3.25	2.88	3.88	4.50
Earnings Per Share	0.15	0.12	0.20	0.14
Price / Earnings Ratio	21.67	24.00	19.40	32.14
Book Value Per Share	2.21	2.03	1.94	1.72
Price / Book Value %	147.06	141.87	200.00	261.63
Dividends Per Share	0.0	0.0	0.0	0.0
Annual Financial Data				
Operating Results (000's)				
Total Revenues	11,801.3	10,325.5	9,943.7	8,383.3
Costs & Expenses	-10,400.8	-9,428.1	-8,300.3	-7,296.2
Income Before Taxes and Other	1,400.5	897.4	1,643.4	1,087.1
Other Items	0.0	0.0	0.0	0.0
Income Tax	-504.0	-312.0	-580.0	-383.0
Net Income	896.5	585.4	1,063.4	704.1
Cash Flow From Operations	86.6	-102.6	201.7	963.7
Balance Sheet (000's)				
Cash & Equivalents	988.6	951.9	247.2	1,593.5
Total Current Assets	9,746.3	8,794.2	8,669.3	8,243.0
Fixed Assets, Net	1,517.4	1,291.9	1,113.3	582.7
Total Assets	12,516.0	11,144.6	10,663.5	8,998.3
Total Current Liabilities	1,311.6	990.3	970.6	408.6
Long-Term Debt	159.5	0.0	0.0	0.0
Stockholders' Equity	11,044.8	10,154.4	9,692.9	8,589.7
Performance & Financial Condition				
Return on Total Revenues %	7.60	5.67	10.69	8.40
Return on Avg Stockholders' Equity %	8.46	5.90	11.63	8.73
Return on Average Assets %	7.58	5.37	10.82	8.11
Current Ratio	7.43	8.88	8.93	20.17
Debt / Equity %	1.44	n.a.	n.a.	n.a.

Compound Growth %'s	EPS %	2.33	Net Income %	8.38	Total Revenues %	12.07

Comments

The 27% revenue increase in fiscal 1998 was attributable to increased volume in the Company's traffic safety products resulting from improved distribution and the introduction of second generation products. Furthermore, despite weaknesses of sales to Pacific Rim countries, international sales advanced 15.6%. Bushnell Corporation has licensing rights to manufacture and market a consumer range finder developed by the Company in cooperation with Bushnell for sporting applications. Royalty and licensing revenue from this arrangement increased to $1,242,732 in fiscal 1998 from $401,121 in fiscal 1996. Management believes that the licensing arrangement will continue to positively impact the Company's results from operations.

Officers	Position	Ownership Information	
Blair Zykan	President, CEO	Number of Shares Outstanding	4,994,551
Dan N. Grothe	Secretary	Market Capitalization	$ 16,232,291
Jeremy G. Dunne	Vice President	Number of Shareholders	639
Richard B. Sayford	Director	Where Listed / Symbol	AMEX / LSR

Other Information			
Transfer Agent	Continental Stock Transfer & Trust Co. New York, NY	SIC Code	3824
Auditor	BDO Seidman LLP	Employees	92
		Web Site	lasertech.com

Let's Talk Cellular & Wireless, Inc.

800 Brickell Avenue, Suite 400 Miami, FL 33131 Telephone (305)358-8255 Fax (305)358-1285

Company Description

Let's Talk Cellular & Wireless, Inc. is the largest independent specialty retailer of cellular and wireless products, services and accessories in the United States, with 248 stores located in 22 states, the District of Columbia and Puerto Rico as of July 31, 1998. The Company also wholesales cellular and wireless products and accessories to more than 500 accounts. Since opening its first store in 1989, the Company has grown through internal expansion and acquisitions. During fiscal 1998, the Company opened 72 new stores and acquired 85 stores. Class action lawsuits have been filed against the Company for alleged false and misleading statements concerning the Company's successful implementation of its business model and integration of newly acquired companies. The Company had its initial public offering in fiscal 1998.

	07/31/98	07/31/97	07/31/96	07/31/95
Per Share Information				
Stock Price as of 12/31	2.87	10.25	n.a.	n.a.
Earnings Per Share	-0.03	-0.07	0.01	0.0
Price / Earnings Ratio	n.a.	n.a.	n.a.	n.a.
Book Value Per Share	3.88	1.08	0.32	0.29
Price / Book Value %	73.97	949.07	n.a.	n.a.
Dividends Per Share	0.0	0.0	0.0	0.0
Annual Financial Data				
Operating Results (000's)				
Total Revenues	122,486.7	30,062.0	13,593.3	8,304.0
Costs & Expenses	-121,577.2	-30,105.0	-13,488.3	-8,296.0
Income Before Taxes and Other	909.4	-43.0	104.9	8.0
Other Items	-631.6	0.0	0.0	0.0
Income Tax	-544.4	-2.8	-38.9	0.0
Net Income	-266.5	-45.8	66.0	8.0
Cash Flow From Operations	-8,629.2	-471.8	252.2	92.0
Balance Sheet (000's)				
Cash & Equivalents	1,697.4	1,080.0	1,357.2	241.8
Total Current Assets	35,451.3	14,132.0	3,321.0	2,265.0
Fixed Assets, Net	12,170.2	5,296.7	3,325.0	1,059.0
Total Assets	86,490.7	34,537.5	6,646.0	3,324.0
Total Current Liabilities	32,178.0	12,519.3	2,542.0	2,375.0
Long-Term Debt	19,250.0	12,350.0	474.0	328.0
Stockholders' Equity	33,920.2	6,610.0	693.0	621.0
Performance & Financial Condition				
Return on Total Revenues %	-0.22	-0.15	0.49	0.10
Return on Avg Stockholders' Equity %	-1.32	-1.26	10.05	1.60
Return on Average Assets %	-0.44	-0.22	1.32	0.20
Current Ratio	1.10	1.13	1.31	0.95
Debt / Equity %	56.75	186.84	68.40	52.82

Compound Growth %'s	EPS % n.a.	Net Income % n.a.	Total Revenues % 145.25

Comments

Fiscal 1998 results include a nonrecurring expense of $631,584 ($.08 per share) related to the retirement of debt. New stores and the acquisitions of Telephone Warehouse on June 30, 1997, of Cellular USA and Cellular Unlimited effective November 1, 1997, and of Cellular Warehouse effective March 1, 1998, were responsible for most of the increase in revenues. Comparable store sales increased 5.1%. At July 31, 1998, the Company had $37.8 million of goodwill reflected as assets which equates to approximately 112% of stockholders' equity and book value per share. For the six months ended January 31, 1999, the Company reported revenues and net income of $85.2 million and $1,839,129 ($.21 per share) as compared to $54.7 million and a loss of $219,660 ($.03 per share) for the same period of fiscal 1998.

Officers	Position	Ownership Information	
Brett Beveridge	Chairman, President	Number of Shares Outstanding	8,749,762
David H. Eisenberg	Chairman, CEO	Market Capitalization	$ 25,111,817
Dan Cammarata	CFO	Number of Shareholders	2,000
John Bolduc	Director	Where Listed / Symbol	NASDAQ / LTCW

Other Information			
Transfer Agent	American Stock Transfer & Trust Company New York, NY	SIC Code	4812
Auditor	Ernst & Young LLP	Employees	989
		Web Site	letstalk.com

Lexington Precision Corporation

767 Third Avenue   New York, NY 10017-2023   Telephone (212)319-4657   Fax (212)319-4659

Company Description

Lexington Precision Corporation manufactures, to customer specifications, rubber and metal component parts used primarily by manufacturers of automobiles, industrial equipment, office equipment, computers, medical devices and home appliances. Operations of two divisions, rubber and metals, are decentralized with each having a management team that is responsible for all aspects of production, sales, and customer service. During 1998, 81.3% of the Company's sales were to the automobile industry. The Company was formed in 1966.

	12/31/98	12/31/97	12/31/96	12/31/95
Per Share Information				
Stock Price	1.37	2.37	2.08	3.13
Earnings Per Share	-0.65	-0.38	-0.02	0.49
Price / Earnings Ratio	n.a.	n.a.	n.a.	6.39
Book Value Per Share	-2.22	-1.56	-1.19	-1.18
Price / Book Value %	n.a.	n.a.	n.a.	n.a.
Dividends Per Share	0.0	0.0	0.0	0.0
Annual Financial Data				
Operating Results (000's)				
Total Revenues	126,717.0	119,056.0	114,872.0	104,939.0
Costs & Expenses	-129,291.0	-119,912.0	-114,849.0	-102,226.0
Income Before Taxes and Other	-2,574.0	-856.0	23.0	2,713.0
Other Items	0.0	0.0	0.0	0.0
Income Tax	-132.0	-672.0	-40.0	-425.0
Net Income	-2,706.0	-1,528.0	-17.0	2,288.0
Cash Flow From Operations	8,013.0	7,529.0	8,054.0	7,860.0
Balance Sheet (000's)				
Cash & Equivalents	103.0	208.0	187.0	118.0
Total Current Assets	32,198.0	31,828.0	30,845.0	24,478.0
Fixed Assets, Net	62,737.0	59,430.0	53,300.0	44,938.0
Total Assets	108,325.0	104,124.0	97,030.0	81,876.0
Total Current Liabilities	40,228.0	36,003.0	35,167.0	29,253.0
Long-Term Debt	74,953.0	72,622.0	65,148.0	56,033.0
Stockholders' Equity	-9,451.0	-6,667.0	-5,057.0	-4,976.0
Performance & Financial Condition				
Return on Total Revenues %	-2.14	-1.28	-0.01	2.18
Return on Avg Stockholders' Equity %	n.a.	n.a.	n.a.	n.a.
Return on Average Assets %	-2.55	-1.52	-0.02	3.07
Current Ratio	0.80	0.88	0.88	0.84
Debt / Equity %	n.a.	n.a.	n.a.	n.a.

Compound Growth %'s	EPS % n.a.	Net Income % n.a.	Total Revenues % 6.49

Comments

The Metals division had a $4.1 million loss from operations in 1998, as compared to a $1.6 million loss in 1997. During 1997 and 1998, the Company implemented a strategy to improve the profitability and growth potential of the Metals division by eliminating the production of a large number of diverse, short-run components and by repositioning productive capacity to manufacture higher-volume components in target markets. The repositioning has caused the Company to experience underabsorption of fixed overhead resulting from the cut-back in short-run business. Furthermore, additional expenses have been incurred in connection with this repositioning. The Rubber division experienced a 16.1% increase in operating income bring its contribution to $13.3 million. At December 31, 1998, the Company had an $8.0 million deficiency in working capital and $38 million of long term debt that required refinancing. The auditors issued a going concern qualification in their report on the last year's financial statement.

Officers	Position	Ownership Information	
Michael A. Lubin	Chairman	Number of Shares Outstanding	4,263,036
Warren Delano Jr.	President	Market Capitalization	$ 5,840,359
Dennis J. Welhouse	Senior VP, CFO	Number of Shareholders	1,000
Kenneth I. Greenstein	Secretary	Where Listed / Symbol	OTC-BB / LEXP

Other Information			
Transfer Agent	Harris Trust & Savings Bank Chicago, IL	SIC Code	3060
Auditor	Ernst & Young LLP	Employees	1,284
Market Maker	Robotti & Co., Inc.	(212)986-0800	
	Carr Securities Corporation	(800)221-2243	

Lincoln Snacks Company

4 High Ridge Park Stamford, CT 06905 Telephone (203)329-4545 Fax (203)329-4555

Company Description

Lincoln Snacks Company is one of the leading manufacturers and marketers in the United States and Canada of caramelized pre-popped popcorn. The primary line includes glazed popcorn/nut mixes and sweet popcorn sold under the brand names Poppycock®, Fiddle Faddle® and Screaming Yellow Zonkers®. In addition, the Company processes, markets and distributes nuts. The Company was formed in 1992 to acquire Lincoln Snacks, a division of Sandoz Ltd.

	06/30/98	06/30/97	06/30/96	06/30/95
Per Share Information				
Stock Price as of 12/31	1.44	1.44	1.37	1.75
Earnings Per Share	0.26	0.23	0.08	-0.25
Price / Earnings Ratio	5.54	6.26	17.13	n.a.
Book Value Per Share	1.83	1.57	1.34	1.26
Price / Book Value %	78.69	91.72	102.24	138.89
Dividends Per Share	0.0	0.0	0.0	0.0
Annual Financial Data				
Operating Results (000's)				
Total Revenues	25,782.2	23,101.7	23,845.8	27,148.8
Costs & Expenses	-23,521.0	-21,619.1	-23,306.0	-28,737.2
Income Before Taxes and Other	1,776.8	1,482.6	539.8	-1,588.4
Other Items	0.0	0.0	0.0	0.0
Income Tax	-110.0	-40.0	-29.0	-14.0
Net Income	1,666.8	1,442.6	510.8	-1,602.4
Cash Flow From Operations	3,508.3	3,140.9	1,272.8	602.8
Balance Sheet (000's)				
Cash & Equivalents	3,726.4	1,606.4	58.5	80.2
Total Current Assets	7,854.7	5,267.6	4,926.3	4,064.9
Fixed Assets, Net	4,312.3	4,555.6	5,409.0	5,926.1
Total Assets	16,073.5	13,289.6	13,978.7	13,850.2
Total Current Liabilities	4,354.8	3,224.8	5,163.0	4,756.2
Long-Term Debt	0.0	0.0	309.3	1,109.3
Stockholders' Equity	11,615.8	9,949.0	8,506.4	7,984.7
Performance & Financial Condition				
Return on Total Revenues %	6.47	6.24	2.14	-5.90
Return on Avg Stockholders' Equity %	15.46	15.63	6.19	-18.48
Return on Average Assets %	11.35	10.58	3.67	-10.62
Current Ratio	1.80	1.63	0.95	0.85
Debt / Equity %	n.a.	n.a.	3.64	13.89

Compound Growth %'s	EPS %	80.28	Net Income %	80.64	Total Revenues %	-1.71

Comments

An exclusive distribution agreement with Planter Company, a unit of Nabisco, Inc., expired on December 31, 1997. Sales to Planters declined to 9% of total revenue in fiscal 1998 as compared to 47% of revenue in fiscal 1997. This took the pop out of income from operations. Termination payments from Planters net of certain expenses, however, totalled $1.4 million, restoring net earnings to a record high. At June 30, 1998, the Company had $3.9 million of intangible assets which equated to approximately 34% of book value. For the six months ended December 31, 1998, the Company reported revenues and a net loss of $15.4 million and $1,064,349 ($.17 per share), including $817,459 of nonrecurring expenses, as compared with $12.9 million and $2,787,159 ($.44 per share) for the same period of the preceding year. As of June 30, 1998, the Company has $3.5 million in tax loss carryforwards to offset future income.

Officers	Position	Ownership Information	
R. Scott Kirk	President, COO	Number of Shares Outstanding	6,331,790
Kristine A. Crabs	Vice President, CFO	Market Capitalization	$ 9,117,778
John T. Gray	Director	Number of Shareholders	500
C. Alan MacDonald	Director	Where Listed / Symbol	NASDAQ / SNAX

Other Information			
Transfer Agent	Continental Stock Transfer & Trust Co. New York, NY	SIC Code	2060
Auditor	Arthur Andersen LLP	Employees	95

Littlefield, Adams & Company

6262 Executive Boulevard   Huber Heights, OH 45424   Telephone (937)236-0660   Fax (937)236-1681

Company Description

Littlefield, Adams & Company, founded in 1949, is principally engaged in the design, imprinting and distribution of young men's and boys' active wear products under various license agreements. In 1995 and 1996, approximately 90% of the Company's revenues were derived from sales of Harley-Davidson Motor Co. licensed products. The Company's Harley-Davidson license agreement expired on December 31, 1996 and was not renewed. Since the expiration of the Harley-Davidson license agreement, the Company has focused its efforts on reducing overhead, on developing and securing new licensing arrangements and on developing new branded products. During April 1998, the Company secured a merchandising license agreement with World Championship Wrestling Inc. (WCW), a Time Warner Company.

	12/31/98	12/31/97	12/31/96	12/31/95
Per Share Information				
Stock Price	4.37	0.12	2.87	1.50
Earnings Per Share	0.60	-0.70	0.30	-0.44
Price / Earnings Ratio	7.28	n.a.	9.57	n.a.
Book Value Per Share	1.03	0.14	1.02	0.01
Price / Book Value %	424.27	85.71	281.37	15,000.00
Dividends Per Share	0.0	0.0	0.0	0.0
Annual Financial Data				
Operating Results (000's)				
Total Revenues	25,917.0	3,314.0	12,649.0	14,735.0
Costs & Expenses	-23,318.0	-5,280.0	-11,880.0	-15,741.0
Income Before Taxes and Other	2,599.0	-1,966.0	769.0	-1,006.0
Other Items	0.0	0.0	94.0	0.0
Income Tax	-133.0	29.0	30.0	14.0
Net Income	2,466.0	-1,937.0	893.0	-992.0
Cash Flow From Operations	-5,325.0	442.0	225.0	-339.0
Balance Sheet (000's)				
Cash & Equivalents	107.0	57.0	54.0	241.0
Total Current Assets	11,511.0	1,073.0	5,088.0	4,789.0
Fixed Assets, Net	486.0	416.0	558.0	1,109.0
Total Assets	12,009.0	1,498.0	6,120.0	6,676.0
Total Current Liabilities	5,963.0	1,052.0	3,752.0	5,084.0
Long-Term Debt	3,137.0	18.0	1.0	1,568.0
Stockholders' Equity	2,867.0	384.0	2,321.0	24.0
Performance & Financial Condition				
Return on Total Revenues %	9.51	-58.45	7.06	-6.55
Return on Avg Stockholders' Equity %	151.71	-143.22	76.16	-165.89
Return on Average Assets %	36.51	-50.85	13.96	-12.47
Current Ratio	1.93	1.02	1.36	0.94
Debt / Equity %	109.42	4.69	0.04	6,533.33

Compound Growth %'s	EPS %	41.42	Net Income %	66.18	Total Revenues %	20.71

Comments

The decline in revenues during 1997 is attributable to the loss of the Harley-Davidson license agreement. So bleak was the outlook that Arthur Andersen issued a going concern qualification in its 1997 auditors report. But the new agreement with WCW saved the day. Sales increased 964% in 1998, the highest revenue level for the Company since 1982. 94% of sales were from WCW products. Artwork depicting professional wrestlers was so popular that major customers placed large initial orders without utilizing the "test order" process common to the industry. 1998 results restored Arthur Andersen's confidence in the future; a clean opinion was issued. $7.5 million of tax loss carryovers remain available to offset future income.

Officers	Position	Ownership Information	
Martin B. Shifrin	Chairman	Number of Shares Outstanding	2,790,057
Michael B. Balber	President, CEO	Market Capitalization	$ 12,192,549
Warren L. Rawls	CFO, Secretary	Number of Shareholders	1,300
William E. Goettelman	Director	Where Listed / Symbol	OTC-BB / FUNW

Other Information			
Transfer Agent	First City Transfer Co. Edison, NJ	SIC Code	5130
Auditor	Arthur Andersen LLP	Employees	50
Market Maker	Troster Singer Corporation (800)222-0890	Web Site	funwear.com
	M.H. Meyerson & Co., Inc. (800)333-3113		

Logitek, Inc.

101 Christopher Street   Ronkonkoma, NY 11779   Telephone (516)467-4200   Fax (516)467-4090

Company Description

Logitek, Inc., organized in 1969, is engaged in the design, development and production of electronic monitors and controls which include electronic time delays, flashers, and voltage, frequency, phase and power monitors and switch mode power supplies. Power monitors are generally used to continuously and automatically monitor the characteristics of electrical power systems for conformance to design limits in order to insure proper and safe operation of equipment which utilize the monitored power. The widest application of the Company's products is in systems such as aircraft and space vehicles, aboard ships, vehicular mobile communications, radar systems, and data processing and telecommunication systems.

	06/30/98	06/30/97	06/30/96	06/30/95
Per Share Information				
Stock Price as of 12/31	0.50	0.62	0.62	0.37
Earnings Per Share	0.11	0.09	0.08	0.03
Price / Earnings Ratio	4.55	6.89	7.75	12.33
Book Value Per Share	0.56	0.44	0.35	0.27
Price / Book Value %	89.29	140.91	177.14	137.04
Dividends Per Share	0.0	0.0	0.0	0.0
Annual Financial Data				
Operating Results (000's)				
Total Revenues	4,834.9	4,218.2	3,527.2	2,979.9
Costs & Expenses	-4,260.1	-3,737.4	-3,191.2	-2,900.5
Income Before Taxes and Other	574.8	399.6	336.0	79.4
Other Items	0.0	0.0	0.0	0.0
Income Tax	-174.0	-75.0	-76.0	14.8
Net Income	400.8	324.6	260.0	94.2
Cash Flow From Operations	258.0	209.6	402.4	-10.5
Balance Sheet (000's)				
Cash & Equivalents	429.7	393.8	349.0	139.8
Total Current Assets	2,182.9	1,927.2	1,760.3	1,334.8
Fixed Assets, Net	680.1	668.9	720.9	694.4
Total Assets	2,953.1	2,666.8	2,555.8	2,100.4
Total Current Liabilities	631.8	697.4	778.1	702.8
Long-Term Debt	300.4	398.6	541.9	461.3
Stockholders' Equity	1,893.6	1,505.4	1,183.0	923.0
Performance & Financial Condition				
Return on Total Revenues %	8.29	7.69	7.37	3.16
Return on Avg Stockholders' Equity %	23.58	24.15	24.69	10.76
Return on Average Assets %	14.26	12.43	11.17	4.34
Current Ratio	3.46	2.76	2.26	1.90
Debt / Equity %	15.86	26.48	45.81	49.97

Compound Growth %'s	EPS %	54.20	Net Income %	62.02	Total Revenues %	17.51

Comments

Fiscal 1998 results reflect an increase of 16% on sales and 23% on earnings. Budgeting and cost control coupled with careful marketing strategies have continued to govern the business planning, according to management. $246,000 and $221,000 were expensed for research and development during fiscal 1998 and 1997, respectively. During the last fiscal year, Boeing Aircraft, the United States Government, Falstrom and Loral accounted for 53% of sales. The Company is gaining financial strength as evidenced by improving current and debt/equity ratios. For the six months ended December 31, 1998, revenue and net income were $2.3 million and $123,638 ($.04 per share) as compared to $2.3 million and $164,259 ($.05 per share) in the preceding year.

Officers	Position	Ownership Information	
Herbert L. Fischer	President, CEO	Number of Shares Outstanding	3,382,859
Jack Pisciotta	Vice President	Market Capitalization	$ 1,691,430
Robert Carson	Vice President	Number of Shareholders	120
Howard Fein	Director	Where Listed / Symbol	OTC-BB / LGTK

Other Information			
Transfer Agent	Continental Stock Transfer & Trust Co. New York, NY	SIC Code	3825
Auditor	Marcum & Kliegman LLP	Employees	50
Market Maker	Paragon Capital Corporation	(800)345-0505	
	Stuart, Coleman & Co., Inc.	(800)261-0498	

Luxtec Corporation

326 Clark Street   Worcester, MA 01606   Telephone (508)856-9454   Fax (508)854-3581

Company Description

Luxtec Corporation, organized in 1981, is engaged in the design, manufacture, marketing and distribution of fiber optic headlight and video camera systems, light sources, cables, retractors, surgical telescopes and other custom made surgical equipment for the medical and dental industries. The Company also manufactures small diameter specialty endoscopes and motion tolerant blood pressure monitors for the medical market.

	10/31/98	10/31/97	10/31/96	10/31/95
Per Share Information				
Stock Price as of 12/31	2.62	2.37	2.62	3.50
Earnings Per Share	0.06	-0.17	-0.22	-4.20
Price / Earnings Ratio	43.67	n.a.	n.a.	n.a.
Book Value Per Share	0.23	0.16	0.29	0.08
Price / Book Value %	1,139.13	1,481.25	903.45	4,375.00
Dividends Per Share	0.0	0.0	0.0	0.0
Annual Financial Data				
Operating Results (000's)				
Total Revenues	12,066.7	10,986.5	9,364.2	7,755.4
Costs & Expenses	-11,801.6	-11,339.2	-9,934.9	-8,651.4
Income Before Taxes and Other	265.1	-352.6	-570.7	-896.0
Other Items	0.0	0.0	0.0	-5,231.0
Income Tax	0.0	0.0	0.0	0.0
Net Income	265.1	-352.6	-570.7	-6,126.9
Cash Flow From Operations	24.3	-555.6	-2,134.2	-355.1
Balance Sheet (000's)				
Cash & Equivalents	43.6	41.7	172.3	11.7
Total Current Assets	5,219.2	4,960.2	4,297.6	3,324.7
Fixed Assets, Net	495.1	586.6	747.8	500.2
Total Assets	5,959.1	5,802.6	5,294.8	4,122.0
Total Current Liabilities	3,484.5	3,565.7	3,363.1	3,924.1
Long-Term Debt	557.9	661.2	118.8	0.0
Stockholders' Equity	665.4	455.9	812.9	197.9
Performance & Financial Condition				
Return on Total Revenues %	2.20	-3.21	-6.09	-79.00
Return on Avg Stockholders' Equity %	47.29	-55.59	-112.92	-518.97
Return on Average Assets %	4.51	-6.36	-12.12	-130.36
Current Ratio	1.50	1.39	1.28	0.85
Debt / Equity %	83.84	145.05	14.61	n.a.

Compound Growth %'s	EPS % n.a.	Net Income % n.a.	Total Revenues % 15.88

Comments

Management believes that the introduction of new and improved products over the last two years was chiefly responsible for the fiscal 1998 revenue growth which came despite lower sales in the Pacific Rim area. Dividends on preferred stock shares are deducted before calculating earnings per common share. Fiscal 1998 produced the first annual profit since fiscal 1994. Fiscal 1995 results include a $5.3 million expense for purchased research and development. Although the compound growth rate is impressive, the Company will have to demonstrate sustainable and increasing profitability to justify a higher stock price.

Officers	Position	Ownership Information	
James W. Hobbs	President, CEO	Number of Shares Outstanding	2,867,592
Samuel M. Stein	CFO, Treasurer	Market Capitalization	$ 7,513,091
James Berardo	Director	Number of Shareholders	1,300
Thomas J. Vander Salm	Director	Where Listed / Symbol	AMEX / LXU

Other Information			
Transfer Agent	Boston EquiServe Boston, MA	SIC Code	3845
Auditor	Arthur Andersen LLP	Employees	63
		Web Site	luxtec.com

MIM Corporation

Company Description

MIM Corporation is a pharmacy benefit management organization that provides a broad range of services to the pharmaceutical health care industry and employers and that promotes the cost-effective delivery of pharmacy benefits to plan members and the public. The Company targets organizations involved in three key industry segments: sponsors of public and private health plans; long-term care facilities such as nursing homes and assisted living facilities; and employers, retail pharmacies and pharmaceutical manufacturers and distributors. The Company offers services providing financial benefits to each of them. The Company completed its initial public offering in August 1996.

	12/31/98	12/31/97	12/31/96	12/31/95
Per Share Information				
Stock Price	3.44	4.75	4.75	13.00
Earnings Per Share	0.26	-1.07	-3.32	-1.43
Price / Earnings Ratio	13.23	n.a.	n.a.	n.a.
Book Value Per Share	2.16	1.26	2.50	-1.44
Price / Book Value %	159.26	376.98	190.00	n.a.
Dividends Per Share	0.0	0.0	0.0	0.0
Annual Financial Data				
Operating Results (000's)				
Total Revenues	452,782.0	244,586.0	284,552.0	214,674.0
Costs & Expenses	-444,811.0	-258,100.0	-289,687.0	-221,446.0
Income Before Taxes and Other	7,971.0	-13,514.0	-5,135.0	-6,772.0
Other Items	-3,700.0	17.0	-26,640.0	0.0
Income Tax	0.0	0.0	21.0	0.0
Net Income	4,271.0	-13,497.0	-31,754.0	-6,772.0
Cash Flow From Operations	-16,377.0	-3,083.0	-7,640.0	1,397.0
Balance Sheet (000's)				
Cash & Equivalents	4,495.0	9,593.0	1,834.0	1,804.0
Total Current Assets	82,980.0	53,382.0	49,722.0	17,108.0
Fixed Assets, Net	4,823.0	3,499.0	2,423.0	1,807.0
Total Assets	110,106.0	62,727.0	61,800.0	18,924.0
Total Current Liabilities	63,157.0	44,049.0	30,153.0	29,188.0
Long-Term Debt	6,185.0	0.0	0.0	0.0
Stockholders' Equity	39,054.0	16,810.0	30,143.0	-11,524.0
Performance & Financial Condition				
Return on Total Revenues %	0.94	-5.52	-11.16	-3.15
Return on Avg Stockholders' Equity %	15.29	-57.49	-341.09	n.a.
Return on Average Assets %	4.94	-21.68	-78.67	-44.50
Current Ratio	1.31	1.21	1.65	0.59
Debt / Equity %	15.84	n.a.	n.a.	n.a.

Compound Growth %'s	EPS % n.a.	Net Income % n.a.	Total Revenues % 28.24

Comments

Revenues increased 86% in 1998. Most of the increase came from managing additional plans and new contracts. Acquisitions accounted for only 9% of revenue growth. 1998 results include $3.7 million of nonrecurring expense in connection with the termination of a contract and the settlement of an investigation. 1996 results include a non-cash expense related to stock options of $26.6 million. At December 31, 1998, the Company had $19.4 million of goodwill recorded as assets which equated to approximately 50% of stockholders' equity and book value per share. At the end of 1998, the Company had tax loss carryovers of $47 million available to offset income of future years.

Officers	Position	Ownership Information	
Richard H. Friedman	Chairman, CEO	Number of Shares Outstanding	18,090,748
Scott R. Yablon	President, COO	Market Capitalization	$ 62,232,173
Ed Sitar	CFO	Number of Shareholders	2,117
Barry A. Posner	Vice President, Secretary	Where Listed / Symbol	NASDAQ / MIMS

Other Information			
Transfer Agent	American Stock Transfer & Trust Co. New York, NY	SIC Code	8090
Auditor	Arthur Andersen LLP	Employees	275
		Web Site	mimhp.com

ML Macadamia Orchards, L.P.

828 Fort Street, Suite 205 Honolulu, HI 96813 Telephone (808)532-4130 Fax (808)532-4131

Company Description

ML Macadamia Orchards, L.P., formerly Mauna Loa Macadamia Partners, L.P., is a limited partnership which owns 4,027 tree acres of macadamia orchards on the Island of Hawaii. After the nuts are harvested, the Partnership sells them pursuant to a twenty-two year nut purchase contract which expires in 2006, to a privately-owned entity, Mauna Loa Macadamia Nut Corporation. The Corporation processes and markets the finished products. Because the Partnership business consists solely of growing macadamia nuts, it captures only the farming profit margin. Macadamia nuts are premium quality nuts that are generally considered to be in a consumer category with cashews, almonds and pistachios. The nuts are also said to be a perfect nutritional match with the Mai Tai, a famous Tahitian cocktail. The Partnership was formed in 1986.

	12/31/98	12/31/97	12/31/96	12/31/95
Per Unit Information				
Price Per Unit	3.19	3.62	3.37	2.50
Earnings Per Unit	0.13	2.06	0.40	0.16
Price / Earnings Ratio	24.54	1.76	8.43	15.63
Book Value Per Unit	7.95	8.13	6.35	6.15
Price / Book Value %	40.13	44.53	53.07	40.65
Distributions Per Unit	0.30	0.30	0.20	0.20
Cash Flow Per Unit	0.34	0.51	0.23	0.37
Annual Financial Data				
Operating Results (000's)				
Total Revenues	12,652.0	12,299.0	13,216.0	10,590.0
Costs & Expenses	-10,494.0	-10,468.0	-10,183.0	-9,398.0
Operating Income	2,158.0	1,831.0	3,033.0	1,192.0
Other Items	-1,119.0	0.0	0.0	0.0
Net Income	963.0	15,581.0	3,033.0	1,192.0
Cash Flow From Operations	3,675.0	4,613.0	2,062.0	3,370.0
Balance Sheet (000's)				
Cash & Equivalents	4,317.0	2,914.0	676.0	421.0
Total Current Assets	9,752.0	9,743.0	7,657.0	4,570.0
Investments	n.a.	n.a.	n.a.	n.a.
Total Assets	64,842.0	66,727.0	65,953.0	64,455.0
Total Current Liabilities	3,967.0	4,530.0	3,315.0	3,335.0
Long-Term Debt	0.0	0.0	0.0	0.0
Partners' Capital	59,655.0	60,965.0	47,656.0	46,138.0
Performance & Financial Condition				
Return on Total Revenues %	7.61	126.69	22.95	11.26
Return on Average Partners' Capital %	1.60	28.69	6.47	2.57
Return on Average Assets %	1.46	23.49	4.65	1.81
Current Ratio	2.46	2.15	2.31	1.37
Debt / Equity %	n.a.	n.a.	n.a.	n.a.

Compound Growth %'s	EPU %	-6.69	Net Income %	-6.86	Total Revenues %	6.11

Comments

In July 1997, Congress passed the Taxpayer Relief Act of 1997. This enables the Partnership to permanently extend its partnership tax status, subject to a 3.5% tax on gross income, beginning in 1998. As a result, the Partnership eliminated most of its deferred tax liability account which produced a tax credit of $13,750,000. Nut yields were down 4% in 1998 as a result of drought caused by El Nino on two of the Partnership's properties. 1998 results included a nonrecurring expense of $1,119,000 relating to the failed acquisition of the Company by C. Brewer Homes, Inc. At December 31, 1998, land, producing orchards and other property were depreciated to 75% of their original cost.

Officers	Position	Ownership Information	
John W. A. Buyers	Chairman, CEO	Number of Units Outstanding	7,500,000
Kent T. Lucien	President	Market Capitalization	$ 23,925,000
Gregory A. Sprecher	Senior VP, CFO	Frequency of Distributions	Quarterly
Daryle S. Nekoba	Secretary	Number of Partners	1,741
		Where Listed / Symbol	NYSE / NUT

Other Information			
Transfer Agent	Chemical Mellon Shareholder Services San Francisco, CA	SIC Code	0100
Auditor	PricewaterhouseCoopers LLP	Employees	0
		Web Site	mlmacadamia.com

MTR Gaming Group, Inc.

State Route 2 South, P.O. Box 356   Chester, WV 26034   Telephone (304)387-5712   Fax (304)387-2167

Company Description

MTR Gaming Group, Inc., founded in 1988, has gone through several corporate restructurings and name changes since inception. Since 1992, the Company's primary business has been the ownership and operation of the Mountaineer Racetrack and Gaming Resort in Chester, West Virginia. This complex currently encompasses a thoroughbred racetrack (including off track betting), 1,300 video lottery terminals, a 101 room hotel, a nine hole executive golf course, and dining and entertainment facilities. The Company also had net assets of approximately $2.5 million representing the operating assets of discontinued oil and gas operations. These assets were liquidated in 1998.

	12/31/98	12/31/97	12/31/96	12/31/95
Per Share Information				
Stock Price	2.37	2.00	0.88	0.66
Earnings Per Share	0.33	0.22	0.06	-0.33
Price / Earnings Ratio	7.18	9.09	14.67	n.a.
Book Value Per Share	1.11	0.76	0.54	0.35
Price / Book Value %	213.51	263.16	162.96	188.57
Dividends Per Share	0.0	0.0	0.0	0.0
Annual Financial Data				
Operating Results (000's)				
Total Revenues	83,511.0	60,329.0	40,963.0	24,979.0
Costs & Expenses	-75,747.0	-57,458.0	-40,694.0	-30,425.0
Income Before Taxes and Other	7,764.0	2,871.0	269.0	-5,446.0
Other Items	-2,735.0	0.0	0.0	0.0
Income Tax	2,659.0	1,823.0	886.0	133.0
Net Income	7,688.0	4,694.0	1,155.0	-5,313.0
Cash Flow From Operations	10,542.0	6,009.0	326.0	553.0
Balance Sheet (000's)				
Cash & Equivalents	9,074.0	7,715.0	4,226.0	807.0
Total Current Assets	15,016.0	13,017.0	7,016.0	1,972.0
Fixed Assets, Net	40,279.0	22,799.0	18,453.0	18,100.0
Total Assets	59,737.0	41,034.0	30,878.0	25,747.0
Total Current Liabilities	2,559.0	3,232.0	3,119.0	9,425.0
Long-Term Debt	33,988.0	21,559.0	16,230.0	8,071.0
Stockholders' Equity	23,190.0	15,113.0	10,266.0	5,984.0
Performance & Financial Condition				
Return on Total Revenues %	9.21	7.78	2.82	-21.27
Return on Avg Stockholders' Equity %	40.14	36.99	14.22	-67.50
Return on Average Assets %	15.26	13.05	4.08	-21.38
Current Ratio	5.87	4.03	2.25	0.21
Debt / Equity %	146.56	142.65	158.09	134.88

Compound Growth %'s   EPS % 134.52   Net Income % 158.00   Total Revenues % 49.53

Comments

The Company has exhibited pronounced revenue growth since its expansion plans began in September, 1994. The emergence of video lottery as the Company's dominant profit center and the 1996 amendment of the West Virginia video lottery law have allowed the Company to generate increased revenues. The loss in 1995 resulted largely from delays encountered in the expansion of the Company's video lottery operations as a result of legal issues as well as from the time required for passage of proper enabling legislation. Once the Company was able to move forward with its plan, revenues increased dramatically. Revenues continued to spiral upward in 1998, 38.2% higher. Approximately 86% of the increase resulted from the video lottery operations. The balance came from other operations of Mountaineer Park. 1998 results include a $2,735,000 loss on the disposal of the oil and gas assets, or $.11 per share.

Officers	Position	Ownership Information	
Edson R. Arneault	President, CEO	Number of Shares Outstanding	20,866,163
Rose Mary Williams	Secretary	Market Capitalization	$ 49,452,806
Robert L. Ruben	Other	Number of Shareholders	3,000
Robert A. Blatt	Other	Where Listed / Symbol	NASDAQ / MNTG

Other Information			
Transfer Agent	Continental Stock Transfer & Trust Co. New York, NY	SIC Code	7990
Auditor	BDO Seidman LLP	Employees	683
		Web Site	mtrgaming.com

Manchester Equipment Co., Inc.

160 Oser Avenue   Hauppauge, NY 11788   Telephone (516)435-1199   Fax (516)435-2113

Company Description

Manchester Equipment Company, Inc. is a systems integrator and reseller of computer hardware, software and networking products, primarily for commercial customers. The Company offers single-source solutions customized to customer information systems needs by combining value-added services with hardware, software, networking products and peripherals from leading vendors. The Company was founded in 1973 and went public in December 1996. In April 1997, the Company purchased the assets of Electrograph Systems, Inc., a distributor of high-end monitors and graphical user interfaces. In January 1998, the Company acquired Coastal Office Products, Inc., a network integrator and reseller of computer products.

	07/31/98	07/31/97	07/31/96	07/31/95
Per Share Information				
Stock Price as of 12/31	2.75	4.00	7.50	5.00
Earnings Per Share	0.26	0.45	0.34	0.27
Price / Earnings Ratio	10.58	8.89	22.06	18.52
Book Value Per Share	4.61	4.33	1.32	0.96
Price / Book Value %	59.65	92.38	568.18	520.83
Dividends Per Share	0.0	0.0	0.0	0.0
Annual Financial Data				
Operating Results (000's)				
Total Revenues	203,117.0	188,421.0	189,693.0	170,832.0
Costs & Expenses	-199,385.0	-182,434.0	-186,125.0	-167,963.0
Income Before Taxes and Other	3,732.0	5,987.0	3,568.0	2,823.0
Other Items	0.0	0.0	0.0	0.0
Income Tax	-1,560.0	-2,450.0	-1,430.0	-1,160.0
Net Income	2,172.0	3,537.0	2,138.0	1,663.0
Cash Flow From Operations	2,340.0	4,568.0	4,162.0	1,570.0
Balance Sheet (000's)				
Cash & Equivalents	7,816.0	15,049.0	5,774.0	1,834.0
Total Current Assets	45,552.0	51,745.0	34,330.0	28,834.0
Fixed Assets, Net	5,975.0	4,073.0	2,244.0	2,000.0
Total Assets	56,894.0	58,208.0	37,761.0	31,635.0
Total Current Liabilities	19,440.0	21,167.0	24,489.0	19,645.0
Long-Term Debt	0.0	77.0	175.0	0.0
Stockholders' Equity	37,345.0	36,877.0	8,175.0	6,037.0
Performance & Financial Condition				
Return on Total Revenues %	1.07	1.88	1.13	0.97
Return on Avg Stockholders' Equity %	5.85	15.70	30.09	31.95
Return on Average Assets %	3.77	7.37	6.16	5.78
Current Ratio	2.34	2.44	1.40	1.47
Debt / Equity %	n.a.	0.21	2.14	n.a.

Compound Growth %'s	EPS %	-1.25	Net Income %	9.31	Total Revenues %	5.94

Comments

The proceeds from the public offering were used to repay debt, upgrade infrastructure, acquire state-of-the-art communications and telecommunications equipment, and for the acquisitions referred to above. The acquisitions have added revenue which has been partially offset by the decline in the average selling price of personal computers. In 1997, the Company was recognized by both Microsoft, Inc. and Cisco Systems, Inc., two of the world's leading high-technology firms. Manchester is now designated as a Microsoft Solution Provider Partner and Cicso has granted the Company Premier Certification status. The Company also sells products from most other major manufacturers. For the six months ended January 31, 1999 revenues and net income were $107.5 million and $641,000 ($.08 per share) as compared to $94.4 million and $993,000 ($.12 per share) in fiscal 1998.

Officers	Position	Ownership Information	
Barry R. Steinberg	President, CEO	Number of Shares Outstanding	8,097,000
Joel G. Stemple	Exec VP, Secretary	Market Capitalization	$ 22,266,750
Joseph Looney	CFO	Number of Shareholders	500
Bert Rudofsky	Director	Where Listed / Symbol	NASDAQ / MANC

Other Information			
Transfer Agent	American Stock Transfer & Trust Co. New York, NY	SIC Code	7371
Auditor	KPMG LLP	Employees	322
		Web Site	mecnet.com

Marlton Technologies, Inc.

2828 Charter Road, Suite 101   Philadelphia, PA 19154   Telephone (215)676-6900   Fax (215)676-1991

Company Description

Marlton Technologies, Inc.'s business was related to computerized electronic telecommunication systems until 1988, when it sold substantially all of its operating assets. In 1990, the Company acquired the business of Sparks Exhibits Corp. Sparks custom designs and manufactures sophisticated trade show exhibits, displays, architectural and museum interiors, graphics and signage, provides trade show services and designs and sells portable exhibits. Management's aggressive growth plan since the acquisition of Sparks has resulted in the dramatic expansion of the Company's client base, the development of new business groups for expansion of its products and services, and the extension into major geographic markets in the United States and internationally.

	12/31/98	12/31/97	12/31/96	12/31/95
Per Share Information				
Stock Price	4.12	6.00	3.87	1.31
Earnings Per Share	0.35	0.36	0.45	0.32
Price / Earnings Ratio	11.77	16.67	8.60	4.09
Book Value Per Share	3.84	3.48	3.00	2.62
Price / Book Value %	107.29	172.41	129.00	50.00
Dividends Per Share	0.0	0.0	0.0	0.0
Annual Financial Data				
Operating Results (000's)				
Total Revenues	91,390.6	49,096.7	38,580.2	27,790.4
Costs & Expenses	-86,840.9	-46,473.4	-37,090.0	-27,075.6
Income Before Taxes and Other	4,549.6	2,623.3	1,490.2	714.8
Other Items	0.0	0.0	1,200.0	0.0
Income Tax	-1,729.0	-620.0	-350.0	538.0
Net Income	2,820.6	2,003.3	2,340.2	1,252.8
Cash Flow From Operations	2,342.0	4,944.1	3,478.0	800.0
Balance Sheet (000's)				
Cash & Equivalents	4,620.1	7,115.1	3,300.0	1,028.6
Total Current Assets	33,662.7	29,935.4	13,940.3	9,128.4
Fixed Assets, Net	3,779.4	2,269.0	2,062.1	2,412.3
Total Assets	62,022.3	54,113.3	22,190.6	16,607.9
Total Current Liabilities	22,632.5	17,916.4	8,157.0	5,299.5
Long-Term Debt	10,927.0	12,243.3	457.4	991.9
Stockholders' Equity	27,645.3	23,953.5	13,576.2	10,316.5
Performance & Financial Condition				
Return on Total Revenues %	3.09	4.08	6.07	4.51
Return on Avg Stockholders' Equity %	10.93	10.68	19.59	11.04
Return on Average Assets %	4.86	5.25	12.06	7.65
Current Ratio	1.49	1.67	1.71	1.72
Debt / Equity %	39.53	51.11	3.37	9.61

Compound Growth %'s	EPS %	3.03	Net Income %	31.06	Total Revenues %	48.71

Comments

Revenues climbed 87% during 1998. Approximately 74% of the increase was acquisition related. The other 26% of the increase was generated by trade show exhibits reflecting the Company's continuing program of client expansion. 1996 results include a $1.2 million gain from a contract amendment. Compound growth in earnings per share is diluted from compound growth in net income because of new common shares issued in connection with acquisitions. At December 31, 1998, the Company had goodwill of $20.6 million reflected as assets which equated to approximately 75% of stockholders' equity and book value per share.

Officers	Position	Ownership Information	
Fred Cohen	Chairman	Number of Shares Outstanding	7,200,905
Robert B. Ginsburg	President	Market Capitalization	$ 29,667,729
E. D. Costantini, Jr.	CFO, Treasurer	Number of Shareholders	971
Alan I. Goldberg	Secretary	Where Listed / Symbol	AMEX / MTY

Other Information			
Transfer Agent	American Stock Transfer & Trust Co. New York, NY	SIC Code	7389
Auditor	PricewaterhouseCoopers LLP	Employees	375
		Web Site	sparksonline.com

McNaughton Apparel Group Inc.

463 Seventh Avenue   New York, NY 10018   Telephone (212)947-2960   Fax (212)563-2766

Company Description

McNaughton Apparel Group Inc, formerly Norton McNaughton, Inc., is one of the leading women's and juniors' branded apparel companies in the United States. The Company designs, sources, markets and distributes moderately-priced separates and collections of career and casual clothing under such well-recognized brand names as Norton McNaughton®, Erika® and Energie®. The Company's products are sold nationwide in over 8,000 individual stores which are operated by over 1,500 department stores, national chains, mass merchants, off-price retail chains and specialty retailers, including   J.C. Penny, May Company, Federated, Sears and T.J. Maxx. The Company was founded in 1981.

	10/31/98	11/01/97	11/02/96	11/04/95
Per Share Information				
Stock Price as of 12/31	2.75	5.25	8.25	10.75
Earnings Per Share	-0.10	-0.63	0.20	1.20
Price / Earnings Ratio	n.a.	n.a.	41.25	8.96
Book Value Per Share	5.59	5.69	6.32	6.29
Price / Book Value %	49.19	92.27	130.54	170.91
Dividends Per Share	0.0	0.0	0.0	0.0
Annual Financial Data				
Operating Results (000's)				
Total Revenues	344,769.0	218,950.0	220,987.0	227,748.0
Costs & Expenses	-342,826.0	-227,055.0	-218,336.0	-211,157.0
Income Before Taxes and Other	1,943.0	-8,105.0	2,651.0	16,591.0
Other Items	-1,161.0	0.0	0.0	0.0
Income Tax	-1,495.0	3,400.0	-1,127.0	-6,888.0
Net Income	-713.0	-4,705.0	1,524.0	9,703.0
Cash Flow From Operations	2,552.0	-26,490.0	5,432.0	1,107.0
Balance Sheet (000's)				
Cash & Equivalents	205.0	529.0	333.0	444.0
Total Current Assets	137,384.0	102,191.0	52,045.0	65,900.0
Fixed Assets, Net	8,261.0	5,899.0	5,077.0	3,800.0
Total Assets	201,589.0	118,762.0	61,109.0	73,500.0
Total Current Liabilities	33,400.0	62,879.0	11,988.0	22,400.0
Long-Term Debt	125,000.0	12,000.0	0.0	0.0
Stockholders' Equity	41,470.0	42,163.0	48,286.0	50,500.0
Performance & Financial Condition				
Return on Total Revenues %	-0.21	-2.15	0.69	4.26
Return on Avg Stockholders' Equity %	-1.71	-10.40	3.09	19.41
Return on Average Assets %	-0.45	-5.23	2.26	13.29
Current Ratio	4.11	1.63	4.34	2.94
Debt / Equity %	301.42	28.46	n.a.	n.a.

Compound Growth %'s	EPS % n.a.	Net Income % n.a.	Total Revenues % 14.82

Comments

Acquisitions were the primary reason for the sharp rise in revenues, up 57.5% during fiscal 1998. A nonrecurring loss of $1,161,000 ($.16 per share), related to the early extinguishment of debt, eliminated a small operating profit. Also included in 1998 expenses is $2.5 million of litigation reserves. Fiscal 1997 results were negatively impacted by the discontinuance of certain operating divisions. If the Company can return to historic levels of profitability, this stock could represent a great buy. However, decisions should not be made on the basis of a low price/book value percentage. At October 31, 1998, the Company had $43.5 million of goodwill recorded as assets which equates to approximately 105% of stockholders' equity and book value per share. Therefore, there is no tangible book value.

Officers	Position	Ownership Information	
Sanford Greenberg	Chairman, CEO	Number of Shares Outstanding	7,414,429
Peter Boneparth	President, COO	Market Capitalization	$ 20,389,680
Amanda J. Bokman	Vice President, CFO	Number of Shareholders	500
David M. Blumberg	Director	Where Listed / Symbol	NASDAQ / NRTY

Other Information			
Transfer Agent	American Stock Transfer & Trust Co. New York, NY	SIC Code	2330
Auditor	Ernst & Young LLP	Employees	340

Measurement Specialties, Inc.

80 Little Falls Road   Fairfield, NJ 07004   Telephone (973)808-1819   Fax (973)808-1787

Company Description

Measurement Specialties, Inc. designs, develops, produces and sells digital electronic measurement products which employ a robust, core technology based on micromachining (the three-dimensional sculpting of silicon), which permits accurate and efficient measurement, resolution and display of ranges of distance, motion, force, pressure or temperature in design-friendly formats. The Company targets high volume, low cost product opportunities. Consumer products, which accounts for 90% of revenues, is comprised of bath scales, kitchen scales, tire pressure gauges and distance measuring devices. The Company was founded in 1981 and has been manufacturing products of its own design since 1986.

	03/31/98	03/31/97	03/31/96	03/31/95
Per Share Information				
Stock Price as of 12/31	4.37	3.75	3.00	4.50
Earnings Per Share	0.21	0.31	0.27	0.09
Price / Earnings Ratio	20.81	12.10	11.11	50.00
Book Value Per Share	1.56	1.31	0.98	0.69
Price / Book Value %	280.13	286.26	306.12	n.a.
Dividends Per Share	0.0	0.0	0.0	0.0
Annual Financial Data				
Operating Results (000's)				
Total Revenues	29,332.0	25,040.7	23,101.1	17,071.0
Costs & Expenses	-28,360.2	-24,216.2	-22,199.0	-16,536.3
Income Before Taxes and Other	878.9	824.5	902.1	339.9
Other Items	0.0	0.0	0.0	0.0
Income Tax	-102.0	350.3	85.0	-6.0
Net Income	776.9	1,174.8	987.0	333.9
Cash Flow From Operations	1,722.4	-531.2	880.3	417.0
Balance Sheet (000's)				
Cash & Equivalents	303.0	238.8	771.0	737.8
Total Current Assets	7,628.4	7,125.2	5,534.2	4,712.5
Fixed Assets, Net	1,763.0	1,386.4	1,078.9	910.7
Total Assets	10,217.3	9,234.2	6,919.6	5,623.2
Total Current Liabilities	4,292.9	3,420.6	3,060.9	2,893.4
Long-Term Debt	0.0	778.0	0.0	297.7
Stockholders' Equity	5,579.8	4,643.3	3,459.4	2,432.1
Performance & Financial Condition				
Return on Total Revenues %	2.65	4.69	4.27	1.96
Return on Avg Stockholders' Equity %	15.20	29.00	33.51	14.79
Return on Average Assets %	7.99	14.55	15.74	7.10
Current Ratio	1.78	2.08	1.81	1.63
Debt / Equity %	n.a.	16.76	n.a.	12.24

Compound Growth %'s	EPS %	32.64	Net Income %	32.51	Total Revenues %	19.77

Comments

Substantial revenue growth is primarily attributable to new product introductions. The Company continues in its efforts towards new product development and increased research and development spending from $833,000 in fiscal 1995 to $1,964,000 in the last year. Fiscal 1997 and 1996 had income tax benefits arising from the utilization of tax loss carryforwards and changes in the valuation of deferred taxes. Earnings per share for these years, as well as for fiscal 1998, would have been substantially lower had a normal tax provision been incurred. For the nine months ended December 31, 1998, revenues and net income were $28.3 million and $1,297,000 ($.36 per share) as compared to $23.2 million and $851,334 ($.23 per share) recorded in the same period of the preceding year.

Officers	Position	Ownership Information	
Joseph R. Mallon Jr.	President, CEO	Number of Shares Outstanding	3,582,287
Damon Germanton	Exec VP, COO	Market Capitalization	$ 15,654,594
Kirk J. Dischino	CFO	Number of Shareholders	141
Mark W. Cappiello	VP - Sales	Where Listed / Symbol	AMEX / MSS

Other Information			
Transfer Agent	American Stock Transfer & Trust Co. New York, NY	SIC Code	3829
Auditor	Grant Thornton LLP	Employees	289
		Web Site	measspec.com

Medicore, Inc.

2337 West 76th Street   Hialeah, FL 33016   Telephone (305)558-4000   Fax (305)825-0961

Company Description

Medicore, Inc. is an international contract manufacturer of electronic, electro-mechanical and plastic insert and injection molded products. The Company primarily serves the data processing, telecommunications and instrumentation industries through its 62% owned public subsidiary, Techdyne, Inc., which is also featured on its own page in this manual. Medicore also owns and operates three kidney dialysis centers through its 68% owned public subsidiary, Dialysis Corporation of America. Medicore was additionally engaged in the sale and lease of home healthcare durables until 1997. The Company was founded in 1961.

		12/31/98	12/31/97	12/31/96	12/31/95
Per Share Information					
	Stock Price	1.12	2.12	2.44	4.75
	Earnings Per Share	0.01	0.36	0.39	0.38
	Price / Earnings Ratio	112.00	5.89	6.26	12.50
	Book Value Per Share	2.63	2.75	2.39	1.79
	Price / Book Value %	42.59	77.09	102.09	265.36
	Dividends Per Share	0.0	0.0	0.0	0.0
Annual Financial Data					
Operating Results (000's)					
	Total Revenues	50,148.5	39,688.8	34,719.4	36,660.1
	Costs & Expenses	-50,177.1	-39,208.0	-30,676.5	-33,067.0
	Income Before Taxes and Other	-28.5	480.8	4,042.9	3,593.1
	Other Items	-225.4	2,713.1	-274.9	-46.2
	Income Tax	352.4	-953.0	-1,350.7	-1,295.6
	Net Income	98.4	2,241.0	2,417.3	2,251.3
	Cash Flow From Operations	-28.1	-3,023.9	-23.3	1,777.0
Balance Sheet (000's)					
	Cash & Equivalents	7,294.7	11,099.4	10,665.8	4,836.5
	Total Current Assets	23,369.1	28,964.6	20,139.5	14,499.1
	Fixed Assets, Net	9,500.3	8,905.0	6,039.2	5,607.7
	Total Assets	36,310.1	40,861.5	27,084.9	21,247.2
	Total Current Liabilities	7,948.6	10,108.0	6,295.4	7,465.5
	Long-Term Debt	5,126.5	5,240.0	1,677.4	964.0
	Stockholders' Equity	15,367.7	16,077.3	13,021.5	9,754.4
Performance & Financial Condition					
	Return on Total Revenues %	0.20	5.08	6.96	6.14
	Return on Avg Stockholders' Equity %	0.63	15.40	21.23	25.32
	Return on Average Assets %	0.26	6.60	10.00	12.10
	Current Ratio	2.94	2.87	3.20	1.94
	Debt / Equity %	33.36	32.59	12.88	9.88

Compound Growth %'s	EPS %	-70.26	Net Income %	-64.77	Total Revenues %	11.01

Comments

The increases in 1998 and 1997 revenues over their preceding years were primarily attributable to an acquisition by Techdyne on August 1, 1997. Approximately 45% of total revenues represents sales to five customers. Higher healthcare salaries and supply costs as well as certain development stage expenses kept the Company only marginally profitable in 1998. 1997 results include a nonrecurring gain of $4.4 million on the sale of certain assets by Dialysis Corporation of America. The financial accounting is critical to evaluating Medicore as an investment. The Company combines the accounts of its two majority-owned subsidiaries with its own books and then backs out an amount designated as minority interest in subsidiaries on both the balance sheet and the income statement. At December 31, 1998, the Company had $3.3 million in intangible assets which equated to only 21% of stockholders' equity and book value per share. The Company reacquired 133,200 of its shares in 1998 at an average price of $1.53 per share.

Officers	Position	Ownership Information	
Thomas K. Langbein	President, CEO	Number of Shares Outstanding	5,848,740
Dennis W. Healey	Senior VP, Treasurer	Market Capitalization	$ 6,550,589
Daniel R. Ouzts	VP - Finance, Controller	Number of Shareholders	2,100
Seymour Friend	Vice President	Where Listed / Symbol	NASDAQ / MDKI

Other Information			
Transfer Agent	Continental Stock Transfer & Trust Co. New York, NY	SIC Code	3679
Auditor	Ernst & Young LLP	Employees	560
		Web Site	medicore.com

Memry Corporation

57 Commerce Drive Brookfield, CT 06804 Telephone (203)740-7311 Fax (203)775-2359

Company Description

Memry Corporation, founded in 1981, is an advanced materials company engaged in the business of developing, manufacturing and marketing semi-finished materials, formed components, and value-added sub-assembled products utilizing the properties exhibited by shape memory alloys, primarily those of nickel titanium. Memry sells its products and services primarily to the medical device, telecommunications, aerospace and automotive industries. The Company conducts its operations from its two operating facilities located in Brookfield, Connecticut and Menlo Park, California. The Company acquired its Menlo Park operations from Raychem Corporation on June 28, 1996, as part of a transaction in which the Company acquired certain assets comprising Raychem's nickel-titanium product line.

	06/30/98	06/30/97	06/30/96	06/30/95
Per Share Information				
Stock Price as of 12/31	2.69	3.50	1.62	0.56
Earnings Per Share	0.14	-0.06	-0.25	-0.45
Price / Earnings Ratio	19.21	n.a.	n.a.	n.a.
Book Value Per Share	0.51	0.33	0.47	-0.13
Price / Book Value %	527.45	1,060.61	344.68	n.a.
Dividends Per Share	0.0	0.0	0.0	0.0
Annual Financial Data				
Operating Results (000's)				
Total Revenues	19,093.0	11,555.0	1,136.0	4,729.0
Costs & Expenses	-15,857.0	-11,815.0	-3,049.0	-7,121.0
Income Before Taxes and Other	3,236.0	-260.0	-1,913.0	-2,392.0
Other Items	-151.0	-751.0	-192.0	0.0
Income Tax	-160.0	0.0	0.0	0.0
Net Income	2,925.0	-1,011.0	-2,105.0	-2,392.0
Cash Flow From Operations	1,690.0	-1,621.0	-2,420.0	-1,869.0
Balance Sheet (000's)				
Cash & Equivalents	1,189.0	25.0	57.0	1,145.0
Total Current Assets	7,656.0	5,413.0	2,732.0	2,709.0
Fixed Assets, Net	2,717.0	2,765.0	3,881.0	1,233.0
Total Assets	13,085.0	11,152.0	9,679.0	3,979.0
Total Current Liabilities	2,361.0	5,428.0	3,584.0	5,003.0
Long-Term Debt	580.0	0.0	0.0	0.0
Stockholders' Equity	10,125.0	5,681.0	6,091.0	-1,031.0
Performance & Financial Condition				
Return on Total Revenues %	15.32	-8.75	-185.30	-50.58
Return on Avg Stockholders' Equity %	37.01	-17.18	-83.20	n.a.
Return on Average Assets %	24.14	-9.71	-30.82	-65.67
Current Ratio	3.24	1.00	0.76	0.54
Debt / Equity %	5.73	n.a.	n.a.	n.a.

Compound Growth %'s	EPS % n.a.	Net Income % n.a.	Total Revenues %	59.23

Comments

The 65% increase in fiscal 1998 revenues over the preceding year was primarily due to additional sales to Raychem pursuant to a private label/distribution agreement. The Company recorded a net profit as a result of increased sales and efficiencies, as well as the elimination of both discontinued operations and special non-recurring expenses. Management expects revenues to continue to increase in future years. For the six months ended December 31, 1998, the Company reported revenues and net income of $9.6 million and $961,000 ($.04 per share) as compared to $8.5 million and $1,148,000 ($.06 per share) in the comparable period of 1997.

Officers	Position	Ownership Information	
James G. Binch	President, CEO	Number of Shares Outstanding	19,949,169
William H. Morton, Jr.	Senior VP, COO	Market Capitalization	$ 53,663,265
Katie Terhune	Secretary	Number of Shareholders	473
James Proft	Vice President	Where Listed / Symbol	OTC-BB / MRMY

Other Information			
Transfer Agent	American Stock Transfer & Trust Co. New York, NY	SIC Code	3541
Auditor	McGladrey & Pullen, LLP	Employees	99
Market Maker	Wilson-Davis & Co., Inc. (800)453-5735	Web Site	memry.com
	Herzog, Heine, Geduld, Inc. (800)221-3600		

Mendocino Brewing Company, Inc.

13351 South Highway 101   Hopland, CA 95449   Telephone (707)744-1015   Fax (707)744-1910

Company Description

Mendocino Brewing Company, Inc. produces domestic specialty beers and sells to distributors and other retailers. The Company's operations are located in Mendocino County, approximately 80 miles north of San Francisco. Distribution is primarily throughout California and in limited quantities to customers in 27 other states. Production has been at capacity from 1988 to 1997. A new brewery in Ukiah began operations in May, 1997, which increased capacity from 18,000 barrels per year to 60,000 barrels in the near-term and 200,000 barrels in the future. The Company owns a brewery in New York as well that presently performs contract brewing services for other brands. The Company also has retail operations consisting of a brewpub and gift shop.

	12/31/98	12/31/97	12/31/96	12/31/95
Per Share Information				
Stock Price	0.56	3.31	7.06	7.56
Earnings Per Share	-0.35	-0.40	-0.05	0.08
Price / Earnings Ratio	n.a.	n.a.	n.a.	94.50
Book Value Per Share	2.26	2.61	1.75	1.81
Price / Book Value %	24.78	126.82	403.43	417.68
Dividends Per Share	0.0	0.0	0.0	0.0
Annual Financial Data				
Operating Results (000's)				
Total Revenues	6,538.2	4,597.3	3,851.3	3,714.1
Costs & Expenses	-9,239.3	-6,296.4	-4,012.1	-3,387.5
Income Before Taxes and Other	-2,701.1	-1,848.6	-202.0	326.6
Other Items	0.0	0.0	0.0	0.0
Income Tax	1,138.8	708.9	78.2	-152.9
Net Income	-1,562.3	-1,139.7	-123.8	173.7
Cash Flow From Operations	-2,666.3	-813.0	224.0	6.4
Balance Sheet (000's)				
Cash & Equivalents	42.0	706.3	494.8	1,696.1
Total Current Assets	1,871.7	1,768.5	1,346.3	2,473.8
Fixed Assets, Net	15,259.8	15,642.5	9,270.3	3,954.1
Total Assets	18,923.2	18,026.4	11,144.6	6,514.0
Total Current Liabilities	2,502.4	2,125.9	4,963.1	1,514.7
Long-Term Debt	4,609.8	2,663.3	0.0	554.9
Stockholders' Equity	10,141.8	11,658.3	4,300.4	4,424.2
Performance & Financial Condition				
Return on Total Revenues %	-23.89	-24.79	-3.21	4.68
Return on Avg Stockholders' Equity %	-14.33	-14.28	-2.84	4.26
Return on Average Assets %	-8.46	-7.81	-1.40	3.29
Current Ratio	0.75	0.83	0.27	1.63
Debt / Equity %	45.45	22.84	n.a.	12.54

Compound Growth %'s	EPS % n.a.	Net Income % n.a.	Total Revenues % 20.74

Comments

In May 1997, beer mogul Vijay Mallya announced plans to invest $3.5 million in the Company and now serves as the chief executive officer. Management attributes the 1998 and 1997 losses to increased overhead associated with the operation of two breweries and increased marketing expenses. New marketing strategies, including new point of sale materials and increased sales personnel, were credited with the increase in revenue. At December 31, 1998, the Company had $4.7 million of tax loss carryovers available to offset future income. But it will take a lot more beer flowing out of the doors before the Company can hope to generate that income. Although there is a working capital deficiency at the last year end, United Breweries of America, the Company's largest shareholder, provided the Company with a credit facility of up to $2 million.

Officers	Position	Ownership Information	
H. Michael Laybourn	President	Number of Shares Outstanding	4,497,059
Vijay Mallya	CEO	Market Capitalization	$ 2,518,353
Yashpal Singh	COO	Number of Shareholders	2,479
P A. Murali	CFO	Where Listed / Symbol	PSE / MBRP

Other Information			
Transfer Agent	Boston EquiServe Boston, MA	SIC Code	2082
Auditor	Moss Adams LLP	Employees	54
		Web Site	mendobrew.com

Mentortech Inc.

462 7th Avenue New York, NY 10018 Telephone (212)736-5870 Fax (212)736-9046

Company Description

Mentortech Inc., formerly PC Etcetera, Inc., develops and offers instructor-led training and technology-based training courses for information technology professionals and end-users. It also provides consulting services in both the State of Israel and the New York tri-state area, primarily to large business and public sector organizations. The Company has been authorized as a training center by a number of software developers including Microsoft, Novell, Corel, Borland, Apple, Lotus and Magic. The Company was founded in 1985.

	12/31/98	12/31/97	12/31/96	12/31/95
Per Share Information				
Stock Price	3.10	0.50	0.25	0.56
Earnings Per Share	-0.29	-0.40	-0.43	-1.36
Price / Earnings Ratio	n.a.	n.a.	n.a.	n.a.
Book Value Per Share	1.64	1.98	-0.63	-0.25
Price / Book Value %	189.02	25.25	n.a.	n.a.
Dividends Per Share	0.0	0.0	0.0	0.0
Annual Financial Data				
Operating Results (000's)				
Total Revenues	19,951.0	17,560.0	9,400.0	11,148.9
Costs & Expenses	-20,740.0	-18,411.0	-10,221.0	-14,847.0
Income Before Taxes and Other	-789.0	-851.0	-821.0	-3,698.1
Other Items	0.0	0.0	68.0	0.0
Income Tax	-221.0	0.0	-45.0	-147.9
Net Income	-1,010.0	-851.0	-798.0	-3,846.0
Cash Flow From Operations	-897.0	-703.0	665.0	-1,447.4
Balance Sheet (000's)				
Cash & Equivalents	220.0	1,659.0	50.4	151.5
Total Current Assets	6,291.0	5,547.0	1,029.8	1,953.9
Fixed Assets, Net	2,347.0	2,364.0	319.7	500.0
Total Assets	13,233.0	13,497.0	1,387.2	2,566.7
Total Current Liabilities	6,559.0	5,694.0	2,976.4	3,188.7
Long-Term Debt	125.0	136.0	0.0	148.0
Stockholders' Equity	5,870.0	6,840.0	-1,987.7	-770.1
Performance & Financial Condition				
Return on Total Revenues %	-5.06	-4.85	-8.49	-34.50
Return on Avg Stockholders' Equity %	-15.89	-35.08	n.a.	-325.24
Return on Average Assets %	-7.56	-11.43	-40.37	-91.68
Current Ratio	0.96	0.97	0.35	0.61
Debt / Equity %	2.13	1.99	n.a.	n.a.

Compound Growth %'s	EPS % n.a.	Net Income % n.a.	Total Revenues %	21.41

Comments

Revenues grew 14% in 1998 largely due to the success in offering more technical courses in Israel. The 87% increase in 1997 revenues as compared to 1996 reflects acquisitions as well as internal growth. Management expected that the increased investment that was made in sales, marketing and research and development would permit the Company to attain profitability in 1998. But this was not to be the case. Even without a $300,000 write-down of goodwill, the Company was far from breakeven. At December 31, 1998, the Company had $4.2 million still recorded as goodwill which equated to approximately 71% of stockholders' equity and book value per share. Also at that date, the Company had a deficiency in working capital.

Officers	Position	Ownership Information	
Roy Machnes	President, CEO	Number of Shares Outstanding	3,578,208
Terry I. Steinberg	Exec VP	Market Capitalization	$ 11,092,445
Elan Penn	CFO	Number of Shareholders	1,000
Adrienne Haber	Controller	Where Listed / Symbol	OTC-BB / MNTK

Other Information			
Transfer Agent	Continental Stock Transfer & Trust Co. New York, NY	SIC Code	8200
Auditor	Ernst & Young LLP	Employees	192
Market Maker	Herzog, Heine, Geduld, Inc. (800)221-3600	Web Site	mentortech.com
	Brean Murray, Co., Inc. (800)223-4132		

Mercury Waste Solutions, Inc.

302 North Riverfront Drive, Suite 100A   Mankato, MN 56001   Telephone (507)345-0522   Fax (507)345-1483

Company Description

Mercury Waste Solutions, Inc. provides services to mercury waste generators to reduce the risk of liability associated with mercury waste disposal. The Company currently operates a mercury waste retorting facility in Union Grove, Wisconsin; a facilities for recycling and storing fluorescent and other mercury-containing lamps in Roseville, Minnesota and Union Grove, Wisconsin; and mercury waste storage and collection facilities in Kenosha, Wisconsin, Indianapolis, Atlanta, Georgia and Albany, New York. The Company was founded in January 1996 and had its initial public offering in 1997 with the issuance of 1.1 million shares at $5.00 per share.

	12/31/98	12/31/97	12/31/96
Per Share Information			
Stock Price	2.87	2.50	5.00
Earnings Per Share	0.11	-0.34	-0.40
Price / Earnings Ratio	26.09	n.a.	n.a.
Book Value Per Share	1.18	1.06	0.13
Price / Book Value %	243.22	235.85	3,846.15
Dividends Per Share	0.0	0.0	0.0
Annual Financial Data			
Operating Results (000's)			
Total Revenues	6,758.6	2,932.1	1,334.7
Costs & Expenses	-6,367.0	-4,105.2	-2,320.2
Income Before Taxes and Other	391.5	-1,173.1	-985.4
Other Items	0.0	0.0	0.0
Income Tax	0.0	0.0	0.0
Net Income	391.5	-1,173.1	-985.4
Cash Flow From Operations	578.9	-878.5	-778.0
Balance Sheet (000's)			
Cash & Equivalents	75.0	779.9	0.0
Total Current Assets	1,799.9	1,843.6	415.2
Fixed Assets, Net	2,145.4	1,315.2	807.1
Total Assets	6,748.5	4,830.2	2,566.6
Total Current Liabilities	1,522.5	908.2	218.0
Long-Term Debt	1,072.6	250.3	1,919.6
Stockholders' Equity	4,123.2	3,661.4	283.7
Performance & Financial Condition			
Return on Total Revenues %	5.79	-40.01	-73.83
Return on Avg Stockholders' Equity %	10.06	-59.47	-698.90
Return on Average Assets %	6.76	-31.72	-76.99
Current Ratio	1.18	2.03	1.90
Debt / Equity %	26.01	6.84	676.63

Compound Growth %'s	EPS % n.a.	Net Income % n.a.	Total Revenues % 125.03

Comments

In just three years, the Company has developed from a start-up enterprise to a profitable business. Sales growth of 142% in 1998 was attributable to the increasing impact of its national sales force implemented in 1997, coupled with increasing processing and storage capability. The Company also acquired a business in May 1998. 1998 results include $445,000 of income from a business interruption insurance claim. At December 31, 1998, the Company had $610,000 of tax loss carryovers available to offset future income. Also at that date, the Company had $2.7 million of goodwill recorded as assets which equated to approximately 66% of stockholders' equity and book value per share.

Officers	Position	Ownership Information	
Brad J. Buscher	Chairman, CEO	Number of Shares Outstanding	3,480,097
Mark G. Edlund	President, Secretary	Market Capitalization	$ 9,987,878
Todd J. Anderson	CFO	Number of Shareholders	450
Alan R. Geiwitz	Director	Where Listed / Symbol	NASDAQ / MWST

Other Information			
Transfer Agent	Norwest Bank Minnesota, N.A. South St. Paul, MN	SIC Code	4955
Auditor	McGladrey & Pullen, LLP	Employees	51
		Web Site	mercurywastesolutions.com

Mesa Laboratories, Inc.

12100 West Sixth Avenue   Lakewood, CO 80228   Telephone (303)987-8000   Fax (303)987-8989

Company Description

Mesa Laboratories, Inc. designs, develops, acquires, manufactures and markets electronic measurement instruments and systems utilized in connection with industrial applications and hemodialysis therapy.   The Company presently markets the DATATRACE? and ELOGG? recording systems, NUSONICS? Concentration Analyzers, Pipeline Interface Detectors and Flow Meter products with are used in various industrial applications, and two product lines used in kidney dialysis (Western Meters and the ECHO Reprocessor).   The Company is also performing research and development to expand the application of its technology.

	03/31/98	03/31/97	03/31/96	03/31/95
Per Share Information				
Stock Price as of 12/31	4.25	6.62	5.37	4.44
Earnings Per Share	0.47	0.39	0.37	0.29
Price / Earnings Ratio	9.04	16.97	14.51	15.31
Book Value Per Share	2.60	2.22	1.86	1.48
Price / Book Value %	163.46	298.20	288.71	300.00
Dividends Per Share	0.0	0.0	0.0	0.0
Annual Financial Data				
Operating Results (000's)				
Total Revenues	8,153.0	7,900.9	8,114.7	6,648.0
Costs & Expenses	-5,019.9	-5,270.4	-5,660.4	-4,790.3
Income Before Taxes and Other	3,133.1	2,630.5	2,454.3	1,857.7
Other Items	0.0	0.0	0.0	0.0
Income Tax	-1,080.8	-910.7	-830.4	-622.0
Net Income	2,052.3	1,719.8	1,624.0	1,235.7
Cash Flow From Operations	2,208.6	2,420.1	1,669.8	891.4
Balance Sheet (000's)				
Cash & Equivalents	3,359.0	3,867.5	1,789.6	402.9
Total Current Assets	9,218.4	7,614.3	6,111.1	4,312.2
Fixed Assets, Net	1,677.0	1,589.9	1,577.5	1,311.2
Total Assets	11,780.1	10,206.4	8,791.9	6,865.7
Total Current Liabilities	544.2	575.5	695.8	515.7
Long-Term Debt	0.0	0.0	0.0	0.0
Stockholders' Equity	11,160.9	9,568.2	8,038.0	6,284.4
Performance & Financial Condition				
Return on Total Revenues %	25.17	21.77	20.01	18.59
Return on Avg Stockholders' Equity %	19.80	19.54	22.68	18.17
Return on Average Assets %	18.67	18.10	20.74	16.48
Current Ratio	16.94	13.23	8.78	8.36
Debt / Equity %	n.a.	n.a.	n.a.	n.a.

Compound Growth %'s	EPS %	17.46	Net Income %	18.42	Total Revenues %	7.04

Comments

The net sales increase during fiscal 1998 was due to strong increases in sales of medical and Datatrace products which were mostly offset by a decrease in Nusonic product sales. In order to correct the decline of the latter, the Company reorganized its sales organization in order to improve its ability to meet the technical demands of its concentration monitor products. The Company has a strong financial position and has been using some of its excess working capital to reacquire shares. For the nine months ended December 31, 1998, the Company reported revenues and net income of $6.0 million and $1,534,951 ($.36 per share) as compared to $5.9 and $1,466,297 ($.33 per share) for the same period of the preceding year.

Officers	Position	Ownership Information	
Luke R. Schmieder	President, CEO	Number of Shares Outstanding	4,284,587
Steven W. Peterson	VP - Finance, CFO	Market Capitalization	$ 18,209,495
Paul D. Duke	Vice President	Number of Shareholders	2,500
Philip D. Quedenfeld	Director	Where Listed / Symbol	NASDAQ / MLAB

Other Information			
Transfer Agent	American Securities Transfer, Inc. Denver, CO	SIC Code	3823
Auditor	Ehrhardt Keefe Steiner Hottman	Employees	42
		Web Site	mesalabs.com

Mesabi Trust

Bankers Trust, P.O. Box 318, Church Street Station   New York, NY 10008-0318   Telephone (212)250-6519   Fax (615)835-2700

Company Description

Mesabi Trust was organized pursuant to a trust agreement dated 1961. The Trust holds all of the interests formerly owned by Mesabi Iron Company, including all of Mesabi Iron Company's right, title and interest in leases, land, and other assets identified in the Trust Agreement. Under the Agreement, the Trustees are specifically prohibited from entering into or engaging in any business. Accordingly, the activities of the Trust in connection with the administration of Trust assets are limited to the collection of income, the payment of expenses and liabilities, the distribution of net income, and the protection and conservation of the assets held. The Trust has a term that will continue twenty-one years after the death of the last survivor of the twenty-five persons named in the Trust. The youngest person on the list is now 38 years old.

	01/31/98	01/31/97	01/31/96	01/31/95
Per Unit Information				
Price Per Unit as of 12/31	3.06	3.75	4.25	3.50
Earnings Per Unit	0.50	0.43	0.28	0.23
Price / Earnings Ratio	6.12	8.72	15.18	15.22
Book Value Per Unit	0.05	0.05	0.05	0.05
Price / Book Value %	6,120.00	7,500.00	8,500.00	7,000.00
Distributions Per Unit	0.49	0.42	0.28	0.24
Cash Flow Per Unit	0.49	0.42	0.28	0.23
Annual Financial Data				
Operating Results (000's)				
Total Revenues	6,860.4	6,001.1	4,061.2	3,485.4
Costs & Expenses	-362.4	-381.5	-387.2	-426.7
Operating Income	6,498.0	5,619.6	3,674.0	3,058.7
Other Items	0.0	0.0	0.0	0.0
Net Income	6,498.0	5,619.6	3,674.0	3,058.7
Cash Flow From Operations	6,474.8	5,513.5	3,691.1	2,999.1
Balance Sheet (000's)				
Cash & Equivalents	3,607.2	0.9	9.2	1,442.6
Total Current Assets	4,286.8	2,603.2	2,286.1	1,991.1
Investments	n.a.	n.a.	n.a.	n.a.
Total Assets	4,286.8	2,603.2	2,286.1	1,991.1
Total Current Liabilities	3,567.0	1,952.6	1,630.4	1,353.6
Long-Term Debt	0.0	0.0	0.0	0.0
Partners' Capital	719.8	650.6	655.8	637.6
Performance & Financial Condition				
Return on Total Revenues %	94.72	93.64	90.47	87.76
Return on Average Partners' Capital %	948.33	860.34	568.15	509.78
Return on Average Assets %	188.62	229.87	171.79	143.06
Current Ratio	1.20	1.33	1.40	1.47
Debt / Equity %	n.a.	n.a.	n.a.	n.a.

Compound Growth %'s	EPU %	29.54	Net Income %	28.55	Total Revenues %	25.32

Comments

The Trust is exempt from income taxes. All income is taxed proportionately by its unit holders. Royalties paid to the Trust are based on the amount of crude ore mined. Crude ore is used to produce iron ore pellets and other products. Royalties are determined by both the volume and selling price of iron ore products sold. Bonuses are received above certain threshold levels. Results of a single year are not necessarily indicative of any trend since factors such as weather can have an impact on mining levels. For the nine months ended October 31, 1998, the Trust reported revenues and net income of $4.6 million and $4,351,472 ($.33 per share) as compared to $3.8 million and $3,623,937 ($.28 per share) for the same portion of fiscal 1998.

Officers	Position	Ownership Information	
David J. Hoffman	Other	Number of Units Outstanding	13,120,010
Richard G. Lareau	Other	Market Capitalization	$ 40,147,231
Ira A. Marshall, Jr.	Other	Frequency of Distributions	Quarterly
Norman F. Sprague III	Other	Number of Partners	3,075
		Where Listed / Symbol	NYSE / MSB

Other Information			
Transfer Agent	Bankers Trust Company New York, NY	SIC Code	6795
Auditor	McGladrey & Pullen, LLP	Employees	0

Met-Coil Systems Corporation

5486 Sixth Street SW   Cedar Rapids, IA 52404   Telephone (319)363-6566   Fax (319)362-0225

Company Description

Met-Coil Systems Corporation designs, engineers, manufactures and markets metal forming and fabrication machinery and computer-controlled fabrication systems which make a wide variety of products from metal coils and sheets. The Company manufactures and markets high-speed automated material handling and press line automation equipment and systems. Although the Company was formed in 1973, its present operating units were acquired thereafter. In fiscal 1999, the Company expects to enter the market place with three completely new computer-controlled material handling machines, all of which are being developed internally.

	05/31/98	05/31/97	05/31/96	05/31/95
Per Share Information				
Stock Price as of 12/31	3.50	2.75	1.44	1.00
Earnings Per Share	0.69	0.01	-0.26	-1.61
Price / Earnings Ratio	5.07	275.00	n.a.	n.a.
Book Value Per Share	0.12	-0.51	-0.63	0.14
Price / Book Value %	2,916.67	n.a.	n.a.	714.29
Dividends Per Share	0.0	0.0	0.0	0.0
Annual Financial Data				
Operating Results (000's)				
Total Revenues	45,009.0	36,844.0	43,702.0	43,775.0
Costs & Expenses	-42,644.0	-36,224.0	-44,120.0	-47,759.0
Income Before Taxes and Other	1,851.0	578.0	-604.0	-4,320.0
Other Items	0.0	0.0	0.0	0.0
Income Tax	1,129.0	0.0	300.0	0.0
Net Income	2,980.0	578.0	-304.0	-4,320.0
Cash Flow From Operations	4,234.0	2,021.0	1,765.0	-1,360.0
Balance Sheet (000's)				
Cash & Equivalents	24.0	594.0	890.0	909.0
Total Current Assets	15,264.0	16,018.0	14,833.0	24,991.0
Fixed Assets, Net	3,448.0	3,093.0	5,507.0	7,953.0
Total Assets	21,462.0	23,525.0	24,663.0	38,735.0
Total Current Liabilities	10,792.0	14,047.0	13,079.0	30,261.0
Long-Term Debt	4,924.0	6,617.0	9,244.0	3,838.0
Stockholders' Equity	5,099.0	2,438.0	1,797.0	3,853.0
Performance & Financial Condition				
Return on Total Revenues %	6.62	1.57	-0.70	-9.87
Return on Avg Stockholders' Equity %	79.08	27.30	-10.76	-105.80
Return on Average Assets %	13.25	2.40	-0.96	-11.39
Current Ratio	1.41	1.14	1.13	0.83
Debt / Equity %	96.57	271.41	514.41	99.61

Compound Growth %'s	EPS % n.a.	Net Income % n.a.	Total Revenues % 0.93

Comments

The strong revenue advance in fiscal 1998 was due in part to an increase in market share for domestic sales of plasma cutting machines as a previous competitor decided to discontinue its line. Net earnings were also helped by the realization of deferred tax assets and the resulting tax credit on the income statement. As of May 31, 1998, the Company had $7 million of tax loss carryovers. Included in equity are 362,000 shares of preferred stock that have certain cumulative dividend and conversion rights. Book value per share is calculated on the common shares only. Earnings per share reflects a deduction for the accrued preferred stock dividends. For the nine months ended February 28, 1999, revenues and net income were $32.3 million and $2,385,000 ($.62 per share) as compared to $33.9 million and $796,000 ($.25 per share) for the same period of the earlier year.

Officers	Position	Ownership Information	
Raymond H. Blakeman	Chairman	Number of Shares Outstanding	3,196,447
James D. Heitt	President, COO	Market Capitalization	$ 11,187,565
Randall J. Stodola	Vice President, Controller	Number of Shareholders	1,500
John J. Toben	Vice President	Where Listed / Symbol	OTC-BB / METS

Other Information			
Transfer Agent	Harris Trust & Savings Bank Chicago, IL	SIC Code	3540
Auditor	McGladrey & Pullen, LLP	Employees	268
Market Maker	Neuberger & Berman, LLC	(800)543-8481	Web Site	iowaprecision.com
	GVR Co.	(800)638-8602		

Metal Arts Company, Inc. (The)

1 American Center   Geneva, NY 14456-1188   Telephone (315)789-2200   Fax (315)789-0100

Company Description

The Metal Arts Company, Inc., established in 1913, has been operated as a holding company for a 70% ownership in Coating Technology, Inc. Coating engages in contract electroless nickel, aluminum anodizing, electroless nickel and gold plating of circuit boards and other surface coating and enhancement operations. Metal Arts also acquired a new patent pending technology for the plating of electroless nickel on aluminum and plans to commercialize that technology. As a result, Metal Arts hopes to become an operating company, marketing its proprietary specialty chemicals to end users nationally under the trade name Microsmooth®.

	06/30/98	06/30/97	06/30/96	06/30/95
Per Share Information				
Stock Price as of 12/31	0.15	0.31	0.28	0.12
Earnings Per Share	-0.02	-0.02	-0.02	-0.05
Price / Earnings Ratio	n.a.	n.a.	n.a.	n.a.
Book Value Per Share	-0.02	-0.01	0.01	0.03
Price / Book Value %	n.a.	n.a.	2,800.00	400.00
Dividends Per Share	0.0	0.0	0.0	0.0
Annual Financial Data				
Operating Results (000's)				
Total Revenues	1,878.9	1,657.0	1,632.4	1,575.8
Costs & Expenses	-2,021.3	-1,736.6	-1,778.5	-1,582.3
Income Before Taxes and Other	-142.3	-127.8	-152.2	-106.5
Other Items	0.0	0.0	-4.9	-279.5
Income Tax	-14.7	1.5	9.8	-14.8
Net Income	-157.0	-126.3	-147.3	-400.7
Cash Flow From Operations	117.1	60.0	44.2	-39.2
Balance Sheet (000's)				
Cash & Equivalents	35.4	53.2	112.2	78.6
Total Current Assets	367.5	347.4	398.3	406.7
Fixed Assets, Net	674.7	460.2	508.3	540.1
Total Assets	1,276.1	1,064.6	1,179.3	1,203.0
Total Current Liabilities	836.1	341.7	338.5	233.8
Long-Term Debt	183.8	348.3	404.9	385.0
Stockholders' Equity	-129.7	-25.6	50.7	198.0
Performance & Financial Condition				
Return on Total Revenues %	-8.36	-7.62	-9.02	-25.43
Return on Avg Stockholders' Equity %	n.a.	-1,008.60	-118.48	-332.44
Return on Average Assets %	-13.41	-11.26	-12.37	-24.77
Current Ratio	0.44	1.02	1.18	1.74
Debt / Equity %	n.a.	n.a.	799.09	194.45

Compound Growth %'s	EPS % n.a.	Net Income % n.a.	Total Revenues % 6.04

Comments

Management reports that Coating Technology has shown steady growth in sales and earnings over the past four years. More important to the potential investor may be the August 12, 1998 agreement with the New York State Energy Research and Development Authority and the United States Department of Labor. The Company will receive funding of $640,000 to demonstrate the Microsmooth® process on aluminum automobile wheels. ALCOA Aluminum is a strategic partner as well and has pledged an additional $100,000 of in-kind material, services and cash. If Metal Arts is successful in commercializing its new technology, it will be necessary to raise additional capital.

Officers	Position	Ownership Information	
Stanley J. Dahle	President, CEO	Number of Shares Outstanding	7,520,802
Albert A. Cauwels	Secretary	Market Capitalization	$ 1,128,120
Geoffrey A. Rich	Vice President	Number of Shareholders	980
		Where Listed / Symbol	OTC-BB / MTRT

Other Information			
Transfer Agent	American Transfer Company New York, NY	SIC Code	3470
Auditor	Davie Kaplan Chapman et al.	Employees	25
Market Maker	Wm. V. Frankel & Co., Inc. (800)631-3091		
	Knight Securities L.P. (800)222-4910		

Meteor Industries, Inc.

216 Sixteenth Street, Suite 730   Denver, CO 80202   Telephone (303)572-1135   Fax (303)572-1803

Company Description

Meteor Industries, Inc. is a wholesale and retail distributor of petroleum products primarily in several western states. It also operates retail gasoline and convenience stores in New Mexico and Colorado. In June 1995, Meteor acquired Hillger Oil Company. This acquisition doubled the Company's gasoline sales and improved cash flows. In November 1995, the Company acquired Capco Resources whose major assets were a California environmental services firm, a $1.5 million promissory note, and an interest in a company that is involved in the development of a power plant in Pakistan. In August 1997, the Company acquired Fleischli Oil Company, Inc., a petroleum marketing and distribution company. In June 1998, the Company acquired Tri-Valley Gas Co., a petroleum marketing and distribution company in Colorado. In November 1998, the Company acquired R & R Oil Company, a petroleum marketing and distribution company in Wyoming. The Company reacquired 113,598 of its common shares during 1998.

	12/31/98	12/31/97	12/31/96	08/31/95
Per Share Information				
Stock Price	3.12	4.25	5.06	2.50
Earnings Per Share	0.31	0.16	0.15	0.12
Price / Earnings Ratio	10.06	26.56	33.73	20.83
Book Value Per Share	2.29	2.24	1.55	0.80
Price / Book Value %	136.24	189.73	326.45	312.50
Dividends Per Share	0.0	0.0	0.0	0.0
Annual Financial Data				
Operating Results (000's)				
Total Revenues	118,842.0	89,440.6	60,380.1	45,372.9
Costs & Expenses	-116,291.0	-87,857.4	-59,237.0	-45,412.2
Income Before Taxes and Other	2,551.0	1,583.2	1,143.0	-39.3
Other Items	-444.0	-399.5	-286.5	0.0
Income Tax	-939.0	-582.6	-394.7	191.7
Net Income	1,168.0	601.1	461.8	152.3
Cash Flow From Operations	2,957.0	1,158.6	842.0	2,177.1
Balance Sheet (000's)				
Cash & Equivalents	380.0	225.7	1,080.3	244.2
Total Current Assets	16,096.0	15,826.1	8,487.9	6,682.5
Fixed Assets, Net	19,235.0	13,939.8	8,277.4	5,767.7
Total Assets	39,390.0	31,941.4	20,433.7	14,581.3
Total Current Liabilities	16,506.0	12,934.6	8,942.9	6,950.6
Long-Term Debt	6,390.0	2,912.2	445.8	2,095.7
Stockholders' Equity	7,856.0	9,291.2	5,119.9	1,014.1
Performance & Financial Condition				
Return on Total Revenues %	0.98	0.67	0.76	0.34
Return on Avg Stockholders' Equity %	13.62	8.34	15.06	20.36
Return on Average Assets %	3.27	2.30	2.64	1.14
Current Ratio	0.98	1.22	0.95	0.96
Debt / Equity %	81.34	31.34	8.71	206.66

Compound Growth %'s	EPS %	37.21	Net Income %	97.19	Total Revenues %	37.85

Comments

The Company has changed fiscal years for reporting. We presented the last four full reporting cycles. In June 1997, the Company raised $3,139,000 through a secondary stock offering of 690,000 common shares. Compound growth in earnings per share is less than that of net income because of additional shares being issued in the offering and for acquisitions. Approximately 26% of stockholders' equity and book value per share is comprised of intangible assets. The Company had a small working capital deficiency at December 31, 1998.

Officers	Position	Ownership Information	
Ilyas Chaudhary	Chairman, CEO	Number of Shares Outstanding	3,423,694
Edward J. Names	President, COO	Market Capitalization	$ 10,681,925
Dennis R. Staal	Secretary, Treasurer	Number of Shareholders	600
Irwin Kaufman	Director	Where Listed / Symbol	NASDAQ / METR

Other Information			
Transfer Agent	American Securities Transfer, Inc. Denver, CO	SIC Code	5170
Auditor	PricewaterhouseCoopers LLP	Employees	320
		Web Site	meteorindustries.com

Miami Subs Corporation

6300 N.W. 31st Avenue   Fort Lauderdale, FL 33309   Telephone (954)973-0000   Fax (954)973-7616

Company Description

Miami Subs Corporation develops, owns, operates and franchises restaurants under the name Miami Subs and Miami Subs Grill. The restaurants are designed to offer fresh quality food delivered in a fast-food environment similar to other fast food restaurants, and the quality, freshness and variety found at casual dining restaurants. The restaurants feature fresh food prepared and cooked to order including hot and cold submarine sandwiches; various ethnic foods such as gyros and greek salads; flame grilled hamburgers and chicken breasts, chicken wings, fresh salads, ice cream and other desserts. The diverse, moderately priced menu is designed to attract a broad customer base and to encourage frequent visits. As of May 31, 1998, the Company's restaurant system consisted of 191 restaurants, of which 130 were located in Florida, 53 were located in 15 other states, and eight were located in Ecuador, Puerto Rico and the Dominican Republic. Of the total restaurants in the system, 17 were Company operated and 174 were operated by franchisees.

	05/31/98	05/31/97	05/31/96	05/31/95
Per Share Information				
Stock Price as of 12/31	0.37	0.44	0.75	1.87
Earnings Per Share	0.02	-0.01	0.01	-0.02
Price / Earnings Ratio	18.50	n.a.	75.00	n.a.
Book Value Per Share	0.59	0.59	0.60	0.57
Price / Book Value %	62.71	74.58	125.00	328.07
Dividends Per Share	0.0	0.0	0.0	0.0
Annual Financial Data				
Operating Results (000's)				
Total Revenues	23,434.0	34,433.0	37,912.0	31,896.0
Costs & Expenses	-22,698.0	-34,824.0	-37,607.0	-32,457.0
Income Before Taxes and Other	736.0	-391.0	305.0	-561.0
Other Items	0.0	0.0	0.0	0.0
Income Tax	-211.0	0.0	0.0	0.0
Net Income	525.0	-391.0	305.0	-561.0
Cash Flow From Operations	1,205.0	-362.0	2,217.0	669.0
Balance Sheet (000's)				
Cash & Equivalents	3,457.0	2,940.0	3,103.0	3,145.0
Total Current Assets	5,456.0	5,209.0	6,066.0	5,180.0
Fixed Assets, Net	11,612.0	11,125.0	17,955.0	14,592.0
Total Assets	30,326.0	32,106.0	36,361.0	33,042.0
Total Current Liabilities	5,368.0	6,443.0	7,645.0	6,785.0
Long-Term Debt	5,613.0	6,288.0	7,955.0	6,000.0
Stockholders' Equity	16,033.0	15,508.0	16,943.0	15,053.0
Performance & Financial Condition				
Return on Total Revenues %	2.24	-1.14	0.80	-1.76
Return on Avg Stockholders' Equity %	3.33	-2.41	1.91	-3.94
Return on Average Assets %	1.68	-1.14	0.88	-1.90
Current Ratio	1.02	0.81	0.79	0.76
Debt / Equity %	35.01	40.55	46.95	39.86

Compound Growth %'s	EPS %	41.42	Net Income %	31.20	Total Revenues %	-9.77

Comments

The decrease in revenues during fiscal 1998 was primarily due to the conversion from Company to franchise operations in a number of locations. Same store sales declined 2.6% during the year. Royalty revenues were adversely affected in both fiscal 1998 and 1997 due to the non-payment and non-accrual of royalty fees from a number of franchised restaurants. At May 31, 1998, the Company had $6.7 million recorded in intangible assets which equated to approximately 42% of shareholders' equity and book value on a per share basis. For the nine months ended February 28, 1999, the Company reported revenue and net income of $17.8 million and $605,000 ($.09 per share) as compared to $17.4 million and $389,000 ($.06 per share) in fiscal 1998.

Officers	Position	Ownership Information	
Gus Boulis	Chairman, CEO	Number of Shares Outstanding	27,119,340
Donald L. Perlyn	President, COO	Market Capitalization	$ 10,034,156
Joseph Zappala	Senior VP	Number of Shareholders	1,800
Jerry W. Woda	Senior VP, CFO	Where Listed / Symbol	NASDAQ / SUBS

Other Information			
Transfer Agent	American Stock Transfer & Trust Co. New York, NY	SIC Code	5812
Auditor	KPMG LLP	Employees	494
		Web Site	miamisubs.com

MicroFrame, Inc.

21 Meridian Road   Edison, NJ 08820   Telephone (732)494-4440   Fax (732)494-4570

Company Description

MicroFrame, Inc. designs, develops and markets a broad range of remote network management and remote maintenance and security products for mission critical voice and data communications networks. The Company's products provide for alarm and fault monitoring, proactive administration and reporting capabilities which are being used as a basis for remote, intranet and internet network management and maintenance. These products can also prevent unauthorized dial-in and/or in-band access to computers, networks and other systems. The Company was founded in 1982.

	03/31/98	03/31/97	03/31/96	03/31/95
Per Share Information				
Stock Price as of 12/31	2.31	1.34	1.56	1.69
Earnings Per Share	0.14	0.07	-0.54	0.10
Price / Earnings Ratio	16.50	19.14	n.a.	16.90
Book Value Per Share	0.83	0.68	0.42	0.94
Price / Book Value %	278.31	197.06	371.43	179.79
Dividends Per Share	0.0	0.0	0.0	0.0
Annual Financial Data				
Operating Results (000's)				
Total Revenues	10,232.8	7,379.2	6,261.9	7,136.8
Costs & Expenses	-9,826.2	-7,177.9	-7,581.6	-6,553.9
Income Before Taxes and Other	406.6	201.3	-1,418.8	582.9
Other Items	0.0	0.0	0.0	0.0
Income Tax	304.7	141.2	-574.9	-218.1
Net Income	711.3	342.5	-1,993.7	364.8
Cash Flow From Operations	332.7	21.0	-469.3	343.2
Balance Sheet (000's)				
Cash & Equivalents	507.7	539.2	48.3	490.3
Total Current Assets	5,120.1	3,903.6	2,751.2	3,602.4
Fixed Assets, Net	421.7	343.1	409.9	317.6
Total Assets	6,375.4	4,682.4	3,558.2	4,337.9
Total Current Liabilities	2,176.1	1,208.2	1,914.1	860.5
Long-Term Debt	0.0	30.4	72.8	0.0
Stockholders' Equity	4,003.0	3,270.7	1,571.2	3,477.4
Performance & Financial Condition				
Return on Total Revenues %	6.95	4.64	-31.84	5.11
Return on Avg Stockholders' Equity %	19.56	14.15	-78.98	11.14
Return on Average Assets %	12.87	8.31	-50.50	8.87
Current Ratio	2.35	3.23	1.44	4.19
Debt / Equity %	n.a.	0.93	4.64	n.a.

Compound Growth %'s	EPS % 11.87	Net Income % 24.93	Total Revenues % 12.76

Comments

Management reports continuing success in the development of new domestic relationships to offset a reduction of sales from its two major customers, MCI and Lucent Technologies. Revenue growth of 39% during fiscal 1998 was primarily due to the Company's Sentinel 2000 product line. During fiscal 1998, the Company continued its development of a new generation of advanced technology products. For the nine months ended December 31, 1998, revenue and net income were $9.5 million and $345,104 ($.05 per share) as compared to $7.1 million and $282,211 ($.06 per share) for the same period of the preceding year.

Officers	Position	Ownership Information	
Stephen M. Deixler	Chairman, Treasurer	Number of Shares Outstanding	4,849,131
Stephen B. Gray	President, CEO	Market Capitalization	$ 11,201,493
Michael Radomsky	Exec VP, Secretary	Number of Shareholders	363
John F. McTigue	Vice President, CFO	Where Listed / Symbol	NASDAQ / MCFR

Other Information			
Transfer Agent	Registrar & Transfer Co. Cranford, NJ	SIC Code	3577
Auditor	PricewaterhouseCoopers LLP	Employees	46
		Web Site	ion-networks.com

Microfluidics International Corporation

30 Ossipee Road, P.O. Box 9101 Newton, MA 02164-9101 Telephone (617)969-5452 Fax (617)965-1213

Company Description

Microfluidics International Corporation specializes in the production and marketing of proprietary Microfluidizer® devices used for the creation of micro droplets and dispersions in liquid streams for very fine mixing and blending applications. These devices have widespread applications in the chemical processing, pharmaceutical, biotechnology, cosmetics and food processing industries. The primary advantage of the Company's equipment is that it mixes materials that are normally difficult to mix while producing higher quality products on a more consistent basis than other blending and mixing techniques. In 1998, the Company acquired two companies, Epworth Mill and Morehouse-COWLES, which specialize in producing and marketing a broad line of proprietary fluid materials processing systems.

	12/31/98	12/31/97	12/31/96	12/31/95
Per Share Information				
Stock Price	0.81	2.44	1.88	1.94
Earnings Per Share	-0.28	0.22	0.10	-0.43
Price / Earnings Ratio	n.a.	11.09	18.80	n.a.
Book Value Per Share	1.64	1.53	1.31	1.22
Price / Book Value %	49.39	159.48	143.51	159.02
Dividends Per Share	0.0	0.0	0.0	0.0
Annual Financial Data				
Operating Results (000's)				
Total Revenues	10,123.8	7,406.8	6,424.4	5,546.9
Costs & Expenses	-11,215.6	-6,702.4	-5,922.9	-6,556.7
Income Before Taxes and Other	-1,091.8	704.4	501.5	-1,009.9
Other Items	0.0	0.0	0.0	0.0
Income Tax	-413.6	403.6	0.0	-1,107.4
Net Income	-1,505.4	1,108.1	501.5	-2,117.3
Cash Flow From Operations	-1,259.4	1,289.9	1,014.6	182.5
Balance Sheet (000's)				
Cash & Equivalents	550.7	4,083.2	2,786.6	1,903.4
Total Current Assets	7,570.3	8,139.6	6,827.4	6,286.6
Fixed Assets, Net	996.3	151.8	144.9	174.4
Total Assets	14,700.0	8,872.2	7,183.3	6,716.0
Total Current Liabilities	5,995.2	1,334.1	754.8	686.9
Long-Term Debt	0.0	0.0	0.0	0.0
Stockholders' Equity	8,029.8	7,538.1	6,428.5	6,029.1
Performance & Financial Condition				
Return on Total Revenues %	-14.87	14.96	7.81	-38.17
Return on Avg Stockholders' Equity %	-19.34	15.87	8.05	-30.04
Return on Average Assets %	-12.77	13.80	7.22	-26.62
Current Ratio	1.26	6.10	9.05	9.15
Debt / Equity %	n.a.	n.a.	n.a.	n.a.

Compound Growth %'s	EPS %	n.a.	Net Income %	n.a.	Total Revenues %	22.21

Comments

The acquisitions referred to above were accounted for using the purchase method of accounting. Therefore, operating results have been combined in the above numbers since August 14, 1998, the date of the transaction. Revenue of $2.8 million came from the acquired companies. Sales of the Microfluidics division declined due to a weak Asian market. At December 31, 1998, the Company had $6.0 million of goodwill reflected as assets which equated to approximately 75% of stockholders' equity and book value per share. The Company also had $4 million of tax loss carryovers available to offset future income. The acquisition and 1998 loss had the effect of substantially weakening the Company's overall financial condition. Working capital is significantly diminished from 1997 levels. Now, profitable operations are critical to the long term viability of the Company.

Officers	Position	Ownership Information	
Irwin J. Gruverman	Chairman, CEO	Number of Shares Outstanding	4,901,585
Michael A. Lento	President, CFO	Market Capitalization	$ 3,970,284
James N. Little	Director	Number of Shareholders	411
Vincent Cortina	Director	Where Listed / Symbol	NASDAQ / MFIC

Other Information			
Transfer Agent	Boston EquiServe Boston, MA	SIC Code	3821
Auditor	Deloitte & Touche LLP	Employees	95
		Web Site	microfluidics.com

Micronetics Wireless, Inc.

26 Hampshire Drive   Hudson, NH 03051   Telephone (603)883-2900   Fax (603)882-8987

Company Description

Micronetics Wireless, Inc. is a manufacturer of specialized radio frequency components and test equipment which are designed to provide solutions for its customers, original equipment manufacturers of wireless communication systems and communication service providers, to enable them to deliver high quality communication systems or offer high quality communication services. The Company's products are used in cellular, microwave, satellite, radar and communications systems around the world. The Company was founded in 1975 and went public in 1988.

	03/31/98	03/31/97	03/31/96	03/31/95
Per Share Information				
Stock Price as of 12/31	1.69	2.37	1.50	2.00
Earnings Per Share	0.13	0.12	0.10	0.08
Price / Earnings Ratio	13.00	19.75	15.00	25.00
Book Value Per Share	1.05	0.95	0.82	0.67
Price / Book Value %	160.95	249.47	182.93	298.51
Dividends Per Share	0.0	0.0	0.0	0.0
Annual Financial Data				
Operating Results (000's)				
Total Revenues	4,909.4	3,852.0	3,703.2	2,542.1
Costs & Expenses	-4,392.1	-3,464.5	-3,400.0	-2,500.8
Income Before Taxes and Other	517.3	387.5	303.1	41.3
Other Items	0.0	71.0	0.0	201.3
Income Tax	-89.2	-63.0	22.6	-3.0
Net Income	428.1	395.5	325.7	239.5
Cash Flow From Operations	96.7	969.2	28.2	49.9
Balance Sheet (000's)				
Cash & Equivalents	1,031.6	961.3	146.7	288.0
Total Current Assets	3,601.4	3,036.7	2,314.9	2,166.7
Fixed Assets, Net	1,521.1	1,512.0	1,419.3	426.4
Total Assets	5,213.9	4,648.2	4,000.4	2,835.9
Total Current Liabilities	719.6	679.0	486.3	520.7
Long-Term Debt	868.7	948.0	947.1	175.0
Stockholders' Equity	3,585.2	3,013.5	2,559.1	1,909.9
Performance & Financial Condition				
Return on Total Revenues %	8.72	10.27	8.80	9.42
Return on Avg Stockholders' Equity %	12.98	14.19	14.58	13.73
Return on Average Assets %	8.68	9.15	9.53	9.51
Current Ratio	5.00	4.47	4.76	4.16
Debt / Equity %	24.23	31.46	37.01	9.16

Compound Growth %'s	EPS %	17.57	Net Income %	21.35	Total Revenues %	24.53

Comments

The 27% jump in fiscal 1998 revenues was primarily due to increased sales of the Company's wireless test instruments. Gross margins also improved and management expects this trend to continue as the Company expands its commercial wireless activities. Fiscal 1997 and 1995 results include nonrecurring gains that added $.02 and $.07 to earnings per share, respectively. This has the result of lowering the compound growth rate of earnings per share and net income from what it would have been without the 1995 nonrecurring gain. For the nine months ended December 31, 1998, the Company reported revenues and net income of $3.3 million and $342,899 ($.10 per share) as compared to $3.5 million and $318,376 ($.09 per share) for the same period of the preceding year.

Officers	Position	Ownership Information	
Richard S. Kalin	President, CEO	Number of Shares Outstanding	3,415,298
David Robbins, Sr.	Senior VP, COO	Market Capitalization	$ 5,771,854
Donna Hillsgrove	Secretary, Treasurer	Number of Shareholders	302
Catherine Marino	Vice President	Where Listed / Symbol	NASDAQ / NOIZ

Other Information			
Transfer Agent	TranSecurities International, Inc. Spokane, WA	SIC Code	3679
Auditor	Paul C. Roberts, C.P.A.	Employees	45
		Web Site	mwireless.com

Micropac Industries, Inc.

905 East Walnut Street   Garland, TX 75040   Telephone (972)272-3571   Fax (972)494-2281

Company Description

Micropac Industries, Inc., founded in 1969, manufactures and sells various types of hybrid microcircuits and optoelectronic components and assemblies. Products are used as components in a broad range of military and industrial systems, including aircraft instrumentation and navigation systems, power supplies, electronic controls, computers and medical devices. A majority of the Company's sales are to the United States Government, primarily to the Department of Defense and NASA. Approximately 10% of 1998 sales were to international customers.

	11/30/98	11/30/97	11/30/96	11/30/95
Per Share Information				
Stock Price as of 12/31	0.70	1.13	1.06	0.69
Earnings Per Share	0.12	0.25	0.23	0.12
Price / Earnings Ratio	5.83	4.52	4.61	5.75
Book Value Per Share	2.00	1.88	1.63	1.40
Price / Book Value %	35.00	60.11	65.03	49.29
Dividends Per Share	0.0	0.0	0.0	0.0
Annual Financial Data				
Operating Results (000's)				
Total Revenues	11,556.0	14,762.0	14,412.0	11,445.0
Costs & Expenses	-10,858.0	-13,357.0	-13,151.0	-10,720.0
Income Before Taxes and Other	698.0	1,405.0	1,261.0	725.0
Other Items	0.0	0.0	0.0	0.0
Income Tax	-253.0	-488.0	-429.0	-282.0
Net Income	445.0	917.0	832.0	443.0
Cash Flow From Operations	768.0	1,563.0	-125.0	10.0
Balance Sheet (000's)				
Cash & Equivalents	420.0	106.0	0.0	213.0
Total Current Assets	7,137.0	7,134.0	6,809.0	5,723.0
Fixed Assets, Net	1,239.0	1,324.0	1,256.0	1,180.0
Total Assets	8,376.0	8,458.0	8,065.0	6,903.0
Total Current Liabilities	1,071.0	1,551.0	2,014.0	1,660.0
Long-Term Debt	0.0	0.0	0.0	0.0
Stockholders' Equity	7,262.0	6,817.0	5,900.0	5,068.0
Performance & Financial Condition				
Return on Total Revenues %	3.85	6.21	5.77	3.87
Return on Avg Stockholders' Equity %	6.32	14.42	15.17	9.14
Return on Average Assets %	5.29	11.10	11.12	6.93
Current Ratio	6.66	4.60	3.38	3.45
Debt / Equity %	n.a.	n.a.	n.a.	n.a.

Compound Growth %'s	EPS %	0.00	Net Income %	0.15	Total Revenues %	0.32

Comments

After record-breaking sales in fiscal 1997, revenues were off 21.5% in fiscal 1998. The decrease was primarily related to a downturn in the Asian economy and the government's "commercial off the shelf" purchasing initiative. Management reports that a 22.4% reduction in its workforce was achieved through attrition and that it was able to maintain its nucleus of experienced personnel. Obtaining new customers and developing new products are the goals for 1999. Although small, the Company has an exceptionally strong balance sheet and trades for a price that deserves some attention.

Officers	Position	Ownership Information	
Nicholas Nadolsky	Chairman, CEO	Number of Shares Outstanding	3,627,151
Connie Wood	Vice President	Market Capitalization	$ 2,539,006
Heinz-Werner Hempel	Director	Number of Shareholders	608
H. Kent Hearn	Director	Where Listed / Symbol	OTC-BB / MPAD

Other Information			
Transfer Agent	Securities Transfer Corp. Dallas, TX	SIC Code	3674
Auditor	Arthur Andersen LLP	Employees	128
Market Maker	Paragon Capital Corporation	(800)345-0505	Web Site	micropac.com
	R.A. Mackie & Co., L.P.	(800)328-1550		

Mikron Instrument Company, Inc.

16 Thornton Road   Oakland, NJ 07436   Telephone (201)405-0900   Fax (201)405-0090

Company Description

Mikron Instrument Company, Inc. develops, manufactures, markets and services equipment and instruments for non-contact temperature measurement. The Company's products are typically used to measure the temperature of moving objects, or statutory objects in environments or situations where contact temperature measurement would be difficult, hazardous or impracticable, and wherever rapid temperature changes must be accurately tracked instantaneously. The predominant market for the Company's hand-held infrared thermometers is industrial quality control applications and maintenance. The Company also manufactures high resolution thermal imaging products. Mikron Instrument was founded in 1969.

	10/31/98	10/31/97	10/31/96	10/31/95
Per Share Information				
Stock Price as of 12/31	1.37	1.25	2.62	3.12
Earnings Per Share	0.05	-0.01	0.0	0.05
Price / Earnings Ratio	27.40	n.a.	n.a.	62.40
Book Value Per Share	0.98	0.93	0.94	0.94
Price / Book Value %	139.80	134.41	278.72	331.91
Dividends Per Share	0.0	0.0	0.0	0.0
Annual Financial Data				
Operating Results (000's)				
Total Revenues	8,451.4	6,827.4	7,135.4	6,500.0
Costs & Expenses	-8,219.7	-6,863.7	-7,116.8	-6,303.6
Income Before Taxes and Other	231.6	-36.3	18.6	196.3
Other Items	0.0	0.0	0.0	0.0
Income Tax	-50.0	0.0	0.0	0.0
Net Income	181.6	-36.3	18.6	196.3
Cash Flow From Operations	-47.2	419.6	-473.1	13.1
Balance Sheet (000's)				
Cash & Equivalents	415.4	548.0	206.4	463.8
Total Current Assets	3,851.0	3,806.0	3,783.8	4,108.5
Fixed Assets, Net	286.5	272.0	293.1	110.4
Total Assets	4,137.5	4,115.5	4,164.4	4,356.3
Total Current Liabilities	541.4	696.7	668.4	830.7
Long-Term Debt	0.0	0.0	37.5	100.0
Stockholders' Equity	3,589.6	3,408.0	3,444.2	3,425.7
Performance & Financial Condition				
Return on Total Revenues %	2.15	-0.53	0.26	3.02
Return on Avg Stockholders' Equity %	5.19	-1.06	0.54	5.90
Return on Average Assets %	4.40	-0.88	0.44	4.83
Current Ratio	7.11	5.46	5.66	4.95
Debt / Equity %	n.a.	n.a.	1.09	2.92

Compound Growth %'s	EPS %	0.00	Net Income %	-2.56	Total Revenues %	9.15

Comments

The 25% increase in revenues in fiscal 1998 was primarily attributable to the introduction and sales of the portable thermal imager Model TH5104. A major portion of the increased expenses was due to promotion, marketing, exhibitions and training associated with the introduction of model TH5104. An additional $75,000 was spent to produce a 250 page general catalog that encompasses descriptions of all Mikron products. $35,000 was spent on the Company's new website. Research and development expenses also increased to $726,241 as compared to $658,070 in the preceding year. Despite the above, the Company recorded a net profit and continues to maintain an excellent financial condition.

Officers	Position	Ownership Information	
Steven N. Bronson	Chairman, CEO	Number of Shares Outstanding	3,654,200
Keikhosrow Irani	President	Market Capitalization	$ 5,006,254
Alex Wu	Vice President, Treasurer	Number of Shareholders	400
Alvin Katz	Director	Where Listed / Symbol	NASDAQ / MIKR

Other Information			
Transfer Agent	American Stock Transfer & Trust Co. New York, NY	SIC Code	3823
Auditor	Feldman Radin & Co., P.C.	Employees	47
		Web Site	mikroninst.com

Milastar Corporation

No. 9 Via Parigi   Palm Beach, FL 33480   Telephone (561)655-9590   Fax (561)833-7253

Company Description

Milastar Corporation sells special metallurgical services to a diversified list of manufacturers primarily located in the greater Midwest and New England regions. The customer base manufactures a wide variety of mechanical end-products and customarily outsources (subcontracts) the processing of some components incorporated in those end-products. The menu of special processing services performed includes metallurgical engineering, heat treating, brazing and surface finishing. Milastar operates four plants, strategically located to expand its geographical reach and to reduce freight charges. The Company was formed in 1969.

	04/30/98	04/30/97	04/30/96	04/30/95
Per Share Information				
Stock Price as of 12/31	0.50	1.03	0.62	0.56
Earnings Per Share	0.17	-0.02	-0.09	-0.22
Price / Earnings Ratio	2.94	n.a.	n.a.	n.a.
Book Value Per Share	1.47	1.29	1.32	1.41
Price / Book Value %	34.01	79.84	46.97	39.72
Dividends Per Share	0.0	0.0	0.0	0.0
Annual Financial Data				
Operating Results (000's)				
Total Revenues	8,280.0	7,379.0	6,673.0	7,208.0
Costs & Expenses	-7,747.0	-7,405.0	-6,882.0	-7,539.0
Income Before Taxes and Other	498.0	-62.0	-252.0	-612.0
Other Items	0.0	0.0	0.0	0.0
Income Tax	-14.0	-1.0	-2.0	-2.0
Net Income	484.0	-63.0	-254.0	-614.0
Cash Flow From Operations	784.0	560.0	483.0	-427.0
Balance Sheet (000's)				
Cash & Equivalents	164.0	71.0	144.0	365.0
Total Current Assets	1,804.0	1,569.0	1,556.0	1,911.0
Fixed Assets, Net	6,737.0	4,453.0	3,966.0	3,020.0
Total Assets	9,022.0	6,093.0	5,902.0	5,315.0
Total Current Liabilities	1,838.0	1,493.0	1,433.0	1,410.0
Long-Term Debt	3,172.0	1,072.0	842.0	40.0
Stockholders' Equity	4,012.0	3,528.0	3,627.0	3,865.0
Performance & Financial Condition				
Return on Total Revenues %	5.85	-0.85	-3.81	-8.52
Return on Avg Stockholders' Equity %	12.84	-1.76	-6.78	-14.75
Return on Average Assets %	6.40	-1.05	-4.53	-6.03
Current Ratio	0.98	1.05	1.09	1.36
Debt / Equity %	79.06	30.39	23.21	1.03

Compound Growth %'s	EPS % n.a.	Net Income % n.a.	Total Revenues % 4.73

Comments

Increasing revenues have finally driven the Company into profitability. Sales volume is being incrementally increased through a combination of acquisitions and capital improvements, extension of market reach and broadening of the customer base. Management expects the rising flow of bookings will increase plant utilization. Income Tax expense has been low due to tax loss carryovers of which $1.4 million remained at the end of fiscal 1998. For the nine months ended January 31, 1999, the Company reported revenues and net income of $6.8 million and $342,000 ($.12 per share) as compared to $6.1 million and $378,000 ($.13 per share) in the same period of the preceding year.

Officers	Position	Ownership Information	
J. Russell Duncan	Chairman	Number of Shares Outstanding	2,738,264
L. Michael McGurk	President, COO	Market Capitalization	$ 1,369,132
Lance H. Duncan	Secretary	Number of Shareholders	5,000
Dennis J. Stevermer	Vice President, Treasurer	Where Listed / Symbol	OTC-BB / MILAA

Other Information

Transfer Agent	American Stock Transfer & Trust Co. New York, NY		SIC Code	3390
Auditor	KPMG LLP		Employees	83
Market Maker	Carr Securities Corporation	(800)221-2243		
	Herzog, Heine, Geduld, Inc.	(800)221-7864		

MileMarker International, Inc.

1450 S.W. 13th Court   Pompano Beach, FL 33069   Telephone (954)782-0604   Fax (954)782-0770

Company Description

MileMarker International, Inc. is a manufacturer and distributor of specialized automobile parts for the 4-wheel drive utility/recreational/military vehicle market. MileMarker and a predecessor company have been in business for over 18 years under the same management. The Company's patented line of hydraulic winches uses a vehicle's power steering pump as its source of energy. The winch kits are very competitively priced against electric winches and have proven performance capabilities not found in electric winches. They offer multiple safety features and durability as well as continuous, reliable and silent operation. MileMarker also markets a patented four-wheel Selectric Drive coupling device.

	12/31/98	12/31/97	12/31/96	12/31/95
Per Share Information				
Stock Price	0.06	0.09	0.12	0.22
Earnings Per Share	-0.01	0.0	-0.01	-0.04
Price / Earnings Ratio	n.a.	n.a.	n.a.	n.a.
Book Value Per Share	0.10	0.10	0.10	0.09
Price / Book Value %	60.00	90.00	120.00	244.44
Dividends Per Share	0.0	0.0	0.0	0.0
Annual Financial Data				
Operating Results (000's)				
Total Revenues	3,754.0	4,008.3	3,772.7	2,432.2
Costs & Expenses	-3,822.7	-4,013.5	-3,910.6	-2,740.9
Income Before Taxes and Other	-68.7	-5.2	-139.1	-383.1
Other Items	0.0	0.0	0.0	0.0
Income Tax	0.0	0.0	0.0	28.7
Net Income	-68.7	-5.2	-139.1	-354.4
Cash Flow From Operations	103.6	-475.6	-130.4	-763.1
Balance Sheet (000's)				
Cash & Equivalents	62.7	102.6	31.9	14.3
Total Current Assets	2,806.7	2,962.9	2,184.6	1,967.9
Fixed Assets, Net	140.5	139.9	155.5	219.4
Total Assets	3,080.7	3,297.2	2,454.5	2,320.9
Total Current Liabilities	1,921.4	1,957.8	1,187.2	1,172.4
Long-Term Debt	45.0	309.0	195.8	195.1
Stockholders' Equity	1,101.7	1,030.4	1,010.5	849.6
Performance & Financial Condition				
Return on Total Revenues %	-1.83	-0.13	-3.69	-14.57
Return on Avg Stockholders' Equity %	-6.45	-0.51	-14.95	-39.38
Return on Average Assets %	-2.15	-0.18	-5.83	-17.72
Current Ratio	1.46	1.51	1.84	1.68
Debt / Equity %	4.08	29.99	19.38	22.96

Compound Growth %'s	EPS % n.a.	Net Income % n.a.	Total Revenues % 15.57

Comments

After several years of improving revenues, 1998 brought a small decline which management attributed to a difficult market brought on by weather conditions. Also absent during 1998 was $177,584 of royalty and licensing income that was recorded in 1997. During 1998, Chairman Richard Aho waived approximately $79,000 of his officer compensation and approximately $6,000 in interest on his shareholder loan. Although small by any standard, operations are dancing with the concept of profitability. What's more, the balance sheet is respectable. MileMarker is one of the lowest priced stocks in this manual and may stay that way unless it can resume its three year compound growth rate.

Officers	Position	Ownership Information	
Richard E. Aho	President, CEO	Number of Shares Outstanding	10,684,354
Leslie J. Aho	Treasurer, Secretary	Market Capitalization	$ 641,061
Joel Aho	Vice President	Number of Shareholders	800
Drew V. Aho	Vice President	Where Listed / Symbol	OTC-BB / MMKR

Other Information			
Transfer Agent	Securities Transfer, Inc. Miami, FL	SIC Code	3714
Auditor	Spear, Safer, Harmon & Co.	Employees	14
Market Maker	Pennsylvania Merchant Group	(800)762-8624	Web Site	milemarker.com
	Paragon Capital Corporation	(800)340-0505		

Millbrook Press Inc. (The)

2 Old New Milford Road Brookfield, CT 06804 Telephone (203)740-2220 Fax (203)740-2223

Company Description

The Millbrook Press Inc. is a publisher of children's nonfiction books, in both hardcover and paperback for the school and library market and the consumer market. The Company has published more than 1,600 books under its Millbrook, Copper Beech, and Twenty-First Century imprints. The Company's books have been placed on numerous recommended lists by libraries, retail bookstores, and educational organizations. The Company went public on December 23, 1996.

	07/31/98	07/31/97	07/31/96	07/31/95
Per Share Information				
Stock Price as of 12/31	4.56	4.62	5.37	4.50
Earnings Per Share	0.19	-0.46	-1.09	-1.60
Price / Earnings Ratio	24.00	n.a.	n.a.	n.a.
Book Value Per Share	4.04	3.85	0.82	1.92
Price / Book Value %	112.87	120.00	654.88	234.38
Dividends Per Share	0.0	0.0	0.0	0.0
Annual Financial Data				
Operating Results (000's)				
Total Revenues	15,615.0	12,573.0	9,940.0	6,866.0
Costs & Expenses	-14,967.0	-13,431.0	-10,403.0	-7,672.0
Income Before Taxes and Other	648.0	-858.0	-463.0	-806.0
Other Items	0.0	0.0	0.0	0.0
Income Tax	0.0	0.0	0.0	0.0
Net Income	648.0	-858.0	-463.0	-806.0
Cash Flow From Operations	-434.0	-2,201.0	-231.0	-1,333.0
Balance Sheet (000's)				
Cash & Equivalents	34.0	323.0	134.0	538.0
Total Current Assets	12,968.0	9,023.0	6,351.0	5,199.0
Fixed Assets, Net	4,484.0	3,380.0	2,852.0	2,298.0
Total Assets	21,476.0	15,769.0	12,574.0	11,078.0
Total Current Liabilities	7,529.0	2,470.0	5,033.0	3,574.0
Long-Term Debt	0.0	0.0	0.0	0.0
Stockholders' Equity	13,947.0	13,299.0	7,041.0	7,504.0
Performance & Financial Condition				
Return on Total Revenues %	4.15	-6.82	-4.66	-11.74
Return on Avg Stockholders' Equity %	4.76	-8.44	-6.37	-11.85
Return on Average Assets %	3.48	-6.05	-3.92	-8.06
Current Ratio	1.72	3.65	1.26	1.45
Debt / Equity %	n.a.	n.a.	n.a.	n.a.

Compound Growth %'s   EPS % n.a.   Net Income % n.a.   Total Revenues % 31.51

Comments

Strong sales growth continued in fiscal 1998 with a 24% advance in revenue. Part of the increase is attributable to the acquisition of Twenty-First Century Books in December 1997, which was accounted for under the purchase method of accounting. Therefore, results have been combined starting with the date of the acquisition. At the time of the initial public offering, all preferred stock and unpaid dividends were converted to common shares. The 1996 loss was attributable to lower gross margins and costs associated with financing, insurance and new personnel. At July 31, 1998, the Company had $3.3 million of goodwill included in assets. For the six months ended January 31, 1999, the Company reported revenues and net income of $9.3 million and $321,000 ($.09 per share) as compared to $7.2 million and $252,000 ($.07 per share) for the same period of the preceding year.

Officers	Position	Ownership Information	
Jeffrey Conrad	President, CEO	Number of Shares Outstanding	3,455,000
Jean E. Reynolds	Senior VP	Market Capitalization	$ 15,754,800
Satish Dua	Vice President, CFO	Number of Shareholders	600
John Whalen	VP - Sales	Where Listed / Symbol	NASDAQ / MILB

Other Information			
Transfer Agent	Continental Stock Transfer & Trust Co. New York, NY	SIC Code	2731
Auditor	Arthur Andersen LLP	Employees	48
		Web Site	millbrookonapproval.com

Miller Diversified Corporation

23360 Weld County Road #35   La Salle, CO 80645   Telephone (970)284-5556   Fax (970)284-6780

Company Description

Miller Diversified Corporation's primary business is operating a feedlot facility near La Salle, Colorado, in which cattle owned by customers are fed and cared for by the Company. Most of its customers operate in the cattle industry or feed cattle as an investment. The Company was formed in 1987 as a result of several transactions and mergers of predecessor companies. Management has reported that the Company is actively seeking additional acquisition and merger candidates and entered into a letter of intent to acquire a 50% interest in a water cooler business for $180,000. Such transaction was completed in fiscal 1999.

	08/31/98	08/31/97	08/31/96	08/31/95
Per Share Information				
Stock Price as of 12/31	0.08	0.10	0.13	0.04
Earnings Per Share	-0.01	0.03	0.07	0.03
Price / Earnings Ratio	n.a.	3.33	1.86	1.33
Book Value Per Share	0.29	0.30	0.27	0.23
Price / Book Value %	27.59	33.33	48.15	17.39
Dividends Per Share	0.0	0.0	0.0	0.0
Annual Financial Data				
Operating Results (000's)				
Total Revenues	11,184.2	11,377.6	12,194.3	9,330.9
Costs & Expenses	-11,294.7	-11,339.6	-11,839.4	-9,149.3
Income Before Taxes and Other	-110.5	38.0	355.0	181.6
Other Items	0.0	0.0	0.0	0.0
Income Tax	56.2	141.3	32.6	-23.5
Net Income	-54.4	179.2	387.5	158.1
Cash Flow From Operations	-1,523.7	333.9	435.3	157.3
Balance Sheet (000's)				
Cash & Equivalents	63.7	359.3	86.6	72.3
Total Current Assets	2,425.4	1,738.3	1,339.7	1,812.1
Fixed Assets, Net	1,155.7	1,204.5	1,993.5	2,109.0
Total Assets	4,341.8	3,450.5	3,828.7	4,292.6
Total Current Liabilities	1,516.2	520.2	1,058.2	1,630.2
Long-Term Debt	0.0	0.0	0.0	0.0
Stockholders' Equity	1,841.1	1,914.4	1,726.0	1,308.4
Performance & Financial Condition				
Return on Total Revenues %	-0.49	1.58	3.18	1.69
Return on Avg Stockholders' Equity %	-2.89	9.85	25.54	12.86
Return on Average Assets %	-1.40	4.92	9.54	3.74
Current Ratio	1.60	3.34	1.27	1.11
Debt / Equity %	n.a.	n.a.	n.a.	n.a.

Compound Growth %'s	EPS % n.a.	Net Income % n.a.	Total Revenues % 6.23

Comments

Managements decision to retain ownership of a significant number of cattle that were fed to slaughter in the Company's feedlot did nothing to fatten corporate profits. The Company realized a loss of the operation of $103,791 and a year end inventory writedown of $140,416. Fiscal 1997 results benefitted from an income tax credit of $141,284 and two nonrecurring income items totalling $115,289 but suffered a nonrecurring loss of $178,452 from the sale of land and water rights. The Company's financial condition is still good. For the six months ended February 28, 1999, the Company reported revenues and net income of $5.4 million and $58,285 ($.01 per share) as compared to $5.3 million and a net loss of $16,730 ($.00 per share) for the same period of the preceding year.

Officers	Position	Ownership Information	
Norman M. Dean	Chairman	Number of Shares Outstanding	6,364,640
James E. Miller	President, CEO	Market Capitalization	$ 509,171
Stephen R. Story	Secretary, Treasurer	Number of Shareholders	1,462
Alan D. Gorden	Director	Where Listed / Symbol	OTC-BB / MILR

Other Information			
Transfer Agent	Interwest Transfer Co., Inc. Salt Lake City, UT	SIC Code	0700
Auditor	Anderson & Whitney, P.C.	Employees	23
Market Maker	Carr Securities Corporation (800)221-2243		
	Sharpe Capital Inc. (800)355-5781		

Miller Industries, Inc.

8503 Hilltop Drive   Ooltewah, TN 37363   Telephone (423)238-4171   Fax (423)238-5371

Company Description

Miller Industries, Inc. is the world's leading integrated provider of vehicle towing and recovery equipment and services. The Company's business is divided into two segments: manufacturing and distributing towing and recovery equipment as well as providing financial and related services to the towing and recovery industry; and providing towing and specialized transportation services. The Company markets its towing and recovery equipment under several well-recognized brand names and markets its towing services under the national brand name of RoadOne®. Since 1990, the Company has developed or acquired several of the most well-recognized brands in the fragmented towing and recovery equipment manufacturing industry. During fiscal 1998, the Company acquired four towing equipment distributors in separate transactions.

	04/30/98	04/30/97	04/30/96	04/30/95
Per Share Information				
Stock Price as of 12/31	4.94	10.87	19.31	5.28
Earnings Per Share	0.27	0.35	0.26	0.26
Price / Earnings Ratio	18.30	31.06	74.27	20.31
Book Value Per Share	3.92	3.27	2.00	1.04
Price / Book Value %	126.02	332.42	965.50	507.69
Dividends Per Share	0.0	0.0	0.0	0.0
Annual Financial Data				
Operating Results (000's)				
Total Revenues	397,213.0	292,394.0	180,463.0	139,779.0
Costs & Expenses	-376,362.0	-269,437.0	-166,328.0	-128,559.0
Income Before Taxes and Other	20,851.0	22,957.0	14,135.0	11,220.0
Other Items	0.0	0.0	0.0	288.0
Income Tax	-8,186.0	-8,436.0	-5,108.0	-3,736.0
Net Income	12,665.0	14,521.0	9,027.0	7,772.0
Cash Flow From Operations	-20,314.0	-11,009.0	n.a.	n.a.
Balance Sheet (000's)				
Cash & Equivalents	7,367.0	8,508.0	25,000.0	21,000.0
Total Current Assets	155,793.0	125,352.0	95,168.0	47,538.0
Fixed Assets, Net	85,849.0	49,171.0	5,000.0	5,000.0
Total Assets	329,730.0	215,297.0	123,978.0	66,018.0
Total Current Liabilities	51,019.0	63,372.0	42,730.0	28,527.0
Long-Term Debt	95,778.0	11,282.0	9,335.0	5,171.0
Stockholders' Equity	180,236.0	138,783.0	71,913.0	32,320.0
Performance & Financial Condition				
Return on Total Revenues %	3.19	4.97	5.00	5.56
Return on Avg Stockholders' Equity %	7.94	13.78	17.32	16.19
Return on Average Assets %	4.65	8.56	9.50	9.72
Current Ratio	3.05	1.98	2.23	1.67
Debt / Equity %	53.14	8.13	12.98	16.00

Compound Growth %'s	EPS %	1.27	Net Income %	17.68	Total Revenues %	41.64

Comments

The Company declared 3 for 2, 2 for 1, and 3 for 2 stock splits in April 1996, September 1996, and December 1996, respectively. All per share amounts have been adjusted for consistency. Some of the Company's acquisitions have been accounted for as pooling of interests. Financial data has been restated accordingly. The 35.8% increase in revenues during fiscal 1998 is a result of higher sales and the inclusion of acquired businesses for a full year that had been accounted for under the purchase method of accounting. At April 30, 1998, the Company had $81.6 million of goodwill recorded as an asset which equated to approximately 45% of book value. For the nine months ended January 31, 1999, the Company reported revenue and net income of $384.4 million and $9,988,000 ($.21 per share) as compared to $285.3 million and $9,988,000 ($.21 per share) for the same period of the preceding year.

Officers	Position	Ownership Information	
William G. MIller	Chairman	Number of Shares Outstanding	45,941,814
Jeffrey I. Badgley	President, CEO	Market Capitalization	$ 226,952,561
Adam L. Dunayer	Vice President, CFO	Number of Shareholders	10,000
Frank Madonia	Vice President, Secretary	Where Listed / Symbol	NYSE / MLR

Other Information			
Transfer Agent	SunTrust Bank Atlanta, GA	SIC Code	3713
Auditor	Arthur Andersen LLP	Employees	4,131
		Web Site	millerind.com

MobiNetix Systems, Inc.

500 Oakmead Parkway Sunnyvale, CA 94086 Telephone (408)524-4200 Fax (408)524-4299

Company Description

MobilNetix Systems, Inc. is the successor to PenUltimate, a company which was engaged in developing and marketing application software products for sales and other mobile professionals. The mission of MobiNetix is to develop and market state-of-the-art interactive electronic (e-) transaction terminals and consumer-friendly applications to the retail, hospitality, financial services, medical and healthcare, insurance and identification/security industries. The Company provides e-transaction networking solutions for the retail industry and contract-based service organizations designed to increase efficiency, expand capabilities and be integrated into the emerging global e-commerce infrastructure.

	06/30/98	06/30/97	06/30/96	06/30/95
Per Share Information				
Stock Price as of 12/31	2.94	1.50	6.50	27.10
Earnings Per Share	-1.36	-2.35	-1.23	-0.29
Price / Earnings Ratio	n.a.	n.a.	n.a.	n.a.
Book Value Per Share	-5.78	-6.94	-5.63	-0.85
Price / Book Value %	n.a.	n.a.	n.a.	n.a.
Dividends Per Share	0.0	0.0	0.0	0.0
Annual Financial Data				
Operating Results (000's)				
Total Revenues	11,156.5	2,156.2	807.2	545.4
Costs & Expenses	-13,278.8	-5,291.8	-2,455.7	-929.9
Income Before Taxes and Other	-2,122.3	-3,135.6	-1,648.4	-384.5
Other Items	0.0	0.0	0.0	0.0
Income Tax	0.0	-2.4	-0.8	-0.8
Net Income	-2,122.3	-3,138.0	-1,649.2	-385.3
Cash Flow From Operations	-4,535.2	-145.1	-1,435.9	-349.1
Balance Sheet (000's)				
Cash & Equivalents	6,465.9	3,421.5	2,438.4	n.a.
Total Current Assets	9,892.1	5,192.4	2,829.3	n.a.
Fixed Assets, Net	309.5	261.2	137.5	n.a.
Total Assets	10,201.6	5,453.6	2,966.8	n.a.
Total Current Liabilities	4,259.4	5,002.0	714.1	n.a.
Long-Term Debt	0.0	0.0	0.0	n.a.
Stockholders' Equity	5,942.2	451.6	2,234.2	n.a.
Performance & Financial Condition				
Return on Total Revenues %	-19.02	-145.53	-204.30	-70.65
Return on Avg Stockholders' Equity %	-66.39	-233.67	-164.92	n.a.
Return on Average Assets %	-27.11	-74.53	-78.53	n.a.
Current Ratio	2.32	1.04	3.96	n.a.
Debt / Equity %	n.a.	n.a.	n.a.	n.a.

Compound Growth %'s	EPS % n.a.	Net Income % n.a.	Total Revenues %	173.49

Comments

Due to continued market acceptance of the Company's signature capture and interactive transaction devices, revenue increased by 449% during the last fiscal year. Research and development expenses also rose 52% to $3.0 million during the last year. The Company has issued three series of preferred stock to provide adequate working capital through fiscal 1998. Management expected that the cash on hand at June 30, 1998, would be adequate to fund operations through fiscal 1999. The liquidation preferences of preferred issues were deducted from equity to calculate the book value of the common shares. For the six months ended December 31, 1998, revenues and net income were $10.1 million and $464,932 ($.07 per share) as compared to $3.9 million and a net loss of $1,306,075 ($.91 per share) in the same period of the preceding year.

Officers	Position	Ownership Information	
Paul Dali	Chairman	Number of Shares Outstanding	1,868,925
Aziz Valliani	President, CEO	Market Capitalization	$ 5,494,640
David M. Licurse, Sr.	Vice President, CFO	Number of Shareholders	350
William L. Powar	Director	Where Listed / Symbol	OTC-BB / NETX

Other Information			
Transfer Agent	U.S. Stock Transfer Corp. Glendale, CA	SIC Code	7372
Auditor	Arthur Andersen LLP	Employees	60
Market Maker	Sharpe Capital Inc. (800)355-5781	Web Site	mobinetix.com
	Paragon Capital Corporation (800)345-0505		

Mobile America Corporation

10475 Fortune Parkway, Suite 110   Jacksonville, FL 32256   Telephone (904)363-6339   Fax (904)363-8338

Company Description

Mobile America Corporation provides property and casualty insurance, life insurance, insurance administrative services to various state underwriting associations on a fee for service basis, and premium financing. The underwriting and marketing of minimum requirement automobile insurance in the state of Florida accounts for more than 80% of the Company's total revenues. In late 1998, the Company disclosed that it had been in a number of discussions for it to be acquired. But a decline in earnings and a volatile stock market caused management to postpone such discussions and refocus on operations. The Company was founded in 1968.

	12/31/98	12/31/97	12/31/96	12/31/95
Per Share Information				
Stock Price	3.75	13.75	10.00	9.75
Earnings Per Share	-0.14	0.86	1.05	0.84
Price / Earnings Ratio	n.a.	15.99	9.52	11.61
Book Value Per Share	5.10	5.54	5.78	8.29
Price / Book Value %	73.53	248.19	173.01	117.61
Dividends Per Share	0.35	0.35	0.30	0.16
Annual Financial Data				
Operating Results (000's)				
Total Revenues	48,302.0	58,810.2	48,163.9	52,925.9
Costs & Expenses	-50,679.8	-49,942.3	-39,177.8	-44,340.2
Income Before Taxes and Other	-2,377.8	8,867.9	8,986.2	8,585.7
Other Items	0.0	0.0	0.0	0.0
Income Tax	1,378.2	-2,692.1	-1,414.8	-2,586.0
Net Income	-999.5	6,175.8	7,571.4	5,999.7
Cash Flow From Operations	-9,756.3	-13,218.6	-2,342.7	12,881.7
Balance Sheet (000's)				
Cash & Equivalents	1,082.4	4,518.0	1,802.6	6,510.5
Total Current Assets	106,248.3	44,170.8	57,550.5	127,329.0
Fixed Assets, Net	2,153.4	1,553.7	1,071.7	900.0
Total Assets	124,663.4	138,242.1	168,414.5	182,771.2
Total Current Liabilities	49,166.2	45,771.5	55,085.0	139,103.2
Long-Term Debt	9,600.0	12,000.0	12,000.0	12,000.0
Stockholders' Equity	36,559.4	39,685.7	36,177.0	31,313.0
Performance & Financial Condition				
Return on Total Revenues %	-2.07	10.50	15.72	11.34
Return on Avg Stockholders' Equity %	-2.62	16.28	22.44	19.35
Return on Average Assets %	-0.76	4.03	4.31	3.67
Current Ratio	2.16	0.97	1.04	0.92
Debt / Equity %	26.26	30.24	33.17	38.32

Compound Growth %'s	EPS %	n.a.	Net Income %	n.a.	Total Revenues %	n.a.

Comments

The reported loss for 1998 is a significant departure from the net income of earlier years. The loss is primarily due to lower earned revenues, increases in loss reserves, less favorable reinsurance recoveries and higher operating expenses. The Company had processing backlogs as a result of computer modification problems during the Year 2000 conversion process which contributed to the loss. Significant expenses were incurred in dealing with the problems. Professional fees were also incurred in 1998 in connection with the possible sale of the Company. Although we should watch very closely, management was optimistic that cash flow would improve as rate increases took effect, premium volume improved, and the settlement of losses returned to a more normal pattern.

Officers	Position	Ownership Information	
Allan J. McCorkle	President, CEO	Number of Shares Outstanding	7,167,542
Thomas L. Stinson	Senior VP, CFO	Market Capitalization	$ 26,878,283
D. A. Sanders	Senior VP	Number of Shareholders	384
T. J. McCorkle	Vice President	Where Listed / Symbol	NASDAQ / MAME

Other Information			
Transfer Agent	ChaseMellon Shareholder Services Ridgefield Park, NJ	SIC Code	6331
Auditor	Cherry Bekaert & Holland, LLP	Employees	300
		Web Site	maig.com

Monterey Pasta Company

1528 Moffett Street   Salinas, CA 93905   Telephone (831)753-6262   Fax (831)753-6987

Company Description

Monterey Pasta Company is a producer and distributor of refrigerated pasta and sauces to grocery store chains nationwide. The Company currently offers 57 varieties of contemporary gourmet pasta products that are produced using the Company's proprietary recipes, including refrigerated cut pasta, ravioli, tortelloni, and pasta sauces. Monterey Pasta believes its pasta products appeal to health-conscious consumers who are seeking excellent quality, convenience and value, as well as innovative taste combinations. As of December 31, 1998, approximately 3,460 grocery and club stores offered Monterey Pasta's products. The Company was founded in 1989.

	12/27/98	12/31/97	12/31/96	12/31/95
Per Share Information				
Stock Price as of 12/31	1.44	1.37	1.62	4.88
Earnings Per Share	0.16	0.02	-1.13	-3.50
Price / Earnings Ratio	9.00	68.50	n.a.	n.a.
Book Value Per Share	0.44	0.48	0.46	0.26
Price / Book Value %	327.27	285.42	352.17	1,876.92
Dividends Per Share	0.0	0.0	0.0	0.0
Annual Financial Data				
Operating Results (000's)				
Total Revenues	26,234.1	23,450.9	24,638.2	18,766.9
Costs & Expenses	-24,166.0	-22,696.3	-32,519.7	-20,064.1
Income Before Taxes and Other	2,068.1	495.1	-8,453.0	-1,297.2
Other Items	0.0	36.9	220.0	-21,279.3
Income Tax	-31.1	-20.7	0.0	0.0
Net Income	2,037.0	511.3	-8,233.0	-22,576.5
Cash Flow From Operations	3,056.9	-1,026.5	-8,083.1	-8,475.5
Balance Sheet (000's)				
Cash & Equivalents	61.6	410.2	724.7	1,937.9
Total Current Assets	5,229.1	5,589.3	4,592.9	5,926.5
Fixed Assets, Net	5,261.7	5,057.8	5,700.9	5,339.0
Total Assets	10,835.3	11,029.0	10,788.8	11,691.0
Total Current Liabilities	3,628.3	3,145.1	4,969.8	5,328.8
Long-Term Debt	497.8	523.7	734.3	4,130.6
Stockholders' Equity	6,709.2	7,360.2	5,084.7	2,231.6
Performance & Financial Condition				
Return on Total Revenues %	7.76	2.18	-33.42	-120.30
Return on Avg Stockholders' Equity %	28.96	8.22	-225.06	-198.02
Return on Average Assets %	18.63	4.69	-73.25	-133.56
Current Ratio	1.44	1.78	0.92	1.11
Debt / Equity %	7.42	7.12	14.44	185.10

Compound Growth %'s	EPS % n.a.	Net Income % n.a.	Total Revenues %	11.81

Comments

The Company discontinued its restaurant operations in 1995, resulting in an $18.5 million loss ($3.30 per share). Capital was raised through the issuance of a preferred class of stock which was converted to common in 1997. The increase in 1998 revenues was attributable to an increase in the number stores carrying Company products. Management reports that gross margins have stabilized at a healthy 41% of sales. Two retail customers, Costco and Sam's, accounted for 46% and 33% of sales, respectively, in 1998. The Company has $11.5 million of tax loss carryovers to offset future taxable income.

Officers	Position	Ownership Information	
R. Lance Hewitt	President, CEO	Number of Shares Outstanding	15,206,259
Stephen L. Brinkman	CFO, Secretary	Market Capitalization	$ 21,897,013
Peter F. Klein	General Manager	Number of Shareholders	4,316
Roy G. Scotton	Other	Where Listed / Symbol	NASDAQ / PSTA

Other Information			
Transfer Agent	Corporate Stock Transfer, Inc. Denver, CO	SIC Code	2098
Auditor	BDO Seidman LLP	Employees	165
		Web Site	montereypasta.com

Movie Star, Inc.

136 Madison Avenue New York, NY 10016 Telephone (212)684-3400 Fax (212)684-3295

Company Description

Movie Star, Inc. designs, manufactures, markets and sells an extensive line of ladies' sleepwear, robes, leisurewear, loungewear, panties and daywear, and also operates retail outlet stores under the names Movie Star Factory Stores, Bargain Box Factory Stores, Bobby's Place, Bobby's Menswear and A Little Xtra from Movie Star. During fiscal 1998, the Company exited the men's, women's and children's screen printed tee shirt business. During fiscal 1996, the Company exited from its men's work and leisure shirt division. The Company was founded in 1935.

	06/30/98	06/30/97	06/30/96	06/30/95
Per Share Information				
Stock Price as of 12/31	1.62	0.62	0.56	0.37
Earnings Per Share	0.08	0.04	-0.38	-0.36
Price / Earnings Ratio	20.25	15.50	n.a.	n.a.
Book Value Per Share	0.37	0.28	0.25	0.62
Price / Book Value %	437.84	221.43	224.00	59.68
Dividends Per Share	0.0	0.0	0.0	0.0
Annual Financial Data				
Operating Results (000's)				
Total Revenues	64,694.0	62,030.0	84,115.0	101,946.0
Costs & Expenses	-63,476.0	-61,446.0	-88,413.0	-106,471.0
Income Before Taxes and Other	1,218.0	584.0	-5,368.0	-5,275.0
Other Items	0.0	0.0	0.0	0.0
Income Tax	-16.0	-65.0	90.0	246.0
Net Income	1,202.0	519.0	-5,278.0	-5,029.0
Cash Flow From Operations	-2,590.0	1,700.0	18,077.0	3,320.0
Balance Sheet (000's)				
Cash & Equivalents	546.0	3,035.0	2,283.0	103.0
Total Current Assets	30,477.0	26,316.0	27,211.0	48,656.0
Fixed Assets, Net	3,551.0	4,262.0	4,569.0	6,053.0
Total Assets	36,743.0	33,957.0	34,610.0	57,204.0
Total Current Liabilities	10,561.0	7,680.0	7,805.0	26,008.0
Long-Term Debt	20,980.0	22,336.0	23,383.0	22,496.0
Stockholders' Equity	5,202.0	3,941.0	3,422.0	8,700.0
Performance & Financial Condition				
Return on Total Revenues %	1.86	0.84	-6.27	-4.93
Return on Avg Stockholders' Equity %	26.29	14.10	-87.08	-44.84
Return on Average Assets %	3.40	1.51	-11.50	-7.92
Current Ratio	2.89	3.43	3.49	1.87
Debt / Equity %	403.31	566.76	683.31	258.57

Compound Growth %'s	EPS %	n.a.	Net Income %	n.a.	Total Revenues %	-14.07

Comments

Between 1992 and 1997, the Company experienced a decline in revenue as a result of consolidations in the retail industry, the high cost of domestic manufacturing and manufacturing difficulties with offshore contractors which resulted in quality control problems. Management appears to have regained the upper hand by maintaining an in-house design staff on location in Mexico which oversees foreign production. With back-to-back profitable years and the first increase in revenues in many years, the Company reports a swelling backlog, $33 million at June 30, 1998 compared to $21.3 million a year earlier. For the six months ended December 31, 1998, the Company reported revenue and net income of $44.7 million and $3,513,000 ($.23 per share) as compared to $37.9 million and $1,825,000 ($.12 per share) for the same period of the preceding year.

Officers	Position	Ownership Information	
Mark M. David	Chairman, CEO	Number of Shares Outstanding	14,117,000
Melvyn Knigin	President, COO	Market Capitalization	$ 22,869,540
Saul Pomerantz	Exec VP, CFO	Number of Shareholders	908
Gary W. Krat	Director	Where Listed / Symbol	NASDAQ / MSI

Other Information			
Transfer Agent	American Stock Transfer & Trust Co. New York, NY	SIC Code	2340
Auditor	Deloitte & Touche LLP	Employees	667

Moyco Technologies, Inc.

200 Commerce Drive Montgomeryville, PA 18936 Telephone (215)855-4300 Fax (215)362-3809

Company Description

Moyco Technologies, Inc. operates in two business segments: Dental Supplies and Precision Abrasives. The Dental Supplies segment involves the manufacturing, marketing and distribution of dental supplies such as waxes, abrasives, medicaments, dental mirrors, endodontic instruments, materials and equipment, sundry dental items, hand instruments and sterilization items, and also involved the repacking of other dental products for the professional dental market. The Precision Abrasives segment involves the manufacturing of commercial coated abrasives, precision submicron coated abrasives, slurries and polishing agents. The Company was founded in 1968.

	06/30/98	06/30/97	06/30/96	06/30/95
Per Share Information				
Stock Price as of 12/31	1.12	5.11	8.41	6.36
Earnings Per Share	0.23	-0.22	0.17	0.12
Price / Earnings Ratio	4.87	n.a.	49.47	53.00
Book Value Per Share	1.29	1.06	1.12	0.96
Price / Book Value %	86.82	482.08	750.89	662.50
Dividends Per Share	0.0	0.0	0.0	0.0
Annual Financial Data				
Operating Results (000's)				
Total Revenues	15,430.6	13,995.6	11,995.7	12,006.8
Costs & Expenses	-15,155.0	-15,383.8	-11,419.7	-10,895.8
Income Before Taxes and Other	275.7	-1,388.2	576.0	1,014.7
Other Items	1,108.5	0.0	355.6	0.0
Income Tax	-322.8	379.6	-186.4	-478.3
Net Income	1,061.3	-1,008.6	745.1	536.3
Cash Flow From Operations	-1,568.0	498.6	1,456.5	864.3
Balance Sheet (000's)				
Cash & Equivalents	1,486.6	1,454.1	1,402.1	1,097.3
Total Current Assets	8,883.1	7,949.2	6,517.1	6,512.5
Fixed Assets, Net	6,035.7	6,473.4	5,893.9	5,991.6
Total Assets	15,739.9	15,044.7	12,544.0	12,983.7
Total Current Liabilities	3,307.7	4,219.9	1,799.7	1,922.8
Long-Term Debt	5,946.3	5,255.3	5,616.1	6,735.5
Stockholders' Equity	5,880.0	4,820.6	4,975.5	4,150.6
Performance & Financial Condition				
Return on Total Revenues %	6.88	-7.21	6.21	4.47
Return on Avg Stockholders' Equity %	19.84	-20.59	16.33	13.82
Return on Average Assets %	6.90	-7.31	5.84	4.72
Current Ratio	2.69	1.88	3.62	3.39
Debt / Equity %	101.13	109.02	112.88	162.28

Compound Growth %'s	EPS %	24.22	Net Income %	25.55	Total Revenues %	8.72

Comments

In September 1998, the Company declared a 10% stock dividend. All per share amounts have been restated for the dividend. On December 31, 1997, the Company sold two of its businesses resulting in nonrecurring gains of $1,883,000 and made nonrecurring payments of $775,000 in connection with the sales that was expensed as research and development. All of these items are reflected in Other Items in the operating results above. Management was pleased with the ending balances noting that working capital and shareholders' equity increased 49% and 22%, respectively. For the six months ended December 31, 1998, the Company reported revenues and a net loss of $7.3 million and $31,156 ($.01 per share) as compared to $7.8 million and a net profit of $782,229 ($.17 per share) in the same period of the preceding year.

Officers	Position	Ownership Information	
Marvin E. Sternberg	Chairman, CEO	Number of Shares Outstanding	4,551,624
William Woodhead	Secretary, Treasurer	Market Capitalization	$ 5,097,819
Joseph S. Sternberg	Vice President	Number of Shareholders	609
Mark E. Sternberg	Vice President	Where Listed / Symbol	NASDAQ / MOYC

Other Information			
Transfer Agent	Company Office Montgomeryville, PA	SIC Code	3843
Auditor	Arthur Andersen LLP	Employees	161
		Web Site	moycotech.com/moyco

Multigraphics, Inc.

431 Lakeview Court   Mt. Prospect, IL 60056   Telephone (800)266-8584   Fax (800)393-4630

Company Description

Multigraphics, Inc. is a distributor of equipment and supplies and a service provider to the U.S. graphic arts industry. The Company has completed its transition from a manufacturer of offset duplicating machines to focus solely on distribution of equipment and supplies and providing service to the graphic arts industry. The Company sells a variety of equipment, systems and supplies under the Multigraphics brand name and increasingly sells products carrying the applicable manufacturers' brand names. Since December 1997, the Company has acquired four regional graphic arts dealers as part of its strategy of expanding its target customer base in the in-plant and smaller to mid-size commercial printing market segments. The Company, founded as Addressograph Securities Corporation in 1924, filed for Chapter 11 bankruptcy protection in 1993 when it was known as AM International, Inc.

	07/31/98	07/31/97	07/31/96	07/31/95
Per Share Information				
Stock Price as of 12/31	3.00	2.94	1.75	0.50
Earnings Per Share	0.38	0.04	-7.19	0.66
Price / Earnings Ratio	7.89	73.50	n.a.	0.76
Book Value Per Share	-3.59	-4.23	0.82	8.02
Price / Book Value %	n.a.	n.a.	213.41	6.31
Dividends Per Share	0.0	0.0	0.0	0.0
Annual Financial Data				
Operating Results (000's)				
Total Revenues	95,462.0	90,069.0	168,221.0	191,707.0
Costs & Expenses	-93,745.0	-89,966.0	-188,263.0	-197,384.0
Income Before Taxes and Other	1,717.0	103.0	-20,254.0	-5,677.0
Other Items	0.0	0.0	-25,342.0	8,764.0
Income Tax	-646.0	0.0	97.0	1,526.0
Net Income	1,071.0	103.0	-45,499.0	4,613.0
Cash Flow From Operations	-2,764.0	-15,639.0	-3,919.0	-4,894.0
Balance Sheet (000's)				
Cash & Equivalents	2,869.0	10,376.0	2,560.0	12,563.0
Total Current Assets	31,412.0	33,759.0	85,643.0	140,427.0
Fixed Assets, Net	9,554.0	10,222.0	10,867.0	12,453.0
Total Assets	45,639.0	44,900.0	97,962.0	163,072.0
Total Current Liabilities	42,615.0	39,683.0	73,923.0	78,925.0
Long-Term Debt	1,048.0	3,352.0	8,527.0	14,915.0
Stockholders' Equity	-10,144.0	-11,900.0	2,296.0	48,301.0
Performance & Financial Condition				
Return on Total Revenues %	1.12	0.11	-27.05	2.41
Return on Avg Stockholders' Equity %	n.a.	n.a.	-179.85	20.06
Return on Average Assets %	2.37	0.14	-34.86	3.42
Current Ratio	0.74	0.85	1.16	1.78
Debt / Equity %	n.a.	n.a.	371.39	30.88

Compound Growth %'s	EPS %	n.a.	Net Income %	n.a.	Total Revenues %	n.a.

Comments

The Company executed a 1 for 2 1/2 reverse stock split in fiscal 1997. All per share amounts have been restated for consistency. Fiscal 1996 results include a $25.3 million loss from discontinued operations whereas fiscal 1995 results include an $8.8 million gain from discontinued operations. As we look at the latest annual report, we see a profitable company operating with a weak financial condition. Although most long term debt has been removed, the Company has a negative working capital. For the six months ended January 31, 1999, the Company reported revenues and a net loss of $50.6 million and $287,000 ($.10 per share) as compared to $42.9 million and $323,000 ($.11 per share) for the same period of fiscal 1998.

Officers	Position	Ownership Information	
Thomas D. Rooney	President, CEO	Number of Shares Outstanding	2,829,526
Steven R. Andrews	Vice President, Secretary	Market Capitalization	$ 8,488,578
Mark F. Duchesne	Vice President	Number of Shareholders	1,000
Donald W. Hanigan	Vice President	Where Listed / Symbol	AMEX / MTI

Other Information			
Transfer Agent	First Chicago Trust Co. of New York Jersey City, NJ	SIC Code	3555
Auditor	Arthur Andersen LLP	Employees	670
		Web Site	multigraphics.com

NBI, Inc.

1880 Industrial Circle, Ste. F   Longmont, CO 80501   Telephone (303)684-2700   Fax (303)684-2804

Company Description

In August 1995, NBI, Inc. acquired L.E. Smith Glass Company, founded in 1907. L.E. Smith was one of the few remaining handmade pressed glass manufacturers in the United States which manufactured and sold an assortment of crystal and colored glass giftware and lighting fixtures for the domestic consumer market. Also in August 1995, the Company acquired Belle Vernon Motel Corporation which owns an 81 room, full service Holiday Inn. The Company also owns 80% of Krazy Colors, Inc., a small children's paint and novelty toy manufacturing company. Previously, the Company operated primarily in the computer industry. Those operations were discontinued after the Company emerged from bankruptcy in 1992.

	06/30/98	06/30/97	06/30/96	06/30/95
Per Share Information				
Stock Price as of 12/31	0.81	0.59	0.75	0.81
Earnings Per Share	0.02	0.13	0.01	-0.07
Price / Earnings Ratio	40.50	4.54	75.00	n.a.
Book Value Per Share	0.16	0.13	n.a.	-0.13
Price / Book Value %	506.25	453.85	n.a.	n.a.
Dividends Per Share	0.0	0.0	n.a.	0.0
Annual Financial Data				
Operating Results (000's)				
Total Revenues	14,698.0	14,495.0	12,199.0	5,506.0
Costs & Expenses	-14,888.0	-13,700.0	-11,802.0	-5,733.0
Income Before Taxes and Other	-190.0	795.0	397.0	-227.0
Other Items	290.0	354.0	-137.0	-256.0
Income Tax	72.0	-105.0	-172.0	0.0
Net Income	172.0	1,044.0	88.0	-483.0
Cash Flow From Operations	367.0	1,499.0	3,410.0	224.0
Balance Sheet (000's)				
Cash & Equivalents	209.0	333.0	782.0	1,931.0
Total Current Assets	4,490.0	4,223.0	5,308.0	7,213.0
Fixed Assets, Net	7,436.0	6,869.0	4,558.0	55.0
Total Assets	12,205.0	11,496.0	10,195.0	7,557.0
Total Current Liabilities	7,369.0	8,420.0	3,844.0	2,717.0
Long-Term Debt	1,351.0	1,604.0	224.0	56.0
Stockholders' Equity	1,300.0	1,025.0	300.0	-854.0
Performance & Financial Condition				
Return on Total Revenues %	1.17	7.20	0.72	-8.77
Return on Avg Stockholders' Equity %	14.80	157.58	n.a.	n.a.
Return on Average Assets %	1.45	9.63	0.99	-5.56
Current Ratio	0.61	0.50	n.a.	2.65
Debt / Equity %	103.92	156.49	n.a.	n.a.

Compound Growth %'s	EPS % n.a.	Net Income % n.a.	Total Revenues % 38.72

Comments

Fiscal 1998 results include $290,000 of income from the Internal Revenue Service. Yes, the IRS agreed to forgive interest as long as it gets its $5.3 million of back taxes in accordance with a new schedule. At June 30, 1998, the Company had a substantial working capital deficiency and the auditor issued a going concern qualification in its report on the Company's financial statement. For the six months ended December 31, 1998, the Company reported revenues and net income of $9.5 million and $684,000 ($.08 per share) as compared to $7.2 million and a net loss of $158,000 ($.02 per share) for the comparable period of the preceding year. At December 31, 1998, the Company had positive working capital.

Officers	Position	Ownership Information	
Jay H. Lustig	Chairman, CEO	Number of Shares Outstanding	8,088,320
Marjorie A. Cogan	Controller, Secretary	Market Capitalization	$ 6,551,539
Martin J. Noonan	Director	Number of Shareholders	1,260
		Where Listed / Symbol	OTC-BB / NBII

Other Information

Transfer Agent	Boston EquiServe Boston, MA		SIC Code	3220
Auditor	BDO Seidman LLP		Employees	237
Market Maker	Thomas Green Securities Inc.	(800)421-0296	Web Site	lesmithglass.com
	Wm. V. Frankel & Co., Inc.	(800)631-3091		

Napco Security Systems, Inc.

333 Bayview Avenue   Amityville, NY 11701   Telephone (516)842-9400   Fax (516)842-8220

Company Description

NAPCO Security Systems, Inc. is engaged in the development, manufacture, distribution and sale of security alarm products and door security devices for commercial and residential installations. The Company's business involves a high technology element. A substantial amount of the Company's efforts are expended to develop and improve the products. During the fiscal years ended June 30, 1998, 1997, and 1996, the Company expended approximately $3,817,000, $3,340,000 and $3,296,000, respectively, on research and development activities. The Company was founded in 1969.

	06/30/98	06/30/97	06/30/96	06/30/95
Per Share Information				
Stock Price as of 12/31	4.00	5.87	3.75	3.50
Earnings Per Share	0.48	0.37	0.23	0.12
Price / Earnings Ratio	8.33	15.86	16.30	29.17
Book Value Per Share	8.26	7.15	6.77	6.54
Price / Book Value %	48.43	82.10	55.39	53.52
Dividends Per Share	0.0	0.0	0.0	0.0
Annual Financial Data				
Operating Results (000's)				
Total Revenues	50,416.0	53,302.0	49,088.0	48,078.0
Costs & Expenses	-48,903.0	-50,738.0	-47,438.0	-47,034.0
Income Before Taxes and Other	1,513.0	2,244.0	1,529.0	1,044.0
Other Items	0.0	0.0	0.0	0.0
Income Tax	525.0	-605.0	-515.0	-532.0
Net Income	2,038.0	1,639.0	1,014.0	512.0
Cash Flow From Operations	-107.0	2,758.0	3,535.0	693.0
Balance Sheet (000's)				
Cash & Equivalents	1,989.0	1,006.0	426.0	368.0
Total Current Assets	44,153.0	42,021.0	41,529.0	39,916.0
Fixed Assets, Net	11,491.0	12,088.0	12,549.0	12,503.0
Total Assets	58,563.0	57,244.0	57,319.0	55,739.0
Total Current Liabilities	10,211.0	11,885.0	12,853.0	11,256.0
Long-Term Debt	18,644.0	13,313.0	14,150.0	15,275.0
Stockholders' Equity	28,833.0	31,218.0	29,574.0	28,560.0
Performance & Financial Condition				
Return on Total Revenues %	4.04	3.07	2.07	1.06
Return on Avg Stockholders' Equity %	6.79	5.39	3.49	1.81
Return on Average Assets %	3.52	2.86	1.79	0.95
Current Ratio	4.32	3.54	3.23	3.55
Debt / Equity %	64.66	42.65	47.85	53.48

Compound Growth %'s	EPS %	58.74	Net Income %	58.48	Total Revenues %	1.60

Comments

Pricing pressures have caused a reduction in revenue as well as gross margins. The loss of a major customer also lowered revenue. Increased export sales offset some of the decline. A settlement with the Internal Revenue Service resulted in a reversal of $900,000 in reserves and a net tax benefit for fiscal 1998. Net income and earnings per share would have approximated one-half of the numbers reported above with a normal tax expense provision. In May 1998, the Company repurchased 889,576 shares of its stock from a co-founder for $5.00 per share to be paid over a four year period. For the six months ended December 31, 1998, the Company reported revenues and net income of $22.0 million and $404,000 ($.11 per share), which includes a net income tax benefit of $561,000, as compared to $23.7 million and $588,000 ($.13 per share) for the same period of the preceding year.

Officers	Position	Ownership Information	
Richard Soloway	President, CEO	Number of Shares Outstanding	3,489,651
Kevin S. Buchel	Senior VP, CFO	Market Capitalization	$ 13,958,604
Randy B. Blaustein	Director	Number of Shareholders	600
Andrew J. Wilder	Director	Where Listed / Symbol	NASDAQ / NSSC

Other Information			
Transfer Agent	Continental Stock Transfer & Trust Co. Jersey City, NJ	SIC Code	3669
Auditor	Arthur Andersen LLP	Employees	1,000
		Web Site	napcosecurity.com

Nastech Pharmaceutical Company Inc.

45 Davids Drive   Hauppauge, NY 11788   Telephone (516)273-0101   Fax (516)273-0252

Company Description

Nastech Pharmaceutical Company is engaged in the research, development, manufacturing and commercialization of nasally administered forms of prescription and over-the-counter pharmaceuticals that are currently delivered in oral, injectable or other dosage forms. The nasal delivery of certain pharmaceuticals may enable more rapid systemic absorption, lower required dosages, and quicker onset of desired effect. The Company's first commercially available pharmaceutical is a prescription pain reliever marketed as Stadol® by Bristol-Myers Squibb for the treatment of moderate to severe pain and the acute pain of migraine. Similarly, Nascobal™, the Company's nasal Vitamin B-12 product, provides both therapeutic and patient benefits over injectable therapy for chronic Vitamin B-12 deficiency anemia. An additional five products are in varying stages of development.

	12/31/98	12/31/97	12/31/96	06/30/95
Per Share Information				
Stock Price	3.31	12.87	20.00	9.75
Earnings Per Share	-0.14	-0.76	-0.01	-0.03
Price / Earnings Ratio	n.a.	n.a.	n.a.	n.a.
Book Value Per Share	4.00	4.09	2.51	1.33
Price / Book Value %	82.75	314.67	796.81	733.08
Dividends Per Share	0.0	0.0	0.0	0.0
Annual Financial Data				
Operating Results (000's)				
Total Revenues	9,590.0	5,522.0	4,331.0	2,938.0
Costs & Expenses	-10,466.0	-10,068.0	-4,385.0	-3,017.0
Income Before Taxes and Other	-876.0	-4,546.0	-54.0	-79.0
Other Items	0.0	0.0	0.0	0.0
Income Tax	0.0	0.0	0.0	0.0
Net Income	-876.0	-4,546.0	-54.0	-79.0
Cash Flow From Operations	-2,591.0	-3,210.0	-272.0	5.0
Balance Sheet (000's)				
Cash & Equivalents	23,515.0	25,294.0	4,494.0	820.0
Total Current Assets	26,470.0	26,648.0	12,396.0	5,046.0
Fixed Assets, Net	1,033.0	708.0	385.0	400.0
Total Assets	27,518.0	27,371.0	12,894.0	6,035.0
Total Current Liabilities	2,016.0	2,427.0	1,054.0	602.0
Long-Term Debt	0.0	15.0	27.0	349.0
Stockholders' Equity	25,502.0	24,929.0	11,813.0	4,288.0
Performance & Financial Condition				
Return on Total Revenues %	-9.13	-82.33	-1.25	-2.69
Return on Avg Stockholders' Equity %	-3.47	-24.75	-0.67	-1.98
Return on Average Assets %	-3.19	-22.58	-0.57	-1.98
Current Ratio	13.13	10.98	11.76	8.38
Debt / Equity %	n.a.	0.06	0.23	8.14

Compound Growth %'s	EPS %	n.a.	Net Income %	n.a.	Total Revenues %	48.34

Comments

1998 revenues were sharply higher but included a nonrecurring minimum royalty payment of $2 million and a nonrecurring milestone payment of $3 million. 1999 revenues are expected to be lower. Research and development costs increased 31% to $6 million in 1998. The net loss was surprisingly small. The Company changed to calendar year reporting in 1996. 1995 results are for the twelve months ended June 30, 1995. Armed with a cash balance of $23.5 million, the Company has plenty of time to advance its products and develop new ones. Stockholders' equity and book value per share are comprised of approximately 92% cash which makes this stock look like a bargain.

Officers	Position	Ownership Information	
Devin N. Wenig	Chairman	Number of Shares Outstanding	6,376,915
Vincent D. Romeo	CEO	Market Capitalization	$ 21,107,589
Andrew Zinzi	CFO	Number of Shareholders	23,000
Joel Girsky	Secretary, Treasurer	Where Listed / Symbol	NASDAQ / NSTK

Other Information			
Transfer Agent	American Stock Transfer & Trust Co. New York, NY	SIC Code	2834
Auditor	KPMG LLP	Employees	46

Nathan's Famous, Inc.

1400 Old Country Road, Suite 400   Westbury, NY 11590   Telephone (516)338-8500   Fax (516)338-7220

Company Description

Nathan's Famous, Inc. develops and operates a chain of retail fast food style restaurants which feature a specialized menu including hot dogs manufactured with a proprietary spice formula, hamburgers, crinkle-cut french fries, and assorted sandwiches and platters. The Company primarily operates in the eastern region of the United States, with 27 Company-owned stores and 156 franchised units as of March 29, 1998. The Nathan's name was first used at the Company's original Coney Island restaurant in 1916. Famous investment journalist Herb Greenberg of The Street.com wrote "Should you relish owning the stock?". Let's take a look at the numbers below:

	03/29/98	03/30/97	03/31/96	03/26/95
Per Share Information				
Stock Price as of 12/31	4.00	3.81	3.69	3.37
Earnings Per Share	0.32	0.17	-1.35	-0.11
Price / Earnings Ratio	12.50	22.41	n.a.	n.a.
Book Value Per Share	4.99	4.65	4.48	5.82
Price / Book Value %	80.16	81.94	82.37	57.90
Dividends Per Share	0.0	0.0	0.0	0.0
Annual Financial Data				
Operating Results (000's)				
Total Revenues	28,877.0	26,575.0	26,441.0	26,201.0
Costs & Expenses	-27,059.0	-25,165.0	-32,914.0	-27,210.0
Income Before Taxes and Other	1,818.0	1,410.0	-6,473.0	-1,009.0
Other Items	0.0	0.0	0.0	0.0
Income Tax	-290.0	-622.0	94.0	492.0
Net Income	1,528.0	788.0	-6,379.0	-517.0
Cash Flow From Operations	2,286.0	762.0	-411.0	4,311.0
Balance Sheet (000's)				
Cash & Equivalents	1,306.0	647.0	801.0	4,086.0
Total Current Assets	11,906.0	10,456.0	9,911.0	11,471.0
Fixed Assets, Net	6,171.0	5,480.0	5,615.0	4,000.0
Total Assets	29,539.0	27,794.0	27,765.0	32,430.0
Total Current Liabilities	5,801.0	5,654.0	5,974.0	4,338.0
Long-Term Debt	0.0	0.0	0.0	63.0
Stockholders' Equity	23,586.0	21,976.0	21,142.0	27,474.0
Performance & Financial Condition				
Return on Total Revenues %	5.29	2.97	-24.13	-1.97
Return on Avg Stockholders' Equity %	6.71	3.66	-26.24	-1.87
Return on Average Assets %	5.33	2.84	-21.19	-1.59
Current Ratio	2.05	1.85	1.66	2.64
Debt / Equity %	n.a.	n.a.	n.a.	0.23

Compound Growth %'s	EPS % n.a.	Net Income % n.a.	Total Revenues % 3.29

Comments

After losses in fiscal 1995 and 1996, the Company took additional charges to clean up its balance sheet. It adopted a new accounting standard and reduced the carrying value of long-lived assets, which included restaurants that were closed, amounting to $3.9 million. Other nonrecurring charges regarding litigation, severance and lease obligations added another $1.2 million in expenses. The financial turnaround seems to be holding firm. Comparable Company-owned unit sales increased 3.8% in fiscal 1998. However, the Company still has intangible assets of $11.3 million on the books, a beefy 48% of book value. For the nine months ended December 31, 1998, the Company reported revenues and net income of $23.2 million and $1,737,000 ($.37 per share) as compared to $22.3 million and $1,325,000 ($.28 per share) for the same period of the preceding year.

Officers	Position	Ownership Information	
Howard M. Lorber	Chairman, CEO	Number of Shares Outstanding	4,722,216
Wayne Norbitz	President, COO	Market Capitalization	$ 18,888,864
Richard E. Boudreaux	Exec VP	Number of Shareholders	329
Carl Paley	Senior VP	Where Listed / Symbol	NASDAQ / NATH

Other Information			
Transfer Agent	American Stock Transfer & Trust Co. New York, NY	SIC Code	5812
Auditor	Arthur Andersen LLP	Employees	690

National Environmental Service Co.

12331 East 60th Street   Tulsa, OK 74146   Telephone (918)250-2227   Fax (918)250-1418

Company Description

National Environmental Service Co. is engaged in the business of providing cathodic protection for underground metal tanks, installation of spill and overfill protection, environmental site assessments, contaminated soil and water remediation, installation and removal of storage tanks, and the construction of fueling systems and related facilities. In the thirteen years since its formation in 1986, the Company has grown from one facility and eight employees to 157 employees operating from eight facilities.

	12/31/98	12/31/97	12/31/96	12/31/95
Per Share Information				
Stock Price	1.37	2.87	1.00	3.00
Earnings Per Share	0.19	0.11	-0.06	0.02
Price / Earnings Ratio	7.21	26.09	n.a.	150.00
Book Value Per Share	0.74	0.57	0.32	0.41
Price / Book Value %	185.14	503.51	312.50	731.71
Dividends Per Share	0.0	0.0	0.0	0.0
Annual Financial Data				
Operating Results (000's)				
Total Revenues	18,346.0	14,856.0	10,315.0	9,077.0
Costs & Expenses	-15,981.0	-13,652.0	-10,846.0	-8,922.0
Income Before Taxes and Other	2,365.0	1,204.0	-531.0	155.0
Other Items	0.0	0.0	0.0	0.0
Income Tax	-895.0	-458.0	160.0	-64.0
Net Income	1,470.0	746.0	-371.0	91.0
Cash Flow From Operations	28.0	-1,496.0	-563.0	-304.0
Balance Sheet (000's)				
Cash & Equivalents	152.0	90.0	119.0	9.0
Total Current Assets	10,639.0	8,245.0	4,771.0	3,613.0
Fixed Assets, Net	2,426.0	1,844.0	1,609.0	1,627.0
Total Assets	13,172.0	10,111.0	6,403.0	5,240.0
Total Current Liabilities	6,215.0	5,311.0	4,239.0	1,397.0
Long-Term Debt	1,007.0	588.0	326.0	1,420.0
Stockholders' Equity	5,753.0	4,099.0	1,822.0	2,371.0
Performance & Financial Condition				
Return on Total Revenues %	8.01	5.02	-3.60	1.00
Return on Avg Stockholders' Equity %	29.84	25.20	-17.70	4.32
Return on Average Assets %	12.63	9.03	-6.37	2.08
Current Ratio	1.71	1.55	1.13	2.59
Debt / Equity %	17.50	14.34	17.89	59.89

Compound Growth %'s	EPS %	111.79	Net Income %	152.79	Total Revenues %	26.43

Comments

Revenue grew 24.1% in 1998 due to increased purchases of cathodic protection kits by the Company's distributor network and increases in the installation of cathodic protection systems by the Company. The increased sales were caused in part by the December 1998 deadline for regulatory compliance by owners and operators of underground storage tanks. The 1996 loss was caused by problems encountered on a government contract and initial costs relating to the acquisition of two small companies. During 1997, 1,450,000 shares were issued in connection with a private placement and the exercise of stock options. These shares have diluted growth in earnings per share as compared to compound growth in net income.

Officers	Position	Ownership Information	
Eddy L. Patterson	Chairman, CEO	Number of Shares Outstanding	7,765,652
James Howell	President	Market Capitalization	$ 10,638,943
Albert A. McCutchan	Exec VP	Number of Shareholders	553
Larry G. Johnson	Secretary, Treasurer	Where Listed / Symbol	NASDAQ / NESC

Other Information			
Transfer Agent	Securities Transfer Corp. Dallas, TX	SIC Code	4955
Auditor	Tullius Taylor Sartain Sartain	Employees	157

National Home Health Care Corp.

700 White Plains Road   Scarsdale, NY 10583   Telephone (914)722-9000   Fax (914)722-9239

Company Description

National Home Health Care Corp. is a provider of home care services throughout the New York Metropolitan area and Long Island in the State of New York as well as in Fairfield and New Haven Counties in the State of Connecticut. The Company provides skilled nursing and para-professional services. The Company was founded and went public in 1983. In 1996, the outpatient medical service business of the Company, formerly known as Brevard Medical Center, Inc. and First Health, Inc., was reorganized as SunStar Healthcare, Inc. SunStar then went public itself, reducing the Company's interest therein to 37.6%. On October 30, 1998, the Company completed the acquisition of Accredited Health Services, Inc., a New Jersey licensed home health care agency with annual revenues approximating $5.3 million.

	07/31/98	07/31/97	07/31/96	07/31/95
Per Share Information				
Stock Price as of 12/31	4.75	4.75	5.37	5.25
Earnings Per Share	0.23	0.35	0.65	0.27
Price / Earnings Ratio	20.65	13.57	8.26	19.44
Book Value Per Share	4.67	4.45	4.22	3.80
Price / Book Value %	101.71	106.74	127.25	138.16
Dividends Per Share	0.0	0.0	0.0	0.0
Annual Financial Data				
Operating Results (000's)				
Total Revenues	35,191.0	35,516.0	40,790.0	24,966.0
Costs & Expenses	-31,394.0	-31,770.0	-35,564.0	-22,414.0
Income Before Taxes and Other	2,167.0	3,134.0	5,216.0	2,552.0
Other Items	0.0	0.0	0.0	0.0
Income Tax	-964.0	-1,278.0	-1,859.0	-1,126.0
Net Income	1,203.0	1,856.0	3,357.0	1,426.0
Cash Flow From Operations	2,016.0	2,398.0	1,066.0	3,496.0
Balance Sheet (000's)				
Cash & Equivalents	10,992.0	9,324.0	8,929.0	9,237.0
Total Current Assets	20,356.0	18,401.0	18,681.0	16,243.0
Fixed Assets, Net	395.0	378.0	319.0	445.0
Total Assets	25,503.0	25,224.0	24,421.0	18,865.0
Total Current Liabilities	1,222.0	1,548.0	2,393.0	937.0
Long-Term Debt	0.0	0.0	0.0	0.0
Stockholders' Equity	24,281.0	23,360.0	21,504.0	17,914.0
Performance & Financial Condition				
Return on Total Revenues %	3.42	5.23	8.23	5.71
Return on Avg Stockholders' Equity %	5.05	8.27	17.03	8.24
Return on Average Assets %	4.74	7.48	15.51	7.75
Current Ratio	16.66	11.89	7.81	17.34
Debt / Equity %	n.a.	n.a.	n.a.	n.a.

Compound Growth %'s	EPS %	-5.20	Net Income %	-5.51	Total Revenues %	12.12

Comments

Fiscal 1996 includes a gain from the public offering of SunStar, referred to above, amounting to $1.5 million, approximately $.20 per share after tax. Revenues decreased in fiscal 1998 as a result of changes to Medicare reimbursement imposed by the Balanced Budget Act of 1997, partially offset by increased revenues from acquisitions. The Company expects a further decline in Medicare related reimbursements in fiscal 1999. The decline in fiscal 1997 revenues is primarily the result of the absence of SunStar revenues which had been consolidated up until 1997. The strong cash balances and the absence of long term debt position the Company for further growth through acquisition. For the six months ended January 31, 1999, the Company reported revenues and net income of $19.2 million and $271,000 ($.05 per share) as compared to $17.9 million and $549,000 ($.10 per share) in 1998.

Officers	Position	Ownership Information	
Steven Fialkow	President, COO	Number of Shares Outstanding	5,199,867
Frederick H. Fialkow	CEO	Market Capitalization	$ 24,699,368
Robert P. Heller	VP - Finance, CFO	Number of Shareholders	147
Ira Greifer	Director	Where Listed / Symbol	NASDAQ / NHHC

Other Information			
Transfer Agent	American Stock Transfer & Trust Co. New York, NY	SIC Code	8082
Auditor	Richard A. Eisner & Co., LLP	Employees	1,800

Netter Digital Entertainment, Inc.

5125 Lankershim Boulevard   North Hollywood, CA 91601   Telephone (818)753-1990   Fax (818)753-7655

Company Description

Netter Digital Entertainment, Inc. is engaged in the acquisition, development and production of television series, made-for-television movies, documentaries, theatrical motion pictures, theme park attractions and multimedia products. The Company specializes in combining live action film production with computer graphics and other digital imaging in the creation of dramatic series, documentaries, and children's programming, utilizing state-of-the-art entertainment production technology. The Company was founded in 1979 and had its initial public offering in 1995.

	06/30/98	06/30/97	06/30/96	06/30/95
Per Share Information				
Stock Price as of 12/31	1.41	2.00	2.50	4.37
Earnings Per Share	0.04	0.06	-0.11	0.05
Price / Earnings Ratio	35.25	33.33	n.a.	87.40
Book Value Per Share	1.46	1.41	1.22	0.07
Price / Book Value %	96.58	141.84	204.92	6,242.86
Dividends Per Share	0.0	0.0	0.0	0.0
Annual Financial Data				
Operating Results (000's)				
Total Revenues	32,344.7	25,828.6	23,768.4	18,880.0
Costs & Expenses	-32,142.7	-25,614.2	-24,025.3	-18,738.3
Income Before Taxes and Other	202.0	214.4	-256.8	141.7
Other Items	0.0	0.0	0.0	0.0
Income Tax	-41.0	-24.0	0.0	-44.4
Net Income	161.0	190.4	-256.8	97.4
Cash Flow From Operations	-878.4	1,449.9	-300.0	140.0
Balance Sheet (000's)				
Cash & Equivalents	1,634.8	2,574.5	2,181.2	650.0
Total Current Assets	6,092.9	4,999.4	2,939.5	960.8
Fixed Assets, Net	3,157.4	1,446.3	569.0	3.5
Total Assets	11,522.5	8,783.2	3,705.4	1,088.0
Total Current Liabilities	4,973.2	3,528.1	290.4	955.8
Long-Term Debt	0.0	0.0	0.0	0.0
Stockholders' Equity	5,211.6	5,015.1	3,414.5	131.6
Performance & Financial Condition				
Return on Total Revenues %	0.50	0.74	-1.08	0.52
Return on Avg Stockholders' Equity %	3.15	4.52	-14.49	74.92
Return on Average Assets %	1.59	3.05	-10.72	9.74
Current Ratio	1.23	1.42	10.12	1.01
Debt / Equity %	n.a.	n.a.	n.a.	n.a.

Compound Growth %'s	EPS %	-7.17	Net Income %	18.24	Total Revenues %	19.66

Comments

The Company acquired Videssence Lighting Products in January 1997, Videssence manufactures and distributes media lighting products which incorporate patented lighting technology. This was the last thing investors wanted to see for this young entertainment company. Management came to the same conclusion by December 31, 1998, when they classified Videssence as a discontinued operation. The loss will eliminate approximately half of stockholders' equity. For the six months ended December 31, 1998, the Company reported revenues of $13.5 million and a net loss of $2,362,818 ($.71 per share), including a loss from discontinued operations of $2,551,700, as compared to revenues and net income of $13.5 million and $8,552 ($.00 per share), respectively, for the same period of the preceding year. Going forward, we should expect the focus to be directly on the core entertainment business.

Officers	Position	Ownership Information	
Douglas Netter	President, CEO	Number of Shares Outstanding	3,334,405
John Copeland	Exec VP, Secretary	Market Capitalization	$ 4,701,511
Thomas L. Jorgenson	Exec VP, COO	Number of Shareholders	1,000
Chad Kalebic	CFO	Where Listed / Symbol	NASDAQ / NETT

Other Information			
Transfer Agent	U.S. Stock Transfer Corp. Glendale, CA	SIC Code	7812
Auditor	Feldman Sherb Ehrlich & Co. PC	Employees	69
		Web Site	netterdigital.com

Network Six, Inc.

475 Kilvert Street   Warwick, RI 02886   Telephone (401)732-9000   Fax (401)732-3948

Company Description

Network Six, Inc., formerly Network Solutions, Inc., is a provider of software development and computer-related consulting services to government and industry. Founded in 1976, the Company focuses on providing its services to state government health and human services agencies. The Company provides a range of information technology services, consisting primarily of systems integration, system design, software development, hardware planning and procurement, and personnel training. More recently, the Company has expanded its customer base to include private sector, non-profit and other organizations.

	12/31/98	12/31/97	12/31/96	12/31/95
Per Share Information				
Stock Price	3.75	2.75	0.62	3.12
Earnings Per Share	0.96	0.25	-2.71	-3.68
Price / Earnings Ratio	3.91	11.00	n.a.	n.a.
Book Value Per Share	0.67	-0.61	0.35	0.74
Price / Book Value %	559.70	n.a.	177.14	421.62
Dividends Per Share	0.0	0.0	0.0	0.0
Annual Financial Data				
Operating Results (000's)				
Total Revenues	10,478.4	11,492.4	7,502.3	20,995.4
Costs & Expenses	-8,804.4	-10,957.4	-10,035.6	-24,250.7
Income Before Taxes and Other	1,674.0	535.0	-2,533.4	-3,792.5
Other Items	0.0	0.0	0.0	0.0
Income Tax	-613.0	-128.0	775.0	1,365.1
Net Income	1,061.0	407.0	-1,758.3	-2,427.4
Cash Flow From Operations	1,066.0	1,854.1	2,230.5	-2,732.8
Balance Sheet (000's)				
Cash & Equivalents	1,442.0	1,291.9	127.6	1,205.7
Total Current Assets	4,741.5	4,936.1	4,196.3	13,606.8
Fixed Assets, Net	172.2	67.1	138.5	150.0
Total Assets	8,700.8	9,292.1	8,273.6	14,945.3
Total Current Liabilities	3,325.3	4,914.0	5,289.3	10,046.4
Long-Term Debt	952.0	742.2	63.9	0.0
Stockholders' Equity	3,808.9	2,955.4	2,748.8	4,644.5
Performance & Financial Condition				
Return on Total Revenues %	10.13	3.54	-23.44	-11.56
Return on Avg Stockholders' Equity %	31.37	14.27	-47.57	-63.88
Return on Average Assets %	11.79	4.63	-15.15	-20.23
Current Ratio	1.43	1.00	0.79	1.35
Debt / Equity %	24.99	25.11	2.32	n.a.

Compound Growth %'s	EPS % n.a.	Net Income % n.a.	Total Revenues % -20.68

Comments

After a number of years of declining revenue, management restructured a return to rising revenues and profits in 1997. Although the substantial completion of several projects reduced revenue in 1998, the lower reliance on subcontractor labor, which comes generally at a higher cost than the Company's internal staff, helped increase margins and net profit. The liquidation value of preferred shares outstanding was deducted from equity in determining the book value per common share and accrued dividends were deducted in computing earnings per share.

Officers	Position	Ownership Information	
Kenneth C. Kirsch	President, CEO	Number of Shares Outstanding	764,663
Joseph Murray	Senior VP	Market Capitalization	$ 2,867,486
Dorothy M. Cipolla	CFO, Treasurer	Number of Shareholders	391
Nicholas R. Supron	Director	Where Listed / Symbol	NASDAQ / NWSS

Other Information			
Transfer Agent	State Street Bank & Trust Co. Boston, MA	SIC Code	7373
Auditor	Sansiveri, Kimball & McNamee	Employees	100
		Web Site	networksix.com

New Horizon Kids Quest, Inc.

13705 First Avenue North   Plymouth, MN 55441   Telephone (612)557-1111   Fax (612)404-1546

Company Description

New Horizon Kids Quest, Inc. develops, owns and operates supervised children's entertainment facilities under the name Kids Quest and premium traditional child care centers under the name New Horizon Child Care. The Company currently operates 18 Kids Quest and 15 New Horizon Child Care centers. Kids Quest combines supervised, hourly child care with children's entertainment and recreational facilities. The Kids Quest concept was developed by the Company in cooperation with Grand Casinos, Inc. (a principal shareholder of the Company) to provide casino guests with quality child care, and the Company opened its first Kids Quest at Grand Casino Hinckley in May 1992. The Company had its initial public offering in 1995 by placing one million shares at $5 per share.

	12/31/98	12/31/97	12/31/96	12/31/95
Per Share Information				
Stock Price	1.50	2.25	4.12	7.25
Earnings Per Share	0.01	0.0	-0.49	-0.16
Price / Earnings Ratio	150.00	n.a.	n.a.	n.a.
Book Value Per Share	1.51	1.51	1.50	1.98
Price / Book Value %	99.34	149.01	274.67	366.16
Dividends Per Share	0.0	0.0	0.0	0.0
Annual Financial Data				
Operating Results (000's)				
Total Revenues	15,734.2	14,008.2	10,055.2	5,667.2
Costs & Expenses	-15,645.9	-14,037.4	-11,213.0	-6,036.2
Income Before Taxes and Other	88.3	-29.2	-1,157.7	-369.0
Other Items	-12.8	31.9	-443.2	0.0
Income Tax	-54.0	0.0	0.0	0.0
Net Income	21.5	2.7	-1,601.0	-369.0
Cash Flow From Operations	2,165.8	1,180.5	48.0	57.1
Balance Sheet (000's)				
Cash & Equivalents	208.7	554.5	150.0	3,865.0
Total Current Assets	1,396.9	1,753.3	1,404.0	4,179.2
Fixed Assets, Net	5,938.5	4,820.6	4,120.0	2,100.9
Total Assets	9,558.6	9,037.3	7,586.0	7,754.8
Total Current Liabilities	2,856.6	1,762.7	1,468.0	634.6
Long-Term Debt	1,719.8	2,314.0	1,184.0	615.2
Stockholders' Equity	4,982.2	4,960.7	4,934.0	6,505.0
Performance & Financial Condition				
Return on Total Revenues %	0.14	0.02	-15.92	-6.51
Return on Avg Stockholders' Equity %	0.43	0.05	-27.99	-10.46
Return on Average Assets %	0.23	0.03	-20.87	-7.38
Current Ratio	0.49	0.99	0.96	6.59
Debt / Equity %	34.52	46.65	24.00	9.46

Compound Growth %'s	EPS %	n.a.	Net Income %	n.a.	Total Revenues %	40.55

Comments

The addition of new locations has led to a continuing rise in revenues. The addition of hotel rooms at some of the adjacent casinos has also benefitted sales. Although operations have only been marginally profitable, the Company has produced operating cash flow as depreciation has been a major expense. At December 31, 1998, the Company had a deficiency in working capital. Despite additional expansion planned for 1999, management believes that it will be able to arrange additional financing to cover whatever shortfall is not funded by cash flow from operations.

Officers	Position	Ownership Information	
William M. Dunkley	Chairman, CEO	Number of Shares Outstanding	3,293,300
Susan K. Dunkley	President	Market Capitalization	$ 4,939,950
Kevin M. Greer	CFO	Number of Shareholders	1,000
Lyle Berman	Director	Where Listed / Symbol	NASDAQ / KIDQ

Other Information			
Transfer Agent	Norwest Bank Minnesota, N.A. South St. Paul, MN	SIC Code	8351
Auditor	Arthur Andersen LLP	Employees	536
		Web Site	careguide.net

New York Health Care, Inc.

1850 McDonald Avenue   Brooklyn, NY 11223   Telephone (718)375-6700   Fax (718)375-1555

Company Description

New York Health Care, Inc. is a licensed home health care agency engaged primarily in supplying the services of paraprofessionals who provide a broad range of health care support services to patients in their homes. The Company operates 24 hours a day, seven days a week to receive referrals and coordinate services with physicians, case managers, patients and their families. The Company operates in all five boroughs of New York City and many of the surrounding counties in the states of New York and New Jersey. The Company was founded in 1983 and went public in 1996. Since its initial public offering, the Company has acquired additional home health care businesses in geographic proximity to its existing operations.

	12/31/98	12/31/97	12/31/96	12/31/95
Per Share Information				
Stock Price	0.75	1.12	4.25	2.00
Earnings Per Share	0.09	-0.05	0.09	0.20
Price / Earnings Ratio	8.33	n.a.	47.22	10.00
Book Value Per Share	1.25	1.15	1.11	1.22
Price / Book Value %	60.00	97.39	382.88	163.93
Dividends Per Share	0.0	0.0	0.0	0.0
Annual Financial Data				
Operating Results (000's)				
Total Revenues	20,297.7	13,302.6	11,944.5	11,809.7
Costs & Expenses	-19,700.5	-12,931.5	-11,185.7	-10,600.7
Income Before Taxes and Other	597.2	371.2	554.6	1,209.0
Other Items	0.0	0.0	0.0	0.0
Income Tax	-256.0	-187.3	-238.0	-520.0
Net Income	341.2	183.9	316.6	689.0
Cash Flow From Operations	-309.4	-1,413.1	-1,430.0	697.8
Balance Sheet (000's)				
Cash & Equivalents	192.7	171.9	1,188.5	177.7
Total Current Assets	6,433.4	5,137.9	4,468.3	4,568.1
Fixed Assets, Net	484.7	254.6	207.6	96.4
Total Assets	9,988.4	6,444.0	4,718.5	4,840.1
Total Current Liabilities	4,097.2	2,020.5	565.3	1,792.9
Long-Term Debt	624.0	100.0	0.0	6.5
Stockholders' Equity	5,213.2	4,323.5	4,151.6	3,040.7
Performance & Financial Condition				
Return on Total Revenues %	1.68	1.38	2.65	5.83
Return on Avg Stockholders' Equity %	7.15	4.34	8.80	21.53
Return on Average Assets %	4.15	3.29	6.63	15.31
Current Ratio	1.57	2.54	7.90	2.55
Debt / Equity %	11.97	2.31	n.a.	0.21

Compound Growth %'s	EPS %	-23.37	Net Income %	-20.89	Total Revenues %	19.78

Comments

The Company was taxed under the provisions of Subchapter S prior to its initial public offering in December, 1996. Income taxes for 1995 and 1996 above are on a pro-forma basis as if the Company has been taxed as a regular corporation for comparative purposes. Most of the increase in revenues reported in 1998 as compared to 1997 result from acquisitions. A small portion of the increase is attributable to increased hours of service provided under existing and new contracts. At December 31, 1998, the Company had $3.0 of intangibles recorded as assets which equated to approximately 66% of common stockholders' equity and book value per common share.

Officers	Position	Ownership Information	
Jerry Braun	President, CEO	Number of Shares Outstanding	3,708,030
David Grossman	CFO	Market Capitalization	$ 2,781,023
Jacob Rosenberg	Vice President, COO	Number of Shareholders	1,000
Charles J. Pendola	Director	Where Listed / Symbol	NASDAQ / NYHC

Other Information			
Transfer Agent	Continental Stock Transfer & Trust Co. New York, NY	SIC Code	8082
Auditor	M.R. Weiser & Co. LLP	Employees	1,335

NewCare Health Corporation

6000 Lake Forrest Drive, Suite 200   Atlanta, GA 30328   Telephone (404)255-7500   Fax (404)843-9677

Company Description

NewCare Health Corporation provides senior residential care services including long-term care, assisted living and independent living services. The Company's long-term care facilities provide skilled nursing care, and ancillary services to patients, while its assisted/independent living center provides services to residents in need of varying degrees of assistance with the activities of daily living. The Company presently owns or leases and operates 24 long-term care facilities with 2,133 skilled nursing beds, and three assisted living/independent living facilities with 294 units. These facilities are located in Alabama, Georgia, Florida, Kansas, Massachusetts and Texas. The Company also manages three long-term care facilities and six assisted living facilities which it does not own or lease.

	12/31/98	12/31/97	12/31/96	12/31/95
Per Share Information				
Stock Price	1.69	3.31	1.25	2.37
Earnings Per Share	-0.65	-0.29	-0.21	-0.02
Price / Earnings Ratio	n.a.	n.a.	n.a.	n.a.
Book Value Per Share	0.14	0.48	0.48	n.a.
Price / Book Value %	1,207.14	689.58	260.42	n.a.
Dividends Per Share	0.0	0.0	0.0	0.0
Annual Financial Data				
Operating Results (000's)				
Total Revenues	77,515.6	33,779.1	28,767.5	23,186.4
Costs & Expenses	-86,293.0	-39,076.5	-28,613.6	-23,491.1
Income Before Taxes and Other	-8,777.4	-5,297.3	153.9	-304.7
Other Items	0.0	866.0	-2,326.2	168.4
Income Tax	968.0	1,331.9	-54.0	-36.0
Net Income	-7,809.3	-3,099.5	-2,226.3	-172.2
Cash Flow From Operations	-12,863.8	-2,198.6	-706.3	1,538.9
Balance Sheet (000's)				
Cash & Equivalents	0.0	2,297.6	3,198.7	201.6
Total Current Assets	31,093.6	21,237.7	7,487.2	6,751.3
Fixed Assets, Net	54,696.9	42,972.7	23,821.6	25,070.7
Total Assets	90,914.3	68,768.4	32,267.1	39,980.7
Total Current Liabilities	47,948.1	23,539.4	20,242.6	16,151.5
Long-Term Debt	41,233.4	39,754.8	6,880.8	16,260.6
Stockholders' Equity	1,732.7	5,460.2	5,143.7	7,370.0
Performance & Financial Condition				
Return on Total Revenues %	-10.07	-9.18	-7.74	-0.74
Return on Avg Stockholders' Equity %	-217.14	-58.46	-35.58	-2.63
Return on Average Assets %	-9.78	-6.14	-6.16	-0.50
Current Ratio	0.65	0.90	0.37	n.a.
Debt / Equity %	2,379.66	728.08	133.77	n.a.

Compound Growth %'s	EPS % n.a.	Net Income % n.a.	Total Revenues % 49.53

Comments

The increase in revenues reported in 1998 is mainly the result of the increase in the number of facilities operated during the current year. But this only made the bottom line worse as there was a significant drop in the average daily census, or percent of beds occupied, at the Company's nursing homes. In addition, a deterioration in the payor mix, which resulted in a greater dependence on lower paying Medicaid residents, also played a major role in the loss. Common shares continued to be issued in connection with acquisitions and in private placements to support working capital requirements. At December 31, 1998, the Company had a significant deficiency in working capital and there was a going concern qualification in the audit report on the Company's financial statements. The Company is also involved in a number of litigation matters.

Officers	Position	Ownership Information	
Chris Brogdon	Chairman	Number of Shares Outstanding	12,128,524
Darrell C. Tucker	President	Market Capitalization	$ 20,497,206
James H. Sanregret	CFO	Number of Shareholders	2,000
Tyrone Walker	Vice President	Where Listed / Symbol	NASDAQ / NWCA

Other Information			
Transfer Agent	Securities Transfer Corp. Dallas, TX	SIC Code	8051
Auditor	Cherry Bekaert & Holland, LLP	Employees	2,662

NewCom, Inc.

31166 via Colinas   Westlake Village, CA 91362   Telephone (818)597-3200   Fax (818)597-3211

Company Description

NewCom, Inc. designs, manufactures, markets and sells high performance computer communication and multimedia products for the personal computer market. NewCom's communication products include a line of high speed external and internal data/fax and voice modems which link PCs through the worldwide web and through direct connections over telephone lines, and NewCom's WebPal, an Internet appliance which enables users to access the worldwide web and perform Internet-specific tasks through their existing television screens. The Company was founded in 1994 and had its initial public offering in September 1997.

	02/28/98	02/28/97	02/29/96	02/28/95
Per Share Information				
Stock Price as of 12/31	3.44	9.50	n.a.	-0.05
Earnings Per Share	0.70	0.44	-0.68	0.0
Price / Earnings Ratio	4.91	21.59	n.a.	n.a.
Book Value Per Share	3.71	1.03	-0.60	-0.04
Price / Book Value %	92.72	922.33	n.a.	125.00
Dividends Per Share	0.0	0.0	0.0	0.0
Annual Financial Data				
Operating Results (000's)				
Total Revenues	93,885.8	50,631.7	31,220.7	2,107.1
Costs & Expenses	-84,251.3	-45,467.7	-36,406.0	-2,487.4
Income Before Taxes and Other	9,634.5	3,770.3	-5,185.3	-380.2
Other Items	0.0	0.0	0.0	0.0
Income Tax	-2,546.6	-433.0	0.0	0.0
Net Income	7,087.8	3,337.3	-5,185.3	-380.2
Cash Flow From Operations	-19,916.9	-9,260.8	-19,377.3	-300.0
Balance Sheet (000's)				
Cash & Equivalents	1,982.4	2,813.6	2,102.2	335.7
Total Current Assets	91,437.2	44,329.1	24,471.2	1,631.7
Fixed Assets, Net	2,347.8	2,271.4	877.1	870.3
Total Assets	96,127.0	47,435.2	25,348.3	2,502.0
Total Current Liabilities	59,022.6	22,412.6	9,726.6	642.9
Long-Term Debt	21.6	0.0	0.0	0.0
Stockholders' Equity	37,082.8	7,772.7	-4,564.5	-290.1
Performance & Financial Condition				
Return on Total Revenues %	7.55	6.59	-16.61	-18.04
Return on Avg Stockholders' Equity %	31.60	208.05	n.a.	n.a.
Return on Average Assets %	9.87	9.17	-37.24	-30.42
Current Ratio	1.55	1.98	2.52	2.54
Debt / Equity %	0.06	n.a.	n.a.	n.a.

Compound Growth %'s	EPS %	59.09	Net Income %	112.38	Total Revenues %	254.52

Comments

The large increase in revenue during fiscal 1998 was due to an increase in the volume of product sales to major mass merchandisers. Fiscal 1995 results are for the nine month period from inception to February 28, 1995. Despite a successful public offering at $9.50 per share, clouds now loom on the horizon. For the nine months ended November 30, 1998, the Company reported revenue and a net loss of $66.1 million and $13.3 million ($1.32 per share) as compared to $67.9 million and a profit of $6.0 million ($.73 per share) for the same period of fiscal 1998. The business reversal was attributable to price pressures which necessitated a $10 million inventory write down. Management is responding with a change in product mix and a tighter control of flows of merchandise into retail channels. Investors would be prudent to wait for proof of a return to profitability before buying shares.

Officers	Position	Ownership Information	
Sultan W. Khan	President, CEO	Number of Shares Outstanding	10,000,000
Asif M. Khan	Exec VP	Market Capitalization	$ 34,400,000
Steve C. Veen	CFO	Number of Shareholders	2,000
David W. Harralson	Vice President	Where Listed / Symbol	NASDAQ / NWCM

Other Information			
Transfer Agent	Interwest Transfer Co., Inc. Salt Lake City, UT	SIC Code	3690
Auditor	Pannell Kerr Forster	Employees	112
		Web Site	newcominc.com

Nicholas Financial, Inc.

2454 McMullen Booth Road, Building C   Clearwater, FL 34619   Telephone (813)726-0763   Fax (813)726-2140

Company Description

Nicholas Financial, Inc. provides direct consumer loans and purchases installment sales contracts from automobile dealers for used cars and light trucks. The finance operation currently has fourteen branch offices throughout the states of Florida and Georgia. As of March 31, 1998, the Company had non-exclusive agreements with approximately 500 dealers for the purchase of retail installment sales contracts. The Company's software subsidiary, Nicholas Data Services, Inc., which accounts for approximately 5% of total revenue, designs, develops, supports and sells accounting software to small businesses. The Company was incorporated in Canada in 1985 and operates through two U.S. subsidiaries based in Florida. Substantially all of the Company's operations are in the United States.

	03/31/98	03/31/97	03/31/96	03/31/95
Per Share Information				
Stock Price as of 12/31	3.12	12.36	8.40	7.89
Earnings Per Share	0.39	0.36	0.33	0.24
Price / Earnings Ratio	8.00	34.33	25.45	32.88
Book Value Per Share	2.96	2.59	1.67	1.14
Price / Book Value %	105.41	477.22	502.99	692.11
Dividends Per Share	0.0	0.0	0.0	0.0
Annual Financial Data				
Operating Results (000's)				
Total Revenues	7,937.0	6,209.1	5,833.2	4,119.0
Costs & Expenses	-6,439.4	-4,919.6	-4,774.3	-3,274.2
Income Before Taxes and Other	1,497.6	1,289.5	1,058.9	844.8
Other Items	0.0	0.0	0.0	0.0
Income Tax	-584.0	-497.3	-396.8	-323.0
Net Income	913.7	792.3	662.2	521.9
Cash Flow From Operations	2,057.3	1,668.0	1,234.6	1,346.8
Balance Sheet (000's)				
Cash & Equivalents	304.0	108.1	490.8	283.3
Total Current Assets	34,172.9	26,427.0	19,135.6	13,294.9
Fixed Assets, Net	0.0	182.3	180.4	186.6
Total Assets	34,172.9	27,020.7	19,801.8	13,784.9
Total Current Liabilities	26,934.5	19,229.4	14,321.4	10,021.1
Long-Term Debt	0.0	0.0	0.0	1,576.1
Stockholders' Equity	6,975.8	6,035.3	3,253.9	2,187.7
Performance & Financial Condition				
Return on Total Revenues %	11.51	12.76	11.35	12.67
Return on Avg Stockholders' Equity %	14.04	17.06	24.34	28.17
Return on Average Assets %	2.99	3.38	3.94	4.70
Current Ratio	1.27	1.37	1.34	1.33
Debt / Equity %	n.a.	n.a.	n.a.	72.04

Compound Growth %'s	EPS %	17.57	Net Income %	20.52	Total Revenues %	24.44

Comments

During fiscal 1998, the Company executed a 1 for 3 reverse stock split. All per share amounts have been restated for consistency. Interest income on finance receivables is the Company's primary source of income and is included in total revenues. The 30% increase in revenues is primarily the result of the opening of three additional branch offices. A placement of 1.1 million shares in the 1997 fiscal year was used to reduce debt and create a significantly stronger capital structure. Quarterly financial statements are posted on the Company's web site. For the nine months ended December 31, 1998, the Company reported revenues and net income of $7.4 million and $1,005,029 ($.41 per share) as compared to $5.8 million and $655,478 ($.28 per share) for the same period of the preceding year.

Officers	Position	Ownership Information	
Peter L. Vosotas	Chairman, President	Number of Shares Outstanding	2,357,013
Ralph T. Finkenbrink	VP - Finance	Market Capitalization	$ 7,353,881
Michael J. Marika	Other	Number of Shareholders	500
Raymond R. Cottrell	Director	Where Listed / Symbol	NASDAQ / NICKF

Other Information			
Transfer Agent	Montreal Trust Co. Vancouver, BC	SIC Code	6153
Auditor	Ernst & Young LLP	Employees	63
		Web Site	nicfn.com

Nitches, Inc.

10280 Camino Santa Fe   San Diego, CA 92121   Telephone (619)625-2633   Fax (619)625-0746

Company Description

Nitches, Inc. has been in the wholesale clothing business since 1973, and imports finished garments manufactured to its specifications from approximately 10 foreign countries. The Company sells all-cotton and cotton blend knit and woven clothing, primarily for the female consumer. Retail customers include J.C. Penney, Kohl's, Mervyn's, Price Costco, Cavendars, and Sheplers. The Company competes primarily on the basis of price, quality, the desirability of its fabrics, and the reliability of its delivery and service.

	08/31/98	08/31/97	08/31/96	08/31/95
Per Share Information				
Stock Price as of 12/31	2.81	6.06	5.00	1.87
Earnings Per Share	0.0	0.08	0.55	0.04
Price / Earnings Ratio	n.a.	75.75	9.09	46.75
Book Value Per Share	5.25	4.98	4.84	4.47
Price / Book Value %	53.52	121.69	103.31	41.83
Dividends Per Share	0.0	0.0	0.0	0.0
Annual Financial Data				
Operating Results (000's)				
Total Revenues	31,409.0	48,565.0	54,700.0	84,764.0
Costs & Expenses	-32,213.0	-48,245.0	-52,995.0	-83,071.0
Income Before Taxes and Other	-804.0	320.0	1,705.0	1,693.0
Other Items	0.0	0.0	0.0	-1,748.0
Income Tax	807.0	-125.0	-279.0	269.0
Net Income	3.0	195.0	1,426.0	214.0
Cash Flow From Operations	1,302.0	281.0	1,713.0	200.0
Balance Sheet (000's)				
Cash & Equivalents	1,338.0	955.0	2,197.0	10,485.0
Total Current Assets	12,871.0	13,885.0	17,568.0	29,971.0
Fixed Assets, Net	137.0	219.0	250.0	325.0
Total Assets	14,058.0	15,079.0	18,179.0	30,966.0
Total Current Liabilities	3,487.0	2,377.0	5,359.0	8,433.0
Long-Term Debt	0.0	0.0	0.0	0.0
Stockholders' Equity	10,571.0	11,681.0	11,724.0	21,437.0
Performance & Financial Condition				
Return on Total Revenues %	0.01	0.40	2.61	0.25
Return on Avg Stockholders' Equity %	0.03	1.67	8.60	1.01
Return on Average Assets %	0.02	1.17	5.80	0.62
Current Ratio	3.69	5.84	3.28	3.55
Debt / Equity %	n.a.	n.a.	n.a.	n.a.

Compound Growth %'s	EPS % n.a.	Net Income % -75.89	Total Revenues % -28.17

Comments

The Company declared a 2 for 1 stock split on September 13, 1996. All per share amounts have been adjusted for consistency. Over the past five years, the apparel market has been marked by deflation and reduced profit margins in certain markets. The success and consolidation of retailers has given retailers leverage to attempt to reduce profit margins to suppliers such as the Company. The Company's response has been to discontinue product lines in areas where it did not believe it could maintain a reasonable profit margin as evident from the declining revenue numbers. Now leaner and meaner, the Company is poised to be highly profitable. For the six months ended February 28, 1999, the Company reported revenues and net income of $15.7 million and $408,000 ($.30 per share) as compared to revenues of $15.3 million and a net loss of $384,000 ($.17 per share) for the same period of the preceding year.

Officers	Position	Ownership Information	
Arjun C. Waney	Chairman	Number of Shares Outstanding	2,012,030
Steven P. Wyandt	President, CEO	Market Capitalization	$ 5,653,804
Diane Ochotsky	VP - Manufacturing	Number of Shareholders	500
Irene Encarnacion	Controller	Where Listed / Symbol	NASDAQ / NICH

Other Information			
Transfer Agent	American Stock Transfer & Trust Co. New York, NY	SIC Code	2330
Auditor	Moss Adams LLP	Employees	48
		Web Site	nitches.com

Nortech Systems Incorporated

641 East Lake Street, Suite 244   Wayzata, MN 55391   Telephone (612)473-0833   Fax (612)404-0227

Company Description

Nortech Systems Incorporated manufactures wire harnesses, cables, electronic sub-assemblies and components, and printed circuit board assemblies, as well as large-screen high resolution video monitors for radar, and document and medical imaging. The Company provides a full "turnkey" contract manufacturing service to its customers. A majority of revenue is derived from products which are built to the customer's design specifications. Nortech Medical Services, Inc., a subsidiary, provides service bureau and office management services to physicians and clinics throughout Minnesota. The Company was organized in 1990. Prior to 1990, the Company operated as DSC Nortech, Inc. which filed a petition for reorganization under Chapter 11 of the Bankruptcy Code.

	12/31/98	12/31/97	12/31/96	12/31/95
Per Share Information				
Stock Price	3.44	4.62	5.25	8.00
Earnings Per Share	0.14	0.28	0.18	0.55
Price / Earnings Ratio	24.57	16.50	29.17	14.55
Book Value Per Share	3.46	3.28	2.99	2.64
Price / Book Value %	99.42	140.85	175.59	303.03
Dividends Per Share	0.0	0.0	0.0	0.0
Annual Financial Data				
Operating Results (000's)				
Total Revenues	40,397.8	36,487.7	26,248.6	18,518.6
Costs & Expenses	-39,943.9	-35,451.0	-25,610.5	-17,186.7
Income Before Taxes and Other	453.9	1,036.7	638.0	1,331.9
Other Items	0.0	0.0	0.0	0.0
Income Tax	-124.0	-359.0	-192.0	0.0
Net Income	329.9	677.7	446.0	1,331.9
Cash Flow From Operations	483.7	162.4	-104.8	510.6
Balance Sheet (000's)				
Cash & Equivalents	415.4	714.2	1,235.1	924.6
Total Current Assets	16,201.5	15,862.7	12,289.2	7,197.7
Fixed Assets, Net	6,765.1	7,299.6	7,870.7	3,839.8
Total Assets	24,728.6	24,694.9	22,152.6	13,223.1
Total Current Liabilities	5,217.5	6,192.5	3,790.7	1,918.2
Long-Term Debt	11,146.5	10,388.6	10,910.8	3,768.7
Stockholders' Equity	8,364.6	7,813.8	7,151.2	6,036.2
Performance & Financial Condition				
Return on Total Revenues %	0.82	1.86	1.70	7.19
Return on Avg Stockholders' Equity %	4.08	9.06	6.76	24.76
Return on Average Assets %	1.33	2.89	2.52	13.41
Current Ratio	3.11	2.56	3.24	3.75
Debt / Equity %	133.26	132.95	152.57	62.44

Compound Growth %'s	EPS %	-36.62	Net Income %	-37.20	Total Revenues %	29.69

Comments

The 10.8 % increase in revenues in 1998 as compared to 1997 was attributable to internal growth of the customer base. The 39.2% increase in revenues experienced in 1997 was primarily generated by acquisitions which were completed in 1996. The Company has experienced gross profit pressure evolving from a change of product mix and material content offset by some improvement in manufacturing productivity. In February 1998, the Company was awarded a significant multi-year contract from Fisher-Rosemount Systems and was named their preferred North American supplier of custom cable assemblies. Fisher-Rosemount Systems is one of nine companies comprising Fisher-Rosemount Group, the world's largest supplier of process automation products and solutions. This contract may lead to opportunities with the other eight companies.

Officers	Position	Ownership Information	
Quentin E. Finkelson	President, CEO	Number of Shares Outstanding	2,351,377
Gregory D. Tweed	Exec VP, COO	Market Capitalization	$ 8,088,737
Garry M. Anderly	Senior VP, CFO	Number of Shareholders	1,301
Peter L. Kucera	Vice President	Where Listed / Symbol	NASDAQ / NSYS

Other Information			
Transfer Agent	American Securities Transfer, Inc. Denver, CO	SIC Code	3679
Auditor	Larson, Allen, Weishair & Co.	Employees	527
		Web Site	nortechsys.com

Norton Drilling Services, Inc.

5211 Brownfield Highway, Suite 230   Lubbock, TX 79407-3501   Telephone (806)785-8400   Fax (806)785-8420

Company Description

Norton Drilling Services, Inc., formerly DSI Industries, Inc., operates sixteen oil and gas drilling rigs and provides contract drilling services to the oil and gas industry, primarily in the Permian Basin of west Texas and eastern New Mexico, the Green River Basin and the Overthrust Belt in the Rocky Mountains and in two states in Mexico. This business was acquired in 1991. The Company was also involved with two other businesses: the ownership and operation of a magnetic resonance imaging center, and a plant supply and nursery business. Both of these businesses sustained substantial losses from operations and were discontinued. The Company was originally formed in 1983.

	11/30/98	11/30/97	11/30/96	11/30/95
Per Share Information				
Stock Price as of 12/31	1.87	10.45	2.35	0.15
Earnings Per Share	0.17	0.50	0.71	-0.55
Price / Earnings Ratio	11.00	20.90	3.31	n.a.
Book Value Per Share	1.75	1.58	1.02	0.27
Price / Book Value %	106.86	661.39	230.39	55.56
Dividends Per Share	0.0	0.0	0.0	0.0
Annual Financial Data				
Operating Results (000's)				
Total Revenues	28,962.1	36,179.3	27,101.3	20,775.4
Costs & Expenses	-27,644.2	-32,481.0	-26,563.4	-21,643.7
Income Before Taxes and Other	1,318.0	3,698.3	537.9	-868.3
Other Items	0.0	253.1	2,893.0	-1,526.1
Income Tax	-490.6	-1,489.4	0.0	0.0
Net Income	827.3	2,461.9	3,430.9	-2,394.4
Cash Flow From Operations	2,181.6	2,435.0	895.9	-94.8
Balance Sheet (000's)				
Cash & Equivalents	172.3	277.1	774.2	283.1
Total Current Assets	7,045.8	7,874.8	6,423.1	3,888.4
Fixed Assets, Net	11,581.3	10,351.5	8,508.5	7,410.6
Total Assets	20,002.9	19,763.1	16,473.0	13,004.5
Total Current Liabilities	6,948.1	8,385.4	8,453.2	10,928.0
Long-Term Debt	3,404.5	2,633.8	3,362.8	763.7
Stockholders' Equity	8,635.5	7,801.6	4,657.0	1,312.7
Performance & Financial Condition				
Return on Total Revenues %	2.86	6.80	12.66	-11.53
Return on Avg Stockholders' Equity %	10.07	39.52	114.95	-98.04
Return on Average Assets %	4.16	13.59	23.28	-18.41
Current Ratio	1.01	0.94	0.76	0.36
Debt / Equity %	39.42	33.76	72.21	58.18

Compound Growth %'s	EPS %	-51.07	Net Income %	-50.89	Total Revenues %	11.71

Comments

The Company executed a 1 for 5 reverse stock split in January 1999. All per share amounts have been adjusted to reflect the split. Weakness in the oil industry caused average rig utilization to decline from 92.4% in fiscal 1997 to 66.4% in fiscal 1998. Rates for the use of the rigs also declined because of competitive pricing pressures. The combination of these factors reduced revenues by 20%. Yet the Company still maintained profitability. Discontinued operations brought income of $2.9 million in fiscal 1996 and losses of $1.5 million in fiscal 1995. In 1997, the last of this activity appears to have been cleared out with $253,000 of income from discontinued operations reported. At November 30, 1998, the Company had goodwill of $1.2 million recorded as assets which equated to approximately 14% of stockholders' equity and book value per share.

Officers	Position	Ownership Information	
Sherman H. Norton Jr.	Chairman	Number of Shares Outstanding	4,934,321
S. Howard Norton, III	President, CEO	Market Capitalization	$ 9,227,180
David W. Ridley	Vice President, CFO	Number of Shareholders	1,000
John W. Norton	Vice President, COO	Where Listed / Symbol	NASDAQ / NORT

Other Information			
Transfer Agent	Continental Stock Transfer & Trust Co. New York, NY	SIC Code	1381
Auditor	Robinson Burdette Martin Cowan	Employees	209
		Web Site	nortondrilling.com

NovaCare,Inc.

1016 West Ninth Street   King of Prussia, PA 19406   Telephone (610)992-7200   Fax (610)992-3341

Company Description

NovaCare, Inc. is a national leader in physical rehabilitation services. The Company treats 47,000 patients per day in cost-effective outpatient and long-term care settings and has achieved number one market shares in long-term care and orthotic and prosthetic rehabilitation. Through its 71% owned subsidiary, NovaCare Employees Services, Inc., it is also the second largest employee services provider or professional employer organization administering the full array of human resource functions, including the management of health care benefits and workers' compensation.

	06/30/98	06/30/97	06/30/96	06/30/95
Per Share Information				
Stock Price as of 12/31	2.87	13.12	11.00	5.12
Earnings Per Share	0.91	0.62	0.24	0.95
Price / Earnings Ratio	3.15	21.16	45.83	5.39
Book Value Per Share	9.29	8.32	7.76	7.44
Price / Book Value %	30.89	157.69	141.75	68.82
Dividends Per Share	0.0	0.0	0.0	0.0
Annual Financial Data				
Operating Results (000's)				
Total Revenues	1,672,755.0	1,068,191.0	798,037.0	905,359.0
Costs & Expenses	-1,610,520.0	-1,001,154.0	-768,075.0	-779,775.0
Income Before Taxes and Other	60,741.0	66,801.0	29,866.0	125,584.0
Other Items	38,805.0	0.0	0.0	0.0
Income Tax	-41,631.0	-27,891.0	-14,585.0	-63,660.0
Net Income	57,915.0	38,910.0	15,281.0	61,924.0
Cash Flow From Operations	73,117.0	47,241.0	57,698.0	43,618.0
Balance Sheet (000's)				
Cash & Equivalents	32,760.0	22,716.0	95,724.0	158,636.0
Total Current Assets	451,853.0	329,895.0	332,159.0	413,820.0
Fixed Assets, Net	80,857.0	69,740.0	63,319.0	63,659.0
Total Assets	1,356,042.0	1,014,304.0	789,731.0	852,557.0
Total Current Liabilities	226,080.0	483,019.0	108,447.0	158,694.0
Long-Term Debt	476,308.0	19,630.0	196,890.0	206,228.0
Stockholders' Equity	580,673.0	508,006.0	484,394.0	487,635.0
Performance & Financial Condition				
Return on Total Revenues %	3.46	3.64	1.91	6.84
Return on Avg Stockholders' Equity %	10.64	7.84	3.14	13.76
Return on Average Assets %	4.89	4.31	1.86	8.26
Current Ratio	2.00	0.68	3.06	2.61
Debt / Equity %	82.03	3.86	40.65	42.29

Compound Growth %'s	EPS %	-1.42	Net Income %	-2.21	Total Revenues %	22.71

Comments

Both fiscal 1998 and 1997 experienced significant revenue and earnings growth resulting from acquisitions and internal growth of its existing businesses. Fiscal 1998 results include a gain of $38.8 million related to the initial public offering of NovaCare Employee Services and the Company's reduction of its interest from 100% to 71%. The Company also recorded a restructuring expense of $23.5 million in fiscal 1998 due to the changes in Medicare related to the Balanced Budget Act of 1997. At June 30, 1998, the Company had $768 million of intangible assets reflected on its books which equated to 132% of book value. Without such intangibles, stockholders' equity and book value per share would be negative. For the six months ended December 31, 1998, the Company reported revenues and a net loss of $961.5 million and $12.8 million ($.20 per share) as compared to $755.5 million and $30.8 million ($.49 per share) for the same period of the preceding year. The interim results include a restructuring expense of $17.8 million.

Officers	Position	Ownership Information	
James W. McLane	President, COO	Number of Shares Outstanding	62,534,000
Daryl A. Dixon	President	Market Capitalization	$ 179,472,580
Ronald G. Hiscock	President	Number of Shareholders	10,000
Timothy E. Foster	CEO	Where Listed / Symbol	NYSE / NOV

Other Information			
Transfer Agent	American Stock Transfer & Trust Co. New York, NY	SIC Code	8090
Auditor	PricewaterhouseCoopers LLP	Employees	20,000
		Web Site	novacare.com

Oakridge Energy, Inc.

4613 Jacksboro Highway   Wichita Falls, TX 76302   Telephone (940)322-4772   Fax (940)322-9452

Company Description

Oakridge Energy, Inc. is engaged in the exploration, development, production and sale of oil and gas primarily in Texas, and to a much lesser extent development of gravel in Colorado. In addition, the Company holds certain real estate and coal deposits in Colorado for development. The Company took initial steps in 1998 toward commencing a golf course/residential lots development on 2,020 acres of land owned by the Company adjacent to Durango, Colorado, and received a land use permit to commence preliminary site work on the golf course portion of the property. The Company was founded in 1969.

	02/28/98	02/28/97	02/29/96	02/28/95
Per Share Information				
Stock Price as of 12/31	2.50	2.75	2.12	1.82
Earnings Per Share	0.08	0.10	-0.17	-0.15
Price / Earnings Ratio	31.25	27.50	n.a.	n.a.
Book Value Per Share	2.12	2.08	1.91	2.16
Price / Book Value %	117.92	132.21	110.99	84.26
Dividends Per Share	0.0	0.0	0.0	0.0
Annual Financial Data				
Operating Results (000's)				
Total Revenues	4,086.4	3,177.0	1,133.1	721.3
Costs & Expenses	-3,385.0	-2,593.2	-2,365.5	-1,679.2
Income Before Taxes and Other	701.4	583.8	-1,232.3	-1,035.3
Other Items	0.0	0.0	0.0	0.0
Income Tax	-290.6	-84.4	329.8	211.2
Net Income	410.8	499.4	-902.5	-824.1
Cash Flow From Operations	2,937.0	1,391.7	-857.3	-648.7
Balance Sheet (000's)				
Cash & Equivalents	877.0	195.6	44.3	982.1
Total Current Assets	3,018.3	2,738.8	3,470.5	4,357.2
Fixed Assets, Net	6,786.3	6,033.0	4,641.0	3,247.9
Total Assets	11,403.6	11,360.4	11,088.3	12,815.2
Total Current Liabilities	340.4	295.9	480.5	1,004.0
Long-Term Debt	0.0	0.0	0.0	0.0
Stockholders' Equity	10,340.9	10,583.2	10,372.6	11,752.7
Performance & Financial Condition				
Return on Total Revenues %	10.05	15.72	-79.65	-114.25
Return on Avg Stockholders' Equity %	3.93	4.77	-8.16	-6.41
Return on Average Assets %	3.61	4.45	-7.55	-5.92
Current Ratio	8.87	9.26	7.22	4.34
Debt / Equity %	n.a.	n.a.	n.a.	n.a.

Compound Growth %'s	EPS % n.a.	Net Income % n.a.	Total Revenues % 78.27

Comments

Significantly higher oil and gas revenues were generated in fiscal 1998 as compared to 1997 despite lower prices. The lower prices also had an adverse effect on the Company's proven oil and gas reserves and their carrying value. Fiscal 1998 results include a $235,168 writedown of asset values. During fiscal 1998, the Company reacquired 211,750 of its common shares for an average price of $3.00 per share. More than one-half of all issued shares are now held as treasury shares. For the nine months ended November 30, 1998, the Company reported net income of $599,075 ($.13 per share) as compared to $716,609 ($.14 per share) for the same period of the preceding year.

Officers	Position	Ownership Information	
Sandra Pautsky	Exec VP, Secretary	Number of Shares Outstanding	4,871,609
Danny Croker	Vice President	Market Capitalization	$ 12,179,023
Randy Camp	Director	Number of Shareholders	524
		Where Listed / Symbol	OTC-BB / OAKR

Other Information

Transfer Agent	Stock Transfer Company of America, Inc. Dallas, TX	SIC Code	1311
Auditor	KPMG LLP	Employees	8
Market Maker	Morgan, Keegan & Company, Inc.	(800)289-5019	
	Sharpe Capital Inc.	(800)355-5781	

Oakridge Holdings, Inc.

4810 120th Street West St. Paul, MN 55124-8628 Telephone (612)686-5495 Fax (612)686-5427

Company Description

Oakridge Holdings, Inc. operates two adjacent cemeteries near Hillside, Illinois, used for the internment of human remains. 37,850 of the burial plots remain in inventory which is estimated to represent a 25 to 34 year supply. There are also 148 niches and 357 crypts in inventory. But on June 29, 1998, the Company acquired Stinar Corporation, a company that designs, engineers and manufactures airline ground equipment, for $4,242,950 including acquisition costs. Will this breathe new life into the financials? Let's take a look.

	06/30/98	06/30/97	06/30/96	06/30/95
Per Share Information				
Stock Price as of 12/31	2.87	0.81	0.50	0.75
Earnings Per Share	0.09	0.16	0.12	0.09
Price / Earnings Ratio	31.89	5.06	4.17	8.33
Book Value Per Share	0.92	0.77	0.60	0.65
Price / Book Value %	311.96	105.19	83.33	115.38
Dividends Per Share	0.0	0.0	0.0	0.0
Annual Financial Data				
Operating Results (000's)				
Total Revenues	2,767.2	2,585.4	2,615.4	2,586.8
Costs & Expenses	-2,334.2	-2,287.8	-2,287.7	-2,228.1
Income Before Taxes and Other	431.9	297.4	244.5	295.1
Other Items	-250.0	0.0	0.0	0.0
Income Tax	-52.0	-83.0	-70.0	-104.6
Net Income	129.9	214.4	174.5	190.5
Cash Flow From Operations	687.7	384.1	454.6	-39.2
Balance Sheet (000's)				
Cash & Equivalents	823.5	382.3	264.7	192.7
Total Current Assets	7,163.9	965.6	778.3	653.0
Fixed Assets, Net	2,285.2	473.9	484.2	416.4
Total Assets	9,509.3	2,682.9	2,613.4	3,125.6
Total Current Liabilities	5,187.0	972.7	835.2	757.4
Long-Term Debt	3,123.8	706.6	989.1	1,315.5
Stockholders' Equity	1,198.5	1,003.6	789.2	1,052.7
Performance & Financial Condition				
Return on Total Revenues %	4.70	8.29	6.67	7.36
Return on Avg Stockholders' Equity %	11.80	23.92	18.95	18.03
Return on Average Assets %	2.13	8.10	6.08	6.96
Current Ratio	1.38	0.99	1.79	0.86
Debt / Equity %	260.64	70.41	125.33	124.96

Compound Growth %'s	EPS %	0.00	Net Income %	-11.98	Total Revenues %	2.27

Comments

Fiscal 1998 results reflect a write-off of $250,000 invested in lease and option rights to develop land adjacent to the Colorado River. Net Income would have otherwise increased for a third consecutive year. All eyes will be on the financial impact of the acquisition of Stinar Corporation which recorded $15.5 million in revenue and $221,000 of net income for the twelve months preceding its acquisition. For the six months ended December 31, 1998, the Company reported revenues and net income of $7.0 million and $598,046 ($.30 per share) as compared to $1.4 million and $168,351 ($.13 per share) for the comparable period in the preceding year.

Officers	Position	Ownership Information	
Robert C. Harvey	Chairman, CEO	Number of Shares Outstanding	1,309,670
Robert B. Gregor	Secretary	Market Capitalization	$ 3,758,753
		Number of Shareholders	1,900
		Where Listed / Symbol	OTC-BB / OKRG

Other Information			
Transfer Agent	Company Office St. Paul, MN	SIC Code	6552
Auditor	Stirtz Bernards Boyden et al.	Employees	110
Market Maker	Carr Securities Corporation	(800)221-2243	
	Paragon Capital Corporation	(800)345-0505	

Omtool, Ltd.

8 Industrial Way   Salem, NH 03079   Telephone (603)898-8900   Fax (603)890-6756

Company Description

Omtool, Ltd. designs, develops, markets and supports open, client/server facsimile software, delivering solutions which automate and integrate fax communication throughout an enterprise. Omtool's Fax Sr. product family, licensed typically on a shrink-wrap basis, provides users with an extensive, flexible feature set for transmitting and receiving faxes and improves an organization's management of its fax communications processes by providing a suite of utility and control functions. Fax Sr. can be deployed on heterogeneous, multi-platform networks and can be integrated with both desktop and enterprise software applications as well as e-mail and groupware systems. To address the needs of large enterprises, Fax Sr. is modular and scaleable as servers, clients and fax lines can be implemented and added over time. Omtool has licensed Fax Sr. to thousands of customers worldwide. The Company was founded in 1991 and had its initial public offering in 1997.

	12/31/98	12/31/97	12/31/96	12/31/95
Per Share Information				
Stock Price	2.69	10.12	9.00	n.a.
Earnings Per Share	0.09	-0.18	0.05	0.07
Price / Earnings Ratio	29.89	n.a.	180.00	n.a.
Book Value Per Share	2.41	2.51	-0.28	n.a.
Price / Book Value %	111.62	403.19	n.a.	n.a.
Dividends Per Share	0.0	0.0	0.0	0.0
Annual Financial Data				
Operating Results (000's)				
Total Revenues	31,876.5	22,019.8	8,444.3	3,935.2
Costs & Expenses	-30,372.3	-19,431.3	-7,766.6	-3,519.1
Income Before Taxes and Other	1,504.2	2,588.5	677.7	416.1
Other Items	0.0	-3,100.0	0.0	0.0
Income Tax	-406.4	-993.3	-238.0	0.0
Net Income	1,097.8	-1,504.8	439.7	416.1
Cash Flow From Operations	1,129.0	1,151.8	-565.6	853.1
Balance Sheet (000's)				
Cash & Equivalents	2,706.0	2,353.7	2,042.1	551.0
Total Current Assets	29,564.1	30,387.8	5,721.7	1,493.0
Fixed Assets, Net	1,770.8	1,788.4	754.4	82.0
Total Assets	36,402.9	37,132.2	6,494.9	1,575.0
Total Current Liabilities	5,954.3	6,415.1	2,370.9	1,543.0
Long-Term Debt	0.0	0.0	212.2	21.0
Stockholders' Equity	29,765.3	29,735.7	-1,466.8	11.0
Performance & Financial Condition				
Return on Total Revenues %	3.44	-6.83	5.21	10.57
Return on Avg Stockholders' Equity %	3.69	-10.65	n.a.	n.a.
Return on Average Assets %	2.99	-6.90	10.90	38.35
Current Ratio	4.97	4.74	2.41	0.97
Debt / Equity %	n.a.	n.a.	n.a.	190.91

Compound Growth %'s	EPS %	8.74	Net Income %	38.18	Total Revenues %	100.83

Comments

The Company completed one acquisition in 1997 and two acquisitions in 1998. Most of the revenue growth, however, comes from greater market acceptance of the Company's facsimile software products and increasing servicing revenues as the Company's installed base grows. 1997 results include $3.1 million in expense related to the write-off of purchased, in-process research and development costs. The compound growth rate of earnings per share is diluted from the compound growth rate of net income because of additional common shares issued in the public offering and the acquisitions. The Company reacquired 660,780 of its common shares in 1998 at an average price of $2.97 per share.

Officers	Position	Ownership Information	
Robert L. Voelk	Chairman, CEO	Number of Shares Outstanding	12,348,592
Martin A. Schultz	President	Market Capitalization	$ 33,217,712
Darioush Mardan	VP - Finance, CFO	Number of Shareholders	1,648
Mark P. Overington	Vice President	Where Listed / Symbol	NASDAQ / OMTL

Other Information

Transfer Agent	American Stock Transfer & Trust Co. New York, NY	SIC Code	7372
Auditor	Arthur Andersen LLP	Employees	195
		Web Site	omtool.com

Optelecom, Inc.

9300 Gaither Road   Gaithersburg, MD 20877   Telephone (301)840-2121   Fax (301)948-6357

Company Description

Optelcom, Inc.'s business consists primarily of the development, manufacture, and sale of fiber optic communications products and laser systems for commercial and military customers. Fiber optic communication equipment is an area of unprecedented growth and change. Technology development is constantly and rapidly improving the capability to transmit ever increasing data rates over even greater distances with fiber-based communication systems. The Company was founded in 1972.

	12/31/98	12/31/97	12/31/96	12/31/95
Per Share Information				
Stock Price	2.50	9.75	5.50	1.83
Earnings Per Share	-1.34	0.48	0.39	-0.12
Price / Earnings Ratio	n.a.	20.31	14.10	n.a.
Book Value Per Share	1.53	2.85	1.68	1.25
Price / Book Value %	163.40	342.11	327.38	146.40
Dividends Per Share	0.0	0.0	0.0	0.0
Annual Financial Data				
Operating Results (000's)				
Total Revenues	16,333.7	12,271.1	8,910.3	6,430.1
Costs & Expenses	-18,001.9	-10,862.7	-7,834.9	-6,857.6
Income Before Taxes and Other	-1,668.2	1,367.2	1,032.2	-442.1
Other Items	-1,462.5	0.0	0.0	0.0
Income Tax	319.3	-418.5	-310.1	233.8
Net Income	-2,811.3	948.7	722.1	-208.4
Cash Flow From Operations	513.1	526.8	387.3	-110.5
Balance Sheet (000's)				
Cash & Equivalents	394.1	242.7	266.6	62.4
Total Current Assets	4,648.6	6,401.8	3,607.7	2,878.6
Fixed Assets, Net	1,361.1	1,265.6	779.1	795.4
Total Assets	8,631.9	12,209.7	4,466.5	3,674.0
Total Current Liabilities	3,467.4	3,945.6	1,221.3	1,223.4
Long-Term Debt	1,726.7	2,291.7	11.6	46.4
Stockholders' Equity	3,290.6	5,799.8	3,041.6	2,188.8
Performance & Financial Condition				
Return on Total Revenues %	-17.21	7.73	8.10	-3.24
Return on Avg Stockholders' Equity %	-61.85	21.46	27.61	-9.12
Return on Average Assets %	-26.98	11.38	17.74	-5.72
Current Ratio	1.34	1.62	2.95	2.35
Debt / Equity %	52.47	39.51	0.38	2.12

Compound Growth %'s	EPS %	n.a.	Net Income %	n.a.	Total Revenues %	36.44

Comments

The Company declared a 3 for 2 stock split on December 1, 1997. All per share amounts have been adjusted for consistency. In December 1997 the Company acquired Paragon Audio Visual Limited. The integration of Paragon proved to be costly in time and resources. As a result of the length of time required to integrate the acquisition, the Paragon operation accumulated a loss of $3.0 million during 1998 including a $1,462,500 write down of intangible assets. The Company has replaced Paragon's management and expects the operation to return to profitability in 1999. Still, at December 31, 1998, the Company had $2.6 million recorded as intangible assets and goodwill which approximated 79% of stockholders' equity and book value per share.

Officers	Position	Ownership Information	
Alexander L. Karpinski	Chairman	Number of Shares Outstanding	2,156,557
Edmund D. Ludwig	President, CEO	Market Capitalization	$ 5,391,393
Carole Argo	CFO	Number of Shareholders	892
Howard Deutch	Secretary	Where Listed / Symbol	NASDAQ / OPTC

Other Information			
Transfer Agent	American Stock Transfer & Trust Co. New York, NY	SIC Code	3663
Auditor	Deloitte & Touche LLP	Employees	84
		Web Site	optelecom.com

Optimumcare Corporation

30011 Ivy Glenn Drive, Suite 219   Laguna Niguel, CA 92677   Telephone (714)495-1100   Fax (714)495-1827

Company Description

Optimumcare Corporation, which was incorporated in 1986, develops health care facility based programs, managed by the Company, for the treatment of certain mental health disorders as well as for alcohol and drug abuse. The Company currently has 10 programs in five hospitals. The host health care facility provides a specified number of beds for the program (usually 20 to 60) as well as all other support services required for its operation. Optimumcare recruits and trains the staff to operate the program which may include a medical director, a program director, a psychologist, a chief therapist and one or more counselors or social workers.

	12/31/98	12/31/97	12/31/96	12/31/95
Per Share Information				
Stock Price	0.83	1.22	1.31	1.13
Earnings Per Share	0.06	0.06	0.14	0.0
Price / Earnings Ratio	13.83	20.33	9.36	n.a.
Book Value Per Share	0.46	0.47	0.40	0.31
Price / Book Value %	180.43	259.57	327.50	364.52
Dividends Per Share	0.0	0.0	0.0	0.0
Annual Financial Data				
Operating Results (000's)				
Total Revenues	11,434.4	12,097.1	10,681.6	6,035.9
Costs & Expenses	-10,819.7	-11,389.7	-9,683.8	-6,033.0
Income Before Taxes and Other	614.8	707.4	997.7	2.9
Other Items	0.0	0.0	0.0	0.0
Income Tax	-237.6	-253.0	-121.0	-0.8
Net Income	377.1	454.4	876.7	2.1
Cash Flow From Operations	500.0	438.6	267.1	159.6
Balance Sheet (000's)				
Cash & Equivalents	188.6	945.4	1,113.8	170.9
Total Current Assets	2,652.0	3,181.6	3,518.0	1,739.1
Fixed Assets, Net	59.5	86.7	73.5	25.6
Total Assets	3,154.7	3,921.2	3,953.1	2,059.5
Total Current Liabilities	429.4	647.7	1,244.9	381.5
Long-Term Debt	0.0	0.0	0.0	166.0
Stockholders' Equity	2,725.4	3,273.5	2,735.4	1,512.0
Performance & Financial Condition				
Return on Total Revenues %	3.30	3.76	8.21	0.03
Return on Avg Stockholders' Equity %	12.57	15.12	41.28	0.14
Return on Average Assets %	10.66	11.54	29.16	0.11
Current Ratio	6.18	4.91	2.83	4.56
Debt / Equity %	n.a.	n.a.	n.a.	10.98

Compound Growth %'s	EPS % n.a.	Net Income % n.a.	Total Revenues %	23.73

Comments

The programs in 1997 generated revenue for longer periods of time than the programs in 1998 which accounts for the decline in income. The Company began 1999 with a 30% drop in total programs. However, management is still hopeful that additional programs can be sold. Uncollectible receivables from one account caused losses of $334,564 and $602,643 during 1998 and 1997, respectively. The Company also wrote off $135,255 of goodwill in 1997. Additionally, there was an increase in the Company's effective tax rate from 12% in 1996 to 36% in 1997, resulting from the utilization in 1996 of tax loss carryforwards. Earnings may have suffered from certain nonrecurring items during 1998 and 1997, but it is essential that the Company stabilize and grow its revenue base for this to be a viable investment.

Officers	Position	Ownership Information	
Edward A. Johnson	President, CFO	Number of Shares Outstanding	5,919,897
Mulemebet E. Michael	Exec VP, COO	Market Capitalization	$ 4,913,515
Michael S. Callison	Vice President	Number of Shareholders	800
Gary L. Dreher	Director	Where Listed / Symbol	OTC-BB / OPMC

Other Information			
Transfer Agent	American Stock Transfer & Trust Co. New York, NY	SIC Code	8060
Auditor	Ernst & Young LLP	Employees	170
Market Maker	Paragon Capital Corporation	(800)521-8877	Web Site	opmc.com
	Wien Securities Corp.	(800)624-0050		

Oralabs Holding Corp.

2901 South Tejon Street   Englewood, CO 80110   Telephone (303)783-9499   Fax (303)783-5759

Company Description

Oralabs Holding Corp. and its wholly-owned subsidiary, OraLabs, Inc., is in the business of manufacturing and distributing lip balm, fresh breath products and other products. The Company was founded in 1990. In 1992 the OraLabs flagship product, Ice Drops®, a breath drop product sold in a small plastic bottle, was introduced as an alternative to breath sprays and candy breath mints. Since that time, the Company has expanded the Ice Drops product line and has expanded into other niche markets ranging from sour candy drops to vitamin sprays. The Company also has private label contracts with Rite-Aid, Thrifty and Payless. The Company supplies numerous airlines and hotels with its products as well, including a specially packaged mouthwash, as part of those businesses' amenity programs.

	12/31/98	12/31/97	12/31/96	12/31/95
Per Share Information				
Stock Price	2.06	4.12	n.a.	n.a.
Earnings Per Share	0.09	0.13	0.16	0.30
Price / Earnings Ratio	22.89	31.69	n.a.	n.a.
Book Value Per Share	0.31	0.22	0.10	0.16
Price / Book Value %	664.52	1,872.73	n.a.	n.a.
Dividends Per Share	0.0	0.0	0.0	0.0
Annual Financial Data				
Operating Results (000's)				
Total Revenues	7,131.1	6,797.1	5,057.3	5,518.1
Costs & Expenses	-5,818.7	-5,146.8	-3,854.1	-2,994.4
Income Before Taxes and Other	1,312.4	1,650.3	1,197.1	2,207.2
Other Items	0.0	0.0	0.0	0.0
Income Tax	-493.8	-522.7	0.0	0.0
Net Income	818.6	1,127.7	1,197.1	2,207.2
Cash Flow From Operations	-373.2	1,240.7	1,338.3	1,840.4
Balance Sheet (000's)				
Cash & Equivalents	349.0	1,023.6	120.4	458.7
Total Current Assets	3,619.8	2,469.2	983.0	1,351.0
Fixed Assets, Net	431.4	214.7	157.8	100.0
Total Assets	4,051.2	2,683.9	1,140.8	1,451.0
Total Current Liabilities	1,162.4	676.5	373.2	292.0
Long-Term Debt	0.0	0.0	0.0	0.0
Stockholders' Equity	2,871.0	2,007.5	767.6	1,159.0
Performance & Financial Condition				
Return on Total Revenues %	11.48	16.59	23.67	40.00
Return on Avg Stockholders' Equity %	33.56	81.27	124.27	209.41
Return on Average Assets %	24.31	58.97	92.38	173.04
Current Ratio	3.11	3.65	2.63	4.63
Debt / Equity %	n.a.	n.a.	n.a.	n.a.

Compound Growth %'s	EPS %	-33.06	Net Income %	-28.15	Total Revenues %	8.92

Comments

In 1998, the Company introduced a line of nutritional supplements and intends to continue to expand its range of products so that it will become less reliant on any individual product. Management did not provide an explanation for flat sales in 1998. The Company recorded approximately $690,000 in returns and allowances for 1998, substantially from cough and cold product returns. No material returns were expected for 1999. Downward pressures on selling prices and increased overhead costs had the impact of lowering 1998 net income as compared to 1997. The Company has adequate working capital and no long term debt.

Officers	Position	Ownership Information	
Gary H. Schlatter	President	Number of Shares Outstanding	9,142,419
Emile Jordan	CFO, Controller	Market Capitalization	$ 18,833,383
Suzan M. Schlatter	Secretary	Number of Shareholders	928
Christopher Farnworth	Other	Where Listed / Symbol	NASDAQ / OLAB

Other Information			
Transfer Agent	Corporate Stock Transfer, Inc. Denver, CO	SIC Code	2844
Auditor	Schumacher & Associates, Inc.	Employees	80
		Web Site	oralabs.com

Orbit International Corp.

80 Cabot Court   Hauppauge, NY 11788   Telephone (516)435-8300   Fax (516)435-8458

Company Description

Orbit International Corp. is engaged in the design, manufacture and sale of customized electronic components and subsystems, distortion free commercial power units, power conversion devices and electronic devices for measurement and display. The Company also manufactures commercial power supplies, AC power sources, frequency converters, uninterruptible power supplies and associated analytical equipment. The primary customers are prime contractors, government procurement agencies and research and development laboratories. The Company discontinued its operations in the apparel business in 1996.

	12/31/98	12/31/97	12/31/96	12/31/95
Per Share Information				
Stock Price	1.50	3.19	2.19	0.81
Earnings Per Share	0.27	0.30	-0.89	-3.75
Price / Earnings Ratio	5.56	10.63	n.a.	n.a.
Book Value Per Share	1.44	1.17	0.83	1.58
Price / Book Value %	104.17	272.65	263.86	51.27
Dividends Per Share	0.0	0.0	0.0	0.0
Annual Financial Data				
Operating Results (000's)				
Total Revenues	16,351.0	17,910.0	18,291.0	14,377.0
Costs & Expenses	-15,170.0	-15,872.0	-14,980.0	-12,039.0
Income Before Taxes and Other	1,181.0	2,038.0	3,311.0	2,338.0
Other Items	-500.0	0.0	-8,800.0	-24,744.0
Income Tax	1,200.0	0.0	0.0	153.0
Net Income	1,881.0	2,038.0	-5,489.0	-22,253.0
Cash Flow From Operations	1,852.0	413.0	1,816.0	4,699.0
Balance Sheet (000's)				
Cash & Equivalents	438.0	1,096.0	927.0	2,274.0
Total Current Assets	13,624.0	13,484.0	14,891.0	25,416.0
Fixed Assets, Net	2,267.0	2,342.0	2,347.0	3,069.0
Total Assets	19,145.0	17,899.0	19,931.0	38,028.0
Total Current Liabilities	5,683.0	6,081.0	8,694.0	25,536.0
Long-Term Debt	3,881.0	864.0	4,352.0	1,097.0
Stockholders' Equity	9,059.0	7,287.0	5,146.0	9,318.0
Performance & Financial Condition				
Return on Total Revenues %	11.50	11.38	-30.01	-154.78
Return on Avg Stockholders' Equity %	23.01	32.78	-75.90	-109.67
Return on Average Assets %	10.16	10.77	-18.94	-43.83
Current Ratio	2.40	2.22	1.71	1.00
Debt / Equity %	42.84	11.86	84.57	11.77

Compound Growth %'s	EPS % n.a.	Net Income % n.a.	Total Revenues %	4.38

Comments

Revenues and gross margins both marginally declined during 1998. In July 1998, the Company reached a settlement with respect to class action securities litigation that has been in process since the closure of the apparel business. The Company's share was $1 million, half of which had been accrued in earlier years. $500,000 was expensed in 1998. The Company benefitted from a tax credit of $1.2 million and still had $24.7 million of tax loss carryovers available to offset future income. The Company incurred substantial losses from discontinued operations in 1996 and 1995. Earnings were reported from continuing operations for each of those years amounting to $.53 and $.42, respectively, on a per share basis. Immediate improvement can be noted in the Company's financial condition after exiting the apparel business by comparing the 1997 and 1996 balance sheets.

Officers	Position	Ownership Information	
Dennis Sunshine	President, CEO	Number of Shares Outstanding	6,270,000
Bruce Reissman	Exec VP, COO	Market Capitalization	$ 9,405,000
Mitchell Binder	VP - Finance, CFO	Number of Shareholders	680
Harlan Sylvan	Secretary, Treasurer	Where Listed / Symbol	NASDAQ / ORBT

Other Information			
Transfer Agent	American Stock Transfer & Trust Co. New York, NY	SIC Code	2330
Auditor	Ernst & Young LLP	Employees	98
		Web Site	orbitintl.com

Orleans Homebuilders, Inc.

One Greenwood Square, Suite 101, 3333 Street Road   Bensalem, PA 19020   Telephone (215)245-7500   Fax (215)947-9312

Company Description

Orleans Homebuilders, Inc., formerly FPA Corporation, operates as both a developer and builder. The Company builds and sells condominiums, townhouses and single-family homes as well as selling land and developed homesites. The Company develops residential communities in southeastern Pennsylvania and central and southern New Jersey. The Orleans family, which has been recognized as the preeminent home builder in the region for the last eighty years, continues to own a majority of the Company's outstanding shares.

	06/30/98	06/30/97	06/30/96	06/30/95
Per Share Information				
Stock Price as of 12/31	2.31	1.00	1.00	1.00
Earnings Per Share	0.15	0.19	0.17	0.10
Price / Earnings Ratio	15.40	5.26	5.88	10.00
Book Value Per Share	1.56	1.41	1.21	1.04
Price / Book Value %	148.08	70.92	82.64	96.15
Dividends Per Share	0.0	0.0	0.0	0.0
Annual Financial Data				
Operating Results (000's)				
Total Revenues	108,998.0	101,996.0	94,359.0	107,840.0
Costs & Expenses	-106,308.0	-99,939.0	-93,506.0	-106,369.0
Income Before Taxes and Other	2,690.0	2,057.0	853.0	1,471.0
Other Items	0.0	594.0	693.0	0.0
Income Tax	-1,022.0	-442.0	382.0	-270.0
Net Income	1,668.0	2,209.0	1,928.0	1,201.0
Cash Flow From Operations	-10,001.0	-13,287.0	-322.0	-2,411.0
Balance Sheet (000's)				
Cash & Equivalents	2,833.0	1,582.0	2,617.0	2,324.0
Total Current Assets	64,589.0	47,039.0	45,744.0	43,391.0
Fixed Assets, Net	1,892.0	507.0	468.0	523.0
Total Assets	130,525.0	107,613.0	92,866.0	102,274.0
Total Current Liabilities	28,592.0	20,433.0	23,257.0	34,087.0
Long-Term Debt	65,737.0	54,238.0	52,898.0	52,778.0
Stockholders' Equity	17,719.0	16,051.0	13,949.0	12,146.0
Performance & Financial Condition				
Return on Total Revenues %	1.53	2.17	2.04	1.11
Return on Avg Stockholders' Equity %	9.88	14.73	14.78	10.40
Return on Average Assets %	1.40	2.20	1.98	1.20
Current Ratio	2.26	2.30	1.97	1.27
Debt / Equity %	371.00	337.91	379.22	434.53

Compound Growth %'s	EPS %	14.47	Net Income %	11.57	Total Revenues %	0.36

Comments

New orders for fiscal 1998 increased by approximately 48%. This increase in new orders resulted from the opening of eight additional selling communities. The dollar backlog at June 30, 1998 increased approximately 86% to $70.1 million on 340 homes, as compared to $38.3 million on 210 homes the year before. The Company is continuing to expand its land acquisition efforts. For the six months ended December 31, 1998, the Company reported revenues and net income of $76.4 million and $2,469,000 ($.18 per share) as compared to $46.8 million and $337,000 ($.03 per share) for the same period of fiscal 1998. Although these numbers look excellent, investors must factor in a strong economy and low interest rates. The economy could weaken and interest rates could rise. The impact that either of these events would have is unpredictable.

Officers	Position	Ownership Information	
Jeffrey P. Orleans	Chairman, CEO	Number of Shares Outstanding	11,356,018
Michael T. Vessey	President, COO	Market Capitalization	$ 26,232,402
Joseph A. Santangelo	CFO, Secretary	Number of Shareholders	2,000
Benjamin D. Goldman	Director	Where Listed / Symbol	AMEX / OHB

Other Information

Transfer Agent	Registrar & Transfer Co. Cranford, NJ	SIC Code	1531
Auditor	PricewaterhouseCoopers LLP	Employees	177
		Web Site	orleanshomes.com

Overseas Filmgroup, Inc.

8800 Sunset Boulevard, Third Floor   Los Angeles, CA 90069   Telephone (310)855-1199   Fax (310)855-0719

Company Description

Overseas Filmgroup, Inc., formerly Entertainment/Media Acquisition Corporation, is an independent film company which specializes in the acquisition and worldwide license or sale of distribution rights to independently produced, feature films in a wide variety of genres (including action, art-house, comedy, drama, foreign language, science fiction and thrillers). The Company was formed in 1993 for the purpose of acquiring an operating business in the entertainment and media industry. An initial public offering was completed in February 1995. On October 31, 1996, Overseas Filmgroup, Inc., a privately-held company which had been operating since 1980, was acquired.

	12/31/98	12/31/97	12/31/96	12/31/95
Per Share Information				
Stock Price	2.00	2.06	4.62	4.56
Earnings Per Share	0.01	-0.09	-0.41	0.42
Price / Earnings Ratio	200.00	n.a.	n.a.	10.86
Book Value Per Share	2.03	2.02	2.11	3.60
Price / Book Value %	98.52	101.98	218.96	126.67
Dividends Per Share	0.0	0.0	0.0	0.0
Annual Financial Data				
Operating Results (000's)				
Total Revenues	25,731.7	22,678.4	28,888.1	22,026.1
Costs & Expenses	-25,619.3	-23,515.6	-27,222.8	-19,132.1
Income Before Taxes and Other	112.5	-837.3	1,665.3	2,894.1
Other Items	0.0	0.0	0.0	0.0
Income Tax	-53.0	293.4	-3,131.4	-432.9
Net Income	59.5	-543.9	-1,466.1	2,461.2
Cash Flow From Operations	20,686.2	n.a.	n.a.	n.a.
Balance Sheet (000's)				
Cash & Equivalents	537.7	1,179.1	353.7	2,433.2
Total Current Assets	20,422.1	16,049.2	11,541.0	11,072.2
Fixed Assets, Net	293.9	408.7	557.1	384.3
Total Assets	50,208.7	46,560.3	40,803.7	28,954.8
Total Current Liabilities	11,054.6	6,392.6	6,335.9	7,773.5
Long-Term Debt	22,013.3	25,304.2	18,693.0	7,421.9
Stockholders' Equity	11,620.6	11,561.1	12,191.8	11,448.4
Performance & Financial Condition				
Return on Total Revenues %	0.23	-2.40	-5.08	11.17
Return on Avg Stockholders' Equity %	0.51	-4.58	-12.40	23.15
Return on Average Assets %	0.12	-1.25	-4.20	9.18
Current Ratio	1.85	2.51	1.82	1.42
Debt / Equity %	189.43	218.87	153.32	64.83

Compound Growth %'s	EPS %	-71.23	Net Income %	-71.09	Total Revenues %	5.32

Comments

The numbers above represent both the Company and the acquired company on a combined basis as if they had been combined for the four year period. The acquired company was taxed as an S corporation under Subchapter S of the Internal Revenue Code. The numbers above reflect a provision for income taxes, had regular corporate income taxes been required. The decrease in revenues during 1997 as compared to 1996 was due to the timing of revenue recognition. Although revenue was not completely restored in 1998, the Company was marginally profitable. The Company is extremely leveraged and remains on a tight leash held by a loan syndicate. The terms of the credit facility were amended and extended on April 9, 1999.

Officers	Position	Ownership Information	
Robert B. Little	Chairman, CEO	Number of Shares Outstanding	5,732,778
Ellen D. Little	President, CEO	Market Capitalization	$ 11,465,556
William F. Lischak	COO, CFO	Number of Shareholders	1,000
MJ Peckos	Senior VP	Where Listed / Symbol	OTC-BB / OSFG

Other Information			
Transfer Agent	Continental Stock Transfer & Trust Co. New York, NY	SIC Code	7812
Auditor	PricewaterhouseCoopers LLP	Employees	24
Market Maker	M.H. Meyerson & Co., Inc.	(800)333-3113	Web Site	ofg.com
	Herzog, Heine, Geduld, Inc.	(800)221-3600		

PDG Environmental, Inc.

300 Oxford Drive   Monroeville, PA 15146   Telephone (412)856-2200   Fax (412)856-6914

Company Description

PDG Environmental, Inc. is engaged primarily in providing asbestos abatement services to the private and public sectors. In 1991, the Company expanded the scope of its business to include environmental remediation services with a specialization in remediating leaking underground storage tanks. It also purchased a thermal desorption plant in 1992 but discontinued that operation in 1996. In December 1997, the Company became a general and limited partner in a venture that is performing a $12 million asbestos abatement contract which is expected to be completed by the end of the second quarter of fiscal 1999. The Company holds a 60% ownership share.

	01/31/98	01/31/97	01/31/96	01/31/95
Per Share Information				
Stock Price as of 12/31	0.81	1.56	1.92	0.31
Earnings Per Share	0.17	-0.09	-0.44	0.07
Price / Earnings Ratio	4.76	n.a.	n.a.	4.43
Book Value Per Share	0.09	-0.18	-0.11	0.23
Price / Book Value %	900.00	n.a.	n.a.	134.78
Dividends Per Share	0.0	0.0	0.0	0.0
Annual Financial Data				
Operating Results (000's)				
Total Revenues	24,662.0	16,292.0	17,602.0	17,707.0
Costs & Expenses	-23,300.0	-16,476.0	-18,249.0	-18,721.0
Income Before Taxes and Other	1,362.0	-184.0	-647.0	-1,014.0
Other Items	-102.0	-302.0	-1,701.0	1,511.0
Income Tax	-20.0	0.0	-103.0	-24.0
Net Income	1,240.0	-486.0	-2,451.0	473.0
Cash Flow From Operations	1,012.0	167.0	2,534.0	-1,817.0
Balance Sheet (000's)				
Cash & Equivalents	892.0	429.0	273.0	681.0
Total Current Assets	8,996.0	5,440.0	6,690.0	16,299.0
Fixed Assets, Net	969.0	688.0	819.0	1,098.0
Total Assets	10,337.0	6,165.0	7,564.0	17,519.0
Total Current Liabilities	6,202.0	5,031.0	3,580.0	9,821.0
Long-Term Debt	1,628.0	372.0	2,766.0	4,089.0
Stockholders' Equity	2,265.0	762.0	1,218.0	3,609.0
Performance & Financial Condition				
Return on Total Revenues %	5.03	-2.98	-13.92	2.67
Return on Avg Stockholders' Equity %	81.93	-49.09	-101.55	14.21
Return on Average Assets %	15.03	-7.08	-19.54	3.72
Current Ratio	1.45	1.08	1.87	1.66
Debt / Equity %	71.88	48.82	227.09	113.30

Compound Growth %'s	EPS %	34.42	Net Income %	37.89	Total Revenues %	11.68

Comments

Fiscal 1998 revenue increased as a result of increased bidding opportunities and contract awards. Higher margins were also experienced. The bottom line was a strong return to profitability. The order backlog at year end was $27.6 million, up from $14.4 million at the end of the preceding year. Book value per common share was calculated after deduction of the liquidation preference of the preferred shares. The Company did not have to record an income tax expense because of tax loss carryovers. At January 31, 1998, the Company had $7.7 million left in tax loss carryovers to offset future income. For the nine months ended October 31, 1998, the Company reported revenues and net income of $31.3 million and $1,064,000 ($.14 per share) as compared to $16.0 million and $783,000 ($.11 per share) for the same portion of fiscal 1998.

Officers	Position	Ownership Information	
John C. Regan	President, CEO	Number of Shares Outstanding	6,474,412
Todd Fortiere	CFO	Market Capitalization	$ 5,244,274
Dulcia Maire	Secretary	Number of Shareholders	2,191
Lawrence J. Horvat	Vice President	Where Listed / Symbol	OTC-BB / PDGE

Other Information			
Transfer Agent	Continental Stock Transfer & Trust Co. New York, NY	SIC Code	4955
Auditor	Ernst & Young LLP	Employees	80
Market Maker	Carr Securities Corporation (800)221-2243	Web Site	pdge.com
	Wien Securities Corp. (800)624-0050		

PDK Labs Inc.

145 Ricefield Lane Hauppauge, NY 11788 Telephone (516)273-2630 Fax (516)273-1582

Company Description

PDK Labs Inc. manufactures and distributes over-the-counter non-prescription pharmaceutical products and vitamins. The Company's line of products primarily consists of non-prescription pain relievers, decongestants, bronchodialators, and a broad range of vitamins and nutritional supplements. The Company markets its products through regional distributors, private label distribution and various licensing and supply agreements. PDK also sells products through its majority-owned public subsidiary, Futurebiotics, Inc. (NASDAQ) and has a supply agreement with Superior Supplements, Inc. (NASDAQ) which is also presented in this manual. On March 3, 1999, the Company and Futurebiotics agreed to sell all of the assets of Futurebiotics to an unrelated party.

	11/30/98	11/30/97	11/30/96	11/30/95
Per Share Information				
Stock Price as of 12/31	3.00	6.87	5.00	4.12
Earnings Per Share	0.16	0.41	0.40	-0.24
Price / Earnings Ratio	18.75	16.76	12.50	n.a.
Book Value Per Share	7.60	7.64	6.96	6.50
Price / Book Value %	39.47	89.92	71.84	63.38
Dividends Per Share	0.0	0.0	0.0	0.0
Annual Financial Data				
Operating Results (000's)				
Total Revenues	47,405.0	51,699.9	47,620.1	32,688.6
Costs & Expenses	-44,516.0	-49,922.7	-45,129.0	-30,815.1
Income Before Taxes and Other	2,889.0	1,671.3	2,491.2	60.5
Other Items	-619.0	498.0	139.6	-190.6
Income Tax	-1,493.0	-610.0	-1,018.0	-50.0
Net Income	777.0	1,559.3	1,612.8	-180.1
Cash Flow From Operations	6,448.0	-503.3	-1,819.3	-4,299.4
Balance Sheet (000's)				
Cash & Equivalents	929.0	3,733.7	2,885.5	928.8
Total Current Assets	38,554.0	44,153.2	39,480.0	26,974.6
Fixed Assets, Net	4,385.0	4,667.4	5,132.5	3,408.1
Total Assets	46,480.0	54,221.5	53,254.5	41,943.1
Total Current Liabilities	9,196.0	5,988.6	7,625.0	3,890.5
Long-Term Debt	4,342.0	15,433.6	13,602.8	8,251.5
Stockholders' Equity	29,504.0	28,304.9	26,661.2	24,437.0
Performance & Financial Condition				
Return on Total Revenues %	1.64	3.02	3.39	-0.55
Return on Avg Stockholders' Equity %	2.69	5.67	6.31	-0.77
Return on Average Assets %	1.54	2.90	3.39	-0.41
Current Ratio	4.19	7.37	5.18	6.93
Debt / Equity %	14.72	54.53	51.02	33.77

Compound Growth %'s	EPS %	-36.75	Net Income %	-30.59	Total Revenues %	13.19

Comments

An increase in the volume of private label sales and the introduction of new products have contributed to a 19.2% advance in revenues. Margins have declined due to product mix and an unfavorable exclusive supply agreement with a non-affiliated customer that was terminated on March 30, 1998. The operating results of Futurebiotics have been separated from normal operations and shown as a loss from discontinued operations, amounting to $619,000 ($.19 per share) for 1998. The effective tax rate climbed to 52% from 32% in 1997 due to state taxes and certain permanent differences. In fiscal 1995, the Company wrote-off $2,374,000 of inventory in ephedrine related products which produced a loss for the year. Intangible assets at December 31, 1998, are immaterial.

Officers	Position	Ownership Information	
Reginald Spinello	President, CEO	Number of Shares Outstanding	3,458,727
Karine Hollander	CFO, Secretary	Market Capitalization	$ 10,376,181
Ira Helman	Director	Number of Shareholders	768
Hartley T. Bernstein	Other	Where Listed / Symbol	NASDAQ / PDKL

Other Information			
Transfer Agent	Continental Stock Transfer & Trust Co. New York, NY	SIC Code	2834
Auditor	Holtz Rubenstein & Co., LLP	Employees	158
		Web Site	pdklabs.com

PREMIS Corporation

13220 County Road 6   Plymouth, MN 55441   Telephone (612)550-1999   Fax (612)550-2999

Company Description

PREMIS Corporation develops, markets and supports enterprise-wide retail automation systems to meet the information needs of multi-store specialty and general merchandise retailing chains. The Company's systems provide retailers with a variety of integrated functions and benefits such as: point of sale data collection; real time sales analysis reporting by store, product, customer and salesperson; enterprise inventory tracking; merchandise management; gross margin improvement, and electronic data interface. The Company's proprietary software products are typically sold in combination with POS terminals, PC workstations and client/server hardware. The Company was founded in 1982.

	03/31/98	03/31/97	03/31/96	03/31/95
Per Share Information				
Stock Price as of 12/31	0.75	1.62	5.25	0.25
Earnings Per Share	-0.51	-1.67	0.28	0.18
Price / Earnings Ratio	n.a.	n.a.	18.75	1.39
Book Value Per Share	0.40	0.92	0.58	0.26
Price / Book Value %	187.50	176.09	905.17	96.15
Dividends Per Share	0.0	0.0	0.0	0.0
Annual Financial Data				
Operating Results (000's)				
Total Revenues	6,044.7	8,807.5	5,902.2	3,017.6
Costs & Expenses	-8,387.0	-14,650.6	-4,547.5	-2,542.9
Income Before Taxes and Other	-2,342.3	-5,843.1	1,354.6	474.7
Other Items	0.0	0.0	0.0	0.0
Income Tax	-83.9	-318.8	-527.0	0.0
Net Income	-2,426.2	-6,161.9	827.6	474.7
Cash Flow From Operations	-366.2	-856.3	713.1	355.4
Balance Sheet (000's)				
Cash & Equivalents	1,359.8	2,433.4	668.1	427.0
Total Current Assets	2,540.0	5,983.3	2,500.2	1,185.0
Fixed Assets, Net	1,316.2	1,395.4	83.5	48.8
Total Assets	4,344.4	8,066.8	2,833.0	1,559.6
Total Current Liabilities	1,610.8	2,534.2	1,208.5	651.5
Long-Term Debt	53.3	152.4	112.1	226.1
Stockholders' Equity	1,862.8	4,338.1	1,512.5	682.0
Performance & Financial Condition				
Return on Total Revenues %	-40.14	-69.96	14.02	15.73
Return on Avg Stockholders' Equity %	-78.25	-210.64	75.43	106.75
Return on Average Assets %	-39.10	-113.06	37.68	49.68
Current Ratio	1.58	2.36	2.07	1.82
Debt / Equity %	2.86	3.51	7.41	33.15

Compound Growth %'s	EPS %	n.a.	Net Income %	n.a.	Total Revenues %	26.06

Comments

A sharp drop in revenues was caused by a change in the relationship of supplying the United States Postal Service Store of the Future systems. The Company has become a subcontractor to NCR with NCR providing the hardware. Management has cut costs to attempt to return the Company to profitability but the auditors issued a going concern exception in their report on the overall financial condition. The large fiscal 1997 loss was due to an acquisition in October 1996, which caused $6.5 million of purchased research and development in process to be expensed. It will be important to watch the financial health of the Company on a quarterly basis. For the nine months ended December 31, 1998, revenues and net income were $4.3 million and $1,593,000 ($.33 per share) as compared to $4.9 million and a net loss of $1,462,000 ($.31 per share) for the same period of the preceding year.

Officers	Position	Ownership Information	
F. T. Biermeier	Chairman, CEO	Number of Shares Outstanding	4,714,177
Richard R. Peterson	CFO	Market Capitalization	$ 3,535,633
Mary Ann Calhoun	Vice President, Secretary	Number of Shareholders	1,252
Gerald F. Schmidt	Director	Where Listed / Symbol	OTC-BB / PMIS

Other Information			
Transfer Agent	Company Office Plymouth, MN	SIC Code	7372
Auditor	PricewaterhouseCoopers LLP	Employees	56
Market Maker	R.J. Steichen and Co.	(800)328-8217	
	Paragon Capital Corporation	(800)345-0505	

PTI Holding Inc.

1 Executive Boulevard, 3rd Floor   Yonkers, NY 10701   Telephone (914)423-8200   Fax (914)423-9610

Company Description

PTI Holding Inc. has three active wholly-owned subsidiaries: Protective Technologies International Inc. (PTI), Flents Products Co., Inc. (Flents), and Zacko Sports, Inc. (Zacko). PTI and Zacko design, manufacture and market bicycle helmets, bicycles and bicycle accessories for sale principally to domestic retailers. Flents designs, manufactures and markets earplugs and other safety and medical supplies such as an eye drop delivery system, styptic devices, and air filter masks. The Company was founded in 1990.

	12/31/98	12/31/97	12/31/96	12/31/95
Per Share Information				
Stock Price	3.37	8.25	8.50	4.69
Earnings Per Share	0.49	-0.23	0.43	0.24
Price / Earnings Ratio	6.88	n.a.	19.77	19.54
Book Value Per Share	3.82	3.40	2.17	1.70
Price / Book Value %	88.22	242.65	391.71	275.88
Dividends Per Share	0.0	0.0	0.0	0.0
Annual Financial Data				
Operating Results (000's)				
Total Revenues	60,522.0	34,566.1	17,529.0	8,216.2
Costs & Expenses	-56,171.3	-29,825.2	-14,858.0	-7,618.2
Income Before Taxes and Other	4,350.7	4,523.5	2,671.0	597.9
Other Items	0.0	-3,636.8	0.0	80.0
Income Tax	-1,858.5	-1,828.0	-980.0	190.0
Net Income	2,492.2	-941.3	1,691.0	867.9
Cash Flow From Operations	-8,273.5	-463.8	-1,691.8	549.9
Balance Sheet (000's)				
Cash & Equivalents	837.6	682.2	361.9	969.3
Total Current Assets	29,755.3	15,016.3	8,496.3	4,367.0
Fixed Assets, Net	3,066.4	1,673.6	470.9	366.6
Total Assets	38,387.0	21,127.0	10,607.6	6,536.9
Total Current Liabilities	19,434.9	4,807.1	2,976.4	773.7
Long-Term Debt	0.0	0.0	0.0	0.0
Stockholders' Equity	18,952.1	16,319.8	7,569.9	5,676.9
Performance & Financial Condition				
Return on Total Revenues %	4.12	-2.72	9.65	10.56
Return on Avg Stockholders' Equity %	14.13	-7.88	25.53	16.77
Return on Average Assets %	8.38	-5.93	19.73	12.40
Current Ratio	1.53	3.12	2.85	5.64
Debt / Equity %	n.a.	n.a.	n.a.	n.a.

Compound Growth %'s	EPS %	26.86	Net Income %	42.13	Total Revenues %	94.57

Comments

The 75% sales increase from 1997 to 1998 resulted predominantly from increased sales to existing customers through the addition of new helmet models, from increased market share at the expense of competitors, from increased sales in existing models due to growth in the overall helmet market, from increased sales of bicycle and bicycle accessory products, and from new licensing arrangements. Income tax expense in 1997 was disproportionate to income due to the nondeductible nature of executive stock-based compensation adjustments in that year. 1997 results included a nonrecurring charge of $3.6 million for this compensation. At December 31, 1998, the Company had $5.3 million of intangible assets recorded on its books which equated to approximately 28% of stockholders' equity and book value per share.

Officers	Position	Ownership Information	
Meredith W. Birrittella	Chairman, CEO	Number of Shares Outstanding	4,956,352
Donald L. Turrell	President	Market Capitalization	$ 16,702,906
Anthony Costanzo	CFO	Number of Shareholders	1,300
Warren Schaeffer	Secretary	Where Listed / Symbol	NASDAQ / PTII

Other Information			
Transfer Agent	Corporate Stock Transfer, Inc. Denver, CO	SIC Code	3949
Auditor	Arthur Andersen LLP	Employees	250

Pacific Aerospace & Electronics, Inc.

434 Olds Station Road   Wenatchee, WA 98801   Telephone (509)667-9600   Fax (509)667-9696

Company Description

Pacific Aerospace & Electronics, Inc. develops, manufactures, markets and sells a broad range of precision electronic components which are designed to operate with a high degree of reliability in harsh environments, and machine or cast metal products for applications in the aerospace, defense, telecommunications, energy, transportation, medical and general electronics industries. The Company was formed in 1986 for the purpose of acquisitions and has been an active consolidator of companies, having integrated eight U.S. operating companies since 1990. On July 30, 1998. the Company nearly doubled its size by acquiring Aeromet International plc, a British company.

	05/31/98	05/31/97	05/31/96	05/31/95
Per Share Information				
Stock Price as of 12/31	2.12	4.81	2.87	4.12
Earnings Per Share	0.27	0.17	-0.16	-0.41
Price / Earnings Ratio	7.85	28.29	n.a.	n.a.
Book Value Per Share	3.65	2.07	1.68	1.05
Price / Book Value %	58.08	232.37	170.83	n.a.
Dividends Per Share	0.0	0.0	0.0	0.0
Annual Financial Data				
Operating Results (000's)				
Total Revenues	54,099.0	34,470.0	20,777.0	11,035.0
Costs & Expenses	-50,114.0	-32,738.0	-21,843.0	-12,148.7
Income Before Taxes and Other	3,132.0	1,732.0	-1,066.0	-1,113.7
Other Items	0.0	0.0	0.0	-538.0
Income Tax	482.0	-50.0	67.0	241.0
Net Income	3,614.0	1,682.0	-999.0	-1,410.7
Cash Flow From Operations	1,500.0	-256.0	-2,692.0	-416.6
Balance Sheet (000's)				
Cash & Equivalents	11,461.0	3,048.0	725.0	1,078.6
Total Current Assets	37,678.0	18,939.0	13,009.0	6,848.3
Fixed Assets, Net	26,335.0	13,190.0	10,656.0	3,008.1
Total Assets	78,580.0	35,752.0	27,649.0	11,629.9
Total Current Liabilities	12,079.0	5,849.0	12,057.0	5,089.5
Long-Term Debt	9,059.0	3,236.0	1,991.0	319.6
Stockholders' Equity	56,142.0	25,619.0	12,539.0	5,454.2
Performance & Financial Condition				
Return on Total Revenues %	6.68	4.88	-4.81	-12.78
Return on Avg Stockholders' Equity %	8.84	8.82	-11.10	-42.24
Return on Average Assets %	6.32	5.31	-5.09	-14.45
Current Ratio	3.12	3.24	1.08	1.35
Debt / Equity %	16.14	12.63	15.88	5.86

Compound Growth %'s	EPS % n.a.	Net Income % n.a.	Total Revenues %	69.88

Comments

Acquisitions and internal growth have propelled revenue to record levels. Better yet, the Company recorded back-to-back profitable years. All of the acquisitions have involved the issuance of additional shares. The acquisition of Aeromet at a cost of $75 million is being accounted for using the purchase method of accounting, which explains the large increase in fiscal 1999 revenues. For the nine months ended February 28, 1999, the Company reported revenues of $76.9 million and a net loss of $8,272,000 ($.49 per share) as compared to revenue of $37.0 million and net income of $2,892,000 ($.23 per share) for the same period of the preceding year. The loss was attributable to goodwill write downs, impaired inventory, a slowdown in Boeing revenue, and acquisition costs.

Officers	Position	Ownership Information	
Donald A. Wright	President, CEO	Number of Shares Outstanding	15,395,723
Nick A. Gerde	VP - Finance, CFO	Market Capitalization	$ 32,638,933
Sheryl A. Symonds	Vice President, Secretary	Number of Shareholders	940
Dale L. Rasmussen	Director	Where Listed / Symbol	NASDAQ / PCTH

Other Information			
Transfer Agent	Interwest Transfer Co., Inc. Salt Lake City, UT	SIC Code	3640
Auditor	KPMG LLP	Employees	748
		Web Site	pcth.com

Paravant Computer Systems, Inc.

1615A West Nasa Boulevard   Melbourne, FL 32901   Telephone (407)727-3672   Fax (407)725-0496

Company Description

Paravant Computer Systems, Inc. is a manufacturer of rugged, portable computers and communication interfaces utilized in outdoor settings. The Company also offers extensive customization services to modify its standard products to the specific needs of the end-users. The Company's laptop and hand-held processors are designed and built to function in adverse environments such as harsh weather, climate and operational conditions. Insulated from temperature extremes, flying debris, shock, vibration, moisture and humidity, its products have a reputation for high-level performance and reliability in difficult circumstances. Paravant products are sold to the United States, foreign military establishments and commercial enterprises. The Company was founded in 1982 and went public in 1996.

	09/30/98	09/30/97	09/30/96	09/30/95
Per Share Information				
Stock Price as of 12/31	2.16	3.75	5.25	3.00
Earnings Per Share	0.14	0.10	0.10	0.13
Price / Earnings Ratio	15.43	37.50	52.50	23.08
Book Value Per Share	1.23	1.03	0.89	0.45
Price / Book Value %	175.61	364.08	589.89	666.67
Dividends Per Share	0.0	0.0	0.0	0.0
Annual Financial Data				
Operating Results (000's)				
Total Revenues	15,635.3	13,240.5	10,506.3	8,652.6
Costs & Expenses	-13,425.7	-11,504.5	-9,428.4	-8,071.1
Income Before Taxes and Other	2,209.6	1,736.0	1,078.0	581.4
Other Items	0.0	0.0	0.0	0.0
Income Tax	-750.0	-594.2	-375.8	0.0
Net Income	1,459.6	1,141.8	702.2	581.4
Cash Flow From Operations	2,049.7	3,448.7	-1,426.1	n.a.
Balance Sheet (000's)				
Cash & Equivalents	1,187.8	1,612.6	65.1	211.4
Total Current Assets	9,881.7	9,709.3	10,084.6	8,486.6
Fixed Assets, Net	1,239.2	914.4	517.5	462.4
Total Assets	12,695.6	11,270.1	10,988.7	9,449.7
Total Current Liabilities	2,225.7	2,901.3	3,248.2	7,136.2
Long-Term Debt	0.0	9.1	619.2	306.4
Stockholders' Equity	10,235.8	8,209.5	7,045.8	2,007.2
Performance & Financial Condition				
Return on Total Revenues %	9.34	8.62	6.68	6.72
Return on Avg Stockholders' Equity %	15.83	14.97	15.51	32.30
Return on Average Assets %	12.18	10.26	6.87	9.69
Current Ratio	4.44	3.35	3.10	1.19
Debt / Equity %	n.a.	0.11	8.79	15.26

Compound Growth %'s	EPS %	2.50	Net Income %	35.91	Total Revenues %	21.80

Comments

The 17% increase in revenues during fiscal 1998 is primarily due to the Company's strong backlog at the beginning of the year, its continued full scale production deliveries to Raytheon in support of the U.S. Marine Corp's HAWK/AVENGER Air Defense missile system upgrade, and to additional requirements of Lockheed Martin in their work on the F-16 Fighter Aircraft and F-117A Stealth Fighter. In addition, significant sales were made to the U.S. Navy of an integrated test and maintenance system for the Phalanx Gun System. The Company is clearly growth oriented as its goal is to become a $100 million technology company by the year 2000. Half of that mark would be very impressive. Subsequent to the last year end, the Company acquired two related electronic defense industry companies.

Officers	Position	Ownership Information	
Krishan K. Joshi	Chairman, CEO	Number of Shares Outstanding	8,343,928
Richard P. McNeight	President, COO	Market Capitalization	$ 18,022,884
William R. Craven	Vice President, Secretary	Number of Shareholders	2,000
Kevin J. Bartczak	Vice President, CFO	Where Listed / Symbol	NASDAQ / PVAT

Other Information			
Transfer Agent	Continental Stock Transfer & Trust Co. New York, NY	SIC Code	3571
Auditor	KPMG LLP	Employees	153
		Web Site	paravant.com

Patterson Energy, Inc.

4510 Lamesa Highway, P.O. Box 1416   Snyder, TX 79550   Telephone (915)573-1104   Fax (915)573-0281

Company Description

Patterson Energy, Inc. is one of the leading providers of domestic land drilling services to major and independent oil and natural gas companies. Formed in 1978, the Company focuses its operations primarily in Texas and southeast New Mexico. The Company currently has a drilling fleet of 119 drilling rigs and has established a reputation for reliability, high quality drilling equipment and well-trained crews. Over the past four years, the Company's operations have expanded significantly through a series of acquisitions. During June 1997, the Company acquired 21 operable contract drilling rigs, related rolling stock, a shop and a yard from Wes-Tex Drilling Company in Abilene, Texas, for the purchase price of approximately $35.4 million. The Company entered the drilling fluid services business in 1998 by acquiring two companies for approximately $55 million.

	12/31/98	12/31/97	12/31/96	12/31/95
Per Share Information				
Stock Price	3.62	38.69	25.75	14.00
Earnings Per Share	-0.01	0.75	0.21	0.18
Price / Earnings Ratio	n.a.	51.59	122.62	77.78
Book Value Per Share	4.95	4.74	2.20	1.07
Price / Book Value %	73.13	816.24	1,170.45	1,308.41
Dividends Per Share	0.0	0.0	0.0	0.0
Annual Financial Data				
Operating Results (000's)				
Total Revenues	188,178.0	193,609.0	84,851.0	65,398.0
Costs & Expenses	-188,410.0	-158,501.0	-80,566.0	-62,984.0
Income Before Taxes and Other	-232.0	35,108.0	4,285.0	2,414.0
Other Items	0.0	0.0	-2,268.0	0.0
Income Tax	-93.0	-12,866.0	2,254.0	787.0
Net Income	-325.0	22,242.0	4,271.0	3,201.0
Cash Flow From Operations	29,992.0	34,442.0	4,655.0	9,533.0
Balance Sheet (000's)				
Cash & Equivalents	8,986.0	23,338.0	3,494.0	9,344.0
Total Current Assets	53,483.0	77,014.0	35,481.0	16,800.2
Fixed Assets, Net	136,677.0	100,405.0	51,308.0	26,470.3
Total Assets	236,605.0	203,200.0	87,913.0	43,790.4
Total Current Liabilities	22,952.0	30,530.0	17,889.0	10,510.8
Long-Term Debt	47,143.0	21,783.0	25,732.0	12,906.5
Stockholders' Equity	156,852.0	146,932.0	43,482.0	20,373.2
Performance & Financial Condition				
Return on Total Revenues %	-0.17	11.49	5.03	4.89
Return on Avg Stockholders' Equity %	-0.21	23.36	13.38	9.42
Return on Average Assets %	-0.15	15.28	6.49	5.69
Current Ratio	2.33	2.52	1.98	1.60
Debt / Equity %	30.06	14.83	59.18	63.35

Compound Growth %'s	EPS % n.a.	Net Income % n.a.	Total Revenues % 42.23

Comments

The decreased profitability in 1998 was largely attributable to a 35% decrease in the Company's rig utilization rates, a change in drilling contracts which required the Company to bear certain costs associated with drilling wells that in 1997 was paid by the Company's customers, and a moderate decrease during 1998 by the Company in its daily drilling rates. These three factors were reflective of the detrimental impact the industry's weakened commodity prices had on the Company's operations. 1996 results include $2,268,000 of nonrecurring acquisition costs. At December 31, 1998, the Company had $45.9 million recorded as goodwill on its books which equated to approximately 29% of stockholders' equity and book value per share.

Officers	Position	Ownership Information	
Cloyce Talbott	Chairman, CEO	Number of Shares Outstanding	31,671,132
A. Glenn Patterson	President, COO	Market Capitalization	$ 114,649,498
James C. Brown	VP - Finance, CFO	Number of Shareholders	18,000
Robert C. Gist	Director	Where Listed / Symbol	NASDAQ / PTEN

Other Information			
Transfer Agent	Continental Stock Transfer & Trust Co. New York, NY	SIC Code	1381
Auditor	PricewaterhouseCoopers LLP	Employees	1,202

Pentacon, Inc.

10375 Richmond Avenue, Suite 700   Houston, TX 77042   Telephone (713)860-1000   Fax (713)463-8997

Company Description

Pentacon, Inc. is the second largest distributor of fasteners and small parts to original equipment manufacturers in the United States. Fasteners and small parts are incorporated into a wide variety of end use applications across a broad spectrum of industries and include screws, bolts, nuts, washers, pins, rings, fittings, springs, electrical connectors and similar small parts, many of which are specialized or highly engineered for particular applications. The Company's largest customers include The Boeing Company, Cummins Engine, General Electric Corporation, Harley-Davidson, Inc., the Hughes Aircraft subsidiary of General Motors Corporation, and Lockheed Martin Corporation.

	09/30/98	09/30/97	12/31/96	12/31/95
Per Share Information				
Stock Price as of 12/31	4.31	12.75	n.a.	n.a.
Earnings Per Share	0.45	0.90	0.85	0.48
Price / Earnings Ratio	9.58	14.17	n.a.	n.a.
Book Value Per Share	6.89	3.35	3.05	2.05
Price / Book Value %	62.55	380.60	n.a.	n.a.
Dividends Per Share	0.0	0.0	0.0	0.0
Annual Financial Data				
Operating Results (000's)				
Total Revenues	141,169.0	42,322.0	44,782.0	41,204.0
Costs & Expenses	-131,109.0	-37,793.0	-40,643.0	-38,785.0
Income Before Taxes and Other	10,060.0	4,529.0	4,139.0	2,419.0
Other Items	0.0	0.0	0.0	0.0
Income Tax	-5,373.0	-1,860.0	-1,628.0	-995.0
Net Income	4,687.0	2,669.0	2,511.0	1,424.0
Cash Flow From Operations	-18,733.0	54.0	-409.0	1,500.0
Balance Sheet (000's)				
Cash & Equivalents	835.0	733.0	256.0	117.0
Total Current Assets	159,250.0	32,996.0	26,431.0	20,717.0
Fixed Assets, Net	7,077.0	1,578.0	2,088.0	2,509.0
Total Assets	304,391.0	34,911.0	28,519.0	23,226.0
Total Current Liabilities	91,096.0	12,841.0	9,301.0	7,409.0
Long-Term Debt	98,381.0	13,686.0	11,588.0	10,698.0
Stockholders' Equity	114,914.0	8,384.0	7,630.0	5,119.0
Performance & Financial Condition				
Return on Total Revenues %	3.32	6.31	5.61	3.46
Return on Avg Stockholders' Equity %	7.60	33.33	39.39	32.31
Return on Average Assets %	2.76	8.42	9.71	6.60
Current Ratio	1.75	2.57	2.84	2.80
Debt / Equity %	85.61	163.24	151.87	208.99

Compound Growth %'s	EPS %	-2.13	Net Income %	48.75	Total Revenues %	50.75

Comments

The Company was formed in March 1997. Simultaneously with the closing of the initial public offering of its common stock, Pentacon acquired five businesses in separate transactions. Alatec Products, Inc. (Alatec) was considered the acquiror under accounting rules. The financial information presented is that of the Company since inception and of Alatec in earlier periods. Operating results for the period ended September 30, 1997 are for a nine month period. The increase in revenues reflected during fiscal 1998 is primarily attributable to acquisitions. At September 30, 1998, the Company had $135.4 million of goodwill reflected on its ledgers which equated to approximately 118% of stockholders' equity and book value per share.

Officers	Position	Ownership Information	
Mark E. Baldwin	Chairman, CEO	Number of Shares Outstanding	16,668,129
Jack L. Fatica	President, COO	Market Capitalization	$ 71,839,636
Brian Fontana	Senior VP, CFO	Number of Shareholders	2,000
Bruce M. Taten	Senior VP, Secretary	Where Listed / Symbol	NYSE / JIT

Other Information			
Transfer Agent	American Securities Transfer, Inc. Lakewood, CO	SIC Code	5072
Auditor	Ernst & Young LLP	Employees	850
		Web Site	pentacon-inc.com

Petroleum Development Corporation

103 East Main Street   Bridgeport, WV 26330   Telephone (304)842-3597   Fax (304)842-0913

Company Description

Petroleum Development Corporation is a regional independent energy company engaged primarily in the development, production and marketing of natural gas. The Company has grown primarily through increased drilling and development activities, the acquisition and subsequent development of natural gas producing wells and the expansion of its natural gas marketing activities. As of December 31, 1998, the Company operated approximately 1,600 wells. The majority of the wells operated by the Company are located in the West Virginia and Pennsylvania portions of the Appalachian Basin. The Appalachian Basin is characterized by shallow developmental wells which generally have provided highly predictable drilling success rates. In addition, because wells drilled in the Appalachian Basin are closer to the large demand centers for natural gas in the northeastern United States, natural gas from this area typically has commanded a price premium relative to natural gas produced in areas such as the Gulf Coast and Mid-Continent regions of the United States. The Company was founded in 1969.

	12/31/98	12/31/97	12/31/96	12/31/95
Per Share Information				
Stock Price	3.06	5.19	4.06	1.44
Earnings Per Share	0.41	0.61	0.31	0.13
Price / Earnings Ratio	7.46	8.51	13.10	11.08
Book Value Per Share	4.05	3.66	2.21	1.78
Price / Book Value %	75.56	141.80	183.71	80.90
Dividends Per Share	0.0	0.0	0.0	0.0
Annual Financial Data				
Operating Results (000's)				
Total Revenues	82,973.6	73,878.0	49,613.7	22,346.5
Costs & Expenses	-74,348.5	-64,195.8	-44,963.7	-20,514.1
Income Before Taxes and Other	8,625.1	9,682.2	4,650.0	1,832.4
Other Items	0.0	0.0	0.0	0.0
Income Tax	-1,967.1	-2,095.4	-1,100.6	-350.9
Net Income	6,658.0	7,586.8	3,549.4	1,481.5
Cash Flow From Operations	13,623.4	18,094.1	16,905.8	5,320.8
Balance Sheet (000's)				
Cash & Equivalents	34,894.6	46,561.0	20,615.4	10,053.6
Total Current Assets	44,008.6	53,858.8	28,619.5	13,156.9
Fixed Assets, Net	65,390.6	43,569.3	34,439.7	27,463.2
Total Assets	111,300.4	98,411.6	63,604.2	40,620.1
Total Current Liabilities	42,483.8	37,375.6	30,976.7	14,676.6
Long-Term Debt	0.0	0.0	5,320.0	6,022.6
Stockholders' Equity	62,746.7	55,766.1	23,072.5	19,920.9
Performance & Financial Condition				
Return on Total Revenues %	8.02	10.27	7.15	6.63
Return on Avg Stockholders' Equity %	11.24	19.25	16.51	7.74
Return on Average Assets %	6.35	9.37	6.81	3.75
Current Ratio	1.04	1.44	0.92	0.90
Debt / Equity %	n.a.	n.a.	23.06	30.23

Compound Growth %'s	EPS %	46.65	Net Income %	65.02	Total Revenues %	54.85

Comments

Revenues increased in 1998 as a result of increased drilling and completion activity. This increase in production was offset in part by lower average sales prices. Costs of production increased as a percent of sales because of lower prices resulting in a lower net profit for the year. Details of estimated reserves are included in each annual report. The Company manages its operations without the use of long term debt.

Officers	Position	Ownership Information	
James N. Ryan	Chairman, CEO	Number of Shares Outstanding	15,510,762
Steven R. Williams	President	Market Capitalization	$ 47,462,932
Dale G. Rettinger	Exec VP, CFO	Number of Shareholders	1,715
Roger J. Morgan	Secretary	Where Listed / Symbol	NASDAQ / PETD

Other Information			
Transfer Agent	Universal Stock Transfer Co. Woodland Hills, CA	SIC Code	1381
Auditor	KPMG LLP	Employees	75
		Web Site	petd.com

Pharmaceutical Formulations, Inc.

460 Plainfield Avenue   Edison, NJ 08818   Telephone (732)985-7100   Fax (732)819-3330

Company Description

Pharmaceutical Formulations, Inc. is primarily engaged in the manufacture and distribution of over-the-counter solid dosage pharmaceutical products in tablet, caplet and capsule form, which are sold under customers' private labels. The Company also supplies bulk products to secondary distributors and repackers as well as smaller competitors who do not have sophisticated research and development departments. The Company also engages in contract manufacturing of selected products for well-known major pharmaceutical companies and testing and research and development of new drug and health care products. Currently, the Company markets more than 120 different types of generic OTC products.

	06/30/98	06/30/97	06/30/96	06/30/95
Per Share Information				
Stock Price as of 12/31	0.35	0.53	0.84	0.47
Earnings Per Share	0.05	0.04	-0.12	0.06
Price / Earnings Ratio	7.00	13.25	n.a.	7.83
Book Value Per Share	0.02	-0.05	-0.10	0.02
Price / Book Value %	1,750.00	n.a.	n.a.	2,350.00
Dividends Per Share	0.0	0.0	0.0	0.0
Annual Financial Data				
Operating Results (000's)				
Total Revenues	80,908.0	71,228.0	54,369.0	59,172.0
Costs & Expenses	-79,080.0	-69,014.0	-58,745.0	-57,643.0
Income Before Taxes and Other	1,828.0	2,214.0	-4,376.0	1,529.0
Other Items	0.0	0.0	0.0	0.0
Income Tax	39.0	-882.0	911.0	517.0
Net Income	1,867.0	1,332.0	-3,465.0	2,046.0
Cash Flow From Operations	2,009.0	1,232.0	3,163.0	-206.0
Balance Sheet (000's)				
Cash & Equivalents	608.0	2,087.0	1,284.0	655.0
Total Current Assets	36,658.0	29,939.0	21,823.0	24,759.0
Fixed Assets, Net	21,441.0	18,075.0	16,802.0	14,346.0
Total Assets	59,864.0	48,734.0	39,661.0	40,456.0
Total Current Liabilities	25,952.0	18,550.0	13,895.0	12,587.0
Long-Term Debt	22,983.0	19,990.0	16,284.0	18,207.0
Stockholders' Equity	3,055.0	1,077.0	-411.0	454.0
Performance & Financial Condition				
Return on Total Revenues %	2.31	1.87	-6.37	3.46
Return on Avg Stockholders' Equity %	90.37	400.00	-16,116.28	n.a.
Return on Average Assets %	3.44	3.01	-8.65	5.51
Current Ratio	1.41	1.61	1.57	1.97
Debt / Equity %	752.31	1,856.08	n.a.	4,010.35

Compound Growth %'s	EPS %	-5.90	Net Income %	-3.01	Total Revenues %	10.99

Comments

The Company posted a second consecutive year of solid revenue growth and profits last year. Increased sales to existing customers and the introduction of new products contributed to the success. Although the Company has significant debt as compared to equity, overall financial strength is improving. A number of new products were also reported in the annual report. For the six months ended December 31, 1998, the Company reported revenues and a net loss of $44.0 million and $1.5 million ($.05 per share) as compared to $41.7 and a net profit of $1,156,000 ($.04 per share) for the same period of the preceding year. The recent loss included nonrecurring expenses of $1,179,000 related to the settlement of a lawsuit.

Officers	Position	Ownership Information	
Charles E. LaRosa	President, CEO	Number of Shares Outstanding	30,253,320
Frank Marchese	VP - Finance, Secretary	Market Capitalization	$ 10,588,662
Brian W. Barbee	Vice President	Number of Shareholders	1,752
Victor J. Biller	Vice President	Where Listed / Symbol	OTC-BB / PHFR

Other Information			
Transfer Agent	Continental Stock Transfer & Trust Co. New York, NY	SIC Code	2834
Auditor	BDO Seidman LLP	Employees	378
Market Maker	Freimak Blair & Company Inc. (201)467-0095		
	RAS Securities Corp. (800)354-7277		

Phoenix Gold International, Inc.

9300 North Decatur   Portland, OR 97203   Telephone (503)288-2008   Fax (503)978-6308

Company Description

Phoenix Gold International, Inc. designs, markets and sells high performance electronics and accessories for the domestic and international car audio aftermarket, the professional sound market, and custom audio/video and home theater markets. These products include speakers for the car audio aftermarket and the home theater market. The Company manufactures substantially all of its electronics and a portion of the accessories and speakers at its facility in Portland, Oregon. The Company was founded in 1991. In November 1995, the Company acquired substantially all of the assets of the professional sound division of Carver Corporation.

	09/30/98	09/30/97	09/30/96	09/30/95
Per Share Information				
Stock Price as of 12/31	1.50	3.87	5.75	10.00
Earnings Per Share	-0.22	0.12	-0.37	0.67
Price / Earnings Ratio	n.a.	32.25	n.a.	14.93
Book Value Per Share	3.03	3.25	3.12	3.49
Price / Book Value %	49.50	119.08	184.29	n.a.
Dividends Per Share	0.0	0.0	0.0	0.0
Annual Financial Data				
Operating Results (000's)				
Total Revenues	26,494.2	27,825.2	26,582.6	20,211.2
Costs & Expenses	-26,843.5	-27,142.1	-27,499.3	-17,167.1
Income Before Taxes and Other	-349.2	683.1	-916.6	3,044.2
Other Items	-878.1	0.0	-1,120.5	0.0
Income Tax	455.0	-273.0	768.0	-1,162.9
Net Income	-772.4	410.1	-1,269.1	1,881.3
Cash Flow From Operations	2,293.4	945.4	-2,818.2	44.7
Balance Sheet (000's)				
Cash & Equivalents	2.6	2.6	2.6	2,101.6
Total Current Assets	11,792.9	12,995.6	14,904.7	10,791.1
Fixed Assets, Net	2,522.0	3,478.8	3,938.8	3,386.7
Total Assets	15,208.1	17,455.1	19,832.5	14,509.2
Total Current Liabilities	3,772.3	5,717.2	8,871.5	1,969.9
Long-Term Debt	938.2	494.9	172.0	526.2
Stockholders' Equity	10,497.6	11,243.0	10,789.0	12,013.2
Performance & Financial Condition				
Return on Total Revenues %	-2.92	1.47	-4.77	9.31
Return on Avg Stockholders' Equity %	-7.11	3.72	-11.13	25.23
Return on Average Assets %	-4.73	2.20	-7.39	15.74
Current Ratio	3.13	2.27	1.68	5.48
Debt / Equity %	8.94	4.40	1.59	4.38

Compound Growth %'s	EPS %	n.a.	Net Income %	n.a.	Total Revenues %	9.44

Comments

While domestic sales increased 6% in fiscal 1998, international sales declined, creating an overall decline of 4.7% for the year. The Company also had a nonrecurring expense of $878,147 related to the implementation of a restructuring plan which included the phase-out of a product line and actions to reduce future operating costs. Fiscal 1996 results included a nonrecurring charge of $1.1 million for in-process research and development associated with the purchase of Carver Corporation's professional sound division. This, combined with lower gross margins, resulted in a loss despite a strong increase in revenue. The balance sheet remains sound with plentiful working capital and a small amount of long term debt.

Officers	Position	Ownership Information	
Keith A. Peterson	President, CEO	Number of Shares Outstanding	3,464,745
Timothy G. Johnson	Exec VP, COO	Market Capitalization	$ 5,197,118
David D. Bills	VP - Finance	Number of Shareholders	500
Joseph K. O'Brien	CFO, Secretary	Where Listed / Symbol	NASDAQ / PGLD

Other Information			
Transfer Agent	Harris Trust Co. of California Chicago, IL	SIC Code	3651
Auditor	Deloitte & Touche LLP	Employees	241
		Web Site	phoenixgold.com

Pioneer Railcorp

1318 S. Johanson Road   Peoria, IL 61607   Telephone (309)697-1400   Fax (309)697-1677

Company Description

Pioneer Railcorp is a short line railroad holding company, operating fifteen railroads totaling over 500 miles in nine states: Alabama, Arkansas, Illinois, Indiana, Iowa, Michigan, Minnesota, Mississippi, and Tennessee. Pioneer currently has a fleet of approximately 980 owned or leased railcars and presently owns 50 locomotives and numerous pieces of specialized track maintenance equipment. The Company also has an equipment leasing company and two service companies. Pioneer was founded in 1986.

	12/31/98	12/31/97	12/31/96	12/31/95
Per Share Information				
Stock Price	1.25	1.56	2.00	3.00
Earnings Per Share	0.09	0.08	0.02	0.10
Price / Earnings Ratio	13.89	19.50	100.00	30.00
Book Value Per Share	0.86	0.79	0.70	0.66
Price / Book Value %	145.35	197.47	285.71	454.55
Dividends Per Share	0.0	0.0	0.0	0.0
Annual Financial Data				
Operating Results (000's)				
Total Revenues	13,796.1	13,190.8	11,282.1	8,580.4
Costs & Expenses	-12,827.4	-12,194.9	-10,920.4	-7,672.0
Income Before Taxes and Other	968.6	894.7	361.7	1,081.6
Other Items	-122.9	-122.7	-123.6	-124.4
Income Tax	-421.0	-405.7	-136.0	-495.4
Net Income	424.8	366.2	102.1	461.7
Cash Flow From Operations	2,463.3	1,849.3	1,807.7	1,442.1
Balance Sheet (000's)				
Cash & Equivalents	469.5	407.4	501.2	276.2
Total Current Assets	3,763.1	3,460.2	3,630.7	2,056.7
Fixed Assets, Net	19,563.4	19,974.7	20,131.6	15,220.2
Total Assets	24,504.0	24,647.7	25,008.3	17,923.9
Total Current Liabilities	5,579.8	5,098.3	6,066.6	2,980.3
Long-Term Debt	11,211.7	12,465.5	12,564.1	9,934.7
Stockholders' Equity	3,980.6	3,647.2	3,221.9	2,970.9
Performance & Financial Condition				
Return on Total Revenues %	3.08	2.78	0.91	5.38
Return on Avg Stockholders' Equity %	11.14	10.66	3.30	19.33
Return on Average Assets %	1.73	1.48	0.48	3.06
Current Ratio	0.67	0.68	0.60	0.69
Debt / Equity %	281.66	341.78	389.96	334.41

Compound Growth %'s	EPS %	-3.45	Net Income %	-2.74	Total Revenues %	17.15

Comments

The Company declared a 2 for 1 stock split in 1995. Per share amounts have been adjusted for consistency. Net income increased by 16% due primarily to increased utilization of the Company's railcar fleet by non-affiliated railroads which lease the cars. Compound revenue growth of 17.15% is largely attributable to the acquisition of new lines. The Company has a consistent cash flow from operations. This is because large depreciation deductions do not affect cash flow. On a cash flow basis, the current valuation of the Company would probably be substantially higher than its market capitalization. But many investors don't even think to look at operating cash flow. Too often this measure is confusing because of all of the adjustments that need to be made to net income in its calculation. Sometimes it's easy.

Officers	Position	Ownership Information	
Guy L. Brenkman	President, CEO	Number of Shares Outstanding	4,610,597
Daniel A. LaKemper	Secretary	Market Capitalization	$ 5,763,246
J. Michael Carr	Treasurer, CFO	Number of Shareholders	1,814
Kevin L. Williams	Shareholder Relations	Where Listed / Symbol	NASDAQ / PRRR

Other Information			
Transfer Agent	Company Office Peoria, IL	SIC Code	4013
Auditor	McGladrey & Pullen, LLP	Employees	108
Market Maker	Paragon Capital Corporation (212)785-4700	Web Site	pioneer-railcorp.com

PlayCore, Inc.

1212 Barberry Drive   Janesville, WI 53545   Telephone (608)755-4768   Fax (608)755-4763

Company Description

PlayCore, Inc., formerly Swing-N-Slide Corp., is manufactures and markets commercial and consumer playground equipment and backyard products. The Swing-N-Slide® product line consists of a broad line of do-it-yourself wooden playground equipment. The Company also manufactures and sells modular and custom commercial playground systems for churches, schools, parks, campgrounds and housing developments. The Company's strategy centers on expanding beyond its core products into commercial products using pre-cut wood and other materials which can be sold through its existing markets. In 1997, the Company acquired GameTime, Inc., a leading manufacturer of modular and custom commercial outdoor playground equipment for schools, parks, and municipalities. On February 16, 1999, the Company acquired Heartland Industries, Inc., a maker of wooden storage buildings.

	12/31/98	12/31/97	12/31/96	12/31/95
Per Share Information				
Stock Price	4.56	4.00	3.25	4.00
Earnings Per Share	0.51	0.18	0.26	0.67
Price / Earnings Ratio	8.94	22.22	12.50	5.97
Book Value Per Share	2.07	1.48	0.13	-0.13
Price / Book Value %	220.29	270.27	2,500.00	n.a.
Dividends Per Share	0.0	0.0	0.0	0.0
Annual Financial Data				
Operating Results (000's)				
Total Revenues	114,792.0	89,494.0	41,872.0	45,077.0
Costs & Expenses	-107,096.0	-85,406.0	-36,185.0	-38,258.0
Income Before Taxes and Other	7,696.0	3,307.0	3,050.0	6,727.0
Other Items	0.0	-860.0	0.0	0.0
Income Tax	-3,020.0	-1,270.0	-1,480.0	-2,600.0
Net Income	4,676.0	1,177.0	1,570.0	4,127.0
Cash Flow From Operations	9,927.0	9,121.0	2,453.0	8,512.0
Balance Sheet (000's)				
Cash & Equivalents	487.0	677.0	1.0	7.0
Total Current Assets	33,587.0	30,175.0	15,077.0	12,163.0
Fixed Assets, Net	20,871.0	20,535.0	5,524.0	6,302.0
Total Assets	103,440.0	101,165.0	46,264.0	44,585.0
Total Current Liabilities	34,310.0	32,417.0	16,602.0	12,244.0
Long-Term Debt	49,309.0	49,590.0	28,873.0	33,137.0
Stockholders' Equity	16,376.0	11,694.0	789.0	-796.0
Performance & Financial Condition				
Return on Total Revenues %	4.07	1.32	3.75	9.16
Return on Avg Stockholders' Equity %	33.32	18.86	n.a.	23.84
Return on Average Assets %	4.57	1.60	3.46	8.95
Current Ratio	0.98	0.93	0.91	0.99
Debt / Equity %	301.11	424.06	3,659.44	n.a.

Compound Growth %'s	EPS %	-8.69	Net Income %	4.25	Total Revenues %	36.56

Comments

The GameTime acquisition referred to above was accounted for under the purchase method of accounting. Therefore, results have been combined with those of the Company starting with the date of the transaction. Revenues were sharply higher in 1998 due to the inclusion of an entire twelve months of GameTime sales and growth in sales of commercial playground equipment. The latter was positively affected by the impact of new playground equipment safety standards. Consumer product sales also rose 10.8%. At December 31, 1998, the Company had $39.2 million of goodwill recorded as an asset which approximated 239% of stockholders' equity and book value per share.

Officers	Position	Ownership Information	
Terence S. Malone	Chairman	Number of Shares Outstanding	7,908,964
Frederic L. Contino	President, CEO	Market Capitalization	$ 36,064,876
Richard E. Ruegger	VP - Finance, CFO	Number of Shareholders	1,000
David H. Hammelman	Vice President	Where Listed / Symbol	AMEX / PCO

Other Information			
Transfer Agent	First Chicago Trust Co. of New York Jersey City, NJ	SIC Code	3949
Auditor	Ernst & Young LLP	Employees	569
		Web Site	swing-n-slide.com

Polymer Research Corp. of America

2186 Mill Avenue   Brooklyn, NY 11234   Telephone (718)444-4300   Fax (718)241-3930

Company Description

Polymer Research Corp. of America's principal business is that of research and development on a contract basis for other companies in the field of polymer chemistry, i.e., the chemical creation and use of polymers. Polymers are essentially compounds of high molecular weight such as plastics and resins. The Company owns several patented processes for chemical "grafting" technology. Chemical grafting refers to processes by which surfaces are bonded together or a coating is affixed to a surface through various polymerization reactions. Almost all of the research and development contracts provide that if the Company successfully develops a patentable new process while working on the contract, the Company will assign patent rights to the customer who will then have the right to use that process. The Company was founded in 1963.

	12/31/98	12/31/97	12/31/96	12/31/95
Per Share Information				
Stock Price	2.87	2.02	2.27	2.79
Earnings Per Share	0.15	0.13	0.11	0.23
Price / Earnings Ratio	19.13	15.54	20.64	12.13
Book Value Per Share	1.93	1.87	1.74	1.49
Price / Book Value %	148.70	108.02	130.46	187.25
Dividends Per Share	0.0	0.0	0.0	0.0
Annual Financial Data				
Operating Results (000's)				
Total Revenues	5,746.9	5,515.8	5,140.4	5,249.4
Costs & Expenses	-5,302.7	-5,080.1	-4,766.2	-4,533.6
Income Before Taxes and Other	444.2	435.6	327.5	715.8
Other Items	0.0	0.0	0.0	0.0
Income Tax	-201.8	-229.1	-157.7	-358.8
Net Income	242.3	206.6	169.8	356.9
Cash Flow From Operations	421.9	297.1	392.9	607.6
Balance Sheet (000's)				
Cash & Equivalents	1,960.6	1,367.0	709.2	1,474.0
Total Current Assets	2,773.9	2,260.2	2,109.5	2,350.3
Fixed Assets, Net	2,814.5	2,863.4	2,939.5	3,014.6
Total Assets	5,600.7	5,135.1	5,060.9	5,377.0
Total Current Liabilities	930.7	765.1	896.1	551.6
Long-Term Debt	1,417.1	1,451.8	1,483.1	2,303.4
Stockholders' Equity	3,252.8	2,918.2	2,681.7	2,522.1
Performance & Financial Condition				
Return on Total Revenues %	4.22	3.75	3.30	6.80
Return on Avg Stockholders' Equity %	7.85	7.38	6.53	15.31
Return on Average Assets %	4.51	4.05	3.25	6.93
Current Ratio	2.98	2.95	2.35	4.26
Debt / Equity %	43.56	49.75	55.30	91.33

Compound Growth %'s	EPS %	-13.28	Net Income %	-12.11	Total Revenues %	3.06

Comments

The Company declared stock dividends of 5%, 5%, 10% and 10% in 1998, 1997, 1996, and 1995, respectively, and a 5 for 4 stock split in 1995. All per share amounts have been adjusted for consistency. This is one company that feels no embarrassment about its stock being priced under $5 per share. Without these dividends and the split, the stock price would have been 63% higher. The Company has a solid balance sheet with no intangible assets. Cash and liquid investments total $2.4 million, approximately 73% of stockholders' equity and book value per share.

Officers	Position	Ownership Information	
Carl Horowitz	President	Number of Shares Outstanding	1,685,784
John M. Ryan	Exec VP	Market Capitalization	$ 4,838,200
Irene Horowitz	Senior VP	Number of Shareholders	900
Anna Dichter	Secretary, Treasurer	Where Listed / Symbol	NASDAQ / PROA

Other Information			
Transfer Agent	Registrar & Transfer Co. Cranford, NJ	SIC Code	8731
Auditor	Castellano, Korenberg & Co.	Employees	53

Prab, Inc.

5944 E. Kilgore Road   Kalamazoo, MI 49003   Telephone (616)382-8200   Fax (616)382-7770

Company Description

Prab, Inc. designs and manufactures complete metal scrap reclamation systems which it sells to die casting, metal stamping, general metal working, and other industries. These systems reduce labor, manufacturing and transportation costs associated with metal scrap disposal as well as reclaiming cutting fluids and increasing the value of scrap metal. The Company's scrap metal reclamation systems are priced from $50,000 to $1,500,000 and range from a single machine to a complex group of machines including conveyors, crushers, centrifuges, and related equipment. The Company was organized in 1961.

	10/31/98	10/31/97	10/31/96	10/31/95
Per Share Information				
Stock Price as of 12/31	2.87	3.62	1.50	1.38
Earnings Per Share	0.41	0.40	0.19	0.27
Price / Earnings Ratio	7.00	9.05	7.89	5.11
Book Value Per Share	1.95	1.02	0.17	0.46
Price / Book Value %	147.18	354.90	882.35	300.00
Dividends Per Share	0.0	0.0	0.0	0.0
Annual Financial Data				
Operating Results (000's)				
Total Revenues	18,244.7	16,920.8	15,418.7	13,845.4
Costs & Expenses	-16,706.5	-15,521.3	-14,187.5	-12,620.1
Income Before Taxes and Other	1,538.2	1,399.5	1,167.2	1,287.9
Other Items	-77.5	0.0	0.0	0.0
Income Tax	-539.6	-501.0	-408.0	0.0
Net Income	921.0	898.5	759.2	1,287.9
Cash Flow From Operations	1,557.4	946.2	1,144.4	1,338.5
Balance Sheet (000's)				
Cash & Equivalents	51.6	26.2	491.4	323.3
Total Current Assets	5,380.5	5,253.9	4,664.0	4,269.5
Fixed Assets, Net	1,085.2	1,041.2	930.7	961.3
Total Assets	6,981.4	6,941.7	5,955.1	5,248.8
Total Current Liabilities	3,120.8	3,515.6	3,480.2	2,049.3
Long-Term Debt	420.0	1,340.8	1,982.1	0.0
Stockholders' Equity	3,423.4	2,069.2	477.7	3,185.6
Performance & Financial Condition				
Return on Total Revenues %	5.05	5.31	4.92	9.30
Return on Avg Stockholders' Equity %	33.54	70.56	41.45	50.72
Return on Average Assets %	13.23	13.93	13.55	26.11
Current Ratio	1.72	1.49	1.34	2.08
Debt / Equity %	12.27	64.80	414.89	n.a.

Compound Growth %'s	EPS %	14.94	Net Income %	-10.57	Total Revenues %	9.63

Comments

The increase in net sales during fiscal 1998 was primarily due to increased sales of the Prab line of conveyors and chip processing systems. The Company's backlog at year end was lower than the prior year. Management projected that sales would decrease in fiscal 1999 and such decline would negatively impact earnings. However, positive cash flow is continuing to be applied against debt thereby greatly reducing interest expense. Fiscal 1998 results include a nonrecurring expense of $77,512 related to the retirement of debt. The Company also retired a substantial block of stock owned by the State of Michigan Retirement System in October, 1996.

Officers	Position	Ownership Information	
John J. Wallace	Chairman	Number of Shares Outstanding	1,757,339
Gary A. Herder	President, CEO	Market Capitalization	$ 5,043,563
Eric V. Brown, Jr.	Secretary	Number of Shareholders	1,062
Robert W. Klinge	Controller	Where Listed / Symbol	OTC-BB / PRAB

Other Information			
Transfer Agent	Illinois Stock Transfer Company Chicago, IL	SIC Code	3569
Auditor	Plante & Moran, LLP	Employees	98
Market Maker	First of Michigan Corporation (800)521-8042	Web Site	prab.com
	Herzog, Heine, Geduld, Inc. (800)221-3600		

Productivity Technologies Corp.

509 Madison Avenue   New York, NY 10022   Telephone (212)843-1480   Fax (212)843-1484

Company Description

Productivity Technologies Corp. is a manufacturer of automated systems, machinery, equipment, components and engineering services. Sales of products have principally been to automobile and automotive parts manufacturers and appliance manufacturers. Other customers include manufacturers of garden and lawn equipment, office furniture, heating, ventilation and air conditioning equipment and aircraft. Export sales amounted to 20% of total revenue in the last fiscal year. The Company was formed in 1993 for the purpose of acquiring a business engaged in the production systems industry. It acquired Atlas Technologies, Inc. in May 1996.

	06/30/98	06/30/97	06/30/96	06/30/95
Per Share Information				
Stock Price as of 12/31	2.62	3.62	3.25	4.75
Earnings Per Share	-0.95	0.28	0.46	1.04
Price / Earnings Ratio	n.a.	12.93	7.07	4.57
Book Value Per Share	4.07	4.69	4.41	1.65
Price / Book Value %	64.37	77.19	73.70	287.88
Dividends Per Share	0.0	0.0	0.0	0.0
Annual Financial Data				
Operating Results (000's)				
Total Revenues	36,328.1	34,593.2	36,163.5	29,482.8
Costs & Expenses	-37,158.5	-33,550.4	-34,423.0	-26,797.9
Income Before Taxes and Other	-830.4	1,042.7	1,740.4	2,685.0
Other Items	-2,131.9	0.0	0.0	0.0
Income Tax	950.0	-450.0	-773.0	-465.0
Net Income	-2,012.4	592.7	967.4	2,220.0
Cash Flow From Operations	5,503.4	-1,389.8	-3,590.2	2,193.8
Balance Sheet (000's)				
Cash & Equivalents	2,172.5	843.7	512.2	17.0
Total Current Assets	15,271.5	22,627.4	18,690.6	11,423.0
Fixed Assets, Net	8,288.8	7,667.4	4,240.4	2,517.0
Total Assets	26,809.4	33,409.7	26,023.8	14,550.0
Total Current Liabilities	5,469.6	7,284.4	13,642.7	8,321.0
Long-Term Debt	11,254.1	15,327.3	2,228.8	2,717.0
Stockholders' Equity	8,649.2	9,966.1	9,373.3	3,513.0
Performance & Financial Condition				
Return on Total Revenues %	-5.54	1.71	2.68	7.53
Return on Avg Stockholders' Equity %	-21.62	6.13	15.01	69.65
Return on Average Assets %	-6.68	1.99	4.77	16.87
Current Ratio	2.79	3.11	1.37	1.37
Debt / Equity %	130.12	153.79	23.78	77.34

Compound Growth %'s	EPS % n.a.	Net Income % n.a.	Total Revenues % 7.21

Comments

The financial information presented includes the accounts of Atlas Technologies, Inc. prior to its acquisition by the Company. Per share calculations in fiscal 1995 are based on the number of shares Productivity Technologies issued in connection with its public offering. The fiscal 1998 loss was mostly attributable to a bonus restructuring with senior executives of Atlas at a cost of $2,131,903. The expense of a legal settlement including fees added an additional $750,000 to general and administrative expenses in fiscal 1998. For the six months ended December 31, 1998, the Company reported revenue and a net loss of $7.8 million and $76,885 ($.03 per share) as compared to $20.7 million and a net profit of $590,077 ($.28 per share) in the same period of the preceding year.

Officers	Position	Ownership Information	
Ray A. Friant, Jr.	Chairman	Number of Shares Outstanding	2,125,000
Samuel N. Seidman	President	Market Capitalization	$ 5,567,500
Jesse A. Levine	Vice President, CFO	Number of Shareholders	500
John S. Strance	Vice President	Where Listed / Symbol	NASDAQ / PRAC

Other Information			
Transfer Agent	Continental Stock Transfer & Trust Co. New York, NY	SIC Code	3540
Auditor	BDO Seidman LLP	Employees	200

Provena Foods Inc.

5010 Eucalyptus Avenue   Chino, CA 91710   Telephone (909)627-1082   Fax (909)627-7315

Company Description

Provena Foods Inc. is a specialty food processor engaged in the supply of food products to other food processors, distributors and canners. Its primary products are pepperoni and Italian-style sausage sold to frozen pizza processors, pizza restaurant chains and food distributors, and dry pasta sold to food processors and canners, private label producers and food distributors. The Company's meat processing business, Swiss American Sausage Co. Division, is a company that was founded in 1922. The Company's pasta business, Royal-Angelus Macaroni Company Division, has two predecessors. They are Royal Macaroni Company and Angelus Macaroni Mfg. Co. which were founded in 1878 and 1946, respectively. Provena Foods acquired these businesses between 1972 and 1975.

	12/31/98	12/31/97	12/31/96	12/31/95
Per Share Information				
Stock Price	2.94	3.00	2.44	3.50
Earnings Per Share	0.77	0.44	0.20	0.03
Price / Earnings Ratio	3.82	6.82	12.20	116.67
Book Value Per Share	3.60	2.94	2.63	2.53
Price / Book Value %	81.67	102.04	92.78	138.89
Dividends Per Share	0.12	0.12	0.10	0.18
Annual Financial Data				
Operating Results (000's)				
Total Revenues	27,846.8	31,245.6	29,008.7	23,608.3
Costs & Expenses	-24,046.9	-29,227.2	-28,114.4	-23,435.3
Income Before Taxes and Other	3,800.0	2,018.4	894.3	173.0
Other Items	0.0	0.0	0.0	0.0
Income Tax	-1,558.2	-763.8	-332.4	-84.2
Net Income	2,241.8	1,254.6	561.9	88.8
Cash Flow From Operations	3,523.1	1,507.8	237.7	1,296.8
Balance Sheet (000's)				
Cash & Equivalents	116.3	1,090.0	265.5	350.8
Total Current Assets	5,476.6	6,927.1	5,652.8	4,717.2
Fixed Assets, Net	7,602.0	4,467.5	4,704.6	5,083.0
Total Assets	17,279.7	11,539.1	10,413.8	10,049.5
Total Current Liabilities	2,215.7	2,352.9	2,088.4	2,085.2
Long-Term Debt	4,000.0	743.3	951.7	969.0
Stockholders' Equity	10,479.4	8,435.1	7,356.6	6,915.1
Performance & Financial Condition				
Return on Total Revenues %	8.05	4.02	1.94	0.38
Return on Avg Stockholders' Equity %	23.70	15.89	7.87	1.25
Return on Average Assets %	15.56	11.43	5.49	0.93
Current Ratio	2.47	2.94	2.71	2.26
Debt / Equity %	38.17	8.81	12.94	14.01

Compound Growth %'s	EPS %	194.98	Net Income %	193.36	Total Revenues %	5.66

Comments

On August 1, 1998, a fire destroyed two of the Company's meat packing facilities. Property and business interruption insurance were both in effect. As of December 31, 1998, the Company processed insurance claims of $5.2 million resulting in income of $3.2 million. Additional claims will be filed in 1999. Lower revenues were attributable to the fire and lower meat prices. The Company has under construction an 85,000 square foot building, planned before the fire and scheduled to be completed in the first half of 1999, intended to provide a more efficient and higher production capacity meat plant. Despite much of the uncertainty in the Company's future having been resolved favorably, the stock still trades at a discount to book value.

Officers	Position	Ownership Information	
John D. Determan	Chairman	Number of Shares Outstanding	2,913,098
Theodore L. Arena	President, CEO	Market Capitalization	$ 8,564,508
Thomas J. Mulroney	CFO	Number of Shareholders	1,040
Santo Zito	Vice President	Where Listed / Symbol	AMEX / PZA

Other Information			
Transfer Agent	ChaseMellon Shareholder Services Ridgefield Park, NJ	SIC Code	2013
Auditor	KPMG LLP	Employees	115

Publishers Equipment Corporation

16660 Dallas Parkway, Suite 1100   Dallas, TX 75248   Telephone (972)931-2312   Fax (972)931-2399

Company Description

Publishers Equipment Corporation manufactures and markets single-width web offset printing presses. Single-width printing equipment prints two newspaper pages across at one time and is generally utilized by daily, weekly, and bi-weekly newspapers, as well as by commercial printers. The market for single-width equipment also includes a large number of individual equipment users who produce a wide variety of products which include flyers, inserts, brochures and catalogs. The Company's revenues are derived from a broad base of customers located worldwide. During 1998, the Company derived approximately 30% of its revenue from foreign sales, down from 43% in 1996. The Company was founded in 1979.

	12/31/98	12/31/97	12/31/96	12/31/95
Per Share Information				
Stock Price	0.25	0.25	0.42	0.12
Earnings Per Share	0.06	0.03	0.09	-0.14
Price / Earnings Ratio	4.17	8.33	4.67	n.a.
Book Value Per Share	0.75	0.65	0.60	0.49
Price / Book Value %	33.33	38.46	70.00	24.49
Dividends Per Share	0.0	0.0	0.0	0.0
Annual Financial Data				
Operating Results (000's)				
Total Revenues	15,277.6	13,559.8	16,580.4	7,548.9
Costs & Expenses	-14,973.1	-13,372.1	-16,115.8	-8,296.1
Income Before Taxes and Other	304.4	180.2	464.6	-747.2
Other Items	0.0	0.0	0.0	0.0
Income Tax	0.0	0.0	0.0	0.0
Net Income	304.4	180.2	464.6	-747.2
Cash Flow From Operations	-949.8	408.3	314.7	447.1
Balance Sheet (000's)				
Cash & Equivalents	42.2	37.8	148.2	91.1
Total Current Assets	9,866.7	9,800.2	8,604.6	10,395.6
Fixed Assets, Net	1,109.1	1,079.6	1,309.5	1,324.5
Total Assets	10,975.8	10,879.8	9,914.1	11,720.1
Total Current Liabilities	4,592.1	6,058.0	6,256.8	4,809.4
Long-Term Debt	2,274.8	1,000.0	0.0	3,703.1
Stockholders' Equity	3,972.3	3,667.9	3,487.7	3,023.1
Performance & Financial Condition				
Return on Total Revenues %	1.99	1.33	2.80	-9.90
Return on Avg Stockholders' Equity %	7.97	5.04	14.27	-22.00
Return on Average Assets %	2.79	1.73	4.30	-6.58
Current Ratio	2.15	1.62	1.38	2.16
Debt / Equity %	57.27	27.26	n.a.	122.49

Compound Growth %'s   EPS % -18.35   Net Income % -19.05   Total Revenues % 26.49

Comments

Revenues increased 12% in 1998 despite continuing weaknesses in foreign markets. Domestic revenues were 21% higher in 1998 compared to 1997. Less dependence on foreign markets may provide a more stable environment. The loss of foreign business caused a net decline in revenue in 1997. Delayed shipments and weak demand caused an operating loss in 1995. During 1998, three customers accounted for approximately 43% of the Company's revenue. As of December 31, 1998, the Company has net operating loss carryovers of $4.6 million and capital loss carryovers of $7.6 million in addition to general business credit carryforwards.

Officers	Position	Ownership Information	
Evans Kostas	President, CEO	Number of Shares Outstanding	5,020,253
Roger R. Baier	VP - Finance, CFO	Market Capitalization	$ 1,255,063
James K. Feeney	Director	Number of Shareholders	422
Reinhart Siewert	Director	Where Listed / Symbol	OTC-BB / PECN

Other Information			
Transfer Agent	KeyCorp Shareholder Services, Inc. Brooklyn, OH	SIC Code	3555
Auditor	Arthur Andersen LLP	Employees	117
Market Maker	Wm. V. Frankel & Co., Inc. (800)631-3091	Web Site	kingpress.com
	Paragon Capital Corporation (800)345-0505		

Puroflow Incorporated

16559 Saticoy Street   Van Nuys, CA 91406   Telephone (818)756-1388   Fax (818)779-3902

Company Description

Puroflow Incorporated designs and manufactures specialized filtration devices used in automobile airbag inflators as well as in aerospace, petrochemical and a wide range of commercial and industrial applications. The Company went into receivership as a result of a default on its loan agreement in 1995 but emerged on August 22, 1996, after the loan was repaid. Puroflow raised additional capital in fiscal 1997, through the placement of 2.5 million shares of common stock. The Company was formed in 1961.

	01/31/98	01/31/97	01/31/96	01/31/95
Per Share Information				
Stock Price as of 12/31	0.72	0.81	0.68	1.00
Earnings Per Share	0.07	0.11	0.19	-0.53
Price / Earnings Ratio	10.29	7.36	3.58	n.a.
Book Value Per Share	0.56	0.49	0.24	0.04
Price / Book Value %	128.57	165.31	283.33	2,500.00
Dividends Per Share	0.0	0.0	0.0	0.0
Annual Financial Data				
Operating Results (000's)				
Total Revenues	8,614.8	8,468.6	8,815.9	9,058.8
Costs & Expenses	-7,760.2	-7,405.9	-7,658.6	-9,585.7
Income Before Taxes and Other	854.6	1,062.8	1,154.4	-526.8
Other Items	-554.1	-394.2	-256.3	-1,845.3
Income Tax	191.4	-5.6	0.0	0.0
Net Income	492.0	663.0	898.1	-2,372.2
Cash Flow From Operations	656.5	-190.0	219.3	728.6
Balance Sheet (000's)				
Cash & Equivalents	361.5	164.4	0.0	74.4
Total Current Assets	3,607.0	3,123.6	2,865.5	3,250.5
Fixed Assets, Net	1,118.6	954.6	1,019.4	1,337.3
Total Assets	5,046.3	4,094.9	3,961.9	4,720.8
Total Current Liabilities	1,065.3	605.9	2,878.8	4,464.4
Long-Term Debt	0.0	0.0	0.0	71.4
Stockholders' Equity	3,981.0	3,489.1	1,083.2	185.1
Performance & Financial Condition				
Return on Total Revenues %	5.71	7.83	10.19	-26.19
Return on Avg Stockholders' Equity %	13.17	29.00	141.63	-190.36
Return on Average Assets %	10.76	16.46	20.69	-39.37
Current Ratio	3.39	5.16	1.00	0.73
Debt / Equity %	n.a.	n.a.	n.a.	38.58

Compound Growth %'s	EPS %	-39.30	Net Income %	-25.99	Total Revenues %	-1.66

Comments

Discontinued operations resulted in a charge of $1.8 million for the year ended January 31, 1995. The Company has had a nice return to profitability and still has $2.7 million in tax loss carryovers to offset future income. At January 31, 1998, the order backlog stood at $6.5 million as compared to $5.8 million in the previous year. Sales to four customers represented approximately 49% of net sales during fiscal 1998 and 58% of net sales in fiscal 1997. Nonrecurring expenses of $554,117, $395,184 and $253,085 in fiscal 1998, 1997 and 1996, respectively, were a direct result of the receivership terminated in fiscal 1997 and the settlement of various litigation actions in fiscal 1998. For the nine months ended October 31, 1998, the Company reported revenues and net income of $6.2 million and $344,587 ($.05 per share) as compared to $6.6 million and $408,417 ($.06 per share) for the same period of the preceding year.

Officers	Position	Ownership Information	
Reuben M. Siwek	Chairman	Number of Shares Outstanding	7,108,821
Michael H. Figoff	President, CEO	Market Capitalization	$ 5,118,351
Gary Rosen	CFO	Number of Shareholders	289
Dale Livingston	Vice President	Where Listed / Symbol	OTC-BB / PURO

Other Information			
Transfer Agent	Continental Stock Transfer & Trust Co. New York, NY	SIC Code	3569
Auditor	Rose, Snyder & Jacobs	Employees	71
Market Maker	Olsen Payne & Co.	(800)453-5321	Web Site	puroflow.com
	Sherwood Securities Corp.	(800)435-1235		

QC Optics, Inc.

46 Jonspin Road   Wilmington, MA 01887   Telephone (978)657-7007   Fax (978)657-6077

Company Description

QC Optics, Inc. (QCO) designs, manufactures and markets laser based defect detection systems for the semiconductor, computer hard disk drive and flat panel display markets. QCO uses its patented and other proprietary technology in lasers and optical systems that scan a computer hard disk, photomask or flat panel display for defects or contamination. The Company's systems combine automatic handling, clean room capability and computer control with reliable laser-based technology. QCO was formed in 1986 to acquire the assets of a division of GCA Corporation. The Company funded its product development primarily with equity investments and debt financing from Kobe Steel Ltd.

	12/31/98	12/31/97	12/31/96	12/31/95
Per Share Information				
Stock Price	1.56	3.61	4.75	6.00
Earnings Per Share	0.06	0.08	-0.09	0.42
Price / Earnings Ratio	26.00	45.13	n.a.	14.29
Book Value Per Share	2.61	2.55	2.47	1.03
Price / Book Value %	59.77	141.57	192.31	582.52
Dividends Per Share	0.0	0.0	0.0	0.0
Annual Financial Data				
Operating Results (000's)				
Total Revenues	10,099.9	10,294.3	13,633.3	10,486.4
Costs & Expenses	-9,770.1	-9,902.1	-12,993.9	-9,498.4
Income Before Taxes and Other	329.9	392.2	639.3	988.0
Other Items	0.0	0.0	0.0	0.0
Income Tax	-118.8	-146.9	-846.2	-79.8
Net Income	211.1	245.3	-206.9	908.2
Cash Flow From Operations	-421.7	-1,074.2	3,569.8	-1,102.6
Balance Sheet (000's)				
Cash & Equivalents	3,313.8	3,766.5	5,022.8	1,431.0
Total Current Assets	9,011.5	10,377.9	10,360.1	7,578.8
Fixed Assets, Net	176.1	227.7	119.9	118.2
Total Assets	9,466.8	11,038.1	10,712.9	7,721.9
Total Current Liabilities	988.1	2,770.5	2,690.6	5,518.1
Long-Term Debt	0.0	0.0	0.0	0.0
Stockholders' Equity	8,478.7	8,267.6	8,022.3	2,203.8
Performance & Financial Condition				
Return on Total Revenues %	2.09	2.38	-1.52	8.66
Return on Avg Stockholders' Equity %	2.97	3.01	-4.05	51.93
Return on Average Assets %	2.22	2.26	-2.24	15.14
Current Ratio	9.12	3.75	3.85	1.37
Debt / Equity %	n.a.	n.a.	n.a.	n.a.

Compound Growth %'s	EPS %	-42.46	Net Income %	-35.36	Total Revenues %	-0.61

Comments

The Company has been adversely affected by a general slowdown in capital equipment spending in the semiconductor and computer disk drive industries as evidenced by the low $258,000 customer order backlog at December 31, 1998. However, the Company still managed to report a profit for 1998. Backlog at March 1, 1999 improved to $3,429,000. Management was still predicting a weak first half of 1999. Although a small company by almost any standards, QCO has one of the soundest balance sheets. Current assets comprise 95% of total assets which means that stockholders' equity and book value are comprised largely of current assets. Yet the stock trades for a deep discount to book value.

Officers	Position	Ownership Information	
Eric T. Chase	President, CEO	Number of Shares Outstanding	3,242,500
Richard Allard	VP - Finance, CFO	Market Capitalization	$ 5,058,300
Abdu Boudour	Vice President	Number of Shareholders	500
Albert E. Tobey	Vice President	Where Listed / Symbol	AMEX / OPC

Other Information			
Transfer Agent	American Securities Transfer, Inc. Denver, CO	SIC Code	3829
Auditor	Arthur Andersen LLP	Employees	46

Quality Products, Inc.

560 Dublin Avenue   Columbus, OH 43215   Telephone (614)228-0185   Fax (614)228-2358

Company Description

Quality Products, Inc. manufactures industrial hydraulic bench presses, floor presses, and accessories through its subsidiary, Multipress. The current Multipress® line consists of 27 different standard models. Multipresses are used in a variety of industries, including automotive, appliance, abrasive materials, electrical and food compaction industries. During the years 1992 through 1994, the Company acquired a number of operating subsidiaries. These acquisitions resulted in revenue growth of more than $36 million. However, the Company later incurred massive operating losses from these subsidiaries and all operations other than Multipress, which was profitable, were subsequently disposed of by sale or bankruptcy. The Company was founded in 1988.

	09/30/98	09/30/97	09/30/96	09/30/95
Per Share Information				
Stock Price as of 12/31	0.37	0.97	0.18	0.05
Earnings Per Share	0.10	0.29	-0.84	-9.40
Price / Earnings Ratio	3.70	3.34	n.a.	n.a.
Book Value Per Share	-0.32	-0.85	-0.81	-0.05
Price / Book Value %	n.a.	n.a.	n.a.	n.a.
Dividends Per Share	0.0	0.0	0.0	0.0
Annual Financial Data				
Operating Results (000's)				
Total Revenues	6,550.7	6,453.6	4,759.6	5,408.0
Costs & Expenses	-6,235.0	-5,374.0	-5,597.9	-6,912.4
Income Before Taxes and Other	315.7	1,043.6	-1,845.8	-2,466.3
Other Items	0.0	0.0	0.0	-16,062.0
Income Tax	-25.9	-33.9	0.0	0.0
Net Income	289.8	1,009.7	-1,845.8	-18,528.3
Cash Flow From Operations	288.5	651.1	5,184.2	-1,106.4
Balance Sheet (000's)				
Cash & Equivalents	669.5	406.6	8.1	94.2
Total Current Assets	2,171.3	1,977.9	1,410.3	7,617.4
Fixed Assets, Net	151.0	36.0	26.9	37.6
Total Assets	2,329.6	2,023.3	1,437.2	7,655.1
Total Current Liabilities	1,276.1	2,437.9	2,866.2	7,759.2
Long-Term Debt	798.2	400.0	500.0	0.0
Stockholders' Equity	-494.8	-814.6	-1,929.0	-104.1
Performance & Financial Condition				
Return on Total Revenues %	4.42	15.65	-38.78	-342.61
Return on Avg Stockholders' Equity %	n.a.	n.a.	n.a.	-400.87
Return on Average Assets %	13.32	58.35	-40.60	-407.21
Current Ratio	1.70	0.81	0.49	0.98
Debt / Equity %	n.a.	n.a.	n.a.	n.a.

Compound Growth %'s	EPS % n.a.	Net Income % n.a.	Total Revenues % 6.60

Comments

Sales remained steady after a 33% increase in revenue in fiscal 1997. The latter was attributable to steadily improving financial conditions, the addition of a new marketing executive, additions to the advertising and marketing budgets and the generally strong overall performance of the machine tool industry. A lower gross margin was realized in fiscal 1998 due to a changing product mix. Management expected margins to improve from cost reductions as well as price increases in October 1998. Cash flow from operations and the placement of long term debt allowed the Company to have a positive working capital in fiscal 1998.

Officers	Position	Ownership Information	
Bruce Weaver	President	Number of Shares Outstanding	1,556,558
Tac Kensler	CFO	Market Capitalization	$ 575,926
Jonathon Reuben	Secretary, Treasurer	Number of Shareholders	323
William Harrison, Jr.	Vice President	Where Listed / Symbol	OTC-BB / QPDC

Other Information			
Transfer Agent	ChaseMellon Shareholder Services Ridgefield Park, NJ	SIC Code	5051
Auditor	Farber and Hass LLP	Employees	35
Market Maker	M.H. Meyerson & Co., Inc.	(800)333-3113	
	Wm. V. Frankel & Co., Inc.	(800)631-3091	

Questron Technology, Inc.

6400 Congress Avenue, Suite 200A   Boca Raton, FL 33487   Telephone (561)241-5251   Fax (561)241-5500

Company Description

Questron Technology, Inc., founded in 1983, is primarily a value-added distribution company specializing in inventory logistics management programs for fasteners and related products sold to original equipment manufacturers. The Company provides its customers with inventory management services, such as bin-stock replenishment and other just-in-time inventory management programs, and is the outsourced materials management function for many of its customers, providing complete supply chain management from procurement to deployment of the products managed. The Company acquired three companies in related businesses during 1998 and two more in early 1999.

	12/31/98	12/31/97	12/31/96	12/31/95
Per Share Information				
Stock Price	4.31	7.75	2.80	27.50
Earnings Per Share	0.60	0.47	0.36	0.26
Price / Earnings Ratio	7.18	16.49	7.78	105.77
Book Value Per Share	5.74	6.47	5.68	5.33
Price / Book Value %	75.09	119.78	49.30	515.95
Dividends Per Share	0.0	0.0	0.0	0.0
Annual Financial Data				
Operating Results (000's)				
Total Revenues	56,968.0	25,710.2	11,036.1	7,259.2
Costs & Expenses	-51,398.5	-22,921.2	-10,422.3	-6,879.8
Income Before Taxes and Other	5,569.5	2,789.0	613.8	379.4
Other Items	0.0	0.0	0.0	0.0
Income Tax	-2,283.5	-1,151.9	-64.4	-27.2
Net Income	3,286.0	1,637.1	549.5	352.2
Cash Flow From Operations	-3,067.1	565.0	498.3	-843.1
Balance Sheet (000's)				
Cash & Equivalents	229.3	875.1	74.4	39.4
Total Current Assets	32,898.0	14,267.9	4,570.0	5,053.8
Fixed Assets, Net	2,042.8	911.0	373.4	419.0
Total Assets	77,725.3	35,194.8	12,031.8	12,433.0
Total Current Liabilities	10,271.0	5,221.0	1,527.3	2,070.1
Long-Term Debt	39,285.7	9,893.5	0.0	2,185.0
Stockholders' Equity	27,464.3	19,274.9	8,719.5	8,177.9
Performance & Financial Condition				
Return on Total Revenues %	5.77	6.37	4.98	4.85
Return on Avg Stockholders' Equity %	14.06	11.70	6.50	5.87
Return on Average Assets %	5.82	6.93	4.49	4.40
Current Ratio	3.20	2.73	2.99	2.44
Debt / Equity %	143.04	51.33	n.a.	26.72

Compound Growth %'s	EPS %	32.15	Net Income %	110.52	Total Revenues %	98.72

Comments

The Company executed a 1 for 10 reverse stock split in early 1997. All per share amounts have been restated for consistency. The three acquisitions in 1998 were all accounted for as purchases. Therefore, operating results have been combined with those of the Company since the date of each respective transaction. The increase in revenue is mostly attributable to acquisitions but also represents internal growth. Net earnings were impressive for a year containing much acquisition activity. The compound growth rate for earnings per share is diluted from the compound growth rate of net income because of additional shares issued in connection with the acquisitions. At December 31, 1998, the Company had $37.6 million of intangible assets recorded on its books which equated to approximately 137% of stockholders' equity and book value per share.

Officers	Position	Ownership Information	
Dominic A. Polimeni	President, CEO	Number of Shares Outstanding	4,783,326
Milton M. Adler	Controller, Secretary	Market Capitalization	$ 20,616,135
Robert V. Gubitosi	Director	Number of Shareholders	1,000
Mitchell Hymowitz	Director	Where Listed / Symbol	NASDAQ / QUST

Other Information			
Transfer Agent	California Stock Transfer Corp. Calabasas Park, CA	SIC Code	5072
Auditor	Ernst & Young LLP	Employees	266
		Web Site	questrontechnology.com

R-B Rubber Products, Inc.

904 East 10th Avenue McMinnville, OR 97128 Telephone (503)472-4691 Fax (503)434-4455

Company Description

R-B Rubber Products, Inc. is a vertically integrated manufacturer of high quality, durable rubber matting and other rubber protective surfaces. The Company processes used tire chips into crumb rubber that is then used to manufacture a variety of rubber products. These products are used for agribusiness, sport and fitness facilities, and other commercial and industrial uses. Products are sold to OEM's, distributors, retailers and end users. Individuals contact the Company (via an 800 number) in response to advertisements or referrals from other users. In most cases, these callers are referred to dealers in their local area. Because of this, only a small percentage of sales have been at retail prices. The Company was founded in 1985 and went public in 1995. There was no trading in the Company's stock prior to 1995.

	12/31/98	12/31/97	12/31/96	12/31/95
Per Share Information				
Stock Price	1.31	3.38	1.69	3.00
Earnings Per Share	-0.04	0.24	0.12	-0.33
Price / Earnings Ratio	n.a.	14.08	14.08	n.a.
Book Value Per Share	2.13	2.13	1.89	1.77
Price / Book Value %	61.50	158.69	89.42	169.49
Dividends Per Share	0.0	0.0	0.0·	0.0
Annual Financial Data				
Operating Results (000's)				
Total Revenues	8,631.5	7,454.8	5,299.1	3,708.3
Costs & Expenses	-8,377.0	-6,598.6	-5,122.7	-4,163.4
Income Before Taxes and Other	254.5	856.2	172.7	-655.1
Other Items	-396.1	0.0	0.0	0.0
Income Tax	56.3	-328.0	91.5	67.1
Net Income	-85.2	528.1	264.2	-588.0
Cash Flow From Operations	802.5	936.2	255.1	-560.6
Balance Sheet (000's)				
Cash & Equivalents	35.0	292.0	26.5	113.3
Total Current Assets	1,912.0	1,932.3	1,459.9	1,088.8
Fixed Assets, Net	5,313.0	4,066.6	4,291.2	4,148.9
Total Assets	7,706.5	6,275.5	5,953.1	5,391.2
Total Current Liabilities	1,234.3	631.0	732.1	515.1
Long-Term Debt	1,573.5	772.9	891.5	880.4
Stockholders' Equity	4,765.1	4,633.6	4,105.5	3,841.2
Performance & Financial Condition				
Return on Total Revenues %	-0.99	7.08	4.99	-15.86
Return on Avg Stockholders' Equity %	-1.81	12.09	6.65	-26.15
Return on Average Assets %	-1.22	8.64	4.66	-14.15
Current Ratio	1.55	3.06	1.99	2.11
Debt / Equity %	33.02	16.68	21.71	22.92

Compound Growth %'s	EPS %	n.a.	Net Income %	n.a.	Total Revenues %	32.53

Comments

Despite lower than expected demand for molded products, revenues advanced another 15% in 1998. Gross margins were lower as the Company incurred costs to increase production capacity. During 1998, the Company acquired certain assets from Iowa Mat Company, adding two new products: rubber weight plates for fitness and a playground surface safety pad. Nonrecurring administrative costs in connection with this acquisition approximated $120,000. The Company also recorded a loss on the impairment of goodwill of $396,050. On January 29, 1999, the Company acquired a tire recovery and processing plant which had been and will continue to provide the Company with most of its required raw material.

Officers	Position	Ownership Information	
Ronald L. Bogh	President, CEO	Number of Shares Outstanding	2,239,167
Paul M. Gilson	Senior VP, COO	Market Capitalization	$ 2,933,309
Brian C. Allen	Treasurer, CFO	Number of Shareholders	617
Edward DeRaeve	Director	Where Listed / Symbol	NASDAQ / RBBR

Other Information			
Transfer Agent	American Securities Transfer, Inc. Denver, CO	SIC Code	3060
Auditor	Morrison & Liebswager, PC	Employees	72
		Web Site	rbrubber.com

R.H. Phillips, Inc.

26836 County Road 12A   Esparto, CA 95627   Telephone (530)662-3215   Fax (530)662-2888

Company Description

R.H. Phillips, Inc. makes and sells premium and super premium varietal table wines. The Company's vineyard, winery and corporate headquarters are located in the Dunnigan Hills region of California, approximately 30 miles northeast of the Napa Valley wine region. The Company specializes in the production of Chardonnay as well as Syrah and Viognier, which are Rhone Valley varietals. The Company owns or leases approximately 1,550 acres of grapes in the Dunnigan Hills viticultural region. The Company's strategy is to combine high quality wine-making technology with low fruit costs from its vineyards in order to increase gross margins and production of its super premium wines. The Company was founded in 1984.

		12/31/98	12/31/97	12/31/96	12/31/95
Per Share Information					
	Stock Price	2.87	3.00	2.87	3.00
	Earnings Per Share	0.27	0.16	0.20	0.17
	Price / Earnings Ratio	10.63	18.75	14.35	17.65
	Book Value Per Share	2.78	2.55	2.34	1.37
	Price / Book Value %	103.24	117.65	122.65	218.98
	Dividends Per Share	0.0	0.0	0.0	0.0
Annual Financial Data					
Operating Results (000's)					
	Total Revenues	21,737.0	17,363.0	16,928.5	15,527.7
	Costs & Expenses	-18,258.0	-15,239.0	-14,852.3	-14,487.9
	Income Before Taxes and Other	3,479.0	2,124.0	1,924.3	1,039.8
	Other Items	0.0	0.0	0.0	0.0
	Income Tax	-1,388.0	-790.0	-631.0	-289.0
	Net Income	2,091.0	1,334.0	1,293.3	750.8
	Cash Flow From Operations	2,119.0	685.0	2,911.2	941.4
Balance Sheet (000's)					
	Cash & Equivalents	151.0	109.0	308.5	317.6
	Total Current Assets	16,924.0	13,396.0	11,719.0	9,955.7
	Fixed Assets, Net	33,213.0	28,870.0	27,429.7	16,578.5
	Total Assets	50,848.0	42,964.0	39,929.4	27,393.5
	Total Current Liabilities	4,139.0	3,397.0	4,702.8	4,586.9
	Long-Term Debt	21,728.0	16,369.0	15,834.5	14,087.5
	Stockholders' Equity	18,133.0	16,385.0	13,970.4	8,040.1
Performance & Financial Condition					
	Return on Total Revenues %	9.62	7.68	7.64	4.83
	Return on Avg Stockholders' Equity %	12.12	8.79	11.75	7.51
	Return on Average Assets %	4.46	3.22	3.84	2.50
	Current Ratio	4.09	3.94	2.49	2.17
	Debt / Equity %	119.83	99.90	113.34	175.22

Compound Growth %'s	EPS %	16.67	Net Income %	40.70	Total Revenues %	11.87

Comments

Despite the high cost of capital required for a vineyard and winery, the Company has grown consistently but without over-extending its credit capabilities. A combination of leases and a redeemable preferred stock have facilitated this effort. Pre-tax profits in excess of 10% of revenue is outstanding for any young winery. The growth evident in 1998 revenues was due primarily to increased sales of higher priced premium wines. Depreciation has reduced fixed assets to approximately 78% of their original cost. The true value of these assets and consistent earnings may indicate that a stock price close to book value is extremely reasonable.

Officers	Position	Ownership Information	
John E. Giguiere	President, CEO	Number of Shares Outstanding	6,531,831
Karl E. Giguiere	President, CEO	Market Capitalization	$ 18,746,355
Michael J. Motroni	VP - Finance, CFO	Number of Shareholders	1,000
Lane C. Giguiere	Vice President, Secretary	Where Listed / Symbol	NASDAQ / RHPS

Other Information			
Transfer Agent	American Stock Transfer & Trust Co. New York, NY	SIC Code	2080
Auditor	KPMG LLP	Employees	110
		Web Site	rhphillips.com

RADVA Corporation

301 First Street, Drawer 2900 First Street Station   Radford, VA 24143   Telephone (540)639-2458   Fax (540)731-3731

Company Description

RADVA Corporation produces and sells molded and fabricated expanded polystyrene foam products such as packaging materials and containers and has also developed and patented housing construction panels utilizing polystyrene foam reinforced with steel. In addition, the Company builds and sells machinery used to manufacture the panels, along with the licensing rights to market the panels. The Company's facilities are located in Radford and Portsmouth, Virginia. The Company was founded in 1962.

	12/31/98	12/31/97	12/31/96	12/31/95
Per Share Information				
Stock Price	0.62	0.47	0.44	1.06
Earnings Per Share	0.37	0.05	0.05	0.13
Price / Earnings Ratio	1.68	9.40	8.80	8.15
Book Value Per Share	1.20	0.83	0.77	0.77
Price / Book Value %	51.67	56.63	57.14	137.66
Dividends Per Share	0.0	0.0	0.0	0.0
Annual Financial Data				
Operating Results (000's)				
Total Revenues	13,253.9	11,049.8	9,727.0	10,793.0
Costs & Expenses	-11,737.0	-10,873.3	-9,726.6	-10,231.8
Income Before Taxes and Other	1,516.9	176.5	0.4	519.9
Other Items	0.0	32.2	0.0	-27.6
Income Tax	0.0	0.0	0.0	-10.4
Net Income	1,516.9	208.6	0.4	482.0
Cash Flow From Operations	-219.2	359.5	-49.4	334.5
Balance Sheet (000's)				
Cash & Equivalents	246.4	79.0	23.6	349.9
Total Current Assets	3,972.0	3,149.3	3,786.6	4,135.4
Fixed Assets, Net	4,443.0	4,687.9	2,497.4	2,307.8
Total Assets	11,890.2	11,192.2	7,773.8	7,997.5
Total Current Liabilities	2,920.6	3,827.9	1,915.9	1,984.9
Long-Term Debt	3,989.0	3,843.4	2,678.1	2,833.2
Stockholders' Equity	4,886.3	3,388.4	3,179.8	3,179.4
Performance & Financial Condition				
Return on Total Revenues %	11.44	1.89	n.a.	4.47
Return on Avg Stockholders' Equity %	36.66	6.35	0.01	17.41
Return on Average Assets %	13.14	2.20	n.a.	5.91
Current Ratio	1.36	0.82	1.98	2.08
Debt / Equity %	81.64	113.43	84.22	89.11

Compound Growth %'s	EPS %	41.72	Net Income %	46.55	Total Revenues %	7.09

Comments

The $1.3 million increase in net income for 1998 included the result of the Company's sale of panel manufacturing and licensing rights which generated a profit of $807,000. The balance of the increase was due to higher manufacturing revenues of $1.6 million. The Company made infrastructure improvements and invested in new molding machines and auxiliary support equipment which became operational in the first half of 1998. Included in revenues for 1995 is a gain of $1.0 million relating to the sale of an 80% interest in its wholly-owned subsidiary. Tax expense has been negligible because of the availability of tax loss carryforwards which have now mostly been utilized.

Officers	Position	Ownership Information	
Stephen L. Dickens	President	Number of Shares Outstanding	4,085,727
Luther I. Dickens	CEO	Market Capitalization	$ 2,533,151
William F. Fry	CFO	Number of Shareholders	334
James M. Hylton	Secretary, Treasurer	Where Listed / Symbol	OTC-BB / RDVA

Other Information

Transfer Agent	American Stock Transfer & Trust Co. New York, NY		SIC Code	3086
Auditor	Persinger & Company L.L.C.		Employees	140
Market Maker	Carr Securities Corporation	(800)221-2243		
	Sharpe Capital Inc.	(800)355-5781		

REXX Environmental Corporation

350 Park Avenue   New York, NY 10022   Telephone (212)750-7755   Fax (212)750-3095

Company Description

REXX Environmental Corporation is a leading regional provider of asbestos-abatement services, demolition and dismantling services, and other related specialty contracting services, including lead paint abatement, to a broad range of governmental, commercial, industrial and institutional clients located primarily in California. The Company was founded in 1967 but was engaged in two other businesses before it acquired a San Diego-based environmental remediation contractor in 1997. The prior businesses were the manufacture and marketing of disposable thermometers and sterilization monitors and the manufacture and marketing of women's apparel and accessories. Both of these businesses were sold.

	12/31/98	12/31/97	12/31/96	12/31/95
Per Share Information				
Stock Price	2.37	3.00	1.50	2.00
Earnings Per Share	-0.20	-0.08	-0.53	-3.32
Price / Earnings Ratio	n.a.	n.a.	n.a.	n.a.
Book Value Per Share	1.88	2.08	2.30	2.94
Price / Book Value %	126.06	144.23	65.22	68.03
Dividends Per Share	0.0	0.0	0.0	0.0
Annual Financial Data				
Operating Results (000's)				
Total Revenues	13,777.0	2,443.0	322.0	159.0
Costs & Expenses	-14,318.0	-2,562.0	-531.0	-215.0
Income Before Taxes and Other	-541.0	-119.0	-209.0	-56.0
Other Items	0.0	0.0	-1,092.0	-6,769.0
Income Tax	45.0	-48.0	-9.0	-14.0
Net Income	-496.0	-167.0	-1,310.0	-6,839.0
Cash Flow From Operations	-2,009.0	-1,422.0	-935.0	-1,743.0
Balance Sheet (000's)				
Cash & Equivalents	68.0	710.0	5,314.0	5,823.0
Total Current Assets	5,984.0	5,155.0	6,880.0	5,823.0
Fixed Assets, Net	1,487.0	718.0	0.0	0.0
Total Assets	10,422.0	9,055.0	6,880.0	9,115.0
Total Current Liabilities	5,041.0	3,686.0	2,144.0	3,069.0
Long-Term Debt	738.0	180.0	0.0	0.0
Stockholders' Equity	4,643.0	5,139.0	4,736.0	6,046.0
Performance & Financial Condition				
Return on Total Revenues %	-3.60	-6.84	-406.83	-4,301.26
Return on Avg Stockholders' Equity %	-10.14	-3.38	-24.30	-72.25
Return on Average Assets %	-5.09	-2.10	-16.38	-37.50
Current Ratio	1.19	1.40	3.21	1.90
Debt / Equity %	15.89	3.50	n.a.	n.a.

Compound Growth %'s	EPS % n.a.	Net Income % n.a.	Total Revenues % 342.51

Comments

Revenues were higher in 1998 as compared to 1997 primarily due to the inclusion of a full year's revenue from the acquired business as well as an expansion of the demolition-related services. Gross profit margins decreased to 25% in 1998 from 42% in 1997, principally due to lower margins on demolition-related projects as compared to higher margins on asbestos projects. 1996 and 1995 results include losses from discontinued operations of $.53 per share and $3.29 per share, respectively. At December 31, 1998, the Company had $2.9 million of goodwill recorded as assets which equated to approximately 63% of stockholders' equity and book value per share.

Officers	Position	Ownership Information	
Arthur L. Asch	Chairman, CEO	Number of Shares Outstanding	2,467,576
Michael A. Asch	President, CFO	Market Capitalization	$ 5,848,155
James L. Hochfelder	Director	Number of Shareholders	680
Joseph Greenberger	Director, Secretary	Where Listed / Symbol	AMEX / REX

Other Information			
Transfer Agent	American Stock Transfer & Trust Co. New York, NY	SIC Code	1795
Auditor	PricewaterhouseCoopers LLP	Employees	159

RF Industries, Ltd.

7610 Miramar Road, Building 6000 San Diego, CA 92126-4202 Telephone (619)549-6340 Fax (619)549-6345

Company Description

RF Industries, Ltd. is engaged in the design, manufacture and distribution of coaxial connectors used in professional radio communication applications as well as in computers, test instruments, personal computer local area networks, and antenna devices. The Company also designs and produces wireless digital transmission products including radio frequency links which transmit and receive control signals for the remote operation and monitoring of equipment. These point to point and point to multi-point wireless data networks are used by banks, casinos, and petrochemical, oil and gas companies, governments, and military agencies, among other users. The Company was founded in 1979.

	10/31/98	10/31/97	10/31/96	10/31/95
Per Share Information				
Stock Price as of 12/31	2.12	2.00	5.00	1.25
Earnings Per Share	0.21	0.19	0.18	0.07
Price / Earnings Ratio	10.10	10.53	27.78	17.86
Book Value Per Share	1.82	1.54	1.30	1.07
Price / Book Value %	116.48	129.87	384.62	116.82
Dividends Per Share	0.0	0.0	0.0	0.0
Annual Financial Data				
Operating Results (000's)				
Total Revenues	6,623.2	6,898.6	6,141.7	3,425.9
Costs & Expenses	-5,337.2	-5,895.1	-5,165.3	-3,150.9
Income Before Taxes and Other	1,286.0	1,003.5	976.4	274.9
Other Items	0.0	0.0	0.0	0.0
Income Tax	-529.0	-402.6	-415.0	-103.3
Net Income	757.0	600.9	561.4	171.6
Cash Flow From Operations	910.9	546.8	212.8	30.0
Balance Sheet (000's)				
Cash & Equivalents	1,209.1	877.6	403.5	211.3
Total Current Assets	5,992.2	4,942.6	3,908.8	2,789.8
Fixed Assets, Net	162.8	119.1	111.8	127.1
Total Assets	6,259.9	5,155.7	4,063.5	2,955.0
Total Current Liabilities	662.3	449.6	454.3	245.1
Long-Term Debt	0.0	0.0	0.0	0.0
Stockholders' Equity	5,597.6	4,706.0	3,609.2	2,709.9
Performance & Financial Condition				
Return on Total Revenues %	11.43	8.71	9.14	5.01
Return on Avg Stockholders' Equity %	14.69	14.45	17.77	6.94
Return on Average Assets %	13.26	13.04	16.00	6.38
Current Ratio	9.05	10.99	8.60	11.38
Debt / Equity %	n.a.	n.a.	n.a.	n.a.

Compound Growth %'s	EPS %	44.22	Net Income %	63.99	Total Revenues %	24.58

Comments

Revenues declined despite a strong order backlog at the beginning of fiscal 1998. But gross margins improved due to a favorable sales mix and tighter inventory controls. The bottom line proved to be the third consecutive improvement in earnings. Fiscal 1999 also looks promising. The sales order backlog was $8.8 million at fiscal year end, up from $4.2 million in the preceding year. With plenty of working capital and no long term debt, the Company has financed its growth internally. The balance sheet is solid and has no intangible assets of any kind. The current size of the Company is too small to attract institutional investors, which may explain the low premium over book value.

Officers	Position	Ownership Information	
Jack A. Benz	Chairman	Number of Shares Outstanding	3,078,598
Howard F. Hill	President, CEO	Market Capitalization	$ 6,526,628
Terrie A. Gross	Secretary, CFO	Number of Shareholders	843
John Ehret	Director	Where Listed / Symbol	NASDAQ / RFIL

Other Information

Transfer Agent	Continental Stock Transfer & Trust Co. New York, NY	SIC Code	3678
Auditor	J.H. Cohn LLP	Employees	33
		Web Site	rfindustries.com

RMH Teleservices, Inc.

40 Morris Avenue   Bryn Mawr, PA 19010   Telephone (610)520-5300   Fax (610)520-5356

Company Description

RMH Teleservices, Inc. provides outbound and inbound teleservices predominantly to major corporations in the insurance, financial services, telecommunications and membership services industries. The Company distinguishes itself through its high quality service and disciplined management approach which has led to long-term client relationships and sustained profitable growth. The Company was founded in 1983. In May 1996, the Company completed a leveraged recapitalization pursuant to which Advanta Partners LP, a venture capital affiliate with Advanta Corp., became the largest equity holder of the Company. In September 1996, the Company completed an initial public offering of 3,220,000 shares of common stock.

	09/30/98	09/30/97	09/30/96	09/30/95
Per Share Information				
Stock Price as of 12/31	2.12	6.00	7.25	12.50
Earnings Per Share	0.06	0.41	-0.55	0.17
Price / Earnings Ratio	35.33	14.63	n.a.	73.53
Book Value Per Share	2.73	2.67	2.26	0.37
Price / Book Value %	77.66	224.72	320.80	3,378.38
Dividends Per Share	0.0	0.0	0.0	0.0
Annual Financial Data				
Operating Results (000's)				
Total Revenues	52,975.0	46,410.0	32,316.0	25,545.0
Costs & Expenses	-52,107.0	-41,218.0	-30,774.0	-23,783.0
Income Before Taxes and Other	868.0	5,192.0	1,542.0	1,762.0
Other Items	0.0	0.0	-6,669.0	0.0
Income Tax	-364.0	-1,825.0	1,222.0	-21.0
Net Income	504.0	3,367.0	-3,905.0	1,741.0
Cash Flow From Operations	144.0	2,470.0	-1,677.0	1,500.0
Balance Sheet (000's)				
Cash & Equivalents	4,179.0	6,882.0	10,047.0	322.0
Total Current Assets	23,160.0	20,698.0	17,139.0	4,988.4
Fixed Assets, Net	4,047.0	4,476.0	5,416.0	3,768.8
Total Assets	27,335.0	25,286.0	22,555.0	8,757.2
Total Current Liabilities	4,998.0	3,314.0	4,240.0	3,927.7
Long-Term Debt	0.0	0.0	0.0	0.0
Stockholders' Equity	22,187.0	21,683.0	18,315.0	3,668.0
Performance & Financial Condition				
Return on Total Revenues %	0.95	7.25	-12.08	6.82
Return on Avg Stockholders' Equity %	2.30	16.84	-35.53	49.74
Return on Average Assets %	1.92	14.08	-24.94	21.76
Current Ratio	4.63	6.25	4.04	1.27
Debt / Equity %	n.a.	n.a.	n.a.	n.a.

Compound Growth %'s	EPS %	-29.33	Net Income %	-33.85	Total Revenues %	27.52

Comments

Compared to 1997, operating income decreased in 1998 when compared to 1997 as a result of the increase in cost of services as a percentage of revenues, partially offset by growth in revenue. Cost of services, which primarily consists of labor, increased from 69.1% of revenues in fiscal 1997 to 75.6% of revenues in fiscal 1998. These costs have increased as a percentage of revenues as the Company has encountered a tight labor market, resulting in higher average hourly pay rates coupled with difficulties in staffing its existing call centers. Fiscal 1996 results include a special bonus to founders of $6.1 million and other nonrecurring items of approximately $600,000. Despite lower income levels, the Company has maintained an excellent financial condition and the balance sheet is free from both intangible assets and long term debt.

Officers	Position	Ownership Information	
John A. Fellows	CEO	Number of Shares Outstanding	8,120,000
Robert M. Berwanger	COO	Market Capitalization	$ 17,214,400
Michael J. Scharff	Exec VP, CFO	Number of Shareholders	1,000
Diane Bowser	Senior VP	Where Listed / Symbol	NASDAQ / RMHT

Other Information			
Transfer Agent	Stocktrans, Inc. Ardmore, PA	SIC Code	7389
Auditor	Arthur Andersen LLP	Employees	2,566
		Web Site	rmhteleservices.com

RMS Titanic, Inc.

17 Battery Place   New York, NY 10004   Telephone (212)558-6300   Fax (212)482-1912

Company Description

RMS Titanic, Inc. acquired all of the assets and assumed all of the liabilities of Titanic Ventures Limited Partnership (TVLP) on May 4, 1993. TVLP was formed in 1987 for the purpose of exploring the wreck and surrounding oceanic areas of the Titanic. The ship sank in 1912 and lies more than 12,500 feet below the surface of the Atlantic Ocean approximately 400 miles off the coast of Newfoundland. Utilizing state-of-the-art technology belonging to the government of France, the Company has been able to retrieve thousands of artifacts through the use of a manned submersible NAUTILE. The Company is engaged in revenue producing activities such as touring exhibitions, television programs and the sale of still photography.

	02/28/98	02/28/97	02/28/96	02/28/95
Per Share Information				
Stock Price as of 12/31	1.16	0.59	0.44	0.28
Earnings Per Share	0.21	0.01	-0.01	-0.11
Price / Earnings Ratio	5.52	59.00	n.a.	n.a.
Book Value Per Share	0.46	0.25	0.24	0.20
Price / Book Value %	252.17	236.00	183.33	140.00
Dividends Per Share	0.0	0.0	0.0	0.0
Annual Financial Data				
Operating Results (000's)				
Total Revenues	4,736.7	1,246.6	724.5	204.4
Costs & Expenses	-1,219.3	-1,089.0	-874.2	-1,735.4
Income Before Taxes and Other	3,517.4	157.5	-149.6	-1,531.0
Other Items	0.0	0.0	0.0	0.0
Income Tax	-150.0	0.0	0.0	0.0
Net Income	3,367.4	157.5	-149.6	-1,531.0
Cash Flow From Operations	1,032.2	909.9	-386.5	77.1
Balance Sheet (000's)				
Cash & Equivalents	1,000.3	105.9	44.0	0.5
Total Current Assets	1,686.9	232.9	74.0	162.1
Fixed Assets, Net	652.6	19.6	26.0	38.5
Total Assets	10,078.7	8,005.4	6,060.0	6,164.6
Total Current Liabilities	2,642.1	3,942.0	2,194.0	3,133.7
Long-Term Debt	0.0	0.0	0.0	300.0
Stockholders' Equity	7,436.6	4,063.4	3,866.0	2,731.0
Performance & Financial Condition				
Return on Total Revenues %	71.09	12.64	-20.65	-749.16
Return on Avg Stockholders' Equity %	58.56	3.97	-4.54	-51.98
Return on Average Assets %	37.24	2.24	-2.45	-27.10
Current Ratio	0.64	0.06	0.03	0.05
Debt / Equity %	n.a.	n.a.	n.a.	10.99

Compound Growth %'s	EPS % n.a.	Net Income % n.a.	Total Revenues % 185.12

Comments

Revenues increased 274% in fiscal 1998 as a result of major exhibitions in Memphis, Tennessee for six months, in Hamburg, Germany for ten months, and in St. Petersburg, Florida for three months. Sales of merchandise and books were also sharply higher. Was this all a result of the movie "Titanic" which was released during the last fiscal year or is this just the tip of the iceberg? For the nine month period ended November 31, 1998, the Company reported revenues and net income of $8.4 million and $2,938,037 ($.18 per share) as compared to $2.9 million and $2,082,797 ($.13 per share) for the same period of the preceding year. More impressive, however, is that the last nine months includes the Company's first full income tax expense of $1.9 million.

Officers	Position	Ownership Information	
William S. Gasparrini	Chairman	Number of Shares Outstanding	16,177,128
George H. Tulloch	President	Market Capitalization	$ 18,765,468
Nicholas Vitti	CFO	Number of Shareholders	1,996
Robert A. Slavitt	Director	Where Listed / Symbol	OTC-BB / SOST

Other Information

Transfer Agent	American Stock Transfer & Trust Co. New York, NY		SIC Code	4400
Auditor	Goldstein Golub Kessler & Co.		Employees	4
Market Maker	M.H. Meyerson & Co., Inc.	(800)333-3113	Web Site	titanic-online.com
	Paragon Capital Corporation	(800)345-0505		

ROHN Industries, Inc.

6718 West Plank Road   Peoria, IL 61604   Telephone (309)697-4400   Fax (309)697-5612

Company Description

ROHN Industries, Inc. is a leading manufacturer of infrastructure products used in the wireless communications markets. The Company's principal products are towers, equipment enclosures/shelters, poles, masts, mounts and cabinets. ROHN's growth in recent years has been due in part to the growth of the cellular phone and other types of wireless communications systems, and the introduction and growth of its equipment enclosure product line. ROHN is the remaining company of the old UNR Industries, Inc. which was formed in 1979 and subject to a bankruptcy reorganization in 1982. As a result of the reorganization, the UNR Asbestos-Disease Claims Trust owns 55.5% of the Company's outstanding shares.

	12/31/98	12/31/97	12/31/96	12/31/95
Per Share Information				
Stock Price	3.25	5.12	5.87	8.62
Earnings Per Share	0.27	0.36	0.89	0.57
Price / Earnings Ratio	12.04	14.22	6.60	15.12
Book Value Per Share	1.39	1.10	0.80	2.45
Price / Book Value %	233.81	465.45	733.75	351.84
Dividends Per Share	0.0	0.10	2.60	2.55
Annual Financial Data				
Operating Results (000's)				
Total Revenues	174,445.0	163,042.0	156,298.0	144,661.0
Costs & Expenses	-150,962.0	-132,972.0	-122,916.0	-112,960.0
Income Before Taxes and Other	23,483.0	30,070.0	33,382.0	31,701.0
Other Items	-540.0	0.0	25,759.0	10,275.0
Income Tax	-8,900.0	-11,151.0	-13,100.0	-12,700.0
Net Income	14,043.0	18,919.0	46,041.0	29,276.0
Cash Flow From Operations	18,908.0	11,270.0	-16,832.0	47,690.0
Balance Sheet (000's)				
Cash & Equivalents	19,690.0	5,994.0	5,030.0	5,878.0
Total Current Assets	80,116.0	78,605.0	68,888.0	141,226.0
Fixed Assets, Net	26,630.0	27,495.0	21,822.0	20,000.0
Total Assets	114,192.0	108,658.0	93,372.0	161,226.0
Total Current Liabilities	29,286.0	39,345.0	38,670.0	28,791.0
Long-Term Debt	10,253.0	11,271.0	12,191.0	4,671.0
Stockholders' Equity	72,579.0	58,042.0	42,511.0	127,764.0
Performance & Financial Condition				
Return on Total Revenues %	8.05	11.60	29.46	20.24
Return on Avg Stockholders' Equity %	21.50	37.63	54.08	16.83
Return on Average Assets %	12.60	18.73	36.17	13.97
Current Ratio	2.74	2.00	1.78	4.91
Debt / Equity %	14.13	19.42	28.68	3.66

Compound Growth %'s	EPS %	-22.05	Net Income %	-21.72	Total Revenues %	6.44

Comments

Revenues gained 10.2% in 1998 as compared to 1997, almost entirely on the strength of enclosure products. Management said that this segment benefited from a wider range of applications for these products both within the communications industry and outside the inventory. But the Company also included $10.7 million of revenue on sales of items that had not yet been shipped. Management maintains that the earnings process was complete on these items. No such amounts were included in income at the end of 1997. The Company sold four of its five operating divisions during 1996. Income from discontinued operations and gains from sale of the divisions amounted to $25.8 million ($.50 per share) and $10.3 million ($.20 per share) in 1996 and 1995, respectively. The Company used the proceeds to pay substantial dividends to shareholders in each of those years.

Officers	Position	Ownership Information	
Brian B. Pemberton	President, CEO	Number of Shares Outstanding	52,181,000
David V. LaRusso	Vice President, CFO	Market Capitalization	$ 169,588,250
Richard L. Rohn	Vice President	Number of Shareholders	3,244
James R. Cote	VP - Sales	Where Listed / Symbol	NASDAQ / ROHN

Other Information			
Transfer Agent	First Chicago Trust Co. of New York Jersey City, NJ	SIC Code	3490
Auditor	Arthur Andersen LLP	Employees	785
		Web Site	rohnindustries.com

Rag Shops, Inc.

111 Wagaraw Road   Hawthorne, NJ 07506-2711   Telephone (973)423-1303   Fax (973)427-6568

Company Description

Rag Shops, Inc. operates retail stores that offer a diverse and extensive assortment of value-priced crafts, fabrics and related items to creative craft and sewing consumers. The Company caters to value conscious consumers who sew and create decorative accessories. At August 29, 1998, the Company operated 33 retail stores in New Jersey, 19 in Florida, 7 in Pennsylvania, 6 in New York and 1 in Connecticut. Fifty-nine of the sixty-six stores also offer picture framing. The Company's expansion strategy is to grow by expanding within areas from which it presently attracts customers and into contiguous market areas, enabling the Company to capitalize on pre-existing advertising and name recognition. The Company was founded in 1963.

	08/29/98	08/30/97	08/31/96	09/02/95
Per Share Information				
Stock Price as of 12/31	2.50	2.69	2.12	2.12
Earnings Per Share	0.21	0.05	0.12	0.12
Price / Earnings Ratio	11.90	53.80	17.67	17.67
Book Value Per Share	4.82	4.61	4.56	4.45
Price / Book Value %	51.87	58.35	46.49	47.64
Dividends Per Share	0.0	0.0	0.0	0.0
Annual Financial Data				
Operating Results (000's)				
Total Revenues	90,566.0	86,527.6	83,766.7	86,089.4
Costs & Expenses	-89,022.0	-86,176.2	-82,987.6	-85,196.9
Income Before Taxes and Other	1,544.0	351.3	779.0	892.5
Other Items	0.0	0.0	0.0	0.0
Income Tax	-602.5	-143.9	-258.7	-350.6
Net Income	941.5	207.4	520.3	541.9
Cash Flow From Operations	2,443.3	1,135.1	2,659.4	1,981.5
Balance Sheet (000's)				
Cash & Equivalents	896.1	763.7	821.0	911.2
Total Current Assets	28,671.1	27,125.0	28,648.6	29,776.9
Fixed Assets, Net	4,327.6	4,885.5	4,462.1	4,725.9
Total Assets	33,318.4	32,263.7	33,555.3	34,821.0
Total Current Liabilities	11,576.6	10,868.8	11,663.5	14,615.8
Long-Term Debt	0.0	554.3	1,230.9	0.0
Stockholders' Equity	21,741.8	20,800.3	20,592.8	20,072.5
Performance & Financial Condition				
Return on Total Revenues %	1.04	0.24	0.62	0.63
Return on Avg Stockholders' Equity %	4.43	1.00	2.56	2.74
Return on Average Assets %	2.87	0.63	1.52	1.53
Current Ratio	2.48	2.50	2.46	2.04
Debt / Equity %	n.a.	2.66	5.98	n.a.

Compound Growth %'s	EPS %	20.51	Net Income %	20.22	Total Revenues %	1.70

Comments

Comparable store sales rose 3.2% during fiscal 1998. Management attributes this success to a point-of-sale system that has been providing valuable information. An automated store ordering system, installed in the spring of 1998, contributed to timely inventory replenishment, improving gross margins because of fewer markdowns. For the six months ended February 28, 1999, the Company reported revenues and net income of $51.8 million and $1,263,000 ($.28 per share) as compared to $51.3 million and $1,413,000 ($.31 per share) for the same period of the preceding year.

Officers	Position	Ownership Information	
Stanley Berenzweig	Chairman, CEO	Number of Shares Outstanding	4,514,400
Michael Aaronson	President, COO	Market Capitalization	$ 11,286,000
Judith Lombardo	Senior VP	Number of Shareholders	800
Steven B. Barnett	Senior VP, CFO	Where Listed / Symbol	NASDAQ / RAGS

Other Information			
Transfer Agent	Continental Stock Transfer & Trust Co. Jersey City, NJ	SIC Code	5949
Auditor	Deloitte & Touche LLP	Employees	1,150

Randers Killam Group Inc. (The)

570 Seminole Road   Norton Shores, MI 49444   Telephone (616)733-0036   Fax (616)733-8137

Company Description

The Randers Killam Group Inc., formerly The Randers Group Incorporated, provides comprehensive engineering and outsourcing services in such areas as water and wastewater treatment, highway and bridge projects, process engineering, construction management, and operational services. In May 1997, Thermo TerraTech, also included in this manual, entered into a definitive agreement to transfer the The Killam Group Inc. to Randers in exchange for additional shares of Randers' common stock. As a result of these transactions, Thermo TerraTech owns 120,551,051 shares of the common stock of the Company, representing 95% of such stock outstanding. Randers was founded in 1974.

	04/04/98	03/29/97	03/30/96
Per Share Information			
Stock Price as of 12/31	2.20	3.45	2.20
Earnings Per Share	0.15	0.15	0.10
Price / Earnings Ratio	14.67	23.00	22.00
Book Value Per Share	3.15	2.86	0.17
Price / Book Value %	69.84	120.63	1,294.12
Dividends Per Share	0.0	0.0	0.0
Annual Financial Data			
Operating Results (000's)			
Total Revenues	71,778.0	64,484.0	58,688.0
Costs & Expenses	-65,822.0	-57,787.0	-53,969.0
Income Before Taxes and Other	5,956.0	6,697.0	4,719.0
Other Items	0.0	0.0	0.0
Income Tax	-2,803.0	-3,117.0	-2,340.0
Net Income	3,153.0	3,580.0	2,379.0
Cash Flow From Operations	4,480.0	3,530.0	5,695.0
Balance Sheet (000's)			
Cash & Equivalents	9,763.0	1,737.0	415.5
Total Current Assets	35,132.0	23,372.0	3,177.7
Fixed Assets, Net	11,664.0	9,035.0	2,670.2
Total Assets	93,193.0	75,434.0	7,327.3
Total Current Liabilities	9,310.0	7,334.0	2,356.4
Long-Term Debt	1,948.0	1,260.0	1,054.4
Stockholders' Equity	79,998.0	64,731.0	3,916.6
Performance & Financial Condition			
Return on Total Revenues %	4.39	5.55	4.05
Return on Avg Stockholders' Equity %	4.36	10.43	7.21
Return on Average Assets %	3.74	8.65	5.95
Current Ratio	3.77	3.19	1.35
Debt / Equity %	2.44	1.95	26.92

Compound Growth %'s	EPS %	22.47	Net Income %	15.12	Total Revenues %	10.59

Comments

The Company executed a 1 for 5 reverse stock split effective February 1, 1999. All per share amounts have been restated for consistency. Operating results for all years presented and the balance sheets for fiscal 1998 and 1997 have been restated to combine The Killam Group for the period prior to the transaction mentioned above. At April 4, 1998, the Company had $45.2 million of goodwill on its books which equated to approximately 57% of stockholders' equity and book value per share. For the nine months ended December 31, 1998, the Company reported revenues and net income of $61.9 million and $2.4 million ($.09 per share) as compared to $53.3 million and $2.7 million ($.11 per share) for the same period of fiscal 1998.

Officers	Position	Ownership Information	
Emil C. Herkert	President, CEO	Number of Shares Outstanding	25,429,346
Theo Melas-Kyriazi	CFO	Market Capitalization	$ 55,944,561
Nicholas M. DeNichilo	Vice President	Number of Shareholders	1,000
Thomas R. Eurich	Vice President	Where Listed / Symbol	AMEX / RGI

Other Information			
Transfer Agent	First Union National Bank of N.C. Charlotte, NC	SIC Code	8711
Auditor	Arthur Andersen LLP	Employees	711
		Web Site	thermo.com

Rankin Automotive Group, Inc.

3709 MacArthur Drive   Alexandria, LA 71302   Telephone (318)487-1081   Fax (318)443-9952

Company Description

Rankin Automotive Group, Inc. is a specialty wholesaler and retailer of automotive replacement parts, maintenance items and accessories for the professional installer and "do it yourself" markets. The Company has 40 auto parts stores and three machine shops located in Louisiana, Mississippi and east Texas. Stores carry an extensive product line of hard parts including brakes, belts, hoses, filters, cooling system parts, tune-up parts, shock absorbers, gaskets, batteries, bearings, engine parts, remanufactured alternators and starters, chassis parts and exhaust systems. The Company was founded in 1978 and went public on November 21, 1996.

	02/25/98	02/25/97	02/25/96	02/25/95
Per Share Information				
Stock Price as of 12/31	2.37	2.50	12.87	n.a.
Earnings Per Share	-0.17	0.04	0.10	n.a.
Price / Earnings Ratio	n.a.	62.50	128.70	n.a.
Book Value Per Share	2.79	3.00	0.16	n.a.
Price / Book Value %	84.95	83.33	n.a.	n.a.
Dividends Per Share	0.0	0.0	0.0	n.a.
Annual Financial Data				
Operating Results (000's)				
Total Revenues	38,655.6	29,946.3	21,032.5	13,957.0
Costs & Expenses	-39,504.4	-29,741.3	-20,717.7	-14,097.0
Income Before Taxes and Other	-848.8	205.0	314.8	-140.0
Other Items	0.0	0.0	0.0	0.0
Income Tax	60.0	-65.0	-5.0	0.0
Net Income	-788.8	140.0	309.8	-140.0
Cash Flow From Operations	-2,235.7	-1,009.6	37.1	n.a.
Balance Sheet (000's)				
Cash & Equivalents	3,962.1	4,022.3	309.1	n.a.
Total Current Assets	19,341.1	16,534.8	7,596.9	n.a.
Fixed Assets, Net	1,994.3	1,342.5	1,013.4	n.a.
Total Assets	21,964.5	18,528.6	8,668.3	n.a.
Total Current Liabilities	4,132.4	3,381.7	2,504.3	n.a.
Long-Term Debt	5,188.2	1,519.0	5,668.8	n.a.
Stockholders' Equity	12,644.0	13,627.8	495.3	n.a.
Performance & Financial Condition				
Return on Total Revenues %	-2.04	0.47	1.47	-1.00
Return on Avg Stockholders' Equity %	-6.01	1.98	90.99	-93.33
Return on Average Assets %	-3.90	1.03	3.60	-1.65
Current Ratio	4.68	4.89	3.03	n.a.
Debt / Equity %	41.03	11.15	1,144.51	n.a.

Compound Growth %'s	EPS % n.a.	Net Income % n.a.	Total Revenues % 40.43

Comments

Approximately 36% of the increase in revenues during fiscal 1997 was attributable to acquisitions. The balance was due to an increase in same store sales and acquisitions that were consummated in the prior year. The loss for fiscal 1998 was attributed entirely to the fourth quarter which had unseasonable weather and problems with a shipper. Working capital remains impressive. For the nine months ended November 25, 1998, the Company reported revenues and net income of $30.3 million and $282,000 ($.06 per share) as compared to $30.3 million and $93,000 ($.02 per share) for the same period of the preceding year.

Officers	Position	Ownership Information	
Randall B. Rankin	President	Number of Shares Outstanding	4,535,000
Deborah N. Eddlemon	CFO	Market Capitalization	$ 10,747,950
Ricky D. Gunn	Vice President	Number of Shareholders	1,500
Harris Lake Smith, Jr.	Vice President	Where Listed / Symbol	NASDAQ / RAVE

Other Information			
Transfer Agent	American Stock Transfer & Trust Co. New York, NY	SIC Code	5013
Auditor	Deloitte & Touche LLP	Employees	420
		Web Site	rankinautomotive.com

Raytel Medical Corporation

2755 Campus Drive, Suite 200   San Mateo, CA 94403   Telephone (650)349-0800   Fax (650)349-8850

Company Description

Raytel Medical Corporation is a provider of healthcare services, focusing on the needs of patients with cardiovascular disease. The Company believes, based on its industry experience, that it is the leading provider of remote cardiac monitoring and testing services utilizing transtelephonic monitoring technology in the United States. The Company's goal is to integrate all of its cardiovascular services in order to become a nationwide provider of cardiac health care services. Raytel intends to accomplish this by complementing its existing nationwide cardiac telephonic testing services with a nationwide network of fixed site cardiac diagnostic and therapeutic service facilities including cardiac catheterization laboratories, heart centers and affiliated cardiology and cardiovascular physician groups. The Company was founded in 1981.

	09/30/98	09/30/97	09/30/96	09/30/95
Per Share Information				
Stock Price as of 12/31	4.50	11.50	10.25	7.00
Earnings Per Share	0.66	0.96	0.75	0.78
Price / Earnings Ratio	6.82	11.98	13.67	8.97
Book Value Per Share	7.67	6.95	5.87	5.00
Price / Book Value %	58.67	165.47	n.a.	140.00
Dividends Per Share	0.0	0.0	0.0	0.0
Annual Financial Data				
Operating Results (000's)				
Total Revenues	108,140.0	86,491.0	73,106.0	63,809.0
Costs & Expenses	-96,905.0	-70,364.0	-62,516.0	-56,327.0
Income Before Taxes and Other	11,235.0	16,127.0	10,590.0	7,482.0
Other Items	-1,273.0	-1,206.0	-1,211.0	-1,161.0
Income Tax	-3,869.0	-6,257.0	-3,248.0	-1,960.0
Net Income	6,093.0	8,664.0	6,131.0	4,361.0
Cash Flow From Operations	8,306.0	12,525.0	14,698.0	8,655.0
Balance Sheet (000's)				
Cash & Equivalents	7,463.0	7,873.0	5,737.0	4,983.0
Total Current Assets	46,963.0	42,188.0	28,962.0	28,684.0
Fixed Assets, Net	19,681.0	19,712.0	9,156.0	8,598.0
Total Assets	122,186.0	119,421.0	68,030.0	46,768.0
Total Current Liabilities	15,795.0	17,797.0	12,758.0	13,137.0
Long-Term Debt	35,035.0	34,461.0	3,842.0	7,718.0
Stockholders' Equity	66,491.0	61,899.0	48,878.0	21,499.0
Performance & Financial Condition				
Return on Total Revenues %	5.63	10.02	8.39	6.83
Return on Avg Stockholders' Equity %	9.49	15.64	17.42	22.56
Return on Average Assets %	5.04	9.24	10.68	8.99
Current Ratio	2.97	2.37	2.27	2.18
Debt / Equity %	52.69	55.67	7.86	35.90

Compound Growth %'s	EPS %	-5.42	Net Income %	11.79	Total Revenues %	19.23

Comments

Fiscal 1998 revenues advanced 29% due to the acquisition of a heart center business on August 15, 1997. A full years revenue from the acquired business was recorded in fiscal 1998. Competitive price pressures and lower reimbursement rates were also reported by management. At September 30, 1998, the Company had $55.5 million of intangible assets recorded on its books which equated to approximately 83% of stockholders' equity and book value per share. Even greater leverage will be needed if the Company is to complete its ambitious expansion plan. So far, the Company has been able to maintain its profitability.

Officers	Position	Ownership Information	
Richard F. Bader	Chairman, CEO	Number of Shares Outstanding	8,663,499
Allan Zinberg	President, COO	Market Capitalization	$ 38,985,746
E. Payson Smith, Jr.	Senior VP, CFO	Number of Shareholders	1,000
David E. Wertheimer	Senior VP	Where Listed / Symbol	NASDAQ / RTEL

Other Information			
Transfer Agent	First National Bank of Boston New York, NY	SIC Code	8090
Auditor	Arthur Andersen LLP	Employees	849
		Web Site	raytel.com

Reconditioned Systems, Inc.

444 West Fairmont Tempe, AZ 85282 Telephone (602)968-1772 Fax (602)894-1907

Company Description

Reconditioned Systems, Inc. reconditions and markets modular office workstations consisting of panels, work surfaces, file drawers, book and binder storage and integrated electrical components (workstations). The Company specializes in reconditioning and marketing workstations that were originally manufactured by Haworth, Inc. The Company purchases used workstations from manufacturers, dealers, brokers, and end-users throughout the United States and transports them to its manufacturing facility in Tempe, Arizona where it disassembles and inventories the workstations by component parts. Upon receipt of purchase orders, the Company reconditions and reassembles the workstations. The Company sells the reconditioned workstations throughout the United States to dealers and end-users. The Company was founded in 1987.

	03/31/98	03/31/97	03/31/96	03/31/95
Per Share Information				
Stock Price as of 12/31	4.28	2.50	1.25	0.75
Earnings Per Share	0.51	0.16	-1.23	-8.28
Price / Earnings Ratio	8.39	15.63	n.a.	n.a.
Book Value Per Share	1.50	0.93	-3.63	2.76
Price / Book Value %	285.33	268.82	n.a.	27.17
Dividends Per Share	0.0	0.0	0.0	0.0
Annual Financial Data				
Operating Results (000's)				
Total Revenues	9,593.2	7,139.8	7,993.3	10,827.7
Costs & Expenses	-8,753.4	-6,881.6	-9,734.3	-11,362.9
Income Before Taxes and Other	839.5	258.1	-1,741.1	-535.2
Other Items	0.0	0.0	0.0	-1,700.0
Income Tax	0.0	0.0	13.0	220.2
Net Income	839.5	258.1	-1,728.1	-2,015.0
Cash Flow From Operations	-167.7	-32.3	746.8	-445.3
Balance Sheet (000's)				
Cash & Equivalents	733.0	142.1	100.7	89.6
Total Current Assets	2,679.3	2,364.5	4,331.3	4,331.3
Fixed Assets, Net	134.7	181.1	420.0	393.3
Total Assets	2,982.2	2,571.2	5,345.9	5,345.9
Total Current Liabilities	766.6	1,162.1	2,257.6	2,257.6
Long-Term Debt	0.0	33.1	166.9	153.9
Stockholders' Equity	2,215.6	1,376.0	2,921.3	2,861.3
Performance & Financial Condition				
Return on Total Revenues %	8.75	3.62	-21.62	-18.61
Return on Avg Stockholders' Equity %	46.75	12.01	-59.77	-51.01
Return on Average Assets %	30.23	6.52	-32.33	-33.58
Current Ratio	3.50	2.03	1.92	1.92
Debt / Equity %	n.a.	2.40	5.71	5.38

Compound Growth %'s	EPS % n.a.	Net Income % n.a.	Total Revenues % -3.95

Comments

The Company executed a 1 for 6 reverse stock split during fiscal 1997. All per share amounts have been restated for consistency. The Company also converted preferred stock to common shares at the same time to complete a financial restructuring. The restructuring also included the elimination of the Steelcase product line, thus enabling the Company to focus on one product line. Expenses in connection with the impairment of assets related to the Steelcase line contributed $1.7 million to the fiscal 1995 loss. The Company now appears to be on a solid financial footing. For the nine months ended December 31, 1998, the Company reported revenues and net income of $8.3 million and $766,387 ($.52 per share) as compared to $7.3 million and $629,798 ($.43 per share) for the same period of the preceding year.

Officers	Position	Ownership Information	
Wayne R. Collingnon	President, CEO	Number of Shares Outstanding	1,473,950
Dirk D. Anderson	CFO	Market Capitalization	$ 6,308,506
Scott W. Ryan	Director	Number of Shareholders	350
Susan J. Zinga	Director	Where Listed / Symbol	NASDAQ / RESY

Other Information			
Transfer Agent	Harris Trust & Savings Bank Chicago, IL	SIC Code	2522
Auditor	Semple & Cooper, LLP	Employees	64

Reflectix, Inc.

P.O. Box 108 Markleville, IN 46056 Telephone (765)533-4332 Fax (765)533-2327

Company Description

Reflectix, Inc. is engaged in the manufacture and sale of reflective insulation products which include insulation for attics, crawl spaces, basement walls, heat ducts, water pipes and wall insulation. Reflectix® insulation reflects 97% of the radiant heat flow that strikes its surface and excels in controlling condensation and humidity. The customer base is the do-it-yourself market (approximately 55%), agriculture market (approximately 15%) and OEM manufacturers nationwide (approximately 30%). Distribution is through sales representatives, distributors, retailers and contractors. The Company was founded in 1980.

	06/30/98	06/30/97	06/30/96	06/30/95
Per Share Information				
Stock Price as of 12/31	0.31	0.31	0.31	0.47
Earnings Per Share	0.01	0.07	0.09	0.06
Price / Earnings Ratio	31.00	4.43	3.44	7.83
Book Value Per Share	0.45	0.44	0.37	0.26
Price / Book Value %	68.89	70.45	83.78	180.77
Dividends Per Share	0.0	0.0	0.0	0.0
Annual Financial Data				
Operating Results (000's)				
Total Revenues	10,119.1	9,511.4	9,085.7	7,766.2
Costs & Expenses	-10,016.5	-8,870.2	-8,252.6	-7,244.6
Income Before Taxes and Other	102.6	641.2	832.0	497.2
Other Items	0.0	0.0	0.0	0.0
Income Tax	-48.6	-250.8	-276.0	-174.0
Net Income	54.0	390.4	555.9	323.2
Cash Flow From Operations	15.1	172.1	577.3	421.9
Balance Sheet (000's)				
Cash & Equivalents	348.9	115.2	204.5	235.1
Total Current Assets	3,326.2	2,538.8	2,048.7	1,807.3
Fixed Assets, Net	2,779.6	2,561.6	2,360.2	1,963.5
Total Assets	6,426.1	5,107.5	4,451.4	3,780.9
Total Current Liabilities	2,186.7	1,175.4	1,198.6	1,630.0
Long-Term Debt	1,526.2	1,384.6	1,069.6	563.1
Stockholders' Equity	2,631.2	2,547.5	2,183.3	1,587.7
Performance & Financial Condition				
Return on Total Revenues %	0.53	4.10	6.12	4.16
Return on Avg Stockholders' Equity %	2.09	16.51	29.49	23.21
Return on Average Assets %	0.94	8.17	13.51	10.05
Current Ratio	1.52	2.16	1.71	1.11
Debt / Equity %	58.00	54.35	48.99	35.47

Compound Growth %'s	EPS %	-44.97	Net Income %	-44.91	Total Revenues %	9.22

Comments

The Company reported its ninth year of consecutive profits in 1998. This was achieved despite El Nino, which reduced the demand for insulation products, a collapse of the foreign markets of the Pacific Rim, and less Canadian demand because of the declining value of Canadian currency. Management estimates that these three factors negatively impacted sales by $1.3 million. For the six months ended December 31, 1998, the Company reported revenues and net income of $5.9 million and $479,752 ($.08 per share) as compared to $5.7 million and $418,429 ($.08 per share) for the same period of the preceding year. Reflectix, Inc. is not required to file reports with the Securities and Exchange Commission but does have a good record in reporting to shareholders.

Officers	Position	Ownership Information	
Stephen C. Painter	Chairman, President	Number of Shares Outstanding	5,791,912
Richard B. Peck, Jr.	Treasurer	Market Capitalization	$ 1,795,493
Arlan H. Landey	VP - Sales, Secretary	Number of Shareholders	Under 500
Charles E. Painter	Other	Where Listed / Symbol	OTC-BB / RECT

Other Information			
Transfer Agent	Western States Transfer & Registrar Salt Lake City, UT	SIC Code	3990
Auditor	Olive LLC	Employees	60
Market Maker	Alpine Securities Corporation (800)521-5588	Web Site	reflectixinc.com
	Paragon Capital Corporation (800)345-0505		

Rehabilicare Inc.

1811 Old Highway Eight   New Brighton, MN 55112   Telephone (651)631-0590   Fax (651)638-0476

Company Description

Rehabilicare Inc. is a designer, manufacturer and provider of electromedical pain management and rehabilitation products and services used for clinical, home health care and occupational medicine applications. Electrotherapy devices such as those marketed by the Company, have broad applications in both the rehabilitation of injured and atrophied muscles and the relief of chronic and acute pain. Transcutaneous electrical nerve stimulation (TENS) devices have been prescribed by physicians and used by physical therapists, athletic trainers and other treating clinicians in pain management for over 25 years. In early 1998, the Company completed the acquisition of Staodyn, Inc. for stock worth $23 million. Staodyn also develops electrotherapy devices. Rehabilicare was founded in 1972.

	06/30/98	06/30/97	06/30/96	06/30/95
Per Share Information				
Stock Price as of 12/31	3.25	3.00	4.00	3.56
Earnings Per Share	-0.10	0.12	0.06	0.14
Price / Earnings Ratio	n.a.	25.00	66.67	25.43
Book Value Per Share	1.92	1.62	1.54	1.46
Price / Book Value %	169.27	185.19	259.74	243.84
Dividends Per Share	0.0	0.0	0.0	0.0
Annual Financial Data				
Operating Results (000's)				
Total Revenues	33,825.7	11,048.4	8,717.8	9,249.0
Costs & Expenses	-36,329.5	-10,219.6	-8,270.5	-8,295.5
Income Before Taxes and Other	-2,503.9	828.7	447.3	953.5
Other Items	0.0	0.0	0.0	-313.4
Income Tax	1,495.2	-265.0	-165.0	0.0
Net Income	-1,008.7	563.7	282.3	640.1
Cash Flow From Operations	-270.2	555.0	-525.0	n.a.
Balance Sheet (000's)				
Cash & Equivalents	919.8	46.5	32.6	56.0
Total Current Assets	22,874.0	9,218.6	8,894.7	7,744.0
Fixed Assets, Net	3,371.2	2,317.8	2,427.1	2,504.3
Total Assets	27,060.4	11,602.1	11,321.8	10,248.3
Total Current Liabilities	3,669.4	1,757.5	1,885.1	1,595.1
Long-Term Debt	3,299.7	1,957.8	2,251.9	1,904.2
Stockholders' Equity	20,091.2	7,886.7	7,184.8	6,749.0
Performance & Financial Condition				
Return on Total Revenues %	-2.98	5.10	3.24	6.92
Return on Avg Stockholders' Equity %	-7.21	7.48	4.05	10.07
Return on Average Assets %	-5.22	4.92	2.62	7.37
Current Ratio	6.23	5.25	4.72	4.85
Debt / Equity %	16.42	24.82	31.34	28.21

Compound Growth %'s	EPS %	n.a.	Net Income %	n.a.	Total Revenues %	54.07

Comments

The acquisition of Staodyn was accounted for as a pooling of interests. We did not restate operating results or balance sheets for years prior to fiscal 1998. On a combined basis, revenue grew at a 5% rate for the last fiscal year. Nonrecurring expenses of $4.4 million related to the acquisition and write-offs of discontinued inventory of Staodyn, amounting to $832,000, resulted in a net loss for the year. For the six months ended December 31, 1998, the Company reported revenues and net income of $20.0 million and $1,413,185 ($.13 per share) as compared to $6.0 million and $341,552 ($.07 per share) for the same period of the preceding year.

Officers	Position	Ownership Information	
Robert C. Wingrove	Chairman	Number of Shares Outstanding	10,443,369
David B. Kaysen	President, CEO	Market Capitalization	$ 33,940,949
W. Glen Winchell	VP - Finance, CFO	Number of Shareholders	1,500
William J. Sweeney	VP - Sales	Where Listed / Symbol	NASDAQ / REHB

Other Information			
Transfer Agent	Norwest Bank Minnesota, N.A. South St. Paul, MN	SIC Code	3845
Auditor	PricewaterhouseCoopers LLP	Employees	252
		Web Site	rehabilicare.com

Reliv International, Inc.

136 Chesterfield Industrial Blvd., P.O. Box 405   Chesterfield, MO 63006   Telephone (314)537-9715   Fax (314)537-9753

Company Description

Reliv International, Inc. produces a line of food products including nutritional supplements, diet management products, granola bars and sports drink mixes. The Company also distributes a line of premium skin care products. These products are marketed directly to consumers through 36,884 independent distributors and licensees in the United States, Australia, New Zealand, Canada, Mexico and the United Kingdom. In addition, the Company provides contract processing and packaging services. Approximately 91% of the Company's sales are derived from operations within the United States. Reliv was founded in 1985.

	12/31/98	12/31/97	12/31/96	12/31/95
Per Share Information				
Stock Price	2.12	3.00	6.00	2.13
Earnings Per Share	0.16	0.20	0.15	0.06
Price / Earnings Ratio	13.25	15.00	40.00	35.50
Book Value Per Share	0.86	0.75	0.63	0.61
Price / Book Value %	246.51	400.00	952.38	349.18
Dividends Per Share	0.02	0.03	0.02	0.01
Annual Financial Data				
Operating Results (000's)				
Total Revenues	52,027.8	46,949.4	40,877.8	29,139.9
Costs & Expenses	-49,529.8	-43,535.4	-38,420.8	-28,383.1
Income Before Taxes and Other	2,497.9	3,414.0	2,457.0	756.8
Other Items	0.0	0.0	0.0	0.0
Income Tax	-941.0	-1,385.0	-950.0	-187.0
Net Income	1,556.9	2,029.0	1,507.0	569.8
Cash Flow From Operations	2,111.4	2,491.3	2,121.5	803.1
Balance Sheet (000's)				
Cash & Equivalents	2,816.8	2,426.4	2,108.8	1,507.2
Total Current Assets	8,357.7	6,744.9	6,553.1	5,498.8
Fixed Assets, Net	10,679.2	9,220.9	4,769.4	4,618.7
Total Assets	20,253.0	15,969.9	11,401.7	10,276.2
Total Current Liabilities	6,174.9	3,653.3	3,866.3	3,351.9
Long-Term Debt	5,216.1	5,109.5	1,464.9	1,341.2
Stockholders' Equity	8,340.2	7,168.1	6,057.3	5,507.6
Performance & Financial Condition				
Return on Total Revenues %	2.05	4.32	3.69	1.96
Return on Avg Stockholders' Equity %	20.08	30.68	26.06	10.24
Return on Average Assets %	8.60	14.83	13.90	5.72
Current Ratio	1.35	1.85	1.69	1.64
Debt / Equity %	62.54	71.28	24.18	24.35

Compound Growth %'s	EPS %	38.67	Net Income %	39.80	Total Revenues %	21.32

Comments

The Company distributed a 10% stock dividend in February 1997. All prior per share amounts have been adjusted for consistency. Revenues from manufacturing and packaging services increased $4.8 million in 1998 due to the return of a major customer and accounted for most of increase in total revenues. The introduction of a new product, SoySentials, a soy-based nutritional supplement, also made a contribution. 1998 was characterized as a year of reorganization for the Company. Geographic business units were folded into a single worldwide organization, and a single executive was placed in charge of each of three critical functions; manufacturing and product development, sales and marketing, and operations and administration.

Officers	Position	Ownership Information	
Robert L. Montgomery	President, CEO	Number of Shares Outstanding	9,653,502
Carl W. Hastings	Exec VP	Market Capitalization	$ 20,465,424
David G. Kreher	Senior VP, COO	Number of Shareholders	1,787
Stephen M. Merrick	Secretary	Where Listed / Symbol	NASDAQ / RELV

Other Information			
Transfer Agent	American Stock Transfer & Trust Co. New York, NY	SIC Code	2834
Auditor	Ernst & Young LLP	Employees	228
		Web Site	reliv.com

Rent-A-Wreck of America, Inc.

Company Description

Rent-A-Wreck of America, Inc. markets and administers one of the nation's largest used vehicle rental fleets through its network of more than 542 franchised locations throughout the United States as well as 16 franchised locations in Europe and Asia. The Company sells, to qualified persons, the right to operate a Rent-A-Wreck and/or PRICELE$$ franchise, allowing them to rent and lease used motor vehicles to the general public at rates that are substantially less than those charged by new car rental companies. The Company was founded in 1977.

	03/31/98	03/31/97	03/31/96	03/31/95
Per Share Information				
Stock Price as of 12/31	1.25	1.00	1.12	1.00
Earnings Per Share	0.09	0.08	0.07	0.06
Price / Earnings Ratio	13.89	12.50	16.00	16.67
Book Value Per Share	0.22	0.14	0.03	0.03
Price / Book Value %	568.18	714.29	3,733.33	3,333.33
Dividends Per Share	0.0	0.0	0.0	0.0
Annual Financial Data				
Operating Results (000's)				
Total Revenues	4,739.0	3,851.6	3,518.2	3,071.6
Costs & Expenses	-4,191.1	-3,251.6	-3,029.4	-2,655.4
Income Before Taxes and Other	547.9	599.9	488.8	416.2
Other Items	0.0	0.0	0.0	0.0
Income Tax	-111.4	-62.4	-30.3	-33.0
Net Income	436.5	537.5	458.6	383.2
Cash Flow From Operations	398.4	857.5	672.7	866.7
Balance Sheet (000's)				
Cash & Equivalents	1,215.6	1,077.6	579.9	566.4
Total Current Assets	3,162.7	1,999.5	1,657.8	1,653.2
Fixed Assets, Net	283.9	342.7	323.9	448.7
Total Assets	3,664.1	2,593.9	2,164.4	2,101.9
Total Current Liabilities	1,635.7	808.5	756.1	803.2
Long-Term Debt	0.0	0.0	0.0	0.0
Stockholders' Equity	2,028.4	1,755.3	1,372.4	1,298.7
Performance & Financial Condition				
Return on Total Revenues %	9.21	13.96	13.03	12.48
Return on Avg Stockholders' Equity %	23.07	34.37	34.34	32.66
Return on Average Assets %	13.95	22.59	21.50	16.46
Current Ratio	1.93	2.47	2.19	2.06
Debt / Equity %	n.a.	n.a.	n.a.	n.a.

Compound Growth %'s	EPS %	14.47	Net Income %	4.43	Total Revenues %	15.55

Comments

Revenues continue to increase due to the addition of new franchises. The liquidation preference of the preferred shares, $1,092,800, was deducted from equity in computing the book value per common share. Dividends on the preferred stock were deducted from net income in computing earnings per share. The Company benefitted from tax loss carryovers that were utilized over the three consecutive years of profits preceding fiscal 1998. Earnings before taxes increased 26% in fiscal 1998. Recognizing an opportunity to increase shareholder value, the Company has been acquiring shares of both common and preferred stock. The Company's financial condition is excellent. For the nine months ended December 31, 1998, revenues and net income were $4.3 million and $677,521 ($.12 per share) as compared to $3.5 million and $439,947 ($.07 per share) for the same period of the preceding year.

Officers	Position	Ownership Information	
Kenneth L. Blum, Sr.	Chairman, CEO	Number of Shares Outstanding	4,189,692
Kenneth L. Blum, Jr.	President, Secretary	Market Capitalization	$ 5,237,115
Mitra Ghahramanlou	CFO	Number of Shareholders	1,400
David Schwartz	Director	Where Listed / Symbol	NASDAQ / RAWA

Other Information			
Transfer Agent	American Stock Transfer & Trust Co. New York, NY	SIC Code	6794
Auditor	Grant Thornton LLP	Employees	21
		Web Site	price-less.com

Response Oncology, Inc.

1775 Moriah Woods Boulevard   Memphis, TN 38117   Telephone (901)761-7000   Fax (901)763-7045

Company Description

Response Oncology, Inc. is a comprehensive cancer management company. The Company provides advanced cancer treatment services through outpatient facilities known as IMPACT® Centers under the direction of practicing oncologists; owns the assets of and manages the nonmedical aspects of oncology practices; and conducts outcomes research on behalf of pharmaceutical manufacturers. Approximately 400 medical oncologists are associated with the Company through these programs. The Company presently operates 54 IMPACT® Centers in 26 states which provide high dose chemotherapy with stem cell support to cancer patients on an outpatient basis. Through its IMPACT® Centers, the Company has developed extensive medical information systems and databases containing clinical and patient information, analysis of treatment results and side effects and clinical care pathways. The Company was founded in 1989.

	12/31/98	12/31/97	12/31/96	12/31/95
Per Share Information				
Stock Price	4.12	8.00	9.50	12.50
Earnings Per Share	-1.45	0.36	0.11	0.32
Price / Earnings Ratio	n.a.	22.22	86.36	39.06
Book Value Per Share	4.08	5.51	4.22	2.60
Price / Book Value %	100.98	145.19	225.12	480.77
Dividends Per Share	0.0	0.0	0.0	0.0
Annual Financial Data				
Operating Results (000's)				
Total Revenues	128,246.0	101,920.0	67,353.0	44,298.0
Costs & Expenses	-125,191.0	-94,551.0	-66,070.0	-41,982.0
Income Before Taxes and Other	3,055.0	7,369.0	1,283.0	2,316.0
Other Items	-25,626.0	-591.0	-373.0	-2.0
Income Tax	5,123.0	-2,576.0	0.0	0.0
Net Income	-17,448.0	4,202.0	910.0	2,314.0
Cash Flow From Operations	2,781.0	6,573.0	-3,723.0	2,000.0
Balance Sheet (000's)				
Cash & Equivalents	1,083.0	2,425.0	415.0	4,205.0
Total Current Assets	52,239.0	41,149.0	31,718.0	20,636.8
Fixed Assets, Net	5,273.0	3,555.0	5,406.0	3,822.4
Total Assets	126,753.0	151,693.0	142,950.0	24,765.3
Total Current Liabilities	35,815.0	22,703.0	17,052.0	4,884.1
Long-Term Debt	32,290.0	35,399.0	25,000.0	0.0
Stockholders' Equity	49,410.0	66,348.0	38,167.0	19,842.6
Performance & Financial Condition				
Return on Total Revenues %	-13.61	4.12	1.35	5.22
Return on Avg Stockholders' Equity %	-30.15	8.04	3.14	15.43
Return on Average Assets %	-12.53	2.85	1.09	10.10
Current Ratio	1.46	1.81	1.86	4.23
Debt / Equity %	65.35	53.35	65.50	n.a.

Compound Growth %'s	EPS %	n.a.	Net Income %	n.a.	Total Revenues %	42.52

Comments

At December 31, 1998, the Company had $68.1 million recorded as management service agreements which is included in assets. This represents the costs of purchasing management service agreements with physician practices in excess of any tangible property. Therefore, this is an intangible asset. The amount equates to approximately 138% of stockholders' equity and book value per share. 1998 results include a $24.9 million write off of management service agreements due to a reappraisal by management of realistic carrying values. Otherwise 1998 would have been a profitable year. Revenue grew 26% as management service fees and pharmaceutical sales were both higher.

Officers	Position	Ownership Information	
William H. West	Chairman	Number of Shares Outstanding	12,049,331
Joseph T. Clark	President, CEO	Market Capitalization	$ 49,643,244
Kenneth L. Scott	COO	Number of Shareholders	1,850
Mary E. Clements	CFO	Where Listed / Symbol	NASDAQ / ROIX

Other Information			
Transfer Agent	SunTrust Bank, Nashville Atlanta, GA	SIC Code	8093
Auditor	KPMG LLP	Employees	700
		Web Site	responseoncology.com

Retrospettiva, Inc.

8825 West Olympic Boulevard   Beverly Hills, CA 90211   Telephone (310)657-1745   Fax (310)657-4499

Company Description

Retrospettiva, Inc. contracts for the manufacture of a variety of garments, primarily basic women's sportswear which includes suits, skirts, blouses, blazers, pants, shorts, vests and dresses, using assorted fabrics including rayons, linens, cotton and wool. The Company arranges for the manufacture of garments for customers under private labels selected by its customers. It markets its products exclusively in the United States directly to large wholesalers. Substantially all of the Company's garments are sold on a package basis pursuant to which the Company markets, at fixed prices, finished garments to the customer's specifications and quantity requirements, arranges for production of the garments and delivers the garments directly to the customer at the port of entry. Since the Company manufactures its finished products only upon receipt of purchase orders from its wholesale and retail customers, it does not maintain an inventory of finished products. The Company was founded in 1990 and had its initial public offering in 1997.

	12/31/98	12/31/97	12/31/96	12/31/95
Per Share Information				
Stock Price	2.50	6.12	7.50	n.a.
Earnings Per Share	0.22	0.50	0.37	0.38
Price / Earnings Ratio	11.36	12.24	20.27	n.a.
Book Value Per Share	3.10	2.82	0.66	0.13
Price / Book Value %	80.65	217.02	1,136.36	n.a.
Dividends Per Share	0.0	0.0	0.0	0.0
Annual Financial Data				
Operating Results (000's)				
Total Revenues	27,642.1	19,792.5	12,913.4	11,384.8
Costs & Expenses	-26,197.2	-17,879.1	-11,794.9	-10,544.3
Income Before Taxes and Other	1,444.9	1,913.4	1,118.5	840.5
Other Items	0.0	0.0	0.0	0.0
Income Tax	-629.4	-775.0	-462.5	-174.0
Net Income	815.5	1,138.4	656.1	666.5
Cash Flow From Operations	-2,616.8	-5,312.1	133.7	-367.3
Balance Sheet (000's)				
Cash & Equivalents	115.9	1,569.9	110.8	38.3
Total Current Assets	12,781.1	11,423.3	5,433.3	3,255.4
Fixed Assets, Net	70.3	183.3	61.4	72.1
Total Assets	12,911.5	11,645.2	5,628.0	3,584.1
Total Current Liabilities	3,923.6	3,472.8	4,698.2	3,260.7
Long-Term Debt	0.0	0.0	0.0	0.0
Stockholders' Equity	8,987.9	8,172.4	929.7	139.7
Performance & Financial Condition				
Return on Total Revenues %	2.95	5.75	5.08	5.85
Return on Avg Stockholders' Equity %	9.51	25.01	122.69	n.a.
Return on Average Assets %	6.64	13.18	14.24	22.83
Current Ratio	3.26	3.29	1.16	1.00
Debt / Equity %	n.a.	n.a.	n.a.	n.a.

Compound Growth %'s	EPS %	-16.65	Net Income %	6.96	Total Revenues %	34.41

Comments

The 39.6% increase in 1998 revenue as compared to 1997 is attributable to an increase in volume of business ordered from existing customers as well as new customers. But operating expenses were sharply higher and reduced net income from the 1997 level. Proceeds of the 1997 stock offering were used to repay debt, to increase working capital and to finance wool manufacturing equipment for use by certain nonaffiliated manufacturers in Macedonia. The negative compound growth rate in earnings per share is diluted from the compound growth rate in net income because of the shares issued in the public offering.

Officers	Position	Ownership Information	
Borivoje Vukadinovic	President, CEO	Number of Shares Outstanding	2,900,000
Michael D. Silberman	CFO, Treasurer	Market Capitalization	$ 7,250,000
Ivan Zogovic	Vice President	Number of Shareholders	850
Mojgan Keywanfar	Director	Where Listed / Symbol	NASDAQ / RTRO

Other Information			
Transfer Agent	U.S. Stock Transfer Corp. Glendale, CA	SIC Code	2330
Auditor	A.J. Robbins, P.C.	Employees	17
		Web Site	rtro.com

Riviera Tool Company

5460 Executive Parkway S E   Grand Rapids, MI 49512   Telephone (616)698-2100   Fax (616)698-2470

Company Description

Riviera Tool Company is a leading designer and manufacturer of large scale, complex stamping die systems used to form sheet metal parts. Most of the stamping die systems sold by the Company are used in the high-speed production of automobile and truck body parts such as doors, door frames, structural components and bumpers. A majority of the Company's sales are to Chrysler Corporation, Ford Motor Company, General Motors Corporation and their tier one suppliers.

	08/31/98	08/31/97	08/31/96	08/31/95
Per Share Information				
Stock Price as of 12/31	4.75	11.00	n.a.	n.a.
Earnings Per Share	0.80	0.60	0.25	0.33
Price / Earnings Ratio	5.94	18.33	n.a.	n.a.
Book Value Per Share	5.18	3.91	3.83	3.58
Price / Book Value %	91.70	281.33	n.a.	n.a.
Dividends Per Share	0.0	0.0	0.0	0.0
Annual Financial Data				
Operating Results (000's)				
Total Revenues	22,581.1	21,960.2	18,334.1	22,224.7
Costs & Expenses	-19,136.1	-20,108.8	-17,734.3	-21,662.2
Income Before Taxes and Other	3,445.0	1,851.4	599.8	562.6
Other Items	0.0	0.0	0.0	0.0
Income Tax	-1,039.9	-666.6	-204.0	-76.7
Net Income	2,405.1	1,184.8	395.8	485.9
Cash Flow From Operations	-20.0	305.0	-977.1	4,991.0
Balance Sheet (000's)				
Cash & Equivalents	4.2	0.0	0.0	3.2
Total Current Assets	13,491.1	9,507.8	11,514.7	10,509.8
Fixed Assets, Net	13,237.5	9,640.3	10,147.1	10,906.0
Total Assets	27,696.4	20,056.2	22,928.4	21,706.1
Total Current Liabilities	2,194.4	2,526.2	15,183.7	13,639.8
Long-Term Debt	8,196.6	7,202.4	883.0	1,433.0
Stockholders' Equity	15,882.0	9,721.9	5,587.7	5,220.4
Performance & Financial Condition				
Return on Total Revenues %	10.65	5.40	2.16	2.19
Return on Avg Stockholders' Equity %	18.79	15.48	7.32	12.32
Return on Average Assets %	10.07	5.51	1.77	2.12
Current Ratio	6.15	3.76	0.76	0.77
Debt / Equity %	51.61	74.08	15.80	27.45

Compound Growth %'s	EPS %	34.34	Net Income %	70.43	Total Revenues %	0.53

Comments

The Company had its initial public offering in March 1997, with the placement of one million shares at $7 per share. Proceeds were used to reduce debt. This had the effect of reducing interest expense by nearly $1 million in fiscal 1998 and caused most of the improvement to the bottom line. Management believes that the automotive industry's trend towards shorter product life cycles and introduction of a greater number of vehicle models will create growing demand for the Company's complex tooling systems. For the six months ended February 28, 1999, the Company reported revenues and net income of $10.6 million and $1,213,000 ($.37 per share) as compared to $11.5 million and $739,171 ($.32 per share) for the same period of fiscal 1998.

Officers	Position	Ownership Information	
Kenneth K. Rieth	President, CEO	Number of Shares Outstanding	3,065,499
Peter C. Canepa	CFO, Secretary	Market Capitalization	$ 14,561,120
Leonard H. Wood	Vice President, General Manager	Number of Shareholders	931
Daniel W. Terpsma	Director	Where Listed / Symbol	AMEX / RTC

Other Information			
Transfer Agent	Continental Stock Transfer & Trust Co. New York, NY	SIC Code	3540
Auditor	Plante & Moran, LLP	Employees	141
		Web Site	rivieratool.com

Ronson Corporation

Corporate Park III, Campus Drive, P.O. Box 6707   Somerset, NJ 08875   Telephone (732)469-8300   Fax (732)469-6079

Company Description

Ronson Corporation and its subsidiary, Ronson Consumer Products Corporation manufactures and distributes consumer packaged products including Ronsonol lighter fluid, MultiFill butane fuel injectors, flints, wicks for lighters, a multi-use penetrant spray lubricant product under the tradename Multi-Lube, a spot remover under the product tradename Kleenol, and a surface protectant under the tradename GlossTek. The consumer products are distributed through distributors, food brokers, automotive and hardware representatives and mass merchandisers, drug chains and convenience stores in the United States and Canada. The Company was founded in 1928 but the Ronson name brand dates back to 1886.

	12/31/98	12/31/97	12/31/96	12/31/95
Per Share Information				
Stock Price	2.69	2.50	2.25	3.62
Earnings Per Share	-0.10	0.25	-0.57	0.24
Price / Earnings Ratio	n.a.	10.00	n.a.	15.08
Book Value Per Share	0.67	0.59	0.67	1.34
Price / Book Value %	401.49	423.73	335.82	270.15
Dividends Per Share	0.0	0.0	0.0	0.0
Annual Financial Data				
Operating Results (000's)				
Total Revenues	23,173.0	23,170.0	25,454.0	26,953.0
Costs & Expenses	-22,653.0	-22,621.0	-25,248.0	-25,950.0
Income Before Taxes and Other	520.0	549.0	206.0	1,003.0
Other Items	-949.0	0.0	-1,190.0	-860.0
Income Tax	140.0	234.0	129.0	497.0
Net Income	-289.0	783.0	-855.0	640.0
Cash Flow From Operations	1,394.0	556.0	1,931.0	-2,590.0
Balance Sheet (000's)				
Cash & Equivalents	146.0	32.0	116.0	64.0
Total Current Assets	6,054.0	5,828.0	5,638.0	9,352.0
Fixed Assets, Net	5,807.0	5,469.0	4,508.0	4,051.0
Total Assets	14,602.0	13,519.0	12,104.0	13,403.0
Total Current Liabilities	8,262.0	7,433.0	7,931.0	9,174.0
Long-Term Debt	3,649.0	3,561.0	2,352.0	2,195.0
Stockholders' Equity	2,145.0	1,864.0	1,210.0	2,034.0
Performance & Financial Condition				
Return on Total Revenues %	-1.25	3.38	-3.36	2.37
Return on Avg Stockholders' Equity %	-14.42	50.94	-52.71	40.00
Return on Average Assets %	-2.06	6.11	-6.70	5.06
Current Ratio	0.73	0.78	0.71	1.02
Debt / Equity %	170.12	191.04	194.38	107.92

Compound Growth %'s	EPS % n.a.	Net Income % n.a.	Total Revenues % -4.91

Comments

Management has not been able to light a fire under revenues or net income. Much attention has been devoted to environmental cleanup matters including a facility that was closed in 1989, underground storage tanks, wastes disposed at a California landfill, and a 1998 spillage of 700 gallons of jet fuel. 1998, 1996 and 1995 results include losses from discontinued operations of $949,000 ($.30 per share), $1,190,000 ($.66 per share) and $860,000 ($.33 per share), respectively. At December 31, 1998, the Company had a deficiency in working capital. The ultimate success of the Company will be dependent on getting the environmental problems behind them. Until such time, the situation can only be described as explosive.

Officers	Position	Ownership Information	
Louis V. Aronson II	President, CEO	Number of Shares Outstanding	3,197,142
Justin P. Walder	Secretary	Market Capitalization	$ 8,600,312
Daryl K. Holcomb	Vice President, CFO	Number of Shareholders	2,772
Saul H. Weisman	Director	Where Listed / Symbol	NASDAQ / RONC

Other Information			
Transfer Agent	Registrar & Transfer Co. Cranford, NJ	SIC Code	2890
Auditor	Demetrius & Company, L.L.C.	Employees	131
		Web Site	ronsoncorp.com

Rotonics Manufacturing Inc.

17022 South Figueroa Street   Gardena, CA 90248   Telephone (310)538-4932   Fax (310)323-9567

Company Description

Rotonics Manufacturing Inc., founded in 1963, manufactures and markets plastic containers and vessels for commercial, agricultural, refuse, pharmaceutical, marine, health care and residential use, as well as an array of custom molded plastic products to customers in a variety of industries located in diverse geographic markets. The Company utilizes the roto-molding process and, on a smaller scale, injection molding and dip molding processes. The Company is recognized as one of the top ten rotational molders in North America. The Company has ten manufacturing locations such that every customer is within 500 miles. On April 1, 1998, the Company acquired and molded Rotocast International, Inc. into its operations.

	06/30/98	06/30/97	06/30/96	06/30/95
Per Share Information				
Stock Price as of 12/31	1.00	1.50	1.50	1.87
Earnings Per Share	0.03	0.10	0.10	0.24
Price / Earnings Ratio	33.33	15.00	15.00	7.79
Book Value Per Share	1.35	1.35	1.29	1.39
Price / Book Value %	74.07	111.11	116.28	134.53
Dividends Per Share	0.04	0.04	0.04	0.0
Annual Financial Data				
Operating Results (000's)				
Total Revenues	38,155.1	39,483.6	35,860.5	36,025.3
Costs & Expenses	-37,389.4	-36,088.2	-33,453.3	-32,833.3
Income Before Taxes and Other	765.7	3,395.4	2,407.2	3,192.0
Other Items	0.0	-1,010.8	0.0	0.0
Income Tax	-348.5	-942.8	-934.5	95.6
Net Income	417.2	1,441.8	1,472.7	3,287.6
Cash Flow From Operations	1,937.3	3,778.9	3,774.1	2,431.4
Balance Sheet (000's)				
Cash & Equivalents	30.7	12.1	11.6	96.7
Total Current Assets	16,463.6	12,814.0	13,023.0	11,903.2
Fixed Assets, Net	18,250.0	10,799.5	8,316.9	8,605.9
Total Assets	40,563.8	30,634.4	29,055.7	30,359.4
Total Current Liabilities	6,452.8	5,099.7	4,864.5	4,766.0
Long-Term Debt	8,976.5	6,490.1	5,864.1	7,711.7
Stockholders' Equity	21,407.9	19,044.6	18,323.1	17,881.7
Performance & Financial Condition				
Return on Total Revenues %	1.09	3.65	4.11	9.13
Return on Avg Stockholders' Equity %	2.06	7.72	8.14	20.09
Return on Average Assets %	1.17	4.83	4.96	11.89
Current Ratio	2.55	2.51	2.68	2.50
Debt / Equity %	41.93	34.08	32.00	43.13

Compound Growth %'s	EPS % -50.00	Net Income % -49.75	Total Revenues % 1.93

Comments

Fiscal 1998 was a transitional year for the Company as it endured difficult market conditions while continuing its internal efforts to increase manufacturing capabilities, promote efficient operations and restructure and build its marketing functions. Operating expenses included $280,000 of plant consolidation costs. Fiscal 1997 results include a nonrecurring expense related to the settlement of a lawsuit of $1 million. At June 30, 1998, the Company had $5.1 million of goodwill recorded as assets which equated to approximately 24% of stockholders' equity and book value per share. For the six months ended December 31, 1998, the Company reported that revenues and net income were $23.2 million and $443,200 ($.03 per share) as compared to $17.2 million and $205,900 ($.02 per share) for the same period of the preceding year.

Officers	Position	Ownership Information	
Sherman McKinniss	President, CEO	Number of Shares Outstanding	15,806,361
Robert E. Gawlik	COO	Market Capitalization	$ 15,806,361
Douglas W. Russell	CFO, Treasurer	Number of Shareholders	6,200
E. Paul Tonkovich	Secretary	Where Listed / Symbol	AMEX / RMI

Other Information			
Transfer Agent	American Stock Transfer & Trust Company New York, NY	SIC Code	3089
Auditor	Arthur Andersen LLP	Employees	600
		Web Site	rotonics.com

Royal Appliance Mfg. Co.

650 Alpha Drive   Cleveland, OH 44143   Telephone (440)449-6150   Fax (216)261-6716

Company Description

Royal Appliance Mfg. Co. develops, assembles and markets a full line of cleaning products for home and commercial use under the Dirt Devil® and Royal® brand names. In 1984, the Company introduced the first in a line of Dirt Devil® hand-held vacuum cleaners, which the Company believes has become the largest selling line of hand-held vacuum cleaners in the United States. The Company has used the Dirt Devil® brand name recognition to gain acceptance for other Dirt Devil® products. The Company continues to market certain metal vacuum cleaners for home and commercial use under the Royal® brand name. The Company has produced durable metal vacuum cleaners since the early 1900's.

	12/31/98	12/31/97	12/31/96	12/31/95
Per Share Information				
Stock Price	3.69	6.62	6.87	2.50
Earnings Per Share	0.12	0.52	0.39	-0.57
Price / Earnings Ratio	30.75	12.73	17.62	n.a.
Book Value Per Share	2.38	2.63	2.34	1.94
Price / Book Value %	155.04	251.71	293.59	128.87
Dividends Per Share	0.0	0.0	0.0	0.0
Annual Financial Data				
Operating Results (000's)				
Total Revenues	282,720.0	325,417.0	286,123.0	270,564.0
Costs & Expenses	-278,588.0	-305,233.0	-270,777.0	-274,513.0
Income Before Taxes and Other	4,132.0	20,184.0	15,346.0	-3,949.0
Other Items	0.0	0.0	0.0	-16,294.0
Income Tax	-1,606.0	-7,777.0	-5,910.0	6,487.0
Net Income	2,526.0	12,407.0	9,436.0	-13,756.0
Cash Flow From Operations	13,606.0	22,741.0	34,890.0	9,014.0
Balance Sheet (000's)				
Cash & Equivalents	0.0	1,355.0	1,001.0	0.0
Total Current Assets	77,344.0	89,006.0	83,802.0	84,732.0
Fixed Assets, Net	36,800.0	42,892.0	37,283.0	35,000.0
Total Assets	117,480.0	134,947.0	126,141.0	131,261.0
Total Current Liabilities	47,104.0	57,870.0	54,164.0	38,687.0
Long-Term Debt	15,593.0	9,098.0	9,550.0	45,999.0
Stockholders' Equity	46,723.0	60,219.0	56,234.0	46,575.0
Performance & Financial Condition				
Return on Total Revenues %	0.89	3.81	3.30	-5.08
Return on Avg Stockholders' Equity %	4.72	21.31	18.36	-25.78
Return on Average Assets %	2.00	9.50	7.33	-10.10
Current Ratio	1.64	1.54	1.55	2.19
Debt / Equity %	33.37	15.11	16.98	98.76

Compound Growth %'s	EPS %	-44.53	Net Income %	-48.26	Total Revenues %	1.48

Comments

The Dirt Devil® Mop Vac® was introduced in 1997 and sparked a sales increase but then reversed course in 1998. Despite lower shipments to retailers in 1998, management believes that retailers' sales to consumers of the Company's products increased over 1997. Overall sales to the top 5 customers for 1998 accounted for approximately 64.2% of revenue. During 1995 the Company ceased its European operations resulting in a non-recurring expense of $16,194,000. The Company reacquired shares worth $3.3 million and $1.2 million during 1998 and 1997, respectively. The average price paid was $4.88 per share in 1998.

Officers	Position	Ownership Information	
Michael J. Merriman	President, CEO	Number of Shares Outstanding	19,621,524
Gary J. Dieterich	Senior VP	Market Capitalization	$ 72,403,424
James A. Holcomb	Vice President	Number of Shareholders	1,200
Jeremiah J. Lynch	Vice President	Where Listed / Symbol	NYSE / RAM

Other Information			
Transfer Agent	National City Bank Cleveland, OH	SIC Code	3630
Auditor	PricewaterhouseCoopers LLP	Employees	680
		Web Site	dirtdevil.com

S2 Golf Inc.

18 Gloria Lane   Fairfield, NJ 07004   Telephone (973)227-7783   Fax (973)227-7018

Company Description

S2 Golf Inc. manufactures and markets a proprietary line of golf equipment including golf clubs, golf bags, golf balls and accessories. The Company markets these products under the tradename and trademark SQUARE TWO® and uses several additional trademarks including S2®, PCX®, XGR®, ZCX®, Totally Matched® and Posiflow®, among others. In the last five years the Company has effectively repositioned itself as one of the top value brands in the women's golf market, which now comprises between 58% and 62% of S2's business. The Company was founded in 1982.

	12/31/98	12/31/97	12/31/96	12/31/95
Per Share Information				
Stock Price	2.50	4.06	0.94	0.81
Earnings Per Share	0.19	0.37	0.05	-0.04
Price / Earnings Ratio	13.16	10.97	18.80	n.a.
Book Value Per Share	1.78	1.58	1.20	1.14
Price / Book Value %	140.45	256.96	78.33	71.05
Dividends Per Share	0.0	0.0	0.0	0.0
Annual Financial Data				
Operating Results (000's)				
Total Revenues	11,505.0	12,077.0	8,563.6	7,247.7
Costs & Expenses	-10,809.9	-11,132.2	-8,406.0	-7,358.8
Income Before Taxes and Other	695.1	944.8	112.7	-111.1
Other Items	0.0	0.0	0.0	0.0
Income Tax	-254.3	-89.2	6.2	30.7
Net Income	440.8	855.6	118.9	-80.5
Cash Flow From Operations	57.4	-1,177.5	-169.0	35.9
Balance Sheet (000's)				
Cash & Equivalents	1.6	121.4	166.6	19.0
Total Current Assets	7,203.0	7,356.2	4,662.0	4,210.8
Fixed Assets, Net	59.4	79.5	112.7	148.4
Total Assets	7,534.1	7,630.2	5,153.7	4,726.4
Total Current Liabilities	3,436.0	3,920.9	2,260.1	1,889.9
Long-Term Debt	0.0	0.0	0.0	0.0
Stockholders' Equity	3,951.9	3,507.1	2,640.1	2,521.2
Performance & Financial Condition				
Return on Total Revenues %	3.83	7.08	1.39	-1.11
Return on Avg Stockholders' Equity %	11.82	27.84	4.61	-3.16
Return on Average Assets %	5.81	13.39	2.41	-1.59
Current Ratio	2.10	1.88	2.06	2.23
Debt / Equity %	n.a.	n.a.	n.a.	n.a.

Compound Growth %'s	EPS %	94.94	Net Income %	92.57	Total Revenues %	16.65

Comments

The 4.7% decrease in revenues during 1998 was primarily due to the Company's decision to halt shipments to retailers with credit problems and the general softness in the golf equipment industry during the year. The strong increase in revenue experienced in 1997 was primarily the result of continued improvement in the sales force, a more cosmetically appealing product line and the addition of a new channel of distribution, specialty sporting goods. Gross margins in 1998 and 1997 benefited from the sales volume and lower material costs. This young company has managed to establish itself while maintaining a good financial condition without the use of long term debt. The balance sheet is clean; intangibles are immaterial.

Officers	Position	Ownership Information	
Robert L. Ross	Chairman, CEO	Number of Shares Outstanding	2,219,313
Douglas A. Buffington	President, COO	Market Capitalization	$ 5,548,283
Randy A. Hamill	Senior VP	Number of Shareholders	1,000
Richard M. Maurer	Secretary	Where Listed / Symbol	NASDAQ / GOLF

Other Information			
Transfer Agent	Continental Stock Transfer & Trust Co. New York, NY	SIC Code	3949
Auditor	Deloitte & Touche LLP	Employees	45
		Web Site	Squaretwo.com

SETECH, Inc.

9035 Industrial Drive   Murfreesboro, TN 37129   Telephone (615)890-1700   Fax (615)890-2914

Company Description

SETECH, Inc. provides integrated supply/inventory management, general line industrial distribution, job shop machining, and engineering products and services to a variety of industries, including the automotive, aviation, and medical industries. General Motors Corporation accounted for 24% of revenues in fiscal 1998. The Company was founded in 1987. In June 1997, the Company acquired Lewis Supply Company, Inc. which provides integrated supply support to 9 key customers through direct management of the maintenance, repair, and operating supply function and tool crib management at over 15 sites. Lewis Supply is also a general line industrial distributor through the operation of five distribution warehouses.

	06/30/98	06/30/97	06/30/96
Per Share Information			
Stock Price as of 12/31	2.94	1.75	1.69
Earnings Per Share	0.01	0.09	0.27
Price / Earnings Ratio	294.00	19.44	6.26
Book Value Per Share	1.40	1.35	1.22
Price / Book Value %	210.00	129.63	138.52
Dividends Per Share	0.0	0.0	0.0
Annual Financial Data			
Operating Results (000's)			
Total Revenues	88,953.0	35,267.6	34,543.2
Costs & Expenses	-88,782.0	-34,326.0	-33,833.4
Income Before Taxes and Other	171.0	941.6	709.9
Other Items	0.0	0.3	-3.5
Income Tax	-116.0	-428.0	692.9
Net Income	55.0	513.9	1,399.2
Cash Flow From Operations	-6,289.0	-34.7	-2,886.2
Balance Sheet (000's)			
Cash & Equivalents	796.0	1,633.6	1,328.9
Total Current Assets	38,375.0	28,413.7	17,955.6
Fixed Assets, Net	2,584.0	1,746.6	587.3
Total Assets	47,836.0	37,272.2	20,973.9
Total Current Liabilities	12,400.0	8,583.8	13,144.5
Long-Term Debt	26,609.0	20,099.8	1,075.5
Stockholders' Equity	7,738.0	7,666.9	6,599.2
Performance & Financial Condition			
Return on Total Revenues %	0.06	1.46	4.05
Return on Avg Stockholders' Equity %	0.71	7.20	20.58
Return on Average Assets %	0.13	1.76	5.60
Current Ratio	3.09	3.31	1.37
Debt / Equity %	343.87	262.16	16.30

Compound Growth %'s	EPS % n.a.	Net Income % n.a.	Total Revenues % 60.47

Comments

Effective as of June 30, 1996, the Company effected a 1 for 20 reverse stock split. All per share amounts have been restated for consistency. The fiscal 1998 increase in revenue was entirely attributable to the acquisition of Lewis Supply. Revenues from operations other than Lewis Supply decreased $746,000. In May 1998, a contract was signed with an existing SETECH customer to establish eight additional sites, with potential annual revenues of up to $30 million. Additional sites, with potential annual revenues of $125 million, were in negotiation. For the six months ended December 31, 1998, revenues and net income were $49.8 million and $708,000 ($.12 per share) as compared to $42.7 million and $361,770 ($.06 per share) in the same period of the preceding year. Intangible assets totalled $6.8 million at June 30, 1998, approximately 88% of book value.

Officers	Position	Ownership Information	
Thomas N. Eisenman	President, CEO	Number of Shares Outstanding	5,515,000
Cindy L. Rollins	Vice President, Secretary	Market Capitalization	$ 16,214,100
Richard Eddinger	Vice President, CFO	Number of Shareholders	180
Martin Oester	Director	Where Listed / Symbol	OTC-BB / SETC

Other Information			
Transfer Agent	American Stock Transfer & Trust Co. New York, NY	SIC Code	4581
Auditor	Arthur Andersen LLP	Employees	251
Market Maker	Fahnestock & Co., Inc.	(800)223-3012	
	Herzog, Heine, Geduld, Inc.	(800)221-3600	

SI Technologies, Inc.

4611 South 134th Place   Tukwila, WA 98168   Telephone (206)244-6100   Fax (206)246-7195

Company Description

SI Technologies, Inc. is a rapidly growing designer, manufacturer and marketer of high-performance industrial sensors, weighing and material-handling equipment and systems. Recent acquisitions have diversified the Company's revenue base and positioned SI Technologies as a consolidator of technologies, products and companies, thus enabling SI to become a leading global provider of devices, equipment and systems that handle, inspect and measure goods and materials. The Company was founded in 1979.

	07/31/98	07/31/97	07/31/96	07/31/95
Per Share Information				
Stock Price as of 12/31	3.12	5.56	2.62	3.75
Earnings Per Share	0.28	0.19	0.25	0.14
Price / Earnings Ratio	11.14	29.26	10.48	26.79
Book Value Per Share	3.30	2.33	2.12	1.87
Price / Book Value %	94.55	238.63	123.58	200.53
Dividends Per Share	0.0	0.0	0.0	0.0
Annual Financial Data				
Operating Results (000's)				
Total Revenues	23,834.4	14,138.6	12,429.6	9,835.4
Costs & Expenses	-22,417.1	-13,288.3	-11,413.6	-9,137.4
Income Before Taxes and Other	1,417.4	850.3	1,016.0	698.0
Other Items	0.0	0.0	0.0	0.0
Income Tax	-587.0	-351.0	-349.4	-187.5
Net Income	830.4	499.3	666.5	510.5
Cash Flow From Operations	1,024.8	141.4	36.2	1,692.7
Balance Sheet (000's)				
Cash & Equivalents	573.9	155.8	57.7	540.0
Total Current Assets	21,107.9	7,857.5	4,519.6	3,262.1
Fixed Assets, Net	8,049.0	1,477.4	821.5	550.6
Total Assets	39,997.0	17,604.7	8,846.8	6,747.1
Total Current Liabilities	14,218.5	7,153.3	1,975.3	1,896.9
Long-Term Debt	12,135.0	4,348.4	1,433.0	53.7
Stockholders' Equity	11,710.9	5,924.7	4,970.4	4,389.3
Performance & Financial Condition				
Return on Total Revenues %	3.48	3.53	5.36	5.19
Return on Avg Stockholders' Equity %	9.42	9.17	14.24	11.50
Return on Average Assets %	2.88	3.78	8.55	6.62
Current Ratio	1.48	1.10	2.29	1.72
Debt / Equity %	103.62	73.39	28.83	1.22

Compound Growth %'s	EPS %	25.99	Net Income %	17.61	Total Revenues %	34.32

Comments

The Company grew significantly in fiscal 1998. Sales, earnings and cash flow increased to record levels. This performance is reflective of the acquisitions completed in 1997 and 1998. Due to the magnitude of these acquisitions, results of operations are not necessarily comparable. At July 31, 1998, the Company had $10.2 million of goodwill reflected as assets on the books which equated to approximately 87% of stockholders' equity and book value per share. Although goodwill and acquisitions are both concerns, the Company has maintained its profitability which is indeed an impressive accomplishment. For the six months ended January 31, 1999, the Company reported revenues and net income of $22.2 million and $334,514 ($.09 per share) as compared to $10.8 million and $435,244 ($.16 per share) for the same period of the preceding year.

Officers	Position	Ownership Information	
Rick A. Beets	President, CEO	Number of Shares Outstanding	3,547,123
Paul V. Cavanaugh	CFO	Market Capitalization	$ 11,067,024
Edward A. Alkire	Secretary	Number of Shareholders	600
S. Scott Crump	Director	Where Listed / Symbol	NASDAQ / SISI

Other Information

Transfer Agent	Continental Stock Transfer & Trust Co. Jersey City, NJ	SIC Code	3590
Auditor	Grant Thornton LLP	Employees	441
		Web Site	sitechnologies.com

SITEL Corporation

111 South Calvert, Suite 1910   Baltimore, MD 21202   Telephone (410)246-1505   Fax (410)659-5754

Company Description

SITEL is a global leader in providing outsourced telephone and Internet-based customer service and sales programs on behalf of large corporations. The Company handles calls in over 25 languages and dialects from more than 14,000 workstations in over 70 call centers located in North America, Europe, Asia Pacific and Latin America. SITEL communicates directly with its clients' customers primarily by responding to customer-initiated telephone calls and electronic mail and by making Company-initiated calls. Approximately 60% of the Company's revenues are currently generated by customer service programs, including technical support activities, with the remainder generated primarily by sales programs and, to a lesser extent, by consulting services.

	12/31/98	12/31/97	12/31/96	12/31/95
Per Share Information				
Stock Price	2.50	9.12	14.25	30.25
Earnings Per Share	-0.02	0.04	0.16	-0.29
Price / Earnings Ratio	n.a.	228.00	89.06	n.a.
Book Value Per Share	2.51	2.51	2.15	3.67
Price / Book Value %	99.60	363.35	662.79	824.25
Dividends Per Share	0.0	0.0	0.0	0.0
Annual Financial Data				
Operating Results (000's)				
Total Revenues	586,318.0	492,161.0	313,890.0	187,946.0
Costs & Expenses	-586,577.0	-462,188.0	-285,747.0	-206,730.0
Income Before Taxes and Other	-259.0	29,973.0	21,155.0	-18,784.0
Other Items	137.0	-15,855.0	-77.0	-1,262.0
Income Tax	-966.0	-11,306.0	-10,221.0	6,593.0
Net Income	-1,088.0	2,812.0	10,857.0	-13,453.0
Cash Flow From Operations	17,743.0	19,014.0	35,843.0	15,273.0
Balance Sheet (000's)				
Cash & Equivalents	14,472.0	24,285.0	25,710.0	4,531.0
Total Current Assets	157,220.0	148,758.0	99,353.0	19,498.0
Fixed Assets, Net	125,615.0	120,600.0	59,109.0	9,305.0
Total Assets	405,610.0	385,880.0	211,684.0	45,968.0
Total Current Liabilities	115,560.0	109,213.0	62,517.0	14,854.0
Long-Term Debt	107,027.0	102,505.0	17,648.0	3,471.0
Stockholders' Equity	161,854.0	158,388.0	126,725.0	27,642.0
Performance & Financial Condition				
Return on Total Revenues %	-0.19	0.57	3.46	-7.16
Return on Avg Stockholders' Equity %	-0.68	1.97	14.07	-34.46
Return on Average Assets %	-0.27	0.94	8.43	-18.04
Current Ratio	1.36	1.36	1.59	1.31
Debt / Equity %	66.13	64.72	13.93	12.56

Compound Growth %'s	EPS % n.a.	Net Income % n.a.	Total Revenues % 46.12

Comments

The Company continued to capture market share in 1998 with a 19.3% increase in revenues. Most of the increase came from new clients but higher calling volumes were also noted in the existing customer base. During 1998 and 1997, the Company expensed $6.6 million and $15.7 million in connection with a restructurings. 1998 also included an extraordinary loss of $514,000 related to refinancing of debt. During 1996, the Company expensed $7 million of transaction related expenses. At December 31, 1998, the Company had $93.3 million of goodwill recorded as an asset which represents approximately 57.6% of stockholders' equity and book value per share.

Officers	Position	Ownership Information	
James F. Lynch	Chairman	Number of Shares Outstanding	64,399,645
Phillip A. Clough	President	Market Capitalization	$ 160,999,113
Michael P. May	CEO	Number of Shareholders	10,000
Alan G. Siemek	Controller	Where Listed / Symbol	NYSE / SWW

Other Information			
Transfer Agent	American Stock Transfer & Trust Co. New York, NY	SIC Code	7389
Auditor	KPMG LLP	Employees	19,000
		Web Site	sitel.com

SYS

Company Description

SYS, formed in 1966, provides management and technical services in systems planning, management and analysis, systems engineering, naval architecture, marine engineering, ordnance engineering, logistics analysis and engineering, operations analysis, design development, reliability engineering and analysis, hazardous materials reduction studies, computer systems analysis, office automation, information management systems and related support services. The Company also provides hardware integration and fabrication.

	06/30/98	06/30/97	06/30/96	06/30/95
Per Share Information				
Stock Price as of 12/31	0.62	0.62	0.25	0.02
Earnings Per Share	0.08	0.07	0.04	-0.08
Price / Earnings Ratio	7.75	8.86	6.25	n.a.
Book Value Per Share	0.24	0.16	0.06	0.02
Price / Book Value %	258.33	387.50	416.67	100.00
Dividends Per Share	0.0	0.0	0.0	0.0
Annual Financial Data				
Operating Results (000's)				
Total Revenues	7,886.1	7,648.6	5,941.7	4,751.0
Costs & Expenses	-7,558.7	-7,419.6	-5,657.5	-4,662.0
Income Before Taxes and Other	327.4	229.0	128.1	-220.0
Other Items	0.0	0.0	0.0	0.0
Income Tax	-43.7	0.0	0.0	-1.0
Net Income	283.7	229.0	128.1	-221.0
Cash Flow From Operations	-98.4	271.4	294.3	-58.0
Balance Sheet (000's)				
Cash & Equivalents	28.1	194.5	24.8	3.0
Total Current Assets	1,552.4	1,451.6	1,152.7	1,045.0
Fixed Assets, Net	246.9	148.4	141.7	99.0
Total Assets	1,815.8	1,615.2	1,310.2	1,180.0
Total Current Liabilities	766.5	877.5	902.6	993.0
Long-Term Debt	101.5	125.4	0.0	35.0
Stockholders' Equity	892.4	612.3	379.6	115.0
Performance & Financial Condition				
Return on Total Revenues %	3.60	2.99	2.16	-4.65
Return on Avg Stockholders' Equity %	37.71	46.18	51.81	-97.57
Return on Average Assets %	16.54	15.66	10.29	-13.27
Current Ratio	2.03	1.65	1.28	1.05
Debt / Equity %	11.37	20.48	n.a.	30.43

Compound Growth %'s	EPS %	41.42	Net Income %	48.80	Total Revenues %	18.40

Comments

The majority of the Company's recent revenues have been derived from contracts with the United States Navy. Essentially all of these contracts are of the cost reimbursable plus fee type. The Company has not had income tax expense due to the available net operating loss carryovers, most of which have now been utilized. Management reported a contract backlog of $22.0 million at June 30, 1998, as compared to $20.3 million one year earlier. For the six months ended December 31, 1998, revenue and net income were $3.7 million and $158,000 ($.05 per share) as compared to $4.0 million and $191,000 ($.06 per share) in the same period of the preceding year. Investor interest in the Company is dampened by a sole dependence related to the defense industry. Still, the Company is an excellent acquisition candidate.

Officers	Position	Ownership Information	
Robert D. Mowry	Chairman, CEO	Number of Shares Outstanding	3,148,518
W. Gerald Newmin	Secretary	Market Capitalization	$ 1,952,081
Michael W. Fink	Vice President	Number of Shareholders	420
Charles E. Vandeveer	Vice President	Where Listed / Symbol	OTC-BB / SYYS

Other Information			
Transfer Agent	ChaseMellon Shareholder Services Ridgefield Park, NJ	SIC Code	7372
Auditor	J.H. Cohn LLP	Employees	93
Market Maker	Carr Securities Corporation	(800)221-2243	Web Site	syys.com
	Drake Capital Securities, Inc.	(800)421-8504		

Safety 1st, Inc.

210 Boylston Street Chestnut Hill, MA 02167 Telephone (617)964-7744 Fax (617)928-3205

Company Description

Safety 1st, Inc., founded in 1984, is a leading developer, marketer and distributor of juvenile products. The Company believes that it has increased consumer awareness of child safety issues and that its flagship brand name, Safety 1st®, is closely associated with child safety among consumers. The Company's first products — the original yellow and black, diamond shaped Baby on Board and Child on Board automobile window displays — provided the Company with national attention and distribution for its juvenile products. The Company has continually broadened its line of safety products from basic items, such as outlet plugs and drawer and cabinet locks, to safety gates, bed rails and balcony guards. The Company believes that it is currently the leading supplier of child safety products in the United States.

	01/02/99	12/31/97	12/31/96	12/31/95
Per Share Information				
Stock Price as of 12/31	3.25	5.87	10.25	14.75
Earnings Per Share	-0.14	0.40	-6.27	0.44
Price / Earnings Ratio	n.a.	14.68	n.a.	33.52
Book Value Per Share	1.40	1.53	0.29	6.44
Price / Book Value %	232.14	383.66	3,534.48	229.04
Dividends Per Share	0.0	0.0	0.0	0.0
Annual Financial Data				
Operating Results (000's)				
Total Revenues	121,279.9	104,977.7	105,752.0	103,218.4
Costs & Expenses	-121,190.6	-101,134.4	-147,463.8	-98,058.8
Income Before Taxes and Other	89.3	3,843.3	-41,711.9	5,159.5
Other Items	0.0	-586.9	-11,596.1	0.0
Income Tax	1,105.1	7,195.2	8,458.8	-1,960.0
Net Income	1,194.5	10,451.6	-44,849.2	3,199.5
Cash Flow From Operations	7,629.2	-5,299.6	-80.5	-11,270.0
Balance Sheet (000's)				
Cash & Equivalents	897.6	838.5	509.4	24.5
Total Current Assets	45,687.1	45,112.4	43,857.4	59,384.8
Fixed Assets, Net	13,393.2	12,665.5	12,163.0	18,000.0
Total Assets	83,735.5	79,533.5	71,276.7	86,318.8
Total Current Liabilities	48,996.5	43,874.6	68,937.8	37,901.7
Long-Term Debt	6,250.0	8,750.0	0.0	0.0
Stockholders' Equity	10,143.7	10,964.0	2,078.2	46,019.1
Performance & Financial Condition				
Return on Total Revenues %	0.98	9.96	-42.41	3.10
Return on Avg Stockholders' Equity %	11.32	160.27	-186.49	7.28
Return on Average Assets %	1.46	13.86	-56.92	4.62
Current Ratio	0.93	1.03	0.64	1.57
Debt / Equity %	61.61	79.81	n.a.	n.a.

Compound Growth %'s	EPS % n.a.	Net Income % -28.00	Total Revenues % 5.52

Comments

In 1996, the Company faced significant financial and operational challenges. The Company recognized that its product offerings had exceeded a manageable level and included products outside its core competency. Approximately 350 of the Company's 650 products were eliminated. 1996 results also include a write-off of the value of impaired assets of $11.6 million. After a return to profitability in 1997, the Company had a difficult 1998. Special charges of $2,069,000 were taken in the fourth quarter most of which related to eliminating the chemical diisononyl phthalate from all of its products intended for the mouth, including pacifiers and teethers. Gross margins were also slightly lower. At December 31, 1998, the Company had $6.3 million recorded as goodwill which equated to approximately 62% of stockholders' equity and book value per share.

Officers	Position	Ownership Information	
Michael Lerner	Chairman, CEO	Number of Shares Outstanding	7,231,122
Richard E. Wenz	President, COO	Market Capitalization	$ 23,501,147
Michael S. Bernstein	Exec VP	Number of Shareholders	2,300
Joseph S. Driscoll	Controller	Where Listed / Symbol	NASDAQ / SAFT

Other Information			
Transfer Agent	State Street Bank & Trust Co. Boston, MA	SIC Code	3089
Auditor	Grant Thornton LLP	Employees	315
		Web Site	safety1st.com

Sandata, Inc.

26 Harbor Park Drive Port Washington, NY 11050 Telephone (516)484-4400 Fax (516)484-6084

Company Description

Sandata, Inc. is engaged in the business of providing computerized data processing services and custom software and programming services, by utilizing Company-developed software, and software acquired or licensed by the Company, principally to the health care industry, but also to the general commercial market. In addition, the Company provides hardware maintenance of personal computers, printers and networks and training on PC software packages. Applications of the Company's software include: a home health care system, computerized preparation of management reports, payroll processing and electronic time card with voice recognition systems. The Company was founded in 1978.

	05/31/98	05/31/97	05/31/96	05/31/95
Per Share Information				
Stock Price as of 12/31	1.44	5.50	7.75	2.25
Earnings Per Share	0.04	0.14	0.16	0.03
Price / Earnings Ratio	36.00	39.29	48.44	75.00
Book Value Per Share	4.68	4.89	5.12	4.78
Price / Book Value %	30.77	112.47	151.37	47.07
Dividends Per Share	0.0	0.0	0.0	0.0
Annual Financial Data				
Operating Results (000's)				
Total Revenues	12,827.0	11,881.5	9,562.2	7,713.9
Costs & Expenses	-12,708.8	-11,311.8	-9,310.7	-7,614.5
Income Before Taxes and Other	118.2	569.7	251.5	99.5
Other Items	0.0	0.0	0.0	0.0
Income Tax	-27.9	-307.0	8.0	-74.4
Net Income	90.3	262.7	259.5	25.0
Cash Flow From Operations	2,170.5	1,483.0	1,985.2	299.5
Balance Sheet (000's)				
Cash & Equivalents	1,794.9	1,200.0	368.4	102.6
Total Current Assets	4,194.0	3,747.9	2,147.0	2,594.0
Fixed Assets, Net	5,814.4	5,279.5	9,399.6	3,564.2
Total Assets	10,633.6	9,538.5	11,957.3	6,708.1
Total Current Liabilities	2,739.1	2,199.3	3,000.0	1,029.7
Long-Term Debt	0.0	1,034.2	4,322.2	1,679.2
Stockholders' Equity	7,296.6	5,691.8	3,912.6	3,653.1
Performance & Financial Condition				
Return on Total Revenues %	0.70	2.21	2.71	0.32
Return on Avg Stockholders' Equity %	1.39	5.47	6.86	0.69
Return on Average Assets %	0.90	2.44	2.78	0.27
Current Ratio	1.53	1.70	0.72	2.52
Debt / Equity %	n.a.	18.17	110.47	45.97

Compound Growth %'s	EPS % 10.06	Net Income % 53.40	Total Revenues % 18.47

Comments

Increased revenue in fiscal 1998 is primarily due to the SANTRAX product line, an automated timekeeping system designed to monitor home health care workers at the visit site. SANTRAX also collects a wide range of additional data from the site visit and is expected to have applications in other industries as well. With only 1.5 million shares outstanding, the Company is not attracting any institutional ownership. This may explain why the stock price is at a deep discount to book value. For the nine months ended February 28, 1999, the Company reported revenues and net income of $10.6 million and $119,174 ($.05 per share) as compared to $9.4 million and $255,861 ($.11 per share) for the same period of the preceding year.

Officers	Position	Ownership Information	
Bert E. Brodsky	President, Treasurer	Number of Shares Outstanding	1,560,149
Hugh Freund	Exec VP, Secretary	Market Capitalization	$ 2,246,615
Gary Stoller	Exec VP	Number of Shareholders	1,075
Paul J. Konigsberg	Director	Where Listed / Symbol	NASDAQ / SAND

Other Information			
Transfer Agent	North American Transfer Co. Freeport, NY	SIC Code	7374
Auditor	Marcum & Kliegman LLP	Employees	134
		Web Site	sandata.com

Saratoga Beverage Group, Inc.

11 Geyser Road Saratoga Springs, NY 12866 Telephone (518)584-6363 Fax (518)584-0380

Company Description

Saratoga Beverage Group, Inc. is primarily engaged in the bottling, marketing and distribution of natural spring water products from naturally free-flowing springs located on the Company's property in Saratoga Springs, New York and elsewhere. It also packages products for others (co-packing). The Company's product line currently includes five water products, including a sparkling spring water product, three sparkling essence-flavored spring water products and a non-carbonated spring water product. All of the Company's products are marketed as premium domestic bottled water under the proprietary brand name Saratoga. The Saratoga brand name has been in existence for over 120 years. On January 29, 1999, the Company acquired The Fresh Juice Company, Inc., which manufactures, markets and distributes fresh squeezed and frozen fresh squeezed citrus juices, fresh fruit smoothies and other non-carbonated beverages.

	12/31/98	12/31/97	12/31/96	12/31/95
Per Share Information				
Stock Price	2.06	2.19	0.94	1.62
Earnings Per Share	0.26	0.25	-0.06	-0.35
Price / Earnings Ratio	7.92	8.76	n.a.	n.a.
Book Value Per Share	1.37	0.98	0.74	0.80
Price / Book Value %	150.36	223.47	127.03	202.50
Dividends Per Share	0.0	0.0	0.0	0.0
Annual Financial Data				
Operating Results (000's)				
Total Revenues	9,154.1	6,449.7	4,455.3	3,407.7
Costs & Expenses	-7,869.4	-5,637.1	-4,602.7	-4,329.5
Income Before Taxes and Other	1,284.7	812.6	-147.5	-923.4
Other Items	-400.0	0.0	0.0	0.0
Income Tax	-17.6	-8.0	0.0	0.0
Net Income	867.1	804.6	-147.5	-923.4
Cash Flow From Operations	665.5	1,706.0	71.8	-312.0
Balance Sheet (000's)				
Cash & Equivalents	2,576.9	1,568.0	387.9	352.8
Total Current Assets	3,957.4	3,802.3	994.6	1,069.3
Fixed Assets, Net	1,502.0	1,501.0	1,618.4	1,813.8
Total Assets	7,499.2	5,704.8	2,629.9	2,990.4
Total Current Liabilities	1,554.6	1,289.6	608.0	814.0
Long-Term Debt	1,500.0	0.0	0.0	0.0
Stockholders' Equity	4,390.1	2,914.0	2,014.5	2,176.4
Performance & Financial Condition				
Return on Total Revenues %	9.47	12.48	-3.31	-27.10
Return on Avg Stockholders' Equity %	23.74	32.65	-7.04	-34.48
Return on Average Assets %	13.13	19.31	-5.25	-26.74
Current Ratio	2.55	2.95	1.64	1.31
Debt / Equity %	34.17	n.a.	n.a.	n.a.

Compound Growth %'s	EPS %	n.a.	Net Income %	n.a.	Total Revenues %	39.01

Comments

1998 was a sparkling year with revenues up 42%, following the 43% increase during 1997. 75% of the 1998 advance was attributable to product sales and 25% was attributable to the expansion of co-packing activities. 1998 results suffered a $400,000 loss on a bad debt to a business associate. The Company restructured its finances during 1997 and placed a $1.5 million convertible debenture. The proceeds of the debenture were added to working capital. Preliminary estimates regarding the 1999 acquisition indicate that goodwill of $15.1 million will be recorded in connection with the transaction. The purchase price of $21.7 million will be paid in cash of $16.4 million and 2,133,553 shares of common stock.

Officers	Position	Ownership Information	
Carl Wolf	Chairman	Number of Shares Outstanding	3,199,094
Robin Prever	President, CEO	Market Capitalization	$ 6,590,134
Adam Madkour	COO	Number of Shareholders	1,716
Gayle Henderson	CFO	Where Listed / Symbol	NASDAQ / TOGA

Other Information			
Transfer Agent	American Stock Transfer & Trust Co. New York, NY	SIC Code	2086
Auditor	PricewaterhouseCoopers LLP	Employees	287
		Web Site	saratogabeverage.com

Sarnia Corporation

6850 Versar Center   Springfield, VA 22151   Telephone (703)642-6800   Fax (703)642-6825

Company Description

Sarnia Corporation is an owner and operator of commercial real estate. Its sole property is an office park of approximately 18.3 acres in Springfield, Virginia known as Versar Center. The Versar Center consists of two four-story office buildings. The Company was formed in 1982 to acquire the property from its then parent, Versar, Inc. On June 30, 1994, Versar spun-off the Company to Versar's shareholders and the Company began to be publicly traded. Versar, Inc. remains as one of five major tenants at Versar Center.

	06/30/98	06/30/97	06/30/96	06/30/95
Per Share Information				
Stock Price as of 12/31	0.41	0.37	0.31	0.25
Earnings Per Share	0.02	0.0	-0.06	-0.06
Price / Earnings Ratio	20.50	n.a.	n.a.	n.a.
Book Value Per Share	-0.33	-0.34	-0.34	-0.28
Price / Book Value %	n.a.	n.a.	n.a.	n.a.
Dividends Per Share	0.0	0.0	0.0	0.0
Annual Financial Data				
Operating Results (000's)				
Total Revenues	3,127.0	2,911.0	2,771.0	2,676.0
Costs & Expenses	-2,879.0	-2,827.0	-3,006.0	-2,946.0
Income Before Taxes and Other	248.0	84.0	-235.0	-270.0
Other Items	0.0	0.0	0.0	0.0
Income Tax	-99.0	0.0	0.0	0.0
Net Income	149.0	84.0	-235.0	-270.0
Cash Flow From Operations	674.0	735.0	508.0	435.0
Balance Sheet (000's)				
Cash & Equivalents	139.0	96.0	55.0	3.0
Total Current Assets	404.0	364.0	397.0	434.0
Fixed Assets, Net	11,443.0	11,944.0	12,365.0	12,871.0
Total Assets	11,847.0	12,308.0	12,762.0	13,305.0
Total Current Liabilities	50.0	351.0	348.0	765.0
Long-Term Debt	9,787.0	10,267.0	10,739.0	12,062.0
Stockholders' Equity	-722.0	-792.0	-797.0	-1,278.0
Performance & Financial Condition				
Return on Total Revenues %	4.76	2.89	-8.48	-10.09
Return on Avg Stockholders' Equity %	n.a.	n.a.	n.a.	n.a.
Return on Average Assets %	1.23	0.67	-1.80	-2.02
Current Ratio	8.08	1.04	1.14	0.57
Debt / Equity %	n.a.	n.a.	n.a.	n.a.

Compound Growth %'s	EPS % n.a.	Net Income % n.a.	Total Revenues % 5.33

Comments

Springfield is located about 14.5 miles southwest of downtown Washington, D.C. The two buildings have about 228,500 square feet of leasable space and had 99% average occupancy during fiscal 1998. The increase in revenue realized in 1998 as compared to 1997 was due to rent escalations and a higher occupancy rate. The Company can build an additional 168,000 square feet under existing zoning regulations and an additional 391,000 square feet by special exception. For the six months ended December 31, 1998, revenues were $1,683,000 as compared to $1,533,000 in the preceding year. The operating cash flow of the properties, without regard to the additional development potential of the acreage, appears to more than justify the price of the stock. However, preferred stock is convertible into another 1,875,000 shares of common and should be included in calculations relative to real value.

Officers	Position	Ownership Information	
Benjamin M. Rawls	Chairman	Number of Shares Outstanding	4,572,545
Charles I. Judkins, Jr.	President, CEO	Market Capitalization	$ 1,874,743
Lawrence W. Sinnott	Treasurer, CFO	Number of Shareholders	743
William G. Denbo	Vice President, General Manager	Where Listed / Symbol	OTC-BB / SARN

Other Information			
Transfer Agent	Bank of New York New York, NY	SIC Code	6512
Auditor	Arthur Andersen LLP	Employees	7
Market Maker	Gabelli & Company, Inc.	(914)921-5154	
	Wachtel & Co. Inc.	(202)898-1018	

Scherer Healthcare, Inc.

120 Interstate Parkway, S.E., Suite 305   Atlanta, GA 30339   Telephone (770)933-1800   Fax (770)933-1880

Company Description

Scherer Healthcare, Inc. was founded in 1981 as successor to Aloe Creme Laboratories, Inc., which dates back to 1953. The Company has two business segments: a waste management services segment assists hospitals, clinics, doctors, and other health care facilities with the control and disposal of infectious medical waste, principally sharp-edged medical waste, which includes needles, scalpels, and syringes; and a consumer healthcare products segment which markets brand name and generic over-the-counter drugs primarily used for treatment of colds and coughs, eye and ear irritations and insect bites. Over the last four years, the Company disposed of a number of other business interests.

	03/31/98	03/31/97	03/31/96	03/31/95
Per Share Information				
Stock Price as of 12/31	3.75	3.37	2.00	2.62
Earnings Per Share	1.33	-0.06	0.40	-2.39
Price / Earnings Ratio	2.82	n.a.	5.00	n.a.
Book Value Per Share	5.08	3.70	3.77	3.40
Price / Book Value %	73.82	91.08	53.05	77.06
Dividends Per Share	0.0	0.0	0.0	0.0
Annual Financial Data				
Operating Results (000's)				
Total Revenues	14,396.0	36,404.0	45,813.0	43,568.0
Costs & Expenses	-12,871.0	-36,394.0	-42,592.0	-49,687.0
Income Before Taxes and Other	1,525.0	-239.0	3,221.0	-6,761.0
Other Items	4,497.0	-16.0	-925.0	-3,607.0
Income Tax	-21.0	-6.0	-548.0	197.0
Net Income	6,001.0	-261.0	1,748.0	-10,171.0
Cash Flow From Operations	3,834.0	576.0	481.0	-2,750.0
Balance Sheet (000's)				
Cash & Equivalents	6,868.0	3,237.0	3,622.0	1,273.0
Total Current Assets	10,241.0	6,412.0	14,374.0	18,231.0
Fixed Assets, Net	4,058.0	3,649.0	10,603.0	18,826.0
Total Assets	25,792.0	21,370.0	34,410.0	41,679.0
Total Current Liabilities	2,865.0	3,036.0	10,468.0	20,640.0
Long-Term Debt	504.0	2,046.0	5,291.0	5,332.0
Stockholders' Equity	21,916.0	15,963.0	16,174.0	14,486.0
Performance & Financial Condition				
Return on Total Revenues %	41.69	-0.72	3.82	-23.35
Return on Avg Stockholders' Equity %	31.69	-1.62	11.40	-50.86
Return on Average Assets %	25.45	-0.94	4.59	-33.18
Current Ratio	3.57	2.11	1.37	0.88
Debt / Equity %	2.30	12.82	32.71	36.81

Compound Growth %'s   EPS % n.a.   Net Income % n.a.   Total Revenues % n.a.

Comments

The decline in fiscal 1998 revenues was attributable to discontinued business interests. Same company sales actually rose 5.6%. Each of the years above include non-recurring items from discontinued operations which are reflected in Other Items in Operating Results. Fiscal 1998 includes a net non-recurring gain of $4,497,000 ($1.00 per share). The Company has a substantially improved financial condition as the result of the divestitures. In addition to a favorable working capital, $6.25 million of marketable securities are classified as non-current assets. For the nine months ended December 31, 1998, the Company reported revenues and net income of $11.2 million and $1,899,000 ($.42 per share) as compared to $10.3 million and $5,689,000 ($1.26 per share) in the same period of the preceding year. However, the prior year's period included income from discontinued operations of $4,572,000 ($1.01 per share).

Officers	Position	Ownership Information	
Robert P. Scherer, Jr.	Chairman, CEO	Number of Shares Outstanding	4,315,759
Gary W. Ruffcorn	Vice President, CFO	Market Capitalization	$ 16,184,096
Kenneth H. Robertson	Director	Number of Shareholders	2,003
Stephen Lukas, Sr.	Director	Where Listed / Symbol	NASDAQ / SCHR

Other Information			
Transfer Agent	Wachovia Bank, N.A. Winston-Salem, NC	SIC Code	3841
Auditor	Arthur Andersen LLP	Employees	120

Scientific Industries, Inc.

70 Orville Drive Bohemia, NY 11716 Telephone (516)567-4700 Fax (516)567-5896

Company Description

Scientific Industries, Inc. is engaged in the manufacture and marketing of laboratory equipment consisting primarily of apparatus such as timers, rotators, pumps and vortex mixers. (Vortex mixers are used to mix the contents of test tubes, beakers and other containers by placing containers on a rotating cup or other attachments that mix the contents at varying speeds.) The Company's products are used by hospital and research laboratories, clinics, pharmaceutical manufacturers, medical device manufacturers and other industries. The Company was formed in 1954.

	06/30/98	06/30/97	06/30/96	06/30/95
Per Share Information				
Stock Price as of 12/31	1.75	1.75	1.06	1.06
Earnings Per Share	0.18	0.14	0.09	0.22
Price / Earnings Ratio	9.72	12.50	11.78	4.82
Book Value Per Share	2.25	2.04	1.87	1.77
Price / Book Value %	77.78	85.78	56.68	59.89
Dividends Per Share	0.0	0.0	0.0	0.0
Annual Financial Data				
Operating Results (000's)				
Total Revenues	3,456.9	3,107.4	2,550.1	2,713.3
Costs & Expenses	-3,246.7	-2,927.9	-2,426.5	-2,414.0
Income Before Taxes and Other	210.2	179.5	123.6	299.3
Other Items	0.0	0.0	0.0	0.0
Income Tax	-29.7	-43.8	-42.1	-93.0
Net Income	180.5	135.7	81.5	206.3
Cash Flow From Operations	230.9	209.5	126.6	149.1
Balance Sheet (000's)				
Cash & Equivalents	165.9	146.6	169.9	315.6
Total Current Assets	1,892.4	1,773.9	1,533.5	1,570.4
Fixed Assets, Net	150.8	143.2	115.8	107.5
Total Assets	2,256.7	2,110.0	1,839.4	1,779.3
Total Current Liabilities	291.7	349.1	229.1	265.7
Long-Term Debt	0.0	0.0	0.0	0.0
Stockholders' Equity	1,877.2	1,683.0	1,545.6	1,463.3
Performance & Financial Condition				
Return on Total Revenues %	5.22	4.37	3.20	7.60
Return on Avg Stockholders' Equity %	10.14	8.41	5.42	15.16
Return on Average Assets %	8.27	6.87	4.50	12.14
Current Ratio	6.49	5.08	6.69	5.91
Debt / Equity %	n.a.	n.a.	n.a.	n.a.

Compound Growth %'s	EPS %	-6.47	Net Income %	-4.36	Total Revenues %	8.41

Comments

Revenues increased 11% in fiscal 1998 which management attributes to increased demand for existing laboratory products. General expenses increased $110,000 resulting from the pursuit of external business opportunities. Although small, the Company has a solid working capital base and no long term debt. Cash and investment securities represent approximately 64% of book value yet the stock was priced at a discount to its book value at December 31, 1998. For the six months ended December 31, 1998, revenues and net income were $1.8 million and $81,400 ($.08 per share) as compared to $1.7 million and $79,000 ($.08) for the equivalent period of the preceding year.

Officers	Position	Ownership Information	
Lowell A. Kleiman	President, Treasurer	Number of Shares Outstanding	834,572
Cathy Pulver-Dugan	Vice President	Market Capitalization	$ 1,460,501
Helena R. Santos	Vice President, Controller	Number of Shareholders	944
Roger B. Knowles	Director	Where Listed / Symbol	OTC-BB / SCND

Other Information			
Transfer Agent	Continental Stock Transfer & Trust Co. New York, NY	SIC Code	3826
Auditor	Nussbaum Yates & Wolpow, P.C.	Employees	22
Market Maker	Paragon Capital Corporation (800)521-8877	Web Site	scind.com
	Troster Singer Corporation (800)526-3160		

Seattle FilmWorks, Inc.

1260 16th Avenue West   Seattle, WA 98119   Telephone (206)281-1390   Fax (206)273-8368

Company Description

Seattle FilmWorks, Inc., founded in 1976, is a leading direct-to-consumer marketer and provider of high-quality amateur photofinishing and digital imaging services and products primarily on a mail-order basis under the brand name Seattle FilmWorks®. The Company was among the first to provide express-mail delivery, cross-referenced data on prints and negatives, a composite photo index and a convenient reorder system. To a lesser extent, the Company provides photofinishing services, products and supplies on a wholesale basis. The Company has developed comprehensive statistical models for the design and analysis of its direct-response marketing programs using proprietary customer data compiled over 17 years.

	09/26/98	09/27/97	09/28/96	09/30/95
Per Share Information				
Stock Price as of 12/31	4.94	11.12	13.33	13.83
Earnings Per Share	0.43	0.57	0.45	0.33
Price / Earnings Ratio	11.49	19.51	29.62	41.91
Book Value Per Share	2.63	2.29	1.64	1.12
Price / Book Value %	187.83	485.59	812.80	1,234.82
Dividends Per Share	0.0	0.0	0.0	0.0
Annual Financial Data				
Operating Results (000's)				
Total Revenues	97,656.0	101,763.0	84,601.0	62,461.0
Costs & Expenses	-86,529.0	-86,376.0	-72,243.0	-53,861.0
Income Before Taxes and Other	11,127.0	15,387.0	12,237.0	8,580.0
Other Items	0.0	0.0	0.0	0.0
Income Tax	-3,552.0	-5,242.0	-4,220.0	-2,898.0
Net Income	7,575.0	10,145.0	8,017.0	5,682.0
Cash Flow From Operations	10,601.0	9,493.0	4,554.0	6,908.0
Balance Sheet (000's)				
Cash & Equivalents	11,780.0	10,252.0	6,135.0	8,560.0
Total Current Assets	27,149.0	29,259.0	20,151.0	16,493.0
Fixed Assets, Net	10,954.0	7,564.0	5,337.0	3,200.0
Total Assets	55,116.0	51,366.0	37,826.0	28,244.0
Total Current Liabilities	5,486.0	9,371.0	7,549.0	8,002.0
Long-Term Debt	0.0	0.0	0.0	0.0
Stockholders' Equity	43,701.0	37,601.0	26,675.0	17,932.0
Performance & Financial Condition				
Return on Total Revenues %	7.76	9.97	9.48	9.10
Return on Avg Stockholders' Equity %	18.63	31.57	35.95	39.19
Return on Average Assets %	14.23	22.75	24.27	24.18
Current Ratio	4.95	3.12	2.67	2.06
Debt / Equity %	n.a.	n.a.	n.a.	n.a.

Compound Growth %'s	EPS %	9.22	Net Income %	10.06	Total Revenues %	16.06

Comments

The Company declared a 3 for 2 stock split in fiscal 1997. All per share amounts have been restated for consistency. Approximately 71% of the decline in revenues experienced in fiscal 1998 was attributable to sales of wholesale film to certain markets in Asia which were discontinued at the beginning of the fourth quarter. The Company also experienced reduced photofinishing volumes due to lower response rates to marketing efforts. The Company has capitalized the direct costs of customer acquisition. Due to a decline in the results from the customer acquisition program, the Company reduced the carrying value of customer acquisition costs by 3.5% at the end of fiscal 1998, amounting to $613,000 in additional expense. At September 26, 1998, there remains $16.8 million of these intangibles on the books which equates to approximately 38% of stockholders' equity and book value per share.

Officers	Position	Ownership Information	
Gary R. Christophersen	President, CEO	Number of Shares Outstanding	16,641,891
Case H. Kuehn	VP - Finance, CFO	Market Capitalization	$ 82,210,942
Michael F. Lass	Vice President	Number of Shareholders	9,700
Annette F. Mack	Vice President	Where Listed / Symbol	NASDAQ / FOTO

Other Information			
Transfer Agent	ChaseMellon Shareholder Services Ridgefield Park, NJ	SIC Code	7384
Auditor	Ernst & Young LLP	Employees	681
		Web Site	filmworks.com

Security National Financial Corporation

5300 South 360 West, Suite 310   Salt Lake City, UT 84123   Telephone (801)264-1060   Fax (801)264-8430

Company Description

Security National Financial Corporation operates in three main business segments: life insurance, cemetery and mortuary, and mortgage loans. The life insurance segment is engaged in the business of selling and servicing selected lines of life insurance, annuity products and accident and health insurance marketed primarily in the intermountain west, California, Texas, and Oklahoma. The cemetery and mortuary segment of the Company consists of five cemeteries in Utah, one cemetery in California, eight mortuaries in Utah and six mortuaries in Arizona. The mortgage loan segment is an approved governmental and conventional lender that originates and underwrites residential and commercial loans for new construction, existing homes and real estate projects primarily in the intermountain west. The Company was founded in 1965.

	12/31/98	12/31/97	12/31/96	12/31/95
Per Share Information				
Stock Price	3.06	3.00	4.31	4.50
Earnings Per Share	0.18	0.32	0.32	0.43
Price / Earnings Ratio	17.00	9.38	13.47	10.47
Book Value Per Share	5.98	6.07	5.95	5.62
Price / Book Value %	51.17	49.42	72.44	80.07
Dividends Per Share	0.0	0.0	0.0	0.0
Annual Financial Data				
Operating Results (000's)				
Total Revenues	32,819.6	28,474.6	29,922.7	26,061.3
Costs & Expenses	-31,793.6	-26,805.6	-28,546.1	-23,801.9
Income Before Taxes and Other	1,026.0	1,669.0	1,376.6	2,259.5
Other Items	0.0	0.0	0.0	20.3
Income Tax	-254.8	-360.1	-139.5	-728.0
Net Income	771.2	1,308.9	1,237.1	1,551.8
Cash Flow From Operations	588.6	7,082.9	11,737.2	-15,713.4
Balance Sheet (000's)				
Cash & Equivalents	6,671.0	3,408.2	3,301.1	7,710.0
Total Current Assets	36,421.2	22,330.9	22,629.0	31,887.0
Fixed Assets, Net	10,682.1	6,641.6	6,514.0	6,500.0
Total Assets	213,265.1	125,451.9	124,709.5	138,212.7
Total Current Liabilities	5,108.9	2,836.9	3,102.0	6,219.0
Long-Term Debt	15,309.3	9,880.0	11,277.0	10,000.0
Stockholders' Equity	26,680.3	25,394.9	23,468.0	21,918.7
Performance & Financial Condition				
Return on Total Revenues %	2.35	4.60	4.13	5.95
Return on Avg Stockholders' Equity %	2.96	5.36	5.45	7.39
Return on Average Assets %	0.46	1.05	0.94	1.24
Current Ratio	7.13	7.87	7.30	5.13
Debt / Equity %	57.38	38.91	48.05	45.62

Compound Growth %'s	EPS %	-25.19	Net Income %	-20.79	Total Revenues %	7.99

Comments

The Company's operations over the last three years have generally reflected three trends or events which management expects will continue: 1) increased attention to "niche" insurance products, such as the Company's funeral plan policies, annuities, and limited pay accident policies; 2) emphasis on high margin cemetery and mortuary business; and 3) capitalizing on the strong economy in the intermountain west by originating and refinancing mortgage loans. Management attributed the decline in 1998 earnings to higher expenses which were primarily the result of the increased number of loan originations by the mortgage division.

Officers	Position	Ownership Information	
George R. Quist	President, CEO	Number of Shares Outstanding	4,463,095
William C. Sargent	Senior VP, Secretary	Market Capitalization	$ 13,657,071
Scott M. Quist	Vice President, CFO	Number of Shareholders	4,837
		Where Listed / Symbol	NASDAQ / SNFCA

Other Information			
Transfer Agent	Company Office Salt Lake City, UT	SIC Code	6311
Auditor	Ernst & Young LLP	Employees	204

Sel-Drum International, Inc.

501 Amherst Street   Buffalo, NY 14207-2913   Telephone (905)335-2766   Fax (905)335-5986

Company Description

The Company's primary business is the distribution of high mortality copier replacement parts, toners and drums. It also manufactures and remanufactures drums, and produces facsimile and printer cartridges. Sel-Drum markets its products in the United States and Canada through a direct network of sales agents and telemarketers. The Company was formed in 1993 and became an operating company in 1995 when it acquired all the outstanding shares of a privately-held Canadian company which had been operating since 1978.

	07/31/98	07/31/97	07/31/96	07/31/95
Per Share Information				
Stock Price as of 12/31	0.31	0.44	0.62	1.50
Earnings Per Share	0.07	0.13	0.10	0.08
Price / Earnings Ratio	4.43	3.38	6.20	18.75
Book Value Per Share	0.08	0.05	-0.07	-0.18
Price / Book Value %	387.50	880.00	n.a.	n.a.
Dividends Per Share	0.0	0.0	0.0	0.0
Annual Financial Data				
Operating Results (000's)				
Total Revenues	14,348.9	16,652.3	14,854.2	14,178.3
Costs & Expenses	-13,399.9	-15,127.9	-13,620.5	-13,224.5
Income Before Taxes and Other	868.1	1,499.9	1,228.9	911.0
Other Items	0.0	0.0	0.0	0.0
Income Tax	-351.6	-538.1	-458.7	-297.1
Net Income	516.5	961.9	770.2	613.9
Cash Flow From Operations	462.6	820.0	456.6	52.5
Balance Sheet (000's)				
Cash & Equivalents	285.8	1,085.0	1,181.4	166.0
Total Current Assets	5,832.3	6,572.8	6,877.4	5,104.2
Fixed Assets, Net	817.9	925.2	1,035.9	1,104.3
Total Assets	7,002.9	7,695.8	8,117.5	6,405.2
Total Current Liabilities	1,598.2	2,340.1	3,732.6	2,627.8
Long-Term Debt	257.7	109.1	129.5	0.0
Stockholders' Equity	5,097.0	5,214.7	4,246.1	3,454.5
Performance & Financial Condition				
Return on Total Revenues %	3.60	5.78	5.18	4.33
Return on Avg Stockholders' Equity %	10.02	20.33	20.00	46.94
Return on Average Assets %	7.03	12.17	10.61	9.96
Current Ratio	3.65	2.81	1.84	1.94
Debt / Equity %	5.06	2.09	3.05	n.a.

Compound Growth %'s	EPS %	-4.35	Net Income %	-5.60	Total Revenues %	0.40

Comments

During fiscal 1997 and 1998, the Company engaged in discussions with two potential acquirors. Employee morale and retention suffered as a result of these talks. Management was then faced with a refocusing effort including a reorganization of key management. The bottom line was a decline in fiscal 1998 revenue and profits. Preferred shares comprise most of stockholders' equity. For the six months ended January 31, 1999, the Company had sales and net income of $6.7 million and $148,998 ($.02 per share) as compared to $7.1 million and $262,417 ($.03 per share), respectively, for the same period of the prior fiscal year.

Officers	Position	Ownership Information	
Raymond C. Sparks	President, CEO	Number of Shares Outstanding	7,642,500
John Hall	VP - Finance, CFO	Market Capitalization	$ 2,369,175
Brian Turnbull	Director	Number of Shareholders	376
Robert Asseltine	Director	Where Listed / Symbol	OTC-BB / SDUM

Other Information			
Transfer Agent	U.S. Stock Transfer Corp. Glendale, CA	SIC Code	3861
Auditor	Mengel, Metsger, Barr & Co.	Employees	68
Market Maker	Paragon Capital Corporation	(800)521-8877	Web Site	seldrum.com
	Sharpe Capital Inc.	(800)355-5781		

Sel-Leb Marketing, Inc.

495 River Street   Paterson, NJ 07524   Telephone (973)225-9880   Fax (973)225-9840

Company Description

Sel-Leb Marketing, Inc. is primarily engaged in the distribution and marketing of consumer merchandise to retail sellers such as mass merchandisers, discount chain stores and food, drug and electronic retailers. The Company's business consists of the following activities: developing, marketing and selling proprietary brands of budget-line health, beauty aid and cosmetic products, which are contract manufactured by others; distributing merchandise on a wholesale basis outside normal distribution channels to retail merchants; and developing, marketing and selling products to be promoted by celebrity spokespersons and sold to mass merchandise retailers. The Company was founded in 1993 and had its initial public offering in 1995.

	12/31/98	12/31/97	12/31/96	12/31/95
Per Share Information				
Stock Price	2.50	7.44	46.00	38.00
Earnings Per Share	0.14	0.03	0.08	0.32
Price / Earnings Ratio	17.86	248.00	575.00	118.75
Book Value Per Share	6.59	6.45	6.04	4.99
Price / Book Value %	37.94	115.35	761.59	761.52
Dividends Per Share	0.0	0.0	0.0	0.0
Annual Financial Data				
Operating Results (000's)				
Total Revenues	17,372.0	17,374.0	13,525.3	11,581.6
Costs & Expenses	-17,146.4	-17,321.6	-13,249.6	-10,968.8
Income Before Taxes and Other	225.6	51.3	275.7	612.8
Other Items	0.0	0.0	0.0	-39.4
Income Tax	-74.7	-23.6	-118.0	-234.0
Net Income	150.9	27.6	157.7	339.4
Cash Flow From Operations	-305.3	-1,838.6	-1,762.5	-1,698.3
Balance Sheet (000's)				
Cash & Equivalents	504.1	249.7	129.5	833.0
Total Current Assets	11,481.6	10,059.0	7,546.5	5,884.4
Fixed Assets, Net	607.7	474.3	356.3	270.7
Total Assets	12,441.3	10,906.6	8,215.0	6,439.6
Total Current Liabilities	4,409.1	2,951.1	1,971.5	1,329.1
Long-Term Debt	859.4	933.6	0.0	469.0
Stockholders' Equity	7,172.8	7,021.9	6,243.5	4,641.5
Performance & Financial Condition				
Return on Total Revenues %	0.87	0.16	1.17	2.93
Return on Avg Stockholders' Equity %	2.13	0.42	2.90	13.43
Return on Average Assets %	1.29	0.29	2.15	11.31
Current Ratio	2.60	3.41	3.83	4.43
Debt / Equity %	11.98	13.30	n.a.	10.10

Compound Growth %'s	EPS %	-24.09	Net Income %	-23.68	Total Revenues %	14.47

Comments

The Company executed a 1 for 8 reverse stock split in 1998. All per share amounts have been adjusted for consistency. During 1997, revenues increased 29.8% as the result of increased sales of the Company's own proprietary brand name line in beauty aids and cosmetics, increased sales of merchandise acquired in connection with the Company's opportunistic purchasing business, and the introduction of a new line of cosmetics which is being sold through electronic media. 1997 results included expenses associated with the building of infrastructure to support anticipated sales growth in 1998. But sales were flat in 1998 making investors wonder what all the hullabaloo was about. During 1998, the Company realigned management and support responsibilities whereby more time of senior management would be spent on purchasing, production and inventory management.

Officers	Position	Ownership Information	
Paul Sharp	President, CEO	Number of Shares Outstanding	1,089,083
Jack Koegel	COO	Market Capitalization	$ 2,722,708
Jan S. Mirsky	Exec VP	Number of Shareholders	500
Jorge Lazaro	Exec VP, Secretary	Where Listed / Symbol	NASDAQ / SELB

Other Information			
Transfer Agent	Continental Stock Transfer & Trust Co. New York, NY	SIC Code	5122
Auditor	J.H. Cohn LLP	Employees	70

Selfcare, Inc.

200 Prospect Street   Waltham, MA 02154   Telephone (781)647-3900   Fax (781)647-3939

Company Description

Selfcare is engaged in the development, manufacture and marketing of self-test diagnostic products for the diabetes, women's health and infectious disease markets, as well as the marketing of nutritional supplement products, several of which are targeted primarily at the women's health market. The Company's existing and planned self-test products are targeted at the two largest existing markets for self-care diagnostics, diabetes management and women's health, as well as the emerging market for self tests for infectious diseases and agents, including HIV. The Company had its initial public offering on August 6, 1996 at $8.50 per share.

	12/31/98	12/31/97	12/31/96	12/31/95
Per Share Information				
Stock Price	2.00	9.44	12.62	8.50
Earnings Per Share	-1.55	-3.36	-6.00	-2.61
Price / Earnings Ratio	n.a.	n.a.	n.a.	n.a.
Book Value Per Share	0.99	0.56	2.02	-1.29
Price / Book Value %	202.02	1,685.71	624.75	n.a.
Dividends Per Share	0.0	0.0	0.0	0.0
Annual Financial Data				
Operating Results (000's)				
Total Revenues	115,530.9	52,830.3	19,872.1	7,276.8
Costs & Expenses	-133,718.6	-77,540.6	-48,449.8	-17,373.7
Income Before Taxes and Other	-18,187.7	-24,710.3	-28,577.6	-10,096.9
Other Items	-45.8	0.0	0.0	0.0
Income Tax	-544.2	0.0	0.0	0.0
Net Income	-18,777.7	-24,710.3	-28,577.6	-10,096.9
Cash Flow From Operations	-11,866.7	-15,857.0	-6,555.4	-4,804.1
Balance Sheet (000's)				
Cash & Equivalents	9,199.6	15,669.9	16,458.7	7,394.8
Total Current Assets	37,816.5	34,679.3	25,238.0	10,307.1
Fixed Assets, Net	8,201.9	10,508.0	7,858.9	2,219.6
Total Assets	115,077.5	95,763.7	41,089.5	13,692.3
Total Current Liabilities	34,708.3	36,960.9	15,374.5	5,989.5
Long-Term Debt	50,409.5	39,476.1	5,895.7	8,166.7
Stockholders' Equity	15,008.9	5,440.7	12,079.3	-5,230.4
Performance & Financial Condition				
Return on Total Revenues %	-16.25	-46.77	-143.81	-138.76
Return on Avg Stockholders' Equity %	-183.65	-282.08	-834.52	n.a.
Return on Average Assets %	-17.81	-36.11	-104.33	-100.97
Current Ratio	1.09	0.94	1.64	1.72
Debt / Equity %	335.86	725.57	48.81	n.a.

Compound Growth %'s	EPS % n.a.	Net Income % n.a.	Total Revenues % 151.34

Comments

The Company has not yet become profitable. However, it has demonstrated a trend towards possible profitability even though the losses remain large. The increase in 1998 revenues as compared to 1997 was primarily due to sales of $57.2 million from the Company's diabetes management segment that realized less than $1 million of revenue in 1997. 1998 results include $7.8 million of charges related to the impairment of asset values. The cash needs to finance the Company have been great. There are various issues of preferred stock outstanding. On January 8, 1999, various additional preferred stock was privately placed to raise $7.4 million of cash for working capital needs. At December 31, 1998, the Company had goodwill and other intangible assets of $66.5 million recorded as assets which approximated 443% of stockholders' equity and book value per share.

Officers	Position	Ownership Information	
Ron Zwanziger	President, CEO	Number of Shares Outstanding	15,108,641
Christopher L. Huntoon	CFO	Market Capitalization	$ 30,217,282
Kenneth D. Legg	Vice President, Secretary	Number of Shareholders	3,000
Richard A. Pinkowitz	Vice President	Where Listed / Symbol	AMEX / SLF

Other Information			
Transfer Agent	State Street Bank & Trust Co. Boston, MA	SIC Code	3826
Auditor	Arthur Andersen LLP	Employees	524
		Web Site	invernessmedical.com

Seven J Stock Farm, Inc.

808 Travis Street, Suite 1453 Houston, TX 77002-5701 Telephone (713)228-8900 Fax (713)228-8913

Company Description

Seven J Stock Farm, Inc. is in the business of producing and selling field crops, leasing pastures, and gathering and transporting natural gas through pipelines. The Company also receives oil and gas royalties on the 11,140 acres of land it owns in Houston County, Texas. In November 1998, the Company invested $100,000 for a 50% interest in Trinity Valley Pecan Company which is in the process of constructing a pecan shelling plant. The other 50% interest is owned by a related party. Seven J Stock Farm was formed in 1948.

	10/31/98	10/31/97	10/31/96	10/31/95
Per Share Information				
Stock Price as of 12/31	3.62	3.50	3.50	3.50
Earnings Per Share	0.05	0.12	0.05	0.11
Price / Earnings Ratio	72.40	29.17	70.00	31.82
Book Value Per Share	1.16	1.15	1.08	1.06
Price / Book Value %	312.07	304.35	324.07	330.19
Dividends Per Share	0.0	0.04	0.04	0.0
Annual Financial Data				
Operating Results (000's)				
Total Revenues	787.0	779.0	561.0	686.0
Costs & Expenses	-683.0	-562.0	-452.0	-459.0
Income Before Taxes and Other	104.0	217.0	109.0	227.0
Other Items	0.0	0.0	0.0	0.0
Income Tax	-30.0	-48.0	-32.0	-65.0
Net Income	74.0	169.0	77.0	162.0
Cash Flow From Operations	292.0	369.0	-74.0	299.0
Balance Sheet (000's)				
Cash & Equivalents	17.0	132.0	97.0	487.0
Total Current Assets	208.0	441.0	437.0	631.0
Fixed Assets, Net	1,641.0	1,492.0	1,353.0	1,168.0
Total Assets	1,921.0	1,978.0	1,798.0	1,807.0
Total Current Liabilities	128.0	208.0	159.0	176.0
Long-Term Debt	0.0	0.0	0.0	0.0
Stockholders' Equity	1,687.0	1,671.0	1,560.0	1,541.0
Performance & Financial Condition				
Return on Total Revenues %	9.40	21.69	13.73	23.62
Return on Avg Stockholders' Equity %	4.41	10.46	4.97	11.10
Return on Average Assets %	3.80	8.95	4.27	9.57
Current Ratio	1.63	2.12	2.75	3.59
Debt / Equity %	n.a.	n.a.	n.a.	n.a.

Compound Growth %'s	EPS %	-23.11	Net Income %	-22.99	Total Revenues %	4.68

Comments

Revenues increased in fiscal 1998 due to pipeline operations. However, higher costs reduced net income. During fiscal 1994, the Company planted 2,500 pecan trees. Management estimates an additional three years before the grove is commercially productive. The estimated future annual yield of the grove is 300,000 pounds. The Company's land is stated at a cost of $288,000, which computes to an average cost of $25.95 per acre. 8,172 acres are presently leased annually for $16 per acre. Another 1,691 acres are leased under a crop sharing arrangement. Another 1,229 acres are not specifically identified. A careful investigation of the properties would be a worthwhile exercise for the serious investor.

Officers	Position	Ownership Information	
John R. Parten	Chairman, President	Number of Shares Outstanding	1,451,000
Valerie Coulter	Secretary	Market Capitalization	$ 5,252,620
R.F. Pratka	Vice President, Treasurer	Number of Shareholders	776
Patrick J. Moran	Director	Where Listed / Symbol	OTC-BB / SEVJ

Other Information			
Transfer Agent	Company Office Houston, TX	SIC Code	0100
Auditor	Mattison and Riquelmy	Employees	8
Market Maker	Carr Securities Corporation	(800)221-2243	
	Hill, Thompson, Magid & Co.	(800)631-3083	

Seventh Generation, Inc.

One Mill Street, Suite A26   Burlington, VT 05401-1530   Telephone (802)658-3773   Fax (802)658-1771

Company Description

Seventh Generation, Inc. is a marketer of environmentally friendly household products. Its brand name products include bathroom and facial towels, napkins, paper plates, cleaning and laundry products, trash bags and other household and personal products. All of the Company's products are made of recycled materials and are biodegradable. The Company's primary strategic objective is to establish Seventh Generation® as the leading brand name for environmentally responsible consumer products. The Company takes its name from the Great Law of the Haudenosaunee (Six Nation Iroquois Confederacy): "In our every deliberation, we must consider the impact of our decisions on the next seven generations." The Company was founded in 1988.

	12/31/98	12/31/97	12/31/96	12/31/95
Per Share Information				
Stock Price	0.72	0.47	0.50	0.31
Earnings Per Share	-0.16	-0.12	-0.11	0.21
Price / Earnings Ratio	n.a.	n.a.	n.a.	1.48
Book Value Per Share	0.11	0.25	0.37	0.48
Price / Book Value %	654.55	188.00	135.14	n.a.
Dividends Per Share	0.0	0.0	0.0	0.0
Annual Financial Data				
Operating Results (000's)				
Total Revenues	8,986.2	6,838.4	5,264.9	3,459.3
Costs & Expenses	-9,388.0	-7,124.9	-5,527.8	-3,591.2
Income Before Taxes and Other	-401.8	-288.0	-263.9	-132.9
Other Items	0.0	0.0	0.0	636.6
Income Tax	0.0	0.0	0.0	0.0
Net Income	-401.8	-288.0	-263.9	503.6
Cash Flow From Operations	-98.0	-753.5	-184.1	-722.3
Balance Sheet (000's)				
Cash & Equivalents	382.0	311.2	1,233.0	1,609.5
Total Current Assets	1,995.2	1,918.8	2,104.9	2,540.5
Fixed Assets, Net	66.6	31.9	23.4	23.1
Total Assets	2,079.5	1,975.7	2,139.7	2,577.7
Total Current Liabilities	789.4	513.6	423.4	597.5
Long-Term Debt	1,016.6	847.5	820.0	820.0
Stockholders' Equity	269.0	608.2	896.3	1,160.2
Performance & Financial Condition				
Return on Total Revenues %	-4.47	-4.21	-5.01	14.56
Return on Avg Stockholders' Equity %	-91.60	-38.29	-25.67	55.44
Return on Average Assets %	-19.81	-14.00	-11.19	17.20
Current Ratio	2.53	3.74	4.97	4.25
Debt / Equity %	377.93	139.34	91.49	70.68

Compound Growth %'s	EPS % n.a.	Net Income % n.a.	Total Revenues % 37.47

Comments

This young energetic company is gradually establishing itself as a recognizable brand name. Revenue was 33.7% higher in 1998 which management credits to continued acceptance of the natural products industry. But advertising also had something to do with it as the Company spent $600,000 more, a total of $1,675,000, on marketing programs. Despite the losses, a reasonably sound financial condition has been maintained, albeit small. At some point management will have to focus on bottom line profitability and perhaps use some of the $11.3 million of tax loss carryovers that have accumulated.

Officers	Position	Ownership Information	
Arthur Gray, Jr.	Chairman	Number of Shares Outstanding	2,428,791
Jeffrey A. Hollender	President, CEO	Market Capitalization	$ 1,748,730
Jeffrey M. Phillips	Exec VP	Number of Shareholders	1,200
Charles J. Hogan	Controller	Where Listed / Symbol	OTC-BB / SVNG

Other Information			
Transfer Agent	Continental Stock Transfer & Trust Co. New York, NY	SIC Code	5961
Auditor	PricewaterhouseCoopers LLP	Employees	8
Market Maker	Paragon Capital Corporation (800)345-0505	Web Site	seventhgen.com
	Wien Securities Corp. (800)624-0050		

Shopsmith, Inc.

6530 Poe Avenue   Dayton, OH 45414   Telephone (937)898-6070   Fax (937)890-5197

Company Description

Shopsmith, Inc. produces and markets power woodworking tools and other woodworking products designed primarily for the home workshop. Products are distributed directly to consumers through demonstration and mail selling channels. The name Shopsmith is a registered trademark which the Company applies to the majority of its products. During fiscal 1994, as an element of a restructuring plan, the Company sold 12 and closed the remainder of its 44 retail stores in order to generate cash for operations. The Shopsmith trademark, which dates back to 1946, was purchased by the Company in 1972.

	04/04/98	04/05/97	03/30/96	04/01/95
Per Share Information				
Stock Price as of 12/31	1.12	2.50	2.37	1.19
Earnings Per Share	0.61	0.66	1.13	0.56
Price / Earnings Ratio	1.84	3.79	2.10	2.13
Book Value Per Share	1.97	1.36	0.68	-0.46
Price / Book Value %	56.85	183.82	348.53	n.a.
Dividends Per Share	0.0	0.0	0.0	0.0
Annual Financial Data				
Operating Results (000's)				
Total Revenues	19,014.8	18,599.5	17,466.7	17,728.9
Costs & Expenses	-17,462.6	-16,797.0	-15,952.8	-16,391.6
Income Before Taxes and Other	1,552.2	1,802.6	1,513.9	1,420.7
Other Items	0.0	0.0	770.8	0.0
Income Tax	120.0	0.0	743.0	0.0
Net Income	1,672.2	1,802.6	3,027.7	1,420.7
Cash Flow From Operations	841.3	1,433.3	1,233.4	2,041.2
Balance Sheet (000's)				
Cash & Equivalents	316.7	1,106.9	560.2	360.9
Total Current Assets	6,945.3	5,435.5	3,849.5	3,799.2
Fixed Assets, Net	486.7	524.2	608.6	613.0
Total Assets	8,076.6	6,548.8	5,024.2	4,415.3
Total Current Liabilities	2,908.1	2,928.1	3,214.7	4,717.0
Long-Term Debt	0.0	0.0	0.0	426.4
Stockholders' Equity	5,168.4	3,620.7	1,809.5	-1,224.7
Performance & Financial Condition				
Return on Total Revenues %	8.79	9.69	17.33	8.01
Return on Avg Stockholders' Equity %	38.05	66.39	1,035.50	n.a.
Return on Average Assets %	22.87	31.15	64.15	24.82
Current Ratio	2.39	1.86	1.20	0.81
Debt / Equity %	n.a.	n.a.	n.a.	n.a.

Compound Growth %'s	EPS %	2.89	Net Income %	5.58	Total Revenues %	2.36

Comments

The Company has not had to incur income tax expense in any of the years above due to tax loss carryovers. Fiscal 1998 and 1996 actually reflect income tax credits. 1996 results include a nonrecurring gain of $770,824 ($.29 per share) from the extinguishment of debt. As a result of its restructuring efforts, the Company showed profits in the last four years and a substantial improvement in working capital, so much so that 62,000 of its shares were reacquired as treasury stock. Is the Company out of the woods? Maybe not. For the nine months ended December 31, 1998, the Company reported revenue and a net loss of $11.0 million and $401,353 ($.15 per share) as compared to $12.8 million and a net profit of $942,443 ($.34 per share) for the same period of fiscal 1998.

Officers	Position	Ownership Information	
John R. Folkerth	President, CEO	Number of Shares Outstanding	2,624,375
William C. Becker	VP - Finance, CFO	Market Capitalization	$ 2,939,300
Robert L. Folkerth	VP - Sales	Number of Shareholders	2,703
J. Michael Herr	Director	Where Listed / Symbol	OTC-BB / SHOP

Other Information			
Transfer Agent	Fifth Third Bank Cincinnati, OH	SIC Code	3550
Auditor	Crowe, Chizek and Company LLP	Employees	112
Market Maker	Wedbush Morgan Securities Inc.	(800)421-0251	Web Site	shopsmith.com
	Wm. V. Frankel & Co., Inc.	(800)631-3091		

Sierra Monitor Corporation

1991 Tarob Court   Milpitas, CA 95035   Telephone (408)262-6611   Fax (408)262-9042

Company Description

Sierra Monitor Corporation designs and develops hazardous gas monitoring devices for the protection of personnel and facilities in industrial work places. Products are sold primarily to oil, gas and chemical companies; waste-water treatment plants; parking garages, and landfill projects. The Company's products are primarily for the fixed installation market which characteristically requires higher levels of technical capability in developing and selling its products. A high level of research and development is maintained to enhance existing products and to develop new products. These expenditures averaged approximately 8% of sales during the past four years.

	12/31/98	12/31/97	12/31/96	12/31/95
Per Share Information				
Stock Price	0.81	0.19	0.34	0.50
Earnings Per Share	0.02	0.02	0.01	0.0
Price / Earnings Ratio	40.50	9.50	34.00	n.a.
Book Value Per Share	0.27	0.24	0.23	0.21
Price / Book Value %	300.00	79.17	147.83	238.10
Dividends Per Share	0.0	0.0	0.0	0.0
Annual Financial Data				
Operating Results (000's)				
Total Revenues	7,013.0	5,158.6	5,068.6	4,803.9
Costs & Expenses	-6,691.6	-5,017.6	-4,928.7	-4,773.4
Income Before Taxes and Other	321.5	141.1	139.9	30.5
Other Items	0.0	0.0	0.0	0.0
Income Tax	-100.7	48.1	9.5	-12.5
Net Income	220.7	189.2	149.4	18.0
Cash Flow From Operations	239.5	134.2	-50.1	13.3
Balance Sheet (000's)				
Cash & Equivalents	393.7	297.5	478.9	310.6
Total Current Assets	3,016.2	2,847.0	2,747.1	2,619.9
Fixed Assets, Net	232.6	137.9	84.7	101.5
Total Assets	3,708.2	3,032.5	2,924.1	2,800.3
Total Current Liabilities	738.3	477.3	568.1	605.7
Long-Term Debt	0.0	0.0	0.0	0.0
Stockholders' Equity	2,969.9	2,555.2	2,356.1	2,194.5
Performance & Financial Condition				
Return on Total Revenues %	3.15	3.67	2.95	0.38
Return on Avg Stockholders' Equity %	7.99	7.70	6.57	0.83
Return on Average Assets %	6.55	6.35	5.22	0.66
Current Ratio	4.09	5.96	4.84	4.33
Debt / Equity %	n.a.	n.a.	n.a.	n.a.

Compound Growth %'s	EPS %	41.42	Net Income %	130.50	Total Revenues %	13.44

Comments

The Company posted a 36.1% increase in revenues for 1998 with no changes in selling practices. A strong construction market caused higher demand for the Company's digital gas monitoring instruments and a single order for analog based gas sensor modules to an international customer accounted for approximately 6.5% of sales. Pre-tax earnings increased 128%. 1998 was the first time in three years that a normal income tax expense was required to be recorded. Although small, the Company maintains a strong balance sheet. With nearly 11 million common shares outstanding, Sierra Monitor should continue to be branded as a penny stock. How many pennies is the only question.

Officers	Position	Ownership Information	
Gordon R. Arnold	CEO, President	Number of Shares Outstanding	10,967,588
Michael C. Farr	Vice President	Market Capitalization	$ 8,883,746
Stephen R. Ferree	Vice President	Number of Shareholders	355
Edward K. Hague	Vice President	Where Listed / Symbol	OTC-BB / SRMC

Other Information			
Transfer Agent	U.S. Stock Transfer Corp. Glendale, CA	SIC Code	3829
Auditor	KPMG LLP	Employees	40
Market Maker	Herzog, Heine, Geduld, Inc.	(800)221-3600	
	Paragon Capital Corporation	(800)521-8877	

Sight Resource Corporation

100 Jeffrey Avenue Holliston, MA 01746 Telephone (508)429-6916 Fax (508)429-6023

Company Description

Sight Resource Corporation manufactures, distributes and sells eyewear and related products and services. As of December 31, 1998 the Company's operations consisted of 93 eye care centers, with three regional optical laboratories and distribution centers, making it the seventeenth largest provider in the primary eye care industry. The Company's eye care centers operate primarily under the brand names Cambridge Eye Doctors, E.B. Brown Opticians, Vision Plaza and Vision World. The Company also provides or administers the business functions of optometrists, ophthalmologists and professional corporations that provide vision-related professional services. In addition, as of December 31, 1998 the Company operates two laser vision correction centers.

	12/31/98	12/31/97	12/31/96	12/31/95
Per Share Information				
Stock Price	2.00	3.62	4.56	10.62
Earnings Per Share	-0.11	-0.46	-0.78	-0.89
Price / Earnings Ratio	n.a.	n.a.	n.a.	n.a.
Book Value Per Share	2.13	2.21	2.63	2.59
Price / Book Value %	93.90	163.80	173.38	410.04
Dividends Per Share	0.0	0.0	0.0	0.0
Annual Financial Data				
Operating Results (000's)				
Total Revenues	55,313.0	45,674.0	30,486.0	18,777.0
Costs & Expenses	-56,228.0	-47,653.0	-36,311.0	-23,665.0
Income Before Taxes and Other	-915.0	-1,979.0	-5,825.0	-4,888.0
Other Items	0.0	0.0	0.0	0.0
Income Tax	-70.0	-25.0	-25.0	0.0
Net Income	-985.0	-2,004.0	-5,850.0	-4,888.0
Cash Flow From Operations	232.0	-2,365.0	-2,557.0	-3,696.0
Balance Sheet (000's)				
Cash & Equivalents	1,860.0	6,076.0	9,924.0	8,035.0
Total Current Assets	9,479.0	12,668.0	14,562.0	10,428.0
Fixed Assets, Net	6,140.0	5,664.0	4,935.0	5,778.0
Total Assets	32,145.0	34,507.0	31,430.0	23,249.0
Total Current Liabilities	6,303.0	8,425.0	6,788.0	5,101.0
Long-Term Debt	184.0	0.0	1,600.0	1,000.0
Stockholders' Equity	18,959.0	19,446.0	22,766.0	16,445.0
Performance & Financial Condition				
Return on Total Revenues %	-1.78	-4.39	-19.19	-26.03
Return on Avg Stockholders' Equity %	-5.13	-9.49	-29.84	-32.80
Return on Average Assets %	-2.96	-6.08	-21.40	-26.31
Current Ratio	1.50	1.50	2.15	2.04
Debt / Equity %	0.97	n.a.	7.03	6.08

Compound Growth %'s	EPS % n.a.	Net Income % n.a.	Total Revenues %	43.35

Comments

The increase in 1998 revenues as compared to 1997 relates to the acquisition of additional centers and the full year operation of centers acquired in 1997. Our general rule of thumb in selecting penny stocks is to identify companies that have demonstrated profitability. One important exception are companies that are heavily trending towards profitability. This is the case with Sight Resource Corporation as can be seen from the declining losses. The prudent investor will pay close attention to quarterly results. At December 31, 1998, the Company had $15.3 million of intangible assets recorded on its ledgers which equated to approximately 81% of stockholders' equity and book value per share. Also at the end of 1998, the Company had tax loss carryforwards of $18.9 million available to offset future income.

Officers	Position	Ownership Information	
William G. McLendon	Chairman	Number of Shares Outstanding	8,905,730
William T. Sullivan	President, CEO	Market Capitalization	$ 17,811,460
James W. Norton	CFO	Number of Shareholders	4,000
Paul Mueller	Controller	Where Listed / Symbol	NASDAQ / VISN

Other Information			
Transfer Agent	American Stock Transfer & Trust Company New York, NY	SIC Code	3845
Auditor	KPMG LLP	Employees	616
		Web Site	sightresource.com

SigmaTron International, Inc.

2201 Landmeier Road   Elk Grove Village, IL 60007   Telephone (847)956-8000   Fax (847)956-8280

Company Description

Sigmatron International, Inc. is an independent contract manufacturer of electronic components, printed circuit board assemblies and completely assembled electronic products. Included among the wide range of services the Company offers its customers are: 1) automatic and manual assembly and testing of products, 2) material sourcing and procurement, 3) design, manufacturing and test engineering support, 4) warehousing and shipment services, and 5) assistance in obtaining product approvals from governmental and other regulatory bodies. The Company provides these services through facilities located in North America and the Far East. The Company operates manufacturing facilities in Elk Grove Village, Illinois; Las Vegas, Nevada; and Acuna, Mexico. The Company was founded in 1993 and had its initial public offering in 1994.

	04/30/98	04/30/97	04/30/96	04/30/95
Per Share Information				
Stock Price as of 12/31	2.69	10.00	n.a.	n.a.
Earnings Per Share	0.18	1.11	0.86	0.69
Price / Earnings Ratio	14.94	9.01	n.a.	n.a.
Book Value Per Share	6.11	5.92	4.66	3.80
Price / Book Value %	44.03	168.92	n.a.	n.a.
Dividends Per Share	0.0	0.0	0.0	0.0
Annual Financial Data				
Operating Results (000's)				
Total Revenues	86,130.1	87,621.1	69,984.3	45,441.0
Costs & Expenses	-84,717.1	-82,385.4	-65,989.8	-42,152.6
Income Before Taxes and Other	836.9	5,160.6	3,751.8	3,031.6
Other Items	0.0	0.0	0.0	0.0
Income Tax	-311.0	-1,905.6	-1,385.0	-1,141.0
Net Income	525.9	3,255.1	2,366.8	1,890.6
Cash Flow From Operations	554.0	1,457.7	-1,536.9	-1,620.5
Balance Sheet (000's)				
Cash & Equivalents	284.7	323.2	2.5	2.5
Total Current Assets	32,204.0	28,719.6	27,946.6	18,002.5
Fixed Assets, Net	11,249.6	10,343.1	7,599.2	7,000.0
Total Assets	48,641.2	42,088.4	38,378.5	28,235.0
Total Current Liabilities	11,495.3	7,070.6	9,662.1	5,070.3
Long-Term Debt	15,177.7	14,714.9	12,533.2	12,763.0
Stockholders' Equity	17,603.4	17,014.6	12,768.5	10,401.7
Performance & Financial Condition				
Return on Total Revenues %	0.61	3.71	3.38	4.16
Return on Avg Stockholders' Equity %	3.04	21.86	20.43	18.91
Return on Average Assets %	1.16	8.09	7.11	8.21
Current Ratio	2.80	4.06	2.89	3.55
Debt / Equity %	86.22	86.48	98.16	122.70

Compound Growth %'s	EPS %	-36.10	Net Income %	-34.72	Total Revenues %	23.76

Comments

After years of solid growth, the Company has experienced a sales decline due to softer sales to some of the Company's key customers. This has occurred at the same time that manufacturing capacity has been increased in order to competitively position the Company for the future. Gross margins were lower in fiscal 1998 because of the costs associated with this expansion. Management's short term objective is to increase sales to take advantage of the structure that is now in place. For the nine months ended January 31, 1999, the Company reported revenues and net income of $64.6 million and $684,837 ($.24 per share) as compared to $65.5 and $472,300 ($.16 per share) for the same period of the preceding year.

Officers	Position	Ownership Information	
Gary R. Fairhead	President, CEO	Number of Shares Outstanding	2,881,227
Linda K. Blake	VP - Finance, CFO	Market Capitalization	$ 7,750,501
Nunzio A. Truppa	Vice President	Number of Shareholders	145
Gregory A. Fairhead	Vice President	Where Listed / Symbol	NASDAQ / SGMA

Other Information			
Transfer Agent	American Stock Transfer & Trust Co. New York, NY	SIC Code	3672
Auditor	Ernst & Young LLP	Employees	1,700
		Web Site	sigmatronintl.com

Signature Eyewear, Inc.

498 North Oak Street Inglewood, CA 90302 Telephone (310)330-2700 Fax (310)330-2770

Company Description

Signature Eyewear, Inc. designs, markets and distributes prescription eyeglass frames primarily under exclusive licenses for Laura Ashley Eyewear, Eddie Bauer Eyewear and Hart Schaffner & Marx Eyewear as well as its own private labels. The Laura Ashley Eyewear collection is one of the leading women's brand-name collections in the United States. The Company attributes its success to its brand-name development process and high quality, creative frame designs. The Company's brand-name development process includes identifying a market niche, obtaining the rights to a carefully selected brand name, producing a comprehensive marketing plan, developing unique in-store displays and creating innovative sales and merchandising programs for independent optical retailers and retail chains. The Company was founded in 1986 and had its initial public offering on September 15, 1997.

	10/31/98	10/31/97	10/31/96	10/31/95
Per Share Information				
Stock Price as of 12/31	4.06	7.75	3.00	n.a.
Earnings Per Share	0.52	0.61	0.36	n.a.
Price / Earnings Ratio	7.81	12.70	8.33	n.a.
Book Value Per Share	3.79	3.29	0.56	n.a.
Price / Book Value %	107.12	235.56	535.71	n.a.
Dividends Per Share	0.0	0.0	0.0	n.a.
Annual Financial Data				
Operating Results (000's)				
Total Revenues	41,303.1	33,238.9	28,309.3	23,606.0
Costs & Expenses	-36,694.5	-29,525.1	-26,296.7	-21,969.9
Income Before Taxes and Other	4,608.6	3,713.8	2,012.6	1,636.1
Other Items	0.0	0.0	0.0	0.0
Income Tax	-1,859.0	-1,374.0	-0.8	-1.4
Net Income	2,749.6	2,339.8	2,011.8	1,634.7
Cash Flow From Operations	-2,279.4	1,055.5	1,393.8	1,000.0
Balance Sheet (000's)				
Cash & Equivalents	4,256.7	8,133.4	214.4	28.7
Total Current Assets	23,548.1	19,963.9	8,988.9	6,462.0
Fixed Assets, Net	1,473.0	1,079.5	1,040.4	798.0
Total Assets	25,151.3	21,175.3	10,293.1	7,260.0
Total Current Liabilities	5,736.4	3,859.5	7,207.0	4,602.0
Long-Term Debt	0.0	0.0	156.9	712.0
Stockholders' Equity	19,414.9	17,311.6	2,929.1	1,946.0
Performance & Financial Condition				
Return on Total Revenues %	6.66	7.04	7.11	n.a.
Return on Avg Stockholders' Equity %	14.97	23.12	82.53	116.47
Return on Average Assets %	11.87	14.87	22.92	26.22
Current Ratio	4.11	5.17	1.25	n.a.
Debt / Equity %	n.a.	n.a.	5.36	n.a.

Compound Growth %'s	EPS %	20.19	Net Income %	18.93	Total Revenues %	20.50

Comments

The increase in sales from fiscal 1997 to fiscal 1998 resulted from the launch of Eddie Bauer Eyewear. Sales in the Laura Ashley Eyewear lines actually decreased 3.8% in the same period. Gross margins improved as lower cost frame manufacturers were utilized in the last year. The Company switched from Subchapter S status at the time of the public offering. For fiscal 1997, income taxes have been provided on a pro forma basis as if the Company had been subject to regular income tax for the entire year. The public offering provided a generous amount of working capital with no long term debt required. The Company is positioned to utilize its creativity to expand existing product lines.

Officers	Position	Ownership Information	
Bernard Weiss	Chairman, CEO	Number of Shares Outstanding	5,119,337
Julie Heldman	Chairman, President	Market Capitalization	$ 20,784,508
Michael Prince	CFO	Number of Shareholders	1,000
Maurice Buchsbaum	Director	Where Listed / Symbol	NASDAQ / SEYE

Other Information			
Transfer Agent	American Stock Transfer & Trust Co. New York, NY	SIC Code	3851
Auditor	Altschuler, Melvoin & Glasser	Employees	130
		Web Site	signatureeyewear.com

Simtek Corporation

1465 Kelly Johnson Boulevard, Suite 301   Colorado Springs, CO 80920   Telephone (719)531-9444   Fax (719)531-9481

Company Description

Simtek Corporation designs, develops, produces and markets high performance nonvolatile semiconductor memories. Nonvolatility prevents loss of programs and data when electrical power is removed. Simtek's products are targeted for use in commercial electronic equipment markets such industrial control systems, office automation, medical instrumentation, telecommunication systems and cable television as well as numerous military systems including communications, radar, sonar and smart weapons. The Company was founded in 1987.

	12/31/98	12/31/97	12/31/96	12/31/95
Per Share Information		•		
Stock Price	0.15	0.35	0.16	0.11
Earnings Per Share	0.01	0.03	0.01	-0.09
Price / Earnings Ratio	15.00	11.67	16.00	n.a.
Book Value Per Share	0.06	0.06	0.03	0.02
Price / Book Value %	250.00	583.33	533.33	n.a.
Dividends Per Share	0.0	0.0	0.0	0.0
Annual Financial Data				
Operating Results (000's)				
Total Revenues	6,388.0	6,690.2	5,219.0	2,670.1
Costs & Expenses	-6,225.3	-5,901.6	-5,074.5	-4,601.1
Income Before Taxes and Other	162.8	788.6	144.5	-1,931.0
Other Items	0.0	0.0	0.0	0.0
Income Tax	0.0	0.0	0.0	0.0
Net Income	162.8	788.6	144.5	-1,931.0
Cash Flow From Operations	-476.3	564.1	291.3	-1,499.9
Balance Sheet (000's)				
Cash & Equivalents	2,149.8	1,475.6	964.5	311.9
Total Current Assets	3,958.2	3,056.6	1,910.9	780.5
Fixed Assets, Net	221.1	177.8	229.0	344.7
Total Assets	4,239.9	3,234.4	2,139.9	1,125.2
Total Current Liabilities	907.7	1,574.2	1,291.6	671.3
Long-Term Debt	1,500.0	0.0	0.0	0.0
Stockholders' Equity	1,832.2	1,660.2	848.3	453.9
Performance & Financial Condition				
Return on Total Revenues %	2.55	11.79	2.77	-72.32
Return on Avg Stockholders' Equity %	9.32	62.88	22.20	-326.79
Return on Average Assets %	4.36	29.35	8.85	-112.00
Current Ratio	4.36	1.94	1.48	1.16
Debt / Equity %	81.87	n.a.	n.a.	n.a.

Compound Growth %'s	EPS %	0.00	Net Income %	6.13	Total Revenues %	33.75

Comments

1998 revenues were negatively affected due to the impact that the struggling Far East economies had on product demand. Still, the Company managed to remain marginally profitable. The reversal of a prior year accrued expense, amounting to approximately $100,000, helped the bottom line. The last three years has seen the Company's conversion from a development stage enterprise to one that can generate net income and positive cash flow from operations. Research and development continued with $1,380,649 in expenses in 1998, up 17.0% from 1997. The long development stage period has left its mark with 28.7 million common shares outstanding.

Officers	Position	Ownership Information	
Richard L. Petritz	Chairman, CFO	Number of Shares Outstanding	28,745,226
Douglas M. Mitchell	President, CEO	Market Capitalization	$ 4,311,784
Klaus C. Wiemer	Director	Number of Shareholders	5,000
Robert Keeley	Director	Where Listed / Symbol	OTC-BB / SRAM

Other Information			
Transfer Agent	Continental Stock Transfer & Trust Co. New York, NY	SIC Code	3674
Auditor	Hein & Associates LLP	Employees	23
Market Maker	Herzog, Heine, Geduld, Inc. (800)221-3600	Web Site	simtek.com
	Josephthal Lyon & Ross Inc. (800)242-4400		

Sizzler International, Inc.

6101 West Centinela Avenue   Culver City, CA 90230   Telephone (310)568-0135   Fax (310)568-8255

Company Description

Sizzler International, Inc. operates 97 and licenses 251 Sizzler restaurants worldwide and operates 98 KFC (formerly Kentucky Fried Chicken) restaurants in Australia. Sizzler restaurants operate in the mid-scale dining market featuring a selection of grilled steak, chicken and seafood entrees, sandwiches and specialty platters, as well as a fresh fruit and salad bar in a family dining environment. Sizzler restaurants follow a semi-service system, whereby guests place their order and pay upon entering the restaurant and then are seated. The Company was founded in 1991 in a transaction whereby Collins Foods, Inc. spun off various operating divisions. On June 2, 1996, in response to continued operating losses, the Company filed for bankruptcy protection under Chapter 11 of the United States Bankruptcy Code. On September 23, 1997, the Company emerged from bankruptcy.

	04/30/98	04/30/97	04/30/96	04/30/95
Per Share Information				
Stock Price as of 12/31	2.31	2.69	2.87	4.25
Earnings Per Share	0.19	0.02	-4.99	0.24
Price / Earnings Ratio	12.16	134.50	n.a.	17.71
Book Value Per Share	1.52	1.54	1.57	6.38
Price / Book Value %	151.97	174.68	182.80	66.61
Dividends Per Share	0.0	0.0	0.08	0.16
Annual Financial Data				
Operating Results (000's)				
Total Revenues	243,604.0	301,106.0	437,185.0	463,465.0
Costs & Expenses	-236,001.0	-307,857.0	-570,782.0	-452,345.0
Income Before Taxes and Other	7,603.0	-6,751.0	-133,597.0	11,120.0
Other Items	0.0	0.0	0.0	0.0
Income Tax	-2,225.0	7,316.0	-4,861.0	-4,425.0
Net Income	5,378.0	565.0	-138,458.0	6,695.0
Cash Flow From Operations	1,618.0	-1,980.0	2,935.0	29,052.0
Balance Sheet (000's)				
Cash & Equivalents	21,167.0	34,085.0	9,216.0	12,220.0
Total Current Assets	29,707.0	46,270.0	23,455.0	33,975.0
Fixed Assets, Net	79,210.0	104,875.0	135,231.0	222,679.0
Total Assets	119,461.0	168,110.0	178,547.0	276,654.0
Total Current Liabilities	26,840.0	30,369.0	63,185.0	39,417.0
Long-Term Debt	35,497.0	329.0	7,041.0	17,100.0
Stockholders' Equity	43,760.0	44,401.0	43,467.0	177,070.0
Performance & Financial Condition				
Return on Total Revenues %	2.21	0.19	-31.67	1.44
Return on Avg Stockholders' Equity %	12.20	1.29	-125.56	3.75
Return on Average Assets %	3.74	0.33	-60.83	2.42
Current Ratio	1.11	1.52	0.37	0.86
Debt / Equity %	81.12	0.74	16.20	9.66

Compound Growth %'s	EPS %	-7.49	Net Income %	-7.04	Total Revenues %	-19.30

Comments

Revenues decreased over the last several years as a result of downsizing. Liabilities subject to compromise under the reorganization proceedings, $83.9 million as of April 30, 1997, have been satisfied. Fiscal 1996 results include a restructuring charge of $108.9 million ($3.92 per share). Although the Company has emerged from bankruptcy and is reporting profits, it still operates with little working capital. For the nine months ended January 31, 1999, revenues and net income were $171.7 million and $4,877,000 ($.17 per share) as compared to $186.2 million and $3,018,000 ($.11 per share) for the same period of the preceding year. Let's throw a steak on the barbie as we wait for year end results.

Officers	Position	Ownership Information	
James A. Collins	Chairman, CEO	Number of Shares Outstanding	28,840,908
Kevin W. Perkins	Exec VP	Market Capitalization	$ 66,622,497
Christopher R. Thomas	Exec VP	Number of Shareholders	2,849
Ryan S. Tondro	Vice President, CFO	Where Listed / Symbol	NYSE / SZ

Other Information			
Transfer Agent	Bank of New York New York, NY	SIC Code	5812
Auditor	Arthur Andersen LLP	Employees	7,000

Smith-Midland Corporation

Route 28, P.O. Box 300   Midland, VA 22728   Telephone (540)439-3266   Fax (540)439-3275

Company Description

Smith-Midland Corporation invents, develops, manufactures, markets, leases, licenses, sells, and installs a broad array of precast concrete products for use primarily in the construction, transportation and utilities industries. The Company's customers are primarily general contractors and federal, state and local transportation authorities located in the Mid-Atlantic and Northeastern regions of the United States. The Company's operating strategy has involved producing innovative and proprietary products, including lightweight, energy efficient concrete and steel exterior wall panel for use in building construction, a positive-connected highway safety barrier, a sound barrier primarily for roadside use, and transportable concrete buildings. The Company was founded in 1960 and had its initial public offering in 1995.

	12/31/98	12/31/97	12/31/96	12/31/95
Per Share Information				
Stock Price	1.00	0.78	1.06	4.62
Earnings Per Share	-0.26	0.09	-0.10	-0.82
Price / Earnings Ratio	n.a.	8.67	n.a.	n.a.
Book Value Per Share	0.42	0.67	0.59	0.58
Price / Book Value %	238.10	116.42	179.66	796.55
Dividends Per Share	0.0	0.0	0.0	0.0
Annual Financial Data				
Operating Results (000's)				
Total Revenues	14,762.0	12,322.9	11,732.2	11,399.3
Costs & Expenses	-15,545.9	-12,059.1	-12,030.6	-12,928.8
Income Before Taxes and Other	-783.9	263.8	-298.5	-1,529.4
Other Items	0.0	0.0	0.0	0.0
Income Tax	0.0	0.0	0.0	0.0
Net Income	-783.9	263.8	-298.5	-1,529.4
Cash Flow From Operations	-284.8	526.0	-428.9	-1,528.6
Balance Sheet (000's)				
Cash & Equivalents	207.7	288.3	438.1	938.1
Total Current Assets	5,859.0	5,452.3	4,880.1	4,985.4
Fixed Assets, Net	2,449.6	1,531.1	1,380.9	1,430.3
Total Assets	9,566.5	7,892.2	7,194.9	7,157.3
Total Current Liabilities	4,172.4	4,964.5	4,222.3	3,526.5
Long-Term Debt	4,020.7	759.4	1,068.1	1,837.5
Stockholders' Equity	1,268.8	2,052.7	1,788.9	1,793.3
Performance & Financial Condition				
Return on Total Revenues %	-5.31	2.14	-2.54	-13.42
Return on Avg Stockholders' Equity %	-47.20	13.73	-16.66	-142.85
Return on Average Assets %	-8.98	3.50	-4.16	-23.53
Current Ratio	1.40	1.10	1.16	1.41
Debt / Equity %	316.89	37.00	59.71	102.46

Compound Growth %'s	EPS % n.a.	Net Income % n.a.	Total Revenues %	9.00

Comments

In 1998, the Company began work on a contract to renovate the Bradley Hall building at Rutgers University. While executing the construction, the original structure was found to be structurally insufficient to support the initial redesign. This lead to cost overruns that have been approximated at $1.2 million and a total loss on the contract of approximately $1.0 million. The loss has been accrued in its entirety in 1998. The Company plans to seek additional compensation of $1.2 million and has accrued $400,000 as accounts receivable at December 31, 1998. At that date, the Company also had $2.7 million of tax loss carryovers available to offset future taxable income.

Officers	Position	Ownership Information	
Rodney I. Smith	President, CEO	Number of Shares Outstanding	3,044,798
Theodore D. Pennington	VP - Finance, CFO	Market Capitalization	$ 3,044,798
Wesley Taylor	Vice President	Number of Shareholders	500
Ashley Smith	Vice President	Where Listed / Symbol	NASDAQ / SMID

Other Information			
Transfer Agent	American Securities Transfer, Inc. Denver, CO	SIC Code	3272
Auditor	BDO Seidman LLP	Employees	136
		Web Site	smithmid.com

SofTech, Inc.

4695 44th Street S.E., Suite B-130   Grand Rapids, MI 49512   Telephone (616)957-2330   Fax (616)956-0077

Company Description

SofTech, Inc. is a provider of Computer Aided Design (CAD), Computer Aided Management (CAM), and Product Data Management (PDM) solutions and was the largest reseller of Parametric Technology Corporation's (PTC) software. During fiscal 1998, the Company terminated its reseller agreement with PTC and acquired four businesses including two CAD/CAM technology companies, a CAD/CAM and PDM services business, and a structural dynamics research company. As a result, the Company has eliminated its dependence upon technology providers and now possesses technology of its own, more than 100 degreed mechanical engineers, and a stable, recurring service business. The Company has 25 offices in 16 states and 4 offices in Western Europe along with indirect distribution relationships in Asia. The Company was founded in 1969 and went public in 1981.

	05/31/98	05/31/97	05/31/96	05/31/95
Per Share Information				
Stock Price as of 12/31	2.31	2.56	2.62	3.75
Earnings Per Share	0.23	0.09	-1.44	-0.60
Price / Earnings Ratio	10.04	28.44	n.a.	n.a.
Book Value Per Share	1.76	1.31	3.65	5.11
Price / Book Value %	131.25	195.42	71.78	73.39
Dividends Per Share	0.0	0.0	0.0	0.0
Annual Financial Data				
Operating Results (000's)				
Total Revenues	20,232.0	16,830.0	13,658.0	10,542.0
Costs & Expenses	-18,771.0	-14,551.0	-14,094.0	-10,466.0
Income Before Taxes and Other	1,461.0	2,279.0	-436.0	76.0
Other Items	0.0	-1,856.0	-5,401.0	-2,303.0
Income Tax	-127.0	3.0	-20.0	-94.0
Net Income	1,334.0	426.0	-5,857.0	-2,321.0
Cash Flow From Operations	-770.0	4,274.0	686.0	-4,335.0
Balance Sheet (000's)				
Cash & Equivalents	429.0	580.0	3,017.0	2,372.9
Total Current Assets	12,221.0	6,069.0	14,271.0	21,666.2
Fixed Assets, Net	2,280.0	1,478.0	994.0	2,338.9
Total Assets	36,060.0	10,158.0	17,037.0	28,745.1
Total Current Liabilities	19,740.0	3,149.0	2,080.0	8,051.3
Long-Term Debt	4,900.0	0.0	0.0	0.0
Stockholders' Equity	11,182.0	6,837.0	14,957.0	20,693.8
Performance & Financial Condition				
Return on Total Revenues %	6.59	2.53	-42.88	-22.02
Return on Avg Stockholders' Equity %	14.81	3.91	-32.86	-11.18
Return on Average Assets %	5.77	3.13	-25.59	-8.62
Current Ratio	0.62	1.93	6.86	2.69
Debt / Equity %	43.82	n.a.	n.a.	n.a.

Compound Growth %'s	EPS % n.a.	Net Income % n.a.	Total Revenues %	24.27

Comments

The large increase in fiscal 1998 revenue was attributable to the acquisitions referred to above which were accounted for under the purchase method of accounting. Therefore, results of operations have been combined starting with the dates of acquisitions. Management was pleased to terminate the relationship with PTC as the Company was too dependent on an uncertain situation. A division known as the Network Systems Group was sold during 1996. Revenues reflected above exclude this discontinued operation. Losses from discontinued operations were $1.9 million, $5.4 million, and $2.3 million in fiscal 1997, 1996 and 1995, respectively. For the nine months ended February 28, 1999, the Company reported revenues of $25.4 million and a net loss of $1,611,000 ($.23 per share) as compared to revenues of $14.3 million and a net profit of $1,073,000 ($.18 per share) in fiscal 1998.

Officers	Position	Ownership Information	
Mark R. Sweetland	President, CEO	Number of Shares Outstanding	6,350,542
Timothy J. Weatherford	Exec VP	Market Capitalization	$ 14,669,752
Joseph P. Mullaney	Vice President, CFO	Number of Shareholders	311
Jeanne Naysmith	Vice President	Where Listed / Symbol	NASDAQ / SOFT

Other Information			
Transfer Agent	State Street Bank & Trust Co. Boston, MA	SIC Code	7373
Auditor	Ernst & Young LLP	Employees	214
		Web Site	softech.com

Solomon-Page Group Ltd. (The)

1140 Avenue of the Americas   New York, NY 10036   Telephone (212)403-6100   Fax (212)764-9261

Company Description

The Solomon-Page Group Ltd. is a specialty niche provider of staffing services organized into two primary operating divisions: executive search/full-time contingency recruitment and temporary staffing and consulting. The executive search and full-time contingency recruitment division has nine lines of business, including four industry (capital markets, publishing and new media, healthcare and fashion services), and five functional (information technology, accounting, human resources, legal and administrative support). The temporary staffing and consulting division provides services to companies seeking personnel in the information technology, accounting and human resources areas. The Company was formed in 1993 and succeeded a predecessor company with the same name through a merger. The predecessor company commenced operations in 1990.

	09/30/98	09/30/97	09/30/96	09/30/95
Per Share Information				
Stock Price as of 12/31	1.50	3.62	1.75	0.56
Earnings Per Share	0.14	0.20	0.13	-0.39
Price / Earnings Ratio	10.71	18.10	13.46	n.a.
Book Value Per Share	1.57	1.62	1.37	1.24
Price / Book Value %	95.54	223.46	127.74	n.a.
Dividends Per Share	0.0	0.0	0.0	0.0
Annual Financial Data				
Operating Results (000's)				
Total Revenues	44,768.5	29,166.7	17,435.3	7,605.4
Costs & Expenses	-43,235.9	-27,331.8	-16,705.7	-9,490.6
Income Before Taxes and Other	1,532.6	1,834.9	729.5	-1,958.3
Other Items	0.0	0.0	0.0	0.0
Income Tax	-710.0	-552.5	-19.2	30.4
Net Income	822.6	1,282.4	710.3	-1,927.8
Cash Flow From Operations	-473.2	292.4	-650.1	-2,094.4
Balance Sheet (000's)				
Cash & Equivalents	935.5	409.9	2,113.6	4,445.2
Total Current Assets	11,945.3	8,985.0	7,713.9	6,254.9
Fixed Assets, Net	2,114.5	1,457.4	938.8	1,072.4
Total Assets	16,735.1	12,815.5	9,613.2	7,641.6
Total Current Liabilities	8,150.9	4,063.7	2,183.6	853.1
Long-Term Debt	0.0	0.0	0.0	0.0
Stockholders' Equity	8,039.6	8,331.5	7,065.4	6,355.0
Performance & Financial Condition				
Return on Total Revenues %	1.84	4.40	4.07	-25.35
Return on Avg Stockholders' Equity %	10.05	16.66	10.59	-55.06
Return on Average Assets %	5.57	11.44	8.23	-38.25
Current Ratio	1.47	2.21	3.53	7.33
Debt / Equity %	n.a.	n.a.	n.a.	n.a.

Compound Growth %'s	EPS %	3.77	Net Income %	7.61	Total Revenues %	80.56

Comments

The 54% increase in fiscal 1998 revenue was comprised of an 86% increase in revenues from the temporary staffing/consulting division and a 22% increase in revenues from the recruiting division. Costs were higher as well, partly caused by the need to provide an infrastructure for business expansion. Fiscal 1998 is the only year presented that had the burden of a full income tax provision. Pre-tax income declined 16.5% from the fiscal 1997 level. However, 1997 net income included charges of approximately $300,000 relating to the startup of its accounting and human resource temporary staffing and consulting business and a $200,000 charge relating to a potentially uncollectible receivable.

Officers	Position	Ownership Information	
Herbert Solomon	Chairman	Number of Shares Outstanding	5,121,282
Scott Page	President	Market Capitalization	$ 7,681,923
Lloyd Solomon	CEO	Number of Shareholders	1,300
Eric M. Davis	VP - Finance, CFO	Where Listed / Symbol	NASDAQ / SOLP

Other Information			
Transfer Agent	American Stock Transfer & Trust Co. New York, NY	SIC Code	7361
Auditor	Moore Stephens, P.C.	Employees	136
		Web Site	solomonpagegroup.com

Sonics & Materials, Inc.

53 Church Hill Road   Newton, CT 06470   Telephone (203)270-4600   Fax (203)270-4610

Company Description

Sonics & Materials, Inc. designs, manufactures and sells 1) ultrasonic bonding equipment for the welding, joining and fastening of thermoplastic components, textiles and other synthetic materials, and 2) ultrasonic liquid processors for dispensing, blending, cleaning, degassing, atomizing and reducing particles as well as expediting chemical reactions. Robert Soloff, president and founder, invented the ultrasonic plastic welding process early in his career and has been granted nine patents. He is considered to be a pioneer in the application of ultrasonic technology to industrial processes. The Company was founded in 1969. On July 25, 1997, the Company acquired Tooltex, Inc., a manufacturer of automated systems used in the plastics industry.

	06/30/98	06/30/97	06/30/96	06/30/95
Per Share Information				
Stock Price as of 12/31	0.56	0.75	4.00	4.00
Earnings Per Share	-0.11	0.01	0.08	0.22
Price / Earnings Ratio	n.a.	75.00	50.00	18.18
Book Value Per Share	1.83	1.94	1.90	2.14
Price / Book Value %	30.60	38.66	210.53	186.92
Dividends Per Share	0.0	0.0	0.0	0.0
Annual Financial Data				
Operating Results (000's)				
Total Revenues	12,331.5	10,938.0	9,421.4	8,602.6
Costs & Expenses	-12,688.4	-10,889.6	-8,985.1	-7,822.9
Income Before Taxes and Other	-356.9	48.4	436.3	939.7
Other Items	0.0	0.0	0.0	0.0
Income Tax	-39.6	-19.4	-174.5	-375.9
Net Income	-396.5	29.1	261.8	563.8
Cash Flow From Operations	-707.3	-773.9	-426.6	56.1
Balance Sheet (000's)				
Cash & Equivalents	503.3	271.6	73.1	187.5
Total Current Assets	8,211.4	7,877.1	8,525.7	4,285.5
Fixed Assets, Net	4,409.9	364.4	301.7	277.8
Total Assets	14,677.8	9,159.1	9,180.5	4,985.4
Total Current Liabilities	3,875.7	1,934.8	2,515.2	2,101.6
Long-Term Debt	4,345.7	406.9	0.0	0.0
Stockholders' Equity	6,456.4	6,817.4	6,665.3	2,883.8
Performance & Financial Condition				
Return on Total Revenues %	-3.22	0.27	2.78	6.55
Return on Avg Stockholders' Equity %	-5.97	0.43	5.48	14.10
Return on Average Assets %	-3.33	0.32	3.70	9.40
Current Ratio	2.12	4.07	3.39	2.04
Debt / Equity %	67.31	5.97	n.a.	n.a.

Compound Growth %'s	EPS % n.a.	Net Income % n.a.	Total Revenues % 12.75

Comments

The increase in revenue is the result of the acquisition of Tooltex. Sales would have otherwise declined 2.5% due to lower sales in Asia and the Pacific Rim partially offset by increased domestic sales volume. The acquisition also resulted in higher administrative costs causing a loss for fiscal 1998. Prior to the Company going public in 1996, it was a subchapter S corporation. The operating results presented above for fiscal 1995 and 1996 are on a pro forma basis as if the corporation had been subject to income tax in those years. For the six months ended December 31, 1998, revenues and net income were $6.4 million and $120,885 ($.03 per share) as compared to $5.9 million and $43,532 ($.01 per share) for the same period of the preceding year.

Officers	Position	Ownership Information	
Robert S. Soloff	President, CEO	Number of Shares Outstanding	3,520,100
Lauren H. Soloff	Vice President, Secretary	Market Capitalization	$ 1,971,256
Richard H. Berger	Vice President	Number of Shareholders	500
Christopher S. Andrade	Controller	Where Listed / Symbol	NASDAQ / SIMA

Other Information			
Transfer Agent	American Stock Transfer & Trust Co. New York, NY	SIC Code	3559
Auditor	Schneider Ehrlich & Wengrover	Employees	120
		Web Site	sonicsandmaterials.com

Sono-Tek Corporation

2012 Route 9W, Building 3   Milton, NY 12547   Telephone (914)795-2020   Fax (914)795-2720

Company Description

Sono-Tek Corporation, since its formation in 1975, has been engaged in the development, manufacture, assembly, and sale of ultrasonic liquid atomizing units (nozzle systems) consisting of 1) a nozzle based on patented technology, and 2) an electrical power supply and related hardware. Nozzle systems atomize low-to-medium viscosity liquids used in industrial spray processes by converting electrical energy into mechanical motion in the form of high-frequency (ultrasonic) vibrations which break liquids into minute drops that can be applied to surfaces at low-velocity. The Company is continuously striving to improve the performance and versatility of its nozzle systems, as well as searching for new industry applications.

	02/28/98	02/28/97	02/29/96	02/28/95
Per Share Information				
Stock Price as of 12/31	0.16	0.56	0.25	0.69
Earnings Per Share	0.05	0.04	0.04	-0.12
Price / Earnings Ratio	3.20	14.00	6.25	n.a.
Book Value Per Share	0.06	-0.01	-0.05	-0.08
Price / Book Value %	266.67	n.a.	n.a.	n.a.
Dividends Per Share	0.0	0.0	0.0	0.0
Annual Financial Data				
Operating Results (000's)				
Total Revenues	3,570.7	3,114.9	2,808.3	2,571.6
Costs & Expenses	-3,318.7	-2,962.2	-2,653.2	-3,054.6
Income Before Taxes and Other	252.0	152.6	155.1	-483.1
Other Items	0.0	0.0	0.0	0.0
Income Tax	0.0	0.0	0.0	0.0
Net Income	252.0	152.6	155.1	-483.1
Cash Flow From Operations	88.2	170.6	56.3	-3.6
Balance Sheet (000's)				
Cash & Equivalents	113.8	107.7	69.0	67.8
Total Current Assets	1,555.6	1,136.2	1,038.4	978.4
Fixed Assets, Net	122.0	56.6	95.9	151.9
Total Assets	1,728.7	1,251.9	1,199.7	1,211.2
Total Current Liabilities	864.2	716.4	725.6	784.3
Long-Term Debt	577.8	576.1	657.9	754.4
Stockholders' Equity	278.6	-41.3	-193.9	-349.0
Performance & Financial Condition				
Return on Total Revenues %	7.06	4.90	5.52	-18.78
Return on Avg Stockholders' Equity %	212.45	n.a.	n.a.	n.a.
Return on Average Assets %	16.91	12.45	12.86	-33.94
Current Ratio	1.80	1.59	1.43	1.25
Debt / Equity %	207.43	n.a.	n.a.	n.a.

Compound Growth %'s	EPS %	11.80	Net Income %	27.49	Total Revenues %	11.56

Comments

Despite several new product introductions in fiscal 1998, most of the 15% advance in revenue was attributable to the SonoFlux 9500 nozzle system, the latest version of which was introduced in 1995. A strong performance allowed the Company to expend $410,000 in research and development costs during the last year, up from $369,000 in the preceding year. $3.2 million in tax loss carryovers remained available at February 28, 1998, to offset future income. For the nine months ended November 30, 1998, there were revenues and a net loss of $2.4 million and $201,053 ($.05 per share) as compared to $2.6 million and a net income of $157,436 ($.04 per share) for the same period of the preceding year.

Officers	Position	Ownership Information	
Samuel Schwartz	Chairman	Number of Shares Outstanding	4,374,387
Harvey L. Berger	President	Market Capitalization	$ 699,902
James L. Kehoe	CEO	Number of Shareholders	309
Kathleen N. Martin	CFO, Treasurer	Where Listed / Symbol	OTC-BB / SOTK

Other Information

Transfer Agent	American Stock Transfer & Trust Co. New York, NY		SIC Code	3559
Auditor	Deloitte & Touche LLP		Employees	28
Market Maker	Carr Securities Corporation	(800)221-2243	Web Site	sono-tek.com
	Herzog, Heine, Geduld, Inc.	(800)221-3600		

Southland Corporation (The)

2711 North Haskell Avenue   Dallas, TX 75204-2906   Telephone (214)828-7011   Fax (214)841-6799

Company Description

The Southland Corporation, soon to become 7-Eleven, Inc., operates 5,560 7-Eleven and 66 other convenience stores in the United States and Canada. Area licensees, or other franchisees, operate approximately 15,300 additional 7-Eleven convenience stores in certain areas of the United States and in 18 foreign countries. The Company's net sales are comprised of sales of groceries, take-out foods and beverages, gasoline (at certain locations), dairy products, non-food merchandise, specialty items and services. Approximately 65% of the Company is owned by IYG Holding Company, a joint venture of two large Japanese companies. The Company traces its roots back to when a Southland Ice Company employee met the needs of his customers by selling bread, milk and eggs from the steps of his ice dock. Hence, the convenience retail industry began.

	12/31/98	12/31/97	12/31/96	12/31/95
Per Share Information				
Stock Price	1.91	2.06	2.94	3.12
Earnings Per Share	0.17	0.16	0.20	0.65
Price / Earnings Ratio	11.24	12.88	14.70	4.80
Book Value Per Share	-1.57	-1.76	-1.92	-2.15
Price / Book Value %	n.a.	n.a.	n.a.	n.a.
Dividends Per Share	0.0	0.0	0.0	0.0
Annual Financial Data				
Operating Results (000's)				
Total Revenues	7,349,811.0	7,060,557.0	6,955,263.0	6,824,278.0
Costs & Expenses	-7,267,198.0	-6,945,262.0	-6,824,439.0	-6,722,749.0
Income Before Taxes and Other	82,613.0	115,295.0	130,824.0	101,529.0
Other Items	23,324.0	0.0	0.0	103,169.0
Income Tax	-31,889.0	-45,253.0	-41,348.0	66,065.0
Net Income	74,048.0	70,042.0	89,476.0	270,763.0
Cash Flow From Operations	232,812.0	197,946.0	261,040.0	236,217.0
Balance Sheet (000's)				
Cash & Equivalents	26,880.0	38,605.0	36,494.0	43,047.0
Total Current Assets	438,602.0	386,641.0	350,900.0	356,107.0
Fixed Assets, Net	1,652,932.0	1,416,687.0	1,349,839.0	1,335,783.0
Total Assets	2,415,844.0	2,090,081.0	2,039,148.0	2,081,117.0
Total Current Liabilities	668,559.0	729,649.0	674,932.0	720,127.0
Long-Term Debt	2,168,843.0	1,594,545.0	1,638,828.0	2,041,782.0
Stockholders' Equity	-642,211.0	-721,527.0	-788,955.0	-880,792.0
Performance & Financial Condition				
Return on Total Revenues %	1.01	0.99	1.29	3.97
Return on Avg Stockholders' Equity %	n.a.	n.a.	n.a.	n.a.
Return on Average Assets %	3.29	3.39	4.34	13.27
Current Ratio	0.66	0.53	0.52	0.49
Debt / Equity %	n.a.	n.a.	n.a.	n.a.

Compound Growth %'s	EPS %	-36.05	Net Income %	-35.09	Total Revenues %	2.50

Comments

Despite having over $2 billion of debt, the Company has reported a net profit in every year since 1992. 1998 and 1995 results include $23.3 million ($.05 per share) and $103.2 million ($.25 per share), respectively, of nonrecurring gains from debt restructuring. 1996 was favorably affected by a $20 million nonrecurring tax settlement. Management knows what they have to do; they must achieve higher merchandise sales increases, lower product cost, and better manage expenses. A major effort to install point-of-sale registers is almost complete, with the system becoming fully operational by the fall of 1999. This should go along way in providing on-line management information. Our conclusion: "7-Eleven, oh thank heaven".

Officers	Position	Ownership Information	
Clark J. Matthews, II	President, CEO	Number of Shares Outstanding	409,922,935
James W. Keyes	Exec VP, CFO	Market Capitalization	$ 782,952,806
Rodney A. Brehm	Senior VP	Number of Shareholders	20,000
Bryan F. Smith, Jr.	Senior VP	Where Listed / Symbol	NASDAQ / SLCM

Other Information			
Transfer Agent	Harris Trust Co. of New York New York, NY	SIC Code	5411
Auditor	PricewaterhouseCoopers LLP	Employees	32,368
		Web Site	7-eleven.com

Spanlink Communications, Inc.

7125 Northland Terrace   Minneapolis, MN 55428   Telephone (612)971-2000   Fax (612)971-2300

Company Description

Spanlink Communications, Inc. designs, develops and markets interactive computer telecommunications software and services that link business computer systems, telephone systems and the Internet. The Company markets its specialized software systems through its sales organization and licensed sales representatives throughout North America. In December 1997, the Company acquired the FastCall product line, including all intellectual property and intangible assets, from Comdial Corporation. The acquisition will be paid for by royalties on future product revenues. The Company was formed in 1988 and went public in 1995.

	12/31/98	12/31/97	12/31/96	12/31/95
Per Share Information				
Stock Price	3.81	2.00	3.25	n.a.
Earnings Per Share	0.05	-0.42	-0.66	0.07
Price / Earnings Ratio	76.20	n.a.	n.a.	n.a.
Book Value Per Share	0.66	0.60	1.02	-0.07
Price / Book Value %	577.27	333.33	318.63	n.a.
Dividends Per Share	0.0	0.0	0.0	0.0
Annual Financial Data				
Operating Results (000's)				
Total Revenues	11,083.2	6,723.0	5,567.2	4,340.4
Costs & Expenses	-10,819.3	-8,868.6	-8,401.8	-4,154.2
Income Before Taxes and Other	264.0	-2,145.5	-2,834.6	186.2
Other Items	0.0	0.0	0.0	0.0
Income Tax	0.0	0.0	0.0	-1.9
Net Income	264.0	-2,145.5	-2,834.6	184.3
Cash Flow From Operations	-982.2	-3,200.0	-2,465.9	402.7
Balance Sheet (000's)				
Cash & Equivalents	11.4	703.7	2,285.0	344.7
Total Current Assets	5,404.5	3,978.8	6,797.2	1,376.8
Fixed Assets, Net	1,227.1	1,264.2	837.5	223.3
Total Assets	7,261.1	5,854.6	7,634.7	1,600.1
Total Current Liabilities	3,538.0	2,378.0	2,457.7	1,779.0
Long-Term Debt	365.9	0.0	0.0	0.0
Stockholders' Equity	3,357.1	3,031.5	5,177.0	-179.0
Performance & Financial Condition				
Return on Total Revenues %	2.38	-31.91	-50.92	4.25
Return on Avg Stockholders' Equity %	8.26	-52.28	-113.43	n.a.
Return on Average Assets %	4.02	-31.81	-61.39	6.14
Current Ratio	1.53	1.67	2.77	0.77
Debt / Equity %	10.90	n.a.	n.a.	n.a.

Compound Growth %'s	EPS %	-10.61	Net Income %	12.72	Total Revenues %	36.68

Comments

Total revenues increased 67% in 1998. All product lines reflected strong growth, with the largest gains occuring in packaged software, hardware and services. This success reflects management's earlier decision to shift focus towards delivering packaged software products rather than customized software. Research and development expense totaled $1,282,549 and $1,463,905 in 1998 and 1997, respectively, from ongoing development of the Company's packaged software products and core software modules. We were pleased to include Spanlink in the first edition of Walker's Manual of Penny Stocks but we are even more pleased that the Company reported a net profit in 1998, something that we were not expecting. At December 31, 1998, the Company had $4.6 million of tax loss carryovers available to offset future income.

Officers	Position	Ownership Information	
Brett A. Shockley	President, CEO	Number of Shares Outstanding	5,105,289
Loren A. Singer, Jr.	Secretary	Market Capitalization	$ 19,451,151
Timothy E. Briggs	Vice President, CFO	Number of Shareholders	1,500
Stephen H. Bostwick	Vice President	Where Listed / Symbol	NASDAQ / SPLK

Other Information			
Transfer Agent	Norwest Bank Minnesota, N.A. South St. Paul, MN	SIC Code	3661
Auditor	PricewaterhouseCoopers LLP	Employees	95
		Web Site	spanlink.com

Sparta Foods, Inc.

1565 First Avenue, N.W. New Brighton, MN 55112 Telephone (612)697-5500 Fax (612)697-0600

Company Description

Sparta Foods, Inc. manufactures a broad line of Mexican food products which include corn and flour tortillas, stone ground and corn flour tortilla chips, picante sauce and other salsas and sauces. These products are distributed under the Company's own brand names and under private labels. The Company's products include Cruz, La Canasta and La Campana Paradiso tortillas; La Canasta, and La Campana Paradiso tortilla chips, and La Canasta and Chapala salsas and picante sauces. The Company's branded retail products are sold in supermarkets located primarily in the midwestern United States.

	09/30/98	09/30/97	09/30/96	09/30/95
Per Share Information				
Stock Price as of 12/31	1.12	1.53	1.25	0.37
Earnings Per Share	0.08	0.05	0.01	-0.24
Price / Earnings Ratio	14.00	30.60	125.00	n.a.
Book Value Per Share	0.60	0.52	0.45	0.43
Price / Book Value %	186.67	294.23	277.78	86.05
Dividends Per Share	0.0	0.0	0.0	0.0
Annual Financial Data				
Operating Results (000's)				
Total Revenues	15,122.2	14,184.6	12,748.8	11,992.0
Costs & Expenses	-14,692.7	-13,351.8	-12,638.5	-12,701.7
Income Before Taxes and Other	429.5	457.7	110.3	-989.2
Other Items	0.0	0.0	0.0	0.0
Income Tax	265.0	-22.0	-5.0	45.4
Net Income	694.5	435.7	105.3	-943.8
Cash Flow From Operations	920.3	1,049.4	305.5	111.2
Balance Sheet (000's)				
Cash & Equivalents	1,131.3	0.6	0.6	0.9
Total Current Assets	3,088.7	2,088.1	1,452.9	1,646.9
Fixed Assets, Net	6,256.9	5,117.7	3,734.7	4,099.1
Total Assets	10,721.2	10,897.3	7,007.0	7,554.5
Total Current Liabilities	1,343.7	3,360.1	1,933.4	3,172.8
Long-Term Debt	2,667.6	4,051.2	2,063.6	2,636.9
Stockholders' Equity	6,709.9	3,486.1	3,010.0	1,744.8
Performance & Financial Condition				
Return on Total Revenues %	4.59	3.07	0.83	-7.87
Return on Avg Stockholders' Equity %	13.62	13.42	4.43	-56.45
Return on Average Assets %	6.43	4.87	1.45	-12.09
Current Ratio	2.30	0.62	0.75	0.52
Debt / Equity %	39.76	116.21	68.56	151.13

Compound Growth %'s	EPS % 182.84	Net Income % 156.81	Total Revenues % 8.04

Comments

Revenues increased 6% despite the loss of the Company's primary private label barbecue sauce customer. Sales to the remaining largest customer represented 25% of total 1998 revenue. Fiscal 1998 was also burdened with costs associated with the move to a new facility. A favorable tax credit arose from the expectation of using tax loss carryovers. Remaining carryovers totaled $2.3 million at September 30, 1998. A $2.5 million preferred stock placement was completed on February 24, 1998, greatly improving working capital and reducing long term debt.

Officers	Position	Ownership Information	
Michael J. Kozlak	Chairman	Number of Shares Outstanding	7,037,172
Joel P. Bachul	President, CEO	Market Capitalization	$ 7,881,633
A. Merrill Ayers	Secretary, Treasurer	Number of Shareholders	182
Thomas C. House	Vice President	Where Listed / Symbol	NASDAQ / SPFO

Other Information			
Transfer Agent	Norwest Bank Minnesota, N.A. South St. Paul, MN	SIC Code	2090
Auditor	McGladrey & Pullen, LLP	Employees	143
		Web Site	spartafoods.com

SpectraLink Corporation

5755 Central Avenue   Boulder, CO 80301   Telephone (303)440-5330   Fax (303)440-5331

Company Description

SpectraLink Corporation designs, manufactures and sells on-premises wireless telephone systems which complement existing telephone systems by providing mobile communications in a building or campus environment. The SpectraLink Pocket Communications System increases the efficiency of employees by enabling them to remain in telephone contact while moving throughout the workplace. The system uses a micro-cellular design consisting of three components: a Master Control Unit (MCU), Remote Cell Units (RCUs) and Pocket Telephones (PTs). The Company's proprietary MCU interfaces directly with a PBX, Centrex or key/hybrid system. The MCU also connects with the system's RCUs, which are small radio transceivers located throughout the customer's facility that relay calls between the six-ounce Pocket Telephones and the telephone system. Calls are handed off from one RCU to another as a user moves throughout the facility. The Company was founded in 1990 and went public in 1996.

	12/31/98	12/31/97	12/31/96	12/31/95
Per Share Information				
Stock Price	3.50	2.81	2.62	7.00
Earnings Per Share	0.11	-0.03	0.14	0.08
Price / Earnings Ratio	31.82	n.a.	18.71	87.50
Book Value Per Share	2.03	1.96	2.01	2.12
Price / Book Value %	172.41	143.37	130.35	330.19
Dividends Per Share	0.0	0.0	0.0	0.0
Annual Financial Data				
Operating Results (000's)				
Total Revenues	36,621.0	29,321.0	22,688.0	16,839.0
Costs & Expenses	-34,413.0	-29,885.0	-20,002.0	-15,603.0
Income Before Taxes and Other	2,208.0	-564.0	2,686.0	1,236.0
Other Items	0.0	0.0	0.0	0.0
Income Tax	-133.0	4.0	-134.0	-57.0
Net Income	2,075.0	-560.0	2,552.0	1,179.0
Cash Flow From Operations	1,446.0	-2,205.0	1,446.0	-428.0
Balance Sheet (000's)				
Cash & Equivalents	9,019.0	5,674.0	7,334.0	1,729.0
Total Current Assets	38,822.0	31,645.0	30,773.0	8,894.0
Fixed Assets, Net	2,780.0	2,628.0	1,621.0	1,000.0
Total Assets	43,716.0	41,299.0	40,464.0	10,026.0
Total Current Liabilities	5,028.0	3,742.0	1,960.0	1,703.0
Long-Term Debt	190.0	0.0	0.0	0.0
Stockholders' Equity	38,498.0	37,426.0	38,504.0	8,004.0
Performance & Financial Condition				
Return on Total Revenues %	5.67	-1.91	11.25	7.00
Return on Avg Stockholders' Equity %	5.47	-1.48	10.97	5.13
Return on Average Assets %	4.88	-1.37	10.11	4.72
Current Ratio	7.72	8.46	15.70	5.22
Debt / Equity %	0.49	n.a.	n.a.	n.a.

Compound Growth %'s	EPS %	11.20	Net Income %	20.74	Total Revenues %	29.56

Comments

The 26% increase in 1998 revenue as compared to 1997 was predominantly due to the continued growing acceptance of SpectraLink systems in the marketplace and the expected improvement in reseller channels. Management is taking nothing for granted as research and development of new products continues. $3.8 million was expended for the R & D effort in 1998, compared to $3.5 million in 1997. The Company is in excellent financial condition with nearly $25 million in cash and investments at December 31, 1998.

Officers	Position	Ownership Information	
Bruce M. Holland	President, CEO	Number of Shares Outstanding	18,951,000
William R. Mansfield	VP - Finance, CFO	Market Capitalization	$ 66,328,500
Gary L. Bliss	Vice President	Number of Shareholders	2,000
E. Ronald Elswick	Vice President	Where Listed / Symbol	NASDAQ / SLNK

Other Information			
Transfer Agent	Boston EquiServe Boston, MA	SIC Code	3663
Auditor	Arthur Andersen LLP	Employees	265
		Web Site	spectralink.com

Spectrum Control, Inc.

6000 West Ridge Road   Erie, PA 16506   Telephone (814)835-4000   Fax (814)835-1600

Company Description

Spectrum Control, Inc. designs, manufactures and markets a broad line of control products and systems. The Company was founded 29 years ago as a solutions-oriented company, designing and manufacturing products to suppress or eliminate electromagnetic interference (EMI). The Company has adapted its core EMI filter technology into a complete line of capacitors, filters, filtered arrays, and filtered connectors. In recent years, the Company has expanded its focus by developing new lines of power products and specialty ceramic products. The Company's products are used in virtually all industries worldwide, including telecommunications, aerospace, military, medical, computer, and industrial controls.

	11/30/98	11/30/97	11/30/96	11/30/95
Per Share Information				
Stock Price as of 12/31	3.75	5.25	3.18	2.87
Earnings Per Share	0.36	0.37	0.32	0.28
Price / Earnings Ratio	10.42	14.19	9.94	10.25
Book Value Per Share	3.10	2.73	2.36	2.05
Price / Book Value %	120.97	192.31	134.75	140.00
Dividends Per Share	0.0	0.0	0.0	0.0
Annual Financial Data				
Operating Results (000's)				
Total Revenues	59,953.0	56,607.0	57,347.0	49,297.0
Costs & Expenses	-53,634.0	-51,097.0	-52,610.0	-45,202.0
Income Before Taxes and Other	6,319.0	5,510.0	4,737.0	4,095.0
Other Items	0.0	0.0	0.0	0.0
Income Tax	-2,385.0	-1,536.0	-1,319.0	-1,111.0
Net Income	3,934.0	3,974.0	3,418.0	2,984.0
Cash Flow From Operations	8,274.0	8,506.0	4,998.0	6,028.0
Balance Sheet (000's)				
Cash & Equivalents	739.0	196.0	413.0	202.0
Total Current Assets	24,379.0	22,837.0	22,995.0	21,115.0
Fixed Assets, Net	16,289.0	15,979.0	16,017.0	16,752.0
Total Assets	44,139.0	40,056.0	40,213.0	39,498.0
Total Current Liabilities	5,760.0	5,956.0	10,461.0	11,148.0
Long-Term Debt	2,500.0	3,330.0	4,072.0	6,569.0
Stockholders' Equity	33,774.0	29,545.0	25,379.0	21,781.0
Performance & Financial Condition				
Return on Total Revenues %	6.56	7.02	5.96	6.05
Return on Avg Stockholders' Equity %	12.43	14.47	14.50	14.79
Return on Average Assets %	9.34	9.90	8.58	7.69
Current Ratio	4.23	3.83	2.20	1.89
Debt / Equity %	7.40	11.27	16.04	30.16

Compound Growth %'s	EPS %	8.74	Net Income %	9.65	Total Revenues %	6.74

Comments

Despite a decline in average selling prices as a result of competitive and market pressures, revenues increased 6% reflecting higher shipment volume of the Company's commercial custom assemblies which consist of telecommunication racks, power supplies, and industrial controls. Changes in the sales mix were responsible for keeping gross margins near fiscal 1997 levels. Income tax expense was higher as a percentage of net income in fiscal 1998. Pre-tax income actually rose 14.7%. The Company has a record of consistent profits and a solid financial condition.

Officers	Position	Ownership Information	
Richard A. Southworth	President, CEO	Number of Shares Outstanding	10,887,008
John P. Freeman	CFO	Market Capitalization	$ 40,826,280
Melvin Kutchin	Director	Number of Shareholders	2,300
John M. Petersen	Director	Where Listed / Symbol	NASDAQ / SPEC

Other Information			
Transfer Agent	ChaseMellon Shareholder Services Ridgefield Park, NJ	SIC Code	3679
Auditor	Ernst & Young LLP	Employees	792
		Web Site	spectrumcontrol.com

Sports Club Company, Inc. (The)

Company Description

The Sports Club Company, Inc. operates sports and fitness clubs under the names the Sports Club, and the Spectrum Club. The Company, founded in 1994, owns interests in thirteen clubs. Eleven of the clubs are located in southern California, and one each in Las Vegas and New York City. An additional nine clubs are under development. The Company's strategy is to expand its business to meet the public's demand for facilities offering a wide variety of sports, fitness and social activities. The Company believes the sports and fitness industry remains highly fragmented, with a predominance of smaller operators at the lower end of the market and that opportunities exist for the Company to operate multi-amenity sports and fitness clubs at the higher end of the market.

	12/31/98	12/31/97	12/31/96	12/31/95
Per Share Information				
Stock Price	4.00	9.25	2.88	3.12
Earnings Per Share	0.21	0.12	0.15	0.14
Price / Earnings Ratio	19.05	77.08	19.20	22.29
Book Value Per Share	5.32	4.11	3.67	3.52
Price / Book Value %	75.19	225.06	78.47	88.64
Dividends Per Share	0.0	0.0	0.0	0.0
Annual Financial Data				
Operating Results (000's)				
Total Revenues	82,803.0	61,850.0	37,549.0	35,519.0
Costs & Expenses	-72,677.0	-57,249.0	-34,213.0	-32,591.0
Income Before Taxes and Other	10,126.0	2,576.0	3,036.0	2,928.0
Other Items	-2,173.0	-22.0	-150.0	-150.0
Income Tax	-3,971.0	-1,014.0	-1,183.0	-1,139.0
Net Income	3,982.0	1,540.0	1,703.0	1,639.0
Cash Flow From Operations	10,020.0	4,548.0	3,625.0	3,466.0
Balance Sheet (000's)				
Cash & Equivalents	2,233.0	1,581.0	3,419.0	1,545.0
Total Current Assets	7,043.0	4,926.0	7,341.0	7,147.0
Fixed Assets, Net	135,269.0	106,791.0	72,736.0	59,956.0
Total Assets	163,757.0	131,561.0	95,584.0	83,106.0
Total Current Liabilities	26,199.0	26,844.0	13,562.0	10,818.0
Long-Term Debt	29,695.0	42,823.0	36,027.0	31,023.0
Stockholders' Equity	104,539.0	58,477.0	41,686.0	39,974.0
Performance & Financial Condition				
Return on Total Revenues %	4.81	2.49	4.54	4.61
Return on Avg Stockholders' Equity %	4.89	3.07	4.17	4.21
Return on Average Assets %	2.70	1.36	1.91	1.99
Current Ratio	0.27	0.18	0.54	0.66
Debt / Equity %	28.41	73.23	86.42	77.61

Compound Growth %'s	EPS %	14.47	Net Income %	34.43	Total Revenues %	32.60

Comments

Revenue grew $20.7 million, or 33.8% during 1998. $14.6 million of the increase resulted from revenue at clubs that were opened during the last six months of 1997 and $6.1 million resulted from the remaining clubs. Bottom line profits were impressive. The Company issued 6.5 million shares during 1998 in connection with a secondary offering. The proceeds were used to pay off debt and increase working capital. 1998 results include a nonrecurring loss of $2,173,000 ($.12 per share) related to the early extinguishment of debt. At December 31, 1998, the Company had $15.4 million of goodwill reflected on the books as assets which equates to only 15% of stockholders' equity and book value per share.

Officers	Position	Ownership Information	
D. Michael Talla	Chairman, CEO	Number of Shares Outstanding	19,637,932
John M. Gibbons	President, COO	Market Capitalization	$ 78,551,728
Nanette P. Francini	Exec VP, Secretary	Number of Shareholders	4,000
Timothy O'Brien	CFO	Where Listed / Symbol	AMEX / SCY

Other Information			
Transfer Agent	American Stock Transfer & Trust Co. New York, NY	SIC Code	7997
Auditor	KPMG LLP	Employees	2,250

Stearns & Lehman, Inc.

30 Paragon Parkway   Mansfield, OH 44903   Telephone (419)522-2722   Fax (419)522-1152

Company Description

Stearns & Lehman, Inc. is engaged in the business of manufacturing and marketing specialty food products, including coffee and espresso flavorings, syrups, oils and toppings, extracts, flavorings, sauces, dressings and specialty sugars. The Company sells its products throughout the United States and in certain foreign countries. Since its incorporation in 1988, the Company has grown from providing a single product line and having two employees, to being a major manufacturer and supplier of flavoring syrups for the specialty coffee industry with 51 employees.

	04/30/98	04/30/97	04/30/96	04/30/95
Per Share Information				
Stock Price as of 12/31	2.50	5.00	6.00	6.50
Earnings Per Share	0.20	0.13	-0.26	0.06
Price / Earnings Ratio	12.50	38.46	n.a.	108.33
Book Value Per Share	1.68	1.47	1.02	1.05
Price / Book Value %	148.81	340.14	588.24	619.05
Dividends Per Share	0.0	0.0	0.0	0.0
Annual Financial Data				
Operating Results (000's)				
Total Revenues	9,259.2	7,395.1	5,514.8	5,558.8
Costs & Expenses	-8,428.0	-7,089.4	-6,247.7	-5,350.3
Income Before Taxes and Other	831.1	305.7	-732.9	206.6
Other Items	0.0	0.0	0.0	0.0
Income Tax	-171.4	96.6	0.0	-49.9
Net Income	659.7	402.3	-732.9	156.7
Cash Flow From Operations	102.6	453.0	-500.0	-335.3
Balance Sheet (000's)				
Cash & Equivalents	272.3	730.8	123.0	640.7
Total Current Assets	3,556.3	2,956.6	1,889.9	2,567.6
Fixed Assets, Net	3,300.2	2,235.5	1,644.3	1,016.8
Total Assets	7,514.2	5,780.4	4,212.0	4,212.0
Total Current Liabilities	1,156.5	1,050.8	924.4	924.4
Long-Term Debt	802.4	0.0	408.4	63.9
Stockholders' Equity	5,504.1	4,727.3	2,879.2	2,879.2
Performance & Financial Condition				
Return on Total Revenues %	7.13	5.44	-13.29	2.82
Return on Avg Stockholders' Equity %	12.90	10.58	-25.46	6.88
Return on Average Assets %	9.92	8.05	-17.40	4.51
Current Ratio	3.08	2.81	2.04	2.78
Debt / Equity %	14.58	n.a.	14.18	2.22

Compound Growth %'s	EPS %	49.38	Net Income %	61.47	Total Revenues %	18.54

Comments

Fiscal 1998 revenues advanced 25.2% led by strong increases in syrup sales. An increase in flavored syrup sales was primarily the result of significant sales growth by several of the Company's private label customers. Branded label syrup sales also increased with the acquisition of three existing labels and the return of a major customer that had been lost in 1996. A new manufacturing facility permitted the Company to improve manufacturing efficiencies which resulted in improved margins. For the nine months ended January 31, 1999, the Company reported revenues and net income of $7.8 million and $389,793 ($.12 per share) as compared to $6.8 million and $412,808 ($.13 per share) for the same period of the preceding year.

Officers	Position	Ownership Information	
William C. Stearns	President	Number of Shares Outstanding	3,272,665
John A. Chuprinko	CFO	Market Capitalization	$ 8,181,663
Sally A. Stearns	Vice President	Number of Shareholders	780
Frank E. Duval	Director	Where Listed / Symbol	NASDAQ / SLHN

Other Information			
Transfer Agent	First-Knox National Bank Mt. Vernon, OH	SIC Code	2087
Auditor	PricewaterhouseCoopers LLP	Employees	51
		Web Site	stearns-lehman.com

Strategic Capital Resources, Inc.

Company Description

Strategic Capital Resources, Inc., formerly JJFN Services, Inc., purchases fully furnished model homes and leases back the units to homebuilders on a triple net basis. The leases are perpetual, providing for payment of rentals without abatement until the model is sold, typically within 18 to 24 months of lease commencement. The Company also has a land acquisition program that is also tied to contracts with homebuilders to purchase the lots. The Company was formed in November 1995.

	06/30/98	06/30/97	06/30/96
Per Share Information			
Stock Price as of 12/31	0.33	0.14	1.97
Earnings Per Share	-0.01	-0.01	-0.02
Price / Earnings Ratio	n.a.	n.a.	n.a.
Book Value Per Share	0.46	0.48	0.50
Price / Book Value %	71.74	29.17	394.00
Dividends Per Share	0.0	0.0	0.0
Annual Financial Data			
Operating Results (000's)			
Total Revenues	21,302.5	7,524.9	965.2
Costs & Expenses	-21,757.8	-7,874.9	-1,127.6
Income Before Taxes and Other	-455.3	-350.0	-162.4
Other Items	0.0	230.4	-22.6
Income Tax	298.0	77.0	0.0
Net Income	-157.3	-42.5	-185.0
Cash Flow From Operations	508.4	665.9	-125.7
Balance Sheet (000's)			
Cash & Equivalents	365.2	831.3	770.7
Total Current Assets	365.2	831.3	2,233.2
Fixed Assets, Net	37,781.1	29,517.0	11,245.5
Total Assets	40,186.1	32,430.3	14,727.4
Total Current Liabilities	685.1	682.6	191.9
Long-Term Debt	30,512.6	22,632.5	6,477.3
Stockholders' Equity	7,962.4	8,089.4	8,058.2
Performance & Financial Condition			
Return on Total Revenues %	-0.74	-0.57	-19.16
Return on Avg Stockholders' Equity %	-1.96	-0.53	-4.62
Return on Average Assets %	-0.43	-0.18	-2.64
Current Ratio	0.53	1.22	11.64
Debt / Equity %	383.21	279.78	80.38

Compound Growth %'s	EPS % n.a.	Net Income % n.a.	Total Revenues % n.a.

Comments

Revenues for fiscal 1998 were substantially higher as the Company recorded revenues from land development sales for the first time and increased its lease revenue and sales of model homes. Fiscal 1996 represents a short year commencing on November 2, 1995. As of June 30, 1998, the Company had purchased 246 model homes of which 75 had been sold. The Company executed a letter of intent with a major publicly-traded homebuilder to acquire four or five tracts of land having a fully-developed cost of approximately $103 million. For the six months ended December 31, 1998, the Company reported total revenues and earnings of $12.8 million and $323,472 ($.02 per share) as compared to $14.5 million (which included $8.6 million from the sale of land) and a net loss of $276,189 ($.02 per share) for the same period of the preceding year.

Officers	Position	Ownership Information	
Samuel G. Weiss	President, Secretary	Number of Shares Outstanding	17,334,085
Richard K. LeBlond III	Senior VP	Market Capitalization	$ 5,720,248
John P. Kushay	Vice President, CFO	Number of Shareholders	1,000
Joan E. Kushay	Vice President	Where Listed / Symbol	OTC-BB / SCRI

Other Information			
Transfer Agent	Company Office Boca Raton, FL	SIC Code	6532
Auditor	Horton & Company, L.L.C.	Employees	6
Market Maker	M.H. Meyerson & Co., Inc.	(800)333-3113	
	Paragon Capital Corporation	(800)345-0505	

Strategic Distribution, Inc.

3220 Tillman Drive, Suite 200   Bensalem, PA 19020   Telephone (215)633-1900   Fax (215)633-4421

Company Description

Strategic Distribution, Inc. is a provider of In-Plant Store® programs for the distribution and sale of maintenance, repair and operating (MRO) supplies to large industrial customers in the United States. The Company's In-Plant Store program permits industrial sites to outsource all aspects of their MRO procurement, storage and internal distribution; the Company takes responsibility for purchasing, receiving, stocking, issuing and delivering MRO supplies at the industrial site. In 1996 and 1997, the Company discontinued two businesses and acquired INTERMAT International Materials Management Engineers, Inc., which provides services that complement those of the In-Plant Store program. The Company was founded in 1968.

	12/31/98	12/31/97	12/31/96	12/31/95
Per Share Information				
Stock Price	2.44	4.50	7.88	7.75
Earnings Per Share	-0.03	-0.52	-0.34	0.05
Price / Earnings Ratio	n.a.	n.a.	n.a.	155.00
Book Value Per Share	1.97	2.00	2.50	1.26
Price / Book Value %	123.86	225.00	315.20	615.08
Dividends Per Share	0.0	0.0	0.0	0.0
Annual Financial Data				
Operating Results (000's)				
Total Revenues	220,087.0	172,241.0	93,888.0	52,995.0
Costs & Expenses	-221,024.0	-183,547.0	-96,477.0	-52,657.0
Income Before Taxes and Other	-937.0	-11,306.0	-2,589.0	338.0
Other Items	0.0	-4,500.0	-6,519.0	815.0
Income Tax	0.0	0.0	0.0	-149.0
Net Income	-937.0	-15,806.0	-9,108.0	1,004.0
Cash Flow From Operations	-13,890.0	-13,414.0	-14,102.0	-6,432.0
Balance Sheet (000's)				
Cash & Equivalents	1,322.0	15,941.0	35,498.0	362.0
Total Current Assets	76,128.0	73,094.0	70,946.0	19,472.2
Fixed Assets, Net	12,854.0	5,290.0	2,251.0	811.1
Total Assets	99,444.0	90,682.0	92,382.0	40,014.3
Total Current Liabilities	27,986.0	27,018.0	17,499.0	7,220.6
Long-Term Debt	7,548.0	1,469.0	587.0	5,053.7
Stockholders' Equity	61,588.0	62,094.0	73,954.0	27,390.9
Performance & Financial Condition				
Return on Total Revenues %	-0.43	-9.18	-9.70	1.89
Return on Avg Stockholders' Equity %	-1.52	-23.24	-17.97	3.85
Return on Average Assets %	-0.99	-17.27	-13.76	2.87
Current Ratio	2.72	2.71	4.05	2.70
Debt / Equity %	12.26	2.37	0.79	18.45

Compound Growth %'s	EPS % n.a.	Net Income % n.a.	Total Revenues % 60.74

Comments

The number of In-Plant Store sites increased from 101 at the end of 1997 to 134 at the end of 1998. These new sites and the growth of revenue in existing In-Plant Store facilities boosted revenue by 28.4% in 1998. The Company's larger purchasing capacity produced an additional 1% in gross margins and almost made the year profitable. Losses from discontinued operations totalled $4.5 million ($.15 per share) and $6.5 million ($.24 per share) in 1997 and 1996, respectively. The Company also expensed $8.0 million ($.27 per share) of acquired in-process research and development expense in 1997. At December 31, 1998, the Company had goodwill of $7.3 million recorded as assets which equated to only 11.8% of stockholders' equity and book value per share.

Officers	Position	Ownership Information	
John M. Sergey	President, CEO	Number of Shares Outstanding	31,281,785
Jeffery O. Beauchamp	Exec VP	Market Capitalization	$ 76,327,555
Michael F. Devine III	CFO, Secretary	Number of Shareholders	1,500
David L. Courtright	Controller	Where Listed / Symbol	NASDAQ / STRD

Other Information

Transfer Agent	Continental Stock Transfer & Trust Co. New York, NY	SIC Code	5080
Auditor	KPMG LLP	Employees	1,030
		Web Site	isacs.com

Streicher Mobile Fueling, Inc.

2720 N.W. 55th Court   Fort Lauderdale, FL 33309   Telephone (954)739-3880   Fax (954)739-3842

Company Description

Streicher Mobile Fueling, Inc. provides mobile fueling services. It primarily serves customers who operate large fleets of vehicles, such as government agencies, utilities, major trucking lines, hauling and delivery services and national courier services. Company-owned custom fuel trucks deliver fuel on a regularly scheduled or as-needed basis directly to vehicles at customers' locations, assuring the customers a dependable supply of fuel at competitive rates. Although the Company was founded in 1983, it did not become public until 1996 when it was spun off from Streicher Enterprises, Inc.

	01/31/98	01/31/97	01/31/96	01/31/95
Per Share Information				
Stock Price as of 12/31	2.50	4.37	4.37	8.37
Earnings Per Share	-0.18	-0.26	0.07	-0.03
Price / Earnings Ratio	n.a.	n.a.	62.43	n.a.
Book Value Per Share	1.72	1.93	0.26	0.19
Price / Book Value %	145.35	226.42	1,680.77	4,405.26
Dividends Per Share	0.0	0.0	0.0	0.0
Annual Financial Data				
Operating Results (000's)				
Total Revenues	43,220.6	33,876.0	24,022.6	16,676.9
Costs & Expenses	-43,516.7	-34,537.8	-23,848.8	-16,735.0
Income Before Taxes and Other	-628.6	-661.8	173.8	-58.1
Other Items	0.0	0.0	0.0	0.0
Income Tax	153.1	232.6	-75.2	7.9
Net Income	-475.4	-429.2	98.6	-50.2
Cash Flow From Operations	-1,406.6	-1,000.6	-298.1	n.a.
Balance Sheet (000's)				
Cash & Equivalents	1,411.1	2,848.0	189.5	258.1
Total Current Assets	7,031.3	7,648.0	3,163.8	2,310.0
Fixed Assets, Net	6,200.7	3,368.8	3,124.7	2,042.7
Total Assets	13,995.5	11,403.0	6,357.9	4,352.7
Total Current Liabilities	3,639.2	5,152.8	2,426.4	2,042.9
Long-Term Debt	5,915.0	1,017.8	1,116.7	2,029.7
Stockholders' Equity	4,441.3	4,961.4	385.1	280.1
Performance & Financial Condition				
Return on Total Revenues %	-1.10	-1.27	0.41	-0.30
Return on Avg Stockholders' Equity %	-10.11	-16.06	29.65	-16.72
Return on Average Assets %	-3.74	-4.83	1.84	-1.25
Current Ratio	1.93	1.48	1.30	1.13
Debt / Equity %	133.18	20.51	290.00	724.54

Compound Growth %'s	EPS % n.a.	Net Income % n.a.	Total Revenues % 37.36

Comments

Revenues increased by 27.2% in fiscal 1998 due to a 41.1% increase in gallons delivered. This increase resulted from a higher volume of fuel sales to existing customers, acquisition of new customers in existing locations, and the introduction of mobile fueling operations into additional metropolitan areas. The Company's net losses in 1998 and 1997 resulted primarily from the Company's expansion into new markets, underutilization of equipment in such markets, and increases in personnel, equipment and facilities to support current and future growth. For the nine months ended October 31, 1998, the Company reported revenues and a net loss of $22.4 million and $577,071 ($.22 per share) as compared to $21.7 million and a net loss of $294,598 ($.11 per share) for the same period of fiscal 1998.

Officers	Position	Ownership Information	
Stanley H. Streicher	President, CEO	Number of Shares Outstanding	2,575,000
Walter B. Barrett	VP - Finance, CFO	Market Capitalization	$ 6,437,500
Timothy Koshollek	Vice President	Number of Shareholders	500
Steven E. Alford	Vice President	Where Listed / Symbol	NASDAQ / FUEL

Other Information			
Transfer Agent	American Stock Transfer & Trust Co. New York, NY	SIC Code	5172
Auditor	Arthur Andersen LLP	Employees	182
		Web Site	mobilefueling.com

Sunair Electronics, Inc.

3101 S.W. Third Avenue Fort Lauderdale, FL 33315   Telephone (954)525-1505 Fax (954)765-1322

Company Description

Sunair Electronics, Inc. is engaged in the design, manufacture and sale of high frequency single sideband communications equipment utilized for long range voice and data communications in fixed station, airborne, mobile and marine para-military applications. Sunair products are marketed both domestically and internationally and are primarily intended for strategic military and other government applications. Sunair's line of equipment is composed of proprietary HF/SSB radio equipment and ancillary items sold as operating units or combined into sophisticated systems. The Company was founded in 1956.

	09/30/98	09/30/97	09/30/96	09/30/95
Per Share Information				
Stock Price as of 12/31	2.62	3.12	2.12	2.37
Earnings Per Share	0.01	0.02	-0.26	0.04
Price / Earnings Ratio	262.00	156.00	n.a.	59.25
Book Value Per Share	3.18	3.16	3.15	3.41
Price / Book Value %	82.39	98.73	67.30	n.a.
Dividends Per Share	0.0	0.0	0.0	0.0
Annual Financial Data				
Operating Results (000's)				
Total Revenues	4,000.7	3,652.4	3,173.8	3,576.6
Costs & Expenses	-3,948.7	-3,547.4	-3,280.8	-3,361.3
Income Before Taxes and Other	52.0	104.9	-107.0	215.3
Other Items	0.0	0.0	0.0	0.0
Income Tax	-14.0	-44.0	-922.2	-47.8
Net Income	38.0	60.9	-1,029.2	167.5
Cash Flow From Operations	727.0	-138.1	589.2	-398.7
Balance Sheet (000's)				
Cash & Equivalents	1,463.7	1,511.0	1,721.8	4,408.1
Total Current Assets	8,786.3	9,588.1	9,455.1	12,970.1
Fixed Assets, Net	1,025.1	915.3	966.8	1,000.0
Total Assets	12,943.2	13,663.8	13,611.0	13,981.3
Total Current Liabilities	273.0	359.2	270.0	410.8
Long-Term Debt	0.0	0.0	0.0	0.0
Stockholders' Equity	11,933.2	12,436.4	12,375.5	13,404.7
Performance & Financial Condition				
Return on Total Revenues %	0.95	1.67	-32.43	4.68
Return on Avg Stockholders' Equity %	0.31	0.49	-7.98	1.26
Return on Average Assets %	0.29	0.45	-7.46	1.21
Current Ratio	32.18	26.69	35.02	31.57
Debt / Equity %	n.a.	n.a.	n.a.	n.a.

Compound Growth %'s	EPS % n.a.	Net Income % n.a.	Total Revenues % 3.81

Comments

Domestic shipments increased 52% during fiscal 1998 but a sluggish export market brought down the overall increase to a more modest 10%. Gross margins were also lower leaving the Company marginally profitable which was all attributable to investment income for two consecutive years. Most of the large loss reported in fiscal 1996 was attributable to deferred income tax that was recorded on the liquidation of a subsidiary. Management reported that a new generation of HF digital radio communication systems is in development. Sunair is still a small company despite its longevity. Its financial condition is excellent. The failure to sustain growth in revenues and profitability is the likely reason for a stock price that is discounted from book value.

Officers	Position	Ownership Information	
Robert Uricho, Jr.	Chairman, President	Number of Shares Outstanding	3,756,270
Shirley Uricho	Secretary	Market Capitalization	$ 9,841,427
Synnott B. Durham	Treasurer, CFO	Number of Shareholders	700
James E. Laurent	Vice President	Where Listed / Symbol	AMEX / SNR

Other Information			
Transfer Agent	American Stock Transfer & Trust Co. New York, NY	SIC Code	3663
Auditor	Puritz and Weintraub, LLP	Employees	44

Sunrise International Leasing Corporation

5500 Wayzata Boulevard, Suite 725 Golden Valley, MN 55416 Telephone (612)593-1904 Fax (612)513-3299

Company Description

Sunrise International Leasing Corporation provides its customers with lease financing for a full range of data processing, telecommunications and other capital equipment. Customers, representing a variety of industry segments, are located throughout the United States. The Company uses master lease agreements with its customers, under which equipment is leased through lease schedules, each of which has its own lease term and constitutes a separate lease agreement. The growth in the equipment leasing industry has occurred principally because users have determined that the benefits of higher productivity and profit can be obtained from the use of capital equipment, not necessarily from its ownership, and that leasing can be significantly more flexible than other methods of acquiring equipment. The Company was founded in 1989.

	03/31/98	03/31/97	03/31/96	03/31/95
Per Share Information				
Stock Price as of 12/31	3.50	2.62	3.50	3.25
Earnings Per Share	0.29	-0.35	0.35	-0.93
Price / Earnings Ratio	12.07	n.a.	10.00	n.a.
Book Value Per Share	3.98	3.72	4.08	3.73
Price / Book Value %	87.94	70.43	85.78	87.13
Dividends Per Share	0.0	0.0	0.0	0.0
Annual Financial Data				
Operating Results (000's)				
Total Revenues	49,272.0	42,978.0	43,488.0	22,055.0
Costs & Expenses	-45,289.0	-45,334.0	-38,601.0	-27,392.0
Income Before Taxes and Other	3,983.0	-2,356.0	4,887.0	-5,337.0
Other Items	0.0	0.0	0.0	0.0
Income Tax	-1,792.0	-191.0	-2,384.0	1,085.0
Net Income	2,191.0	-2,547.0	2,503.0	-4,252.0
Cash Flow From Operations	20,195.0	25,131.0	16,858.0	n.a.
Balance Sheet (000's)				
Cash & Equivalents	2,140.0	2,191.0	1,629.0	2,398.0
Total Current Assets	9,760.0	13,255.0	17,703.0	22,766.0
Fixed Assets, Net	326.0	411.0	450.0	500.0
Total Assets	93,940.0	109,748.0	123,085.0	120,147.0
Total Current Liabilities	4,542.0	11,649.0	12,000.0	13,000.0
Long-Term Debt	21,647.0	13,329.0	18,298.0	15,608.0
Stockholders' Equity	31,008.0	26,757.0	29,304.0	26,800.0
Performance & Financial Condition				
Return on Total Revenues %	4.45	-5.93	5.76	-19.28
Return on Avg Stockholders' Equity %	7.59	-9.09	8.92	-15.19
Return on Average Assets %	2.15	-2.19	2.06	-3.40
Current Ratio	2.15	1.14	1.48	1.75
Debt / Equity %	69.81	49.82	62.44	58.24

Compound Growth %'s	EPS %	-8.97	Net Income %	-6.44	Total Revenues %	30.73

Comments

A single vendor leasing program generated 52.6% of the Company's total leasing revenue during fiscal 1998. Management believes that it has the ability and capacity to develop additional large vendor leasing programs. Fluctuations in loan loss reserves and the costs of an arbitration settlement resulted in losses in both fiscal 1997 and 1995. Estimating the residual value of equipment that may revert back to the Company also presents valuation challenges. On the surface, this may be a great value investment. But, without dividends, any prospective shareholder should see how a return on investment would manifest itself. For the nine months ended December 31, 1998, the Company reported revenues and net income of $36.6 million and $2,444,000 ($.31 per share) as compared to $36.3 million and $2,669,000 ($.35 per share) for the same period of the preceding year.

Officers	Position	Ownership Information	
Peter J. King	President, CEO	Number of Shares Outstanding	7,788,000
Jeffrey G. Jacobsen	Exec VP	Market Capitalization	$ 27,258,000
R. Bradley Pike	Vice President	Number of Shareholders	1,427
Thomas R. King	Director	Where Listed / Symbol	NASDAQ / SUNL

Other Information			
Transfer Agent	Norwest Bank Minnesota, N.A. South St. Paul, MN	SIC Code	7377
Auditor	Deloitte & Touche LLP	Employees	40

Sunshine Mining and Refining Company

877 W. Main Street, Suite 600   Boise, ID 83702   Telephone (208)345-0660   Fax (208)342-0004

Company Description

Sunshine Mining and Refining Company owns the Pirquitas Mine in northwest Argentina and the Sunshine Mine in northern Idaho. The Pirquitas Mine has estimated resources of 101 million ounces of silver, 116 million pounds of tin, and 194 million pounds of zinc. The Company expects future development work at the site will expand these reserves. The Sunshine Mine, located in northern Idaho, has been a leading silver producer for more than a century, with over 350 million ounces of silver production. Its silver reserves and resources total 365 million ounces. It produced approximately 5.8 million ounces of silver in 1998. What would a penny stock manual be without a mining stock, especially one from the New York Stock Exchange?

	12/31/98	12/31/97	12/31/96	12/31/95
Per Share Information				
Stock Price	0.56	1.00	0.94	1.50
Earnings Per Share	-0.25	-0.08	0.05	-0.13
Price / Earnings Ratio	n.a.	n.a.	18.80	n.a.
Book Value Per Share	-0.07	0.17	0.25	-0.22
Price / Book Value %	n.a.	588.24	376.00	n.a.
Dividends Per Share	0.0	0.0	0.0	0.0
Annual Financial Data				
Operating Results (000's)				
Total Revenues	35,396.0	29,033.0	16,484.0	18,535.0
Costs & Expenses	-49,816.0	-48,341.0	-42,386.0	-34,018.0
Income Before Taxes and Other	-14,420.0	-19,308.0	-25,902.0	-15,483.0
Other Items	-50,425.0	0.0	37,502.0	-10,089.0
Income Tax	0.0	0.0	0.0	0.0
Net Income	-64,845.0	-19,308.0	11,600.0	-25,572.0
Cash Flow From Operations	-9,539.0	-15,102.0	-22,174.0	-6,965.0
Balance Sheet (000's)				
Cash & Equivalents	1,412.0	15,985.0	16,317.0	12,837.0
Total Current Assets	15,497.0	31,891.0	30,561.0	26,478.0
Fixed Assets, Net	20,414.0	65,465.0	69,285.0	70,919.0
Total Assets	39,897.0	101,601.0	105,486.0	101,134.0
Total Current Liabilities	5,781.0	4,932.0	5,002.0	2,928.0
Long-Term Debt	42,597.0	42,265.0	25,780.0	1,519.0
Stockholders' Equity	-17,466.0	44,496.0	63,598.0	85,082.0
Performance & Financial Condition				
Return on Total Revenues %	-183.20	-66.50	70.37	-137.97
Return on Avg Stockholders' Equity %	-479.80	-35.72	15.60	-27.57
Return on Average Assets %	-91.66	-18.65	11.23	-23.48
Current Ratio	2.68	6.47	6.11	9.04
Debt / Equity %	n.a.	94.99	40.54	1.79

Compound Growth %'s	EPS % n.a.	Net Income % n.a.	Total Revenues % 24.07

Comments

The Company has incurred an operating loss each year since 1992. Net income for 1996 was the result of a gain from the retirement and exchange of preferred stock. It is the size of the Company's recoverable reserves of silver, and to a lesser degree other metals, as well as their related price which will govern the Company's financial future. The Company believes that the price of silver has been inordinately low for many years. But without firm evidence of an imminent rebound, the Company wrote down mining properties by $50.4 million in 1998 due to continued low silver prices. Higher production has enabled the Company to steadily decrease the cost of mining per ounce from $6.61 in 1995 to $4.43 in 1998. But higher silver prices are still needed to return the Company to profitability.

Officers	Position	Ownership Information	
John S. Simko	Chairman, CEO	Number of Shares Outstanding	259,408,000
William W. Davis	Exec VP, CFO	Market Capitalization	$ 145,268,480
Robert H. Peterson	Senior VP, COO	Number of Shareholders	32,000
Rebecca L. Saunders	Secretary	Where Listed / Symbol	NYSE / SSC

Other Information			
Transfer Agent	American Stock Transfer & Trust Co. New York, NY	SIC Code	1400
Auditor	Ernst & Young LLP	Employees	335
		Web Site	sunshinemining.com

Superior Energy Services, Inc.

1105 Peters Road Harvey, LA 70058 Telephone (504)362-4321 Fax (504)362-1430

Company Description

Superior Energy Services, Inc. provides a broad range of specialized oilfield services and equipment, primarily to major and independent oil and gas companies engaged in the exploration, production and development of oil and gas properties offshore in the Gulf of Mexico and throughout the Gulf Coast region. These services and equipment include the rental of specialized oilfield equipment, oil and gas well plug and abandonment services, electric and mechanical wireline services, the manufacture, sale and rental of drilling instrumentation and the manufacture and sale of oil spill containment equipment. Over the last three years, the Company has significantly expanded its operations through both internal growth and strategic acquisitions.

	12/31/98	12/31/97	12/31/96	12/31/95
Per Share Information				
Stock Price	2.56	10.06	2.94	2.50
Earnings Per Share	-0.14	0.43	0.22	-0.38
Price / Earnings Ratio	n.a.	23.40	13.36	n.a.
Book Value Per Share	2.87	3.05	1.09	0.70
Price / Book Value %	89.20	329.84	269.72	357.14
Dividends Per Share	0.0	0.0	0.0	0.0
Annual Financial Data				
Operating Results (000's)				
Total Revenues	91,334.0	54,256.0	23,638.0	12,338.0
Costs & Expenses	-76,700.0	-39,740.0	-18,021.0	-11,011.0
Income Before Taxes and Other	14,634.0	14,516.0	5,617.0	1,327.0
Other Items	-13,763.0	0.0	0.0	-4,042.0
Income Tax	-4,979.0	-5,061.0	-1,685.0	-131.0
Net Income	-4,108.0	9,455.0	3,932.0	-2,846.0
Cash Flow From Operations	18,126.0	2,343.0	2,676.0	3,616.0
Balance Sheet (000's)				
Cash & Equivalents	737.0	1,902.0	433.0	5,068.0
Total Current Assets	30,655.0	29,247.0	8,941.0	10,278.0
Fixed Assets, Net	76,187.0	51,797.0	9,894.0	6,904.0
Total Assets	131,144.0	118,060.0	28,200.0	22,984.0
Total Current Liabilities	11,873.0	10,741.0	6,484.0	9,302.0
Long-Term Debt	27,955.0	11,339.0	250.0	180.0
Stockholders' Equity	82,704.0	88,853.0	20,349.0	13,094.0
Performance & Financial Condition				
Return on Total Revenues %	-4.50	17.43	16.63	-23.07
Return on Avg Stockholders' Equity %	-4.79	17.32	23.51	-37.04
Return on Average Assets %	-3.30	12.93	15.36	-23.72
Current Ratio	2.58	2.72	1.38	1.10
Debt / Equity %	33.80	12.76	1.23	1.37

Compound Growth %'s	EPS % n.a.	Net Income % n.a.	Total Revenues % 94.89

Comments

The 68% increase in revenues experienced in 1998 was attributable to acquisitions. 1998 results were impacted by the decline in activity in the oilfield services industry as a result of a decline in oil prices. In addition, work in the Gulf of Mexico, which is the Company's primary operating area, was virtually shut down during September 1998 by a series of storms and hurricanes. The Company incurred a special charge during 1998 of $13.7 million, most of which related to the impairment of goodwill. Since the bulk of this was nondeductible for income tax purposes, income tax expense appears disproportionately large. The Company has been under new management since a reverse acquisition took place in 1995. 1995 results include a nonrecurring expense of $4,042,000 related to the impairment of long-lived assets. At December 31, 1998, the Company had $24.3 million of goodwill recorded as assets which equated to approximately 29% of stockholders' equity and book value per share.

Officers	Position	Ownership Information	
Terence E. Hall	President, CEO	Number of Shares Outstanding	28,792,523
Robert S. Taylor	CFO	Market Capitalization	$ 73,708,859
Ernest J. Yancey, Jr.	Vice President	Number of Shareholders	5,000
James E. Ravannack	Vice President	Where Listed / Symbol	NASDAQ / SESI

Other Information			
Transfer Agent	American Stock Transfer & Trust Co. New York, NY	SIC Code	1389
Auditor	KPMG LLP	Employees	560
		Web Site	superiorenergy.com

Superior Supplements, Inc.

270 Oser Avenue   Hauppauge, NY 11788   Telephone (516)231-0783   Fax (516)231-3515

Company Description

Superior Supplements, Inc. was formed on April 24, 1996. The Company is engaged in the development, manufacture, marketing and sale of dietary supplements including vitamins, minerals, herbs and specialty nutritional supplements, in bulk tablet, capsule and powder form. The Company manufactures a wide variety of products for companies which package and sell through many different channels of distribution, including health food, drug, convenience and mass market stores. The Company's manufacturing facility has the annual capacity to produce 1.2 billion tablets and capsules of various sizes and shapes.

	06/30/98	06/30/97	06/30/96
Per Share Information			
Stock Price as of 12/31	0.75	7.12	12.00
Earnings Per Share	0.01	-0.15	0.01
Price / Earnings Ratio	75.00	n.a.	1,200.00
Book Value Per Share	0.67	0.66	0.37
Price / Book Value %	111.94	1,078.79	3,243.24
Dividends Per Share	0.0	0.0	0.0
Annual Financial Data			
Operating Results (000's)			
Total Revenues	10,284.3	4,628.1	857.4
Costs & Expenses	-10,231.1	-4,724.1	-809.0
Income Before Taxes and Other	53.3	-538.5	48.4
Other Items	0.0	0.0	0.0
Income Tax	-2.0	-20.2	-13.2
Net Income	51.3	-558.7	35.2
Cash Flow From Operations	-666.8	-851.8	280.5
Balance Sheet (000's)			
Cash & Equivalents	37.0	412.9	594.2
Total Current Assets	5,077.8	4,043.6	1,086.0
Fixed Assets, Net	1,526.0	1,039.6	341.3
Total Assets	6,674.4	5,221.5	2,565.5
Total Current Liabilities	3,991.4	2,579.6	1,085.4
Long-Term Debt	0.0	0.0	200.0
Stockholders' Equity	2,674.1	2,632.9	1,280.1
Performance & Financial Condition			
Return on Total Revenues %	0.50	-12.07	4.10
Return on Avg Stockholders' Equity %	1.93	-28.56	5.50
Return on Average Assets %	0.86	-14.35	2.71
Current Ratio	1.27	1.57	1.00
Debt / Equity %	n.a.	n.a.	15.62

Compound Growth %'s	EPS % n.a.	Net Income % n.a.	Total Revenues % n.a.

Comments

Management attributes the increase in revenue to the expansion of the Company's product line. The earliest year presented was a partial year from April 24, 1996 through June 30, 1996. Accordingly, compound growth rates were not displayed. In the 1998 fiscal year, approximately 88% of sales were derived from PDK Labs Inc. (NASDAQ), also included in this manual. Reginald Spinello, who is a director of the Company, is the executive vice president of PDK. Although these sales are not reported as a related party transaction, the material impact to the Company should be noted. For the six months ended December 31, 1998, the Company reported sales of $2.5 million and a net loss of $664,660 ($.17 per share) as compared to $3.2 million and a net income of $169,352 ($.04 per share) in the same period of the preceding year.

Officers	Position	Ownership Information	
Lawrence D. Simon	President, CFO	Number of Shares Outstanding	4,000,000
Matthew L. Harriton	Secretary	Market Capitalization	$ 3,000,000
Reginald Spinello	Director	Number of Shareholders	1,000
Raveendra Nandigam	Director	Where Listed / Symbol	OTC-BB / SPSU

Other Information			
Transfer Agent	American Stock Transfer & Trust Co. New York, NY	SIC Code	2833
Auditor	Holtz Rubenstein & Co., LLP	Employees	61
Market Maker	J. Alexander Securities Inc. (800)421-0258		
	I.A. Rabinowitz & Co. (212)809-0018		

Suprema Specialties, Inc.

510 East 35th Street   Paterson, NJ 07543-0280   Telephone (973)684-2900   Fax (973)684-8680

Company Description

Suprema Specialties, Inc., manufactures and markets a variety of premium gourmet natural cheese products from high quality cheese produced in the United States, Europe and South America. Suprema's product line encompasses grated and shredded parmesan and pecorino romano cheeses, mozzarella and ricotta cheese products including "lite" versions of these products with less fat and fewer calories, and provolone cheese. The Company's products are sold to retail customers and service industry distributors. The Company was founded in 1983 and went public in 1991.

	06/30/98	06/30/97	06/30/96	06/30/95
Per Share Information				
Stock Price as of 12/31	4.94	3.19	4.37	4.37
Earnings Per Share	0.30	0.02	0.40	0.32
Price / Earnings Ratio	16.47	159.50	10.93	13.66
Book Value Per Share	3.66	3.35	3.28	3.02
Price / Book Value %	134.97	95.22	133.23	144.70
Dividends Per Share	0.0	0.0	0.0	0.0
Annual Financial Data				
Operating Results (000's)				
Total Revenues	108,140.0	88,311.5	65,516.4	52,629.2
Costs & Expenses	-103,973.0	-86,851.1	-63,103.1	-51,084.6
Income Before Taxes and Other	4,167.0	201.3	2,413.3	1,544.5
Other Items	-1,011.0	0.0	0.0	0.0
Income Tax	-1,750.2	-80.5	-1,004.0	-633.0
Net Income	1,405.9	120.8	1,409.3	911.5
Cash Flow From Operations	-7,055.8	-8,148.5	-7,287.0	-2,061.8
Balance Sheet (000's)				
Cash & Equivalents	489.9	480.2	528.9	494.2
Total Current Assets	53,117.7	39,379.0	28,374.2	18,179.5
Fixed Assets, Net	6,999.7	6,135.1	11,444.5	8,536.2
Total Assets	61,846.1	47,042.5	41,662.6	27,212.2
Total Current Liabilities	9,726.4	6,832.6	9,000.1	6,970.9
Long-Term Debt	31,762.0	5,268.5	5,066.2	5,000.0
Stockholders' Equity	16,694.8	15,289.0	14,085.7	7,401.2
Performance & Financial Condition				
Return on Total Revenues %	1.30	0.14	2.15	1.73
Return on Avg Stockholders' Equity %	8.79	0.82	13.12	14.53
Return on Average Assets %	2.58	0.27	4.09	4.15
Current Ratio	5.46	5.76	3.15	2.61
Debt / Equity %	190.25	34.46	35.97	67.56

Compound Growth %'s	EPS %	-2.13	Net Income %	15.54	Total Revenues %	27.13

Comments

Revenue growth of 22.5% was attributable to a higher sales volume for food service products manufactured by the Company. Record operating results were lowered as the Company took an extraordinary charge of $1 million ($.21 per share) on the extinguishment of debt. The charge was the result of prepayment penalties and associated fees. For the six months ended December 31, 1998, revenues and net income were $81.6 million and $1,856,086 ($.39 per share) as compared to $51.3 million and $77,081 ($.01 per share) for the same period of the preceding year. Included in the prior year's results was the extraordinary loss of $1.0 million ($.22 per share) related to the extinguishment of debt.

Officers	Position	Ownership Information	
Mark Cocchiola	President, CEO	Number of Shares Outstanding	4,562,800
Paul Lauriero	Exec VP	Market Capitalization	$ 22,540,232
Thomas Egan	Senior VP	Number of Shareholders	1,000
Steven Venechanos	CFO, Secretary	Where Listed / Symbol	NASDAQ / CHEZ

Other Information

Transfer Agent	Continental Stock Transfer & Trust Co. New York, NY	SIC Code	5140
Auditor	BDO Seidman LLP	Employees	140
		Web Site	chez.com

Swank, Inc.

6 Hazel Street   Attleboro, MA 02703   Telephone (508)222-3400   Fax (508)226-9598

Company Description

Swank, Inc. is engaged in the manufacture, sale and distribution of men's jewelry, belts, leather accessories and suspenders and women's jewelry. Its products are sold both domestically and internationally, principally through department stores and also through specialty stores and mass merchandisers. The Company operates a number of factory outlet stores, primarily to distribute excess and out-of-line merchandise. Products are sold under the names Swank, Pierre Cardin, Geoffrey Been, Yves Saint Laurent, Kenneth Cole, Anne Klein and Guess?, among others. Swank has been in business since 1936.

	12/31/98	12/31/97	12/31/96	12/31/95
Per Share Information				
Stock Price	1.91	1.06	0.56	0.75
Earnings Per Share	0.22	0.29	0.08	-0.55
Price / Earnings Ratio	8.68	3.66	7.00	n.a.
Book Value Per Share	1.88	1.59	1.29	1.24
Price / Book Value %	101.60	66.67	43.41	60.48
Dividends Per Share	0.0	0.0	0.0	0.0
Annual Financial Data				
Operating Results (000's)				
Total Revenues	151,770.0	137,074.0	132,642.0	140,102.0
Costs & Expenses	-145,673.0	-132,226.0	-130,483.0	-148,052.0
Income Before Taxes and Other	6,097.0	4,848.0	2,159.0	-7,950.0
Other Items	0.0	0.0	0.0	0.0
Income Tax	-2,435.0	-1.0	-860.0	-994.0
Net Income	3,662.0	4,847.0	1,299.0	-8,944.0
Cash Flow From Operations	-3,655.0	-6,131.0	15,386.0	-6,051.0
Balance Sheet (000's)				
Cash & Equivalents	757.0	1,235.0	2,871.0	1,121.0
Total Current Assets	61,733.0	48,840.0	37,905.0	45,768.0
Fixed Assets, Net	5,574.0	6,157.0	6,760.0	7,457.0
Total Assets	72,969.0	59,949.0	48,787.0	57,324.0
Total Current Liabilities	32,228.0	24,485.0	18,865.0	29,218.0
Long-Term Debt	9,563.0	0.0	0.0	0.0
Stockholders' Equity	31,178.0	26,861.0	21,331.0	20,533.0
Performance & Financial Condition				
Return on Total Revenues %	2.41	3.54	0.98	-6.38
Return on Avg Stockholders' Equity %	12.62	20.12	6.21	-35.25
Return on Average Assets %	5.51	8.92	2.45	-15.58
Current Ratio	1.92	1.99	2.01	1.57
Debt / Equity %	30.67	n.a.	n.a.	n.a.

Compound Growth %'s	EPS %	65.83	Net Income %	67.90	Total Revenues %	2.70

Comments

The Company was caught off guard in 1995 by a lackluster retail environment. Heavier than normal returns were experienced as the Company was in the midst of a shift in emphasis in women's jewelry from higher margin fashion products to more competitively priced career-oriented products. A net loss for the year was the bottom line. Management has since completed three years of tight cost controls, becoming more efficient and improving profit margins. Revenues increased in both 1998 and 1997 after two years of decline. The 10.7% advance registered during 1998 was excellent, especially considering a 1.5% decline related to export sales.

Officers	Position	Ownership Information	
John Tulin	President, CEO	Number of Shares Outstanding	16,554,423
Richard V. Byrnes, Jr.	Senior VP	Market Capitalization	$ 31,618,948
Arthur T. Gately, Jr.	Senior VP	Number of Shareholders	5,000
Christopher F. Wolf	Senior VP, CFO	Where Listed / Symbol	NASDAQ / SNKI

Other Information			
Transfer Agent	American Stock Transfer & Trust Co. New York, NY	SIC Code	3960
Auditor	PricewaterhouseCoopers LLP	Employees	1,490

Synbiotics Corporation

11011 Via Frontera   San Diego, CA 92127   Telephone (619)451-3771   Fax (619)451-5719

Company Description

Synbiotics Corporation, founded in 1982, is an animal health business which develops, manufactures and markets diagnostic products and biological products primarily for companion animals. The Company's principal customers are veterinarians and veterinary clinical laboratories in the United States and Europe. The Company's products are sold primarily to wholesale distributors. On October 25, 1996, the Company acquired substantially all of the assets of International Canine Genetics, Inc. (Canine). Canine's operations consisted of the manufacturing and marketing of canine reproduction diagnostic products and services, nutritional supplements, and a line of coat and skin care products. On July 9, 1997, the Company acquired the worldwide veterinary diagnostic business of Rhone Merieux S.A.S. On March 6, 1998, the Company acquired Prisma Acquisition Corp. which develops, manufactures and markets instruments and reagents used by veterinarians to measure blood chemistry information at the point-of-care.

	12/31/98	12/31/97	12/31/96	12/31/95
Per Share Information				
Stock Price	2.44	3.06	3.06	2.12
Earnings Per Share	-0.23	0.02	1.47	0.09
Price / Earnings Ratio	n.a.	153.00	2.08	23.56
Book Value Per Share	3.38	3.60	3.47	1.57
Price / Book Value %	72.19	85.00	88.18	135.03
Dividends Per Share	0.0	0.0	0.0	0.0
Annual Financial Data				
Operating Results (000's)				
Total Revenues	31,696.0	23,618.0	17,831.0	14,118.0
Costs & Expenses	-30,429.0	-22,852.0	-16,806.0	-14,548.0
Income Before Taxes and Other	1,914.0	766.0	1,025.0	-430.0
Other Items	-4,600.0	0.0	1,159.0	931.0
Income Tax	1,422.0	-559.0	7,094.0	0.0
Net Income	-1,264.0	207.0	9,278.0	501.0
Cash Flow From Operations	1,403.0	2,800.0	-625.0	229.0
Balance Sheet (000's)				
Cash & Equivalents	4,357.0	2,190.0	3,050.0	1,017.0
Total Current Assets	16,445.0	15,829.0	14,896.0	6,464.0
Fixed Assets, Net	1,774.0	1,102.0	656.0	879.0
Total Assets	45,446.0	41,627.0	28,567.0	11,458.0
Total Current Liabilities	7,217.0	4,571.0	2,891.0	2,310.0
Long-Term Debt	6,716.0	7,543.0	0.0	0.0
Stockholders' Equity	27,857.0	26,757.0	25,676.0	9,148.0
Performance & Financial Condition				
Return on Total Revenues %	-3.99	0.88	52.03	3.55
Return on Avg Stockholders' Equity %	-4.63	0.79	53.29	5.86
Return on Average Assets %	-2.90	0.59	46.36	4.60
Current Ratio	2.28	3.46	5.15	2.80
Debt / Equity %	24.11	28.19	n.a.	n.a.

Compound Growth %'s	EPS % n.a.	Net Income % n.a.	Total Revenues % 30.94

Comments

The increase in 1998 revenue as compared to 1997 was attributable to acquisitions and a $4 million increase in sales of diagnostic products. A $4.6 million nonrecurring expense caused a loss for the year. The expense was a settlement of a patent infringement lawsuit against the Company. 1996 results include a gain of $1,159,000 on the sale of securities and a benefit from income taxes of $7,094,000. 1995 results include a gain of $931,000 on the sale of securities. Research and development expense increased from $1,692,000 in 1997 to $2,386,000 in 1998. At December 31, 1998, the Company had $13.4 million of goodwill recorded as assets which equated to approximately 48% of stockholders' equity and book value per share.

Officers	Position	Ownership Information	
Donald E. Phillips	Chairman	Number of Shares Outstanding	8,246,000
Kenneth M. Cohen	President, CEO	Market Capitalization	$ 20,120,240
Michael K. Green	VP - Finance, CFO	Number of Shareholders	578
Keith A. Butler	Controller	Where Listed / Symbol	NASDAQ / SBIO

Other Information			
Transfer Agent	ChaseMellon Shareholder Services Los Angeles, CA	SIC Code	2835
Auditor	PricewaterhouseCoopers LLP	Employees	135
		Web Site	synbiotics.com

Synergy Brands, Inc.

40 Underhill Boulevard   Syosset, NY 11791   Telephone (516)682-1980   Fax (516)682-1990

Company Description

Synergy Brands, Inc., formerly Krantor Corporation, is a distributor of groceries, general household merchandise and health and beauty aids in the promotional wholesale industry. In addition, the Company distributes squid and premium handmade cigars throughout the United States. In 1996, the Company terminated its Kosher Foods and Specialty Foods business and significantly curtailed its wholesale operations in general. The Company is presently attempting to re-focus on its traditional business as a Promotional Grocery Product distributor as well as on its expansion into distribution, presently on an agency basis, of frozen squid and other seafood products under a distribution agreement with a Chinese company.

	12/31/98	12/31/97	12/31/96	12/31/95
Per Share Information				
Stock Price	3.06	1.62	3.00	32.75
Earnings Per Share	0.05	0.11	-34.12	1.75
Price / Earnings Ratio	61.20	14.73	n.a.	18.71
Book Value Per Share	0.11	0.47	0.68	35.10
Price / Book Value %	2,781.82	344.68	441.18	93.30
Dividends Per Share	0.0	0.0	0.0	0.0
Annual Financial Data				
Operating Results (000's)				
Total Revenues	11,301.7	5,524.2	7,388.2	43,936.2
Costs & Expenses	-10,990.9	-5,132.3	-7,733.9	-42,537.6
Income Before Taxes and Other	310.8	305.8	-345.6	1,058.4
Other Items	0.0	-130.6	-9,690.1	-150.7
Income Tax	-13.3	0.0	-23.1	-354.8
Net Income	297.5	175.2	-10,058.9	552.9
Cash Flow From Operations	-1,877.4	-599.3	1,034.4	-1,290.5
Balance Sheet (000's)				
Cash & Equivalents	325.7	189.6	2.9	370.0
Total Current Assets	4,774.2	1,724.3	2,013.4	16,946.5
Fixed Assets, Net	120.1	117.4	30.6	834.1
Total Assets	6,754.1	4,094.7	4,350.3	18,318.5
Total Current Liabilities	2,727.9	1,639.1	3,396.2	11,319.5
Long-Term Debt	400.0	395.0	377.0	50.0
Stockholders' Equity	3,362.2	1,955.6	577.1	6,949.0
Performance & Financial Condition				
Return on Total Revenues %	2.63	3.17	-136.15	1.26
Return on Avg Stockholders' Equity %	11.19	13.83	-267.31	15.71
Return on Average Assets %	5.48	4.15	-88.75	5.03
Current Ratio	1.75	1.05	0.59	1.50
Debt / Equity %	11.90	20.20	65.33	0.72

Compound Growth %'s	EPS % -69.43	Net Income % -18.66	Total Revenues % -36.40

Comments

In May 1997, the Company executed a 1 for 25 reverse stock split. All per share amounts have been adjusted for consistency. Revenues increased 120.7% in 1998 as compared to 1997. The Company attributes this increase to a significant increase in the grocery and health and beauty aid businesses and to increased business with Proctor & Gamble in particular. The Company was able to achieve its first year of profitability since its reorganization. The Company recorded a loss from discontinued operations of $9.7 million ($29.25 per share) in 1996. The 1997 loss from discontinued operations was only $130,632 ($.08 per share). In 1999 the Company is developing E-commerce sites for the purpose of expanding its distribution to the consumer market through on-line channels. The Company will devote a significant amount of resources to this and may require additional capital to achieve its goals.

Officers	Position	Ownership Information	
Henry J. Platek Jr.	President	Number of Shares Outstanding	29,898,600
Mair Fabish	Exec VP, CFO	Market Capitalization	$ 91,489,716
Mitchell Gerstein	Vice President, Controller	Number of Shareholders	5,000
Dominic A. Marsicovetere	Director	Where Listed / Symbol	NASDAQ / SYBR

Other Information			
Transfer Agent	American Stock Transfer & Trust Company New York, NY	SIC Code	5141
Auditor	Belew Averitt LLP	Employees	30
		Web Site	synergybrands.com

T.J.T., Inc.

843 North Washington   Emmett, ID 83617   Telephone (208)365-5321   Fax (208)365-3983

Company Description

T.J.T., Inc. is engaged in the business of repairing and reconditioning axles and tires for the manufactured housing industry. The Company also distributes vinyl and steel siding primarily to the constructed or site-built housing market and supplies skirting and other after-market accessory products to manufactured housing dealers and set-up contractors. The Company was founded in 1977. Following a geographic expansion, the Company was forced to sell unprofitable operations when the manufactured housing industry experienced a significant decline from 1983 to 1991.

	09/30/98	09/30/97	09/30/96	09/30/95
Per Share Information				
Stock Price as of 12/31	1.06	1.56	2.56	5.81
Earnings Per Share	0.09	0.11	0.10	0.10
Price / Earnings Ratio	11.78	14.18	25.60	58.10
Book Value Per Share	1.84	1.75	1.72	1.05
Price / Book Value %	57.61	89.14	148.84	553.33
Dividends Per Share	0.0	0.0	0.0	0.0
Annual Financial Data				
Operating Results (000's)				
Total Revenues	34,158.0	25,634.0	12,859.0	12,350.3
Costs & Expenses	-33,348.0	-24,806.0	-12,335.0	-11,918.3
Income Before Taxes and Other	810.0	827.0	524.0	432.0
Other Items	0.0	0.0	0.0	0.0
Income Tax	-364.0	-350.0	-206.0	-183.7
Net Income	446.0	477.0	318.0	248.3
Cash Flow From Operations	678.0	228.0	294.0	20.1
Balance Sheet (000's)				
Cash & Equivalents	204.0	835.0	2,737.0	0.9
Total Current Assets	6,606.0	6,306.0	5,591.0	2,739.6
Fixed Assets, Net	1,944.0	1,318.0	511.0	506.0
Total Assets	11,054.0	10,140.0	6,998.0	3,546.2
Total Current Liabilities	1,929.0	1,470.0	647.0	1,047.5
Long-Term Debt	0.0	0.0	0.0	58.1
Stockholders' Equity	8,929.0	8,471.0	6,224.0	2,316.5
Performance & Financial Condition				
Return on Total Revenues %	1.31	1.86	2.47	2.01
Return on Avg Stockholders' Equity %	5.13	6.49	7.45	11.35
Return on Average Assets %	4.21	5.57	6.03	7.50
Current Ratio	3.42	4.29	8.64	2.62
Debt / Equity %	n.a.	n.a.	n.a.	2.51

Compound Growth %'s	EPS %	-3.45	Net Income %	21.56	Total Revenues %	40.37

Comments

Acquisitions continue to play an important role in revenue growth. However, the Company also experienced a manufactured housing market that grew at a 7% rate during 1998. Despite the many acquisitions, goodwill totaled only $1,440,000 at September 30, 1998, approximating 16% of stockholders' equity and book value per share. The Company maintains a solid working capital and does not have any long term debt. In November 1998, the Company announced that it will buy back up to 5%, or 240,000 shares, of its common stock. A turbulent stock market that was unkind to small companies is the apparent reason for the loss of one-third of the stock's trading price in calendar 1998.

Officers	Position	Ownership Information	
Terrence J. Sheldon	President, CEO	Number of Shares Outstanding	4,843,832
Patricia Bradley	Exec VP	Market Capitalization	$ 5,134,462
Ulysses B. Mori	Senior VP	Number of Shareholders	1,411
April L. Kierstead	Secretary, Controller	Where Listed / Symbol	NASDAQ / AXLE

Other Information			
Transfer Agent	Corporate Stock Transfer, Inc. Denver, CO	SIC Code	3790
Auditor	Balukoff, Lindstrom & Co.	Employees	200

TBA Entertainment Corporation

402 Heritage Plantation Way   Hickory Valley, TN 38042   Telephone (901)764-2300   Fax (901)764-6107

Company Description

TBA Entertainment Corporation, founded in 1995, is a diversified entertainment company. The Company currently produces live entertainment for corporate meetings and special events, develops and produces integrated music marketing programs for corporate clients, manages entertainers and owns and operates concert amphitheaters, produces and promotes concerts and manages merchandising for concerts and sporting events. The Company also owned and operated the Village at Breckenridge Resort, a year-round destination resort, until it was sold in 1998. The Company has embarked on an aggressive acquisition program, completing its first transaction in 1997 followed by three more in 1998.

	12/31/98	12/31/97	12/31/96	12/31/95
Per Share Information				
Stock Price	4.19	3.81	n.a.	n.a.
Earnings Per Share	0.32	0.06	-0.87	-0.54
Price / Earnings Ratio	13.09	63.50	n.a.	n.a.
Book Value Per Share	3.30	2.88	2.66	n.a.
Price / Book Value %	126.97	132.29	n.a.	n.a.
Dividends Per Share	0.0	0.0	0.0	0.0
Annual Financial Data				
Operating Results (000's)				
Total Revenues	27,417.2	30,307.8	10,809.0	2,299.6
Costs & Expenses	-25,737.4	-30,267.1	-13,936.3	-3,093.5
Income Before Taxes and Other	1,679.8	40.7	-3,127.3	-793.9
Other Items	1,180.9	361.6	0.0	0.0
Income Tax	-189.7	0.0	0.0	0.0
Net Income	2,671.0	402.3	-3,127.3	-793.9
Cash Flow From Operations	1,476.9	949.4	-9.5	-995.1
Balance Sheet (000's)				
Cash & Equivalents	15,583.8	3,369.3	2,659.9	235.7
Total Current Assets	22,107.7	5,301.2	3,841.0	363.5
Fixed Assets, Net	1,853.6	33,670.9	34,043.6	2,530.7
Total Assets	40,445.2	52,561.5	38,108.1	3,032.6
Total Current Liabilities	7,173.8	9,475.6	5,640.0	504.6
Long-Term Debt	4,755.7	21,632.5	19,521.7	0.0
Stockholders' Equity	28,515.7	20,720.4	12,213.3	1,795.0
Performance & Financial Condition				
Return on Total Revenues %	9.74	1.33	-28.93	-34.52
Return on Avg Stockholders' Equity %	10.85	2.44	-44.65	-99.24
Return on Average Assets %	5.74	0.89	-15.20	-52.93
Current Ratio	3.08	0.56	0.68	n.a.
Debt / Equity %	16.68	104.40	159.84	n.a.

Compound Growth %'s	EPS % n.a.	Net Income % n.a.	Total Revenues % 128.45

Comments

The 324% increase in revenues reported for 1998 as compared to 1997 resulted from the production of 406 events in 1998, as compared to 108 in 1997, and to a lesser extent on acquisitions. The increase in the number of events is primarily attributable to an increase in the Company's sales force. 1998 results include a gain from discontinued operations of $1,180,900 ($.14 per share). 1997 results included income from discontinued operations of $361,600 ($.05 per share). The sale of the Breckenridge resort restored the Company's financial condition after it closed 1997 with a deficiency in working capital. At December 31, 1998, the Company had $16 million of goodwill recorded as assets which equated to approximately 56% of stockholders' equity and book value per share.

Officers	Position	Ownership Information	
Thomas Jackson Weaver III	President, CEO	Number of Shares Outstanding	8,634,800
Brian J. Cusworth	CFO	Market Capitalization	$ 36,179,812
Frank A. McKinnie Weaver Sr.	Secretary	Number of Shareholders	2,000
Prab Nallamilli	General Manager	Where Listed / Symbol	NASDAQ / TBAE

Other Information			
Transfer Agent	American Stock Transfer & Trust Co. New York, NY	SIC Code	7011
Auditor	Arthur Andersen LLP	Employees	120
		Web Site	tbaent.com

TENERA, Inc.

One Market, Spear Tower, Suite 1850   San Francisco, CA 94105-1018   Telephone (415)536-4744   Fax (415)536-4714

Company Description

TENERA, Inc. provides a broad range of professional consulting, management, and technical services to solve complex management, engineering, environmental, and safety challenges associated with the operation, asset management, and maintenance of power plants, federal government properties, and capital intensive industries. The Company has developed expertise in providing solutions to complex technical and regulatory issues facing the commercial electric power industry, particularly with respect to nuclear facilities.

	12/31/98	12/31/97	12/31/96	12/31/95
Per Share Information				
Stock Price	1.87	0.75	0.69	0.94
Earnings Per Share	0.16	-0.19	-0.11	0.07
Price / Earnings Ratio	11.69	n.a.	n.a.	13.43
Book Value Per Share	0.46	0.30	0.48	0.60
Price / Book Value %	406.52	250.00	143.75	156.67
Dividends Per Share	0.0	0.0	0.0	0.0
Annual Financial Data				
Operating Results (000's)				
Total Revenues	28,087.0	21,231.0	24,168.0	25,546.0
Costs & Expenses	-26,084.0	-23,260.0	-25,385.0	-24,322.0
Income Before Taxes and Other	2,003.0	-2,029.0	-1,217.0	1,204.0
Other Items	0.0	0.0	0.0	0.0
Income Tax	-329.0	139.0	137.0	-306.0
Net Income	1,674.0	-1,890.0	-1,080.0	898.0
Cash Flow From Operations	906.0	-2,681.0	2,954.0	-286.0
Balance Sheet (000's)				
Cash & Equivalents	3,361.0	2,292.0	3,964.0	1,474.0
Total Current Assets	9,012.0	5,896.0	7,617.0	9,730.0
Fixed Assets, Net	194.0	156.0	323.0	340.0
Total Assets	9,206.0	6,052.0	7,940.0	10,087.0
Total Current Liabilities	4,538.0	3,065.0	3,062.0	3,894.0
Long-Term Debt	0.0	0.0	0.0	0.0
Stockholders' Equity	4,668.0	2,987.0	4,878.0	6,175.0
Performance & Financial Condition				
Return on Total Revenues %	5.96	-8.90	-4.47	3.52
Return on Avg Stockholders' Equity %	43.74	-48.06	-19.54	16.75
Return on Average Assets %	21.94	-27.02	-11.98	9.60
Current Ratio	1.99	1.92	2.49	2.50
Debt / Equity %	n.a.	n.a.	n.a.	n.a.

Compound Growth %'s	EPS %	31.73	Net Income %	23.07	Total Revenues %	3.21

Comments

On November 14, 1997, the Company sold its interest in a subsidiary which generated $2,870,000 of revenue during the first 10 months of 1997. The business was not generating profits nor was it expected to within the following twelve months. But this may be what was needed to restore the Company to profitability. Revenues made a strong advance on core business activity and more than replaced revenues of the sold subsidiary. Although gross margins dropped from 38% to 25%, mainly due to an increase in the proportion of revenues derived from lower margin government projects, net earnings were solidly in the black. The Company maintains an excellent financial condition without the need for any long term debt.

Officers	Position	Ownership Information	
Robert C. McKay	President, CEO	Number of Shares Outstanding	10,129,403
Jeffrey R. Hazarian	CFO	Market Capitalization	$ 18,941,984
James A. Robison, Jr.	Controller, Treasurer	Number of Shareholders	500
William A. Hasler	Director	Where Listed / Symbol	AMEX / TNR

Other Information			
Transfer Agent	Chemical Mellon Shareholder Services San Francisco, CA	SIC Code	8711
Auditor	Ernst & Young LLP	Employees	196
		Web Site	tenera.com

THT Inc.

33 Riverside Avenue   Westport, CT 06880   Telephone (203)226-6408   Fax (203)226-8022

Company Description

THT Inc. conducts business through two operating subsidiaries: Jackburn Mfg., Inc. is engaged in the business of manufacturing stove-top grills, fabricated steel parts and other wire forming products and Setterstix Corporation is engaged in the manufacture of rolled paper products used principally in the confectionery and health-related industries. For fiscal 1998, Setterstix accounted for 64% of THT's revenues. The Company was formed in 1983.

	09/30/98	09/30/97	09/30/96	09/30/95
Per Share Information				
Stock Price as of 12/31	3.31	3.12	2.56	1.81
Earnings Per Share	0.44	0.55	0.45	0.36
Price / Earnings Ratio	7.52	5.67	5.69	5.03
Book Value Per Share	2.35	1.91	1.36	0.91
Price / Book Value %	140.85	163.35	188.24	198.90
Dividends Per Share	0.0	0.0	0.0	0.0
Annual Financial Data				
Operating Results (000's)				
Total Revenues	19,763.5	18,693.1	18,657.2	18,503.5
Costs & Expenses	-16,726.8	-15,879.0	-16,375.2	-16,171.4
Income Before Taxes and Other	2,905.1	2,732.6	2,167.8	2,132.5
Other Items	0.0	0.0	0.0	0.0
Income Tax	-1,119.0	-341.0	-115.0	-317.0
Net Income	1,786.1	2,391.6	2,052.8	1,815.5
Cash Flow From Operations	2,750.0	2,468.3	3,797.6	2,809.3
Balance Sheet (000's)				
Cash & Equivalents	1,200.0	1,659.1	914.3	458.8
Total Current Assets	5,256.5	5,689.3	4,492.1	4,651.3
Fixed Assets, Net	3,460.7	3,568.7	3,073.5	2,854.3
Total Assets	12,487.5	13,095.4	11,034.1	11,038.0
Total Current Liabilities	2,099.5	2,175.8	1,867.1	2,661.7
Long-Term Debt	0.0	1,400.0	0.0	24.1
Stockholders' Equity	9,349.0	8,597.9	7,416.3	5,643.4
Performance & Financial Condition				
Return on Total Revenues %	9.04	12.79	11.00	9.81
Return on Avg Stockholders' Equity %	19.90	29.87	31.44	40.23
Return on Average Assets %	13.96	19.82	18.60	15.96
Current Ratio	2.50	2.61	2.41	1.75
Debt / Equity %	n.a.	16.28	n.a.	0.43

Compound Growth %'s	EPS %	6.92	Net Income %	-0.54	Total Revenues %	2.22

Comments

The increase in revenue was primarily attributable to Jackburn which benefited from increased demand, an expanded sales effort, and new product developments. Jackburn has three major customers which accounted for 57% of fiscal 1998 revenues. No such concentration applies to Setterstix. Although operating profit improved, fiscal 1998 was the only year presented above that was subject to a normal income tax provision. Therefore, net earnings declined after the impact of income taxes. Income taxes had been significantly lower than the statutory rate in earlier years because of the availability of tax loss carryforwards. Cash flows from operations enabled the Company to repay $1.8 million of long term debt and redeem $1.0 million of preferred stock.

Officers	Position	Ownership Information	
Paul K. Kelly	Chairman, CEO	Number of Shares Outstanding	3,982,605
Frederick A. Rossetti	President, CEO	Market Capitalization	$ 13,182,423
Jeffrey B. Gaynor	Exec VP, Secretary	Number of Shareholders	1,960
Salvatore V. Porio	Director	Where Listed / Symbol	NASDAQ / TXHI

Other Information			
Transfer Agent	American Securities Transfer, Inc. Denver, CO	SIC Code	2679
Auditor	Grant Thornton LLP	Employees	137
		Web Site	jackburn.com

TMS, Inc.

206 West Sixth Avenue   Stillwater, OK 74074   Telephone (405)377-0880   Fax (405)377-0452

Company Description

TMS, Inc., doing business as TMSSequoia since the 1996 acquisition of Sequoia Computer Corporation, is involved in the research, design, development, and marketing of software tools and applications for document capture, image enhancement, image viewing, forms processing, intranets and the Internet. The Company also provides software development and document conversion services to corporations and government organizations worldwide to assist them in their migration from paper to electronic information systems. The Company was formed in 1981.

	08/31/98	08/31/97	08/31/96	08/31/95
Per Share Information				
Stock Price as of 12/31	0.28	0.41	1.50	0.66
Earnings Per Share	0.04	0.0	0.03	0.08
Price / Earnings Ratio	7.00	n.a.	50.00	8.25
Book Value Per Share	0.32	0.28	0.28	0.27
Price / Book Value %	87.50	146.43	535.71	244.44
Dividends Per Share	0.0	0.0	0.0	0.0
Annual Financial Data				
Operating Results (000's)				
Total Revenues	7,367.8	5,721.8	5,683.7	4,221.1
Costs & Expenses	-6,918.7	-5,654.6	-5,471.5	-3,796.6
Income Before Taxes and Other	442.1	67.1	212.2	455.6
Other Items	0.0	0.0	0.0	0.0
Income Tax	46.9	-23.6	170.9	315.8
Net Income	489.0	43.5	383.2	771.5
Cash Flow From Operations	998.7	505.1	389.6	622.2
Balance Sheet (000's)				
Cash & Equivalents	491.7	426.2	542.1	114.2
Total Current Assets	2,748.0	2,562.8	2,480.6	1,326.0
Fixed Assets, Net	1,659.9	1,546.4	1,482.3	1,446.8
Total Assets	5,285.6	4,847.0	4,708.4	3,131.7
Total Current Liabilities	652.0	767.9	642.4	499.0
Long-Term Debt	310.0	333.6	355.8	378.3
Stockholders' Equity	4,245.0	3,745.5	3,710.2	2,254.4
Performance & Financial Condition				
Return on Total Revenues %	6.64	0.76	6.74	18.28
Return on Avg Stockholders' Equity %	12.24	1.17	12.85	41.58
Return on Average Assets %	9.65	0.91	9.77	31.40
Current Ratio	4.21	3.34	3.86	2.66
Debt / Equity %	7.30	8.91	9.59	16.78

Compound Growth %'s	EPS %	-20.63	Net Income %	-14.10	Total Revenues %	20.40

Comments

Revenues are comprised mostly of software license fees and royalties, which made up 59%, 63% to 65% of revenues in fiscal 1998, 1997 and 1996, respectively. Document conversion services increased 127% to $1.7 million, leading the overall growth in revenue to a 30% advance. The higher revenue and related significant increases in gross margins were the primary factors that caused an increase in net income. For the six months ended February 28, 1999, the Company had revenues of $2.5 million and a net loss of $573,536 ($.04 per share) as compared to revenue of $4.1 million and net income of $356,098 ($.03 per share) for the same period of the prior year. The poor results were attributed to revenue and related operating margin shortfalls, and asset write-offs and restructuring charges of $182,000.

Officers	Position	Ownership Information	
Doyle E. Cherry	Chairman	Number of Shares Outstanding	13,431,049
Arthur D. Crotzer	CEO	Market Capitalization	$ 3,760,694
Dana R. Allen	Exec VP	Number of Shareholders	1,730
Deborah D. Mosier	CFO	Where Listed / Symbol	OTC-BB / TMSS

Other Information			
Transfer Agent	American Securities Transfer, Inc. Denver, CO	SIC Code	7372
Auditor	KPMG LLP	Employees	90
Market Maker	Herzog, Heine, Geduld, Inc. (800)221-3600	Web Site	tmssequoia.com
	Paragon Capital Corporation (800)345-0505		

Taitron Components Incorporated

25202 Anza Drive   Santa Clarita, CA 91355   Telephone (805)257-6060   Fax (805)257-6415

Company Description

Taitron Components Incorporated, founded in 1989, distributes a wide variety of transistors, diodes and other discrete semiconductors and optoelectronic devices to other electronic distributors and to original equipment manufacturers who incorporate them into their products. In order to meet the rapid delivery requirements of its customers, the Company maintains an inventory of over 1.4 billion components. The Company distributes over 12,000 different products manufactured by more than 65 different suppliers with an average unit sales price of approximately 3.1 cents each. Because of its large inventory, good prices and one stop shopping, the Company sees itself as a discrete components super store. The Company went public in 1995.

	12/31/98	12/31/97	12/31/96	12/31/95
Per Share Information				
Stock Price	1.53	2.62	2.38	7.75
Earnings Per Share	0.24	0.27	0.31	0.68
Price / Earnings Ratio	6.38	9.70	7.68	11.40
Book Value Per Share	4.09	3.78	3.48	3.17
Price / Book Value %	37.41	69.31	68.39	244.48
Dividends Per Share	0.0	0.0	0.0	0.0
Annual Financial Data				
Operating Results (000's)				
Total Revenues	30,911.0	33,960.0	30,166.0	36,156.0
Costs & Expenses	-28,389.0	-30,890.0	-26,584.0	-29,045.0
Income Before Taxes and Other	2,522.0	3,070.0	3,582.0	7,111.0
Other Items	0.0	0.0	0.0	0.0
Income Tax	-1,023.0	-1,220.0	-1,424.0	-2,807.0
Net Income	1,499.0	1,850.0	2,158.0	4,304.0
Cash Flow From Operations	4,220.0	-478.0	-13,658.0	-4,010.0
Balance Sheet (000's)				
Cash & Equivalents	364.0	163.0	300.0	1,145.0
Total Current Assets	41,271.0	41,923.0	40,020.0	34,352.0
Fixed Assets, Net	2,976.0	2,309.0	1,660.0	1,627.0
Total Assets	44,583.0	44,985.0	42,315.0	36,380.0
Total Current Liabilities	16,032.0	17,139.0	14,709.0	13,914.0
Long-Term Debt	3,455.0	3,475.0	3,493.0	511.0
Stockholders' Equity	25,096.0	24,371.0	24,113.0	21,955.0
Performance & Financial Condition				
Return on Total Revenues %	4.85	5.45	7.15	11.90
Return on Avg Stockholders' Equity %	6.06	7.63	9.37	30.42
Return on Average Assets %	3.35	4.24	5.48	15.69
Current Ratio	2.57	2.45	2.72	2.47
Debt / Equity %	13.77	14.26	14.49	2.33

Compound Growth %'s	EPS %	-29.33	Net Income %	-29.64	Total Revenues %	-5.09

Comments

The decline in sales experienced in 1998 was principally the result of an industry wide decline in demand for discrete semiconductors. A decrease of $1.5 million in export sales also contributed to the decline. The Company continued to add new customers in 1998, but at a slower rate than during previous years. Management was able to respond with a reduction in selling, general and administrative expenses by eliminating non-essential expenditures and reducing other non-essential overhead. With an excellent financial condition and a stock price that has dropped below book value, management has found the purchase of its own shares to be a pretty good value. Nearly 11.5% of all outstanding shares were reacquired during 1998 and 1997.

Officers	Position	Ownership Information	
Stewart Wang	President, CEO	Number of Shares Outstanding	6,138,708
Bill Lloyd	Senior VP	Market Capitalization	$ 9,392,223
Steven H. Dong	CFO	Number of Shareholders	1,815
Sally Manley	Vice President	Where Listed / Symbol	NASDAQ / TAIT

Other Information			
Transfer Agent	American Stock Transfer & Trust Co. New York, NY	SIC Code	5065
Auditor	Grant Thornton LLP	Employees	51
		Web Site	taitron.net

Tandycrafts, Inc.

1400 Everman Parkway   Fort Worth, TX 76140   Telephone (817)551-9600   Fax (817)551-9795

Company Description

Tandycrafts, Inc. operates in two primary industry segments: specialty retail and specialty manufacturing. The specialty retail segment consists of two distinct retail concepts: Tandy Leather & Crafts, which sells leathercraft and related products through 128 stores located in 42 states; and Sav-On Office Supplies, which sells office supplies and related products through a chain of 41 stores in eleven states. The specialty manufacturing segment is comprised of Picture Frames and Framed Art. Joshua's Christian Stores, a retail chain of Christian bookstores, was sold by the Company in May 1998. The Company was founded in 1975 to operate the handycrafts segment previously operated by Tandy Corporation.

	06/30/98	06/30/97	06/30/96	06/30/95
Per Share Information				
Stock Price as of 12/31	3.69	4.56	6.00	7.87
Earnings Per Share	0.37	-0.15	-0.89	0.46
Price / Earnings Ratio	9.97	n.a.	n.a.	17.11
Book Value Per Share	7.05	6.69	6.86	7.74
Price / Book Value %	52.34	68.16	87.46	101.68
Dividends Per Share	0.0	0.0	0.0	0.0
Annual Financial Data				
Operating Results (000's)				
Total Revenues	232,582.0	244,963.0	254,335.0	256,590.0
Costs & Expenses	-225,463.0	-248,008.0	-251,901.0	-248,563.0
Income Before Taxes and Other	7,119.0	-3,045.0	-15,883.0	8,027.0
Other Items	0.0	0.0	0.0	0.0
Income Tax	-2,502.0	1,127.0	5,174.0	-2,810.0
Net Income	4,617.0	-1,918.0	-10,709.0	5,217.0
Cash Flow From Operations	7,936.0	9,373.0	8,425.0	-4,030.0
Balance Sheet (000's)				
Cash & Equivalents	1,216.0	1,005.0	1,512.0	1,807.0
Total Current Assets	83,077.0	90,017.0	99,771.0	101,980.0
Fixed Assets, Net	22,886.0	25,505.0	26,783.0	28,707.0
Total Assets	150,691.0	156,529.0	168,579.0	178,803.0
Total Current Liabilities	24,675.0	28,961.0	33,751.0	27,113.0
Long-Term Debt	34,230.0	40,840.0	50,000.0	0.0
Stockholders' Equity	88,964.0	84,274.0	83,598.0	90,661.0
Performance & Financial Condition				
Return on Total Revenues %	1.99	-0.78	-4.21	2.03
Return on Avg Stockholders' Equity %	5.33	-2.29	-12.29	6.15
Return on Average Assets %	3.01	-1.18	-6.17	3.17
Current Ratio	3.37	3.11	2.96	3.76
Debt / Equity %	38.48	48.46	59.81	n.a.

Compound Growth %'s	EPS %	-7.00	Net Income %	-3.99	Total Revenues %	-3.22

Comments

Last year's decline in revenue was due to divested operations. Net sales increased 1.3% on continuing operations. Fiscal 1996 results include a restructuring charge of $18.3 million that was supposed to set the course for profitable growth. Management explained the fiscal 1997 loss as attributable to a $5 million charge for repositioning the Joshua's Christian Stores chain, severance expenses and store closings. At June 30, 1998, the Company had $37.8 million of goodwill recorded as assets, which equates to approximately 42% of book value. For the six months ended December 31, 1998, the Company reported revenues of $103.9 million and a net loss of $11.2 million ($.91 per share) which included additional restructuring charges of $8.1 million.

Officers	Position	Ownership Information	
R. Earl Cox III	Chairman	Number of Shares Outstanding	12,610,569
Michael J. Walsh	President, CEO	Market Capitalization	$ 46,533,000
James D. Allen	Exec VP, CFO	Number of Shareholders	7,200
Russell L. Price	Vice President, Secretary	Where Listed / Symbol	NYSE / TAC

Other Information

Transfer Agent	ChaseMellon Shareholder Services Ridgefield Park, NJ	SIC Code	5940
Auditor	PricewaterhouseCoopers LLP	Employees	2,800
		Web Site	tandycrafts.com

Tangram Enterprise Solutions, Inc.

11000 Regency Parkway, Suite 401 Cary, NC 27511 Telephone (919)653-6000 Fax (919)653-6004

Company Description

Tangram Enterprise Solutions, Inc. develops and markets asset tracking software and software distribution solutions that enable automated enterprise-wide information system management. Since early 1996, the Company has focused its business on the asset tracking market and the launch of Asset Insight. Asset Insight is designed to enable corporations to proactively manage their base of distributed assets without disruption to their business. The Company also offers AM:PM® software, which provides automatic software distribution, data distribution and data collection within a heterogeneous business environment. The Company was founded in 1984.

	12/31/98	12/31/97	12/31/96	12/31/95
Per Share Information				
Stock Price	4.50	6.25	5.62	1.75
Earnings Per Share	0.06	-0.22	-0.02	-0.08
Price / Earnings Ratio	75.00	n.a.	n.a.	n.a.
Book Value Per Share	0.37	0.29	0.53	0.57
Price / Book Value %	1,216.22	2,155.17	1,060.38	307.02
Dividends Per Share	0.0	0.0	0.0	0.0
Annual Financial Data				
Operating Results (000's)				
Total Revenues	20,678.0	14,074.0	11,142.0	12,538.0
Costs & Expenses	-19,542.0	-17,535.0	-11,395.0	-12,845.0
Income Before Taxes and Other	1,136.0	-3,461.0	-253.0	-307.0
Other Items	0.0	0.0	0.0	0.0
Income Tax	-20.0	0.0	0.0	-878.0
Net Income	1,116.0	-3,461.0	-253.0	-1,185.0
Cash Flow From Operations	1,403.0	463.0	2,807.0	2,123.0
Balance Sheet (000's)				
Cash & Equivalents	245.0	246.0	176.0	92.0
Total Current Assets	6,829.0	3,478.0	3,434.0	3,202.0
Fixed Assets, Net	381.0	466.0	488.0	278.0
Total Assets	15,170.0	12,961.0	12,946.0	12,829.0
Total Current Liabilities	5,358.0	5,021.0	4,289.0	4,581.0
Long-Term Debt	3,576.0	3,006.0	400.0	0.0
Stockholders' Equity	5,764.0	4,483.0	8,257.0	8,246.0
Performance & Financial Condition				
Return on Total Revenues %	5.40	-24.59	-2.27	-9.45
Return on Avg Stockholders' Equity %	21.78	-54.33	-3.07	-13.46
Return on Average Assets %	7.93	-26.72	-1.96	-8.50
Current Ratio	1.27	0.69	0.80	0.70
Debt / Equity %	62.04	67.05	4.84	n.a.

Compound Growth %'s	EPS % n.a.	Net Income % n.a.	Total Revenues %	18.15

Comments

Revenues increased 47% in 1998 driven by a three-fold increase in Asset Insight product line revenue. The Company has developed a total of 63 channel partner relationships to date for the promotion of Asset Insight as compared to 22 partners at the end of 1997. Despite expensing $3,340,000 for research and development, the Company was profitable in 1998. At December 31, 1998, the Company had $29 million of tax loss carryovers to offset future taxable income. The 1997 loss reflects a reserve charge as a result of the uncertain collection of a receivable and as a result of a substantial increase in expenditures for research and development, a sales and marketing campaign, and increased staffing to support the Asset Insight product rollout.

Officers	Position	Ownership Information	
Charles A. Root	Chairman	Number of Shares Outstanding	15,767,747
W. Christopher Jesse	President, CEO	Market Capitalization	$ 70,954,862
Steven F. Kuekes	Senior VP	Number of Shareholders	3,000
John N. Nelli	Senior VP, CFO	Where Listed / Symbol	NASDAQ / TESI

Other Information			
Transfer Agent	ChaseMellon Shareholder Services Ridgefield Park, NJ	SIC Code	7372
Auditor	Ernst & Young LLP	Employees	141
		Web Site	tangram.com

Tanknology-NDE International, Inc.

8900 Shoal Creek, Building 200   Austin, TX 78757   Telephone (512)451-6334   Fax (512)459-1459

Company Description

Tanknology-NDE International, Inc., formerly NDE Environmental Corporation, provides environmental compliance services, installation of products, and consulting to owners and operators of aboveground and underground storage tanks. Operations are conducted in the United States, Puerto Rico, and the District of Columbia. The Company expects that over the next two years it will see a significant decline in its precision tank testing services as government regulations and enforcement thereof are taking over. Accordingly, it has begun to diversify into the construction services field, has expanded its participation in the installation of Automatic Tank Gauges, and has entered new businesses. The Company has grown significantly through acquisitions, financed primarily by debt. On August 7, 1998, the Company acquired OSI, a company engaged in the business of providing site service management to retail fuel and food service providers.

	12/31/98	12/31/97	12/31/96	12/31/95
Per Share Information				
Stock Price	0.87	0.13	0.41	0.05
Earnings Per Share	0.16	-0.09	-0.21	-1.45
Price / Earnings Ratio	5.44	n.a.	n.a.	n.a.
Book Value Per Share	0.14	-0.11	-0.05	-0.11
Price / Book Value %	621.43	n.a.	n.a.	n.a.
Dividends Per Share	0.0	0.0	0.0	0.0
Annual Financial Data				
Operating Results (000's)				
Total Revenues	67,034.0	38,780.9	16,153.8	11,503.8
Costs & Expenses	-62,320.4	-40,304.6	-18,728.8	-14,396.4
Income Before Taxes and Other	4,713.5	-1,535.1	-3,408.4	-2,892.6
Other Items	0.0	220.5	1,813.1	0.0
Income Tax	-809.7	-39.1	-43.8	0.0
Net Income	3,903.8	-1,353.6	-1,639.0	-2,892.6
Cash Flow From Operations	2,239.6	-2,225.2	868.0	-1,181.4
Balance Sheet (000's)				
Cash & Equivalents	416.2	193.6	2,412.2	327.0
Total Current Assets	20,227.6	11,682.5	10,093.2	2,910.4
Fixed Assets, Net	8,109.1	4,812.5	5,736.4	4,027.0
Total Assets	35,482.8	21,748.8	25,049.6	8,229.8
Total Current Liabilities	13,201.5	10,938.9	9,992.1	4,729.2
Long-Term Debt	18,271.7	0.0	14,192.0	3,739.7
Stockholders' Equity	2,302.5	-1,804.3	-734.5	-239.0
Performance & Financial Condition				
Return on Total Revenues %	5.82	-3.49	-10.15	-25.15
Return on Avg Stockholders' Equity %	1,567.42	n.a.	n.a.	-520.64
Return on Average Assets %	13.64	-5.78	-9.85	-34.64
Current Ratio	1.53	1.07	1.01	0.62
Debt / Equity %	793.58	n.a.	n.a.	n.a.

Compound Growth %'s	EPS %	n.a.	Net Income %	n.a.	Total Revenues %	79.95

Comments

Regulatory deadlines caused a flurry of activity in 1998. This combined with a $5.7 million upgrade program for a major customer and the inclusion of acquired companies in operating results generated a 73% increase in total revenues. A refinancing of debt reduced interest expense from $3.2 million in 1997 to $1.8 million in 1998. Increased utilization of equipment and personnel had the impact of increasing gross margins. This welcome combination of factors allowed the Company to report solid profits for 1998. Goodwill of $2.4 million approximates stockholders' equity and book value per share.

Officers	Position	Ownership Information	
Jay Allen Chaffee	Chairman	Number of Shares Outstanding	16,735,040
A. Daniel Sharplin	President, CEO	Market Capitalization	$ 14,559,485
David G. Osowski	Vice President, CFO	Number of Shareholders	2,000
H. Baxter Nairon	Vice President	Where Listed / Symbol	OTC-BB / TNDE

Other Information

Transfer Agent	Continental Stock Transfer & Trust Co. New York, NY		SIC Code	8734
Auditor	Ernst & Young LLP		Employees	460
Market Maker	Troster Singer Corporation	(800)526-3160	Web Site	tanknde.com
	M.H. Meyerson & Co., Inc.	(800)333-3113		

Tapistron International, Inc.

6203 Alabama Highway Ringgold, GA 30736 Telephone (706)965-9300 Fax (706)965-9310

Company Description

Tapistron International, Inc. is in the business of developing or acquiring proprietary technologies in the textile industry. Since inception in 1986, the Company's efforts have been focused on the continued development, production and marketing of the computerized yarn placement machine (CYP machine) for producing tufted carpets and rugs in highly versatile patterns, colors and textures. The Company is also involved in the exploration of a second technology involving the dyeing of textile materials. Tapistron filed a voluntary petition for relief under Chapter 11 of the United States Bankruptcy Code on June 21, 1996. The Court approved the plan of reorganization in August 1997 after a successful private placement of $2.5 million earlier that month.

	07/31/98	07/31/97	07/31/96	07/31/95
Per Share Information				
Stock Price as of 12/31	0.21	0.25	0.12	0.47
Earnings Per Share	-0.01	0.03	-0.45	-0.69
Price / Earnings Ratio	n.a.	8.33	n.a.	n.a.
Book Value Per Share	0.13	0.09	0.06	0.50
Price / Book Value %	161.54	277.78	200.00	94.00
Dividends Per Share	0.0	0.0	0.0	0.0
Annual Financial Data				
Operating Results (000's)				
Total Revenues	5,693.6	3,626.2	1,331.8	2,608.1
Costs & Expenses	-5,880.8	-4,516.2	-4,958.4	-8,068.4
Income Before Taxes and Other	-208.6	-1,683.6	-4,649.1	-6,053.2
Other Items	0.0	0.0	171.0	0.0
Income Tax	0.0	2,000.0	0.0	0.0
Net Income	-208.6	316.4	-4,478.1	-6,053.2
Cash Flow From Operations	-2,221.7	446.2	-1,002.0	-3,608.3
Balance Sheet (000's)				
Cash & Equivalents	247.1	27.9	17.1	99.4
Total Current Assets	3,138.4	2,532.1	2,840.2	3,895.7
Fixed Assets, Net	572.4	564.3	877.3	4,771.3
Total Assets	5,882.9	5,267.8	4,016.5	9,655.9
Total Current Liabilities	668.8	1,774.0	1,755.7	4,802.7
Long-Term Debt	0.0	0.0	1,604.7	14.0
Stockholders' Equity	4,511.9	972.4	656.1	4,839.2
Performance & Financial Condition				
Return on Total Revenues %	-3.66	8.72	-336.25	-232.09
Return on Avg Stockholders' Equity %	-7.61	38.85	-162.98	-96.91
Return on Average Assets %	-3.74	6.82	-65.51	-58.66
Current Ratio	4.69	1.43	1.62	0.81
Debt / Equity %	n.a.	n.a.	244.60	0.29

Compound Growth %'s	EPS % n.a.	Net Income % n.a.	Total Revenues %	29.72

Comments

Sales jumped 55.9% in fiscal 1998 as the CYP machine received general acceptance by the carpet industry. The operating loss of only $208,608 was the smallest in years. In fiscal 1997, the Company booked a $2 million income tax benefit, resulting in a net profit for the year. At July 31, 1998, the Company had $21.4 million in tax loss carryovers should it generate future profits. For the six months ended January 31, 1999, the Company reported revenues and a net loss of $2.7 million and $254,979 ($.007 per share) as compared to $2.7 million and a net loss of $50,078 ($.002 per share) in the same period of the preceding year.

Officers	Position	Ownership Information	
J. Darwin Poe	President, CEO	Number of Shares Outstanding	34,785,611
Rodney C. Hardeman, Jr.	Exec VP	Market Capitalization	$ 7,304,978
Gary L. Coulter	Secretary	Number of Shareholders	3,000
Kim K. Amos	Vice President	Where Listed / Symbol	OTC-BB / TAPI

Other Information

Transfer Agent	Continental Stock Transfer & Trust Co. New York, NY		SIC Code	3550
Auditor	Dudley, Hopton-Jones et al.		Employees	28
Market Maker	Troster Singer Corporation	(800)526-3160	Web Site	tapistron.com
	Paragon Capital Corporation	(800)345-0505		

Techdyne, Inc.

2230 W. 77th Street   Hialeah, FL 33016   Telephone (305)556-9210   Fax (305)364-1350

Company Description

Techdyne, Inc. is an international contract manufacturer of electronic and electro-mechanical products, primarily manufactured to customer specifications and designed for original equipment manufacturers (OEMs) and distributors in the data processing, telecommunications, instrumentation and food preparation equipment industries. Custom-designed products primarily include conventional and molded cables and wire harnesses, and complex printed circuit boards and electro-mechanical assemblies. The Company also provides OEMs with value-added, turnkey contract manufacturing services and total systems assembly and integration. In addition, the Company delivers manufacturing and test engineering services and materials management, with flexible and service-oriented manufacturing and assembly services for its customers' high-tech and rapidly changing products. The Company was founded in 1976.

	12/31/98	12/31/97	12/31/96	12/31/95
Per Share Information				
Stock Price	2.00	4.37	5.62	6.12
Earnings Per Share	0.15	0.24	0.14	0.27
Price / Earnings Ratio	13.33	18.21	40.14	22.67
Book Value Per Share	1.80	1.85	1.20	0.91
Price / Book Value %	111.11	236.22	468.33	672.53
Dividends Per Share	0.0	0.0	0.0	0.0
Annual Financial Data				
Operating Results (000's)				
Total Revenues	44,926.7	33,168.8	24,434.2	30,424.4
Costs & Expenses	-44,001.8	-32,307.5	-23,423.7	-28,577.5
Income Before Taxes and Other	924.9	861.2	1,010.5	1,846.9
Other Items	0.0	0.0	0.0	0.0
Income Tax	-127.2	564.3	-267.7	-531.6
Net Income	797.7	1,425.5	742.7	1,315.3
Cash Flow From Operations	1,544.2	-3,570.7	-486.6	2,085.4
Balance Sheet (000's)				
Cash & Equivalents	1,659.7	1,451.6	3,954.0	3,131.5
Total Current Assets	15,936.3	17,069.2	10,546.7	10,471.1
Fixed Assets, Net	5,076.0	5,240.5	2,506.0	2,242.5
Total Assets	23,817.8	24,625.1	13,224.2	12,879.1
Total Current Liabilities	6,615.0	7,521.9	3,950.1	5,550.1
Long-Term Debt	4,450.6	4,619.1	1,384.6	729.8
Stockholders' Equity	9,460.7	9,508.9	5,168.3	3,662.9
Performance & Financial Condition				
Return on Total Revenues %	1.78	4.30	3.04	4.32
Return on Avg Stockholders' Equity %	8.41	19.42	16.82	57.10
Return on Average Assets %	3.29	7.53	5.69	12.17
Current Ratio	2.41	2.27	2.67	1.89
Debt / Equity %	47.04	48.58	26.79	19.92

Compound Growth %'s	EPS %	-17.79	Net Income %	-15.35	Total Revenues %	13.87

Comments

The Company entered the food preparation equipment business through the acquisition of Lytton in July 1997. 1998 revenues increased primarily due to recording a full year of Lytton revenues. Approximately 50% of sales for 1998 were made to five customers. Significant reductions or delays from any of these major customers could have a material adverse effect on the Company's results of operations. The Company recorded a deferred tax credit relating to foreign operations in 1997 which resulted in a net tax benefit for the year. Goodwill on the books at December 31, 1998, approximated 28% of stockholders' equity and book value per share.

Officers	Position	Ownership Information	
Thomas K. Langbein	Chairman, CEO	Number of Shares Outstanding	5,250,167
Barry Pardon	President	Market Capitalization	$ 10,500,334
Joseph Verga	Senior VP, Treasurer	Number of Shareholders	820
Daniel R. Ouzts	VP - Finance, Controller	Where Listed / Symbol	NASDAQ / TCDN

Other Information			
Transfer Agent	Continental Stock Transfer & Trust Co. New York, NY	SIC Code	3679
Auditor	Ernst & Young LLP	Employees	573
		Web Site	tcdn.com

Technology Research Corporation

5250 140th Avenue North   Clearwater, FL 33760   Telephone (727)535-0572   Fax (727)535-4828

Company Description

Technology Research Corporation designs, develops, manufactures and markets electronic control and measurement devices related to the distribution of electric power and specializes in electrical safety products that protect against shock, electrocution and fires. Such products include ground fault protective devices, fire prevention devices for fires caused by aging appliance and extension cords, controls for electrical power generating systems, transformers and magnetics. These products are used in providing safe and efficient utilization and controlled distribution of electricity. The Company was founded in 1981.

	03/31/98	03/31/97	03/31/96	03/31/95
Per Share Information				
Stock Price as of 12/31	1.22	3.50	4.31	11.25
Earnings Per Share	-0.04	0.10	0.38	0.35
Price / Earnings Ratio	n.a.	35.00	11.34	32.14
Book Value Per Share	2.13	2.35	2.49	2.35
Price / Book Value %	57.28	148.94	173.09	478.72
Dividends Per Share	0.18	0.24	0.24	0.0
Annual Financial Data				
Operating Results (000's)				
Total Revenues	18,562.9	15,592.5	17,641.8	21,949.0
Costs & Expenses	-18,648.5	-14,895.4	-14,437.2	-19,536.0
Income Before Taxes and Other	-85.6	697.1	3,204.6	2,413.0
Other Items	0.0	0.0	0.0	0.0
Income Tax	-110.7	-130.5	-1,165.8	-545.0
Net Income	-196.3	566.7	2,038.8	1,868.0
Cash Flow From Operations	-585.7	1,512.8	1,235.2	2,467.1
Balance Sheet (000's)				
Cash & Equivalents	1,153.8	1,307.6	341.6	1,707.9
Total Current Assets	11,118.9	12,554.3	12,799.4	12,208.7
Fixed Assets, Net	4,557.1	2,957.5	2,421.6	2,323.9
Total Assets	15,746.8	15,637.9	15,380.6	14,813.9
Total Current Liabilities	4,243.2	2,903.2	1,867.7	2,119.0
Long-Term Debt	131.3	206.3	281.4	356.4
Stockholders' Equity	11,372.4	12,528.5	13,231.6	12,338.6
Performance & Financial Condition				
Return on Total Revenues %	-1.06	3.63	11.56	8.51
Return on Avg Stockholders' Equity %	-1.64	4.40	15.95	16.49
Return on Average Assets %	-1.25	3.65	13.50	13.22
Current Ratio	2.62	4.32	6.85	5.76
Debt / Equity %	1.15	1.65	2.13	2.89

Compound Growth %'s   EPS % n.a.   Net Income % n.a.   Total Revenues % -5.43

Comments

The Company executed a 1 for 3 reverse split in fiscal 1996. All per share amounts have been restated for consistency. A new manufacturing facility in Honduras was expected to improve the Company's cost structure but got off to a rocky start. Manufacturing complexities caused the facility not to meet its production shipment plan. The result was that additional product continued to be produced at the Company's Clearwater facility causing the use of temporary employees and heavy overtime as well as higher labor rates in order to meet customer delivery commitments. Management estimates a total of $1.2 million in manufacturing cost variances for fiscal 1998. The 20% increase in revenue in fiscal 1998 was largely attributable to military sales which were expected to decrease in fiscal 1999. For the nine months ended December 31, 1998, revenues and net income were $12.9 million and $253,870 ($.05 per share) as compared to $14.0 million and $269,890 ($.05 per share) for the same period of the preceding year.

Officers	Position	Ownership Information	
Robert S. Wiggins	Chairman, CEO	Number of Shares Outstanding	5,332,571
Raymond H. Legatti	President	Market Capitalization	$ 6,505,737
Raymond B. Wood	Senior VP	Number of Shareholders	3,200
Scott J. Loucks	VP - Finance	Where Listed / Symbol	NASDAQ / TRCI

Other Information			
Transfer Agent	ChaseMellon Shareholder Services Ridgefield Park, NJ	SIC Code	3613
Auditor	KPMG LLP	Employees	145
		Web Site	techrsrch.com

Tekgraf, Inc.

6000 Lake Forrest Drive, Suite 110 Atlanta, GA 30328 Telephone (404)252-0201 Fax (404)459-8288

Company Description

Tekgraf, Inc. is engaged in the manufacture, configuration, distribution and servicing of computers and computer peripherals, hardware and software. The Company commenced operations in February 1993 for the purpose of engaging in the manufacture of custom or made-to-order premium servers and network workstations under the brand name Crescent Computer. In December 1994, the Company acquired a controlling interest in Prisym Technologies, Inc. of Georgia, an authorized reseller of equipment. In June 1997, the Company completed the acquisition of six regional distributors specializing in computer graphics technologies. In 1998 the Company acquired an additional three distributors.

	12/31/98	12/31/97	12/31/96	12/31/95
Per Share Information				
Stock Price	1.56	2.31	n.a.	n.a.
Earnings Per Share	0.02	-0.15	0.04	0.0
Price / Earnings Ratio	78.00	n.a.	n.a.	n.a.
Book Value Per Share	3.42	6.02	0.01	0.01
Price / Book Value %	45.61	38.37	n.a.	n.a.
Dividends Per Share	0.0	0.0	0.0	0.0
Annual Financial Data				
Operating Results (000's)				
Total Revenues	99,295.4	48,800.0	13,429.0	12,277.0
Costs & Expenses	-98,717.2	-49,234.0	-13,373.0	-12,282.0
Income Before Taxes and Other	578.2	-434.0	56.0	-5.0
Other Items	0.0	0.0	0.0	0.0
Income Tax	-487.0	41.0	-13.0	1.0
Net Income	91.2	-393.0	43.0	-4.0
Cash Flow From Operations	-3,128.9	1,585.7	-199.1	-170.4
Balance Sheet (000's)				
Cash & Equivalents	1,702.8	8,600.3	633.0	306.0
Total Current Assets	27,219.1	22,950.4	2,891.7	2,893.0
Fixed Assets, Net	824.7	344.7	56.8	114.0
Total Assets	37,155.6	29,952.3	3,007.1	3,007.0
Total Current Liabilities	15,397.9	9,884.3	2,995.8	2,997.0
Long-Term Debt	0.0	12.8	0.0	0.0
Stockholders' Equity	21,661.7	20,055.2	10.1	10.0
Performance & Financial Condition				
Return on Total Revenues %	0.09	-0.81	0.32	-0.03
Return on Avg Stockholders' Equity %	0.44	-3.92	427.61	n.a.
Return on Average Assets %	0.27	-2.38	1.43	-0.20
Current Ratio	1.77	2.32	0.97	0.97
Debt / Equity %	n.a.	0.06	n.a.	n.a.

Compound Growth %'s	EPS %	-29.29	Net Income %	45.61	Total Revenues %	100.73

Comments

All acquisitions were accounted for under the purchase method of accounting. Therefore, results of the acquired companies have been included starting with the dates of the respective transactions. All of the 1998 growth in revenue was attributable to the acquisitions. The compound negative growth in earnings per share is diluted from the compound growth in net income because of the issuance of new shares in connection with the acquisitions. At December 31, 1998, the Company had $9 million of goodwill reflected on its books as assets which equated to approximately 42% of stockholders' equity and book value per share. Management's strategy of increasing market share may pay off once the Company's focus shifts to bottom line profitability. But there is no way to be sure until the proof is in hand.

Officers	Position	Ownership Information	
William M. Rychel	President, CEO	Number of Shares Outstanding	6,328,331
Martyn L. Cooper	COO	Market Capitalization	$ 9,872,196
W. Jeffrey Camp	CFO	Number of Shareholders	2,000
Albert E. Sisto	Director	Where Listed / Symbol	NASDAQ / TKGFA

Other Information			
Transfer Agent	American Stock Transfer & Trust Co. New York, NY	SIC Code	5045
Auditor	PricewaterhouseCoopers LLP	Employees	121
		Web Site	tekgraf.com

Tel-Instrument Electronics Corp.

728 Garden Street   Carlstadt, NJ 07072   Telephone (201)933-1600   Fax (201)933-7340

Company Description

Tel-Instrument Electronics Corp., founded in 1947, designs, manufactures and markets avionic test equipment for the general, commercial, and government/military aviation markets. The Company's instruments are used to test navigation and communications equipment installed in aircraft. The Company sells its equipment to both the domestic and international markets. On August 12, 1997, the Company received notice that it was awarded a major contract from the U.S. Navy. The initial order is for $950,000 to provide five T-47M IFF (Identification Friend or Foe) test sets for navy evaluation and for the associated documentation. This work represents a major milestone for the Company and its engineering efforts since the contract could be a significant source of future revenues. The contract includes options for up to 1,300 units which the Navy can exercise through calendar year 2001.

	03/31/98	03/31/97	03/31/96	03/31/95
Per Share Information				
Stock Price as of 12/31	1.50	1.50	0.75	0.19
Earnings Per Share	0.28	0.41	0.04	0.01
Price / Earnings Ratio	5.36	3.66	18.75	19.00
Book Value Per Share	0.51	0.22	-0.70	-0.74
Price / Book Value %	294.12	681.82	n.a.	n.a.
Dividends Per Share	0.0	0.0	0.0	0.0
Annual Financial Data				
Operating Results (000's)				
Total Revenues	3,987.1	3,170.9	2,318.6	1,865.5
Costs & Expenses	-3,432.0	-2,729.8	-2,222.9	-1,855.0
Income Before Taxes and Other	519.1	441.1	95.7	10.5
Other Items	0.0	0.0	0.0	12.0
Income Tax	58.7	340.2	0.0	0.0
Net Income	577.8	781.3	95.7	22.5
Cash Flow From Operations	98.4	464.6	20.1	103.3
Balance Sheet (000's)				
Cash & Equivalents	585.3	528.6	22.6	38.8
Total Current Assets	1,445.1	1,268.8	736.1	795.6
Fixed Assets, Net	79.3	45.5	41.8	40.2
Total Assets	1,941.1	1,648.1	824.6	872.4
Total Current Liabilities	581.1	827.8	1,236.3	1,314.8
Long-Term Debt	300.0	350.0	100.0	165.0
Stockholders' Equity	1,060.1	455.3	-511.7	-607.4
Performance & Financial Condition				
Return on Total Revenues %	14.49	24.64	4.13	1.20
Return on Avg Stockholders' Equity %	76.26	n.a.	n.a.	n.a.
Return on Average Assets %	32.20	63.19	11.28	2.72
Current Ratio	2.49	1.53	0.60	0.61
Debt / Equity %	28.30	76.88	n.a.	n.a.

Compound Growth %'s	EPS %	203.66	Net Income %	195.14	Total Revenues %	28.81

Comments

Included in fiscal 1998 and 1997 results are income tax benefits of $58,700 and $340,200, respectively, related to the use of tax loss carryovers. The 25% increase in sales is attributable to the government segment, specifically to sales associated with a contract with the United States Air Force which was completed during the year. Management predicted lower revenue in the first half of fiscal 1999. Research and development costs rose to $902,000 in fiscal 1998 from $487,000 in the prior year. For the nine months ended December 31, 1998, the Company reported revenues and a net loss of $2.7 million and $11,954 ($.01 per share) as compared to $3.2 million and a net profit of $348,593 ($.17 per share) for the equivalent period of the preceding year.

Officers	Position	Ownership Information	
Harold K. Fletcher	President, CEO	Number of Shares Outstanding	2,094,735
Donald S. Bab	Exec VP, Secretary	Market Capitalization	$ 3,142,103
Richard J. Wixson	VP - Manufacturing	Number of Shareholders	838
George J. Leon	Director	Where Listed / Symbol	OTC-BB / TINE

Other Information			
Transfer Agent	Registrar & Transfer Co. Cranford, NJ	SIC Code	3670
Auditor	PricewaterhouseCoopers LLP	Employees	21
Market Maker	Herzog, Heine, Geduld, Inc.	(800)221-3600	
	Carr Securities Corporation	(800)221-2243	

Telebyte Technology, Inc.

270 East Pulaski Road   Greenlawn, NY 11740   Telephone (516)423-3232   Fax (516)385-8184

Company Description

Telebyte Technology, Inc. designs, manufactures and markets electronic data communications products that operate over copper and fiber cables. The products are sold to end users, dealers, distributors and original equipment manufacturers. The Company's data communications equipment is used principally to provide connectivity solutions and maintain data communications networks. Telebyte addresses the needs of customers who have computer systems with data communications applications with distances ranging from a few feet to a few miles. Accordingly, Telebyte's products are used in data communication networks in facilities such as industrial plants, factories, high rise office buildings, and campus-like environments. The Company was founded in 1983.

	12/31/98	12/31/97	12/31/96	12/31/95
Per Share Information				
Stock Price	1.75	1.75	0.81	0.75
Earnings Per Share	0.22	0.31	0.02	0.07
Price / Earnings Ratio	7.95	5.65	40.50	10.71
Book Value Per Share	1.94	1.74	1.42	1.39
Price / Book Value %	90.21	100.57	57.04	53.96
Dividends Per Share	0.0	0.0	0.0	0.0
Annual Financial Data				
Operating Results (000's)				
Total Revenues	5,643.7	5,542.0	4,203.3	3,827.5
Costs & Expenses	-5,274.2	-5,068.1	-4,171.8	-3,723.9
Income Before Taxes and Other	369.5	473.8	31.5	103.6
Other Items	0.0	0.0	0.0	0.0
Income Tax	-36.0	-7.0	-1.0	-2.0
Net Income	333.5	466.8	30.5	101.6
Cash Flow From Operations	274.3	254.5	107.8	320.1
Balance Sheet (000's)				
Cash & Equivalents	919.6	730.3	583.7	609.5
Total Current Assets	3,111.0	2,823.4	2,234.9	2,205.4
Fixed Assets, Net	1,064.1	1,120.4	1,170.0	1,198.5
Total Assets	4,332.3	4,113.5	3,448.3	3,451.4
Total Current Liabilities	553.2	613.2	358.3	313.6
Long-Term Debt	862.8	926.6	983.1	1,046.3
Stockholders' Equity	2,916.3	2,573.7	2,106.8	2,091.5
Performance & Financial Condition				
Return on Total Revenues %	5.91	8.42	0.72	2.65
Return on Avg Stockholders' Equity %	12.15	19.95	1.45	4.97
Return on Average Assets %	7.90	12.35	0.88	2.99
Current Ratio	5.62	4.60	6.24	7.03
Debt / Equity %	29.59	36.00	46.66	50.03

Compound Growth %'s	EPS %	46.48	Net Income %	48.62	Total Revenues %	13.82

Comments

The 1998 numbers may look a little sleepy but more was happening than meets the eye. Negotiations were conducted and concluded to remove the Company's chairman and CEO Joel Kramer, effective January 20, 1999. Total consideration of $1,075,190 will be paid in the package which includes $867,510 for his shares of Company stock. The Company may be small but its financial condition is relatively strong. Research and development expense increased to $469,415 in 1998 from $319,996 in 1997. The 32% increase in revenue in 1997 was attributable to expanded sales and marketing efforts begun in 1996. The Company is about to run out of tax loss carryovers and credits as only $176,000 and $66,000, respectively, remained at the end of 1998.

Officers	Position	Ownership Information	
Kenneth S. Schneider	Chairman, CEO	Number of Shares Outstanding	1,506,266
Michael Breneisen	President, CFO	Market Capitalization	$ 2,635,966
Alan Pfeffer	Vice President	Number of Shareholders	268
Anthony Horber	Vice President	Where Listed / Symbol	OTC-BB / TBTI

Other Information

Transfer Agent	American Stock Transfer & Trust Co. New York, NY		SIC Code	3576
Auditor	Grant Thornton LLP		Employees	39
Market Maker	Wien Securities Corp.	(800)624-0050	Web Site	telebyteusa.com
	Wm. V. Frankel & Co., Inc.	(800)631-3091		

Telecomm Industries Corp.

1743 Quincy Avenue Naperville, IL 60540 Telephone (630)369-7111 Fax (630)369-7193

Company Description

Telecomm Industries Corp. is one of the nation's largest Regional Bell Operating Company distributors. As such, Telecomm sells voice, data, cellular, video and telephone information network solutions to business customers throughout its five-state region. Ameritech and BellSouth are Telecomm's primary partners. In addition, the Company represents numerous telecommunications manufacturers and suppliers including Nortel, Lucent, NEC, Comdial, and Toshiba. The Company also offers services including system networking, installation, and maintenance. The Company was incorporated as Scotco Data Leasing in 1967. It was inactive from 1984 to 1993. Acquisitions are an important element in the Company's growth strategy. Three acquisitions were made during 1997 and one in 1998. In February 1999, the Company entered into letters of intent to acquire six Internet companies.

	12/31/98	12/31/97	12/31/96	12/31/95
Per Share Information				
Stock Price	0.47	1.16	1.25	2.25
Earnings Per Share	-0.12	0.10	0.06	0.02
Price / Earnings Ratio	n.a.	11.60	20.83	112.50
Book Value Per Share	0.31	0.40	0.26	0.19
Price / Book Value %	151.61	290.00	480.77	1,184.21
Dividends Per Share	0.0	0.0	0.0	0.0
Annual Financial Data				
Operating Results (000's)				
Total Revenues	24,023.2	17,062.8	10,586.9	5,713.3
Costs & Expenses	-26,069.9	-15,148.6	-9,662.6	-5,370.6
Income Before Taxes and Other	-2,046.7	1,914.1	923.4	342.7
Other Items	0.0	0.0	0.0	0.0
Income Tax	586.4	-792.7	-371.2	-137.6
Net Income	-1,460.3	1,121.5	552.2	205.1
Cash Flow From Operations	-2,800.3	-806.4	-55.6	-548.7
Balance Sheet (000's)				
Cash & Equivalents	0.0	97.8	238.3	575.4
Total Current Assets	6,856.9	5,239.0	4,030.2	2,360.2
Fixed Assets, Net	1,609.9	1,481.6	482.7	364.3
Total Assets	16,239.9	13,175.7	5,607.7	3,187.8
Total Current Liabilities	5,954.6	4,660.2	2,336.9	1,024.7
Long-Term Debt	6,066.7	2,863.0	389.4	137.1
Stockholders' Equity	3,768.0	4,735.2	2,478.5	1,867.0
Performance & Financial Condition				
Return on Total Revenues %	-6.08	6.57	5.22	3.59
Return on Avg Stockholders' Equity %	-34.35	31.09	25.42	14.98
Return on Average Assets %	-9.93	11.94	12.56	8.27
Current Ratio	1.15	1.12	1.72	2.30
Debt / Equity %	161.01	60.46	15.71	7.34

Compound Growth %'s	EPS % n.a.	Net Income % n.a.	Total Revenues % 61.40

Comments

In 1998 Telecomm underwent some major changes to consolidate and centralize the Company's operations and redefine the information technology and accounting departments. Management believes that these changes will better position the Company to integrate acquisitions and to achieve continued growth and enhanced profitability in the future. The loss in 1998 is due to restructuring, lower margins due to pricing pressures, higher interest expense, and the write down of certain assets. At December 31, 1998, the Company had $3.7 million of intangibles on its balance sheet which equated to approximately 97% of stockholders' equity and book value per share.

Officers	Position	Ownership Information	
James M. Lowery	Chairman, CEO	Number of Shares Outstanding	12,121,559
Mark A. Travi	CFO	Market Capitalization	$ 5,697,133
Paul J. Satterthwaite	Vice President, Secretary	Number of Shareholders	405
Rita Koridek	Vice President	Where Listed / Symbol	OTC-BB / TCMM

Other Information

Transfer Agent	Continental Stock Transfer & Trust Co. New York, NY		SIC Code	4813
Auditor	PricewaterhouseCoopers LLP		Employees	200
Market Maker	Wilson-Davis & Co., Inc.	(800)453-5735	Web Site	tcmm.com
	Herzog, Heine, Geduld, Inc.	(800)221-3600		

Texas Equipment Corporation

1305 Hobbs Highway   Seminole, TX 79360   Telephone (915)758-3643   Fax (915)758-1215

Company Description

Texas Equipment Corporation operates eight retail stores in two states, specializing in the distribution, sales, service and rental of agricultural equipment. Deere & Company, a leading manufacturer and supplier of agricultural equipment in the United States since 1837, is the primary supplier of the equipment and parts sold by the Company. The Company's stores are located in west Texas and eastern New Mexico. Four of the stores were acquired during 1997 and two were acquired in 1998. The Company's customers are primarily farmers growing cotton, peanuts, corn, wheat and other grains.

	12/31/98	12/31/97	12/31/96	12/31/95
Per Share Information				
Stock Price	0.19	0.75	2.13	7.00
Earnings Per Share	0.04	0.01	0.04	0.02
Price / Earnings Ratio	4.75	75.00	53.25	350.00
Book Value Per Share	0.32	0.27	0.25	58.11
Price / Book Value %	59.38	277.78	852.00	12.05
Dividends Per Share	0.0	0.0	0.0	0.0
Annual Financial Data				
Operating Results (000's)				
Total Revenues	68,253.5	58,674.4	28,308.4	25,244.0
Costs & Expenses	-66,772.9	-56,998.3	-27,217.7	-24,827.3
Income Before Taxes and Other	1,480.6	1,387.9	1,090.7	416.7
Other Items	0.0	-540.4	0.0	0.0
Income Tax	-528.0	-572.5	-354.4	-163.3
Net Income	952.6	275.0	736.4	253.4
Cash Flow From Operations	-690.8	-2,473.0	469.0	634.3
Balance Sheet (000's)				
Cash & Equivalents	494.1	104.8	2,661.1	250.0
Total Current Assets	40,816.9	23,296.2	9,131.2	6,917.1
Fixed Assets, Net	5,725.9	4,027.7	1,244.4	1,444.9
Total Assets	47,845.6	28,528.6	11,612.3	9,624.7
Total Current Liabilities	34,883.3	19,729.7	4,316.5	4,790.7
Long-Term Debt	4,665.4	1,819.8	1,005.8	1,195.4
Stockholders' Equity	8,063.8	6,746.0	6,182.8	3,486.6
Performance & Financial Condition				
Return on Total Revenues %	1.40	0.47	2.60	1.00
Return on Avg Stockholders' Equity %	12.86	4.25	15.23	14.48
Return on Average Assets %	2.49	1.37	6.93	5.28
Current Ratio	1.17	1.18	2.12	1.44
Debt / Equity %	57.86	26.98	16.27	34.28

Compound Growth %'s	EPS %	25.99	Net Income %	55.49	Total Revenues %	39.31

Comments

The increases in revenue during the last two years were primarily due to the new stores acquired during those years. The severe 1998 drought made overall conditions somewhat unfavorable. In 1998 and 1997, the Company recorded non-cash charges of $154,724 and $288,211, respectively, which were related to the personal guarantee by three major shareholders and one executive officer of approximately $30 million of accounts payable to Deere & Company, and a $3.9 million credit facility at the Company's bank. Guarantee fees related to such arrangements were paid in the form of stock options. 1997 results include a nonrecurring expense of $540,398 ($.02 per share), related to a discontinued operation. The Company also incurred $323,462 in litigation expenses in connection with the discontinued operation. All matters were settled during 1997.

Officers	Position	Ownership Information	
Paul Condit	President, CEO	Number of Shares Outstanding	24,824,808
John T. Condit	Secretary, Treasurer	Market Capitalization	$ 4,716,714
E.A. Milo Mattorano	Vice President, CFO	Number of Shareholders	5,000
Robert T. Maynard	Director	Where Listed / Symbol	OTC-BB / TEXQ

Other Information			
Transfer Agent	American Securities Transfer, Inc. Lakewood, CO	SIC Code	5590
Auditor	Ernst & Young LLP	Employees	152
Market Maker	Wien Securities Corp. (800)624-0050		
	Paragon Capital Corporation (800)345-0505		

Texas Vanguard Oil Company

9811 Anderson Mill Road, Suite 202   Austin, TX 78750   Telephone (512)331-6781   Fax (512)331-4011

Company Description

Texas Vanguard Oil Company is engaged in the acquisition, exploration, development and operation of onshore oil and gas properties in the United States, principally in Texas. Generally the Company acquires working interests in producing oil and natural gas properties which it further develops. The Company owns a working interest in 180 oil wells and 56 gas wells. These are located on land leases totalling 7,101 acres in Texas, New Mexico, Wyoming and Oklahoma. Texas Vanguard Oil Company was founded in 1979 and completed its initial public offering in 1980.

	12/31/98	12/31/97	12/31/96	12/31/95
Per Share Information				
Stock Price	0.75	0.87	0.63	1.00
Earnings Per Share	0.12	0.17	0.18	0.06
Price / Earnings Ratio	6.25	5.12	3.50	16.67
Book Value Per Share	1.33	1.22	1.05	0.87
Price / Book Value %	56.39	71.31	60.00	114.94
Dividends Per Share	0.0	0.0	0.0	0.0
Annual Financial Data				
Operating Results (000's)				
Total Revenues	1,493.5	1,664.0	1,403.8	896.6
Costs & Expenses	-1,279.1	-1,305.2	-1,014.6	-739.9
Income Before Taxes and Other	214.3	358.8	303.6	128.8
Other Items	0.0	0.0	0.0	0.0
Income Tax	-45.0	-122.0	-45.4	-42.1
Net Income	169.3	236.8	258.2	86.7
Cash Flow From Operations	355.7	625.5	613.2	118.8
Balance Sheet (000's)				
Cash & Equivalents	1,099.8	1,105.3	985.2	383.3
Total Current Assets	1,187.7	1,185.7	1,021.8	409.7
Fixed Assets, Net	3,142.9	2,513.9	2,197.9	1,997.4
Total Assets	4,332.8	3,704.6	3,235.5	2,473.8
Total Current Liabilities	1,791.4	1,057.8	1,189.1	982.1
Long-Term Debt	482.6	802.4	560.8	252.2
Stockholders' Equity	1,891.8	1,722.4	1,485.6	1,239.4
Performance & Financial Condition				
Return on Total Revenues %	11.34	14.23	18.39	9.67
Return on Avg Stockholders' Equity %	9.37	14.76	18.95	7.25
Return on Average Assets %	4.21	6.82	9.04	3.83
Current Ratio	0.66	1.12	0.86	0.42
Debt / Equity %	25.51	46.58	37.75	20.35

Compound Growth %'s	EPS %	25.99	Net Income %	25.00	Total Revenues %	18.54

Comments

The Company increased production and realized higher prices per barrel for both oil and gas in 1996 and 1997. But the worldwide crude oil prices declined from approximately $16.50 per barrel at December 31, 1997 to approximately $10.00 per barrel at December 31, 1998. The average price per barrel realized in 1998 was $12.16 which caused a decline in total revenues. An improvement in oil prices was noted in early 1999. Management is focused on the long term and continues to make additional investments in proven oil and gas properties. Cash flow from operations is typically higher than net income because of deferred income taxes and depletion. The three officers listed above are active in management but do not take a salary.

Officers	Position	Ownership Information	
Robert N. Watson, Jr.	President, CEO	Number of Shares Outstanding	1,417,087
Linda R. Watson	Secretary, Treasurer	Market Capitalization	$ 1,062,815
Robert L. Patterson	Director	Number of Shareholders	553
		Where Listed / Symbol	OTC-BB / TVOC

Other Information			
Transfer Agent	American Securities Transfer, Inc. Denver, CO	SIC Code	1311
Auditor	Sprouse & Winn, L.L.P.	Employees	1
Market Maker	Paragon Capital Corporation	(800)521-8877	
	Boenning & Scattergood, Inc.	(800)883-8383	

Thermo TerraTech Inc.

81 Wyman Street, P.O. Box 9046   Waltham, MA 02254-9046   Telephone (781)622-1000   Fax (781)622-1123

Company Description

Thermo TerraTech Inc., founded in 1986, provides industrial outsourcing services and manufacturing support encompassing a broad range of specializations, including infrastructure engineering, design and construction, environmental compliance, laboratory testing, and metal treating. The Company's majority-owned, publicly held Thermo Remediation Inc. subsidiary is a national provider of environmental-liability management services. In May 1997, the Company purchased a controlling interest in The Randers Group Incorporated, also a publicly traded company.

	04/04/98	03/29/97	03/30/96	04/01/95
Per Share Information				
Stock Price as of 12/31	4.37	8.12	9.87	11.37
Earnings Per Share	0.18	-0.01	0.18	0.24
Price / Earnings Ratio	24.28	n.a.	54.83	47.38
Book Value Per Share	4.97	4.67	4.92	4.47
Price / Book Value %	87.93	173.88	200.61	254.36
Dividends Per Share	0.0	0.0	0.0	0.0
Annual Financial Data				
Operating Results (000's)				
Total Revenues	306,284.0	288,497.0	229,893.0	139,560.0
Costs & Expenses	-297,770.0	-288,788.0	-221,579.0	-128,547.0
Income Before Taxes and Other	8,514.0	-291.0	8,314.0	11,013.0
Other Items	-95.0	1,834.0	-1,223.0	-4,268.0
Income Tax	-5,146.0	-1,705.0	-3,644.0	-2,630.0
Net Income	3,273.0	-162.0	3,447.0	4,115.0
Cash Flow From Operations	6,528.0	8,953.0	9,072.0	7,385.0
Balance Sheet (000's)				
Cash & Equivalents	34,711.0	63,172.0	31,182.0	35,808.0
Total Current Assets	142,782.0	187,038.0	121,080.0	100,141.0
Fixed Assets, Net	91,709.0	83,566.0	81,845.0	59,737.0
Total Assets	360,526.0	393,784.0	332,009.0	271,673.0
Total Current Liabilities	73,463.0	109,723.0	53,632.0	35,445.0
Long-Term Debt	149,800.0	149,800.0	155,384.0	96,851.0
Stockholders' Equity	97,130.0	83,526.0	86,341.0	77,601.0
Performance & Financial Condition				
Return on Total Revenues %	1.07	-0.06	1.50	2.95
Return on Avg Stockholders' Equity %	3.62	-0.19	4.21	5.74
Return on Average Assets %	0.87	-0.04	1.14	1.47
Current Ratio	1.94	1.70	2.26	2.83
Debt / Equity %	154.23	179.35	179.97	124.81

Compound Growth %'s	EPS %	-9.14	Net Income %	-7.35	Total Revenues %	29.95

Comments

Thermo Electron Corp. (NYSE) owns an 82% interest in the Company. The Company consolidates the information of its two majority-owned public companies, ThermRetec (AMEX) and The Randers Killam Group (AMEX), with its own financial information. Fiscal 1998 results include a nonrecurring $3 million gain from the sale of a business. Fiscal 1997, 1996 and 1995 results include gains on the issuance of stock by subsidiaries of $1.5 million, $4.1 million and $1.3 million, respectively. At April 4, 1998, the Company had $107.8 million of intangible assets related to acquisitions on its books which equated to approximately 111% of stockholders' equity and book value per share. For the nine months ended December 31, 1998, the Company reported revenues and a net loss of $234.3 million and $1,924,000 ($.10 per share), which included $10.2 million of restructuring costs, as compared to $227.6 million and a net profit of $4,555,000 ($.24 per share) for the same period of the preceding year.

Officers	Position	Ownership Information	
John P. Appleton	President, CEO	Number of Shares Outstanding	19,532,585
John N. Hatsopoulos	Senior VP, CFO	Market Capitalization	$ 85,357,396
Emil C. Herkert	Vice President	Number of Shareholders	2,000
Jeffrey L. Powell	Vice President	Where Listed / Symbol	AMEX / TTT

Other Information			
Transfer Agent	American Stock Transfer & Trust Co. New York, NY	SIC Code	8734
Auditor	Arthur Andersen LLP	Employees	2,736
		Web Site	thermo.com

Thermo Vision Corporation

8E Forge Parkway   Franklin, MA 02038   Telephone (781)622-1000   Fax (781)553-1922

Company Description

Thermo Vision Corporation designs, manufactures, and markets a diverse array of photonics products. These are light-based technologies that are embedded as enabling technologies in a wide range of applications, including medical diagnostic and analytical instrumentation; semiconductor manufacturing; X-ray imaging; and physics, chemistry, and biology research. The Company was incorporated in November 1995 as a wholly-owned subsidiary of Thermo Optek Corporation (AMEX). In December 1997, the Company was spun out as a tax-free dividend to all Thermo Optek shareholders. Thermal Vision also sold 1.1 million shares to the public at the same time in an initial public offering.

	12/31/98	12/31/97	12/31/96	12/31/95
Per Share Information				
Stock Price	3.12	8.12	n.a.	n.a.
Earnings Per Share	0.03	0.34	0.21	0.02
Price / Earnings Ratio	104.00	23.88	n.a.	n.a.
Book Value Per Share	4.00	3.98	2.99	0.69
Price / Book Value %	78.00	204.02	n.a.	n.a.
Dividends Per Share	0.0	0.0	0.0	0.0
Annual Financial Data				
Operating Results (000's)				
Total Revenues	38,421.0	39,735.0	30,434.0	6,026.0
Costs & Expenses	-37,933.0	-35,686.0	-28,011.0	-5,775.0
Income Before Taxes and Other	488.0	4,049.0	2,423.0	251.0
Other Items	0.0	0.0	0.0	0.0
Income Tax	-267.0	-1,701.0	-1,005.0	-104.0
Net Income	221.0	2,348.0	1,418.0	147.0
Cash Flow From Operations	2,590.0	3,311.0	1,679.0	-126.0
Balance Sheet (000's)				
Cash & Equivalents	9,457.0	9,604.0	306.0	171.0
Total Current Assets	25,592.0	27,216.0	13,711.0	1,171.0
Fixed Assets, Net	5,855.0	4,757.0	3,901.0	800.0
Total Assets	46,280.0	47,401.0	28,362.0	6,971.0
Total Current Liabilities	6,137.0	7,577.0	8,110.0	200.0
Long-Term Debt	7,747.0	7,747.0	0.0	2,074.0
Stockholders' Equity	32,179.0	32,055.0	20,252.0	4,697.0
Performance & Financial Condition				
Return on Total Revenues %	0.58	5.91	4.66	2.44
Return on Avg Stockholders' Equity %	0.69	8.98	11.37	6.39
Return on Average Assets %	0.47	6.20	8.03	4.20
Current Ratio	4.17	3.59	1.69	5.86
Debt / Equity %	24.07	24.17	n.a.	44.16

Compound Growth %'s	EPS %	14.47	Net Income %	14.56	Total Revenues %	85.43

Comments

The compound growth of revenues is primarily attributable to acquisitions. Excluding the impact of acquisitions, revenues decreased $4.9 million in 1998 primarily as a result of a slowdown in the semiconductor industry and the economic crisis in Asia. Gross margins decreased as well largely due to a $2.2 million inventory write-down. Research and development costs totalled $4.2 million, $4.1 million and $3.5 million in 1998, 1997 and 1996, respectively. At December 31, 1998, the Company had $14.0 million of goodwill recorded as assets which equated to approximately 44% of stockholders' equity and book value per share.

Officers	Position	Ownership Information	
Kristine Stotz Langdon	President, CEO	Number of Shares Outstanding	8,048,276
Theo Melas-Kyriazi	CFO	Market Capitalization	$ 25,110,621
Allen J. Smith	Vice President	Number of Shareholders	1,000
Paul F. Kelleher	Controller	Where Listed / Symbol	AMEX / VIZ

Other Information			
Transfer Agent	American Stock Transfer & Trust Co. New York, NY	SIC Code	3826
Auditor	Arthur Andersen LLP	Employees	243
		Web Site	tvcinstruments.com

Thousand Trails, Inc.

2711 LBJ Freeway, Suite 200   Dallas, TX 75234   Telephone (972)243-2228   Fax (972)488-5008

Company Description

Thousand Trails, Inc., formerly USTrails Inc., owns and operates a system of 53 membership-based campgrounds located in 17 states and British Columbia, Canada, serving 111,000 members as of June 30, 1998. The Company also provides a reciprocal use program for members of approximately 325 recreational facilities and manages 130 public campgrounds for the United States Forest Service. The Company's current business strategy is to improve its campground operations and stabilize its campground membership base through increased sales and marketing efforts. The Company was founded in 1984.

	06/30/98	06/30/97	06/30/96	06/30/95
Per Share Information				
Stock Price as of 12/31	4.12	4.50	0.40	0.40
Earnings Per Share	2.96	0.89	0.30	-3.19
Price / Earnings Ratio	1.39	5.06	1.33	n.a.
Book Value Per Share	0.37	-3.00	-8.63	-8.93
Price / Book Value %	1,113.51	n.a.	n.a.	n.a.
Dividends Per Share	0.0	0.0	0.0	0.0
Annual Financial Data				
Operating Results (000's)				
Total Revenues	76,509.0	78,413.0	91,022.0	91,392.0
Costs & Expenses	-60,793.0	-71,244.0	-91,262.0	-102,965.0
Income Before Taxes and Other	15,716.0	7,169.0	-240.0	-11,573.0
Other Items	0.0	0.0	1,390.0	0.0
Income Tax	9,163.0	-370.0	-41.0	-255.0
Net Income	24,879.0	6,799.0	1,109.0	-11,828.0
Cash Flow From Operations	19,356.0	12,551.0	5,597.0	5,887.0
Balance Sheet (000's)				
Cash & Equivalents	13,631.0	1,343.0	37,403.0	50,596.0
Total Current Assets	21,453.0	9,033.0	47,224.0	73,294.0
Fixed Assets, Net	35,217.0	36,912.0	42,390.0	29,000.0
Total Assets	74,262.0	63,302.0	111,631.0	137,517.0
Total Current Liabilities	31,948.0	39,170.0	68,925.0	50,328.0
Long-Term Debt	32,973.0	38,230.0	66,922.0	120,243.0
Stockholders' Equity	2,754.0	-22,168.0	-31,952.0	-33,054.0
Performance & Financial Condition				
Return on Total Revenues %	32.52	8.67	1.22	-12.94
Return on Avg Stockholders' Equity %	n.a.	n.a.	n.a.	n.a.
Return on Average Assets %	36.17	7.77	0.89	-8.24
Current Ratio	0.67	0.23	0.69	1.46
Debt / Equity %	1,197.28	n.a.	n.a.	n.a.

Compound Growth %'s	EPS % n.a.	Net Income % n.a.	Total Revenues % -5.75

Comments

Management reports that it intends to continue to keep the size of its campground system in an appropriate relation to the size of its membership base. In this regard, if the membership base continues to decline, the Company may close and dispose of additional campgrounds and it will seek to decrease other expenses. Fiscal 1996 results included a nonrecurring gain from debt restructuring. The Company also recorded gains on the sale of assets of $5.3 million, $2.9 million, and $4.0 million in fiscal 1998, 1997 and 1996, respectively. The downsizing has resulted in an improved financial condition. The Company recorded a net income tax benefit of $9,163,000 in fiscal 1998 by booking the benefit of $26.9 million in tax loss carryforwards, now that their use is more likely than not. For the six months ended December 31, 1998, revenue and net income were $36.2 million and $3,515,000 ($.42 per share) as compared to $39.3 million and $8,486,000 ($1.01 per share) for the same period of the preceding year.

Officers	Position	Ownership Information	
William J. Shaw	President, CEO	Number of Shares Outstanding	7,437,083
Bryan Reed	CFO	Market Capitalization	$ 30,640,782
		Number of Shareholders	400
		Where Listed / Symbol	AMEX / TRV

Other Information			
Transfer Agent	American Stock Transfer & Trust Co. New York, NY	SIC Code	7000
Auditor	Arthur Andersen LLP	Employees	1,355
		Web Site	1000trials.com

Tidel Technologies, Inc.

5847 San Felipe, Suite 900   Houston, TX 77057   Telephone (713)783-8200   Fax (713)783-6003

Company Description

Tidel Technologies, Inc., formerly American Medical Technologies, Inc., develops, manufactures, sells and supports products designed for specialty retail marketers, including automated teller machines and related software (the ATM products) and electronic cash security systems (the Timed Access Cash Controller or TACC products). The TACC products have been instrumental in the reduction of losses due to crime in many segments of the retail industry, including convenience stores, retail gasoline, specialty retailers, hospitality and entertainment. The Company was founded in 1984.

	09/30/98	09/30/97	09/30/96	09/30/95
Per Share Information				
Stock Price as of 12/31	1.56	3.87	2.44	0.91
Earnings Per Share	0.25	0.14	0.09	-0.29
Price / Earnings Ratio	6.24	27.64	27.11	n.a.
Book Value Per Share	0.85	0.54	0.33	0.17
Price / Book Value %	183.53	716.67	739.39	535.29
Dividends Per Share	0.0	0.0	0.0	0.0
Annual Financial Data				
Operating Results (000's)				
Total Revenues	33,607.5	30,152.9	20,111.2	11,612.4
Costs & Expenses	-29,675.2	-28,035.7	-18,896.1	-15,030.3
Income Before Taxes and Other	3,932.4	2,117.2	1,215.1	-3,417.9
Other Items	0.0	0.0	0.0	0.0
Income Tax	307.3	0.0	0.0	0.0
Net Income	4,239.6	2,117.2	1,215.1	-3,417.9
Cash Flow From Operations	-1,175.0	-114.0	-1,740.6	-737.0
Balance Sheet (000's)				
Cash & Equivalents	1,400.1	1,549.3	582.1	233.8
Total Current Assets	20,966.3	15,894.4	9,815.2	6,165.0
Fixed Assets, Net	1,293.3	937.3	672.4	519.1
Total Assets	24,246.6	18,263.5	12,363.1	8,193.0
Total Current Liabilities	5,528.2	6,517.0	7,594.4	5,526.1
Long-Term Debt	5,234.6	3,654.6	640.0	640.0
Stockholders' Equity	13,483.8	8,091.8	4,128.8	2,026.9
Performance & Financial Condition				
Return on Total Revenues %	12.62	7.02	6.04	-29.43
Return on Avg Stockholders' Equity %	39.30	34.65	39.48	-92.61
Return on Average Assets %	19.95	13.83	11.82	-46.31
Current Ratio	3.79	2.44	1.29	1.12
Debt / Equity %	38.82	45.16	15.50	31.58

Compound Growth %'s	EPS %	66.67	Net Income %	86.79	Total Revenues %	42.51

Comments

Significant sales growth was primarily due to the continued strong demand for the Company's ATM products. The gross profit from these sales, together with efficiencies in cost management, were primary factors in the overall improvement in net income. TACC sales have increased gradually over the last three years as sales efforts have intensified. Despite an improving performance, Tidel has not yet captured the heart of investors. $100 invested on September 30, 1993, was worth only $83.33 on September 30, 1998, as compared to $211.88 for the overall NASDAQ market index.

Officers	Position	Ownership Information	
James T. Rash	President, CEO	Number of Shares Outstanding	15,860,468
Mark K. Levenick	COO	Market Capitalization	$ 24,742,330
Michael F. Hudson	Exec VP	Number of Shareholders	2,850
Leonard L. Carr Jr.	Vice President	Where Listed / Symbol	NASDAQ / ATMS

Other Information			
Transfer Agent	Harris Trust & Savings Bank Chicago, IL	SIC Code	3578
Auditor	KPMG LLP	Employees	122
		Web Site	tidel.com

Tivoli Industries, Inc.

1513 E. Saint Gertrude Place   Santa Ana, CA 92705   Telephone (714)957-6101   Fax (714)957-1501

Company Description

Tivoli Industries, Inc. designs, develops, manufactures, markets, sells and distributes specialty lighting and related products worldwide. These products are designed to fulfill architectural applications where specific requirements dictate the use of energy efficient, economical, precision, decorative, integrated and high performance lighting equipment. The Company has expanded its product lines and markets to serve general and specialized commercial construction projects and applications which require a combination of specialty lighting and related product features. Over 30 years ago, Tivoli introduced a series of low voltage miniature lamps encased in a variety of plastic extrusions. These "tube lighting" products established the Company as an innovator in lighting applications. The Company was acquired by its present management in 1991 and went public in 1994.

	09/30/98	09/30/97	09/30/96	09/30/95
Per Share Information				
Stock Price as of 12/31	0.34	1.94	1.78	2.37
Earnings Per Share	-0.16	0.13	0.04	-0.03
Price / Earnings Ratio	n.a.	14.92	44.50	n.a.
Book Value Per Share	1.02	1.14	1.01	0.97
Price / Book Value %	33.33	170.18	176.24	244.33
Dividends Per Share	0.0	0.0	0.0	0.0
Annual Financial Data				
Operating Results (000's)				
Total Revenues	9,642.2	9,921.1	6,721.2	4,633.2
Costs & Expenses	-10,457.1	-9,352.7	-6,557.2	-4,848.7
Income Before Taxes and Other	-814.9	568.4	164.0	-215.5
Other Items	188.6	0.0	0.0	98.0
Income Tax	-0.8	-56.6	2.2	8.2
Net Income	-627.1	511.8	166.2	-109.3
Cash Flow From Operations	-208.3	98.8	21.0	-1,010.4
Balance Sheet (000's)				
Cash & Equivalents	1,362.6	1,389.7	1,692.9	1,972.0
Total Current Assets	5,266.8	5,120.9	4,515.5	4,254.0
Fixed Assets, Net	688.2	793.0	295.5	645.0
Total Assets	6,846.0	6,888.2	5,725.8	5,260.0
Total Current Liabilities	1,710.8	1,395.6	1,770.1	1,462.0
Long-Term Debt	833.7	667.5	0.0	13.0
Stockholders' Equity	3,931.8	4,501.6	3,950.8	3,785.0
Performance & Financial Condition				
Return on Total Revenues %	-6.50	5.16	2.47	-2.36
Return on Avg Stockholders' Equity %	-14.87	12.11	4.30	-3.01
Return on Average Assets %	-9.13	8.11	3.03	-2.15
Current Ratio	3.08	3.67	2.55	2.91
Debt / Equity %	21.20	14.83	n.a.	0.34

Compound Growth %'s	EPS % n.a.	Net Income % n.a.	Total Revenues % 27.67

Comments

The decline in fiscal 1998 revenue was attributable to a large product order from a national customer in fiscal 1997 that was not repeated. Sales exclusive of this order rose 12% according to management. New product introductions and heightened sales and marketing activities caused a substantial increase to overhead expenses and resulted in a loss for the year. The Company's financial condition remains strong. If an investor believes that management will be successful in profitably growing the Company, the stock price at one-third of book value is very attractive. Interesting to note is that the Company may be delisted from the NASDAQ because of its price even though the underlying quality is better than half of what remains on NASDAQ.

Officers	Position	Ownership Information	
Terrence C. Walsh	Chairman, CEO	Number of Shares Outstanding	3,843,871
Charles Kimmel	President, COO	Market Capitalization	$ 1,306,916
Gerald Morris	Director	Number of Shareholders	1,550
Vincent F. Monte	Director	Where Listed / Symbol	NASDAQ / TVLI

Other Information			
Transfer Agent	U.S. Stock Transfer Corp. Glendale, CA	SIC Code	3640
Auditor	Corbin & Wertz	Employees	55

Todd Shipyards Corporation

1801-16th Avenue SW   Seattle, WA 98134-1089   Telephone (206)623-1635   Fax (206)442-8505

Company Description

Todd Shipyards Corporation was organized in 1916 and has operated a shipyard in Seattle, Washington since incorporation. It is engaged in the repair/overhaul, conversion and construction of commercial and military vessels. Until early this decade, a substantial portion of the Company's revenues and profits were attributable to long term United States Government contracts. This business declined along with the Department of the Navy's greatly reduced budget. Excess shipyard capacity, both nationally and locally, has resulted in intense price competition. The Company has responded to this competition by carefully reviewing its overhead, streamlining its operations and implementing advanced shipyard production techniques. All aboard for a visit to the financial statements.

	03/29/98	03/30/97	03/30/96	04/02/95
Per Share Information				
Stock Price as of 12/31	4.75	4.19	6.50	5.87
Earnings Per Share	0.82	-2.14	0.42	0.36
Price / Earnings Ratio	5.79	n.a.	15.48	16.31
Book Value Per Share	5.73	4.84	6.80	6.28
Price / Book Value %	82.90	86.57	95.59	93.47
Dividends Per Share	0.0	0.0	0.0	0.0
Annual Financial Data				
Operating Results (000's)				
Total Revenues	112,966.0	118,938.0	104,802.0	72,891.0
Costs & Expenses	-106,340.0	-140,191.0	-100,670.0	-69,489.0
Income Before Taxes and Other	6,626.0	-21,253.0	4,132.0	3,402.0
Other Items	0.0	0.0	0.0	438.0
Income Tax	1,477.0	0.0	0.0	0.0
Net Income	8,103.0	-21,253.0	4,132.0	3,840.0
Cash Flow From Operations	-5,537.0	3,942.0	-601.0	1,997.0
Balance Sheet (000's)				
Cash & Equivalents	5,317.0	4,233.0	8,552.0	11,966.0
Total Current Assets	66,775.0	63,157.0	68,706.0	68,462.0
Fixed Assets, Net	21,565.0	24,477.0	26,499.0	24,552.0
Total Assets	116,873.0	115,789.0	120,571.0	110,924.0
Total Current Liabilities	22,378.0	29,912.0	19,826.0	17,758.0
Long-Term Debt	0.0	0.0	0.0	0.0
Stockholders' Equity	56,813.0	47,940.0	67,380.0	62,433.0
Performance & Financial Condition				
Return on Total Revenues %	7.17	-17.87	3.94	5.27
Return on Avg Stockholders' Equity %	15.47	-36.86	6.37	6.09
Return on Average Assets %	6.97	-17.98	3.57	3.45
Current Ratio	2.98	2.11	3.47	3.86
Debt / Equity %	n.a.	n.a.	n.a.	n.a.

Compound Growth %'s	EPS % n.a.	Net Income % n.a.	Total Revenues % 15.72

Comments

Fiscal 1998 results look better than they really are because an insurance recovery of $6.1 million and the reversal of a contract reserve of $6.1 million created the accounting profit. Also included in net income is $3.2 million of investment portfolio gains. The benefit of tax loss carryovers was also booked to further enhance earnings per share. The Company still has a long way to go before real profitability is restored. For the nine months ended December 31, 1998, the Company reported revenues and a net loss of $60.5 million and $1,729,000 ($.17 per share) as compared to $88.7 million and a net profit of $1,533,000 ($.16 per share) as reported in the same period of the preceding year.

Officers	Position	Ownership Information	
Patrick W. E. Hodgson	Chairman	Number of Shares Outstanding	9,910,180
Stephen G. Welch	CEO	Market Capitalization	$ 47,073,355
Scott H. Wiscomb	CFO, Treasurer	Number of Shareholders	5,000
Brent D. Baird	Director	Where Listed / Symbol	NYSE / TOD

Other Information			
Transfer Agent	ChaseMellon Shareholder Services South Hackensack, NJ	SIC Code	3731
Auditor	Ernst & Young LLP	Employees	1,120

Tofutti Brands Inc.

50 Jackson Drive   Cranford, NJ 07016   Telephone (908)272-2400   Fax (908)272-9492

Company Description

Tofutti Brands Inc. is engaged in the development, production and marketing of TOFUTTI® brand non-dairy frozen desserts and other food products. TOFUTTI® products are non-diary, soya-based products which contain no butterfat, cholesterol or lactose. The products are an alternative for dairy-conscious individuals with lactose intolerance or for those health-oriented people with a desire to keep cholesterol intake in check. The Company's products enable such individuals to enjoy products similar to dairy products without their downside health risks. Effective March 31, 1996, the Company terminated the services of the Haagen-Dazs Company and appointed the Mattus Ice Cream Company to be its New York area master distributor. The Company was founded in 1982.

	12/26/98	12/27/97	12/28/96	12/30/95
Per Share Information				
Stock Price as of 12/31	0.87	1.50	0.56	0.75
Earnings Per Share	0.08	0.08	0.02	0.01
Price / Earnings Ratio	10.88	18.75	28.00	75.00
Book Value Per Share	0.37	0.27	0.17	0.15
Price / Book Value %	235.14	555.56	329.41	500.00
Dividends Per Share	0.0	0.0	0.0	0.0
Annual Financial Data				
Operating Results (000's)				
Total Revenues	8,991.0	7,440.0	5,842.0	5,023.0
Costs & Expenses	-8,476.0	-6,988.0	-5,752.0	-4,995.0
Income Before Taxes and Other	515.0	452.0	90.0	28.0
Other Items	0.0	0.0	0.0	0.0
Income Tax	45.0	83.0	45.0	19.0
Net Income	560.0	535.0	135.0	47.0
Cash Flow From Operations	393.0	-71.0	12.0	7.0
Balance Sheet (000's)				
Cash & Equivalents	407.0	54.0	11.0	12.0
Total Current Assets	2,353.0	1,521.0	1,349.0	1,225.0
Fixed Assets, Net	0.0	0.0	0.0	0.0
Total Assets	2,652.0	2,068.0	1,736.0	1,545.0
Total Current Liabilities	363.0	319.0	634.0	563.0
Long-Term Debt	29.0	49.0	66.0	81.0
Stockholders' Equity	2,260.0	1,700.0	1,036.0	901.0
Performance & Financial Condition				
Return on Total Revenues %	6.23	7.19	2.31	0.94
Return on Avg Stockholders' Equity %	28.28	39.11	13.94	5.22
Return on Average Assets %	23.73	28.13	8.23	3.13
Current Ratio	6.48	4.77	2.13	2.18
Debt / Equity %	1.28	2.88	6.37	8.99

Compound Growth %'s	EPS %	100.00	Net Income %	128.40	Total Revenues %	21.42

Comments

A significant improvement in the distribution of its products during 1997 resulted in a substantial increase in revenues and profits. The Company's 1998 gross profit percentage was adversely affected by the start-up manufacturing costs associated with new products and marketing costs associated with the introduction of new products. More is expected for 1999 but the Company remains comfortably profitable with an excellent financial condition. Tax loss carryovers have allowed the Company to escape normal income tax over the four years presented. Instead tax benefits have been booked as the carryovers have been utilized. $1 million of carryovers remained at December 31, 1998.

Officers	Position	Ownership Information	
David Mintz	Chairman, CEO	Number of Shares Outstanding	6,183,567
Steven Kass	CFO, Secretary	Market Capitalization	$ 5,379,703
Reuben Rapoport	Vice President	Number of Shareholders	1,042
Franklyn Snitow	Director	Where Listed / Symbol	AMEX / TOF

Other Information			
Transfer Agent	American Stock Transfer & Trust Co. New York, NY	SIC Code	2024
Auditor	KPMG LLP	Employees	9
		Web Site tofutti.com koshermall.com	

Tone Products, Inc.

2129 North 15th Street   Melrose Park, IL 60160   Telephone (708)681-3660   Fax (708)681-2368

Company Description

Tone Products, Inc. manufactures, distributes and markets under its own proprietary brand names, as well as under private labels developed for others, a line of specialty beverages, snack foods and condiments. The Company's product lines include fruit and other drink concentrates; juices and juice blends; bar mixes and cocktail bases; snow cone syrups; pancake, waffle, corn and molasses syrups; barbeque and steak sauces; marinades and dressings; and popcorn, cookies, nuts and other snack food. On October 15, 1996, the Company acquired, in a reverse merger transaction, Minute Man of America, Inc. Tone Products started business in 1947.

	09/30/98	09/30/97	09/30/96	09/30/95
Per Share Information				
Stock Price as of 12/31	1.00	1.47	0.75	0.44
Earnings Per Share	0.15	0.08	0.02	-0.01
Price / Earnings Ratio	6.67	18.38	37.50	n.a.
Book Value Per Share	0.98	0.79	0.75	0.24
Price / Book Value %	102.04	186.08	100.00	183.33
Dividends Per Share	0.0	0.0	0.0	0.0
Annual Financial Data				
Operating Results (000's)				
Total Revenues	11,024.7	9,948.4	6,248.1	1,205.6
Costs & Expenses	-10,261.9	-9,387.2	-6,113.7	-1,239.0
Income Before Taxes and Other	762.9	561.2	134.3	-33.4
Other Items	0.0	0.0	0.0	0.0
Income Tax	-201.4	-257.1	-75.3	-0.2
Net Income	561.4	304.2	59.1	-33.7
Cash Flow From Operations	765.3	713.1	-448.5	-12.7
Balance Sheet (000's)				
Cash & Equivalents	458.3	349.6	155.7	24.7
Total Current Assets	2,564.1	2,386.4	2,220.2	537.6
Fixed Assets, Net	1,485.4	1,460.9	1,464.7	209.7
Total Assets	4,819.7	4,248.2	4,117.1	859.6
Total Current Liabilities	1,093.6	1,099.8	1,716.4	105.4
Long-Term Debt	166.0	140.2	14.3	0.0
Stockholders' Equity	3,498.0	2,915.5	2,318.6	734.2
Performance & Financial Condition				
Return on Total Revenues %	5.09	3.06	0.95	-2.79
Return on Avg Stockholders' Equity %	17.51	11.62	3.87	-2.41
Return on Average Assets %	12.38	7.27	2.37	-1.53
Current Ratio	2.34	2.17	1.29	5.10
Debt / Equity %	4.74	4.81	0.62	n.a.

Compound Growth %'s	EPS % n.a.	Net Income % n.a.	Total Revenues % n.a.

Comments

The increase in fiscal 1998 revenue was the result of new private packaging contracts for sauces and beverage concentrates. This added additional profit to the bottom line as operating expenses were held constant with only a slight decrease in gross margins. The fiscal 1996 results and balance sheet have been restated to reflect the predecessor company that was acquired in the reverse merger. The results of operations are for a nine month period. Fiscal 1995 numbers are those of Minute Man of America, Inc. prior to the reverse merger and are not comparable. Because of the lack of comparability, compound growth rates are not displayed. Tone Products represents a good example of what can happen to the pricing of stock in a small company. Despite improved results and financial condition, the stock has declined approximately one-third in value.

Officers	Position	Ownership Information	
Timothy E. Evon	President, General Manager	Number of Shares Outstanding	3,579,612
William H. Hamen	CFO, Secretary	Market Capitalization	$ 3,579,612
Thomas J. Evon	Secretary, Treasurer	Number of Shareholders	600
Michael W. Evon	VP - Sales	Where Listed / Symbol	OTC-BB / TNPD

Other Information			
Transfer Agent	Securities Transfer Corp. Dallas, TX		SIC Code	2090
Auditor	Kelly & Company		Employees	45
Market Maker	First Albany Corporation	(800)541-5061	Web Site	toneproducts.com
	Paragon Capital Corporation	(800)345-0505		

Top Air Manufacturing, Inc.

317 Savannah Park Road   Cedar Falls, IA 50613   Telephone (319)268-0473   Fax (319)268-1435

Company Description

Top Air Manufacturing, Inc. is engaged in the manufacturing and marketing of several agricultural products including sprayers, liquid manure handling equipment, grain carts and wagons, milking parlors, seed conveyors, feeding and forage equipment and a complete line of attachments and replacement parts for each line of equipment. On January 15, 1997, the Company acquired Ficklin Machine Co. for 1.15 million shares of Company stock. Ficklin brings an autumn product line that is expected to even out the overall production schedule as well as provide additional uses of the Top Air's marketing resources and dealer network. The Company was founded in 1981.

	05/31/98	05/31/97	05/31/96	05/31/95
Per Share Information				
Stock Price as of 12/31	1.00	2.62	1.25	1.25
Earnings Per Share	0.19	0.19	0.17	0.12
Price / Earnings Ratio	5.26	13.79	7.35	10.42
Book Value Per Share	1.47	1.28	1.03	0.91
Price / Book Value %	68.03	204.69	121.36	137.36
Dividends Per Share	0.0	0.0	0.0	0.0
Annual Financial Data				
Operating Results (000's)				
Total Revenues	16,582.8	13,821.7	11,678.6	6,224.1
Costs & Expenses	-15,021.8	-12,482.0	-10,628.2	-5,616.6
Income Before Taxes and Other	1,561.0	1,339.7	1,050.4	607.6
Other Items	0.0	0.0	0.0	0.0
Income Tax	-561.0	-482.3	-373.0	-236.6
Net Income	1,000.0	857.4	677.4	371.0
Cash Flow From Operations	-663.7	-336.1	741.0	129.6
Balance Sheet (000's)				
Cash & Equivalents	5.1	263.5	0.5	414.7
Total Current Assets	9,553.7	7,846.0	5,265.9	3,341.8
Fixed Assets, Net	2,676.3	2,059.1	1,007.7	778.7
Total Assets	13,641.3	11,385.5	6,499.7	4,248.9
Total Current Liabilities	3,856.1	2,705.4	1,537.2	1,025.3
Long-Term Debt	2,323.6	2,108.4	830.1	270.2
Stockholders' Equity	7,461.6	6,571.7	4,132.5	2,874.5
Performance & Financial Condition				
Return on Total Revenues %	6.03	6.20	5.80	5.96
Return on Avg Stockholders' Equity %	14.25	16.02	19.33	13.80
Return on Average Assets %	7.99	9.59	12.60	9.50
Current Ratio	2.48	2.90	3.43	3.26
Debt / Equity %	31.14	32.08	20.09	9.40

Compound Growth %'s	EPS %	16.55	Net Income %	39.17	Total Revenues %	38.63

Comments

1997 revenues and earnings increased for the sixth consecutive year. Most of the revenue advance in fiscal 1998 was credited to a continued geographic expansion of the Company's dealer network. Both the Ficklin acquisition and a fiscal 1996 acquisition were accounted for under the purchase method of accounting. Accordingly, the results of those operations have been included only since the dates of acquisition. The Company acquired 54,425 shares of treasury stock during fiscal 1998. For the nine months ended February 28, 1999, the Company reported revenues of $7.0 million and a net loss of $458,601 ($.09 per share) as compared to revenues of $10.8 million and net income of $383,394 ($.07 per share) for the same period of the preceding year. The poor results were attributable to softness in the agricultural economy.

Officers	Position	Ownership Information	
Steven R. Lind	President, CEO	Number of Shares Outstanding	5,083,456
Thaddeus P. Vannice, Sr.	CFO	Market Capitalization	$ 5,083,456
Steven F. Bahlmann	Treasurer, Secretary	Number of Shareholders	850
James R. Harken	Vice President	Where Listed / Symbol	AMEX / TPC

Other Information			
Transfer Agent	Firstar Trust Company Milwaukee, WI	SIC Code	3523
Auditor	McGladrey & Pullen, LLP	Employees	150

Total Research Corporation

5 Independence Way, CN 5305   Princeton, NJ 08543-5305   Telephone (609)520-9100   Fax (609)987-8839

Company Description

Total Research Corporation is a full-service consultative marketing research organization that provides marketing research and information to assist its clients with the pricing and positioning of new or existing products, customer loyalty measurements, brand equity issues, organizational structure and other marketing concerns. The Company provides services for its clients by using proprietary market research technologies developed by the Company as well as other standard market research techniques. The Company's clients consist principally of Fortune 100 corporations operating in a wide array of industries. The Company's professional staff has business experience in each industry for which it conducts market research. The Company was founded in 1975.

	06/30/98	06/30/97	06/30/96	06/30/95
Per Share Information				
Stock Price as of 12/31	2.25	1.47	0.77	1.50
Earnings Per Share	0.10	0.06	-0.15	0.08
Price / Earnings Ratio	22.50	24.50	n.a.	18.75
Book Value Per Share	0.48	0.36	0.29	0.44
Price / Book Value %	468.75	408.33	265.52	340.91
Dividends Per Share	0.0	0.0	0.0	0.0
Annual Financial Data				
Operating Results (000's)				
Total Revenues	34,117.5	29,493.4	23,802.1	19,309.0
Costs & Expenses	-31,509.2	-28,365.2	-25,026.1	-17,997.0
Income Before Taxes and Other	1,885.3	1,128.2	-2,325.4	1,312.0
Other Items	0.0	0.0	0.0	0.0
Income Tax	-760.5	-490.0	842.4	-552.0
Net Income	1,124.8	638.2	-1,483.0	760.0
Cash Flow From Operations	1,712.2	4,934.1	801.6	n.a.
Balance Sheet (000's)				
Cash & Equivalents	2,097.3	678.4	4.2	128.1
Total Current Assets	10,708.5	7,870.5	7,936.2	6,037.3
Fixed Assets, Net	2,110.9	2,316.6	2,230.2	2,458.8
Total Assets	15,469.2	12,948.3	13,154.6	11,742.6
Total Current Liabilities	9,907.5	9,021.2	7,953.3	5,826.5
Long-Term Debt	0.0	0.0	2,142.0	1,593.4
Stockholders' Equity	5,077.5	3,648.1	2,821.2	4,322.7
Performance & Financial Condition				
Return on Total Revenues %	3.30	2.16	-6.23	3.94
Return on Avg Stockholders' Equity %	25.78	19.73	-41.52	23.75
Return on Average Assets %	7.92	4.89	-11.91	6.33
Current Ratio	1.08	0.87	1.00	1.04
Debt / Equity %	n.a.	n.a.	75.92	36.86

Compound Growth %'s	EPS %	7.72	Net Income %	13.96	Total Revenues %	20.89

Comments

Beginning in 1996, the Company planned to aggressively increase revenues through geographic expansion as well as through new product introduction. As a result, the Company incurred significant planned as well as unanticipated expenses beyond those normally incurred for recurring operations, resulting in a net loss for the year. Since then, the Company has produced respectable profits. For the six months ended December 31, 1998, the Company reported revenues and net income of $19.7 million and $1,060,419 ($.08 per share) as compared to $17.0 million and $760,040 ($.07 per share) for the same period of the preceding year.

Officers	Position	Ownership Information	
David Brodsky	Chairman	Number of Shares Outstanding	10,476,108
Albert Angrisani	President, CEO	Market Capitalization	$ 23,571,243
Eric C. Zissman	CFO	Number of Shareholders	500
George Lindemann	Director	Where Listed / Symbol	NASDAQ / TOTL

Other Information			
Transfer Agent	American Stock Transfer & Trust Co. New York, NY	SIC Code	8732
Auditor	Amper, Politziner & Mattia	Employees	229
		Web Site	totalres.com

Touchstone Applied Science Associates, Inc.

4 Hardscrabble Heights, P.O. Box 382   Brewster, NY 10509   Telephone (914)277-8100   Fax (914)277-3548

Company Description

Touchstone Applied Science Associates, Inc. serves the education market with assessment and instructional products. Prior to new executive management in 1994, the Company's primary business was reading assessment through the publishing and sale of its proprietary tests and related assessment tools. Since 1994, the Company's current management has implemented a strategy to broaden the Company's services in the education market. In the Company's 1997 and 1998 fiscal years and through the beginning of fiscal 1999, the Company completed four acquisitions in three core segments of the education market: assessment, instruction and delivery. The Company was founded in 1976.

	10/31/98	10/31/97	10/31/96	10/31/95
Per Share Information				
Stock Price as of 12/31	0.50	0.97	0.50	2.62
Earnings Per Share	0.02	-0.17	0.03	0.02
Price / Earnings Ratio	25.00	n.a.	16.67	131.00
Book Value Per Share	0.76	0.74	0.95	0.97
Price / Book Value %	65.79	131.08	52.63	270.10
Dividends Per Share	0.0	0.0	0.0	0.0
Annual Financial Data				
Operating Results (000's)				
Total Revenues	6,364.6	4,699.3	2,686.9	2,478.3
Costs & Expenses	-6,204.4	-6,893.1	-2,475.6	-2,348.7
Income Before Taxes and Other	160.2	-2,193.8	211.3	129.6
Other Items	0.0	0.0	0.0	0.0
Income Tax	-29.0	830.0	-19.2	25.5
Net Income	131.2	-1,363.8	192.0	155.1
Cash Flow From Operations	896.8	641.3	428.4	483.2
Balance Sheet (000's)				
Cash & Equivalents	4,980.2	1,156.7	1,049.8	617.3
Total Current Assets	7,106.4	3,078.9	4,458.5	3,449.4
Fixed Assets, Net	1,753.8	1,739.9	1,795.2	1,869.1
Total Assets	14,074.6	9,592.9	8,975.5	8,416.7
Total Current Liabilities	1,281.6	834.4	342.3	526.1
Long-Term Debt	6,267.2	2,529.0	728.3	571.3
Stockholders' Equity	6,525.8	6,229.6	7,383.7	6,717.2
Performance & Financial Condition				
Return on Total Revenues %	2.06	-29.02	7.15	6.26
Return on Avg Stockholders' Equity %	2.06	-20.04	2.72	2.37
Return on Average Assets %	1.11	-14.69	2.21	1.94
Current Ratio	5.54	3.69	13.02	6.56
Debt / Equity %	96.04	40.60	9.86	8.50

Compound Growth %'s	EPS %	0.00	Net Income %	-5.43	Total Revenues %	36.94

Comments

One-third of the fiscal 1998 increase in revenues was attributed to the net internal growth from the Company's traditional test business. The balance related to two businesses acquired during fiscal 1997. The acquisitions are not without cost. At October 31, 1998, intangible assets recorded on the ledgers totalled $4.5 million which equated to approximately 69% of stockholders' equity and book value per share. In November 1998, the Company acquired Mildred Elley as a platform for the Company's entrance into the post-secondary school market. Mildred Elley is a two-year, New York State degree-granting institution and has been in operation for over 80 years.

Officers	Position	Ownership Information	
Andrew L. Simon	President, CEO	Number of Shares Outstanding	8,567,222
Linda G. Straley	Vice President, Secretary	Market Capitalization	$ 4,283,611
Miachael D. Beck	Vice President	Number of Shareholders	1,500
Walter B. Barbe	Director	Where Listed / Symbol	NASDAQ / TASA

Other Information			
Transfer Agent	American Stock Transfer & Trust Co. New York, NY	SIC Code	8200
Auditor	Lazar, Levine & Felix LLP	Employees	32
		Web Site	tasa.com

TransCoastal Marine Services, Inc.

2925 Briarpark Drive, Suite 930   Houston, TX 77042   Telephone (713)784-7429   Fax (713)781-6364

Company Description

TransCoastal Marine Services, Inc. (TCMS) is a marine construction company with operations focused in the transition zone (water depths up to 20 feet) and shallow water (from 20 to 200 feet) in the Gulf of Mexico. The Company's primary services include pipeline construction, repair, maintenance, trenching, testing, commissioning and related services, and fabrication and refurbishment of offshore drilling rigs, barge drilling rigs and structural components of fixed platforms. TCMS commenced operations concurrently with the acquisition of four privately owned marine construction businesses and the completion of an initial public offering in November, 1997.

	12/31/98	12/31/97	12/31/96	12/31/95
Per Share Information				
Stock Price	2.91	13.75	n.a.	n.a.
Earnings Per Share	0.29	0.40	0.44	1.22
Price / Earnings Ratio	10.03	34.38	n.a.	n.a.
Book Value Per Share	11.51	12.59	3.42	3.38
Price / Book Value %	25.28	109.21	n.a.	n.a.
Dividends Per Share	0.0	0.0	0.0	0.0
Annual Financial Data				
Operating Results (000's)				
Total Revenues	188,878.0	57,992.0	18,341.0	18,144.0
Costs & Expenses	-184,562.0	-55,448.0	-17,091.0	-16,046.0
Income Before Taxes and Other	4,316.0	2,544.0	1,250.0	2,098.0
Other Items	0.0	0.0	0.0	0.0
Income Tax	-1,511.0	-527.0	-91.0	-839.0
Net Income	2,805.0	2,017.0	1,159.0	1,259.0
Cash Flow From Operations	5,879.0	5,761.0	2,657.0	2,812.0
Balance Sheet (000's)				
Cash & Equivalents	9,020.0	2,416.0	1,117.0	852.0
Total Current Assets	55,060.0	27,866.0	5,242.0	6,000.0
Fixed Assets, Net	96,135.0	66,907.0	2,956.0	3,007.0
Total Assets	236,597.0	171,817.0	9,157.0	9,007.0
Total Current Liabilities	39,544.0	24,427.0	1,439.0	1,372.0
Long-Term Debt	55,096.0	13,471.0	0.0	19.0
Stockholders' Equity	120,228.0	115,145.0	7,718.0	7,616.0
Performance & Financial Condition				
Return on Total Revenues %	1.49	3.48	6.32	6.94
Return on Avg Stockholders' Equity %	2.38	3.28	15.12	19.04
Return on Average Assets %	1.37	2.23	12.76	15.73
Current Ratio	1.39	1.14	3.64	4.37
Debt / Equity %	45.83	11.70	n.a.	0.25

Compound Growth %'s	EPS %	-38.05	Net Income %	30.61	Total Revenues %	118.35

Comments

Operating results prior to the acquisitions mentioned above are presented for the founding company that was identified as the "accounting acquiror" for financial statement presentation purposes. The other four companies were accounted for using the purchase method of accounting. Approximately 90% of the increase in revenues reported in 1998 as compared to 1997 is attributable to the inclusion of the four deemed acquired companies for a full year. The balance is attributable to internal growth. 1998 results include restructuring charges of $2.4 million. 1997 results include a non-cash expense of $2.2 million related to the issuance of common shares to management of the Company. At December 31, 1998, the Company had $80.4 million recorded as goodwill on its ledgers which equated to approximately 67% of stockholders' equity and book value per share.

Officers	Position	Ownership Information	
Bill E. Stallworth	Chairman, CEO	Number of Shares Outstanding	10,448,441
Thad Smith	President, COO	Market Capitalization	$ 30,404,963
Johnnie W. Domingue	Senior VP, CFO	Number of Shareholders	2,200
Allyson B. Fox	Secretary	Where Listed / Symbol	NASDAQ / TCMS

Other Information			
Transfer Agent	American Stock Transfer & Trust Co. New York, NY	SIC Code	1389
Auditor	Arthur Andersen LLP	Employees	950
		Web Site	transcoastal.com

Transcend Services, Inc.

3353 Peachtree Road, N.E., Suite 1000   Atlanta, GA 30326   Telephone (404)836-8000   Fax (404)364-8009

Company Description

Transcend Services, Inc. provides healthcare information management (HIM) solutions to hospitals and other associated healthcare providers. The Company's range of HIM services includes 1) contract management, or "Co-Sourcing", of medical records and other HIM functions; 2) transcription of physicians' dictated medical notes; and 3) consulting relating to medical records and reimbursement coding. The Company currently operates the medical records and certain other HIM functions of 25 general acute care hospitals located in 11 states and the District of Columbia. The Company was founded in 1976.

	12/31/98	12/31/97	12/31/96	12/31/95
Per Share Information				
Stock Price	1.87	2.25	5.00	5.62
Earnings Per Share	-0.01	-0.20	-0.37	-0.22
Price / Earnings Ratio	n.a.	n.a.	n.a.	n.a.
Book Value Per Share	0.10	0.14	0.30	0.51
Price / Book Value %	1,870.00	1,607.14	1,666.67	1,101.96
Dividends Per Share	0.0	0.0	0.0	0.0
Annual Financial Data				
Operating Results (000's)				
Total Revenues	53,314.0	43,413.0	39,633.0	28,009.0
Costs & Expenses	-52,932.0	-47,205.0	-45,294.0	-31,674.0
Income Before Taxes and Other	382.0	-3,792.0	-5,661.0	-3,665.0
Other Items	-100.0	-147.0	-1,582.0	-479.0
Income Tax	0.0	0.0	0.0	0.0
Net Income	282.0	-3,939.0	-7,243.0	-4,144.0
Cash Flow From Operations	-191.0	-2,315.0	-3,153.0	-4,004.0
Balance Sheet (000's)				
Cash & Equivalents	450.0	5,541.0	1,663.0	1,124.0
Total Current Assets	9,596.0	11,485.0	6,015.0	4,438.0
Fixed Assets, Net	7,302.0	3,422.0	2,615.0	2,740.0
Total Assets	22,971.0	20,650.0	16,557.0	16,833.0
Total Current Liabilities	7,372.0	5,214.0	7,591.0	3,977.0
Long-Term Debt	7,547.0	4,983.0	464.0	2,796.0
Stockholders' Equity	7,512.0	7,913.0	5,961.0	9,698.0
Performance & Financial Condition				
Return on Total Revenues %	0.53	-9.07	-18.28	-14.80
Return on Avg Stockholders' Equity %	3.66	-56.78	-92.51	-97.19
Return on Average Assets %	1.29	-21.17	-43.38	-41.89
Current Ratio	1.30	2.20	0.79	1.12
Debt / Equity %	100.47	62.97	7.78	28.83

Compound Growth %'s	EPS % n.a.	Net Income % n.a.	Total Revenues % 23.93

Comments

Revenues rose 22.8% in 1998 resulting primarily from new contracts, net of terminations. Gross profits also increased as a result of the higher sales. Not only is the Company trending towards profitability, it made it. The Company reported its first annual profit despite a $100,000 loss from discontinued operations. Preferred stock dividends of $479,000, however, exceeded the net income thereby eliminating any earnings for common stockholders. At December 31, 1998, the Company had tax loss carryovers of $18.5 million available to offset future income. Preferred stock and convertible debentures will continue to be the cost of growth. The Company's challenge will be to remain profitable and strengthen its financial condition.

Officers	Position	Ownership Information	
Donald L. Lucas	Chairman	Number of Shares Outstanding	21,500,000
Larry G. Gerdes	President, CEO	Market Capitalization	$ 40,205,000
Doug Shamon	Exec VP, CFO	Number of Shareholders	2,000
Todd S. Mann	Exec VP	Where Listed / Symbol	NASDAQ / TRCR

Other Information

Transfer Agent	SunTrust of Atlanta Atlanta, GA	SIC Code	8090
Auditor	Arthur Andersen LLP	Employees	943
		Web Site	transcendservices.com

Travel Ports of America, Inc.

3495 Winton Place, Building C   Rochester, NY 14623   Telephone (716)272-1810   Fax (716)272-9952

Company Description

Travel Ports of America, Inc. is primarily engaged in the operation of travel plazas and has sixteen service plazas located in the states of New York, Pennsylvania, New Jersey, Indiana, Maryland, North Carolina and New Hampshire. The service travel plazas sell, both to the trucking industry and to others, petroleum products (such as diesel fuel, gasoline and lubricants), and generally include a truck service and repair shop, a tire and parts center, a truck wash, scales for weighing trucks, parking facilities, motel rooms, a family-style restaurant, a travel store, shower and laundry facilities, and a convenience store. The Company went public in 1986.

	04/30/98	04/30/97	04/30/96	04/30/95
Per Share Information				
Stock Price as of 12/31	2.87	3.12	2.13	2.19
Earnings Per Share	0.30	0.24	0.24	0.30
Price / Earnings Ratio	9.57	13.00	8.88	7.30
Book Value Per Share	3.00	2.63	2.35	2.07
Price / Book Value %	95.67	118.63	90.64	105.80
Dividends Per Share	0.0	0.0	0.0	0.0
Annual Financial Data				
Operating Results (000's)				
Total Revenues	211,943.5	207,489.7	165,701.8	153,532.9
Costs & Expenses	-207,983.0	-204,586.5	-162,817.3	-150,512.3
Income Before Taxes and Other	3,960.5	2,903.2	2,884.5	3,020.6
Other Items	0.0	0.0	0.0	0.0
Income Tax	-1,622.8	-1,203.0	-1,194.0	-1,130.6
Net Income	2,337.7	1,700.2	1,690.5	1,890.0
Cash Flow From Operations	7,657.7	5,038.3	3,207.8	3,913.7
Balance Sheet (000's)				
Cash & Equivalents	4,082.2	3,134.9	1,667.1	7,593.8
Total Current Assets	15,638.6	15,790.8	12,839.5	18,315.3
Fixed Assets, Net	44,597.2	41,686.3	35,976.8	27,052.5
Total Assets	64,812.7	62,436.0	55,278.6	51,370.8
Total Current Liabilities	14,888.1	14,536.5	13,364.1	13,295.1
Long-Term Debt	28,376.5	30,176.9	26,934.3	24,979.0
Stockholders' Equity	18,900.7	15,817.0	14,086.1	12,349.6
Performance & Financial Condition				
Return on Total Revenues %	1.10	0.82	1.02	1.23
Return on Avg Stockholders' Equity %	13.47	11.37	12.79	16.60
Return on Average Assets %	3.67	2.89	3.17	4.06
Current Ratio	1.05	1.09	0.96	1.38
Debt / Equity %	150.14	190.79	191.21	202.27

Compound Growth %'s	EPS %	0.00	Net Income %	7.34	Total Revenues %	11.35

Comments

The Company declared 8% and 6% stock dividends in 1998 and 1997, respectively. All per share amounts have been restated for consistency. Lower diesel fuel and gasoline prices held revenues to a small gain in fiscal 1998. There would have been a 9.1% sales increase if fuel prices had remained constant with the prior year level. However, this didn't stop the Company from pumping more profits as net earnings reached a record level. The surge in fiscal 1997 sales volume was attributable to two new plazas that were opened during most of the year and $13 million in increased sales at existing plazas. For the nine months ended January 31, 1999, revenues and net income were $154.3 million and $1,834,709 ($.24 per share) as compared to $161.8 million and $1,970,092 ($.26 per share) for the same period of the preceding year.

Officers	Position	Ownership Information	
E. Philip Saunders	Chairman, CEO	Number of Shares Outstanding	6,302,596
John M. Holahan	President, COO	Market Capitalization	$ 18,088,451
William Burslem III	Vice President, Secretary	Number of Shareholders	1,900
William A. DeNight	Director	Where Listed / Symbol	NASDAQ / TPOA

Other Information			
Transfer Agent	American Stock Transfer & Trust Co. New York, NY	SIC Code	5500
Auditor	PricewaterhouseCoopers LLP	Employees	1,447
		Web Site	tpoa.com

Triple S Plastics, Inc.

14320 Portage Road   Vicksburg, MI 49097-0905   Telephone (616)649-0545   Fax (616)649-3427

Company Description

Triple S Plastics, Inc. is a full-service custom injection molder, providing mold design and engineering services, mold manufacturing, injection molding, and post-molding assembly and finishing operations to a diverse base of customers. Its customers are primarily in the consumer products, telecommunications, medical/pharmaceutical, information technologies and automotive markets. The Company was founded in 1969 and had its initial public offering in March 1994. Proceeds of the offering were used to finance building expansions, purchase new equipment for those facilities, retire existing debt and fund working capital needs.

	03/31/98	03/31/97	03/31/96	03/31/95
Per Share Information				
Stock Price as of 12/31	4.12	6.06	7.75	6.50
Earnings Per Share	0.43	0.36	0.28	0.92
Price / Earnings Ratio	9.58	16.83	27.68	7.07
Book Value Per Share	8.55	8.12	7.77	7.49
Price / Book Value %	48.19	74.63	99.74	86.78
Dividends Per Share	0.0	0.0	0.0	0.0
Annual Financial Data				
Operating Results (000's)				
Total Revenues	67,692.0	64,844.0	61,469.0	54,051.0
Costs & Expenses	-65,235.0	-62,755.0	-59,882.0	-48,759.0
Income Before Taxes and Other	2,457.0	2,089.0	1,587.0	5,292.0
Other Items	0.0	0.0	0.0	0.0
Income Tax	-860.0	-760.0	-549.0	-1,866.0
Net Income	1,597.0	1,329.0	1,038.0	3,426.0
Cash Flow From Operations	5,056.0	5,436.0	1,371.0	2,802.0
Balance Sheet (000's)				
Cash & Equivalents	3,783.0	2,681.0	1,382.0	3,947.0
Total Current Assets	21,254.0	19,537.0	16,308.0	19,161.2
Fixed Assets, Net	25,025.0	24,587.0	24,928.0	22,000.0
Total Assets	50,030.0	48,870.0	46,150.0	42,339.4
Total Current Liabilities	9,086.0	8,854.0	6,747.0	6,920.7
Long-Term Debt	6,603.0	7,251.0	8,747.0	6,516.1
Stockholders' Equity	31,981.0	30,353.0	28,981.0	27,902.5
Performance & Financial Condition				
Return on Total Revenues %	2.36	2.05	1.69	6.34
Return on Avg Stockholders' Equity %	5.12	4.48	3.65	12.69
Return on Average Assets %	3.23	2.80	2.35	8.16
Current Ratio	2.34	2.21	2.42	2.77
Debt / Equity %	20.65	23.89	30.18	23.35

Compound Growth %'s	EPS %	-22.39	Net Income %	-22.46	Total Revenues %	7.79

Comments

1998 sales increased modestly but included strong advances in both the telecommunications market and the consumer products markets, 49% and 22%, respectively. Gross margins also improved as management was successful in installing manufacturing efficiency improvement initiatives. The stock market has not been kind to the Company's shareholders as the stock trades at prices substantially below book value. For the nine months ended December 31, 1998, the Company reported revenues and a net loss of $48.2 million and $341,000 ($.09 per share) as compared to $48.5 million and a net profit of $920,000 ($.25 per share) for the same period of the preceding year.

Officers	Position	Ownership Information	
Daniel B. Canavan	Chairman, CEO	Number of Shares Outstanding	3,741,951
Victor V. Valentine, Jr.	President	Market Capitalization	$ 15,416,838
Robert D. Monk	VP - Finance, CFO	Number of Shareholders	2,280
Michael E. Zaagman	Vice President	Where Listed / Symbol	NASDAQ / TSSS

Other Information			
Transfer Agent	American Stock Transfer & Trust Company New York, NY	SIC Code	3089
Auditor	BDO Seidman LLP	Employees	627

Tubby's, Inc.

6029 East Fourteen Mile Road   Sterling Heights, MI 48312   Telephone (810)978-8829   Fax (810)978-8850

Company Description

Tubby's, Inc. develops, operates, franchises and services a system of restaurants which prepare and serve a comprehensive menu of submarine sandwiches and related items. Tubby's submarine sandwiches are all prepared to order and many of its sandwiches are cooked on a grill. As of November 30, 1998, a total of eighty-eight restaurants were in operation consisting of two Stuff-Yer-Face restaurants, three Tubby's Express restaurants, (of which one was owned by the Company), and eighty-three Tubby's Sub Shop restaurants (of which two were owned by the Company). In the first half of fiscal 1999, twelve additional franchisee owned Tubby's Sub Shops were opened. Tubby's was founded in 1968.

	11/30/98	11/30/97	11/30/96	11/30/95
Per Share Information				
Stock Price as of 12/31	0.44	0.25	0.31	0.12
Earnings Per Share	-0.01	0.04	0.01	0.01
Price / Earnings Ratio	n.a.	6.25	31.00	12.00
Book Value Per Share	1.01	1.02	0.10	0.09
Price / Book Value %	43.56	24.51	310.00	133.33
Dividends Per Share	0.0	0.0	0.0	0.0
Annual Financial Data				
Operating Results (000's)				
Total Revenues	7,485.0	3,708.5	3,218.1	3,871.9
Costs & Expenses	-7,510.6	-3,505.7	-3,086.0	-3,568.3
Income Before Taxes and Other	-31.2	202.8	117.4	274.4
Other Items	0.0	0.0	0.0	0.0
Income Tax	0.0	-95.3	0.0	0.0
Net Income	-31.2	107.5	117.4	274.4
Cash Flow From Operations	-84.1	169.8	46.5	181.2
Balance Sheet (000's)				
Cash & Equivalents	692.2	864.2	793.5	951.1
Total Current Assets	1,987.7	1,655.9	1,449.3	1,658.9
Fixed Assets, Net	666.2	896.2	1,039.6	673.5
Total Assets	3,326.3	3,325.4	3,332.5	3,269.9
Total Current Liabilities	551.0	478.5	578.1	564.6
Long-Term Debt	120.3	139.9	175.8	246.2
Stockholders' Equity	2,614.9	2,646.1	2,538.6	2,365.0
Performance & Financial Condition				
Return on Total Revenues %	-0.42	2.90	3.65	7.09
Return on Avg Stockholders' Equity %	-1.19	4.15	4.79	13.74
Return on Average Assets %	-0.94	3.23	3.55	9.22
Current Ratio	3.61	3.46	2.51	2.94
Debt / Equity %	4.60	5.29	6.92	10.41

Compound Growth %'s	EPS % n.a.	Net Income % n.a.	Total Revenues % 24.57

Comments

The 107.2% increase in fiscal 1998 revenues was primarily attributable to revenues generated by a new food and restaurant supplies distribution company that was launched in February 1998. The new company supplies all franchised and Company-owned stores. This may be the kind of excitement the Company needs to change its image from a sleepy little business with marginal profits. Fortunately, the Company has always maintained a reasonably strong balance sheet. More growth is on the horizon. In December 1998, the Company announced the proposed acquisition of Interfoods of America, Inc. and a planned 1 for 5 reverse split. Due diligence will include checking on the status of this transaction.

Officers	Position	Ownership Information	
Peter T. Paganes	Chairman	Number of Shares Outstanding	2,583,114
Robert M. Paganes	President, CEO	Market Capitalization	$ 1,136,570
Theresa M. Borto	CFO	Number of Shareholders	7,000
Vincent J. Tatone	Secretary	Where Listed / Symbol	NASDAQ / TUBY

Other Information			
Transfer Agent	Continental Stock Transfer & Trust Co. New York, NY	SIC Code	5812
Auditor	BDO Seidman LLP	Employees	45
		Web Site	tubby.com

Tufco International, Inc.

12575 Pioneer Lane   Gentry, AR 72734   Telephone (501)736-2201   Fax (501)736-2947

Company Description

Tufco International, Inc. is engaged in the business of installing industrial floors and selling floor products, supplies and techniques to its franchisees and licensees. The products are popular with industrial, meat processing, food service and retailing customers throughout the continental United States, Canada and Mexico. Certain of the independent franchises are owned by relatives of the primary stockholders. Management reports that all transactions with these franchises are engaged in for a profit. The Company's primary product is the FLOOR. This industrial flooring surface is offered in a variety of colors and formulations designed to meet the specific needs and requirements of its customers. The Company was founded in 1976.

	05/31/98	05/31/97	05/31/96	05/31/95
Per Share Information				
Stock Price as of 12/31	0.06	0.06	0.37	0.19
Earnings Per Share	0.04	-0.01	0.03	0.04
Price / Earnings Ratio	1.50	n.a.	12.33	4.75
Book Value Per Share	0.16	0.16	0.19	0.15
Price / Book Value %	37.50	37.50	194.74	n.a.
Dividends Per Share	0.0	0.0	0.0	0.0
Annual Financial Data				
Operating Results (000's)				
Total Revenues	6,663.0	7,615.8	7,473.9	6,382.8
Costs & Expenses	-6,212.8	-7,682.9	-7,036.9	-5,867.4
Income Before Taxes and Other	450.1	-135.8	437.0	515.4
Other Items	0.0	0.0	0.0	0.0
Income Tax	-197.7	29.7	-177.1	-203.5
Net Income	252.5	-106.1	259.9	311.8
Cash Flow From Operations	213.8	42.1	48.9	14.4
Balance Sheet (000's)				
Cash & Equivalents	1.1	21.4	14.6	0.8
Total Current Assets	2,227.9	2,410.2	2,583.1	1,685.0
Fixed Assets, Net	704.2	773.8	772.8	645.0
Total Assets	3,040.8	3,298.4	3,527.5	2,617.2
Total Current Liabilities	1,398.2	2,092.4	1,776.2	1,116.2
Long-Term Debt	482.9	27.1	210.8	319.0
Stockholders' Equity	1,125.5	1,147.8	1,450.6	1,182.0
Performance & Financial Condition				
Return on Total Revenues %	3.79	-1.39	3.48	4.89
Return on Avg Stockholders' Equity %	22.21	-8.16	19.75	30.64
Return on Average Assets %	7.97	-3.11	8.46	12.73
Current Ratio	1.59	1.15	1.45	1.51
Debt / Equity %	42.90	2.36	14.53	26.99

Compound Growth %'s	EPS %	0.00	Net Income %	-6.80	Total Revenues %	1.44

Comments

The Company discontinued offering wall and ceiling products in fiscal 1997. Although fiscal 1998 revenue declined as a result, the Company was able to reduce overhead expenses by nearly 25% and return to profitability. The Company reacquired 937,000 shares of its common stock during fiscal 1997. For the six months ended November 30, 1998, revenues and net income were $2.9 million and $190,222 ($.027 per share) as compared to $3.2 million and $125,639 ($.018 per share) as reported in the same period of the preceding year. The $.06 per share presented above as the stock price as of December 31, 1998, is the bid price. The ask price was $.45 as of the same date, making the spread a whopping 750%.

Officers	Position	Ownership Information	
Donald L. Cox	President, CEO	Number of Shares Outstanding	6,965,800
Lucille M. Cox	Secretary	Market Capitalization	$ 417,948
Brent Mills	Treasurer, CFO	Number of Shareholders	1,000
Russell D. Cox	Vice President	Where Listed / Symbol	OTC-BB / TUFC

Other Information			
Transfer Agent	Jersey Transfer & Trust Co. Verona, NJ	SIC Code	2273
Auditor	Moore Stephens Frost	Employees	1,976
Market Maker	M.H. Meyerson & Co., Inc. (800)333-3113	Web Site	tufcoflooring.com
	N.American Instutional Brokers (800)952-6559		

U.S. Home & Garden Inc.

655 Montgomery Street, Suite 830   San Francisco, CA 94111   Telephone (415)616-8111   Fax (415)616-8110

Company Description

U.S. Home & Garden Inc., formerly Natural Earth Technologies, Inc., is a leading manufacturer and marketer of a broad range of consumer lawn and garden products. Products include weed preventive landscape fabrics, fertilizer spikes, decorative landscape edging, shade cloth and root feeders, which are sold under recognized brand names. The Company markets its products through most large national home improvement and mass merchant retailers including Home Depot, Kmart, Wal-Mart and Home Base. The Company was founded in 1990. Since 1992, the Company has consummated eight acquisitions of other companies or product lines.

	06/30/98	06/30/97	06/30/96	06/30/95
Per Share Information				
Stock Price as of 12/31	4.69	4.13	2.50	2.50
Earnings Per Share	0.24	0.20	0.25	0.19
Price / Earnings Ratio	19.54	20.65	10.00	13.16
Book Value Per Share	2.56	2.27	1.84	1.58
Price / Book Value %	183.20	181.94	135.87	158.23
Dividends Per Share	0.0	0.0	0.0	0.0
Annual Financial Data				
Operating Results (000's)				
Total Revenues	67,635.0	52,122.0	27,100.0	19,726.0
Costs & Expenses	-57,059.0	-44,732.0	-25,291.0	-18,113.0
Income Before Taxes and Other	10,576.0	7,390.0	1,809.0	1,613.0
Other Items	-1,450.0	-1,007.0	0.0	0.0
Income Tax	-3,600.0	-3,200.0	715.0	-38.0
Net Income	5,526.0	3,183.0	2,524.0	1,575.0
Cash Flow From Operations	7,796.0	10,545.0	618.0	438.0
Balance Sheet (000's)				
Cash & Equivalents	27,130.0	2,083.0	680.0	970.0
Total Current Assets	57,895.0	19,746.0	12,976.0	8,126.0
Fixed Assets, Net	3,590.0	2,315.0	1,216.0	961.0
Total Assets	126,813.0	68,475.0	33,584.0	28,140.0
Total Current Liabilities	11,152.0	17,454.0	7,648.0	4,800.0
Long-Term Debt	0.0	17,570.0	6,238.0	8,000.0
Stockholders' Equity	51,599.0	31,926.0	19,370.0	15,340.0
Performance & Financial Condition				
Return on Total Revenues %	8.17	6.11	9.31	7.98
Return on Avg Stockholders' Equity %	13.23	12.41	14.54	17.04
Return on Average Assets %	5.66	6.24	8.18	9.32
Current Ratio	5.19	1.13	1.70	1.69
Debt / Equity %	n.a.	55.03	32.20	52.15

Compound Growth %'s	EPS %	8.10	Net Income %	51.95	Total Revenues %	50.79

Comments

Recent growth was largely due to acquisitions. The Company raised $63.3 million during fiscal 1998 through the placement of subordinated debentures. As a result of a refinancings, the Company recorded extraordinary expenses of $.07 per share and $.06 per share in 1998 and 1997, respectively. Acquisitions are not without a price. The Company had $58.9 million of goodwill recorded on its balance sheet as of the last year end. Therefore, tangible net equity and book value per share are nonexistent. Furthermore, the debentures carry an interest rate of 9.4%. For the six months ended December 31, 1998, revenues and the net loss were $26.8 million and $1.9 million ($.09 per share) as compared to $15.5 million and $1.1 million ($.07 per share) for the same period of the preceding year.

Officers	Position	Ownership Information	
Robert L. Kassel	President, CEO	Number of Shares Outstanding	20,133,000
Richard Raleigh	COO	Market Capitalization	$ 94,423,770
Lynda Gustafson	VP - Finance	Number of Shareholders	700
Maureen Kassel	Vice President, Secretary	Where Listed / Symbol	NASDAQ / USHG

Other Information			
Transfer Agent	North American Transfer Co. Freeport, NY	SIC Code	2879
Auditor	BDO Seidman LLP	Employees	210

U.S. Plastic Lumber Corporation

2300 Glades Road, Suite 440 W.   Boca Raton, FL 33431   Telephone (561)394-3511   Fax (561)394-5335

Company Description

U.S. Plastic Lumber Corporation is engaged in the manufacturing of recycled plastic lumber products from plastic waste. The Company is also a provider of environmental recycling services including the processing of soils which have been exposed to hydrocarbons. Within the plastic lumber division, the Company owns and operates seven manufacturing, processing and fabrication facilities in the United States. Within the environmental services division, the Company operates three facilities. The Company has been pursuing an aggressive growth strategy through acquisitions with single acquisitions occurring in both 1996 and 1997, followed by seven acquisitions in 1998. On January 7, 1999, the Company acquired Soil Remediation of Philadelphia and Allied Waste, Inc. On January 28, 1999, the Company acquired its largest competitor in the recycled plastic lumber business, Eaglebrook Plastics, Inc.

	12/31/98	12/31/97	12/31/96	12/31/95
Per Share Information				
Stock Price	4.87	4.50	4.62	2.00
Earnings Per Share	-0.03	-0.05	-0.32	-0.19
Price / Earnings Ratio	n.a.	n.a.	n.a.	n.a.
Book Value Per Share	0.84	0.46	0.05	0.47
Price / Book Value %	579.76	978.26	9,240.00	425.53
Dividends Per Share	0.0	0.0	0.0	0.0
Annual Financial Data				
Operating Results (000's)				
Total Revenues	45,745.7	24,790.3	6,683.5	7,258.0
Costs & Expenses	-45,649.9	-25,368.3	-10,363.0	-8,393.9
Income Before Taxes and Other	95.8	-710.0	-3,679.5	-1,135.9
Other Items	0.0	0.0	66.9	0.0
Income Tax	0.0	4.3	61.5	-310.0
Net Income	95.8	-705.6	-3,551.1	-1,445.9
Cash Flow From Operations	-6,251.6	-2,453.9	-606.7	-1,164.0
Balance Sheet (000's)				
Cash & Equivalents	902.0	1,170.1	854.3	1,199.6
Total Current Assets	19,384.3	9,833.8	3,087.6	4,702.3
Fixed Assets, Net	17,890.6	5,775.4	1,198.2	1,486.0
Total Assets	52,205.0	23,171.4	4,510.7	6,434.9
Total Current Liabilities	10,528.0	10,307.7	2,376.0	2,214.8
Long-Term Debt	14,669.1	817.0	6.7	0.0
Stockholders' Equity	23,071.9	11,466.2	2,127.9	4,220.1
Performance & Financial Condition				
Return on Total Revenues %	0.21	-2.85	-53.13	-19.92
Return on Avg Stockholders' Equity %	0.55	-10.38	-111.88	-39.03
Return on Average Assets %	0.25	-5.10	-64.89	-72.30
Current Ratio	1.84	0.95	1.30	2.12
Debt / Equity %	63.58	7.13	0.32	n.a.

Compound Growth %'s	EPS % n.a.	Net Income % n.a.	Total Revenues % 84.72

Comments

The Company experienced an 85% increase in net sales in 1998 as compared to 1997. Approximately one-half of the increase was attributable to acquisitions. The remainder was due to the start up of dredging operations and other internal growth. Approximately $516,000 of the net loss incurred in 1997 was due to certain one-time charges for consolidating the operations of the Tennessee and Michigan manufacturing facilities as well as other general and administrative expenses. At December 31, 1998, the Company had $9.6 million of intangible assets which equated to approximately 41% of stockholders' equity and book value per share. The Company is highly leveraged using convertible debentures and preferred shares to finance its growth.

Officers	Position	Ownership Information	
Mark S. Alsentzer	President, CEO	Number of Shares Outstanding	18,230,528
Michael D. Schmidt	Treasurer, CFO	Market Capitalization	$ 88,782,671
Bruce C. Rosetto	Vice President, Secretary	Number of Shareholders	2,400
Gary J. Ziegler	Director	Where Listed / Symbol	NASDAQ / USPL

Other Information			
Transfer Agent	Interwest Transfer Co., Inc. Salt Lake City, UT	SIC Code	3080
Auditor	Arthur Andersen LLP	Employees	489
		Web Site	usplasticlumber.com

UFP Technologies, Inc.

172 East Main Street   Georgetown, MA 91833-2107   Telephone (978)352-2200   Fax (978)352-5616

Company Description

UFP Technologies, Inc. designs and manufactures a broad range of high-performance cushion packaging and specialty foam products as well as 100% recycled molded fiber packaging products for a variety of industrial and consumer markets. The Company is a leading manufacturer of custom-designed cushion foam packaging products and highly engineered specialty foam and laminated products. Its molded fiber products offer a functionally and environmentally responsible alternative to plastic packaging products in the high volume consumer packaging market. The Company was founded in 1963. On January 1, 1997, the Company acquired Foam Cutting Engineers, Inc., an Illinois company engaged in the business of designing and manufacturing engineered foam plastics for packaging and specialty applications. On November 30, 1998, the Company acquired Pacific Foam Technologies, Inc., which is engaged in the business of designing and manufacturing a line of specialty foam products for the health and beauty industry.

	12/31/98	12/31/97	12/31/96	12/31/95
Per Share Information				
Stock Price	3.00	3.50	4.75	4.00
Earnings Per Share	0.34	0.27	0.26	0.19
Price / Earnings Ratio	8.82	12.96	18.27	21.05
Book Value Per Share	3.38	3.03	2.75	2.47
Price / Book Value %	88.76	115.51	172.73	161.94
Dividends Per Share	0.0	0.0	0.0	0.0
Annual Financial Data				
Operating Results (000's)				
Total Revenues	47,281.0	45,472.0	39,418.8	34,113.8
Costs & Expenses	-44,493.0	-43,167.7	-37,750.4	-33,439.6
Income Before Taxes and Other	2,788.0	2,304.3	1,668.5	655.5
Other Items	0.0	0.0	0.0	0.0
Income Tax	-1,141.0	-995.0	-406.0	232.2
Net Income	1,647.0	1,309.3	1,262.5	887.7
Cash Flow From Operations	4,294.8	3,089.5	2,968.3	1,075.6
Balance Sheet (000's)				
Cash & Equivalents	512.4	233.5	143.5	524.5
Total Current Assets	13,160.0	9,846.8	8,935.4	8,453.2
Fixed Assets, Net	10,938.9	11,190.1	9,715.6	7,622.0
Total Assets	29,948.8	25,194.8	22,899.9	20,794.5
Total Current Liabilities	11,060.9	7,268.3	6,447.0	6,501.7
Long-Term Debt	568.7	624.6	764.3	1,161.4
Stockholders' Equity	15,895.4	14,133.2	12,729.5	11,438.3
Performance & Financial Condition				
Return on Total Revenues %	3.48	2.88	3.20	2.60
Return on Avg Stockholders' Equity %	10.97	9.75	10.45	8.08
Return on Average Assets %	5.97	5.44	5.78	4.45
Current Ratio	1.19	1.35	1.39	1.30
Debt / Equity %	3.58	4.42	6.00	10.15

Compound Growth %'s	EPS % 21.41	Net Income % 22.88	Total Revenues % 11.49

Comments

1998 was a modest sales growth year for the Company due to the challenging situation many of its customers faced in Asia. However, management was able to adapt to the changing needs and effectively manage the business to deliver strong earnings growth. 1997 net income improved over its preceding year despite a one time write-off of receivables associated with a customer that filed for bankruptcy protection, acquisition related expenses, and additions to the management team. At December 31, 1998, the Company had $4.7 million of goodwill recorded as assets which equated to approximately 30% of stockholders' equity and book value per share.

Officers	Position	Ownership Information	
William H. Shaw	Chairman	Number of Shares Outstanding	4,707,354
R. Jeffrey Bailly	President, CEO	Market Capitalization	$ 14,122,062
Richard L. Bailly	Exec VP, Secretary	Number of Shareholders	1,000
Ronald J. Lataille	Vice President, CFO	Where Listed / Symbol	NASDAQ / UFPT

Other Information			
Transfer Agent	American Stock Transfer & Trust Co. New York, NY	SIC Code	3086
Auditor	KPMG LLP	Employees	500
		Web Site	ufpt.com

Unapix Entertainment, Inc.

200 Madison Avenue, 24th Floor   New York, NY 10016   Telephone (212)252-7600   Fax (212)252-7630

Company Description

Unapix Entertainment, Inc., founded in 1986, is a worldwide licensor and distributor of feature films and television programs. The Company also produces and distributes music videos and audio recordings primarily to the new contemporary market. Since 1996 the Company has developed and produced documentary and educational non-fiction programming including *Nelson Mandela* which was broadcast on PBS on Frontline in May 1999. During the second quarter of 1998, the Company expanded its television programming production operation to include development of reality based and creative television programming that is principally designed to have a mass audience appeal including *Shocking Behavior: Caught on Tape* which was broadcast on the Fox network in February 1999. Also during 1998, the Company launched a number of E-Commerce web sites on the Internet.

	12/31/98	12/31/97	12/31/96	12/31/95
Per Share Information				
Stock Price	2.19	4.00	4.13	5.24
Earnings Per Share	-0.01	0.19	0.09	0.22
Price / Earnings Ratio	n.a.	21.05	45.89	23.82
Book Value Per Share	3.10	2.41	2.10	1.86
Price / Book Value %	70.65	165.98	196.67	281.72
Dividends Per Share	0.0	0.0	0.0	0.0
Annual Financial Data				
Operating Results (000's)				
Total Revenues	36,481.0	32,608.0	22,831.0	18,582.0
Costs & Expenses	-36,205.0	-30,315.0	-21,842.0	-17,632.0
Income Before Taxes and Other	276.0	2,293.0	989.0	950.0
Other Items	0.0	0.0	0.0	0.0
Income Tax	-166.0	-946.0	-400.0	-15.0
Net Income	110.0	1,347.0	589.0	935.0
Cash Flow From Operations	11,178.0	10,791.0	-7,240.0	-6,164.0
Balance Sheet (000's)				
Cash & Equivalents	1,707.0	425.0	659.0	2,028.0
Total Current Assets	20,675.0	16,433.0	11,501.0	10,416.0
Fixed Assets, Net	1,037.0	685.0	485.0	279.0
Total Assets	65,883.0	47,071.0	31,248.0	21,833.0
Total Current Liabilities	24,057.0	20,176.0	10,015.0	7,433.0
Long-Term Debt	15,951.0	0.0	1,236.0	2,785.0
Stockholders' Equity	24,771.0	16,030.0	12,814.0	11,615.0
Performance & Financial Condition				
Return on Total Revenues %	0.30	4.13	2.58	5.03
Return on Avg Stockholders' Equity %	0.54	9.34	4.82	11.37
Return on Average Assets %	0.19	3.44	2.22	5.28
Current Ratio	0.86	0.81	1.15	1.40
Debt / Equity %	64.39	n.a.	9.65	23.98

Compound Growth %'s	EPS %	n.a.	Net Income %	-51.00	Total Revenues %	25.22

Comments

General and administrative expenses increased 72% to $12.7 million in 1998 as compared to 1997. The increase was attributable to costs related to the infrastructure required to support the Company's expansion and diversification. 1998 results also included $333,000 of nonrecurring costs related to termination and relocation expenses. During 1997, net income increased almost 130% over 1996. This increase was due in large part to the increase in sales volume, offset by increases in general and administrative expenses and interest costs. Included in stockholders' equity at December 31, 1998, is preferred stock with a liquidation preference of $1.5 million. Included in long term debt is $13.3 million in convertible notes.

Officers	Position	Ownership Information	
David M. Fox	President, CEO	Number of Shares Outstanding	7,515,000
Cheryl Freeman	VP - Finance	Market Capitalization	$ 16,457,850
David S. Lawi	Treasurer, Secretary	Number of Shareholders	1,000
Daniel T. Murphy	Vice President, CFO	Where Listed / Symbol	AMEX / UPX

Other Information			
Transfer Agent	American Stock Transfer & Trust Co. New York, NY	SIC Code	7822
Auditor	Richard A. Eisner & Co., LLP	Employees	91
		Web Site	unapixent.com

Unidigital Inc.

229 West 28th Street   New York, NY 10001   Telephone (212)244-7820   Fax (212)244-7814

Company Description

Unidigital Inc. is a service business within the graphic arts industry that provides imaging, reproduction and integrated media solution services to advertising agencies, retailers, corporations, marketing/communications firms, publishers, government agencies and financial institutions in the New York City, Boston, San Francisco and London markets. The Company continues to review opportunities to expand its business and markets in the large format, digital prepress and digital printing markets. The Company had its initial public offering in fiscal 1996.

	08/31/98	08/31/97	08/31/96	08/31/95
Per Share Information				
Stock Price as of 12/31	4.81	5.53	5.00	n.a.
Earnings Per Share	0.30	0.41	0.31	0.57
Price / Earnings Ratio	16.03	13.49	16.13	n.a.
Book Value Per Share	3.69	2.92	2.31	0.82
Price / Book Value %	130.35	189.38	216.45	n.a.
Dividends Per Share	0.0	0.0	0.0	0.0
Annual Financial Data				
Operating Results (000's)				
Total Revenues	47,389.0	27,290.0	11,892.0	8,542.0
Costs & Expenses	-44,361.0	-25,356.0	-9,998.0	-7,042.3
Income Before Taxes and Other	3,028.0	1,934.0	1,894.0	1,499.7
Other Items	-914.0	0.0	0.0	0.0
Income Tax	-978.0	-593.0	-1,064.0	-356.0
Net Income	1,136.0	1,341.0	830.0	1,143.7
Cash Flow From Operations	-1,498.0	489.0	1,488.0	713.4
Balance Sheet (000's)				
Cash & Equivalents	287.0	3,203.0	4,145.5	186.8
Total Current Assets	24,304.0	15,715.0	8,188.5	2,787.2
Fixed Assets, Net	14,591.0	11,899.0	8,595.0	2,965.4
Total Assets	67,315.0	33,033.0	17,623.3	6,550.0
Total Current Liabilities	15,407.0	17,904.0	5,869.2	2,765.8
Long-Term Debt	33,978.0	2,128.0	1,898.9	139.5
Stockholders' Equity	14,393.0	9,473.0	7,364.7	2,604.6
Performance & Financial Condition				
Return on Total Revenues %	2.40	4.91	6.98	13.39
Return on Avg Stockholders' Equity %	9.52	15.93	16.65	n.a.
Return on Average Assets %	2.26	5.29	6.87	n.a.
Current Ratio	1.58	0.88	1.40	1.01
Debt / Equity %	236.07	22.46	25.78	5.36

Compound Growth %'s	EPS %	-19.26	Net Income %	-0.22	Total Revenues %	77.03

Comments

Fiscal 1998 results include expenses of $771,000 due to restructuring and $143,000 related to the early retirement of debt. The 74% increase in revenue over the preceding year was primarily attributable to acquisitions. Two additional acquisitions were completed in early fiscal 1999 including SuperGraphics Holding Company for $15.9 million. Acquisitions are being financed through additional long-term debt which totalled $40.0 million at the last year end. At August 31, 1998, the Company also had $28.1 million of intangible assets which equated to approximately 195% of stockholders' equity and book value per share. For the six months ended February 28, 1999, the Company reported revenues and net income of $34.3 million and $824,000 ($.16 per share) as compared to $19.3 million and $698,000 ($.20 per share) for the same period of the preceding year.

Officers	Position	Ownership Information	
William E. Dye	Chairman, CEO	Number of Shares Outstanding	3,902,634
Peter Saad	President	Market Capitalization	$ 18,771,670
Richard J. Sirota	Senior VP, COO	Number of Shareholders	400
Anthony Manser	Vice President	Where Listed / Symbol	NYSE / UNDG

Other Information			
Transfer Agent	Continental Stock Transfer & Trust Co. New York, NY	SIC Code	2790
Auditor	Ernst & Young LLP	Employees	391
		Web Site	unidigital.net

Unilab Corporation

18448 Oxnard Street   Tarzana, CA 91356   Telephone (818)996-7300   Fax (818)757-3809

Company Description

Unilab Corporation is the largest independent clinical laboratory testing company in California, providing laboratory testing services to physicians, managed care groups, hospitals and other health care providers. As of December 31, 1998, the Company operated three centrally located full-service laboratories, approximately 40 strategically located short turn around laboratories and approximately 270 conveniently located patient service centers. Also as of December 31, 1998, on an average workday, Unilab processed approximately 37,000 patient specimens and performed over 85,000 tests batteries. Tests performed by Unilab measure the levels of, and analyze chemical and cellular components in human body fluids and tissue and are used in the diagnosis, monitoring and treatment of disease.

	12/31/98	12/31/97	12/31/96	12/31/95
Per Share Information				
Stock Price	2.37	1.88	0.44	2.62
Earnings Per Share	0.25	0.01	-2.53	-1.17
Price / Earnings Ratio	9.48	188.00	n.a.	n.a.
Book Value Per Share	-0.58	-0.86	-0.99	1.55
Price / Book Value %	n.a.	n.a.	n.a.	169.03
Dividends Per Share	0.0	0.0	0.0	0.0
Annual Financial Data				
Operating Results (000's)				
Total Revenues	217,370.0	214,001.0	206,496.0	189,953.0
Costs & Expenses	-206,667.0	-213,465.0	-225,805.0	-193,497.0
Income Before Taxes and Other	10,703.0	536.0	-23,838.0	-3,544.0
Other Items	0.0	0.0	-69,106.0	-38,231.0
Income Tax	0.0	0.0	0.0	0.0
Net Income	10,703.0	536.0	-92,944.0	-41,775.0
Cash Flow From Operations	13,996.0	3,715.0	-5,128.0	-7,400.0
Balance Sheet (000's)				
Cash & Equivalents	20,137.0	11,652.0	12,176.0	70.0
Total Current Assets	65,563.0	52,341.0	54,665.0	59,584.0
Fixed Assets, Net	11,277.0	13,160.0	17,264.0	18,326.0
Total Assets	142,460.0	118,700.0	125,919.0	196,174.0
Total Current Liabilities	22,631.0	23,791.0	29,752.0	49,273.0
Long-Term Debt	137,170.0	124,285.0	126,120.0	87,207.0
Stockholders' Equity	-21,367.0	-32,283.0	-34,688.0	56,330.0
Performance & Financial Condition				
Return on Total Revenues %	4.92	0.25	-45.01	-21.99
Return on Avg Stockholders' Equity %	n.a.	n.a.	-858.92	-55.09
Return on Average Assets %	8.20	0.44	-57.71	-20.89
Current Ratio	2.90	2.20	1.84	1.21
Debt / Equity %	n.a.	n.a.	n.a.	154.81

Compound Growth %'s	EPS %	n.a.	Net Income %	n.a.	Total Revenues %	4.60

Comments

Most of the increase in 1998 revenues was attributable to the acquisition of Meris Laboratories, Inc. on November 5, 1998. Tight control over all expense categories resulted in an impressive improvement to net earnings. 1996 results include restructuring and other nonrecurring expense of $69,106,000. At December 31, 1998, the Company had $59.3 million of intangibles recorded as assets which would increase the deficit in stockholders' equity if restated on a tangible asset basis. The Company also had $60 million in operating loss carryovers and $36.5 million in capital loss carryovers available to offset future income.

Officers	Position	Ownership Information	
David C. Weavil	President, CEO	Number of Shares Outstanding	40,708,000
Mark L. Bibi	Exec VP, Secretary	Market Capitalization	$ 96,477,960
Ian J. Brotchie	Exec VP	Number of Shareholders	2,940
Brian D. Urban	Vice President, CFO	Where Listed / Symbol	AMEX / ULB

Other Information			
Transfer Agent	ChaseMellon Shareholder Services New York, NY	SIC Code	8071
Auditor	Arthur Andersen LLP	Employees	2,600
		Web Site	unilab.com

United-Guardian, Inc.

230 Marcus Boulevard   Hauppauge, NY 11788   Telephone (516)273-0900   Fax (516)273-0858

Company Description

United-Guardian, Inc. conducts research, product development, manufacturing, and marketing of pharmaceuticals, cosmetics, health care products, medical devices, and proprietary industrial products. The Company also distributes a line of over 3,000 organic chemicals, research chemicals, test solutions, indicators, dyes and reagents. Sales from the Company's two major product lines, Lubrajel and Renacidin, account for approximately 70% of the Company's sales. Lubrajel is a non-drying water based lubricating jelly which has applications in the medical field as a lubricant and in the cosmetic industry as a moisturizer. Renacidin is a urological prescription drug.

	12/31/98	12/31/97	12/31/96	12/31/95
Per Share Information				
Stock Price	4.50	4.25	1.75	1.63
Earnings Per Share	0.21	0.17	0.11	0.06
Price / Earnings Ratio	21.43	25.00	15.91	27.17
Book Value Per Share	1.22	1.08	0.95	0.89
Price / Book Value %	368.85	393.52	184.21	183.15
Dividends Per Share	0.07	0.06	0.05	0.0
Annual Financial Data				
Operating Results (000's)				
Total Revenues	8,867.2	8,790.6	8,097.8	6,971.8
Costs & Expenses	-7,221.0	-7,463.8	-7,245.7	-6,521.0
Income Before Taxes and Other	1,646.2	1,326.9	852.1	450.8
Other Items	0.0	0.0	0.0	0.0
Income Tax	-632.7	-502.6	-324.8	-178.0
Net Income	1,013.5	824.2	527.3	272.8
Cash Flow From Operations	1,234.3	1,497.1	1,059.6	260.1
Balance Sheet (000's)				
Cash & Equivalents	1,320.6	822.6	826.1	307.1
Total Current Assets	4,721.3	3,795.2	3,813.6	3,849.2
Fixed Assets, Net	1,532.7	1,532.9	1,511.6	1,516.6
Total Assets	6,794.3	6,125.8	5,854.1	5,915.8
Total Current Liabilities	795.2	821.5	831.1	913.0
Long-Term Debt	16.2	0.0	475.0	727.5
Stockholders' Equity	5,972.9	5,284.3	4,516.4	4,227.2
Performance & Financial Condition				
Return on Total Revenues %	11.43	9.38	6.51	3.91
Return on Avg Stockholders' Equity %	18.01	16.82	12.06	6.67
Return on Average Assets %	15.69	13.76	8.96	4.57
Current Ratio	5.94	4.62	4.59	4.22
Debt / Equity %	0.27	n.a.	10.52	17.21

Compound Growth %'s	EPS %	51.83	Net Income %	54.87	Total Revenues %	8.35

Comments

Revenues were almost flat in 1998 due to a weakness in the Asian market and downsizing of certain product lines. But operating revenue improved despite a $204,000 nonrecurring noncash charge related to unamortized costs of certain technology. Revenue growth in 1997 resulted primarily from increased sales of the Company's lubricating products. Along with the improved operating results came another year of good cash flow. As a result, the Company's financial position is improving with increased levels of working capital and equity. Stockholders have been rewarded with cash dividends for three consecutive years.

Officers	Position	Ownership Information	
Alfred R. Globus	Chairman, CEO	Number of Shares Outstanding	4,883,139
Kenneth H. Globus	President, CFO	Market Capitalization	$ 21,974,126
Robert S. Rubinger	Exec VP, Secretary	Number of Shareholders	1,604
Charles W. Castanza	Vice President	Where Listed / Symbol	AMEX / UG

Other Information			
Transfer Agent	Continental Stock Transfer & Trust Co. New York, NY	SIC Code	2834
Auditor	Grant Thornton LLP	Employees	44

Universal American Financial Corp.

Six International Drive, Suite 190   Rye Brook, NY 10573-1068   Telephone (914)934-5200   Fax (914)934-9123

Company Description

Universal American Financial Corp. is an insurance holding company, providing supplemental health insurance, life insurance and annuities to senior citizens and customized insurance programs for market niches. Marketing efforts are primarily focused in Florida, New York and Texas. The Company was founded in 1981 and originally conducted business through a single subsidiary, John Adams Life Insurance Company of New York. Through a series of acquisitions, the Company has grown from one subsidiary with less than $2 million in annual premiums in 1990 to four subsidiaries with total premiums today in excess of $131 million. On March 19, 1998, the Company acquired a $12.6 million block of annual premiums in force of Medicare Supplemental business from Dallas General. Not yet reflected in the financial information below is an agreement by the Company to acquire six insurance companies from PennCorp Financial Group, Inc. in 1999.

	12/31/98	12/31/97	12/31/96	12/31/95
Per Share Information				
Stock Price	2.41	2.75	1.87	2.25
Earnings Per Share	0.20	0.18	0.01	0.25
Price / Earnings Ratio	12.05	15.28	187.00	9.00
Book Value Per Share	3.19	2.96	2.53	2.89
Price / Book Value %	75.55	92.91	73.91	77.85
Dividends Per Share	0.0	0.0	0.0	0.0
Annual Financial Data				
Operating Results (000's)				
Total Revenues	56,089.1	51,330.5	53,387.2	49,811.6
Costs & Expenses	-52,157.5	-48,119.3	-53,014.3	-47,160.7
Income Before Taxes and Other	3,931.6	3,211.2	372.9	2,650.9
Other Items	0.0	0.0	0.0	0.0
Income Tax	-1,324.0	-1,091.8	-269.0	-9.0
Net Income	2,607.6	2,119.4	103.9	2,641.8
Cash Flow From Operations	-374.3	-6,873.3	-9,908.9	-6,081.2
Balance Sheet (000's)				
Cash & Equivalents	17,092.9	25,014.0	15,403.5	12,289.8
Total Current Assets	245,606.0	250,858.8	222,446.5	151,593.7
Fixed Assets, Net	0.0	0.0	0.0	0.0
Total Assets	283,302.3	272,575.3	242,236.7	182,994.4
Total Current Liabilities	184,544.9	186,615.0	172,282.9	135,772.8
Long-Term Debt	4,750.0	0.0	0.0	0.0
Stockholders' Equity	28,317.9	25,706.4	22,078.5	24,114.3
Performance & Financial Condition				
Return on Total Revenues %	4.65	4.13	0.19	5.30
Return on Avg Stockholders' Equity %	9.65	8.87	0.45	13.40
Return on Average Assets %	0.94	0.82	0.05	1.52
Current Ratio	1.33	1.34	1.29	1.12
Debt / Equity %	16.77	n.a.	n.a.	n.a.

Compound Growth %'s	EPS %	-7.17	Net Income %	-0.43	Total Revenues %	4.04

Comments

Management attributes the improvement in results to the fact that premium revenues are increasing faster than expenses. Acquisitions are largely responsible for the additional premiums. Considerable efficiencies have been realized over recent years including the consolidation of administrative functions. At December 31, 1998, the Company had $6.1 million of intangible assets recorded as assets which equated to approximately 25% of common stockholders' equity and book value per common share. To partially fund the cash of $136 million required for the PennCorp acquisition mentioned above, the Company will be privately placing 26 million additional common shares at an average price of $3.15 per share.

Officers	Position	Ownership Information	
Richard A. Barasch	Chairman, CEO	Number of Shares Outstanding	7,638,057
Gary W. Bryant	Senior VP	Market Capitalization	$ 18,407,717
Robert A. Waegelein	Senior VP, CFO	Number of Shareholders	1,700
Joan M. Ferrarone	Secretary	Where Listed / Symbol	NASDAQ / UHCO

Other Information			
Transfer Agent	American Stock Transfer & Trust Co. New York, NY	SIC Code	6311
Auditor	Ernst & Young LLP	Employees	265

Vermont Pure Holdings, Ltd.

P.O. Box C, Route 66, Catamount Industrial Park   Randolph, VT 05060   Telephone (802)728-3600   Fax (802)728-4614

Company Description

Vermont Pure Holdings, Ltd. is engaged in the bottling, marketing and distribution of natural spring water obtained from Company-owned properties in Randolph, Vermont, and other properties in Vermont. The Company's products are sold primarily in the New England, Mid-Atlantic and Midwestern states, through a network of independent beverage distributors. The Company was founded in 1990. Beginning in 1996, the Company embarked on an aggressive growth through acquisition strategy. Since May 1996, the Company has acquired seven companies, made many small acquisitions of home and office customer bases, and expanded into the coffee service market.

	10/31/98	10/25/97	10/26/96	10/28/95
Per Share Information				
Stock Price as of 12/31	4.94	4.00	2.18	1.87
Earnings Per Share	0.26	0.11	-0.13	-0.30
Price / Earnings Ratio	19.00	36.36	n.a.	n.a.
Book Value Per Share	0.97	0.66	0.47	0.69
Price / Book Value %	509.28	606.06	463.83	271.01
Dividends Per Share	0.0	0.0	0.0	0.0
Annual Financial Data				
Operating Results (000's)				
Total Revenues	29,271.5	17,739.2	11,878.8	8,517.5
Costs & Expenses	-27,859.7	-17,215.8	-13,085.1	-11,275.0
Income Before Taxes and Other	1,411.8	523.4	-1,267.3	-2,804.1
Other Items	0.0	0.0	0.0	0.0
Income Tax	1,447.0	544.0	0.0	0.0
Net Income	2,858.8	1,067.4	-1,267.3	-2,804.1
Cash Flow From Operations	2,806.4	1,430.5	-225.0	-2,748.2
Balance Sheet (000's)				
Cash & Equivalents	161.3	93.8	783.1	1,543.3
Total Current Assets	5,627.9	3,661.7	2,885.2	3,437.9
Fixed Assets, Net	9,174.1	7,332.9	5,536.2	5,659.2
Total Assets	26,173.5	16,546.8	9,971.4	9,266.5
Total Current Liabilities	4,892.4	3,404.3	2,176.6	1,590.6
Long-Term Debt	10,212.6	5,435.3	2,779.4	1,682.2
Stockholders' Equity	9,965.1	6,642.0	4,526.5	5,793.8
Performance & Financial Condition				
Return on Total Revenues %	9.77	6.02	-10.67	-32.92
Return on Avg Stockholders' Equity %	34.43	19.11	-24.56	-62.31
Return on Average Assets %	13.38	8.05	-13.18	-35.05
Current Ratio	1.15	1.08	1.33	2.16
Debt / Equity %	102.48	81.83	61.40	29.03

Compound Growth %'s   EPS % n.a.   Net Income % n.a.   Total Revenues % 50.91

Comments

Only half of the strong 65% increase in revenues during fiscal 1998 was attributable to acquisitions, with the balance coming from internal growth. For fiscal 1998 and 1997, the Company recorded tax benefits of $1,447,000 and $544,000, respectively, which reflects partial recognition of the use of tax loss carryforwards. The Company has $13.1 million of tax loss carryforwards available to offset future taxable income. At October 31, 1998, the Company had intangible assets totalling $9.6 million on its books which equated to approximately 96% of stockholders' equity and book value per share. (So much for book value being a meaningful number.) The Company is highly leveraged and will likely issue additional shares if it is to continue its growth strategy.

Officers	Position	Ownership Information	
Timothy G. Fallon	President, CEO	Number of Shares Outstanding	10,237,187
Bruce S. MacDonald	Vice President, CFO	Market Capitalization	$ 50,571,704
Frank G. McDougall, Jr.	Director	Number of Shareholders	1,500
Beat Schlagenhauf	Director	Where Listed / Symbol	NASDAQ / VPUR

Other Information			
Transfer Agent	American Stock Transfer & Trust Co. New York, NY	SIC Code	5149
Auditor	Feldman Sherb Ehrlich & Co. PC	Employees	163
		Web Site	vermontpure.com

Vicon Fiber Optics Corp.

90 Secor Lane   Pelham Manor, NY 10803   Telephone (914)738-5006   Fax (914)738-6920

Company Description

Vicon Fiber Optics Corp., founded in 1969, manufactures fiber optic illuminating systems and components for use in conjunction with dental equipment and instruments. Fiber optics are glass fibers through which light is transmitted. Each fiber is composed of an inner glass core with one index of refraction, covered by an outer glass cladding or coating with a higher index of refraction. These fibers are bundled in different ways to transmit images in industrial and medical inspection scopes. The Company believes that it is one of the leading domestic manufacturers of fiber optic components and systems for use in the dental industry. The Company also manufactures a line of decorative fiber optic lamps under the tradename Fantasia Products.

	12/31/98	12/31/97	12/31/96	12/31/95
Per Share Information				
Stock Price as of 12/31	0.69	1.00	0.81	0.88
Earnings Per Share	0.01	0.05	0.04	0.06
Price / Earnings Ratio	69.00	20.00	20.25	14.67
Book Value Per Share	0.36	0.35	0.30	0.26
Price / Book Value %	191.67	285.71	270.00	338.46
Dividends Per Share	0.0	0.0	0.0	0.0
Annual Financial Data				
Operating Results (000's)				
Total Revenues	3,368.7	4,067.9	2,833.6	2,825.9
Costs & Expenses	-3,163.8	-3,413.3	-2,285.5	-2,151.1
Income Before Taxes and Other	204.9	654.5	548.2	674.8
Other Items	0.0	0.0	4.1	126.7
Income Tax	-89.9	-235.6	-208.8	-236.9
Net Income	115.0	418.9	343.5	564.6
Cash Flow From Operations	109.7	-33.9	533.8	274.1
Balance Sheet (000's)				
Cash & Equivalents	254.6	834.2	1,049.2	858.7
Total Current Assets	2,713.2	3,144.1	2,491.4	2,169.3
Fixed Assets, Net	425.3	413.0	399.0	95.8
Total Assets	4,019.5	3,933.6	3,264.5	2,836.7
Total Current Liabilities	754.8	686.2	436.2	257.4
Long-Term Debt	99.1	234.5	258.0	424.2
Stockholders' Equity	3,108.6	2,965.5	2,535.3	2,155.1
Performance & Financial Condition				
Return on Total Revenues %	3.41	10.30	12.12	19.98
Return on Avg Stockholders' Equity %	3.79	15.23	14.65	30.15
Return on Average Assets %	2.89	11.64	11.26	20.40
Current Ratio	3.59	4.58	5.71	8.43
Debt / Equity %	3.19	7.91	10.18	19.68

Compound Growth %'s	EPS % -44.97	Net Income % -41.16	Total Revenues % 6.03

Comments

Revenue decreased 17% in 1998 as compared to 1997. Management attributes this decline to late deliveries of new and existing models of the Fantasia decorative lamps by the Company's Chinese vendors. These delays were due to shortages of shipping containers from the Pacific rim and other related economic factors in China. Net income declined because of lower revenue and a $160,000 settlement expense in a patent infringement lawsuit against the Company. During 1998, the Company made a $500,000 investment in American Entertainment Group, Inc., an Internet company. Although the stock had declined in value to $17,500 at December 31, 1998, the investment was still being carried at its original cost. However, the Company's financial condition was not in jeopardy.

Officers	Position	Ownership Information	
Leonard Scrivo	President, CEO	Number of Shares Outstanding	8,679,069
Les Wasser	Secretary, Controller	Market Capitalization	$ 5,988,558
Michael Scrivo	Vice President	Number of Shareholders	1,600
Robert J. Figliozzi	Director	Where Listed / Symbol	OTC-BB / VFOX

Other Information			
Transfer Agent	Continental Stock Transfer & Trust Co. Jersey City, NJ	SIC Code	3843
Auditor	Sheft, Kahn & Company LLP	Employees	25
Market Maker	Paragon Capital Corporation (800)345-0505		
	Herzog, Heine, Geduld, Inc. (800)221-3600		

Wade Cook Financial Corporation

14675 Interurban Avenue South Seattle, WA 98168 Telephone (206)901-3000 Fax (206)901-3100

Company Description

Wade Cook Financial Corporation through its subsidiary, Wade Cook Seminars (WCSI), conducts educational investment seminars. WCSI produces video tapes, audio tapes, and written materials designed to teach various investment and cash flow strategies for investors in the stock market. The Company also publishes books and other written materials relating to personal finance, inspirational themes and other topics. Additionally, the Company provides subscription Internet access and paging services and maintains an investment information network on the Internet. The company also owns interests in hotels and hold interests in marketable securities, real estate, gold, oil and gas, and other venture capital partnerships and private companies.

	12/31/98	12/31/97	12/31/96	12/31/95
Per Share Information				
Stock Price	0.41	4.13	0.29	0.21
Earnings Per Share	0.06	0.14	0.05	0.0
Price / Earnings Ratio	6.83	29.50	5.80	n.a.
Book Value Per Share	0.31	0.25	0.06	0.01
Price / Book Value %	132.26	1,652.00	483.33	2,100.00
Dividends Per Share	0.0	0.0	0.0	0.0
Annual Financial Data				
Operating Results (000's)				
Total Revenues	121,751.0	105,421.2	40,913.8	7,560.8
Costs & Expenses	-116,541.0	-89,476.0	-36,247.9	-7,253.3
Income Before Taxes and Other	5,210.0	15,034.6	4,665.9	307.5
Other Items	890.0	21.3	0.0	0.0
Income Tax	-2,346.0	-6,063.4	-1,601.2	-183.7
Net Income	3,754.0	8,992.5	3,064.6	123.8
Cash Flow From Operations	15,261.0	13,947.8	4,388.4	910.9
Balance Sheet (000's)				
Cash & Equivalents	1,742.0	540.8	635.1	26.8
Total Current Assets	11,998.0	12,778.2	6,958.9	577.4
Fixed Assets, Net	29,203.0	10,425.2	7,135.2	345.0
Total Assets	58,698.0	41,404.1	16,937.7	2,283.1
Total Current Liabilities	28,602.0	23,827.9	10,849.6	1,340.6
Long-Term Debt	9,473.0	821.2	1,768.8	117.8
Stockholders' Equity	19,687.0	16,067.1	3,702.0	528.9
Performance & Financial Condition				
Return on Total Revenues %	3.08	8.53	7.49	1.64
Return on Avg Stockholders' Equity %	21.00	90.97	144.87	5.85
Return on Average Assets %	7.50	30.83	31.89	1.29
Current Ratio	0.42	0.54	0.64	0.43
Debt / Equity %	48.12	5.11	47.78	22.27

Compound Growth %'s	EPS %	9.54	Net Income %	211.84	Total Revenues %	152.52

Comments

The Company declared two 3 for 1 stock splits in 1997 and a 2 for 1 stock split in 1996. All per share amounts have been adjusted for consistency. During 1998, the number of seminars that the Company held increased to 3,737 seminars as compared to 2,416 seminars during 1997. However, due to a reduction in participants per seminar, revenue per seminar decreased from $25,150 in 1997 to $21,000 per seminar in 1998. A large deficiency in working capital would be troublesome to any potential investor even though some of the money is owed to Mr. Wade Cook himself. At December 31, 1998, goodwill of $3.1 million equals about 16% of stockholders' equity.

Officers	Position	Ownership Information	
Wade B. Cook	President, CEO	Number of Shares Outstanding	64,094,630
Richard Smith	CFO	Market Capitalization	$ 26,278,798
Laura M. Cook	Secretary	Number of Shareholders	11,308
Robin Anderson	Director	Where Listed / Symbol	OTC-BB / WADE

Other Information			
Transfer Agent	National Stock Transfer, Inc. Salt Lake City, UT	SIC Code	8200
Auditor	Miller and Co.	Employees	434
Market Maker	Fahnestock & Co., Inc. (800)223-3012	Web Site	wadecook.com
	Wilson-Davis & Co., Inc. (800)453-5735		

Waterlink, Inc.

4100 Holiday Street N. W., Suite 201   Canton, OH 44718-2532   Telephone (330)649-4000   Fax (330)649-4008

Company Description

Waterlink, Inc., founded in 1994, is an international provider of integrated water purification and wastewater treatment solutions, treating process water and wastewater for its industrial customers, and drinking water and wastewater for its municipal customers. In order to participate in the consolidation of this highly fragmented industry, the Company is executing an acquisition program which targets businesses in two principal markets (wastewater and pure water) as well as in two geographic areas (the United States and Europe). The Company completed three acquisitions, five acquisitions, and three acquisitions during fiscal 1998, 1997 and 1996, respectively. The Company went public on June 24, 1997.

	09/30/98	09/30/97	09/30/96	09/30/95
Per Share Information				
Stock Price as of 12/31	3.69	16.50	5.00	n.a.
Earnings Per Share	-1.46	0.05	0.06	-0.42
Price / Earnings Ratio	n.a.	330.00	83.33	n.a.
Book Value Per Share	4.49	5.95	0.31	n.a.
Price / Book Value %	82.18	277.31	1,612.90	n.a.
Dividends Per Share	0.0	0.0	0.0	0.0
Annual Financial Data				
Operating Results (000's)				
Total Revenues	135,204.0	64,962.0	19,801.0	2,717.0
Costs & Expenses	-129,604.0	-61,105.0	-19,446.0	-3,194.0
Income Before Taxes and Other	5,600.0	3,857.0	311.0	-477.0
Other Items	-21,636.0	-3,015.0	0.0	0.0
Income Tax	-1,468.0	-470.0	-5.0	-35.0
Net Income	-17,504.0	372.0	306.0	-512.0
Cash Flow From Operations	-9,453.0	-6,708.0	-14.0	-500.0
Balance Sheet (000's)				
Cash & Equivalents	3,925.0	2,482.0	119.0	995.0
Total Current Assets	79,894.0	46,795.0	17,877.0	6,855.0
Fixed Assets, Net	13,730.0	5,811.0	5,000.0	2,000.0
Total Assets	183,561.0	115,860.0	28,991.0	10,819.0
Total Current Liabilities	49,157.0	27,365.0	14,439.0	4,791.0
Long-Term Debt	73,639.0	12,502.0	12,145.0	6,039.0
Stockholders' Equity	54,878.0	70,873.0	2,407.0	-11.0
Performance & Financial Condition				
Return on Total Revenues %	-12.95	0.57	1.55	-18.84
Return on Avg Stockholders' Equity %	-27.84	1.02	25.54	-64.00
Return on Average Assets %	-11.69	0.51	1.54	-3.41
Current Ratio	1.63	1.71	1.24	1.43
Debt / Equity %	134.19	17.64	504.57	n.a.

Compound Growth %'s	EPS % n.a.	Net Income % n.a.	Total Revenues % 267.82

Comments

The Company reports an internal negative growth rate of 10.8% during fiscal 1998. The net increase in revenues was attributable to acquisitions. During fiscal 1998, the Company recorded special charges totaling $21,636,000 related to the closure of a facility, the impairment of goodwill, and the costs associated with the resignation of the Company's former president. But the Company is not under water yet as all resources are now focused on a single objective - to achieve sustainable, profitable growth in 1999. Growth via acquisition has its costs. At September 30, 1998, the Company had $80 million of goodwill reflected as assets which equates to approximately 146% of stockholders' equity and book value per share. $73.6 million of long term debt at the same date means the Company is highly leveraged.

Officers	Position	Ownership Information	
Theodore F. Savastano	Chairman	Number of Shares Outstanding	12,225,604
T. Scott King	President, CEO	Market Capitalization	$ 45,112,479
Michael J. Vantusko	CFO	Number of Shareholders	2,707
Rollin S. Reiter	Director	Where Listed / Symbol	NYSE / WLK

Other Information			
Transfer Agent	American Stock Transfer & Trust Co. New York, NY	SIC Code	3590
Auditor	Ernst & Young LLP	Employees	750
		Web Site	waterlink.com

Wegener Corporation

11350 Technology Circle   Duluth, GA 30155-1528   Telephone (770)623-0096   Fax (770)623-9648

Company Description

Wegener Corporation designs and manufactures communications transmission and receiving equipment for the business broadcast, data communications, cable and broadcast radio and television markets. The Company considers itself a leader in digital and analog compression technology. Its digital products are in use worldwide in distance learning, radio, cable television, and private business networks. In terms of new orders, compressed digital products are the fastest growing product segment. As expected, demand for the Company's analog products has continued to decline following market demand, and the Company's emphasis on, digital technology. The Company was founded in 1977.

	08/28/98	08/29/97	08/30/96	09/01/95
Per Share Information				
Stock Price as of 12/31	1.84	1.50	3.81	11.75
Earnings Per Share	0.23	-0.19	0.16	0.05
Price / Earnings Ratio	8.00	n.a.	23.81	235.00
Book Value Per Share	1.60	1.36	1.48	1.29
Price / Book Value %	115.00	110.29	257.43	910.85
Dividends Per Share	0.0	0.0	0.0	0.0
Annual Financial Data				
Operating Results (000's)				
Total Revenues	34,719.9	21,836.6	23,263.4	19,512.3
Costs & Expenses	-30,254.7	-24,591.8	-22,655.3	-19,127.0
Income Before Taxes and Other	4,465.2	-2,755.2	608.1	384.9
Other Items	0.0	0.0	0.0	0.0
Income Tax	-1,705.0	946.0	848.0	0.0
Net Income	2,760.2	-1,809.2	1,456.1	384.9
Cash Flow From Operations	5,787.3	6,324.9	-6,041.3	-2,488.1
Balance Sheet (000's)				
Cash & Equivalents	6,492.8	2,242.4	171.7	4,914.0
Total Current Assets	19,962.8	18,110.1	21,150.5	16,775.4
Fixed Assets, Net	4,523.3	4,979.9	4,727.7	4,412.2
Total Assets	25,905.0	25,614.0	27,736.7	22,018.1
Total Current Liabilities	4,985.5	7,627.4	7,140.1	8,833.8
Long-Term Debt	1,231.3	1,782.5	2,331.4	0.0
Stockholders' Equity	19,080.1	14,918.9	12,956.2	11,220.0
Performance & Financial Condition				
Return on Total Revenues %	7.95	-8.29	6.26	1.97
Return on Avg Stockholders' Equity %	16.24	-12.98	12.05	5.40
Return on Average Assets %	10.72	-6.78	5.85	2.27
Current Ratio	4.00	2.37	2.96	1.90
Debt / Equity %	6.45	11.95	17.99	n.a.

Compound Growth %'s	EPS %	66.31	Net Income %	92.84	Total Revenues %	21.18

Comments

The demand for digital products is being driven by the high cost of satellite capacity. Digital compression technology allows a four to ten-fold, or more, increase in the throughput of a satellite channel. Management attributes the 57% growth in fiscal 1998 revenues to improved product quality and the development of new products. The solid bottom line performance was after $2.6 million of research and development costs. This was a nice rebound after the Company stumbled in fiscal 1997. Management had a lengthy explanation at that time, all of which pointed to lower demand and late deliveries in products. For the six months ended February 28, 1999, the Company reported revenues and net income of $13.5 million and $626,611 ($.05 per share) as compared to $16.9 million and $1,457,730 ($.12 per share) for the same period in the preceding year.

Officers	Position	Ownership Information	
Robert A. Placek	President, CEO	Number of Shares Outstanding	11,956,029
C. Troy Woodbury, Jr.	Treasurer, CFO	Market Capitalization	$ 21,999,093
James T. Traicoff	Controller	Number of Shareholders	426
James H. Morgan, Jr.	Director	Where Listed / Symbol	NASDAQ / WGNR

Other Information			
Transfer Agent	Securities Transfer Corp. Dallas, TX	SIC Code	3663
Auditor	BDO Seidman LLP	Employees	137
		Web Site	wegener.com

Weirton Steel Corporation

400 Three Springs Drive   Weirton, WV 26062-4989   Telephone (304)797-2000   Fax (304)797-2904

Company Description

Weirton Steel Corporation, a major integrated steel producer, was formed in 1982 for the purpose of acquiring the assets of the Weirton Steel Division of National Steel Corporation. In 1984, the Company completed the acquisition in a transaction financed through an Employee Stock Ownership Plan. The Company and its predecessors have operated as an integrated steel producer in the Weirton, West Virginia area since 1909. The Company has an annual raw steel production capacity of three million tons and produces flat rolled, cold rolled or coated products, including hot dipped and electro-galvanized steels and tin mill products. Food and beverage cans, general packaging, pipe and tube, service centers, construction, and shipping containers are the major market sectors supplied by the Company.

	12/31/98	12/31/97	12/31/96	12/31/95
Per Share Information				
Stock Price	1.56	2.69	3.50	4.12
Earnings Per Share	-0.15	-0.42	-1.18	1.10
Price / Earnings Ratio	n.a.	n.a.	n.a.	3.75
Book Value Per Share	2.95	2.61	3.08	4.35
Price / Book Value %	52.88	103.07	113.64	94.71
Dividends Per Share	0.0	0.0	0.0	0.0
Annual Financial Data				
Operating Results (000's)				
Total Revenues	1,259,514.0	1,401,451.0	1,388,716.0	1,365,326.0
Costs & Expenses	-1,267,325.0	-1,420,881.0	-1,441,369.0	-1,294,387.0
Income Before Taxes and Other	-7,811.0	-22,040.0	-55,263.0	68,329.0
Other Items	293.0	0.0	-5,431.0	-6,718.0
Income Tax	1,391.0	4,298.0	10,776.0	-13,255.0
Net Income	-6,127.0	-17,742.0	-49,918.0	48,356.0
Cash Flow From Operations	50,224.0	72,104.0	34,608.0	109,219.0
Balance Sheet (000's)				
Cash & Equivalents	68,389.0	124,690.0	112,092.0	131,811.0
Total Current Assets	487,696.0	565,706.0	580,798.0	594,029.0
Fixed Assets, Net	576,238.0	591,389.0	610,494.0	586,430.0
Total Assets	1,195,699.0	1,282,540.0	1,300,621.0	1,314,021.0
Total Current Liabilities	294,724.0	271,617.0	271,305.0	253,726.0
Long-Term Debt	304,626.0	388,997.0	430,820.0	407,869.0
Stockholders' Equity	121,543.0	132,527.0	149,204.0	198,628.0
Performance & Financial Condition				
Return on Total Revenues %	-0.49	-1.27	-3.59	3.54
Return on Avg Stockholders' Equity %	-4.82	-12.59	-28.70	26.69
Return on Average Assets %	-0.49	-1.37	-3.82	3.80
Current Ratio	1.65	2.08	2.14	2.34
Debt / Equity %	250.63	293.52	288.75	205.34

Compound Growth %'s	EPS %	n.a.	Net Income %	n.a.	Total Revenues %	-2.65

Comments

In 1997, the Company significantly reduced operating costs, enhanced the quality of iron and produced more of it, negotiated constructive labor agreements, and formed new alliances to help grow the business. 1997 results include $17.0 million of restructuring charges associated with employee reduction programs. These programs were extended to the managerial level in 1998 and another $2.9 million was expensed. Hindering the Company's return to profitability in 1998 were lower shipments and selling prices of steel which were the result, according to management, of unfairly priced imports which drastically weakened the domestic steel market in the second half of 1998.

Officers	Position	Ownership Information	
Richard K. Riederer	President, CEO	Number of Shares Outstanding	41,194,573
Craig T. Costello	Exec VP, COO	Market Capitalization	$ 64,263,534
David L. Robertson	Exec VP	Number of Shareholders	10,000
Earl E. Davis, Jr.	Exec VP	Where Listed / Symbol	NYSE / WS

Other Information			
Transfer Agent	Harris Trust & Savings Bank Chicago, IL	SIC Code	3312
Auditor	Arthur Andersen LLP	Employees	4,329
		Web Site	weirton.com

Westerbeke Corporation

411 Ledan Drive   Avon, MA 02322   Telephone (508)588-7700   Fax (508)559-9323

Company Description

Westerbeke Corporation is primarily engaged in the business of designing, manufacturing and marketing marine engine and air-conditioning products. The Company's marine products consist of diesel and gasoline engine-driven electrical generator sets, inboard propulsion engines, self-contained, reverse cycle air-conditioners, and associated spare parts and accessories. Generator sets are installed in powerboats, houseboats, large sailboats and other types of pleasure and commercial boats to provide electricity for operating, safety and convenience needs. Propulsion engines are installed as auxiliary power systems for sailboats. The Company was founded in 1932.

	10/24/98	10/25/97	10/26/96	10/28/95
Per Share Information				
Stock Price as of 12/31	2.62	4.12	2.37	2.62
Earnings Per Share	0.31	0.37	0.33	0.31
Price / Earnings Ratio	8.45	11.14	7.18	8.45
Book Value Per Share	5.59	5.37	4.73	4.40
Price / Book Value %	46.87	76.72	50.11	59.55
Dividends Per Share	0.0	0.0	0.0	0.0
Annual Financial Data				
Operating Results (000's)				
Total Revenues	26,202.0	24,620.3	20,700.3	18,837.1
Costs & Expenses	-25,111.8	-23,271.4	-19,465.7	-17,695.1
Income Before Taxes and Other	1,090.2	1,348.9	1,234.6	1,142.0
Other Items	0.0	0.0	0.0	0.0
Income Tax	-446.7	-550.0	-497.2	-444.4
Net Income	643.5	798.9	737.4	697.6
Cash Flow From Operations	1,191.6	924.0	-581.1	336.7
Balance Sheet (000's)				
Cash & Equivalents	101.9	156.9	200.5	1,322.2
Total Current Assets	8,708.0	9,406.0	8,635.4	7,627.4
Fixed Assets, Net	2,161.5	2,139.3	1,782.3	1,594.9
Total Assets	14,670.3	14,810.7	12,681.2	10,998.6
Total Current Liabilities	3,058.4	3,605.6	2,320.0	1,719.0
Long-Term Debt	417.4	605.4	396.3	189.0
Stockholders' Equity	10,718.9	10,135.9	9,841.0	9,090.6
Performance & Financial Condition				
Return on Total Revenues %	2.46	3.24	3.56	3.70
Return on Avg Stockholders' Equity %	6.17	8.00	7.79	8.01
Return on Average Assets %	4.37	5.81	6.23	6.56
Current Ratio	2.85	2.61	3.72	4.44
Debt / Equity %	3.89	5.97	4.03	2.08

Compound Growth %'s	EPS %	0.00	Net Income %	-2.65	Total Revenues %	11.63

Comments

Despite a $538,000 decline in international sales resulting from less than favorable economic conditions in the Far East, overall revenue grew 6.4% due to more favorable economic conditions benefiting the pleasure boat industry. Higher legal costs in the Company's suit against Daihatsu Motor Company and an increase in research and development to $1,180,900 from $1,030,300 in fiscal 1997, had the impact of reducing earnings. Westerbeke reacquired 223,738 common shares, about 10% of shares outstanding, during 1997. But the stock is trading at approximately half of book value. The Company's balance sheet continues to be strong and profits have been consistent.

Officers	Position	Ownership Information	
John H. Westerbeke, Jr.	Chairman, President	Number of Shares Outstanding	1,917,812
Carleton F. Bryant, III	Exec VP, COO	Market Capitalization	$ 5,024,667
Gerald Bench	Director	Number of Shareholders	400
Thomas M. Haythe	Director	Where Listed / Symbol	NASDAQ / WTBK

Other Information			
Transfer Agent	Boston EquiServe Boston, MA	SIC Code	3621
Auditor	KPMG LLP	Employees	104
		Web Site westerbeke.com boatdiesel.com	

Westminster Capital, Inc.

9665 Wilshire Boulevard, M-10   Beverly Hills, CA 90212   Telephone (310)278-1930   Fax (310)271-6274

Company Description

Until 1991, the Company's business consisted primarily of the operations of its subsidiary, FarWest Savings and Loan Association. In 1991, the S & L was taken over by the Resolution Trust Company (RTC) and the Company's interest terminated. Since RTC's take over of FarWest, the Company's significant continuing operations and assets have consisted of cash, marketable securities, a 100% interest in a company which provides group purchasing of goods and services for new car dealers (acquired on November 12, 1997), a majority interest in a telephone company serving military personnel, and a substantial interest in a home delivery shopping company (which was sold on February 26, 1998). The Company also engages in the secured lending business. The acquisitions of a 50% interest in Touch Controls, Inc. and an 80% interest in One Source Industries were announced in early 1999.

	12/31/98	12/31/97	12/31/96	12/31/95
Per Share Information				
Stock Price	2.69	2.25	1.84	2.31
Earnings Per Share	0.73	0.17	0.20	0.17
Price / Earnings Ratio	3.68	13.24	9.20	13.59
Book Value Per Share	4.06	3.31	3.25	2.96
Price / Book Value %	66.26	67.98	56.62	78.04
Dividends Per Share	0.0	0.0	0.0	0.0
Annual Financial Data				
Operating Results (000's)				
Total Revenues	30,925.0	7,996.0	5,234.0	4,596.0
Costs & Expenses	-23,007.0	-5,667.0	-2,763.0	-2,819.0
Income Before Taxes and Other	7,918.0	2,329.0	2,471.0	1,777.0
Other Items	-51.0	-26.0	-60.0	-49.0
Income Tax	-2,040.0	-932.0	-840.0	-420.0
Net Income	5,827.0	1,371.0	1,571.0	1,308.0
Cash Flow From Operations	7,843.0	1,851.0	2,904.0	-1,484.0
Balance Sheet (000's)				
Cash & Equivalents	291.0	1,738.0	2,310.0	1,715.0
Total Current Assets	28,130.0	21,946.0	27,119.0	24,305.0
Fixed Assets, Net	147.0	1,544.0	1,128.0	1,378.0
Total Assets	42,597.0	34,870.0	33,212.0	28,199.0
Total Current Liabilities	2,500.0	7,950.0	7,391.0	4,634.0
Long-Term Debt	0.0	655.0	0.0	0.0
Stockholders' Equity	31,847.0	25,968.0	25,467.0	23,100.0
Performance & Financial Condition				
Return on Total Revenues %	18.84	17.15	30.02	28.46
Return on Avg Stockholders' Equity %	20.16	5.33	6.47	5.87
Return on Average Assets %	15.04	4.03	5.12	4.54
Current Ratio	11.25	2.76	3.67	5.24
Debt / Equity %	n.a.	2.52	n.a.	n.a.

Compound Growth %'s	EPS %	62.54	Net Income %	64.54	Total Revenues %	88.79

Comments

Income for 1998, 1997, 1996, 1995, 1994 and 1993, included $52,000, $950,000, $813,000, $1,209,000, $3,528,000 and $16,819,000, respectively, from the settlement of a lawsuit against Drexel Burnham Lambert securities firm and the infamous Michael Milken in connection with alleged violations of various federal and state securities laws. The increase in revenues reported in 1998 is primarily attributable to the newly acquired business mentioned above and a $5.9 million gain on the sale of the interest in the home delivery shopping company. Because it has been trading at a price below book value, calculating what might be the real value of the Company, with its many different assets, is an accountant's picnic.

Officers	Position	Ownership Information	
William Belzberg	Chairman, CEO	Number of Shares Outstanding	7,835,000
Keenan Behrle	Exec VP, CFO	Market Capitalization	$ 21,076,150
Hyman Belzberg	Director	Number of Shareholders	967
Samuel Belzberg	Director	Where Listed / Symbol	OTC-BB / WMCP

Other Information			
Transfer Agent	Boston EquiServe Boston, MA	SIC Code	4899
Auditor	Deloitte & Touche LLP	Employees	21
Market Maker	Paragon Capital Corporation	(212)785-4700	
	Koonce Securities, Inc.	(800)368-2802	

Westmoreland Coal Company

2 North Cascade Avenue, 14th Floor   Colorado Springs, CO 80903   Telephone (719)442-2600   Fax (719)448-5824

Company Description

Westmoreland Coal Company's principal activities are the production and sale of coal from the Powder River Basin in eastern Montana, the ownership of interests in cogeneration and other non-regulated independent power plants, the provision of repair and maintenance services to utilities and power projects, and the leasing of capacity at Dominion Terminal Associates which is a coal storage and vessel loading facility. On December 23, 1996, the Company filed a voluntary petition for reorganization under Chapter 11 of the United States Bankruptcy Code. The shares were suspended from being traded on the New York Stock Exchange. In 1998 it emerged from bankruptcy but not with a clean slate as noted below.

	12/31/98	12/31/97	12/31/96	12/31/95
Per Share Information				
Stock Price	3.81	1.25	1.00	6.37
Earnings Per Share	-1.64	3.34	4.80	-13.11
Price / Earnings Ratio	n.a.	0.37	0.21	n.a.
Book Value Per Share	0.16	1.80	-1.07	-5.47
Price / Book Value %	2,381.25	69.44	n.a.	n.a.
Dividends Per Share	0.0	0.0	0.0	0.0
Annual Financial Data				
Operating Results (000's)				
Total Revenues	111,043.0	69,066.0	97,533.0	140,831.0
Costs & Expenses	-92,462.0	-66,703.0	-72,097.0	-224,361.0
Income Before Taxes and Other	18,581.0	-121.0	25,436.0	-83,530.0
Other Items	-21,342.0	28,277.0	13,482.0	-1,368.0
Income Tax	-3,787.0	0.0	-575.0	-1,488.0
Net Income	-6,548.0	28,156.0	38,343.0	-86,386.0
Cash Flow From Operations	49,639.0	19,931.0	-14,949.0	8,174.0
Balance Sheet (000's)				
Cash & Equivalents	84,073.0	30,664.0	8,791.0	11,711.0
Total Current Assets	90,560.0	49,615.0	17,090.0	18,985.0
Fixed Assets, Net	36,950.0	35,687.0	42,700.0	59,868.0
Total Assets	215,606.0	181,997.0	153,971.0	167,107.0
Total Current Liabilities	75,506.0	11,103.0	6,905.0	35,443.0
Long-Term Debt	1,562.0	407.0	881.0	3,131.0
Stockholders' Equity	21,845.0	28,393.0	237.0	-38,106.0
Performance & Financial Condition				
Return on Total Revenues %	-5.90	40.77	39.31	-61.34
Return on Avg Stockholders' Equity %	-26.07	196.69	n.a.	-1,369.25
Return on Average Assets %	-3.29	16.76	23.88	-43.54
Current Ratio	1.20	4.47	2.48	0.54
Debt / Equity %	7.15	1.43	371.73	n.a.

Compound Growth %'s	EPS %	n.a.	Net Income %	n.a.	Total Revenues %	-7.62

Comments

Recognizing that it would not be able to meet its retiree benefit obligations to the United Mine Workers pension funds, the Company tried to renegotiate its agreements but failed. Filing under Chapter 11 became the only possible way to save the Company. Court decisions generally in favor of the Company determined the liabilities during 1998 which permitted the Company to remove itself from Chapter 11. In the meantime, arrears in preferred stock dividends total $20.8 million which are not reflected as liabilities. We deducted the arrears in the calculation of book value per common share. 1998 results include $21,342,000 of nonrecurring expenses related to the reorganization and accounting changes. Also included in 1998 Costs and Expenses is $12.2 million of impairment charges.

Officers	Position	Ownership Information	
Christopher K. Seglem	President, CEO	Number of Shares Outstanding	6,965,328
Theodore E. Worcester	Senior VP, Secretary	Market Capitalization	$ 26,537,900
Robert J. Jaeger	Senior VP, CFO	Number of Shareholders	1,723
Larry W. Mikkola	Controller	Where Listed / Symbol	OTC-BB / WMCL

Other Information			
Transfer Agent	First Chicago Trust Co. of New York Jersey City, NJ	SIC Code	1220
Auditor	KPMG LLP	Employees	35
Market Maker	Herzog, Heine, Geduld, Inc. (800)221-3600		
	Oscar Gruss & Son, Inc. (212)943-6418		

Westwood Corporation

5134 South Yale Avenue, Suite 1100   Tulsa, OK 74135   Telephone (918)524-0002   Fax (918)524-0006

Company Description

Westwood Corporation is engaged in the design, manufacture, and sale of electrical generation and distribution equipment and automated control equipment and products, including marine switchboards and panelboards, safety cable sealing and transit systems, electrical generation equipment, automated power control systems, and related electrical hardware. Much of the Company's electrical switchgear is designed in accordance with specifications of the United States Navy for use on combat vessels. In May 1997, the Company announced the acquisitions of: 1) the marine division of Tano Automation, Inc., a leading and long-standing provider of automated machinery plant control systems for the Coast Guard, Navy and Military Seacliff Command, and 2) MCII Electric Co., a designer and manufacturer of a broad family of diesel, gas, natural gas and turbine mobile electrical generator sets for both military and commercial applications. Westwood Corporation was formed in 1986.

	03/31/98	03/31/97	03/31/96	03/31/95
Per Share Information				
Stock Price as of 12/31	0.87	1.50	1.62	2.87
Earnings Per Share	-0.19	0.27	0.20	0.26
Price / Earnings Ratio	n.a.	5.56	8.10	11.04
Book Value Per Share	1.46	1.87	1.80	1.78
Price / Book Value %	59.59	80.21	90.00	161.24
Dividends Per Share	0.0	0.04	0.03	0.03
Annual Financial Data				
Operating Results (000's)				
Total Revenues	30,232.0	33,441.0	29,538.0	31,932.0
Costs & Expenses	-32,191.0	-30,777.0	-27,524.0	-29,310.0
Income Before Taxes and Other	-2,032.0	2,664.0	2,014.0	2,622.0
Other Items	0.0	0.0	0.0	0.0
Income Tax	715.0	-1,033.0	-777.0	-997.0
Net Income	-1,317.0	1,631.0	1,237.0	1,625.0
Cash Flow From Operations	-3,247.0	2,315.0	3,488.0	397.0
Balance Sheet (000's)				
Cash & Equivalents	574.0	1,165.0	598.0	103.0
Total Current Assets	14,494.0	12,621.0	12,526.0	15,536.0
Fixed Assets, Net	2,733.0	2,296.0	1,472.0	1,256.0
Total Assets	24,831.0	16,156.0	15,724.0	18,492.0
Total Current Liabilities	11,363.0	3,384.0	5,407.0	9,297.0
Long-Term Debt	3,152.0	600.0	67.0	0.0
Stockholders' Equity	10,083.0	11,475.0	10,073.0	9,044.0
Performance & Financial Condition				
Return on Total Revenues %	-4.36	4.88	4.19	5.09
Return on Avg Stockholders' Equity %	-12.22	15.14	12.94	19.52
Return on Average Assets %	-6.43	10.23	7.23	9.38
Current Ratio	1.28	3.73	2.32	1.67
Debt / Equity %	31.26	5.23	0.67	n.a.

Compound Growth %'s	EPS % n.a.	Net Income % n.a.	Total Revenues % -1.81

Comments

The acquisitions referred to above, particularly MCII Electric, caused significant expense as the Company repositioned itself for the next phase of growth. The Company also has debt and not nearly the cushion it once had in working capital. As of March 31, 1998, the Company had goodwill of $6.7 million on its books from the acquisitions, which equates to approximately 67% of stockholders' equity and book value per share. But whether or not management took the right course with these acquisitions will be reflected in future operating results. For the nine months ended December 31, 1998, revenues and a net loss of $23.8 million and $818,000 ($.12 per share) were recorded as compared to $22.2 million and a net income of $74,000 ($.01 per share) for the same period of the preceding year.

Officers	Position	Ownership Information	
Ernest H. McKee	President, CEO	Number of Shares Outstanding	6,891,647
Paul R. Carolus	Secretary, Treasurer	Market Capitalization	$ 5,995,733
Richard E. Minshall	Director	Number of Shareholders	700
Anthony Pantaleoni	Director	Where Listed / Symbol	NASDAQ / WNMP

Other Information			
Transfer Agent	Progressive Transfer Company Salt Lake City, UT	SIC Code	3610
Auditor	Ernst & Young LLP	Employees	274

White Electronic Designs Corporation

3601 East University Drive   Phoenix, AZ 85034   Telephone (602)437-1520   Fax (602)437-1731

Company Description

White Electronic Designs Corporation, formerly Bowmar Instrument Corporation, is a designer and manufacturer of high density, solid state memory modules, multichip modules, interface products, and electromechanical components and packages. The Company's customers include both domestic and international government contractors as well as commercial businesses. The majority of the sales are generated by the memory and multichip module product lines. After the end of the last year, the Company decided to divest itself of its Technologies division and is in the process of finding a buyer. This left the Company with its White Microelectronics division, hence the name change. The Company was founded in 1951.

	10/03/98	09/27/97	09/28/96	09/30/95
Per Share Information				
Stock Price as of 12/31	1.37	2.62	1.69	2.50
Earnings Per Share	-0.02	0.02	0.14	0.48
Price / Earnings Ratio	n.a.	131.00	12.07	5.21
Book Value Per Share	1.37	1.39	1.36	1.20
Price / Book Value %	100.00	188.49	124.26	208.33
Dividends Per Share	0.0	0.0	0.0	0.0
Annual Financial Data				
Operating Results (000's)				
Total Revenues	29,119.0	22,189.0	19,363.0	18,570.0
Costs & Expenses	-29,394.0	-20,070.0	-17,307.0	-17,016.0
Income Before Taxes and Other	-275.0	2,088.0	2,056.0	1,554.0
Other Items	780.0	-780.0	18.0	-207.0
Income Tax	-292.0	-786.0	-784.0	2,556.0
Net Income	213.0	522.0	1,290.0	3,903.0
Cash Flow From Operations	2,156.0	1,295.0	309.0	3,017.0
Balance Sheet (000's)				
Cash & Equivalents	1,069.0	1,218.0	108.0	739.0
Total Current Assets	11,248.0	17,173.0	12,213.0	12,196.0
Fixed Assets, Net	2,361.0	2,642.0	1,122.0	1,335.0
Total Assets	14,898.0	21,509.0	16,538.0	17,432.0
Total Current Liabilities	3,066.0	7,351.0	3,711.0	5,307.0
Long-Term Debt	2,366.0	4,546.0	3,675.0	3,992.0
Stockholders' Equity	9,127.0	9,273.0	8,813.0	7,795.0
Performance & Financial Condition				
Return on Total Revenues %	0.73	2.35	6.66	21.02
Return on Avg Stockholders' Equity %	2.32	5.77	15.53	65.90
Return on Average Assets %	1.17	2.74	7.59	25.01
Current Ratio	3.67	2.34	3.29	2.30
Debt / Equity %	25.92	49.02	41.70	51.21

Compound Growth %'s	EPS % n.a.	Net Income % n.a.	Total Revenues %	16.18

Comments

The results of the Technology division are reported as a discontinued operation. A loss was provided for the disposition of the division in fiscal 1997 in the amount of $780,000 ($.12 per share) after tax benefits. But the item was reversed in fiscal 1998, having a positive impact of the same amount. Fiscal 1998 revenues were favorably impacted by additional sales of new interface products in the electromechanical segment. Gross margins declined as a result of the adverse effect on sales resulting from a strong downward pricing pressure, in turn due to competition and general downturn in the semiconductor industry as a whole. The Company also reported a $1 million merger expense in connection with its reorganization.

Officers	Position	Ownership Information	
Donald McGuinness	Chairman	Number of Shares Outstanding	6,674,992
Hamid Shokrgozar	President, CEO	Market Capitalization	$ 9,144,739
Joseph G. Warren, Jr.	VP - Finance, CFO	Number of Shareholders	6,775
Kenneth Buckley	Vice President	Where Listed / Symbol	AMEX / WHT

Other Information			
Transfer Agent	American Stock Transfer & Trust Company New York, NY	SIC Code	3674
Auditor	PricewaterhouseCoopers LLP	Employees	160
		Web Site	whitemicro.com

Whitman Education Group, Inc.

4400 Biscayne Boulevard   Miami, FL 33137   Telephone (305)575-6510   Fax (305)575-6537

Company Description

Whitman Education Group, Inc. is a proprietary provider of career-oriented postsecondary education. Whitman currently operates 24 schools in 13 states offering a range of graduate, undergraduate and non-degree certificate or diploma programs primarily in the fields of information technology, healthcare and business to more than 7,500 students. Whitman's students are predominantly adults, generally between the ages of 24 and 35, who commute to its schools and require limited ancillary student services. The students are seeking to acquire basic knowledge and skills necessary for entry-level employment in technical careers or to acquire new or additional skills to either change careers or advance in their current careers. Whitman was founded in 1979.

	03/31/98	03/31/97	03/31/96	03/31/95
Per Share Information				
Stock Price as of 12/31	3.50	5.75	7.25	6.00
Earnings Per Share	0.01	-0.38	-0.01	-0.02
Price / Earnings Ratio	350.00	n.a.	n.a.	n.a.
Book Value Per Share	1.35	1.27	0.72	0.71
Price / Book Value %	259.26	452.76	1,006.94	845.07
Dividends Per Share	0.0	0.0	0.0	0.0
Annual Financial Data				
Operating Results (000's)				
Total Revenues	60,509.9	47,123.1	39,874.9	19,332.0
Costs & Expenses	-60,856.2	-51,895.3	-40,112.0	-19,479.0
Income Before Taxes and Other	-346.3	-4,772.2	-237.0	-147.0
Other Items	0.0	0.0	0.0	0.0
Income Tax	489.5	408.8	136.5	0.0
Net Income	143.1	-4,363.4	-100.6	-147.0
Cash Flow From Operations	110.1	-2,211.6	2,206.6	-200.0
Balance Sheet (000's)				
Cash & Equivalents	3,384.3	3,853.9	2,762.1	1,787.3
Total Current Assets	28,982.8	25,535.1	20,842.9	19,787.3
Fixed Assets, Net	12,925.2	10,062.8	7,017.2	6,000.0
Total Assets	53,821.2	48,017.5	35,326.9	31,600.0
Total Current Liabilities	21,029.0	19,879.3	16,060.1	14,877.0
Long-Term Debt	11,813.6	9,096.0	11,881.5	9,467.0
Stockholders' Equity	17,833.2	16,107.2	7,385.3	7,256.0
Performance & Financial Condition				
Return on Total Revenues %	0.24	-9.26	-0.25	-0.76
Return on Avg Stockholders' Equity %	0.84	-37.15	-1.37	-2.27
Return on Average Assets %	0.28	-10.47	-0.30	-0.66
Current Ratio	1.38	1.28	1.30	1.33
Debt / Equity %	66.25	56.47	160.88	130.47

Compound Growth %'s	EPS % n.a.	Net Income % n.a.	Total Revenues % 46.28

Comments

The Company declared a 2 for 1 stock split on May 13, 1996. All per share amounts have been restated for consistency. Strong revenue growth in fiscal 1998 was attributed to a new campus opening at Colorado Tech, the acquisition of Huron University, and new medical assisting programs that were offered on twelve different campuses for the first time. At March 31, 1998, the Company had $10.2 million of goodwill recorded as assets which equated to approximately 57% of stockholders' equity and book value per share. For the nine months ended December 31, 1998, the Company reported revenues and net income of $53.1 million and $536,787 ($.04 per share) as compared to $43.9 million and a net loss of $1,345,974 ($.11 per share) for the same period of the preceding year.

Officers	Position	Ownership Information	
Phillip Frost	Chairman	Number of Shares Outstanding	13,193,582
R. Proto	President, COO	Market Capitalization	$ 46,177,537
Richard C. Pfenniger, Jr.	CEO	Number of Shareholders	2,000
Fernando L. Fernandez	VP - Finance, CFO	Where Listed / Symbol	AMEX / WIX

Other Information			
Transfer Agent	Continental Stock Transfer & Trust Co. Jersey City, NJ	SIC Code	8200
Auditor	Ernst & Young LLP	Employees	591

Willamette Valley Vineyards, Inc.

8800 Enchanted Way, S.E. Turner, OR 97392 Telephone (503)588-9463 Fax (503)588-8894

Company Description

Willamette Valley Vineyards, Inc. owns and operates vineyards and wineries. It produces and distributes premium and super premium wines, primarily pinot noir, chardonnay, and white riesling. Tualatin Vineyards, Inc. was acquired in April 1997. O'Connor Vineyards was also leased that year on a ten-year contract. At the end of 1998, the Company controlled 170 producing acres, 52 acres in development and 19 plantable acres. The majority of the Company's wine is sold to grocery stores and restaurants in the state of Oregon through the Company's own sales force. The Company also sells its wine from hospitality rooms at its wineries and at festivals and events throughout the year. Direct sales to consumers are highly profitable because retail prices are charged rather than wholesale prices. For 1998, direct sales made up approximately 24% of the Company's revenues. Let's check out the liquid assets below:

	12/31/98	12/31/97	12/31/96	12/31/95
Per Share Information				
Stock Price	2.00	1.44	2.75	2.75
Earnings Per Share	-0.02	0.02	0.05	0.0
Price / Earnings Ratio	n.a.	72.00	55.00	n.a.
Book Value Per Share	1.66	1.68	1.49	1.44
Price / Book Value %	120.48	85.71	184.56	190.97
Dividends Per Share	0.0	0.0	0.0	0.0
Annual Financial Data				
Operating Results (000's)				
Total Revenues	6,165.3	5,764.9	4,288.4	3,658.8
Costs & Expenses	-6,264.9	-5,644.7	-4,019.3	-3,622.7
Income Before Taxes and Other	-99.6	120.2	269.1	36.1
Other Items	0.0	0.0	0.0	0.0
Income Tax	27.6	-52.3	-98.7	-29.8
Net Income	-72.0	67.9	170.4	6.3
Cash Flow From Operations	623.1	-684.1	-274.1	-16.3
Balance Sheet (000's)				
Cash & Equivalents	149.4	13.5	794.9	599.9
Total Current Assets	5,468.4	5,202.6	4,145.5	2,798.8
Fixed Assets, Net	8,683.5	6,859.8	5,421.0	4,849.7
Total Assets	14,390.9	13,945.7	10,263.7	8,340.6
Total Current Liabilities	2,953.5	2,731.4	1,449.3	818.0
Long-Term Debt	4,101.8	3,920.8	3,072.2	2,007.9
Stockholders' Equity	7,035.5	7,105.3	5,628.2	5,457.8
Performance & Financial Condition				
Return on Total Revenues %	-1.17	1.18	3.97	0.17
Return on Avg Stockholders' Equity %	-1.02	1.07	3.07	0.12
Return on Average Assets %	-0.51	0.56	1.83	0.08
Current Ratio	1.85	1.90	2.86	3.42
Debt / Equity %	58.30	55.18	54.59	36.79

Compound Growth %'s	EPS % n.a.	Net Income % n.a.	Total Revenues %	19.00

Comments

A full year's interest expense in connection with the Tualatin acquisition, borrowings to finance vineyard development and a potential $81,000 bad debt caused the Company to report a loss for 1998. Vineyard and winery stocks are a long term investment and can be a great value. Reported income is usually low in comparison to what is accumulating in the ground. Even when acreage becomes productive, full productivity is not reached for many more years. The vineyards are depreciated for accounting purposes when, in fact, they are appreciating in value. There are risks as well. Overproduction of a certain varietals or crush volumes in excess of demand can reduce prices and cause a decline in the value of the vineyard as well.

Officers	Position	Ownership Information	
James W. Bernau	Chairman, President	Number of Shares Outstanding	4,232,681
James L. Ellis	Vice President, Secretary	Market Capitalization	$ 8,465,362
John E. Moore	Controller	Number of Shareholders	3,503
William H. Malkmus	Director	Where Listed / Symbol	NASDAQ / WVVI

Other Information			
Transfer Agent	Company Office Turner, OR	SIC Code	2080
Auditor	PricewaterhouseCoopers LLP	Employees	41
		Web Site	wvv.com

Williams Controls, Inc.

14100 SW 72nd Avenue   Portland, OR 97224   Telephone (503)684-8600   Fax (503)684-8675

Company Description

Williams Controls, Inc. is a manufacturer and integrator of sensors, controls and communications systems for the transportation, communications and agriculture industries. The Company's primary business segment was founded in 1939 and acquired by the Company in 1988. The Company also went public in 1988. Through fiscal 1996, the Company pursued an acquisition strategy to diversify its operations. During fiscal 1997, the Company discontinued its diversification in order to focus its corporate and financial resources on opportunities emerging in the vehicle components and train tracking markets as well as on the development of commercial applications of sensor related products.

	09/30/98	09/30/97	09/30/96	09/30/95
Per Share Information				
Stock Price as of 12/31	2.37	2.47	2.00	2.35
Earnings Per Share	0.0	-0.12	-0.03	0.26
Price / Earnings Ratio	n.a.	n.a.	n.a.	9.04
Book Value Per Share	1.34	0.95	1.02	1.06
Price / Book Value %	176.87	260.00	196.08	221.70
Dividends Per Share	0.0	0.0	0.0	0.0
Annual Financial Data				
Operating Results (000's)				
Total Revenues	57,646.0	56,254.0	51,279.0	45,073.0
Costs & Expenses	-50,163.0	-53,830.0	-47,292.0	-36,648.0
Income Before Taxes and Other	6,977.0	2,040.0	3,812.0	8,143.0
Other Items	-4,299.0	-2,922.0	-2,868.0	-523.0
Income Tax	-2,366.0	-1,155.0	-1,505.0	-3,108.0
Net Income	312.0	-2,037.0	-561.0	4,512.0
Cash Flow From Operations	2,430.0	2,117.0	415.0	4,756.0
Balance Sheet (000's)				
Cash & Equivalents	1,281.0	700.0	1,379.0	1,653.0
Total Current Assets	31,087.0	25,156.0	30,926.0	25,788.0
Fixed Assets, Net	20,013.0	14,533.0	19,801.0	20,000.0
Total Assets	66,359.0	48,313.0	53,049.0	47,182.0
Total Current Liabilities	11,901.0	9,028.0	29,600.0	7,881.0
Long-Term Debt	27,846.0	21,235.0	2,782.0	20,244.0
Stockholders' Equity	24,411.0	16,835.0	18,010.0	18,293.0
Performance & Financial Condition				
Return on Total Revenues %	0.54	-3.62	-1.09	10.01
Return on Avg Stockholders' Equity %	1.51	-11.69	-3.09	29.11
Return on Average Assets %	0.54	-4.02	-1.12	11.28
Current Ratio	2.61	2.79	1.04	3.27
Debt / Equity %	114.07	126.14	15.45	110.67

Compound Growth %'s	EPS % n.a.	Net Income % -58.95	Total Revenues % 8.55

Comments

Losses from discontinued operations are reflected in Other Items included in Operating Results above. For fiscal 1998, a loss from discontinued operations totalled $4.3 million ($.24 per share) as compared to $4.6 million ($.26 per share) for fiscal 1997. The decline in fiscal 1998 revenues is due to discontinued operations. Management reports a 24% increase in revenue from continuing operations for the same period. The financial condition of the Company is much improved from what it was at the end of fiscal 1996, indicating success in management's strategy to end diversification. But historical numbers are not necessarily comparable. Special emphasis should be placed on the present. For the three months ended December 31, 1998, the Company reported revenue and net income of $14.9 million and $1,031,000 ($.05 per share) as compared to $12.7 million and $694,000 ($.04 per share) for the same period of the preceding year.

Officers	Position	Ownership Information	
Thomas W. Itin	President, CEO	Number of Shares Outstanding	18,181,088
Gerard A. Herlihy	CFO	Market Capitalization	$ 43,089,179
R. William Caldwell	Director	Number of Shareholders	524
H. Samuel Greenawalt	Director	Where Listed / Symbol	NASDAQ / WMCO

Other Information			
Transfer Agent	American Securities Transfer, Inc. Denver, CO	SIC Code	3714
Auditor	Arthur Andersen LLP	Employees	511
		Web Site	wmco.com

Wiltek, Inc.

542 Westport Avenue Norwalk, CT 06851 Telephone (203)853-7400 Fax (203)846-3177

Company Description

Wiltek, Inc. is involved in the design and management of data communication networks and services. Specifically, the Company provides outsourcing connectivity services to companies migrating between or coexisting with multiple disparate messaging platforms. Wiltek performs all design required for the implementation and operation of its worldwide message and data communication services. These services enable its customers to seamlessly communicate with electronic mail, among all intra-and inter-company messaging systems both public and private. The Company was founded in 1947.

	10/31/98	10/31/97	10/31/96	10/31/95
Per Share Information				
Stock Price as of 12/31	0.47	0.80	0.25	0.31
Earnings Per Share	0.07	0.01	0.02	-0.24
Price / Earnings Ratio	6.71	80.00	12.50	n.a.
Book Value Per Share	0.37	0.29	0.26	0.23
Price / Book Value %	127.03	275.86	96.15	134.78
Dividends Per Share	0.0	0.0	0.0	0.0
Annual Financial Data				
Operating Results (000's)				
Total Revenues	7,584.3	6,036.7	5,004.2	4,943.3
Costs & Expenses	-7,276.9	-5,997.5	-4,913.9	-5,110.6
Income Before Taxes and Other	307.4	39.2	90.3	-870.0
Other Items	0.0	0.0	0.0	0.0
Income Tax	0.0	0.0	0.0	0.0
Net Income	307.4	39.2	90.3	-870.0
Cash Flow From Operations	557.5	350.4	194.2	56.9
Balance Sheet (000's)				
Cash & Equivalents	667.9	526.7	407.6	444.2
Total Current Assets	1,847.9	1,738.9	1,293.5	1,289.3
Fixed Assets, Net	897.2	630.6	539.0	430.7
Total Assets	2,745.1	2,369.5	1,832.5	1,720.0
Total Current Liabilities	1,201.8	1,163.3	787.9	828.6
Long-Term Debt	0.0	0.0	0.0	0.0
Stockholders' Equity	1,450.9	1,094.1	956.3	851.9
Performance & Financial Condition				
Return on Total Revenues %	4.05	0.65	1.80	-17.60
Return on Avg Stockholders' Equity %	24.16	3.82	9.99	-68.23
Return on Average Assets %	12.02	1.87	5.08	-42.66
Current Ratio	1.54	1.49	1.64	1.56
Debt / Equity %	n.a.	n.a.	n.a.	n.a.

Compound Growth %'s	EPS %	87.08	Net Income %	84.50	Total Revenues %	15.34

Comments

Consulting revenues rose 125.5% during fiscal 1998 whereas messaging services revenue declined 3.9%. Early in fiscal 1998, the Company successfully completed several large-scale and complex consulting engagements. As a result, the Company has earned and now enjoys a reputation as a provider of technically superior project management and consulting services related to Microsoft BackOffice® product installations where demand for qualified and competent service providers remains high. Operations appear to have stabilized after a restructuring of the workforce in fiscal 1995. Wiltek's customer list contains over 50 large corporations, most of which are Fortune 500 companies. General Electric and Sea-Land Service, Inc. accounted for 11.6% and 11.1% of revenues, respectively, in fiscal 1998.

Officers	Position	Ownership Information	
Jay W. Fitzpatrick	Chairman	Number of Shares Outstanding	3,892,128
David S. Teitelman	President, CEO	Market Capitalization	$ 1,829,300
Boris Frenkiel	Secretary	Number of Shareholders	742
David Holst-Grubbe	Vice President	Where Listed / Symbol	OTC-BB / WLTK

Other Information			
Transfer Agent	ChaseMellon Shareholder Services Ridgefield Park, NJ	SIC Code	4822
Auditor	Grant Thornton LLP	Employees	50
Market Maker	Wm. V. Frankel & Co., Inc. (800)631-3091	Web Site	wiltek.com
	Drake Capital Securities, Inc. (800)421-8504		

Winston Resources, Inc.

535 Fifth Avenue   New York, NY 10017   Telephone (212)557-5000   Fax (212)682-4073

Company Description

Winston Resources, Inc. provides a wide range of personnel supply services to businesses, institutions and governmental agencies, through its own offices and through offices operated by independent franchisees under licenses from the Company. The Company also provides recruitment advertising services to businesses and other institutions. The Company recruits and places employees in entry-to-high level permanent salaried positions. Temporary employees with professional, secretarial, clerical, medical, allied health, nursing, light industrial, information technology and word processing skills are supplied to business clients and governmental agencies in the New York City, Long Island and New Jersey areas, as well as in Florida's Fort Lauderdale area. The Company was founded in 1967.

	12/31/98	12/31/97	12/31/96	12/31/95
Per Share Information				
Stock Price	3.78	5.62	3.44	1.31
Earnings Per Share	0.52	0.41	0.34	-0.15
Price / Earnings Ratio	7.27	13.71	10.12	n.a.
Book Value Per Share	2.26	1.68	1.22	0.91
Price / Book Value %	167.26	334.52	281.97	143.96
Dividends Per Share	0.0	0.0	0.0	0.0
Annual Financial Data				
Operating Results (000's)				
Total Revenues	60,899.0	49,268.0	39,442.0	31,206.0
Costs & Expenses	-57,651.0	-46,688.0	-37,992.0	-31,638.0
Income Before Taxes and Other	3,248.0	2,580.0	1,450.0	-432.0
Other Items	0.0	0.0	0.0	0.0
Income Tax	-1,419.0	-1,136.0	-312.0	0.0
Net Income	1,829.0	1,444.0	1,138.0	-432.0
Cash Flow From Operations	1,913.0	-190.0	2,242.0	-33.0
Balance Sheet (000's)				
Cash & Equivalents	2,047.0	445.0	1,068.0	144.0
Total Current Assets	11,656.0	8,405.0	7,423.0	6,474.0
Fixed Assets, Net	649.0	540.0	311.0	672.0
Total Assets	12,919.0	9,451.0	8,438.0	7,146.0
Total Current Liabilities	5,360.0	3,709.0	4,576.0	3,446.0
Long-Term Debt	0.0	0.0	0.0	606.0
Stockholders' Equity	7,287.0	5,404.0	3,862.0	2,654.0
Performance & Financial Condition				
Return on Total Revenues %	3.00	2.93	2.89	-1.38
Return on Avg Stockholders' Equity %	28.82	31.17	34.93	-15.13
Return on Average Assets %	16.35	16.14	14.60	-6.05
Current Ratio	2.17	2.27	1.62	1.88
Debt / Equity %	n.a.	n.a.	n.a.	22.83

Compound Growth %'s	EPS %	23.67	Net Income %	26.78	Total Revenues %	24.97

Comments

1998 was a banner year with revenues gaining 24% over 1997 levels. Most of the increase came in the temporary staffing arena with permanent placement revenues gaining a mere 3%. Management believes that a majority of the clients to whom it supplied temporary staffing during 1998 were repeat customers. The Company realized a 26.6% increase in net income as the higher revenues were only partially offset by additional costs. The Company's financial condition is excellent with no long term debt and no intangible assets.

Officers	Position	Ownership Information	
Seymour Kugler	President, CEO	Number of Shares Outstanding	3,228,121
Jesse Ulezalka	CFO	Market Capitalization	$ 12,202,297
David Silver	Vice President, Secretary	Number of Shareholders	1,000
Todd Kugler	Vice President	Where Listed / Symbol	AMEX / WRS

Other Information			
Transfer Agent	Continental Stock Transfer & Trust Co. Jersey City, NJ	SIC Code	7363
Auditor	Ernst & Young LLP	Employees	123
		Web Site	winston-data.com

Worksafe Industries Inc.

130 West 10th Street   Huntington, NY 11746   Telephone (516)427-1802   Fax (516)427-1840

Company Description

Worksafe Industries Inc., formerly Eastco Industrial Safety Corp., manufactures and sells industrial protective clothing products to distributors throughout the United States and Puerto Rico and to end users located primarily in the northeastern United States. The Company's manufacturing division uses Tyvek® to produce disposable clothing which accounted for 52% of sales in the last fiscal year. Tyvek® is sold solely by E.I. Dupont Industries. Management believes that its current relationship with DuPont is satisfactory. The Company was organized in 1958.

	06/30/98	06/30/97	06/30/96	06/30/95
Per Share Information				
Stock Price as of 12/31	3.00	1.87	4.56	1.25
Earnings Per Share	-0.29	-0.98	0.02	0.17
Price / Earnings Ratio	n.a.	n.a.	228.00	7.35
Book Value Per Share	2.32	2.61	3.40	5.83
Price / Book Value %	129.31	71.65	134.12	n.a.
Dividends Per Share	0.0	0.0	0.0	0.0
Annual Financial Data				
Operating Results (000's)				
Total Revenues	34,383.2	27,997.0	26,982.7	24,064.7
Costs & Expenses	-34,871.7	-29,388.9	-26,878.3	-23,986.8
Income Before Taxes and Other	-488.5	-1,391.8	10.0	77.9
Other Items	0.0	0.0	0.0	0.0
Income Tax	0.0	0.0	0.0	0.0
Net Income	-488.5	-1,391.8	10.0	77.9
Cash Flow From Operations	-2,102.4	-2,205.8	-1,153.4	-1,142.4
Balance Sheet (000's)				
Cash & Equivalents	223.1	112.3	646.0	521.0
Total Current Assets	14,957.3	11,316.4	10,987.1	9,265.0
Fixed Assets, Net	2,276.7	2,214.0	1,278.1	1,319.0
Total Assets	17,685.0	14,040.6	12,472.1	10,716.0
Total Current Liabilities	13,247.9	8,841.9	9,434.6	8,201.0
Long-Term Debt	538.3	811.4	433.7	489.0
Stockholders' Equity	3,898.8	4,387.3	2,603.8	2,026.0
Performance & Financial Condition				
Return on Total Revenues %	-1.42	-4.97	0.04	0.32
Return on Avg Stockholders' Equity %	-11.79	-39.82	0.43	3.92
Return on Average Assets %	-3.08	-10.50	0.09	0.79
Current Ratio	1.13	1.28	1.16	1.13
Debt / Equity %	13.81	18.49	16.66	24.14

Compound Growth %'s	EPS % n.a.	Net Income % n.a.	Total Revenues % 12.63

Comments

The strong increase in fiscal 1998 revenues was not enough to return the Company to profitability. The large loss in fiscal 1997 was attributable to a hurricane in Puerto Rico that affected production, a deliberate switch away from the end user business, higher payroll and other costs, and increased competition. The Company is involved in numerous legal actions because of its use of asbestos in the manufacture of its products up until the mid-1980's. The Company is unable to ascertain the total extent of insurance applicable to these claims or to what amount the Company will be held liable. No reserves for this possible liability have been accrued on the Company's books. For the six months ended December 31, 1998, revenue and the net loss were $11.6 million and $510,204 ($.30 per share) as compared to $11.3 million and $72,751 ($.04 per share) for the same period of the preceding year.

Officers	Position	Ownership Information	
Lawrence Densen	President, CEO	Number of Shares Outstanding	1,683,079
Alan E. Densen	Senior VP	Market Capitalization	$ 5,049,237
Anthony P. Towell	Senior VP, Secretary	Number of Shareholders	1,200
Arthur Wasserspring	VP - Finance, CFO	Where Listed / Symbol	NASDAQ / WRKS

Other Information			
Transfer Agent	American Stock Transfer & Trust Co. New York, NY	SIC Code	3841
Auditor	Arthur Andersen LLP	Employees	300
		Web Site	eastco.com

Worldtex, Inc.

212 12th Avenue, N.E. Hickory, NC 28601 Telephone (828)328-5381 Fax (828)328-4936

Company Description

Worldtex, Inc. is engaged in the manufacture of covered elastic yarn and narrow elastic fabrics, which are used in the production of a broad range of apparel products. Worldtex was organized in July, 1992 to acquire the covered yarn manufacturing operations of Willcox & Gibbs, Inc., a New York corporation that later changed its name to Rexel, Inc. The Company believes that it is the largest manufacturer of woven and knitted narrow elastic fabrics in the world. Narrow elastic fabrics are elasticized fabric bands, typically under six inches in width, that are used as components in the production of a broad range of apparel products, such as waistbands for men's, women's and children's underwear, athletic apparel and other garments, straps, facing and edgings in women's intimate apparel and elastic bands in women's hosiery.

	12/31/98	12/31/97	12/31/96	12/31/95
Per Share Information				
Stock Price	3.69	7.94	8.87	5.75
Earnings Per Share	-0.41	0.35	0.75	0.36
Price / Earnings Ratio	n.a.	22.69	11.83	15.97
Book Value Per Share	5.15	5.37	5.91	5.45
Price / Book Value %	71.65	147.86	150.08	105.50
Dividends Per Share	0.0	0.0	0.0	0.0
Annual Financial Data				
Operating Results (000's)				
Total Revenues	258,537.0	203,256.0	208,523.0	188,151.0
Costs & Expenses	-264,929.0	-191,085.0	-191,162.0	-177,920.0
Income Before Taxes and Other	-6,392.0	11,869.0	17,361.0	10,231.0
Other Items	0.0	-1,344.0	0.0	0.0
Income Tax	494.0	-5,377.0	-6,415.0	-4,979.0
Net Income	-5,898.0	5,148.0	10,946.0	5,252.0
Cash Flow From Operations	10,470.0	-1,497.0	15,032.0	12,046.0
Balance Sheet (000's)				
Cash & Equivalents	6,715.0	14,872.0	2,117.0	1,845.0
Total Current Assets	112,097.0	118,418.0	82,225.0	75,880.0
Fixed Assets, Net	113,652.0	99,160.0	90,282.0	83,991.0
Total Assets	324,120.0	312,439.0	206,032.0	194,389.0
Total Current Liabilities	38,945.0	30,675.0	34,755.0	30,734.0
Long-Term Debt	198,246.0	185,780.0	67,754.0	84,716.0
Stockholders' Equity	73,482.0	77,502.0	85,178.0	78,939.0
Performance & Financial Condition				
Return on Total Revenues %	-2.28	2.53	5.25	2.79
Return on Avg Stockholders' Equity %	-7.81	6.33	13.34	7.10
Return on Average Assets %	-1.85	1.99	5.47	2.90
Current Ratio	2.88	3.86	2.37	2.47
Debt / Equity %	269.79	239.71	79.54	107.32

Compound Growth %'s	EPS % n.a.	Net Income % n.a.	Total Revenues % 11.17

Comments

Revenue growth in 1998 reflects acquisitions. Because of softness in the European textile market and overall problems relating to Asian economic issues, results were less than expected. The Company recorded $7.8 million of expenses related to restructuring and to underutilized equipment. Management expects to complete the restructuring in the fourth quarter of 1999. An additional $400,000 is expected to be expensed in 1999. 1997 results include an extraordinary expense of $1,344,000 ($.09 per share) related to a refinancing of debt. At December 31 1998, the Company had $85.5 million of goodwill reflected on the books as assets which equated to approximately 116% of stockholders' equity and book value per share. The good news, if you wish to call it that, is $20 million of tax loss carryovers that are available if and when the Company becomes profitable.

Officers	Position	Ownership Information	
Barry D. Setzer	President, CEO	Number of Shares Outstanding	14,271,171
Mitchell R. Setzer	Treasurer, Secretary	Market Capitalization	$ 52,660,621
A. Orrin Maldoff	Vice President	Number of Shareholders	956
Donald W. Pruitt	Controller	Where Listed / Symbol	NYSE / WTX

Other Information			
Transfer Agent	ChaseMellon Shareholder Services Ridgefield Park, NJ	SIC Code	2200
Auditor	KPMG LLP	Employees	1,000

Writer Corporation (The)

6061 S. Willow Drive, Suite 232   Englewood, CO 80112   Telephone (303)779-4100   Fax (303)779-1199

Company Description

The Writer Corporation is a developer and builder of planned residential communities in the greater metropolitan area of Denver, Colorado. The homes are marketed to a broad spectrum of middle and upper middle income buyers. The Company has received national recognition for the design of its residential communities. Single family homes and townhomes are integrated with extensive greenbelts, bicycle and walking paths, winding streets and family recreational facilities to create a beneficial lifestyle for residents. Home prices range from $129,000 to $337,000. The Company has sold a total of 9,925 homes in 35 communities since its inception in 1982.

	12/31/98	12/31/97	12/31/96	12/31/95
Per Share Information				
Stock Price	1.75	1.34	1.01	1.13
Earnings Per Share	0.29	0.46	0.18	0.17
Price / Earnings Ratio	6.03	2.91	5.61	6.65
Book Value Per Share	2.64	2.44	1.89	1.73
Price / Book Value %	66.29	54.92	53.44	65.32
Dividends Per Share	0.0	0.0	0.0	0.0
Annual Financial Data				
Operating Results (000's)				
Total Revenues	64,302.0	45,338.0	46,488.0	32,129.0
Costs & Expenses	-61,290.0	-42,779.0	-45,211.0	-33,159.0
Income Before Taxes and Other	3,012.0	2,559.0	1,277.0	-1,030.0
Other Items	0.0	0.0	0.0	1,437.0
Income Tax	-830.0	901.0	24.0	714.0
Net Income	2,182.0	3,460.0	1,301.0	1,121.0
Cash Flow From Operations	3,879.0	-2,462.0	5,100.0	-907.0
Balance Sheet (000's)				
Cash & Equivalents	3,363.0	1,015.0	995.0	1,094.0
Total Current Assets	21,910.0	21,650.0	17,553.0	21,489.0
Fixed Assets, Net	597.0	470.0	604.0	649.0
Total Assets	44,478.0	41,580.0	36,650.0	41,070.0
Total Current Liabilities	21,108.0	19,094.0	16,420.0	18,145.0
Long-Term Debt	3,721.0	2,946.0	6,309.0	10,388.0
Stockholders' Equity	19,649.0	17,917.0	13,921.0	12,537.0
Performance & Financial Condition				
Return on Total Revenues %	3.39	7.63	2.80	3.49
Return on Avg Stockholders' Equity %	11.62	21.74	9.83	10.35
Return on Average Assets %	5.07	8.85	3.35	2.70
Current Ratio	1.04	1.13	1.07	1.18
Debt / Equity %	18.94	16.44	45.32	82.86

Compound Growth %'s	EPS %	19.49	Net Income %	24.86	Total Revenues %	26.02

Comments

The Company's inventory of real estate held for sale, $17.6 million in 1998, has been included in current assets; related debt of $14.2 million has been included in current liabilities. In 1998 the Company recorded the highest levels of sales, revenue, gross profit, and income from residential operations in the last decade of its history. This improved performance reflects the Company's continued efforts to maximize the efficiencies in its purchasing, construction and development processes. Income before taxes rose 17.7% in 1998 as compared to 1997. An income tax credit recorded in 1997 favorably distorts the bottom line performance. As a result of the restructuring of debt arrangements, the Company recognized a gain on the extinguishment of debt of $1,437,000 million in 1995. At December 31, 1998, the Company had 188 homes under construction as compared to 146 at December 31, 1997.

Officers	Position	Ownership Information	
George S. Writer, Jr.	Chairman, CEO	Number of Shares Outstanding	7,432,600
Daniel J. Nickless	Exec VP, CFO	Market Capitalization	$ 13,007,050
Robert R. Reid	Senior VP	Number of Shareholders	400
Derrell Schreiner	Vice President	Where Listed / Symbol	OTC-BB / WRTC

Other Information			
Transfer Agent	Harris Trust & Savings Bank Chicago, IL	SIC Code	1531
Auditor	Deloitte & Touche LLP	Employees	101
Market Maker	Herzog, Heine, Geduld, Inc.	(800)221-3600	Web Site	writerhomes.com
	Paragon Capital Corporation	(800)521-8877		

XeTel Corporation

2105 Gracy Farms Lane Austin, TX 78758 Telephone (512)435-1000 Fax (512)834-9250

Company Description

XeTel Corporation provides advanced design and prototype services, manufactures sophisticated surface mount assemblies and supplies full-service manufacturing solutions to original equipment manufacturers, primarily in the telecommunications, networking and computer industries. The Company's design and prototype services support customers in the product development phase and assist in their efforts to reduce time to market and time to volume as well as production costs. The Company incorporates its design and prototype services and assembly capabilities, together with materials management, advanced testing, systems integration and order fulfillment services, to provide turnkey solutions for its customers. The Company was founded in 1984 and had its initial public offering in fiscal 1996.

	03/28/98	03/29/97	03/30/96	04/01/95
Per Share Information				
Stock Price as of 12/31	1.81	3.69	3.75	8.00
Earnings Per Share	0.07	0.05	0.85	0.14
Price / Earnings Ratio	25.86	73.80	4.41	57.14
Book Value Per Share	3.10	3.03	2.92	1.74
Price / Book Value %	58.39	121.78	128.42	459.77
Dividends Per Share	0.0	0.0	0.0	0.0
Annual Financial Data				
Operating Results (000's)				
Total Revenues	112,685.0	90,721.0	117,846.0	64,507.0
Costs & Expenses	-111,670.0	-90,015.0	-108,480.0	-63,246.0
Income Before Taxes and Other	1,015.0	706.0	8,761.0	1,261.0
Other Items	0.0	0.0	0.0	0.0
Income Tax	-386.0	-257.0	-3,106.0	-319.0
Net Income	629.0	449.0	5,655.0	942.0
Cash Flow From Operations	-2,747.0	4,924.0	-1,512.0	1,928.0
Balance Sheet (000's)				
Cash & Equivalents	7,239.0	7,032.0	5,142.0	1,322.0
Total Current Assets	49,114.0	33,253.0	40,630.0	19,393.0
Fixed Assets, Net	8,955.0	5,599.0	4,488.0	3,519.0
Total Assets	58,806.0	39,802.0	45,156.0	22,950.0
Total Current Liabilities	28,161.0	12,869.0	20,070.0	18,386.0
Long-Term Debt	2,667.0	42.0	0.0	0.0
Stockholders' Equity	27,744.0	26,661.0	24,922.0	4,400.0
Performance & Financial Condition				
Return on Total Revenues %	0.56	0.49	4.80	1.46
Return on Avg Stockholders' Equity %	2.31	1.74	38.57	24.00
Return on Average Assets %	1.28	1.06	16.61	4.93
Current Ratio	1.74	2.58	2.02	1.05
Debt / Equity %	9.61	0.16	n.a.	n.a.

Compound Growth %'s	EPS %	-20.63	Net Income %	-12.60	Total Revenues %	20.44

Comments

Revenue increased 24.6% in fiscal 1998 primarily as a result of increased shipments to the Company's major computer, telecommunications, and networking customers. The Company's sales to its three largest customers for fiscal 1998 represented 20%, 16% and 9% respectively, of total net sales. The Company experienced a decrease in gross margin mainly due to higher costs associated with strategic investments made to expand and upgrade equipment and facilities. For the nine months ended December 26, 1998, the Company reported revenues and net income of $111.1 million and $134,000 ($.01 per share) as compared to $75.0 million and $128,000 ($.01 per share) for the same period of fiscal 1998. Despite an impressive revenue growth, low earnings have depressed the trading value of the stock to a substantial discount from book value.

Officers	Position	Ownership Information	
Ronald W. Guire	Chairman	Number of Shares Outstanding	8,936,400
Angelo A. Decaro, Jr.	President, CEO	Market Capitalization	$ 16,174,884
Stephen D. Sauter	Vice President	Number of Shareholders	1,864
Norman E. O'Shea	Vice President	Where Listed / Symbol	NASDAQ / XTEL

Other Information			
Transfer Agent	American Stock Transfer & Trust Co. New York, NY	SIC Code	3670
Auditor	PricewaterhouseCoopers LLP	Employees	650
		Web Site	xetel.com

Z-Axis Corporation

7395 East Orchard Road, Suite A100   Greenwood Village, CO 80111-2509   Telephone (303)713-0200   Fax (303)713-0299

Company Description

Z-Axis Corporation, founded in 1983, operates in the development and production of computer-generated video graphics and other presentation materials. The primary market for the Company's services is the litigation industry. These services include the strategic analysis of complex litigation issues, the design of demonstrative evidence, the production of such evidence and courtroom presentation. The Company has also developed two types of courtroom presentation systems for its clients: a touchscreen video presentation system and an electronic image presentation system (VuPoint).

	03/31/98	03/31/97	03/31/96	03/31/95
Per Share Information				
Stock Price as of 12/31	0.25	0.06	0.12	0.12
Earnings Per Share	0.01	0.0	0.0	0.12
Price / Earnings Ratio	25.00	n.a.	n.a.	1.00
Book Value Per Share	0.30	0.28	0.28	0.28
Price / Book Value %	83.33	21.43	42.86	42.86
Dividends Per Share	0.0	0.0	0.0	0.0
Annual Financial Data				
Operating Results (000's)				
Total Revenues	3,902.3	2,507.9	2,833.8	3,279.3
Costs & Expenses	-3,815.1	-2,496.5	-2,829.4	-2,646.4
Income Before Taxes and Other	87.3	11.4	4.4	632.9
Other Items	0.0	0.0	0.0	0.0
Income Tax	-33.9	-3.5	-1.5	-179.0
Net Income	53.4	7.9	2.9	453.9
Cash Flow From Operations	385.7	-8.1	136.0	668.2
Balance Sheet (000's)				
Cash & Equivalents	139.3	24.7	118.8	285.2
Total Current Assets	1,308.0	914.8	877.3	1,102.0
Fixed Assets, Net	473.3	325.0	456.6	500.0
Total Assets	1,927.6	1,735.9	1,651.1	1,836.2
Total Current Liabilities	691.6	584.6	484.1	596.6
Long-Term Debt	114.6	85.8	110.1	187.2
Stockholders' Equity	1,121.4	1,065.5	1,056.9	1,052.4
Performance & Financial Condition				
Return on Total Revenues %	1.37	0.31	0.10	13.84
Return on Avg Stockholders' Equity %	4.88	0.74	0.28	55.01
Return on Average Assets %	2.92	0.46	0.17	29.28
Current Ratio	1.89	1.56	1.81	1.85
Debt / Equity %	10.22	8.05	10.42	17.78

Compound Growth %'s	EPS %	-56.32	Net Income %	-51.00	Total Revenues %	5.97

Comments

During the past three years, the Company has developed proprietary software and has filed for trademark protection of the name and patent protection for the software. This product was introduced to the market in the first quarter of fiscal 1998. During fiscal 1998, the Company was involved in three high-profile cases of international significance including work for the United States Department of Justice in the trials of Timothy McVeigh and Terry Nichols for the Oklahoma City bombing. The prominent use of VuPoint in these trials and the Company's design and development of sophisticated demonstrative exhibits proved very valuable to the trial team. Revenues have been explosive. For the nine months ended December 31, 1997, the Company reported revenues and a net loss of $2.9 million and $189 ($.00 per share) as compared to $2.7 million and a net profit of $88,036 ($.02 per share) for the same period of the preceding year.

Officers	Position	Ownership Information	
Alan Treibitz	President, COO	Number of Shares Outstanding	3,785,000
Steven H. Cohen	CEO	Market Capitalization	$ 946,250
Marilyn T. Heller	Secretary	Number of Shareholders	447
Jon D. Ackelson	Vice President	Where Listed / Symbol	OTC-BB / AXIS

Other Information			
Transfer Agent	American Securities Transfer, Inc. Denver, CO	SIC Code	7812
Auditor	BDO Seidman LLP	Employees	27
Market Maker	Paragon Capital Corporation	(800)345-0505	Web Site	zaxis.com
	Financial American Securities	(800)873-7045		

ZEON Corporation

1500 Cherry Street   Louisville, CO 80027   Telephone (303)666-9400   Fax (303)666-5400

Company Description

ZEON Corporation, founded in 1980, is engaged in the manufacture and sale of neon and fluorescent backlit illuminated signs and related products under the name Neon Glassworks. The Company entered into the neon glass tubebending business in July 1998 by acquiring the assets of a local neon business. The Company converted this business from a wholesale operation (primarily forming neon tubes for local sign companies) to a volume production shop, manufacturing finished neon window and interior signs for national accounts. In May 1995, the Company sold its Electronic Display Division to Colorado Time System, Inc.

	12/31/98	12/31/97	12/31/96	12/31/95
Per Share Information				
Stock Price	2.75	0.50	1.00	1.00
Earnings Per Share	0.33	0.51	-0.02	0.33
Price / Earnings Ratio	8.33	0.98	n.a.	3.03
Book Value Per Share	2.38	2.05	1.53	1.55
Price / Book Value %	115.55	24.39	65.36	64.52
Dividends Per Share	0.0	0.0	0.0	0.0
Annual Financial Data				
Operating Results (000's)				
Total Revenues	2,906.8	2,703.8	2,181.5	2,302.4
Costs & Expenses	-2,785.1	-2,523.8	-2,187.0	-2,184.9
Income Before Taxes and Other	121.7	180.0	-5.5	117.4
Other Items	0.0	0.0	0.0	0.0
Income Tax	-6.2	0.0	0.0	0.0
Net Income	115.5	180.0	-5.5	117.4
Cash Flow From Operations	46.3	79.7	21.0	73.5
Balance Sheet (000's)				
Cash & Equivalents	169.9	181.5	133.8	n.a.
Total Current Assets	820.3	827.7	606.7	n.a.
Fixed Assets, Net	173.4	82.2	75.6	n.a.
Total Assets	1,019.5	943.7	724.1	n.a.
Total Current Liabilities	164.2	228.3	187.8	n.a.
Long-Term Debt	24.6	0.0	0.0	n.a.
Stockholders' Equity	830.7	715.3	536.3	n.a.
Performance & Financial Condition				
Return on Total Revenues %	3.97	18.31	-0.25	5.10
Return on Avg Stockholders' Equity %	14.94	28.77	-1.02	24.26
Return on Average Assets %	11.76	21.59	-0.92	21.35
Current Ratio	4.99	3.62	3.23	n.a.
Debt / Equity %	2.96	n.a.	n.a.	n.a.

Compound Growth %'s	EPS %	0.00	Net Income %	-0.56	Total Revenues %	8.08

Comments

Demand for Company products continued to be strong and pushed revenue to another record level in 1998, 7% higher than in 1997. We presented ZEON in last year's edition of Walker's manual of Penny Stocks to prove that we do not discriminate as to company size. Might we have anything to do with the stock price rising 550%? Maybe a little but the Company deserves the credit for producing a decent income stream. Shareholders should be quite proud of their company. With only 349,137 shares outstanding, market makers can take advantage of the thin float by demanding a large spread between what they are willing to pay and what they will sell it for. But investors can capitalize on this phenomenon by posting their own bid price. If you like situations like this, Walker's Manual of Unlisted Stocks contains many inactively traded securities.

Officers	Position	Ownership Information	
T. Bryan Alu	President, CEO	Number of Shares Outstanding	349,137
Alan M. Bloom	Exec VP, Secretary	Market Capitalization	$ 960,127
Ruel G. Routt	Controller	Number of Shareholders	500
Jay R. Beyer	Director	Where Listed / Symbol	OTC-BB / ZEON

Other Information			
Transfer Agent	Securities Transfer Corp. Dallas, TX	SIC Code	3990
Auditor	BDO Seidman LLP	Employees	27
Market Maker	Hill, Thompson, Magid & Co. (800)631-3083	Web Site	zeon.com
	Paragon Capital Corporation (800)345-0505		

¢¢

INDICES

¢¢

I

J

K

L

M

¢ ¢

This page intentionally left blank.

North Carolina

Ohio

Oklahoma

Oregon

Pennsylvania

Rhode Island

South Carolina

Tennessee

Texas

Utah

Vermont

Virginia

Washington

West Virigina

Wisconsin

¢ ¢

4000 - 4999
Transportation & Public Utilities

5000 - 5199
Wholesale Trade

5200 - 5999 Retail Trade	

6000 - 6299 Finance & Banking	

6300 - 6499 Insurance	

6500 - 6799 Real Estate & Other Investing	

7000 - 8999 Services	

¢ ¢

This page intentionally left blank.

Under $1	
CareAdvantage, Inc.	0.03
MileMarker International, Inc.	0.06
Tufco International, Inc.	0.06
Miller Diversified Corporation.	0.08
Celox Laboratories, Inc.	0.09
AM Communications, Inc.	0.12
Compare Generiks, Inc.	0.12
FiberCore, Inc.	0.13
InterWest Medical Corporation	0.15
Metal Arts Company, Inc. (The)	0.15
Simtek Corporation	0.15
HIA, Inc.	0.16
Sono-Tek Corporation	0.16
Fairmount Chemical Co., Inc.	0.18
Laser Master International, Inc.	0.18
Texas Equipment Corporation	0.19
Cistron Biotechnology, Inc.	0.20
Tapistron International, Inc.	0.21
Bingo & Gaming International, Inc.	0.25
Canyon Resources Corporation	0.25
Publishers Equipment Corporation.	0.25
Z-Axis Corporation	0.25
Coeur d' Alenes Company (The)	0.26
Astrex, Inc.	0.27
Creative Technologies Corp.	0.28
Electronic Systems Technology, Inc.	0.28
TMS, Inc.	0.28
Avesis Incorporated	0.29
Dynamic International, Ltd.	0.30
CPT Holdings, Inc.	0.31
Reflectix, Inc.	0.31
Sel-Drum International, Inc.	0.31
Strategic Capital Resources, Inc.	0.33
Tivoli Industries, Inc.	0.34
Pharmaceutical Formulations, Inc.	0.35
Miami Subs Corporation	0.37
Quality Products, Inc.	0.37
Butler National Corporation	0.38
Ag-Bag International Limited	0.41
Sarnia Corporation	0.41
Wade Cook Financial Corporation	0.41
Bollinger Industries, Inc.	0.44
Tubby's, Inc.	0.44
Cambridge Holdings, Ltd.	0.45
HemaCare Corporation.	0.46
Bristol Retail Solutions, Inc.	0.47
Telecomm Industries Corp.	0.47
Wiltek, Inc.	0.47
Firecom, Inc.	0.48
American Consumers, Inc.	0.50
CAS Medical Systems, Inc.	0.50
HEARx Ltd.	0.50
Logitek, Inc.	0.50
Milastar Corporation	0.50
Touchstone Applied Science Associates, Inc.	0.50
Boonton Electronics Corporation	0.51
Champion Parts, Inc.	0.55
ERC Industries, Inc.	0.56
Emerson Radio Corp.	0.56
Kyzen Corporation	0.56

Mendocino Brewing Company, Inc.	0.56
Sonics & Materials, Inc.	0.56
Sunshine Mining and Refining Company	0.56
Amtech Systems, Inc.	0.59
DeVlieg-Bullard, Inc.	0.59
Galaxy Foods Company	0.59
Arthur Treacher's, Inc.	0.62
Eldorado Artesian Springs, Inc.	0.62
Electronic Tele-Communications, Inc.	0.62
Health Fitness Corporation.	0.62
Intellectual Technology, Inc.	0.62
RADVA Corporation.	0.62
SYS.	0.62
Advanced Photonix, Inc.	0.69
All Communications Corporation	0.69
Hydromer, Inc.	0.69
Vicon Fiber Optics Corp.	0.69
Micropac Industries, Inc.	0.70
Hemagen Diagnostics, Inc.	0.71
Puroflow Incorporated	0.72
Seventh Generation, Inc.	0.72
New York Health Care, Inc.	0.75
PREMIS Corporation	0.75
Superior Supplements, Inc.	0.75
Texas Vanguard Oil Company	0.75
Accuhealth, Inc.	0.81
All American Semiconductor, Inc.	0.81
Arizona Instrument Corporation	0.81
Computer Research, Inc.	0.81
Comtrex Systems Corporation	0.81
Microfluidics International Corporation	0.81
NBI, Inc.	0.81
PDG Environmental, Inc.	0.81
Sierra Monitor Corporation	0.81
Optimumcare Corporation	0.83
Advanced Tobacco Products, Inc.	0.84
Guardian International, Inc.	0.84
EFI Electronics Corporation	0.87
Grill Concepts, Inc.	0.87
Interfoods of America, Inc.	0.87
Tanknology-NDE International, Inc.	0.87
Tofutti Brands Inc.	0.87
Westwood Corporation.	0.87
ATS Money Systems, Inc.	0.91
FAFCO, Inc.	0.94
GlobeNet International I, Inc.	0.94

Under $2	
AMBI Inc.	1.00
Bio-Reference Laboratories, Inc.	1.00
InterSystems, Inc.	1.00
Jetronic Industries, Inc.	1.00
Rotonics Manufacturing Inc.	1.00
Smith-Midland Corporation	1.00
Tone Products, Inc.	1.00
Top Air Manufacturing, Inc.	1.00
Image Systems Corporation	1.03
ACR Group, Inc.	1.06
BAB Holdings, Inc.	1.06
Carlyle Industries, Inc.	1.06
T.J.T., Inc.	1.06

Under $3

Under $4

Applied Innovation Inc.	3.22
American Residential Services, Inc.	3.25
Apple Orthodontix, Inc.	3.25
Capital Associates, Inc.	3.25
Command Systems, Inc.	3.25
FTI Consulting, Inc.	3.25
First Alliance Corporation	3.25
Hawaiian Airlines, Inc.	3.25
Laser Technology, Inc.	3.25
ROHN Industries, Inc.	3.25
Rehabilicare Inc.	3.25
Safety 1st, Inc.	3.25
CompuCom Systems, Inc.	3.28
Consumer Portfolio Services, Inc.	3.31
DMI Furniture, Inc.	3.31
JLM Couture, Inc.	3.31
Nastech Pharmaceutical Company Inc.	3.31
THT Inc.	3.31
Capital Title Group, Inc.	3.37
Eagle Geophysical, Inc.	3.37
Endogen, Inc.	3.37
PTI Holding Inc.	3.37
Abatix Environmental Corp.	3.44
Birner Dental Management Services, Inc.	3.44
Candie's, Inc.	3.44
MIM Corporation	3.44
NewCom, Inc.	3.44
Nortech Systems Incorporated	3.44
Applied Cellular Technology, Inc.	3.50
Flour City International, Inc.	3.50
Met-Coil Systems Corporation	3.50
SpectraLink Corporation	3.50
Sunrise International Leasing Corporation	3.50
Whitman Education Group, Inc.	3.50
Elantec Semiconductor, Inc.	3.56
American Dental Technologies, Inc.	3.62
Hawker Pacific Aerospace	3.62
I.C.H. Corporation	3.62
IRIDEX Corporation	3.62
Patterson Energy, Inc.	3.62
Seven J Stock Farm, Inc.	3.62
Diamond Home Services, Inc.	3.66
Jaco Electronics, Inc.	3.69
Royal Appliance Mfg. Co.	3.69
Tandycrafts, Inc.	3.69
Waterlink, Inc.	3.69
Worldtex, Inc.	3.69
B.B. Walker Company	3.75
BioSpecifics Technologies Corp.	3.75
Cylink Corporation	3.75
EKCO Group, Inc.	3.75
Fiberstars, Inc.	3.75
Hi-Tech Pharmacal Co., Inc.	3.75
Mobile America Corporation	3.75
Network Six, Inc.	3.75
Scherer Healthcare, Inc.	3.75
Spectrum Control, Inc.	3.75
Winston Resources, Inc.	3.78
First American Health Concepts, Inc.	3.81
Spanlink Communications, Inc.	3.81
Westmoreland Coal Company	3.81
Cache, Inc.	3.87
Central Financial Acceptance Corporation	3.87

Flanders Corporation	3.87
Gentner Communications Corporation	3.87
Horizon Medical Products, Inc.	3.87
Collins Industries, Inc.	3.94
Comprehensive Care Corporation	3.94
FARO Technologies, Inc.	3.94
GZA GeoEnvironmental Technologies, Inc.	3.94

Under $5

Aasche Transportation Services, Inc.	4.00
Casa Ole' Restaurants, Inc.	4.00
Dynamex Inc.	4.00
EcoScience Corporation	4.00
Equivest Finance, Inc.	4.00
Gundle/SLT Environmental, Inc.	4.00
Napco Security Systems, Inc.	4.00
Nathan's Famous, Inc.	4.00
Sports Club Company, Inc. (The)	4.00
Integrity Incorporated	4.03
Kreisler Manufacturing Corporation	4.03
Adams Golf, Inc.	4.06
Kaneb Services, Inc.	4.06
Signature Eyewear, Inc.	4.06
Bayou Steel Corporation	4.12
Canterbury Park Holding Corporation	4.12
Marlton Technologies, Inc.	4.12
Response Oncology, Inc.	4.12
Thousand Trails, Inc.	4.12
Triple S Plastics, Inc.	4.12
Charming Shoppes, Inc.	4.19
Esquire Communications Ltd.	4.19
IRI International Corporation	4.19
TBA Entertainment Corporation	4.19
Autologic Information International, Inc.	4.25
Disc Graphics, Inc.	4.25
Mesa Laboratories, Inc.	4.25
Reconditioned Systems, Inc.	4.28
Arrow-Magnolia International, Inc.	4.31
Pentacon, Inc.	4.31
Questron Technology, Inc.	4.31
Littlefield, Adams & Company	4.37
Measurement Specialties, Inc.	4.37
Thermo TerraTech Inc.	4.37
Interlink Electronics, Inc.	4.50
Raytel Medical Corporation	4.50
Tangram Enterprise Solutions, Inc.	4.50
United-Guardian, Inc.	4.50
Frontier Airlines, Inc.	4.53
Government Technology Services, Inc.	4.53
International Total Services, Inc.	4.53
InterDigital Communications Corporation	4.56
Millbrook Press Inc. (The)	4.56
PlayCore, Inc.	4.56
Conrad Industries, Inc.	4.62
Edac Technologies Corporation	4.62
Horizon Offshore, Inc.	4.62
International Airline Support Group, Inc.	4.62
Impac Mortgage Holdings, Inc.	4.69
U.S. Home & Garden Inc.	4.69
Acme Electric Corporation	4.75
National Home Health Care Corp.	4.75

¢ ¢

This page intentionally left blank.

Over $100,000,000

Southland Corporation (The)	7,349,811,000
CompuCom Systems, Inc.	2,254,465,000
NovaCare,Inc.	1,672,755,000
Weirton Steel Corporation	1,259,514,000
Charming Shoppes, Inc.	1,032,523,000
Eagle Food Centers, Inc.	967,090,000
Fortress Group, Inc. (The)	696,330,000
Halter Marine Group, Inc.	670,238,000
Government Technology Services, Inc.	605,884,000
SITEL Corporation	586,318,000
Argosy Gaming Company	510,250,000
American Residential Services, Inc.	506,439,000
MIM Corporation	452,782,000
Guess ?, Inc.	435,128,000
Hawaiian Airlines, Inc.	428,054,000
Miller Industries, Inc.	397,213,000
Kaneb Services, Inc.	376,725,000
McNaughton Apparel Group Inc.	344,769,000
Drypers Corporation	337,106,000
EKCO Group, Inc.	329,235,000
Thermo TerraTech Inc.	306,284,000
Royal Appliance Mfg. Co.	282,720,000
Capital Associates, Inc.	281,074,000
Worldtex, Inc.	258,537,000
DenAmerica Corp.	255,956,000
Bayou Steel Corporation	250,880,835
All American Semiconductor, Inc.	250,044,000
Diamond Home Services, Inc.	245,393,000
Sizzler International, Inc.	243,604,000
Ithaca Industries, Inc.	237,021,000
Tandycrafts, Inc.	232,582,000
Strategic Distribution, Inc.	220,087,000
Unilab Corporation	217,370,000
Travel Ports of America, Inc.	211,943,501
Dynamex Inc.	207,746,000
Applied Cellular Technology, Inc.	207,501,000
Manchester Equipment Co., Inc.	203,117,000
Capital Pacific Holdings, Inc.	193,253,000
Bernard Chaus, Inc.	191,604,000
TransCoastal Marine Services, Inc.	188,878,000
Patterson Energy, Inc.	188,178,000
Consolidated Delivery & Logistics, Inc.	185,865,000
Atlantic Premium Brands, Ltd.	181,138,378
Gundle/SLT Environmental, Inc.	180,822,000
IRI International Corporation	177,258,000
ROHN Industries, Inc.	174,445,000
International Total Services, Inc.	173,235,000
AlphaNet Solutions, Inc.	171,972,000
Impac Mortgage Holdings, Inc.	168,104,000
Allstar Systems, Inc.	167,173,000
Emerson Radio Corp.	164,254,000
Flanders Corporation	159,680,608
Gristede's Sloan's, Inc.	158,024,840
Collins Industries, Inc.	156,805,236
Innovative Valve Technologies, Inc.	154,864,000
Jaco Electronics, Inc.	153,674,226
Swank, Inc.	151,770,000
Friedman Industries, Incorporated	148,893,804
Coast Distribution System (The)	148,680,000
Frontier Airlines, Inc.	147,950,658

Cache, Inc.	147,058,000
Pentacon, Inc.	141,169,000
I.C.H. Corporation	140,032,000
Digital Solutions, Inc.	139,758,000
Waterlink, Inc.	135,204,000
Hahn Automotive Warehouse, Inc.	133,914,000
EMCON	130,508,000
Response Oncology, Inc.	128,246,000
Lexington Precision Corporation	126,717,000
Consumer Portfolio Services, Inc.	126,280,000
Eagle Geophysical, Inc.	123,597,000
Let's Talk Cellular & Wireless, Inc.	122,486,671
Wade Cook Financial Corporation	121,751,000
ICT Group, Inc.	121,595,572
Safety 1st, Inc.	121,279,933
G-III Apparel Group, Ltd.	120,136,000
Horizon Offshore, Inc.	119,840,000
Meteor Industries, Inc.	118,842,000
Aerovox Incorporated	117,714,000
DeVlieg-Bullard, Inc.	116,767,000
Selfcare, Inc.	115,530,933
PlayCore, Inc.	114,792,000
Judge Group, Inc. (The)	114,498,397
Aasche Transportation Services, Inc.	114,312,000
Great Lakes Aviation, Ltd.	114,031,960
Todd Shipyards Corporation	112,966,000
XeTel Corporation	112,685,000
Jennifer Convertibles, Inc.	112,306,000
Westmoreland Coal Company	111,043,000
CPT Holdings, Inc.	110,830,000
Esquire Communications Ltd.	110,586,000
Kentucky Electric Steel, Inc.	109,536,000
Orleans Homebuilders, Inc.	108,998,000
Suprema Specialties, Inc.	108,140,007
Raytel Medical Corporation	108,140,000
ERC Industries, Inc.	107,111,000
InterDigital Communications Corporation	101,675,000
Big Dog Holdings, Inc.	100,677,000

$100,000,000 - $50,000,000

LaBarge, Inc.	99,405,000
Tekgraf, Inc.	99,295,408
Farrel Corporation	98,580,000
Seattle FilmWorks, Inc.	97,656,000
BridgeStreet Accomodations, Inc.	96,941,679
ACR Group, Inc.	96,682,424
Cade Industries, Inc.	95,792,417
Multigraphics, Inc.	95,462,000
NewCom, Inc.	93,885,782
Business Resource Group	93,565,000
Comstock Resources, Inc.	93,235,000
Candie's, Inc.	92,976,416
Marlton Technologies, Inc.	91,390,562
Superior Energy Services, Inc.	91,334,000
Acme Electric Corporation	90,916,000
Rag Shops, Inc.	90,565,996
Boundless Corporation	90,202,000
SETECH, Inc.	88,953,000
Autologic Information International, Inc.	87,616,000
SigmaTron International, Inc.	86,130,106
Adams Golf, Inc.	85,978,000

First Alliance Corporation	83,808,000
MTR Gaming Group, Inc.	83,511,000
Petroleum Development Corporation	82,973,600
Sports Club Company, Inc. (The)	82,803,000
L.A. T Sportswear, Inc.	81,874,000
Pharmaceutical Formulations, Inc.	80,908,000
Centrum Industries, Inc.	79,793,697
NewCare Health Corporation	77,515,605
Thousand Trails, Inc.	76,509,000
Circuit Systems, Inc.	75,618,076
Holiday RV Superstores, Incorporated.	74,809,842
Eagle Pacific Industries, Inc.	74,090,192
Randers Killam Group Inc. (The)	71,778,000
HMG Worldwide Corporation	68,744,000
Texas Equipment Corporation	68,253,548
Triple S Plastics, Inc.	67,692,000
U.S. Home & Garden Inc.	67,635,000
JB Oxford Holdings, Inc.	67,268,325
Tanknology-NDE International, Inc.	67,033,969
Jerry's Famous Deli, Inc.	66,619,756
Industrial Services of America, Inc.	65,272,973
Hawker Pacific Aerospace	65,225,000
DMI Furniture, Inc.	64,841,924
Movie Star, Inc.	64,694,000
Writer Corporation (The)	64,302,000
Aldila, Inc.	62,705,000
Diodes Incorporated	61,116,000
Winston Resources, Inc.	60,899,000
PTI Holding Inc.	60,522,011
Whitman Education Group, Inc.	60,509,916
EA Engineering, Science, and Technology, Inc.	60,086,000
GZA GeoEnvironmental Technologies, Inc.	59,989,000
Spectrum Control, Inc.	59,953,000
Disc Graphics, Inc.	59,031,202
FTI Consulting, Inc.	58,934,000
Bollinger Industries, Inc.	58,793,757
Williams Controls, Inc.	57,646,000
Questron Technology, Inc.	56,968,007
BTU International, Inc.	56,946,000
Universal American Financial Corp.	56,089,106
Sight Resource Corporation	55,313,000
Joule Inc.	55,301,000
Applied Innovation Inc.	55,292,624
Pacific Aerospace & Electronics, Inc.	54,099,000
Transcend Services, Inc.	53,314,000
Edac Technologies Corporation	53,253,217
RMH Teleservices, Inc.	52,975,000
Canisco Resources, Inc.	52,304,272
Command Security Corporation	52,061,375
Reliv International, Inc.	52,027,760
Napco Security Systems, Inc.	50,416,000
Medicore, Inc.	50,148,529

$49,999,999 - $20,000,000

Sunrise International Leasing Corporation.	49,272,000
Go-Video, Inc.	48,909,089
Kinark Corporation.	48,313,000
Mobile America Corporation	48,302,029
Apple Orthodontix, Inc.	47,517,000
PDK Labs Inc.	47,405,000
Unidigital Inc.	47,389,000

UFP Technologies, Inc.	47,281,000
Casa Ole' Restaurants, Inc.	47,139,370
Bio-Reference Laboratories, Inc.	46,993,885
Central Financial Acceptance Corporation	46,888,000
Elantec Semiconductor, Inc.	46,884,000
Comprehensive Care Corporation	46,833,000
Conrad Industries, Inc.	46,597,000
U.S. Plastic Lumber Corporation	45,745,741
Cylink Corporation.	45,107,000
Met-Coil Systems Corporation.	45,009,000
Diagnostic Health Services, Inc.	44,928,220
Techdyne, Inc.	44,926,731
Solomon-Page Group Ltd. (The).	44,768,501
Bontex, Inc.	43,571,000
Golden Genesis Company	43,555,000
Streicher Mobile Fueling, Inc.	43,220,625
Jenna Lane, Inc.	42,561,796
Burke Mills, Inc.	42,335,800
First Montauk Financial Corp.	41,876,378
CCA Industries, Inc.	41,402,270
Signature Eyewear, Inc.	41,303,065
Nortech Systems Incorporated	40,397,752
Horizon Medical Products, Inc.	39,445,623
Educational Insights, Inc.	39,310,000
Bull Run Corporation	39,285,000
Integrity Incorporated	38,847,000
Blimpie International, Inc.	38,721,000
Rankin Automotive Group, Inc.	38,655,609
Thermo Vision Corporation	38,421,000
Rotonics Manufacturing Inc.	38,155,100
Abatix Environmental Corp.	37,345,853
ILX Resorts Incorporated	36,871,570
SpectraLink Corporation	36,621,000
Unapix Entertainment, Inc.	36,481,000
Canyon Resources Corporation	36,363,200
Productivity Technologies Corp.	36,328,052
Command Systems, Inc.	36,208,889
Alfa Leisure, Inc.	36,025,591
Berger Holdings, Ltd.	35,744,952
ASA International Ltd.	35,608,993
Sunshine Mining and Refining Company	35,396,000
National Home Health Care Corp.	35,191,000
Grill Concepts, Inc.	34,908,105
Wegener Corporation	34,719,858
Worksafe Industries Inc.	34,383,204
T.J.T., Inc.	34,158,000
Total Research Corporation	34,117,508
Rehabilicare Inc.	33,825,688
Tidel Technologies, Inc.	33,607,533
InterSystems, Inc.	33,345,000
Calprop Corporation	33,071,722
Flour City International, Inc.	32,965,000
Security National Financial Corporation.	32,819,603
Netter Digital Entertainment, Inc.	32,344,673
Bristol Retail Solutions, Inc.	32,297,248
Hi-Rise Recycling Systems, Inc.	31,956,401
Omtool, Ltd.	31,876,506
Synbiotics Corporation.	31,696,000
Nitches, Inc.	31,409,000
Exigent International, Inc.	31,185,200
Westminster Capital, Inc.	30,925,000
Taitron Components Incorporated	30,911,000
Foilmark, Inc.	30,909,498

Westwood Corporation.	30,232,000
Janus American Group, Inc.	30,194,331
Chicago Pizza & Brewery, Inc.	30,051,503
Equivest Finance, Inc.	29,636,500
Measurement Specialties, Inc.	29,331,961
Vermont Pure Holdings, Ltd.	29,271,467
White Electronic Designs Corporation.	29,119,000
Encore Medical Corporation.	28,990,000
Norton Drilling Services, Inc.	28,962,132
Nathan's Famous, Inc.	28,877,000
B.B. Walker Company.	28,852,000
Interwest Home Medical, Inc.	28,842,000
FARO Technologies, Inc.	28,731,767
Colonial Commercial Corp.	28,458,664
American Dental Technologies, Inc.	28,426,786
TENERA, Inc.	28,087,000
Ag-Bag International Limited	28,084,403
International Airline Support Group, Inc.	27,963,000
Provena Foods Inc.	27,846,844
Farmstead Telephone Group, Inc.	27,810,000
Retrospettiva, Inc.	27,642,140
HEARx Ltd.	27,493,849
TBA Entertainment Corporation.	27,417,200
Back Yard Burgers, Inc.	27,395,000
GlobeNet International I, Inc.	27,188,800
Aero Systems Engineering, Inc.	27,181,457
Calloway's Nursery, Inc.	27,069,000
American Consumers, Inc.	26,984,471
Champion Parts, Inc.	26,798,000
Phoenix Gold International, Inc.	26,494,231
Monterey Pasta Company	26,234,140
Westerbeke Corporation	26,202,000
Littlefield, Adams & Company	25,917,000
Jetronic Industries, Inc.	25,873,000
Lincoln Snacks Company	25,782,224
Health Fitness Corporation.	25,752,902
Overseas Filmgroup, Inc.	25,731,736
PDG Environmental, Inc.	24,662,000
JMAR Industries, Inc.	24,622,797
Glassmaster Company	24,548,803
Interfoods of America, Inc.	24,219,609
IRIDEX Corporation.	24,096,000
Telecomm Industries Corp.	24,023,226
Advanced Deposition Technologies, Inc.	23,853,000
SI Technologies, Inc.	23,834,449
Carlyle Industries, Inc.	23,801,000
Fiberstars, Inc.	23,707,000
Athanor Group, Inc.	23,646,334
Miami Subs Corporation.	23,434,000
Capital Title Group, Inc.	23,206,225
Ronson Corporation	23,173,000
Arthur Treacher's, Inc.	22,986,762
Riviera Tool Company.	22,581,100
EcoScience Corporation	22,435,000
Hi-Tech Pharmacal Co., Inc.	22,366,000
Interlink Electronics, Inc.	22,095,000
Birner Dental Management Services, Inc.	21,740,665
R.H. Phillips, Inc.	21,737,000
Financial Performance Corporation	21,572,666
EXX INC.	21,454,000
Strategic Capital Resources, Inc.	21,302,522
Hadron, Inc.	21,139,400
Amistar Corporation	20,954,077

AMBI Inc.	20,829,000
Tangram Enterprise Solutions, Inc.	20,678,000
Cable Link, Inc.	20,570,821
Galaxy Foods Company	20,569,232
New York Health Care, Inc.	20,297,667
SofTech, Inc.	20,232,000

$19,999,999 - $10,000,000

Mentortech Inc.	19,951,000
THT Inc.	19,763,549
BCT International, Inc.	19,405,000
Canterbury Park Holding Corporation	19,203,164
Fotoball USA, Inc.	19,157,856
Memry Corporation	19,093,000
Shopsmith, Inc.	19,014,834
CareAdvantage, Inc.	18,903,000
HIA, Inc.	18,830,330
Accuhealth, Inc.	18,603,823
Technology Research Corporation	18,562,869
Allied Devices Corporation	18,448,483
Continental Information Systems Corporation.	18,419,000
National Environmental Service Co.	18,346,000
Prab, Inc.	18,244,714
Emons Transportation Group, Inc.	17,787,189
GameTech International, Inc.	17,545,696
Sel-Leb Marketing, Inc.	17,371,999
Gentner Communications Corporation.	17,294,550
AM Communications, Inc.	16,854,000
Top Air Manufacturing, Inc.	16,582,823
InnerDyne, Inc.	16,561,602
Healthcare Imaging Services, Inc.	16,451,057
EFI Electronics Corporation	16,377,224
Orbit International Corp.	16,351,000
Optelecom, Inc.	16,333,749
Intelligent Controls, Inc.	16,280,902
Amtech Systems, Inc.	16,268,351
Bradley Pharmaceuticals, Inc.	15,900,686
New Horizon Kids Quest, Inc.	15,734,247
BLC Financial Services, Inc.	15,729,000
JLM Couture, Inc.	15,704,889
Paravant Computer Systems, Inc.	15,635,313
Millbrook Press Inc. (The)	15,615,000
Moyco Technologies, Inc.	15,430,634
Publishers Equipment Corporation.	15,277,562
Creative Technologies Corp.	15,263,000
Guardian International, Inc.	15,165,755
Sparta Foods, Inc.	15,122,234
Smith-Midland Corporation	14,761,972
BAB Holdings, Inc.	14,722,506
Creative Host Services, Inc.	14,720,350
NBI, Inc.	14,698,000
Coeur d'Alenes Company (The)	14,430,428
Scherer Healthcare, Inc.	14,396,000
Sel-Drum International, Inc.	14,348,875
Firecom, Inc.	14,275,000
Astrex, Inc.	14,263,697
Kids Stuff, Inc.	14,172,864
Laser Master International, Inc.	14,102,367
Dynamic Homes, Inc.	14,003,600
Arrow-Magnolia International, Inc.	13,856,623
Arizona Instrument Corporation	13,809,271

Pioneer Railcorp	13,796,056
REXX Environmental Corporation	13,777,000
Armanino Foods of Distinction, Inc.	13,670,768
Advantage Marketing Systems, Inc.	13,637,012
All Communications Corporation	13,273,529
RADVA Corporation.	13,253,913
AML Communications, Inc.	13,155,000
Electronic Tele-Communications, Inc..	13,150,209
Kreisler Manufacturing Corporation	13,127,602
HemaCare Corporation.	13,124,000
Fairmount Chemical Co., Inc.	12,887,800
Sandata, Inc.	12,826,970
ML Macadamia Orchards, L.P.	12,652,000
Hytek Microsystems, Inc.	12,533,045
Hemagen Diagnostics, Inc..	12,408,094
Dynatronics Corporation	12,359,873
Sonics & Materials, Inc.	12,331,525
Luxtec Corporation.	12,066,700
Cohesant Technologies Inc.	11,896,442
Hitox Corporation of America	11,833,666
ATS Money Systems, Inc.	11,811,484
Laser Technology, Inc..	11,801,293
George Risk Industries, Inc.	11,799,000
Micropac Industries, Inc..	11,556,000
S2 Golf Inc.	11,505,000
Optimumcare Corporation	11,434,426
Electric & Gas Technology, Inc..	11,375,936
InterWest Medical Corporation	11,353,817
Synergy Brands, Inc.	11,301,733
FAFCO, Inc.	11,266,400
Miller Diversified Corporation.	11,184,161
MobiNetix Systems, Inc..	11,156,480
Spanlink Communications, Inc.	11,083,239
Tone Products, Inc..	11,024,747
Environmental Safeguards, Inc.	11,002,000
Everest Medical Corporation.	10,727,773
Network Six, Inc..	10,478,416
Genelabs Technologies, Inc..	10,359,000
Superior Supplements, Inc..	10,284,340
MicroFrame, Inc..	10,232,799
Boatracs, Inc..	10,220,743
Microfluidics International Corporation	10,123,837
Reflectix, Inc.	10,119,126
QC Optics, Inc..	10,099,940
Endogen, Inc..	10,033,451

Under $10,000,000

Goddard Industries, Inc.	9,764,701
International Electronics, Inc..	9,689,526
Tivoli Industries, Inc.	9,642,184
Reconditioned Systems, Inc.	9,593,212
Nastech Pharmaceutical Company Inc..	9,590,000
Lannett Company, Inc.	9,464,814
Isomet Corporation	9,412,539
ChoiceTel Communications, Inc.	9,344,248
Stearns & Lehman, Inc..	9,259,171
Compare Generiks, Inc..	9,160,121
Saratoga Beverage Group, Inc.	9,154,111
Cumberland Technologies, Inc..	9,010,377
Tofutti Brands Inc.	8,991,000
Seventh Generation, Inc.	8,986,236

United-Guardian, Inc..	8,867,226
R-B Rubber Products, Inc.	8,631,546
Puroflow Incorporated	8,614,838
FiberCore, Inc.	8,459,000
Mikron Instrument Company, Inc.	8,451,358
Avesis Incorporated.	8,367,613
Milastar Corporation	8,280,000
Image Systems Corporation	8,201,091
DCI Telecommunications, Inc.	8,183,841
Mesa Laboratories, Inc..	8,152,995
Dynamic International, Ltd.	8,043,076
First American Health Concepts, Inc.	7,972,286
Big Sky Transportation Co..	7,947,131
Nicholas Financial, Inc..	7,937,022
SYS	7,886,075
HealthStar Corp.	7,853,996
CAS Medical Systems, Inc..	7,851,366
Diehl Graphsoft, Inc.	7,767,578
Wiltek, Inc.	7,584,300
Tubby's, Inc.	7,484,953
TMS, Inc.	7,367,839
Advanced Photonix, Inc.	7,133,000
Oralabs Holding Corp.	7,131,096
Sierra Monitor Corporation	7,013,023
Boonton Electronics Corporation.	6,872,635
Mesabi Trust	6,860,369
Computer Research, Inc.	6,778,518
Mercury Waste Solutions, Inc.	6,758,552
Tufco International, Inc.	6,662,969
RF Industries, Ltd.	6,623,217
K2 Design, Inc..	6,580,744
Quality Products, Inc..	6,550,704
Mendocino Brewing Company, Inc.	6,538,200
Coda Music Technology, Inc.	6,501,715
Simtek Corporation	6,388,043
Comtrex Systems Corporation	6,382,948
Touchstone Applied Science Associates, Inc.	6,364,636
Global Maintech Corporation.	6,356,095
BioSpecifics Technologies Corp..	6,338,124
Willamette Valley Vineyards, Inc.	6,165,335
PREMIS Corporation	6,044,717
Frontier Adjusters of America, Inc..	5,968,809
Kyzen Corporation	5,946,245
Polymer Research Corp. of America	5,746,913
Tapistron International, Inc.	5,693,598
Ceramics Process Systems Corporation	5,657,523
Telebyte Technology, Inc.	5,643,726
Intellectual Technology, Inc.	5,525,343
Butler National Corporation	5,475,230
Micronetics Wireless, Inc.	4,909,384
Logitek, Inc..	4,834,879
Rent-A-Wreck of America, Inc.	4,738,992
RMS Titanic, Inc.	4,736,731
Bingo & Gaming International, Inc.	4,207,297
Oakridge Energy, Inc..	4,086,395
Sunair Electronics, Inc.	4,000,691
Tel-Instrument Electronics Corp..	3,987,114
Z-Axis Corporation	3,902,316
Farm Fish, Inc.	3,773,668
MileMarker International, Inc.	3,754,022
Sono-Tek Corporation	3,570,748
Scientific Industries, Inc.	3,456,900
Vicon Fiber Optics Corp.	3,368,734

Eldorado Artesian Springs, Inc.	3,333,164
Sarnia Corporation	3,127,000
ZEON Corporation	2,906,764
CREDO Petroleum Corporation	2,835,000
Oakridge Holdings, Inc.	2,767,214
Hydromer, Inc.	2,394,095
Metal Arts Company, Inc. (The)	1,878,922
Electronic Systems Technology, Inc.	1,564,877
Cell Robotics International, Inc.	1,514,430
Texas Vanguard Oil Company	1,493,456
Seven J Stock Farm, Inc.	787,000
Cistron Biotechnology, Inc.	760,205
Advanced Tobacco Products, Inc.	593,917
Celox Laboratories, Inc.	335,564
Cambridge Holdings, Ltd.	178,068

¢ ¢

This page intentionally left blank.

Over $100,000,000

Southland Corporation (The)	782,952,806
Charming Shoppes, Inc.	421,804,723
Miller Industries, Inc.	226,952,561
InterDigital Communications Corporation	220,827,120
Guess ?, Inc.	206,380,433
NovaCare,Inc.	179,472,580
ROHN Industries, Inc.	169,588,250
IRI International Corporation	167,181,000
SITEL Corporation	160,999,113
CompuCom Systems, Inc.	155,609,170
Sunshine Mining and Refining Company	145,268,480
Halter Marine Group, Inc.	140,363,140
Hawaiian Airlines, Inc.	133,241,339
Kaneb Services, Inc.	127,523,065
Applied Cellular Technology, Inc.	124,519,500
Impac Mortgage Holdings, Inc.	115,175,411
Patterson Energy, Inc.	114,649,498
Cylink Corporation	109,181,250
Genelabs Technologies, Inc.	108,084,640
Equivest Finance, Inc.	100,793,404

$100,000,000 - $50,000,000

Flanders Corporation.	99,166,192
Unilab Corporation.	96,477,960
U.S. Home & Garden Inc.	94,423,770
Horizon Offshore, Inc.	91,598,338
Synergy Brands, Inc.	91,489,716
Adams Golf, Inc.	91,265,885
U.S. Plastic Lumber Corporation	88,782,671
Thermo TerraTech Inc.	85,357,396
Seattle FilmWorks, Inc.	82,210,942
Sports Club Company, Inc. (The)	78,551,728
Strategic Distribution, Inc.	76,327,555
Comstock Resources, Inc.	75,973,410
Superior Energy Services, Inc.	73,708,859
Royal Appliance Mfg. Co.	72,403,424
Pentacon, Inc.	71,839,636
EKCO Group, Inc.	71,493,750
Argosy Gaming Company	71,033,361
Tangram Enterprise Solutions, Inc.	70,954,862
Bull Run Corporation	66,729,000
Sizzler International, Inc.	66,622,497
SpectraLink Corporation.	66,328,500
Weirton Steel Corporation	64,263,534
MIM Corporation	62,232,173
Bernard Chaus, Inc.	61,010,791
First Alliance Corporation	58,953,336
Big Dog Holdings, Inc.	58,928,705
Capital Title Group, Inc.	57,043,286
Randers Killam Group Inc. (The)	55,944,561
Memry Corporation	53,663,265
Bayou Steel Corporation	53,108,889
Worldtex, Inc.	52,660,621
Gundle/SLT Environmental, Inc.	52,510,588
Consumer Portfolio Services, Inc.	51,829,638
HEARx Ltd.	51,809,166
Horizon Medical Products, Inc.	51,727,496
Applied Innovation Inc.	50,831,345

Drypers Corporation	50,818,114
Vermont Pure Holdings, Ltd.	50,571,704

$49,999,999 - $25,000,000

American Residential Services, Inc.	49,794,297
Response Oncology, Inc.	49,643,244
MTR Gaming Group, Inc.	49,452,806
Petroleum Development Corporation	47,462,932
Cade Industries, Inc.	47,085,034
Todd Shipyards Corporation	47,073,355
Tandycrafts, Inc.	46,533,000
Whitman Education Group, Inc.	46,177,537
Apple Orthodontix, Inc.	46,163,000
Waterlink, Inc.	45,112,479
BLC Financial Services, Inc.	44,501,510
Government Technology Services, Inc.	44,391,690
FARO Technologies, Inc.	43,372,060
Williams Controls, Inc.	43,089,179
Candie's, Inc.	42,742,048
LaBarge, Inc.	42,612,020
EcoScience Corporation	41,953,820
Frontier Airlines, Inc.	41,918,640
Spectrum Control, Inc.	40,826,280
Dynamex Inc.	40,276,000
Transcend Services, Inc.	40,205,000
Mesabi Trust	40,147,231
Gristede's Sloan's, Inc.	39,273,148
Raytel Medical Corporation	38,985,746
JMAR Industries, Inc.	38,331,408
DCI Telecommunications, Inc.	37,909,161
Aldila, Inc.	37,263,912
Capital Pacific Holdings, Inc.	36,622,108
Galaxy Foods Company	36,406,865
Go-Video, Inc.	36,286,262
TBA Entertainment Corporation	36,179,812
PlayCore, Inc.	36,064,876
Cache, Inc.	35,183,478
NewCom, Inc.	34,400,000
Eagle Food Centers, Inc.	34,154,244
Rehabilicare Inc.	33,940,949
Omtool, Ltd.	33,217,712
Boatracs, Inc.	32,959,556
Elantec Semiconductor, Inc.	32,709,280
Conrad Industries, Inc.	32,699,080
Pacific Aerospace & Electronics, Inc.	32,638,933
Swank, Inc.	31,618,948
G-III Apparel Group, Ltd.	31,295,188
Friedman Industries, Incorporated	31,225,596
Diamond Home Services, Inc.	31,136,993
Thousand Trails, Inc.	30,640,782
TransCoastal Marine Services, Inc.	30,404,963
Selfcare, Inc.	30,217,282
International Total Services, Inc.	30,178,860
Gentner Communications Corporation.	29,793,284
Marlton Technologies, Inc.	29,667,729
Eagle Geophysical, Inc.	29,616,605
JB Oxford Holdings, Inc.	29,482,215
Collins Industries, Inc.	29,277,671
ICT Group, Inc.	29,106,188
InnerDyne, Inc.	28,677,718
Emerson Radio Corp.	28,585,049

Central Financial Acceptance Corporation	28,161,990
Sunrise International Leasing Corporation.	27,258,000
Hi-Rise Recycling Systems, Inc..	27,049,644
Mobile America Corporation	26,878,283
American Dental Technologies, Inc..	26,857,718
Fortress Group, Inc. (The)	26,793,241
Westmoreland Coal Company	26,537,900
EMCON	26,526,123
Wade Cook Financial Corporation.	26,278,798
Orleans Homebuilders, Inc.	26,232,402
Judge Group, Inc. (The)	26,192,526
BridgeStreet Accomodations, Inc..	26,061,774
Global Maintech Corporation	25,773,156
Encore Medical Corporation	25,129,500
Let's Talk Cellular & Wireless, Inc..	25,111,817
Thermo Vision Corporation	25,110,621

$24,999,999 - $10,000,000

Command Systems, Inc..	24,884,438
Diagnostic Health Services, Inc..	24,798,174
Tidel Technologies, Inc.	24,742,330
National Home Health Care Corp..	24,699,368
Autologic Information International, Inc..	24,598,873
Diodes Incorporated	24,580,044
Acme Electric Corporation.	23,991,039
ML Macadamia Orchards, L.P..	23,925,000
Total Research Corporation	23,571,243
IRIDEX Corporation	23,551,756
Safety 1st, Inc.	23,501,147
Interlink Electronics, Inc.	23,472,000
Disc Graphics, Inc..	23,453,251
Movie Star, Inc.	22,869,540
Birner Dental Management Services, Inc..	22,831,211
Suprema Specialties, Inc.	22,540,232
Golden Genesis Company	22,469,052
Manchester Equipment Co., Inc..	22,266,750
Integrity Incorporated	22,221,420
Wegener Corporation.	21,999,093
Great Lakes Aviation, Ltd..	21,992,558
United-Guardian, Inc.	21,974,126
Flour City International, Inc..	21,936,387
Monterey Pasta Company	21,897,013
Janus American Group, Inc.	21,727,730
Digital Solutions, Inc.	21,679,653
Boundless Corporation.	21,569,230
Esquire Communications Ltd.	21,461,092
Consolidated Delivery & Logistics, Inc..	21,260,725
Dynatronics Corporation	21,118,358
Nastech Pharmaceutical Company Inc.	21,107,589
GameTech International, Inc.	21,084,359
Hawker Pacific Aerospace	21,076,444
Westminster Capital, Inc..	21,076,150
AMBI Inc.	20,898,297
Blimpie International, Inc..	20,822,520
Signature Eyewear, Inc.	20,784,508
Questron Technology, Inc..	20,616,135
NewCare Health Corporation	20,497,206
Reliv International, Inc.	20,465,424
BTU International, Inc..	20,420,289
McNaughton Apparel Group Inc.	20,389,680
Synbiotics Corporation.	20,120,240

Edac Technologies Corporation	19,688,500
Innovative Valve Technologies, Inc..	19,619,061
Spanlink Communications, Inc.	19,451,151
AlphaNet Solutions, Inc.	19,098,684
TENERA, Inc.	18,941,984
Nathan's Famous, Inc.	18,888,864
Oralabs Holding Corp.	18,833,383
Aasche Transportation Services, Inc.	18,784,520
Unidigital Inc.	18,771,670
RMS Titanic, Inc.	18,765,468
R.H. Phillips, Inc.	18,746,355
Universal American Financial Corp..	18,407,717
HMG Worldwide Corporation	18,378,534
Mesa Laboratories, Inc.	18,209,495
Travel Ports of America, Inc.	18,088,451
Paravant Computer Systems, Inc.	18,022,884
BioSpecifics Technologies Corp.	17,959,860
Sight Resource Corporation	17,811,460
Ithaca Industries, Inc.	17,500,000
Jerry's Famous Deli, Inc..	17,265,593
Cell Robotics International, Inc.	17,252,475
RMH Teleservices, Inc.	17,214,400
Hi-Tech Pharmacal Co., Inc..	16,921,875
PTI Holding Inc.	16,702,906
Capital Associates, Inc.	16,649,750
Berger Holdings, Ltd.	16,540,150
Unapix Entertainment, Inc..	16,457,850
Laser Technology, Inc..	16,232,291
SETECH, Inc.	16,214,100
Scherer Healthcare, Inc.	16,184,096
XeTel Corporation	16,174,884
All American Semiconductor, Inc..	16,092,194
DenAmerica Corp..	16,047,480
Holiday RV Superstores, Incorporated.	16,013,526
Financial Performance Corporation	16,006,892
Rotonics Manufacturing Inc..	15,806,361
Millbrook Press Inc. (The)	15,754,800
Measurement Specialties, Inc.	15,654,594
FTI Consulting, Inc.	15,541,159
Triple S Plastics, Inc..	15,416,838
ERC Industries, Inc.	15,399,032
Ceramics Process Systems Corporation	15,357,461
Coast Distribution System (The).	15,153,181
Business Resource Group	15,071,334
BCT International, Inc..	14,954,820
Fiberstars, Inc..	14,822,254
Kinark Corporation.	14,820,913
Calprop Corporation	14,809,154
Emons Transportation Group, Inc..	14,737,139
SofTech, Inc..	14,669,752
Riviera Tool Company	14,561,120
Tanknology-NDE International, Inc..	14,559,485
Casa Ole' Restaurants, Inc.	14,390,820
GZA GeoEnvironmental Technologies, Inc..	14,290,242
Circuit Systems, Inc..	14,280,780
Jaco Electronics, Inc..	14,266,355
Jennifer Convertibles, Inc..	14,251,813
UFP Technologies, Inc.	14,122,062
First Montauk Financial Corp..	14,114,150
Napco Security Systems, Inc.	13,958,604
Grill Concepts, Inc..	13,933,531
Atlantic Premium Brands, Ltd..	13,861,530
Security National Financial Corporation.	13,657,071

Comprehensive Care Corporation	13,456,684
THT Inc.	13,182,423
Healthcare Imaging Services, Inc.	13,174,090
GlobeNet International I, Inc.	13,030,473
Writer Corporation (The)	13,007,050
DMI Furniture, Inc.	12,882,563
Interwest Home Medical, Inc.	12,757,770
Arrow-Magnolia International, Inc.	12,695,062
Environmental Safeguards, Inc.	12,615,555
Canterbury Park Holding Corporation	12,443,088
Eagle Pacific Industries, Inc.	12,407,515
Farrel Corporation	12,235,341
Winston Resources, Inc.	12,202,297
Littlefield, Adams & Company	12,192,549
Oakridge Energy, Inc.	12,179,023
Centrum Industries, Inc.	12,101,041
International Airline Support Group, Inc.	11,839,522
Intelligent Controls, Inc.	11,719,197
Kentucky Electric Steel, Inc.	11,682,425
Endogen, Inc.	11,602,243
Canyon Resources Corporation	11,534,275
Frontier Adjusters of America, Inc.	11,513,395
Overseas Filmgroup, Inc.	11,465,556
Rag Shops, Inc.	11,286,000
ACR Group, Inc.	11,272,058
Exigent International, Inc.	11,233,880
MicroFrame, Inc.	11,201,493
Met-Coil Systems Corporation	11,187,565
Aerovox Incorporated	11,110,035
Mentortech Inc.	11,092,445
SI Technologies, Inc.	11,067,024
George Risk Industries, Inc.	10,957,935
Cumberland Technologies, Inc.	10,889,916
Educational Insights, Inc.	10,771,200
Rankin Automotive Group, Inc.	10,747,950
Meteor Industries, Inc.	10,681,925
National Environmental Service Co.	10,638,943
Pharmaceutical Formulations, Inc.	10,588,662
Everest Medical Corporation	10,526,884
Techdyne, Inc.	10,500,334
PDK Labs Inc.	10,376,181
Continental Information Systems Corporation	10,200,418
Hahn Automotive Warehouse, Inc.	10,059,430
Miami Subs Corporation	10,034,156

$9,999,999 - $5,000,000

Mercury Waste Solutions, Inc.	9,987,878
Tekgraf, Inc.	9,872,196
Sunair Electronics, Inc.	9,841,427
First American Health Concepts, Inc.	9,771,644
Electric & Gas Technology, Inc.	9,755,887
Jenna Lane, Inc.	9,741,726
I.C.H. Corporation	9,653,146
Kids Stuff, Inc.	9,449,583
Orbit International Corp.	9,405,000
Taitron Components Incorporated	9,392,223
Command Security Corporation	9,295,710
Chicago Pizza & Brewery, Inc.	9,227,982
Norton Drilling Services, Inc.	9,227,180
Arthur Treacher's, Inc.	9,219,244
White Electronic Designs Corporation	9,144,739

HealthStar Corp.	9,135,051
Lincoln Snacks Company	9,117,778
Bradley Pharmaceuticals, Inc.	9,077,834
Sierra Monitor Corporation	8,883,746
CCA Industries, Inc.	8,856,689
Ronson Corporation	8,600,312
Back Yard Burgers, Inc.	8,595,401
Provena Foods Inc.	8,564,508
BAB Holdings, Inc.	8,552,510
Advantage Marketing Systems, Inc.	8,530,489
Multigraphics, Inc.	8,488,578
Diehl Graphsoft, Inc.	8,467,144
Willamette Valley Vineyards, Inc.	8,465,362
ILX Resorts Incorporated	8,464,933
Joule Inc.	8,257,500
Stearns & Lehman, Inc.	8,181,663
K2 Design, Inc.	8,168,364
Farmstead Telephone Group, Inc.	8,161,448
Fotoball USA, Inc.	8,097,726
Nortech Systems Incorporated	8,088,737
AML Communications, Inc.	8,053,670
Allied Devices Corporation	8,015,666
Sparta Foods, Inc.	7,881,633
Hitox Corporation of America	7,871,153
EA Engineering, Science, and Technology, Inc.	7,856,250
InterSystems, Inc.	7,828,000
Kreisler Manufacturing Corporation	7,826,453
Carlyle Industries, Inc.	7,825,749
SigmaTron International, Inc.	7,750,501
Coda Music Technology, Inc.	7,743,415
Guardian International, Inc.	7,741,672
Solomon-Page Group Ltd. (The)	7,681,923
Hytek Microsystems, Inc.	7,599,395
ASA International Ltd.	7,534,040
Luxtec Corporation	7,513,091
Advanced Photonix, Inc.	7,478,399
Allstar Systems, Inc.	7,406,369
Health Fitness Corporation	7,368,336
Nicholas Financial, Inc.	7,353,881
Tapistron International, Inc.	7,304,978
ChoiceTel Communications, Inc.	7,287,515
DeVlieg-Bullard, Inc.	7,277,591
Retrospettiva, Inc.	7,250,000
Bio-Reference Laboratories, Inc.	7,212,910
Advanced Tobacco Products, Inc.	6,797,394
Foilmark, Inc.	6,770,954
Saratoga Beverage Group, Inc.	6,590,134
NBI, Inc.	6,551,539
Medicore, Inc.	6,550,589
RF Industries, Ltd.	6,526,628
Abatix Environmental Corp.	6,522,632
Technology Research Corporation	6,505,737
B.B. Walker Company	6,453,578
Streicher Mobile Fueling, Inc.	6,437,500
Aero Systems Engineering, Inc.	6,338,460
Reconditioned Systems, Inc.	6,308,506
Intellectual Technology, Inc.	6,200,001
Amistar Corporation	6,178,905
Burke Mills, Inc.	6,167,628
Calloway's Nursery, Inc.	6,143,978
JLM Couture, Inc.	6,134,029
Westwood Corporation	5,995,733
Vicon Fiber Optics Corp.	5,988,558

REXX Environmental Corporation	5,848,155
Lexington Precision Corporation	5,840,359
Lannett Company, Inc.	5,830,863
Isomet Corporation	5,782,770
Micronetics Wireless, Inc.	5,771,854
Pioneer Railcorp	5,763,246
Strategic Capital Resources, Inc.	5,720,248
Telecomm Industries Corp.	5,697,133
Firecom, Inc.	5,671,866
Nitches, Inc.	5,653,804
Hemagen Diagnostics, Inc.	5,574,842
Armanino Foods of Distinction, Inc.	5,570,491
Productivity Technologies Corp.	5,567,500
S2 Golf Inc.	5,548,283
MobiNetix Systems, Inc.	5,494,640
Arizona Instrument Corporation	5,478,862
Optelecom, Inc.	5,391,393
Tofutti Brands Inc.	5,379,703
CREDO Petroleum Corporation	5,302,500
Seven J Stock Farm, Inc.	5,252,620
PDG Environmental, Inc.	5,244,274
Rent-A-Wreck of America, Inc.	5,237,115
Creative Host Services, Inc.	5,201,873
Phoenix Gold International, Inc.	5,197,118
Advanced Deposition Technologies, Inc.	5,189,819
ATS Money Systems, Inc.	5,150,643
T.J.T., Inc.	5,134,462
Puroflow Incorporated	5,118,351
Moyco Technologies, Inc.	5,097,819
Top Air Manufacturing, Inc.	5,083,456
QC Optics, Inc.	5,058,300
Worksafe Industries Inc.	5,049,237
Prab, Inc.	5,043,563
Westerbeke Corporation	5,024,667
Mikron Instrument Company, Inc.	5,006,254

Under $5,000,000

Interfoods of America, Inc.	4,966,893
Ag-Bag International Limited	4,945,416
New Horizon Kids Quest, Inc.	4,939,950
Goddard Industries, Inc.	4,920,258
Optimumcare Corporation	4,913,515
EXX INC	4,850,802
Polymer Research Corp. of America	4,838,200
EFI Electronics Corporation	4,789,040
Texas Equipment Corporation	4,716,714
L.A. T Sportswear, Inc.	4,704,001
Netter Digital Entertainment, Inc.	4,701,511
FiberCore, Inc.	4,671,740
CAS Medical Systems, Inc.	4,664,639
Cistron Biotechnology, Inc.	4,596,737
Image Systems Corporation	4,586,175
Industrial Services of America, Inc.	4,341,600
Simtek Corporation	4,311,784
Touchstone Applied Science Associates, Inc.	4,283,611
Butler National Corporation	4,141,266
Microfluidics International Corporation	3,970,284
Cohesant Technologies Inc.	3,900,544
Alfa Leisure, Inc.	3,810,171
TMS, Inc.	3,760,694
Oakridge Holdings, Inc.	3,758,753

AM Communications, Inc.	3,728,676
Jetronic Industries, Inc.	3,604,499
Canisco Resources, Inc.	3,589,175
Tone Products, Inc.	3,579,612
PREMIS Corporation	3,535,633
All Communications Corporation	3,387,900
Cable Link, Inc.	3,378,272
Dynamic Homes, Inc.	3,361,380
Farm Fish, Inc.	3,360,756
HemaCare Corporation	3,349,315
Colonial Commercial Corp.	3,335,759
Computer Research, Inc.	3,270,177
Bristol Retail Solutions, Inc.	3,247,944
Tel-Instrument Electronics Corp.	3,142,103
FAFCO, Inc.	3,105,112
Smith-Midland Corporation	3,044,798
Hydromer, Inc.	3,013,911
Superior Supplements, Inc.	3,000,000
Shopsmith, Inc.	2,939,300
R-B Rubber Products, Inc.	2,933,309
Comtrex Systems Corporation	2,902,693
Network Six, Inc.	2,867,486
Hadron, Inc.	2,805,769
Kyzen Corporation	2,803,797
New York Health Care, Inc.	2,781,023
Sel-Leb Marketing, Inc.	2,722,708
Telebyte Technology, Inc.	2,635,966
Bontex, Inc.	2,547,975
Micropac Industries, Inc.	2,539,006
RADVA Corporation	2,533,151
Mendocino Brewing Company, Inc.	2,518,353
Amtech Systems, Inc.	2,490,158
CareAdvantage, Inc.	2,465,696
Glassmaster Company	2,441,844
Athanor Group, Inc.	2,421,698
Sel-Drum International, Inc.	2,369,175
Sandata, Inc.	2,246,615
Big Sky Transportation Co.	2,148,816
InterWest Medical Corporation	2,129,349
Bingo & Gaming International, Inc.	2,106,250
Champion Parts, Inc.	2,010,396
Sonics & Materials, Inc.	1,971,256
SYS	1,952,081
Laser Master International, Inc.	1,910,768
Sarnia Corporation	1,874,743
International Electronics, Inc.	1,866,626
Wiltek, Inc.	1,829,300
Reflectix, Inc.	1,795,493
Bollinger Industries, Inc.	1,760,092
Seventh Generation, Inc.	1,748,730
Logitek, Inc.	1,691,430
Eldorado Artesian Springs, Inc.	1,671,155
Electronic Tele-Communications, Inc.	1,555,547
Cambridge Holdings, Ltd.	1,529,280
Fairmount Chemical Co., Inc.	1,492,716
Scientific Industries, Inc.	1,460,501
Accuhealth, Inc.	1,458,906
Astrex, Inc.	1,450,673
Coeur d'Alenes Company (The)	1,391,088
Electronic Systems Technology, Inc.	1,387,027
Milastar Corporation	1,369,132
Dynamic International, Ltd.	1,325,477
Tivoli Industries, Inc.	1,306,916

Publishers Equipment Corporation	1,255,063
Avesis Incorporated	1,238,627
Creative Technologies Corp.	1,155,560
Tubby's, Inc.	1,136,570
Metal Arts Company, Inc. (The)	1,128,120
Texas Vanguard Oil Company	1,062,815
ZEON Corporation	960,127
Z-Axis Corporation	946,250
HIA, Inc.	908,875
Boonton Electronics Corporation	838,594
Sono-Tek Corporation	699,902
MileMarker International, Inc.	641,061
Quality Products, Inc.	575,926
Miller Diversified Corporation	509,171
CPT Holdings, Inc.	468,126
Compare Generiks, Inc.	466,800
American Consumers, Inc.	460,754
Tufco International, Inc.	417,948
Celox Laboratories, Inc.	246,975

¢ ¢

This page intentionally left blank.

Over 20%	

Sono-Tek Corporation	212.45
Littlefield, Adams & Company	151.71
Calprop Corporation	95.72
Pharmaceutical Formulations, Inc.	90.37
PDG Environmental, Inc.	81.93
Met-Coil Systems Corporation	79.08
Great Lakes Aviation, Ltd.	78.03
Tel-Instrument Electronics Corp.	76.26
International Airline Support Group, Inc.	73.22
Financial Performance Corporation	71.26
Bollinger Industries, Inc.	70.49
AM Communications, Inc.	68.54
InterDigital Communications Corporation	64.68
RMS Titanic, Inc.	58.56
Alfa Leisure, Inc.	56.37
Emons Transportation Group, Inc.	54.42
Luxtec Corporation	47.29
Reconditioned Systems, Inc.	46.75
TENERA, Inc.	43.74
Digital Solutions, Inc.	42.41
Avesis Incorporated	42.36
InterWest Medical Corporation	40.31
MTR Gaming Group, Inc.	40.14
Tidel Technologies, Inc.	39.30
Colonial Commercial Corp.	38.99
Shopsmith, Inc.	38.05
SYS	37.71
Memry Corporation	37.01
RADVA Corporation	36.66
Bayou Steel Corporation	35.65
Bingo & Gaming International, Inc.	34.62
Vermont Pure Holdings, Ltd.	34.43
Hytek Microsystems, Inc.	34.25
FAFCO, Inc.	34.15
American Dental Technologies, Inc.	33.99
Go-Video, Inc.	33.82
Oralabs Holding Corp.	33.56
Prab, Inc.	33.54
PlayCore, Inc.	33.32
International Electronics, Inc.	32.68
Scherer Healthcare, Inc.	31.69
NewCom, Inc.	31.60
Network Six, Inc.	31.37
Gentner Communications Corporation	31.08
Boundless Corporation	30.61
BLC Financial Services, Inc.	30.07
National Environmental Service Co.	29.84
Kreisler Manufacturing Corporation	29.51
K2 Design, Inc.	29.09
Monterey Pasta Company.	28.96
Capital Title Group, Inc.	28.88
Winston Resources, Inc.	28.82
Guess ?, Inc.	28.58
Everest Medical Corporation	28.37
Tofutti Brands Inc.	28.28
Edac Technologies Corporation.	27.64
Fairmount Chemical Co., Inc.	27.42
Candie's, Inc.	27.25
Movie Star, Inc.	26.29
HemaCare Corporation	26.17

Adams Golf, Inc.	25.92
Total Research Corporation.	25.78
Advanced Tobacco Products, Inc.	25.56
Consumer Portfolio Services, Inc.	25.49
Elantec Semiconductor, Inc.	25.25
I.C.H. Corporation	25.21
International Total Services, Inc.	24.80
HMG Worldwide Corporation	24.51
Wiltek, Inc.	24.16
Saratoga Beverage Group, Inc.	23.74
Provena Foods Inc.	23.70
Logitek, Inc.	23.58
Flour City International, Inc.	23.49
Consolidated Delivery & Logistics, Inc.	23.09
Rent-A-Wreck of America, Inc.	23.07
George Risk Industries, Inc.	23.02
Orbit International Corp.	23.01
Disc Graphics, Inc.	22.87
Tufco International, Inc.	22.21
Arrow-Magnolia International, Inc.	21.91
Tangram Enterprise Solutions, Inc.	21.78
Horizon Offshore, Inc.	21.76
ROHN Industries, Inc.	21.50
Isomet Corporation	21.48
Wade Cook Financial Corporation	21.00
CAS Medical Systems, Inc.	20.76
Abatix Environmental Corp.	20.54
Westminster Capital, Inc.	20.16
Reliv International, Inc.	20.08

20 - 10%	

THT Inc.	19.90
Moyco Technologies, Inc.	19.84
Friedman Industries, Incorporated	19.83
Mesa Laboratories, Inc.	19.80
Hydromer, Inc.	19.71
MicroFrame, Inc.	19.56
Riviera Tool Company	18.79
Healthcare Imaging Services, Inc.	18.67
Seattle FilmWorks, Inc.	18.63
Halter Marine Group, Inc.	18.43
United-Guardian, Inc.	18.01
Argosy Gaming Company	17.85
ATS Money Systems, Inc.	17.61
Tone Products, Inc.	17.51
Eagle Food Centers, Inc.	17.28
LaBarge, Inc.	17.27
First Alliance Corporation	17.14
Canisco Resources, Inc.	16.98
Cade Industries, Inc.	16.84
DMI Furniture, Inc.	16.80
Fortress Group, Inc. (The)	16.66
Hi-Rise Recycling Systems, Inc.	16.60
Interwest Home Medical, Inc.	16.60
Kaneb Services, Inc.	16.37
Eldorado Artesian Springs, Inc.	16.34
Wegener Corporation	16.24
Goddard Industries, Inc.	16.14
Paravant Computer Systems, Inc.	15.83
Casa Ole' Restaurants, Inc.	15.60
Todd Shipyards Corporation	15.47

Lincoln Snacks Company.	15.46
Integrity Incorporated.	15.34
BCT International, Inc.	15.31
MIM Corporation.	15.29
Measurement Specialties, Inc.	15.20
Cache, Inc.	15.18
Collins Industries, Inc.	15.09
Cohesant Technologies Inc..	14.99
Signature Eyewear, Inc..	14.97
ZEON Corporation	14.94
SofTech, Inc.	14.81
NBI, Inc.	14.80
RF Industries, Ltd.	14.69
Eagle Pacific Industries, Inc.	14.60
Aero Systems Engineering, Inc.	14.52
Big Sky Transportation Co..	14.46
HIA, Inc.	14.30
Athanor Group, Inc..	14.26
Top Air Manufacturing, Inc.	14.25
Acme Electric Corporation	14.22
PTI Holding Inc.	14.13
Questron Technology, Inc.	14.06
Nicholas Financial, Inc..	14.04
Centrum Industries, Inc.	13.84
JLM Couture, Inc..	13.69
Meteor Industries, Inc.	13.62
Sparta Foods, Inc..	13.62
Horizon Medical Products, Inc..	13.53
Travel Ports of America, Inc..	13.47
Intelligent Controls, Inc.	13.33
U.S. Home & Garden Inc.	13.23
Puroflow Incorporated	13.17
Back Yard Burgers, Inc.	13.10
Micronetics Wireless, Inc.	12.98
Stearns & Lehman, Inc..	12.90
Texas Equipment Corporation	12.86
Milastar Corporation	12.84
Allied Devices Corporation.	12.77
Swank, Inc.	12.62
Optimumcare Corporation	12.57
Spectrum Control, Inc.	12.43
Dynatronics Corporation	12.42
Blimpie International, Inc.	12.38
TMS, Inc.	12.24
Sizzler International, Inc.	12.20
Equivest Finance, Inc.	12.19
Telebyte Technology, Inc.	12.15
Berger Holdings, Ltd..	12.14
R.H. Phillips, Inc.	12.12
ACR Group, Inc.	12.07
InterSystems, Inc..	12.05
S2 Golf Inc..	11.82
Oakridge Holdings, Inc.	11.80
AMBI Inc..	11.75
Hi-Tech Pharmacal Co., Inc.	11.69
Writer Corporation (The).	11.62
CCA Industries, Inc.	11.33
Safety 1st, Inc.	11.32
Diehl Graphsoft, Inc.	11.30
Petroleum Development Corporation.	11.24
Business Resource Group.	11.20
Synergy Brands, Inc.	11.19
L.A. T Sportswear, Inc..	11.15

Pioneer Railcorp	11.14
GlobeNet International I, Inc..	11.11
FTI Consulting, Inc.	11.02
DCI Telecommunications, Inc.	10.99
UFP Technologies, Inc..	10.97
Marlton Technologies, Inc.	10.93
TBA Entertainment Corporation	10.85
Joule Inc.	10.80
Fotoball USA, Inc.	10.72
Firecom, Inc.	10.68
NovaCare,Inc..	10.64
Astrex, Inc.	10.41
Cable Link, Inc..	10.35
Diodes Incorporated	10.30
HealthStar Corp.	10.16
Hitox Corporation of America	10.15
Scientific Industries, Inc.	10.14
Norton Drilling Services, Inc.	10.07
Mercury Waste Solutions, Inc.	10.06
Holiday RV Superstores, Incorporated	10.05
Solomon-Page Group Ltd. (The)	10.05
Sel-Drum International, Inc.	10.02

10 - 0%

Creative Host Services, Inc..	9.92
Orleans Homebuilders, Inc.	9.88
Comtrex Systems Corporation	9.67
Universal American Financial Corp.	9.65
Unidigital Inc..	9.52
Retrospettiva, Inc..	9.51
Raytel Medical Corporation.	9.49
Farmstead Telephone Group, Inc.	9.43
SI Technologies, Inc.	9.42
Frontier Adjusters of America, Inc.	9.41
Encore Medical Corporation	9.39
Texas Vanguard Oil Company.	9.37
GameTech International, Inc.	9.35
Simtek Corporation	9.32
Ag-Bag International Limited.	9.28
Hawaiian Airlines, Inc.	9.23
Big Dog Holdings, Inc.	9.09
BioSpecifics Technologies Corp.	9.08
Applied Cellular Technology, Inc..	9.03
Coeur d'Alenes Company (The)	8.87
Pacific Aerospace & Electronics, Inc..	8.84
Suprema Specialties, Inc.	8.79
Farrel Corporation.	8.74
Bull Run Corporation	8.61
Laser Technology, Inc..	8.46
Techdyne, Inc.	8.41
EXX INC	8.36
Spanlink Communications, Inc..	8.26
G-III Apparel Group, Ltd..	8.17
Hahn Automotive Warehouse, Inc.	8.02
Sierra Monitor Corporation	7.99
Publishers Equipment Corporation	7.97
Miller Industries, Inc.	7.94
Computer Research, Inc.	7.89
Polymer Research Corp. of America	7.85
Ithaca Industries, Inc.	7.63
Dynamic Homes, Inc.	7.61

Sunair Electronics, Inc.	0.31
ILX Resorts Incorporated	0.29
Diamond Home Services, Inc.	0.25
Advanced Photonix, Inc.	0.20
CompuCom Systems, Inc.	0.19
Hemagen Diagnostics, Inc.	0.10
Nitches, Inc.	0.03

Under 0%

Patterson Energy, Inc.	-0.21
SITEL Corporation	-0.68
Willamette Valley Vineyards, Inc.	-1.02
Jerry's Famous Deli, Inc.	-1.05
Impac Mortgage Holdings, Inc.	-1.06
Tubby's, Inc.	-1.19
Let's Talk Cellular & Wireless, Inc.	-1.32
Strategic Distribution, Inc.	-1.52
Technology Research Corporation	-1.64
McNaughton Apparel Group Inc.	-1.71
R-B Rubber Products, Inc.	-1.81
Strategic Capital Resources, Inc.	-1.96
Kids Stuff, Inc.	-1.98
Innovative Valve Technologies, Inc.	-2.04
Gristede's Sloan's, Inc.	-2.56
Mobile America Corporation	-2.62
Esquire Communications Ltd.	-2.64
Miller Diversified Corporation	-2.89
Capital Pacific Holdings, Inc.	-3.37
Nastech Pharmaceutical Company Inc.	-3.47
EKCO Group, Inc.	-3.60
Calloway's Nursery, Inc.	-3.80
Cambridge Holdings, Ltd.	-3.80
ERC Industries, Inc.	-3.83
Cistron Biotechnology, Inc.	-4.20
Interfoods of America, Inc.	-4.23
Synbiotics Corporation	-4.63
Superior Energy Services, Inc.	-4.79
Circuit Systems, Inc.	-4.80
Weirton Steel Corporation	-4.82
Sight Resource Corporation	-5.13
Bontex, Inc.	-5.57
Cumberland Technologies, Inc.	-5.66
American Residential Services, Inc.	-5.90
Sonics & Materials, Inc.	-5.97
Rankin Automotive Group, Inc.	-6.01
MileMarker International, Inc.	-6.45
Phoenix Gold International, Inc.	-7.11
Rehabilicare Inc.	-7.21
Tapistron International, Inc.	-7.61
Worldtex, Inc.	-7.81
Allstar Systems, Inc.	-8.01
Amtech Systems, Inc.	-8.82
Environmental Safeguards, Inc.	-9.39
Emerson Radio Corp.	-9.54
Streicher Mobile Fueling, Inc.	-10.11
REXX Environmental Corporation	-10.14
Educational Insights, Inc.	-10.19
Compare Generiks, Inc.	-11.30
FARO Technologies, Inc.	-11.70
Worksafe Industries Inc.	-11.79
Command Systems, Inc.	-11.89

JB Oxford Holdings, Inc.	-11.96
Westwood Corporation	-12.22
Golden Genesis Company	-13.10
Accuhealth, Inc.	-13.40
Industrial Services of America, Inc.	-13.87
Mendocino Brewing Company, Inc.	-14.33
Ronson Corporation	-14.42
Comstock Resources, Inc.	-14.66
Tivoli Industries, Inc.	-14.87
Drypers Corporation	-15.31
Mentortech Inc.	-15.89
Continental Information Systems Corporation	-16.91
Hawker Pacific Aerospace	-17.80
All Communications Corporation	-17.86
Microfluidics International Corporation	-19.34
Judge Group, Inc. (The)	-20.74
Productivity Technologies Corp.	-21.62
Coda Music Technology, Inc.	-24.02
Canyon Resources Corporation	-24.04
Guardian International, Inc.	-24.14
Westmoreland Coal Company	-26.07
Celox Laboratories, Inc.	-26.41
EcoScience Corporation	-27.05
FiberCore, Inc.	-27.26
Waterlink, Inc.	-27.84
DeVlieg-Bullard, Inc.	-28.40
Bristol Retail Solutions, Inc.	-28.74
Grill Concepts, Inc.	-30.01
Response Oncology, Inc.	-30.15
Advanced Deposition Technologies, Inc.	-31.04
Apple Orthodontix, Inc.	-31.70
Genelabs Technologies, Inc.	-32.22
Telecomm Industries Corp.	-34.35
First Montauk Financial Corp.	-42.25
Global Maintech Corporation	-45.92
Smith-Midland Corporation	-47.20
HEARx Ltd.	-60.84
Optelecom, Inc.	-61.85
MobiNetix Systems, Inc.	-66.39
PREMIS Corporation	-78.25
Command Security Corporation	-90.56
Seventh Generation, Inc.	-91.60
Arthur Treacher's, Inc.	-96.04
Health Fitness Corporation	-101.41
Diagnostic Health Services, Inc.	-126.99
Cell Robotics International, Inc.	-142.98
Selfcare, Inc.	-183.65
NewCare Health Corporation	-217.14
Sunshine Mining and Refining Company	-479.80
Frontier Airlines, Inc.	-843.11

¢ ¢

Digital Solutions, Inc.	8.00
Nicholas Financial, Inc.	8.00
Wegener Corporation	8.00
Bernard Chaus, Inc.	8.04
Hitox Corporation of America	8.05
Canisco Resources, Inc.	8.10
Guess ?, Inc.	8.15
Disc Graphics, Inc.	8.17
Kentucky Electric Steel, Inc.	8.19
Great Lakes Aviation, Ltd.	8.26
Napco Security Systems, Inc.	8.33
New York Health Care, Inc.	8.33
ZEON Corporation	8.33
Reconditioned Systems, Inc.	8.39
Diehl Graphsoft, Inc.	8.41
Blimpie International, Inc.	8.42
Westerbeke Corporation	8.45
Swank, Inc.	8.68
Hi-Rise Recycling Systems, Inc.	8.78
Dynamic Homes, Inc.	8.82
UFP Technologies, Inc.	8.82
Interwest Home Medical, Inc.	8.91
Ceramics Process Systems Corporation	8.93
PlayCore, Inc.	8.94
Cache, Inc.	9.00
Monterey Pasta Company	9.00
Mesa Laboratories, Inc.	9.04
ATS Money Systems, Inc.	9.10
LaBarge, Inc.	9.17
Consolidated Delivery & Logistics, Inc.	9.18
Edac Technologies Corporation	9.24
Electronic Systems Technology, Inc.	9.33
Unilab Corporation	9.48
Acme Electric Corporation	9.50
Dynamex Inc.	9.52
Travel Ports of America, Inc.	9.57
Pentacon, Inc.	9.58
Triple S Plastics, Inc.	9.58
Aero Systems Engineering, Inc.	9.60
Centrum Industries, Inc.	9.60
Firecom, Inc.	9.60
Hahn Automotive Warehouse, Inc.	9.64
Holiday RV Superstores, Incorporated.	9.65
Scientific Industries, Inc.	9.72
Diodes Incorporated	9.74
Hi-Tech Pharmacal Co., Inc.	9.87
Autologic Information International, Inc.	9.88
Tandycrafts, Inc.	9.97

10 - 20

Business Resource Group	10.00
Dynamic International, Ltd.	10.00
TransCoastal Marine Services, Inc.	10.03
BCT International, Inc.	10.04
SofTech, Inc.	10.04
Meteor Industries, Inc.	10.06
Collins Industries, Inc.	10.10
RF Industries, Ltd.	10.10
Kaneb Services, Inc.	10.15
Puroflow Incorporated.	10.29
HMG Worldwide Corporation.	10.37

Candie's, Inc.	10.42
Spectrum Control, Inc.	10.42
Manchester Equipment Co., Inc.	10.58
R.H. Phillips, Inc.	10.63
Solomon-Page Group Ltd. (The)	10.71
Creative Host Services, Inc.	10.80
Tofutti Brands Inc.	10.88
Norton Drilling Services, Inc.	11.00
SI Technologies, Inc.	11.14
Southland Corporation (The)	11.24
GameTech International, Inc.	11.25
Retrospettiva, Inc.	11.36
Cade Industries, Inc.	11.37
Seattle FilmWorks, Inc.	11.49
GZA GeoEnvironmental Technologies, Inc.	11.59
Healthcare Imaging Services, Inc.	11.60
Capital Associates, Inc.	11.61
AML Communications, Inc.	11.64
Ithaca Industries, Inc.	11.67
TENERA, Inc.	11.69
Marlton Technologies, Inc.	11.77
T.J.T., Inc.	11.78
JLM Couture, Inc.	11.82
Joule Inc.	11.84
Bradley Pharmaceuticals, Inc.	11.90
Rag Shops, Inc.	11.90
Argosy Gaming Company.	11.96
Arrow-Magnolia International, Inc.	11.97
G-III Apparel Group, Ltd.	12.03
ROHN Industries, Inc.	12.04
Universal American Financial Corp.	12.05
Sunrise International Leasing Corporation	12.07
Big Sky Transportation Co.	12.13
Sizzler International, Inc.	12.16
Jaco Electronics, Inc.	12.30
Go-Video, Inc.	12.48
EA Engineering, Science, and Technology, Inc.	12.50
ICT Group, Inc.	12.50
Nathan's Famous, Inc.	12.50
Stearns & Lehman, Inc.	12.50
Integrity Incorporated	12.59
Berger Holdings, Ltd.	13.00
Micronetics Wireless, Inc.	13.00
TBA Entertainment Corporation	13.09
S2 Golf Inc.	13.16
MIM Corporation	13.23
ACR Group, Inc.	13.25
Reliv International, Inc.	13.25
Gundle/SLT Environmental, Inc.	13.33
Techdyne, Inc.	13.33
Aldila, Inc.	13.39
Computer Research, Inc.	13.50
IRI International Corporation	13.52
BTU International, Inc.	13.64
Fotoball USA, Inc.	13.64
Optimumcare Corporation.	13.83
Pioneer Railcorp.	13.89
Rent-A-Wreck of America, Inc.	13.89
IRIDEX Corporation	13.92
Advanced Tobacco Products, Inc.	14.00
Lannett Company, Inc.	14.00
Sparta Foods, Inc.	14.00
Bio-Reference Laboratories, Inc.	14.29

Randers Killam Group Inc. (The)	14.67
Farmstead Telephone Group, Inc.	14.71
SigmaTron International, Inc.	14.94
BLC Financial Services, Inc.	15.00
Simtek Corporation	15.00
Big Dog Holdings, Inc.	15.22
Orleans Homebuilders, Inc.	15.40
Paravant Computer Systems, Inc.	15.43
Intelligent Controls, Inc.	15.80
CREDO Petroleum Corporation	15.91
Unidigital Inc.	16.03
Encore Medical Corporation	16.18
Suprema Specialties, Inc.	16.47
MicroFrame, Inc.	16.50
EMCON	16.79
Security National Financial Corporation	17.00
Hawaiian Airlines, Inc.	17.11
Government Technology Services, Inc.	17.42
BAB Holdings, Inc.	17.67
BridgeStreet Accomodations, Inc.	17.72
Fiberstars, Inc.	17.86
Sel-Leb Marketing, Inc.	17.86
Foilmark, Inc.	18.00
Cable Link, Inc.	18.18
Miller Industries, Inc.	18.30
Miami Subs Corporation	18.50
PDK Labs Inc.	18.75
Vermont Pure Holdings, Ltd.	19.00
Sports Club Company, Inc. (The)	19.05
Polymer Research Corp. of America	19.13
Memry Corporation	19.21
Frontier Adjusters of America, Inc.	19.23
Janus American Group, Inc.	19.23
Flanders Corporation	19.35
U.S. Home & Garden Inc.	19.54
Equivest Finance, Inc.	20.00
InterSystems, Inc.	20.00

Over 20

All American Semiconductor, Inc.	20.25
Movie Star, Inc.	20.25
ASA International Ltd.	20.45
Sarnia Corporation.	20.50
Image Systems Corporation	20.60
National Home Health Care Corp.	20.65
Eldorado Artesian Springs, Inc.	20.67
Measurement Specialties, Inc.	20.81
Cylink Corporation	20.83
Glassmaster Company	21.43
United-Guardian, Inc.	21.43
Gentner Communications Corporation	21.50
Laser Technology, Inc.	21.67
BioSpecifics Technologies Corp.	22.06
Total Research Corporation	22.50
Horizon Medical Products, Inc.	22.76
Advantage Marketing Systems, Inc.	22.89
Jenna Lane, Inc.	22.89
Oralabs Holding Corp.	22.89
Applied Innovation Inc.	23.00
Charming Shoppes, Inc.	23.28
Electric & Gas Technology, Inc.	23.80

Millbrook Press Inc. (The)	24.00
Thermo TerraTech Inc.	24.28
Kinark Corporation	24.33
ML Macadamia Orchards, L.P.	24.54
Nortech Systems Incorporated	24.57
Bingo & Gaming International, Inc.	25.00
Touchstone Applied Science Associates, Inc.	25.00
Z-Axis Corporation	25.00
XeTel Corporation.	25.86
Endogen, Inc.	25.92
QC Optics, Inc.	26.00
Mercury Waste Solutions, Inc.	26.09
Applied Cellular Technology, Inc.	26.92
First American Health Concepts, Inc.	27.21
AlphaNet Solutions, Inc.	27.27
Bull Run Corporation	27.27
Mikron Instrument Company, Inc.	27.40
Armanino Foods of Distinction, Inc.	28.10
Amistar Corporation.	28.14
Canterbury Park Holding Corporation	29.43
Omtool, Ltd.	29.89
Capital Title Group, Inc.	30.64
Royal Appliance Mfg. Co.	30.75
Reflectix, Inc.	31.00
HealthStar Corp.	31.20
Oakridge Energy, Inc.	31.25
GlobeNet International I, Inc.	31.33
SpectraLink Corporation	31.82
Oakridge Holdings, Inc.	31.89
Rotonics Manufacturing Inc.	33.33
Exigent International, Inc.	34.00
Birner Dental Management Services, Inc.	34.40
Everest Medical Corporation	35.25
Netter Digital Entertainment, Inc.	35.25
RMH Teleservices, Inc.	35.33
Dynatronics Corporation	35.71
Sandata, Inc.	36.00
Eagle Pacific Industries, Inc.	37.40
Butler National Corporation.	38.00
Arizona Instrument Corporation.	40.50
NBI, Inc.	40.50
Sierra Monitor Corporation	40.50
Luxtec Corporation	43.67
Atlantic Premium Brands, Ltd.	46.75
DMI Furniture, Inc.	47.29
JMAR Industries, Inc.	53.00
Kyzen Corporation	56.00
Interlink Electronics, Inc.	56.25
Galaxy Foods Company	59.00
Jerry's Famous Deli, Inc.	59.50
Synergy Brands, Inc.	61.20
ChoiceTel Communications, Inc.	62.50
Farm Fish, Inc.	62.50
InnerDyne, Inc.	65.50
Vicon Fiber Optics Corp.	69.00
Seven J Stock Farm, Inc.	72.40
Superior Supplements, Inc.	75.00
Tangram Enterprise Solutions, Inc.	75.00
Spanlink Communications, Inc.	76.20
Tekgraf, Inc.	78.00
EFI Electronics Corporation.	87.00
Boatracs, Inc.	87.50
B.B. Walker Company	93.75

¢ ¢

Under 50 %	
Bollinger Industries, Inc.	16.79
Compare Generiks, Inc.	16.90
American Consumers, Inc.	17.48
Laser Master International, Inc.	23.38
Bontex, Inc.	23.41
Innovative Valve Technologies, Inc.	24.76
Mendocino Brewing Company, Inc.	24.78
Celox Laboratories, Inc.	25.00
TransCoastal Marine Services, Inc.	25.28
Canyon Resources Corporation	25.51
Dynamic International, Ltd.	25.64
Electronic Tele-Communications, Inc.	25.94
Miller Diversified Corporation	27.59
HIA, Inc.	28.57
Sonics & Materials, Inc.	30.60
Sandata, Inc.	30.77
NovaCare,Inc.	30.89
Boonton Electronics Corporation	32.08
Eagle Geophysical, Inc.	32.97
Kentucky Electric Steel, Inc.	33.21
Publishers Equipment Corporation	33.33
Tivoli Industries, Inc.	33.33
Milastar Corporation	34.01
Micropac Industries, Inc.	35.00
Continental Information Systems Corporation	35.25
Taitron Components Incorporated	37.41
Tufco International, Inc.	37.50
DeVlieg-Bullard, Inc.	37.58
American Residential Services, Inc.	37.75
Sel-Leb Marketing, Inc.	37.94
ILX Resorts Incorporated	38.55
Amtech Systems, Inc.	38.56
Jaco Electronics, Inc.	38.97
PDK Labs Inc.	39.47
Amistar Corporation	40.04
ML Macadamia Orchards, L.P.	40.13
Central Financial Acceptance Corporation	40.15
L.A. T Sportswear, Inc.	41.18
Cistron Biotechnology, Inc.	41.67
Medicore, Inc.	42.59
Burke Mills, Inc.	43.35
Consumer Portfolio Services, Inc.	43.55
Tubby's, Inc.	43.56
Cambridge Holdings, Ltd.	43.69
Aerovox Incorporated	43.92
Foilmark, Inc.	44.02
SigmaTron International, Inc.	44.03
Bio-Reference Laboratories, Inc.	44.44
Coast Distribution System (The)	44.77
EMCON	44.87
AlphaNet Solutions, Inc.	44.91
Tekgraf, Inc.	45.61
Aldila, Inc.	46.44
Farrel Corporation	46.50
Astrex, Inc.	46.55
Westerbeke Corporation	46.87
Coeur d'Alenes Company (The)	47.27
ERC Industries, Inc.	47.46
Triple S Plastics, Inc.	48.19
Napco Security Systems, Inc.	48.43

McNaughton Apparel Group Inc.	49.19
Microfluidics International Corporation	49.39
Phoenix Gold International, Inc.	49.50

50 - 100 %	
Educational Insights, Inc.	50.66
Security National Financial Corporation	51.17
RADVA Corporation	51.67
Rag Shops, Inc.	51.87
Impac Mortgage Holdings, Inc.	51.94
EXX INC	52.23
GameTech International, Inc.	52.33
Tandycrafts, Inc.	52.34
Weirton Steel Corporation	52.88
Nitches, Inc.	53.52
Dynamex Inc.	53.76
Janus American Group, Inc.	54.00
Bayou Steel Corporation	54.57
Hemagen Diagnostics, Inc.	55.04
Bristol Retail Solutions, Inc.	55.29
EA Engineering, Science, and Technology, Inc.	56.05
Armanino Foods of Distinction, Inc.	56.31
Texas Vanguard Oil Company	56.39
CCA Industries, Inc.	56.74
Shopsmith, Inc.	56.85
Technology Research Corporation	57.28
T.J.T., Inc.	57.61
Capital Pacific Holdings, Inc.	58.05
Pacific Aerospace & Electronics, Inc.	58.08
Allstar Systems, Inc.	58.33
XeTel Corporation	58.39
Gundle/SLT Environmental, Inc.	58.48
Raytel Medical Corporation	58.67
AML Communications, Inc.	58.72
Texas Equipment Corporation	59.38
Ag-Bag International Limited	59.42
Westwood Corporation	59.59
Manchester Equipment Co., Inc.	59.65
QC Optics, Inc.	59.77
MileMarker International, Inc.	60.00
New York Health Care, Inc.	60.00
Fortress Group, Inc. (The)	60.48
BridgeStreet Accomodations, Inc.	60.65
FTI Consulting, Inc.	60.75
All American Semiconductor, Inc.	60.90
R-B Rubber Products, Inc.	61.50
Autologic Information International, Inc.	61.59
FiberCore, Inc.	61.90
Electronic Systems Technology, Inc.	62.22
GZA GeoEnvironmental Technologies, Inc.	62.44
InterWest Medical Corporation	62.50
Pentacon, Inc.	62.55
Miami Subs Corporation	62.71
CREDO Petroleum Corporation	62.72
Glassmaster Company	63.56
ICT Group, Inc.	63.61
Electric & Gas Technology, Inc.	63.98
Fairmount Chemical Co., Inc.	64.29
I.C.H. Corporation	64.30
Productivity Technologies Corp.	64.37
Bradley Pharmaceuticals, Inc.	65.38

Dynamic Homes, Inc.	65.79
Touchstone Applied Science Associates, Inc.	65.79
EKCO Group, Inc.	66.02
Capital Associates, Inc.	66.06
Westminster Capital, Inc.	66.26
Writer Corporation (The)	66.29
Jerry's Famous Deli, Inc.	66.85
Top Air Manufacturing, Inc.	68.03
Reflectix, Inc.	68.89
Comstock Resources, Inc.	69.33
Randers Killam Group Inc. (The)	69.84
Advanced Deposition Technologies, Inc.	70.11
Unapix Entertainment, Inc.	70.65
Athanor Group, Inc.	71.24
Worldtex, Inc.	71.65
Strategic Capital Resources, Inc.	71.74
Synbiotics Corporation	72.19
Arizona Instrument Corporation.	72.97
Patterson Energy, Inc.	73.13
Mobile America Corporation	73.53
Scherer Healthcare, Inc.	73.82
Let's Talk Cellular & Wireless, Inc.	73.97
CompuCom Systems, Inc.	74.04
Rotonics Manufacturing Inc.	74.07
Hahn Automotive Warehouse, Inc.	74.13
CareAdvantage, Inc.	75.00
Questron Technology, Inc.	75.09
Sports Club Company, Inc. (The)	75.19
Universal American Financial Corp.	75.55
Petroleum Development Corporation	75.56
Circuit Systems, Inc.	77.04
International Total Services, Inc.	77.17
Chicago Pizza & Brewery, Inc.	77.42
RMH Teleservices, Inc.	77.66
Scientific Industries, Inc.	77.78
Thermo Vision Corporation	78.00
Farm Fish, Inc.	78.13
Hitox Corporation of America.	78.24
Healthcare Imaging Services, Inc.	78.38
Lincoln Snacks Company	78.69
First Alliance Corporation.	79.08
IRI International Corporation	79.51
Nathan's Famous, Inc.	80.16
Government Technology Services, Inc.	80.18
Retrospettiva, Inc.	80.65
Command Systems, Inc.	81.66
Provena Foods Inc.	81.67
Waterlink, Inc.	82.18
Cohesant Technologies Inc.	82.23
Calloway's Nursery, Inc.	82.35
Sunair Electronics, Inc.	82.39
Nastech Pharmaceutical Company Inc.	82.75
Todd Shipyards Corporation	82.90
Kinark Corporation	83.27
Z-Axis Corporation	83.33
Ithaca Industries, Inc.	83.73
Flour City International, Inc.	83.93
American Dental Technologies, Inc.	84.38
Guardian International, Inc.	84.85
Rankin Automotive Group, Inc.	84.95
All Communications Corporation	85.19
ASA International Ltd.	85.55
Moyco Technologies, Inc.	86.82

TMS, Inc.	87.50
G-III Apparel Group, Ltd.	87.77
Thermo TerraTech Inc.	87.93
Sunrise International Leasing Corporation	87.94
Allied Devices Corporation	88.04
PTI Holding Inc.	88.22
BTU International, Inc.	88.24
UFP Technologies, Inc.	88.76
Superior Energy Services, Inc.	89.20
Logitek, Inc.	89.29
Back Yard Burgers, Inc.	89.47
Diodes Incorporated	89.52
Telebyte Technology, Inc.	90.21
Flanders Corporation	90.42
Diamond Home Services, Inc.	90.59
IRIDEX Corporation	90.95
Diehl Graphsoft, Inc.	91.19
Holiday RV Superstores, Incorporated	91.36
Riviera Tool Company	91.70
Advantage Marketing Systems, Inc.	92.38
NewCom, Inc.	92.72
Halter Marine Group, Inc.	92.94
Isomet Corporation	93.17
Sight Resource Corporation	93.90
SI Technologies, Inc.	94.55
Butler National Corporation.	95.00
Computer Research, Inc.	95.29
Solomon-Page Group Ltd. (The)	95.54
FARO Technologies, Inc.	95.63
Travel Ports of America, Inc.	95.67
Netter Digital Entertainment, Inc.	96.58
Horizon Offshore, Inc.	97.06
International Electronics, Inc.	98.43
Overseas Filmgroup, Inc.	98.52
Goddard Industries, Inc.	98.72
New Horizon Kids Quest, Inc.	99.34
Nortech Systems Incorporated	99.42
SITEL Corporation	99.60
Creative Host Services, Inc.	100.00
White Electronic Designs Corporation	100.00
Drypers Corporation	100.70
Blimpie International, Inc.	100.92
Response Oncology, Inc.	100.98

101 - 150 %

Charming Shoppes, Inc.	101.21
Elantec Semiconductor, Inc.	101.42
Swank, Inc.	101.60
National Home Health Care Corp.	101.71
Tone Products, Inc.	102.04
Firecom, Inc.	102.13
HemaCare Corporation	102.22
R.H. Phillips, Inc.	103.24
Hawker Pacific Aerospace	103.43
Adams Golf, Inc.	103.57
Orbit International Corp.	104.17
Business Resource Group.	104.53
Comtrex Systems Corporation	105.19
Nicholas Financial, Inc.	105.41
Abatix Environmental Corp.	105.52
Hi-Rise Recycling Systems, Inc.	105.80

Hytek Microsystems, Inc..	105.93
Casa Ole' Restaurants, Inc..	106.10
Eagle Food Centers, Inc.	106.12
CAS Medical Systems, Inc..	106.38
Norton Drilling Services, Inc.	106.86
Signature Eyewear, Inc..	107.12
Conrad Industries, Inc.	107.19
Marlton Technologies, Inc.	107.29
Berger Holdings, Ltd..	107.59
Hi-Tech Pharmacal Co., Inc.	107.76
FAFCO, Inc.	108.05
International Airline Support Group, Inc.	109.48
Fiberstars, Inc.	110.95
Techdyne, Inc.	111.11
BAB Holdings, Inc..	111.58
Omtool, Ltd.	111.62
Superior Supplements, Inc..	111.94
Kyzen Corporation	112.00
Millbrook Press Inc. (The)	112.87
Canisco Resources, Inc..	113.29
Judge Group, Inc. (The).	113.45
Wegener Corporation	115.00
ZEON Corporation	115.55
RF Industries, Ltd.	116.48
Colonial Commercial Corp..	116.92
Oakridge Energy, Inc..	117.92
Esquire Communications Ltd.	119.37
Joule Inc.	119.68
Jenna Lane, Inc..	120.47
Willamette Valley Vineyards, Inc.	120.48
Spectrum Control, Inc.	120.97
Friedman Industries, Incorporated	121.46
ChoiceTel Communications, Inc..	121.95
Birner Dental Management Services, Inc.	121.99
Alfa Leisure, Inc.	122.55
Strategic Distribution, Inc.	123.86
Image Systems Corporation	124.10
Horizon Medical Products, Inc..	124.84
DMI Furniture, Inc..	125.38
Acme Electric Corporation	125.66
George Risk Industries, Inc.	125.69
Miller Industries, Inc..	126.02
Cache, Inc.	126.06
REXX Environmental Corporation	126.06
Health Fitness Corporation	126.53
Encore Medical Corporation	126.73
TBA Entertainment Corporation	126.97
Wiltek, Inc.	127.03
Industrial Services of America, Inc.	127.12
Aero Systems Engineering, Inc.	128.57
Centrum Industries, Inc.	128.57
Puroflow Incorporated	128.57
Farmstead Telephone Group, Inc.	128.87
Worksafe Industries Inc.	129.31
Boundless Corporation	129.52
Kreisler Manufacturing Corporation	130.00
Exigent International, Inc.	130.14
Aasche Transportation Services, Inc..	130.29
Unidigital Inc..	130.35
SofTech, Inc.	131.25
Wade Cook Financial Corporation	132.26
Suprema Specialties, Inc..	134.97
BCT International, Inc.	135.10

Meteor Industries, Inc.	136.24
Big Dog Holdings, Inc..	136.41
Interwest Home Medical, Inc.	136.84
Fotoball USA, Inc.	137.61
B.B. Walker Company	138.89
Mikron Instrument Company, Inc.	139.80
S2 Golf Inc.	140.45
Atlantic Premium Brands, Ltd.	140.60
THT Inc.	140.85
ACR Group, Inc.	141.33
JLM Couture, Inc..	143.91
LaBarge, Inc.	143.98
Collins Industries, Inc.	144.32
Cylink Corporation	145.35
Pioneer Railcorp	145.35
Streicher Mobile Fueling, Inc.	145.35
Hawaiian Airlines, Inc.	146.40
Advanced Photonix, Inc.	146.81
Big Sky Transportation Co..	146.97
Laser Technology, Inc.	147.06
Prab, Inc.	147.18
Interfoods of America, Inc..	147.46
Orleans Homebuilders, Inc..	148.08
Polymer Research Corp. of America	148.70
Stearns & Lehman, Inc..	148.81
ATS Money Systems, Inc.	149.18
Hydromer, Inc.	150.00
Saratoga Beverage Group, Inc.	150.36

151 - 200 %

Telecomm Industries Corp.	151.61
Sizzler International, Inc..	151.97
Kaneb Services, Inc.	154.37
Royal Appliance Mfg. Co.	155.04
EFI Electronics Corporation	155.36
Apple Orthodontix, Inc..	155.50
Eagle Pacific Industries, Inc.	158.47
MIM Corporation	159.26
Cable Link, Inc..	160.00
Intelligent Controls, Inc.	160.14
Interlink Electronics, Inc..	160.14
Micronetics Wireless, Inc.	160.95
Applied Innovation Inc..	161.00
Tapistron International, Inc..	161.54
Optelecom, Inc..	163.40
Mesa Laboratories, Inc..	163.46
Winston Resources, Inc.	167.26
Disc Graphics, Inc..	167.98
Rehabilicare Inc.	169.27
Integrity Incorporated.	171.49
Emons Transportation Group, Inc.	171.83
SpectraLink Corporation	172.41
Candie's, Inc.	172.86
K2 Design, Inc.	172.99
Argosy Gaming Company	174.05
Cade Industries, Inc.	174.19
Calprop Corporation	175.61
Paravant Computer Systems, Inc..	175.61
Williams Controls, Inc.	176.87
Frontier Adjusters of America, Inc..	178.57
Endogen, Inc.	180.21

Optimumcare Corporation	180.43
HealthStar Corp.	182.46
U.S. Home & Garden Inc.	183.20
Tidel Technologies, Inc.	183.53
Applied Cellular Technology, Inc.	184.21
First American Health Concepts, Inc.	184.95
National Environmental Service Co.	185.14
Sparta Foods, Inc..	186.67
Consolidated Delivery & Logistics, Inc.	186.83
Canterbury Park Holding Corporation	187.27
PREMIS Corporation	187.50
Seattle FilmWorks, Inc..	187.83
Equivest Finance, Inc.	188.68
Mentortech Inc.	189.02
JB Oxford Holdings, Inc..	189.29
BioSpecifics Technologies Corp..	190.36
Vicon Fiber Optics Corp..	191.67
InterSystems, Inc..	200.00

Over 200 %

Selfcare, Inc.	202.02
HMG Worldwide Corporation	203.09
Cumberland Technologies, Inc..	204.08
Golden Genesis Company	204.69
Edac Technologies Corporation.	205.33
Guess ?, Inc.	205.56
Arrow-Magnolia International, Inc.	208.21
SETECH, Inc..	210.00
MTR Gaming Group, Inc.	213.51
PlayCore, Inc..	220.29
Bull Run Corporation	223.88
Boatracs, Inc.	227.27
First Montauk Financial Corp.	228.57
Safety 1st, Inc.	232.14
ROHN Industries, Inc.	233.81
Tofutti Brands Inc.	235.14
Smith-Midland Corporation	238.10
Mercury Waste Solutions, Inc.	243.22
Reliv International, Inc..	246.51
Simtek Corporation	250.00
RMS Titanic, Inc..	252.17
SYS	258.33
Whitman Education Group, Inc.	259.26
Coda Music Technology, Inc..	260.42
Diagnostic Health Services, Inc.	266.67
Sono-Tek Corporation	266.67
Digital Solutions, Inc..	273.17
Gristede's Sloan's, Inc.	273.97
AMBI Inc..	277.78
MicroFrame, Inc.	278.31
Measurement Specialties, Inc.	280.13
Reconditioned Systems, Inc.	285.33
JMAR Industries, Inc..	290.41
InterDigital Communications Corporation	290.45
HEARx Ltd..	294.12
Tel-Instrument Electronics Corp..	294.12
Sierra Monitor Corporation	300.00
GlobeNet International I, Inc..	303.23
Eldorado Artesian Springs, Inc..	310.00
Emerson Radio Corp.	311.11
Oakridge Holdings, Inc..	311.96

Seven J Stock Farm, Inc.	312.07
BLC Financial Services, Inc.	312.50
Go-Video, Inc.	326.14
Monterey Pasta Company.	327.27
InnerDyne, Inc.	327.50
Advanced Tobacco Products, Inc.	336.00
Galaxy Foods Company	347.06
DCI Telecommunications, Inc..	349.35
Bingo & Gaming International, Inc.	357.14
Grill Concepts, Inc.	362.50
United-Guardian, Inc..	368.85
Jetronic Industries, Inc.	370.37
Dynatronics Corporation	373.13
Great Lakes Aviation, Ltd.	376.47
Financial Performance Corporation	384.09
Sel-Drum International, Inc.	387.50
Ronson Corporation.	401.49
TENERA, Inc.	406.52
Littlefield, Adams & Company	424.27
Movie Star, Inc..	437.84
Total Research Corporation.	468.75
NBI, Inc.	506.25
Vermont Pure Holdings, Ltd..	509.28
Capital Title Group, Inc.	526.56
Kids Stuff, Inc.	527.45
Memry Corporation.	527.45
Network Six, Inc.	559.70
Rent-A-Wreck of America, Inc.	568.18
Gentner Communications Corporation	569.12
Spanlink Communications, Inc.	577.27
U.S. Plastic Lumber Corporation	579.76
AM Communications, Inc.	600.00
Genelabs Technologies, Inc.	604.44
Tanknology-NDE International, Inc.	621.43
Seventh Generation, Inc.	654.55
Ceramics Process Systems Corporation	657.89
Oralabs Holding Corp.	664.52
Command Security Corporation	773.33
Global Maintech Corporation.	777.78
Bernard Chaus, Inc..	865.38
PDG Environmental, Inc..	900.00
Thousand Trails, Inc..	1,113.51
Luxtec Corporation.	1,139.13
NewCare Health Corporation	1,207.14
Tangram Enterprise Solutions, Inc.	1,216.22
Arthur Treacher's, Inc..	1,240.00
EcoScience Corporation	1,333.33
Environmental Safeguards, Inc.	1,388.89
Pharmaceutical Formulations, Inc..	1,750.00
Transcend Services, Inc..	1,870.00
Westmoreland Coal Company	2,381.25
Synergy Brands, Inc..	2,781.82
Met-Coil Systems Corporation.	2,916.67
Mesabi Trust	6,120.00
Hadron, Inc..	16,200.00

¢ ¢

Based on the years presented

Over 25 %	
Intellectual Technology, Inc.	780.79
Interfoods of America, Inc.	342.52
REXX Environmental Corporation	342.51
Applied Cellular Technology, Inc.	341.52
Adams Golf, Inc.	324.20
DCI Telecommunications, Inc.	320.10
Birner Dental Management Services, Inc.	316.94
Compare Generiks, Inc.	309.72
Innovative Valve Technologies, Inc.	278.21
Waterlink, Inc.	267.82
NewCom, Inc.	254.52
Impac Mortgage Holdings, Inc.	232.23
Capital Title Group, Inc.	199.76
Horizon Offshore, Inc.	191.25
RMS Titanic, Inc.	185.12
Bristol Retail Solutions, Inc.	177.43
MobiNetix Systems, Inc.	173.49
Wade Cook Financial Corporation	152.52
Selfcare, Inc.	151.34
HealthStar Corp.	147.13
Financial Performance Corporation	146.36
Let's Talk Cellular & Wireless, Inc.	145.25
Apple Orthodontix, Inc.	145.03
Guardian International, Inc.	140.37
TBA Entertainment Corporation	128.45
Mercury Waste Solutions, Inc.	125.03
TransCoastal Marine Services, Inc.	118.35
BridgeStreet Accomodations, Inc.	114.63
Dynamex Inc.	114.56
Hi-Rise Recycling Systems, Inc.	110.97
Atlantic Premium Brands, Ltd.	106.38
Omtool, Ltd.	100.83
Tekgraf, Inc.	100.73
Horizon Medical Products, Inc.	99.02
Questron Technology, Inc.	98.72
Superior Energy Services, Inc.	94.89
PTI Holding Inc.	94.57
BAB Holdings, Inc.	92.98
Creative Host Services, Inc.	92.62
Flour City International, Inc.	90.00
Westminster Capital, Inc.	88.79
Bingo & Gaming International, Inc.	88.05
Thermo Vision Corporation	85.43
U.S. Plastic Lumber Corporation	84.72
BLC Financial Services, Inc.	83.73
Frontier Airlines, Inc.	81.33
Advanced Tobacco Products, Inc.	80.89
Solomon-Page Group Ltd. (The)	80.56
Tanknology-NDE International, Inc.	79.95
Oakridge Energy, Inc.	78.27
Unidigital Inc.	77.03
K2 Design, Inc.	76.53
Global Maintech Corporation	75.24
GameTech International, Inc.	73.66
Consumer Portfolio Services, Inc.	73.32
American Residential Services, Inc.	72.95
AML Communications, Inc.	71.54
All Communications Corporation	71.27
Pacific Aerospace & Electronics, Inc.	69.88
Consolidated Delivery & Logistics, Inc.	67.71
Chicago Pizza & Brewery, Inc.	65.86
GlobeNet International I, Inc.	64.73
Centrum Industries, Inc.	63.21
Eagle Geophysical, Inc.	61.62
Telecomm Industries Corp.	61.40
Galaxy Foods Company	61.23
Comstock Resources, Inc.	60.92
Strategic Distribution, Inc.	60.74
SETECH, Inc.	60.47
Flanders Corporation	60.42
Esquire Communications Ltd.	60.41
Ceramics Process Systems Corporation	59.73
Memry Corporation	59.23
Candie's, Inc.	56.64
Boatracs, Inc.	55.70
Canyon Resources Corporation	55.30
Petroleum Development Corporation	54.85
Rehabilicare Inc.	54.07
Fortress Group, Inc. (The)	51.76
Vermont Pure Holdings, Ltd.	50.91
U.S. Home & Garden Inc.	50.79
DenAmerica Corp.	50.77
Pentacon, Inc.	50.75
IRI International Corporation	49.66
MTR Gaming Group, Inc.	49.53
NewCare Health Corporation	49.53
ChoiceTel Communications, Inc.	49.14
Marlton Technologies, Inc.	48.71
Gristede's Sloan's, Inc.	48.34
Nastech Pharmaceutical Company Inc.	48.34
AM Communications, Inc.	47.15
Cade Industries, Inc.	46.51
Arthur Treacher's, Inc.	46.45
Whitman Education Group, Inc.	46.28
SITEL Corporation	46.12
ERC Industries, Inc.	45.32
Hemagen Diagnostics, Inc.	44.86
Advantage Marketing Systems, Inc.	44.52
InnerDyne, Inc.	44.18
Sight Resource Corporation	43.35
Command Systems, Inc.	42.78
FARO Technologies, Inc.	42.52
Response Oncology, Inc.	42.52
Tidel Technologies, Inc.	42.51
Patterson Energy, Inc.	42.23
Miller Industries, Inc.	41.64
New Horizon Kids Quest, Inc.	40.55
Rankin Automotive Group, Inc.	40.43
T.J.T., Inc.	40.37
IRIDEX Corporation	39.51
Texas Equipment Corporation	39.31
Cable Link, Inc.	39.06
Saratoga Beverage Group, Inc.	39.01
Capital Associates, Inc.	38.87
Halter Marine Group, Inc.	38.81
NBI, Inc.	38.72
Top Air Manufacturing, Inc.	38.63
Casa Ole' Restaurants, Inc.	38.45
Meteor Industries, Inc.	37.85
Diagnostic Health Services, Inc.	37.77
FiberCore, Inc.	37.67
Seventh Generation, Inc.	37.47

Streicher Mobile Fueling, Inc.	37.36
Touchstone Applied Science Associates, Inc.	36.94
Spanlink Communications, Inc.	36.68
PlayCore, Inc..	36.56
Optelecom, Inc..	36.44
FTI Consulting, Inc.	36.01
Advanced Deposition Technologies, Inc..	35.66
Kids Stuff, Inc.	35.22
HEARx Ltd..	35.02
Everest Medical Corporation	34.72
Retrospettiva, Inc..	34.41
SI Technologies, Inc.	34.32
Kreisler Manufacturing Corporation	34.06
Fotoball USA, Inc.	33.94
Simtek Corporation	33.75
Jerry's Famous Deli, Inc..	33.23
ICT Group, Inc..	32.63
Sports Club Company, Inc. (The).	32.60
R-B Rubber Products, Inc.	32.53
ACR Group, Inc.	32.52
AlphaNet Solutions, Inc.	32.42
Hytek Microsystems, Inc..	32.30
Business Resource Group.	32.05
Amtech Systems, Inc..	31.92
Berger Holdings, Ltd..	31.60
Millbrook Press Inc. (The)	31.51
Equivest Finance, Inc.	30.96
Synbiotics Corporation	30.94
Sunrise International Leasing Corporation	30.73
Conrad Industries, Inc.	30.53
Thermo TerraTech Inc..	29.95
Tapistron International, Inc.	29.72
Nortech Systems Incorporated	29.69
SpectraLink Corporation	29.56
Lannett Company, Inc.	29.54
Edac Technologies Corporation	29.35
Tel-Instrument Electronics Corp..	28.81
Industrial Services of America, Inc.	28.72
Central Financial Acceptance Corporation	28.37
Jenna Lane, Inc..	28.36
Golden Genesis Company	28.31
MIM Corporation.	28.24
CareAdvantage, Inc.	28.20
Cylink Corporation	27.85
Encore Medical Corporation	27.84
American Dental Technologies, Inc.	27.80
Tivoli Industries, Inc.	27.67
RMH Teleservices, Inc..	27.52
Drypers Corporation	27.16
Suprema Specialties, Inc.	27.13
Interlink Electronics, Inc..	26.62
Publishers Equipment Corporation	26.49
National Environmental Service Co.	26.43
JMAR Industries, Inc..	26.34
Argosy Gaming Company	26.32
InterSystems, Inc..	26.12
PREMIS Corporation.	26.06
Writer Corporation (The).	26.02
JLM Couture, Inc..	25.99
Hydromer, Inc.	25.39
Endogen, Inc.	25.38
Mesabi Trust	25.32
Diamond Home Services, Inc.	25.26

Unapix Entertainment, Inc.	25.22
Isomet Corporation	25.17
Fiberstars, Inc.	25.11
Dynatronics Corporation	25.09

25 - 10 %

Big Dog Holdings, Inc..	25.00
Winston Resources, Inc.	24.97
Calprop Corporation	24.67
Colonial Commercial Corp..	24.63
RF Industries, Ltd.	24.58
Tubby's, Inc.	24.57
Micronetics Wireless, Inc.	24.53
Nicholas Financial, Inc..	24.44
SofTech, Inc.	24.27
Kinark Corporation	24.15
Sunshine Mining and Refining Company	24.07
Transcend Services, Inc.	23.93
SigmaTron International, Inc..	23.76
Optimumcare Corporation	23.73
Digital Solutions, Inc..	23.64
International Total Services, Inc.	23.19
Hawker Pacific Aerospace	23.05
Interwest Home Medical, Inc.	22.88
NovaCare,Inc..	22.71
Allstar Systems, Inc.	22.44
Eldorado Artesian Springs, Inc..	22.39
Microfluidics International Corporation	22.21
EcoScience Corporation	22.07
Farmstead Telephone Group, Inc..	21.96
Judge Group, Inc. (The).	21.84
Paravant Computer Systems, Inc..	21.80
Tofutti Brands Inc.	21.42
Mentortech Inc.	21.41
Reliv International, Inc..	21.32
Wegener Corporation	21.18
Healthcare Imaging Services, Inc.	21.16
Kaneb Services, Inc.	20.95
Total Research Corporation.	20.89
Mendocino Brewing Company, Inc.	20.74
Littlefield, Adams & Company.	20.71
AMBI Inc..	20.60
Signature Eyewear, Inc..	20.50
Intelligent Controls, Inc.	20.49
XeTel Corporation	20.44
TMS, Inc..	20.40
Elantec Semiconductor, Inc.	20.08
Grill Concepts, Inc..	19.90
New York Health Care, Inc.	19.78
Measurement Specialties, Inc.	19.77
Netter Digital Entertainment, Inc.	19.66
First American Health Concepts, Inc.	19.63
JB Oxford Holdings, Inc.	19.31
Raytel Medical Corporation	19.23
Aasche Transportation Services, Inc..	19.05
Willamette Valley Vineyards, Inc.	19.00
Stearns & Lehman, Inc..	18.54
Texas Vanguard Oil Company	18.54
Sandata, Inc.	18.47
SYS	18.40
Tangram Enterprise Solutions, Inc..	18.15
Arrow-Magnolia International, Inc.	18.06
Disc Graphics, Inc.	17.76

Image Systems Corporation	17.72
Logitek, Inc.	17.51
Pioneer Railcorp	17.15
LaBarge, Inc.	17.08
Ag-Bag International Limited	17.07
Laser Master International, Inc.	16.78
S2 Golf Inc.	16.65
Cell Robotics International, Inc.	16.42
White Electronic Designs Corporation	16.18
Continental Information Systems Corporation	16.13
CompuCom Systems, Inc.	16.07
Seattle FilmWorks, Inc.	16.06
Luxtec Corporation	15.88
Gentner Communications Corporation	15.87
Comprehensive Care Corporation	15.80
Todd Shipyards Corporation	15.72
MileMarker International, Inc.	15.57
Rent-A-Wreck of America, Inc.	15.55
Wiltek, Inc.	15.34
Big Sky Transportation Co.	15.30
Friedman Industries, Incorporated	14.94
Applied Innovation Inc.	14.92
McNaughton Apparel Group Inc.	14.82
Sel-Leb Marketing, Inc.	14.47
Bradley Pharmaceuticals, Inc.	14.40
International Electronics, Inc.	14.39
DeVlieg-Bullard, Inc.	14.16
Diehl Graphsoft, Inc.	13.96
Bio-Reference Laboratories, Inc.	13.91
First Montauk Financial Corp.	13.90
Techdyne, Inc.	13.87
Telebyte Technology, Inc.	13.82
Kyzen Corporation	13.52
Sierra Monitor Corporation	13.44
PDK Labs Inc.	13.19
Eagle Pacific Industries, Inc.	12.91
Bull Run Corporation	12.90
BioSpecifics Technologies Corp.	12.85
Blimpie International, Inc.	12.84
Health Fitness Corporation	12.80
MicroFrame, Inc.	12.76
Sonics & Materials, Inc.	12.75
Goddard Industries, Inc.	12.72
BCT International, Inc.	12.65
Worksafe Industries Inc.	12.63
HMG Worldwide Corporation	12.55
FAFCO, Inc.	12.49
First Alliance Corporation	12.49
All American Semiconductor, Inc.	12.13
National Home Health Care Corp.	12.12
Laser Technology, Inc.	12.07
R.H. Phillips, Inc.	11.87
ATS Money Systems, Inc.	11.86
Monterey Pasta Company.	11.81
Norton Drilling Services, Inc.	11.71
PDG Environmental, Inc.	11.68
Westerbeke Corporation	11.63
Sono-Tek Corporation	11.56
UFP Technologies, Inc.	11.49
Travel Ports of America, Inc.	11.35
Jetronic Industries, Inc.	11.18
Worldtex, Inc.	11.17
Medicore, Inc.	11.01

Pharmaceutical Formulations, Inc.	10.99
Bayou Steel Corporation	10.97
Randers Killam Group Inc. (The)	10.59
Abatix Environmental Corp.	10.54
Capital Pacific Holdings, Inc.	10.54
Hi-Tech Pharmacal Co., Inc.	10.05
EKCO Group, Inc.	10.04
CREDO Petroleum Corporation	10.02

10 - 0 %

Cumberland Technologies, Inc.	9.90
Prab, Inc.	9.63
Alfa Leisure, Inc.	9.62
Command Security Corporation	9.46
Phoenix Gold International, Inc.	9.44
Coda Music Technology, Inc.	9.23
Reflectix, Inc.	9.22
HIA, Inc.	9.17
Mikron Instrument Company, Inc.	9.15
InterWest Medical Corporation	9.11
Great Lakes Aviation, Ltd.	9.00
Smith-Midland Corporation	9.00
Oralabs Holding Corp.	8.92
Moyco Technologies, Inc.	8.72
Dynamic Homes, Inc.	8.67
Avesis Incorporated	8.62
Williams Controls, Inc.	8.55
Scientific Industries, Inc.	8.41
United-Guardian, Inc.	8.35
Joule Inc.	8.21
Emons Transportation Group, Inc.	8.15
ZEON Corporation	8.08
Sparta Foods, Inc.	8.04
EFI Electronics Corporation	8.02
Security National Financial Corporation	7.99
EMCON	7.93
Triple S Plastics, Inc.	7.79
Circuit Systems, Inc.	7.78
Autologic Information International, Inc.	7.43
Burke Mills, Inc.	7.34
Hawaiian Airlines, Inc.	7.26
Productivity Technologies Corp.	7.21
Exigent International, Inc.	7.20
RADVA Corporation	7.09
Mesa Laboratories, Inc.	7.04
Farrel Corporation	7.03
Athanor Group, Inc.	6.95
Cache, Inc.	6.82
CAS Medical Systems, Inc.	6.81
HemaCare Corporation	6.77
Spectrum Control, Inc.	6.74
I.C.H. Corporation	6.62
Quality Products, Inc.	6.60
George Risk Industries, Inc.	6.50
Lexington Precision Corporation	6.49
ROHN Industries, Inc.	6.44
Accuhealth, Inc.	6.35
Back Yard Burgers, Inc.	6.35
Calloway's Nursery, Inc.	6.31
Miller Diversified Corporation	6.23
ML Macadamia Orchards, L.P.	6.11
Metal Arts Company, Inc. (The)	6.04
Vicon Fiber Optics Corp.	6.03

Z-Axis Corporation	5.97
Manchester Equipment Co., Inc.	5.94
Allied Devices Corporation	5.93
Provena Foods Inc.	5.66
Coeur d'Alenes Company (The)	5.64
Safety 1st, Inc.	5.52
Carlyle Industries, Inc.	5.36
Sarnia Corporation.	5.33
Overseas Filmgroup, Inc.	5.32
Astrex, Inc.	5.02
InterDigital Communications Corporation	4.92
Celox Laboratories, Inc.	4.77
Government Technology Services, Inc.	4.76
Milastar Corporation	4.73
ASA International Ltd.	4.68
Seven J Stock Farm, Inc.	4.68
Unilab Corporation	4.60
Orbit International Corp.	4.38
ILX Resorts Incorporated	4.08
Universal American Financial Corp.	4.04
Comtrex Systems Corporation	3.91
International Airline Support Group, Inc.	3.83
Sunair Electronics, Inc.	3.81
Collins Industries, Inc.	3.67
CCA Industries, Inc.	3.66
Jaco Electronics, Inc.	3.48
Nathan's Famous, Inc.	3.29
Frontier Adjusters of America, Inc.	3.28
TENERA, Inc.	3.21
Polymer Research Corp. of America	3.06
Aldila, Inc.	2.99
Computer Research, Inc.	2.92
Canterbury Park Holding Corporation	2.82
Swank, Inc.	2.70
Hitox Corporation of America.	2.61
Creative Technologies Corp.	2.58
Southland Corporation (The)	2.50
Shopsmith, Inc.	2.36
Integrity Incorporated	2.31
Oakridge Holdings, Inc.	2.27
THT Inc.	2.22
Holiday RV Superstores, Incorporated	2.04
Rotonics Manufacturing Inc.	1.93
Bernard Chaus, Inc.	1.77
Rag Shops, Inc.	1.70
Napco Security Systems, Inc.	1.60
Royal Appliance Mfg. Co.	1.48
Arizona Instrument Corporation.	1.45
Tufco International, Inc.	1.44
Aero Systems Engineering, Inc.	1.38
Diodes Incorporated	1.33
Advanced Photonix, Inc.	1.23
Fairmount Chemical Co., Inc.	1.18
Hadron, Inc.	0.94
Met-Coil Systems Corporation	0.93
Kentucky Electric Steel, Inc.	0.64
Electronic Tele-Communications, Inc.	0.63
Glassmaster Company.	0.63
Riviera Tool Company	0.53
Firecom, Inc.	0.44
Sel-Drum International, Inc.	0.40
Orleans Homebuilders, Inc.	0.36
Micropac Industries, Inc.	0.32

Armanino Foods of Distinction, Inc.	0.08
Boonton Electronics Corporation	0.07

0 - (10) %

Acme Electric Corporation	-0.08
QC Optics, Inc.	-0.61
Farm Fish, Inc.	-0.64
Educational Insights, Inc.	-0.80
BTU International, Inc.	-0.97
Electronic Systems Technology, Inc.	-1.10
DMI Furniture, Inc.	-1.47
Eagle Food Centers, Inc.	-1.60
Puroflow Incorporated	-1.66
Boundless Corporation	-1.70
Lincoln Snacks Company	-1.71
Westwood Corporation	-1.81
American Consumers, Inc.	-2.23
Weirton Steel Corporation.	-2.65
GZA GeoEnvironmental Technologies, Inc.	-2.71
Aerovox Incorporated	-3.15
Tandycrafts, Inc.	-3.22
Guess ?, Inc.	-3.67
Reconditioned Systems, Inc.	-3.95
Jennifer Convertibles, Inc.	-4.41
Coast Distribution System (The)	-4.51
Ronson Corporation	-4.91
Taitron Components Incorporated.	-5.09
Bontex, Inc.	-5.38
Technology Research Corporation	-5.43
Cohesant Technologies Inc.	-5.63
Foilmark, Inc.	-5.75
Thousand Trails, Inc.	-5.75
Amistar Corporation.	-6.38
Charming Shoppes, Inc.	-6.96
Bollinger Industries, Inc.	-7.03
Westmoreland Coal Company.	-7.62
Miami Subs Corporation	-9.77

Over (10) %

Gundle/SLT Environmental, Inc.	-10.13
Canisco Resources, Inc.	-11.12
G-III Apparel Group, Ltd.	-11.18
EXX INC	-11.49
B.B. Walker Company	-12.76
L.A. T Sportswear, Inc.	-13.13
EA Engineering, Science, and Technology, Inc.	-13.38
Movie Star, Inc.	-14.07
Ithaca Industries, Inc.	-17.02
Genelabs Technologies, Inc.	-18.49
Sizzler International, Inc.	-19.30
Champion Parts, Inc.	-20.31
Network Six, Inc.	-20.68
Butler National Corporation	-25.53
Electric & Gas Technology, Inc.	-26.36
Nitches, Inc.	-28.17
Synergy Brands, Inc.	-36.40
Emerson Radio Corp.	-36.93

¢ ¢

Based on the years presented

Sports Club Company, Inc. (The).	14.47
Thermo Vision Corporation	14.47
Allied Devices Corporation.	13.62
Applied Cellular Technology, Inc.	13.04
MicroFrame, Inc.	11.87
Laser Master International, Inc..	11.80
Sono-Tek Corporation	11.80
BridgeStreet Accomodations, Inc.	11.46
CREDO Petroleum Corporation	11.20
SpectraLink Corporation	11.20
Halter Marine Group, Inc.	10.38
Capital Associates, Inc..	10.06
HIA, Inc.	10.06
Sandata, Inc.	10.06

10 - 0 %

Wade Cook Financial Corporation	9.54
Hitox Corporation of America.	9.49
Seattle FilmWorks, Inc.	9.22
Omtool, Ltd..	8.74
Spectrum Control, Inc.	8.74
U.S. Home & Garden Inc.	8.10
Total Research Corporation	7.72
THT Inc..	6.92
Business Resource Group	4.89
Holiday RV Superstores, Incorporated	4.77
IRI International Corporation	4.71
IRIDEX Corporation	4.17
Solomon-Page Group Ltd. (The)	3.77
Aerovox Incorporated	3.23
Marlton Technologies, Inc.	3.03
Shopsmith, Inc.	2.89
Paravant Computer Systems, Inc.	2.50
Laser Technology, Inc..	2.33
Miller Industries, Inc.	1.27
Casa Ole' Restaurants, Inc.	0.94
ASA International Ltd.	0.00
Advantage Marketing Systems, Inc..	0.00
CAS Medical Systems, Inc.	0.00
ChoiceTel Communications, Inc.	0.00
Coeur d'Alenes Company (The)	0.00
Eldorado Artesian Springs, Inc.	0.00
Hi-Tech Pharmacal Co., Inc.	0.00
Hydromer, Inc..	0.00
Micropac Industries, Inc.	0.00
Mikron Instrument Company, Inc.	0.00
Oakridge Holdings, Inc..	0.00
Simtek Corporation	0.00
Touchstone Applied Science Associates, Inc.	0.00
Travel Ports of America, Inc.	0.00
Tufco International, Inc..	0.00
Westerbeke Corporation.	0.00
ZEON Corporation	0.00

0 - (10) %

Central Financial Acceptance Corporation	-0.55
Eagle Geophysical, Inc..	-0.71
Blimpie International, Inc.	-1.25
Manchester Equipment Co., Inc.	-1.25

InterDigital Communications Corporation	-1.30
NovaCare,Inc..	-1.42
Pentacon, Inc.	-2.13
Suprema Specialties, Inc.	-2.13
EMCON .	-3.28
Pioneer Railcorp.	-3.45
T.J.T., Inc.	-3.45
Sel-Drum International, Inc.	-4.35
Burke Mills, Inc.	-5.16
National Home Health Care Corp.	-5.20
Raytel Medical Corporation.	-5.42
Interwest Home Medical, Inc..	-5.90
Pharmaceutical Formulations, Inc.	-5.90
Scientific Industries, Inc.	-6.47
ML Macadamia Orchards, L.P.	-6.69
Tandycrafts, Inc..	-7.00
Netter Digital Entertainment, Inc..	-7.17
Universal American Financial Corp.	-7.17
Argosy Gaming Company.	-7.44
Sizzler International, Inc.	-7.49
Fortress Group, Inc. (The).	-8.60
PlayCore, Inc..	-8.69
Sunrise International Leasing Corporation	-8.97
Thermo TerraTech Inc.	-9.14
Encore Medical Corporation	-9.59
Joule Inc..	-9.93

Over (10) %

Spanlink Communications, Inc.	-10.61
Polymer Research Corp. of America	-13.28
Diehl Graphsoft, Inc.	-13.82
Image Systems Corporation	-14.50
Guess ?, Inc.	-14.98
HealthStar Corp.	-15.48
Computer Research, Inc.	-15.66
Electronic Systems Technology, Inc..	-15.66
Frontier Adjusters of America, Inc.	-16.08
Retrospettiva, Inc.	-16.65
First American Health Concepts, Inc.	-17.57
Diodes Incorporated	-17.79
Techdyne, Inc.	-17.79
Electronic Tele-Communications, Inc.	-18.35
Publishers Equipment Corporation	-18.35
Boonton Electronics Corporation.	-19.10
Unidigital Inc.	-19.26
American Consumers, Inc.	-20.63
DMI Furniture, Inc..	-20.63
TMS, Inc..	-20.63
XeTel Corporation	-20.63
Carlyle Industries, Inc.	-20.76
Aldila, Inc.	-21.35
ROHN Industries, Inc.	-22.05
Triple S Plastics, Inc..	-22.39
Dynamic Homes, Inc.	-22.84
Electric & Gas Technology, Inc.	-23.11
Seven J Stock Farm, Inc.	-23.11
Collins Industries, Inc.	-23.13
New York Health Care, Inc.	-23.37
Berger Holdings, Ltd..	-23.49
Sel-Leb Marketing, Inc.	-24.09
Charming Shoppes, Inc.	-24.61

¢ ¢

This page intentionally left blank.

OTC

OTHER

¢ ¢

Notes

Notes

Notes

Notes

Notes